THE UNIVERSITY OF
WINCHESTER

Martial Rose Library
Tel: 01962 827306

To be returned on or before the day marked above, subject to recall.

MEDIEVAL GRAMMAR AND RHETORIC
LANGUAGE ARTS AND LITERARY THEORY,
AD 300–1475

MEDIEVAL GRAMMAR AND RHETORIC

LANGUAGE ARTS AND LITERARY THEORY, AD 300–1475

EDITED BY
RITA COPELAND
AND
INEKE SLUITER

OXFORD
UNIVERSITY PRESS

OXFORD

UNIVERSITY PRESS

Great Clarendon Street, Oxford OX2 6DP

Oxford University Press is a department of the University of Oxford.
It furthers the University's objective of excellence in research, scholarship,
and education by publishing worldwide in

Oxford New York

Auckland Cape Town Dar es Salaam Hong Kong Karachi
Kuala Lumpur Madrid Melbourne Mexico City Nairobi
New Delhi Shanghai Taipei Toronto

With offices in

Argentina Austria Brazil Chile Czech Republic France Greece
Guatemala Hungary Italy Japan Poland Portugal Singapore
South Korea Switzerland Thailand Turkey Ukraine Vietnam

Oxford is a registered trade mark of Oxford University Press
in the UK and in certain other countries

Published in the United States
by Oxford University Press Inc., New York

© Rita Copeland and Ineke Sluiter 2009

The moral rights of the authors have been asserted
Database right Oxford University Press (maker)

First published 2009

British Library Cataloguing in Publication Data

Data available

Library of Congress Cataloging in Publication Data

Data available

Typeset by SPI Publisher Services, Pondicherry, India
Printed in Great Britain
on acid-free paper by
CPI Antony Rowe, Chippenham, Wiltshire

ISBN 978–0–19–818341–9

1 3 5 7 9 10 8 6 4 2

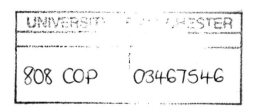

PREFACE AND ACKNOWLEDGMENTS

From the earliest stages of its conception, this book was intended as a contribution to two fields, the history of the language arts and the history of literary theory. Through the different stages of the book's development, these two objectives have remained fixed and have guided the selection and treatment of the primary texts. Overall, our principle has been to include two kinds of texts: those that were essential sources for any medieval understandings of grammar and rhetoric, and those that used grammatical or rhetorical knowledge in ways that pertain to the understanding of literary form and language or the teaching of literary composition. Some of the later texts included here were important for transmitting new kinds of sources and registering sharp changes in the development of the language arts, whether they illustrate new apprehensions of grammar or rhetoric as a theoretical tool, or the emergence of vernacular instruction in the language arts, or the impact of new additions (such as Aristotle's *Rhetoric*) to the canon of sources.

Well over half of the items here have never been translated into English; in some cases we have also provided fresh translations of texts that already existed in English. Where using an existing translation or working from a critical edition, we have tended to provide new annotation to take account of the most recent scholarship as well as situate the text for our readers. New annotation was deemed to be especially important when the only edition of a work was very old (and also of course when texts were not annotated). But in the course of updating and re-annotating these texts we have been profoundly indebted to the labors and scholarly vision of those editors and translators who went before us. It is our hope that this volume will make newly visible to its readers, as comprehensively as possible, the long roots of medieval literary culture in the interrelated traditions of grammar and rhetoric, the arts of language.

The international community of scholars is a generous one, and we take great pleasure here in recording the debts we have incurred over the years during which we have both collaborated on this project. We are most grateful to the following colleagues for their advice and help with specific textual questions as well as larger critical issues: Roger Allen, Adriano Aymonino, Christopher Baswell, Charles Briggs, Charles Burnett, Martin Camargo, Christopher Cannon, Mary Carruthers, Laura Cleaver, Virginia Cox, Cynthia Damon, Shane Duarte, Joseph Farrell, Alexander Fidora, Margareta Fredborg, Anne Grondeux,

Holger Gzella, Stephanie Gibbs Kamath, Michelle Karnes, C. H. Kneepkens, Sheila Lindenbaum, Peter Mack, Ann Matter, Constant Mews, Christoph Pieper, Ralph Rosen, Franz Schupp, James Simpson, D. Vance Smith, Justin Steinberg, David Wallace, John O. Ward, Olga Weijers, Marjorie Curry Woods, and Nicolette Zeeman. We also wish to thank Alastair Minnis, Martin Irvine, Suzanne Reynolds, and especially James J. Murphy for their invaluable advice and contributions at the inception of this project.

It is a pleasure to record our debts to the institutions that made our work possible, especially the libraries that welcomed us for extended periods of research. Ineke Sluiter wishes to thank Oliver Berggötz and the staff of the Staatsbibliothek zu Berlin, Haus Potsdamer Platz, for generous library assistance and a wonderful research environment during two longer visits in the springs of 2003 and 2005; Gregory Nagy and the library staff of the Center for Hellenic Studies in Washington DC for generous help and academic hospitality whenever the need was greatest; and librarians and staff at the Leiden University Libraries for gracious and competent assistance. Rita Copeland's work during several long periods was carried out mainly at the Warburg Institute in London, which provided the ideal conditions for research on classical learning and its later receptions: profound thanks are due to the Librarian of the Warburg, Jill Kraye, to François Quiviger, and to the generous staff of the Institute. The librarians and staff at the British Library and the Bodleian Library were also unfailingly helpful, as were those at the University of Pennsylvania Libraries, in particular Daniel Traister. Rita Copeland would also like to thank the American Philosophical Society for a sabbatical fellowship in 2004–5.

Many others have facilitated our work over the years. We note with gratitude the remarkable work of Susan Forsyth, who coordinated the complex permissions for this book. The editorial offices at Oxford University Press have graciously overseen this project at its various stages. We wish particularly to thank Jacqueline Baker for speeding this project through production with the greatest efficiency. Malcolm Todd brought graceful expertise to the large and small matters of copy-editing. Finally, we are indebted to two senior commissioning editors for literature, Sophie Goldsworthy and Andrew McNeillie, whose enthusiastic and generous guidance enabled us to bring this work to completion.

Although every effort has been made to trace and contact copyright holders prior to publication, this has not been possible in every case. If notified, the publisher will be pleased to rectify any errors or omissions at the earliest opportunity.

Rita Copeland
Ineke Sluiter

October, 2008

CONTENTS

PART 2 DOSSIERS ON THE ABLATIVE ABSOLUTE AND ETYMOLOGY

PART 3 SCIENCES AND CURRICULA OF LANGUAGE IN THE TWELFTH CENTURY

PART 6   RECEPTIONS OF THE TRADITIONS: THE LANGUAGE ARTS AND POETICS IN THE LATER MIDDLE AGES, CA. 1369–CA. 1475

LIST OF ABBREVIATIONS

AHDLMA	*Archives d'histoire doctrinale et littéraire au moyen âge*
ALMA	*Bulletin du Cange. Archivum latinitatis medii aevii*
CAG	*Commentaria in Aristotelem graeca*
CCCM	*Corpus christianorum, continuatio medievalis*
CCSL	*Corpus christianorum, series latina*
CIMAGL	*Cahiers de l'institut du moyen âge grec et latin*
CP	*Classical Philology*
CSEL	*Corpus scriptorum ecclesiasticorum latinorum*
Du Cange	C. du Cange. *Glossarium mediae et infimae Latinitatis.* 10 vols. Graz: Akademische Druck-u. Verlagsanstalt, 1954.
GG	A. Hilgard et al., eds. *Grammatici graeci.* 4 vols. Leipzig: Teubner 1878–1910 (rpt. Hildesheim: G. Olms, 1965)
GL	H. Keil, ed. *Grammatici latini.* 8 vols. Leipzig: Teubner, 1855–80 (rpt. Hildesheim: G. Olms, 1961)
HL	*Historiographia linguistica*
MRS	*Mediaeval and Renaissance Studies* (Warburg Institute, London)
MS	*Mediaeval Studies*
PL	J.-P. Migne, ed. *Patrologia latina, cursus completus.* 221 vols. Paris, 1844–65
RHT	*Revue d'histoire des textes*
RTAM	*Recherches de théologie ancienne et médiévale*
StM	*Studi medievali*
TAPA	*Transactions of the American Philological Association*

A note on Translations

Unless otherwise noted, translations of frequently cited classical rhetorical sources are from the following:

Cicero, *De inventione*, trans. Hubbell. Loeb edition.
[Cicero], *Rhetorica ad Herennium*, trans. Caplan. Loeb edition.
Horace, *Ars poetica*, trans. Fairclough. Loeb edition.
Quintilian, *Institutio oratoria*, trans. Butler. Loeb edition.
Translations of the Bible are those of the Douai version in Challoner's revision.

GENERAL INTRODUCTION

The texts brought together in this book represent the contributions of the arts of grammar and rhetoric to literary theory over the course of the Middle Ages, from late Latin antiquity to the fifteenth century. Grammar and rhetoric, the language disciplines, formed the basis of any medieval education, no matter what future career a student would want to pursue. However, given the importance of literature as the subject matter of the *ars grammatica* and the emphasis on literary form and structure in ancient rhetoric, these were also the disciplines that would prepare students for an understanding of literary language and form. It is this specific connection between grammatical and rhetorical theory and theoretical approaches to literature that is the central concern of this book. Whether one was to approach texts from the perspective of a poet or an exegete, whether the texts to be considered were secular or sacred, whether one was to compose a text or teach others how to compose, an education in the principles of grammar and rhetoric was the entryway into literary thought. But more than just the point of entry, these arts constituted the abiding theoretical toolbox for anyone engaged in a life of letters.

In the Middle Ages, the arts of grammar and rhetoric were often more inclusive than their modern-day counterparts. The art of grammar embraced not only language and linguistic thought but literature and the analysis of literary texts. The art of rhetoric entailed mastery of form and style in any kind of writing, prose or poetry, and any literary genre. Thus these arts were the source and often the primary substance of critical thought about literature, the literary canon, the mechanics of literary representation, the efficacy of poetic language or narrative structure, and even the purpose of literature. Moreover, such critical questions were not the arcane preserve of poets and academic exegetes. They were basic components of pedagogy at almost every level, so that one who was educated into Latin letters from an early age absorbed these principles throughout the course of study.

Because grammar and rhetoric were the perennial curricular subjects, many of the foundational texts of these disciplines were pedagogical in their purpose, and this is reflected in the selection of texts here. The pedagogical texts included range from the rank elementary, such as Donatus' *Ars minor*, an introduction to grammar composed in the fourth century AD and known in some form to virtually every medieval schoolboy for the next one thousand years, to the most ambitious theoretical explorations of the language arts, such as the encyclopedic synthesis of Western and Arabic science in *De divisione philosophiae* (On the Division of Philosophy) by the twelfth-century archbishop of Toledo, Dominicus Gundissalinus. The principles of selection have been, first, to present foundational texts for the arts in each period, especially those texts that set a new standard for analysis of the grammar and rhetoric, and then to give texts that exemplify the impact of newer disciplinary approaches.

The primary organization of the book is diachronic: medieval grammar and rhetoric valued their own traditions in ancient and late antique sources, and tended to emphasize continuity even when there were in fact significant changes in curricular or pedagogical environment or intellectual interests. The texts present a surface of slow and continuous development. Accordingly, we lay out a groundwork of grammatical and rhetorical thought in late antiquity and the early Middle Ages before entering the periods of the greatest expansion and innovation in these fields, the twelfth and the thirteenth centuries. We close with examples of late medieval teaching about the language arts in Latin and the vernacular, in didactic treatises and poetic fictions. The exceptions to the strict diachronic progression are two parts where we trace developments of subtraditions or themes that play out across a larger historical framework: the "dossiers" on the ablative absolute and etymology (Part 2), where short illustrative selections are arranged chronologically, and the large grouping of texts representing classroom pedagogies and the arts of poetry in the twelfth and thirteenth centuries (Part 4).

The book is divided into six parts: Part 1 covers the period from AD 300 to about 950; Part 2 surveys theoretical traditions of the ablative absolute and etymology; Part 3 presents the new scientific approaches to grammar and rhetoric in the twelfth century; Part 4 deals with the new genres of pedagogical treatises between about 1150 and the late thirteenth century; Part 5 presents the new theoretical and practical outlooks of the thirteenth century, both within and beyond university cultures; and Part 6 surveys some of the poetic and pedagogical implications of the language arts traditions in the fourteenth and fifteenth centuries, especially in vernacular writings. Our focus throughout is on texts that concern the language arts in their application to literary culture. For this reason we have not followed the history of grammar through its definitive break from literature and its incorporation into philosophy, in the academic movement known as speculative grammar, although some of the texts included here represent aspects of that movement. For the same reason we do not trace the specializations of rhetoric into the technical areas of the *ars dictaminis* (the art of letter writing) or the *ars praedicandi* (the art of preaching), although several of our selections are relevant to these fields. Similarly, because our focus is on the application of language arts to literary theory and and poetics, we do not cover the development of dialectic, even though that art was typically classified along with grammar and rhetoric as part of the trivium or one of the arts of "verbal logic." Our concern is with those arts, grammar and rhetoric, that not only directly taught a knowledge of language and facility of expression, but also incorporated the analysis or production of literary texts into their teaching.

We have reserved descriptive historical overviews of each period for the introductions to each Part. Here we consider the educational and institutional conditions that produced the critical outlook of each period, its continuities with, and innovative departures from, earlier periods. The highest level of contextual detail is provided in the headnote to each individual selection. The headnotes serve two purposes: to augment the historical overviews by giving a fuller account of the text's production and later influence; and to highlight important issues in the text, whether treatment of certain traditional themes or radical break with precedent. The relationship between the historical overviews and the individual headnotes is somewhat analogous to the medieval convention of "extrinsic" and "intrinsic" prologues to the arts: like the extrinsic prologues, the overviews allow readers to grasp the subject (here, the historical period) as a whole, from the outside, while the headnotes, like the intrinsic prologues, focus on the character of a particular text.

The sections of the General Introduction that follow here offer synthetic perspectives on the large questions generated by the texts in this volume. These essays are thematic rather than strictly historical, illustrating how the language arts enabled systematic reflection on disciplinary structures, on language itself, on the production of meaning in literary texts, on the special status of literary representation, on the formal properties of poetic fiction, on hermeneutics, and on the cognitive and ethical functions of literature. In these thematic essays we discuss many of the texts that are in this volume; but our discussion also ranges more widely to some philosophical and literary texts not included here, in order to suggest how the arts of grammar and rhetoric extended beyond their strict disciplinary limits to inform literary and intellectual expression at large.

CLASSIFICATION OF KNOWLEDGE

Many of the texts included here present classifications of knowledge or the sciences (*ordo* or *divisio scientiarum*). In some cases, for example Martianus Capella's *De nuptiis Philologiae et Mercurii* (*Marriage of Philology and Mercury*) from the end of the fifth century, and Cassiodorus' *Institutiones* from the late sixth century, the treatments of grammar and rhetoric are sections of a large classificatory enterprise. Why was classification of the sciences so important a tool in medieval representations of knowledge, and why in particular for the language sciences and for understanding the systems of grammar and rhetoric? We find such classifications in many forms and contexts. We are most likely to encounter them in encyclopedic surveys which set out to define and examine the branches of knowledge, such as the texts mentioned above, as well as Isidore of Seville's *Etymologiae* (seventh century), Thierry of Chartres' *Heptateuchon* (twelfth century), Gundissalinus' *De divisione philosophiae* (twelfth century), Vincent of Beauvais' *Speculum historiale* (thirteenth century), and the anonymous Middle English treatise on the arts from the later fifteenth century (see Part 6 of this book). They also appear in commentaries on a particular text which use a classifying scheme in order to situate the science represented by that text in relation to other branches of knowledge, such as Aquinas' preface to his commentary on the *Posterior Analytics*, Giles of Rome's commentary on Aristotle's *Rhetoric*, and Brunetto Latini's commentative translation of Cicero's *De inventione* (all from the later thirteenth century). Scientific classifications play a role in free-standing theoretical treatises on the nature of a certain kind of knowledge, such as Boethius' *De topicis differentiis* (On Different [kinds of] Topics) (AD 523), which devotes its fourth book to explaining the difference between rhetoric and dialectic, and John of Salisbury's *Metalogicon* (1159), which is a defense of the trivium that entails close accounts of grammar and dialectic. They also have a place in curricular handbooks, such as the treatise by Alexander Neckam (ca. 1210) which gives a reading list for elementary and advanced sciences. Finally, various kinds of poetic fictions build on or incorporate a division of knowledge as a thematic and structural device, as represented here by Alan of Lille's *Anticlaudianus* (1180s), Henri d'Andeli's satirical *Bataille des VII ars* (Battle of the Seven Liberal Arts, ca. 1230) and John Gower's *Confessio amantis* (1386–90). These are some of the most explicit forms that such classification takes; the idea of scientific classification underlies many other kinds of texts as well, including treatises devoted to one particular art or author.[1] Moreover, just as classification of the sciences can take many different textual forms, so the classifications also reflect the influences of various philosophical systems that determine how knowledge can be divided.

Classification of the sciences or of knowledge was, above all, a speculative and theoretical enterprise. We cannot explain the popularity of such schematic systems, the frequency with which authors of all kinds and from all eras in the Middle Ages recurred to these schemes, on the grounds of any specific prescriptive force that the schemes were meant to have. While some classifying treatments would have had a practical application (for example, Boethius certainly intended for his readers to grasp the difference between

---

[1] Commentaries on Boethius provided occasion for scientific classification, as did commentaries on the Bible. See, for example, questions V and VI of Aquinas' commentary on Boethius' *De trinitate*, trans. Maurer, *The Division and Methods of the Sciences*; and on biblical commentary, see Dahan, "Origène et Jean Cassien dans un *Liber de philosophia Salomonis*."

dialectical topics and rhetorical topics, or between the thesis and the hypothesis, so that they could apply this understanding when they learned the two arts), comprehensive accounts of the divisions of knowledge had a role akin to that of a world map or the modern atlas: to give visible contours to a vast inheritance about the very nature of knowledge itself, so that it could be at once externally systematized and internally assimilated. Martin Grabmann speaks of the literature of classification as a form of reflection on the purpose and method of scientific endeavor,[2] and indeed these schemes represent a constant development and refinement of an epistemology or theory of knowledge rather than, necessarily, actual programs of study.[3]

The philosophical and pedagogical systems for classifying knowledge have their origins in ancient thought, and were transmitted sometimes directly, and more often through various mediations, to the Middle Ages.[4] In the *Metaphysics*, Aristotle laid out a division of knowledge or science into theoretical, practical, and productive, that is, the study of those things which are independent of us, those which depend upon us (because we effect change in them), and those which are produced by us.[5] For Aristotle, this was not intended as a program of study, but rather as a means of defining the nature of the highest science, theology or divine science, which takes as its object that which neither moves nor is moved. The schematic distinction between theoretical and practical sciences was transmitted to the Middle Ages chiefly by Boethius in his two commentaries on Porphyry's *Isagoge*, as well as in the iconic π (*practica*) and θ (*theoria*) woven into the hem of Philosophy's cloak in the *Consolation of Philosophy* 1 pr. 1. The threefold division into theoretical, practical, and mechanical (or productive) was also transmitted through Boethius' translation of Aristotle's *Topics*, where the three branches of knowledge are mentioned,[6] and, among various other sources, through Cassiodorus' *Institutiones* and Isidore of Seville's *Etymologiae*. In this system, the theoretical sciences comprised theology, mathematics (or the measuring sciences of the quadrivium), and the natural sciences; the practical sciences would include ethics, economics, and politics; and the productive sciences came to include "mechanical" arts such as building or navigation. A second classification scheme was

---

[2] Grabmann, *Die Geschichte der scholastischen Methode*, 2: 28.

[3] See Hadot, *Arts libéraux et philosophie dans la pensée antique*, 59, 136.

[4] Useful studies include: Hadot, "Les divisions des parties de la philosophie dans l'Antiquité"; Taylor's introduction to his translation of Hugh of St. Victor's *Didascalicon*, 7–19, and 161–2; Weisheipl, "Classification of the Sciences in Medieval Thought"; Dahan, "Les classifications du savoir aux XIIe et XIIIe siècles"; see also Kelley, ed., *History and the Disciplines: The Reclassification of Knowledge in Early Modern Europe*.

[5] *Metaphysics* 6.1–2 (1025b–1027a), 11.7 (1064b) and cf. book 2.1 (993b); cf. Plato, *Politics* 258e.

[6] *Topics* 6.6 (145a15) and 8.1 (157a10): for Boethius' translation, see *PL* 64: 978B and 996B.

descended from Stoic thought, which divided philosophy into logic, physics, and ethics.[7] Under this system, which received its medieval imprint in Isidore's *Etymologiae*, logic comprised rhetoric and dialectic, physics incorporated the quadrivium, and ethics was most often represented as the four cardinal virtues. Yet another system entered medieval discourse in the twelfth century through Arabic receptions of Aristotle's logical texts, known collectively as the *Organon*. This system divided the parts of logic as represented by each of the books of the *Organon*: *Categories*, *De interpretatione*, *Prior Analytics*, *Posterior Analytics*, *Topics*, and *Sophistical Refutations*. But to these six "categories" were added two further forms of "logical" inquiry represented by two other books by Aristotle, the *Rhetoric* and the *Poetics*.[8] This scheme of eight parts of logic placed rhetoric and poetics under the aegis of logic, so that they were understood as extensions of the tools of logic with their own particular syllogistic forms (the enthymeme and the "imaginative syllogism," respectively). Finally, underlying all the medieval epistemological schemes and their countless mutations was the simplest and most commonplace form of scientific classification, the seven liberal arts, or the trivium (arts of language, *artes sermocinales*) and the quadrivium (the arts of numerical measurement), which achieved its conventional form in late antiquity.[9] While the trivium and quadrivium together formed a coherent scheme for organizing knowledge, they were also easily detached from one another, like movable parts that could be adjoined to other systems. Indeed, as much as these schemes carried the weight of traditional authority, they were also plastic and mutable. For example, where a scheme, such as the Aristotelian division into theoretical, practical, and mechanical sciences, did not obviously make a place for the language sciences of the trivium, it could be adjusted, extended, or combined with another scheme in order to accommodate the crucial roles of grammar, rhetoric, and dialectic, as in Hugh of St. Victor's synthetic classification of theoretical (including the quadrivium), practical, mechanical, and logical arts (incorporating the trivium).[10]

But if these schemes were not used to prescribe specific courses of study, what function did they serve? Every iteration of a *divisio scientiarum*, whether part of an encyclopedic overview or explanation of a particular text, represents a claim to participate in a broad

---

[7] The doctrine is described in Diogenes Laertius, *Lives of Eminent Philosophers* 7.39; see Hadot, "Les divisions des parties de la philosophie," 208–12.

[8] See Walzer, *Greek into Arabic: Essays on Islamic Philosophy*, 129–36; Black, *Logic and Aristotle's Rhetoric and Poetics in Medieval Arabic Philosophy*, 17–51.

[9] See Hadot, *Arts libéraux*, 137–55 on Martianus Capella and the Neoplatonist thought that lies behind this structure of the liberal arts.

[10] *Didascalicon* 2.1; cf. Hugh's other division of the parts of logic, 2.28–30, where grammar (here seen as the study of words) is split off from the sciences of discourse (which concern understanding or reasoning); but dialectic and rhetoric are a subcategory of discourse under probable reasoning.

institutional power, which in turn can be given a concrete visibility through the outlines of the epistemology that stands for it. For example, a classification scheme may formally announce the outlook of a particular school, or at least a curriculum associated with a particular master, as in Thierry of Chartres' prologue to his *Heptateuchon,* which aimed to be a compilation of curricular texts on a grand scale, or John of Salisbury's magisterial defense of the role of the language arts and the teaching of the northern French cathedral schools, or Aquinas' representation of the divisions of logic in connection with a Parisian curriculum that led from the arts of logic to theology. But institutional power is more often an intangible entity: the power of learning, the authority of the classical legacy of the arts, and the notion of *translatio studii* or the transfer of learning from ancients to moderns, from the old centers of pagan learning to the cities, courts, and schools of Christian Europe, or indeed from Latin to vernacular. Brunetto Latini incorporates scientific classification into his Tuscan exposition of Cicero's *De inventione* in order to instruct his lay vernacular audience on the place of rhetoric within the divisions of philosophy. And the fifteenth-century Middle English text on the liberal arts wears its classical learning with enormous pride, even as it enacts a *translatio studii*—a transferring of knowledge—from academic or even bureaucratic Latinity to the wealthy merchant gentry of London, and reorients the traditional treatment of grammar to account for the pronunciation of sounds in the English language.

However, the power lies not just in being able to reproduce a scheme of knowledge that is invested with traditional authority, but in participating in the enterprise that such schemes represent: to theorize and understand cognition itself. This is perhaps why the simple scheme of the seven liberal arts is not always a satisfactory system for describing the interrelation of the parts of knowledge, even though the trivium and quadrivium are omnipresent in many guises in other schemes. Indeed, Aquinas has a remark on the insufficiency of this system for classifying the theoretical sciences.[11] The model of the seven liberal arts, ascending through the language sciences to the parts of the quadrivium, is sequential and progressive, but the relation between the parts is based more on contiguity (they are next to each other on a continuum) than on inherent similarities. Moreover, the system of the seven liberal arts emphasizes the individual art as a doctrinal totality (i.e. these are the rules of grammar, these are the rules of rhetoric), rather than the cognitive process involved in the art, the method of knowing it, and the ontological nature of the object to be known. We might see a response to these limitations in Thierry of Chartres' prologue to his *Heptateuchon.* Thierry speaks of two instruments of philosophy: under-standing, which is the province of the quadrivium, and expression in language of the truths

---

[11] Aquinas, *Expositio super librum Boethii de Trinitate*, ed. Decker, 167 (ques. 5, art. 1).

that have been understood, for which the trivium was devised. Here he applies a principle that can be traced back to late antique thought, that the arts of the quadrivium are instruments for the knowledge of eternal truths.[12] Thierry thus uses an inherited vocabulary about scientific order while also trying to resolve the question of how the arts are interrelated.

By contrast, the Aristotelian division into theoretical and practical sciences is a supple system for examining the nature of the object to be known, the relation of the knower to the object, and the method that is specific to each science.[13] Yet this system as it came down to the Middle Ages gives no place to the arts of language. While Aristotle's writings, especially the works of the *Organon,* give ample attention to the language disciplines, his division of the sciences into theoretical and practical did not make explicit provision for the language arts, in particular for grammar and rhetoric. Thus when later medieval authors using this system wished to take account of the language arts and extend the Aristotelian model to include them, the very structure of the model forced them to theorize the method, object, and even cognitive process of the *artes sermocinales,* that is, to reflect on the place of language within an analytical model of learning. Various twelfth-century schemes find a place for the language arts under a new category, eloquence, while another category, wisdom (*sapientia*), contains the traditional theoretical and practical sciences.[14] But Gundissalinus takes the category of *scientiae eloquentiae* (i.e. grammar, poetics, and rhetoric) and places it under practical science as a form of civil science, by which one organizes one's communication with all people. Moreover, for Gundissalinus, grammar is an instrument of philosophy, but not a part of it: it is an instrument for the teaching of philosophy, for without words, philosophy cannot be taught.[15]

The trivium can also be seen as a synthetic and dynamic unit of "logic" in which words, however treated, are linked to *logos* as reasoning. The notion that language and reasoning are unified is certainly essential to the Stoic understanding of "logic" as a division of knowledge. It is also implicit in Boethius' treatment of the topics of dialectic and rhetoric: the same reasoning is involved, but the two arts use different methods (the syllogism versus the enthymeme) and are aimed at different kinds of objects (the thesis versus the hypothesis). John of Salisbury's defense of the trivium as a methodological and curricular unity in his *Metalogicon* further articulates this outlook. This imperative, to see the arts of the trivium linked together as forms of reasoning, has its apogee in certain thirteenth-century

---

[12] Hadot, *Arts libéraux,* p. 99.   [13] Hadot, "Les divisions des parties de la philosophie," 205.

[14] See the examples in Dahan, "Notes et textes sur la poétique au moyen âge," 178, which reflect a tradition of Neoplatonist exegesis.

[15] Gundissalinus, within, p. 469.

schemes in which the division between theoretical, practical, and mechanical sciences is folded into an expanded and comprehensive system of the human sciences, and the theoretical (or speculative) sciences are now divided into two categories: the "principal" sciences, comprising the quadrivium, and the sciences that are "instrumental" to theoretical knowledge, comprising the trivium. This division is clearly based on an ancient and deeper distinction between things and words, wisdom and eloquence. In the thirteenth century, Giles of Rome elaborated such a scheme, just a few years after he wrote his commentary on Aristotle's *Rhetoric*.[16] But in his *Rhetoric* commentary Giles was moved to make a distinction within the trivium between dialectic and rhetoric in terms of the different motions of the intellect, on the part of the one reasoning, but also on the part of the auditor. Moreover, if rhetoric is also to be understood as a part of civil science (as Aristotle suggests), rhetoric must be distinguished from the science of politics in terms of what it actually produces: rhetoric creates reasoning, not political realities.[17]

In terms of tangible institutional power, classifying knowledge served to keep a curriculum intact, keep the arts apart when they threatened to blur, and determine the criteria for what should be considered competence in an art. To the extent that classification schemes perform these functions, they can be considered to have a normative force, establishing a curricular standard. Certainly the works of late antiquity and the early Middle Ages, exemplified here by Martianus Capella's *De nuptiis Philologiae et Mercurii*, Cassiodorus' *Institutiones*, and Isidore's *Etymologiae*, use the structure of scientific classification to erect encyclopedic defenses against the dispersal and loss of ancient learning (in the cases of Martianus and Isidore), or as a *translatio studii* from the pagan to the Christian imperium (in the case of Cassiodorus). Seen in this way, we can say that the classification scheme is used as a kind of library or other holding structure in whose empty compartments may be stored the archives of knowledge pertaining to each of the disciplines. This archival storage must be imagined as complete and unified, although also discrete in its parts. Its power lies in its claim to store and preserve what is already known, not to advance new knowledge. Of course the conservationist rhetoric gives such encyclopedic classifications the status of textbooks in themselves, so that they are not just keepers of the curriculum, but become authoritative components of later curricula.[18] Moreover, in

---

[16] For Giles' scheme and the dating of the text in which it is found, see Siemiatkowska, "Avant l'exil de Gilles de Rome: au sujet d'une dispute sur les 'theoremata de esse et essentia' de Gilles de Rome," at 48–63 ("Exposé sur les sciences"); and see the analytical chart produced in Dahan, "Notes et textes sur la poétique," 177; for other examples see Dahan, "Les classifications du savoir," 17–18.

[17] See Giles of Rome, within, p. 810.

[18] This is witnessed, for example, in the tradition of commentaries on Martianus Capella from the Carolingian period through the twelfth century.

storing the archives of disciplinary knowledge in discrete compartments (as in Martianus Capella's individual books each given over to the exposition of one art), the classification system can reinforce the differences among the arts, keeping separate their respective competences and therefore (at least implicitly) regulating the teaching of each art. Martianus Capella turns this perennial institutional question about who is competent to teach a given art into comic fiction when he has Minerva interrupt Grammar's discourse just at the point at which Grammar is about to take up tropes and figures, as well as rhythm and meter, that is, the point at which the grammarian's teaching might overlap with the fields of rhetoric and music. The "boredom" that Grammar's lecture on her art produces in the celestial senate, and the very elementary nature of her teaching, must not be allowed to overflow into the presentations of the other arts. Of course, it is precisely through such a dramatized enforcement of boundaries that the ulterior relationship between various arts becomes most visible. In some later medieval texts, in this volume notably Thierry of Chartres' *Heptateuchon* and Alexander Neckam's *Sacerdos ad altare*, we find a more elaborated model of disciplinary and curricular preservation in the actual presentation or listing of texts appropriate to each science. Thierry's compilation provided each art with its own library of primary texts, taking the notion of discrete disciplinary archives to its most ambitious extreme. Along similar lines, Alexander Neckam uses the structure of scientific classification in order to prescribe an ideal reading list for each art, substituting an idealized library of primary sources for the archive of knowledge about the discipline that we find in earlier classifications. Moreover, the *Sacerdos ad altare* presents its reading lists as a set of criteria towards mastery of the individual arts: to know certain texts is to know the art that they represent. As a curricular survey, the *Sacerdos ad altare* is close in spirit (if not in structure) to Hugh of Trimberg's *Registrum multorum auctorum* (Register of Many Authors), written in the late thirteenth century, which offers a complete initiation into the grammatical study of canonical authors. In a different vein, the *Bataille des VII ars* by Henri d'Andeli explores the real institutional consequences of allowing an older curriculum to be edged out by new science, as he places the old grammatical and literary curriculum of Orleans in combat with the newer, voguish, dialectical curriculum of Paris; the battle ends with Grammar retreating to her home in Egypt to bide her time, while Logic now holds sway.

The schemes of scientific classification are repetitive, in part because they represent a supposedly atemporal system, a discourse of universal truths about knowledge that is seen to be outside of historical change. But even though they are seen as atemporal—or perhaps because of this—the schemes are surprisingly flexible forms that lend themselves to different kinds of interests, that is, different philosophical influences and curricular outlooks, as we have seen. Their formulaic character also enables them to accommodate quite radical change under the pressure of new historical interests, even though the overall continuity of the schemes seems to disavow the mutability of history. Gower's treatment of the Aristotelian division of theoretical and practical sciences presents just such radical change, under the guise of absolute continuity with convention. Gower's treatment of the theoretical and practical sciences is thoroughly conventional. But between these two divisions he has created a third category called "Rethorique" (i.e. "Rhetorique" or Rhetoric), which contains grammar and logic "that serven bothe unto the speche" (line 1529). The exposition of this category is given over almost completely to rhetoric, that is, eloquent speech. Gower's innovation certainly recalls earlier attempts to find a place for the language arts within the Aristotelian scheme of theoretical, practical, and mechanical sciences: for example, as noted above, Hugh of St. Victor adds the category of "logical arts" which comprises the trivium, and other twelfth-century thinkers introduce the category of "eloquence" (or *artes sermocinales*). But Gower's change is quite different in its effects. Gower elevates the particular discipline of rhetoric to the status of an epistemo-logical category: rhetoric is not just a specific knowledge, but now a way of knowing, on a par with theoretical knowledge and practical knowledge. The motivation for this change can be found in earlier vernacular treatments of the sciences, especially Brunetto Latini's *Trésor*, where rhetoric as an instrument of civil science assumes new importance in light of the self-governance of the urban communes. Gower may not be imagining an Italian-style *vernacular* civic discourse in England; but his explosive revision of the scientific model reflects a new political reality in which vernacular culture must rely upon rhetoric to mediate between ethics and public affairs.

Finally, how is the project of scientific classification allied to literary thought? In antiquity, there was no doubt that the discipline that dealt with analysis of poetry was grammar, and in pedagogical practice this continued throughout the Middle Ages: poetry remained the object of grammatical explication. On the other hand, the twelfth and especially thirteenth centuries also saw a competing move within the art of grammar to look at language, not as literature, but as the object of logic.[19] This created an opportunity for a disciplinary practice filling the place of the "literary" on the theoretical level of scientific classification: poetics. We have already seen how the challenge of adapting inherited systems of classification to new interests invited medieval thinkers to consider how the language arts fit together. The repetition along with modification of traditional schemes produced further articulations of the relation between eloquence and wisdom or about the instrumentality of the language arts. Such new articulations also helped to make a new place for poetics in academic thought. We see this in the twelfth century, as in a

---

[19] See the following section of this introduction.

commentary on Porphyry that introduces the category *poesis,* separate from *eloquentia,* and gives its parts as the ancient poetic genres.[20] Of more significance, Gundissalinus gives two treatments of poetics as a department of knowledge: the first as part of an expanded "trivium," the "sciences of eloquence," which he places under practical science; the second in accordance with the Al-Farabian model of the logical sciences based on an extension of the Aristotelian *Organon* to include the *Rhetoric* and the *Poetics.* The extended *Organon* was taken up in thirteenth-century Aristotelian thought, as we see in Aquinas' prologue to his commentary on the *Posterior Analytics,* where poetics has a place under "inventive logic," along with dialectic and rhetoric. So important was the idea of poetry as a kind of logic that Hermannus Alemannus decided to translate the commentary of Averroes on the *Poetics* in order to complete the corpus of the *Organon.*[21] The idea that poetics belongs under logic gave rise to a large body of academic commentary and argument.[22]

But there is another dimension of the role of literary thought in scientific classification. Beyond treating questions specific to the category of poetics, scientific classification is itself a textual form that regulates approaches to other texts. For example, it lies behind the textual convention of the double prologue, the "extrinsic art" and the "intrinsic art," that accompanies many commentaries, as in Thierry of Chartres' exposition (from the 1130s) of Cicero's *De inventione* and the pseudo-Ciceronian *Rhetorica ad Herennium.* The "extrinsic" prologue describes the art in terms of its parts and its external attributes, including its relationship with other adjacent sciences: thus Thierry's extrinsic prologue gives the traditional definition of rhetoric as a department of civil science, and also considers whether rhetoric is a part of logic. The "intrinsic" prologue describes the internal characteristics of the art. Not only does the prologue determine the approach to a text: the prologue itself is a complex literary form that calls attention to its own parts and composition. Even without the apparatus of extrinsic and intrinsic prologues, we find that scientific classification can structure the entry into any kind of precept, even at fairly elementary levels. For example, John of Garland's *Parisiana poetria,* which is not a commentary but a preceptive manual, opens with a prologue in which John places his book in relation to grammar, rhetoric, and ethics. And even Hugh of Trimberg's elementary guide to the authors insinuates the structure of scientific classification into his introduction by distinguishing his grammatical teaching from the high-flown realms of dialectic and the advanced skills of law, suggesting that his own teaching pertains mostly to

---

[20]   *Ysagoge in theologiam,* ed. Landgraf, 70–3. It gives the genres satire, comedy, and tragedy.

[21]   Dahan, "Notes et textes sur la poétique," 178; Hermannus Alemannus, *Averrois expositio poeticae,* ed. Minio-Paluello, 41.

[22]   See Dahan, "Notes et textes sur la poétique," 193–239 for a series of texts that speak to this issue.

ethics, because the literary texts recommended here will instill good morals by example and counter-example.

Beyond these pedagogical adaptations, scientific classification lends itself to poetic construction. It provides a picture of a concept, a macro-structure; by its nature it is a kind of fictive form itself, an imagining of an integrated whole. For this reason, the most obvious and memorable poetic uses of scientific classification are those that emphasize an iconic value. Martianus Capella's *De nuptiis Philologiae et Mercurii* set the standard for medieval visual representations and literary personifications of the arts. The iconic status of the arts also finds its complex way into literary ekphrasis, for example, as mentioned above, in the π and θ woven into the hem of Philosophy's garment in Boethius' *Consolation of Philosophy*, or indeed in the depiction of the arts of the quadrivium which adorn Erec's beautiful cloak at the end of Chrétien de Troyes' *Erec et Enide* (6674–6731). The arts are also an architectural metaphor, as in Alcuin's *De grammatica* (ca. 790–800), which expresses the notion of the seven liberal arts as "seven pillars" or columns that support the house of Wisdom (and of course it is not far from architectural metaphor to the iconic embedding of the liberal arts in real architectural forms, such as columns and carvings).[23]

Just as they are "pictures" of a conceptual order, scientific classifications also have an architecture that can be charted, outlined, and schematized, like a narrative plot, a verse form, or a metrical scheme. Thus it is not surprising that we find it taken up as a key structuring device in mythographic and allegorical narratives. The Neoplatonist mythography of the twelfth-century schools had found in Plato's account of cosmic order in the *Timaeus* a way of using mythic narrative as a vehicle of scientific explanation. Bernardus Silvestris' *Cosmographia* personifies the epistemological categories of *Physis* (physics), *Theoria*, and *Practica*, making them the deputies charged with the task of creating a man. So also in this tradition, Alan of Lille's *Anticlaudianus* builds its allegorical plot around the idea that the human mind is formed in the image of the arts. The seven liberal arts are called forth in sequence to contribute their skills to the building of the chariot which will take Prudence to heaven where she will ask for a soul for man. Here the categories of science are not the object of explanation: rather, they have been incorporated into a mythography which is itself the instrument for explaining the cosmological truth of human formation in body and intellect. The macro-structure of scientific classification, its imagining of an integrated wholeness, provides the narrative system whereby an integrated cosmology can be rendered in its totality.

---

[23] See d'Alverny, "La Sagesse et ses sept filles: recherches sur les allégories de la philosophie et des arts libéraux du IXe au XIIe siècle."

Henri d'Andeli's *Bataille des VII ars* deals in a lighter vein with no less serious matters. Here the sciences (the seven liberal arts, but also some of the practical and mechanical sciences such as law and medicine) are realized in their actual institutional forms as teaching faculties or curricula in a state of conflict. Taking the allegorical form of a psychomachia, a war of opposing moral or spiritual forces, the poem positions itself in the historical moment of the early thirteenth century, when the study of dialectic at Paris reigned supreme, displacing grammar (the grammarians at Paris have gone over to the side of Logic, lines 93–6) and degrading rhetoric (which has become nothing but a subfield of law for the writing of legal documents, lines 68–74). Orleans, with its humanistic grammar curriculum, is at war with Paris, where logic dominates; the forces of Logic unhappily prevail over Grammar and her curricular forces. If the division of the sciences is a macro-structure, holding all epistemological categories and their disciplines in delicate suspension, its imagined unity also tends to conceal the historical conflicts among academic disciplines, as the reputations of masters and schools rose and fell. Henri's narrative is driven by the dynamic conflicts that are hidden within the static depiction of the sciences as a unified system. Its plot is not the unity of the sciences (as in the *Anticlaudianus*), but the dissolution of that unity under the various historical pressures of institutional prestige and power, academic fashion, and economic interest.

GRAMMAR: THE LOGIC OF LANGUAGE AND THE "READING ROAD"

John of Salisbury spoke of grammar as the "cradle of all philosophy."[24] The technical field of grammar was a foundation for explanatory systems of how language signifies and meaning is produced. Through grammatical theory, ancient and medieval readers could move from questions of signification to questions of meaning, from signs to semantics, and ultimately to questions of literary representation, that is, the relationship of poetic language to different kinds of truth, including the possibilities that the poetic language of Scripture offered to speculative theology. Because of its concern with signification, grammar was linked closely with the logical science of dialectic. In its turn, dialectic, which teaches how to determine true and false, was understood as a language science. For medieval thinkers, Aristotle's *De interpretatione* (*Peri hermeneias*), his logical investigation of language as a conventional system of signifying "mental impressions," provided a link

---

[24] *Metalogicon*, ch. 13; see within, p. 493.

between grammar as a science of correct usage and philosophical study of how knowledge of the world is signified through language. Thus John of Salisbury could also reiterate the notion that "logic" (for him, the trivium) is the science of verbal expression and reasoning. Rhetoric, too, traveled with dialectic, both being regarded as sciences of verbal reasoning which used the same fund of "topics" for the invention of arguments. Thus grammar and rhetoric were each understood to have a philosophical dimension; but equally, the whole of the trivium, that is, the three sciences of grammar, rhetoric, and dialectic, came to be known as the *artes sermocinales*, arts of discourse or speech.

In this section, we explore how grammar in particular was linked, often intimately, with the functions of logic, and how the questions of verbal signification that emerged from this linkage could open out into the broadest questions of literary representation. We consider how questions that were important to the logical analysis of language were also important to grammarians in their approaches to literary texts; conversely we also look at how the problems addressed by grammarians could inform philosophical investigations about the relationship between words and the mental operations of cognition, especially the link between words and mental images of things. We exemplify these questions by means of works that are included in this collection; but at the end of this section we also consider some philosophical and literary texts not in this collection in order to illustrate the broadest implications of grammatical thought about language and its "logic."

Up to the period of the speculative grammarians of the thirteenth and fourteenth centuries, the philosophical orientation of grammar was still also a textual orientation: the dialectical scope of grammar and philosophical commentary on grammatical teaching were framed within a larger context of application to spoken and written language, and especially of preparation for the reading of the authoritative texts of sacred and secular tradition. With the flourishing of speculative or modistic grammar in the universities of the thirteenth century, the interest in modes of signifying led to conceptual, ontological questions that no longer depended on speaking or writing or on the nature, structure, or usage of individual languages.[25] For the most part, these later developments of grammatical philosophy, in which grammar as a field of theoretical reflection decisively parts company with literary or

[25] Kneepkens, "The Priscianic Tradition," 251–2. In the fourteenth century, a critic of the modists still claimed that even if there were only concepts and no spoken or written languages, there would still be "grammatical government in men's mind and knowledge of grammatical government," quoted in Kneepkens, 252; Pinborg, "Some Syntactical Concepts in Medieval Grammar"; Pinborg, "Speculative Grammar."

textual concerns, lie outside the scope of the present volume. However, we have included some examples of speculative grammar in relation to studies on the ablative absolute,[26] and some of the commentaries on Priscian from the twelfth century included here look forward in certain respects to the later development of a fully modistic grammar.[27]

In antiquity, grammatical theory was not an independent discipline from the moment the Greeks became interested in language. In fact, technical grammar does not seem to have emerged as an independent discipline before the late second and first centuries BC. Before that time, however, many ideas about language were developed in different contexts: the interpretation of the poets and a philological interest in literary texts; the art of persuasive speech, stimulated by the necessity to persuade one's fellow-citizens in law courts and assemblies in democratic Athens; and finally, and arguably most influentially, in a philosophical context. Aristotle's heritage is a good example: in his work we often find ideas about language, but always in the service of his local philosophical interests.[28] That is why his logical study of propositions, *De interpretatione*, for instance, starts from an analysis of those linguistic elements that will feed into the construction of the proposition. Although this short section at the beginning of *De interpretatione* would arguably become the most influential passage in the history of linguistics, it did not start out *as* linguistics.[29] Aristotelian influence on the language arts did not start immediately, although in the Middle Ages it would overwhelm that of any other philosophical school. In antiquity, the philosophical ideas that would most penetrate later grammatical thought were those developed in the Stoa. To the Stoics, logic was one of the three parts into which they divided philosophy, while at the same time insisting that their philosophy should be considered a unity. Theories developed in one part may bear surprisingly direct relationships to those in the others. Logic itself was divided into rhetoric (continuous use of speech, as in oratory) and dialectic. Logic provided a complete analysis of "rational speech," the instrument by which to conduct philosophy, from phonetic aspects to semantics and

[26] See within, in the ablative absolute dossier, Siger of Courtrai on *modus significandi* and the gloss *Admirantes* on Alexander of Villa Dei.

[27] See within, the introduction to Part 3, and the selections from the gloss *Promisimus*. On this, see Fredborg, "The *Promisimus*."

[28] E.g. in his *Rhetoric*, he is interested in the analysis of persuasion, occasioning a study of prose style in book 3; in *Poetics* 1456b–1457a (section 20), he looks at language as the instrument of poetry, and analyzes eight parts in chapter 20—not parts of speech, but parts of the "expression"; in *De anima* and the *Historia animalium*, Aristotle attempts to demarcate the line between human speech and other sounds, including those made by animals.

[29] On discontinuities in the history of ancient linguistics, see Taylor, "Rethinking the History of Language Sciences in Classical Antiquity," and Schenkeveld, "Studies in the History of Ancient Linguistics IV: Developments in the Study of Ancient Linguistics."

epistemology. Dialectic was itself also divided into two parts: one dealing with form and sound (*phônê*, voice or sound), and one with meaning and signification (*sêmaino-mena*, "things signified"). This bipartition, and the emphasis on semantics, exercised a profound influence on later grammarians, and in all likelihood so did the systematic and hierarchical structure of the Stoic *Tekhnê peri phônês* ("*ars* on the formal aspects of language / on sound").[30] Importantly, however, while grammarians would take over terminology and basic orientation, they were under no compulsion to preserve the philosophical integrity of these ideas—and indeed they did not.[31] Stoic influence can be seen (with explicit mention of its provenance) in the Greek syntactician / semantician Apollonius Dyscolus (second century AD). It reached the Middle Ages in the authoritative form of Priscian's *Institutiones grammaticae*, which relied extensively on Apollonius Dyscolus. Priscian's definitions of the noun and verb, for instance, are a good illustration: the noun signifies substance and quality, the verb signifies action and being affected (i.e, "passion").[32]

But such a highly differentiated background—a mixture of Platonic, Aristotelian, Stoic, Hellenistic, and Alexandrian contributions—was not visible as such to the early medieval grammarians of the Latin West.[33] These post-classical grammarians saw in Priscian's text a clear and open route to the dialectical considerations that were familiar to them through their knowledge of Aristotle's writings on logic (which had come down to them through the Latin translations by Boethius). They read their knowledge of Aristotelian logic back into the grammatical theory they inherited from antiquity.[34] The parallels with their conception of dialectical studies were manifest to them. Both grammarians and dialecticians treated the noun and the verb, the difference being that grammarians regarded these terms as classes of words while dialecticians considered them in terms of the logical functions of subject and predicate in a proposition (as seen in the opening chapters of Aristotle's *De interpretatione*).[35] Grammar and dialectic covered the same territory,

---

[30] Note that this Stoic *Techne* is not a grammar; it is a philosophical treatise on language.

[31] By the time of the Roman empire, Stoic thought (especially their ethics) had become a part of the common knowledge of the educated. One did not have to be a Stoic to have some ideas that (originally) were Stoic. When dealing with later antiquity and especially the Middle Ages (when no independent Stoic sources were available any more) one should be very precise in defining what one means when labeling certain ideas "Stoic."

[32] See within, selection from Priscian.

[33] For a resumé of these traditions, see Irvine, *The Making of Textual Culture: Grammatica and Literary Theory*, 23–48.

[34] And thus they ran into trouble (cf. William of Conches' famous pronouncement, "Priscian's definitions are obscure"; see William of Conches within, p. 384) because there is no one-to-one match with Aristotelian ideas (the main philosophical provenance being Stoic—through Apollonius Dyscolus).

[35] Luhtala, "Early Medieval Commentary on Priscian's *Institutiones grammaticae*," 118; see also Luhtala, "'Priscian's Definitions are Obscure,': Carolingian Commentators on the *Institutiones grammaticae*," 57–63.

towards different but complementary ends: grammarians were concerned with correct speech, while dialecticians focused on precision and accuracy for the sake of logical arguments.[36] It is to Alcuin (ca. 730–804) that we probably owe the revival of interest in Priscian's *Institutiones grammaticae* and the parallels between grammar and dialectic implicit there.[37] In his *De grammatica*, Alcuin introduced the Priscianic definitions of the parts of speech, with their philosophical vocabulary derived from the Stoics, alongside earlier Roman grammatical definitions, and supplemented these in turn with definitions taken from Boethius' commentary on Aristotle's *De interpretatione*: "[Teacher]: It is characteristic of a noun to signify a substance or a quality or a quantity... The noun is a sound with arbitrary [i.e. conventional] meaning, without tense, signifying something definite in the nominative, when it *is* or *is not*, e.g. 'man is,' 'man is not.'"[38] The seeming obscurities or inconsistencies in Priscian's definitions prompted early medieval grammarians to master dialectical techniques in order to explicate his grammatical doctrine.[39] Alcuin was to take such concerns further when, in his own treatise on dialectic, in his definition of the term *interpretatio*, he attributed to the noun and the verb an extraordinary ontological value, such that these two parts of speech truly signify all substance and all action.[40]

Carolingian commentary on Priscian developed an extensive system of philosophical elaboration, using dialectic to provide typologies of definitions, or applying the Aristotelian categories to the parts of speech. The apogee of such philosophical interest in grammar is the sophisticated commentary on Priscian by the ninth-century scholar John Scotus Eriugena.[41] We also find such interests reflected in the anonymous gloss (included in this volume) representing Carolingian thought about syntax, which shows the influence of Aristotelian thought about combined expressions or propositions (the tradition descending from the *De interpretatione*).[42]

But the other dimension of grammar that was always complementary to linguistic logic is the powerful notion of written language as the "road of reading." Priscian etymologizes

---

[36] Law, *Grammar and Grammarians in the Early Middle Ages*, 138.

[37] Law, "Linguistics in the Earlier Middle Ages: the Insular and Carolingian Grammarians;" *Grammar and Grammarians*, 82–3, 136–7.

[38] See Alcuin, within. On the complex history of the philosophical vocabulary behind Alcuin's uses of Priscian (Alcuin's attempt to reconcile a known Aristotelian vocabulary with the puzzling character of Priscian's Stoic-derived vocabulary), see Luhtala, " 'Priscian's Definitions are Obscure,' " 57–63.

[39] Law, *Grammar and Grammarians,* 138; Luhtala, " 'Priscian's Definitions are Obscure.' "

[40] *De dialectica, PL* 101: 972D, in a passage based on Isidore, but elaborated. See Luhtala, " 'Priscian's Definitions are Obscure,' " 62–3.

[41] See Eriugena in Dutton and Luhtala, eds., "*Eriugena in Priscianum.*"

[42] See within, the gloss from Paris BN MS lat 7501 p. 310.

litera ("letter") as *leg-iter-a*, the "reading road": "The letter is the smallest part of a compound sound, i.e. sound that consists of the combination of letters; it is 'the smallest' with reference to the whole complex made up of a literate sound...It is called *litera*, " 'letter' either as a *leg-iter-a*, 'reading-road,' because it provides a path for reading..." This derivation is reiterated in Isidore of Seville.[43] The derivation is certainly linked to the fact that literature (not logic) was the oldest domain for the study of language, and that grammarians were not just "guardians of language"[44] but "guardians of literature." Along these lines, Martianus Capella spins a series of tropes on letters, literature, the *litteratus* or man of letters, and writing *litterate* or in a skillful literary style.[45] Early commentators did not lose sight of the relevance of their linguistic concerns to spoken and written language: for example, the tenth-century scholar Remigius of Auxerre, commenting on Priscian's *De nomine pronomine verbo*, insists upon the relationship of technical grammatical knowledge to eloquence itself, distinguishing between the general notion of "language," in which there can be "deficient" forms, and "eloquence," that is, "copiousness of expression" (or alternatively, "ornamented speech," "exuberant facility of speech"), in which there can be no deficiency. And Remigius' explanation of why the names of letters are indeclinable develops an elaborate image of the letters as unmovable (that is, uninflected) "foundations of the arts."[46] Remigius himself was an indefatigable commentator on secular and Christian texts whose attention to literary detail (notably in his commentaries on Martianus Capella and Boethius) contributed to the long-lasting popularity of his work.

Thus the philosophical dimension of grammar worked in concert with textual analysis. Indeed, the very process of commenting on a grammatical or rhetorical author, even towards the most abstruse philosophical purposes, would be conceived first as an exercise in literary analysis. In this respect, then, theories of language are themselves the products of textual exposition: from a medieval standpoint, a theory of signification *emerges* from the careful exposition of a grammatical text, and would then be adduced in resolving difficult passages in other secular and sacred texts. In this way, the *artes sermocinales* provided a metadiscourse: they enabled scholars to construct the apparatus for analyzing systems of meaning, and such construction began with attention to the textual articulation of the art itself.

The high point of grammatical "logic" in the twelfth century is of a piece with sustained application to literary exegesis of philosophical, mythographical, and scriptural texts.

---

[43] See within, pp. 173, 179 of Priscian text and Isidore of Seville, p. 235.

[44] An appellation made famous by the title of Kaster's book, *Guardians of Language: The Grammarian and Society in Late Antiquity*.

[45] See within, Martianus text, p. 154.

[46] See Remigius within, pp. 308; cf. Isidore of Seville, within, p. 235: letters were invented to "tie things down."

In his commentary on Priscian, written during the first half of the twelfth century, William of Conches describes a threefold curriculum based on study of the authors: *genus didascalicum*, that is, instruction; *genus dramaticum*, debate along with question and answer among equals; and *genus enarrativum* or *hermeneuticum*, discourse to an audience.[47] This threefold curricular division is clearly based on the contemporary terminology for the genres of literary narrative: dramatic, hermeneutic, and didactic.[48] Exposition of Priscian's grammatical thought according to scientific methods based on the logic of Aristotle, Porphyry, and Boethius would take place within this generous curricular structure.

Some of the most interesting theoretical discussions about the nature of linguistic usage found their application in explaining theological discourse.[49] For example, William of Conches, commenting on Priscian's description of the relation of relative pronouns to their antecedents, analyzes the phrase "woman who damned [the world] saved [the world]," a phrase that had already been used by Abelard to illustrate the formal logical structure of certain more difficult kinds of propositions involving relative pronouns, a notion that logicians began to treat under the classification *relatio simplex*. But William's treatment of the problem is more literary than philosophical, even though he shows himself to be fully acquainted with the dialectical backgrounds of this problem.

> [At Priscian, *Institutiones grammaticae* 17.5.30: "If a nominative is joined to a nominative, the verbs refer to the same person, as 'the man who wrote, came.'"]: But some would say this is false, because we may find the phrase "woman who damned [the world] saved [the world]"; and yet the same woman did not damn and save the world. To such people we respond either that the sacred page is not subject to any art, because it is the queen of the arts, or that this expression is figurative. The sense of it is this: the same sex damned and saved. And so here the noun "woman" names the [female] sex, not a person.

William suggests how a more flexible, indeed ingenious, understanding of figurative expression may bring the grammatical usage of a pronouncement into accord with theological principles. What the logicians, pursuing questions of universals, would analyze under the technical problem of *relatio* (the term "woman" and its relative pronoun denote different persons, but the relative pronoun refers back to the antecedent's general or *simplex* meaning, the class "woman"), the grammatical commentator treats as a figurative

---

[47] Reilly, ed., introduction to Petrus Helias, *Summa super Priscianum* 1: 15.

[48] See within, John of Garland, *Parisiana poetria*, p. 655.

[49] Kneepkens, "The Priscianic Tradition," 242. See also Evans, *The Language and Logic of the Bible: The Earlier Middle Ages*, 85–7; de Rijk, *Logica modernorum: A Contribution to the History of Early Terminist Logic*, II.i: 221–63.

expression in which the two "women," Eve and Mary, who damned and saved the world respectively, are two types of womanhood or the female sex.[50] Ralph of Beauvais' commentary on Donatus' *Ars minor* (from the later part of the twelfth century) can also serve to illustrate the application of grammar to theological discourse. Ralph presents a grammatical solution to a crucial passage in Scripture which had apparently presented readers with problems. In a discussion of the noun and its various "accidents," Ralph addresses a question on the comparative form in the verse at 1 Corinthians 13,13: *horum autem maior est caritas* (but the greater of these is charity). Can *maior* (greater) govern the genitive *horum* (of these)? He acknowledges that this presents a problem for the rules of the comparative, but he rejects emending the text to read "but greater than these." Instead, his solution is to propose that the word actually governing the genitive is "charity," because here the genitive is being used to "distinguish" charity from the other two virtues.[51]

Grammatical theory has its *raison d'être* in reading, as William of Conches points out: "the knowledge of construing is necessary for the correct exposition of the authors."[52] Grammar, logic, and rhetoric may be seen as three divisions of the genus of eloquence, of which grammar concerns "how to write correctly for the enlightenment of those who are not present and to make men's recollection more enduring, and to know how to pronounce corrrectly that which has been written, in order to enlighten those present."[53] But alternatively, grammar may be seen to belong to the genus of logic: it is "logic applied through the medium of words. One form of logic is that which works through reason, the other that which works through words... [I]t is the task of the grammarian to lead his pupil towards the construction of a sentence. But it is the task of a logician to define and divide a sentence."[54] The desire to know the absolute nature of grammar is a response to

---

[50] "Sed dicerent hoc esse falsum cum inveniatur 'mulier que dapnavit salvavit', nec tamen eadem mulier dapnavit et salvavit. Quibus respondemus vel quod divina pagina ut domina arcium nulli arti subiacet, vel quod illa locutio sit figurativa. Est enim sensus illius: idem sexus et dapnavit et salvavit. Et sic hoc nomen 'mulier' ibi est nomen sexus, non persone." Jeauneau, "Deux rédactions des gloses de Guillaume de Conches sur Priscien," 240. This is one of various interpretations of Priscian's rule at 17 V. 30. ("Si nominativo nominativus adiungitur, ad eandem personam verba referuntur: 'homo venit, qui scripsit'"). On the use of this famous example in twelfth-century discussions of the *relatio simplex* or *relatio generalis* see Kneepkens, "'Mulier quae damnavit, salvavit': A Note on the Early Development of the *Relatio simplex*," and for the development and clarification of this principle in later grammatical and logical thought, Kneepkens, "The *Relatio simplex* in the Grammatical Tracts of the Late Twelfth and Early Thirteenth Century."

[51] Ralph of Beauvais, *Glose super Donatum*, ed. Kneepkens, 10.

[52] See within, William of Conches, p. 389. For further examples of the application of grammatical theory to interpretive questions in literary texts, see within, selections from Servius on Virgil, Ralph of Beauvais' *Liber Tytan*, and the texts excerpted in the ablative absolute dossier.

[53] See within, William of Conches, p. 386.   [54] See within, William of Conches, pp. 387–8.

the imperatives of logic. But alongside this, there is the grammatical-literary commentator's desire to explain the text of the *auctor* (whether a literary author or even a textbook author such as an ancient grammarian) with the greatest accuracy:

> Since grammar takes priority in all learning, we have made it our topic to talk about it, for, although Priscian says enough at a later point, yet he gives obscure definitions and does not explain them, and he omits the "causes of invention" of the different parts and of the different accidents within each part... So we have made it our topic to say what has not been said by them, to expound what they left obscure.[55]

Grammatical theory, even when applied to literary criticism, was everywhere permeated with the most fundamental logical questions of substance and accident, matter and form, what can be expressed and what is meant, signification and reference, ambiguity and equivocation. Logicians such as Peter Abelard and Gilbert of Poitiers mined the dialectical vein of Priscian's *Institutiones* while grammatical commentators such as William of Conches and Petrus Helias (mid twelfth century) integrated this specialist field into a broader approach to language;[56] although Petrus Helias is not primarily interested in literature when he writes his vast *summa* on Priscian, he does insist on separating grammar and logic, when affirming that the grammaticality (correct usage) of a sentence is not the same as its being true or false. The early-twelfth-century *Glosule* on Priscian determine in the most finely calibrated ways how substance inheres in a verb, and therefore how the difference between a noun and a verb allows us to understand the difference between signifying substance in itself (noun) and substance that coheres with action (verb); the *Glosule* similarly show how ontology infuses every pronouncement when they address the status of the "substantive" verb "to be," asking whether such "being" is a substance or an action.[57] Such grammatical-logical thought presupposed the referential function of language, that language was part of a chain of reference from word to concept to thing, or from sign to another sign to an extra-linguistic reality.[58] Such concerns had also been at the root of Augustine's numerous statements about signification: words are signs instituted by convention to signify things or sometimes to refer to other signs that designate things (for example, *nomen* can mean "noun," that is, the part of speech by which something is

---

[55] William of Conches, *Philosophia mundi*; see within, p. 384.

[56] See de Libera and Rosier, "La Pensée linguistique médiévale" (note especially the material on the twelfth century); and Pinzani, *The Logical Grammar of Abelard*, 7–10.

[57] *Glosule*, in William of Conches, pp. 379–82.

[58] The idea of the referential function of language does not diminish even in late medieval modistic grammar, although the application to written language and literary texts is no longer crucial.

named, and it can also mean "name").[59] Thus Augustine too had believed that grammar needs dialectic, which is the science of disputation about things, so that one can move beyond discourse about words to discourse about things, including the nature of language itself.[60] It is in light of such long-held assumptions about language as a referential tool that we should understand how grammatical theory was seen to support the very unity of the arts. As Thierry of Chartres tells us in his majestic introduction to the *Heptateuchon*, that which can be known by studying the arts of the quadrivium will be expressed elegantly and clearly through the arts of the trivium. This theme recurs throughout medieval thought about the language sciences.[61]

The understanding of language in terms of its referential function opens out into questions about the mechanics of representation. Logicians were not directly or primarily concerned with poetic ("artistic" or "fictive") representation; but the question of how words relate to things led commentators on logical texts to consideration of the status of fictive (or "imaginative") constructs that mediate between the things that we perceive and the language that we use to express thought. Thus the questions that were addressed in grammatical thought also took hold in discussions of logic, especially where there appeared to be a natural "bridge" between the concerns of the one discipline and the other. This was the case with the reception of Aristotle's *De interpretatione*. Aristotle's logical analysis of linguistic structure in this text—his analysis of how meaningful expressions are formed—provided a fruitful opportunity for thinking about the referential and representational functions of language, because of the importance Aristotle attaches to the notion of (spoken) words as symbols of "mental impressions" or "impressions in the soul," which are, in turn, the images of things. For Aristotle, as his medieval commentators recognized, language produces meaning by conventional imposition of signs on universal mental operations, not directly on reality.[62] The challenge was to clarify and

---

[59] *De doctrina christiana* 2.1.1–3; *De magistro*, ch. 4; cf. *De dialectica*, chs. 5–10. On the incorporation of Augustinian sign theory into later medieval conjunctions between semiotics, theology, and logic, especially in the thought of Roger Bacon, see Rosier, *La Parole comme acte: sur la grammaire et la sémantique au XIIIe siècle*, chapters 3–4.

[60] *De dialectica*, ch. 5 and see notes in Jackson, trans.; see Amsler, *Etymology and Grammatical Discourse in Late Antiquity and the Early Middle Ages*, 44–55, esp. 51.

[61] See Fredborg, "The Unity of the Trivium."

[62] Aristotle's *De interpretatione* and later commentaries on it, including those by Boethius and Abelard, are brought together in Arens, trans., *Aristotle's Theory of Language and its Tradition*. See Sluiter, "The Greek Tradition," 188–200; Amsler, *Etymology and Grammatical Discourse*, 34; Kretzmann, "Aristotle on Spoken Sound Significant by Convention."

define the nature of those mental operations. The commentaries on the *De interpretatione* by Boethius and Abelard attempted to explain *passiones in anima* or mental impressions and their relation to the words that we use. Boethius and Abelard thus elaborated theories of cognition in which the process of reasoning or conceptualizing must be differentiated from the sensory apprehension of things. In the course of their commentaries, they emerge into discussions of "imaginative" representation that have striking parallels in rhetorical and hermeneutical writings, and ultimately in poetic thought about mimesis.

Boethius attempts to clarify what Aristotle meant by "mental impressions" by differentiating this carefully from "imaginations, which the Greeks call *phantasias*,"[63] and in the course of his commentary he introduces a vocabulary of representation and mental imagery that is shared with rhetoric, psychology, and the art of memory. Mental concepts (to which words refer) cannot come into being, Boethius asserts, without *imaginationes* (imaginations or images); according to Boethius, an *imaginatio* (a mental image, associated with the mental faculty of processing what is taken in by the senses) is a *prima figura* (a "first outline"), just like the outlines or archetypes (*lineae*) that painters first make of their subjects.[64] As he goes on to explain, to understand a thing one must first receive in the imagination the "form" and "property" (*forma, proprietas*) of that thing; the mental impression created from this form is like an *impressio figurae*, the "imprint of a figure," or indeed it is a *similitudo*, a "likeness" of the thing. It is "settled and stored in the seats of the mind" (*posita et in mentis sedibus conlocata*).[65] Here Boethius develops a program of mental representation by drawing on a language familiar from rhetorical teaching about composition and memory: mental archetypes, figures, and forms, and even the notion of locational "storage" in the mind, which conjures up associations both with the rhetorical theory of invention from "places" (*topoi, loci*) or "seats" (*sedes*) of argument, and teaching about the "seats" or "places" of memory.[66]

---

[63] Arens, *Aristotle's Theory of Language*, 168.

[64] Arens, *Aristotle's Theory of Language*, 169; Boethius, *Commentarii in librum Aristotelis Peri hermeneias*, 29. On the Neoplatonist backgrounds of *imaginatio* in Boethius' commentary, see Watson, *Phantasia in Classical Thought*, 153–5.

[65] Arens, *Aristotle's Theory of Language*, 172–3; Boethius, *Commentarii*, 34–5. For the background to this notion of "likeness" in Aristotle's treatments of perception, both in the *De interpretatione* and in the *De anima*, see Sluiter, "The Greek Tradition," 192–3, and Denyer, *Language, Thought, and Falsehood in Ancient Greek Philosophy*, 185–206.

[66] On *lineae* see Carruthers, *The Book of Memory*, 129, 147, 347 note 3; on *formae*, 180, 251, 346 notes 76, 77, and see also "memory: images" in the index; on phantasia and *imaginatio*, see Carruthers, *The Craft of Thought*, 14, and for an excellent introduction to the "seats" of memory, 10–46. See also Eden, *Poetic and Legal Fiction in the Aristotelian Tradition*, 85–96.

Abelard's commentary on the *De interpretatione* adds more force to this vocabulary, heightening the resonances with the art of memory, as if taking a cue from the suggestions in Boethius' commentary. Abelard elaborates the notion of mental images that are stored in the mind, what he calls an "effigy [*effigies*] of the thing which the mind devises, even after the thing is removed or completely destroyed," by invoking the instruction on the art of memory in the *Rhetorica ad Herennium*: "Tullius, writing on memory in the third book of the *Rhetorica ad Herennium*, calls these effigies of the things which the mind forms for itself instead of the real things so as to contemplate the latter in the former, images, forms, signs [*notae*], semblances [*simulacra*] of the things."[67] By way of comparison with Plato's notion of the incorporeal forms that existed providentially in the divine mind before they were embodied, Abelard introduces one of the great commonplaces of the arts of invention and memory, the metaphor of the architect:

> ... because [just as] an architect who is going to build a house, before he begins to work, conceives an imaginary house in his mind equal to the one he wants to build, so Plato has spoken in a human way of God's providence, showing that he composed this world not improvidently, but deliberately and with premeditation, after the first picture that was only in his mind...[68]

The metaphor of the master-builder has a long history in Christian mnemonics and hermeneutics, handed down from a key text in St. Paul ("as a wise master-builder, I have laid the foundation, and another buildeth thereon," 1 Corinthians 3:10), and linked back to the architectural mnemonics of ancient rhetoric. Abelard's contemporary, Hugh of St. Victor, gave the metaphor one of its most influential uses in the *Didascalicon*, where the master-builder is shown stretching out his measuring line, his *linea*, which is compared with the internal archetype or diagram, the outline or *linea*, with which the reader of Scripture must begin.[69] Perhaps Abelard was developing Boethius' comparison of *imaginatio* or similitude with the painter's "outline" (*linea*) of the person.[70] Abelard pursues the notion of mental images as *formae* or archetypes through a series of extraordinary similitudes: one who is going away from Rome keeps "an image of the city in his mind,

[67] Arens, *Aristotle's Theory of Language*, 238–9; Abelard, *Die Glossen zu Peri hermeneias*, 314. William of Champeaux, one of Abelard's teachers in Paris, lectured on the *Ad Herennium*, and is probably the author of one of the earliest extant commentaries we have on it and its precepts on the art of memory. See Carruthers, "Rhetorical *memoria* in Commentary and Practice," and Fredborg, "The Commentaries on Cicero's *De inventione* and *Rhetorica ad Herennium* by William of Champeaux."

[68] Arens, *Aristotle's Theory of Language*, 239; Abelard, *Die Glossen zu Peri hermeneias*, 314.

[69] *Didascalicon*, book 6, chapter 4; cf. Gregory the Great, *Moralium libri*, PL 75: 513C.

[70] Carruthers, *The Craft of Thought*, 16–24; see also Carruthers, "The Poet as Master-Builder: Composition and Locational Memory in the Middle Ages."

in which he contemplates the faraway city"; in the mind's eye one remembers a tower that one has seen, even if it has been completely destroyed, in its "immense, high, and quadrangular likeness," which is not substance but rather a mental form, a representation; and a statue of Achilles must refer us to some meaning, either Achilles as a person, or the fact that it is a statue, an "effigy." These illustrations culminate in the idea that such mental images, like the effigy of Achilles, are "intersigns," which we use to form concepts of the things to which our words refer. Thus representations have a curious intermediate status between sensory apprehension and concept: they are nothing in themselves, but they are necessary to the process of forming the concepts that our words generate about particular things.[71]

Boethius and Abelard deploy the vocabularies of mnemonics, textual hermeneutics, and even literary composition in order to explain why making images is necessary to the faculties of cognition that find meaningful expression in propositions. Theirs is the approach of logicians: they examine the relationship of words to mental images from the perspective of logic. Arguments about the cognitive value of images also took shape in studies of ethics, theology, natural science, and cosmology.

But such arguments also have important corollaries in medieval poetic thought about the cognitive nature of image-making, the necessary role of integuments or fictive constructs in human understanding. As a summation of such thought we may look to one medieval poetic text that achieved the status of "literary masterpiece" in the grammatical curriculum, Bernardus Silvestris' *Cosmographia*, from the middle of the twelfth century. The teacher Gervase of Melkley regarded the *Cosmographia* as an exemplary text because it illustrated a wealth of grammatical teaching about compositional principles such as ornamented language and beautiful structure.[72] While it is not a theoretical text about grammar per se, it brings together many of the themes about language, cognition, reasoning, and representation that, as we have just seen, could play out in grammatical thought. The *Cosmographia* is an allegory that offers an apotheosis of mimesis, in which human poetic artifice is understood as an extension or reflection of divine making. It describes the creation of the world and of the human being in terms derived from the vast tradition of Plato's myth-making in the *Timaeus* and the medieval commentaries on its divine and natural philosophy, as well as from other late-antique and early medieval

---

[71] Arens, *Aristotle's Theory of Language*, 238–42; Abelard, *Die Glossen zu Peri hermeneias*, 313–16. For further references, see Luscombe, "Peter Abelard"; for philosophical background, see also Pasnau, *Theories of Cognition in the Later Middle Ages*, 254–89.

[72] Kelly, *The Arts of Poetry and Prose*, 57–68; see within, Gervase of Melkley, p. 609.

Neoplatonist writings.[73] In the course of this extraordinary text, in which allegorical poetics and philosophical argument are virtually inextricable from one another, Bernardus describes how the goddesses Urania and Physis are assigned to make the human soul and body respectively, and how Natura is to conjoin soul and body. Each goddess is given her own special instrument: a *monumentum*, a token or means of recognition, of the divine plan for her particular task, which she can contemplate as an *aide-mémoire* while she performs her creative labors. For the goddess Physis, who must create the human body and mind, the model is the "book of memory" (*liber recordationis*), which is written, not with ordinary letters, but with "marks and signs." The book of memory, we are told, is nothing but the intellect applying itself to things and summoning memory, basing its understanding often on true reasoning but more often on probable conjecture. The book of memory contains a shadowy summary of Providence and Destiny (the tools provided to the other goddesses), but a clear visual record of the embodied world of creation.[74] This is not only an image of the divine plan for the creation of humanity: it is also an image of the human mind which Physis is going to produce, just as she creates the human being by taking as her model a "similitude" or likeness of the greater universe.[75] The human mind is so constructed that images of things (*imagines rerum*) can easily impress themselves on the brain through a soft and liquid covering. Within the skull are three chambers comprising the mental functions: at the front, *fantasia* or imagination receives images, which it transmits to the reason; memory is located in the back chamber, where it will not be constantly invaded by new images; and reason's chamber is placed between the two, where it can impose judgment on both imagination and memory.[76]

This picture of the mind and its processing of images is not just the making of a myth or the poetic imaginary. It is a moment of highly self-conscious mythopoesis in which the poetic, figurative terms of Bernardus' own allegory are fully implicated. It is an imagining

---

[73] On sources and background of the *Cosmographia*, see Bernardus Silvestris, *Cosmographia*, ed. Dronke, 70–91; *The Cosmographia of Bernardus Silvestris*, trans. Wetherbee, 29–34; Silverstein, "The Fabulous Cosmogony of Bernardus Silvestris."

[74] *Cosmographia*, ed. Dronke, 144; *The Cosmographia*, trans. Wetherbee, 116–17; Dronke, *Fabula : Explorations into the Uses of Myth in Medieval Platonism*, 122–6.

[75] *Cosmographia*, ed. Dronke, 148; *The Cosmographia*, trans. Wetherbee, 121.

[76] *Cosmographia*, ed. Dronke, 149; *The Cosmographia*, trans. Wetherbee, 122; On literary and philosophical sources for the mind as three chambers, see Silverstein, "Fabulous Cosmogony," 97–8; Wetherbee, *Platonism and Poetry in the Twelfth Century*, 94–7, 116–18. On the medieval history and use more generally of "imagination" as a mental faculty see Kelly, *Medieval Imagination: Rhetoric and the Poetry of Courtly Love*, 26–56; Carruthers, *The Book of Memory*, 46–71. These issues are explored in the treatise by Robert Kilwardby, *De spiritu fantastico* (On Imagination): see Kilwardby, *On Time and Imagination: De tempore, De spiritu fantastico*, ed. Lewry, trans. Broadie.

of the very conditions of poetic making or the production of images. Poetic making is not just artifice: on the poetic logic of Bernardus' allegory, it is organic to the functioning of the mind. The image-making of the book of memory is the divine plan from which Physis fabricates and constructs the image-making faculties of the human mind. The mind is "hard-wired" to produce representations, and by extension, to produce poetic representations, as Bernardus' own philosophical "making" about mimesis argues. Behind such an expression of the signature principles of poetic theory lies a tradition of logical inquiry into the nature and function of language as the system that signifies the mind's formation of concepts out of images. The logic of language lays the foundation for other functions of the language sciences, and is always immanent, in some form, to medieval literary explorations of how textual meaning is produced.[77]

FIGURATIVE LANGUAGE IN GRAMMAR AND RHETORIC

Grammar and rhetoric shared the study of the figures and tropes. Earlier in the Middle Ages, the definitions of the figures and tropes derived from the grammatical tradition of Donatus' *Ars maior*, but by about 1100 commentators and teachers had begun to make more use of a rhetorical source, book 4 of the *Rhetorica ad Herennium*.[78] For both arts, the figures and tropes constituted the territory for the treatment of style. But while rhetorical theory treated the figures and tropes under stylistic ornamentation, grammarians from Donatus onwards treated them under departures from normal usage, that is, under or along with "faults" of style such as solecisms and metaplasms. Despite this crucial distinction, it was generally understood that this body of knowledge is common to both disciplines: for example, in his influential account of rhetoric, Isidore of Seville sends his readers back to his chapter on grammar for definitions of many of the figures of speech. Each of these models of textual figuration, in grammar as deviation from orthopraxis, and in rhetoric as outward enrichment or embellishment, demands further examination on its own terms. In light of this analysis we can arrive at some larger understanding of how each

---

[77] See, for example, Irvine, "Medieval Grammatical Theory and Chaucer's *House of Fame*," which considers how Priscianic theory on voice or *vox* lies behind Chaucer's exploration of words, rumor, and fame. On logical categories and narrative technique, see Hunt, "Aristotle, Dialectic, and Courtly Literature."

[78] On the ascendancy of the *Ad Herennium* as an authority on the figures and tropes, see Camargo, "Latin Composition Textbooks." However, the shift from grammatical to rhetorical sources is not always clear-cut: for example, the definition of metaphor in Matthew of Vendôme's *Ars versificatoria*, ca. 1175, derives from grammatical sources (see 3.18–24; and see within, p. 569 n. 55).

discipline exerted control over what its practitioners considered to be the nature of poetic language, and from that to how each discipline understood the status of poetic fiction.

The third book of Donatus' *Ars maior*, known from the ninth century on as the *Barbarismus* because of its first word, treats grammatical deviations as well as figures of speech and tropes. The main divisions of grammatical deviations or "faults" (*vitia*) of style are barbarism and solecism, which come under the grammarian's task of teaching correct usage, and metaplasm and figures, which are in reality the calculated or "poetic" deployment of barbarism and solecism.[79] This represents a double attitude towards language: inadvertent error as opposed to controlled and deliberate distortion for the sake of a certain stylistic effect.[80] But whether reflecting ignorance or enabling poetic effect, these forms are all regarded as departures from normal usage.[81] Tropes too are deviations from proper or dominant meaning or application of words, although Donatus' definition stresses "transference" or "carrying over" from proper meaning rather than the original Greek idea of a "turning" (*tropos*):[82] "A trope is a word [*dictio*] 'transferred' [*translata*] from its proper signification to a likeness that is not its own, for the sake of ornamentation or necessity."[83] The definitions of metaphor and allegory similarly emphasize movement "away" from something. Metaphor is defined in terms that recall systems of logical predication: "Metaphor is a transferring of things and words. This occurs in four ways: from animate to animate, from inanimate to inanimate, from animate to inanimate, from inanimate to animate."[84] Donatus' definition of allegory as a deviation in verbal meaning was influential: "Allegory is a trope in which something other than what is said is

[79] Donatus, *Ars maior* 3.1, *GL* 4: 392.5–6: *Barbarismus est una pars orationis vitiosa in communi sermone. In poemate metaplasmus*; 3.2, *GL* 4: 394.23–4: *Soloecismus in prosa oratione, in poemate schema nominatur.* See Baratin and Desbordes, "La 'troisième partie' de l'*ars grammatica*."

[80] Holtz, *Donat et la tradition de l'enseignement grammatical*, 147–50.

[81] Ibid., 148; Grondeux, "Les Figures dans le *Doctrinale* d'Alexandre de Villedieu et le *Graecismus* d'Évrard de Béthune."

[82] On the history of the trope within Stoic thought, see Holtz, *Donat et la tradition*, 199–201, and on Donatus' recasting of "turning" into "carrying over," 202; the background is studied in depth by Barwick, *Probleme der stoischen Sprachlehre und Rhetorik*, 88–97; and see also Irvine, *The Making of Textual Culture*, 104–7, 247–50. See Holtz, "Grammairiens et rhéteurs romains en concurrence pour l'enseignement des figures de rhétorique," and Schenkeveld, "Figures and Tropes: A Border Case between Grammar and Rhetoric." See also within, introduction to Part 1.

[83] *Ars maior* 3.6, *GL* 4: 399.13–14: *Tropus est dictio translata a propria significatione ad non propriam similitudinem, ornatus necessitative causa.*

[84] *Ars maior* 3.6, *GL* 4: 399.17–19; cf. Aristotle, *Poetics* 3.21, 1457b ("the transference being either from genus to species, or from species to genus, or from species to species, or on grounds of analogy" [trans. Bywater, in *Complete Works of Aristotle* 2, ed. Barnes]). But where Donatus' grammar preserves a philosophical structure, this disappears from the rhetorical definition in *Rhetorica ad Herennium* 4.34.45.

signified . . . It has many species, among which seven stand out: irony, antiphrasis, enigma, charming politeness, proverb [*paroemia*], sarcasm, humor [*astismos*]."[85]

The grammatical notion of the figure as deviation is richly thematized in later medieval thought about poetics. The grammatical treatise *Doctrinale* (1199) by Alexander of Villa Dei had given a great deal of attention to the figures of speech, helping to make it a very popular teaching text. Expounding the section on figures in the *Doctrinale*, a thirteenth-century commentary known as the *Admirantes* gloss offers its own series of explanations for the term *figura*. The glossator recognizes that the grammatical term itself is metaphorical, the product of various possible "similitudes":

> All words that transpose themselves do so with reference to a certain likeness. But "figure" in nature [i.e. a form, a shape] has been transposed to "figure" in grammar.[86] So the question is: on account of what likeness did this transference come about? Some say that the word "figure" is used in grammar because of a likeness to form [*figura*] in natural and man-made objects, because just as a form, whether it is natural or made by artifice, conceals the baseness of matter, so there are reasons that justify such a mutation (in speech), as if it were a kind of decorousness or veil over improper or faulty diction. Others say that "figure" is used here by likeness to a semicircular figure, construed over the straight diameter line, and so delimited:[87] for, just as in a figure of this sort there is something straight, like the diameter line, which is intrinsic in some way, and there is something curved ["oblique"], like the circumference of a semicircle, which is extrinsic in some way, so in every figurative speech there is a straight element, which is intrinsic when one looks to the meaning, and there is a curved ["oblique"] element, which is extrinsic when one looks to the word or to the primary arrangement of the words or to the primary signification.[88]

In this geometric model, the meaning or reference is unchanged by the outward curvature of the figure of speech. We can see what is at stake here when we compare it with the mid-twentieth-century New Critical model of "tenor" (basic idea) and "vehicle" (the figure itself). New Criticism would see the meaning of a poetic figure generated through a "transaction between contexts," that is, the exchange between tenor and vehicle.[89] In contrast, the medieval grammatical model sees an intrinsic "rectitude" that governs the extrinsic deviation. The meaning has been established and fixed prior to the figurative

---

[85] *Ars maior* 3.6, *GL* 4: 401.26–30.   [86] I.e. "figure" is itself an example of a figure, or figurative speech.

[87] *disposite tali modo*, i.e. the ends of the diameter line go as far as, but not beyond, the circumference of the circle. Cf. Adelard of Bath's translation of Euclid's *Elements*, book I, definition xvii: "*diametros circuli recta linea est supra centrum eius transiens . . . extremitates suas circumferentie applicans . . .*" H. L. L. Busard, *The First Latin Translation of Euclid's Elements commonly ascribed to Adelard of Bath* (Toronto: Pontifical Institute of Mediaeval Studies, 1983), 136f.

[88] Quoted in Thurot, *Notices et extraits*, 460.   [89] Richards, *The Philosophy of Rhetoric*, 95.

deviation. The *Admirantes* gloss suggests a certain spatial likeness between semantics and geometric form: the external word can curve away from an established, intrinsic meaning in the same way that an outer circumference curves away from the inner rectilinear base.[90]

But the notion of grammatical deviation can also be rendered in moral rather than spatial terms. In Alan of Lille's *De planctu Naturae* (Plaint of Nature), written in the middle of the twelfth century, the term "fault" or *vitium* comes to life through one of its own common tropological usages, "sin" or "vice." The weeping poet-narrator bemoans certain sexual crimes against nature, which are represented as violations of the laws regulating the language sciences, especially grammar:

> Gramatice leges ampliat ille nimis.
> Se negat esse virum Nature factus in arte
> Barbarus. Ars illi non placet, immo tropus.
> Non tamen ista tropus poterit translatio dici;
> In vicium melius ista figura cadit.[91]

He over-extends the laws of grammar. A barbarian [or (living) barbarism] in the art of nature, he denies that he is a man. Art does not please him, trope does.[92] But that trope cannot be called a metaphor; better to say that this figure sinks into vice.[93]

Gloss as we will, the exact nature of this "crime" does not reveal itself readily, so dense is the thicket of playful, academic allusion in which the laws of grammatical gender are mapped—ambiguously—onto the sexual "laws" of nature, and in which the Donatan grammatical "vices" or faults, from barbarism to figure or trope, are invoked as if their names already stood for the moral dimension of *vitium*. The "likeness" between grammatical and sexual vice that Alan's wordplays conjure up must rest on the idea of deviation from orthopraxis which is inherent to grammatical theories of figuration. In other words, the likeness between grammatical and sexual "vices" lies in their common "otherness," their unlikeness to their respective orthopraxes.[94]

---

[90] In this derivation of *figura* from likeness to geometric forms or figures, there may also be some reminiscence of the status of geometry itself as the science of forms in their most true and proper sense. See, for example, Cassiodorus, *Institutiones* 2.5.11, on geometry: "geometry is the theoretical description of forms and the visible proof of philosophers" (ed. Mynors, 150).

[91] Ed. Häring, meter 1, lines 20—4; our translation (reflecting a slight modification in the punctuation suggested by Häring for the clauses).

[92] I.e. in grammar, as in nature, he "tropes."

[93] Metaphor is not a *vitium* or "fault" of grammar, because it is a permitted deviation; thus this trope cannot be called a "metaphor," but rather is a "vicious" turning: it "falls into vice" and "falls under the vices/faults [of usage]."

[94] Compare Alan of Lille's description of scriptural language in the preface to his *Distinctiones*, *PL* 210: 687–8; see Valente, "Langage et théologie pendant la seconde moitié du XIIe siècle."

In rhetoric, the terms of figuration, especially of tropes, relate less to the individual word (*dictio*) than to the expression (*sermo*) more broadly understood. Quintilian is clear about the effect of tropes: the trope changes not just individual words, but the conception and nature of the composition, adding new force.[95] Of course, since ancient rhetorical treatises often took their basic definition of figures and tropes from the grammarians, this cannot always be an absolute distinction.[96] But even where definitions of figures and tropes are similar, rhetoric and grammar will approach figurative language in fundamentally different ways, because the arts have radically different orientations. Rhetoric is an architectonic system: it looks at large structures, at the composition as a whole from conceptual plan to its realization in the orator's delivery of the speech, and at the effects of discourse on the audience. Rhetoric treats figurative language under style or *elocutio*, as the third component of the production of a discourse, after invention and arrangement, and before memory and delivery. This continuum of instruction simulates the stages in which a composition would come into being, from inception to public presentation. Rhetorical instruction aims at generating and completing the verbal artifact, and the position of *elocutio* in the continuum marks the point at which the work nears completion (at least as a mental construct).[97] By contrast, the movement of grammatical instruction is towards correctness of usage, and the order of grammatical treatises simulates the order in which linguistic precept is mastered. Thus the placing of *vitia* (including licensed poetic deviation) at the ends of grammatical treatises, as in Donatus' *Ars maior* and Alexander's *Doctrinale*, follows on the presumed mastery of correct usage. But whereas grammar, in its drive towards correctness, treats the figures and tropes last as a form of deviation from correctness, rhetoric, in its drive towards completeness, treats figurative style as the last of its compositional components or canons, as if to suggest that the edifice under construction is now ready for its surface, its outer walls, its uppermost layers.

But rhetorical ornament is not extrinsic in the sense of being an afterthought or unnecessary addition. This is despite the fact that it is regularly spoken of as clothing,

---

[95] *Institutio oratoria* 8.6.1–2; Holtz, *Donat et la tradition de l'enseignement*, 201–2.

[96] See Holtz, *Donat et la tradition de l'enseignement*, 201. The difference between *dictio* and *sermo*, rendering Greek *lexis* and *logos*, is not always firm, and *sermo* can be an ambiguous term; see Holtz, 139–40.

[97] It is important to keep in mind that classical rhetorical instruction aims at delivery of an oration which has been composed mentally, from inventing (discovering) the argument to arrangement to verbal style (*elocutio*), but which will be actualized (not recited or read) in oral presentation by drawing on the techniques of memory and delivery. Thus in classical teaching, the oration has only a hypothetical existence until it achieves public delivery. When rhetorical theory is applied to written compositions, as in the medieval arts of poetry and prose, the sequence of instruction, from invention to arrangement to style, can have a much closer correspondence to the stages in which the composition actually emerges, from finding material to ordering it and committing it to writing.

or as beautiful surface or form (for example, a complexion), or appropriate decoration.[98] Such metaphors about metaphor and other verbal ornaments (tropes, figures of thought, and figures of speech) have made *elocutio* an easy hostage to rhetoric's fortunes, an obvious focus of ambivalence about rhetorical artifice.[99] As the surface of composition, *elocutio* is the most visible part of the rhetorical process, and sometimes (as if on the order of the trope synecdoche) figuration seems to stand for the art of rhetoric as a whole, as we see especially in late medieval representations of the art: in his *Fall of Princes* (1430s) John Lydgate speaks of rhetoric as "sugared language," and more effusively Nicolaus Dybinus, the teacher of grammar and rhetoric in mid-fourteenth-century Prague, commends rhetoric as a queen clothed in the golden raiment of pleasing eloquence.[100] Seen in this way as surface, *elocutio* can fall victim to philosophical condemnations of exteriority and superfluity, and to moral condemnations of appearance, either in the sense of deception or the sense of beauty for its own sake. However, its real place in rhetorical thought is not as an artificial surface but rather as the completion of a process of artifice that begins with the conceptual orientation of invention and the division of argument into its parts and culminates in the technical control of effective language.[101] Even the "faults" of style are understood in relation to the necessity of figurative device: according to the *Rhetorica ad Herennium*, the *vitia* of style represent either the insufficiency or excess of good effect, never the deviation from a norm.[102]

The most obvious place to look for the tropes and figures is in the arts of poetry of the early thirteenth century and the teaching of what commonly came to be known as the

---

[98] See, notably, Geoffrey of Vinsauf, *Poetria nova*, introduction: "Let the art of poetry come to clothe the matter with words."

[99] This ambivalence can already be found in classical rhetoric, with its concern to link wisdom with eloquence (as in the influential opening sections of Cicero's *De inventione*); it is a recurrent theme in Augustine's writing, for example *De doctrina christiana* 4.10.24. For an overview of early Christian suspicion of rhetoric as eloquence, see Cameron, *Christianity and the Rhetoric of Empire*, 15–88. John of Garland deploys this theme in one of his model letters in the *Parisiana poetria* (5. 147–61): "True love knows not how to be painted in the ornaments of words and brilliant figures, knows not how to spread paint over plain soil . . . I go along on the path of this decision, writing to you rather in the open air of truth than in the shade of vanity, by no means under the mask of a Ciceronian tongue a hunter after artifice, but an embracer of Christian integrity, free of the subtleties of dissimulation" (trans. Lawler, *The Parisiana poetria of John of Garland*, 91, 93).

[100] Lydgate and Dybinus, pp. 855, 825 within.

[101] See Quintilian, *Institutio oratoria* 8.3.1 and sq.: "But ornamentation of speech contributes no small thing to the argument as well" (8.3.5). Quintilian's account gives perhaps the most explicit attention to the culminative role of verbal ornament. Compare Cicero, *De oratore* 1.31.142 on the five parts of rhetoric.

[102] *Rhetorica ad Herennium* 4.8.10–4.13.18. The difference between rhetorical and grammatical fault can readily be seen in John of Garland's *Parisiana poetria*: John puts the two kinds of fault together in one section towards the end of the treatise, but he also marks the distinction between faults of style, derived from the *Ad Herennium* or the later Horatian commentaries, and the faults of language, which are based on Donatus' grammar. See also Kelly, *The Arts of Poetry and Prose*, 143.

rhetorical *colores*.[103] The arts of poetry assign the figures a clearly compositional function in the rhetorical sense. Their position in the manuals indicates that they generate meaning or complete a technical process (or both). They are used as devices of generating meaning when they appear under the heading of "amplification," which is a stage in the process of developing inherited literary material by transforming it stylistically.[104] In Geoffrey of Vinsauf's *Poetria nova* (ca. 1208–1213) the eight devices of amplification of material include six figures of diction and thought.[105] John of Garland's *Parisiana poetria* (1231–1235) places amplification and embellishment under his treatment of invention, and lists seven figures (six of diction, one of thought) through which one approaches the question of "how" one invents. Matthew of Vendôme's *Ars versificatoria* (ca. 1175) treats the stylistic device of *descriptio* (vivid description) as a form of topical invention (drawing on the Ciceronian inventional scheme of attributes of the person).[106] Matthew also offers an extended account of the relation between the "inner sweetness" and the outer adornment of poetry. Under various rubrics, the treatises typically devote a section to embellishment on its own terms. The teaching of the *colores* reaches an apex in the late Middle Ages, in the work of masters like Nicolaus Dybinus, who offers a systematic theory and practice of the tropes possibly aimed at advanced students.[107] Dybinus is the inheritor of the earlier arts of poetry (his work is imbued with the influence of Geoffrey of Vinsauf, on whose *Poetria nova* he wrote a commentary): for him, rhetoric is nothing less than magnificent speech that imposes determinate form on raw matter. Where he goes beyond his early medieval predecessors is in what he calls his "theoretical speculation about the colors of diction and ideas": to understand the workings of a trope is to gain a purchase on the operations of language itself, from its logical content to its material form and to its persuasive or rhetorical purpose.[108]

---

[103] The term "colors of rhetoric" (*colores rhetorici*) came to stand in more regularly for *figurae et tropi* or *schemata* after the eleventh century, during the period when there was a shift from the use of Donatus' *Barbarismus* as the source of information to *Ad Herennium*, book 4. The mid-eleventh-century treatise by Onulf of Speyer is entitled *Colores rhetorici*; and by the late twelfth century, the use of this term is widespread. The fact that the term *colores* is typically modified by *rhetorici* may be a sign of the ascendancy of the *Rhetorica ad Herennium*; while that work uses the word *exornationes* as the term for verbal ornaments, it also compares *exornationes* to *colores* (4.11.16). We are grateful to Martin Camargo for his suggestions on this question.

[104] Kelly, "La Spécialité dans l'invention des topiques," 104; Kelly, *The Arts of Poetry and Prose*, 64–8; Woods, "In a Nutshell: *Verba* and *Sententia* and Matter and Form in Medieval Composition Theory."

[105] Cf. Geoffrey's *Documentum de modo et arte dictandi et versificandi*, ed. Faral, *Les Arts poétiques*, which presents amplification through various figures as one of the primary devices of composition, followed by stylistic embellishment through "difficult" and "easy" ornament.

[106] For this view of Matthew's approach, see Kelly, *The Arts of Poetry and Prose*, 71–2.

[107] See within, Dybinus, *Declaracio oraciones de beata Dorothea*, pp. 830–3.

[108] Jaffe, "Commentary as Exposition: The *Declaracio oracionis de beata Dorothea* of Nicolaus Dybinus."

Grammar and rhetoric present different orientations to the role of figurative language: in grammar it is deviation from a proper "norm" of "correctness" and "proper words," and in rhetoric it is amplification of form and meaning. These orientations carry over, broadly speaking, to each discipline's perspective on the nature and production of poetic fiction as a whole. As we will show here, grammatical thought provides the terms for theories of what fiction does as a special kind of representation and deviation from truth. Rhetorical theory, on the other hand, is concerned with the form that representation actually takes: the generic and stylistic properties of texts, the artifice and effect of structure. In other words, the grammatical orientation can be said to define what poets do in terms of the standards of what is truth and what is fiction; the rhetorical model presents a complementary vision of how poets accomplish their aims, in a generative sense. We should not see these as merely parallel perspectives: they are mutually reinforcing, along the same lines that grammatical and rhetorical thought continually inform each other. They interact in producing an understanding of fiction as a total enterprise.

Writing in the fourth century, the theologian (and former rhetorician) Lactantius took up the question of whether the fables of poets should be considered lies, and produced an influential formulation which extends the grammatical notion of figurative language to fiction as a whole. Perhaps rather surprisingly, he claims that poets (in this case, the mythographers of pagan antiquity who wrote stories about the gods) do not lie, but rather are "licensed" to refigure truth according to what is, in fact, their function: "it is the office of the poet to transpose events that really happened, and turn them with a certain elegance into other appearances, using oblique figures."[109] On Lactantius' terms, poetic fiction does exactly what individual figures and tropes do: it "turns" the events of history along an oblique or curved line away from their proper form into other representations (*in alias species*). Understood in this way as an "oblique" mode of discourse, fiction is not necessarily false, but it turns away from truth.[110] Like the poetic figure of speech in grammatical teaching, fictive deviation is "licensed," the *modus poeticae licentiae*. Poetic fiction is not really made up (*fictum*): "something is perhaps transferred (*traductum*) and obscured by oblique figuration in which an enfolded truth is hidden."[111]

---

[109] *Divinarum institutiones* 1.11, *PL* 6: 171B; or see the critical edition with French translation by Monat, *Institutions divines* 1. The idea is repeated in Lactantius' *Epitome institutionum divinarum*, chapter 11.

[110] Zeeman, "The Schools Give a License to Poets," 157. The present discussion of "licensed deviation" in poetic figures and poetic fiction is greatly indebted to Zeeman's essay. On this passage in Lactantius and comparison with similar attitudes to poetic fiction in Augustine's *City of God*, see Demats, *Fabula*, 50–4; and see also Chinca, *History, Fiction, Verisimilitude*, 74–5.

[111] *PL* 6: 171B–2A.

Lactantius' formulation of poetic office was taken up by Isidore of Seville and many later writers, including Vincent of Beauvais, Pierre Bersuire, and Boccaccio.[112] The notion that it is poetic license to render things obliquely takes the grammatical view of tropes as deviation from the proper and enlarges it to a whole epistemology of fiction as refiguration, "re-presentation." Indeed, from this perspective, the very theory of literary representation itself would seem to trace its roots back through grammatical thought about linguistic deviation. Such is the etymological journey of *fictio* or *fictum* and *figura*, both derived from *fingere*, to make, to fashion, but also to devise, feign, and represent. The grammatical notion of deviation from the proper admits the slipperiness of language, its ambiguity and multiplicity, even though the proper meaning is not changed by the oblique figuration. Like the figure, poetry is neither correct nor incorrect, neither truth nor lies.[113]

So we move from figures and tropes as forms of grammatical fault to a notion of poetry as a deviation from, or sometimes ambiguation of, a proper signification. In this we also move from focus on individual words which have deviated from their meaning to the architectonics of fiction. So powerful were these explanatory models of figuration and fiction that they were also brought to bear on theological discussions of the nature of scriptural discourse. It should not be surprising to find that medieval theorists mapped grammatical and rhetorical notions of figures and tropes onto theological categories of truth and reality, for as we have already seen, theologians regularly deployed the vocabularies and explanatory structures of the *artes sermocinales* when interpreting the mysteries of scriptural language.

But Scripture presented a very challenging case, because it was understood to be singularly invested with the capacity to signify both through words and through things. It required successive theoretical innovations to explain the nature of figurative language in Scripture. In his treatise on schemes and tropes (early eighth century), Bede makes one of the earliest and most important theoretical contributions to the history of the notion of allegory, in his distinction between "verbal allegory" and "factual allegory" (*allegoria in verbis, allegoria in factis*) in Scripture. In the former, a verbal expression without literal or historical meaning must be interpreted figuratively to yield a historical or spiritual truth; in the latter, an event in Scripture will be read to refer to another historical or spiritual reality beyond itself.[114] This distinction between allegory of words and allegory of events in

[112] Isidore, *Etymologiae* 8.7.10; Vincent of Beauvais, *Speculum doctrinale* 3.110; Pierre Bersuire, *Reductorium morale* (ed. J. Engels, 3 vols., [Utrecht : Rijksuniversiteit, Instituut voor Laat Latijn, 1960–6], prologue [1: 1]); Boccaccio, *De genealogia deorum gentilium*, book 14, chs. 9 and 13. See also von Moos, "*Poeta* und *historicus* im Mittelalter."

[113] Zeeman, "The Schools Give a License to Poets," 161–2.   [114] See Bede, within, pp. 269–71.

Scripture had purchase especially among twelfth-century exegetes: we find an extensive reformulation of it in the *Allegoriae super tabernaculum Moysi* of Peter of Poitiers, Chancellor of Paris (d. 1205).[115] But on the other hand, Thierry of Chartres seems to collapse the distinction between verbal and factual allegory, when he glosses the rhetorical definition of allegory (*permutatio*) in the *Rhetorica ad Herennium* by means of an example that Bede uses for factual allegory: "*Permutatio* is the arrangement of words in their proper meaning, but through which meaning the signification of another thing emerges, as in this example: 'It is written that Abraham had two sons: the one by a bondwoman, the other by a free woman.' By 'Abraham' the one who wrote these verses intended, that is signified, God, and by 'two sons' the Jewish and gentile peoples."[116] On the terms of Thierry's definition here, the verbal trope "allegory" seems to be no different from a figuration of one event through another.

Thomas of Chobham, however, approaches this problem systematically, synthesizing different theoretical sources in his *Summa de arte praedicandi* (ca. 1220) in order to clarify the distinction between secular and sacred, literary and theological, approaches to figuration.[117] Under the heading of "the mode of signifying in theology," Thomas presents an account of the signification of words and things, drawing from Augustine's *De doctrina christiana* and twelfth-century thought on the nature of scriptural discourse, especially Hugh of St. Victor's *De sacramentis* and *Didascalicon*. He shows himself to be aware of contemporary studies of grammar and of sign-theory, citing Aristotle's *De interpretatione* as well as examples of non-verbal signification.[118] Making a strong distinction between the concerns of secular language arts, which deal with the significations of words, and of theology, which deals with the signification of things as well as words, he is able to differentiate clearly between the level of verbal figuration in Scripture and the level of mystical signification of things (the moral, allegorical, and anagogical senses). Here Thomas also appears to add further clarification to earlier discussions of the kinds of literary narrative that we may encounter in Scripture—*fabula, argumentum* or realistic fiction, and history—drawing on a tradition that goes back to narrative classifications in Ciceronian rhetoric.[119] On the authority of Macrobius, he asserts that *fabula* has no more place in Scripture than in philosophy. *Argumentum* can be found in the form of parables. But the harder question is history, which is sometimes told directly by words that correspond to the thing (*analogia*), and sometimes metaphorically. Peter of Poitiers had

[115] *Allegoriae super tabernaculum Moysi*, ed. Moore and Corbett, 100–1.
[116] See Thierry of Chartres, within, p. 438.   [117] See Thomas of Chobham, within, pp. 617–18.
[118] See Evans, "Thomas of Chobham on Preaching and Exegesis."
[119] *Ad Herennium* 1.8.13; *De inventione* 1.19.27. Cf. Peter of Poitiers, *Allegoriae super tabernaculum Moysi*, ed. Moore and Corbett, 100.

proposed a distinction between "metaphorical" and "allegorical" history (through words and things) which left some obscurity in its wake, because verbal allegory could be the same thing as metaphor.[120] Thomas resolves such obscurity by separating verbal signification entirely from the signification of things, and reserving allegory for later treatment under theological meanings. History can be presented through proper or literal speech, in which the statement corresponds with the fact. This, he tells us, is the domain of grammar and dialectic, which "govern words in their proper significations, in the meanings they are instituted to signify." But "metaphorical" history works figuratively. Thus expressions such as "A thistle [of Lebanon] sent to a cedar tree" are to be read as metaphor, yielding up a historical or moral truth, as long as we understand the principles of the trope. Metaphor is the domain of rhetoric, "because rhetoric teaches how to transform words from their proper significations to non-proper meanings by various colors of discourse." And finally, when he moves to consider the theological categories by which things signify other things, he adds a clear distinction: "And here, tropology is interpreted in a different way than we saw earlier, when we spoke about transumption of a historical narration. In the present case, the tropological level [i.e. moral sense] is where night signifies sin and day signifies virtue." Thus Thomas of Chobham deploys an understanding of the language sciences on their own terms, whereby, as he sees it, grammar and dialectic deal with a stability of meaning, and rhetoric governs the ambiguation of meaning. In this way he captures the literary and linguistic properties of Scripture as separate from the sacred *realia* of Scripture. That he assigns to grammar the domain of "proper" meaning (and thus literal historical narrative) is consistent with the grammatical treatment of figurative speech as deviation (permissible or not) from a norm.

RHETORIC, POETICS, AND THE FORMS OF FICTION

Poetry was the object of choice for grammatical analysis: grammarians dealt with the given text, its devices of image-making, and its alteration of the proper or the true. But how does fiction or poetry achieve its power of representation in formal terms? How does the process of figuration or deviation take on form, such as a beginning, middle, and end, or the contours of genre? Rhetorical thought about composition establishes the architectonic principles of form that representation takes. Here we consider several types of formal

---

[120] *Allegoriae super tabernaculum Moysi*, ed. Moore and Corbett, 101, and see introduction, xx–xxiii.

analysis associated with rhetoric, from the structure and organization of a text to the classificatory principles of genre itself.

At first glance, *dispositio* or arrangement, the second component of rhetoric, might seem to be the part of rhetorical theory most concerned with structure and organization. But in classical rhetorical teaching, invention, the first component of rhetoric, also proceeds through division and ordering of parts, that is, the elements of the oration itself: exordium, narration, partition, proof (confirmation), refutation, peroration. Cicero's *De inventione* begins its instruction with a section on what is known as "status" theory (the *constitutiones* or "issues" of the case), which will entail questions of fact, definition, genus, or legal process (1.8.10–1.14.19). But at the heart of Cicero's theory of invention lies the structure of the speech itself, for each section of the speech requires the devising and marshaling of certain kinds of arguments based on understanding the case from different structural perspectives. Thus the overall characteristics of a case (strange, scandalous, difficult) may be handled through insinuation in the exordium. But the most important divisions of the oration, proof and refutation, are the sites for the exercise of rhetoric's most technical procedure: invention through rhetorical topics, that is, the *circumstantiae* or attributes of the person and the act (1.24.34–1.52.98). The complexity of this structural system allows for some variation of its treatment from one manual to another, and some amplification of its terms. Thus, for example, Boethius' *De topicis differentiis* insists that each of the five canons of rhetoric must be in each of the divisions of the oration, because the elements of the discipline must inhere in each of the instruments of the discipline.[121]

This architectonic principle, invention understood through the division of the parts of the oration, finds various expressions in post-classical and medieval treatments of rhetoric. We call attention to two distinctive examples in this volume. In Tiberius Claudius Donatus' *Interpretationes Vergilianae* (Interpretations of Virgil), the principle becomes a strategy for critical reading of a canonical text. According to Tiberius Claudius Donatus, Virgil's inimitable art must be understood as an art of rhetoric, and specifically the master genre of late antique rhetoric, epideictic. The poem is to be read as a consummate example of encomium, an oration in praise of Aeneas. This requires no small skill on Virgil's part, because Aeneas has many faults, having lost a war, fled his country and kingdom, and suffered the enmity of gods and men. The excellence of Virgil's skill in praising Aeneas despite such deficiencies is revealed by discovering in the poem the subdivisions of a speech, so that Virgil is seen to advance the case of Aeneas by expert distribution of arguments across the "parts" of the

---

[121] Boethius, *De topicis differentiis*, within, p. 197; another important example of variation is the teaching of status theory in the *Ad Herennium*, where this subject is treated under the two main parts of the oration, proof and refutation: see *Rhetorica ad Herennium* 1.10.18–2.18.27.

"oration" (exordium, partition, narration and proof, and refutation). In the early twelfth century, Rupert of Deutz used the divisions of the oration as a hermeneutical and scientific program. In his encyclopedic *De sancta trinitate* (On the Holy Trinity), Rupert presents an account of rhetoric (along with the other liberal arts), in a grand attempt to show how the human sciences are the work of the trinity. In this chapter, his aim is to discover the principles of technical rhetoric in Scripture, so as to show that Scripture contained the human sciences before secular (or pagan) teachers ever drafted surveys of the arts. The precepts of rhetorical invention may be discovered by reading Scripture as if it contains and illustrates all the parts of the oration through which the process of invention takes shape. Thus the beginning of Rupert's treatment of rhetoric follows the pattern of instruction in book 1 of Cicero's *De inventione*, but with the added dimension of a hermeneutical objective: not only will Scripture illustrate the stages of inventing arguments according to the individual parts of the oration, but the principles of technical rhetoric serve in turn to illuminate the discursive power of Scripture.

In classical rhetorical theory, formal structure is the apprehension and realization of the matter of a speech. Thus Quintilian introduces his treatment of arrangement (*dispositio*):

> But just as it is not sufficient for those who are erecting a building merely to collect stone and timber and other building materials, but skilled masons are required to arrange and place them, so in speaking, however abundant the matter may be, it will merely form a confused heap unless arrangement be employed to reduce it to order and to give it connexion and firmness of structure.[122]

Form is thus the manifestation of thought. Quintilian uses the metaphor of building an edifice in order to suggest how the artifice of form is part of the technical process of discovering and devising arguments. When this outlook is translated into later theory, especially about poetic composition, we see how the articulation of form is treated as a dimension of representation, not as a separate process. We have already seen how medieval writers used the metaphor of the architect in association with cognition through images, and this is how the mental planning of the architect is identified with the process of invention, as most famously in the opening of Geoffrey of Vinsuaf's *Poetria nova*.[123] But even in Geoffrey's brief opening allusions to the process of invention, the metaphor impinges on arrangement: "When, in the recesses of the mind, order has arranged the matter . . ." In other words, representation as both mental cognition and as articulation of form is seen as product of a technical construction.[124]

---

[122] *Institutio oratoria* 7 pr. 1.   [123] See Geoffrey of Vinsauf, within, p. 596.
[124] Compare also metaphors of military *taxis* or arrangement of troops: *Ad Herennium* 3.10.18, from whence Thomas of Chobham, within, p. 633.

Allied to the architectural metaphor is the image of the well-arranged text as a harmonious, well-proportioned body. Again, Quintilian's approach to arrangement in the *Institutio oratoria* can serve as a *locus classicus*:

> For the fact that all the limbs of a statue have been cast does not make it a statue: they must be put together; and if you were to interchange some one portion of our bodies or of those of other animals with another, although the body would be in possession of all the same members as before, you would none the less have produced a monster. (7pr. 2–3)

This gives us the linkage between arrangement and decorum, a principle whose expression derived in large part from the tradition of Horace's *Ars poetica*, whose opening image of a monstrous body, made up of the parts of human, horse, bird, and fish, was a touchstone for medieval poetic arts. Such poetic precept about decorum was conveyed to the Middle Ages through commentaries on Horace's *Ars*. Among the many glosses and commentaries on Horace's *Ars*, the "Materia" commentary of the mid twelfth century is particularly important for its presentation of the faults or violations of structural and stylistic decorum and for its clear influence on the poetic arts of Matthew of Vendôme, Geoffrey of Vinsauf, John of Garland, and others.[125]

To some extent, and more often in classical sources than in medieval rhetorics and poetics, the imagery that conveys the perfection of form is organic, typically images of the harmonious body or its opposite, the monstrous body (which is meant to evoke the norm of the well-formed body), as we see in Quintilian and Horace. But this should not be taken as a version of a Platonic or indeed Romantic or nineteenth-century aesthetic of "organic form." The "organicism" of such medieval references to the well-proportioned body should be understood in terms of ideas of the body as a well-designed machine (as in *organon*, "tool" or "instrument") whose "organs"—exterior and interior parts—work together effectively to perform a function, whether that of sustaining life or comprising a coherent representation. It is worth recalling that Plato's comparison of a harmonious discourse to a "living being" (*zoön*) is part of a larger rejection of technical rhetoric, especially in its written forms: the Platonic model of "organicism" opposes itself to the instrumentality of a reproducible rhetorical *tekhnê*.[126] By contrast, the notions of poetic decorum or harmonious form that the Middle Ages received from classical theory are

---

[125] See the "Materia" commentary, within, pp. 551–6, and Friis-Jensen, "Horace and the Early Writers of Arts of Poetry."

[126] *Phaedrus* 264c. See Sicking, "Organische Komposition und Verwandtes," and for the "organic" model of grammar corresponding to it, Sluiter, "Textual Therapy: On the Relationship between Medicine and Grammar in Galen." On the reception of the aesthetic principle of organic form and its modern avatars, see Rousseau, ed., *Organic Form*.

grounded in technical rhetoric, in precept about arrangement. In the medieval *artes poetriae*, consideration of the beginning, middle, and end of a poem, or of natural and artificial order, correspond to the treatment of *dispositio* in classical rhetorical treatises. Thus in the *Parisiana poetria*, John of Garland clearly links his discussion of narrative order with the traditional position of *dispositio* in rhetorical treatises: "The next subject after Invention and Selection of subject matter is how to begin and arrange it. Any subject has three aspects: beginning, middle, and end . . . In poetry, we can launch the subject with either the natural or the artificial beginning."[127] Geoffrey of Vinsauf presents the choice of artificial order by means of an extravagant natural image, the many-branched tree: "This order, though reversed, is more pleasant and by far better than the straightforward order . . . [It is] fertile, from its marvelous source sending out more branches from the parent trunk, changing one branch into many, a single into several, one into eight." But we are reminded that the achievement of such a complex form is an art which can be mastered by observing the rules for amplification of beginnings that Geoffrey's treatise is about to set out: "Behold, the way lies open! Guide the reins of the mind by my explanation of the way."[128] This is not far short of an apotheosis of technical rhetoric, a guarantee of the teachability of poetic artifice.

The architectonic principles of rhetorical theory take us from the divisions and arrangement of the speech to the division and classification of narrative into genres, and the division of rhetoric itself into genres. The emergence of the very concept of literary genre as a system of classification based on formal properties as well as content can be traced in the passage of ancient rhetorical thought into the Middle Ages.[129]

Throughout medieval poetics and theories of fiction we find the triad *fabula–argumentum–historia*: *fabula* is a story that has no truth and no resemblance to truth (consisting of fantasies); *argumentum* is a "realistic" fiction that is not true but has verisimilitude; and *historia* is an account of true events, usually of the remote past. We encounter the triad in Martianus Capella, Isidore of Seville, William of Conches' commentaries on Plato and Macrobius, Bernardus Silvestris' commentary on Martianus Capella, Gundissalinus, John of Salisbury's *Metalogicon*, Geoffrey of Vinsauf, John of Garland, Thomas of Chobham, and other writers. This threefold classification of narratives according to the degree of truthfulness in content is the oldest and most constant generic taxonomy in the Middle Ages. It is an important point of origin for independent definitions of *historia* and

---

[127] John of Garland, *Parisiana poetria*, within, p. 650.

[128] Geoffrey of Vinsauf, *Poetria nova*, within, p. 598.

[129] The concept of genre has even earlier classical antecedents in the Hellenistic period; see Harder et al., *Genre in Hellenistic Poetry*; Sluiter, "The Dialectics of Genre."

fabula.[130] But the sources for the triad are in rhetorical precept: the medieval knowledge of this classification derives from the *Rhetorica ad Herennium* and Cicero's *De inventione*. In the Ciceronian texts, the triad appears as a relatively minor subdivision of the part of the oration known as the narration, in which the speaker sets forth events that have occurred or are supposed to have occurred.[131] These "genres" represent a wholly digressive form of narrative, not connected at all with the facts of a case to be pleaded in court, but used in oratorical training as exercises (*praeexercitamina* or *progymnasmata*) in shaping a plot, so that the orator can develop facility in presenting a sequence of events. This form of exercise is clearly distinguished from training in the presentation of character. In classical pedagogy, *narratio* was the first exercise that students would encounter in the rhetorical schoolroom, just as they passed from the study of grammar to that of rhetoric, although for Quintilian it is only historical narration that belongs in rhetorical training, the poetic types being more appropriate to the grammarians.[132]

As a whole, this triad of *narratio* is also associated with literary study, and indeed its application, in elementary pedagogy, to mastering plot structure links it with descriptive poetics such as Aristotle's treatment of verisimilitude in the *Poetics* (1451a) and Horace's discussions of plot in the *Ars poetica* (179, 338). In its medieval uses it was progressively detached from its rhetorical context, becoming simply a literary commonplace. It could be integrated into more complex distinctions of literary genre (for example, the thirteenth-century encyclopedist Vincent of Beauvais gives a list of seven "species" of poetry: comedy, tragedy, invective, satire, fable, history, and argument);[133] it was a useful way of characterizing the epistemology or knowledge-content of poetry as an object of scientific study (as in Gundissalinus' discussion); and it served as a way of identifying the matter of literary genres.[134] Medieval precept tended to associate these generic distinctions with the content of narrative (degree of verisimilitude). But the teaching of genre was also intimately related to ancient and medieval grammatical exercises in *enarratio poetarum*,

---

[130] See the exhaustive study by Mehtonen, *Old Concepts and New Poetics: Historia, Argumentum, and Fabula in the Twelfth- and Early Thirteenth-Century Latin Poetics of Fiction*. See also von Moos, "*Poeta* und *historicus* im Mittelalter"; on medieval literary notions of history see Morse, *Truth and Convention in the Middle Ages*; on Hellenistic antecedents, see Meijering, *Literary and Rhetorical Theories in Greek Scholia*.

[131] *Rhetorica ad Herennium* 1.8.12–13; *De inventione* 1.19.27; cf. Quintilian, *Institutio oratoria* 2.4.2. In these texts the triad appears as a subdivision of a subdivision of the *narratio*: a kind of narration which is unconnected with the case and which is further divided into that concerned with events (*in negotiis*) and that concerned with persons or character. Each genre of the narrative of events is yet a further subdivision.

[132] *Institutio oratoria* 2.4.2. See Cousin, *Études sur Quintilien* 1: 113–21; and Viljamaa, "From Grammar to Rhetoric: First Exercises in Composition According to Quintilian."

[133] *Speculum doctrinale* 3.109

[134] Mehtonen, *Old Concepts and New Poetics*, 30–61; see Gundissalinus, within, pp. 478–9.

the interpretation (literally "narrating out") of the poets and authors, in which students mastered not just the content but the formal and stylistic aspects of a text, through practice in paraphrase, amplification, and abbreviation.[135] In other words, while genre theory tended to focus on content, the practical application to narrative genres involved proficiency in developing and sustaining a plot, in just the way that ancient training used fictive or historical plots as compositional practice towards the rhetorical *narratio*.[136]

It is just such an exercise in plot construction, the stripping down or building up of a narrative, that Geoffrey of Vinsauf illustrates in his famous example of the story of the "Snow-Child," in which he shows how to compress a complicated plot into two lines of verse.[137] John of Garland's *Parisiana poetria* gives a consummate illustration of the passage of generic content into precept about form and structure. In chapter 5, John presents the Ciceronian triad as a subdivision of "expository" discourse, and proceeds to define *fabula*, *historia*, and *argumentum*. His treatment of *historia* offers more than the commonplace about its content (events remote from our time). Having stated the standard definition, he proceeds to offer instruction on how to build such a narrative in order for it to be properly structured: "whoever deals in it, to escape fault, should include, in order, proposition, invocation, and narration; then he should use the rhetorical figure called Transition, a figure whereby the mind of the listener, with the aid of the preceding narration, understands what is to come."[138] Here is advice whereby a notion of genre emerges into a notion of narrative architecture, where genre is defined not only through content, but through the exigencies of form. Although most medieval treatments of the triad *fabula–argumentum–historia* do not make the overt gestures towards formal composition that we see in this example, we should understand that John of Garland is drawing here on a strong tradition in which the practical understanding of the genres of narrative is indissociable from training in the formal structures of plot and arrangement, from natural and artificial order to the devices for beginning a narrative.[139] Here we see how categories of genre can be generative as well as analytic.

The concept of genre structures rhetoric itself. Aristotle, and following him the Latin rhetoricians, divided rhetoric into the three genres of epideictic (demonstrative),

[135] See Copeland, *Rhetoric, Hermeneutics, and Translation*, 21–32, 56–62, 82–96, 158–78; Kelly, "The Scope of the Treatment of Composition in the Twelfth- and Thirteenth-Century Arts of Poetry."

[136] On the related question of oratorical exercises and narrative invention, see Edwards, "Poetic Invention and the Medieval *Causae*."

[137] Geoffrey of Vinsauf, within, p. 601.

[138] John of Garland, within, p. 656. Cf. Thomas of Chobham's use of these terms (within, pp. 623–5), comparing divisions of poetry with the divisions of a sermon (based on the divisions of the oration).

[139] Mehtonen, *Old Concepts and New Poetics*, 72–9; on this passage in the *Parisiana poetria*, see also Klopsch, *Einfürung in die Dichtungslehren des lateinischen Mittelalters*, 119, 155–6.

deliberative (political), and judicial (forensic).[140] These generic categories, which in antiquity were understood to mark the purpose, construction, and content of the speech, could also find new leverage in medieval rhetorical commentary on Scripture, as analytical rather than generative categories. Cassiodorus' commentary on the Psalms (mid sixth century) reads the eloquence of the Psalter by applying these largest of generic divisions to the whole corpus of the Psalms, grouping them according to the genres of rhetoric, but at the same time allowing the Psalms to redefine the genres of rhetoric. Thus the deliberative genre now mediates between God and humanity; epideictic is revelation; and judicial is petitionary and penitential. Rupert of Deutz similarly reads the genres of rhetoric into Scripture as a whole, using the categories as an exegetical vehicle for understanding the fundamental moral imperatives of Scripture.[141]

Finally, the vocabulary and conceptual structure of rhetoric lie behind medieval conventions of generic classification based on textual form or method as well as content. There are various traditions through which the Middle Ages received and articulated its understandings of individual genres: for example, the Averroistic commentaries on Aristotle's *Poetics* informed medieval theories of tragedy.[142] But to think across large theoretical questions of form, method, and effect on an audience requires a vocabulary of classification, and it is to this that the rhetorical tradition made an important contribution. We have considered how ancient theory divided rhetoric into three types or "genres," epideictic, deliberative, and judicial, each of them incorporating the whole of rhetorical doctrine, but each proceeding in somewhat different ways, towards different ends. With its roots in dialectic, rhetorical theory applied the logical term *genus*, redefining it along certain formal or methodological lines, to arrive at this notion of the *genera* or "genres" of rhetoric. *Genus* is used in this way with some consistency in later writings, for example Cassiodorus' use of the term when he classifies the Psalms according to the *genera* of rhetoric. But the term that provides the most important link between rhetorical theory and the formal or rhetorical properties of literary genre is *modus*.

In ancient rhetoric, *modus* is the equivalent sometimes of manner or method, and sometimes of *genus*.[143] In Cicero's system of topical invention in the *De inventione*, *modus* is a topic connected with the attributes of the action, the questions that determine how the act was committed or performed (place, time, occasion, manner or *modus*, and facilities).

---

[140] Aristotle, *Rhetoric* 1358b7; *De inventione* 1.5.7; *Rhetorica ad Herennium* 1.2.2; Quintilian, *Institutio oratoria* 3.4.1–16.

[141] See within, Cassiodorus, and Rupert of Deutz, pp. 399–400.

[142] See Kelly, "Aristotle-Averroes-Alemannus on Tragedy."

[143] As method, see, e.g. *De inventione* 1.51.96; as the equivalent of *genus*, see, e.g. *De inventione* 1.29.45 and *Ad Herennium* 4.45.59.

He states: "Manner [*modus*], again, is the category under which one inquires how and in what state of mind the act was performed" (1.27.41). If the act was committed unintentionally (without premeditation), there might be various reasons for this, including emotional states such as annoyance, anger, and love. Thus *modus* as manner is here connected with affect, with the emotional or mental state of the person who performed the action. The early commentators on this preserved Cicero's general meaning, adding only that *modus* could also signify the way that something was done in a given state of mind.[144] By the twelfth century, however, the term *modus* had acquired clearer associations with form or method. This would not have been foreign to Cicero's original meaning, but the vocabulary of twelfth-century commentary gives this dimension of meaning greater prominence. In his commentary on Cicero, Thierry of Chartres gives three definitions of *modus*. First of all, as we would expect, he preserves the force of *modus* as a state of mind in which the action is performed.[145] But he also closely identifies *modus* with the term *modus tractandi*, form or method of treatment: *modus tractandi* was in common use by the middle of the twelfth century to designate the stylistic, formal, and rhetorical procedure of a text.[146] At *De inventione* 1.24.34, Thierry describes the particular *modus* that Cicero follows at this point in the text, using the term to describe Cicero's method of approach.[147] And third, a few sections later, Thierry explains Cicero's own use of the word *modus* by equating it with *genus*: "By *modi* he indicates the *genera* of arguments."[148] In other words, *modus* has acquired a more precise affiliation with literary form or method, as well as with genre, while also retaining the association with mental condition or emotional state.

This chain of associations sets the stage for the technical use of *modus* in the thirteenth century as a term designating distinctions among different scriptural styles according to their different emotional force or appeal. In scholastic discussions of Scripture, the term *modus* serves the same classifying function that we moderns would assign to the word "genre." The term's classical ancestry takes us back to questions of emotional state, but in thirteenth-century discourse, the emotion is associated not with an act, but with a text, with the kind of emotion that a text produces in the reader. According to Alexander of Hales, the various "literary" or poetic forms that Scripture takes are each associated with a

---

[144] See Victorinus, *Explanationes*, in Halm, *Rhetores latini minores*, 225; and Fortunatianus, *Ars rhetorica*, in Halm, 104.

[145] At 1.27.41; see Fredborg, ed., *The Latin Rhetorical Commentaries by Thierry of Chartres*, 141.38–9.

[146] On its use in the twelfth century, see Minnis, *Medieval Theory of Authorship*, 17–23 and 41–68 *passim*; and Hunt, "The Introductions to the *Artes* in the Twelfth Century."

[147] See Fredborg, ed., *The Latin Rhetorical Commentaries by Thierry of Chartres*, 127.78–83.

[148] At 1.30.49; Fredborg, ed., *The Latin Rhetorical Commentaries*, 153.23–4.

kind of emotional appeal. Scripture is meant to work through "pious affect," and its various *modi* are precept, example, exhortation, revelation, prayer. The different books of Scripture can be classified according to the *modus* used: precept in the Law and the Gospels, example in the historical books, exhortation in the books of Solomon and the Epistles, revelation in the prophetic books, and prayer in the Psalms.[149] Here we can also see continuity with, and development from, Cassiodorus' classification of the Psalms into the genres of rhetoric according to their emotional and preceptive purpose. Throughout the scholastic period, the term *modus* acquires even more distinctive applications to the forms of scriptural writing: for example, the *modus* of history, the *modus* of prophecy, and other *modi*, which produce different affective responses in readers. Thus we can trace a passage from Ciceronian theory of invention, where *modus* represents a state of mind or emotion on the part of someone performing an action, to commentary on Cicero, where *modus* is equated with genre as form or method, to the later Middle Ages, where *modus* is a generic term used to differentiate literary forms or methods according to their emotional impact on readers.[150]

HERMENEUTICS AND RHETORIC: READING AS INVENTION

Augustine's *De doctrina christiana* can justly be called the first systematic Christian rhetoric. It sets into motion a theological tradition of rhetoric which embraces not only preaching, but scriptural interpretation, grammar and theories of the sign, and the spiritual disciplines of reading and meditation. Its unique accomplishment is its transformation of rhetorical terminology into hermeneutical language, and its redesigning of a rhetorical treatise into a program for reading. Its approach to traditional rhetorical theory is to strip it down to its simplest components and then build it back up to a new purpose. Thus instead of the traditional five parts of rhetoric, it divides its teaching into two parts: invention, the *modus inveniendi* or the means of discovering what is to be understood; and delivery, the *modus proferendi* or the means of setting forth what has been understood. The object of understanding is not a legal or political case or logical arguments or technical proofs, but a text, Scripture. Thus invention or discovery, which is the most powerful engine of ancient rhetorical theory, the intellectual "control room" for the assessment and

---

[149] Alexander of Hales, *Summa theologica*, ed. Klumper, I: 7–8 (question 1, ch. 4, art. 1, *ad obiecta* 2). This is discussed in Minnis, *Medieval Theory of Authorship*, 119–22. These passages are also translated in Minnis et al., eds., *Medieval Literary Theory and Criticism*, 212–23.

[150] See Copeland, "The Ciceronian Rhetorical Tradition and Medieval Literary Theory," 260–4.

production of meaning through language, linking rhetorical composition with philosophical categories of being and thought, is recast in Augustine's treatise as the "means of discovering" the truths that are contained and often concealed in Scripture. On Augustine's terms, invention is still generative, but its function now is to generate understanding of a text in which all truth has already been revealed, and whose correct interpretation is ultimately the responsibility of informed readers committed to its spiritual and moral teachings.[151] Thus we can say that Augustine shifts the responsibility for invention or discovery from writer to reader, or from the production to the interpretation of meaning. This does not imply that invention has been weakened or even necessarily changed in terms of the nature of the classical precept that would continue to guide it. Rather, its weight has been shifted from generating arguments about a case to generating arguments about a text. In this way the *De doctrina christiana* captures and sums up the crucial orientation of Christian culture to hermeneutical strategies. Under the rhetorical *modus inveniendi* Augustine synthesizes grammar and dialectic, thus anticipating what would later be the disciplinary unity of the trivium. Grammar (including philology) is necessary to an understanding of the literal signs of Scripture (2.11–16; 3.2–3), and dialectic is implicit in the treatment of signification, where a theory of signs is joined to a theory of predication.[152] Most important, the treatise gives powerful expression to the interconnection of grammar and rhetoric in the exegetical outlook of Christian culture. It offers a new justification for the notion of the "reading-road."[153] We can trace the theoretical significance of this move across various fields of medieval literary and critical practice.

The semiotic thought of the *De doctrina christiana* remained a basis for grammatical exposition, including that of the technical Prisicanic tradition. In his exposition of the difference between things and signs, Augustine provided an authoritative Christian restatement of ancient theories of the sign, now enfolding these principles in a theological purpose (*caritas* or love of God) which gave an absolute primacy to the things signified by the signs or words of Scripture, both as real and as symbolic entities.

We see the transformation of rhetorical into hermeneutical strategies at many levels of textual practice. The system of invention finds new application in exegetical procedures. In Cassiodorus' *Expositio Psalmorum*, in Bede's *De schematibus et tropis*, and in Rupert of Deutz' *De sancta trinitate*, rhetoric is a body of knowledge revealed in Scripture, and the

---

[151] On the question of exegetical truth claims in Augustine's *De doctrina christiana*, see Sluiter, "Metatexts and the Principle of Charity."

[152] Jackson, "The Theory of Signs in St. Augustine's *De doctrina christiana*."

[153] In fact, reading is explicitly compared to following a road, or making a journey, cf. *De doctrina christiana* 1.36.41; Stock, *Augustine the Reader*, 168.

discovery of rhetorical forms and techniques is also an instrument for further exposition of scriptural meaning. More complex is the transposition of inventional schemes to expository purposes. One notable example of this involves the inventional system of the circumstances, the topics of person, act, cause, time, place, manner, and means, concisely laid out in Boethius' *De topicis differentiis* 4. This system was used in the Carolingian era as a way of organizing the *accessus ad auctores* (introductions to the authors). Remigius of Auxerre uses this scheme in the *accessus* to his commentary on Martianus Capella:

> First to be considered are the seven topics, that is circumstances, which are established at the beginning of every authentic book: who, what, why, in what manner, where, when, by what faculties. Thus the question "who" refers to the person of the author: who wrote it? Martianus. The second topic is "what," which refers to the matter at hand, which is announced by the title of the work itself. Martianus thus wrote of the marriage of Philology and Mercury. The third topic is "why," which refers to the cause: why did he write about the marriage of Philology and Mercury? Clearly because he wanted to examine the seven liberal arts. The fourth topic is "in what manner," which refers to the method. Literary discourses are created through the modes of either verse or prose: Martianus has used both in this work. The fifth topic is "where," which refers to the place: where was it written? In Carthage. The sixth topic is "when," which refers to the time at which it was written; this the author has left to be investigated by future generations and to this day the answer remains uncertain. The seventh topic is "by what means," which refers to the materials used: by what means did he write it? Clearly by means of the marriage of Philology and Mercury and of the seven liberal arts.[154]

As this scheme suggests, the work of commentary, even of secular texts, takes on the argumentative, topical character of rhetorical invention.

In the arts of preaching, exegesis and invention could be said to occupy the same position or perform the same function: these preceptive guides are of course the late-medieval elaborations of Augustine's program for reading and preaching. While many of the later preaching manuals are very schematic and give little explicit attention to broader hermeneutical questions, Thomas of Chobham's *Summa* gives a forceful account of what one is to discover in Scripture and the methods of discovery one is to bring to the reading of the text. On the model of Augustine's treatise, Thomas considers the modes of signification in Scripture, extending this to include an account of how the interpretation of levels of meaning can be amplified. His system of amplification is in fact based on the Ciceronian system of topical invention out of the attributes of the person and the act,

---

[154] Translated from Lutz, ed., *Remigii Autissiodorensis commentum in Martianum Capellam*, 1: 65. On the prologue form, see Copeland, *Rhetoric, Hermeneutics, and Translation*, 66–76.

which is closely related to the seven *circumstantiae* of topical invention as presented by Boethius. Thus, for example, we can amplify our interpretation of scriptural significa-tion through the topic of "quality": "through Rachel, who was beautiful, the contem-plative life is signified; through Leah, who was bleary-eyed and ugly, the active life is signified."[155] The Prologue to the Wycliffite Bible from the 1390s takes us to yet another level of hermeneutical production towards an evangelical purpose. The writer of the Prologue borrowed and quoted extensively from *De doctrina christiana* books 2 and 3 (on literal and figurative signs). In this way the Prologue text gave vernacular readers the same theoretical equipment that academically trained clerical readers had long enjoyed. The passages chosen were in fact those in which Augustine is most dependent upon Ciceronian precept for interpreting the intention of legal documents (such as wills or laws), that is, for distinguishing between the "letter" and the "spirit" of a document. In this oblique way, via Augustine's treatment of scriptural signs, Ciceronian inventional theory found its way into one of the most ambitious projects in vernacular hermeneutics of the later Middle Ages.

The transformation of rhetorical systems into interpretive methods also finds influential and consistent expression in approaches to poetic composition. It is reflected in precept and theory as well as in literary practice, where engagement with literary tradition takes on primary aesthetic value through the study and imitation of poetic models. The twelfth- and thirteenth-century arts of poetry prize imitation both as exercise and as an end in itself. They present the imitation of models as a combination of grammatical commentary on canonical texts and rhetorical orientation to the future text. In the arts of Matthew of Vendôme, Geoffrey of Vinsauf, John of Garland, and Gervase of Melkley, as well as in the anonymous *Tria sunt*, the space allocated to inventional precept is occupied by questions of literary analysis: grammatical exposition, amplification, and stylistic devices. John of Garland's treatise can serve here as an example: John takes over the Ciceronian apparatus for invention of argument out of the circumstances of the case, but his explanations of these procedures draw from the categories of *enarratio poetarum*, where answers to the questions "what" and "why" concern a text and an author's purpose, rather than an action and a motivation for it.[156]

Although the arts of poetry may themselves represent the elementary side of poetic theory, assuming an unskilled audience working closely with its textual models, they articulate a compositional outlook that went far beyond the classroom, and which placed a

---

[155] See within, p. 620.
[156] See Copeland, *Rhetoric, Hermeneutics, and Translation*, 161–78. On the role of the "masterpiece" as source text, see Kelly, "The Scope of Medieval Instruction in the Art of Poetry and Prose."

premium on commentary and the interpretive drawing out of truths to be restated. As Marie de France puts it in her famous pronouncement on the power of exposition:

> Custume fu as ancïens,
> Ceo testimoine Precïens,
> Es livres ke jadis feseient
> Assez oscurement diseient
> Pur ceus ki a venir esteient
> E ki aprendre les deveient,
> K'i peüssent gloser la lettre
> E de lur sen le surplus mettre.

[It was the custom among the Ancients—so testifies Priscian—in the books which they wrote in olden days to put their thoughts somewhat obscurely, so that those who were to come after them and who were to learn them, might construe their writing and add to it from their own ingenuity.][157]

This statement distantly echoes Priscian's own prefatory remarks about the grammarian's relation to his forebears.[158] But more importantly, it expresses a fundamental medieval outlook in which the interpretive work of *enarratio poetarum* becomes an inventional strategy oriented to the future text.

THE ETHICS OF GRAMMAR AND RHETORIC

In a classic essay on grammar and ethics in the twelfth century, Philippe Delhaye notes that the common scheme of the seven liberal arts did not present an obvious way of accounting for the scientific category of ethics.[159] The ancient but still popular division of fields of knowledge into logic, physics (or sometimes theoretical sciences), and ethics could be mapped only partially onto the seven liberal arts: the trivium represented "logic," the arts of the quadrivium accounted for "physics," but none of the seven arts clearly corresponded to "ethics." This could be solved by juxtaposing ethics with the seven liberal arts, suggesting that it constituted yet another field or dimension of study alongside of the trivium. But more commonly this seeming inconsistency was resolved by a process of integration, enlarging the function of the art of grammar and making it the carrier of all ethical import. This integrative solution emphasized the literary applications of grammatical

---

[157] Text and translation from Marie de France, *Lais*, ed. Ewert, 1 (Prologue, lines 9–16) and 163.
[158] *GL* 2: 1.   [159] Delhaye, "*Grammatica* et *ethica* au XIIe siècle."

study. The content of the canonical texts which grammarians taught and expounded was itself ethics: the texts exemplified moral behavior to be imitated or immoral behavior to be avoided.[160] As has often been noted, this integrative strategy protected the study of the classical authors: the claim of ethics provided a buffer zone for secular literature and learning against criticisms that it was irrelevant or inappropriate to Christian learning.[161]

But it was not only the object to which grammar applied itself, that is, the literary texts taught and expounded, that served ethics. The very terms of the art itself, the intellectual system that it comprised, was understood as a cultivation and preparation of the mind through language. This is an extension and late elaboration of the program in the earlier cathedral schools of cultivating virtue through learning, what has memorably been called the teaching of "letters and manners."[162] John of Salisbury gives expression to its broadest philosophical ambitions in his defense of the study of grammar:

> From what has been said, it is clear that the function of grammar is not narrowly confined to one subject. Rather, grammar prepares the mind to understand everything that can be taught in words...For grammar equips us both to receive and impart knowledge...It is accordingly evident that grammar, which is the basis and root of scientific knowledge, implants, as it were, the seed in nature's furrow after grace has readied the ground.[163]

And John of Salisbury's description of the teaching of Bernard of Chartres is far more than an account of the content or even method of instruction. The picture of Bernard's pedagogy is that of an ethical performance itself, the teacher and his teaching formed together in the image of this "moral art." Here the ethical model to be imitated is not found in the authors whom Bernard teaches; rather it is Bernard the teacher who embodies the ethical truth, the moral lesson of the art of grammar.[164] As the teacher of grammar, Bernard emerges from the iconographic tradition of Lady Grammar who both nurtures and disciplines her young students. But as an embodiment of the ideal of teaching, the image of Bernard also derives from the Neoplatonic tradition of the language arts as a form of spiritual ennoblement. In his commentary on Cicero, Victorinus (fourth century)

---

[160] See, for example, Conrad of Hirsau, *Dialogus super auctores* (ed. Huygens, *Accessus ad auctores*; trans. Minnis, *Medieval Literary Theory*).

[161] Minnis, *Medieval Theory of Authorship*, 23–7, 182–3, and for the later twelfth century, Baldwin, *Masters, Princes, and Merchants*, 1:77–83; 2:269.

[162] Jaeger, *The Envy of Angels*, 2–4, 49–117.   [163] See within, *Metalogicon*, p. 503.

[164] See Jaeger, *The Envy of Angels*, 128–31, for comparison of the portrait of Bernard of Chartres with the portrait of an eleventh-century master at Würzburg (see also 66–73). On the continuation of this traditional pedagogy through the later Middle Ages, see Gehl, *A Moral Art*, 20–42.

understood discipline or art as a form of moral ascesis through which the soul can return to its transcendent origins: through the arts, and especially through the language arts, the soul seeks emancipation, and the inner essence of the perfect good, wisdom, is imaged forth in the eloquence that is thereby achieved.[165]

The idea of spiritual perfection through the arts informs Augustine's *De doctrina christiana* as well as the Arabic reception of Greek thought, exemplified in this volume by the Al-Farabian *Didascalia* on the *Rhetoric* of Aristotle translated into Latin by Hermannus Alemannus.[166] This notion of spiritual perfection finds some of its most beautiful expressions in twelfth-century thought about the study of grammar. For Thierry of Chartres in his *Heptateuchon*, the language arts have an ethical and not merely decorative role in expressing scientific truths. In a similar vein, William of Conches describes the order of learning at the end of his *Philosophia mundi* (World [or Natural] Philosophy): we come to knowledge through eloquence, the arts of the trivium, into which grammar initiates us. These furnish us with the equipment with which to approach philosophy, the arts of the quadrivium, and from there we approach sacred Scripture. Thus through knowledge of creation we arrive at knowledge of the Creator. Here William announces his own treatise on grammar, "since grammar takes priority in all learning": on these grounds it is no negligible contribution to expound what has been left obscure by Priscian and his commentators.[167] Another perspective on the distinctive ethical power of grammar can be found in the work of the early-twelfth-century English scientist Adelard of Bath. In his *De eodem et diverso* (On the Same and the Different), Adelard presents a myth of grammar's founding of civilization: when men first roamed the countryside like beasts, without linguistic communication, a personified *Grammatica*, "by putting names to single objects, first blessed mortals with the distinction of mutual conversation."[168] As the science of imposing names, grammar created the social world. If Thierry of Chartres, William of Conches, and John of Salisbury present grammar as the point of the individual's ethical initiation into an intellectual ascent, Adelard depicts grammar as the origin of ethical contact between people. But these two perspectives are nevertheless part of the same picture: grammar is an ethical beginning.

---

[165] See Victorinus, within, p. 107; see also Copeland, "The Ciceronian Rhetorical Tradition," and for its Neoplatonist background, Hadot, *Arts libéraux et philosophie dans la pensée antique*, 101–36.

[166] *De doctrina christiana* 2, 7; see Copeland, "The Ciceronian Rhetorical Tradition," and van Fleteren, "St. Augustine, Neoplatonism, and the Liberal Arts: the Background to *De doctrina christiana*." For the Al-Farabian *Didascalia*, see within, pp. 735–52 and references there.

[167] *Philosophia*, ed. Maurach, 115–16, §§ 58–9 (or *PL* 172: 100 C–D); and see within, p. 384.

[168] Adelard of Bath, *De eodem et diverso*, ed. Burnett, 36, 37; see also Reynolds, *Medieval Reading*, 46. This myth of the origin of civilization through the arts is close in spirit and in content with the Ciceronian myth of the origins of rhetoric: see within, the commentaries by Victorinus, Thierry of Chartres, and Brunetto Latini.

The twelfth century is the high point for the scientific and philosophical expression of grammar's ethical function. But this linkage has important consequences for the cultural outlook of later authors across different academic environments. In the essay on classification of knowledge (above), we considered how the *Bataille des VII ars* by Henri d'Andeli represents the competition between Orleans and Paris in terms of a struggle between grammar and logic for institutional supremacy. On Henri's terms, this is also a conflict between old and new ways of knowing, between the genuine moral content of the art of grammar, which has a long pedagogical history on its side, and the intellectual autonomy of the new dialectical study which has detached itself from the traditional aims of the trivium. Grammatical study is represented by the canonical authors who are assembled in the sense both of a curricular "list" and the "lists" of a tournament. The effects of logical study, on the other hand, are pointedly represented by a messenger who is so ungrammatical that he mangles the peace offerings that he was meant to convey: "He did not know the sense / Of the presents nor the preterits . . . The boy did not know how to come to the point, / And came back in shame" (377–93). The new dominance of a facile logic signals the degradation of all the arts that attend it: rhetoric is nothing but the writing of legal formularies (represented by the mercenary Lombard knights of the poem); civil and canon law, and even the arts of the quadrivium, are emptied of their content in a world no longer cultivated by grammar.

We find similar attitudes in Italy, whose schools had long been dominated by legal professionalism. In the autobiographical preface to his *Rota nova* written around 1225, Guido Faba, master of *dictamen* in Bologna, tells us that he abandoned and then gratefully returned to his "literary studies" (*litterae*). By this term he most likely means a broad-based study drawing from the curricula of both grammar and rhetoric, that is, study of language and literary authors along with rhetorical theory and training in the art of prose composition. When he abandons this study it is to work in the law courts of Bologna; and later on, in order to earn money, he takes up a post as a notary. In both these professional spheres, the law courts and the notarial business, he has had to narrow his focus to the very specialized *ars dictaminis*, the writing of bureaucratic letters and legal prose. When he returns from his intellectual exile to establish his own school, he sets out to reorganize the curriculum in dictaminal study. He presents his new textbook, the *Rota nova* (New Wheel), as the signature of that new curriculum. His innovation, as he suggests in his ostentatious praise of his own achievements, is to have reunited the art of *dictamen* with Latin eloquence: "Watching over Latin eloquence, which was abandoned by the purple science of *dictamen*, the Celestial Piety, in her holy royal chamber on high, mercifully agreed to listen to the prayers of her suppliant servants." He has restored the literary value of the *ars dictaminis*, re-establishing its links with *litterae* and rescuing rhetorical training from the specialized professionalism of legal and notarial studies.[169] The *Rota nova* and its blockbuster successor, the *Summa dictaminis*, reflect this restorative aim: they offer a virtually complete curriculum in both grammar and rhetoric.[170] Thus grammatical learning, celebrated by John of Salisbury as cultivation of the mind and intellectual preparation, finds its ethical function even in the high-pressured environment of the Bolognese schools of rhetoric. For Guido Faba, the study of letters is the key to the renaissance of Latin eloquence in the dictaminal art.

A similar effect could be achieved by inverse means, incorporating the *ars dictaminis* into existing grammatical teaching about the composition of poetry. This is what some grammarians in northern Europe did, during the same era in which Guido flourished in Italy. John of Garland modeled his *Parisiana poetria* on the new and vibrant tradition of the *artes poetriae*, but his course was more comprehensive because he also included prose composition, that is, letter writing, in his treatise. The anonymous treatise known by its opening words as *Tria sunt*, which was composed sometime after 1256, could be seen as the culmination of this process of placing professional instruction on *dictamen* within the larger frame of *litterae* or cultivation of letters. The *Tria sunt* is an expansion of a treatise (thought to be by Geoffrey of Vinsauf) on verse and prose composition: into the existing structure of an *ars poetriae* destined for the grammar classroom, the *Tria sunt* inserts a complete dictaminal treatise, suggesting that instruction in business communication can be integrated into the older study of letters and literary composition.[171]

The theme of grammatical ethics also remains a constant of elementary teaching. Hugh of Trimberg's *Registrum multorum auctorum*, written in 1280 for the instruction of younger students, carries forward the notion of the ethical content of the literary canon. If the beginning of grammar is the beginning of ethics, there is also a justification for reasserting the prior claim of older traditions of learning in the face of modern interests. Thus while acknowledging the powerful attractions of dialectic, which can represent one kind of perfection through the arts, Hugh presents a survey of the curricular authors as a less glamorous but equally valuable form of knowledge. Proficiency in the ancient and modern authors, secular and Christian, demands both a knowledge of Latin and a firm sense of historical development.[172] To some extent like Henri d'Andeli's *Bataille des VII ars*, Hugh's register is a restatement of a literary canon; but the sense of an intellectual psychomachia, of a struggle among the disciplines for preeminence, is not part of Hugh's outlook. Rather, Hugh's orientation is closer to that of the twelfth-century *Dialogus super auctores* by Conrad of Hirsau and the *artes poetriae* of the twelfth and

---

[169] Copeland, "Medieval Intellectual Biography: the Case of Guido Faba"; and see within, Guido Faba, pp. 702–5.
[170] See Faulhaber, "The *Summa dictaminis* of Guido Faba."   [171] See within, *Tria sunt*, pp. 672–81.
[172] See Hugh of Trimberg, within, p. 659 (prologue).

thirteenth centuries. In Hugh's work, as in these earlier texts, the weight of inducting students into an entire cultural inheritance is borne by the grammar teacher. The most important distinctions among the texts will rest, not on the kind of knowledge they contain, but on their suitability for different levels of intellectual preparation, and thus different degrees of ethical maturity.

The ethical application of rhetoric has a more technical history than that of grammar. Grammar was understood to have a general ethical import: as an art it cultivated the mind, while its literary content reinforced good behavior. To a great extent it shared this general ethical value with the other arts of the trivium. All three arts were most often classed together, whether under "logic," "eloquence," or "arts of discourse" (*artes sermocinales*). But rhetoric also had an inheritance from classical political culture, and this made it subject to a somewhat more specialized and varying treatment, so that it could be classed both with the "arts of discourse" and under the headings of politics or ethics.[173] According to Cicero's influential statement at *De inventione* 1.5.6, rhetoric is a part of civil science, a definition repeated or elaborated in the late antique commentaries on Cicero.[174] The Aristotelian tradition of rhetoric also exerted an influence, first through the mediation of Arab philosophers and then directly when Aristotle's *Rhetoric* was translated into Latin by William of Moerbeke in the later thirteenth century. Aristotle says that rhetoric is a counterpart of dialectic, but he also says that rhetoric is a part of ethics which is justly called politics, and that it assumes the appearance of politics (*Rhetoric* 1356a25).

The Ciceronian tradition had the longer reach, because it was continuous from late antiquity. Among the earliest authors, Cassiodorus, Isidore of Seville, and Alcuin follow Cicero in defining rhetoric as discourse on civil questions, although they do not classify it as a branch of politics. But Thierry of Chartres' extrinsic prologue to his commentaries on the *De inventione* and *Rhetorica ad Herennium* presents rhetoric quite explicitly as the "greater part of civil science." Developing Cicero's conjunction of wisdom and eloquence, and also enlarging on the notion, from Victorinus' late antique commentary, that eloquence is the outer form of wisdom, Thierry says that wisdom and rhetoric together make up civil science. But he also goes on to state that rhetoric plays the greater role in civil affairs.[175] Even though the study of Ciceronian rhetoric in the northern cathedral schools served largely as a supplement to the study of dialectic (giving students another handle on how to discover "topics" for dialectical arguments), Thierry still wishes to identify rhetoric

---

[173]   For more background, see Copeland, "Lydgate, Hawes, and the Science of Rhetoric."
[174]   For example, Victorinus, *Explanationes*, ed. Halm, 156 (and see within, p. 109).
[175]   Thierry of Chartres, p. 412 within.

with a moral and political application. Gundissalinus borrows wholesale Thierry's extrinsic prologue for his section on rhetoric in the *De divisione philosophiae*, and thus this political classification of rhetoric sits side by side, in Gundissalinus' text, with other schemes of knowledge. Gundissalinus also classifies grammar, poetic, and rhetoric together as the sciences of eloquence, which he regards as a branch of practical science ("civil reasoning"), because they teach how to conduct one's civil affairs in language. Robert Kilwardby's *De ortu scientiarum* (On the Origin of the Sciences), written between 1246 and 1250, carries forward the Ciceronian notion of rhetoric as a form of civil science. Kilwardby considers rhetoric a civil science which pertains to ethics.[176] But he also makes an unusual distinction between rhetoric as a theoretical and as a practical science, based on the difference between the rhetor (the teacher of rhetoric) and the orator: the theoretical science is what the rhetor teaches, but the practical science is what the orator practices in his civil cases.[177]

In the writings of Brunetto Latini and John Gower we see the great vernacular culminations of this Ciceronian tradition of rhetoric as civil reasoning, rhetoric as the ethical discourse of politics. In the essay on the classification of knowledge, we considered how Gower's *Confessio amantis* represents a monumental change in the status of rhetoric, elevating it to a new position as a whole division of knowledge unto itself, not simply one of many sciences. In terms of the instructive poetics of the *Confessio amantis*, this radical move offers an emblem for the moral-political turn of the work, from the ethics of self-knowledge to the teaching of moral responsibility. But in terms of the history of its ideas, Gower's enlargement of the scope of rhetoric has an immediate background in vernacular political discourse.

During the 1260s, in exile during the civil wars in Florence, Brunetto Latini produced a number of learned texts in the vernacular. One of these, the French *Trésor*, was Gower's direct source for much of book 7 of the *Confessio amantis*, and Brunetto's extended treatment there of rhetoric and politics was certainly the prompt for Gower's enhancement of the role of rhetoric. Along with the *Trésor*, Brunetto also produced his *Rettorica*, his translation and exposition of the beginning of Cicero's *De inventione* in the Tuscan dialect of Florence. Brunetto's greater attention here is to commenting on Cicero's text and extending its application to the *ars dictaminis*. The Ciceronian notion of rhetoric as the political activity of the *res publica* had taken on new meaning in the educational environments of the Italian cities, where dictaminal practice had represented an extension of academic rhetorical

---

[176] Kilwardby, *De ortu scientiarum*, ed. Judy, §§ 473, 587–8, and 623 (rhetoric is reasoning about civil ethics). See Dahan, "L'entrée de la *Rhétorique* d'Aristote dans le monde latin," 79–80.

[177] *De ortu scientiarum*, ed. Judy, § 597.

training into the secular, public sphere. For Brunetto in particular, rhetoric is not just a *tekhnê*, but a form of political analysis. The chronicler Giovanni Villani recalls Brunetto as "the master who first taught refinement to the Florentines and the arts of speaking well and of guiding and ruling our republic according to the science of politics."[178] Brunetto insists that the technical system of rhetoric is relevant to any kind of public discourse or dispute, whether oral or written, whether legal, bureaucratic, political, or personal, whether a debate between councilmen or a petitionary poem written to one's beloved.[179] Thus the vernacular project of the *Rettorica* finds its broadly educative directive within the traditional terms of rhetoric as a civil science. In the *Rettorica*, Brunetto also gives a division of the sciences which has much in common with earlier schemes in which the language arts are identified as "civil reasoning" because they involve verbal communication. According to Brunetto, grammar, rhetoric, and dialectic constitute that part of politics which works in words as opposed to actions. If for the Neoplatonists Victorinus and Thierry of Chartres the conjunction of wisdom and eloquence represents a spiritual ascesis, for Brunetto this Ciceronian conjunction has a tangible application to communication of all kinds.

The Aristotelian tradition of rhetoric is represented in this volume by the Al-Farabian *Didascalia* on Aristotle's *Rhetoric* and the influential commentary on the *Rhetoric* by Giles of Rome. Commentators on the *Rhetoric* had to negotiate Aristotle's double placement of rhetoric, both as a counterpart of dialectic and as a part of ethics whose concern is politics. Moreover, readers and commentators would encounter Aristotle's extensive consideration of the kinds of ethical issues appropriate to each of the genres of oratory: deliberative (political) rhetoric deals with questions of the good; epideictic with virtue and vice; and forensic (judicial) with wrongdoing. In the Al-Farabian *Didascalia* on Aristotle's *Rhetoric*, preserved in the Latin translation produced by Hermannus Alemannus in 1256, the purpose of rhetoric is equated with the sum of the moral issues treated by the three genres of rhetoric. In the Arabic philosophical framework of the expanded *Organon*, rhetoric and poetics together are seen as important dimensions of logic. Thus with respect to Aristotle's *Rhetoric*, the Arabic commentators build their discussions around the formal questions of argumentation and proof, as well as the psychology of belief and opinion. But within that governing structure, the ethical import of rhetoric takes prominence. Rhetoric is not itself the system for ethical reasoning, but one of its chief uses is to communicate the products of such reasoning to a non-philosophical public.[180] For example, the *Didascalia* considers the practice of rhetoric in terms that are specific to moral teaching: rhetorical discourse finds its perfection in oratory that appeals to the emotions and moral sensibility, for oratorical

---

[178] Quoted from Davis, "Brunetto Latini and Dante," 422–3.   [179] see within, pp. 774–6.
[180] Cf. *Rhetoric*, 1357a1–4.

propositions are drawn from matters that derive from moral science and the science of governing a state (i.e. politics). Thus affective oratory derives from the topics of moral and civil science.[181]

One of the important themes that runs through Al-Farabi's commentaries is that rhetoric, with its focus on the particular as opposed to the general, is especially useful in the religious as well as the political sphere. If Aristotle positions rhetoric in relation to ethics and politics, Al-Farabi extends ethical thought to religious instruction, so that rhetoric, like poetics, is an instrument for the popularization of the speculative truths of religious knowledge. According to the *Didascalia*, "rhetoric is counted among the noble and celebrated arts, and it is an excellent instrument for governance of the state, and necessary for ordering religious laws."[182] Similarly, in another philosophical work, *The Attainment of Happiness*, Al-Farabi posits the usefulness of both poetics and rhetoric for teaching the general public: "what is established in the souls of the multitude is through an image and a persuasive argument."[183] In the Arab tradition of philosophy, the association of rhetoric and poetics together under logic had the effect of bringing the ethical application of rhetoric closer to that of poetics, so that both could be understood as instruments of popular instruction. In the Latin West, we find the legacy of this double association with logic and ethics in Gundissalinus' treatment of rhetoric and poetics under the *Organon*, and similarly in Aquinas' famous preface to the *Posterior Analytics*. In both these Latin texts, rhetoric and poetics are treated along the lines of the Al-Farabian discussions as relating to certain faculties of understanding and certain cognitive responses produced in the minds of the listeners: rhetoric produces belief or opinion that still has an element of doubt (*suspicio*), while poetics can lead to desire or to virtue by arousing an "estimation" of something.[184]

---

[181] *Didascalia*, section 26 (see within, p. 747).   [182] See within, *Didascalia*, section 1, p. 741.

[183] Al-Farabi, *The Attainment of Happiness*, trans. Mahdi, in *Philosophy of Plato and Aristotle*, 47. See also Black, *Logic and Aristotle's Rhetoric and Poetics*, 62, 66, 125, 131–6, 185. Thus we also find that in the *Kitâb al-khatâbah* (The Book of Rhetoric), Al-Farabi develops Aristotle's suggestive linkage between persuasion and instruction (*Rhetoric* 1355a) into a program for a psychology of teaching: "And persuading in the art of rhetoric is like instruction in the arts of demonstration, whereas persuasion corresponds to the knowledge which is produced in the learner by the instruction. And the attention of the audience to the speaker, its search for confirmation, and its consideration of what he says, corresponds to learning," translated by Black, 104; and see *Deux ouvrages inédits sur la Rhétorique*, ed. Langhade, 32–3.

[184] See Gundissalinus and Aquinas, within, pp. 482–3, 791. On the poetic faculty of "estimation" and its logical tool, the "imaginative syllogism," see Black, *Logic and Aristotle's Rhetoric and Poetics*, 209–46, and Black, "The 'Imaginative Syllogism' in Arabic Philosophy." For a general study of this tradition, see Hardison, "The Place of Averroes' Commentary on the *Poetics* in the History of Medieval Criticism"; and see the introductions to Gundissalinus and to Part 5, within.

In the medieval Latin West, Aristotle's *Rhetoric* emerges as a forceful presence on the intellectual scene with the exhaustive and influential commentary on the text by Giles of Rome, produced around 1272. Giles is at pains to work out the implications of Aristotle's double classification of rhetoric—as "counterpart" (*assecutiva* in William of Moerbeke's translation) of dialectic and as part of ethics as politics. In his commentary as well as in his treatise *De differentia rhetoricae, ethicae et politicae* (On the Difference between Rhetoric, Ethics, and Politics), Giles clearly holds that as method, rhetoric is more closely linked with dialectic than with ethics, and should indeed be considered part of (although not subordinate to) dialectic. In his short treatise, he explicitly prefers Aristotle's opening position (rhetoric to be classified with dialectic) over Cicero's (rhetoric to be classed as part of politics).[185] On the other hand, in his commentary Giles also recognizes and stresses that the reasonings generated by rhetoric are applicable to civil affairs "as something like rhetoric's proper material." Thus, if not in a strict disciplinary sense, then in a general but important sense, rhetoric has a claim to be linked with ethics.

Towards the beginning of his commentary, Giles outlines a number of important distinctions between rhetoric and dialectic, some of which have to do with method, but some of which concern the context and subject matter of rhetorical discourse: the rhetorician deals in moral issues whereas the dialectician works in abstractions; the rhetorician should appeal to emotions; and the audience of rhetorical discourse is simple and unsophisticated.[186] In other words, like Al-Farabi, Giles recognizes that rhetoric appeals to popular outlooks. Whether one is teaching princes the art of governance, or extending that teaching to the populace, the subject matter requires the very procedures and contextual understanding by which Giles defines rhetoric, as an art whose reasonings pertain to the field of ethics. As mediated by Giles in this work and in his vastly influential book *De regimine principum* (On the Rule of Princes), this is the outlook on public rhetoric that stands behind much vernacular advice literature, for example Hoccleve's *Regiment of Princes*, and ultimately texts in the visionary mode of Christine de Pizan's *L'Avision*.[187] Such texts sought justification for their recourse to the "figurative and general" procedures of fiction, that is, for their literary method of exemplarity.[188] From moral philosophy to poetry, the ethical application of rhetoric justifies the affective appeal of fiction and its similitudes.

[185] See within, Commentary on Aristotle's *Rhetoric*, esp. pp. 805–10; and see *De differentia rhetoricae, ethicae et politicae*, ed. Bruni.

[186] See Giles' commentary on the *Rhetoric* within, pp. 799–800.

[187] See Perkins, *Hoccleve's Regiment of Princes*, 88–90; Knapp, *The Bureaucratic Muse: Thomas Hoccleve and the Literature of Late Medieval England*, 81–3; Forhan, *The Political Theory of Christine de Pizan*, 116–17.

[188] On exemplarity in advice literature and Giles' influence, see Scanlon, *Narrative, Authority, and Power: The Medieval Exemplum and the Chaucerian Tradition*, 105–18.

PART I
ARTS OF LANGUAGE, CA. 300–CA. 950

INTRODUCTION

The ancient traditions of grammar and rhetoric remained the foundations of language curricula throughout the Middle Ages. The Middle Ages erected its curricula on a relatively small group of essential texts from Latin antiquity. In Greek antiquity, rhetoric may have come into being as a systematic discipline a little earlier than grammar: first Gorgias and then, more decisively, Aristotle imposed a disciplinary method on rhetoric before Stoic thinkers from the third century BC onwards produced the first coherent theoretical systems of grammar. Even though the methods of grammar and rhetoric were distinctive, there was much commonality between the two disciplines, and from the early Christian period onwards they were more and more entwined in terms of curricular practices and literary applications. But even in view of this commonality, it will be useful here to begin by outlining each discipline separately, surveying their foundational texts from late antiquity and early medieval developments (up to about 1100).

In antiquity, grammar had two functions: to teach language and to teach as well as make judgments about literature: *ars recte loquendi et scribendi* and *enarratio poetarum*. Three linked treatises by the retired poet Terentianus Maurus (late third century AD), *De litteris*, *De syllabis*, and *De metris*, constitute our oldest grammar in verse form. It links the most elementary material from grammar, the theory on letter and syllable, with metrical theory, and thus illustrates how the principles of grammar were seen as the key to understanding poetic form. It also demonstrates the self-reflexive interest in pedagogy and didactic genre of both the late antique and medieval teaching traditions. As to grammar proper, the preeminent textbooks of late antique and medieval grammar were the *Ars minor* and the *Ars maior* of Aelius Donatus (fl. 350), mainstays of curricula and commentaries for the next millennium. Taken together, the *Ars minor* (an elementary classroom handbook on the parts of speech) and the *Ars maior* (a more advanced and complete handbook of rules) form an *Ars grammatica*. In terms of a regularized discipline of grammar in Latin antiquity, Donatus is an intermediate figure, summing up a long tradition of Greek grammatical theory and its Latin adaptations. The universal authority that Donatus' *Ars grammatica* achieved is due in part to Donatus' own renown as a grammarian and as the teacher of St. Jerome, and in part to the highly practical and rationalized structure of the textbooks themselves. The contents of the *Ars maior* are arranged for ready pedagogical reference and are easily summarized: in book 1, definitions of speech or voice (*vox*), and then the letters, syllables, metrical feet, and accents; in book 2, the parts of speech; and in book 3, barbarisms and solecisms, and figures of speech (*schemata*) and tropes. Thus of all the Latin grammatical arts of the fourth century, including the richer encyclopedic treatises by Diomedes and Charisius,[1] it was Donatus' *Ars* that had the most sustained impact on later eras.

Donatus' *Ars maior* draws nearly all of its examples of usage from Virgil's poetry, but in the context of his grammatical handbook no aesthetic or literary analysis takes place beyond enumeration. However, the closeness of the two traditional strands of *grammatica*, language study and literary analysis, is obvious from what is left of his commentary on Virgil and his extant work on Terence.[2] Donatus became the model for later grammarians, and also the object of extensive commentary activity in his own right in the centuries to come. Many of the grammatical handbooks of the fourth and fifth centuries, including the grammars by Servius and Pompeius,[3] are commentaries on, or developments of, the *Ars maior*. The imprint of the *Ars maior*, along with that of Priscian's *Institutiones*, is to be found in the vastly influential early medieval encyclopedias (represented here by Martianus Capella, Cassiodorus, and Isidore of Seville). Donatus' *Ars grammatica* and Virgil commentary together represented a complete course in grammatical theory, rules, and literary application. The close link between these works gave rise to a number of subtraditions of grammar (also closely linked to each other): grammatical commentaries on Virgil; specialized attention to the figures and tropes, taking its rules from book 3 of the *Ars maior* and its examples from Virgil; and a Christianized tradition of Donatus' grammar, which substituted or added examples from Scripture and the Church Fathers. To some extent, Donatus' teaching on Virgil survives in Servius' vast Virgilian commentary (from the later fourth century), which was to supersede Donatus' commentary in long-term influence and establish itself as the unrivaled late antique authority on Virgil. Yet another strand of Virgilian commentary from the fourth century is the rhetorical approach to the *Aeneid* exemplified by the interpretation of the poem by Tiberius Claudius Donatus, possibly a contemporary of the grammarian Aelius Donatus.[4]

The traditions of specialized attention to the figures and tropes, and of Christianizing the textual examples in Aelius Donatus' grammar, also interbred: while the early textual

---

[1] The art by Diomedes is edited in *GL* 1. The standard edition of Charisius is by Barwick.

[2] See Holtz, "À l'école de Donat, de saint Augustin à Bède," 523 and references there. For the dedication and the life of Virgil from this commentary, see the selections from Aelius Donatus below.

[3] Pompeius, *Commentum artis Donati, GL* 5:81–312; Marius Servius Honoratus, *Commentarius in artem Donati, GL* 4:403–48.

[4] See discussion below.

stages of this relationship have not survived and have had to be reconstructed painstakingly from later examples, one remarkable surviving product of this contact between traditions was Bede's *De schematibus et tropis* (On Figures and Tropes), which reproduced Donatus' catalogue of figures and tropes exactly, but substitutes Scripture and Christian examples throughout. Thus we can say that Bede's *De schematibus et tropis*, which proved one of the most successful contributions to medieval study of figurative language, had its roots in the Virgil commentaries of late antiquity.

If for centuries Donatus' *Ars maior* was the anchor of Latin grammar, the reference and framework for further investigation of grammar, the story of Priscian's *Institutiones* is one of a more delayed impact. Priscian's comprehensive and theoretically advanced grammar was written in Constantinople in the first quarter of the sixth century. Books 1–16 of the *Institutiones grammaticae* (Institutes of Grammar), which treat voice and the elements of words, and then the classes of words (or parts of speech), came to be known as *Priscianus maior*; books 17–18 on syntax came to be known as *Priscianus minor*. The two sections could circulate separately. The *Priscianus minor* had its own particular fortunes because it was the only systematic work on Latin syntax produced in antiquity. The whole work began to make its mark in the medieval West during the eighth century: Alcuin was very interested in Priscian's grammar and may have contributed directly to its revival, although his primary source for his *De grammatica* (On Grammar) remained Donatus.[5] But it was in the ninth century, probably with Alcuin's pupil Rabanus Maurus (abbot of Fulda in 822 and archbishop of Mainz in 847), and definitely with Rabanus' pupil Lupus of Ferrières, that the *Institutiones* began to receive sustained attention and attracted explanatory glosses. Many copies of the *Institutiones* issued from the monastic scriptoria in the ninth and tenth centuries, and had some currency among scholars associated with the court schools of the ninth century, including John Scotus Eriugena, to whom a commentary on Priscian has been attributed.[6] Sedulius Scotus, another Irish scholar of the ninth century, also wrote a continuous commentary which survives only in fragmentary form.[7] The nature of Carolingian approaches to Priscian is exemplified here by the glosses from the school of Remigius (late ninth century). But the profound influence of the *Institutiones* on linguistic thought had to await the era around 1100, when Priscian's work was received into a scholarly context newly energized by the methods of logic.[8]

---

[5] Law, *Insular Latin Grammarians*, 21; Luhtala, "Priscian's Definitions are Obscure," 56; Gibson, "Milestones in the Study of Priscian, circa 800–circa 1200," 18.

[6] "*Eriugena in Priscianum*," Dutton and Luhtala, eds. For more general overview, see Kneepkens, "The Priscianic Tradition," 241 and references there.

[7] Ed. Löfstedt, *CCCM* 40C.   [8] See the introduction to Part 3, below.

As noted above, key witnesses to the continuity of Donatan grammatical pedagogy are the encyclopedists, Martianus Capella (fifth century), Cassiodorus (sixth century), and Isidore of Seville (seventh century). Their summaries of grammar draw from the older repositories of grammatical teaching in the Latin West, that is, on the pre-Priscianic tradition that culminated in Donatus' *Ars grammatica*. The importance and ubiquity of these early compendia may have been one factor in the supremacy of Donatus' *Ars* for many centuries, despite the emerging interest in Priscian in the ninth century.

Grammatical work is often characterized by conscious choices of genre and general form, never far removed from the foundational task of teaching about language. We have already mentioned the *De litteris*, *De syllabis*, and *De metris* of Terentianus Maurus, who imposes verse form on his work and who puts the general theory of the letter and the syllable to the service of teaching elements of prosody. While the work was influential in late antiquity, it seems to have been unknown in the later Middle Ages. By contrast, Servius' commentary on the *Aeneid* is the outstanding example of a professional grammarian's approach to a literary classic. The elements and form of his commentary, from the divisions of its prologue to its expository procedure of breaking the text into the smallest lexical units, set the standard for medieval practices of *enarratio poetarum*. The commentary is both explanatory and prescriptive: its explanatory scope is not limited to language use, but encompasses historical, cultural, and intertextual information, as well as teaching about poetic form and literary devices. Two further examples here of the literary, or form-conscious, dimensions of grammatical teaching both come from the Insular Latin tradition: the *Epistola* and *Epitome* of Virgilius Maro grammaticus (seventh century) and Bede's *De arte metrica* (Metrical Art or Art of Poetry) and *De schematibus et tropis* (early eighth century). Virgilius Maro's erudite grammatical fancies did not have a significant influence on later teaching, but represent rather an exuberant appropriation of classical learning. By contrast, Bede's literary-grammatical writings were widely disseminated throughout European monasteries over many centuries. Apart from these more extravagant examples, even the economic handbook style of Donatus' *Ars maior*, or the question-and-answer format of his *Ars minor*, are stylistic and literary choices, related to a specific pedagogy. We will see more examples of such choices, notably in the grammar of Alcuin.

While the Latin grammars that were known and preserved in the medieval West were the products of late antiquity, the main sources of technical rhetorical knowledge were produced in republican Rome, and so offered a direct link to the earlier stages of the discipline. The two signature works that generated the medieval knowledge of rhetoric were Cicero's youthful *De inventione* (On Invention) and the Pseudo-Ciceronian *Rhetorica ad Herennium* (Rhetoric to Herennius), which, until the fifteenth century, was thought to be by Cicero. These works were written within a few years of one another, both around 90 BC.

The works of Cicero's maturity, the *Orator* (55 BC) and the *De oratore* (On the Orator; 46 BC), were for the most part unknown to the Middle Ages. A few passages from the *Orator*, on the levels of style, were known from Augustine's quotation of them in *De doctrina christiana* 4, which was quoted in turn by Rabanus Maurus in his *De institutione clericorum* (On the Instruction of Clerics). The *De oratore*, which was rediscovered by Humanist scholars and in modern times has become the centerpiece of Cicero's rhetorical teaching, was not widely copied or used in the Middle Ages, although it was known to some degree in excerpts. Similarly, Quintilian's *Institutio oratoria* (Institutes of Oratory), written in the first century AD, was not widely known or appreciated until the fifteenth century.[9]

To speak of "Ciceronian rhetoric" in the Middle Ages is to speak of the *De inventione* and *Rhetorica ad Herennium*, but also of the tradition of commentaries, compendia, and handbooks based on the doctrine contained in these two Ciceronian works. The main difference between the two works is that the *Ad Herennium* covers the whole of the art of rhetoric in four books, while the *De inventione*, as its title indicates, deals with only one part of rhetoric, invention. Ancient rhetorical doctrine, as fixed in the two Ciceronian manuals, was a five-part system for generating a speech: invention (*inventio*), which is the discovery (*invenire* "to come upon, to find") of valid or seemingly valid arguments to make one's case plausible; arrangement (*dispositio*), which is the ordering of the arguments that have been discovered; style (*elocutio*), which is the fitting of suitable and expressive language to the invented matter; memory (*memoria*), the method of remembering and calling up the ordered arguments and words so that the orator can speak without a text, as if extemporaneously; and delivery (*pronuntiatio*), the control of voice, body, and physical gesture. These five parts or "canons" of rhetoric all go into the making of three kinds or "genres" of oratory: judicial or forensic, that is, speeches (in prosecution or defense) in law courts; deliberative or political, that is, speeches delivered before political bodies on matters of state policy; and epideictic or demonstrative (ceremonial or "occasional") oratory, that is, speeches devoted to praise or censure of some person.

Of the two works, the *De inventione* had a more continuous influence, the *Ad Herennium* going underground for some centuries and only coming into ascendancy as a preferred authority in the twelfth century. Because of its importance, and because we do not provide selections from it here, a short summary of the *De inventione* will be useful. Cicero begins with an elegant myth about the origins of rhetoric, which he links with the origins of civilization: an eloquent wise man persuaded a savage population to accept the rule of law and to cooperate among themselves. Cicero then gives the genres of oratory and the canons of rhetoric, and announces that this treatise will concern itself with

---

[9] On some limited knowledge of *Institutio oratoria*, see Ward, *Ciceronian Rhetoric*, 78.

invention, the most important of all the divisions of the art. At the heart of invention is the "controversy" (*controversia*) or "issue" (*constitutio*), also known as "status" (*status*, Greek *stasis*), around which any dispute revolves. This may be a question about a fact, a definition, the nature of an action, or legal procedure. One of these issues or *constitutiones* will always be applicable to every kind of case, because a case always involves some controversy. (Did an action occur? How is the action to be defined, e.g. what crime? How is it to be classified, e.g. as justified? Under what legal procedures should the act be tried?) When the issue at stake has been determined through the complex process known as "status theory," and the subordinate legal arguments discovered, the separate divisions of the case must be considered. These divisions of the case correspond to the divisions of the speech, each of which requires its own inventional procedure. The six divisions of the speech are: the *exordium*, in which the good will and attention of the audience are secured; the *narratio*, an exposition of events that have occurred or are supposed to have occurred; the *partitio,* where the structure of the whole speech and the controversy under debate are rendered clear; the *confirmatio* or proof, where the speaker marshals supporting arguments that he derives or "discovers" by exploiting a system of "topics," that is, "places" or "commonplaces" (*loci*, Greek *topoi*), known as the "attributes of the person and the act"; *refutatio*, where the opponent's proof is weakened or refuted; and the *peroratio* (peroration), which is the conclusion of the speech. Book 2 sets out these rules of invention in relation to the three different genres of oratory, with special attention to the forensic or judicial genre.

Book 1 of the *Rhetorica ad Herennium* gives a similar but shorter account of invention; books 2–3 deal with arrangement, memory, and delivery; and book 4 gives an expansive and ultimately influential treatment of style, with a list of figures, here called *exornationes verborum* ("embellishments of words") and *exornationes sententiarum* ("embellishments of thought"). Beginning in the twelfth century, the catalogue of figures in book 4 came to be widely copied or used as a template in treatises on composition.

The study of rhetoric in late antiquity and the early Middle Ages, up through the eighth century and Alcuin's dialogue with Charlemagne on rhetoric, can be characterized in terms of either of two related concerns: a highly technical approach to the subject stressing the rules and elements of invention, especially the system of topics or "commonplaces" of invention and the legal theory that underlies the Ciceronian exposition of this field; or an attention to the dialectical (that is, logical) aspects of the art, also placing an overwhelming emphasis on invention.

The first of these orientations is found in the various independent handbooks on rhetoric that were produced in the Latin West from the fourth to the sixth centuries by the so-called "minor Latin rhetoricians" (after the title of Halm's edition published in 1863,

Rhetores latini minores), including the larger arts by Fortunatianus (a source for Cassiodorus' summary of rhetoric) and C. Julius Victor (a source for Alcuin's treatise). This technographic approach is also exemplified in the chapters on rhetoric of late antique and early medieval encyclopedias: Martianus Capella's *De nuptiis*, Cassiodorus' *Institutiones*, and the *Etymologiae* of Isidore of Seville. The proliferation of such handbooks on rhetoric during this period may have been an effect of the linguistic rupture between the Greek East and the Latin West of the late Empire: the Latin handbooks would have replaced Greek works which students in the West could no longer easily read.[10] Why the technographers present invention almost as if it were an autonomous art that overshadows the other parts of rhetoric is not easily answered. The special interest in status theory may reflect changes in legal systems, the decline of juries, and the need to train students to identify the correct issues of legal situations rather than prepare them for public speaking and presenting briefs.[11] It is also unclear whether the popularity of the *De inventione* was a cause or effect of this narrowing of scope to inventional matters. The encyclopedists carry forward many of the tendencies of their technographic predecessors, although at least Martianus Capella and Isidore of Seville transmit complete, if somewhat unbalanced, outlines of the art.

The second orientation, to the dialectical dimensions of the art, is at the root of the more intellectual tradition of rhetoric, in which the art could be received as an academic science. There is much in the *De inventione* that overlaps with the field of dialectic, especially its treatment of syllogistic reasoning under the heading of probable arguments (part of the section on proof or *confirmatio*, 1.34.57–1.41.77). Late antiquity produced two towering responses to the *De inventione* which ensured the lasting academic influence of Cicero's youthful treatise: the massive commentary on *De inventione* by the Neoplatonist philosopher Marius Victorinus (middle of the fourth century) and book 4 of Boethius' *De topicis differentiis* (On the Different Topics), written about 523. These two works, separately or in tandem, paved the way for Cicero's text, acccompanied Cicero's text, or even substituted for the Ciceronian *ipsa verba* for nearly the next thousand years. The philosophical approaches to rhetoric, and the prestige of these late antique authorities, shaped the understanding of the discipline. The influence of Victorinus and Boethius could be said to be both cause and effect of the tendency to attach rhetoric to dialectic.[12]

It is obvious, therefore, that early medieval Europe, up through 1100, never lost touch with Ciceronian rhetoric, finding it either through the many copies of the works or through various epitomes. This familiarity was not universal throughout Europe: it has

---

[10] Fontaine, *Isidore de Séville et la culture classique*, 1:212; Leff, "The Topics of Argumentative Invention," 35.
[11] Ward, *Ciceronian Rhetoric*, 78.
[12] Ward, "From Antiquity to the Renaissance," 44, and *Ciceronian Rhetoric*, 97.

been argued, for example, that Anglo-Saxon England had no direct knowledge of Cicero, but rather took its rhetorical doctrine from grammatical texts which carried some imprint of rhetorical teaching.[13] But Alcuin, who had a continental career, knew the *De inventione* as well as one or more of the "minor Latin rhetoricians." The earliest surviving manuscripts of the *De inventione* and the *Rhetorica ad Herennium* date from the ninth century. Ciceronian rhetoric found a receptive audience among the prominent scholars of the court and monastic schools of the early Middle Ages. For Alcuin, writing his *Disputatio de rhetorica et de virtutibus* (Disputation on Rhetoric and the Virtues) as an imagined dialogue with Charlemagne sometime before 800, rhetoric was both a technical art of inventing arguments and a public, formal art of presentation. We find similar responses among later Carolingian scholars. For Gunzo of Novara (writing about 965), Notker III of St. Gall (writing around the year 1000), and Anselm of Besate (writing in the middle of the eleventh century), rhetoric is also an art of adjudicating controversies in public or institutional spheres, as suggested by their attention to the inventional method of status theory. But for them rhetoric is also a kind of classical learning to be prized, adapted, and even (in the case of Gunzo especially) paraded.[14]

While grammar and rhetoric each had its own disciplinary development and high points, it is important to remember that in practical as well as even in theoretical contexts they often occupied the same sphere and could share the same body of teaching. The long medieval tradition of Horace's *Ars poetica* suggests the commonality of grammatical and rhetorical interests. The *Ars poetica* lays down precepts for composition: thus its orientation, like that of rhetorical manuals, is towards the future text. But as generations of medieval grammar teachers knew, it also taught recognition and appreciation of the formal properties of poetic style, and thus earned its place as a fixture in the grammar classroom.[15]

To be sure, in Roman antiquity there were theoretically rather firm institutional distinctions made between grammatical and rhetorical curricula and teachers.[16] But neither in ancient practice nor in the early medieval West were such strict distinctions maintained.[17] One important piece of material evidence for the curricular interplay of grammar and rhetoric is an outstanding manuscript, Paris BN MS lat. 7530, written at the abbey of Montecassino between 779 and 796. This manuscript of over 300 folios contains

[13] Knappe, "The Rhetorical Aspect of Grammar Teaching in Anglo-Saxon England." By contrast, Ray has argued from Bede's apparent theoretical knowledge that Cicero was known to him; see below, p. 258, note 10.

[14] On the letter of Gunzo of Novara, see Ward, *Ciceronian Rhetoric*, 85–6; on Notker's *Nova rhetorica*, see Jaffe, "Antiquity and Innovation in Notker's *Nova rhetorica*" and Conley, *Rhetoric in the European Tradition*, 88–90, 106–7; on Anselm of Besate, see Bennett, "The Significance of the *Rhetorimachia* of Anselm de Besate."

[15] See below, introduction to Part 4.

[16] Kaster, "The Grammarian's Authority"; Holtz, "Grammairiens et rhéteurs romains."

[17] See for example Schenkeveld, "Figures and tropes. A Border-case between Grammar and Rhetoric," 149.

forty texts on grammar, nine on rhetoric, one on dialectic, seven texts related to the arts of the quadrivium, a hymn, and an outline of the liberal arts.[18] The manuscript has been linked with the historiographer and court figure Paul the Deacon, and it almost certainly witnesses or even constitutes a curriculum, a book that furnished material for teaching. While its contents are predominantly grammatical (commentaries on sections of Donatus' *Ars maior* as well as selections from late antique grammarians such as Charisius and Pompeius), its rhetorical contents are impressive, including a complete text of Fortunatianus' *Ars rhetorica*. No matter which art prevails in terms of numbers of items, the whole collection seems to be the product of a single and coherent curricular vision.

The teaching of the figures and tropes is a large area where rhetoric and grammar share much ground despite their separate handbook traditions. Not only was there, by late antiquity, a common pool of figures (schemes) and tropes taught by grammarians and rhetoricians, but the history of how figurative language came to be classified reveals an intermingling of rhetorical and grammatical theory at various junctures in the tradition.[19] In the early medieval West, it was the tradition of Donatus and other Latin grammarians that purveyed the teaching of figures, because the major rhetorical works that offered similar information—the *Rhetorica ad Herennium* and Quintilian's *Institutio oratoria*— dropped out of use. The ubiquitous book 3 of Donatus' *Ars maior*, known separately as the *Barbarismus* on account of its first word, filled this role until the late Carolingian period, when the *Ad Herennium* came back into circulation. In the latter part of the eleventh century, Marbod of Rennes produced his *De ornamentis verborum* (On the Ornaments of Language), based on book 4 of the *Ad Herennium*. Marbod's treatise was to influence the teaching of figures for generations to come.[20] The impact of this later shift to the *Ad Herennium* and its rhetorical approach to the teaching of "ornaments of language" can be seen, from the late twelfth century onwards, in a growing emphasis on the discursive power of figurative language, and a particular fascination with the transformative power of the tropes, especially metaphor.

Rhetoric also found a role in another "preserve" of grammatical teaching, learned commentary on poetic texts. The grammarians Donatus and Servius produced vast "grammatical" commentaries on Virgil's poetry, affirming the canonical status of Virgil by subjecting his work to minute analysis of its linguistic usage, literary effects, and mythological lore. But such an enterprise could also advance the formal claims of rhetoric on a work. Tiberius Claudius Donatus contributed yet another massive Virgil commentary

---

[18] Holtz, "Le Parisinus latinus 7530"; Ward, "The Medieval and Early Renaissance Study," 12–16.

[19] On this complex history of grammatical and rhetorical figures, see Holtz, "Grammairiens et rhéteurs romains."

[20] See Camargo, "Latin Composition Textbooks."

to the era, treating the *Aeneid* as a form of epideictic rhetoric, a praise of Aeneas and of the emperor Augustus. A century and a half later, Cassiodorus (himself a consummate product of late antique rhetorical training) was to take a similar approach, but now to a sacred text, the Psalms, which he reads as inspired exercises in the three genres of rhetoric, political, judicial, and epideictic.

Neither the tradition of grammar nor of rhetoric can fully claim Augustine's *De doctrina christiana* for itself. *De doctrina christiana* is the kind of revolutionary book that recasts everything that preceded it and shapes everything to come. It can be treated as a systematic rhetoric, but not an *ars rhetorica* in the classical Ciceronian tradition. Its linguistic thought is continuous with ancient grammar: it emphatically restates grammatical doctrines of language as a system of "conventional" signs by which humans make their thoughts known, and further emphasizes written over spoken language as the object of its analysis. (2.1.1–2.4.5). Augustine also includes the whole system of the language arts (including textual criticism) as a remedy for readers' ignorance or uncertainty about aspects of the language of Scripture (2.11.16–2.15.22; 3.2.2–3.4.8). But the semiotic scope of the *De doctrina christiana* is much greater than that of the grammars of its age because it lays out a theory of sacred signs as well as human language, incorporating an approach to the spiritual *realia* or truths of Scripture as the critical ground for any correct understanding of scriptural discourse (1.1.1–4). It could also be treated as a "grammaticizing" of rhetoric: it conspicuously redefines the principal part of rhetoric, invention or discovery (*modus inveniendi*), as a hermeneutical tool, a method of understanding or discovering what Scripture means (1.1.1: the "means of discovering" what is to be understood in Scripture). In its overwhelming stress on invention or discovery, it is structurally parallel with the Latin rhetorical handbooks of late antiquity; but its technical content bears no relation to the handbooks of that era, because it has evacuated traditional legal and logical procedures of invention and replaced them with a program of close reading informed by Pauline notions of letter and spirit (3.5.9–3.15.23). It is a new paradigm for medieval arts of language. It did not replace the older pagan traditions of grammar and rhetoric, but in its powerful implications as a Christian art of language and art of reading, it at once contained and exceeded the pagan arts that preceded it.[21]

---

[21] Because of the wide availability of the work in multiple translations, selections from the *De doctrina christiana* were not included in the present volume. For further discussion of its influence see above, General Introduction, pp. 47–51, as well as the selection from the Wycliffite Bible, Part 6 within, pp. 845–53. See also Copeland, "The Ciceronian Rhetorical Tradition and Medieval Literary Theory," 239–47, and Sluiter, "Communication, Eloquence and Entertainment in Augustine's *De doctrina christiana*," and further references in these; and Stock, *Augustine the Reader*, 190–206.

TERENTIANUS MAURUS, *DE LITTERIS* AND *DE SYLLABIS*, CA. 300

INTRODUCTION

The North African Terentianus Maurus lived sometime between 150 and 350, most probably end of the third, beginning of the fourth century.[1] He wrote three treatises in verse form on metrics—*De litteris*, *De syllabis*, and *De metris*—originally separate,[2] but transmitted as a whole with continuous verse numbering.[3] Like Tiberius Claudius Donatus, he was probably not a professional grammarian, but rather a retired poet, writing as an old man.[4] He presents the work to his son and son-in-law to correct and criticize. It was probably not intended as a manual for students or teachers, but rather aimed at an audience of poets and versifiers;[5] it was not so much a work of didactic poetry as a "versifiziertes Fachbuch."[6] Terentianus' work is the oldest "verse grammar" we have. The verse form performs several functions. It could certainly assist memorization and pedagogy, especially in the third part of the work, where every meter is discussed in verses that exemplify it. Thus exposition and form reinforce each other. Yet the main purpose of the verse form in this case was probably not mnemonic, but rather to make the dry subject matter more palatable to the reader, and the work of writing up such materials more

[1] Cf. *De syllabis*, ed. and trans. Beck, 10; *De litteris, de syllabis, de metris*, ed. Cignolo, xxvii (end second, beginning third century); Beck, "Terentianus Maurus *non paenitendus inter ceteros artis metricae auctor*," 3214 (end third, beginning fourth century), and see further references there.

[2] Cf. *De litteris, de syllabis, de metris*, ed. Cignolo, xxxviii.

[3] The *De litteris* (vs. 85–278) is written in sotadei, *De syllabis* (vs. 279–1299) in trochaic tetrameters and dactylic hexameters, and *De metris* (1300–2981) first in trochaic tetrameters, then in the meter of the type of verse under discussion. The *praefatio* (vs. 1–84) is in glyconics.

[4] Beck, "Terentianus Maurus," 3215. The work shows signs of its author being grounded in poetic practice, rather than a theoretician: Terentianus Maurus avoids technical terms, and diverges from the grammatical tradition in favor of empirical data of linguistic usage. See e.g. Beck's commentary on *De syllabis*, 384ff. For the type of the layman grammarian, see also below, the introduction to the section on Tiberius Claudius Donatus (who also dedicates his work to his son).

[5] Cf. Beck, "Terentianus Maurus," 3236; 3253.   [6] Cf. Beck, "Terentianus Maurus," 3217.

interesting and challenging for the author himself.[7] In fact, the author insists on the difficulty of the exercise.[8]

The focus of the treatise *De litteris* is very different from that of the grammatical tradition. Basic knowledge is taken for granted, and the poem concentrates on the pronunciation of the different letters. Much attention is paid to the consonantic use of the letters I and U. The poem ends with the use of letters to represent numbers, from which predictions of the future may be derived.

De syllabis deals with the qualities and combinatory possibilities of letters in forming syllables, and with the prosodic qualities of the syllable in the dactylic hexameter. Terentianus' metrical theory is based on the derivation of all meters from the iambic trimeter and the dactylic hexameter, through a familiar set of four categories of change.[9] This theory goes back to Varro and Caesius Bassus (first century AD, Terentianus' main source). Terentianus was very influential between the fourth and sixth centuries (toward the later part of this period, probably through indirect use):[10] he was much admired by, among others, Servius, Augustine, Martianus Capella, Priscian, and Bede. He was unknown in the later Middle Ages (when the alternative metrical theory, working with eight or nine "prototypical meters" represented, for example, by Servius' *De metris Horatii* [On the Meters of Horace], gained the upper hand). He was only rediscovered through a Codex Bobiensis in 1493 (*editio princeps* 1497).

The preface is notable for the comparison between the writer on metrics and a former Olympic champion. The ending of *De syllabis* also adds a personal touch by describing the author's struggle with sickness. It contains the one quote that made Terentianus famous (*habent sua fata libelli*). The other passages excerpted here are the formal and the actual opening of the treatise on syllables (*On Syllables* 279ff.; 342ff.).

Translated from Terentianus Maurus, *De litteris, de syllabis, de metris*, ed. Cignolo, by permission.[11]

[7] Cf. Beck, "Terentianus Maurus," 3218 (adducing among other passages *De syllabis* 281f. and 305f., and the preface).

[8] For verse grammars, see also the sections on Alexander of Villa Dei and Eberhard of Béthune (Part 4). Law, "Why Write a Verse Grammar?", points out the usefulness of verse when the material does not obviously lend itself to a logically structured division. However, for Terentianus this is not the most important factor in his choice of genre.

[9] Cf. Beck, "Terentianus Maurus," 3244ff. The four categories are: *adiectio, detractio, concinnatio, mutatio*. Cf. Usener, "Ein altes Lehrgebäude der Philologie"; Ax, "*Quadripertita ratio*: Bemerkungen zur Geschichte eines aktuellen Kategoriensystems (*adiectio-detractio-transmutatio-immutatio*)"; and see below in the etymology dossier.

[10] Cf. *De syllabis*, ed. and trans. Beck, 11.

[11] See also *GL* 6:325ff.; *De syllabis*, ed. and trans. Beck, and review by Sluiter in *Mnemosyne* 48; Beck, "Terentianus Maurus."

FROM *DE LITTERIS*

[Preface, *De litteris* 1–84]

 I heard an old man
 tell a story in public:
 a threefold Olympic victor
 under the protection of Zeus
5 saw grey old age
 approaching his strength
 while still being spoken of as the victor of all.
 He hurried to break off
 the duties of training and diet,
10 but to prevent the sudden leisure
 from bringing about the ruin of his physique,
 he claimed to have thought up
 the following type of exercise
 which he would engage in at home by himself.
15 He connected to each other
 fine pieces of string to form a smooth line
 just like a Parthian or Scythian
 connects a fine string
 to the ends of his bow:
20 he kept tying these together
 until he had a length of rope
 that would be long enough for the well.
 From there, then, he would pull up
 full jars of waters, from the deepest darkness
25 by such a fine line
 that it couldn't be gripped with the full palm of the hand,
 by concentrating the efforts from all parts of the body
 in the tips of his fingers.
 And holding a tight grip
30 until the slippery burden
 emerged into the light above
 through the space of such a large hollow shaft,
 by the alternate pinching with his thumbs
 he struggled to prevent the easy escape

35   of the weight into the depth.
      You may think he did not do anything of importance
      and that the effort was in his fingers only.
      Yet in all the innermost parts of his body
      the hidden effort is aquiver.
40   You can see all, yet it is not apparent
      where it is all achieved:
      By invisible breaths the innermost
      corners of the lungs are extended,
      his knee and knee-hollow are shaking,
45   and his feet cannot remain stable.
      Nothing is left unaffected,
      and (yet) all these powers have but a small outlet.[12]
      The habit and manner are those of a fight,
      while the customary sweat pours down,
50   without the effort of the wrestling arena.

      Thus our old age too
      —now that our mature talent
      refuses to speak of grand subjects
      and our organism does not have the breath—
55   treads the narrow path of study
      and its subtle track,
      only to prevent our mouth from wrongly
      accustoming itself to the silence of inactivity.

      What is a letter, what are two,
60   what are syllables, when they are joined,[13]
      we will pursue between thorny bushes and rough terrain
      in shallow waters with sharp rocks.
      It looks like a humble activity
      one you may think fit for children,

---

[12] Namely, just thumb and index finger.

[13] This is where the topic of the whole treatise seems to be announced. However, a simple equation of the three parts with the parts on the letter, the syllable, and meters, will not do, because it would be odd to announce the part on the syllable as the combination of two letters, since a syllable could be said to consist of one letter, but would usually be defined as a combination of two or more letters. However, the tripartition could refer to a division in phonetics, prosody (always a function of letters in combination) and metrics. See comments by Cignolo in *De litteris, de syllabis, de metris*, ed. Cignolo, 237f.

65   but for the one who has undertaken it, the work is hard
    and the weight unmanageable.[14]
    But the mind makes a greater effort
    in order not to content itself with what is common,
    and in order that subtle clues do not escape
70   the man who is on the search for what is hidden,
    or that he make false distinctions
    in such subtle subject matter.
    Skillful caution is on the alert
    to prevent the discourse from sounding ambiguous,
75   or too archaic or too smooth;
    a series of sounds should not produce hiatus,
    nor should the structure be disjointed,
    nor may it have anything unclear.
    While we are going forward with steady foot,
80   the [metrical] feet themselves should not be shaky.[15]
    The testing is equally fervent
    as if you were discussing elevated subject matter,
    the time necessary to pronounce verdict is the same.
    The glory of ostentation is cheap.[16]

    [*De litteris* 85–107.]

85   The elements [*elementa*][17] which schoolteachers teach to boys who are beginners,
    some of them they call vowels [*vocalia*], and some of them consonants [*consona*]:
    "vowels" because they are capable of making a sound [*vox*] by themselves
    and because no word can come into being without them.
    But the ones that are consonants, unless you join them to vowels,
90   will partly produce by themselves half the work of a sound [*vox*],[18]
    and partly they will clamp shut and deprive of sound the mouths of those trying to
        pronounce them.
    The former have a sound that is darker and more obstructed,
    yet it can be produced with the mouth half-closed,
    and it is less than that of the vowels and more than that of the mutes.

---

[14]   The expression is obviously meant to recall the Olympic athlete.

[15]   Jokes on the basis of the homonymy between a (human) foot and a metrical foot were topical ever since Aristophanes, *Frogs* 1323f. For other jokes on meter and body parts, see Sluiter, "Textual Therapy: On the Relationship between Medicine and Grammar in Galen."

[16]   I.e. the ostentation of those dealing with grandiose subject matter.

[17]   The theme of the section is its first word.   [18]   Circumlocution for "semi-vowels."

95 These latter have a sound value [*soni vis*] that is completely imperceptible and hidden:
its exertion cannot open up through the lips, nor sound through the tongue,
or open up for itself any path
unless vowels are connected to it and unlock the mouth.
Since the material is subtle, hence hard to demonstrate in words,
100 examples usually illuminate our understanding.
When I wish to say *B* to you, or *C, D,* or *G,*
if I withhold *E* from them, which provides them with sound,
the lips will be pressed together and the tongue will be tied:
When this vowel [*e*] is connected with them, it spontaneously renders
105 their silent and too mute force capable of expressing the sound hiding within them,
and it gives to the ears the double sensation from both letters
if one has been instructed in their correct rendering [*proprietas*][19] and if the rules are
known.

FROM *DE SYLLABIS*

[*De syllabis* 279–326 (the opening of the treatise on syllables)]

Syllables which rightly fit the heroic meter
280 I have brought together and expounded, according to my capacity,[20]
in verses, hoping of course that adding the sonorous smoothness of the measures
might alleviate the tedium of a rather dry subject matter.
You must first refine this, my son Bassinus, and you, my son-in-law Novatus,
as much as you can, by frequent application of the fine file.
285 Not as if I am your father and father-in-law, but as if I were a stranger
you must check to see whether for each individual letter
the original force [*nativitas*] of each has been distinguished correctly;
whether the force of syllables joined out of two vowels[21]
has not been found and set out scrupulously;
290 whether I expressed with too little precision or clarity
how much of a difference it makes if one consonant precedes a vowel,
or, when one vowel is put in front of two consonants,
how much of a difference this produces for the [metrical] feet;
see if my speech is clear and keeps to prosaic modesty,

[19] Cf. comments by Cignolo, *ad loc.* in *De litteris, de syllabis, de metris*, ed. Cignolo.
[20] *Captus ut meus ferebat*; cf. vs. 1286 below: *pro captu lectoris habent sua fata libelli.*   [21] i.e. diphthongs.

295 the tone learned scholars recommend for teaching;[22]
whether the wording without being far-fetched and unknown to most,
but rather in common use, yet not commonplace,
preserves the dignity of a poem, not of a lowly song,
with which one marks the beat of the turns, when sitting at an olive press.

300 It suffices to avoid defects and to remain free from meanness,
to struggle for a stylistic level adequate to the contents,[23]
free from the shine of the schools [of rhetoric], having taken off the poet's cloak,
a style which leaves behind all tropes [*tropos*] and proud figures [*schemata*],
in order that by neglecting itself it may be praised for its lack of refinement:

305 as long as it manages for this subtle material,
which even without meter our language could barely set out without giving offense,
to bring it to a safe conclusion in this tricky verse form,
preserving everywhere the rule that the ending of the fourth foot
brings the first verse-part [*comma*] to a close with the end of a noun or verb.

310 For that caesura is the test of this trochaic meter.
Whether my pen has managed this measure competently,
or whether the result of my work has fallen short of its intended course,
that you should weigh more sharply than hostile readers would.
My work will remain locked up at home, nor will I allow it to become known

315 before your judgment will deliver me from this worry,
whether my trouble has been taken in vain or to some useful purpose.
The effort you will have to make in reading is enormous:
for through a cursory or careless reading no one will be able to follow
these subtle complexities, but for the reader

320 the same long concentration is needed that we also had,
we who kept looking for difficulties, conquered boredom,
and dug out from its hiding place what many perhaps have ignored,
aiming to be praised for something hard, not to get approval for what is ordinary.
If some elements will appear to you to be in need of correction,

325 I will not stupidly resist, nor be wrongly in love with my own ideas,
so that I would not immediately delete what comes in for reproach in order to make
place for what is right.

[After the introductory remarks and an observation about method, the treatise on syllables begins (lines 342–89).].

[22] *Disputandi . . . tenorem.* For teaching and the simple style, see Cicero, *Orator* 29.101; Augustine, *De doctrina christiana* 4.19.38.
[23] According to the rhetorical principle of aiming at *to prepon*.

The mother and nurse of the arts is the diligence of the Greeks:
no people, then, has found an interest in letters with more care,
and refined it to the very end in all detail.

345 Yet the Latins, through imitation, without a great deal of self-confidence
(for our language does not admit so many possibilities),[24]
have produced a linguistic abundance which is not inferior.
Therefore I have thought it appropriate to put in this work, on syllables,
which I have just begun to write, the origins of letters,

350 which are derived from there, in order to show more clearly
at the same time both how many of our things do not correspond to the Greek ones,
and that what does correspond has been handed down by them to us.
The origin of the art[25] spreads from there, the language however is not so
     influential.[26]
So then, we know that among their seven vowels the Greeks have

355 *êta* and *ô*, which each provide two beats to [metrical] feet,[27]
and that [Gr.] *e* and [Gr.] *o* are called short, with one beat each.
The remaining three they call *dikhronoi* ["of two measures/beats"]
because the same letters can be taken now short, now long.
Alpha is the first, then *iôta*, and the third the one they call *u*.

360 However since our language takes all of its five vowels,
the same ones, now short and now long,
it uses them as long ones, and applies the same ones equally as short;
and it does not require a vowel always to be short, or always long,
but always uses all five vowels as *dikhronoi*.

365 This is the origin of the multitude of different syllables,
since not even those three which the Greek calls *dikhronoi*
always exhibit the same sounds as our letters:[28]
alpha we call *A*, and equally *iôta* we call *I*;
But the third one, which they call *u*[*psilon*] the Roman language does not have.

---

[24] Cf. Fögen, *Patrii sermonis egestas: Einstellungen lateinischer Autoren zu ihrer Muttersprache.* See also the etymology dossier for the relationship between Latin and Greek.

[25] Namely, of grammar, cf. vs. 342 *artium parens*.

[26] *Lingua non tantum patet*: we follow *De syllabis*, ed. and trans. Beck *ad loc.*, in referring this to the limited sphere of influence of the Greek language (*non tantum* = "not that far"); hence his translation: "Von dort kommt der Ursprung der Kunst, die Sprache <aber> findet nicht so weite Anwendung." Compare Cignolo, ed., *ad loc.*, who takes *non tantum* as a postponed "not only," and translates: "Da lì non soltanto si sviluppa la lingua, ma scaturisce l'origine di questa disciplina."

[27] *Tempus* is a length-unit; it is usually translated "beat" here.

[28] "Sound" (*sonus*) refers to the expression of quantity here.

370   In its stead it seems the Latin *U* has been substituted,[29]
      which at times for us takes the place of the lacking *u*[*psilon*],
      namely when it renders a sound that is common to Latin and Greek,
      but at times does not even preserve its character of a vowel, because of which
      it was adopted [among the vowels], and often changes the rule of the syllables—[30]

375   not, of course, when as a vowel it ties up a consonant,[31]
      but when we produce a syllable with two vowels,
      and this one is put in first position, it becomes a consonant.[32]
      Further, if it follows a vowel, it preserves the force of vowels
      and connects both sounds, whence these are called "diphthongs"

380   by the masters of Greece, because two [vowels] are connected with each other
      and produce the sound of one syllable;[33] being provided with a double force[34]
      they always preserve the effect of two measures/beats,
      whether they are pronounced with lengthened or shortened sound.[35]
      This may perhaps seem astonishing at first sight,

385   that I claim that a syllable pronounced short can be of two beats,
      but it will become probable if one examines the form of the feet.
      For we do not pronounce the Latin [diphthongs] less frequently with short sound
      [than the Greek ones],[36] although they are produced by two vowels,
      which themselves, too, equally provide the feet with two beats.[37]

[The end of the treatise on syllables, with the one quote that made Terentianus famous (lines 1282–99)]

      Maybe someone will not hesitate to call this book verbose.
      Maybe someone much more excellent will think
      that only few things have been found here, while he himself found more.

---

[29] Cf. *De litteris* 135–41. Reference in what follows is to three usages of the letter U: 1. Similar to Greek *u*; 2. U + consonant (where U is a vowel); 3. vowel + U (where U helps form a diphthong). Terentius then goes on to discuss diphthongs.

[30] Namely, when U changes from a vowel into a consonant, affecting the syllable structure.

[31] I.e. when a syllable consists of U followed by consonant (e.g. *pu-to*).   [32] As in UIS (*vis*).

[33] E.g. *au, eu*.   [34] Namely of the two vowels.

[35] This theory is unique for Terentianus. Normally, a diphthong is held to be long "by nature." According to Terentianus, it just counts as long for metrical purposes, but may in fact be pronounced short, something Terentianus surely derived from the practice of normal (possibly local) usage. Cf. Beck, ed. and trans., 182. Terentianus himself calls this astonishing. According to Cignolo, ed. (*ad loc.*), what he finds surprising is not the shortened pronunciation, but the fact that the diphthong nevertheless counts as long for metrical purposes!

[36] There are various circumstances under which a Greek diphthong (e.g. *ai*) counts as short for the purposes of accentuation or meter.

[37] I.e. two individual vowels produce two beats, as one would then also expect from their combination into a diphthong.

1285 The slow and impatient will think that this is much too obscure:
Books have their fates according to what the reader can grasp.[38]
But I do not regret my judgment: it is good that I committed this
to you,[39] who have both love and wisdom,
and in whom is always firmly planted your usual industriousness.

1290 You I will follow, when you have examined this, that's caution enough.
While I wrote this, I was sick for two times five months
and was hanging as an ambiguous[40] body in the judging scales,
swaying in alternate directions, but not sinking down through either weight.
For neither did Death avidly open its black gaping holes

1295 nor did the Parcae[41] hold on to my life with a strong thread.
In that way such a long time led to the present day,
renewing the different pains, and always threatening without end.
Yet, when I could, I crept up and finished what I had begun,
so that, uncertain of my life, even so people could see I had lived.

---

[38] *Pro captu lectoris habent sua fata libelli*, usually quoted without the first three words.
[39] His son and son-in-law, cf. vs. 283 above.
[40] *Ambiguum . . . corpus*, i.e. it was unclear whether he was alive or dead.   [41] Goddesses of fate.

AELIUS DONATUS, *ARS MINOR, ARS MAIOR, LIFE OF VIRGIL*, CA. 350

INTRODUCTION

Aelius Donatus (ca. 350)[1] is the figure who looms largest in late antique and medieval grammar. The *Ars minor* by this teacher of Saint Jerome would become the standard Latin primer throughout the Middle Ages. His three-part *Ars maior* also remained a classic, providing the standard structure for any treatment of grammar until it was replaced with the fourfold division into *ortographia*, *prosodia*, *ethimologia*, *diasintastica* ("syntax") current in the later Middle Ages. Its status as a classic is underlined by the fact that it instantly became the subject of many commentaries.[2] From late antiquity there are commentaries by Servius, Sergius, Cledonius, and Pompeius.

Latin grammar under the Roman Empire ultimately goes back to Greek contributions to linguistic thought, made in the context of reading the poets (philology), philosophy, and rhetoric. The first teaching manuals were written during the Hellenistic period. During the late second and first centuries BC, Rome became a new center of intellectual activity where Greek and Roman intellectuals exchanged ideas. In this setting, the first major encyclopedic theory of Latin was compiled by Varro, and the first (now lost) *ars grammatica* by Q. Remmius Palaemon, the teacher of Quintilian (first century AD). While Greek grammar reached an intellectual peak in the second century AD with the theoretically sophisticated work of Apollonius Dyscolus and his son Herodian;[3] there is a gap in our sources for this period on the Roman side. But under the later Empire, from the third century onwards, and especially in the fourth and fifth centuries AD, a new type of *ars*

---

[1] Kaster, *Guardians of Language*, number 52. Along with all students of Donatus, we are deeply indebted to the masterful study by Holtz, *Donat et la tradition de l'enseignement*.

[2] Beck, *Zur Zuverlässigkeit der bedeutendsten lateinischen Grammatik*, points out that the universal praise heaped on Donatus should be evaluated critically and proceeds in a rather polemical spirit to show passages where Donatus is either incorrect or unclear or both.

[3] On Apollonius Dyscolus, see Blank, *Ancient Philosophy and Grammar*; Sluiter, *Ancient Grammar in Context*; Ildefonse, *La naissance de la grammaire dans l'Antiquité grecque*; and bibliography at http://schmidhauser.us/apollonius/bibliography. What we consider "syntactic" information was part of the "meaning" half of the opposition form—meaning in ancient grammar.

grammatica, clearly designed for use in teaching (now designated as *Schulgrammatik*) became very popular. On the Greek side, however, we lack this type of source.[4] Ultimately, the *Schulgrammatik* goes back to Greek (philosophical) ideas, but these were filtered through their reception in Varro and Palaemon, and any original philosophical connections not already watered down in Hellenistic philology were now largely lost. In thinking about the history of linguistic thought it is imperative to keep in mind these different contexts and the discontinuities even within seeming continuity.

Donatus' work represents this *Schulgrammatik* or "school grammar" of the Empire.[5] The *Schulgrammatik* is a word-and-accident grammar with very little sense of "syntax" beyond the basic concept of "combining parts of speech" into larger units.[6] Donatus' *Ars minor*, most likely composed after and excerpted from the *Ars maior*, aims at beginners and rehearses the main concepts of the theory of the parts of speech in question and answer format. The *Ars maior* consists of three parts: I. *vox, littera, syllaba, pedes, toni, positurae*; II. *partes orationis, nomen, pronomen, verbum, adverbium, participium, praepositio, coniunctio, interiectio*; III. *barbarismus, soloecismus, cetera vitia, metaplasmus, schemata, tropi*.

Donatus' two *artes* are characterized by a number of pedagogically inspired principles:[7] they represent two stages in teaching, one for beginners, one for more advanced students; they aim at concision, leaving out material that would be unnecessarily burdensome; even the advanced *Ars* omits the identification of sources; and all exceptions and miscellaneous considerations are relegated to the end of each section. Although one of the purposes of grammar is to offer a framework for reading the poets, this structure makes the direct connection with poetry virtually invisible.[8] The structure is entirely hierarchical, and rigidly articulated, building up from the most basic units smaller than the word to the heart of the theory, the parts of speech, to the rhetorical superstructure dealing with

[4] Within the *Schulgrammatik*, closely related grammars are considered to form "groups." Donatus' grammar is the head of the "Donatus-group," which also comprises the grammars by Diomedes (370–380), clearly aimed at a Greek audience, and Consentius (400–410); the commentaries on Donatus also belong to this group. See Holtz, *Donat et la tradition de l'enseignement*, 82–4, who claims that Diomedes and Consentius are directly dependent on Donatus, rather than on a common ancestor of all three.

[5] The term is not quite logical, since obviously other types of grammar would also be used in teaching, but it has been traditional ever since Barwick, *Remmius Palaemon und die römische Ars grammatica* (1922), who also defended the claim that the *Schulgrammatik* goes back to Remmius Palaemon in the first century AD. Whereas Barwick restricted the use of the term to primers such as the *Ars minor*, it is now used for all hierarchically ordered and rigidly structured Latin grammars, especially including texts such as the *Ars maior*, destined for the more advanced student. Cf. Schenkeveld, in C. Julius Romanus: Schenkeveld, ed., *A Rhetorical Grammar*, 14–17 for the older distinction, Law, *The History of Linguistics*, 65–6 for the more general usage.

[6] On Latin grammar see especially Baratin, *La Naissance de la Syntaxe à Rome*, and Baratin and Desbordes, "La 'troisième partie' de l'*ars grammatica*."

[7] Holtz, *Donat et la tradition de l'enseignement*, 91–3.

[8] See within, section on Priscian, for a grammarian who gives ample space to poetic examples.

stylistics. The organizing principle of the work is a structure *per divisionem*: it consists mostly of definitions and subdivisions;[9] it gives lists; and each of the items on the list is discussed systematically. The compelling logic of the organization seems to presuppose a view of language as a rational, logical system, but (unlike Greek grammars as well as Priscian's grammar) the *Ars* does not articulate any philosophical principles.[10]

The presence of the "third part" of the *Ars maior*, dealing with linguistic error and stylistic enrichment deserves special mention: it characterizes imperial *Schulgrammatik*, not only differentiating this type of text from beginners' manuals, but also setting it apart from its Greek predecessors.[11] Donatus' pedagogical aim is to help his students avoid mistakes. He distinguishes barbarisms, solecisms, and "other mistakes." Barbarisms occur in single words in ordinary language, solecisms are errors in the connection of words. Both are the result of ignorance. But they can also be the result of the extraordinary linguistic mastery of great poets—in which case they are called "transformation" (*metaplasmus*) or "figures" (*schemata*) respectively. This is not just a matter of the difference between prose and poetry: what is at stake is the difference between ignorance and mastery, inadvertent mistake and conscious and purposeful deviation.[12] Donatus does not discuss these from the perspective of aesthetic appreciation, but just gives a technical description. We will see how this same distinction plays out in Servius to indicate the difference between what does and what does not lend itself for imitation.

The tropes and figures are an ambiguous area in the delineation of the domains of grammarians and rhetoricians. Grammarians as "guardians of language" were the traditional authority in matters of linguistic correctness.[13] And linguistic correctness is a

---

[9] Luhtala, "On definitions in ancient grammar," shows that only with Donatus does the grammatical definition acquire this formalized format. Earlier definitions would often introduce etymological information. But in defining the different parts of speech, Donatus will systematically give the "substantial definition" first (i.e. "x is a part of speech") and then add the "accidentia." His definitions are focused on semantic content of the term at issue. See Law, "Memory and the Structure of Grammars in Antiquity and the Middle Ages," and Law, *The History of Linguistics in Europe*, on the systematic nature of Donatus' *per divisionem* organization of his grammar and its pedagogical value.

[10] Law, *The History of Linguistics in Europe* (discussion of Donatus, 65–80) mentions the link between logical organization and the idea that language itself is logical by nature.

[11] Barwick, *Remmius Palaemon und die römische Ars grammatica*, 89–111 and "Probleme der stoischen Sprachlehre," had suggested that Stoic ideas on virtues of style were at the basis of the "third part"; this was refuted conclusively by Baratin and Desbordes, "La 'troisième partie' de l'*ars grammatica*." In Stoic theory, correct Greek constitutes the norm, and this leaves no space for "outdoing" the norm. On figures of speech, see Flobert, "La théorie du solécisme," discussing links with logical theory; Baratin, *La naissance de la syntaxe à Rome*, 261–322; Schenkeveld, "Figures and Tropes: A Border Case between Grammar and Rhetoric"; Calboli "The *Schemata lexeos*: A Grammatical and Rhetorical Tool."

[12] So Holtz, *Donat et la tradition de l'enseignement*, 170.

[13] Cf. Kaster, *Guardians of Language*, especially 169–96; Siebenborn, *Die Lehre von der Sprachrichtigkeit und ihren Kriterien*.

starting point for the rhetorician. But poetic exegesis and rhetorical text production sometimes require similar tools, and this is where the theory of tropes and figures belongs. The "figures" themselves are divided into "figures of speech" (*lexeos*) and "figures of thought" (*dianoeas*). This is not the same distinction as that between changes "in one word" or "in more words," which is relevant for the distinction between "metaplasm" and "figure." The "figures" all occur in combinations of words, but within them there is a distinction between figures that work on the level of the expression, and figures that affect the level of thought or meaning.[14]

Whereas the *Ars maior* just provides names, definitions, and examples of the figures, the text by Donatus that seems to have exercised most influence on the "theory of figures" in the earliest commentaries on his grammar was not the *Ars* itself, but rather his exegetical and more expansive work in the commentaries he wrote on Virgil and Terence.[15] Donatus' commentary on Terence is extant; but from his work on Virgil we have only the dedicatory letter to Lucius Munatius, translated below, a "Life of Virgil" heavily dependent on Suetonius' *vita* of Virgil,[16] and an introduction to his commentary on the *Eclogues*. There is much debate about the extent to which Donatan material was adopted in the extended version of the Virgil commentary by Servius.[17] But in any case, Virgil is the most important literary source in Donatus' *Ars maior*, although his name is constantly omitted. The Donatan Life is constructed as the perfect corollary of Virgil's work: there are omens connected with his birth that indicate future poetic greatness (e.g. mention of the laurel which is sacred to Apollo). Poetic tradition and continuity are hinted at by the synchronicity of Virgil's coming of age and the death of Lucretius. And in spite of connections with boys and a woman, there is an overall sense of moral greatness.

Translated from *GL* 4 ed. Keil, and *Vitae Vergilianae Antiquae*, ed. Hardie, by **permission.**

---

[14] *Lexis* has the more general sense of "expression" here (Holtz, *Donat et la tradition de l'enseignement*, 183).

[15] Schindel, *Die lateinischen Figurenlehren des 5. bis 7. Jahrhunderts*, discusses the commentaries by Pompeius (fifth century), "Sergius" (fifth–sixth century), and the lost examples of the work by Isidore of Seville, Julian of Toledo, and "Isidore junior." Holtz, *Donat et la tradition de l'enseignement*, 49ff. discusses the difference between treatments of similar phenomena in the schoolbook version of the *Ars* and the more expansive, academic genre of the *variorum* commentary.

[16] See Ziolkowski and Putnam, *The Virgilian Tradition*, 189–99; 227, 406, 424.

[17] See section on Servius, pp. 125–40, within. The extended version is known as "Servius *auctus*" or "Servius Danielis." Daintree, "The Virgil commentary of Aelius Donatus: Black Hole or *éminence grise*?" argues that a correct assessment of commentary practices and medieval intellectual practice in general should make us wary of straight attributions to Donatus of material found in the Servius *auctus*.

FROM *ARS MINOR*[18]

1. On the Parts of Speech

How many parts of speech are there? Eight. Which ones? Noun, pronoun, verb, adverb, participle, conjunction, preposition, interjection.

2. On the Noun

What is a noun? A part of speech with case signifying a body or a thing as a proper name [uniquely] or as a common name [generally]. How many *accidentia*[19] does the noun have? Six. Which ones? Quality, comparison, gender, number, figure, case.

In what consists the quality of nouns? It is twofold: for either it is the name of one thing and is called "proper name," or it is that of many things and is called "appellative" [common name].

How many degrees of comparison are there? Three. What are they? The positive degree, e.g. "learned," the comparative, e.g. "more learned," the superlative, e.g. "most learned." What nouns undergo comparison? Appellative nouns as long as they signify a quality or a quantity: a quality, like "good"; a quantity, like "great," "small." What case does the comparative degree serve? The ablative without a preposition: for we say *doctior illo* "more learned **than he**" [pron.abl.]. And the superlative? The genitive plural only: for we say *doctissimus poetarum* "most learned **of the poets**" [gen.plur.].

How many genders does the noun have? Four. What are they? Masculine, e.g. *hic magister* "this master," feminine, e.g. *haec Musa* "this Muse," neuter, e.g. *hoc scamnum* "this bench,"[20] common, e.g. *hic et haec sacerdos* "this priest/ess."[21] There are also nouns of three genders, called "everything," as *hic/haec/hoc felix* "happy m/f/n"; and there is the *epicoenon*, i.e. "indiscriminate," e.g. *passer aquila* "sparrow, eagle."[22]

---

[18] *GL* 4: 355. 1–27 (= Holtz, *Donat et la tradition de l'enseignement*, 585f.).

[19] The features or properties of a part of speech are called *accidentia*. They are "what happens to" (*accidit*) the word.

[20] Note the common didactic practice of choosing as examples of the grammatical genders words which are easily identified as male, female, or "neither" (*neutrum*), i.e. a thing, in the real world. Note further the use of the demonstrative pronoun *hic haec hoc* for quick identification of what gender is meant. The forms of *hic* are used where, for the same purpose, the Greek would have used the article, which Latin does not have.

[21] "Common" nouns have the same form in the masculine and feminine, but their modifiers will take the masculine or feminine form.

[22] *Passer* "sparrow" is always grammatically masculine, whether it denotes a female or a male bird; similarly, *aquila* "eagle" is always feminine. The difference with the common noun *sacerdos* is that common nouns can either

How many numbers does the noun have? Two. What are they? Singular, e.g. *hic magister* "this master," plural, e.g. *hi magistri* "these masters."

How many figures does the noun have? Two. What are they? Simple, e.g. *decens* "fitting," *potens* "powerful," compound, e.g. *in-decens* "un-fitting," *in-potens* "powerless." How do nouns form compounds? In four ways: from two intact [*integer*] words, e.g. *sub-urbanus* "suburban";[23] from two affected [*corruptus*] words, e.g. *ef-ficax* "effient," *muni-ceps* "citizen";[24] from an intact and an affected word, e.g. *in-sulsus* "tasteless";[25] from an affected and an intact word, e.g. *nugigerulus* "dealer in women's stuff";[26] sometimes from several words, e.g. *in-ex-pugna-bilis* "inexpugnable," *in-per-territus* "unterrified."

How many cases does the noun have? Six. What are they? Nominative, genitive, dative, accusative, vocative, ablative. Nouns, pronouns, and participles of all genders are declined in these cases as follows . . .

[Following this introduction of the noun, the *Ars minor* has a survey of the declensions and similar, but shorter discussions of the other parts of speech.]

From *Ars maior*[27]

I 1. On Sound [Voice][28]

Sound[29] is air that is struck which is perceptible to the ear, in and by itself.[30] Every sound is either articulate or confused. Articulate sound can be captured in letters, confused sound cannot be written.

---

behave as masculine nouns, when they denote a male, or as feminine nouns, when they denote a female. This will appear, e.g. from the gender of accompanying adjectives.

[23]   The two halves of the compound are each complete words in Latin: *sub* and *urbanus*.

[24]   Neither of the two halves of the compound is a complete and unchanged word: *ef-ficax*, comes from *ex* and *facio*; *muni-ceps* comes from *munia* and *capio*.

[25]   *In* is a complete Latin word, *sulsus* relates to *salsus*.   [26]   *Gerulus* is complete, *nugi* relates to *nugae* "trifles."

[27]   *GL* 4:367.1–4.369.15 = *de voce, littera, syllaba* (=Holtz, *Donat et la tradition de l'enseignement*, 603,1ff.)

[28]   On the chapter *De voce* see: Ax, *Laut, Stimme und Sprache: Studien zu drei Grundbegriffe der antiken Sprachtheorie*; Schenkeveld, "Studies in the History of Ancient Linguistics IV: Developments in the Study of Ancient Linguistics"; Stroh, "De vocis definitione quadam Stoica"; Ax, "Zum *de voce*-Kapitel der römischen Grammatik."

[29]   *Vox* is "voice," "sound," "utterance" (articulate/inarticulate), "word." The emphasis in using this term is always on the form of the word as opposed to its meaning. We will not strive after totally consistent translation, since that could be misleading, but indicate what Latin word hides behind the English terminology.

[30]   "In and by itself": *quantum in ipso est*. There are two competing interpretations of this phrase: (1) "in as far as it depends on the air that has been struck," that is, independent of the question whether the sound is actually perceived. This disambiguates the phrase "perceptible to the ear." Thus Stroh, "De vocis definitione quadam

I 2. *On the Letter*[31]

The letter is the smallest part of articulate sound [*vox articulata*]. Of the letters, some are vowels, others consonants. Of the consonants, some are semi-vowels, others are mute.

Vowels are letters that can be brought forth by themselves and that make a syllable by themselves. They are five in number, *a e i o u*. Two of these, *i* and *u*, cross over to the value of consonants, when they are either repeated themselves, or are combined with other vowels, e.g. *Iuno* "Juno," *uates* "vates, seer." They are also called "middle" letters, because in certain words they do not have an explicit sound, *i*, as in *uir* "man," *u*, as in *optumus* "best."[32] Apart from having its form the letter *u* is sometimes considered neither a vowel nor a consonant,[33] when it is put between the consonant *q* and a vowel, e.g. *quoniam, quidem*. A digammon [F/W] is also commonly written next to it, when it is put in front of itself, e.g. *seruus* > *servus, uulgus* > *vulgus*.[34] For most people deny that the letter *i* can be doubled in one syllable.[35]

All Latin vowels can be taken long or short. And some people think that these alone can take an aspiration.

Semi-vowels are letters that, although they can be pronounced by themselves, do not produce a syllable by themselves. There are seven of them, *f l m n r s x*. One of these is double, *x*, four are liquids, *l m n r*, and of these *l* and *r* produce a syllable that is common;[36] the letter *s* has a peculiar force of its own: in meter it usually loses its force as a consonant.

Stoica." (2) "in and by itself," "in isolation," "an und für sich": thus Ax, *Laut, Stimme und Sprache* and "Zum *de voce*-Kapitel der römischen Grammatik"; Schenkeveld, "The Stoic *techne peri phōnês*: Studies in the History of Ancient Linguistics III." See also the section on Priscian, within, pp. 172–3.

[31] The term *littera* can easily be misleading. It corresponds to our "letter," but also to "speech sound," i.e. it can refer both to a phonological or phonetic entity and to a part of our writing system. See also selection from Isidore of Seville, within, pp. 235–40. For a critical reading of the sections on letters and syllables of Donatus, see Beck, *Zur Zuverlässigkeit der bedeutendsten lateinischen Grammatik*, 6ff.

[32] The point here is that *i* and *u* are fairly close together and hard to distinguish in pronunciation in these two examples. The *i* in *uir* is colored by the preceding *u* and the middle *u* in *optumus* even forms an alternative spelling for *optimus*. Cf. Quintilian, *Institutio oratoria* 1.4.8; Priscian, *Institutiones grammaticae* 1.3, GL 2:7.15ff.; Isidore, *Etymologiae* 1.4.7.

[33] I.e. it is an empty graphic form. Cf. Holtz, *Donat et la tradition de l'enseignement*, 53 for an analysis of the structure of this part of the chapter.

[34] *Huic item digammon adscribi solet, cum sibi ipsa praeponitur.* I.e. the first of two /u/, taken as a consonant, can be replaced with the Aeolic sign, "wau." Beck, *Zur Zuverlässigkeit der bedeutendsten lateinischen Grammatik*, 21 and 28 points out that in fact /u/ also stands in for the fricative in front of a vowel, not just in front of another *u*.

[35] I.e. even if, phonetically, the consonant *i* is followed by the vowel *i*, it is written only once. Cicero liked doubling it (Quintilian, *Institutio oratoria* 1.4.11).

[36] I.e. metrically either long or short.

Further, of these letters *f* can be put in front of the liquids *l* or *r*, just like whichever mute consonant, and then produces a syllable that is common.[37]

Mute letters cannot be pronounced by themselves, and do not produce a syllable by themselves. There are nine of them: *b c d g h k p q t*. Some people think *k* and *q* are redundant.[38] These people do not know that whenever an *a* follows, the letter *k* should precede, not *c*. And whenever *u* follows, spelling should be with *q*, not *c*. It is sometimes believed that the consonant *h* is the sign of aspiration [rough breathing].

The remaining letters are *y* and *z*, letters which we have admitted because of Greek names:[39] the former is a vowel, the latter a double consonant. This explains that according to some there are only seventeen Latin letters, since out of the twenty-three one is the sign of aspiration, one is double, two are redundant, and two are Greek.

Every letter has three accidents, name [*nomen*], form [*figura*], and force [*potestas*]. For it is asked what the letter is called, what its form is, and what effect it has.

I 3.   On the Syllable[40]

A syllable is the combination of letters or the pronunciation of one vowel capable of containing [metrical] beats. Some syllables are short, others are long, others again are "common."

Short syllables have a vowel with short pronunciation and do not end in two consonants or in one double consonant or in something that stands in for two consonants. Long syllables are either long by nature or become so by position: by nature, when either their vowel is pronounced long, as *ā ō*, or when two vowels are combined to make a diphthong, as in *ae, oe, au, eu, ei*; [they are long] by position, when a vowel with short pronunciation ends in two consonants, e.g. *arma* "weapons," *arcus* "bow," or in one double consonant, e.g. *axis* "axis," or in one consonant and one vowel that is used instead of a consonant, e.g. *at Iuno* "but Juno," *at Venus* "but Venus," or in just the letter *i* when used as a consonant, which is written twice by some, e.g. *aio te, Aeacida, Romanos vincere posse.*[41]

---

[37] I.e. the syllable preceding the *fl/fr* combination counts for metrical purposes as either long or short.

[38] Namely because of the existence of "c." For discussion of this passage, see Beck, *Zur Zuverlässigkeit der bedeutendsten lateinischen Grammatik*, 38–42.

[39] I.e. in order to be able to spell Greek names with them.

[40] On this chapter, see the critical discussion by Beck, *Zur Zuverlässigkeit der bedeutendsten lateinischen Grammatik*, 42–5.

[41] Ennius, *Annales* 179. This is a famously ambiguous oracle, meaning either "I say that you, descendant of Aeacus, can vanquish the Romans" or: "I say that the Romans can vanquish you, descendant of Aeacus." Reference here is to the length of the initial *a* of *aio*, which is claimed to be long "by position."

There are also syllables which are called "common," when either two consonants follow a short vowel, of which the first is either any mute consonant or the semi-vowel *f*, and the second a liquid consonant; or when a short vowel ends in one consonant followed by *h*, which to most people is the sign of a rough breathing; or when a short vowel is followed by two consonants, of which the first is the letter *s*; or when a short syllable ending in one consonant is the end of a part of speech; or when a part of speech ends in a long syllable, called a diphthong,[42] and a vowel follows immediately; or when there is a long vowel, followed by another vowel; or when a pronoun ending in the letter *c* is immediately followed by a vowel; or when a vowel with short pronunciation is taken up by the Greek double consonant *z*.

A long syllable has two beats, a short one one. The metricians call the syllable "half-foot."

[The end of chapter I continues with discussion of metrical feet, accents, and punctuation.]

II 1. On the Parts of Speech[43]

There are eight parts of speech, noun, pronoun, verb, adverb, participle, conjunction, preposition, interjection. Of these, two are the principal parts of speech, noun and verb. The Latin authors do not count the article, the Greeks do not count the interjection.[44] Many people think there are more parts of speech, many that there are fewer. Of all parts of speech there are three that are declined through six cases, noun, pronoun, and participle.

II 2. On the Noun

The noun is a part of speech with case signifying a body or a thing as a proper name [uniquely] or as a common name [generally], as a proper name, e.g. *Roma* "Rome," *Tiberis* "Tiber," as a common name, e.g. *urbs* "city," *flumen* "river."[45] The noun has six accidents, quality, comparison, gender, number, figure, case. A name belongs to one person, an appellative [common noun] to many, a designation [*vocabulum*] to things. But we use only the word "nouns" generally.[46]

---

[42] Rather imprecisely put in Latin—and thus also in English: reference is to metrical correption.

[43] *GL* 4:372.25–30 (= Holtz, *Donat et la tradition de l'enseignement*, 613.1ff.)

[44] Latin does not have the article. The suspicion is justified that the Latin grammarians added the interjection as a separate part of speech in order to bring their list up to eight, a number which had acquired canonical standing (e.g. through the *Tekhnê* ascribed to Dionysius Thrax). Cf. Sluiter, *Ancient Grammar in Context*, chapter 4.

[45] Note that the examples belong together. Rome is a city, the Tiber a river.

[46] I.e. for all of these: proper names, common names, and words for things.

II 3

The quality of nouns is twofold. Nouns are either proper nouns or appellatives. According to the Latins there are four kinds of proper names, *praenomen* "first name," *nomen* "family name," *cognomen* "surname," and *agnomen* "nick-name," e.g. *Publius Cornelius Scipio Africanus*. All first names are either written as single letters, e.g. *C.* [Gaius], *P.* [Publius], or with two letters, e.g. *Cn.* [Gnaeus], or with three, e.g. *Sex.* [Sextus].

There are many kinds of appellative nouns: some denote corporeal things, e.g. *homo* "man," *terra* "land," *mare* "sea," others are incorporeal, e.g. *pietas* "piety," *iustitia* "justice," *dignitas* "dignity."

Some are original [*primae positionis*],[47] e.g. *mons* "mountain," *schola* "school," others derivative, e.g. *montanus* "of a mountain," *scholasticus* "belonging to a school," others diminutive, e.g. *monticulus* "little mountain," *scholasticulus* "little schoolmaster." There are three degrees of diminutives; the smaller the shape gets, the more syllables there are.[48] There are also quasi-diminutives, whose origin is unclear, e.g. *fabula* "story," *macula* "stain," *tabula* "table," *vinculum* "tie."[49]

There are nouns that are completely Greek in declension, e.g. *Themisto, Calypso, Pan*; there are nouns that are totally adapted to the Latin rules, e.g. *Polydeuces* into *Pollux*, *Odysseus* into *Ulixes*. There are also nouns which are intermediate between Greek and Latin in form, called "bastards," like *Achilles Agamemno*.

Some nouns are homonyms, which signify several things with one appellative, e.g. *nepos* "grandson/spendthrift," *acies* "keenness of sight/line of battle," *aries* "ram/battering ram." Others are synonyms or polynyms, e.g. *terra humus tellus* [all three: "earth"], *ensis mucro gladius* [all three: "sword"].[50]

Others are patronymics, like *Atrides* "son of Atreus," *Pelides* "son of Peleus": these are also often formed on the basis of the name of the grandparents and mothers. The Greek

---

[47] I.e. not reducible to any other nouns; they are "the way they were on first imposition" (*primae positionis*); cf. Charisius, *Ars grammatica* 196.10f. Barwick = *GL* 1:154.26–155.1 "some nouns are spoken as they were at birth, like *mons* "mountain," *schola* "school," others are derivative."

[48] I.e. the strongest sense of diminution is created by adding more syllables (along the principle that makes teeny tiny smaller than tiny). The three degrees may be reflected in series like *homo, homuncio, homunculus* or *homo, homullus, homullulus*, for which cf. Priscian, *Institutiones grammaticae* 3.27, *GL* 2:102.2ff. (diminution of words already diminutive). They would parallel the three *gradus comparationis*.

[49] These words have the ending of a diminutive, but there is no corresponding non-diminutive word.

[50] The examples are highly traditional, and ultimately derive from the Greek tradition (along the lines of the *Tekhnê* attributed to Dionysius Thrax, *GG* I:i).

ones among them, whether masculine or feminine, will rather preserve the Greek rules.[51] The masculine forms then end in -*des*, e.g. *Atrides* from Atreus, or in -*ius*, e.g. *Peleius* from Peleus, or in -*ion*, e.g. *Nerion* from Nereus. The feminine ones end in -*is*, like *Atreis*, or in -*as*, like *Peleias*, or in -*ne*, like *Nerine*. There are also *ktetika* [Gr.], i.e. possessives, which end in -*ius*, like *Euandrius ensis* "the sword of Euander," *Agamemnoniae*que *Mycenae* "[and] Agamemnon's Mycenae."[52]

Other nouns are of middle meaning[53] and are added to [substantive] nouns, like *magnus* "great," *fortis* "brave." For we say *magnus vir* "a great man," *fortis exercitus* "a brave army": these are also called epithets.

Some indicate quality, like *bonus* "good," *malus* "bad"; others quantity, like *magnus* "great," *parvus* "small"; others ethnicity, like *Graecus* "Greek," *Hispanus* "Spanish"; others fatherland, like *Thebanus* "Theban," *Romanus* "Roman"; others number, like *unus* "one," *duo* "two"; others order, like *primus* "first," *secundus* "second": but we use *primus* "first" when we're dealing with many, *prior* "former" when we're dealing with two, like we say *alter* "the other" when we're dealing with two, *alius* "another" when we're dealing with many.

Some are relative [*ad aliquid*], like *pater* "father," *frater* "brother"; others express relative quality [*ad aliquid qualiter se habentia*], like *dexter* "right," *sinister* "left." These also admit the comparative degree, like *dexterior* "more to the right," *sinisterior* "more to the left."

Others are general, like *corpus* "body," *animal* "animal," others particular, like *lapis* "stone," *homo* "man," *lignum* "wood." Some are made from verbs, like *doctor* "teacher," *lector* "reader," others resemble participles, like *demens* "demented," *sapiens* "wise," *potens* "powerful," others resemble verbs, like *comedo* "glutton" [also: "to eat"] *palpo* "flatterer" [also: "to touch"] *contemplator* "contemplator" [also looks like deponent verb "to contemplate" (*contemplor*)], *speculator* "explorer" [also looks like deponent verb "to explore" (*speculor*)]: but the former group [those resembling participles] are distinguished [from real participles] by their comparative grade, the latter [are distinguished from verbs] by their cases.

[We omit the remaining discussion of the noun and the other parts of speech, resuming with the short section on the interjection.]

---

[51] I.e. they keep their Greek declension.

[52] *Agamemnoniae Mycenae*, with the nom. f. plur. of the possessive adjective noun *Agamemnonius*.

[53] Cf. Priscian, *Institutiones grammaticae* 2.28, *GL* 2:60.6ff. *adiectivum . . . significat laudem vel vituperationem vel medium . . . medium, ut magnus—dicimus enim magnus imperator laudantes et magnus latro . . . vituperantes*: "an adjective signifies praise or blame or something in the middle . . . in the middle, e.g. "great, big": for we say "a big chief" in praise, and "a big thief" in blame."

II 17. On the Interjection[54]

The interjection is a part of speech thrown in between the other parts of speech to express the affects of the soul; either of someone who fears, like *ei*; or of someone who wishes, like *o*; or of someone in pain, like *heu*; or of someone merry, like *evax*.

But among the Greeks these are joined to the adverbs.[55] The Latins do not do that for the reason that the verb does not immediately follow this kind of words.[56]

Instead of an interjection it is also allowed to substitute one or more other parts of speech, e.g. *nefas* "dreadful!" *pro nefas* "o terrible!"

There can be no certain accents in the interjections—this also goes for other words that are of a crude sound-form.[57]

[From the beginning of book 3 of the *Ars Maior*, the so-called *Barbarismus*.[58]]

III 1. On Barbarism[59]

A barbarism is one wrong word in common speech.[60] In a poem, it is called "metaplasm" ["transformation"], occurring within our own language it is "barbarism," in a foreign language it is called "barbarolexis" ["barbaric speech"], e.g. *mastruga* "a sheepskin coat [Sardinian]," *cateia* "boomerang [Gallic]," *magalia* "huts, tents [Punic]."[61]

Barbarisms occur in two ways, in pronunciation and in writing. Four species are subordinated to these two categories: addition [*adiectio*], omission [*detractio*], substitution

---

[54] *GL* 4:391.25–392.3 *de interiectione* (= Holtz, *Donat et la tradition de l'enseignement*, 652.4–13). The interjection was the part of speech added by the Latin grammarians to the Greek list.

[55] I.e. they are not (yet) separated out from the class of adverbs, which in Greek grammar functions as a "rest" category.

[56] I.e. it does not feature the most eye-catching characteristic of the ad-verb, namely that it is construed "with the verb."

[57] In order to accommodate these words, of which the form is often not completely articulate and which behave irregularly, in an *Ars grammatica*, their very irregularity is made into a rule. Cf. Sluiter, *Ancient Grammar in Context*, chapter 4.

[58] *GL* 4:392.4–393.3 *de barbarismo* (= Holtz, *Donat et la tradition de l'enseignement*, 653.1–655.2).

[59] See on this section Holtz, *Donat et la tradition de l'enseignement*, 136ff.; cf. Quintilian, *Institutio oratoria* 1.5.6.

[60] Cf. *Rhetorica ad Herennium* 4.12.17.

[61] Donatus will focus on the "regular mistake" within Latin, i.e. barbarism in the narrow sense. What in normal language would be called a mistake is considered a purposeful alteration protected by poetic license in poetry—not to be imitated by the student of language. The use of loan-words (barbarolexis) within a Latin context was considered a stylistic mistake that Cicero reflects upon often in the *prooemia* of his philosophical work. See e.g. *Tusculanae disputationes* 1.15. This does not prevent Donatus from citing poetic examples that use the different categories of (corrupting) change. For *mastruga*, see Cicero, *Pro Scauro* 20; for *cateia*, see *Aeneid* 7.741; *magalia*, see *Aeneid* 1.421.

[*inmutatio*], transposition [*transmutatio*].[62] [These four species can affect] the letter, the syllable, the quantity, the accent, and the aspiration.

Barbarism through addition of a letter occurs, e.g. in *relliquias Danaum* "what had been left over by the Danaans,"[63] since we should spell *reliquias* with one L.

[Barbarism through addition] of a syllable, e.g. *nos abiisse rati* "we thought they had left," instead of *abisse*;[64] of quantity, e.g. *Ītaliam fato profugus* "through fate fleeing to Italy,"[65] since we should pronounce *Italiam* with the first letter taken short.

[Barbarism] through omission of a letter [occurs], e.g. in *infantibu parvis* "from little children,"[66] instead of *infantibus*; of a syllable, e.g. *salmentum* "salted fish" instead of *salsamentum*;[67] of quantity, e.g. *unŭs ob noxam* "because of one man's wrongdoing,"[68] instead of *unīus*.

[Barbarism] through substitution of a letter, e.g. *olli* "they [arch.]" instead of *illi*; of a syllable, e.g. *permities* instead of *pernicies* "ruin"; of quantity, e.g. *fervĕre Leucaten* "that Leucate was seething,"[69] although *fervēre* is of the second conjugation and should be pronounced long.

[Barbarism] through transposition of a letter, e.g. *Euandre* instead of *Euander*;[70] of a syllable, e.g. *displicina* instead of *disciplina*;[71] of quantity, as when one pronounces *dĕōs* "gods [acc.plur.]" with long first syllable and short last syllable.

The accents are similarly changed through these four species. For they, too, are added, omitted, substituted, or transposed. The examples will present themselves spontaneously, if one looks into it.

In the same number of ways barbarism is also detected in aspiration. Some think this ought to be ascribed to errors of writing, others of pronunciation, because of the H, of course, which some consider a letter, others the sign of aspiration.[72]

Barbarism can also occur through hiatus. For there are bad compositions, *cacosyntheta* [Gr. "badly put together"], which some consider barbarisms. They include mytacisms, labdacisms, iotacisms,[73] hiatus, collisions, and all the other phenomena that produce an excess of sound or too little of it, which are rejected by trained ears. We will state clearly that these mistakes are to be avoided, but leave the dispute about the name to the intransigent.

---

[62] These four categories of change also underlie etymological procedures: see the etymology dossier (Part 2); Usener, "Ein altes Lehrgebäude der Philologie"; and Ax, "*Quadripertita ratio*: Bemerkungen zur Geschichte eines aktuellen Kategoriensystems."

[63] E.g. *Aeneid* 1.30. The example is also discussed under metaplasm (Holtz, *Donat et la tradition de l'enseignement*, 661.1f.).

[64] *Aeneid* 2.25.　　[65] *Aeneid* 1.2.　　[66] Lucretius, *De rerum natura* 1.186.

[67] An interesting example of "new" contemporary Latin adopted as an example in Donatus.

[68] *Aeneid* 1.41.　　[69] *Aeneid* 8.677.　　[70] In both cases vocative. See *Aeneid* 11.55.

[71] The ancient version of the spoonerism.　　[72] Cf. *Ars maior* 1.2, above, pp. 88–9.

[73] Labdacisms, mytacisms, and iotacisms are associated with various mistakes to do with the letters L (Gr. labda), M (Gr. my/mu), and I (Gr. iota). They are either pronounced too thickly or not clearly enough, or the sounds are used too frequently. The grammatical tradition varies. Cf. e.g. Quintilian, *Institutio oratoria* 1.5.32.

III 2. On Solecism[74]

Solecism is the mistake that is committed against the rules of grammar in a combination [*contextus*] of parts of speech.

The difference between a solecism and a barbarism is that a solecism contains words which are in conflict or incongruent among themselves, while barbarisms occur in individual written or spoken words. Yet many people err, who believe that a solecism can also occur in one part of speech, if we either say "she" while pointing out a man, or "he" when pointing out a woman;[75] or when we are asked where we are going and we answer *Romae* "in Rome";[76] or when we greet one man and say *salvete* "hello [to second pers. plur.]": in fact, the preceding pointing, or the question or the greeting provide the effect of context.[77] Many people have also hesitated about whether *scala* "stairs," *quadriga* "team of four," *scopa* "broom" is a solecism or a barbarism,[78] but of course the fact that this sort of word is a barbarism can easily be recognized from the very definition of that mistake.

Solecism occurs in two ways, either through the parts of speech or through the accidents of the parts of speech . . .

III 3. On the Other Faults[79]

Including barbarism and solecism the faults are twelve in number,[80] as follows: barbarism, solecism, improper choice of words [*acyrologia*], obscenity [*cacemphaton*], fullness of

---

[74] *GL* 4:393.5–19 *de soloecismo* (= Holtz, *Donat et la tradition de l'enseignement*, 655.3–16). On this section see also Holtz, 136 ff.

[75] The example derives from Greek grammar (see Apollonius Dyscolus, *On Syntax* III 8ff.); on this passage, cf. I. Sluiter, review of Jean Lallot's translation of the *Syntax* of Apollonius Dyscolus.

[76] The correct form would have been *Romam* "to Rome."

[77] So the cases discussed are indeed solecisms: they are not mistakes within one word, but function within a wider context, to which linguistic and non-linguistic (or pre-linguistic) elements contribute. Thus far, Donatus agrees with Apollonius Dyscolus, who also points out that in fact these one-word sentences presuppose more linguistic elements. However, as long as the sentence is grammatically well-formed, Apollonius will deny that the mistake in reference has anything to do with grammar. So according to him, the one-word reply "she" while pointing to a man, could qualify as a solecism, since in fact theoretically more words are involved, but as long as the grammar is in order, it is in fact not the grammarian's problem.

[78] The "correct" forms are the pluralia tantum *scalae, quadrigae, scopae.*

[79] *GL* 4:394.24ff. *de ceteris vitiis* (= Holtz, *Donat et la tradition de l'enseignement*, 658.4f.).

[80] Holtz, *Donat et la tradition de l'enseignement*, 163, points out that from here the different categories (e.g. "other faults") get a fixed *number* of subcategories (here twelve), which are then systematically presented.

expression [*pleonasmus*], redundancy [*perissologia*], long-windedness [*macrologia*], tautology, eclipse, bathos [*tapinosis*], bad composition [*cacosyntheton*], ambiguity [*amphibolia*].

[definitions follow] . . .

III 4. *On Transformation* [metaplasmus] [81]

"Transformation" [*metaplasmus*] is a certain change in form of straight prose speech into another kind for the sake of meter or embellishment. It has fourteen species: addition [*prosthesis*], epenthesis, and paragoge;[82] aphaeresis, syncope, and apocope;[83] ectasis and systole,[84] diaeresis and episynaloephe;[85] synaloephe and ecthlipsis;[86] antithesis and metathesis.[87]

[Donatus then goes on to discuss the so-called *schemata* ("figures") and the *tropi* ("tropes"). From the latter chapter, we translate the sections on metaphor and allegory.]

III 5. *On* Schemata *[Figures]*

There are figures of speech [*schemata lexeos*] and of thought [*schemata dianoeas*], but figures of thought pertain to the orators, those of speech to the grammarian.

There are seventeen figures: prolepsis,[88] zeugma,[89] hypozeuxis,[90] syllepsis,[91] anadiplosis, anaphora, epanalepsis, epizeuxis,[92] paronomasia,[93] schesis onomaton,[94]

---

[81] *GL* 4:395.25ff. *de metaplasmo* (= Holtz, *Donat et la tradition de l'enseignement*, 660.7ff.).

[82] These first three kinds refer to an addition at the beginning, in the middle, or at the ending of a word.

[83] The second group of three refers to elements left out from the beginning, the middle, or the ending of a word.

[84] These are metrical abnormalities: abnormal metrical lengthening versus abnormal metrical shortening.

[85] The splitting of one syllable into two and conversely the combining of two syllables into one.

[86] A gentle gliding over colliding vowels through elision of one of them versus the harsh expulsion of a syllable when consonants "collide" with vowels (i.e. when the meter cannot accommodate them all) (e.g. the elision of the last syllable of *multum* in *Aeneid* 1.3, *multum ille*).

[87] Substitution of a letter, called *immutatio* ("substitution") in the section on barbarism, see above, pp. 93–4; versus transposition of letters, called *transmutatio* in the section on barbarism, see above, p. 94.

[88] "Anticipation."   [89] One verb added to different objects.

[90] Repetition of verb with each complement.

[91] One verb connected with more nouns, but only agreeing with one.

[92] These last four are all forms of "addition": *anadiplosis*, the repetition of the last word of the preceding verse at the beginning of a verse; *anaphora*, the repetition of the same word at the beginning of several verses; *epanalepsis*, the repetition at the end of a verse of a word from the beginning of the same verse; *epizeuxis*, the instant repetition of the same word.

[93] "Punning."   [94] Amplification through heaping of synonyms.

parhomoeon, homoeoptoton, homoeoteleuton, polyptoton,[95] hirmos,[96] polysyndeton, dialyton.[97]

III 6. On Tropes[98]

A trope is a word transferred from its proper signification to a likeness that is not proper to it for reasons of embellishment [*ornatus*] or necessity. There are thirteen tropes: metaphor, catachresis, metalepsis, metonymy, antonomasia, synecdoche, epitheton, onomatopoeia, periphrasis, hyperbaton, hyperbole, allegory, homoeosis.

Metaphor is the transfer of things and words. This happens in four ways: from animate to animate, from inanimate to inanimate, from animate to inanimate, from inanimate to animate.[99]

From animate to animate, as in "They made Tiphys the charioteer [*auriga*] of the fast ship."[100] For both a charioteer [*auriga*] and a steersman [*gubernator*] have a soul. From inanimate to inanimate, as in "As the rafts [*rates*] sailed the sea."[101] For neither rafts [*rates*] nor ships [*naves*] have a soul.

From animate to inanimate, as in "of Atlas, whose pine-bearing head is constantly surrounded by dense clouds" etc.[102] For as these features belong to an animate being,[103] so a mountain does not have a soul, yet the parts of a human body are ascribed to it. From inanimate to animate, as in "if you have such oaktree-(strength) [*robur*] in your breast."[104] For an "oak tree" [*robur*] does not have a soul, but Turnus, to whom this is said, definitely does.

We should know that some metaphors are reciprocal, some are one-sided.[105]

[. . .]

---

[95] Four figures associated with the Greek intellectual Gorgias (fifth century BC): *parhomoeon*, similarity of words; *homoeoptoton*, similarity of cases (often with same endings); *homoeoteleuton*, similarity of word-endings; *polyptoton*, the use of one word in several case forms.

[96] "Concatenation."

[97] The use of many connectors (*polysyndeton*), or the use of none (*asyndeton*, or *dialyton*). See on this whole section Holtz, *Donat et la tradition de l'enseignement*, 183–99.

[98] GL 4:399.12ff. (= Holtz, *Donat et la tradition de l'enseignement*, 667.1ff.); GL 4:401 (= Holtz, 671.14ff.).

[99] Cf. Aristotle, *Poetics* 21.1457b7; Quintilian, *Institutio oratoria* 8.6.9–13.

[100] A fragment from the work of P. Terentius Varro Atacinus (82–ca. 35 BC); see A. S. Hollis, ed. and trans., *Fragments of Roman Poetry c. 60 BC–AD 20* (Oxford: Oxford University Press, 2007), 172–3 (fragment 124).

[101] *Aeneid* 5.8.   [102] *Aeneid* 4.248f.

[103] The passage does not only give Atlas a head, but also discusses its shoulders, chin, and beard.

[104] *Aeneid* 11.368ff.

[105] Not explained in Donatus' text. Cf. Diomedes, *Ars grammatica*, GL 1:457.32f. Standard example is that wings may be described as oars, and vice versa, so that the metaphor may work both ways. Other metaphors are unidirectional.

Allegory is a trope, by which something else is signified [*significatur*] than is said [*dicitur*], as in "and now it is time to unharness the steaming necks of the horses,"[106] that is, "to finish up the poem." There are many kinds of allegory, of which seven stand out: irony, antiphrasis, enigma, charming politeness, proverb [*paroemia*], sarcasm, humor [*astismos*].

Irony is the trope that shows what it attempts to say through the contrary, as in "Truly wonderful praise and ample spoils you are winning, you and that boy of yours" etc.[107] If the speaker is not assisted by the seriousness of her intonation, she will seem to agree to what she intends to deny.

Antiphrasis is irony in one word,[108] e.g. *bellum* "war," *lucus* "sacred grove," *Parcae* "the goddesses of Fate." *Bellum*, i.e. not at all *bellus* "pretty"; *lucus* from the fact that there is no light [*luceat*] there; *Parcae*, because they spare [*parcant*] nobody.

Enigma is a sentence that is obscure through the hidden similarity of the referents, as in *mater me genuit, eadem mox gignitur ex me* ["my mother brought me forth, and will soon be born from me"]: this means that water congeals into ice and will stream forth from it again.

Charming politeness [*charientismos*] is a trope which proffers things that are harsh to say in a more acceptable way. For instance, if we ask "was anyone looking for us?," and we are given the answer "you're lucky." We understand that nobody wanted us.

A proverb [*paroemia*] is a saying which is appropriate to the times and circumstances, for example, "kicking against the goad"[109] and "the wolf in the story."[110]

Sarcasm is hostile derision full of hatred, as in "There! Lying down you can measure out, Trojan, the lands and Hesperia, which you tried to conquer through war."[111]

Humor [*astismos*][112] is a varied trope with many virtues. It describes whatever is free of rustic simplicity, and is polished by a rather witty urbanity [*urbanitas*], as in the

---

[106] Virgil, *Georgics* 2.542.

[107] *Aeneid* 4.93f. Juno speaking to Venus, who, with the help of her son Cupid, has made Dido fall in love with Aeneas.

[108] This paragraph is related to the theory of etymology that specifies that in some cases the semantic relationship between the word that is to be explained and its explanation is a negative or inverse one. In fact, this view is not entirely nonsensical, since it is the basis of the phenomenon of euphemism. Thus, the explanation for *lucus* may very well be right; cf. further the name of the Eumenides. See the etymology dossier (Part 2).

[109] Terence, *Phormio* 77, meant as a comforting "resistance is futile."

[110] Terence, *Adelphi* 537, said when the person about whom one is talking all of a sudden shows up ("talking of the devil...").

[111] *Aeneid* 12.359f., the hateful words of Turnus as he kills one of his enemies in battle.

[112] See D. M. Schenkeveld, "asteïsmos," in G. Ueding, ed., *Historisches Wörterbuch der Rhetorik*, I (1992), s.v.; on the stylistic opposition expressed in terms of city and countryside, see I. Sluiter and R. Rosen, "General Introduction" to *City, Countryside, and the Spatial Organization of Value*.

well-known "He who does not hate Bavius, must love your songs, Maevius, and he must also bring foxes under the yoke and milk he-goats."[113]

FROM THE *VITAE VERGILIANAE ANTIQUAE*[114]

Aelius Donatus sends his greetings to his dear friend Lucius Munatius.

After having looked at almost every author versed in Virgil's work before me, I have excerpted, in a concerted effort to be brief (I know you appreciate that), so few things out of the many that I would rather expect the justified indignation of the reader because I have knowingly skipped a lot of information from older authors, than because I have filled a page with unnecessary matter. In this work of a collector you may frequently recognize the authentic voice of an ancient authority. Of course I was free to put in my own views: but I have preferred in good faith to retain the words also of those to whom the ideas belonged.[115] So what did we achieve? This, to be sure, that by presenting what we have collected from the massive material, mixed with our own understanding, the few things presented here give us more pleasure than others have from the many things written down elsewhere. An additional advantage is that, for those authors whose views we took over with our full approval, we have secured the attention of all in the parts that we chose, while we removed boredom by having left out the rest.[116] So see if we succeeded in following your instructions. For if this work will show the way and lend a hand to a grammarian who, as you put it, is inexperienced and a beginner, we will have fulfilled your orders.[117] If not, you will have to demand from yourself what you wished from us. Greetings.

---

[113] Virgil, *Eclogues* 3.90f.

[114] The so-called *VSD* (*Vita Suetoniana-Donatiana*) is a fourth-century AD version of the Life of Virgil by Suetonius (in his *De poetis*, now lost), dating from the end of the first century AD. Most recent edition by Brugnoli and Stok. For translations of the letter to Munatius, see Holtz, *Donat et la tradition de l'enseignement*, 29f. (into French); Hardie (2nd edn., 1963), x (into English); Ziolkowski and Putnam, *The Virgilian Tradition*, 643f. (into English). The *Life of Virgil* itself has been translated into English by D. S. Wilson-Okamura, available at www.virgil.org/vitae/a-donatus.htm; Ziolkowski and Putnam, *The Virgilian tradition*, 189–99; 227–8; 406; 424–5. See further Stok, "Virgil between the Middle Ages and the Renaissance," 15, describing the medieval reception of the "Life" tradition; and for a skeptical view on the reliability of the *Vita*, Horsfall, "Virgil: His Life and Times."

[115] Note that he does not claim to have given full credit in the commentary. If we look at Servius' practice (who must have relied on Donatus very heavily), we notice that the only times he mentions Donatus by name is to disagree with him.

[116] Donatus claims to have done a service to his sources: he picked out what was best and strongest and thus made sure that people noticed it fully—and at the same time he made sure nobody could get bored with the rest.

[117] Donatus' commentary was indeed so used by later commentators on Virgil, who freely excerpted it. See Schindel, *Die lateinischen Figurenlehren des 5. bis 7. Jahrhunderts*.

DONATUS' LIFE OF VIRGIL[118]

1. Publius Vergilius Maro of Mantua was born from humble parents, especially his father, who according to some was a potter. Most claim that initially he was the hired hand of a certain Magus, a traveling agent, but soon became his son-in-law through his diligence. They say he did an excellent job of increasing his small estate by buying forests and keeping bees.

2. Virgil was born under the first consulate of Cn. Pompey the Great and M. Licinius Crassus, on the Ides of October in a village called Andes, not far from Mantua. 3. When his mother was pregnant with him, she dreamed that she gave birth to a branch of laurel that was fed through contact with the earth and grew instantly into a fully mature tree, filled with all kinds of fruits and flowers. The next day while on her way with her husband to a nearby estate, she had to turn off the road and delivered her child in a lower-lying ditch. 4. They claim the baby never cried from the time it was born, and that it had such a sweet face that he provided even then the hope, without room for doubt, of having been born under a rather favorable sign. 5. There was also another prophetic indication, for the young branch of a poplar which had instantly been planted on the very place of his birth according to the habits of the region, shot up in such a short time, that it was equal to poplars that had been sown long before. From that time it is called "Virgil's tree," and it is hallowed with the utmost religious awe by pregnant and newly delivered women, who go there to have the child recognized and to fulfill what they promised in prayer.

6. His first years he spent in Cremona until he took up the *toga virilis*, which happened on his seventeenth birthday, when the same people as at his birth were consuls for the second time—and it happened that on that same day the poet Lucretius died. 7. But Virgil moved from Cremona to Milano, and from there a little bit later to the city.[119] 8. Of body and build he was big, of swarthy color, with a farmer's face, and fragile health. For he suffered most of the time from stomach and throat and headaches, and also threw up blood a lot. 9. He ate and drank very little. He was sexually rather inclined to boys, of whom he loved Cebes and Alexander most (in the second eclogue he calls him Alexis); the latter was given to him by Asinius Pollio, both boys were well trained, and Cebes was a poet too. It is widely known that he also had a relationship with Plotia Hieria. 10. But Asconius Pedianus[120] claims that later, when she was older, she would habitually tell the

---

[118] Paragraphs 1–11; 21–5; 30–2; 35–6; 39–42; 46.   [119] I.e. to Rome.

[120] Asconius Pedianus (AD 3–88) is best known for his commentaries on the speeches of Cicero, in which he provides a wealth of historical background information.

story that although he had been invited by Varius to sleep with her, he had refused most pertinently. 11. It is certainly true that in the rest of his conduct, what he said, and what he thought, he was so good that in Naples he was generally called "Parthenias" ["the Virgin-boy"]. And whenever he was seen in public in Rome, where he seldom went, he would take refuge in the nearest house from his followers and people who would point him out.

[In sections 12–20 Virgil's economic situation and his family are described. He studied medicine and mathematics, and once he gave his own defense speech in court, but just once: he was not a very fluent speaker. As a boy he writes his first poem: a distichon on a schoolmaster who was stoned to death for his thievery. There follows a list of the minor poems attributed to Virgil, and a short description of the *Bucolica* and *Georgica*. The biographer then turns to the *Aeneid*:]

21. As his last project he embarked on the *Aeneid*, a diverse and multi-layered theme [*argumentum*], almost the equivalent of both Homeric epics,[121] and furthermore common to Greeks and Romans in names and subject matter. Moreover, something he aimed at most, it could contain simultaneously the origin of the city of Rome and of Augustus. 22. When he was writing the *Georgics*, people say that every day he would dictate some verses that he had thought up in the morning, and would then through constant revision throughout the day reduce them to just a few, claiming (not an absurd claim either) that he gave birth to verses like a she-bear, and got them into shape only through licking. 23. He first gave shape to the *Aeneid* as prose, roughly divided into twelve books, and he then started working on it in chunks, just as he was inclined, without getting to grips with it in order. 24. And lest his drive would slow down, he passed some things on unfinished, others he supported as it were with the lightest of verses. As a joke he said that those were put in between instead of flute play to sustain the work until the solid columns would arrive. 25. He finished the *Bucolics* in three years, the *Georgics* in seven, and the *Aeneid* in eleven.

[After discussing the initial reception of *Bucolica* and *Georgica*, the *Vita* turns to the *Aeneid* again: it was instantly recognized as a "classic," a worthy Roman challenge to Homer.]

30. Hardly had he begun the *Aeneid* when its fame became such that Sextus Propertius declared without hesitation [ii 34.65]: "make place, Roman authors, make place, ye Greeks: / something, I don't know what, that is greater than the Iliad is being born." 31. And Augustus (he happened to be away on an expedition to Cantabria) demanded in letters that were begging and even jokingly menacing that, to give his own words, "he

---

[121] The first six books deal with Aeneas' travels and are compared to the *Odyssey*, the last six deal with the wars over Latium and are considered the equivalent of the *Iliad*.

would be sent from the Aeneid either the first *hupographê* [Gr.: "sketch"] of the epic, or any *kôlon* [Gr.: "verse-part"] whatsoever." 32. A lot later, and only when the subject matter had been finished, Virgil recited to him three books, the second, fourth, and sixth, the latter the occasion of the remarkable emotion of Octavia. She was present at the recital and the story goes that at those verses about her son [*Aeneid* 6.884]: "you will be Marcellus," she fainted and could hardly be brought to.

[After some remarks on Virgil as a declaimer of his own verses, the *Vita* continues:]

35. At the age of fifty-two, when he was about to put the last touches on the *Aeneid*, he decided to withdraw to Greece and Asia, and to do nothing else for three continuous years but correct it, so that the rest of his life could be dedicated to philosophy exclusively. But having set out on his trip, he ran into Augustus in Athens, who was just returning to Rome from the East, and he resolved not to leave him but to return together with him. He then visited the neighboring city of Megara under an absolutely burning hot sun, and contracted a faintness, which he made so much worse through not interrupting his sea-journey that he finally had to land at Brundisium in a very much worsened state. And there he died within a few days on the 21st of September under the consulate of Cn. Sentius and Q. Lucretius. 36. His body was brought to Naples and buried in a tomb on the road to Puteoli within two miles from the city. He made the following distichon for it:

> Mantua bore me, Calabria took me, and now
> Parthenope is keeping me; I sang of pastures, farms, generals.[122]

[The *Vita* discusses the fate of the *Aeneid* after Virgil's death.]

39. He had agreed with Varius, before leaving Italy, that should anything happen to him, Varius should burn the Aeneid. But Varius had refused to do this. Therefore, on his deathbed he constantly asked for his book-box, meaning to burn them himself. But when nobody volunteered, he made no provisions about it to anyone by name. 40. He left his writings to this same man Varius and also to Tucca on this condition that they would not publish anything that had not been published by himself. 41. But at the instigation of Augustus, Varius did publish it, only slightly corrected, for he left even incomplete verses the way they were. Soon many people attempted to supplement them, but did not succeed very well because of the difficulty of the task: for just about all half-verses in his work have an absolute and complete meaning except for this one [*Aeneid* 3.340]: "which for you already Troy." 42. The grammarian Nisus[123] claims to have heard from older people that

---

[122] The reference is to *Bucolics*, *Georgics*, and *Aeneid*, respectively.
[123] Usually dated to the second half of the first century AD. Mentioned by various later Latin grammarians.

Varius had changed the order of two books, and that he had put the original second book in third place. Besides he allegedly corrected the beginning of the first book, by removing the following verses:

> I am the man who once having played a song on the slender flute,
> and having left the woods, forced the neighboring fields
> to obey to the farmer, however eager he was,
> a work pleasing to countrymen, but now of Mars' grueling
> weapons I sing and the man [*arma virumque cano*].

[The *Vita* mentions several of Virgil's critics and parodists: a book with the title *Aeneidomastix* "Scourge of the *Aeneid*" is clearly so named to parallel the nickname of the Greek grammarian Zoilus: *Homeromastix* "Scourge of Homer." The *Vita* then discusses Virgil's defenders:]

46. In the book he wrote against the critics of Virgil, Asconius Pedianus[124] presents only few objections made against him. Mostly they have to do with *Realien* and the fact that he had taken most of his material from Homer. But he claims that very accusation can usually be fended off as follows: "Why don't they attempt those same thefts? Then they would understand that it is easier to steal the club of Hercules than to cheat Homer of a verse." And yet, he said, he had decided to give up so that he would have ruined everything just to satisfy the malevolent.

End of the *Vita*.

---

[124] See above, note 120.

MARIUS VICTORINUS, COMMENTARY ON THE *DE INVENTIONE*, BEFORE 355

INTRODUCTION

The celebrated Roman rhetorician Gaius Marius Victorinus (born ca. 285?) converted to Christianity in about the year 355, and died most likely during the next decade. There is a famous testimony to his rhetorical teachings and Christian writings by Jerome, who also remembers him as a contemporary of his own teacher, the grammarian Donatus.[1] Augustine uses the dramatic story of Victorinus' conversion as an *exemplum* in his own conversion narrative.[2] Before converting to Christianity, Victorinus wrote on dialectic and Neoplatonist philosophy, rhetoric, and grammar, although many of his dialectical and philosophical writings are lost.[3] After his conversion, he wrote theological treatises and scriptural commentaries, which are extant.

The commentary on the *De inventione* would have derived from Victorinus' activity as an orator and teacher of rhetoric. It is the earliest complete commentary on Cicero's *De inventione* that survives, and it had a continuous influence on rhetorical teaching and the reception of Cicero from late antiquity through the early and later Middle Ages, and into the early age of print.[4] It is a very lengthy commentary, linked to the text by *lemmata*, quotes from the text that function as the entries in the commentary. It incorporates many paraphrases to enable students to understand the text, as well as philosophical explanations and digressions which give the interpretation a distinctively Neoplatonist character. Its orientation is pedagogical and practical, to complete the general education of students after the initial teaching of the grammarian.[5] But its

---

[1] Jerome, *De viris illustribus* 101; *Chronicon* (continuation of Eusebius' chronicle), year 2370, 283rd Olympiad, XVII.

[2] *Confessions* 8.2.

[3] Most of the *Ars grammatica*, as edited by Keil in *GL* 6, has now been recognized as the *De metris* of Aphthonius. See Hadot, *Marius Victorinus*, 62–70. Only the opening section of the treatise (corresponding to *GL* 6:3–31) is the work of Victorinus, and this has now been edited by Mariotti (Victorinus, *Ars grammatica*).

[4] Ward, *Ciceronian Rhetoric*, 76, 97. See also the description of the forty-six extant manuscripts (and fragments) and eighteen early printed texts in the recent edition by Ippolito (which appeared when the present book was in its final stages of preparation), xxv–xxxiv.

[5] Hadot, *Marius Victorinus*, 78.

practical leanings are not in the direction of courtroom oratory.[6] Ward notes that its outlook is to the academic or schoolroom environment: the student imagined here is one who "writes" rhetoric.[7] As much as it teaches an application of particular skills, rhetoric is more importantly an intellectual exercise, an understanding of how knowledge is formed.[8] Thus Victorinus sets out a distinction (which medieval authors found extremely useful) between the extrinsic art, which teaches the nature of a particular field of knowledge, that is, "what is rhetoric, what is its genus, its function, its goal, its material, its parts?", and the intrinsic art, which teaches us how to apply the precepts taught by the art. The extrinsic art teaches "only knowledge" (*scientiam solam tradit*).[9]

Victorinus devotes attention to the relation between rhetoric and logic, the terminology of the *De inventione*, the theory of genus and species, and the syllogism. His treatment of the subject is determined by the highly dialectical terminology of the *De inventione*; this is also the case with Boethius' *De topicis differentiis*. The overwhelmingly theoretical nature of his interests can be gauged from the much greater attention that he pays to book 1 of the *De inventione* than to book two.[10]

Victorinus' magnificent introduction to the *De inventione*, including his interpretation of Cicero's pairing of wisdom and eloquence and the mythical account of the origin of civilization (*De inventione* 1.1.1–1.3.5), provides the essence of the commentary's Neoplatonist perspective. Hadot shows how Victorinus transforms the Ciceronian notion of virtue from conformity with reason and natural order (*De inventione* 2.53.159: "Virtue may be defined as a habit of mind in harmony with reason and the order of nature") into a Neoplatonist notion of the transcendent essence of the soul before its entrance into the body: "Virtue is a state of the soul, directed towards the order of nature in accordance with reason—that is why it is directed towards the order of nature."[11] Nature, for Victorinus, corresponds to the transcendent state of the soul separated from the body, and on this model, "study" and "discipline" (*studium, disciplina*) are the two parts of philosophy, contemplation and moral ascesis, which return humans to their spiritual "nature" or transcendent origins. "Virtue" is "wisdom" and ultimately "philosophy." This redefinition of virtue permits Victorinus to reinterpret Cicero's myth

---

[6] On the general academic character of the *rhetores latini minores*, as opposed to active courtroom context, see the introduction to Part 1, above; cf. Ward, *Ciceronian Rhetoric*, 78.

[7] *Explanationes*, ed. Halm, 216.9; 244.28.   [8] Cox and Ward, eds., *The Rhetoric of Cicero*, 410.

[9] *Explanationes*, ed. Halm, 170, 26–42.

[10] Cox and Ward, eds., *The Rhetoric of Cicero*, 410. Both books of *De inventione* teach the canon of invention, but book one focuses on the dialectical underpinnings of invention, while book two takes a more applied approach to the kinds of legal or political situations in which the techniques of invention would be used.

[11] *Explanationes*, ed. Halm, 155, 28–9; Hadot, *Marius Victorinus*, 82.

of the civilizing power of rhetoric, in which a wise man rose above the savagery of the earliest people to recognize the untapped virtue inherent in them and used his eloquence to bring order to their lives. He transforms Cicero's political myth into an account of spiritual ascent. The soul has divine origins: with the formation of the sensible world, the soul is enveloped and oppressed by the body and forgets its divine origins; but some souls that inhabit chaste bodies are able to retain an understanding of their divine nature. Hence there could be a sage who rose above the savagery of his fellow humans and recalled them to their spiritual potentials.[12] The adjoining of eloquence to wisdom is here understood as the exterior manifestation (eloquence) of the inner substance (wisdom): "Every perfect good, that is, what nature gives—free from unsuitable alloy—to the human condition, attains its full essence through two things: the thing itself, and its external form and image . . . Therefore this great and wise man, whoever he was, and the people who followed after him and preserved the lessons for life that they had received, in order to be perfect had the thing itself, namely wisdom; and they also had an external form, namely eloquence." Eloquence is the manifested form of wisdom, which is the soul.[13] If, for Cicero, a "mute and voiceless wisdom" has no meaning for political life, for Victorinus wisdom is the soul itself seeking emancipation through the discipline of the arts, here through eloquence or rhetoric. What Ward has called the "metaphysical antinomy between body and soul" is the driving, organizing principle of Victorinus' commentary.[14] Victorinus' Neoplatonist doctrine of spiritual ascent through intellectual discipline may have colored Augustine's theological re-evaluation of the arts in his *De doctrina christiana*.[15] Victorinus' philosophical interpretation of Cicero's pairing of wisdom and eloquence was a key source for Thierry of Chartres' treatment of this theme in both his *Heptateuchon* prologue and his commentary on the *De inventione*; Thierry was also indebted to Victorinus for his own understanding of Cicero's myth about the origins of rhetoric and the founding of civilization.[16]

Translated from *Rhetores Latini Minores*, ed. Halm, by permission.[17]

---

[12] Hadot, *Marius Victorinus*, 83–6.

[13] *Explanationes*, ed. Halm, 165, 32–44; Hadot, *Marius Victorinus*, 87. For details about the theme of wisdom in the commentary, see Bergner, *Der Sapientia-Begriff im Kommentar des Marius Victorinus*, and on this passage, 84–8; and see Préaux, "Le couple de 'sapientia' et 'eloquentia.'" For this coupling of *sapientia* and *eloquentia* Victorinus may also have built on the theory set out by Licinius Crassus in Cicero's *De oratore* 3.20f.

[14] Ward, "From Antiquity to the Renaissance," 43, n. 49.

[15] See Copeland, "The Ciceronian Rhetorical Tradition," 241–4.

[16] See within, Thierry of Chartres, pp. 405–43.

[17] In the interests of making Victorinus' text clear, the translations of Cicero's text here depart from Hubbell's translation in the Loeb edition in order to follow Victorinus' interpretations more closely.

Book I

Anyone beginning a speech of whatever type should start with three things: he should make his audience alert, well disposed, and receptive to instruction. In this case, Cicero makes his audience receptive to instruction by showing what eloquence is; alert, by saying he will speak about eloquence, clearly an important subject; well disposed, since he shows that anyone trained in these techniques is going to profit from the instruction. He does not show the inherent quality of eloquence: it can absorb from its practitioner a quality that it does not intrinsically have. For he shows that its quality or effect is in accordance with the natural capacity of whoever uses it. Because anyone of even average sense can see that eloquence in the hands of a fool is bad, and in the hands of a wise man is good, therefore Cicero does not raise the question whether eloquence is bad or good, but shows whether it has more that is good or more that is bad.

In the beginning he deals with four theses: first, that one should strive for wisdom with eloquence; second, that wisdom by itself is not very useful, although it has some use; third, that eloquence devoid of wisdom is very harmful. And since one could say "then should one not study eloquence? For wisdom you praise everywhere," the answer is that one should indeed study eloquence, because it is necessarily through eloquence that wisdom can exercise its power. Fourth thesis: one should study eloquence, but only eloquence that is mixed with wisdom. We should note in the beginning the setting of the theme for debate, the parts of the theme-setting, their execution, and its conclusion. When one pays attention these are easy to distinguish. However, before we get on to Cicero's opening, we think we need to discuss first what art [*ars*] is, and then what the difference is between art and virtue. "Art" is a term that does not yield its complete sense, but is understood to refer to something. When we hear the word *codex*, we know straightaway what a codex is—but we cannot know immediately what "art" is, unless we add "of what" it is the art: for example, poetics, grammar, rhetoric. Virtue is a state of the soul, directed towards the order of nature in accordance with reason—that is why it is directed towards the order of nature.[18] For we consist of two things, soul and body. The soul is immortal. If it is immortal, it is descended from the gods. If it is descended from the gods, it is perfect. But however perfect the soul, its keenness is entangled and surrounded by a certain thick covering, the body, and thus it becomes forgetful of itself in a certain way. But when through study and discipline it starts to uncover and lay itself bare, then the state of the soul returns and is called back to its natural order. This is virtue, and Plato sometimes says that it comes into

---

[18] *De inventione* 2.53.159. See also Cox and Ward, eds., *The Rhetoric of Cicero*, 411 and note.

being through art, sometimes that it is born with human beings, sometimes that it is produced by exercise [*exercitatio*], sometimes that it is given by God. In his rhetorical works, Cicero equates this virtue with wisdom. Elsewhere, however, namely in the books on the Republic, this same Cicero equates virtue with prudence. Virtue has four parts, prudence, justice, courage, temperance. Prudence is the permanent knowledge of what is good and bad. Justice is the state of the soul that is so formed that it assigns dignity to all merits. Courage is the well-considered undertaking of dangers and the enduring of suffering. Temperance is the victorious and chaste rule over the soul where useless and indecent things are concerned. In what follows we will examine the subdivisions of these parts.

Let us return now to what we had proposed to show, namely the difference between art and virtue. Of these four parts which we said are in virtue, none at all falls under art. For art only hands down precepts, not what one should do with them.[19] That means no art of wisdom can be taught. Wisdom exists completely and permanently all by itself. It is perfect if it has these four, prudence, justice, courage, and temperance. But an art of eloquence is imparted [*datur*], and rightly imparted.[20] For since eloquence is based on four things, nature [*natura*], usage [*usus*], training [*exercitatio*], and art [*ars*], it is necessary that the precepts of the art be imparted so as to attain eloquence. If art is lacking, the other three can sometimes definitely do great harm, but never any good.

Further, I think we also need to state the difference between a rhetor, a sophist, and an orator. A rhetor teaches literature and the techniques of eloquence. With a sophist, one learns the practice of speaking. An orator uses full and perfect eloquence in public and private cases. And so that we may know that a rhetor is different from an orator, he called those books in which he teaches the art of speaking the "Art of Rhetoric," but those other three, in which he shows what an orator needs "On the Orator."[21] At this point, then, where he considers what he is going to discuss, that is eloquence, and how important it is, he rightly introduces himself as having pondered for a long time, not the question whether eloquence is good or bad, but whether it has more that is good or more that is bad.[22]

De Inventione 1.1.1

LONG AND OFTEN HAVE I THOUGHT TO MYSELF If only one of these were the case, it would not show really long-term cogitation. For we could think about something frequently, but

---

[19] I.e. unlike virtue, an *ars* does not have an ethical direction or object. Virtue, by contrast, deals with good and evil, merit, and the like. *Ars* can show what one *can* do with such things, but not what *should* be done with them.

[20] Cf. Cox and Ward, *The Rhetoric of Cicero*, 412.   [21] The latter reference is to the *De oratore*.

[22] This is already part of the paraphrase of the opening of the *De inventione*.

stop thinking straightaway; we could also think about something for a long time, but do so one day only. He is right, therefore, to combine the two: "*long* and *often* have I thought to myself." And since he should never have published on the topic unless he had it worked out in deliberation, he rightly says "I thought to myself."

MORE THAT IS GOOD OR MORE THAT IS BAD The topic of debate is not whether eloquence is good or bad, but whether is has more that is good or more that is bad. The order is no coincidence. For he could also have said "more that is bad or more that is good." But Cicero keeps to the nature of eloquence, which as soon as it began, was of use to people. For it "drove them together and assembled them." Later, however, when it had been corrupted by bad characters, it caused the state much harm. It is good therefore that he keeps to the order, so that he said "more that is good or more that is bad."

IT GAVE TO PEOPLE AND CITIES[23] A state is based on two things: the public and the private. Therefore he says "to people and cities." We should also note this in the Verrine orations, how Cicero is everywhere either defending people or cities.

THE ABILITY TO SPEAK [*COPIA DICENDI*] The word "eloquence" makes the assertion and claim for itself that whoever hears it will only take it to be the best kind. That is why he preferred to give a definition of eloquence: for fear that anybody, on hearing "eloquence"—which by its very sound has secured the reputation of being mixed with wisdom—for fear, I say, that anybody should believe that there is no argument about whether eloquence has more that is good or more that is bad, but would think that it is adequate in itself. That is why he preferred to define eloquence by calling it "the ability to speak." Since that expression could be bent either way, it justifies full discussion.

AND THE GREATEST ZEAL [TO ATTAIN] ELOQUENCE Now that he has taught what eloquence is through a definition, he can safely call it eloquence later, since he has already determined the outlook of his audience. But it is correct that he says "and the greatest zeal [to attain] eloquence": for it is impossible to state what power eloquence has unless somebody has it, and it has reached its full capacity.

FOR WHEN I CONSIDER BOTH THE HARM DONE TO OUR STATE As he is about to show how much good or evil eloquence can do, he talks about the state, and he is right: for eloquence should not be put to the test in private affairs, but in public ones. That is what he does himself in the Verrine orations when he is most strongly recommending himself or his eloquence. He mentions his public cases, and is silent about the private ones: "I who have been so involved for so many years in public cases and trials."[24] At this point, then, he talks about the disadvantages and advantages to the state, in order to demonstrate the good that eloquence does. Notice that he does not follow up on the parts in the same order in

---

[23] *Civitas*, which can mean city, state, or community.   [24] Cicero, *Divinatio in Q. Caecilium* §1.

which he announced them. For above he said "whether more that is good or more that is bad"; but here he starts from the bad aspects of eloquence. Above, he followed a natural order, as we said; here he preserves the logical organization of thought. For those things occur to us first that are close in memory. And so he is choosing from recent events and what is nearer when he says "I consider the harm done to our state": for what he is considering is the present state. And since so far much harm has come to the state entirely through eloquence, he is right to take his starting point from the bad aspects of eloquence; later he will come to speak of the good and bad things that happened in earlier times.

AND RECOLLECT IN MY MIND THE OLD DISASTERS THAT BEFELL THE GREATEST STATES He gradually steps back from our state to foreign ones, and he rightly mentions the greatest states after Rome. Because the examples of these greatest states are older, he says he "recollects them in his mind." But what happened in our state, he "considers." So it is right that he has recollected the disasters of the greatest states: for eloquence is effective in those cases where there are a large people.

I SEE THAT IT IS NOT THE SMALLEST Since the point of debate here is quantity, i.e. whether eloquence brings more that is good or more that is bad, therefore he says "I see that it is not the smallest part of the harm that has been brought about."

PART OF THE HARM THAT HAS BEEN BROUGHT ABOUT BY THE MOST ELOQUENT MEN As we discussed before, he did not want to say "by eloquence," but rather "by the most eloquent men," i.e. who only possess the ability to speak. "Brought about" [*invectam,* lit. "sailed in"] is a metaphor from a ship. For one can say that someone "holds the helm of state."

WHEN THINGS THAT ARE FAR REMOVED FROM WHAT WE CAN REMEMBER BECAUSE OF THEIR AGE Now that he has set out the bad things, he begins to talk about the good that eloquence has. "Far removed from what we can remember," he says, and in order to excuse our memory for what might be deemed its negligence, he adds "because of their age." So how can we know the things that are very far removed from what we can remember? "I began to retrieve them," he says, "from the memorials of literature." We should take these memorials in two ways: either as annals or as histories. For the annals were there first, and histories were written later.

MANY CITIES WERE FOUNDED, NUMEROUS WARS EXTINGUISHED, THE FIRMEST ALLIANCES, THE MOST SACRED OF FRIENDSHIPS Here we should say what a state [*civitas*] is. A state is a large group of people brought together to live justly. So when a state is founded, it should suffer war first, and then live in peace. For the word *pax* ["peace"] comes from "pact." But there cannot be a pact, without a prior reason, i.e. war. This was also Sallust's view, when he was discussing Roman history; for he said that first wars were fought, and then peace was made. "The Roman state," he says, "was at its most powerful under the consulate of Servius Sulpicius and Marcus Marcellus, when all of Gallia on this side of the Rhine and between Our Sea and the Ocean was under control, except the parts that were impassable because of swamps." Here war is being waged and then he mentions that peace follows. "The state knew perfect morality and the greatest concord between the second and last Punic war."[25] Now the question is whether eloquence has any power in wars. The answer is undoubtedly yes, just as much as manly courage [*virtus*]. For if manly courage can finish a war, so can eloquence. That is why he [Cicero] says "numerous wars extinguished." Now it is well known that wars can be said to "flame": "all of Hispania on this side of the Alps was aflame";[26] and "who [has not heard of] the fires of such a great war."[27]

THE FIRMEST ALLIANCES [*SOCIETATES*], THE MOST SACRED OF FRIENDSHIPS [*AMICITIAS*] This is the difference between an ally [*socius*] and a friend [*amicus*]. An ally is tied to us by some agreement to do something with us; a friend is connected to me through a similar lifestyle in pious and loyal love. And because an ally does something with us, that is why he said "the firmest alliances." Because a friend is connected to us by pious love, that is why he said "the most sacred of friendships." So sometimes one can be a friend, but not an ally, if the person is not doing anything with me. Inversely, although one is an ally, he is not a friend, if he does something with me without really wanting to. Therefore Cicero combines these two everywhere, "allies of the Roman people and friends": in this way we have here, too, "the firmest alliances, the most sacred of friendships."

I UNDERSTAND "Understanding" is right: for above he says "from the memorials of literature I began to retrieve them": what one reads, one needs to understand.

WERE STRUCK UP BY REASONABLE THOUGHT, BUT ALL THE MORE READILY BY ELOQUENCE He connects these two things everywhere. But when two things produce an effect, they do so in three ways: either they are equal, or in some cases one is worth more, or in some cases the other. Here he attributes to wisdom its own reasonable actions. But since all virtue is slow because of its size, therefore he also added something about time, so that what wisdom has discovered is readily completed by eloquence. So in order to achieve something fast, each needs the help of the other. Therefore he correctly has the good of the state arise out of the combination of both forces.

AND AFTER LONG THOUGHT, REASON ITSELF BRINGS ME ABOVE ALL TO THIS VIEW: THAT WISDOM WITHOUT ELOQUENCE DOES TOO LITTLE GOOD FOR STATES, BUT ELOQUENCE WITHOUT WISDOM IS MOSTLY VERY HARMFUL, AND NEVER HELPFUL Above he has shown how much harm eloquence could do, and how much good, but only when mixed with wisdom. Now he wishes to show, point by point, how much good wisdom by itself can do, and how much harm eloquence by itself. When he has shown both that wisdom by itself

[25] Sallust, *Historiae*, book 1.1, fragment 11, ed. B. Maurenbrecher (Leipzig: Teubner, 1891).
[26] Cf. Sallust, *Historiae*, book 1.4, fragment 85   [27] *Aeneid* 1.566.

does too little good, and that eloquence by itself is very harmful, he will state once again that eloquence should be coupled with wisdom. Every thing is either of great use or of little use, it is either extremely harmful or less harmful: he assigns one of these to wisdom, that by itself it is of too little use to the state, but does no harm. Of eloquence by itself he often says that it is too harmful, meaning it is always harmful, but sometimes just rather harmful. The other half, though, he denies to eloquence only, namely that it benefits the state too little, but does not do any harm. As for his words "and after long thought reason itself brings me": he says "reason itself," namely the reason of wisdom, which we say should be connected with eloquence.

THEREFORE IF SOMEONE NEGLECTS THE BEST AND MOST HONORABLE EFFORTS TOWARDS REASON AND DUTY He shows what complete wisdom is. For he is wise who has the best knowledge of divine and human things. Therefore we should associate "the effort towards good reason" with things divine, and "the effort towards honorable duty" with things human. That he said "effort" is better than if he had said "therefore if someone neglects reason and duty." For these words describe perfect philosophy; since no orator can fully achieve that, therefore he shows that we should make at least an effort towards reason and duty.

AND SPENDS ALL HIS ENERGY IN THE PRACTICE OF SPEAKING "Spends [*consumit*]," he says: the word itself indicates the uselessness of the labor. What he refers to as "in the practice of speaking," he is afraid to call "eloquence," as we said above, for fear of offending the feelings of his audience. This then is the definition of eloquence: eloquence is the practice of speaking.

THAT MAN IS RAISED A USELESS CITIZEN TO HIMSELF, A DANGEROUS ONE TO HIS FATHERLAND Every man either looks out for himself, or for his fatherland, or more for himself than for his fatherland. So it is right that people are invited to mix these two, wisdom and eloquence, first on the strength of the usefulness to themselves, and then also the public usefulness. "The man," he says, "who will have spent his time only on the practice of speaking, having neglected efforts towards reason and duty, is raised a useless citizen to himself, a dangerous one to his fatherland." "But the man who arms himself with eloquence in such a way": "arms" is good, as if wisdom stands for strength, eloquence for arms. Let us notice, though, that although earlier he used "the ability to speak," "practice," or "skill in speaking," now he feels it is safe to call it "eloquence," since he is also speaking about wisdom. Here too he preserves the two points we mentioned above: "he who will have mixed eloquence with wisdom, that man will be, I think, a very useful and friendly citizen for his own affairs and the public ones": we should take "useful" to be about private affairs, "friendly" about the public ones.

AND IF WE WISH [TO CONSIDER THE BEGINNING] OF THIS THING WHICH IS CALLED ELOQUENCE First he sets up an entity, on which he imposes the name "eloquence," and he shows the origins of eloquence. "Either from art or from striving or from exercise or from nature": "if we wish to consider the beginning," he says, of this eloquence, whose origin is uncertain, "we discover," he says, "that it arose out of the most honorable causes, and proceeded from the best reasonings." A cause is an impulse of the soul to do something; a reasoning is the order of things to do, which come from a cause, so that you understand what you should do or say in any situation.[28] So, he says, if we wish to consider the beginning of eloquence, we should first pay attention to its cause. This cause is honorable. Next we find the reasonings, and discover that they are the best. The difference between striving and exercise is the following: striving is the stubborn determination of the soul to do something, exercise is the continuation of an act that was begun. We have said above that eloquence can also originate from these.

De Inventione 1.2.2–1.2.3

FOR ONCE UPON A TIME, HUMAN BEINGS WERE ROAMING OVER THE FIELDS EVERYWHERE LIKE ANIMALS He starts to relate that there had been honorable causes, not through which eloquence was born in its essence, but took its beginning in terms of action. As we said before, the philosophers claim that a human being consists of two things, body and soul. The soul is perfect, but is hindered by the grossness of the body in revealing itself as it is by nature. So when the world was made, human beings were too much bothered by their bodies, and in such a condition that the power of their souls was buried and overwhelmed. At that time they had to live from theft, they behaved badly because the goodness of the soul was suppressed, and they misused their bodily strength in everything. But since nature does not distribute itself evenly over everyone, at some point one man stood out who understood himself well and who could see that there is this divine soul in human beings, with most valuable potential, if only somebody could lure it from its hiding place and bring it forth. This then was not the cause of birth for eloquence, but the cause for its action. "For once upon a time, human beings were roaming over the fields everywhere like animals." Virgil has this too: "These forests were occupied by local Fauns and nymphs/ and a race of men born from trees and hard oak: / who had neither custom nor culture, nor did they know how to yoke bulls / or collect riches or preserve it once they got it."[29]

---

[28] This explanation is reprised and developed in Thierry of Chartres' commentary on *De inventione*, which depends heavily on Victorinus. See within, p. 421.

[29] *Aeneid* 8.314–17.

AND THEY SUBSISTED ON WILD FARE Every wise man strives to be remembered. But people whose power of soul is languishing, overwhelmed by the weight of their bodies, do not strive to be remembered, but look for help day by day like wild animals. So Sallust: "And since the life itself, which we enjoy, is short, it is right to make the memory of ourselves as long-lived as possible, not to live like beasts which nature has made bent downwards and obedient to their stomachs,"[30] like those people who subsisted on wild fare.

NO ONE YET RESPECTED A SENSE OF AWE TOWARDS THE GODS, OR DUTY TOWARDS MAN This is perfect philosophy, consisting of two parts, physics and ethics. Physics deals with the divine, ethics with what is human. Since here he is teaching what is necessary for an orator, he is pursuing ethics. If ethics was unknown to the people at that time, even more so was physics unknown to them. So he indicates the way of life of those people, who knew nothing of the good of their souls, but did everything by bodily force.

NO ONE HAD SEEN A LEGITIMATE MARRIAGE, NO ONE HAD LOOKED UPON CHILDREN CERTAINLY HIS OWN Both marriages and children were the product of a vague and uncertain Venus; there were no laws to forbid this either.

THEY HAD NOT ACCEPTED THE USE OF EQUITABLE LAW Life is led without injustice to anyone, where there is equality of law, equal liberty, where it is either allowed to all, or not allowed to all to do something.

THE MOST PERNICIOUS ASSISTANTS He says that the strengths of the body are the helpers of desire, who exercise a certain tyranny in the souls of human beings.

IN THAT DAY, A CERTAIN MAN, OBVIOUSLY GREAT AND WISE In order to facilitate understanding, we need a comparison. The soul is like wine. For just as wine can either preserve or lose its strength depending on its container, so the soul preserves its nature if it happens to have found a very good and chaste body, but if not, it is as if it loses it. So when the mortal race, which was brutish and ignorant of everything, was wandering around, there was a certain great man whose soul retained its nature. He understood that all human beings have something divine in themselves, but that this is oppressed and ruined by the faults of the body. If that aspect could be teased out, the greatest benefits could accrue to humankind.

REALIZED WHAT A POTENTIAL [MATERIES] AND HOW GREAT AN OPPORTUNITY FOR THE GREATEST THINGS EXISTED IN THE SOULS OF HUMAN BEINGS Materia ["matter," "potential"] is not "matter" for that which is called "matter," but for that which can come about from it. Opportunitas ["opportunity"] is not an accident, and is not in something else, but is in the same material. In wood there can be the potential [materies] to make something,

---

[30] Sallust, *Bellum Catilinae* 1.

but if it rots, there is no opportunity [*opportunitas*] in the material [*materia*]. We can say something similar about other "materials." This means it was not enough to have found the material/potential in human beings, unless there was also the opportunity in the same material for the greatest things.

IF SOMEONE WOULD BE ABLE TO TEASE IT OUT [*ELICERE*]   So there is somebody capable of teasing it out, and something capable of being teased out. Let us pay attention to this next point. A man can see that something can be done, yet not do it. In fact, Cicero says that this wise and great man too had seen the potential in human beings, but harbored doubts about its effectiveness. For he says: "if someone would be able to tease it out." Yet he gives both capacities to this man: to understand and to put into effect. For he is both wise and eloquent.

AND MAKE IT BETTER AGAIN BY TEACHING   So human beings had a soul, but he says "make . . . again," because it seemed to have been lost: it was a good soul, that is why he says "make it better again by teaching." It is, then, for these very honorable reasons, as we see, that that man was compelled to be eloquent, i.e. to do that from which eloquence first began to come alive and into action. What more honorable cause could there be than to bring human beings, who were living like animals, to a human and divine insight through useful and honorable instruction? Let us accept then this great and wise man, whoever he was: for many want him to be understood as Saturnus, Plato, Aristotle or others—but they are wrong.

IN ACCORDANCE WITH A CERTAIN PLAN [*RATIO*] HE DROVE THE PEOPLE WHO WERE DISPERSED OVER THE FIELDS AND WERE HIDING IN FOREST SHELTERS TOGETHER IN ONE PLACE AND ASSEMBLED THEM   He [Cicero] had already posited two things, that there had been the most honorable causes and the best of reasons for eloquence to come into being and action. Having explained the most honorable causes he now starts to show that the reasons for eloquence to come into action were the best. And so that you understand that he has already dealt with the causes he says, "in accordance with a certain plan [*ratio*] he drove them together in one place and assembled them." We said that *ratio* ["plan," "reason"] is a necessary order of doing something, e.g. this must happen first, then this, thirdly this, for example, now men are driven together first, then they are assembled, then they are brought to do every individual useful and honorable thing.

HE DROVE TOGETHER IN ONE PLACE AND ASSEMBLED   "Drove together" is said as it were of unwilling people, "assembled" of people who are already willing. We need to know what "drove together and assembled" means: it is as if he created a *civitas* ["state" or "community"]. For as we said above, a *civitas* is a large group of people brought together to live justly. Therefore eloquence is most useful: it creates a *civitas* and introduces whatever is useful and honorable.

AND HE GOT THEM TO DO EVERY INDIVIDUAL USEFUL AND HONORABLE THING Cicero teaches that the honorable is two things: first, the pure thing by itself; second, that which is introduced in combination with what is useful. The thing by itself is to be found in few people, namely those who care for honor [*gloria*] only and do nothing to benefit themselves. Whatever they sanction, they sanction generally on considering what is good and what is bad, not for the sake of the people involved in it. The combination of the honorable and the useful is called "honorable" [*honestum*], because anything combined and double takes its name from the predominant element. The first *honestum* is that of the philosophers, the second that of those wise men who aim their efforts at the state, who are active in state business [*in civitate*]. But the honorable is always connected with the useful, and usefulness with the honorable. This is also something Socrates says, that there is nothing useful which is not honorable; nothing honorable, which is not useful. But we need examples so that we may understand him. It is honorable to be a judge, yet usefulness is coupled with the honorable: for nobody will do such a person, or his servants, an injustice. He is useful to posterity, he is of use to his offspring. If he helps his friends in any way, that is useful too. But although the two are mixed, they are not mixed the way water is mixed with wine, namely in such a way that it is impossible to separate them. No, they are mixed in such a way that they seem to be separable again, just as if a heap is made of wheat and barley. Although those two are mixed, still they can also be separated in some way. Now, if I render a service to someone, and do not claim gratitude back, that is honorable; but my very service becomes useful when I do claim gratitude back. So let the honorable by itself be primary, that which is pleasing by itself, without any gratitude connected to it; the intermediate honorable is connected with usefulness. And let the third be commodity, which concentrates on profits only and rejects all that is honorable. However, what is philosophically honorable strives after honor only, and rejects even usefulness. Now then, since a community has been founded by collecting people and assembling them, what should they be made to believe? What should be introduced to those people? Not that which is honorable by itself, which is the characteristic of philosophers, not commodity, which is characteristic of depraved people, but that intermediate version of honorable and useful, which is around in every state [*re publica*], in every community [*civitate*].

AT FIRST THEY WERE PROTESTING AGAINST IT BECAUSE THEY WERE NOT USED TO IT He would not have needed eloquence if he had persuaded them the minute he started to introduce the notions of the honorable and the useful to them. But he shows that eloquence has great powers, since it brought them against their will to what was best. He wishes to avoid the impression that they were protesting against it because it was not the best: that is why he adds "because they were not used to it" and "at first they were protesting." Then he avoids the impression that the poison of eloquence had also brought them to something bad by saying "they listened more attentively to his reason and his speech." Where there is reason and wisdom, there can be no malice. Let us realize that "reason" should be referred to the gravity of his opinions, "speech" to the ornateness of his diction.

[AND SO] FROM WILD AND FIERCE HE MADE THEM MILD AND GENTLE It is hard to take something away from somebody, it is even harder to give them something else. Here both are done: their wildness and ferocity are taken away from human beings, and they are given humanity [*humanitas*] and gentleness [*mansuetudo*].[31]

AND IT WOULD SEEM TO ME AT LEAST THAT NO SILENT WISDOM, NOR ONE DEPRIVED OF SPEECH COULD HAVE PERFECTED THIS There are many things that are perfected by nothing but their own natural condition [*habitus*], many by their natural condition and by practice. Even if an athlete has a massive body, he is not instantly perfect, unless it is reinforced by practice [*usus*]. And even when an orator has a grasp of the natural condition of all knowledge, he is not instantly perfect, unless it is reinforced by practice. Wisdom however is perfect by its own natural condition, and it does not need speaking, i.e. practice. It is enough for it to be contained within souls; therefore it does not achieve anything by practice. And even if he will wish to point out his thoughts by verbalizing them, the wise man does not become any wiser because he points out that he is wise. No, his wisdom is perfect and intact, yet something reinforces it in order to perform other actions. So human beings, having been made mild and gentle from wild and fierce, little by little learned the honorable and the useful. But since he is speaking about the beginning of eloquence, let us see whether wisdom brought this about all by itself, or whether wisdom did it, but together with eloquence. First, then, we need to understand how many ways wisdom can be persuasive about something. We can understand that eloquence is very valuable in this area. Wisdom by itself can be persuasive about something in two ways. It may be silent, and somebody else imitates something that wisdom does, because it is good, that is, whatever a wise man does in silence, somebody else imitates, led by the thing itself, not by words. Or it may persuade through words that something should be done or not done, and this happens in two ways: sometimes by natural words, sometimes through eloquence. Here Cicero denies that a silent wisdom could have brought this about: he denies that a wisdom deprived of speech could have brought this about, that is, one that uses natural words—but he claims that the wisdom coupled with eloquence could have perfected it.

---

[31] The Ciceronian terms (1.2.2) are *mites* and *mansuetos* (both meaning "kind," "mild," "gentle"); Victorinus introduces the term (and notion) *humanitas*.

AND IT WOULD SEEM TO ME AT LEAST THAT NO SILENT WISDOM, NOR ONE DEPRIVED OF SPEECH COULD HAVE PERFECTED THIS "Perfect," he says: elsewhere it is the duty of full-blown wisdom to discover, for example, as above, "in that day, a certain man, obviously great and wise, realized what a potential [*materies*] and how great an opportunity for the greatest things existed in the souls of human beings, if someone would be able to tease it out and make it better again by teaching." Thus wisdom realized that there was a soul in human beings. It may have been wisdom that made them assemble and be brought to do every individual useful and honorable thing, but it accomplished this through the help of eloquence.

NAMELY THAT IT SUDDENLY TURNED THEM AWAY FROM WHAT THEY WERE USED TO AND LED THEM TO A VERY DIFFERENT WAY OF LIFE Great is the power of eloquence, if it causes a sudden conversion—this is what wisdom cannot do. Elsewhere, wisdom too is effective, but not suddenly. As for what he says "and led them to a very different way of life": as we said above, it is hard to break habits; all the harder then even to make a different way of life acceptable.

CONSIDER THEN, WHEN CITIES HAD BEEN FOUNDED Above, when talking about the benefits of eloquence, he also used this order "many cities were founded, numerous wars extinguished, the firmest alliances, the most sacred of friendships." And although in this passage human beings were first brought out of their savagery and made equals, and then even started to obey spontaneously, yet we can find the order mentioned above preserved. So first states were formed through the services of eloquence, as above, "many cities were founded." One speaks of the birth of a civic community [*civitas*], when people are brought together into one place to live justly.

THAT THEY LEARNED TO PRESERVE GOOD FAITH This is where wars are extinguished.[32] As long as desire was misusing bodily strength to satisfy itself, it is as if wars were being waged. So when good faith is preserved, this either happens in order to prevent wars, or the wars that were there already are extinguished.

AND MAINTAIN JUSTICE All justice that derives from us is concerned with others, that we assign to everyone what they deserve. This is where it is possible for a community [*societas*] to be, as it were, protected. For a society should be made or preserved in just circumstances.

AND BECOME USED TO OBEYING OTHERS VOLUNTARILY Justice makes human beings equals; here, however, they even voluntarily endure being inferior. Yet here they can be bound together in friendship: for we do not obey anybody voluntarily unless we are friends. Before, however, as long as everything was conducted through physical force, nobody obeyed another person voluntarily, nor could anybody who was coerced be a friend.

---

[32] A reference to Cicero, *De inventione* I.I.I *bella restincta* and Victorinus' own comments above.

AND THEY THOUGHT THEY SHOULD NOT JUST TAKE ON WORK FOR THE COMMON GOOD
Through eloquence, he says, it was achieved that all would readily take on work for the welfare of the state [*pro publica salute*], and not just that they would take on work, but even lose their lives. Eloquence, then, achieved a great deal, so that they would count their lives for little, who for such a long time had subsisted on wild fare.[33]

HOW COULD THIS HAVE HAPPENED? The question is, whether human beings were brought to these ways of life by nature, or whether they seem to have been induced to it by instruction. There used to be a better nature in humankind, but it was oppressed by the faults of the body and deteriorated into evil. However, since nothing exists with utter uniformity, there is always something that lets us see what is missing in others.[34] So that great and wise man realized that there was a good nature in human beings which would be very useful if it was made better by instruction. Therefore, everything that is perfect is so by nature and instruction. But since that first man could not get instruction, he was perfect by nature and practice. For once he had recognized his natural disposition [*habitus*], he also discovered after long ruminations that there was a good nature in human beings, and in order to make its perfection possible he applied instruction to it. So the potential [*materies*], i.e. the nature, was there in human beings, which was made perfect by instruction that had been discovered through wisdom, and introduced through eloquence.

TO BE SURE, NO ONE, UNLESS MOVED BY A SERIOUS AND PLEASANT SPEECH Although nature is suitable for the perfect life, yet he says that nature itself was brought to these ways of life by instruction. "Moved by a serious and pleasant speech," he says. Let us connect seriousness with wisdom, pleasantness with eloquence, or better: seriousness with the content, pleasantness with the verbal ornamentation.

WHEN HE WAS VERY POWERFUL THROUGH STRENGTH, WOULD WISH TO AGREE TO LAW WITHOUT VIOLENCE Everything is defeated by something similar. For example, an eloquent man is excelled by the man who will be more eloquent; a strong man is not defeated unless by somebody who is stronger; an intelligent man is not defeated unless by somebody who is more intelligent. Notice, therefore, Cicero's subtlety: the strongest people, he says, are not brought to a life of equality by strength (by which inferior strength would normally be defeated), but by eloquence. Thus, eloquence is beyond all powers, but only eloquence that is combined with wisdom.

---

[33] That is, a people so accustomed to surviving by brute force, and to placing mere survival above all else, could now be willing to sacrifice their lives for the good of their communities.

[34] That is, human nature was not so uniformly corrupt that no glimpse of goodness could be seen. So the wise man was able to glimpse the enormous potential that appears to be missing from human nature. Similarly, as Victorinus understands this myth of origins, some souls, when encased in human bodies, are able to retain a deeper memory of the divine, and hence (like the sage) can rise above ordinary human circumstances: see Hadot, *Marius Victorinus*, 83–6.

SO THAT HE WOULD ENDURE TO BE MADE THE EQUAL OF PEOPLE AMONG WHOM HE COULD EXCEL "Excel," in strength, of course. "Endure to be made the equal of people," so above: "they had not accepted the use of equitable law."

AND OF HIS OWN WILL Not forced by bodily strength. But the will had already been created in them by the persuasiveness of eloquence.

WOULD RELINQUISH THEIR VERY AGREEABLE LIFE-STYLE [CONSUETUDO] He does not say "relinquish their life-style" but "their very agreeable life-style": for all things, even bad ones, make a very agreeable life-style to the ones who are cherishing them.

ALL THE MORE SO, SINCE THAT LIFE-STYLE HAD ALREADY ACQUIRED FORCE OF NATURE THROUGH ITS GREAT AGE So the nature of human beings is good, but evil had taken the place of nature through habit [consuetudo].

THIS IS HOW AT FIRST ELOQUENCE ORIGINATED AND DEVELOPED FURTHER He has made good on his proposed theme. For above he said: "if we wish to consider the beginning of this thing called 'eloquence,' we will discover that it arose out of the most honorable causes, and proceeded from the best reasoning." Similarly, he says here "this is how at first eloquence originated and developed further."

AND SIMILARLY LATER IN THE MOST IMPORTANT MATTERS OF WAR AND PEACE He shows that eloquence has long been useful. As to his words "in the most important matters," see what he said above, "he realized what a potential [materies] and how great an opportunity for the greatest things existed in the souls of human beings, if someone would be able to tease it out": so the greatest things are war and peace.

WITH THE GREATEST USEFULNESS FOR HUMANKIND Namely that usefulness that is coupled with the honorable.

BUT AFTER A CERTAIN OPPORTUNISM, THE EVIL IMITATOR OF VIRTUE Every perfect good, that is, what nature gives—free from unsuitable alloy—to the human condition, attains its full essence through two things: the thing itself, and its external form and image. For example: honey has the thing itself, namely sweetness; it also has an external form, i.e. a color and the way it looks: this is as it were its face, which makes people believe it is sweet, as it is indeed. Similarly, a strong man has the thing itself, namely virtue; he also has an external form, i.e. corporeal beauty. For in members that are misshapen and not fittingly positioned according to their nature, there can be no place for virtue: accordingly, Virgil and others have said that whoever was strong was also beautiful. So a cloak has the thing itself, the usefulness of the cloth; it also has an external form, namely gracefulness of external aspect. Therefore this great and wise man, whoever he was, and the people who followed after him and preserved the lessons for life that they had received, in order to be perfect had the thing itself, namely wisdom; and they also had an external form, namely eloquence. As a reward for their virtue, these people received the worthiest prizes, magistracies and other useful things. Therefore many who wanted the same rewards for themselves ignored the thing itself and started to follow the external aspect only, that is, they skipped wisdom and attained only the capacity to speak. So seduced by the rewards only, opportunism ignored the substance and started to imitate the external aspect of virtue. And this is how it happened that evil characters acquired the ability to speak and, to the detriment of the state, made a wrongful use of eloquence by itself, without wisdom. Opportunism, that is, the evil imitator of virtue, is that third element, opposed to the honorable by itself.[35]

GREW ACCUSTOMED TO DESTROY THE CITIES AND DISRUPT THE LIVES OF HUMAN BEINGS Cf. above: "whether it gave to people and cities more that is good or more that is bad." The public cause is a combination of these two elements.

De Inventione 1.3.4–5

IT SEEMS TO ME MOST LIKELY Here begins the passage on the disadvantages of eloquence. The question is raised how it is possible that eloquence mixed with wisdom, which assembled people, persuaded them to do what was useful and honorable, founded cities, taught law, which benefited people greatly—that eloquence, I say, mixed with wisdom began to be a liability to people and states [*civitatibus*]. That was, of course, "the beginning of evil." After the cities had been founded it was necessary that first these same states grew by their own population or neighboring ones. Then, not everyone in the states was wise and eloquent, but only few—although all had the potential to have these qualities. Therefore it was necessary that, once the states had grown and expanded, the wise and eloquent men should govern state affairs, and occupy themselves with these matters exclusively. Since the wise men were occupied with state business then, shrewd and talkative people started to deal with private business. First they handled small conflicts, later they began to be the patrons of everyone's fortunes. Since these shrewd men would now and then defend bad cases against justice, and would win them frequently too, those wise men who had been concentrating on the state were forced to stand up to those clever and well-spoken men in the interests of their citizens and relatives. In the meantime the latter, through their assiduous public speaking, had become very well known to the people and very friendly with them. That is how those clever men, when speaking against the wise men, would often be judged by the people to be equal to the wise men, sometimes even superior, and they

---

[35] Cf. the discussion above on the honorable and the useful; this conclusion about opportunism parallels the idea of the useful alone, without the honorable.

began to be judged worthy of governing the state. After the state had been entrusted to them, much trouble arose, and many shipwrecks occurred. That is how eloquence, which had originally been useful as long as it was mixed with wisdom, later, on its own, did great harm to the state interest. But when everything was being controlled by those who were eloquent in a bad way, the wise men were distressed and started to write down what they had used to put into practice. These people are considered philosophers, and it is through them that the memory and imitation of goodness is still remembered in our time.

IT SEEMS TO ME MOST LIKELY THAT AT A CERTAIN TIME   In his mind, he is dwelling in the past and he is calling back to mind many aspects of the state [*rei publicae*]. And this confirms his opinion that without doubt there had been a time when the state was governed by the wise, and private affairs conducted by the clever. Afterwards the masses judged the clever men equal to and sometimes better than the wise men; and so the clever were entrusted with state affairs and ruined them.

NOR THAT GREAT AND WELL-SPOKEN MEN WOULD TAKE UP PRIVATE CAUSES   This is because public affairs were to be preferred to private ones. We should refer "great" to wisdom, "well-spoken" to eloquence.

I THINK THERE WERE OTHER, NOT UNCLEVER MEN   Clever [*callidi*] are those who imitate the effect of virtue through evil intent [*dolo*] and deception [*fraude*].

SINCE PEOPLE OFTEN GREW ACCUSTOMED BY FALSEHOOD TO RESIST TRUTH[36]   It is much better that he names the things themselves than when he had named them as attributes, for example, "since they often got used to resist the true cause with a deceitful speech."

SO WHEN IN SPEAKING HE WOULD OFTEN SEEM EQUAL   "In speaking," he says. Therefore wisdom is already left out here, if the judgment is about the ability to speak only.

SOMETIMES EVEN SUPERIOR   He shows that the verdict was not true, since somebody "seems" to have lost, rather than "is proven" to have lost.

IT HAPPENED THAT BOTH IN THE EYES OF THE MASSES AND OF HIMSELF HE SEEMED WORTHY OF GOVERNING THE STATE   "In the eyes of the masses," he says: in the masses the variety itself is something cheap. As for "in the eyes of himself," that is useless too: who can or should have a judgment about himself? Finally "he seemed worthy," cf. supra: "and so, since in speaking he would often seem equal, sometimes even superior."[37]

OF COURSE THIS MEANT THAT NOT WITHOUT CAUSE THE GREATEST AND MOST MISERABLE SHIPWRECKS OCCURRED, WHEN THOUGHTLESS AND AUDACIOUS CHARACTERS HAD STEPPED UP TO THE HELM OF STATE   He perseveres in his metaphor: "helm" and "shipwreck" both

---

[36] Translating Victorinus' reading *saepe mendacio contra verum stare homines consuescerent*; Our Cicero editions read *a mendacio*, "(to be) on the side of falsehood (against truth)".

[37] Victorinus' comments continue to focus on the irony implicit in Cicero's disparaging language.

apply to ships. Thus he says that it should seem surprising to nobody that the state was ruined, when its government is taken over by thoughtless and audacious men. This is the difference: "audacious" can sometimes also be interpreted as something good, "thoughtless" is only bad. "Audacity" is double, therefore: for both the man who undertakes something rashly when everything was going well is "audacious," and the man who courageously starts something with due forethought is "audacious." Since "audacity," then, has two aspects, he has preceded it by "thoughtless," so that we might understand "audacious." For thoughtlessness and lack of consideration are causes, and "audacity" is their effect.

THROUGH THESE THINGS ELOQUENCE ATTRACTED SO MUCH HATRED AND ILL WILL Every cause has its effect, and every effect its cause. For example, when fire is thrown into wood, it is necessary that the wood will be set ablaze. The fire [*ignis*] thrown into the wood is the cause, the blaze [*incendium*] is the effect of the cause. Similarly, then, eloquence first attracted hatred. Then some effect necessarily follows from the hatred, that is, from the cause. So ill will follows, since ill will mostly originates from hatred— "mostly," I say. For it can also have a different effect. If you hate an enemy, you do not bear him ill will, but you are hostile to him. If you hate a slave, you don't bear him ill will, but you are angry with him. So the result of hatred is not always ill will. There are causes which sometimes have non-necessary effects, for example, if you hit somebody with your fist and you kill him. There are also causes that do have necessary effects, for example, if you throw fire into a hay-stack it necessarily causes a fire.

THAT THE MOST TALENTED PEOPLE Talent is a power naturally implanted in souls, prevailing through its own powers. Talent therefore contains both wisdom and eloquence, and so it is also among those whom he calls "most talented." Talent also contains eloquence by itself, cf. supra "then, malice confiding in its talent."

BUT THAT THIS ONE WAS DESERTED BY MOST OF THEM AND BECAME OBSOLETE AT A TIME . . . "This one" is used absolutely, that is, the position in which wise and eloquent men spent their time in the state was lost and reduced to oblivion, at that time of all times when there should have been the greatest help offered against the dangers threatening the state. "This one" should almost be pronounced with indignation. As for his saying "by most," this is right! For not all wise men withdrew from state business. Solon wrote laws for the Athenians, and because he knew there were many most corrupt elements in the state, he went into exile of his own free will.[38] Draco also wrote laws for those same Athenians, and they use the laws of both men. Similarly, Lycurgus wrote laws for the

---

[38] I.e. in order not to be forced to change his laws again. See Plutarch, *Vita Solonis* 25.

Spartans. Therefore, not all wise men withdrew from state business, but because most of them had withdrawn, the few left over easily either left or were oppressed.

FOR THE MORE SHAMEFULLY THE THOUGHTLESSNESS AND AUDACITY OF FOOLISH AND EVIL PEOPLE WAS VIOLATING THE NOBLEST AND FAIREST THING When we are persuading people that something needs to be done, we base our persuasion on the honorable, the useful and the possible. Sometimes we also posit the necessary. According to the same precepts we are also critical about something that has not been done, just as Cicero is complaining here that the wise have withdrawn from state business. For the honorable was at hand to prevent them from doing so: "for the more shamefully the noblest and fairest thing was violated"; usefulness was at hand "with the greatest damage to the state"—it goes without saying that removing a danger from the state is useful; opportunity was at hand: "the thoughtlessness and audacity," he says, "of foolish and evil people"; for foolish and thoughtless people are easily overcome.

THE MORE ASSIDUOUSLY THESE PEOPLE SHOULD HAVE MET WITH RESISTANCE AND THE STATE SHOULD HAVE BEEN CARED FOR Here, too, he has preserved the honorable and useful. For it is honorable to resist the evil, useful to defend the state in which one lives.

SERVIUS, COMMENTARY ON THE *AENEID*, CA. 400–420

INTRODUCTION

Servius was born ca. AD 360/370, so his *floruit* fell in the last quarter of the fourth and the beginning of the fifth century.[1] We have a literary representation of Servius, revealing his status and the social role of grammarians, in Macrobius' *Saturnalia*. A number of works are connected with him (although the ascription varies): work on metrics (*De centum metris* [On the Hundred Meters],[2] *De finalibus* [On final syllables], *De metris Horatii* [On the Meters in Horace]), a commentary on the *Ars* of Donatus,[3] and the commentary on Virgil, from which we present excerpts here.[4] This commentary must have depended heavily on the Virgil commentary of Donatus, which has been lost.

The commentary to book one begins with an introductory section dealing with topical *accessus* issues: before proceeding to the *expositio/explanatio* of the text the commentator offers comments on the life of the poet, title of work, quality or nature of the poem, author's intention, number of books, and order of books. The topical form of this prologue was to remain influential on the medieval conventions of the *accessus ad auctores* in the Middle Ages: several forms of the medieval *accessus* preserve a core of topics found here, including author and work, the author's intention, and the subject matter of the

---

[1] See especially the article by Brugnoli s.v. Servio in the *Enciclopedia Virgiliana* 4 (1988): 805–13 (with very full references to scholarship, 812f.); Kaster, *Guardians of Language*, 168–97; Uhl, *Servius als Sprachlehrer*; Ziolkowski and Putnam, *The Virgilian Tradition,* 628–35; and bibliography at http://virgil.org/bibliography/servius.htm. For the question of Servius' precise name, and the relation between the different Servii and Sergii, see Brugnoli (as above), 805f.

[2] *GL* 4:456–67.

[3] The commentary in *GL* 4:403–48 in Servius' name is a compressed version of a longer commentary (*Servius plenior*) which is no longer extant, but which must have been the common ancestor of the expansive commentaries of the fifth century AD (see Jeep, *Zur Geschichte der Lehre von den Redetheilen bei den lateinischen Grammatikern,* 28–56; Holtz, *Donat et la tradition de l'enseignement,* 228). The shorter version was possibly written by Servius himself as well. The commentary that we have takes on all of Donatus: it deals with the parts of speech on the basis of the *Ars minor* (*GL* 4:406–21) and then proceeds to commentary on the *Ars maior* (from 4:421). The last part, on Donatus' *Barbarismus*, is very truncated. See also the *Explanationes in artem Donati* (in the name of Sergius), *GL* 4:486–565, which likely postdates Servius.

[4] The date of the commentary is unknown. Uhl, *Servius als Sprachlehrer*, 594, suggests 415–20.

book.[5] We translate the introduction, leaving out the section on the poet's life, which is much shorter than the life by Donatus. It also contains the story about the original beginning being deleted by the editors, Tucca and Varius.[6] Servius pictures Virgil as a source of encyclopedic knowledge; he even calls him divine.[7] In his defence of the moral excellence of the poet, Servius also uses allegorical interpretation.[8]

Servius' commentary thoroughly reflects the teaching practice of his time: it proceeds on a word-by-word and line-by-line basis. While the commentator offers a panoply of information, including facts about philosophy, history, religion, and the sources of literary allusions,[9] his primary focus is language. Here he devotes special attention to more technical linguistic and rhetorical aspects of language use rather than literary or aesthetic matters. His other main focus is the function of the poet as a potential model for students. *Auctoritas* has a double character: the authoritative author is both an example and an exception.[10] That means that Servius is very explicit about when *not* to follow the poet, namely when he is at his most poetic and making use of his poetic license.[11] It is likely that Servius' commentary was primarily meant for schoolteachers, not for schoolboys. Like most ancient grammarians, Servius is highly prescriptive. In his judgments on whether or not a linguistic utterance is correct, he makes use of the traditional criteria:[12] nature, analogy, the authority of canonical authors (*auctoritas*), and educated usage or convention (*usus, consuetudo*).

The commentary is often also revealing in what it does *not* discuss. When commenting on Anchises' great prophecy in book six, for example, with its famous mention of Caesar and Augustus, the result of the fragmentation that is typical of these commentaries becomes clear: Servius strings together innocent remarks on meter and other technical issues without making any mention of the larger implications of this text for the meaning of the poem as a whole—and this in spite of his having diagnosed the "praise of Augustus" as part of the

---

[5] The classic form of the Servian prologue descended to the Middle Ages, although in the twelfth century its use diminished. R. W. Hunt classifies the medieval imitation of the Servian prologue as the "Type B" prologue: see Hunt, "The Introductions to the 'Artes' in the Twelfth Century," and Minnis, *Medieval Theory of Authorship*, 15–18. For examples see Bernard of Utrecht, *Commentum in Theodolum*, ed. Huygens, 59, and Conrad of Hirsau, *Dialogus super auctores*, ed. Huygens, 79 (and trans. Minnis and Scott, *Medieval Literary Theory*, 46). Some features of the Servian prologue were incorporated into other prologue forms, notably the most popular version used in the twelfth century (Hunt's "Type C" prologue); see Minnis (as above), 18–27. On ancient prologue conventions, see Mansfeld, *Prolegomena: Questions to be Settled Before the Study of an Author or a Text*.

[6] See the *Life* by Donatus in the section on Donatus, within, pp. 102–3.

[7] Encyclopedic knowledge: see below the opening of the commentary on book 6; "divine" (*divinum poetam*) at *Aeneid* 3.349, cf. Ziolkowski and Putnam, *The Virgilian Tradition*, 408.

[8] Cf. Jones, "Allegorical Interpretation in Servius"; Fowler, "The Virgil Commentary of Servius," 73-9; Ziolkowski and Putnam, *The Virgilian Tradition*, 631–5.

[9] Cf. Ziolkowski and Putnam, *The Virgilian Tradition*, 630.   [10] Cf. Uhl, *Servius als Sprachlehrer*, 224ff.

[11] Kaster, *Guardians of Language*, 173; Uhl, *Servius als Sprachlehrer*, 287, see below on *Aeneid* 1.4.

[12] Correctness is the traditional province of the grammarian: see Siebenborn, *Die Lehre von der Sprachrichtigkeit und ihren Kriterien*; Kaster, *Guardians of Language*.

intention of the poet in his introduction (see below). Some other pregnant verses in book six, heavily commented on in modern scholarship, are of no interest to Servius because there are no linguistic or metrical difficulties, and there is no need to elucidate *Realien* (i.e. no need to provide factual background information on people, places, history, or myth).[13]

It is worth noting that, despite its overall, long-range significance for the reception of Virgil, Servius' commentary on the *Aeneid* does not seem to have had an important impact on the teaching of the figures of speech through the early Middle Ages. On the other hand, the Servian commentaries on Donatus seem to have carried great authority among late antique and early medieval grammarians.[14]

Servius' text of the Virgil commentary has come down to us in a "normal" (S) and an expanded (DS) version, although the transmission is contaminated. This latter version, *Servius auctus*, has additions probably going back to the Virgil commentary by Donatus;[15] this text version was used first by Servius editor Pierre Daniel (1600), and hence this version is known as Servius Danielis (DS). According to scholarly convention, the sections deriving from DS are printed in italics in the translation below.[16]

Translated from *Servii grammatici qui feruntur in Vergilii carmina commentarii*, volumes 1 and 2, ed. Thilo and Hagen, by permission.

COMMENTARY ON THE FIRST BOOK OF VIRGIL'S *AENEID* BY THE GRAMMARIAN SERVIUS

In explaining an author, the following elements must be taken into consideration: the poet's life, the title of the work, the nature [*qualitas*] of the poem, the intention of the author, the number of books, the order of the books, the explanation [*explanatio*].

---

[13] E.g. *Aeneid* 6.851–2, in which the mission of the Roman people is formulated (*tu regere imperio populos, Romane, memento / (hae tibi erunt artes), pacique imponere morem, / parcere subiectis et debellare superbos*. Cf. the dramatic reference to Marcellus at the end of Anchises' prophecy, the hope of Rome, who would die prematurely. When Marcellus' mother Octavia heard Virgil recite these verses, she fainted (*Life of Virgil* 32; see section on Donatus, within, p. 102). The total extent of Servius' comments on 6.883 *tu Marcellus eris* "you will be Marcellus" is: "such as Marcellus is."

[14] See Holtz, "À l'école de Donat, de saint Augustin à Bede," 530, referring to Schindel, *Die lateinischen Figurenlehren*. Among fifth-century grammarians, the lost *Servius plenior* commentary on Donatus' grammar (see note 3 above) appears to have been an important resource for exemplification of the figures.

[15] However, Daintree, "The Virgil Commentary," does not want to rule out additions by early-medieval schoolmen. See section on Donatus, above, p. 85.

[16] Brugnoli, in *Enciclopedia Virgiliana* 4:811 characterizes DS as insecure in matters of prosody and metrical theory. DS also evinces a certain "tendenza a interpretare in modo complicato, e spesso del tutto assurdo, passi che non presentano difficoltà, o ne presentano di facilmente solubili."

This is Virgil's biography...

The title is *the Aeneid*, a name derived from Aeneas, just as *Theseis* is derived from Theseus. So Juvenal: "vexed so many times by the *Theseis* of hoarse Cordus."[17]

The nature [*qualitas*] of the work is clear. The meter is heroic and the action mixed, for the poet speaks himself and introduces others as speaking characters. The poem is heroic: it has divine and human characters and contains both truth and fiction. For it is obvious that Aeneas did come to Italy, but it is certainly fiction [*compositum*] that Venus spoke with Jove[18] or that Mercury was sent.[19] The style is grandiloquent. It consists of high discourse and grand thoughts (*sententiae*). We know that there are three kinds of style [*genera dicendi*], low [*humile*], middle [*medium*], and grandiloquent [*grandiloquum*].[20]

Virgil's intention is the following: to imitate Homer and to praise Augustus on account of his parents.[21] For he is the son of Atia, the daughter of Julia, who was the sister of Caesar. Julius Caesar derives his origin from Iulus, the son of Aeneas, as Virgil himself confirms: "a name handed down from the great Iulus."[22]

There is no problem here with the number of books, although that problem is found in other authors. For some say that Plautus wrote twenty-one plays, others forty, others one hundred.

The order [of books] is also manifest, although some say, unnecessarily, that the second book is the first, the third the second, and the first the third, because first Troy fell, then Aeneas wandered around, then he came to queen Dido: they don't know that it is poetic artistry to start with what happened in the middle and then to use narrative to relate what happened first, or sometimes to anticipate what will happen in the future, for example through prophecies. Horace too gave this instruction in the *Ars Poetica*, to "say now what needs to be said now, but sometimes to postpone and to omit for the time being."[23] Hence it is apparent that Virgil wrote expertly.

The only topic remaining is the explanation [*explanatio*], which will be set forth in the following exposition. As for the *Aeneid*, this should suffice, for with the *Bucolics* and *Georgics* it is another story. Note further that, just as we now propose our theme [*thema*] when we are about to speak, so the ancients started a poem with its heading [*titulus*],[24] for example *arma virumque cano* "I sing of weapons and the man,"[25] or Lucan: "Wars throughout the Emathian fields,"[26] or Statius: "Battle-lines of brothers and alternate reigns."[27]

[17] Juvenal, *Satires* 1.2.   [18] *Aeneid* 1.229ff.   [19] E.g. *Aeneid* 1.297; 4.223ff.

[20] For the theory of the three levels of style, see *Rhetorica ad Herennium* 4.8.11; Cicero, *Orator* 20–2; 69; 128ff.; Augustine, *De doctrina christiana* 4.17.34–4.25.55.

[21] Cf. section on Tib. Claudius Donatus, within, pp. 141–7: Servius also recognizes "praise" as one of Virgil's goals (if not the exclusive one).

[22] *Aeneid* 1.288.   [23] Horace, *Ars poetica* 43f.

[24] I.e. the first words served as an indication of the contents.   [25] *Aeneid* 1.1.

[26] Lucan, *De bello civili* 1.1. Reference is to Thessaly (where Pharsalus lies).   [27] Statius, *Thebaid* 1.1.

1 ARMA ["WEAPONS"] Many people have discussed in various ways why Virgil begins with "arms." But it is clear that all their opinions are nonsense, since it is certain that he in fact had taken a different starting point, as was shown in his biography above.[28] By "weapons" he means "war," and the trope is called metonymy. For he substituted for "war" the "weapons" which we use in a war, just as "toga," which we wear in peacetime, can be used for "peace," as in Cicero's "let arms cede to the toga,"[29] i.e. let "war" cede to "peace." *Others accept that "arms" is used in its proper sense in this place, first because they were victorious, second because they were divine, third because he almost always adds "man" to "weapons," as in "carrying the weapons and the man," "weapons to be made for a vehement man."*[30] ARMA VIRUMQUE ("WEAPONS AND THE MAN") it is a common figure of speech not to give the corresponding items in the same order in which we announced topics; for he speaks first about the wanderings of Aeneas,[31] and later about the war.[32] This figure of speech we also use in prose.[33] E.g. Cicero in the Verrine orations, "for without any cost to ourselves having provided helmets, tunics, and wheat, he clothed, fed, and armed our greatest armies."[34]*Some people however believe there is hyperbaton, so that the sense would be as follows: "I sing of the weapons and the man, from whom the Latin race, the Alban fathers and the walls of high Rome sprang," and then you have to recall "who first left the coasts of Troy." For in this way, the reason for the work is stated, why he came to Latium through the force of fate. And a poetic beginning contains an announcement ("I sing of the weapons and the man"), an invocation ("Muse, tell me the reasons"),*[35]*and a narrative ("there was an ancient city").*[36]*And the announcement he makes in four ways: about the leader ("I sing of the weapons and the man"), the journey ("who first left the coasts of Troy"), the war ("after having suffered a lot also in war"), and the race of descendants ("from where the Latin race").* VIRUM ["MAN"] he does not name him, but makes clear it is Aeneas by the attendant circumstances. *It is good that he added "man" after "weapons," since the instruments of other arts may also be called "weapons," e.g. the weapons of Ceres.*[37] CANO ["I SING"] the language is polysemous.[38] For it means three things: sometimes it means "I praise," e.g. "and they praised the king";[39] sometimes "I foretell," as in "I beg you to foretell us yourself";[40] sometimes "I sing," as

---

[28] Servius starts his commentary with a brief discussion of Virgil's life in which he takes over from Donatus the tradition that the original beginning of the *Aeneid* was suppressed by the editors, and that *arma virumque* was in fact the beginning of the fifth verse.

[29] Cicero, *De officiis* 1.77.   [30] *Aeneid* 11.747 and 8.441.   [31] In books 1–6.   [32] In books 7–12.

[33] This is the permission for the students to imitate Virgil in this respect, cf. Uhl, *Servius als Sprachlehrer*, 299.

[34] Cicero, *Verrines* act. sec. II 2.5.   [35] *Aeneid* 1.8.

[36] *Aeneid* 1.12. For this tripartition of poetic song into "proposition," invocation, and narrative, see on vs. 8 below.

[37] I.e. ploughs: *Aeneid* 1.177.

[38] The use of this Greek technical term betrays Servius' knowledge of the Greek grammatical tradition. Cf. Uhl, *Servius als Sprachlehrer*, 540.

[39] *Aeneid* 7.698.   [40] *Aeneid* 6.76.

here. This is its proper meaning, because songs have to be sung. TROIAE ["OF TROY"] Troia is a region of Asia, Ilium is the city of Troy. Mostly, though, the poets use it freely, and employ the region or province instead of the state, e.g. Juvenal "and Asia falling through flames and iron."[41] *Probus says that* Troia, Graios *"Greeks," and* Aiax, *should not be written with one* i.[42] QUI PRIMUS many people ask why he says that Aeneas was the first to have come to Italy, when a little later he says that Antenor had founded a community there before the arrival of Aeneas. That is a fact, yet if one takes the chronology into account Virgil's statement is expert. For at the time when Aeneas came to Italy, the border of Italy was at the river Rubicon. Lucan mentions that: "a fixed border separates the Gallic meadows from the Ausonian farmers."[43] Hence it appears that Antenor had not come to Italy, but to Gallia Cisalpina, where Venice is.[44] Later, however, the borders of Italy were moved to the Alps, and that new situation created the mistake. Most people though would like to solve this problem from what follows, so that it would seem to have been for this reason that Virgil added "to the Lavinian coasts," in order to avoid the reference to Antenor. But the first explanation is better. PRIMUS *["FIRST"] not "before whom nobody else," but "after whom nobody else," e.g. "O you, for whom the earth, hit by your great trident, first gave birth to a fiery horse,"[45] and "he was the first to answer me." "First" can also be used in praise, e.g. "who will found the first city based on laws, from little Cures."[46]* AB ORIS ["FROM THE COAST"] *species instead of genus. For we should take "coasts" for "lands" generally. He did change the preposition, for he could have better said* ex oris *"from the coasts."*[47]

2 ITALIAM ["<TO> ITALY"] The art [of grammar] requires that we add prepositions to the names of provinces, but never to those of cities. Yet we often read the reverse. For, look, here he left out the preposition with a province *Italiam venit instead of* ad Italiam venit *"he came to Italy."* Tully in the Verrine orations: "on that day Verres came *ad Messanam"* instead of *Messanam* "to Messana."[48] Know that it belongs to the usage of the *auctores* ["great authors"]to either add or omit prepositions. For Virgil says *silvis* "Did you think,

[41] Juvenal, *Satires* 10.266.

[42] Cf. Diomedes, *Ars grammatica, GL* 1:428.10; Priscian, *Partitiones XII versuum, GL* 3:467.16 (= Passalacqua, ed., *Prisciani opuscula*, 58.4ff.). On the letter i, cf. sections on Donatus and Isidore, pp. 88, 238, 240.

[43] Lucan, *Pharsalia* 1.215.

[44] Gallia "on this side of the Alps" was a Roman province. Note that in this instance Virgil is supposed to have taken the perspective of his characters; elsewhere critics spot an anachronism (called "an anticipation" because it is not held against the poet), cf. on line 1.2 *Lavinaque venit litora*. Servius himself notes one on 6.900.

[45] Virgil, *Georgics* 1.12.

[46] *Aeneid* 6.810. Reference is to king Numa Pompilius, from the little Sabine town of Cures.

[47] This remark is meant as a "don't try this at home" piece of advice for the students.

[48] The quotation is not found in this form. Cf. Cicero, *Verrines* act. sec. 5.5 *ne . . . fugitivi ad Messanam transire possent.*

Tyrrhenian, that you were hunting the wild animals in the woods [*silvis*]?," instead of *in silvis*.[49] So just like he omitted the preposition there with the word indicating a place, so he omitted it here with the province. This is a figure of speech. Italy is a part of Europe. For Italus, the king of Sicily, left Sicily and came to the place beside the river Tiber, and Italy was called after him. That the Sicilians lived where Laurolavinium is, is clear, as he says himself somewhere else:[50] "The Sicilians and the old Sicanians and the Sicanian people came often." *The i of* Italiam *is taken long against its natural value. By nature it is short.*[51] FATO PROFUGUS ["FLEEING/BANISHED BY FATE"] "by fate" refers to both aspects, both to the fact that he fled, and that he came to Italy. He did well to add "by fate," lest he seemed either to have deserted his fatherland because of a crime or out of greed for a new empire. "Banished" is used properly for someone who strays far from his home, as if "chased far away."[52] However, many define it thus, that they call "fleeing" those who are still wandering around after having been excluded by necessity from their homes, and as soon as they have found a place to stay, they are no longer called "fleeing," but "exiles." But both are false. For (1) somebody who has already acquired a place to stay may be called "fleeing," as in Lucan, "the Celts, fleeing from their old Gallic tribe, mixing their name with the Spanish,"[53] and (2) someone who is still wandering about may be called "exile," as in Sallust, "who were wandering in uncertain exile": here "exile" is the wandering itself. *Some people wish to take* profugus *as a participle here. And he certainly did not call Aeneas "fleeing by fate" idly, but on the basis of the Etruscans' learning. For in the book called "Etruscan law literature" it is written under the words of Taga, "that he who derives his lineage from perjurers, must be exiled by fate [*fato*] and fleeing [*profugus*]. Aeneas derives his lineage from the perjurer Laomedon, for elsewhere he says "a long time ago we have paid with our blood for the perjuries of Laomedon's Troy").*[54] LAVINAQUE VENIT LITORA ["AND CAME TO THE LAVINAN COASTS"] This city had three names. First, it is called Lavinum after Lavinus, the brother of Latinus; second, it is called Laurentum, after the laurel tree found by Latinus, when he had acquired the power after the death of his brother and was increasing the city. Finally, it is called Lavinium after Lavinia, Aeneas' wife. So we should read *Lavina*, not *Lavinia*, because it took the name Lavinium after the arrival of Aeneas, and he should have said either *Lavinum* (as he in fact did), or *Laurentum*. Some people though wish to have an anticipation, but this is unnecessary. *It is very good of him to have added Lavina, so that he could show what part of Italy Aeneas had come to. For*

---

[49] *Aeneid* 11.686.   [50] *Aeneid* 7.795 only has *Rutuli veteresque Sicani*.
[51] This passage is used as a standard example for this phenomenon in the *Artes*, cf. e.g. section on Donatus, p. 94.
[52] *Porro fugatus*, etymological explanation of *profugus*.   [53] Lucan, 4.9.   [54] *Georgics* 1.501.

many others had also come to Italy at this time, like Capys, who founded Capua, and Polites, who founded Politorium.

3 LITORA ["COASTS"] It is certain that Laurolavinium is eight miles removed from the sea. And we should not be misled by the fact that he says "Lavinian coasts": for land in the vicinity of the sea may also be called "coast," like Virgil himself does in the fourth book "to whom [we gave] the coast for plowing,"[55] seeing that by nature [true] coastland cannot be plowed. So we need to know that land too can be called "coast." *Fabius Maximus [i.e. Fabius Pictor] writes in the first book of the Annals "Aeneas took it hard that he had arrived on that soil, barren as could be and right next to the shore [litorosissimus]."* MULTUM ILLE ["MUCH HE"] *mult-ille* is a case of collision.[56] *Ille* is redundant here. The word has been inserted because of metrical necessity, *so that the verse will scan.* For if one removes *ille*, the meaning is complete—we can refer *qui primus* "who as the first" to everything.[57] Similarly he says somewhere else: "now doubling the blow with his right, now [*ille* "he"] with his left."[58] This is an archaism. *Or he has used* ille *because that particle was used according to ancient custom to bestow nobility or magnitude, e.g. "and just like he . . . gray,"[59] and "he, wounded."[60]* ET TERRIS IACTATUS ["AND TOSSED ABOUT BY LAND"] for he is wearied in Thracia by that monster, which the blood sent up from the tomb of Polydorus, in Crete by pestilence, at the Strophadic Isles[61] by the Harpies, and by storm in the first and third books. At sea we are tossed about by the streams, on land we are wearied.[62] And he combined the miseries of the two elements well in one expression. ET ALTO ["AND AT SEA"] now at sea, *because he escaped from Scylla and Polyphemus by sailing, Orontes was lost, Palinurus and Misenus went missing.* Notice that *altum* can indicate both height [higher *altitudo*], as in "Maia sends her child down from on high,"[63] and depth [lower *altitudo*]. For *altitudo* is a name for a measure.[64]

4 VI SUPERUM ["BY THE FORCE OF THOSE ABOVE"] By the violence of the gods,[65] according to Homer, who says that the gods have been asked by Juno to hate the Trojans. Virgil, too,

<hr />

[55] *Aeneid* 4.212.

[56] I.e. after the final *m* of *multum* has been elided, the final vowel of *multum* collides with the first one of *ille*.

[57] I.e. *qui primus* from line 1 could be connected to *iactatus* (line 3) directly, without there being any grammatical necessity for *ille*.

[58] *Aeneid* 5.457. The same man is referred to, hitting with both right and left hand.

[59] *Aeneid* 10.707.   [60] *Aeneid* 12.5.

[61] Two islands off the coast of Messenia, residence of the harpies: *Aeneid* 3. 210.

[62] This is a note about proper usage and *differentiae* (semantic distinctions): *iactari*: "to be tossed about," properly said of occurrences at sea, *fatigari*: "to be wearied," properly said of events on land. Virgil combines the two here.

[63] *Aeneid* 1.297.

[64] *altus* [from *alo, alĕre*] is "grown," hence "great," and then as a polar word both "high" and "deep." So it is true that *altitudo* in a way denotes size or distance.

[65] This is the paraphrase: *vi = violentia; superum = deorum.*

touches on this, saying "it is right now that you, too, spare the people of Pergamon, all ye gods and goddesses."⁶⁶ In secret he defends the Trojans by this argument, that the divine powers were not persecuting them by their own fault, but at the instigation of Juno. *Many say that* vi superum *can be accepted to mean Iris, Aeolus, Iuturna, Juno. But the better judgment is "'the power', namely that those above have."* SAEVAE ["SAVAGE"] Since Juno gets her name from *iuvare* "to help," many wonder why he calls her "savage," and they think the epithet is only momentary, as it were "savage where the Trojans are concerned," but they do not know that the ancients meant "great" by *saeva*. E.g. Ennius, "she was dressed in a great [*saeva*] stola." Similarly Virgil says, although he always presents Aeneas as pious, "Aeneas, *saevus* in the weapons of his mother," that is "great." MEMOREM IUNONIS OB IRAM ["BECAUSE OF THE UNFORGETTING WRATH OF JUNO"] It is well-known that many expressions are found in the *auctores* that convey their meaning through the opposite [*per contrarium*]. Passive forms instead of active ones, e.g. "the Amazons wage war with painted armour";⁶⁷ active instead of passive, e.g. "and plunders a huge heap of spelt."⁶⁸ This variety, or rather, contrariety is found also in the other parts of speech, e.g. adverb instead of adverb, like "the fire-master then descended here [*hoc*] from high heaven,"⁶⁹ where *hoc* is used instead of *huc* ["(to) here"]; and in the participle, e.g. "and [the ship] in which Abas [was] transported [*vectus*]"⁷⁰ instead of *qua vehebatur* ["in which he was transported"]; and in the noun, as in "because of the unforgetting wrath of Juno," not "the wrath which remembered," but "which remained in memory." Of these cases, we just cite the ones we have read, but we do not form different ones based on those examples.⁷¹*Memor is not just used by the ancients to denote "ho memnêmenos"* [Greek: "he who has remembered"], *but also "ho mnêmôn"* [Greek: "he who has a good memory."] *This is because of the confusion between verb and noun. For* memorem *has the meaning of a verb, when it is not a noun.*⁷²

5 MULTA QUOQUE ET BELLO PASSUS ["AFTER HAVING SUFFERED MANY THINGS ALSO IN WAR"] *This refers to the last six books.* Nobody naturally connects two separate conjunctions.⁷³ But this happens often in the poets because of the meter. So one of them is redundant here, just as elsewhere *dixit**que** et proelia voce diremit* "so he spoke and interrupted the fighting with his voice."⁷⁴ *Sallust:* tyrannum**que** et Cinnam "*the tyrant*

---

⁶⁶ *Aeneid* 6.63.   ⁶⁷ *Aeneid* 11.660: *bellantur*, passive, whereas *bellant*, active, would have been "normal."

⁶⁸ Virgil, *Georgics* 1.185: *populat* act., where the deponent *populatur* is more common.

⁶⁹ *Aeneid* 8.423.   ⁷⁰ *Aeneid* 1.121.

⁷¹ Note the implied warning to young students again: this is an area of poetic license, which must not be imitated.

⁷² Possibly a reference to the fact that *memorem* can both be the accusative of *memor* or the first person singular subjunctive of *memorare*.

⁷³ Namely *quoque et*.   ⁷⁴ *Aeneid* 5.467.

and Cinna." BELLO PASSUS ["HAVING SUFFERED IN WAR"] against Turnus. DUM CONDERET URBEM ["UNTIL HE FOUNDED A CITY"] this means three things. Either he means Troy, which Aeneas created as soon as he came to Italy, and about which he says "like a camp he surrounded it with pinnacles and a wall,"[75] and elsewhere (Mercury speaking) "Troy cannot contain you."[76] That it was called Troy as soon as Aeneas had founded it is maintained by Livy in his first book,[77] and by Cato in his *Origins*—for while [*dum*] this happened,[78] a war was started by the country-people because the royal stag had been wounded. Or he means Laurolavinium, and *dum* means *donec* ["until"]; for he battled for as long as it took to come to the time to found a city, i.e. until [*donec*] Turnus died. Or he means Rome, and the meaning is *dummodo* "in order to found a city."

6 INFERRETQUE DEOS LATIO ["AND HE BROUGHT HIS GODS INTO LATIUM"] Latium is two things, the first stretching from the Tiber to Fundi, the other from there until Vulturnum. He did say himself "the old Latini,"[79] because he knows there are also "new ones," namely between Fundi and Vulturnum. It is called "Latium," because Saturnus "hid" [*latuerit*] there. *Saufeius*[80] *says it is called Latium because the inhabitants hid [*latuerant*] there, who are called Cascei*[81] *because they used to hide in mountain caves or hidden places to protect themselves against wild animals, or stronger people, or the weather. Later people called them Aboriginals, because they knew they were born somewhere else.*[82] *They also called them Latins.* INFERRETQUE DEOS LATIO ["AND HE BROUGHT HIS GODS INTO LATIUM"] [*Latio*] i.e. *in Latium* ["into Latium"]. This is a frequent figure of speech in Virgil. For what we express through the accusative with a preposition, he states in the dative without a preposition, like elsewhere *it clamor caelo* ["the shouting goes up to heaven"][83] for *in caelum* ["to heaven"]. Are the "gods" the penates, as in "astonished by such sights and the voice of the gods",[84] or are they himself, Ascanius and his off-spring, about whom it is said "son of the gods, who will produce gods."[85] GENUS UNDE LATINUM ["FROM WHERE THE LATIN RACE"]. If the Latini already existed and the place was already called Latium, it is a contradiction that he says that the Latins derived their origin from Aeneas. The first solution is clever: you don't refer *unde* "from where" to a person, but to the place. For *unde* is an adverb indicating "place whence," not derivation from a person. Yet, in the *Origins* Cato says (and Sallust follows his authority in *The Catiline War*),[86] "that Italy was first held by certain people who were called Aboriginals. When these had later been connected to Phrygians

---

[75] *Aeneid* 7.159.   [76] *Aeneid* 9.644.   [77] Livy, *Ab urbe condita* 1.1.5.

[78] Servius claims that *dum* should be translated "while" in this interpretation. See the next one.

[79] Not in fact attested in Virgil.   [80] Not otherwise known.

[81] Only attested here. *Cascei* is here related etymologically with *cavus* "cave" or *cavere* "to watch out for."

[82] Textual transmission corrupt.   [83] *Aeneid* 5.451.   [84] *Aeneid* 3.172.   [85] *Aeneid* 9.639.

[86] Sallust, *Bellum Catilinae* 6.1f.

through the arrival of Aeneas, they were called by one name: 'Latins.'" So the Latins are not just descended from the Trojans, but also from the Aboriginals. The true explanation then is the following. We know that the defeated take over the name of the victors. Through the victory of Aeneas, the Latin name could therefore have perished. But since he wanted to curry favor in Latium, not only did he not take away the Latin name from them, but he even imposed it on the Trojans. It is well deserved, therefore, that he ascribed the power to him to make it perish. That is why in the twelfth book he presents Juno's request not to have the Latin name perish. And similarly in Dido's curse we read "nor when he will have given himself over under the conditions of an unfair peace":[87] an unfair peace is one in which the winner loses his name. *But the older authors apply* unde *also to a person, as they do to any gender and number. In this case he has connected* genus unde Latinum *to the masculine gender and the singular number, elsewhere he refers it to the feminine gender and the plural number, e.g. "nymphs, Laurentian nymphs, from whom [*unde*] the rivers derive their race."[88] Similarly, Terence in the old style transferred the particle* hinc *["from here"], although it is an adverb of place, to a person: "but look there I see Syrus come: from him [*hinc*] I will find out what is the matter."[89]*

7 ALBANIQUE PATRES ["AND THE ALBANIAN FATHERS"] It is well-known that Alba was founded by Ascanius, but it is uncertain which Ascanius: the son of Creusa or that of Lavinia. Even Livy hesitates about the matter. After Tullus Hostilius had destroyed the city, he transferred all noble families to Rome. Take good note that Virgil *always* preserves this order: Latium was first, then Alba, then Rome. He does that here as well and also in the fifth book, namely "he taught the ancient Latins to celebrate" and then "the Albans taught their own, now great great Rome has taken it over and has preserved the rites of its fathers."[90] Similarly in the seventh book "it was customary in Hesperian Latium, a custom then held sacred by the cities Alba, and now held in honor by the ruler of all, Rome."[91] ATQUE ALTAE MOENIA ROMAE ["AND THE WALLS OF HIGH ROME"] either because of its glory, or because of the giant buildings, or because it is built on mountains.

8 MUSA MIHI CAUSAS MEMORA ["MUSE, TELL ME THE REASONS"] mihī *is long here, elsewhere it is short, e.g.* mihĭque haec edissere vera roganti *["and on my asking they gave the following true reply"].[92]* Poets divide their song in three parts: they propose, they invoke, they narrate.[93] Mostly, however, they do two out of the three and mix the proposition proper with the invocation, as Homer did in both his works. For this is better. Lucan, however, inverts the order: he proposed first, then narrated, and invoked afterwards, as in: "nor if I the singer accept you in my heart."[94] It should be observed that a divinity is not invoked in every song,

---

[87] *Aeneid* 4.618.   [88] *Aeneid* 8.71.   [89] Terence, *Adelphoe* 361, with minor textual variations.
[90] *Aeneid* 5.598ff.   [91] *Aeneid* 7.601–3.   [92] *Aeneid* 2.149.   [93] Cf. supra on verse 1.1.
[94] Lucan, 1.63.

unless we ask for something that is beyond human capacity. That is why in the *Ars poetica*, Horace says "let no god intervene, unless we come to a knotty juncture worthy of a deliverer."[95] Thus, Virgil's invocation is good, for he could not have known by himself the wrath of a divinity. Similarly in the ninth book, if he did not add "Juno gave strength and courage,"[96] who could have believed that Turnus had escaped from the camp? MUSA ["MUSE"] *he did not add which one, just as in "Goddess, sing of the wrath."*[97] *"Muse, tell me of the causes" is instead of "help me tell."*[98] *Many people say there are nine Muses,*[99] *many that there are seven. Numa had built a little bronze temple for them, which was later hit by lightning and placed in the temple of Honos and Virtus [Honor and Virtue], and then was moved by Fulvius Nobilior to the temple of Heracles, hence the name: temple of Heracles and the Muses. Some people maintain they are virgins. They say that that is the reason why a female pig is offered to them, because they are so fertile. Some on the other hand give them off-spring, Orpheus, Linus, the Sirens. Some people say they are eight, the way they are seen in Athens,*[100] *others four,*[101] *some Boeotian ones, some Attic ones, and some Sicilian ones. The Sicilian Epicharmus does not call these muses "muses," but homonoousas "the unanimous ones."* QUO NUMINE LAESO "BY OFFEND- ING WHAT DIVINITY" *quo* equals *in quo* ["in what respect (having offended a divinity)"], *in qua causa* ["in what cause" (having offended a divinity)].[102] It is in the seventh case,[103] and a common expression. For we say "how [*quo*] have I offended you?"[104] There is also a different explanation. For Juno has many divine powers: she is Juno Curitis, who uses a chariot [*currus*] and a spear, as in "this was her armour, this her chariot";[105] she is Lucina, who is in charge of child-birth, e.g. "Juno Lucina, help!"[106] She is the queen, e.g. "I who walk majestically as the queen of the gods."[107] She also has other divine powers. The poet therefore rightfully doubts which of her divine powers Aeneas has offended.[108] Others, however, say it should be separated, so that there is no doubt about the hatred of Juno, but

---

[95] *Ars poetica* 191.   [96] *Aeneid* 9.761.

[97] Textual corruption here. The translation follows a suggestion proposed in Thilo-Hagen's apparatus criticus. See *Iliad* 1.1.

[98] Text emended to "adesto ut memorem."

[99] On the number of Muses, see Arnobius, *Adversus nationes* 3.37.

[100] Servius is referring to a group of eight statues on display in Athens. It is entirely possible that the Romans brought one statue out of an original group of nine to Rome for copying, but Servius believes the group was meant to represent eight Muses only. See H. Kees, art. s.v. Musai in Pauly-Wissowa's *Real-Encyclopedie*, col. 738.

[101] This is said about Aratus. Cf. also Cicero, *De natura deorum* 3.54.

[102] In both these interpretations *quo* does not modify *numine*.

[103] The seventh case is the ablative used without the preposition *ab*, so, for example, the ablative with a verb that takes that case, cf. Donatus *Ars maior* 2.9, *GL* 4:377.20–3.

[104] The expression *communis elocutio* is taken up by a first person plural, indicating that this is general and correct usage (*usus*). Cf. Uhl, *Servius als Sprachlehrer*, 330, 332.

[105] *Aeneid* 1.16.   [106] Terence, *Andria* 473.   [107] *Aeneid* 1.46.

[108] I.e. in this reading *quo* is directly connected with *numine*.

the question is what other divine power has been offended.[109] QUO NUMINE LAESO ["BY OFFENDING WHAT DIVINITY"] therefore becomes ambiguous and the poet asks in what respect has Aeneas offended the divine power of Juno, because there were no definite grounds for hatred against him personally, but against his people for the reasons which will be discussed in a little while. *Some people take* numen *"divinity" as "will." By using the very word* laeso *"offended," the poet shows that even if there was guilt, it was minimal. For he did not say* violato *"violated" or* iniuriam passo *"having suffered injustice."*

9 QUIDVE DOLENS ["OR BY WHAT PAIN"] *Philosophically a good doubt. For according to some nothing matters to the gods.* VOLVERE CASUS ["TO ROLL ON ACCIDENTS"] i.e. to be involved in accidents. The figure of speech is "hypallage"; this occurs whenever words are understood in a contrary sense. Thus he says elsewhere "to give the southern winds to the fleet,"[110] when in fact we give the ships over to the winds, not the winds to the ships. Similarly "he forced my undecided mind,"[111] i.e. by forcing he made my mind undecided.

10 INSIGNEM PIETATE VIRUM ["THE MAN WHO STOOD OUT BY HIS PIETAS"] Because he saved his father and the penates from Troy. And here he shows that it was right for him to have invoked the muse. For if Aeneas is just, why does he suffer from the hatred of the gods?

11 TANTAENE ANIMIS CAELESTIBUS IRAE ["DO THE HEAVENLY MINDS HEDGE SUCH GREAT ANGERS?"] The question here is not about the quality of the anger, but about its quantity: For anger that takes no account of *pietas* is too great. This he says in accordance with the Stoics, for the Epicureans claim that the gods do not care about human things at all. *tantaene* ["such great!?"] is as it were the exclamation of someone who is wondering, *when we draw a conclusion from the narrative itself and interject our own persona, e.g. "did they want to clash together with such vehemence?"*[112] Some people read *tantaene* as a question rather than an exclamation. ANIMIS CAELESTIBUS ["HEAVENLY MINDS"] the gods above, for it is certain that the gods below do have anger—that is where the Furies are. animis *is "tois thumois"* (Greek: "in their minds").

[There are two major prophetic passages in the *Aeneid* which are important in interpreting Virgil's relation to Augustus. The first is the prophecy by Jupiter himself in book one, while comforting Venus. The following selection is the commentary on lines 1.286–8: *nascetur pulchra Troianus origine Caesar, / imperium Oceano, famam qui terminet astris / Iulius, a magno demissum nomen Iulo* ... 294 *claudentur Belli portae.*]

---

[109] I.e. *quo* is again directly connected with *numine*, but the word group is not taken to refer to Juno.
[110] *Aeneid* 3.61.   [111] *Aeneid* 4.22f.   [112] *Aeneid* 12.503.

286 NASCETUR ["THERE WILL BE BORN"] this corresponds to the verse "Surely from them the Romans would one day..."[113] All of the poet's intention, as we said when discussing the quality of the song,[114] is directed at the praise of Augustus, just as in the catalogue of the sixth book and in the description of the shield. This speech of Jupiter partly cleanses away objections, partly consists of promises. PULCHRA ["BEAUTIFUL"] an allusion because of Venus. TROIANUS ["TROJAN"] as if he said, Caesar is also a Trojan. CAESAR this is the man called Gaius Iulius Caesar. Gaius is his first name, Iulius comes from Iulus, and he is called Caesar either because he was born through his mother's belly being cut open [*caeso*],[115] or because his grandfather killed an elephant in Africa with his own hands—and elephant is called *caesa* in Punic.[116] *This Gaius Iulius Caesar vanquished sixty-four Gallic communities and then asked the senate for a consulate and a triumphal procession. When he got neither he waged civil war in Pharsalia against Cn. Pompey the Great and his friends, who envied Caesar his successes. Pompey was defeated there and was killed in Alexandria. Caesar returned to Rome after things had been put in order and Alexandria had been taken, and was killed in the Pompeian curia by Cassius, Brutus, and other followers of Pompey. When his heir Augustus had entered the city, he forced the senate to the judgment that the killers of Caesar were parricides and state enemies, and that Caesar himself was adopted among the gods and got the name divus "divine."*
287 IMPERIUM OCEANO, FAMAM QUI TERMINET ASTRIS ["WHO BOUNDS HIS EMPIRE BY THE OCEAN, HIS FAME BY THE STARS"] This is either said in praise, or certainly in accordance with factual data [*historia*]. For, indeed, he vanquished the Britanni, who live in the ocean, and after his death, when his funeral games were organized by Augustus his adoptive son, a star was seen in the middle of the day, which explains the verse "see the star of Dione's offspring Caesar has moved forward."[117] 288 A MAGNO ["FROM THE GREAT"] like Alexander, like Pompey. *The Greeks call everything magnificent "great," e.g. "the great mother," "the great gods."*

COMMENTARY ON THE SIXTH BOOK OF VIRGIL'S *AENEID* BY THE GRAMMARIAN SERVIUS[118]

All of Virgil is full of wisdom, but this book most of all. The greater part of it derives from Homer. Some things said in it are simple, many come from knowledge of factual

---

[113] *Aeneid* 1.234 (the request by Venus to which Jupiter is here responding).

[114] See the *accessus* about the *intentio poetae*.   [115] Hence "caesarian."

[116] See Uhl, *Servius als Sprachlehrer*, 497 on the different etymologies of Caesar's *cognomen*.

[117] Virgil, *Eclogues* 9.47.

[118] Vol. 2:1. Text also in Ziolkowski and Putnam, *The Virgilian Tradition*, 464–5. For translations of other passages from book 6, see Ziolkowski and Putnam, 545–7.

occurrences [*historia*],[119] many have come down through the high wisdom of philosophers, theologians, and Egyptians, to the point where most people have written complete treatises on these individual aspects of this book. Note that although Probus and others left the first two verses at the end of book five, they have been transferred to the beginning of book six for a good reason. For this way, the connection of the poem is better, and Homer too began this way "so he said while shedding a tear."[120]

[The following selection is taken from Servius' comments on Anchises' great prophecy in book six, in particular on lines 789ff., where Caesar and Augustus are mentioned: *hic Caesar et omnis Iuli / progenies, magnum caeli ventura sub axem. / hic vir, hic est, tibi quem promitti saepius audis, / Augustus Caesar, divi genus, aurea condet / saecula*. See the introduction to this section.]

789 HIC CAESAR ET OMNIS IULI PROGENIES ["HERE IS CAESAR AND THE WHOLE PROGENY OF IULUS"] Compare [1.288] "Julius, the name derived from the great Julus."

790 MAGNUM CAELI VENTURA SUB AXEM ["THAT WILL COME UNDER THE AXIS OF HEAVEN"] For when Augustus organized funeral games for his father Caesar, there appeared a star during daytime. Augustus persuaded the people to believe that it belonged to Caesar. Hence "look the star of Dionaean[121] Caesar has moved."[122] "Under the axis," therefore, i.e, "to divine honors." 791 HIC VIR HIC EST "THIS IS THE MAN, THIS IS HE" The letter *c* is only used for a double consonant in monosyllabic words, e.g. [2.664] *hoc erat alma parens*,[123] because of their privilege, of course.[124] Therefore, what Terentianus says is false,[125] that it is considered double or single in relation to the meter. For if this were true, it should also have been taken for two consonants in disyllabic words—but we have never encountered that. For it is proper that a letter retains its natural characteristics also in polysyllabic words. 792 DIVI GENUS ["SON OF THE DIVINE"] Of Caesar, who was made a god. He calls him *genus* "son" not just by right of adoption, but also of blood-relationship: for he was the son of Atia, who was a sister of Caesar. This Augustus Caesar took his name

---

[119] Cf. Dietz, "*Historia* in the Commentary of Servius."

[120] The beginning of book 6 is: *sic fatur lacrimans* "so he spoke crying." The Homeric phrase in the form quoted by Servius occurs e.g. *Iliad* 1.357. But the beginning of *Odyssey* 11, which has the Homeric equivalent to the *katabasis* scene of *Aeneid* 6, also features tears (*Odyssey* 11.5, *kata dakru kheontes*). After this introductory section, the lemmatic commentary on book 6 follows.

[121] "Of Dione," i..e. Venus (Caesar's divine forebear).   [122] Virgil, *Eclogues* 9.47.

[123] Where *hoc* forms a long syllable in spite of the fact that it has a short *o*.

[124] Monosyllabic words were the headache of the ancient grammarians—they "regularly" behaved "irregularly" and rejected analogy. So the normal rules do not hold for them: they are "privileged." Cf. at *Aeneid* 3.91 . . . *quia omnia monosyllaba ad artem non pertinent et his licenter uti possumus*.

[125] Terentianus Maurus (see pp. 72–81), *De litteris, syllabis, metris* 1657f.

from his adoptive father. For before he was called Octavianus after his father Octavius, Atia's husband.

> [When Aeneas leaves the underworld, he passes through the gate of false dreams: 6.893ff. "There are two gates of Sleep [*geminae somni portae*]: the one is said/ to be of horn [*cornea*], through it an easy exit/ is given to true Shades [*veris umbris*]; the other is made/ of polished ivory [*elephanto*], perfect, glittering,/ but through that way the Spirits send false dreams/ into the world above. And here Anchises,/ when he is done with words, accompanies/ the Sibyl and his son together; and/ he sends them through the gates of ivory."[126] Modern scholarship worries over Aeneas' connection with the gate of false dreams here. What does it mean for the status of the prophecy he received? Is there a subversive message hidden in the *Aeneid* which is not so favorable to Augustus after all? This is what Servius has to say:]

893 SUNT GEMINAE SOMNI PORTAE ["THERE ARE TWO GATES OF SLEEP"] Instead of "of dreams" [*somniorum*] In this passage he follows Homer, with this difference that Homer says that dreams leave through both gates, Virgil says that true *shades* leave *through the gate of horn*—by these *shades* he means true dreams. And in poetic terms the meaning is clear: he wishes it to be understood that everything he has said is false. Physiologically things are as follows: by the gate of horn the eyes are meant, which have a horn-like color and are tougher than the other body parts: for they don't feel the cold, as Cicero also says in his books on the nature of the gods.[127] By the gate of ivory the mouth is indicated, because of the teeth. And we know that what we say may be false, but what we see is true without any doubt. That is why Aeneas is let out by the gate of ivory. There is also another meaning: we know that "sleep" is depicted with a horn. And writers about dreams say that dreams which fit the fortune and possibilities of the person will come true. And these are close to a horn.[128] That's why the poet creates the true gate as made from horn. But dreams of what is beyond one's fortunes and has too much decoration and empty display are false, as they say: hence the ivory gate, as the more ornate one, is thought of by the poet as the false one.

896 INSOMNIA ["DREAMS"] i.e. *somnia* ["dreams"]

899 SECAT ["CUTS"] *tenet* ["holds"]: this is also why we use the name "sects": they "hold" on to their beliefs.

900 TO THE HARBOR OF CAIETA A prolepsis [anticipation] spoken from [the point of view of] the person of the poet: for the name Caieta did not exist yet.

---

[126] Translation from A. Mandelbaum, *The Aeneid of Virgil* (New York: Bantam, 1961).

[127] Cicero, *De natura deorum* 2.57, which is about ears, however.

[128] Either because this is considered an honest, unadorned, and see-through (hence "realistic"?) material (see below on ivory), or possibly because someone's personal courage and capacities are as it were his "horn," cf. Lewis & Short, *A Latin Dictionary*, s.v. *cornu* II.

TIBERIUS CLAUDIUS DONATUS, *INTERPRETATIONES VERGILIANAE*, CA. 400

INTRODUCTION

Tiberius Claudius Donatus, not to be confused with the more famous grammarian Aelius Donatus, was an amateur interpreter of Virgil, probably ca. 400.[1] His *Interpretationes Vergilianae* (Interpretations of Virgil), a 1,200-page paraphrase dedicated to his son,[2] is remarkable for its unified scope. It is Tib. Claudius Donatus' thesis that the whole poem has one purpose, the praise of Aeneas, and through him of Augustus. From this perspective, the poem belongs to the *genus laudativum* and hence Tib. Claudius Donatus defends the claim that the interpretation of Virgil belongs to the domain of the rhetorician rather than the grammarian. In this way the *Aeneid* becomes part of a much larger and longer tradition of competition between the language disciplines, with participants registering anxieties about the boundaries and legitimate domain of each. This instance of such competition is of particular interest for the history of literary theory, in that what is at stake is who gets to speak authoritatively about the *literary* domain.

Literature was traditionally the domain of the grammarian, but Tib. Claudius Donatus believes that the question of what discipline may claim interpretive competence should be determined by the authorial intentions of the poet. Since he holds that Virgil's inspiration was rhetorical, Tib. Claudius Donatus recognizes the expertise only of the exegete trained in rhetoric. The interpretive strategy that he adopts, however, is remarkably reductive in that it excludes all historical and political interests,[3] and creates a monochromatic Aeneas and *Aeneid*.[4] The rhetorical principle is the starting point for

---

[1] Cf. Kaster, *Guardians of Language*, 400 (no. 209).

[2] For other ancient educational works dedicated to sons, see e.g. Cato, Cicero's *De finibus*, Aulus Gellius, Charisius, Terentianus Maurus, Nonius Marcellus, Martianus Capella, Macrobius; see Squillante Saccone, *Le Interpretationes Vergilianae di Tiberio Claudio Donato*, 18 note 38.

[3] Cf. Starr, "An Epic of Praise," 159, 166.

[4] Cf. ibid., 171; Squillante Saccone, *Le Interpretationes Vergilianae*, 105–6.

interpretation (the poet is a product of rhetorical training) and at the same time the criterion for correctness of interpretation (the exegete explains the work as the consummate realization of rhetorical purpose and doctrine; if the interpretation fails to reveal the underlying rhetorical principles, it must be wrong). A comparison with Augustine's rhetorical hermeneutics may be instructive here. Augustine also enlists a rhetorical program in his reading of Scripture: Augustine does this by redefining the fundamental principle of rhetoric, the device of invention, as a hermeneutical tool. To invent is to "find," and Augustine conceives rhetorical invention as a tool for "discovering" multiple layers of meaning in Scripture. Augustine's hermeneutical starting point is the *regula dilectionis* (the rule of love) and this is also the object of interpretation: in this respect there is a singular mission in Augustine's reading, and the correctness of interpretation is measured by how well it conforms to that principle. But the net effect of Augustine's rhetorical "method of discovery" is to open rather than restrict interpretive possibilities: it enables the finding of multiple interpretations of Scripture, as long as they can be compatible with the command to love God and one's neighbor.[5] Perhaps somewhat closer (in effect, if not necessarily in spirit) to the rhetorical reading of Tib. Claudius Donatus are the rhetorical readings that Cassiodorus brings to the Psalms. For Cassiodorus, the Psalms are exemplifications of the genres of rhetoric, and the meanings that he finds the Psalms yielding up are closely correlated with his rhetorical classification of their forms.

Despite his proclaimed rhetorical approach, however, Tib. Claudius Donatus cannot help applying some of the principles of grammar, which must have constituted his own basic formation.[6] Thus his work gives us a glimpse of the grammatical competence of an educated layman.[7]

Translated from Tiberius Claudius Donatus, *Interpretationes Vergilianae*, ed. Georges, by permission.[8]

[5] Augustine, *De doctrina christiana* 1.22.21 § 42; 1.35.39 § 84ff. *Caritas* is the *finis praecepti*: *De doctrina christiana* 1.36. 41 § 88; 1.40. 44 § 95.

[6] Note that he cites only school authors, e.g. Terence, Cicero, Sallust; cf. Starr, "Explaining Dido to your Son," 27.

[7] Cf. Gioseffi, "Ut sit integra locutio: esegesi e grammatica in Tiberio Claudio Donato," 143.

[8] A missing part from ms V was discovered and edited by Peter K. Marshall, "Tiberius Claudius Donatus on Virgil *Aeneid* 6.1–157," *Manuscripta* 37 (1993): 3–20. We have not seen Pirovano, *Le interpretationes vergilianae* or Gnoza, "Finding an Orator in the Poet." See also Ziolkowski and Putnam, eds., *The Virgilian Tradition*, 644–9 with translation of a different selection of excerpts than the one presented here. They also notice Tib. Claudius Donatus' focus on Virgil's speeches (169) and put him in the context of the commentary tradition (623–6, esp. 625).

INTERPRETATIONES VERGILIANAE

To My Son Tib. Claudius Maximus Donatianus

Aeneid Book I

After those who taught me the songs of the poet from Mantua, after those whose works express a virtually unique and pure understanding of the books entitled "the Aeneid," it would have been better to remain silent than to incur the accusation of arrogance by speaking out. However, I noticed that the schoolmasters are not teaching their students anything sensible, and that the authors of commentaries are not driven by the desire to teach, but just to be remembered themselves, and while they have treated some themes felicitously, yet they have left many problems unresolved. Therefore, my dearest son, I have written this for you, not in order for you to read nothing else, but to compare it with other work and thus to come to an understanding of what should be followed in their work, and what in that of your father. For neither have they dealt with everything, as is apparent, nor have I written so much that it could instruct you properly with complete understanding as a result. Therefore, read everything, as I said, and if perhaps our work does not please others, hopefully what I, your father, have passed on to you, my son, with the best of intentions, will please you.[9]

First and foremost notice what kind of subject matter [*materiae genus*][10] our Maro has taken on. For if you do not realize this right from the start, bad mistakes will be the result. It certainly belongs to the genre of praise [*laudativum*], but this is not recognized and remains hidden for the following reason. Through his wonderful technique of praise, while treating the deeds of Aeneas he also embraced (as can be demonstrated) genres that belong to a different subject matter without therefore, however, being alien to the roles of praise. For they have been adopted for this very reason that they should assist in the praise of Aeneas.

At this point, whoever will wish to take the measure of Virgil's talent, his morality, his language, knowledge, character, and experience with the art of rhetoric, must necessarily

---

[9] This encouragement to take an active part in reading and interpretation is also implied in the common practice in ancient commentaries of presenting several possible readings side by side without the commentator expressing a preference; cf. Starr, "The Flexibility of Literary Meaning."

[10] Cf. *De inventione* 1.5.7. Cicero distinguishes three kinds, *genus demonstrativum* (here called *laudativum*), dealing with praise and blame, *genus deliberativum*, and *genus iudiciale*. The term *laudativum* is found in Quintilian, *Institutio oratoria* 3.7.28 (for the epideictic genre).

notice first who it is that he has undertaken to praise in his epic, what a huge job and what a dangerous work he has begun. For he had to show that Aeneas was such as to provide a worthy parent and founder of the family for Caesar, in whose honor the work was written. And since he was going to put it to future generations that he had been the founder of the Roman empire, there was no doubt that he had to demonstrate, as in fact he did, that he was free of all guilt and his praise to be loudly proclaimed.

Let us therefore state what could have been detrimental to the image of Aeneas himself. For the nature of Virgil's epic will not at all be apparent, unless the disadvantages in the character of the hero are enumerated. Well, there can be no doubt that Aeneas left Asia, after having lost his fatherland, which he had been unable to defend, and having lost the riches of a kingdom, with tremendous suffering both there at Troy and when he was thrust forth from his native land. These circumstances would lead anyone to believe that he would not have suffered such things, unless he rightly had all the gods as his enemies: without doubt that is gravely incriminating to him, and if anyone conducts his life in such a way that he falls into disgrace with all the gods, and is unable to find any protector, not even his grandfather Jupiter...[11] Virgil cleanses this away with astonishing art: not only does he bring together formulations that offer excuses in the first verses, as will appear soon, but he has also spread these out over all the books, and, a sign of a truly great orator,[12] he confesses what cannot be denied and having removed the incriminating aspect turns it into praise:[13] thus he made Aeneas stand out in many ways in those very respects which could have led to his criticism.

He composed, not, as others think,[14] the beginning of a poem [*carminis caput*], but, as we assert, its theme,[15] with such subtle artistry that within that theme, i.e. in its brevity, he demonstrated the great breadth of the work that was getting started. In the first proposition [*propositio*][16] he recommends his poem and the character and the deeds which he had undertaken to cleanse and praise. At the same time he gives a partition [*partitur*]: what did he suffer through fate,[17] what beyond fate, demonstrating subtly that things that happen by fate are beyond anybody's powers to overcome, and that therefore no blame attached to

---

[11] The text seems to be lacunose here: supplement something like: "he might easily seem not to be a very worthy founder of the Roman people."

[12] Here Tib. Claudius Donatus stakes his claim that Virgil is an orator, and hence part of the rhetorical, not the grammatical domain.

[13] Reference to *status* theory: the *status qualitatis* does not dispute the fact or the definition, but considers whether the facts are culpable; cf. *Ad Herennium* 1.14.24, *De inventione* 1.11.15. See the introduction to Part 1 (p. 67) and e.g. pp. 225–6 within.

[14] Marked competition with the grammarians again.

[15] *carminis thema*; Tib. Claudius Donatus uses the term *thema* for the rhetorical *propositum* of the case.

[16] *Aeneid* 1.1–7.   [17] *Aeneid* 1.2.

his inability to defeat fate; but that through his patience and virtue he did overcome the difficulties that were imposed on him over and beyond his fate through the enmity of the gods and Juno.[18] Meanwhile he also demonstrates that Aeneas had not done anything in particular to deserve the enmity of Juno first, and then of all the gods. His version is (mentioned in passing in the Theme,[19] worked out more fully in the poem) that Juno had conceived a hatred against Aeneas for nothing, and that the other gods had not been irritated by the perverse misdoings of Aeneas, but had followed their queen with however much or little enthusiasm. He also added this subdivision [*divisio*] there that he promised to speak about the adversity suffered by Aeneas by land as well as at sea.[20] After Virgil had cleansed the character he was protecting through his own speech of defense, the next task of the orator was to disgrace the other party, i.e. the enemy.[21] Her he reproaches with the accusation of cruelty,[22] adds the culpably long cultivation of the hostility, and subjoins at the end of the Theme the enormous jealousy,[23] namely that the happiness of the Roman empire would never have emerged, if Aeneas, its inventor and founder, had been fully crushed by Juno's party.

This is what you need to know, son, in rough outline, and do not think that I have been using superfluous words. For since I realized that you, as a beginner, cannot be instructed by novel and brief instructions, I have had to extend my exposition a bit. Thus, I too have as it were set out first the Theme of the interpretation I will give,[24] thinking it better to actually make you wiser through a certain verbosity than to leave you in error through the fault of dark brevity. For I want you to make progress and I am making over to you by right this little product of my labor, as if it were a hereditary gift of personal "mind-capital" [*peculiaris animi*]. And if perchance you do not know what good can come to you from this delivery of possession, let me tell you in a few words.

If you pay careful attention to the epic of Maro and grasp its meaning correctly, you will discover in the poet a perfect rhetor, and hence you will understand that Virgil should not have been taught by grammarians, but by the best of orators. For he will show you the art of speech at its fullest, as we have posited at several places by way of examples. When you love him who embraces the writings of many different people, your reward will be not to have to wander erratically through a great many of them.[25] And if you agree, you will praise him who could run through everything, who made himself available as a benevolent

---

[18] *Aeneid* 1.4.   [19] *Aeneid* 1.4.   [20] *Aeneid* 1.3.   [21] I.e. the goddess Juno.   [22] *Aeneid* 1.4.
[23] *Aeneid* 1.8–11.   [24] Note how the commentator here claims to follow the example of his author.
[25] I.e. Virgil is a shortcut to a whole library. This view of Virgil as an encyclopedic source of knowledge is parallel to similar views about Homer (in an ironic way in Plato's *Ion*, wholly seriously in the pseudo-Plutarchean *De Vita et Poesi Homeri II*). Cf. Squillante Saccone, *Le Interpretationes Vergilianae*, 19–23; Kaster, *Guardians of Language*, 237–8.

and most experienced teacher to the followers of various professions and different disciplines. In short, the sailor can learn from him how to deal with his duties, fathers and sons, husbands and wives, the emperor and the soldier, the best citizen and the most honored devotee to his fatherland will find something to imitate, namely that in labors and dangers to the state the very best man in high standing with his people should regard as unimportant his own fortunes and well-being. By his teaching those can be instructed who are preparing to celebrate the rites of the gods, and to know the future. Here people who love unhurt friendships find a praise that deserves imitation, here people who have deceived a friend or relative through fickle faith find a reproach to fear. He teaches how people should be when their help is asked in times of necessity, in order to avoid the charges of arrogance or inhumanity. There is no ground for shame if a better man asks a lesser one, when there is a close connection. Finally, since we cannot go through all the tales of Maronian virtue, let it suffice to have said this by way of example. For you will rather easily discover the rest through reading and reconsidering, if you have followed what has been said so far. Certainly, we will discuss in its own place everything that we have now simply pulled together from his work and explain it.

Do not be disturbed by the hostile voices of people who do not know Virgil's poetry or criticize it. For I know that some people falsely claim that Virgil undoes his own statements by also claiming the opposite. Among them are found people who ignore the obvious and wish to assert the opposite themselves in their arguments, and so they show through their claims that they are far removed from true understanding. For if Virgil says that the gods exist, and later mentions that they do not, somewhere else again he claims that they exist but do not care for anything, and at yet another place that they exist and do care what people do, that fate exists and that it does not, that people die at a fixed day and that they sometimes are killed before the pre-set time, that the dead feel something or that there is nothing after death, then he is not led by the job of making claims, but either defends or refutes those things in relation to the time, the character, the place, the cause. Finally, if we return to the proposed theme, we shall discover that Virgil has declared that he would deal with the deeds of Aeneas, not that he would take on the case of some secret science or philosophy as its defender.

In the meantime, this is also something admirable and remarkable that the praise of Aeneas is organized in such a way that in it through exquisite technique the styles of all kinds of subject matter [*materiarum genera*] come together.[26] This is how the reader of Virgil's poetry can be instructed in the lessons of rhetoric and can find there all the duties of life and action. What remains before the beginning of the in-depth discussion is that

---

[26] *De inventione* 1.5.7; see also at note 10 of this section.

you should know that Virgil has arranged his work so that he put what happened later first and vice versa. For the shipwreck which is described in the Sicilian part was not counted among Aeneas' first adventures, to the point where he himself says (1.29): "The Trojans, thrown about over the whole sea, what the Greeks and savage Achilles left over, she kept away far from Latium, and during many years they wandered over all the seas driven by their fate." And in the character of Aeneas (1.198): "friends—we have known suffering before, you who have suffered worse, god will end this also. You have approached the fury of Scylla and the rocks with their awful din, you have been to the Cyclopean rocks." And in the character of Dido (1.755): "For this is the seventh summer to carry you in your wanderings over all the lands and the seas." So he put first what belonged at a later moment, and displaced what had happened before to a different time, in order for them to be told at dinner at Dido's. In this way he avoids the boredom of having to repeat these same things, if he had put them before, when Dido was asking after them. In order to avoid prolixity it was fitting to just tell them once.

MARTIANUS CAPELLA, *DE NUPTIIS PHILOLOGIAE ET MERCURII*, ca. 420–490

INTRODUCTION

No late antique or early medieval compendium of the arts had as comprehensive an influence as *De nuptiis Philologiae et Mercurii* (The Marriage of Philology and Mercury) by the fifth-century author Martianus Capella.[1] It was ideal as a source of complete and reliable information about the seven liberal arts because it presented each of them in detail but also at manageable length. It quickly achieved canonical status: Martianus Capella's text is mentioned by the mythographer Fulgentius (sixth century), Cassiodorus, and Gregory of Tours, and may also have been a source for the *Liber de numeris* attributed to Isidore of Seville. It was certainly known and read in the monastic and palace schools of the early Middle Ages.[2] Its striking descriptions of each of the personified arts informed the visual imagery of those arts in manuscript illuminations, wood and stone carvings, stained glass, and verbal ekphrases throughout the Middle Ages. Martianus' work comes down to us in 241 known manuscripts, the earliest of which date from the ninth century.[3]

De nuptiis Philologiae et Mercurii is not unique as an influential early encyclopedia. But unlike the other encyclopedic compendia that had similarly vast reach, the *Institutiones* of Cassiodorus and the *Etymologiae* of Isidore of Seville, Martianus Capella's work also had a literary-philosophical influence, because of its form, the *prosimetrum*, and its framework, an allegorized mythography and cosmology.[4] Perhaps on this account the work early on acquired a distinctive commentary tradition, and remained attractive to commentators

---

[1] Modern scholarship has traditionally placed the text within the early decades of the fifth century, ca. 410–430; for a recent defense of this, see Cameron, "Martianus and his First Editor," who settles on the 420s or 430s. However, Shanzer makes a strong argument for a date later in the century, the 470s or 480s; see *A Philosophical and Literary Commentary*, 1–28. Grebe, *Martianus Capella 'De nuptiis Philologiae et Mercurii,'* 21, puts the date even later, between 496 and 523. We indicate here a range of dates.

[2] See the excellent overview by Stahl, "To a Better Understanding of Martianus Capella."

[3] Leonardi, "I codici di Marziano Capella." See also the extensive bibliography on the medieval influence of Martianus Capella in Willis' edition of *De nuptiis Philologiae et Mercurii*, xxiii–xxvi and Ramelli, *Tutti i commenti a Marziano Capella: Scoto Eriugena, Remigio di Auxerre, Bernardo Silvestre e Anonimi*.

[4] On the literary character of the text, see Shanzer, *A Philosophical and Literary Commentary*, and Lemoine, *Martianus Capella*.

even after its doctrinal value had been superseded by more modern developments in scientific thought.[5] The Carolingian period saw an explosive interest in the text: over twenty-five of the extant manuscripts are from this period, all of them complete, and nearly all of them glossed. Two important kinds of commentary emerge from the Carolingian context. There are the commentaries dedicated to philosophical and cosmographical questions, represented by the glosses first attributed to Dunchad and later to Martin of Laon, but in fact the collaborative product of a group of scholars from the 820s or 830s, and of which John Scotus Eriugena is the most important representative.[6] On the other hand, there is the systematic pedagogical explanation presented in the commentary by Remigius of Auxerre, a work clearly destined for the schoolroom, where its influence long held sway.[7] Remigius' commentary not only treats the moral and conceptual questions of the arts and their doctrinal content, but attempts to open up the textual elements, that is, the hybrid genre, the difficult style, the allusive language, and the mythographical lore of the work. This suggests that the text could be used to generate a literary command of Latinity as well as to teach the essentials of the arts. Martianus' work also penetrated into the schoolroom through interlingual teaching. At the end of the tenth century, Notker III, of the monastery of St. Gall, made a German translation of the allegorical introduction (the first two books) that combined Martianus' text with the Remigian commentary.[8] In tenth-century Italy as well there was a revival of learned and literary interest in Martianus Capella.[9]

Study of *De nuptiis Philologiae et Mercurii* reached its literary-philosophical apex among the Platonists of the twelfth century. Paradoxically, the value of the text as a model for classification of the sciences or for the content of each art would have begun to wane in this period because of the increasing impact of Aristotelian epistemology, and because of the new reception of Aristotelian logic (the "new logic") and the increasing transmission of Greco-Arab science. In grammatical and rhetorical studies, emphasis shifted notably from the old reliable compendia, such as Martianus' text, to the authoritative (and longer) primary texts: Priscian's *Institutiones* and the Ciceronian *De inventione* and *Rhetorica ad Herennium*. But the interest in Martianus' work shifted too, as scholars now prized it for the acrobatics of its allegory and its cosmological principles, that is, the allegory of the celestial marriage and

---

[5] Cf. Ramelli, *Tutti i commenti a Marziano Capella*.

[6] Dunchad, *Glossae in Martianum*, ed. Lutz; *Johannis Scotti annotationes in Marcianum*, ed. Lutz; see Contreni, "John Scottus, Martin Hiberniensis, the Liberal Arts, and Teaching." For the attribution, see Préaux, "Les manuscrits principaux du *De nuptiis Philologiae et Mercurii* de Martianus Capella"; Teeuwen, *Harmony and the Music of the Spheres: The Ars musica in Ninth-Century Commentaries on Martianus Capella*, 145–50; Teeuwen, "The Study of Martianus Capella's *De nuptiis* in the Ninth Century"; M. Teeuwen, review of Ramelli, *Tutti i commenti*, Bryn Mawr Classical Review 2007.09.39, correcting Ramelli on the status of these glosses.

[7] *Commentum in Martianum Capellam*, ed. Lutz.

[8] Book-length studies are Glauch, *Die Martianus-Capella Bearbeitung Notkers des Deutschen*, and Backes, *Die Hochzeit Merkurs und der Philologie*. See also Copeland, *Rhetoric, Hermeneutics, and Translation*, 97–107.

[9] Leonardi, "Raterio e Marziano Capella."

ascent to the heavens. It finds direct literary influence in the *Philosophia mundi* (World [or Natural] Philosophy) of William of Conches, the *Heptateuchon* of Thierry of Chartres (Thierry's account of wisdom and eloquence, and his presentation of Grammar), the *Cosmographia* of Bernardus Silvestris, the *De eodem et diverso* (On the Same and the Different) of Adelard of Bath, and perhaps most spectacularly, the *Anticlaudianus* of Alan of Lille. It was also the subject of commentaries associated with the intellectual and literary milieu of William of Conches and Bernardus Silvestris.[10] At the end of the century, the polymath teacher and scholar Alexander Neckam produced a mythographic commentary on the first two books in which he interpreted the mythic marriage of Mercury and Philology in terms of contemporary Song of Songs allegories and the union of Christ with the church.[11]

In the "plot" that frames the exposition of the arts, Mercury and Philology are to be united in marriage through the efforts of Apollo. Philology is adopted among the gods, and at the wedding celebration, Apollo brings forth seven female figures who personify each of the seven liberal arts. Over books three to nine, each art presents a distilled account of her content, "with true intellectual nourishment ... [putting] aside all fable and for the most part [explaining] serious studies."[12]

The precise models of the doctrinal elements of book three on grammar are not known, although the contents are consistent with the grammatical knowledge of the fourth and fifth centuries, including Varro's *De lingua latina* and the works of Donatus. Grammar is first identified, through dense etymologizing, with both the elements and attributes of literacy: she is at once letters, the access to literacy, and the literary product of literacy. Grammar's discourse covers the elements of speech (letters and their pronunciation, §§ 232–63; syllables, §§ 264–7; accent, §§ 268–74; (metrical) length, §§ 275–88; and analogy and anomaly, §§ 289–325).[13] But she is stopped before she can discuss elementary matters that smack of the schoolroom and would bore the celestial senate: these (cleverly summarized in Minerva's *occultatio* at § 326) are the fundamental eight parts of speech and the "faults" described in book three of the *Ars maior* of Donatus (the *Barbarismus*).

The models of book five on rhetoric are easier to identify because Martianus' treatment of the art is of a piece with other late antique compendia which were based on the

---

[10] Westra, ed. *The Commentary on Martianus Capella's De Nuptiis Philologiae et Mercurii Attributed to Bernardus Silvestris*; Westra et al., eds., *The Berlin Commentary on Martianus Capella's De Nuptiis Philologiae et Mercurii*; Dronke, "William of Conches' Commentary on Martianus Capella." For the commentary tradition, see Ramelli, *Tutti i commenti*; more commentaries enumerated in M. Teeuwen, review of Ramelli, *Tutti i commenti*, Bryn Mawr Classical Review 2007.09.39.

[11] Neckam, *Commentum super Martianum*, ed. McDonough, xii–xiii. See also Chance, *Medieval Mythography* 2:139.

[12] *Martianus Capella and the Seven Liberal Arts*, trans. Stahl and Johnson, 2:63 (§ 220). On Martianus' sources for the presentations of the arts, see Lutz, "Remigius' Ideas on the Origin of the Seven Liberal Arts."

[13] On possible sources and parallels for the treatment of grammatical theory, see Grebe, *Martianus Capella*, 54–108.

De inventione. Along the lines of Fortunatianus' *Ars rhetorica* (fourth century), and according to the same principles of distribution that are found in other rhetorical technographers of the fourth century (e.g. Sulpicius Victor, C. Julius Victor) Martianus' chapter on rhetoric gives the bulk of its treatment to invention and within that, to the intricacies of the theory of status or issues (*constitutiones*).[14] Of 146 sections in the chapter on rhetoric, fifty-five are devoted to invention (443–97) and another twenty-two to a subset of invention, the parts of the oration (544–65); two each are given to arrangement and to memory, and four to delivery; and thirty are dedicated to *elocutio* (508–37), including a list of figures from the handbook by the technographer Aquila Romanus.[15] Although Martianus covers rhetoric in more detail than the other encyclopedists of late antiquity and the early Middle Ages, his treatment of it is consistent with the other technical rhetorics, betraying the overwhelming influence of the *De inventione* and approaching the art in terms of its theoretical interests.

Where Martianus' treatments of grammar and rhetoric found perhaps their greatest impact for later periods was in his personifications: elderly, maternal Grammar with her surgical instruments for cleaning the mouth, and bold, elegant Rhetoric with her noisy, percussive entry and martial attire.[16] Martianus himself has the Muse emphasize the pedagogic usefulness of "clothing" the naked disciplines like this (III 222).

Translation reprinted from *Martianus Capella and the Seven Liberal Arts, 2: The Marriage of Philology and Mercury*, trans. Stahl and Johnson (with minor adaptations), by permission.[17]

Book III. Grammar

[The introduction of Grammar]

[223] So Latona's son [Apollo] moved forward from her former place one of the servants of Mercury, an old woman indeed but of great charm, who said that she had been born in

---

[14] Leff, "The Topics of Argumentative Invention." Note that at §§ 557–9 Martianus reproduces the list of topics of invention from Fortunatianus' *Ars rhetorica*, in Halm, ed., *Rhetores latini minores*, 115.9–116.21.

[15] §§ 523–537; Aquila Romanus, *De figuris sententiarum et elocutionis liber*, in Halm, ed., *Rhetores latini minores*, and apparatus in *De nuptiis* ed. Willis, 182–9.

[16] For the tradition of the personifications of the liberal arts in classical Antiquity, see Gabriela Moretti, 'Il manuale e l'allegoria.'

[17] Edition used for reference: *De nuptiis* ed. Willis. We have taken over some of the annotations in Stahl and Johnson.

Memphis when Osiris was still king; when she had been a long time in hiding, she was found and brought up by the Cyllenian [Mercury] himself. This woman claimed that in Attica, where she had lived and prospered for the greater part of her life, she moved about in Greek dress; but because of the Latin gods and the Capitol and the race of Mars and descendants of Venus, according to the custom of Romulus [i.e. Roman custom] she entered the senate of the gods dressed in a Roman cloak. She carried in her hands a polished box, a fine piece of cabinet-making, which shone on the outside with light ivory, from which like a skilled physician the woman took out the emblems of wounds that need to be healed.[18] [224] Out of this box she took first a pruning knife with a shining point,[19] with which she said she could prune the faults of pronunciation in children; then they could be restored to health with a certain black powder carried through reeds, a powder which was thought to be made of ash or the ink of cuttlefish.[20] Then she took out a very sharp medicine which she had made of fennelflower and the clippings from a goat's back,[21] a medicine of purest red color, which she said should be applied to the throat when it was suffering from bucolic ignorance and was blowing out the vile breaths of a corrupt pronunciation. She showed too a delicious savory,[22] the work of many late nights and vigils, with which she said the harshness of the most unpleasant voice could be made melodious. [225] She also cleaned the windpipes and the lungs by the application of a medicine in which were observed wax smeared on beechwood and a mixture of gallnuts and gum and rolls of the Nilotic plant [papyrus].[23] Although this poultice was effective in assisting memory and attention, yet by its nature it kept people awake.[24] [226] She also brought out a file[25] fashioned with great skill, which was divided into eight[26] golden parts joined in different ways, and which darted back and forth—with which by gentle rubbing she gradually cleaned dirty teeth and ailments of the tongue and the filth which had been picked up in the town of Soloe.[27]

[227] She is reckoned to know by the effort of frequent calculations arcane poems and manifold rhythms. Whenever she accepted patients,[28] it was her custom to start them with

---

[18] Here begins an extended analogy between grammar and medicine, playing on the ambiguity of technical terms. Cf. Sluiter, "Textual Therapy: On the Relationship between Medicine and Grammar in Galen."

[19] *Scalprum* is a surgical instrument, but also a pen-knife, see e.g. Tacitus, *Annales* 5.8 (there used to commit suicide).

[20] Ingredients for ink.

[21] Fennel-giant (*ferula*). *Ferula* is the normal term for the rod or whip of the schoolmaster.

[22] *Gustus* "taste" for an appetizer or for literary taste (or a specimen or foretaste of literary work).

[23] Ambiguous between a medicinal drug and writing materials (wax tablets; papyrus).

[24] A reference to scholars burning the midnight oil while reading or writing.

[25] The *lima* to be applied to one's literary work: e.g. Horace, *Ars poetica* 291.

[26] Suggestive of the number of the parts of speech.

[27] Traditionally, "soloecisms" were said to be part of the peculiar use of language of the inhabitants of Soloe.

[28] *Curandos*, "wards" (with the suggestion of medical care).

the noun. She mentioned also how many cases could cause faults or could be declined accurately. Then, appealing to her patients' powers of reasoning, she kept a firm grasp on the different classes[29] of things and the words for them, so that, as is often done by the sick, they would not change one name for another. Then she used to ask them the moods of the verbs and their tenses and the figures,[30] and she ordered others, on whom complete dullness and inert laziness had settled, to run through the steps and to climb upon as many works as possible,[31] treading on the prepositions or conjunctions or participles, and for these patients to be exercised to exhaustion by the whole art.[32]

[228] Because of different aspects of her work some of the gods thought this woman, the clever nurse of so many, was Iatrice, others took her for Genethliace.[33] Their conviction was shored by her expertise in healing: neither Pallas nor Maia's son himself[34] would deny that she could remedy faults of pronunciation. Yet it seemed incongruous that a female doctor in Roman dress should be entering the meeting. So she was asked for her name and her profession and an explanation of her whole field of study.

[229] As if it was normal for her to explain what had been asked and easy to instruct about what was wanted of her,[35] she modestly and decently folded back her cloak from her right hand and began: "In Greece I am called *Grammatikê*, because a line is called *grammê* and letters are called *grammata* and it is my province to form the letters in their proper shapes and lines. For this reason Romulus gave me the name *Litteratura*, although when I was a child he had wanted to call me *Litteratio*, just as amongst the Greeks I was at first called *Grammatistikê*; and then Romulus gave me a priest and collected some boys to be my attendants. Nowadays, my advocate is called *Litteratus*, who was formerly called *Litterator*. This is recalled by a certain Catullus,[36] a poet not without charm, when he says 'The Litterator Sylla renders you his service.' Such a man was called by the Greeks *Grammatodidaskalos*.[37]

---

[29] *Genera.* Thus, for the *nomen*, the accidents of *casus* and *genus* have been mentioned here.

[30] *Figura*: whether they are simple or compound.

[31] This sounds like a fitness program, but in fact the "steps" also refer to the *gradus comparationis*, one of the accidents of the noun, see e.g. Donatus, *Ars minor* 1, *GL* 4:355.9; the climbing (*scandere*) refers to the metrical reading, scanning, of verses.

[32] I.e. "of grammar."

[33] *Iatrice* is Greek for (the art of) medicine; *Genethliace* is Greek for "belonging to one's birthday": it refers to horoscopes and astrology. Grebe, *Martianus Capella*, 61 points out that the name "Grammar" is withheld for a long time.

[34] Hermes.   [35] This is of course indeed the case, since Grammar is the teacher *par excellence*.

[36] Catullus, *Carmina* 14.9.

[37] This section represents the chapter *de grammatica*, see e.g. [Sergius] *Explanationes in Donatum*, *GL* 4:486.16–487.2. For the link between *grammatica* and *litteratura*, see Grebe, *Martianus Capella*, 64 note 33; Varro according to M. Victorinus, *GL* 6:4.4f. and below § 231.

[230] My duty in the early stages was to read and write correctly; but now there is the added duty of understanding and criticizing knowledgeably.[38] These two aspects seem to me to be shared with the philosophers and the critics. Two of these four functions may be called active, and two contemplative, since indeed we are active when we write or read anything, but we are engaged in the contemplation of the result when we understand or assess what has been written, although these four functions are all linked by a certain affinity, just as is shown to happen in other studies also. For the actor understands at the beginning what he is capable of acting, and the astronomer does certain things in order to know through them what he needs to assess. The geometrician also combines those functions, in that he both produces and comprehends the shapes of the theorems, assisted by sure calculation.

[231] I have four parts: letters, literature, the man of letters, and literary style. Letters are what I teach, literature is I who teach,[39] the man of letters is the person whom I have taught, and literary style is the skill of a person whom I form. I claim to speak also about the nature and practice of speech. Nature is that from which speech is formed. Practice occurs when we put that material into use. To these we add the matter, so as to know what we must talk about. Speech itself is taught in three steps; that is, form letters, syllables, and words.[40]

[232] In respect of letters, two questions arise. Letters are either natural or artificial. The names of letters are formed into the substance of speaking by the operation of nature; artificial formation has laid down their written forms to the end that people in each other's presence could use one form, those absent another.[41] From the point of view of the writer they are called mute, from the reader's they are called sounds, if indeed the latter can be taken in only by hearing and the former only by sight.[42]

[233] There are some letters which can form a complete sound by themselves, others which by themselves can form none. For there are the vowels, of which the Greeks say there are seven, Romulus[43] says six, later usage five—rejecting *y*, as a Greek letter. These vowels in Latin can be pronounced long or short, acute, grave, or even circumflex in accent, combined and separated without losing their names. Sometimes single vowels form syllables, sometimes they accept consonants and certain vowels on either side,

---

[38] Four tasks of grammar: *scribere, legere, intellegere, probare*. Cf. Dionysius Thrax, *Tekhnê grammatikê, GG* I i 5.4–6.3. See also below on § 263.

[39] See above, note 37 (on the connection between *grammatica* and *litteratura*).

[40] This division will be worked out in §§ 232–6 (letters); 262–78 (syllables); 279–325 (words).

[41] A "letter" in ancient theory is always the combination of a sound and a shape. The sound is here held to be natural, the shape conventional and artificial.

[42] Note the common ancient practice of reading out loud.   [43] I.e. early Latin.

sometimes they change among themselves, then again they follow themselves with pleasing effect." . . .

[End of the section on letters, beginning of the section on syllables.[44]]

[258] "Out of all these, eighteen letters completely cover the needs of any piece of composition.[45] I am satisfied to include *y* amongst the vowels; without it one cannot write *Hyacinthus* or *Cyllenius*. This gives us a total of six vowels, six semi-vowels, and six mutes. [259] For if *h* is treated as an aspirate symbol; and *q* and *k* are unnecessary; and *x*, being a double letter, lacks the simplicity prerequisite for the basic letters; and *z* is excluded from Latin; then, as I said, eighteen letters remain.

[260] All these letters, including those classed as unnecessary or not genuine, are formed by the sound of any single voice; and in the harmony of the voice they have uncovered the various elements of the concord of nature.

[261] We utter *A* with the mouth open, with a single suitable breath.

We make *B* by the outburst of breath from closed lips.

C is made by the back teeth brought forward over the back of the tongue.

D is made by bringing the tongue against the top teeth.

E is made by a breath with the tongue a little depressed.

F is made by the teeth pressing on the lower lip.

G by a breath against the palate.

H is made by an exhalation with the throat a little closed.

I is made by a breath with the teeth kept close together.

K is made with the palate against the top of the throat.

L is a soft sound made with the tongue and the palate.

M is a pressing together of the lips.

N is formed by the contact of the tongue on the teeth.

O is made by a breath with the mouth rounded.

P is a forceful exhalation from the lips.

Q is a contraction of the palate with the mouth half-closed.

R is a rough exhalation with the tongue curled against the roof of the mouth.

S is a hissing sound with the teeth in contact.

T is a blow of the tongue against the teeth.

U is made with the mouth almost closed and the lips forward a little.

---

[44] Cf. Varro according to Cassiodorus, *De orthographia*, *GL* 7:153.1–3; Charisius, *Ars grammatica*, ed. Barwick, 5.19–29; Donatus, *Ars maior* 1.2, *GL* 4:368.6–16; Grebe, *Martianus Capella*, 73 note 51.

[45] I.e. one can write any text with them without needing additional letters.

X is the sibilant combination of *C* and *S*.

Y is a breath with the lips close together.

Z was abhorrent to Appius Claudius, because it resembles in its expression the teeth of a corpse.

[262]⁴⁶ The rules of literacy, the primary study, which usually are spread

over many volumes, are quickly brought into a small compass:

in it we see what any letter connects together by its association on either side;

on which side it accepts or demands an accompanying letter;

how a letter customarily is altered by the laws of transformation

and thus accepts a different name;

what sounds of the mouth or movements of the tongue

or outbursts from the lips form the letters.

Now we must survey the syllable, composed of letters in combination:

how it is accented; when it is long or short.

I shall survey these two points, since the preceding study of the letter

has at the same time taught the connections.

The order of studies takes this at the next matter to be dealt with,

if that meets with your divine approval."

[263] While Grammar was saying this, and Jupiter and the Delian⁴⁷ were urging her forward, Pallas spoke up: "While Literature here is hurrying on to discuss the connection of syllables, she has passed over the historical aspect."⁴⁸ At this objection by the maiden goddess, Grammar in great agitation answered: "I know I must pass over a great deal, so as not to incur the distaste of the blessed by getting entangled in details. So I shall perform my purpose, hastening along the shortest ways, to avoid getting lost, hidden in thick undergrowth or a dense mass of briars." . . .

[289]⁴⁹ "The topic of syllables has now been quickly covered;

we must come on to words. This is the proper order

for such matters, and this topic in turn will divide

into two. First we must discuss *proportio*,

which the Greeks call *analogia* [analogy];

and then what the scholars commonly call *anomalia* [anomalies],

---

⁴⁶ Grammar here bursts into a bit of poetry (distichs).　　⁴⁷ Apollo.

⁴⁸ Perhaps a reference to one of the traditional tasks of grammar as defined in Greek grammar (Dionysius Thrax, *Tekhnê grammatikê*, *GG* I i 6.1).

⁴⁹ The end of the section on syllables (dealing with the parts of speech) is again marked by a bit of poetry— Grammar is again worried that she may be boring the gods.

the innovations which set the rule aside;[50]

in them half of our speech consists,

or rather, the integrity of our speech is injured;

these I shall discuss within the scope of this one small book,

and as far as your distaste for serious topics will permit.

[290] Analogy, which in Latin is called *proportio*, is the observance of agreement between similar words. In the first place, all Latin nouns end in one of twelve letters: five vowels, the six semi-vowels, and one mute, *t*, as in *caput* 'head.'" . . .

[324] "Those are enough examples of analogy. The forms that are not included above must certainly be reckoned as anomalies. I shall discuss these very briefly to show that usage [*usus*] has in some words prevailed over analogy [*ratio*], or in defiance of the rules [*regula*] lacks certain forms.[51]

[325] When *reus* and *deus* are similar in the nominative singular, why do we say *hi rei* in the plural for one and is *hi di* normal usage for the other, against the rule—we ought to say *dei* only—especially when no genitive should be longer by two syllables than its nominative, as happens when we say *deorum*? When *Thoas*, *Aeas*, and *Aeneas* are similar, why do two form the genitives *Thoantis* and *Aeantis*, yet *Aeneas* forms not *Aeneantis*, but *Aeneae*? When we say *hic biceps* and *triceps*, why is the genitive form two syllables longer, contrary to the norm, so that we say *bicipitis* or *tricipitis*, and not *bicipis* or *tricipis*? How does it happen that *aliger*, *frugifer*, *accipiter* have all the case terminations, but *Iuppiter* has only two?[52] When *sanctus*, *pius*, and *bonus* are all similar, why do we say *sanctior* but not *piior*? Why do we say *sanctior*, *sanctissimus*, but not *bonior*, *bonissimus*? When Vergil says *fandi atque nefandi*[53] why do we form *nefarius* from *nefando* but not *farius* from *fando*? Why can *seiunctus* lose its prefix and form *iunctus*, while if you take *se-* away from *securus* and *sedulus* you cannot use what is left? When we may say, in the plural, *singuli viri*, *singulae mulieres*, *singula scrinia*, why may we not say, in the singular *singulus vir*, *singula mulier*, *singulum scrinium*? When the verbs *venor*, *piscor*, and *aucupor* are similar, why do we form from them the nouns *venator* and *piscator*, yet not *aucupator* but *auceps*? Why does *volo* have no imperative?[54] Why does the verb *fari* have no first person singular in the present

---

[50] In the section on the morphology of words, grammar focuses on the debate about grammatical regularity or irregularity, in which *usus* "(empirically established) usage" is pitted against *ratio* (the system of rules). The debate was framed in these stark terms by Varro in *De lingua latina* [On the Latin Language], in which it becomes the organizing principle of the work (*argumentatio in utramque partem*, the work is framed as a debate for and against analogy).

[51] Namely, when e.g. a verb or noun is "defective" in conjugation or declension; see the examples quoted below.

[52] An example of "deficient" declination, cf. III 324.   [53] *Aeneid* 1.543

[54] An example of a deficient conjugation.

indicative?[55] Why does *soleo* have no perfect tense? When *canta* and *lava* are similar, why does one form *cantavi* but the other not form *lavavi*? Again, *corusca* forms *coruscavi*, but *tona* does not form *tonavi*. Why does *ego* have no other case? When *calceatus*, *armatus*, *togatus*, and *paenulatus* all seem the same, why do we say *calceo* and *armo* and cannot say *togo* and *paenulo*? Adjectives whose nominative singular ends in -*us* all form the adverb in the positive degree of comparison ending in long -*ē*, as *doctus* forms *docte*; *avarus*, *avare*; *parcus*, *parce*; then why do *bonus* and *malus* have the *e* of the adverb short in *bene* and *male*? When we form the adverb *habiliter* from *habilis*, why do we not form *faciliter* from *facilis*? Again, when we say *difficulter*, why can we not say *faculter*? When from *audax* we form *audacter*, why do we form from *verax* not *veracter* but *veraciter*? Why do we say *singulatim* but not *binatim* or *ternatim*? There are innumerable things of this kind, which I could mention if I did not have to hurry on to other topics."

[326] When Grammar had said this as if she was getting ready for a fresh introduction of her subject, Minerva intervened,[56] because of the boredom that had come upon Jove and the celestial senate, and said: "Unless I am mistaken, you are getting ready to go back to the basics and tell us in depth about the eight parts of speech, adding also the causes of solecisms, the barbarisms, and the other faults of speech which are very frequent in celebrated poets. Those you will call now tropes, now metaplasms, now *schemata* or figures, and all the faults which flow, as it were, from the same fountain of embellishment, illustrating either the misconception of the writer who does not understand them or the labored ornamentation of the pedant. If you bring such matters from the elementary school before the celestial senate, you will nip in the bud the good will you have won by this display of knowledge. If you were to take up a discussion of rhythm and meter, as you would venture to do with young pupils, Music would surely tear you apart for usurping her office. The teaching you have given us will be well-proportioned and complete if after having set out its main points you do not cheapen them by commonplace and elementary instruction."

The Delian and his spouse nodded in approval of these words of his sister, and they made Grammar walk across to the attendants of Philology. Then the Clarian introduced another of the women who would form part of the nuptial exchange of gifts.

[The second figure introduced is Dialectic, and after she has set out the principles of her discipline, it is the turn of Rhetoric, who makes a most impressive entrance (book V). Once

---

[55] We are again dealing with deficient conjugation: the form *for "I say" is never attested (but *faris* and *fatur* are). See for this example Diomedes, *Ars grammatica*, *GL* 1:379.24f.

[56] Minerva deals with the whole "third part" of grammar in one section. Cf. Baratin and Desbordes, "La 'troisième partie' de l' *Ars grammatica*."

again, the beginning of the book is highly allegorical. Rhetoric is described throughout in military terminology and with associations of loud and powerful sounds and noise.]

Book V. Rhetoric

[426] But while a great group of the earth-gods was disturbed by such thoughts,[57] in strode a woman of the tallest stature and abounding self-confidence, a woman of outstanding beauty; she wore a helmet, and her head was wreathed with royal grandeur; in her hands the arms with which she used either to defend herself or to wound her enemies, shone with the brightness of lightning. The garment under her arms was covered by a robe wound about her shoulders in the Latin fashion; this robe was adorned with the light [*lumine*] of all kinds of devices [*figurarum*] and showed the figures [*schemata*] of them all, while she had a belt under her breast adorned with the rarest colors [*coloribus*] of jewels [*gemmarum*].[58] [427] When she clashed her weapons on entering, you would say that the broken booming of thunder was rolling forth with the shattering clash of a lightning cloud; indeed it was thought that she could hurl thunderbolts like Jove.[59] For like a queen with power over everything, she could drive any host of people where she wanted and draw them back from where she wanted; she could sway them to tears and whip them to a frenzy, and change the countenance and senses not only of cities but of armies in battle. She was said to have brought under her control, amongst the people of Romulus, the senate, the public platforms, and the law courts, and in Athens had at will swayed the legislative assembly, the schools, and the theaters, and had caused the utmost confusion throughout Greece.

[428] What countenance and voice she had as she spoke, what excellence and exaltation of speech! It was worth even the gods' effort to hear such genius of argument,[60] so rich a wealth of diction,[61] so vast a store of memory and recollection.[62] What order in structure,[63] what harmonious delivery,[64] what movement of gesture,[65] what profundity of concept! She was light in treating small topics, ready with middling topics, and with

---

[57] Of resisting the Olympians.

[58] As Johnson points out, this passage exploits the ambiguity of a number of technical rhetorical terms: *lumen*, *figurae*, *schemata*, *colores*, *gemmae* all apply to rhetorical ornamentation and are here used for the literal adornment of a woman.

[59] Johnson *ad loc* refers to Pericles' nickname "the Olympian," earned by his "oratory with the force of a thunderbolt."

[60] A reference to *inventio* "invention."   [61] A reference to *elocutio* "style."

[62] A reference to *memoria* "memory."   [63] A reference to *dispositio* "disposition."

[64] A reference to *pronuntiatio* "delivery."   [65] A reference to *actio/gestus*, the non-verbal aspects of delivery.

exalted ones a firebrand.[66] In discussion she made her whole audience attentive, in persuasion amenable, full of conflict in disagreements, full of pride in speeches of praise. But when she had, through the testimony of some public figure, proclaimed some matter of dispute, everything seemed to be in turbulence, confusion, and on fire. [429] This golden-voiced woman, pouring out some of the jewels of crowns and kingdoms, was followed by a mighty army of famous men, amongst whom the two nearest her outshone the rest. These two[67] were of different nationalities and styles of dress, one wearing the Greek pallium, the other the Roman trabea. Each spoke a different language, though one professed to have studied Greek culture at Athens and was considered quick in the studies of the Greek schools and in the constant disputes and discussions of the Academy. Both were men from poor families, who rose to fame from humble beginnings.[68] And although a Roman *eques* fathered one, and a toiling workman the other,[69] both grew to such fame through their oratorical prowess that after their destinies in public life and their unmerited deaths they rose by their excellence to the stars and now outlast the ages through their eternal glory. [430] The one whom the people of Athens and the whole stream of Greeks followed had the reputation of being most forceful, more vigorous than the storms and the raging of the angry ocean.[70] He was described in verse such as this: "A man to fear, who might find fault even with the innocent".[71] [431] But the other, who wore the purple of a consul, and a laurel wreath for suppressing a conspiracy,[72] came into the senate of heaven, and, delighted to have come into Jove's presence, joyfully began to declaim: "How blessed we are, how fortunate the State, how brilliant the fame of my consulship!"[73] [432] After these two in different lines there came the great orators of the past, bearing before them the highest honors and the rewards of their eloquence: one could see Aeschines, Isocrates, and Lysias, and then, in the Roman ranks, the *Sosantii*,[74] the Gracchi, Regulus, Pliny, and Fronto. [433] But before them all, even before the woman who led the whole array, went an old man bearing the mark of office and the preceding rod, after the manner of a Roman lictor, and on the top of the rod there flew a golden-mouthed crow as a sign of the woman who was coming. [434] But the man who was carrying the rod was called Tisias, and

---

[66] Cf. Cicero, *Orator* 101 for such correspondences between topic and style.

[67] Demosthenes (384–322 BC) and Cicero (106–43 BC).

[68] Johnson's note *ad loc*: "Martianus says 'both were new men,' which in Latin means the first of a family to reach senatorial rank."

[69] Johnson's note *ad loc.*: "Demosthenes' father had been, in fact, quite wealthy; but the estate was embezzled by Demosthenes' guardian."

[70] According to Plutarch, *Life of Demosthenes* 11, Demosthenes had overcome a speech deficiency by trying to be heard over the waves of the sea while speaking with his mouth full of pebbles.

[71] *Iliad* 11.654 (Patroclus describing Achilles).

[72] The conspiracy of Catiline, suppressed by Cicero as consul 63 BC.   [73] Cicero, *In Catilinam* 2.10.

[74] The text is corrupt here.

seemed older and more important than all of them; for with a glance at the crow perched above him,[75] he called the others, his inferiors, their common bond, and the woman in the lead their daughter. [435] Stirred by this thought, very many of the gods believed that this woman was indeed of high nobility, but that, if a Greek, then she was the sister of Apollo, and if one of Romulus' people,[76] one of the Corvinian family.[77] Added to this mystery was the fact that fearlessly and with very ready self-confidence she kissed the breast of Pallas and of the Cyllenian himself,[78] thus giving clear signs of her almost sisterly intimacy with them. Indeed some of the gods—who between their fear of the heralding trumpet and their wonder at her friendship with the heavenly beings, had long been uncertain, and wanted to learn from foresighted Phoebus, since great Jove was not yet making any inquiry—asked her loudly who she was.

[436] She then, looking at the whole assembly of gods, with some emotion began to speak: "I call to witness great father Jove and the other dwellers in heaven, whom I have often invoked in a great many cases, and the very assembly of the celestial senate, that nothing could be deemed more unsuitable or more inappropriate for me than that I, who have constantly been the accuser in many political and legal disputes and who in many other instances have been the defender and have striven with all my might for the glory of the contest and have obtained for myself from the hazardous fates the fame of a well-earned result, should now amongst you gods, to please whom seemed the price of immortality, be compelled against my will to recall the advice given to school children and the jejune rules of a timeworn subject.[79] Nor does poverty bring me to this, since I have thronging hordes of followers.[80] But apart from those who break the benches and bring turmoil to the hearts and senses of all those who know me, I have other devotees also, who have written detailed instructions and commentaries on the most esoteric points of the subject; under each category of my followers my Cicero shines out, since he not only has thundered forth with the grandeur of impressive speech in forum, senate, and public assembly, but also in writing the rules of the subject has committed many books to use by future generations. [437] Since this is so, regard for the dignity I have earned and the fame of a reputation as widespread as I believe mine to be, would deter me from expounding these elementary first principles, were it not that you command me, and that command contributes to my reward of immortality, and the pledge of everlasting fame inspires me to

---

[75] "Crow" is *korax* in Greek, and Tisias and Corax allegedly had invented rhetoric in the fifth century BC (which also explains why rhetoric is here called their daughter).

[76] i.e. a Roman   [77] *Corvus* is Latin for "crow" (Corax), see note 75.   [78] Hermes.

[79] Johnson *ad loc.*: "this is a particularly long and elaborate sentence, like many first sentences in Cicero's speeches; this effect has been retained in the translation." Note the high rhetoric on introducing rhetoric herself (iconic relationship between subject matter and style).

[80] A sly dig at grammar, which famously kept its practitioners in poverty.

set forth even the rudiments of my subject when Jove and the gods ordain it. So I prepare myself to traverse these arid topics, giving less pleasure, indeed, than I usually do in public performances; although if the approbation of His Gracious Majesty has allowed Pallas and the Arcadian to participate, then in your assembly, mighty deities, shall I cause displeasure? [438] For I am Rhetoric herself, whom some term an art [*artem*], some a virtue, some a study [*disciplina*]; an art, because I am the object of teaching, although Plato disputes the title.[81] Those who have discovered that I possess the knowledge of how to speak well call me a virtue. Those who are aware that the innermost secrets of speaking can be studied and learned proclaim confidently that I am a study.

[439][82] My duty is to speak appropriately in order to persuade; my object is through speech to persuade the hearer of the subject proposed. I invoke these words of Cicero, whose examples I will also be using while going through all the branches of instruction in turn. [440] My material is twofold—namely, in what circumstances and from what resources a speech is made; in what circumstances, when I approach the elements of the *quaestio* itself; from what resources, when the matter and words of a speech are put together.

[441] The *quaestio* is either limited or unlimited. It is limited when it arises from a particular action and concerns a given individual; for instance, in Cicero's speech for Roscius, the issue is whether Roscius killed his father. The *quaestio* is unlimited when it asks as a general question whether one ought to do something; for example, the *Hortensius* discusses whether one ought to pursue philosophy. I am often vigorously engaged in the former, which the Greeks chose to call *hypothesis*. In the unlimited *quaestio*, which has the boldness to make a universal affirmation, I engage mainly when I have in prospect leisure and argument, although generally that aspect of it which is called *thesis* would have often furnished me with sturdy javelins and far-ranging spears in the more exalted parts of my lawsuits. Is not this what happens in the speech for Scaurus, when Cicero interpolates a discussion on 'the possible causes of sudden death', or again in the speech for Milo, 'whether the world is governed by providence'? And then, some of my followers, inspired by most keen and subtle reasoning, assert that no issue is a hypothesis, but that all that may be argued in defense of the accused or against them in prosecution will be applicable to general issues.

[442] There is no doubt that my duty has five parts:[83] invention, arrangement, style, memory, and delivery. For judgment, which some include, is required in all the parts, and therefore cannot itself properly be considered a part, although it is the province of

---

[81] Namely, of being a *tekhnê*, e.g. in Plato's *Gorgias*.   [82] Cf. *De inventione* 1.5.6.
[83] Cf. *De inventione* 1.7.9; *Rhetorica ad Herennium* 1.3.4.

judgment to weigh what should and what should not be said. Invention is the prudent and searching collection of issues and arguments. Arrangement is that which puts the matter in order. Style chooses words that are proper or figurative, invents new usages, and arranges words of traditional usage. Memory is the firm guardian of our matter and our diction. Delivery is the control of our voice, movement, and gesture according to the importance of our matter and our words. Of these, the most powerful surely is invention, which has the task of discovering the issues in a case and finding suitable arguments to prove it." . . .

[470] [84] "Now we must examine the direction [*ductus*] of the case. The direction is a consistency in a particular approach, held throughout a case. There are five types of direction: the simple, the subtle, the figurative, the oblique, and the mixed. The simple exists when the speaker's words reflect what is in his mind directly; for example, if one praises the deserving and accuses the objectionable. The subtle exists when the words do not directly reflect the mind; for example, a man disowns his son because the son has no friends. The man is not really disowning his son, but is frightening him into acquiring friends. The figurative exists when modesty forbids us to say something openly because of its obscenity and it is expressed under some other representation, dressed in clothing, as it were. The oblique exists when fear prevents us from saying something freely and we show that it must be presented in an underground manner of speaking. For example: A tyrant who had given up his tyranny under condition of amnesty has performed valiantly, and asks as his reward the custody of the armory and the citadel. The magistrates oppose him. The mixed kind is made up of both these two, when both shame and fear inhibit freedom of speech. For example: A tyrant has two sons; with the wife of one the father committed adultery; her husband hanged himself; the father ordered the other son to marry her. He refused. In this case one cannot speak freely either about the incest or the tyranny. [471] These are the directions, which need to be worked out with care and should inconspicuously permeate the whole speech. They are distinguished from 'color' by the fact that color is observed in only one part of a speech, whereas direction is held throughout the case." . . .

[473] "Having covered all these points, we turn to look at arguments, by which credence can be brought to a disputed aspect of a question.[85] Credence is formed in three ways: by winning good will [*conciliando*], by instruction [*docendo*], and by emotional appeal [*permovendo*]. The first is called the ethical approach, the second the demonstrative, the third the emotional. Although one ought to win good will throughout the case, it should

---

[84] Cf. Fortunatianus, *Ars rhetorica* I 5–7, ed. Halm, 84.24–86.33.

[85] This is a discussion of the three "means of persuasion," cf. Cicero, *De oratore* 2.115 and 310. See Wisse, *Ethos and Pathos from Aristotle to Cicero*, 210–14, who describes the historical confusion between these three means of persuasion and the three tasks of the orator (to instruct, delight, and move).

be pursued most of all at the commencement, while the end should be most vigorous with appeal to the emotions. Instruction should come particularly from the narrative section of the speech, although by resolving questions and putting forward accusations the argumentative section of a speech works in much the same way. Now I shall begin to discuss arguments." . . .

> [After the discussion of invention, Rhetorica now takes up the other tasks of the orator, first disposition (presented completely here), then style (the beginning of this section is given here).]

[506] "To these devices, which have been cleverly worked out to create credibility, we must add the order in which our material is presented: this is called 'disposition'. By it we pay careful attention to what to say in which place in the speech; what should be left out altogether; and how and when and where something should be said. This part of rhetoric has two aspects, for the structure follows either a natural order or an artificial one devised by the skill of the orator. The natural order occurs when, after the introduction, there follows the narrative [*narratio*], the outline of main points [*partitio*], the presentation of one's thesis [*propositio*], the argument [*argumentatio*], the conclusion drawn [*conclusio*], and the peroration [*epilogus*]. The skill of the orator is employed when we distribute the points to be made throughout the speech. Our arrangement, then, is not in chronological order but in the most advantageous order for our case, as was done in the speech for Milo, when Cicero, to dispel the hostile predispositions of the jury, brought in certain questions before his narrative; he made this change from the natural order because of the advantage it brought his case.[86] In the first speech for Cornelius, Cicero rebutted the accusations concerning the period after Cornelius' tribunate, then went back to discuss the tribunate; this, as I have said, is called an artificial arrangement. [507] But in the speech against Verres he kept the natural, chronological order so that he presented first Verres' quaestorship, then the legateship, then the two praetorships, keeping the chronological order which we inevitably follow unless the advantage of the case rejects this approach. But when great and heinous accusations require thorough refutation, the speech for the defense ought to begin with the accusations; for example, in the speech for Cluentius, he first gets the matters of fact out of the way and then comes to discuss the letter of the law, changing the usual order, so as not to give the impression of shirking the issue by defending Cluentius with an appeal to the law.

[508] Having dealt with these two parts of my duties,[87] I must turn my attention to style. Since this consists in the consideration of individual words, it is distinguished from

---

[86] For this classical analysis of the *pro Milone*, see Quintilian, *Institutio oratoria* 6.5.10.
[87] Invention and disposition; Rhetorica is still speaking.

eloquence, because the latter is the caliber of the whole rhetorical work, while the former is one part of rhetoric, and, according to Cicero, has two foundations, as it were, and two summits. The two fundamentals are, to speak Latin correctly and clearly; the first of these you learned from Grammar, when you absorbed her cleverness. The summits are, to speak with fluency and embellishment, which come not from natural ability but from the utmost effort and daily practice, which gives our style not only more richness but greater clarity and brilliance.

[509] There are two aspects of this subject: one adds luster [*lumen*] to the individual words used, the other enhances the quality of the speech by the attractive combination of the words. In examining individual words, we consider whether they are proper, transferred, or borrowed." . . .

[557][88] "The section of proof [*argumentatio*] is the delivery of the arguments themselves in words; the arguments are the means to prove the case.[89] This section is divided into two parts: proof and refutation. There are two kinds of arguments: artificial and inartificial. The artificial kind has four chief sources of argument: before the act, in the act, around the act, after the act. 'Before the act' is divided into seven sources of argument: from the person, from the act, from the cause, the time, the place, the manner, the matter. 'In the act' there are twelve sources of argument: from the whole; the part; the genus; the species; from difference, using the seven circumstances (this source of argument contains those from greater to lesser and from lesser to greater); from property; from definition; from name; from synonymy; from the beginning; from the development, or advancement; from the conclusion, or consummation. [558] 'Around the act' there are ten sources of argument:[90] from likeness—of which there are five kinds: example, similitude, tale, image, and vignette, which is taken from comedy. Some also add allegories, like those of Aesop—to resume: around the act there are sources of argument from the dissimilar; the equal; the contrary by affirmation and negation; and with respect to something, which is represented by four cases, the genitive, the dative, the accusative, and the ablative; by conflicts through possession and loss; from greater to lesser, from lesser to greater; from what precedes; from

---

[88] For this section, see Fortunatianus, *Ars rhetorica* 2.23–4, ed. Halm, 115.9–116.21; cf. *Rhetoria ad Herennium* 1.10.18.

[89] *Argumentatio est elocutio, qua argumenta ipsa verbis exsequimur, argumenta vero quibus causa probatur.* The arguments or *loci argumentorum* are part of invention and were discussed there (V 474ff.). The *argumentatio*, here distinguished from the arguments themselves, are part of *elocutio* or delivery. Cf. Grebe, *Martianus Capella*, 271. For the "circumstances" discussed in this section, see also the headnote to the section on Boethius' *De differentiis topicis*, within, pp. 190–3.

[90] Helpfully listed by Johnson (210 note 245): (1) from the like; (2) from the dissimilar; (3) from the equal; (4) from the contrary; (5) with respect to something; (6) by conflict; (7) from greater to lesser, and vice versa; (8) from what precedes; (9) from the simultaneous; (10) from what follows.

what is simultaneous, or conjoint; from what follows. There are two sources of argument after the act: from the result and from the decision. [559] There are other sources of argument from syzygy [*apo tes syzygias*]—that is, from conjunction or from union—which is, as it were, joined to a quality of a person; for example, if we call one who feels hostile sentiments 'an enemy'. Again, from quality; for example: 'If he acted in anger, he acted without reason'. From quantity; for example: 'If he is a serious man, the action was the same'. From conjunct matters; that is, from forms and covenants [*apo typoseos kai syntheton*]—as the rods and chair of office are the insignia of magistrates.[91] Again, from partition: that is, from division [*apo tes diareseos*], through all the circumstances; that is, when we subdivide by persons, times, and the other things which are distinguished and acceptable by diversity." . . .

> [Very fittingly, when Rhetorica has dealt with "the conclusion'" she is made to terminate her speech—here is the end of her teaching, performed in accordance with her (loud) character.]

[565] "The conclusion has three parts: the recapitulation, just mentioned; the exciting of indignation, which we call exacerbation; and the arousing of pity, which we call commiseration and compassion.[92] Exacerbation comes from the sources of the arguments; for by these we not only prove things but enhance them. But the arousing of pity (that is, commiseration) is taken from the same sources of argument as exacerbation. Peroration should be used not only at the end of a speech but wherever the subject permits it; that is, by way of digression from the opening remarks or from constant narrative, and even sometimes from the discussion of the basic issues. In the conclusion, on the whole, we should take care that it is brief, since the judge is to be sent straight away with his emotions stirred to cast his verdict, while he is either angry with our adversary or in sympathy with your tears or moved by compassion for the accused."

But as Rhetoric reached this point, the Cyllenian nodded to her to move across into the company of her sisters and the service of the bride. Seeing his signal, she concluded her address and with ready confidence went to Philology's throne, kissed her forehead noisily—for she did nothing quietly, even if she wanted to—and mingled with the company and fellowship of her sisters.

---

[91] And can hence be adduced as proof of magistrate status.

[92] Note by Johnson *ad loc.*: "Martianus uses the Greek words *deinosis* [exacerbation], *oiktos* [commiseration], and *eleos* [compassion]."

PRISCIAN, *INSTITUTIONES GRAMMATICAE* AND *INSTITUTIO DE NOMINE PRONOMINE VERBO*, CA. 520

INTRODUCTION

Priscian of Caesarea, who flourished in the late fifth and early sixth centuries, was professor of grammar in Constantinopolis, in the Greek-speaking part of the Roman Empire.[1] His work was aimed at native speakers of Greek with advanced competence in Latin.[2] His main achievement, the *Institutio de arte grammatica* or *Institutiones grammaticae* (Institutes of grammar) in eighteen books (ca. 520?) is the largest and most theoretical handbook transmitted from Latin antiquity. It would acquire enormous authority in the Middle Ages, although initially Donatus remained the most popular textbook.

Priscian's grammar stands out among the representatives of Roman *Schulgrammatik* for various reasons. First, he combined the strictly hierarchical and systematic structure of the *Schulgrammatik* type with long lists of examples of morphological phenomena: this reflects an alternative organization of grammatical information that we associate with the so-called *Regulae* type of grammar.[3] Since these different structures cannot easily be integrated, Priscian switches between the two modes.[4] Second, Priscian used as his main sources two very important Greek grammarians from the second century AD, the

---

[1] Cf. Kaster, *Guardians of Language*, 346–48; M. Baratin, "Priscian," in *Lexicon grammaticorum*, ed. Stammerjohann et al., 756–9. Other works by Priscian are *De figuris numerorum* (On the Forms of Numerals), *De metris fabularum Terentii* (On the Meters of the Plays of Terence), and *Praeexercitamina* (Preliminary Exercises). For the *Institutiones* we use the edition in G*L* 2–3, ed. Keil. For the *Institutio* and the *Partitiones*, we have used the edition by Passalacqua. For bibliography on Priscian, see the *Corpus grammaticorum latinorum* at http://kaali.linguist.jussieu.fr/CGL/bgl.jsp?query = Priscianus.

[2] Salamon, "Priscianus und sein Schülerkreis," argues that the intellectuals around Priscian did not regard Latin just as the language of imperial administration and Greek as the language of culture, but rather that Priscian's project indicates the status of Latin as a *Kultursprache*.

[3] For a discussion of the *Schulgrammatik*, see introduction to section on Aelius Donatus. For the distinction between these two types of grammar, see Law, *The History of Linguistics in Europe*, 65–6, 83.

[4] Law, *The History of Linguistics in Europe*, 86. For example, books 1–5 belong to the *Schulgrammatik* type, but books 6 and 7 on noun inflection belong to the *Regulae* type. Book 8 gives the *Schulgrammatik* version of the doctrine of the verb, while books 9 and 10 provide the *Regulae*-type lists of information.

syntactician Apollonius Dyscolus, and his son Herodian, a specialist in morphology and accentuation,[5] thus trying to improve on traditional Latin grammar by applying Greek theoretical (philosophically inspired) notions.[6] He translated large parts of Apollonius' and Herodian's work and adapted them to a Latin context. This adaptation included the addition of very rich illustrative examples from Roman literature, most prominently Virgil,[7] a third feature that sets him apart from Donatus, whose grammar has comparatively little illustrative literary matter. Providing theoretical justification for the *expositio auctorum* is an explicit goal of Priscian: his syntax is an instrument to that end. A fourth important point is that his use of Apollonius and Herodian keeps Greek constantly in the background, so that Priscian has a more independent metalanguage at his disposal than the colleagues who tried to explain Latin by means of Latin itself.[8] Fifth, inspired by Apollonius Dyscolus, Priscian is unique among Latin grammarians in his concern for questions of syntax, to which the last two books (known in the Middle Ages as *Priscianus minor*) are dedicated.

Like all traditional Roman *artes* of the *Schulgrammatik* type, the *Institutiones grammaticae* begin with chapters on *vox* (voice, sound), letters, and syllables; this part became known as the *Ortographia* in the Middle Ages. The section on *dictio* and *oratio*, and the long section on the *partes orationis*, the heart of any Roman *ars*, was called *Ethimologia* in the Middle Ages. The elements of this section represent an organic progression of levels:[9] syllables constitute words, and words constitute sentences. This then raises the question of how many "parts of speech" there are as constituents of a complete sentence. There is a tendency throughout antiquity to regard all efforts to distinguish linguistic "parts" as contributions to one developmental story leading to a final outcome of a fixed

    [5] On Apollonius Dyscolus, see especially Blank, *Ancient Philosophy and Grammar*; Sluiter, *Ancient Grammar in Context*. His works are partly available in translation. For the *Syntax*, there is an English translation by F. W. Householder, *The Syntax of Apollonius Dyscolus* (Amsterdam: Benjamins, 1981); the standard translation however is the excellent French one with commentary by Lallot, *Apollonius Dyscole, De la Construction (syntaxe)*. The treatise on conjunctions has been translated by Dalimier, *Apollonius Dyscole, Traité des Conjonctions*; the treatise *De pronominibus* by P. Brandenburg, *Apollonios Dyskolos, Über das Pronomen* (Leipzig: Teubner, 2005); A. Schmidhauser, *Apollonius Dyscolus on the Pronoun* [in preparation].

    [6] Luhtala, *Grammar and Philosophy in Late Antiquity*, emphasizes the fact that the interaction between grammar and rhetoric does not stop in the first century BC. She argues that there is continued influence during the first three centuries AD, with a status quo being reached in the fourth century. Priscian not only reflects the mix of (predominantly) Stoic and (to a lesser extent) Peripatetic elements that he found in Apollonius, but also betrays (Neo-)platonist influences, particularly in some of his definitions. See Luhtala, 8–10, 82, 153–4.

    [7] Ziolkowski and Putnam, *The Virgilian Tradition*, 649–60

    [8] Cf. P. L. Schmidt, "Priscianus," in *Der Neue Pauly* (2001), 10: 338–9.

    [9] The hierarchical structure of Priscian's grammar implies that each higher level embraces the previous ones: letters make up syllables, syllables make up words, words make up sentences. The internal structure of each level is also constructed in a similar way ("isomorphism").

number of "parts of speech." This construction ignores the very different contexts in which philosophers, rhetoricians, philologists, and grammarians thought about this question. Establishing the minimum number of constituents of a proposition is a very different enterprise from parsing a verse of poetry or drawing up an exhaustive list of all possible parts of speech.[10] Priscian himself offers a version of such a development story.[11] In his own grammar, he does not offer a different number of parts of speech than the now standard eight, but he does alter Donatus' order of discussion of these parts because of the logical priority of noun and verb.[12]

Priscian's discussion of all parts of speech, supplemented with *Regulae*-style morphological information, completes the *Priscianus maior*, the first sixteen books of the *Institutiones grammaticae*. Books 17 and 18 of the *Institutiones* (the *Priscianus minor*), represented the part called *Diasynthetica* or *Diasintastica* [Syntax] in the Middle Ages. This part relies heavily on Apollonius Dyscolus. The driving notion in the syntactic theory of Apollonius Dyscolus is that of *katallêlotês*, a perfectly regular syntax in which all semantic (and morphological) features of the sentence are congruent with each other. Priscian adopts this concept under labels such as *congruentia*, *apta coniunctio*, or *apta structura* of elements that are *conveniens* or *consequens*. The complete, self-contained, and grammatically perfect sentence is grammar's best result. Apollonius Dyscolus' theory is strongly based on semantics, and on a strict separation between the levels of form and meaning, which he took over from Stoic observations on language. The semantic level is always more important in settling questions of grammatical correctness. Changes and corruption affect the word-forms, but not their meanings.[13] Apollonius Dyscolus' theory of grammatical irregularity is equally based on a semantic analysis of words: if words are marked for a grammatical category, such as tense, this restricts their combinatory possibilities.[14] If they are not so marked, they can combine freely with words that do have such marking. That explains why an adverb like "well" (not marked for "tense") can be combined with present, past, and future tenses, whereas an adverb like "yesterday" can only be combined

---

[10] Important sources for the developmental story are the Greek rhetorician Dionysius of Halicarnassus (working in Rome in the time of Augustus) and the Roman rhetorician Quintilian (*Institutio oratoria* 1.4.17ff.). Priscian offers his own version, *Institutiones* 2.15–18, *GL* 2:54.5–55.3. The developmental model was taken over by Robins, *A Short History of Linguistics*; for a more contextualizing approach, see Sluiter, "Antieke grammatica: autonoom of instrument?"; de Jonge, *Between Grammar and Rhetoric: Dionysius of Halicarnassus on Language, Linguistics and Literature*, chapter 3.

[11] For Priscian's awareness of a difference between the philosophers' two parts and the grammarians' eight, see Luhtala, *Grammar and Philosophy in Late Antiquity*, 129–37, referring especially to Priscian, *Institutiones* 11.3–7, *GL* 2:549.21–552.17.

[12] In the later tradition, the "Donatus" grammars start with noun, pronoun, verb, the "Priscian" grammars with noun, verb, participle. See within, section on Eberhard of Béthune, p. 585, with note 9.

[13] Also the principle on which etymology is based.   [14] Cf. Apollonius Dyscolus, *Syntax* III 6ff.

with tenses that are compatible with its marking as "past." Semantic analysis should underlie a judgment about the viability of combinations. Semantic clashes must be avoided, but if the same semantic feature is contributed by more words, that is not a problem. When applied to literary examples, analyses such as these allow the grammarian to pronounce a verdict on the merits of poetic speech with more authority and on explicit grounds. The grammarian can now demonstrate which expressions are in "perfect order," and which are not. Some instances of the latter category may be explained by poetic license, which automatically disqualifies them from being suitable for imitation.[15]

Because of its massive dimensions and complexity, the *Institutiones grammaticae* were not suitable for beginners. Priscian's shorter work, the *Institutio de nomine pronomine verbo* (Instruction on the Noun, Pronoun, and Verb), came to fulfill a prominent role as beginners' textbook in medieval grammatical teaching, as a competitor to Donatus' *Ars minor*. The work is mostly morphological in orientation. The instruction on the noun, which serves as an example in the excerpts presented here, starts from the observation that the noun has five declensions. Priscian takes us through the nominatives of the first through fifth declensions, then the oblique cases of every single declension. The morphology of pronoun and verb are presented in a similarly systematic way.

Priscian also wrote the *Partitiones*, a word-by-word discussion, in question-and-answer format, of the first verses of the twelve books of Vergil's *Aeneid*. In this work, Priscian assigns to each word its correct grammatical category and he pays attention to the metrical features of the poem.[16] The *Partitiones* demonstrate a pedagogical approach to poetry aimed at beginners: no attention is paid to interpretation, but rather, the text offers an occasion for grammatical exercises.

The *Institutiones grammaticae* is introduced by a letter of dedication to the consul Julian. During the Middle Ages, confusion of this consul with the earlier Emperor Julian the Apostate (AD 361–363) led to some misperceptions of Priscian as himself an apostate.[17] The end of the letter consists of a table of contents of the whole work, which follows below.

Translated from *Institutiones grammaticae*, *GL* 2 and 3, ed. Keil, and *Prisciani Caesariensis opuscula*, ed. Passalacqua, by permission.

---

[15] Baratin, *Naissance de la syntaxe*, 435–53, also relates Priscian's evaluation of abnormal language that goes under the guise of rhetorical figures to his engagement with the *auctores*.

[16] See Glück, *Priscians Partitiones und ihre Stellung in der spätantiken Schule*; Ziolkowski and Putnam, *The Virgilian Tradition*, 649–51.

[17] See within, sections on Alan of Lille (*Anticlaudianus*), p. 526 with note 61, and Hugh of Trimberg, p. 661 with note 9. Priscian was in fact a Christian; see Schmidt, "Priscianus," *Der Neue Pauly* 10.

PRISCIAN'S "TABLE OF CONTENTS"

[From the dedicatory letter of the *Institutiones grammaticae*, Priscian's table of contents:][18]

I have also added the titles of the sections of the whole work throughout the individual books, so that when one is looking for a specific topic, it may be found more easily in its several places.

The first book contains chapters on sound [*vox*] and its species; on the letter [*litera*]: what a letter is, on its kinds and species, on the force [*potestas*] of each single one, which ones change into which ones when the parts of speech are declined or compounded.

Book II is on the syllable: what a syllable is, of how many letters it can consist, and in what order and with what sound, on the accidents of the individual syllables; on the word [*dictio*]: what a word is, how it differs from a syllable; on speech [*oratio*]: what speech is, how many parts it has, on the characteristics of the parts of speech; on the noun/name [*nomen*]: what a noun is, on its accidents, how many kinds of proper names are there, how many kinds of common names, how many kinds of adjectives, how many derivatives; on patronyms: how many forms do they have, how are they derived, from what primitive forms; on the different endings of possessives and their rules.

Book III is on the comparatives and superlatives and their different endings: from what positive forms are they formed, and in what way? on diminutives: how many kinds are there, from what declensions of nouns, how are they formed?

Book IV is on words derived from nouns, from verbs, from participles, and from adverbs: how many kinds are there, from what primitive forms, how do they originate?

Book V is on how to recognize gender through the individual endings; on numbers; on forms [*figura*] and their compound structure;[19] on case.

Book VI deals with the nominative case through the individual endings of all nouns, both the ones ending in vowels and the ones in consonants, in [alphabetical] order; on the last and penultimate syllables of the genitives.

Book VII is on the other oblique cases, in the singular and plural.

---

[18] *GL* 2:3.3–4, 10.

[19] "Form" here refers to whether a noun is "simplex" (e.g. *magnus*), "compound" (e.g. *magn-animus*), or "derived from a compound" (*decompositus*, e.g. *magn-animi-tas*). "Compound structure" refers to the question of whether the newly formed word behaves as one compact whole, with case-endings only at the end of the whole word, or whether the parts of the compound continue to be felt as such, as in *respublica, reipublicae*. Cf. *Institutiones* 5.61, *GL* 2:180.12ff., and cf. *compago compositionis* "compound structure," ibid. 180.24f.

Book VIII is on the verb and its accidents.

Book IX is on the general rules for all conjugations.

Book X is on the perfect [past] tense.

Book XI is on the participle.

Books XII and XIII are on the pronoun.

Book XIV is on the preposition.

Book XV is on the adverb and the interjection.

Book XVI is on the conjunction.

Books XVII and XVIII are on syntax or the ordering of the parts of speech among themselves.

[The opening of the *Institutiones grammaticae* proper: we translate the chapter on sound and the beginning of the chapter on letters.[20]]

ON SOUND (VOICE) [*VOX*][21]

[1.1] According to the definition of the philosophers, sound (voice) is "very fine air when it is struck," or "that which it is the property of ears to perceive," i.e. the characteristic accident of ears.[22] The former definition is taken from the substance, the latter from the concept [*notio*], which the Greeks call *ennoia*, i.e. from the accidents. For it is an accident of sound to be heard, in as far as it depends on the sound itself.[23]

There are four different kinds of sound: "articulate," "inarticulate," "literate," "illiterate": "articulate" sound is compressed, that is to say it is expressed in combination with a mental meaning of the speaker. "Inarticulate" is the opposite, namely sound that does not originate in any mental affection. "Literate" sound can be written, "illiterate" sound cannot. Thus one may find certain articulate sounds that can be written and understood, e.g.: "I sing of the weapons and the man" (*Aeneid* 1.1), some that cannot be written, but can be understood, e.g. when human beings hiss or groan: for although these sounds indicate some intention of the person who delivers them, they cannot be written.

---

[20] Cf. the section on Aelius Donatus.   [21] *GL* 2:5.1–6.5

[22] These definitions ultimately derive from Stoic sources. See K. Hülser, *Die Fragmente zur Dialektik der Stoiker*, Fr. 479 (our text), 480 (Simplicius, on Aristotle, *Physics*, 425.31–426.6), 481 (Scholia on Dionysius Thrax, *GG* 1.3:482.5ff.).

[23] *Accidit enim voci auditus, quantum in ipsa est.* Cf. section on Aelius Donatus p. 87–8, note 30.

[1.2] But there are others that are called "inarticulate," because they do not signify anything, although they can be written, e.g. *coax*,[24]*cra*. Others are "inarticulate" and "illiterate": they can neither be written nor understood, e.g. creaking, lowing, and so on. We should know that these four types of sounds are produced by the four different general features of sound mentioned above, two different characteristics combining to produce each individual type.[25] The word *vox* ["sound," "voice"] comes either from *vocare* ["to call"], as *dux* ["leader"] comes from *ducere* ["to lead"], or *apo tou boô* [Greek "from the word 'to call' "], as some think.[26]

ON THE LETTER[27]

[1.3] The letter is the smallest part of a compound sound, i.e. sound that consists of the combination of letters; it is "the smallest" with reference to the whole complex made up of literate sound. For if that is the framework of reference, even long vowels can be found to be the shortest parts. Or [it may be called "smallest"] because, of all the things that can be divided, the shortest is that which cannot be divided. We can also describe it as follows: a letter is a sound that can be written separately.

It is called *litera* ["letter"] either as a *leg-iter-a* ["reading-road"],[28] because it provides a path for reading, or derived from *litura* ["erasure"], as some prefer, because the ancients used to write mostly on wax tablets. [1.4] They also called letters "elements" with an eye to the similarity with the elements of the world: as those elements combine to form any body, so these too when combined compose sound made up of letters as if it were a body, or rather as a real body. For if air is a body, it is also demonstrated that sound, which consists of air that is struck, is a body, since it both touches the ear, and can be divided three ways, which is a characteristic of a body, namely in height, breadth, and length—this explains why it can be heard everywhere. Moreover, individual syllables have height in their tone [*tenor*], thickness or breadth in their breathings, length in their measure [*tempus*].

---

[24] Conventional notation of the sounds of frogs, cf. Aristophanes, *Frogs* 209–10.

[25]

	articulate	literate
type 1	+	+
type 2	+	−
type 3	−	+
type 4	−	−

[26] Cf. the section on etymology, Part 2, p. 352; this etymology was a very successful one.

[27] *GL* 2:6.6–7.14 (beginning of *De litera*). Cf. sections on Donatus, Martianus Capella, and Isidore.

[28] Cf. section on Isidore, p. 235.

Thus, a letter is the notation of an element and as it were a picture of literate sound, which may be recognized by the quality and quantity of the form of the lines. Therefore, the difference between elements and letters is that "elements" are properly speaking the pronunciations themselves, while "letters" are the notations of those pronunciations. By a less proper use, however, we also call "elements" "letters" and vice versa. [1.5] For when we say that *r* cannot precede *p* in the same syllable, we are not speaking about letters, but about their pronunciations: for they can be so combined as far as the writing is concerned, but they cannot also be pronounced, unless the *r* comes after the *p*.

The forms of the letters that we use are twenty three in number, but there are many more pronunciations, since each individual vowel is found to have ten or more pronunciations each.[29] For example, the short letter *a* has four different sounds, when it has an aspiration and either an acute or a grave accent, and when it has an acute or grave accent without aspiration, like *hábĕo, habēmus* "I have, we have", *ábĕo, àbīmus* "I go away, we go away." The long *a* sounds six different ways: with aspiration and acute, grave, or circumflex accent, and again without aspiration with acute, grave, or circumflex accent, as in *hámīs, hàmōrum, hâmŭs* ["hook": dat./abl. plur., gen. plur., nom. sing.], *árae, àrārum, ârä* ["altar": nom. plur., gen. plur., nom. sing.]. Other vowels can be pronounced similarly.

ON THE SYLLABLE[30]

[2.1] A syllable is the consecutive combination of letters pronounced under one accent and in one breath; less properly, however, we also call the sounds of single vowels "syllables."[31] Yet, we can also define the syllable as follows: a syllable is sound expressed in letters, pronounced under one accent and in one breath without interruption.[32] Beginning from single letters, the syllable in Latin cannot proceed beyond six letters, as in *a* ["from"], *ab* ["from"], *arx* ["citadel"], *mars* ["Mars"], *stans* ["standing"], *stirps* ["stalk"].

---

[29] This whole section and its examples heavily rely on the model of Greek with its three accents (*acutus, gravis, circumflexus*) and its breathings. The accents originally represented a musical accent. However, by Priscian's time, the accent has long been turned into a stress accent, as in Latin.

[30] *GL* 2:44.1–7, the beginning of book 2.

[31] The etymology of Greek *sul-labê* suggests "taking together, combination": therefore a single letter can only be called a "syllable" in a less proper use of the term.

[32] In that case, the notion of "combination" is eliminated, hence single letters can also legitimately count as syllables.

ON THE WORD[33]

[2.14] A word is the smallest part of construed speech, i.e. speech that is put together in order: it is "a part" with reference to the whole understanding, i.e. the understanding of the complete sense. The reason this is stipulated is in order to avoid that somebody try to divide *vires* "powers" in two parts, namely *vi* and *res*, or something of the kind.[34] For this division does not happen with reference to the whole understanding. The difference between a word and a syllable is not just that a syllable is a part of a word, but also that a *dictio* ["word"], has something *dicendum* ["to be said"], i.e. to be understood. A syllable does not necessarily signify anything by itself. Therefore monosyllabic words can also be syllables in a way, but not really, since a syllable can never signify anything by itself: that is peculiar to words. Thus, if I say *a*, I know that this in itself is a syllable, but I do not recognize its length, nor its tone, nor its breathing, nor its meaning, until I will have recognized the word to which it belongs. For in *ara* "altar" of the gods, the penultimate *a* is long, bears the circumflex accent in the nominative case, and does not have an aspiration. But when it signifies a stable for swine,[35] the same penultimate syllable is short, it takes the acute accent, and is aspirated. When this same *a* is the preposition "from," it takes the grave accent, is long, and is not aspirated. So you see that the syllable by itself is deficient in the way just indicated, and cannot be discussed with precision, unless it be placed in a word.

ON SPEECH[36]

[2.15] Speech is the congruent ordering of words, displaying a complete meaning [*sententia*]. This is a definition of that kind of *oratio*, which is general, i.e. which is divided into kinds or parts.[37] For *oratio* is also the name for a work of rhetoric,[38] and also any individual word is often called by this name if it displays a complete meaning, as in imperatives and

---

[33] *GL* 2:53.8–26 (*de dictione*).

[34] I.e. in a case like this, *vi* and *res* are meaningless; they do not form part of the meaning of the whole *oratio*. We are discouraged to read "through power" and "things" in them, respectively.

[35] Priscian is referring to the word *hăra* "hog-stye"; of course, this word is written differently from *ara*, but Priscian is discussing Latin as if it were Greek. In both cases, people might be somewhat uncertain about which words should be aspirated and which ones should not, but in Greek the only difference would be not in the spelling proper of the words, but in the prosodic signs added to them: either a rough or a smooth breathing. Accordingly, some Roman grammarians considered the H not a separate letter, but just the sign of aspiration. Cf. e.g. sections on Aelius Donatus and Isidore, pp. 89 and 239.

[36] *GL* 2:53.27–56.27 (*de oratione*).   [37] I.e. "speech," "discourse."   [38] I.e. "a speech."

answers, which often consist of one word.[39] For example when I say "what is the highest good in life?," and someone answers "the honorable," I may react: "He answered with a good *oratio*."

According to the dialecticians, there are two parts of speech, noun and verb, because these by themselves, when combined with each other, may form a complete sentence [*oratio*]. The other parts they called *syncategoremata*, i.e. co-signifiers.

[2.16] According to the Stoics, however, there are five parts of speech: proper name [*nomen*], common name [*appellatio*], verb, pronoun or article, conjunction. For they took the participle with the verbs and called it "participial verb" or "verb with cases"; the adverbs they counted with the nouns or the verbs, and they called them as it were the adjectives of verbs. Pronouns they counted as articles, and called them definite articles, and the articles proper, which we do not have,[40] they named indefinite articles.

Alternatively, as others say, they counted the articles among the pronouns and called them articular pronouns. In this respect we Latins are still following them, although we do not find actual articles in our language. For when we say *idem* ["the same"], [Greek:] *ho autos*, we do not only produce the meaning of the prepositive article [the], but also of the pronoun in the same word. Similarly, *qui* ["who"], [Greek:] *hostis*, is understood as a postposed article together with a pronoun, an indefinite one according to some, or rather with a noun, as Apollonius has demonstrated with the best of arguments. [2.17] The preposition also the Stoics coupled with the conjunction, and they called it a prepositive conjunction.

Some people said there were nine parts of speech, adding the common noun separately from the proper nouns, others claimed there were ten, positing the infinitive verbs as a separate part, others again eleven, who counted the pronouns that cannot be combined with articles as a part to themselves. To these, others among the Greeks also added the designation [*vocabulum*] and the interjection, which we still preserve, but among the Latins some added the article, which in its pure separate form is not found in our language, as we demonstrated above.

There is, then, no other way to discriminate among the parts of speech, unless we pay attention to the specific meanings conveyed by each.

[2.18] The characteristic [*proprium*] of the noun is to signify substance and quality.[41] This is also true for the common noun [*appellatio*] and the designation [*vocabulum*]: those three are therefore one part of speech.

---

[39] *Oratio* is "a sentence," "a (complete) utterance" here. It translates Greek *logos*.

[40] Latin does not have articles.

[41] For the philosophical background to this definition, see Luhtala, *Grammar and Philosophy in Late Antiquity*, 84–90.

The characteristic of the verb is to signify action or passion or both, with moods and forms and tenses without case. This also goes for the infinitives, which should thus not be separated from the verb. The participle, however, is rightly separated from the verb, since it has both cases—which the verb lacks—and genders, like the nouns, but no moods, which the verb does have.

The characteristic of the pronoun is to replace a proper noun and to indicate definite persons. Therefore *quis* ["someone," "who?"] and *qui* ["who"] and *qualis* ["such as"] and *talis* ["such"] and *quantus* ["how great"] and *tantus* ["so great"] etc., which are indefinite or interrogative, or relative, or correlative,[42] should rather be called nouns than pronouns: for they are neither used to replace proper nouns, nor do they indicate definite persons, but they also have substance, although indefinite, and quality, although general—and this is the peculiar characteristic of the noun. [2.19] Therefore, they should be called nouns, although some of them are declined as pronouns. For it is not the declension, but the value [*vis*] and meaning [*significatio*] of every part of speech that needs to be considered.[43] For we find many nouns that are declined as pronouns and vice versa, indifferently. What would be more stupid than to call all the words that signify numbers "nouns," but one of them, *unus unius* ["one"], a pronoun because of its declension? But if the declension were proof of what kind of word one is dealing with, then all possessive pronouns and all participles should be counted as nouns, since they follow the nominal declension—but that lacks all sense. Therefore, it is not the declension, but the characteristic meaning that needs to be examined.

Since we have now spoken briefly about the characteristics of noun, verb, participle, and pronoun, I think it would not be out of place to go cursorily through what is peculiar to the other parts of speech as well.

[2.20] The characteristic of the adverb is to be put with the verb and not to be able to have a complete meaning without a verb, e.g. *bene facio* ["I do well"], *docte lego* ["I read learnedly"].[44] The difference between an adverb and a preposition is that the adverb can be put before and after verbs with or without words that have cases, e.g. *pone currit* [literally: "behind he is running"] and *currit pone* ["he is running behind"], *venit tempore longo post* ["he came a long time later"] and *post longo tempore venit* [literally: "later by a long time he came"]. Terence in *the Brothers*:[45] *post faceret tamen* ["he would do it later anyway"]. So if you find an adverb with a noun without a verb, you may know that this

---

[42] *Infinita* (indefinite): *quis*, "someone"; *interrogativa* (interrogative): *quis?*, "who?"; *relativa* (relative): *quantus*, "so great as"; *redditiva* (correlative): *tantus*, "so great."

[43] This important principle, which states that meaning is more important than form, was taken over from Apollonius Dyscolus: see Sluiter, *Ancient Grammar in Context*, 24, 64.

[44] For Priscian's work on the adverb, see Baratin and Garcea, *Autour du De Adverbio de Priscien*.

[45] Terence, *Adelphoe* 110.

has happened through an ellipse, as when I say *non bonus homo* ["not [adv.]—good man"] instead of *malus* ["bad"], I supply *est* ["is"].[46]

The characteristic of the preposition is to be preposed to words with cases, separately, [i.e.] by being put next to it, e.g. *de rege* ["about the king"], *apud amicum* ["with a friend"], but also connected to them by composition, both to words with cases and to words without them, e.g. *indoctus* ["not learned"], *interritus* ["not scared"], *intercurro* ["to run between"], *proconsul* ["proconsul"], *induco* ["to lead into"], *inspiciens* ["looking into"].

[2.21] The characteristic of the conjunction is to connect different nouns or whatever kinds of words with cases, or different verbs or adverbs, e.g. *et Terentius et Cicero* ["both Terence and Cicero"], *vel Terentius vel Cicero* ["either Terence or Cicero"], *et formosus et sapiens* ["both beautiful and wise"], *vel formosus vel sapiens* ["either beautiful or wise"]; *et legens et scribens* ["both reading and writing"], *vel legens vel scribens* ["either reading or writing"], *et ego et tu* ["both you and I"], *vel ego vel tu* ["either you or I"], *et facio et dico* ["I both do and say"], *vel facio vel dico* ["I either do or say"], *et bene et celeriter* ["both well and quickly"], *vel bene vel celeriter* ["either well or quickly"]; the preposition does not do this. Another difference is that prepositions can form compounds with verbs,[47] e.g. *sub-traho* ["to subtract"], *ad-dico* ["to say to"], *prae-pono* ["to put before"], *pro-duco* ["to draw out"], *de-hortor* ["to advise against"]. However, although the conjunction is a prepositive word, it is not found in compounds with verbs, e.g. *at, ast, sed* ["but"]. Another point: the preposition is always put before words with cases as a separate word, but the conjunction can be connected with all words either in pre- or in postposition.

ON CONSTRUCTION[48]

[17.1] In the previous books dealing with the parts of speech we have mostly followed the authority of Apollonius,[49] without omitting what was necessary from other sources, either Roman or Greek, or any additional new insight of our own. In the same way we will now also follow his tracks in dealing with the ordering [*ordinatio*] or construction

---

[46] *Non* is an adverb. According to Priscian, it is supposed to modify the verb *est*, which has been omitted through ellipse (although the explanation seems to waver in replacing *non bonus* with *malus*).

[47] Conjunctions can never do this.

[48] *GL* 3:107.24–109.3, the beginning of the *Syntax* (*Institutiones* books 17–18, known later as the *Priscianus minor*).

[49] Apollonius Dyscolus.

[*constructiones*] of words, which the Greeks call *suntaxis*, without refusing to add anything fitting found in others or by ourselves.[50]

[17.2] In what went before we discussed the individual sounds of words, as their system required. Now, however, we will be speaking about their ordering, which normally takes place in order to achieve the construction of complete speech.[51] We will have to look into this very carefully since it is most necessary for the discussion of all important authors [*auctores*].[52] For in the same way that the fitting combination of letters produces syllables, and syllables words, so too words produce speech [or: a sentence].[53] The traditional theory of the letters has also demonstrated this. Apollonius rightly declares that they are the first indivisible matter of the human voice.[54] That theory shows that combinations of letters do not happen randomly, but according to a most fitting ordering, hence the likelihood of the explanation of the name [of "letter"] as *leg-iter-ae* ["reading-road"], since they provide a road for reading when they are put into fitting order.[55] And the same thing happens to syllables, which are bigger items than letters, when the combinations made from their joining produce a complete word the way they should.

[17.3] It is clear, therefore, and logical that words too, being parts "for the construction of a complete sentence," that is [Greek:] *tou kata suntaxin autotelous logou*,[56] should accept a fitting structure. For the meaning [*sensibile*][57] produced by the individual words is as it were an element of the complete sentence. As the elements produce syllables by their combinations, so, too, the ordering of intelligibles produces an image of a syllable by the combination of words.[58] For a sentence is the grasp-as-a-whole of words[59] that are ordered

---

[50] Note that both the Greek word *sun-taxis* and the Latin *con-structio* refer primarily to the combination of words into greater wholes. This does not imply a concept of what we would call "syntactic relationships."

[51] This corresponds to Apollonius Dyscolus: [in Greek] "the *suntaxis* ('construction, combination') of these parts, in order to achieve the regularity [*katallêlotês*] of complete speech [*logos autotelês*]," Apollonius Dyscolus, *Syntax* I.1, see introductory note to this section.

[52] As is the case with Apollonius (*Syntax* I.1), so also for Priscian grammar is emphatically in the service of the interpretation of texts.

[53] A description of the "implicative hierarchy," an important structural element in Priscian (as in Apollonius Dyscolus); see introductory note.

[54] I.e. they are the smallest elements which cannot be divided into smaller ones still. Cf. Apollonius Dyscolus, *Syntax* I.2, and Scholia in Dionysius Thrax, *GG* I.iii, e.g. 31.6; 45.33 etc. (whenever Priscian and the Scholia on Dionysius Thrax coincide, this is usually taken to imply that they both go back to Apollonius Dyscolus as a common source, since neither can be shown to be directly dependent on the other).

[55] For this etymology, see above, Priscian, *Institutiones* 1.3, *GL* 2:6.12, and section on Isidore within, p. 235.

[56] Priscian closely follows Apollonius Dyscolus, *Syntax* I.2, here.

[57] *Sensibile* is used as a substantivized adjective: "that which is (mentally) perceived."

[58] I.e. what syllables are in morphology is what the (intelligible) meaning of individual words is in semantico/syntax: put together, the former produce a complete word, the latter a complete meaningful sentence.

[59] *Com-prehensio* is formed as a *calque* on *sul-labê* "taking, grasping together" (*sullabê* is, of course, the Greek term for syllable).

in the most fitting way, the way a syllable is the grasp-as-a-whole of letters that are most fittingly joined. And as the word consists of the conjunction of syllables, so the complete sentence consists of the conjunctions of words.

[The importance of the notion of parallelism, identity of structure (isomorphism) of different levels of linguistic description, is demonstrated in the following passages, which try to explain the rationale behind the order of different linguistic elements.[60]]

[17.12] A familiar question is that of the reason for the order of the elements, why "a" comes before "b" and so on. In the same way people also tend to inquire about the order of the cases, the genders, the tenses, and the parts of speech themselves.[61] It remains therefore to discuss those, and first of all the order of the parts of speech, although some, trying to find comfort for their lack of expertise, claim that one should not ask about those things, and suspect that the assignments of rank order are random. But as far as their opinion is concerned, it would turn out that in general nothing would be acceptable for its order or its mistake against order, and this is a completely stupid thing to think. But if they admit that there is order in some things, they have to admit it for all things.[62] Therefore, just as a complete sentence is produced by a fitting order, so the parts of speech have been handed down in a fitting order by the most learned authors of grammars [*artium scriptores*]: they put the noun first, the verb second, obviously because no sentence is complete without them. It is possible to demonstrate this from a construction that contains virtually all parts of speech. If one removes the noun or the verb from it, the sentence becomes incomplete. But if one takes away all the others, the sentence is not necessarily deficient. Example: *idem homo lapsus heu hodie concidit* ["the same [pron.] man [subst.] having slipped [part.], alas [interj.], today [adv.] has fallen down [verb + prep.]"].[63] See, it contains all parts of speech apart from the conjunction—if one added that, it would require [the addition of] another sentence.

[17.13] Therefore, if you remove the noun or the verb, the sentence will be incomplete, and will require a noun or a verb, e.g.[64] "the same Ø having slipped, alas, today has fallen down" or "the same man having slipped, alas, today Ø"; but if you take out the adverb, the sentence will not be incomplete at all, as in "the same man having slipped, alas, Ø has fallen down." Neither will it be incomplete after removal of the participle: "the same man Ø, alas,

---

[60]   *GL* 3:115.20–121.15, the order of the parts of speech.
[61]   Source here is Apollonius Dyscolus, *Syntax* I.13.
[62]   Stated forcefully, but obviously a logical fallacy: it does demonstrate the importance of the notion of "order" though.
[63]   Apollonius Dyscolus, *Syntax* I.14.
[64]   In the following the omitted part of speech has been indicated in the translation by Ø.

(today)[65] has fallen down." Nor after that of the preposition and the interjection: "the same man Ø Ø Ø has fallen Ø." Nor after that of the pronoun "the Ø man ØØØ has fallen." I am not saying, however, that a complete sentence cannot also consist of a pronoun and a verb, when we say "*I* am walking, *you* are walking." For completion of a sentence is achieved when a pronoun is used instead of a noun, and it fulfills the value of a noun in good order; at what times it may be put by itself instead of a noun will be demonstrated in the following, and I will also show what verbs are combined with just the nominatives, and which ones require oblique cases.

[17.14][66] The noun is also necessarily put before the verb, because acting and being acted on are characteristic of substance, which is named by nouns; from them[67] the characteristic of the verb, that is "action" and "passion,"[68] originates. The nominative is therefore present through understanding in the verbs themselves: without the nominative it is impossible to signify substance. The nominative is definite in the first and second persons, indefinite in the third, since the number of third persons are innumerable, unless an action is unique, as "Ø lightens, Ø thunders": even when we do not add the noun, these seem to be definite, since they refer to Jupiter alone. It has become usual also to call the other parts of speech by the name of this one: "verbs"—or, conversely, the common name of all of them is carried *par excellence* by this part of speech, which, as it were by its distinction, claims its ownership.[69]

[17.15] However, it is not unreasonable to ask why we do not arrange after the noun that part of speech that is being used instead of the noun, i.e. the pronoun, which takes the place of a noun to form a complete sentence together with a verb. The obvious justification for this state of affairs will be that pronouns, too, have been invented for the sake of verbs . . .[70]

[A discussion of the role of pronouns in constructions with verbs is omitted here.]

---

[65] The adverb "today" is read here in the text as edited by Keil. We suspect it should be omitted, since Priscian is showing that the successive removals of all the parts of speech except the noun and the verb will eventually leave a complete sentence.

[66] Cf. Apollonius Dyscolus, *Syntax* I.16.

[67] I.e. from nouns: they indicate the substances which are the source of any action or passion.

[68] *Actio* and *passio* refer to what verbs express, namely "action" and "passion," the latter in the technical sense of the passive correlate of action ("undergoing"). Substances "act" or "are acted upon." The action or the state of being acted upon (*actio, passio*) are expressed by the verb. Note that there is not necessarily a straightforward correspondence with the active and passive verb forms, i.e. logic (or semantics) and morphology may not coincide. We will normally translate *actio* and *passio* by "action" and "passion."

[69] Either the semantic range of "verb" has been extended from the verb *stricto sensu* to all the parts of speech, or it has been restricted from originally denoting all of them to being used specifically to denote the "best" of them. (Reference is, of course, to the common use of *verbum* to mean "word.")

[70] Priscian is offering arguments here for an ordering of the parts of speech that deviates from Donatus' order. Donatus has noun, pronoun, verb, and then the other parts; Priscian starts with the parts that are most crucial to

[17.18] The participle, too, is suitably placed after the verb, the part from which it also takes its origin as we demonstrated in our discussion of the verb. For it was necessary to procure a transfer of verbs into forms that have cases with genders—and these are accidents of the participle—so that they can be added even through oblique cases and be linked without a conjunction, as in *me legente proficio* ["while I am reading [abl. abs. partic.] I am making progress"][71] for *lego et proficio* "I am reading and I am making progress," because verbs can present no congruence with themselves.

[17.19] However, it is clear that [the value of] the very name attached to the participle[72] would not be preserved rightly, unless the participle were placed after the noun and the verb, since this part of speech is generally held to be dependent by positive confirmation on both of these. In the same way the neuter gender is placed after the masculine and feminine, which it both denies.[73] For unless we accept the priority of the parts placed before it, we could not use the names "participle" or "neuter," because this "neither" [*neutrum*] denies the two genders that precede it. The *parti-cipium* must also take part [*partem capiens*] in certain elements that go before it, and thus come into being, but it would be wrong to interpose a different part, i.e. the pronoun, adverb, conjunction, or something else, since the participle does not take any part in their characteristics. After the participle, the Greeks put the article, which we do not have, as I showed in the part on the pronoun . . .

[17.20] There is no question that the pronoun should follow the participle since, but for the reasons mentioned above, it almost had to be placed after the noun. But it also turns out that the preposition does not have the first position,[74] nor an older one than the other words, but follows the ones mentioned above. Thus it did not get its name from some peculiar meaning of its own, but because it may be put "before" the parts named above: if they did not have the earlier position in the list, the preposition cannot come into being—this is the same argument we used with respect to the participle. And this is, then, the reason for its place in the order: namely that it is put before the aforementioned parts either by combination or by compounding. So it is later by nature, but *qua* construction belongs in the beginning.

---

logic and the formation of propositions: noun and verb (followed by the other parts). Later grammarians have to choose between the Donatan and the Priscianic order, see for example the section on Eberhard of Béthune within, pp. 585, 591.

[71] Ablative absolute, although in classical Latin one would have expected a *participium coniunctum*. See within, the dossier on the ablative absolute, pp. 314–38.

[72] Namely as "taking part in."

[73] The participle "gives positive confirmation" to noun and verb, because it shares the characteristics of both, the neuter "denies" masculine and feminine, because it is "neither."

[74] I.e. the name *prae-positio* "placed before" has no influence on its ranking among the parts of speech.

[17.21] That the adverb is potentially an adjective of a verb is made clear too by its name. Therefore, just as the verb is in second position after the noun, so the adverb is rightly placed in second position after the preposition which, when used in combination, defends its own power as a word and is put before nouns or other words with cases. For in compounds it does not have the value of a word, but cedes that to the word to which it is added.

It is right that the conjunction be accepted after all the parts mentioned above, since it cannot signify any sense by itself without the material of the words that are mentioned before, just as chains for the body are useless if there are no bodies that can be chained by them.

We can also hold forth on the ordering of the parts through fuller arguments; but since this is not our main topic, let it suffice to say this much.

[The following selection presents Priscian's theory of grammatical irregularity, which is based on a notion of semantic incompatibility of the parts of speech in a construction.[75]]

[17.84] Note that some parts of speech contain the notions of others, for example, if I say *Ajax*, I also understand "one," in the singular. If I say *Anchisiades* ["Anchisiad, or son of Anchises"], I understand the genitive singular of the underived form of the name and "son" in the nominative singular. If I say *divinitus* "by divine providence, from the side of the gods" [adv.], I understand a noun with the preposition *ex* ["from"]. If I say *fortior* ["stronger"], I understand "more" and the positive grade of the underived form.

[17.85] The number of examples of this kind is endless. And it is not correct to say that, if I say *Anchisiades*, there is a deficiency, and the word "son" needs to be added to it.[76] . . . Nor is the word "one" lacking if I say *Ajax*, which is singular.[77]

[17.86] Thus, similarly, there are accidents in verbs, which are understood together with them, as in the indicative the "indication" itself, and the affirmation, which is understood from it.[78] That is why in response to a question we answer with the confirmative adverb *etiam* ["yes"], or with "no" or with the indicative verb, since that carries the affirmation within itself. To the question "are you reading?" we answer "yes," "no," or "I am reading." About these matters too we will speak in greater detail in the [part on] the construction of verbs.

---

[75] *GL* 3:155.16–24; 156.12–157.16. Cf. Apollonius Dyscolus, *Syntax* II.50ff.

[76] If such fullness of diction is cultivated and the word "son" is added, that is an example of poetic license. Examples follow of the addition or omission of prepositions by poets. After this digression, the argument picks up again a few lines later (at *GL* 3:156.12), where we continue the translation.

[77] I.e. there is no problem of ellipse or a deficiency in the expression here.

[78] An indicative verb such as "he walks" communicates the positive affirmation "that he walks."

The singular number is also comprised in the verb *scribo* "I am writing," and there is no need to add "one person." Clearly, the nominative of the pronoun is also part of the verb. Therefore, if the aforementioned elements are not lacking, because they are understood, the same goes for the pronoun. However, that does not mean that if it is added, the construction should be criticized.

[17.87] For sometimes elements that can be understood even if they are not added, are added in order to produce a fuller meaning. Example: "are you writing?" "yes, I am writing." Here, even though the adverb "yes" by itself evokes the understanding of the verb that precedes in the question, yet the addition of that verb does not make the speech faulty, but more certain. The promise becomes firmer by the double confirmation. Similarly we say "one man is walking" to distinguish him from the multitude of others, not because the word "man," when said in the singular, would not inherently also contain the notion of the number "one." Again, to deny a claim for everyone we say "nobody is walking, I haven't found anybody," and we add a singular number to a singular. So in the same way, when the statement is absolute and not meant to draw distinctions, we say *disputo, disputas* ["[I] debate, [you] debate"] without pronouns;[79] [17.88] but if we wish to make manifest the distinction from something else, we add the pronoun, whose characteristic it is to distinguish persons. For we do not add them in order to *indicate* persons, since the verbs already contain them. That is why infinitive verbs, since they lack the indication of persons, need verbs in the indicative, in order to get what is lacking from them. Thus, it is for the sake of distinctions, especially if a conjunction is used, that the pronoun is added to the verb, e.g. *ego quidem affui, tu vero non* ["*I* was present, but *you* were not"], or *ego quidem scripsi, ille vero legit* ["*I* wrote, but *he* read]—or [the pronoun is added] in order to produce a fuller meaning, but then too a distinction seems to be drawn from all others, e.g. Cicero in the first of his invectives [*In Catilinam* 1.1.3] *nos, nos, dico aperte, nos consules desumus* "we, we, I'm telling you openly, we consuls are failing." For we understand "nobody else but us."

[Priscian's discussion of the *causa incongruentiae*, or the explanation of irregularity:[80]]

[17.153] Some of the parts of speech have among their general accidents numbers and cases and genders, like the noun, pronoun, participle; some have persons and number, like the verb and the pronoun; some have tenses, like the verb and the participle; some have

---

[79] Of course the pronouns had to be added in the English translation. Priscian is discussing the difference between *disputo* and *ego disputo*. The latter is used when the person acting needs to be emphasized or distinguished from someone else.

[80] *GL* 3:182.23–186.16. Cf. Apollonius Dyscolus, *Syntax* III.13ff.

none of these, like the preposition, the adverb, the conjunction, and the interjection: these do not have any kind of flexion. The declinable parts of speech are accepted, on the basis of their own forms, into a congruent regularity [*ad convenientes consequentias*] of the numbers, genders, cases, persons, or tenses mentioned above; they must be brought to the right combination [*ad aptam coniunctionem*] by the construction, i.e. the disposition of the sentence. For example, a singular with a singular and a plural with a plural, when reference is made without transition to one and the same person,[81] as in *ego Priscianus scribo intellegens* ["I Priscian am writing, (while) understanding (nom. sing. participle)"] and *nos oratores scribimus intellegentes* ["we orators are writing (while) understanding (nom. plur. participle)"].

[17.154] When the verbs are transitive or reflexive [*refractiva*],[82] one may use different numbers, as in *docemus discipulum* ["we are teaching the student"] *docemus discipulos* ["we are teaching the students"]; *doceo discipulum* ["I am teaching the student"] and *doceo discipulos* ["I am teaching the students"]; *accuso vos* ["I am accusing you (plur.)"] and *prosum nobis* ["I am benefiting us"]. The same goes for genders:[83] *bonus homo et iustus et rectus est ille* ["he is a good man and just and straight," all marked for m. (sing.)], *bona mulier et casta et pudica est illa* ["she is a good woman and chaste and modest," all marked for f. (sing.)], *boni homines et iusti et recti sunt illi* ["they are good men and just and straight," all marked for m. (plur.)], *bonae mulieres et castae et pudicae sunt illae* ["they are good women and chaste and modest," all marked for f. (plur.)].

Similarly with the cases: *mei ipsius dolentis misereor* ["I am sorry for myself in my suffering," genitives], and *illius vel tui dolentis misereor* ["I am sorry for him or you in his/your suffering," genitives]; *te ipsum legentem video* ["I see you yourself (while you're) reading" ("I see that you yourself are reading")] and *me ipsum intellegentem sentio* ["I notice that I myself understand"]. So, when cases and genders and numbers refer to one and the same person, the congruence mentioned above should be observed.

[The opening of the *Institutio de nomine pronomine verbo*[84]]

---

[81] "Without transition," i.e. when the same person is not both the agent and the person acted upon (if the same person were to be both the agent and the person acted upon, s/he could be referred to by using different cases). For Priscian's theory of transitivity, see Luhtala, "On the Concept of Transitivity in Greek and Latin Grammars."

[82] For the term *refractivus* referring to reflexive action (i.e. where agent and patient are the same), cf. Priscian, *Institutiones* 17.136 (said of pronouns there), *GL* 3:176.17f.

[83] I.e. every element in the sentence referring to the same entity ("without transition") must be congruent in gender also.

[84] Passalacqua, ed., 5.1ff (= *GL* 3:443.1–444.4).

BOOK OF INSTRUCTION BY THE GRAMMARIAN PRISCIAN ON THE NOUN, THE PRONOUN, AND THE VERB

All the nouns that Latin eloquence uses undergo flection in five declensions, which are ordered on the basis of the order of the vowels used to form the genitive. The first declension then, has a genitive ending in the diphthong *ae*, e.g. *hic poeta huius poetae* ["the poet (nom.)," "of the poet (gen.)"]; the second is the one of which the case mentioned above ends in a long *ī*, e.g. *hic doctus huius doctī* ["learned (nom.)," "of the learned (gen.)"].[85] The third one [has a genitive ending] in short *ĭs*, e.g. *hic pater, huius patrĭs* ["the father (nom.)" "of the father (gen.)"]. The fourth [has a genitive ending] in long *ūs*, e.g. *hic senatus huius senatūs* ["the senate (nom.)" "of the senate (gen.)"]. The fifth [has a genitive ending] in *e-i* divided over two syllables, e.g. *hic meridies huius meridie-i* ["the afternoon (nom.)," "of the afternoon (gen.)"].

Now, the nominative of the first declension can have two final letters, *a* and *s*, but three endings, *a*, *as*, and long *ēs*, e.g. *haec syllab-a huius syllab-ae* ["the syllable (nom.)," "of the syllable (gen.)"], *hic Aene-as huius Aene-ae* ["Aeneas (nom.)," "of Aeneas (gen.)"], *hic Anchis-ēs huius Anchis-ae* ["Anchises (nom.)," "of Anchises (gen.)"]. Words ending in *a*, whether Greek or Latin, that are masculine, feminine, or common,[86] belong to the first declension, e.g. *hic citharista huius citharistae* ["the lyre-player (nom.)," "of the lyre-player (gen.)": Greek word; masculine], *hic scriba huius scribae* ["the scribe (nom.)," "of the scribe (gen.)": Latin word; masculine], *haec Calliopea huius Calliopeae* ["Calliopea (nom.)," "of Calliopea (gen.)": Greek word; feminine], *haec regina huius reginae* ["the queen (nom.)," "of the queen (gen.)": Latin word; feminine], *hic* and *haec advena, huius advenae* ["the foreigner (m./f., nom.)," "of the foreigner (m./f., gen.)": Latin word; masculine and feminine]. Exceptions are *una ulla nulla sola tota alia utra altera* ["one, any, none, one only, all of one, other, which one (of two), the other (of two); all f.]," which follow the declension of pronouns that have a genitive ending in *ius*; just like the ones that are compounds: *ali-qua ne-qua si-qua* ["someone, lest one, if one (all f.)"]. Neuter words ending in *a* are Greek and belong to the third declension: for the Greek genitive *tos* changes to *tis* in our language, e.g. *hoc poema huius poema-tis* ["the poem (nom.)," "of the poem (gen.)"], *hoc emblema huius emblematis* ["the emblem (nom.)," "of the emblem (gen.)"], *hoc toreuma huius toreumatis* ["the carved relief (nom.)," "of the carved relief

---

[85] Note again the use of the deictic pronoun *hic*, gen. *huius* to indicate the difference in case, gender, number: it is used where the Greek examples use the article, which Latin of course does not have.

[86] I.e. either masculine or feminine in the same form.

(gen.)"].[87] The names of the letters are indeclinable both in Greek and in Latin, and they are neuter, e.g. *alpha, beta, a, b.*

The Greek words that end in *as* or *es* have a genitive in Greek that ends in the diphthong *ou* or in *a;* in Latin they belong to the first declension, e.g. [Greek] *ho Lusias tou Lusiou,* [Latin] *hic Lysias huius Lysiae* ["Lysias (nom.)," "of Lysias (gen.)"], [Greek] *ho Antas tou Anta,* [Latin] *hic Antas huius Antae* ["Antas (nom.)," "of Antas (gen.)"], [Greek] *ho Priamidês tou Priamidou,* [Latin] *hic Priamides huius Priamidae* ["The son of Priam (nom.)," "of the son of Priam (gen.)"]. Take note though that if one finds proper names of the same form as patronymics, the ancients tend to pronounce them rather according to the third declension, e.g. *hic Thucydides huius Thucydid-is* ["Thucydides (nom.)," "of Thucydides (gen.)"], *hic Euripides huius Euripid-is* ["Euripides (nom.)," "of Euripides (gen.)"]. They do the same with foreign names of the same ending, e.g. *hic Tigranes huius Tigran-is* ["Tigranes (nom.)," "of Tigranes (gen.)"], *hic Mithridates huius Mithridat-is* ["Mithridates (nom.)," "of Mithridates (gen.)"], *hic Ariobarzanes huius Ariobarzan-is* ["Ariobarzanes (nom.)," "of Ariobarzanes (gen.)"]. There are also a couple of other cases in which one may find that they have done the same.[88]

[The transition between the section on nouns and that on pronouns:[89]]

For brevity's sake, let it suffice to say this much for now for the instruction of boys. A more penetrating explanation of the rules both for penultimate and last syllables, relevant for the declension of every noun, you may find in the seven books that we wrote about the noun, especially in books VI and VII. They discuss the nominative and the oblique cases and base themselves on the testimony of many authors.

Pronouns about which there is no dispute are fifteen in number in Latin. There are eight primitive ones,[90] one of the first person: *ego* ["I"] one of the second person: *tu* ["you"], and six of the third person: *sui* ["of oneself"], *ille* ["he"], *ipse* ["he himself"], *hic* ["he"], *iste* ["that man"], *is* ["he"]. There are seven derivative ones: *meus* ["my"], *tuus* ["your"], *suus* ["his/her/its"], *noster* ["our"], *vester* ["your (plur.)"], *nostras* ["of our country"], *vestras* ["of your country"].

---

[87] An article decorated by engraving in relief.

[88] This is Keil's text. Passalacqua reads: *et in aliis tamen quibusdam Graecis auctoritate idem fecisse inveniuntur, ut hic Orontes huius Orontis* "There are also a couple of other Greek words where they have done the same, on the strength of the usage of the great authors, e.g. *hic Orontes huius Orontis* ['Orontes (nom.)' 'of Orontes (gen.)']," referring to *Institutiones* 6.61 (*GL* 2:245.13–14). However, the parallel is not very persuasive (in the latter text, reference is to names being declined both according to the first and the third declension), and the use of *auctoritate* by itself seems strange in this context.

[89] Passalacqua, ed., 21.3ff. (= *GL* 3:449.1–35).   [90] "Primitive," i.e. that are not derived from other forms.

The primitive ones have two declensions, the derivative ones three. One of the declensions of the primitive pronouns has both genitive and dative ending in *i*, and accusative and ablative in long *ē*, e.g. *ego tu*, [gen.:] *mei tui sui*, [dat.:] *mihi tibi sibi*, [acc.:] *me te se*, [abl.:] *a me a te a se* ["from me, from you, from him-/her-/itself"].[91] The vocative only occurs in the second person, and is similar to the nominative: *o tu*! The plural pronouns of the first and second person are declined similarly[92] (the pronoun of the third person that was mentioned above, *sui*, which does not have a nominative, is shared by both numbers):[93] [nom./acc.:] *nos vos*, [gen.:] *nostrum* or *nostri vestrum* or *vestri*, [dat./abl.:] *nobis vobis*. In the plural, only the second person has a vocative, which is the same as the nominative and accusative: *o vos*. The reason why *sui* does not have a nominative is that in Greek neither does *hautou* or *heautou*, *huius sui* ["of him-/her-/itself"].[94] We have discussed this at greater length in the [second] book on the pronoun. The other type of declension occurs in the remaining five primitive pronouns, whose genitive ends in *ius* and whose dative ends in *i* in all three genders. The accusative and ablative singular and all the plural cases retain, at least in the masculine and neuter forms, the endings of the nouns of the second declension, and in the feminine those of the first declension: *ille illius illi* [m.: "he," nom. gen. dat.]; *illa illius illi* [f.: "she," nom. gen. dat.]; *illud illius illi* [n.: "it," nom. gen. dat.]; *illum illam illud* [acc. sing.: "he, she, it"] (for it is necessary that the neuters have the same nominative and accusative);[95] *ab illo ab illa ab illo* [abl. "he, she, it"]. Note that *hic haec hoc* [gen. *huius*, dat. *huic*] always have their dative end in *c* to distinguish it from the interjection *hui* ["hey!"].

From the seven derivative pronouns, five are declined according to the rule of the mobile [adjective] nouns:[96] i.e. the masculine and neuter are of the second declension, the feminine of the first; they are the following: *meus tuus suus noster vester* ["my, your, his/her/its, our, your (plur.)"]. The remaining two pronouns are common,[97] and belong to

[91] The ablative forms are preceded by the preposition *a(b)* "from," in order to disambiguate the case: *a* only takes the ablative.

[92] I.e. to each other.

[93] I.e. the same forms are used for the plural and the singular, so there is no need for Priscian to discuss them separately here.

[94] The reflexive pronoun is only used in the oblique cases. Apollonius Dyscolus devotes a long section to this problem. Priscian discusses the same issue at more length in the *Institutiones* 13.22, *GL* 3:14.18ff.; the lacking nominative at 13.23, *GL* 3:15.6ff. *Huius sui* is a fairly bizarre-looking calque on Greek *he-autou*.

[95] This remarks explains the form *illud*, where the acc. neuter is, according to the general rule, equal to the nom.—this explains why it does not look like a second-declension ending.

[96] The *nomina mobilia* are the adjectives of three endings like *bonus bona bonum*. (The term *nomina* can refer to both substantives and adjectives.)

[97] I.e. its forms are shared by the masculine and feminine. Passalacqua reads "*id est nostras vestras*" here, but that rather looks like a gloss.

the third declension: *hic* and *haec*[98] *nostras vestras, huius nostratis vestratis* ["belonging to our country, belonging to your country" (nom. m. and nom. f.), "of the one belonging to our country, of the one belonging to your country" (gen. m. and gen. f.)].

---

[98] *Hic etc.* used instead of the article again, to indicate that the following word can be either masculine or feminine.

BOETHIUS, *DE TOPICIS DIFFERENTIIS*, BOOK 4, CA. 523

INTRODUCTION

De topicis differentiis (On the Different Topics) was most likely the last of the works on logic that Boethius wrote before his arrest in 523 and execution in 524.[1] In addition to his translations of Aristotle's logic, Boethius' logical works consist of two commentaries on Porphyry's *Isagoge*, treatises on categorical and hypothetical syllogisms, a commentary on Aristotle's *Categories*, two commentaries on Aristotle's *De interpretatione*, a book on methods of analysis (*Liber de divisione*), a commentary on Cicero's *Topica*, a commentary (lost) on Aristotle's *Topics*, and *De topicis differentiis*. Boethius' study of dialectical and rhetorical topics in *De topicis differentiis* was not intended primarily as a contribution to rhetorical theory, but rather as a further examination of dialectical method and its use of topics or "seats" of arguments, that is, the conceptual "places" (literally *topoi* or *loci*) from which arguments can be discovered ("invented"). In Aristotelian dialectic, a topic is either a strategy of argumentation that can be used to construct arguments, or a principle that can support arguments.[2] In *De topicis differentiis*, Boethius devotes books 1–3 to dialectical topics. In the final part of the treatise, book 4, he considers rhetorical topics of invention as comparanda with the methods of dialectic.

But in its medieval reception, *De topicis differentiis* achieved great authority not only as a reference work on dialectic, but also as a primary textbook on rhetoric. De Rijk counts about 170 extant manuscripts of the work dating from the tenth to the fifteenth centuries, a number that attests to its wide influence across medieval academic communities.[3] Book 4, however, came to have a life of its own as a technical manual on rhetoric, frequently included as a separate rhetorical text in manuscripts with copies of the *De inventione* and the *Rhetorica ad Herennium*. From the tenth century onwards it provided the information

---

[1] De Rijk, "On the Chronology of Boethius' Works on Logic," 154.
[2] *Boethius's De topicis differentiis*, trans. Stump, 16.
[3] De Rijk, "On the Chronology of Boethius' Works on Logic," 153 note.

for glosses on the Ciceronian rhetorics.[4] Fulbert of Chartres (d. 1028) wrote a pedagogical poem summarizing book 4.[5] Abelard's commentary on the dialectical books of *De topicis differentiis* includes an excursus on rhetorical argument that develops the ideas contained in book 4.[6] By the early thirteenth century, book 4 had in effect supplanted the Ciceronian rhetorics as the approved textbook for extra-curricular reading and lectures on rhetoric at Paris, and during the thirteenth and fourteenth centuries, it was the subject of a small number of *quaestio* commentaries.[7]

Book 4 of *De topicis differentiis* was an important conduit for the Ciceronian theory of the *circumstantiae*, that is, the circumstances or attributes that define (delimit) the case to be argued and that could serve as topics of rhetorical invention. Boethius lists these seven circumstances as who, what, where, when, why, how, and by what means (1205D). The theory of the circumstances derives from the (lost) handbook of Hermagoras of Temnos, a Greek rhetorician of the second century BC. Hermagoras used the seven circumstances to distinguish the thesis, an abstract or unlimited question, from the hypothesis, a controversy that was limited to a particular situation.[8] In his *De inventione*, Cicero incorporated the seven circumstances into an elaborate system of topics for the attributes of the person and the act, to be used for inventing arguments in the part of the oration known as "proof" (*confirmatio*).[9] Boethius' contribution was twofold. First, he simplified Cicero's intricately calibrated system of topics. Second, and more important, he elevated the seven circumstances to a comprehensive position so that they define the essence of rhetorical method and represent the whole discipline of rhetoric. For Boethius, as for Cicero, rhetoric should only treat the hypothesis, that is, "questions hedged in by a multitude of circumstances" (1205D). But where previously the circumstances were absorbed into a larger apparatus of topics, Boethius brings them forward as the feature that distinguishes rhetorical method conclusively from dialectic. The circumstances now represent the key procedure of rhetoric, topical invention.

For medieval rhetorical and literary theory, the implications of *De topicis differentiis* 4—a text that may strike modern readers as arcane or excessively technical—were

---

[4] Ward, *Ciceronian Rhetoric*, 80, 100; Ward, "From Antiquity to the Renaissance," 54. Munk Olsen finds eighteen copies of book 4 on its own, mostly in manuscripts containing one or both of the Ciceronian rhetorics: see his *L'Étude des auteurs classiques latins aux XIe et XIIe siècles*, 132.

[5] *The Letters and Poems of Fulbert of Chartres*, ed. and trans. Behrends, 266–7.

[6] For discussion and edition, see Fredborg, "Abelard on Rhetoric."

[7] On the commentaries, see Fredborg, "Rhetoric and Dialectic," 179–87.

[8] In Hermagoras' theory, the thesis and hypothesis were both accepted as matter for rhetoric; but in later theory, only the hypothesis was admitted as a proper rhetorical question. See *De inventione* 1.6.8, and for details and references, see Leff, "Boethius' *De differentiis topicis*, Book IV," 10, and Copeland, *Rhetoric, Hermeneutics, and Translation*, 67–9.

[9] *De inventione* 1. 24.34–1.28.43.

profound. Boethius' interest, of course, was not to generate a theory of rhetoric, but rather to examine rhetorical topics as special forms of dialectical topics, and rhetoric as an art subordinate to the master logic of dialectic. Yet his influential treatise presents the *circumstantiae* as a coherent principle that sums up the art of rhetorical invention.

The art of invention based on a manageable and concrete set of topics that relate to persons and their actions was applicable to any kind of discourse that involved discovering arguments. The inventional scheme of the *circumstantiae* found its way into commentary and hermeneutics, rhetorical teaching on composition and literary portraiture, preaching manuals, and even confession. Bede even finds the system useful in his scriptural commentaries, as a way of apprehending methods of narrative proof in the Bible.[10] The circumstances make a vivid appearance in Carolingian commentaries, as a scheme that structures the *accessus ad auctores*. Remigius of Auxerre uses the full apparatus of seven circumstances in his *accessus* to Martianus Capella, applying the questions to the author and his work:

> First to be considered are the seven topics, that is circumstances, which are established at the beginning of every authentic book: who, what, why, in what manner, where, when, by what faculties.

The topic "who" corresponds to the author, Martianus; "what" to the work and its title; "why" to Martianus' motivation for writing the work; "in what manner" to his method or form (verse and prose); "where" to the place of composition; "when" to the time it was written; and "by what faculties" to the matter or material, that is, the subject matter of the work.[11] The elements of this system lie behind many of the later forms of the *accessus ad auctores* as well, and allowed the commentator to generate new arguments about authorial intention and the work's meaning. The circumstantial scheme is embedded in the *artes poetriae*: Matthew of Vendôme uses it to teach how to produce a *descriptio* of a person based on the attributes of character and action, and John of Garland uses it in his account of invention.[12] The Ciceronian–Boethian system of circumstances of the person and the act lies behind the subtle crafting of character portraits (*descriptiones*) in the *General Prologue* of the *Canterbury Tales*. It can be found as a preacher's device for inventing an argument, as in Thomas of Chobham's art of preaching, and it enters even into the

---

[10] See, for example, *Explanatio Apocalypsis*, PL 93: 135C. See Ray, "Bede, the Exegete, as Historian."

[11] *Commentum in Martianum Capellam*, ed. Lutz, 1:65; and see Lutz, "One Form of *Accessus* in Remigius' Works," and Silvestre, "Le schéma 'moderne' des *accessus*."

[12] See within, Matthew of Vendôme, *Ars versificatoria*, and John of Garland, *Parisiana poetria*.

psychology of penitential casuistry ("who, what, where, with whom, how often, why, in what way, when").[13]

The system of the rhetorical circumstances penetrates so deeply and broadly into medieval literary and persuasive discourse that it would be impossible and unnecessary to trace every use of it directly to Boethius' *De topicis differentiis*. Rather, we should say that Boethius' work gave this inventional system a coherence that accounted for its lasting popularity and the multiplicity of its applications. The centrality of book 4 of *De topicis differentiis* as a textbook ensured the pervasive power of its definition of rhetoric.

Translation reprinted from *Boethius's De topicis differentiis*, trans. Stump (with minor adaptations), by permission.[14]

DE TOPICIS DIFFERENTIIS, BOOK 4

[1205C] If anyone carefully examines and considers the title of [this] work, since we wrote *De topicis differentiis*, he will be bound to expect from us not only that we give the differentiae [which distinguish] the dialectical Topics from one another, or even that we give the differentiae [which distinguish] the rhetorical Topics [from one another], but much more that we separate the dialectical from the rhetorical Topics. And we consider that we can undertake this more effectively if we begin the discussion with the very nature of the disciplines [*facultatum*].[15] For when the similarity and dissimilarity of dialectic and rhetoric have been shown, we must draw the likenesses and differences of the Topics which serve the disciplines from the forms of the disciplines themselves.

The dialectical discipline examines the thesis only; a thesis is a question not involved in circumstances. The rhetorical [discipline], on the other hand, investigates [1205D] and discusses hypotheses, that is, questions hedged in by a multitude of circumstances. Circumstances are who, what, where, when, why, how, by what means.[16]

Again, if dialectic ever does admit circumstances, such as some deed or person, into the disputation, it does not do so for their own sake [*principaliter*], but it transfers the whole

---

[13] For Thomas of Chobham, see within, *Summa de arte praedicandi*. For examples of casuistries, see Robertson, "A Note on the Classical Origin of 'Circumstances' in the Medieval Confessional."

[14] 79–95 of Stump's translation. Source in *PL* 64:1205–16 (references to the *PL* column numbers are noted in Stump's text and here). We have not reproduced Stump's extensive notes in full, but many of the annotations here are based on Stump's explanations. Stump's outline of this book is reproduced at the end.

[15] Stump, 141–2 note 3, points out that *De inventione* provides the structure of discussion of rhetoric in the first half of this book.

[16] I.e. who did it, what was done, where, when, why, how was it done, with what aid or by what means was it done?

force of the circumstances to the thesis it is discussing. But if rhetoric takes up a thesis, [1206C] it draws it into the hypothesis.[17] Each investigates its own material but takes up that of the other so that the matter depends on the discipline more suited to it.

Again, dialectic is restricted to question and answer. Rhetoric, on the other hand, goes through the subject proposed in unbroken discourse. Similarly, dialectic uses complete syllogisms. Rhetoric is content with the brevity of enthymemes.[18]

This, too, produces a differentia, namely, that the rhetorician has as judge someone other than his opponent, someone who decides between them. But for the dialectician, the one who is the opponent also gives the decision because a reply [which is], as it were, a decision is elicited from the opponent by the cunning of the questioning.

So every difference between these [disciplines] consists in matter, use, or end. In matter, because thesis and hypothesis are the matter put under the two of them. [1206D] In use, because one disputes by question, the other by unbroken discourse, or because one delights in complete syllogisms, the other in enthymemes. In end, because one attempts to persuade a judge, the other attempt to wrest what it wants from the opponent.

With these things considered beforehand, we will enumerate a little later both rhetorical questions which are posited in issues [constitutionibus][19] [1207A] and Topics of the appropriate kind. For the immediate present, it seems to me that we must examine the whole discipline quite briefly, [and this is] a great and difficult task. The internal complication of the rhetorical art is so great that it cannot easily be examined; and it can scarcely even be understood by [one] hearing [it explained], still less is it easily understood by [one] discovering [it for himself]. We have received no tradition from the ancient authors on this subject, for they taught the particulars but did not work at the whole at all.[20] Let us undertake this missing part of [their] teaching as best we can.

---

[17] Rhetoric deals in particulars, particular actions by particular people at particular times; dialectic deals with abstract questions not tied to individuals. Rhetoric may deal with abstractions in order to make a case about an individual person or action; dialectic may use particulars to help illustrate or establish a general point (Stump, 142 note 6).

[18] Aristotle, *Rhetoric*, 1255b15–16.

[19] I.e. status. Stump, 142 note 8, at 1209A, "Boethius says that the technical terms *quaestio* and *constitutio* are synonymous: both refer to the issue that occasions a debate or legal case."

[20] Cf. Aristotle, *Rhetoric*, 1354a: "As things are now, those who have composed *Arts of Speech* have worked on a small part of the subject . . . they give most of their attention to matters external to the subject" (Kennedy, trans., *Aristotle on Rhetoric*, 29–30). Stump, 143 note 12, points to the oddness of Boethius' statement, given that his account of the genus and species of rhetoric is a standard element of the Ciceronian tradition. Perhaps, as Stump suggests, his claim to originality should be restricted to his attempt to relate the divisions of rhetoric to one another. In these terms, the contribution of his treatise is unprecedented: to place the circumstances at the theoretical center of rhetoric.

Accordingly, we will talk about the genus of the art, [its] species, matter, parts, instrument, parts of the instrument, work, function of the speaker, the end—and after that, about questions and Topics.[21]

So let us take the beginning of the discussion from what is to be observed [about the subject] in general.

The genus of rhetoric [1207B] is discipline. [Its] species are [these] three: judicial, epideictic, and deliberative.[22]

It is clear that the genus is what we said it is. The species are those we mentioned above because the whole discipline of rhetoric is in them. It is complete in the judicial genus of cases, likewise in the epideictic or the deliberative. But these are the genera of cases; for all cases, whether special or individual, fall under one of these three genera.[23] For example, special cases, such as that of an offense against the sovereignty of the people or that of extortion by a provincial governor, fall under the judicial genus. Under deliberative, every case that involves consultation [*consultatio*]: for example, in special cases, if you treat of war or peace, in individual cases, if you treat of the war or peace of Pyrrhus. Similarly in epideictic [cases], every one that has to do with praise or censure is put under the epideictic genus: for example, in a special case, the praise of a brave [1207C] man, in an individual case, the praise of Scipio.

The matter of this discipline is every subject proposed for a speech. But, for the most part, it is a political question.

The species of rhetoric come into this [matter, namely, the political question] and take [the] matter to themselves as if they were forms of a certain sort; and in a threefold way they constitute the form [of rhetoric], as will be clear later, so that the political question, which heretofore was without form as far as the species go, accepts bounds and becomes

---

[21] The elements considered here in Boethius' influential text—genus of the art, its species, matter, parts, instrument, parts of the instrument, work, function, and end (or purpose)—came to form the matter of the "extrinsic prologue" of twelfth-century academic commentary: see within, introduction to Thierry of Chartres' commentary on Cicero's rhetoric, pp. 407–11.

[22] I.e. what in Ciceronian rhetoric are called the three "genres" of rhetoric or "classes" of rhetorical subjects: *De inventione* 1.5.7. However, Cicero places the discipline of rhetoric as a whole under the genus of politics or civil science (*De inventione* 1.5.6); rhetoric is then divided into "kinds" or genres, the subdivisions of which, in turn, would be species of cases. Cf. Stump, 144 note 17.

[23] The definition of "case," as transmitted through Cicero from his source, the Greek rhetorician Hermagoras of Temnos, is "a matter involving a controversy conducted by a speech with the introduction of definite individuals" (*De inventione* 1.6.8), that is, a dispute conducted verbally involving specific persons. Boethius' terms here are difficult to follow because he now seems to have made what he previously called the "species" of rhetoric into "genera" of cases. But this seeming inconsistency can be clarified. Stump's explanation is helpful: "[J]udicial, epideictic, and deliberative occur in two different schemes of division and are species (and subaltern genera) of two different genera—of *rhetoric*, in one division, and of *case*, in the other" (144 note 17).

subject to one or another of the species of rhetoric.[24] For example, a political question heretofore without form becomes a political question established in the judicial genus when it has accepted from the judicial genus the bounds [which are] the just. When it has taken the advantageous or the proper from the deliberative genus, then it will become a political question established in the deliberative genus of cases. If it has taken the good from the epideictic genus, then it is an epideictic [1207D] political question.[25] The species come from rhetoric into the matter, because no discipline can work on its matter except insofar as it employs its parts. For if all its parts were absent, rhetoric itself would also be absent. But since it has been said that the species of rhetoric are the genera of cases, they are so in this way. Of all the actions [*negotiorum*] involved in the political question, the genus is judicial when they have been bounded by the just; and of all those involved in the political question, the genus is deliberative when they have been bounded by the proper or the advantageous; and also of all those involved in the political question, the genus is epideictic when they have been bounded by the proper only or by the good. But this suffices for these things.

[1208A] Now we must give our attention to the parts of rhetoric. There are five parts of rhetoric: invention, arrangement, style, memorization, delivery. They are called parts because if an orator lacks any of these, the discipline is incomplete, and therefore it is right to call those things which make the oratorical discipline a whole the parts of that discipline.

Since these are the parts of the rhetorical discipline and make the rhetorical discipline whole, it must be that where rhetoric is whole (namely, in the appropriate species), the parts themselves also follow. So, all the parts of rhetoric will be in the species of rhetoric.[26] And therefore they are also employed in the discussion of political actions, which are given form by the aforementioned species of rhetoric. So, invention, arrangement, style, [1208B] memorization, and delivery are equally suitable for a judicial, deliberative, or epideictic action.

Since almost every discipline uses an instrument to do what it is able to do, there will also be an instrument for the rhetorical discipline. This is discourse; and it is used partly in the political genus and partly not.[27] But we are talking now about discourse which involves

[24] See Stump, 145 note 21: "Boethius here is playing with the Aristotelian analysis of things into matter and form. The 'matter' of rhetoric is the political question, and the 'form' of rhetoric is the three species into which rhetoric is divided."

[25] See *De inventione* 2.4.12: the inquiry in a trial (judicial genre) is about the just; in epideictic, about the honorable; in deliberative (political), about the advantageous and honorable.

[26] That is, all the five parts of rhetoric will be found in each of its species (or in Ciceronian language, "genres" or classes): each kind of speech needs all five parts of rhetoric.

[27] "Political genus": the meaning here is most likely political cases; see Stump, 145 note 28.

a question or which is suitable for the purpose of untangling a question. Discourse used in the political genus runs along without a break; but that which is not used in political cases unfolds in questions and answers. The first is called rhetorical; the second, dialectical. The latter differs from the former, first because the former examines a political hypothesis [but] the latter, a thesis; [and] then because the former is carried on by unbroken discourse [but] the latter, by interrupted discourse, and because rhetorical discourse has a judge in addition [1208C] to an opponent, but dialectical discourse uses the same person as both judge and opponent.

This rhetorical discourse has six parts: the prooemium, which is the exordium, the narrative, the partition, the confirmation, the refutation, the peroration; and these are the parts of the instrument of the rhetorical discipline. Since rhetoric is in all its species, [these] will be in all the species. Nor will they be in [the species more] than they will assist the things that are carried on by means of those same [species].[28] So, the series of prooemium, narrative, and the rest must be in the judicial genus of cases, and [these things] must be in the epideictic and deliberative genera as well.

The work of the rhetorical discipline is to teach and to move; but this is accomplished by just those same six instruments, that is, the parts of discourse.

Since the parts of rhetoric are parts of a discipline, [1208D] they are themselves also disciplines. Therefore, they themselves also take a share in the use of the parts of discourse as instruments; and in order that the parts of the instrument may function by the parts of rhetoric [*his operentur*], it will be in the parts of the instrument [*eisdem inerit*]. For unless the five aforementioned parts of rhetoric are in exordia, so that the orator invents, arranges, expresses, memorizes, and delivers, the orator accomplishes nothing. And in the same way, unless all the remaining parts of the instrument have all the parts of rhetoric, they are futile.

The practitioner of this discipline is the orator, whose function is to speak appropriately for persuasion.

The end is both within the orator himself and within another. Within the orator himself, it is to have spoken well, that is, to have spoken in a way appropriate for persuasion; within another, it is to have persuaded. For it is not the case that if something hinders the orator in persuading, the end has not been achieved, when his function has been performed.[29] [1209A] The end which was near and related to the function is

---

[28] Stump, 146, note 32: "Boethius' point is that the six parts of discourse are in rhetoric's species and are also the instrument used by the three genera of cases" (for this distinction, see note 22 above).

[29] On this distinction between the orator's function and the purpose of the art (i.e. that the orator may fulfill his function even if persuasion does not occur), see Aristotle, *Rhetoric*, 1355b (the function of the orator is to see the available means of persuasion in each case).

achieved when the function has been performed; the end which is external, however, often is not achieved. But rhetoric, which has striven for its end, is not thereby deprived of [its] honor.

These things are mixed in such a way that rhetoric is in [its] species, and the species are in the cases. The parts of cases are called "issues" [*status*]; one may call these also by other names, sometimes "points in dispute" [*constitutiones*], sometimes "questions" [*quaestiones*].

Issues are divided as the nature of things is divided. But let us describe the differentiae of questions [that is, issues] from the beginning.[30] Since rhetorical questions are all involved with circumstances, either they involve debate over some document or they take the beginning [*exordium*] of the dispute from outside the document, from the thing itself.

Those that have to do with a document can arise in five ways. First, when [1209B] one man argues from the words of a writer; another, from the writer's meaning. This is called "what is written and what is intended." In another way, if laws disagree among themselves by a certain opposition, and [two men each] argue from an opposed part, the documents produce a controversy. This is called "an issue from opposed laws." Third, when the document about which there is some dispute contains an ambiguous meaning. This is called by the [corresponding] name "ambiguity." Fourthly, when from what is written, something different which is not written is understood. This is called "reasoning" or "syllogism," because it is found by reasoning and as a consequent [*consequentia*] of a syllogism. Fifthly, when a word is written whose force and nature is not easily made clear unless it is discovered by definition. This is called "limit" or "circumscribing" [*finis, inscriptio*].

To differentiate all these things is a part not of our task but of the rhetorician's; [1209C] for we put these things forth to be examined by the learned, not to teach the ignorant, although we have discussed their differentiae in passing in the commentaries on the *Topics.*

The differentiae of the issues external to documents and put forth in dispute about things themselves are divided according to the diversity of the nature of the things themselves, for in every rhetorical question what is in doubt is whether it is [*an sit*], what kind of thing it is [*quid sit*], what qualities it has [*quale sit*], and in addition, whether judgment can be lawfully [*lege*] or morally [*more*] administered.[31]

---

[30] The following discussion reprises information in *De inventione* 1.12.16ff, 1.11.14ff., and 1.8.9ff.

[31] These four "controversies," fact, definition, quality, and legal procedure, form the basis of "status theory" or the issue with which the case will be be concerned. Every case will arise from one of these issues (*constitutiones*; [Greek] *staseis*). Status theory is the core of the Ciceronian theory of invention. See *De inventione* 1.8.10.

If the deed or matter which is alleged is denied by the opponent, the question is "whether it is or not." This is called "a conjectural issue." If it is established that the deed occurred but what it is [*quid sit*] is not known, the issue is called "definitional" since the import of the deed must be shown by definition. If it is established that [the deed] occurred and if there is agreement on the definition of the matter [1209D] but there is some question about the qualities of the deed, then because there is doubt about what genus it ought to be put under, [the issue] is called "generic qualitative." In this question, an account [*ratio*] of quality, quantity, and comparison is employed.

Since the question is about genus, this [last] issue must be divided into many parts according to the nature of genus. Every generic question—when one asks about the genus, quality, and quantity of a deed—is divided into two parts. One asks about the quality of what is under discussion either with respect to the past or with respect to the present or future. If with respect to the past, the issue is called "juridical." If it contains a question of present or future time, the issue is called "legal" [*negotialis*].[32]

A juridical inquiry considers what is past; it is divided into two parts. [1210A] Either the force of the defense is in the deed itself, and the quality is called "absolute"; or the force of the defense is assumed from without, and the issue is called "assumptive."

The latter is distributed into four parts; the charge[33] is acknowledged, removed, transferred, or, finally, compared.

The charge is acknowledged when one introduces no defense of the deed but asks for pardon. This can happen in two ways: if you entreat or if you justify. You entreat when you produce no excuse. You justify when the blame for the deed is ascribed to things which cannot be withstood or prevented but are not people (for that falls under another issue[34]). These things are ignorance, chance events, and necessity.

The charge is removed when it is shifted from him who is accused to someone else. Removal of the charge can occur in two ways: [1210B] if the responsibility or the deed is removed. The responsibility is removed when it is argued that something was done by someone else's power. The deed is removed when it is shown that someone else either could have or ought to have done it—these things are of most use if the indictment brought against us is of this sort, that we have not done what we ought to have done.

---

[32] On the "legal" issue (*negotialis*) see *De inventione* 1.11.14–15; 2.21.62. Boethius does not pursue the legal issue, but goes on to consider the "juridical" issue.

[33] The word used in Boethius and Cicero is *crimen*. Stump translates this as "crime," but we have translated it as "charge," to convey its particular legal force in this rhetorical context.

[34] Namely to the following issue, where the blame is shifted to someone else.

The charge is transferred when it is argued that the misdeed was justly committed against someone since the one against whom it was committed was often unjust and deserved to suffer what it is charged [that the defendant did].

A comparison occurs when the deed which the opponent argues was committed is defended [as having been done] for the sake of what is better or more advantageous.[35]

There are appropriate differentiae of all these and also very minute divisions; the books of the rhetoricians, written to teach and explain these things, contain them more thoroughly. [1210C] For us, it is enough to have taken these things from Cicero, for the whole plan of the work hurries on to something else, all of which we must now examine.

Cicero shows that issues are parts of cases in the passage in which he argues against Hermagoras: "if they cannot rightly be thought parts of a genus of cases, still less will they rightly be thought parts of a part of a case. But every issue is part of a case"—indicating that issues are parts of cases.[36]

Hence there is considerable question about the way in which issues were considered to be parts of a case. If they are parts in the way species are parts, how can it be that there are many issues in one case? For species cannot mingle with each other, but many issues enter into a case. Therefore, issues are not parts of cases as species. [1210D] There is this also: no species aids the substance of another species opposed to it, but one issue strengthens belief for another. Nor can it be that they are parts of cases as parts of a whole, for there can be no whole and complete thing composed of one part, and in a case one issue is enough to constitute a case.

The road to reason therefore shows us what to say.

An issue [*constitutio*] is not said to be part of a case which comes into dispute and which is constituted by an issue [*status*], especially since an issue [*status*] added to a case which is already established by one issue [*constitutio*] is not a principal issue but an accidental one.[37] And in one action there occur as many disputes as issues, and as many cases as disputes. Although one action may contain these, nevertheless the cases do not mingle [1211A] but are different from each other. For example, someone sees a young man coming out of a brothel and a little later sees his wife coming out of the same place, and he accuses the young man of adultery. What is involved here is one action but two cases: one conjectural if he denies that he did it, the other definitional if he says that copulation in a brothel

---

[35] I.e. not something to the defendant's "advantage," but rather that the defendant's deed was the best choice among several courses of action. See Stump, 147 note 48.

[36] *De inventione* 1.10.13. Boethius cites this, not because he will pursue the differences between Cicero and Hermagoras, but because he wishes to discuss the idea that issues are parts of a case. See Stump, 148–9 note 50.

[37] Stump, 148 note 54: "In any given actual case there may be more than one issue: but if so, one issue will be the primary or principal one and whatever others there are will be accidental." This is proof, for Boethius, that issues of a case are not species of a genus, because species are on a par with each other.

cannot be thought adultery. But the conjectural issue is not a part of this dispute if he denies [that he did it], nor is the definitional issue a part if [his defense is] in defining; for [either way] the issue contains the whole case.[38] I am using "case" not generally but [only] as a dispute formed by some issue.

But issues are parts of a case in general in this way.[39] If the whole case were conjectural and no other issue were found, the conjectural status would not be part of the case, but the case itself would without doubt be conjectural. But since [1211B] all cases are comprised partly by what is conjectural, partly not, partly by quality, partly by transference,[40] an issue is part not of the case which it informs by comprising it but rather of the case in general which it divides. Separating from such a case as a kind of part, any one issue produces its own [case]. So issues are parts which are species of a case in general but not of a case which any one issue has informed and comprised.

So the genus of rhetoric is discipline. There are three species of rhetoric: judicial, epideictic, and deliberative. The matter [of rhetoric] is the political question, which is called a case. The parts of this matter are issues. The parts of rhetoric are invention, arrangement, style, memorization, and delivery. [Its] instrument is discourse. The parts of the instrument are exordium, narration, partition, confirmation, refutation, and peroration. [Its] work is [1211C] to teach and to move. The one who does this work is the orator. [Its] function is to speak well. [Its] end is sometimes to have spoken well, sometimes to persuade.

All of rhetoric is in [its] species. The species inform all the matter in such a way that they in turn appropriate all the matter for themselves; and this can be understood from the fact that the individual species contain all the parts of the matter, for you will find four issues in the judicial [species], and you can find the same four in the epideictic and deliberative [species]. And so, if the individual species have all the parts of a case in general, which is a political question, and the case itself is all the parts, then it is shown that the species in turn appropriate the whole case (that is, the political question) in the same way as an utterance simultaneously comes to the ears of many, complete and with its parts (namely, the letters); for the whole case [1211D] with its parts simultaneously goes through to the different species.

---

[38] Stump, 149 note 57: "And a whole cannot be composed of only one part. Since the whole case is composed of or constituted by its issue, the issue cannot be a part of that case." In other words, the issue is constitutive of the case, rather than being just a part of the case, so there cannot be several issues constituting a single case. As Boethius acknowledges, one action could produce different kinds of cases, each informed by a different issue.

[39] Here, despite what he has just proposed, Boethius attempts to rescue Cicero's argument that issues *are* parts of cases by distinguishing a broader and a narrower sense of "case." See Stump, 149 note 59.

[40] Transference is the issue in which there is a dispute about whether the right person has brought the suit, or whether the suit is being tried in the right court, or under the right law. See *De inventione* 1.8.10.

When the species have come into the matter, that is, into the political question, and have obtained it with their parts, they bring with themselves also the rhetorical discipline itself. So the parts of rhetoric too will be in the individual issues. Once the matter has been introduced, it brings with it its instrument; so it brings with it discourse, and discourse brings with it its own parts. And so in the issues to be discussed there will be exordium, narration, and the rest.

When the instrument has come into the political question, it also brings with it at the same time its work; so in every issue there will be teaching and persuading. These cannot occur by themselves; there must be someone who moves them like a craftsman or builder. This is the orator. When he [1212A] has come to a case, he will fulfill his function. So he will speak well in every genus of cases. And in every issue, he will produce the end also: sometimes, to have spoken well in every issue; sometimes, to have persuaded.

We have now dealt with the particulars in general. Later, if it is convenient, we will also discuss them separately. And that is enough about these things.

Now we must examine discovery.[41] For previously we gave the dialectical Topics, and now we are bringing the rhetorical Topics to light;[42] and these must come from the attributes of the person and the action.[43]

The person is the one brought to trial, some deed or speech of whose is censured. The action is the person's deed or speech for which he is brought to trial. Every division of Topics is comprised in these two. For unless the things that give occasion for censure [1212B] verge on the altogether inexcusable, they also provide an abundance of defense; for every accusation and every defense are established from the same Topics. If a person is brought to trial and no deed or speech [of his] is censured, there can be no case. Nor can any deed or speech be brought into a trial if there is no person. And so every account [*ratio*] of trials involves these two, namely, person and action.

As was said, the person is the one who is brought to trial; the action is the person's deed or speech, for which he, the defendant, is judged. Therefore, the person and the action cannot supply arguments, for the question is about them, and the things brought into question cannot produce belief for what is in question. But an argument was a reason [1212C] producing belief regarding what is in doubt. Belief regarding an action is produced by the attributes of persons and actions. And whenever a person produces belief regarding an action—for example, if someone believes that Catiline plotted against the republic because Catiline is a person marked by the baseness of vices—then it is not insofar as he is

---

[41] i.e. invention.   [42] The dialectical topics were treated ("previously") in books 1–3.
[43] Stump, 151 note 69: "The person and the action are for rhetoric what the subject and predicate of the question under discussion are for dialectic: they are the givens around which one's case has to be built."

a person and brought to trial that he produces belief regarding the action but rather insofar as he has a certain nature, from the attributes of the person.

To show the order of [these] things more clearly, I think circumstances must be discussed. Circumstances are things which, by coming together, produce the substance of the issue [*quaestio*]. For unless there is someone who did [something] and something which he did, and a reason why he did it, and a place and time in which he did it, and manner and means [*facultates*] [in and by which he did it], there will be no case.[44]

Cicero divides these circumstances in two. The circumstance [1212D] "who [did it]" he puts among the attributes of the person. The other circumstances, according to him, consist in the attributes of the action.

The first of the circumstances, which is "who" and attributed to the person, he divides into eleven parts: name (for example, "Verres"); nature (for example, foreigner); mode of life (for example, friend of nobles); fortune (for example, rich); studies (for example, geometrician); luck (for example, exile); feelings (for example, loving); disposition (for example, wise); purpose; deeds; and words (deeds and words other than the deed and speech now brought into the trial).

The remaining circumstances—what, why, how, where, when, with what means—he puts among the attributes of the action.

"What" and "why" he says are connected with the action itself. "Why" is comprised in the reason, according to him, for the reason [1213A] for any deed is that on account of which it was done. He divides "what" into four parts: the gist of the deed, for example, the killing of a parent (from this the Topic of amplification is most often taken); before the deed, for example, he seized a sword in a state of excitement; while [the deed] occurs, [for example,] he struck violently; after the deed, [for example,] he hid in a secret place. All these things are deeds; nevertheless, since they pertain to the performed action in question, they are not the deeds which are counted among the attributes of the person. For these latter deeds, posited outside the action at issue and forming the person, provide belief regarding the action which the accusation deals with; but the deeds connected with the action itself pertain to the very action in question.

Cicero puts the last four circumstances among the performing of the action, which is [1213B] the second part of the attributes of actions.[45] The circumstance "when" he divides

---

[44] The circumstances are discussed at length in *De inventione* 1.24.34–1.51.77, under the part of the oration called *confirmatio* or proof; here the circumstances are embedded in a scheme of attributes of the person and the act. By contrast, Boethius' treatment strips away most of Cicero's detail about the construction of the actual speech, thus allowing the circumstances a more prominent role.

[45] The "first part" referred to here is the preceding "what" and "why," which are part of the action itself. The next four, now under discussion (when, where, how, with what aid) are connected with the performance of the action, but do not inhere in the action itself.

into time, for example, he carried it out by night, and opportunity, for example, when everyone was sleeping. The circumstance "where" he calls place, for example, he carried it out in the bedroom. Of the circumstances, "how" is the method, for example, he carried it out secretly. He calls the means the circumstance "with what aid," for example, with a large band of men. Even if the differences among these Topics[46] are clear from the nature of the circumstances, we will show more good will if we present the differentiae among them more abundantly.

Cicero maintained that some of the circumstances are connected with the action itself and others are connected with the performing of the action. Among those connected with the action itself he numbered the Topic which he called "while it occurs"; from the signification [1213C] of the expression, this Topic "while it occurs" seems to be the same Topic as that which is in the performing of the action. But such is not the case, because the former "while it occurs" is what is committed at the time while the crime is being perpetrated, for example, he struck. In the performing of the action there are things which contain what is done before the deed which was performed, while that deed occurs, and after that deed; for in all of these there is a question about time, place, opportunity, method, and means. Again, the "while it occurs" is the deed by which the action is accomplished. So the things which are in the performing of the action are not deeds but adherents to the deed, for no one would agree that time, opportunity, place, method, and means are deeds, but they are equally adherents to any deed whatever, as was said. And this is not in any way altered because in a certain relationship [*relatio*] they are subsumed under the action which was performed.

Similarly, the things which are in the performing [1213D] of the action can be without the things which are connected with the action. The place, time, opportunity, method, and means of any deed can be understood even if no one does the deed, which could occur in that place or time or opportunity or by that method or those means. So the things which are in the performing of the action can be without the things which are connected with the action itself; but the latter cannot be without the former, for there cannot be a deed without place, time, opportunity, method, and means.

Those things which consist in the attributes of the person and the action [1214A] [are] like those among the dialectical Topics which inhere in the very things asked about. The remainder, however, which either are associated with the action or follow from the action performed, are (in Themistius' division) partly like those among the dialectical Topics which follow from the substance of the thing, partly like those from without, and partly like those used as intermediates—or (in Cicero's division) like those numbered among

---

[46] The Topics are the seven circumstances and their subdivisions.

things involved [with the action] or those posited from without.[47] They are associated with the action and equally produce belief regarding the question, being related in a certain way to what is in question and having regard to the action at issue.

Seven circumstances are numbered among the attributes of the person or the action. When these begin to be compared and to come into a relationship, as it were, then if [what is being compared] is held up to that which contains or to that which is contained, it is either species or genus [of whatever it is held up to]; if it is held up to [1214B] what is most different from it, it is a contrary, and if it is held up to its own goal and end, it is a result. In the same way, they are compared to things that are greater, lesser, and equal. In general these Topics are considered whenever something is relative [to something else] [*ad aliquid*], for greater and less than, or similar to, or equally great as, or different from are accidents of the circumstances which are numbered among the attributes of the person and the action, so that when these circumstances are compared to others, an argument about the speech or deed brought into the trial arises from them.

They are different from the preceding Topics, because the preceding Topics either contained deeds or adhered to deeds in such a way that they could not be separated, as place, time, and the rest, which do not desert the action performed. But those things that are associated with the action do not adhere to the [1214C] action itself but are accidents of the circumstances, and they provide an argument only when they enter into comparison. The arguments, however, are taken not from contrariety but from a contrary, and not from similarity but from a similar, so that the argument seems to be taken not from a relationship [such as contrariety] but from things associated with the action [such as contraries]. Those things are associated with the action which are related to the very action at issue.

Consequence is the fourth part of the attributes of the action. It is not in the things which do not leave the substance of things nor is it derived from comparison, but it precedes or even follows the thing performed. And this whole Topic is extrinsic. In this Topic one asks first by what name it is fitting to call what has been done; and here one takes pains not with [1214D] the thing but with the word. Then one asks who the doers of this deed are and who approve of its having been thought up and are emulators of it. This whole [Topic] comes together from judgment and from a kind of witness which is extrinsic in order to aid the argument. Then one asks also what is the law, custom, agreement, judgment, opinion [*sententia*], and theory [*artificium*] for the thing [in

---

[47] Themistius (ca. 320–390), a Greek commentator on dialectical topics whose work survives in fragmentary form. In book 2 of *De topicis differentiis*, Boethius gives an account of Themistius' division of the topics; in book 3, he considers the division of the topics in Cicero's *Topica*. "Things involved [with the action]," translating *affecta*. Stump's translation here slightly modified to reflect this.

question]. Then one asks if the kind of thing involved generally befalls the mass of men or whether it happens contrary to custom and rarely; [also] whether men in these matters are accustomed to agree to and defend this by [giving it] their authority; and [so on with] other things which in the same way generally follow some deed either immediately or after a time, which are extrinsic [1215A] and must tend more to opinion than to the very nature of the things.

So one can divide the attributes of actions into the following four. In part, they are connected with the action itself and, as was said above, these are deeds. In part, they are in the performing of the action; and, as we showed previously, these are not deeds but the adherents to deeds. In part, they are associated with the action. And these, as was said, partly are put forth in a relationship and partly follow from the action performed; belief regarding these is taken from without. And enough has been said about rhetorical Topics.

Now we must explain the similarity and the difference between these and dialectical Topics. When I have shown this sufficiently and appropriately, then the plan of the work proposed will be completed.

First of all, according to Themistius, among the dialectical Topics there are some which inhere in the very things in question, some which [1215B] are taken from without, and some which are placed intermediate between these two. So also among the rhetorical Topics, some are in the persons and the action which are in contention, some are from without, such as those which follow from the action performed, and some are intermediate.

Of these [i.e. rhetorical topics], the closest to the action are those which, from among the circumstances, are thought to be in the performance of the action.[48] Those which are associated with the action are also placed among the intermediate Topics since they are tied to the action at issue by a certain relationship. Or, someone might say that the attributes of the person or the things connected with the action itself or those considered to be in the performing of the action are similar to the dialectical Topics which are drawn from the very things asked about in the question; the things following from the action [1215C] he might consider extrinsic, and the things associated with the action he might designate as intermediate between those two.

---

[48] *Quorum proximi quidem negotio sunt hi qui ex circumstantiis reliqui in gestatione negotii considerantur.* Translation of this sentence slightly adapted from Stump's, to emphasize the transition from the preceding passage: i.e. after eliminating all of those *circumstantiae* that are not part of the performance of the action, two rhetorical topics which are inherent in the performance of the action ("what was done," "why") remain among the list of seven *circumstantiae*.

It is similar to Cicero's division in this way.[49] The things connected with the action itself or those which are considered to be in the performing of the action inhere in the things in question. The things associated with the action are placed within [Cicero's Topic of] related things. The things that follow from the action performed are taken from without. Or, someone might think that the things connected with the action [are like those of Cicero's Topics which] inhere in the things themselves, that those which are in the performing of the action or are associated with the action are [like Cicero's Topic of] related things, and that those which follow from the action performed are from without.

The likenesses are already clear, because almost the same Topics are used in both disciplines, such as genus, part, similarity, contrary, and greater and lesser. [1215D] Enough has been said about likenesses.

The differences are that dialectical Topics are suited also for theses, but rhetorical Topics are suited for hypotheses only, that is, they are arrogated to questions informed by circumstances. For as the disciplines are distinguished from one another by the universality [of the one] and the particularity [of the other], so also their Topics differ in range and [1216A] restriction.[50] For the range of dialectical Topics is greater, and since they are independent of circumstances, which produce individual cases, they are useful not only for theses but also for arguments put forth in hypotheses, whose Topics, composed of circumstances, they include and range over.

So the rhetorician always proceeds from dialectical Topics, but the dialectician can be content with his own Topics. For since a rhetorician draws cases from circumstances, he takes arguments from the same circumstances; but these must be confirmed by the universal and simple, namely, the dialectical [Topics]. The dialectician, on the other hand, is prior and has no need of anything posterior, unless on occasion there happens to be a question about a person, as when a dialectician happens to prove his thesis by a case involving circumstances, then only [1216B] does he use rhetorical Topics.

So in dialectical Topics, arguments are taken from, say, the genus, that is, from the very nature of genus. But in rhetorical Topics, arguments are taken from the particular genus which is the genus at issue; they are not taken from the nature of genus, but from the generic thing, from the thing that is the genus. But in order to proceed, the argument [*ratio*] depends on the fact that the nature of genus is known beforehand. For example, suppose there is a question whether someone was drunk. If we want to refute [the charge],

---

[49] This refers to the division of topics in Cicero's *Topica*.

[50] Stump, 154 note 104: "In other words, dialectic deals with what is universal (theses) and rhetoric with what is particular (hypotheses)."

we will say that he was not since he had never before been dissipated. Therefore, since dissipation is, as it were, a genus of drunkenness, and since there was no dissipation, there certainly was no drunkenness. But this depends on something else. For the fact that there could be no drunkenness since there was no dissipation is shown from the nature of genus, and this the dialectical argument [*ratio*] provides. For where the genus is absent, there [1216C] the species must also be absent, since the genus does not leave the species.

And in the same way for similars and contraries. In these things there is a very great difference between rhetorical and dialectical Topics. Dialectic discovers arguments from qualities themselves; rhetoric, from things taking on a quality. So the dialectician [discovers arguments] from genus, that is, from the nature of genus; the rhetorician, from the thing that is the genus. The dialectician [discovers arguments] from similarity; the rhetorician, from a similar, that is, from the thing which takes on similarity. In the same way, the former [discovers arguments] from contrariety; the latter, from a contrary.

Now that all the things which we proposed above have been explained, I think we ought to add this. Cicero's *Topica*, which he published for C. Trebatius, who was skilled at law, does not examine how one can dispute about these things themselves but how arguments of the rhetorical discipline [1216D] may be produced, which we explained more thoroughly in the commentaries we wrote on Cicero's *Topica*. How one disputes about them with dialectical arguments [*rationibus*], we explained in the commentaries we wrote on Aristotle's *Topics*, translated by us.

Outline of Book 4 [51]

[51] Outline by Stump, 155.

CASSIODORUS, *EXPOSITIO PSALMORUM*, CA. 540, AND *INSTITUTIONES*, CA. 562

INTRODUCTION

Cassiodorus Senator, "one of the last completely rhetorical men,"[1] was born ca. 484–90 at Squillace (Scyllacium) in southern Italy, from a distinguished Roman family. He was educated in the elite schools of Roman rhetoric and letters, and first came to the attention of Theodoric, the ruler of the Ostrogothic kingdom, through a panegyric that he delivered in Theodoric's praise. From his young adulthood through his fifties he pursued an illustrious career in public office at Ravenna, appointed first as quaestor, then as consul ordinarius, then as *magister officiorum* (as the successor of Boethius), and finally (in the 530s) as praetorian prefect.[2] The record that he left of this long period is his selection of his official correspondence, the *Variae*, compiled during the closing years of his public life, in 537–8. When the Ostrogothic kingdom came under increasing attack from the eastern Empire, Cassiodorus left public office and removed to Constantinople, where he remained for more than a decade. It was there that he turned his efforts to spiritual and theological writings, producing his treatise *De anima* (On the Soul) and his *Expositio Psalmorum* (Exposition of the Psalms). He returned to Italy about 554, to the pursuit that was to occupy him until his death (well into his nineties), the monastic foundation at Vivarium on his family's estates at Squillace. It was for this monastic community that he produced the *Institutiones* in two books, "Divine Readings" and "Secular Readings," which he first completed around 562. In his late old age, at the request of the monks at Vivarium, he produced an elementary grammatical treatise, *De orthographia*.

In the new institutional and pedagogic setting of Vivarium with its library, Cassiodorus made use of recent developments in book production. The *codex* was now more and more replacing the *volumen*, which usually only contained one book of a given work. The *codex* made it possible to collect works on related topics in one volume. Cassiodorus exploited this possibility systematically and self-consciously: in *Institutiones* 2.2.10, included below,

---

[1] O'Donnell, *Cassiodorus*, 180.
[2] O'Donnell, *Cassiodorus*, 13–32; *An Introduction to Divine and Human Readings*, trans. Jones, 3–18.

for instance, he reports how he organized rhetorical reference works in one such codex.[3] His constant activities in updating his work through marginal notes also testifies to the importance of the library as the central archive of secular and Christian learning.[4]

The commentary on the Psalms and the *Institutiones* may be taken together as exegetical practice followed by the exposition of the theory on which the practice is based.[5] The *Expositio Psalmorum* is a remarkable attempt to marry the rhetorical learning of late Roman culture to the theological revelation of the Psalms. In the broadest sense, Cassiodorus believes that the secular arts had their origin in sacred Scripture, and thus that the methods of secular learning brought to Scripture are no more than an elucidation of the knowledge sequestered there. The idea that the arts were first implanted in Scripture and that the knowledge of the learned pagans was a belated one was shared by early exegetes like Augustine, and was reiterated by various medieval writers on the arts, including Bede in his *De schematibus et tropis* and, to grand effect, Rupert of Deutz in his *De sancta trinitate*.[6] But even in a restricted sense as a rhetorical reading, the *Expositio Psalmorum* is a *tour de force*. Cassiodorus treats the Psalms as a rhetorical laboratory, a complement to the theoretical statements about rhetoric (and about grammar and logic) in the *Institutiones*. In his hands, the Psalms become the consummate statement of rhetorical doctrine: "Cassiodorus' Commentary provides us with an *ars rhetorica* that is simultaneously an *ars poetriae*."[7] Cassiodorus classifies the Psalms according to the genres of oratory: deliberative (political), judicial (forensic), and epideictic (demonstrative, or praise and blame). He recasts these genres in terms of prayer and spiritual knowledge: the deliberative genre is meditation and the seeking of instruction; the judicial is for penitence; and the epideictic is for inspiration and revelation, or showing. Each psalm is given a "division," as in the divisions of a speech. Throughout the *Expositio*, Cassiodorus deploys the terminology of rhetorical tropes in order to justify revelatory, or indeed allegorical, readings, a feature that ensured the enduring usefulness of the work.[8] In this way he used his knowledge of rhetoric as a tool to understand the mystery of the Psalms. In applying his secular rhetorical training to a reading of the Psalms, he was seeking an exegetical mastery, to reveal the text's profound truths, which, he says, had formerly lain hidden to him beneath a veil of parables.[9]

---

[3] Van de Vyver, "Cassiodore et son oeuvre," 276 with note 2.

[4] Van de Vyver, "Cassiodore et son oeuvre," 278.   [5] O'Donnell, *Cassiodorus*, 213–14.

[6] Augustine, *De doctrina christiana* 3.29.40; see the selections from Bede and Rupert of Deutz, below.

[7] Astell, "Cassiodorus's *Commentary on the Psalms*," 75.

[8] Adriaen lists over eighty manuscripts from the ninth to the thirteenth centuries, *Expositio Psalmorum* ed. Adriaen, 1:viii–xi. On the impact of Cassiodorus' Psalm commentaries on studies of the figures and tropes through the following centuries, see Grondeux, *À la frontière entre grammaire et rhétorique*.

[9] *Expositio Psalmorum*, ed. Adriaen, *praefatio* 7.

The two books of the *Institutiones*, the first devoted to sacred matters and the second a true compendium of the secular liberal arts, were often copied separately, and the second book had a somewhat wider dissemination because of its sheer usefulness.[10] In short compass (seventy-four pages in the modern edition) it covers the whole of the seven liberal arts, so that it could form the basis of any library, even the poorest, that aspired to some coverage in the liberal arts. Book 2 follows the pattern of Augustine's *De doctrina christiana* in presenting the scientific knowledge of the learned pagans as an equipment for scriptural study. Perhaps surprisingly, Cassiodorus' treatment of grammar is extremely brief, reducing his main source, the *Ars maior* of Donatus, to a series of concepts and definitions, and leaving out all discussions and examples. He also refers the reader to two commentaries on Donatus for further explanation. Yet despite his use of Donatus as his main source, he gives no pagan literary references or examples.[11] Cassiodorus devotes greater space and detailed attention to rhetoric. He cites as his sources not only Cicero's *De inventione*, but also the *De oratore* and Quintilian's *Institutio oratoria*. He mentions Martianus' *De nuptiis*, once in the chapter on rhetoric and once later in the treatise (book 2, § 20, where he notes that he has only heard of the work, but has not obtained it). He also reveals the learned culture of his own youthful rhetorical training, citing as a "modern" authority Fortunatianus, and referring to Victorinus' commentary on the *De inventione* as a work "in my library" which can be consulted if his own readers require further detail. It is sometimes noted that Cassiodorus' treatment of rhetoric amounts to little more than a technographic handbook on inventional theory, like that of Fortunatianus and many of the other *rhetores latini minores* of late antiquity.[12] This is in part a function of the overwhelming influence of the *De inventione* and its attention to theories of invention. But beyond this lies the fact that Cassiodorus was a product of the era in which the teaching of rhetoric had such pervasive currency that the art could be reduced to an outline of theory in anticipation or alongside of its fuller realization in classroom or administrative practice. Certainly in its medieval reception, the chapter on rhetoric seems to have served this purpose: it is often found by itself in manuscripts as a kind of preface or supplement to the *De inventione* and *Ad Herennium*.[13] Moreover, it would oversimplify to assume that Cassiodorus, who devoted the first half of his adult life to civil administration and who

[10] Cassiodorus, *An Introduction to Divine and Human Readings*, trans. Jones, 52, 58–63; and see Mynors' list of the more important manuscripts of the whole or parts, *Cassiodori Senatoris Institutiones*, ed. Mynors, x–xlix.

[11] For Cassiodorus' knowledge of literature, see Bacherler, "Cassiodors Dichterkenntnisse und Dichterzitate"; van de Vyver, "Cassiodore et son oeuvre," 279, and see *ibid.*, 280f. for an overview of literary knowledge and activity in the early sixth century.

[12] Murphy, *Rhetoric in the Middle Ages*, 66; Kennedy, *Classical Rhetoric and its Christian and Secular Traditions*, 177–8; Ward, "From Antiquity to the Renaissance," 44.

[13] Ward, *Ciceronian Rhetoric*, 83.

compiled his own correspondence as a model of state epistolography, would not have considered the applied value of rhetoric when he delivered the outlines of the art to his monks at Vivarium.[14] In his own *Expositio Psalmorum* we see one example of this application, the turning of rhetoric to an interpretive function, as a foundation for sacred reading.

Translations reprinted from Cassiodorus, *Explanation of the Psalms*, trans. Walsh (vol. 1), by permission, and *An Introduction to Divine and Human Readings*, trans. Jones (with minor adaptations), by permission.[15]

FROM *EXPOSITIO PSALMORUM*

[From Cassiodorus' preface.]

Chapter 15: The Eloquence of the Entire Divine Law

The eloquence of the divine law has not been fashioned by human speech. Its impact is not doubtful, confused, or ambiguous. So it does not forgetfully contradict what has gone before; it is not in turmoil through confusion of present events; and it is not deceived by the uncertainties of the future. It speaks to the heart, not to the body's ears. It judges everything with great truth and great force of prescience. It comprises the truth of its Author. For this is how the Gospel speaks of the Lord Christ's preaching: *Now he was speaking as one having power, and not as the scribes and Pharisees.*[16] He speaks of certainties, for all things are present to Him, and the outcome of events is seen to be subject to Him.

Now eloquence is the right and fitting exposition of any particular matter. But the eloquence of the divine law is a chaste, secure, truthful, and eternal proclamation. It gleams with the purest possible expression. Its usefulness shines out, the splendor of its power stands out, and its saving work smiles out. As David is to say in Psalm 118: *For thy eloquence will enliven me*, and again: *Thy word is a lamp to my feet, O my Lord, and a light to my paths.*[17] It is truly a light, because it always prescribes what brings life, and forbids what harms; it removes things earthly, and advances things heavenly. This is why the teacher of

---

[14] Ward, "The Medieval and Early Renaissance Study," 19.
[15] Translations of Scripture are those used in the translations. Notes for the *Expositio Psalmorum* are those of the translator, with some additions. Notes for the *Institutiones* are based on those of the Jones translation. Editions used for reference: *Expositio Psalmorum*, ed. Adriaen; *Cassiodori Senatoris Institutiones*, ed. Mynors.
[16] Matthew 7:29.   [17] Psalm 119 (118):50 and 107.

the Gentiles is a further witness in a letter to the Corinthians: *For the kingdom of God is not in speech, but in power.*[18] In his second letter to Timothy, Paul further recalls: *All Scripture, inspired of God, is profitable to teach, to reprove, to instruct, to correct in the discipline which is of justice, that the man of God be perfect, furnished to every good work.*[19]

As the authority of father Jerome attests,[20] divine eloquence among the Jews is composed according to rhythms or metrical law, which the Jews describe as ordered in *fastucia*, a *fastucium* being a fully elaborated concept developed phrase by phrase to draw out the sense.[21] If, careful reader, you wish to examine the force of this, listen to Paul speaking to the Hebrews: *For the word of God is living and effectual, and keener than any two-edged sword, and reaching unto the division of the soul and the spirit, of the joints also and the marrows; and is a discerner of the thoughts and intents of the heart.*[22] Now the holy depth of divine Scripture is expressed in such common language that everyone immediately takes it in, but buried within it are hidden senses of truth, so that the vital meaning must be most carefully sought out. What contributes most of all to our understanding that it is really divine is the fact that ignorant men are known to have been able to explain most subtle things, and moral men eternal things, but only when filled with the divine Spirit.

Finally, how many successive miracles were performed so that Scripture might become diffused and fill the extent of the world? As Scripture says: *Their sound hath gone forth into all the earth, and their words unto the ends of the world.*[23] So the greatest proof lies in the fact that the divine law is known to have been received through every part of the world. It exploits its varieties of language in sundry ways, being clothed in definitions adorned by figures, marked by its special vocabulary, equipped with the conclusions of syllogisms, gleaming with forms of instruction. But it does not appropriate from these a beauty adopted from elsewhere, but rather bestows upon them its own high status. For when these techniques shine in the divine Scriptures, they are precise and wholly without fault, but once enmeshed in men's opinions and the emptiest problems, they are disturbed by obscure waves of argument. What in the Scriptures is unshakeably true often becomes uncertain elsewhere. So while our tongues sing a psalmody, they are adorned with the nobility of truth, but once they turn to foolish fictions and blasphemous words they are cut off from the glory of integrity. As the apostle James says: *From our very mouths we bless God and the Father, and from our very mouths we curse man who is made after the image and likeness of God.*[24]

---

[18] 1 Corinthians 4:20.   [19] 2 Timothy 3:16 ff.   [20] Jerome, *Praef. in Job*, *PL* 28:1,140ff.
[21] G. Card. Mercati, "Fastucium," *Biblica* 29 (1948): 282–3 reintroduces (based on *Thes. Ling. Lat.* t. VI pars prior, col. 325.52) the emendation *phas(s)ucium*, meant to represent Hebrew *pasuq*, which is a verse with a clearly marked boundary; the end of such a verse is indicated by a so-called *sof pasuq*, literally "end of verse," a punctuation mark resembling a colon. We thank Professor Holger Gzella for discussion of this passage.
[22] Hebrews 4:12.   [23] Psalm 19 (18) 5.   [24] James 3:9.

Those experienced in the secular arts, clearly living long after the time when the first words of the divine books were penned, transferred these techniques to the collections of arguments which the Greeks call topics, and to the arts of dialectic and rhetoric.[25] So it is crystal clear to all that the minds of the just were endowed to express the truth with the techniques which pagans subsequently decided should be exploited for human wisdom. In the sacred readings they shine like the brightest of stars, aptly clarifying the meanings of passages most usefully and profitably. I shall draw attention to them briefly at the most suitable places, for it will be most convenient to cite the passage in which the expression of the meaning will shine out more clearly.

Moreover, father Augustine in the third book of *De doctrina christiana* maintained the following: "The learned must realize that our authors have employed the modes of all the forms of expression which grammarians using the Greek term call tropes." And a little later: "Those who know these tropes or modes of expression recognize them in sacred literature, and by knowledge of them are assisted to some extent towards understanding of it."[26] This point he makes very clearly in other books as well; for in the volumes which he calls *De modis locutionum* (On Modes of Expression),[27] he showed that the various figures belonging to secular literature are found in the sacred books, and he declared that there are other modes peculiar to divine eloquence which *grammatici* and rhetors have not mentioned at all. Other most learned fathers of our number have also stated this, namely Jerome, Ambrose, and Hilary, so that clearly I am in no sense the originator of this idea, but a follower of others. Someone however may say: the premises of syllogisms, the names of figures, the terms for the disciplines, and other items of this kind are not found at all in the psalms. But they are clearly found in force of meaning, not in the utterance of words; in this sense we see wine in vines, a harvest in the seed, foliage in roots, fruits in branches, and trees conceptually in nuts. Moreover, succulent fish though invisible to the human eye before being hooked are caught from the deepest pools. So we rightly proclaim the existence of the techniques which we feel are equally present because of their force. Paul bids us not to be seduced by the empty wisdom of the world,[28] but he does not deny the presence of these techniques in the divine letters. At any rate, let us turn to the psalms, and investigate the reliability of the facts, which is superior to any contention.

---

[25] This is the frequently voiced claim (see e.g. the comments of Augustine cited in the next paragraph and the remarks of Cassiodorus, *Institutiones* preface 6 and 1.4.2) that the rhetorical and literary devices found in Greek and Latin literature were anticipated in and borrowed from the Old Testament. Cicero's *Topica* is a summary of Aristotle's treatise of that name.

[26] *De doctrina christiana* 3.29.40.

[27] *Locutiones in Heptateuchum*, ed. J. Fraipont, *CCSL* 33 (Turnhout: Brepols 1958), 379–465.

[28] Cf. 1 Corinthians 3:18.

The main force of eloquence in the scriptures, previously untried and a pointer to salvation, frequently recounts certain things yet is often explaining matters greatly different from the words heard. This is a simplicity which is at two levels, a guileless form of double speaking such as Joseph employed; though he recognized his brothers by their faces and native speech, he seemed to them to speak as if there could have been absolutely no recognition.[29] The device is not adopted in the interests of deception, but to achieve a most useful effect. It employs the Hebrew language to intimate the deepest of issues. It often uses the one concept in both the bad and the good sense, so that what has a shared name is seen to differ in its qualities. It compares heavenly things with earthly, so that the understanding forbidden by the incomprehensible Majesty can be attained by comparison with objects totally familiar. It has a marvelous faculty of interweaving words, so that suddenly things which are measureless and beyond understanding are expounded in two or three words.

To put it succinctly, often even a single syllable shows the Lord's indescribable nature, as in the phrase: *He who is hath sent me.*[30] Every word of that phrase is subtly sought out, and swarms with numerous meanings. Just as the most fertile land bears perfumed plants to aid our health, so when the divine reading is examined word by word, one always finds there the cure for a wounded heart. (Many of the Fathers have spoken at greater breadth and length on the forms of the eloquence, and I have ensured that their names are mentioned in the introductory books.)[31] But the more constantly the heavenly spring is drunk, the more it knows no drying up. Let us not delay longer on generalities, but with God's help touch on the particular issues of the Psalter, for individual points are clearly recognized when described in particular cases after the preliminary generalizations.

Chapter 16: The Particular Eloquence of the Psalter

The first fact to note is that only the psalms are cited by individual numbers.[32] I have consulted those with the greatest knowledge of Scripture, and after consideration of the psalms and their extent I considered that the practice of those who sing the psalms should be continued, and that they should be set down by their verses, so that the mingling of authorities should not cause confusion in the choice of order adopted. Secondly, there is

[29] Cf. Genesis 42:23.   [30] Exodus 3:14.

[31] The "introductory books" refer to Cassiodorus' own *Institutiones*, which were written after the *Expositio*. This sentence is evidence for Cassiodorus' updating, through marginal notes that in later copying became part of the main text, of his works in the library of Vivarium. See van de Vyver, "Cassiodore et son Oeuvre," 272 with note 2.

[32] I.e. among the biblical books.

the fact that no other work with divine authority is divided into a hundred and fifty parts. In what other book do we find so diverse a variety of headings? In one place the votive word *Alleluia* comes first in the titles; elsewhere an allusion to the narrative of the Book of Kings is put at the very beginning, and is seen to denote the powers of psalms. Again, in other places there are merely diapsalms interposed,[33] while elsewhere psalms maintain numerical order following the powers which they possess.

The book starts with Christ's blessedness, runs through the mysteries of the New and Old Testaments, and concludes with sacred praises and holy joy. Hence the church rightly consoles herself with such a gift, wounded as she clearly is here on earth with the afflictions of many disasters. Weighed down as she is, she can triumph over her disasters by the Lord's kindness, for she grows by persecutions, constantly swells through afflictions, is watered by the blood of martyrs, raised higher by grief, enlarged by want, fed by tears, refreshed by fasting. She thrives on the things which weaken the world.

What will you not find in that book for provision of the means by which the human race must obtain sweet consolation? It is a treasure ever increasing in a pure heart, a great consolation for those who grieve, a blessed hope for the just, a useful refuge for those in danger. One always takes from it what is helpful, yet its stream continues enduring and unfailing. The blessed Athanasius, bishop of the city of Alexandria, in the book which he addressed to his dearest Marcellinus about the peculiar nature of the Psalter says: "Whoever recites the words of a psalm seems to be repeating his own words, to be singing in solitude words composed by himself; it does not seem to be another speaking or explaining what he takes up and reads. It is as though he were speaking from his own person, such is the nature of the words he utters. He seems to be expressing the kind of language used as if spoken from the heart. He seems to offer words to God."[34]

A further peculiarity of the Psalter is that it is the entry into the divine law. Novices do not begin with Genesis or St. Paul; initially we do not knock on the door of the sacred authority of the gospel. Though the Psalter is the fourth book authorized by God, it is fittingly the first with which novices begin when embarking on the Holy Scriptures.[35]

[The deliberative genre]

[33] In chapter 11 of his Preface, Cassiodorus defines "diapsalm" as follows: "The fact is that sympsalm is the Greek for the combining and linking of expressions, and diapsalm for a break in the flow of them. Wherever it is found it informs us that a change of spokesman or of situation is taking place. So such a term is aptly inserted where meanings or speakers are clearly to be separated. So I too shall divide the psalms appositely wherever a diapsalm can be discovered in them." (33).

[34] Athanasius, *Epistola ad Marcellinum* 11.

[35] So earlier Jerome, *Epistle* 107.12. In his *Institutiones* 1, Cassiodorus surveys the Octateuch, Kings, Prophets, and Psalms (1.4), the fourth book in this sense of the Old Testament.

From Commentary on Psalm 2

Ps. 2.11 (10): *And now, O ye kings, understand.* The third limb of the psalm is reached here, in which the prophet now urges the human race humbly to obey the Creator at the revelation of these fearful mysteries. Here the deliberative type of utterance begins, expressed most beautifully; for when men's hearts are paralyzed by the unfolding of the mystery, this most salutary and vital adviser appears, urging us to serve the true Lord with fear and trembling, and showing us that the words spoken are valuable from the viewpoint of the useful and the honorable, motifs extremely effective in deliberative speeches.[36] The useful appears in: *Lest at any time the Lord be angry, and you perish from the just way*; the honorable in: *Blessed are all they that trust in him.*[37] So the deliberative type of speech is achieved by a perfect disquisition. Now let us return to explanation of the words. By *kings* we must understand masters of vices, for they can both *understand* and with the Lord's help fulfill the command. Kings need not invariably denote men in the purple, for the term is applied also to those who have private status, for example, in Paul's description: *Now you reign without us, and would to God you did reign, that we also may reign with you.*[38]

Receive instruction, you that judge the earth. Erudire (instruct) means to teach, for the word denotes the grasping of knowledge, because *rudis* means new. One instructed is raised from an unformed state, in other words removed from ignorance and set in the boundaries of learning. This is a good description for those who have now subdued their faults of the flesh, for they *judge the earth* well when after subjugation of faults they impose the precepts of the law on their bodies with the support of the Lord. *Terra* (earth) is derived from *terere*, to wear away, because the earth is worn by the steps of journeying men.[39]

[The judicial (forensic) genre]

From Commentary on Psalm 6

Conclusion drawn from the Psalm

Though we should apply our eager intelligence to all the psalms, since the greatest resources for living are sought from them, yet we ought to pay particular attention to the psalms of the penitents, for they are like suitable medicine prescribed for the human race. From them we obtain most health-giving baths for our souls, from them we are

---

[36] In the deliberative genre, the useful and honorable are stock motifs; see *De inventione* 2.51.156; Quintilian, *Institutio oratoria* 3.8.10ff., who subdivides them into subsidiary motifs and adds a third, the possible.

[37] Psalms 2:13–14 (12–13).   [38] 2 Corinthians 4:8.

[39] This etymology was offered by Aelius Stilo, cited by Varro, *De lingua latina* 5.21 (= *Grammaticae romanae fragmenta,* ed. Funaioli, 67.39). Isidore (*Etymologiae* 14.1.1) would take it over from Cassiodorus.

restored to life when dead through sins, from them when grief-stricken we attain eternal joys. They form a sort of judicial genre, in which the defendant appears before the sight of the Judge, atoning for his sin with tears, and dissolving it by confessing it.[40] He offers the best type of defense by condemning himself. Here there is no outside person acting as prosecutor; he is his own accuser. He merits pardon because he does not excuse himself from blame. No other approach is possible before such a Judge, for before Him no man can deny his sins. Here conjecture[41] gives place, definition[42] is not sought, other aspects of the case are not in evidence, since the whole situation is exposed by the brightness of truth. So the only approach necessary is that called concession,[43] in which the defendant does not defend what has been done, but asks to be pardoned. How immeasurable is the Creator's father love? The defendant caused sentence to be passed in his favour because he accused himself more fiercely. Yet in vain could the cleverest of orators have sought to obtain from the Judge what the psalmist deserved to get from Him out of the fullness of his simplicity.

[The epideictic (demonstrative) genre]

From Commentary on Psalm 28

1. *A psalm of David at the finishing of the tabernacle.* Since the first words are now familiar, it remains for us to investigate rather more carefully the words: *The finishing of the tabernacle.* The phrase connotes the perfection of the Catholic Church, now known to be established throughout the whole world. By the term *tabernacle* the Church is said to have been founded in the world; as it wages war on the vices of the flesh, it has deservedly won the title of "expedition-dwelling."[44] So the prophet sings this psalm, so rich in the glory of Christian teaching, in praise of the holy Spirit, once he has hymned the perfection of the Church as a whole; since so important a subject as the Church's perfection has been fulfilled by prophets and apostles in their blessed teaching, he wants it to be adorned fittingly with the Spirit's praises. The whole psalm is teeming with praise of the holy Spirit, and by various allusions it issues proclamations of His majesty. This is what orators call the demonstrative type, when someone is revealed and acknowledged by description of

---

[40] Here Cassiodorus brings in classical rhetorical status theory: the Psalm chooses the position where the "defendant" does not deny the fact, nor disputes its definition, but admits it and seeks forgiveness through confession.

[41] Translator has "inference." Cassiodorus here rules out the other types of *status* as viable choices: we are dealing with the "conjectural status" (*coniectura*) when the defendant denies the fact (yes/no question): *De inventione* 1.8.10; Quintilian, *Institutio oratoria* 7.2.

[42] *Finis* here is the alternative form of *definitio*: if this *status* is adopted, the defendant contests the definition of the fact (e.g. is it murder or manslaughter?). *De inventione* 1.8.10; Quintilian, *Institutio oratoria* 7.3. See Martin, *Antike Rhetorik*, 31 ff.

[43] *Concessio*, admission of guilt, is a subdivision of the *status qualitatis*, in which fact and definition are admitted, but culpability is at issue. *De inventione* 1.9.12; Quintilian, *Institutio oratoria* 7.4. See Martin, *Antike Rhetorik*, 40. See below, selection from Cassiodorus *Institutiones* 2.2, on rhetoric.

[44] A tabernacle is properly a tent, which can serve as dwelling for men on military expeditions; here the expedition is against the vices of the flesh.

this kind. But what could anyone say appropriately about Him, except what He deigns to utter about Himself? . . .

4. *The voice of the Lord is in power.* What remarkable brevity, three words[45] expressing so great a thought! By the voice of the Lord in power he means the Spirit of understanding, who casts down and lays low all opposition. As Scripture says: *And there is none who can resist thy will.*[46] So the voice of the Lord is rightly said to be in power, for it is blocked by no obstacles.

The voice of the Lord is magnificence. Here the spirit of counsel breathes its fragrance. What is more magnificent than He who illuminates the heart, and brings the realization that good things are to be sought and all most wicked things avoided, who makes provision that the impious man becomes pious, the captive free, the slave a son? There is no doubt that this accrues to those in whom the holy Spirit dwells with the power of His majesty.

From Commentary on Psalm 32 [33]

Explanation of the psalm

Rejoice in the Lord, ye just: joint praise becometh the upright. The blessed David dissociates the Catholic Church from the contagion of heretics, and advises upright Christians to rejoice not in earthly delights but in the Lord, where their joys are perfected in unbroken sweetness. Though this world's afflictions are appropriate to the faithful, the just are told *rejoice.* But with what joy? It could only be that of which the Lord advises us: *When men persecute you and speak all that is evil against you untruly for my name's sake, be glad and rejoice, for your reward is very great in heaven.*[47] In the same way Paul mentions that we must rejoice unceasingly, for he says: *Rejoice in the Lord: again I say, rejoice.*[48] This repetition makes the point that we should rejoice here in afflictions, and be glad in the undying peace of the kingdom to come. This is why the Lord says in the gospel: *I will see you again, and your heart shall rejoice, and your joy no man shall take from you.*[49] The psalmist added: *Joint praise becometh the upright.* Who these upright are he is to tell us in the second part. In this phrase, *Joint praise becometh the upright,* he shows that such praise does not become debased heretics. As another prophet has also said: *Praise is not seemly in the mouth of a sinner.*[50] *Joint praise* is the same praise uttered in the mouths of many; the expression is used to denote the unity of the Church, which he proclaims is preserved

---

[45] In Latin, *vox Domini in virtute.*   [46] Esther 13:9.   [47] Matthew 5:11ff.
[48] Philippians 4:4.   [49] John 16:22.   [50] Ecclesiastes 15:9.

everywhere. When he says *becometh*, he demonstrates that it is appropriate and suitable that one who sings the praise of the Lord is likewise pleasing to Him both in uprightness of faith and in worth of deeds. . . .

4. *For the word of the Lord is right: and all his works are done with faithfulness.* From this point he begins to hasten through the praises of the Lord by different statements made in the demonstrative genre, so that all His deeds and commands may grow sweet in our eyes. So *the word of the Lord is right*, that is, for the guidance of men. It is truly called right for it makes men right; a marvelous epithet, a true-spoken word. Since we are corrected by the divine law, we are detached by it from our wickedness, and then we live according to the law since we obey its commands. This is the fifth type of definition, called by the Greeks *kata ten lexin* and in Latin *ad verbum*;[51] for one part of the prayer defines what the word of the Lord is, namely *right*. He attaches the phrase, *And all his works are done with faithfulness*; this is especially so when He works in those who by His gift have gained the merit of fidelity. As He says in the gospel: *Thy faith hath made thee safe*.[52] That woman would not have deserved the Lord's help if faith bestowed through gratuitous generosity had not preceded it.

FROM *INSTITUTIONES* BOOK 2, SECULAR LETTERS

[In the opening of book 2 Cassiodorus explains that he will divide this book into seven chapters to reflect the notions of continuity and perpetuity that that number can evoke (pref. 2).]

1. On Grammar

1. Grammar gets its name from the letters as the derived character of the word itself shows.[53] The first inventor of only sixteen of them is said to have been Cadmus,[54] who

---

[51] "By the word."   [52] Luke 7:50, describing how Christ rewarded Magdalen for anointing his feet.
[53] Greek *grammatikê* (Latin *grammatica*) comes from *grammata* "letters."
[54] Pliny, *Naturalis historia* 7.192.

handed them down to the studious Greeks, who in turn supplied the rest by their liveliness of mind. On the positions and values of the letters Helenus has written a subtle treatise in Greek and Priscian another in Latin.[55] Grammar is skill in the art of cultivated speech— skill acquired from famous writers of poetry and of prose; its function [*officium*] is the creation of faultless prose and verse; its end [*finis*] is to please through skill in finished speech and blameless writing. But although such authors of earlier times as Palaemon,[56] Phocas,[57] Probus,[58] and Censorinus[59] have written on the art of grammar with variety of method and have been highly esteemed in their own day, nevertheless we intend to bring Donatus to everyone's attention,[60] who is considered to be especially appropriate for boys and suitable for novices;[61] we have left you two commentaries on his work in order that a twofold explanation may make even clearer him who is already clear.[62] We have also discovered that St. Augustine has written a short course of instruction on the same topic for the simple brothers; and we have left you this work to read, lest anything seem to be lacking to the inexperienced, who are being made ready for high achievement in this great study.

2. In the second part of his work[63] Donatus discusses the following topics: articulate sound,[64] the letter, the syllable, [metrical] feet, accentuation, punctuation or proper phrasing, the eight parts of speech (for the second time),[65] figures of speech, etymologies, and orthography. Articulate sound is air that is struck which is perceptible to the ear, in and by itself.[66] The *letter* is the smallest part of articulate sound.[67] A *syllable* is the combination of letters or the pronunciation of one vowel capable of containing (metrical) beats.[68] A *foot* is a definite reckoning of syllables and of quantity.[69] *Accentuation* is the artistic pronunciation of a word without mistake. *Punctuation* or *proper phrasing* is a clear pausing

---

[55] Reference is to book I of Priscian's *Institutiones* (*GL* 2), see pp. 173–4 on Priscian.

[56] Q. Remmius Palaemon, famous grammarian of the first century AD. This work is lost. See Barwick, *Remmius Palaemon und die römische Ars grammatica*.

[57] Author of an *ars de nomine et verbo*, fifth century AD.

[58] M. Valerius Probus, grammarian of the first century AD.

[59] Wrote a book on accentuation in the third century AD.

[60] For Donatus, see pp. 62–3 and 82–103.

[61] Boys study the *ars minor*, novices the *ars maior*, cf. Holtz, *Donat et la tradition de l'enseignement*, 247.

[62] Jones translates as if the *Ars minor* and *maior* themselves are meant. However, reference is probably to commentaries based on the work by Servius, cf. Holtz, *Donat et la tradition de l'enseignement*, 248f. Possibly one of them dealt with the *Ars minor* and one with the *Ars maior*. Cassiodorus himself may have been their compiler. Cf. for the codex with helpful material on grammar put together by Cassiodorus in *De orthographia* 144.7ff. *post codicem, in quo Artes Donati cum commentis suis et librum de etymologiis et alium librum Sacerdotis de schematibus Domino praestante collegi* (Holtz, *Donat et la tradition de l'enseignement*, 249).

[63] I.e. in his *Ars maior*. This whole section is based on Donatus, except for the definitions of accents and punctuation.

[64] *de voce articulata.*   [65] Donatus had also discussed these in the much shorter *Ars minor.*

[66] Cf. Donatus *Ars maior* I.1, *GL* 4:367.5–7.   [67] Cf. Donatus *Ars maior* I.2, *GL* 4:367.9.

[68] Cf. Donatus *Ars maior* I.3, *GL* 4:368.18–19.   [69] *temporum.* Cf. Donatus *Ars maior* I.4, *GL* 4:369.17.

in well-regulated pronunciation. The parts of speech are eight in number: noun, pronoun, verb, adverb, participle, conjunction, preposition, and interjection.[70] The *noun* is a part of speech with case signifying a body or a thing as a proper name (uniquely) or as a common name (generally); as a proper name, e.g. *Roma* ["Rome"], *Tiberis* ["Tiber"], as a common name, e.g. *urbs* ["city"], *flumen* ["river"].[71] A *pronoun* is a part of speech which is used instead of a noun without causing any perceptible change in meaning and which sometimes admits person.[72] A *verb* is a part of speech which has tense and person, but no case.[73] An *adverb* is a part of speech added to a verb to clarify and complete its meaning, as in such an expression as "I shall *now* make," or "I shall *not* make."[74] A *participle* is a part of speech so called because it partakes of the functions of a noun and of a verb; it receives gender and case from the noun, tense and meaning from the verb, number and form[75] from both.[76] A *conjunction* is a part of speech which binds a sentence together and sets it in order.[77] A *preposition* is a part of speech placed before other parts of speech to change, complete, or curtail their meaning.[78] An *interjection* is a part of speech, which signifies a disposition of mind through uncultivated sound.[79] *Figures of speech* are transformations of words or thoughts, used for the sake of adornment;[80] in the collection made by the grammatical writer Sacerdos[81] they are ninety-eight in number. But this number includes those which are considered faults by Donatus. Like Sacerdos, I too feel that it is unfortunate to label as faults those figures which are supported by the example of established authors and particularly by the authority of the divine law.[82] Figures of speech are common to professors of literature[83] and to orators, and they are recognized as being well suited to both. I must also add something on etymologies and orthography, concerning which I am sure several men have written. *Etymology* is the true or probable demonstration of the origin of a word.[84] *Orthography* is the art of composing correctly and without error; it applies alike to writing and to speaking.

3. Let these words, which concern brief definitions alone, suffice. But let him who desires wider and fuller knowledge of these matters read both preface and body of the

[70] Cf. Donatus *Ars maior* 2.1, *GL* 4:372.25–6.   [71] Cf. Donatus *Ars maior* 2.2, *GL* 4:373.1–2.

[72] Cf. Donatus *Ars maior* 2.11, *GL* 4:379.23–4.   [73] Cf. Donatus *Ars maior* 2.12, *GL* 4:381.14.

[74] Cf. Donatus, *Ars maior* 2.13, *GL* 4:385.11–12.

[75] *figura*. I.e. the characteristic of being either simple or compound.

[76] Cf. Donatus, *Ars maior* 2.14, *GL* 4:387.18–20.   [77] Cf. Donatus, *Ars maior* 2.15, *GL* 4:388.28.

[78] Cf. Donatus, *Ars maior* 2.16, *GL* 4:389.19–20.   [79] Cf. Donatus, *Ars maior* 2.17, *GL* 4:391.26–7.

[80] Here Cassiodorus abandons Donatus, who does not give a simple definition, but gives a more complex statement unsuitable for the text Cassiodorus is composing (see *Ars maior* 3.5, *GL* 4:397.5ff.).

[81] M. Plotius Sacerdos, third century AD. A short selection from his work may be found in the ablative absolute dossier in Part 2.

[82] On this passage, cf. Holtz, *Donat et la tradition de l'enseignement*, 251f.   [83] *grammatici*.

[84] See the etymology dossier, Part 2, pp. 339–66.

codex which I have had written on the art of grammar, in order that the careful reader may find the facts which he knows are considered to belong to this subject. Let us now come to the divisions and definitions of the art of rhetoric; as its extensiveness and richness deserve, it has been amply treated by many illustrious writers.

2. *On Rhetoric*

1. Rhetoric is said to be derived *apo tou rhêtoreuein*, that is, from skill in making a set speech. The art of rhetoric, moreover, according to the teaching of professors of secular letters, is expertness in discourse on civil questions.[85] The orator, then, is a good man skilled in discoursing on civil questions,[86] as has just been said. The function[87] of an orator is speaking suitably in order to persuade; his purpose[88] is to persuade, by speaking on civil questions, to the extent permitted by the nature of things and persons.[89] Let us now, therefore, take up a few matters briefly in order that we may understand the main points of almost the entire art and the excellence of the art from a description of several of its parts. According to Fortunatianus,[90] a modern writer on rhetoric, civil questions are questions "which can fall within the range of common understanding, that is, questions which everyone can comprehend, since they concern what is fair and good."[91]

2. Rhetoric has five parts:[92] invention, arrangement, style, memorization, delivery. *Invention* is the devising of arguments which are true or which resemble true arguments to make a case appear credible. *Arrangement* is the excellent distribution in regular order of the arguments devised. *Style* is the use of suitable words adapted to the arguments. *Memorization* is a lasting comprehension by the mind of the arguments and the language. *Delivery* is the harmonious adjustment of voice and gesture in keeping with the dignity of the arguments and the language.

3. The three principal kinds of rhetorical case are these:[93]

[85] Quintilian, *Institutio oratoria* 2.15.33, 38; Isidore, *Etymologiae* 2.1.1 (based on this passage).
[86] Fortunatianus 1.1, in Halm, ed., *Rhetores latini minores*, 81. [87] *officium.* [88] *finis.*
[89] Quintilian 2.15.5; cf. Cicero, *De inventione* 1.5.6; Fortunatianus 1.1 (= Halm, 81).
[90] *Artis rhetoricae libri III* (second half of the fourth century, in Halm, ed., *Rhetores latini minores*, 79–134), largely based on Quintilian. The work is in erotapokritic (question-and-answer) format.
[91] Fortunatianus 1.1 (= Halm, 81). [92] Main source for this section: Cicero, *De inventione* 1.7.9.
[93] Main source: Fortunatianus 1.1; cf. Aristotle, *Rhetoric*, 1358b8.

The *demonstrative* kind is that which points out a particular matter and contains praise or blame. The *deliberative* kind is that which contains persuasion and dissuasion. The *judicial* kind is that which contains accusation and defense, or the seeking and refusing of a penalty.

4. The central issue of a case is called its "position."[94] The position arises out of the complaint and the answer. The positions of cases are either rational or legal.[95] There are four rational positions which are general:

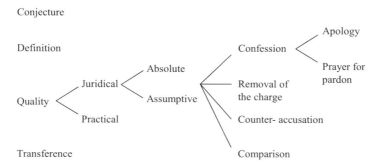

But, as Cicero relates in his work *On the Orator*[96] in correction of his own statements, transference ought to be classed among the legal positions, for Fortunatianus says,[97] we "accept transference as merely legal. Why? Because no transference, that is, no demurrer, can exist without law." There are five legal positions:[98] letter and spirit, contradictory laws, ambiguity, reasoning or deduction, and legal definition.

5. The *conjectural* position[99] is that in which the fact charged by one side is vigorously denied by the other. The *definitive* position[100] is that in which we hold that the fact is not as charged, but in which we demonstrate its nature by the use of definitions. *Quality*[101] is the position in which the character of an act is sought; and, since the controversy concerns the import and essential nature of the act, it is called the general position. When a case depends either upon the fact that the proper man does not seem to be bringing the action or the fact that the action is not being brought against the proper man, or in the proper court, or at the proper time, or under the proper law, or with the proper charge, or with the proper penalty, the position in which the case rests is called *translative*, because the

---

[94] *status*. Sections 4–7 are taken over by Isidore, *Etymologiae* 2.5–6. Source here is Fortunatianus 1.11 and 12, in Halm, ed., *Rhetores latini minores*, 89ff.

[95] I.e. either based on argument, or on legal documents or written law.

[96] In fact *Rhetorica ad Herennium* 1.2.   [97] Fortunatianus 1.11, (Halm, 89).

[98] Fortunatianus 1.22, (Halm, 97).   [99] Fortunatianus 1.11, (Halm, 90).

[100] Fortunatianus 1.13, (Halm, 91).   [101] Cf. *De inventione* 1.8.10.

action seems to require transference and change. The *juridical* position[102] is that in which the nature of the justice and right involved and the reasonableness of the fine or punishment are sought. The *practical* position is that in which one considers what is right in accordance with civil custom and equity.[103] The *absolute* position is that which contains the question of justice and injury in itself. The *assumptive* position is that which has no strength of defense in itself but assumes some defense from without. The *confession* is the position in which the accused does not defend that which has been done but begs to be pardoned; we have pointed out that this has to do with penitents.[104] *Removal of the charge* is the position in which the accused attempts by force of argument or influence to transfer the charge from himself and his own culpability to another. A *counter accusation* is the position in which an act is said to have been lawfully done because the doer was previously provoked unjustly. *Comparison* is the position in which it is contended that as a result of the commission of the act charged some other worthy and useful deed has been done by one of the two parties to the dispute.[105] *Apology* is the position in which the act is admitted but the blame set aside; it has three parts: ignorance, chance, necessity. A *prayer for pardon* is the position in which the defendant admits that he has been guilty and deliberately guilty and yet begs that he be pardoned; this type of plea will happen very rarely.

6. *Letter and spirit*[106] is the position in which the actual language of a written document seems to be at variance with the writer's intention. The position of a *contradictory law* is that in which two or more laws are recognized as disagreeing. *Ambiguity* is the position in which a written document seems to have two or more meanings. *Reasoning*, also called *deduction*, is the position in which something that is not written in the law is ascertained from that which is written therein. *Legal definition* is the position in which the force of a word on which the definition depends is sought, just as in the definitive position. According to some men, therefore, the total number of both rational and legal positions is quite surely eighteen.[107] According to Tully's *Rhetorical Books*,[108] on the other hand, the number is found to be nineteen, because the author has, for the most part, assigned transference to the rational positions; in correction of his own classification, however, as has been stated above, he has later joined transference to the legal positions.

7. Every subject for dispute, as Cicero says,[109] is either simple or complex; and if it is complex, one must consider whether it is made so because of the joining of several points

---

[102] From here to end of section 5, see *De inventione* 1.10.14–1.11.15.

[103] Cf. Quintilian, *Institutio oratoria* 2.21.3.

[104] Cf. Cassiodorus, *Expositio Psalmorum.* 31.1; 16.13; 50.1f. (ed. Adriaen, CCSL 97:148; 275; 454).

[105] I.e. if something bad was done, it was for the sake of a greater good.   [106] Cf. *De inventione* 1.12.17.

[107] Not counting transference.   [108] *De inventione* (see 1.11.16).   [109] *De inventione* 1.12.17.

or because of some comparison. A *simple* subject is that which contains a single complete point, as in the following question: "Shall we declare war against Corinth or not?" A *complex subject arising from the joining of several points* is that in which an inquiry is made concerning several matters, for example, whether Carthage should be destroyed, or whether it should be given back to the Carthaginians, or whether a colony should be transplanted there. A *complex subject arising from a comparison* is that in which an inquiry is made concerning the relative desirability of two or more acts; for example, whether an army should be sent into Macedonia against Philip to help our allies or whether it should be held in Italy to provide us with as many men as possible against Hannibal.

8. There are five kinds of legal cases: honorable, paradoxical, insignificant, uncertain, obscure. An *honorable* case is one toward which the mind of the hearer is favorably disposed at once without any utterance of ours. A *paradoxical* case is one by which the minds of those who are about to hear is made hostile. An *insignificant* case is one which is neglected by the hearer and seems unworthy of very much attention. An *uncertain* case is one in which either the judgment is doubtful or the cause partly honorable and partly discreditable so that it begets both good will and displeasure. An *obscure* case is one in which either the hearers are dull or the cause is apparently entangled in affairs which are somewhat hard to understand.

9. A rhetorical composition has six parts: exordium, narration, partition, direct argument, refutation, conclusion.[110] The *exordium* is an utterance which suitably prepares the hearer's mind for the rest of the discourse.[111] The *narration* is an exposition of the acts done or supposed to have been done.[112] The *partition* is that which, if properly made, renders the whole speech clear and intelligible.[113] The *direct argument* is that by means of whose proofs the speech induces belief and adds strength and support to our cause.[114] The *refutation* is that by means of whose proofs the direct argument of adversaries is destroyed or weakened.[115] The *conclusion* is the termination and end of the entire speech, and in it there is sometimes employed a concluding plea calculated to bring forth tears.[116]

10. Now, Cicero, the distinguished light of Latin eloquence, has set these matters forth abundantly and carefully in his various works and seems to have included them in the two books of his *Art of Rhetoric*,[117] on which I have left you, in my library, a commentary composed by Marius Victorinus.[118] But nevertheless, Quintilian, a surpassing instructor, after the streams of Tully's learning was still able to enrich his teachings. He took into his care at an early age that man morally good and skilled in speaking, and has pointed out that this

---

[110] *De inventione* I.14.19. [111] *De inventione* I.15.20. [112] *De inventione* I.19.27.
[113] *De inventione* I.22.31. [114] *De inventione* I.24.34. [115] *De inventione* I.42.78.
[116] *De inventione* I.52.98. [117] Namely, the two books of *De inventione*.
[118] See above, section on Marius Victorinus, pp. 104–24.

man ought to be trained in all the arts and disciplines of noble letters in order that the prayers of the entire state may justly seek him out as a champion. We have concluded that the two books of Cicero's work *On the Art of Rhetoric*,[119] and the twelve books of Quintilian's *Manual* ought to be joined in such a way that they fit into one big codex, and that both works may be at hand when they are needed. Fortunatianus, a recent teacher, who has discussed this subject subtly and minutely in three books, we have reduced to one neat handy volume, in order that he may put an end to the reader's aversion and may fittingly cause him to arrive at the essentials. Let the lover of brevity read this author, for, though he has not extended his work to many books, he has nevertheless discussed a large number of topics with an exceedingly acute reasoning. You will discover that these codices, together with a special preface, have been assembled in a single corpus.[120]

11. Rhetorical argumentation is treated as follows:[121]

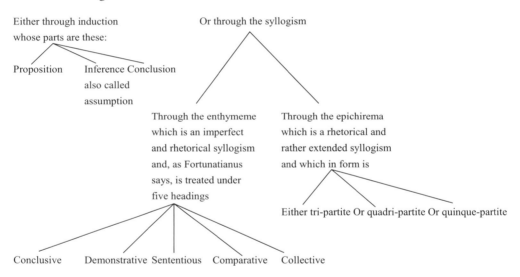

Argumentation [*argu-ment-atio*] is the term used, as it were, for the verbal expression of a clear mind [**argutae mentis oratio**];[122] it is a statement by means of which we maintain that

---

[119] Namely, the two books of *De inventione*.

[120] Van de Vyver, "Cassiodore et son oeuvre," 257f. notes the discrepancy between the two statements about the books by Cicero, Quintilian, and Fortunatianus. This is another sign of revision of the texts in the library at Vivarium. After having completed the *Institutiones*, Cassiodorus created a corpus (which is nothing but a large codex: van de Vyver, "Cassiodore et son oeuvre," 276 note 3) of rhetorical texts with a special preface, just as he provided other collected volumes on the introductory disciplines (grammar, orthography, logic).

[121] *De inventione* 1.31.51; Fortunatianus, 2.28f. (Halm, 118f.).

[122] Cf. Fortunatianus 2.28, (Halm, 118). The etymology was taken over by Isidore, *Etymologiae* 2.9.1. For such syllabic etymologies, see the etymology dossier in Part 2.

a proof which has been discovered is probable. An *induction* is a statement which by the use of clearly known particulars seeks to gain approval for the generalization with which the induction was begun, whether among philosophers or rhetoricians or conversationalists.[123] A *proposition* is the part of an induction which of necessity introduces one or more points similar to the point to be admitted. An *inference*, also called an "assumption," is the part of an induction that introduces the point which is at issue and on account of which the similarities have been used.[124] A *conclusion* is the part of an induction which establishes the admission made in the *inference* or points out what is established from the admission.

12. A *syllogism* is a form of statement by means of which we prove a point at issue. An *enthymeme* is rendered into Latin as a mental concept and is usually called an imperfect syllogism by rhetorical writers.[125] For this form of proof consists of two parts, since to gain credence it employs an argument which disregards the law of the syllogism; for example: "If the tempest is to be avoided, one must therefore not sail upon the sea." It is indeed considered complete in possessing merely a major premise and a conclusion, and consequently it has been deemed suitable for orators rather than for dialecticians. We shall, however, speak of dialectical syllogisms in the proper place.

13. A *conclusive* enthymeme is one which proves something beyond doubt, as in the following example from Cicero's defense of Milo: "You sit here, then, to avenge the death of one to whom you would refuse to restore life, even if you thought you had the power."[126] A *demonstrative* enthymeme is one which is compelling through the certain demonstration of a point, as in the following example from Cicero's *Orations against Catiline*: "And yet this man lives. He lives? Why, he even comes into the Senate."[127] A *sententious* enthymeme is one whose authority is increased by the use of a maxim, as in the following example from Terence:[128] "Complaisance makes friends, and truthfulness is the mother of unpopularity." A *comparative* enthymeme is one which by a comparison to something used as an example portends a similar outcome, as in the following illustration from Cicero's *Philippics*:[129] "I wonder that you, Antonius, while you copy their deeds, do not shudder at their end." A *collective* enthymeme is one in which all the proofs are collected into a single statement, as in the following example from Cicero's defense of Milo: "Did he then desire, when some people were sure to protest, to do what he refused to do when all would have been delighted? And did he have no hesitation in slaying

---

[123] *De inventione* 1.31.51; Fortunatianus 2.28.   [124] *De inventione* 1.32.54.

[125] For the enthymeme as an abbreviated syllogism, cf. e.g. Quintilian, *Institutio oratoria* 5.14.24.

[126] Cicero's *Pro Milone* 79. The *Pro Milone* was the classic of rhetorical theory (the rhetorical equivalent of the *Oedipus Rex* for the theory of tragedy): Quintilian, *Institutio oratoria* 5.14.2.

[127] Cicero, *In Catilinam* I 1.2.   [128] Terence, *Andria* 68.   [129] Cicero, *Philippics* II 1.1.

Clodius unlawfully, inopportunely, and at the risk of his own life, when he did not venture to slay him when he might have done so lawfully, advantageously, and opportunely?"[130]

14. According to Victorinus, moreover, there is another definition of the enthymeme. It consists of a major premise alone, as has already been stated; for example: "If the tempest is to be avoided, one must not sail upon the sea"; or of a minor premise alone; for example: "There are those who say that the world moves without divine direction"; or of a conclusion alone; for example: "A divine judgment is therefore true"; or of a major and minor premise; for example: "If he is unfriendly, he will perish,[131] and he is unfriendly," and because a conclusion is lacking in the last case, the argument is called an enthymeme.

15. The epichirema follows. An *epichirema*, as we have said above, is a rather extended treatment of the rhetorical syllogism, proceeding from deduction and differing from the dialectical syllogism in amplitude and length of language, on account of which it is assigned to rhetoricians.[132] A *tripartite* epichirematic syllogism is one which consists of three parts: major premise, minor premise, and conclusion. A *quadripartite* epichirematic syllogism is one which consists of four parts: major premise, minor premise, additional proof joined to either, and conclusion. In like manner, a *quinquepartite* syllogism is one which consists of five parts: major premise and additional proof, minor premise and additional proof, and conclusion. This is the type of syllogism used in the following quotation from Cicero's *Art of Rhetoric*:[133] "If deliberative and demonstrative oratory are types of speech, they cannot rightly be considered as subdivisions of one type, for the same object may be called a type by some people and a subdivision by others, but it cannot be called both a type and a subdivision by the same person"; more follows which falls within the limits of this syllogism. But I shall see to what extent the reader can exercise his ingenuity concerning the parts which I have omitted.

16. In his third book,[134] the aforesaid Fortunatianus has made mention of the orator's memorization and of his delivery and use of voice; the monk will derive a certain advantage from this book,[135] since it seems not improper for him to adapt to his own uses that which orators have profitably applied to disputation. Duly cautious, he will pay heed to memorization, as applied to divine reading, when he has learned its force and nature from the afore-mentioned book; he will foster the art of delivery in reading the divine law aloud; and he will, moreover, preserve a careful manner of using the voice in

[130] Cicero, *Pro Milone* 41; Quintilian, *Institutio oratoria* 5.14.3.   [131] or: "he will kill."

[132] Cassiodorus, *Expositio Psalmorum* 26.2 (ed. Adriaen, *CCSL* 97:235); 36.2 (*CCSL* 97:325).

[133] Cicero, *De inventione* 1.9.12.   [134] Fortunatianus, 3.13ff. (Halm, ed., *Rhetores latini minores*, 128).

[135] Note explicit indication of intended audience.

chanting the psalms. Thus, though he be somewhat occupied by secular books, he will be restored to holy work upon the completion of his instruction.

17. Let us now in due order come to logic, which is also called dialectic. Some have preferred to name it a science,[136] and some an art[137], saying that when it uses demonstrative, that is, true arguments in discussing a subject, it ought to be called a science and when it treats something probable and conjectural it is called an art. Each of these terms is properly used because of the nature of proof in each case. For Father Augustine, impressed, I believe, by this consideration, has followed Varro in naming grammar and rhetoric sciences;[138] and, in addition, Felix Capella[139] has given the title *On the Seven Sciences* to his own work. A science[140] is so named because it is a subject completely known[141] and the name is justly applied, since the immutable rule of truth always follows in its track.

[136] *disciplinam.*   [137] *artem.*   [138] Augustinus, *De ordine* 2.22.37; *Retractiones* 1.6.

[139] This is Martianus [Minneus Felix] Capella, author of the *De nuptiis Philologiae et Mercurii*. See Part 1, section on Martianus Capella, above, pp. 148–66.

[140] *disciplina.*

[141] *quia **discitur plena**.* Taken over by Isidore, *Etymologiae* 1.1.1. See also the etymology dossier, Part 2, pp. 339–66.

ISIDORE OF SEVILLE, *ETYMOLOGIAE*, CA. 625

INTRODUCTION

Isidore, bishop of Seville (ca. 560–636), left an intellectual heritage marked out by his interest in grammar and philology. His massive encyclopedic work, the *Etymologiae* (or *Origines*), had a vast influence across the Middle Ages as a lasting authoritative resource, giving rise in turn to other encyclopedias and lexicons.[1] The work dates to the first quarter of the seventh century. It was left unfinished at Isidore's death and was edited posthumously in twenty books by his friend Braulio, who also authored an important bibliographical essay of Isidore's works.[2]

Intended as a Christian alternative to the comprehensive pagan works of learning such as Pliny's *Natural History*, the *Etymologiae* dealt with all aspects of knowledge (books 1–4 on the *artes liberales* and medicine; 5 and 6 on law, time, books and libraries, organization of the religious year, cult), and in addition covered theological, moral, and natural sciences. In the words of the translators of the recent (and only) complete English version of the text, "[Isidore's] aims were not novelty but authority, not originality but accessibility, not augmenting but preserving and transmitting knowledge."[3] The work belongs in the context of a monastic educational program, but was also destined for the governing classes of the Visigothic kingdom, consisting of political and ecclesiastical administrators. For both parts of his intended audience, the work would impart the "preliminary skills that make intelligent reading, especially of Scripture, possible."[4]

---

[1] On Isidore, see especially Fontaine, *Isidore de Séville et la culture classique* and *Isidore de Séville: genèse et originalité*; Amsler, *Etymology and Grammatical Discourse*, 133–72. On the *Etymologies*, see now the new translation by Barney et al., *The Etymologies of Isidore of Seville* (this appeared when the present book was nearing completion). For the title of the *Etymologiae*, cf. Codoñer Merino, "'Origines' o 'Etymologiae'?"

[2] The so-called *Renotatio*: see the edition by Martin, *La renotatio . . . de Braulio de Zaragoza*, CCSL 113B.

[3] *The Etymologies*, trans. Barney et al., 10–11.   [4] Ibid., 18.

The *Etymologiae* derives from three distinctive ancient intellectual traditions: etymology, encyclopedia, and lexicography (of which etymology may also be considered a part).[5] The etymological tradition thrives throughout classical antiquity.[6] Isidore's most important predecessor in the encyclopedic tradition was Varro (116–27 BC), whose *Disciplinae* (covering what became the seven liberal arts, along with medicine and architecture) does not survive. Pliny's *Natural History* (AD 77) is another important precedent for encyclopedism. In fact, Pliny may be one of only four named sources that Isidore used directly (with Jerome, Augustine, and, importantly, Donatus).[7] Isidore's main sources remain unacknowledged. They are Solinus, Servius, and Cassiodorus.[8]

Isidore sets great conceptual store on beginnings (*exordium, primordium, origo, etymologia*).[9] The discursive strategy of etymology is used as an organizing principle in his work, which means that disciplines are dissected into their constituent terms, and the etymologies serve to gain epistemological access to the underlying concepts by explaining why something has the name it has. The name works first heuristically, but then functions as an epistemological archive. The etymologies thus also serve a mnemonic function.[10] Language itself will reveal the truth of the world and is thus an instrument of divine providence.[11] Apart from etymologizing, Isidore also avails himself of the technique of distinguishing *differentiae*: apparent synonyms,[12] words easily confused, are given their distinctive semantic properties.[13] This contributes to a proper use of words, and to a better grasp and more precise knowledge of the world.[14] Apart from briefly discussing *differentiae*

---

[5] See the overview ibid., 12.   [6] See also the introduction to the etymology dossier, Part 2, pp. 339–44.

[7] For the importance of Donatus, see Magallon, *La tradicion gramatical de differentia y etymologia hasta Isidoro de Sevilla*, and Gasti, "Isidore e la tradizione grammaticale." On the "Christianized" Donatus see below, p. 257.

[8] *The Etymologies*, trans. Barney et al., 14.   [9] Fontaine, *Isidore de Séville: genèse et originalité*, 283ff.

[10] See Carruthers, "Inventional Mnemonics and the Ornaments of Style: the Case of Etymology."

[11] Cf. Valastro Canale, "Isidoro di Siviglia: la vis verbi come riflesso dell' omnipotenza divina."

[12] Cf. Pérez Castro, "Acerca de los *verba idem significantia*, la *synonymia*, y la sinonimia." In ancient rhetoric, the figure of *synonymia* was a combination of words with complementary (not same or similar) meanings: they combine to express one thing (from different angles).

[13] See Codoñer Merino, "Differentia y etymologia, dos modos de aproximación a la realidad, II," and *Isidoro de Sevilla, Diferencias, Libro I*, ed. and trans. Codoñer Merino.

[14] Cf. Codoñer Merino, "Differentia y etymologia," emphasizing the *differentiae rerum*, the distinctions in the ordering of the universe on the level of the "significates," rather than the signifiers. In the preface to his work *Differentiae*, Isidore states that words that are now confused are in fact distinguished by their proper "origins" [*propria origine*]. This shows the relation between etymology and *differentiae*. The confusion was brought about by the metrical exigencies of poetry, which then became normal usage also for the *auctores*: "plerique veterum sermonum *differentias distinguere* studuerunt subtilius inter verba et verba aliquid indagantes. Poetae autem gentilium necessitate metrica *confuderunt* sermonum *proprietatem*. Sicque ex his consuetudo obtinuit pleraque ab auctoribus *indifferenter accipi*, quae quidem quamvis similia videantur *quadam tamen propria inter se origine distinguuntur*" (*Isidoro de Sevilla, Diferencias, Libro I*, ed. Codoñer Merino, 84 [emphasis added]).

in the context of the first book of the *Etymologiae*, Isidore also wrote separate treatises on *Differentiae* and on synonyms.[15]

We present excerpts from the first book (*De grammatica*) and excerpts on rhetoric from the second book (*De rhetorica et dialectica*). In the first book, Isidore combines a technical approach to grammar with a more mystical view on the value of letters as an indication of moral truth.[16] The summary of rhetorical doctrine in book 2 is a product of the late antique preference for rhetorical compendia, and in turn served as an authoritative compendium of the art for many centuries. It is important to note that Isidore's treatment of the figures and tropes is to a large extent based in grammatical sources.[17]

Selections from book 1 (Grammar) translated from *Etymologiarum sive originum libri xx*, ed. Lindsay, by permission; translation of selections from book 2 (sections on Rhetoric) reprinted (with minor adaptations) from *Etymologies book II: Rhetoric*, ed. and trans. Marshall, by permission.

FROM BOOK 1: GRAMMAR

i. Discipline and Art

1. *Disciplina* ["discipline"] has got its name from *discere* ["to learn"]; hence it can also be called *scientia* ["knowledge"]. For *scire* ["to know"] is named after *discere* ["to learn"], since none of us *scit* ["knows"] unless he *di-scit* ["learns"]. Or else *disciplina* ["discipline"] <has got its name> because it *discitur plena* ["is learned fully"].[18]

2. *Ars* ["art"] has got its name because it consists of *artis* ["strict"] instructions and rules.[19] Others say that this word is derived from the Greek *apo tês aretês*, i.e. from virtue, the name they used for knowledge.[20]

---

[15] See Fontaine, *Isidore de Séville: genèse et originalité*, 167ff. for these different types of grammatical works.

[16] On the structure of Isidore's "grammar," cf. Holtz, *Donat et la tradition de l'enseignement*, 259–60.; see also Amsler, *Etymology and Grammatical Discourse*, 133–72, esp. 147–58. For the chapter on etymology itself (a part of grammar, *Etymologies* I 29), see the etymology dossier in Part 2, pp. 349–51.

[17] See excerpt from 2.xxi below and note; and see the introduction to Part 1, above, p. 70.

[18] This etymology also accounts for the second half of the word *disci-plina*.

[19] *Ars* connected to *artus* ["narrow, strict"].

[20] Based on the identification by Plato's Socrates of virtue and knowledge.

3. Plato and Aristotle drew this distinction (*differentia*) between art and discipline: that art is in things that can also be different; but discipline deals with those things which cannot happen differently. For when something is set out in true disputations, it will be a discipline; when something is discussed which is likely and subject to opinion, it will have the name of art.

ii. *The Seven Liberal Disciplines*

1. There are seven disciplines of the liberal arts. First, grammar, i.e. the expertise of speech. Second, rhetoric, which is held necessary especially in civil controversies because of its beauty and the abundance [*copia*] of its eloquence. Third, dialectic, also named logic, which distinguishes what is true from what is false through the subtlest argumentations.

2. Four, arithmetic, which includes the causes and divisions of numbers. Five, music, which consists of tunes and songs.

3. Six, geometry, embracing the measures and dimensions of the earth. Seven, astronomy, which is about the laws of the stars.

iii. *Common Letters*[21]

1. The basis of the art of grammar are the common letters, used by elementary teachers of writing and arithmetic.[22] Learning them is as it were the infancy of the art of grammar. That is why Varro calls this stage *litteratio* ["letter-learning": instruction in reading and writing]. Letters are indices of things, and signs for words. They are so powerful that the words of those who are absent speak to us without a voice. [For they introduce words through our eyes, not our ears].[23]

2. The use of letters was invented in order to remember things. To prevent them from fleeing away through oblivion, they are tied down by letters. For given the great variety of things they could neither all be learned by hearing about them, nor be contained in memory.

3. Letters are so called as if they were *leg-iter-ae* ["reading-roads"],[24] because they offer a path to the readers, or because they (*in*) *leg-endo iter-entur* ["are repeated in reading"].

---

[21] On the chapters on letters, see Fontaine, *Isidore de Séville et la culture classique*, chapter 2.
[22] Letters would also be used in arithmetic, see also below 1.iii.10 and 11.
[23] Text bracketed as inauthentic by editor.   [24] Cf. section on Priscian, above, pp. 173–4.

4.   It seems that the Latin and Greek letters originate from the Hebrew ones. For they had the name "aleph" first, then alpha was derived from that among the Greeks on the basis of its similar pronunciation, then the A among the Latins. For a translator set up that letter on the basis of a similar sound in the other language, so that we may know that the Hebrew language is the mother of all languages and letters. Now the Hebrews use twenty-two letter elements according to the number of books of the Old Testament; the Greeks have twenty-four. The Latins take the middle road between the two languages, and have twenty-three elements.

5.   Hebrew literature starts from the Law by Moses. Syrian and Chaldaean literature starts through Abraham. That is why they agree with the Hebrews in number and sound of the letters, and differ in the shapes only. The Egyptian letters were invented and handed down to the Egyptians by queen Isis, the daughter of Inachos,[25] who came from Greece to Egypt. Among the Egyptians, the priests had one set of letters, the people a different set. The priestly letters are the *hierai* [Greek: "holy ones"], the vulgar ones are the *pandêmoi* ["demotic"] ones.[26] The use of the Greek letters was first invented by the Phoenicians. Hence Lucan: "If one believes the stories, the Phoenicians were the first / who dared to mark voice that was to be preserved with rough shapes."[27]

6.   This is the reason why chapter headings of books are also written in the Phoenician color, because letters originated with them.[28] Cadmus, the son of Agenor, was the first to import seventeen Greek letters from Phoenicia into Greece: *A B Γ Δ E Z I K Λ M N O Π P Σ T Φ* [a b g d e z i k l m n o p r s t ph]. In the Trojan War Palamedes added three: *H X Ω* [ê kh ô]. After him Simonides from Melos added another three: *Ψ Ξ Θ* [ps ks th].

7.   The letter *Y* [u/y] was first given shape by Pythagoras of Samos to exemplify human life.[29] Its lower stem signifies the first years, evidently uncertain and not yet devoted to vices or virtues. The cross roads, which form the upper part, starts from adolescence. Its right-hand part is steep, but leads to the happy life. The left-hand side is easier, but leads down to destruction and death. Persius says the following about it: "and where the letter had led its Samian branches for you, / it showed an ascending road on the path to the right."[30]

8.   The Greeks have five letters that are mystical. First the upsilon [u/y], which signifies human life—the one we just spoke about. The second is theta [th], which signifies death.[31]

---

[25] This rests on a late antique identification between Isis and Io.
[26] Correct distinction between hieroglyphics and demotic script.   [27] Lucan, *Pharsalia*, 3.220.
[28] Reference to the decorations in red ink of first letters or section headings ("rubrics").
[29] Amsler, *Etymology and Grammatical Discourse*, 151 speaks about the "moral orthography" of this letter.
[30] Persius, *Satires* 3.56.   [31] First letter of the Greek word for "death," *thanatos*.

For judges would put the same letter theta by the names of those whom they were sentencing to death. It is called theta *apo tou thanatou* [Greek, "from death"], i.e. from death. That is why it has a stroke through the middle, which is the sign of death. Someone wrote about it: "O letter theta, much unhappier than the rest (of the letters)."

9. The third is the letter T which exhibits the shape of the cross of the Lord, which is why it is translated "sign" in Hebrew. In Ezechiel the angel is told about this letter [Ezechiel 9,4]: "Go through the midst of the city, through the midst of Jerusalem: and mark [the sign of] TAU upon the foreheads of the men that sigh and mourn."[32] The other two Christ claims as the earliest and last. For he is the beginning and he is the end, in his words [Apocalypse 22,13] "I am Alpha and Omega." For they meet among themselves as A rolls down all the way to Omega, and Omega turns back to A, so the Lord shows within himself the course of beginning to end and of the end to the beginning.

10. Among the Greeks all the letters form words and make up numbers. For with them the letter Alpha is called "one" as a number. When they write Beta, it is called two. When they write Gamma, among their numbers it is called three. When they write Delta, among their numbers it is called four. And in this way all the letters betoken numbers for the Greeks.

11. The Latins however do not count their numbers with letters, but letters form words only, with the exception of the letters I and X; the latter signifies both the shape of the cross and as a number represents "ten."

iv. Latin Letters[33]

1. The nymph Carmentis was the first to teach the Latin letters to the Italians.[34] She is called Carmentis, because she sings of the future in her *carmina* ["songs"].[35] Her proper name, however, is Nicostrate.

2. The letters are either common or liberal. Common letters are so called because many people use them "in common," for reading and writing. They are called "liberal," because they are known only by those people who write books and know how to speak correctly and to compose in writing.[36]

---

[32] T is the last letter of the Hebrew alphabet. This sign (in the shape of a cross) would save the ones so marked from the general destruction.

[33] On the letters, cf. e.g. Quintilian, *Institutio oratoria* 1.4.6ff.

[34] Cf. Hyginus, *Fabulae* 277.2; Tacitus, *Annales* 11.14.   [35] Cf. Ovid, *Fasti* 1.467.

[36] *Litterae* can refer both to the letters of the alphabet ("common letters") or to "literature" ("liberal letters").

3. There are two types of letters: for their main division is into two parts, vowels and consonants. Vowels are the ones that are pronounced in different ways through a controlled opening of the throat without any collision. They are called *vocales* ["vowels"] because they fill out the sound [*vocem*] all by themselves, and form a syllable by themselves without any consonant being connected to them. Consonants are the ones that are produced through different motions of the tongue or the pressing together of the lips. And they are called *consonantes* ["consonants"], because they do not *sonant* ["sound"] by themselves, but they *con-sonant* ["sound in conjunction with"] the vowels which are connected with them.

4. These are divided in two parts: semi-vowels and mutes. The semi-vowels are called that name because they have some half [*semi*] [of the characteristics] of the vowels. For they start with the vowel E, and end in their natural sound [e.g. F, L, M etc.].[37] The mutes are called that name because they never break forth unless a vowel is added to them. For if you take away from them the last sound, that of a vowel, their murmuring sound will be locked up within the letter [e.g. B, G, D etc.]. Vowels, semi-vowels, and mutes were called "sounding" [*sonae*], "half-sounding" [*semisonae*] and "not-sounding" [*insonae*] by the ancients.

5. Among the vowels, the grammarians attribute various values [*significationes*] to *i* and *u*.

6. Sometimes they are vowels, sometimes semi-vowels, sometimes "intermediary." They are vowels because they can form a syllable by themselves, and because they are connected with other [letters, namely] consonants. They are considered consonants because they are sometimes followed by vowels which form part of the same syllable, e.g. *Ia-nus*, *va-tes*,[38] and then they are considered consonants.

7. They are called "intermediary," because they are the only ones that have an intermediary sound by nature, e.g. *illius*, *unius*.[39] When they are joined with others, they have a thicker sound, e.g. *Ianus*, *vanus*. For they sound one way when by themselves, and another way when joined. *I* is called double sometimes for this reason because whenever it is found between two vowels, it is regarded as two consonants, e.g. *Troia*.[40] For there its sound is doubled.

8. Similarly, the letter *v* is sometimes nothing, because in some places it is neither a vowel nor a consonant, as in *quis*: it is not a vowel, for it is followed by *i*; it is not a consonant, for it is preceded by *q*. Therefore, when it is neither a vowel nor a consonant,

---

[37] I.e. if one pronounces the name of the semi-vowel it will be EF, EM, EL etc.

[38] /v/ and /u/ both written [u] in Latin.

[39] The point here is that *i* and *u* are fairly close together and hard to distinguish in pronunciation. Cf. Quintilian, *Institutio oratoria* 1.4.8; Donatus, *Ars maior* 1.2, *GL* 4:367.12ff; Priscian, *Institutiones* 1, *GL* 2:7.15ff.

[40] Heard as Troi-j-a.

it is without doubt nothing. This same letter is also called digamma [*digammon*] by the Greeks when it is joined to itself or to other vowels. It is called digamma because it is double, just like the letter F, which has two gammas [on top of each other]. By analogy the grammarians tended to call conjoined vowels "digamma," as in *votum* ["prayer"], *virgo* ["maiden"].[41]

9. Among the semi-vowels some are called *liquidae* ["fluid"] because sometimes when they follow other consonants in one syllable they do not count and are excluded from the meter [*deficiunt et a metro excluduntur*].[42] Two of them are fluid [*liquescunt*] among the Latins, L and R, as in *fragor, flatus*. The other two, M and N, are "fluid" to the Greeks, as in Mnesitheus.

10. The old script consisted of 17 Latin letters. They are called "legitimate," on the grounds that they either start with the vowel E and end in a mute sound, as happens with the consonants, or they start with their own sound and end in the vowel E, as happens with the mutes [and they are A.B.C.D.E.F.G.I.L.M.N.O.P.R.S.T. and U].

11. The letter H was added later to stand for aspiration only. Therefore, most people consider it an aspiration, not a letter. Accordingly, they call it the "sign of aspiration,"[43] because it elevates the voice. For aspiration is a sound proffered more broadly; its opposite is prosody, a sound evenly modulated.

12. The letter K was first added to the Latin ones by the schoolmaster Salvius, in order to make a sound distinction in between the two letters C and Q. People call it superfluous, because with the exception of *Kalendae* ("first day of the month") it is deemed redundant; for we express everything through the letter C.

13. Neither Greeks nor Hebrews make the sound of Q. No language besides Latin has it. First it did not exist. Therefore that letter too is called redundant, because the ancients wrote everything with C.

14. The letter X was not in use in Latin until the time of Augustus [and it rightly appeared then, in the time when the name of Christ became renowned; for through this letter the written sign is made that forms the sign of the cross].[44] In its stead they wrote C and S, which is why it is called "double," because it is used for C plus S. That also explains why its name is composed of those same letters.

---

[41] I.e. where "u" is understood as a fricative consonant (our "v") when placed next to another vowel.

[42] When *muta* + *liquida* "do not make position," i.e. are taken together as the beginning of a syllable, they are ignored for metrical purposes, i.e. they cannot make the preceding syllable long "by position." The alternative is that muta and liquida are divided over two syllables, in which case a preceding short vowel could yield a long syllable still for metrical purposes.

[43] Cf. Donatus, *Ars maior* 1.2, *GL* 4:368.9–10.   [44] Editor's brackets.

15. Latin borrowed two letters from the Greeks, Y and Z, because of Greek names of course, which were not written among the Romans until the time of Augustus. Instead of Z they put two Ss, e.g. *hilarissat* [*"he makes happy"].[45] For Y they wrote I.

16. Every letter has three *accidentia*: its name [*nomen*], what it is called; its form [*figura*], how it is drawn; and its force [*potestas*], which one is a vowel, which a consonant. Some also add "order" [*ordo*], that is which letter comes first, which one follows, so that A comes first, then B.[46] The A is the first letter among all people, because it is the beginning of speech for babies.

17. People gave names to the letters on the basis of the sound of their own language, having taken note of and distinguished the sounds they produced. For having noticed the letters, they imposed names and forms. The forms are partly imposed at will, partly on the basis of the sound of the letters, e.g. I and O: the former has a slight sound, and thus also a slight line, the latter has a fat sound, and thus also a full form.[47] The force [of the letters] was given by nature, the order and *apex* by will.[48]

18. The ancients also put the *apex* among the forms of the letters. It is called *apex* ["top," "peak"] because it is far from the feet [*a pedibus*],[49] and is put on the top of a letter. It is a line lying straight over the letter. [The "form" is the way the whole letter is written].[50]

v. On Grammar

1. Grammar is the knowledge [*scientia*] of correct speaking, and it is the origin and foundation of the liberal arts [*liberalium litterarum*]. Among the disciplines this one was

---

[45] From *hilaris*, connected with Greek *hilaros* "cheerful," "happy"; a Greek verb *hilarizô is not otherwise attested.

[46] Originally, this fourth distinction referred to the combinatory possibilities of the letters, i.e. which ones are "prepositive" to which other ones and which ones are "postpositive." For instance, R can follow T at the beginning of a word, but not at the end. Cf. e.g. Priscian, *Institutiones grammaticae* I, *GL* 2:7.2ff.; 37.4ff.

[47] Several attempts were made in antiquity and later to construe a natural relationship between the shape of letters in writing, and the sound they represent, motions accompanying them, position of the organs of articulation etc. See e.g. the section on the Middle English treatise on the Seven Liberal Arts (within, pp. 869–70) for iconicity between position of the organs of articulation and the written shape; and Sluiter, *Ancient Grammar in Context*, 239–40 and note 267 for Greek examples.

[48] *Oxford Latin Dictionary*, s.v. *apex* 5: "a mark placed over a vowel to show that it is long." These marks are not compulsory parts of orthography, and in fact Quintilian points out that it is useless to write them over vowels that everyone knows are long; they can be added for clarity's sake (*Institutio oratoria* 1.4.10; 1.7.2).

[49] This is, of course, an attempt at etymology: *a-pe(dibus): apex*.   [50] Editor's brackets.

invented after the common letters, so that whoever had learned how to read and write would know the theory of speaking correctly through grammar. Grammar has taken its name from the letters. For *grammata* is what the Greeks call letters.

2. *Ars* "art" is called by that name because it consists of *artis* "narrow" instructions and rules.[51] Others say that this word is taken over from the Greeks, *apo tês aretês*, i.e. "from virtue," the name they used for knowledge [*scientia*].

3. *Oratio* "speech" is called as it were *oris ratio* "oral account." For *orare* is to speak and to say. *Oratio* is the coherent structure [*contextus*] of words with meaning. Structure without meaning is not *oratio*, because it is not "an oral account." Complete *oratio* consists of meaning, sound, and letter.

4. The divisions of the art of grammar are counted to be thirty by some, namely the eight parts of speech; articulate sound, the letter, the syllable, the [metrical] feet, accents, punctuation marks [*positurae*],[52] critical signs [*notae*], orthography, analogy, etymology, glosses, differences [*differentiae*],[53] barbarisms, solecisms, errors, metaplasms, schemata, tropes, prose, meters, fables, histories.

From Book 2: Rhetoric

[In his account of rhetoric Isidore mostly follows Cassiodorus, but reorganizes that material to conform to the etymological *quod*/*quia* format.[54] Other sources are Augustine, Boethius, Diomedes, Jerome, Lactantius, Marius Victorinus, Martianus Capella, and Tertullian. Notable through absence are Cicero and Quintilian.[55]]

i. Rhetoric and its Name

1. Rhetoric[56] is the science of speaking well on civil questions; eloquence is a flow of words, designed to persuade people to the just and the good.[57] The name "rhetoric" is

---

[51] See above, at 1.1.2, with note 19. [52] Also called *distinctiones*, cf. Donatus, *Ars maior* 1.6, *GL* 4:372.16.
[53] The distinction of near-synonyms. [54] Amsler, *Etymology and Grammatical Discourse*, 158.
[55] See *Etymologies Book II*, trans. Marshall, 5–7. [56] Cf. Cassiodorus, *Institutiones* 2.2.1.
[57] Note the addition of this moral element (not in Cassiodorus), cf. Augustine, *De doctrina christiana* 4.17.34.

Greek, from the word *retoresin*,[58] that is to say a flow of expression. For the Greek call expression *resis*, and an orator *retor*.[59]

2. Rhetoric is allied to the art of grammar. For in grammar we learn the science of speaking correctly; while in rhetoric we are taught how to express what we have learned.[60]

ii. *The Discoverers of the Art of Rhetoric*

1. This discipline was discovered by the Greeks, by Gorgias, Aristotle, and Hermagoras, and translated into Latin by Tullius,[61] of course, and Quintilian, but with such detail and variety that the reader can readily wonder at it, but under no circumstances grasp it.

2. For when he has the books in his hands, the order of the words sticks in his memory, but as soon as he lays them aside all recollection disappears. The perfect knowledge of this discipline makes the orator.

iii. *The Name of the Orator and the Parts of Rhetoric*

1. The orator, then, is a good man skilled in speaking.[62] His goodness comes from nature, character, and accomplishments. His skill in speaking comes from studied eloquence,[63] which is divisible into five parts:[64] invention, arrangement, style, memory, delivery, and purpose (which is to persuade the listener of something).

2. Skill in speaking itself contains three elements:[65] nature, learning, and experience. "Nature" means the ability, "learning" the knowledge, and "experience" the constant practice. These qualities one looks for not merely in the orator, but in any master of an art if he is to accomplish anything.

---

[58] Greek: *rhêtorizein*.   [59] Greek: *rhêsis*; *rhêtôr*.

[60] Cf. Augustine, *De doctrina christiana* 1.1.1.

[61] Particularly, Cicero, *De inventione*. Cf. for this history of the discipline, *De inventione*, 1.5.7–1.6.8.

[62] Cf. Cassiodorus, *Institutiones* 2.2.1; the definition goes back to Cato the Censor (Quintilian, *Institutio oratoria* 12.1.1).

[63] This ultimately goes back to *De inventione* 1.5.6 (*artificiosa eloquentia*).

[64] Cf. Cassiodorus, *Institutiones* 2.2.2. Isidore has taken over the number five from Cassiodorus, but has in fact added a sixth element (purpose).

[65] Source: Augustine, *De civitate Dei*, 11.25 (ed. Dombart and Kalb, *CCSL* 48:344.20).

iv. The Three Kinds of Cases

1. There are three kinds of cases:[66] deliberative, demonstrative, and judicial. The deliberative is that which discusses what ought or ought not to be done in the affairs of life. The demonstrative is that in which a praiseworthy or reprehensible character is held up to view.

2. The judicial is that in which a sentence of punishment or reward is rendered on the actions of the character involved. It is called "judicial" because it "judges" a man, and by its sentence shows whether he is praiseworthy and deserving of reward, or whether the defendant should be condemned or acquitted.

3. The deliberative kind is so called, because in it one "deliberates" about each point. This kind is twofold, being divisible into persuasion and dissuasion, involving ends to seek and ends to avoid, that is to say things which ought to be done, and things which ought not.

4. The persuasive is subdivided into three areas:[67] the honorable, the useful, and the possible. This differs somewhat from the deliberative in that the persuasive needs another person, whereas at times the deliberative is self-contained.[68] In the persuasive there are two powerful elements: hope and fear.

5. The demonstrative is so called, because it "demonstrates" each thing by praising or censuring it.[69] This kind has the two subdivisions of praise and censure. Praise has three chronological divisions, before, during, or after the event.

6. Before, as: "what age so fortunate bore you."[70] During, as: "you who alone took pity on the unspeakable trials of Troy."[71] After, as: "as long as the rivers shall run into the seas, as long as the shadows shall range across the mountains, your glory, name, and praise shall always remain."[72]

7. The same order must also be preserved in the opposite procedure, in censuring a person: before, during, and after. The commonplace belongs to the demonstrative kind of condemnation,[73] but it differs from it in some respects. For censure, which is the opposite of praise, is directed specifically against the individual;

---

[66] Source: Cassiodorus, *Instutiones* 2.2.3; it goes back ultimately to *De inventione* 1.5.7 and *Rhetorica ad Herennium* 1.2.2, and before that to Aristotle, *Rhetoric* 1358b.

[67] Cf. Quintilian, *Institutio oratoria* 3.8.22.   [68] I.e. one may deliberate within oneself.

[69] Source: Cassiodorus 2.2.3, cf. *De inventione* 1.5.7.

[70] *Aeneid* 1.605. This example and the two following ones are all taken from one speech (Aeneas to Dido).

[71] *Aeneid* 1.597.   [72] *Aeneid* 1.607.

[73] The classification of the "commonplace" under demonstrative oratory is awkward and confusing (Marshall's note in Isidore, *Etymologies* II, *ad loc.*).

8. while a commonplace is proffered generally against an evil deed. This is the reason why it is called a "commonplace," since, with no person involved, it is directed not so much against the man, as against the crime itself. For every evil is not found only in one person, but is common to many.

xvi. Style

1. Now, as far as style is concerned,[74] in response to the demands of the topic [*res*], the place, the time, the character of the audience, we should avoid mixing profane matters with sacred, impure matters with chaste, the trivial with the important, the frivolous with the serious, the humorous with the sad. We must speak with good Latinity, and with clarity.

2. A speaker employs good Latinity if he chooses the genuine and natural words for things, and does not depart from the speech and practice of the present day. Such a man must not be content simply to watch what he is saying; he must also say it unambiguously and attractively. He must also be prepared not merely to talk, but also to act upon what he says.

xvii. The Three Varieties of Oratory

1. In addition, matters involving little emotion should be presented calmly; those inviting much feeling should be presented gravely; while a moderate style is appropriate for plaintive matters.[75] For this is the well known threefold division of style [*genus dicendi*]: the lowly, the medium, the grandiloquent. For when we speak of great subjects, they should be expressed in a grand style; when we speak of unimportant subjects, a fine style should be used; when the subject lies in between, a mixed style.[76]

2. For in unimportant cases we should say nothing grand or sublime, but we should speak in a calm and everyday fashion. But in cases of greater importance,[77] where God or the salvation of men is concerned, we should show more magnificence and fire.

---

[74] The main emphasis here is on *to prepon*, propriety, cf. Aristotle, *Rhetoric* 1408a.

[75] Cf. Cicero, *Orator* 56, connecting tone of voice and manner of speaking (or content); and *Orator* 100, *et humilia subtiliter et alta graviter et mediocria temperate . . . dicere*, with style reflecting content.

[76] Cf. Augustine, *De doctrina christiana* 4.17.34 (and, indirectly, Cicero, *Orator* 101). For the relation between subject, style, and rhetorical function, cf. Sluiter, "Communication, Eloquence," 256–67.

[77] Cf. Augustine, *De doctrina christiana* 4.18.35.

3. But in middling cases, where the pleading is not an end in itself, but serves to delight the listener, we should speak in a moderate fashion in between the two extremes. Yet even though someone may be speaking on important themes,[78] nevertheless he must not always instruct the audience in the grand style, but in the low style when he is instructing; in the moderate style when he is praising or censuring something; in the grand style when he is seeking to convert a hostile audience. Now, in the lowly style the vocabulary should be adequate, in the middling style it should be brilliant, in the grand style it should be forceful.[79]

xviii.   *The Colon, the Comma, and the Period*

1. All utterance is made up of words, commas [*komma*], colons [*kôlon*], and periods [*periodos*].[80] A "comma" is a small part of a sentence. A "colon" is a member (clause). A "period" is a "going around" [*ambitus*], or "rounding off" [*circuitus*]. A comma is composed of words, a colon is composed of commas, a period is composed of colons.[81] A comma is the completion of a combination of words, for example:[82]

2. "Although I am afraid, gentlemen of the jury."[83] There you have one comma. There follows another comma: "that it might be disgraceful to speak on behalf of a very brave man," and a colon, or member (clause), has been produced, which affords a meaning. Yet the sentence is still left hanging, and so after this, from several such members, is created the period, that is to say, the completion of the sentence as follows: "they look for the well established habit of the courts." However, a period should be short enough to be uttered in one breath.

xix.   *The Avoidance of Faults in Letters, Words, and Sentences*

1. Moreover, the pure and dignified style of the orator should be free of all faults in letters, as well as in words and also in sentences.

2. In letters[84] the joining should be fitting and appropriate; and care should be taken that the final vowel of one word should not collide with the same initial vowel in the next

---

[78] Cf. ibid., 4.19.38.   [79] Cf. ibid., 4.28.61.   [80] Source: Diomedes, *GL* 1:465.23.
[81] Source: ibid., 466.3.   [82] Source: ibid., 466.15.   [83] Cicero, *Pro Milone* 1.
[84] Cf. Diomedes, *GL* 1:466.26.

word, as *feminae Aegyptiae* ["Egyptian women"]. This kind of arrangement is better if consonants come after the vowels. You should also avoid the combination of the three consonants *R*, *S*, and *X*, each of which, when it collides with any of the same consonants, seems to grate and to fight, as it were; as in the examples *ars studiorum* ["the art of study"], *rex Xerxes* ["King Xerxes"], *error Romuli* ["the error of Romulus"].[85] Take care also not to have the consonant *M* colliding into a vowel, as in *verum enim* "but yet."[86]

xx. *Combinations of Words*

1. In words also faults should be avoided, so that words are not improperly used (which the Greeks call *akurologia*). You should therefore show a fondness for proper signification; however, at times, non-literal words [*verba translata*] must be used to avoid the vulgarity of a sordid or dirty word—provided that they are not far-fetched, but seem closely related to the true [*veris*] terms.

2. You should also avoid transpositions [*hyperbata*] over too great a distance,[87] as these inevitably involve confusion of meaning. In addition, you must guard against ambiguity, and that fault by which some people, attracted by ostentatious eloquence, add empty phrases and indulge in ornate periphrasis, where they could have made their meaning clear in one or two words. This fault is called *perissologia*.

3. The opposite fault is to remove even necessary words in aiming at brevity. As in letters and words, so also in sentences you should avoid those vices which teachers train you to recognize in their very first lessons.[88]

4. These are: ugly-sounding expressions [*kakemphaton*], tautology [*tautologia*], omission [*ellipsis*], the use of inexact words [*akurologia*], long-windedness [*makrologia*], wordiness [*perissologia*], redundancy [*pleonasmos*], and suchlike. On the other hand, vividness [*enargeia*] elevates and adorns a speech, as does innuendo [*emphasis*], as it enables you to hint at more than is actually said. An example would be, if you were to say: "He rose to the glory of Scipio," and Virgil's "sliding down the rope."[89] For when he says "sliding," he suggests a picture of height. The opposite quality to this is, by one's choice of vocabulary, to detract from things naturally great.

---

[85] Cf. ibid., 467.14.   [86] Cf. ibid., 467.12.   [87] Cf. *Rhetorica ad Herennium* 4.18; Quint. 8.6.65–7.
[88] Cf. the list in *Etymologiae* 1.34.1 (*barbarismus, soloecismus, acyrologia, cacenphaton et reliqua*).
[89] *Aeneid* 2.262

xxi. *Figures of Speech and Thought*[90]

1. Speech is also elevated and adorned by figures of speech and of thought.[91] For since straightforward and uninterrupted speech produces weariness and boredom, as much for the speaker as for the audience, you must change it and direct it to other patterns. In this way, the speaker is refreshed, the speech is more ornate, and the judge's attention is gained by the variety of expression. Very many of these have been noted in the previous book,[92] as given by Donatus amongst the grammatical figures.[93]

2. It seemed necessary to mention here only those which can never, or only with difficulty, be used in poetry, but which can be used freely in a speech.

---

[90] This is the second time Isidore deals with figures. Book I.32–7 also has sections on *vitia, metaplasmi, schemata,* and *tropi,* corresponding to the third part of the traditional Roman grammar and going back to a Christian theory of figures dating from the fifth or sixth century (cf. Schindel, *Die lateinischen Figurenlehren des 5. bis 7. Jhs. und Donats Vergil-Kommentar,* 53ff. and "Die Quelle von Isidors 'rhetorischer' Figurenlehre," 374). This is the "rhetorical" (as opposed to "grammatical") treatment of the material, yet according to Schindel ("Die Quelle," 382) both parts probably go back to the same "Donatus christianus" of the fifth–sixth centuries. This would be a type of figure-theory, unattested until Isidore, that combines grammatical and rhetorical figures. See also the introduction to Part I, above, pp. 63–4, 70.

[91] Marshall refers to the Greek *skhêmata lexeôs* and *skhêmata dianoias,* cf. Quintilian, *Institutio oratoria* 9.1.17; 9.2 and 3.

[92] *Etymologiae* 1.37.   [93] Donatus, *Ars maior* 3.5ff., *GL* 4:397.4–402.34.

VIRGILIUS MARO GRAMMATICUS, *EPISTOLAE* AND *EPITOMAE*, CA. 650

INTRODUCTION

The enigmatic work of Virgilius Maro grammaticus probably originated in Ireland in the mid-seventh century.[1] He wrote fifteen *Epitomae* (of which we have twelve) and eight *Epistolae* on the eight parts of speech, with a preface.[2] Both *Epitomae* and *Epistolae* present themselves as grammatical works, but of a very peculiar nature. The *Epitomae* are based on Donatus' *Ars maior*, discussing letter, syllable, metrical feet, and the eight parts of speech. Where Donatus then goes on to his *Barbarismus*, Virgilius discusses "word-splitting," etymology, and the history of his discipline. The *Epistulae* are based on Donatus' *Ars minor*.[3]

The work is a wonderfully inventive and creative text, with obvious elements of parody: it abounds with odd characters, puts an old man called Donatus at the scene of Troy, and gives him a student called Virgil. The teacher of our "Virgil" (Virgilius Maro grammaticus), who is the third of three Virgilii, is called Aeneas. Virgilius also discusses twelve kinds of Latin, only one of which looks familiar,[4] and seems to freely invent words, sources, and authorities.[5]

The question is whether parody exhausts the functions and purposes of the work. Vivien Law has argued that the grammatical form may function as the vehicle for some of the substance of the work, which may be found in the digressions.[6] One such recurring theme is wisdom, and Virgilius may be expressing the traditional idea that grammar and

---

[1] On Irish provenance, see Herren, "Notes on the life," 253–7; "Some New Light," 27–71; accepted by Law, *Wisdom, Authority, and Grammar*, 3.

[2] In much of the secondary literature, the *Epitomae* and *Epistulae* are referred to by the sigla A and B respectively (followed by a number).

[3] See Law, *Wisdom*, 1; Polara, "A proposito delle dottrine grammaticali di Virgilio Marone," gives a detailed comparison of the grammatical doctrine of these works and their late antique grammatical sources, especially Donatus.

[4] Cf. Law, *Wisdom*, 53f. for the theory of the twelve kinds of Latin.

[5] Lehmann, *Die Parodie im Mittelalter*, 9ff., treats him as a parodist ("eine Schulparodie") and "ein arger Schalk."

[6] Law, *Wisdom*, 22ff.

the liberal arts are just one step on the road to true wisdom in an unconventional manner.[7] Wisdom literature is one of the generic influences in the text; other generic affinities noted by Law are autobiography, the *disputatio* (especially in the *Epistolae*), allegory, precepts, maxims, gnomic sayings, and riddles.[8] A particularly important theme is that of Creation, where "grammar, the key to the scriptures, parallels natural philosophy, the key to God's Creation."[9] In general, Virgilius' emphasis on multiplicity, the possibility that language has several meanings, seems an important unifying theme.[10]

An intriguing section is Virgilius' presentation of the history of his discipline (A XV), which turns out to be all-encompassing. Donatus is the first character mentioned, and he lived at Troy, and thence came to Rome where he met Romulus. Donatus was a teacher and someone who discussed Wisdom in riddling form. His pupil was Virgil, one of three successive Virgils (just as Virgilius Maro grammaticus knows of three Lucans). The highest authority of the discipline of grammar (Donatus, here presented as a teacher of wisdom!) and the poet, who is the foremost object of study of the grammarian, are connected here, and this happens "*ab urbe condita*": history of the world, of literature (if only evoked by the poet's name), and of grammar (Donatus) coincide.[11] This obviously constitutes a strong bid for intellectual and moral authority for the "grammarian."

Translation reprinted from Law, *Wisdom, Authority, and Grammar*, by permission.[12]

[The following discussion of the morphological problems of the first-person pronoun gives a good impression of the unusual nature of Virgilius' work. Emotions run high among the grammarians and a host of unsubstantiated sources are invoked.[13] We also encounter Virgilius' teacher, Aeneas, and a woman grammarian called Fassica. This text formed the inspiration for a passage from Umberto Eco's *The Name of the Rose*.[14]]

---

[7] See also Luhtala, "Linguistics and theology," 516. Virgilius stands in the tradition of Augustine, Cassiodorus, and Bede here, in the Christianization of grammar.

[8] Law, *Wisdom*, 27.

[9] Law, *Wisdom*, 107; cf. Luhtala, "Linguistics and Theology," 517.

[10] Law, *Wisdom*, 55; cf. Luhtala, "Linguistics and Theology," 516.

[11] Note that Aeneas also figures as a character: he is the teacher of our Virgilius, see below.

[12] 109–15. For the base texts, see *Virgilio Marone grammatico, Epitomi ed Epistole*, ed. Polara, Italian translation by Caruso and Polara, and *Virgilius Maro grammaticus: Opera omnia*, ed. Löfstedt.

[13] On this passage see further Law, *Wisdom*, 7–10, who concludes that Virgilius exaggerates elements already present in the Latin grammatical tradition (e.g. Pompeius, *GL* 5:209.1–25) and pushes them "over the brink of parody" (10).

[14] Umberto Eco's *The Name of the Rose* (trans. W. Weaver [San Diego: Harcourt Brace Jovanovich, 1983]) mentions the grammarians Priscian, Honoratus, Donatus, Victorinus, Metrorius, Eutyches, Servius, Phocas, Asper, and then "Virgil of Toulouse": "was he crazy?—I don't know: he didn't come from my islands . . . I was told that in that period, for fifteen days and fifteen nights, the rhetoricians Gabundus and Terentius argued on the vocative of

Epistola II 14–93: The vocative of ego (=B II)

The first pronoun to be discussed is the finite pronoun *ego*, "I," on which so many people raise countless questions, looking into how and why one and the same pronoun is made up of such dissimilar letters, e.g. *ego mei* "I, mine." Many people have wanted to calm the dispute with erudition, affirming that *ego* "I" should always be considered an uninflected noun, so that in every number, gender, and case one should use *ego* alone. Terrentius believed that *ego* should be judged to be among the defectives, so that apart from the nominative it has no case. Nonetheless, they agreed in a joint exhortation and definitive pronouncement that *mius* should be used for *ego* and is to be declined thus: *mius, mei* or *mis, mihi, o, a me*.[15] Galbungus' followers, objecting from their contrary stance, said: "If this is the case, why is this sequence of letters not also observed in the plural, where we say *nos nostrum*? In any case there are quite a large number of words which, although they do not retain the same sequence of letters, nonetheless indubitably agree in sense and meaning. Hence, this pronoun is to be defended on similar grounds, namely, that it is correctly declined in the way that most people observe[16]—*ego mei*, and in the plural *nos nostrum*."

When I relayed this question to my Aeneas,[17] we spent the better part of a day pondering this at length. He concluded in the end that according to the opinion of Galbungus and his followers, the most correct form was *mius mei mihi*. However, we are compelled by extensive reading in the works of reliable authors to believe that *ego*, like *nequam* and other such indeclinable words, has only one form throughout its cases. Servilius, for example, writes: "They took away *I* (*ego*) field," that is to say "they took away *my* (*mei*) field"; and Galbungus, a retired veteran of the Indian forces, said this at the end of one of his works: "You won't cheat *I*, my son, of my well-earned reward, will you?,"

'ego', and in the end they attacked each other, with weapons" (311–12). Virgil is placed with the authors from the British isles, as the speaker William explains: "the books are arranged according to the country of their origin, or the place where their authors were born, or, as in this instance, the place where they should have been born. The librarians told themselves Virgil the grammarian was born in Toulouse by mistake: he should have been born in the western islands. They corrected the errors of nature" (314).

[15] With *o* (*me*) standing for the vocative, and *a me* for the ablative.

[16] Hence the debate is made to focus on the question of whether adherence to the system of rules (*ratio*) or normal usage (*consuetudo*) should determine the issue of "correctness."

[17] From A 15 section 8 (see below), it turns out that this "Aeneas" proposed "Virgilius Maro" as a nickname for our author. In general, it is conceivable that the identification of grammarians and literature, as their primary object of study, could have led to the imposition of such nicknames. For nicknames, see also the section on Alcuin, who was called Albinus, but also Flaccus (cf. Horace), just as Charlemagne was called "David" (after King David); each nickname is relevant to the bearer's area of expertise.

putting *ego* for *mihi* "me." Virgilius of Asia wrote thus in the fourth book of his records of the genesis of man: "Who formed *I*, that I should be thus?," that is, "Who formed me?" And Sarbon, Glengus' father, said this in a song on Queen Rigas: "Worthy of being praised by *I* in a wondrous song," that is, *a me* "by me." But in case anyone should attempt to deny that *ego* has a plural, we shall set down some examples found all over the place. Latomius, my fellow student, spoke thus in a querulous song: "What are *I* to do, now that our fields have been taken away?" Here *ego* stands for *nos* "we." Fassica too, a woman so wise and so learned that her name will without a shadow of doubt be celebrated as long as the world exists,[18] used this example among others: "The fathers handed down to *I* all the instruments of learning which we use," that is to say, I think, "the fathers handed down to *us*"; similarly, Sarricius, Cicero's father, said: "Why is *I* life lived?" that is to say *nostrum* or *nostri* "our life." But these examples will suffice, for the same applies to other such cases.

They say that Galbungus and Terrentius continued in debate for fourteen days and as many nights in an attempt to ascertain from the teachings of the ancients whether or not *ego* had a vocative case.[19] Terrentius denied that *ego* could have a vocative, for the vocative must always be attached to the second person, whereas *ego* will always pertain to the first person. Galbungus claimed that the vocative case could be found in this pronoun, and particularly when a first-person verb in the interrogative mood was used, as when you say, "O me (*ego*), have I done or spoken rightly?" But this vocative, that is, *ego*, cannot stand without the aid of the *o* and the [interrogative] *ne* on either side of it. When this question was referred to Aeneas with me acting as the intermediary, he held forth with utter veracity to the effect that since *ego* is a pronoun of the first person, and a verb of the first person does not have the imperative mood, which is the one with which the vocative is always associated, then this pronoun can only have a vocative case when "O me (*ego*), have I done or spoken rightly?" is uttered in the interrogative mood. That the vocative case occurs in the plural number is doubted by no one, even on the part of the adversaries, i.e. *nos, o, a nobis* "us, O us, by us," especially since the imperative mood is routinely inflected in the first person plural. For when you say *nos dicamus* "let us say," *nos* "us" is here in the vocative case, even though it cannot be denied that it is also nominative. But let this suffice on this pronoun.

[The following excerpt contains Virgilius' vision of the history of everything.]

---

[18] Law, *Wisdom*,12–13 relates this name to Jerome's etymology according to which *Fase* is *pascha*, "Passover," "Easter." "Naturally, then, Fassica's *name* will be celebrated to the end of time" (13).

[19] The vocative of *ego* was actually a real concern to the Latin grammarians. For a complete set of references see Pseudo-Palaemon, *Regulae*, ed. Rossellini, 122–3, and the remarks by L. Holford-Strevens in *Bryn Mawr Classical Review* 2003.03.24 n. 10.

EPITOME XV: THE CATALOGUE OF GRAMMARIANS (=A XV)

1. The first was an aged man by the name of Donatus, at Troy, who lived, they say, for a thousand years. When he came to Romulus, the founder of the city of Rome, he was received with the greatest rejoicing and stayed there for four years. During this time he built up a school and left innumerable works in which he posed various riddles, saying: "My son, who is the woman who offers her breasts to countless offspring, and however much they are sucked they flow just as richly?" The answer is Wisdom.[20] "What is the difference between word (*verbum*), speech (*sermo*), sentence (*sententia*), utterance (*loquela*) and discourse (*oratio*)?" Whatever the tongue and voice produce is *word*; *speech*, however, which gets its name from the combination of two words, *SERendo* "sowing" and *MOnendo* "admonishing," is more ornate and diligent; a *sentence* is what is conceived with one's sense; an *utterance* is when the sequence of speech (*dictio*) is woven with a certain degree of elegance; and *discourse* is when oratorical speech reaches the point of elaboration with the hands.[21]

2. Likewise at Troy was Virgilius, a pupil of that Donatus. He was extremely energetic at copying out verses. It was he who wrote seventy books on meter and a letter on the verb sent to Virgilius of Asia. The third Virgilius is myself.

3. Virgilius of Asia was the student of the aforesaid. He was a man so solicitous to the needs of holy persons that a call never found him sitting idly. I saw him with my own eyes, and when I was a boy he wrote out signs for me. He wrote a splendid book on the twelve Latins,[22] which he called by these names:

   I The first is the kind in common use in Roman eloquence.

   II *Assena*, i.e. shorthand, which represents a whole word (*fonum*) with a single letter in a prescribed form.[23]

   III *Semedia*, i.e. neither wholly strange nor wholly familiar, like *monta glosa*, which is *mons altus* "tall mountain" and *gilmola* for *gula* "gullet."

---

[20] Law, *Wisdom*, 34 (see also 124 n. 27) notes parallels in Sedulius Scotus, *Collectaneum miscellaneum* II 1, ed. D. Simpson, *CCCM* 67 (Turnhout: Brepols, 1988), and pseudo-Bede, *Collectanea*, *PL* 94:539D.

[21] Law *Wisdom*, 34, points out that this second riddle is only one "in a parodistic sense: it is a *differentia*, a type of definition which distinguishes between synonyms and near-synonyms."

[22] Also discussed in the first *Epitoma*, where the twelve Latins deal with different aspects of fire (Law, *Wisdom*, 54). Here, they are different kinds of language use which expand and collapse language to the point of unrecognizability. On the two versions of the twelve Latins, see Law, *Wisdom*, 88ff.

[23] Law, *Wisdom*, 88, links this with Roman shorthand, the so-called "Tironian notes," used for legal purposes.

IV *Numeria* has its own numbers: *nim* 1, *dun* 2, *tor* 3, *quir* 4, *quan* 5, *ses* 6, *sen* 7, *onx* 8, *amin* 9, *ple* 10, which is so called from "plenitude"; and in this manner from *nimple* 11 to *plasin* 20, *torlasin* 30, *quirlasin* 40, up to *bectan* 100, and on up to *colephin* 1,000, etc.

V *Metrofia*,[24] i.e. pertaining to the understanding, e.g. *dicantabat* "beginning," *bora* "fortitude," *gcno* "utility," *sade* "justice," *teer* "conjugal pair," *rfoph* "veneration," *brops* "piety," *rihph* "hilarity," *gal* "kingdom," *fkal* "religion," *clitps* "nobility," *mrmos* "dignity," *fann* "recognition," *ulioa* "honor," *gabpal* "compliance," *blaqth* "light of the sun," *merc* "rain," *pal* "day and night," *gatrb* "peace," *biun* "water and fire," *spadx* "longevity." The whole world is ruled by these things and prospers in them.

VI *Lumbrosa*, i.e. excessively long, when a whole phrase is written for a single common word. Here are some examples: *gabitariuum bresin galsiste ion* for "to read"; similarly *nebesium almigero pater panniba* for "life."[25]

VII *Sincolla*, i.e. excessively short, is the opposite: a whole common phrase is contained in one word, as in the following examples: *gears* "mend your ways and love good things"; similarly *biro* "it is not expedient to abandon one's parents."[26]

VIII *Belsavia*, i.e. upside down, when the case of nouns and moods of verbs are altered, as in these examples: *lex* for *legibus*, *legibus* for *lex*, *rogo* for *rogate*, *rogant* for *rogo*.[27]

IX *Presina*, i.e. comprehensive, when one word-form signifies many normal words, like *sur*, which means "field" or "gelding" or "sword" or "stream."[28]

X *Militana*, i.e. manifold, when many words are used in the place of one common word-form, as for example for "running," *gammon, saulin, selon, rabath*.

XI *Spela*, i.e. extremely humble, which always speaks about earthly matters, e.g. *sobon* "hare," *gabul* "fox," *gariga* "crane," *lena* "hen." Ursinus used this kind.[29]

XII *Polema*, i.e. supernatural, which treats of higher matters, e.g. *affla* for "soul," *spiridon* for "spirit," *repota* for certain "supernal virtues," *sanamiana anus* for the "unity of God on high." Virgilius always used this kind.

---

[24] Law, *Wisdom*, 89ff, attempts several keys to explain this kind of Latin: she discerns an alphabet in them (*a* in *dicantabat*, *b* in *bora*, *c* in *gcno* etc)., relates some words to Latin words or to the names of Hebrew letters, and connects them with an orally transmitted esoteric arithmology.

[25] Law, *Wisdom*, 92, relates this to "rhetorical expansion." One could also think of the etymological practice of explaining single words by phrases that would contain and hide within themselves the relevant sounds or syllables.

[26] This may parody mnemonic words concealing whole sentences.

[27] Here we are on slightly more familiar ground again: substitution of case for case or mood for mood is a recognized description of figures—although the examples again suggest wild parody.

[28] IX and X are reminiscent of the doctrine of homonyms and synonyms (Law, *Wisdom*, 92).

[29] Law, *Wisdom*, 93, connects XI and XII: the theory of the three styles could be related to subject matter: here, the same is done for the lexicon. The humble Latinity, exemplified by Ursinus ("Bear," Law, 93, cf. 12), uses words for things related to the earth, while Virgil of course exemplifies an elevated lexicon for elevated topics.

This is what Virgilius of Asia had to say.

4. Primogenus, who lived in Cappadocia, was a very gentle man, quite learned in natural science and of inimitable judgment in the computation of lunar cycles and the months. When his students asked him about thunder, he said that it was the breath of an abnormal wind which roars at the world at predetermined times and has a thunderous sound. Its nature is such that it is the only wind which is visible to the human gaze; it has not so much breath as a brilliant flame. He maintained that it was higher than any wind and penetrated the deepest of all. When I asked him whether this wind was governed by its own command or by that of another, he took a page and composed four poetic verses, thus: "Who is the mighty one who governs the loftiest things in the heights of heaven and the towering summits of heaven itself?" That is, the god of the Hebrews.

5. Estrius, a Spaniard of quite dazzling eloquence in the composition of (hi)stories, gave me an analogy, saying, "The verb plays the part of the sun in sentences, for just as a day with no sun is not radiant, so a sentence without a main verb is not clear." He said too: "O king, know that just as your handmaid has chosen to share this life with you, so you will share a common death with her." And this question: "O miser, why is it that the sky, the earth and the sea bring their gifts to you and yet you will not give your goods to your neighbor?" Similarly: "Look, there is a fish in the sea which devours whatever comes its way and yet it is never satiated: in just the same way the mind of the miser cannot be satiated by the whole world." These are Estrius' sayings.

6. In Egypt there was Gregory, devoted to Greek studies, who wrote three thousand books on the (hi)stories of the Greeks.

7. In Nicomedia there was Balapsidus, alive until recently, who at my command translated the books of our law, which I heard read in Greek, into Latin. They begin thus: "In the beginning the spirit brooded within itself heaven, earth, sea, and all the stars."

8. There were in addition three Vulcans, one in Arabia, another in India, and a third in Africa. My Aeneas had them as his teachers and made a fair copy of their books via the art of shorthand. In them he found that there was a man called Maro near the Flood whose wisdom no age will be able to relate. Hence, when Aeneas saw that I was possessed of a modicum of wit, he ordered that I should be called by this name, saying: "This my son shall be called Maro, for in him the spirit of the ancient Maro has come back to life."[30]

---

[30] Law, *Wisdom*, 75 rightly points out that "this name-giving incident has all the ingredients of the esoteric tradition: the teacher bestows on the pupil a name which reveals something of his spiritual nature, a name with true symbolic value." Cf. 138 n. 68 on the late ancient associations of the name Virgilius with manhood and wisdom.

9. There was also my grandfather Martulis,[31] a man of considerable learning and noble features. He was most active in the study of grammar.

Let it suffice, friends and pupils, that I have placed on record these excerpts from the books of the laws of our fathers for the edification and benefit of all our readers.

---

[31] Martianus Capella.

BEDE, *DE ARTE METRICA* AND *DE SCHEMATIBUS ET TROPIS*, CA.710

INTRODUCTION

Bede's *De arte metrica* (Metrical Art or Art of Poetry) and *De schematibus et tropis* (On Schemes [or Figures] and Tropes) constitute a unified grammatical work, containing rules designed to help a student recognize the formal literary devices he would encounter in his reading of sacred (as well as to some extent classical) texts.[1] The two works were intended to be taken together, as the epilogue of the *De arte metrica* shows: here Bede tells his dedicatee Cuthbert that he has produced another little treatise on what "the Greeks call schemes and tropes," which he "subjoins" to his treatise on metrics. The treatise on metrics gives instruction on how to pronounce syllables according to their correct length, and how to recognize and scan meters. Correct reading is also the aim of *De schematibus et tropis*, not in the technical sense of forming syllables and rhythmic patterns, but in the exegetical sense of recognizing and interpreting figurative speech and the theological significances with which Scripture can invest certain kinds of figures.[2]

The sources of both the works are grammatical writings. The sources of *De arte metrica* include Diomedes' *Ars grammatica*, Donatus' *Ars maior*, Servius' *De finalibus*, the commentary on Donatus' *Ars* by the grammarian known as Sergius (fifth century?), the commentary on Donatus by the grammarian Pompeius (fifth century), and the grammatical art by Audax (seventh century).[3] The treatise gives sound coverage of the classical and post-classical meters. Its value as a long-enduring textbook lies in Bede's judicious selection and synthesis of his authorities, and his modification of classical metrics to account for "modern" usage, that is, the Christian Latin poets whose hymns were a central part of

---

[1] On internal evidence for dating in the period after 709, see Franklin, "Grammar and Exegesis: Bede's *Liber de schematibus et tropis*."

[2] Irvine, *The Making of Textual Culture*, 293. The most complete treatment of *De schematibus et tropis* is Knappe, *Traditionen der klassischen Rhetorik*, 234–43, placing it in its grammatical context. For extensive analysis of its exegetical purpose and its relationship to Cassiodorus' exposition of the Psalms, see Franklin, "Grammar and Exegesis." On both works see Brown, *Bede the Venerable*, 31–5.

[3] Sergius' commentary in *GL* 4:475–85; Pompeius in *GL* 5:81–312; Audax's *Excerpta* in *GL* 7:320–62; on these sources see Palmer, "Bede as a Textbook Writer," and *GL* 7:220–1.

monastic life and learning.[4] The treatise is divided into three parts, the first (chapters i–viii) dealing with the quantities of syllables, the second (ix–xxiii) discussing different poetic forms, especially the dactylic hexameter and pentameter, and the third (xxiv–xxv) describing rhythmic verse, i.e. verse that is not based on quantities, but on word-accent, and the three main genres of poetry.[5]

The sources of *De schematibus et tropis* present a more complex picture of the transmission of grammatical doctrine. Bede's treatise is the early culminating point of an important development within the tradition of grammatical teaching and commentary on classical poetry: the "Christianization" of Donatus' *Ars*, especially its teaching of the figures and tropes. Bede's list of seventeen figures and twenty-eight tropes is identical with the list in Donatus' *Ars maior* 3, so it is clear that the essence of his system derives from this late classical authority. But Bede, like his early Christian predecessors, also read Donatus through a "Christianized" version or augmentation of the *Ars* that added examples from Scripture and the Christian authors to illustrate the theory. This Christianized Donatan *ars grammatica*, no longer itself extant, has been shown to be the common ancestor of a number of texts from the sixth to the eighth centuries, most prominently Isidore of Seville's treatment of grammar in book I of the *Etymologiae* and Bede's *De schematibus et tropis*.[6] Largely through the influence of Bede's *De schematibus et tropis* (but also the influence of Cassiodorus' *Expositio Psalmorum*), the scriptural or broadly Christianized exemplification of schemes and tropes recurs throughout later medieval grammatical teaching.[7] The emergence of a Christianized Donatus is, in turn, part of a larger tradition of grammatical commentaries on Virgil's poetry. Inevitably, studies of the figures and tropes played a large role in these commentaries. In this tradition, the early and important influence was Donatus' Virgil commentary, the greater part of which is now lost, although it may have survived into the Carolingian period. The Christianized teachings on the figures and tropes, which derive ultimately from Donatus' *Ars maior*, have also helped to provide a picture of the contents of this lost commentary.[8]

Bede's Christianizing of the figures and tropes is more decisive and complete than that of any of his predecessors in the tradition of Donatan grammatical teaching. In this respect

---

[4] See chapters xvi–xxiii; and see Coronati, "La dottrina del tetrametro trocaico in Bede."

[5] We give a sample here from all three parts.

[6] The other surviving works derived from this common ancestor are the treatise *De vitiis et figuris* by Julian of Toledo (seventh century), and the anonymous *De vitiis et virtutibus orationis liber*, found in a unique eighth-century manuscript in which it is attributed to a mysterious "Isidorus Iunior." See Schindel, *Die lateinischen Figurenlehren des 5. bis 7. Jahrhunderts und Donats Vergilkommentar*, 19–95 (also containing an edition of "Isidorus Iunior"); Schindel, "Die Quellen von Bedas Figurenlehre"; Holtz, "À l'école de Donat, de saint Augustin à Bède," 524–9.

[7] In this volume see Rupert of Deutz and Nicolaus Dybinus.

[8] Schindel, *Die lateinischen Figurenlehren*, 96–183.

Bede comes closest to the outlook of Cassiodorus in the *Expositio Psalmorum*. At the beginning of *De schematibus et tropis*, Bede echoes Cassiodorus in declaring that the enhancement and beautification of language was a sacred knowledge of Scripture before it was appropriated as a worldly science by the pagan doctors. But beyond claiming the schemes and tropes for Scripture, Bede's purpose is to reconstruct the textbook tradition of grammar itself. That this effort was successful can be seen in the long influence of both *De arte metrica* and *De schematibus et tropis* on grammatical teaching in England and the Continent.[9]

The two treatises thus form a single textbook anchored securely in grammatical authorities. Yet among modern scholars, *De schematibus et tropis* has sometimes been treated as a rhetorical text, and Bede considered a rhetorician. [10] The earliest modern edition of *De schematibus et tropis* was by Halm, in his influential collection *Rhetores latini minores*. And certainly *De schematibus et tropis* enters into the space shared between grammar and rhetoric: if the ancient Greek grammarians were the first to systematize the study of figures and tropes, the Roman rhetoricians appropriated much of that material and augmented it to serve their own theoretical interests.[11] The two traditions, grammatical and rhetorical, were always likely to mingle throughout the Middle Ages because there was a great deal of overlap between grammatical catalogues of schemes and tropes and rhetorical catalogues of verbal ornaments. But rather than quibbling over their disciplinary attachments or uses, or about how to classify Bede's treatise, it may be simplest to say that the difference between grammar- and rhetoric-based catalogues was largely an effect of changing fashions and availability of sources.[12] The grammatical model of the figures, as in Bede's consummate treatise, held sway at least until the late eleventh century, when there was a revival of interest in the *Rhetorica ad Herennium* and teachers began to make use of the catalogue of figures of speech and thought in book 4. Lists of figures drawn from the rhetorical source became increasingly

[9] On the role of Bede in English grammatical thought, see Gneuss, "The Study of Language in Anglo-Saxon England," and Murphy, "The Rhetorical Lore of the *Boceras* in Byhrtferth's *Manual*." See also the edition of the two texts by Kendall, *CCSL* 123A:61–72, for the diffusion of manuscripts of the treatises.

[10] So Kendall treats him in his edition and translation of *De arte metrica* and *De schematibus et tropis* (*The Art of Poetry and Rhetoric*); this is also the assumption of Tannenhaus, the first English translator of Bede's *De schematibus*. Most prominently among modern scholars, Roger Ray has argued that Bede knew Ciceronian rhetorical theory and used it catalytically in his scriptural commentaries and historical writing: see his "Bede and Cicero," and "Bede, Rhetoric, and the Creation of Christian Latin Culture."

[11] Holtz, "Grammairiens et rhéteurs romains en concurrence pour l'enseignement des figures de rhétorique."

[12] As Knappe argues of Anglo-Saxon England, grammatical sources could readily be substituted for rhetorical teaching on some compositional points: "The Rhetorical Aspect of Grammar-Teaching in Anglo-Saxon England," 20.

popular, especially for composition handbooks, culminating of course in Geoffrey of Vinsauf's *Poetria nova*.[13] And even the influential grammar of Eberhard of Béthune, the *Graecismus*, expands its list of figures beyond the Donatan standards to include some of the "colors of rhetoric" taken from the *Ad Herennium*. At the same time, textbooks that used the "rhetorical" lists of figures made use of other formulas taken directly from the grammarians, for example the classification of three kinds of poetry (dramatic, narrative, mixed), derived from Diomedes' *Ars grammatica* and included in Bede's *De arte metrica*.[14] So while it is fair to say that Bede's work was not composed as a rhetoric, certain pedagogical functions that his catalogue of figures would have served came to be filled by catalogues based on rhetorical sources. And in terms of the largest framework, Bede has a significant place in the tradition of Augustine and Cassiodorus, as an exegete who attended to the rhetoricity of Scripture, whether at the level of language or of argument.

One element of *De schematibus et tropis* that has attracted considerable attention is Bede's elaborate explication of the term *allegoria*, and his invention of a new terminology, *allegoria in verbis* and *allegoria in factis* ("verbal" allegory or "allegory in words" and "historical" allegory or "allegory in facts"). In this famous passage, Bede attempts to explain the complexity that had grown around the term *allegoria*, which was a grammatical and rhetorical term for a category of trope as well as a theological term for a category of sacred meaning in scripture. The history behind these dual meanings for one Latin word involves the Latin appropriation of Greek terminology. In both classical Latin and Greek, *allegoria* (*allēgoria*) had the meaning of veiled language or speaking under figures, and in Latin rhetorical use (the *Ad Herennium*, Quintilian's *Institutio oratoria*) the trope *allegoria* was defined narrowly as saying one thing and meaning another for the purposes of embellishing discourse. This was also the definition that Donatus gave in the *Ars maior*. But in early and later Greek philosophical and religious language, it also had a hermeneutical value, the notion of mystical truths that lie hidden beneath the surface but that can be disclosed through allegorical interpretation. This is the value that *allēgoria* took on in Greek Christian writings, that is, a method of exegesis that contrasts with the literal level, and that finds profound meaning in the content of the text rather than in its form or words. It was this second, theological meaning of *allegoria* that was imported from the Greek into the Latin Church. *Allegoria* in its spiritual sense had become a crucial term for

---

[13] See Camargo, "Latin Composition Textbooks and *Ad Herennium* Glossing," 268–71; see introductions to Parts 1, 3, and 4, and references to Marbod of Rennes' *De ornamentis verborum* (late eleventh or early twelfth century), based on the figures and tropes in the *Ad Herennium*.

[14] See John of Garland, within, p. 630.

the interpretation of Scripture, sometimes as the generic term for the various mystical or spiritual senses of Scripture.

It is testimony to Bede's acuity as a thinker that he saw the essence of the problem when trying to reconcile the value of the trope *allegoria* with the needs of scriptural interpretation. His solution is the distinction between allegory that has a historical referent in events, and allegory that has no literal meaning, but must immediately be interpreted for its mystical content. After first paying due attention to the definitions of *allegoria* that he finds in Donatus (with its subgenres, irony, antiphrasis, enigma, and charientismos), Bede announces: "It is important to observe that allegory is sometimes factual and sometimes purely verbal" (*allegoria quando factis, aliquando verbis tantum modo fit*). This looks back to the questions that Augustine raises about allegory in *De trinitate* 15.9, and more generally about ambiguous figurative signs in *De doctrina christiana* 3. But Bede takes this further by expressly expanding the compass of the grammatical trope *allegoria*, in effect doubling its value. In his exposition he creates two bipartitions. The first, the distinction between factual and verbal allegory, refers to the vehicle of the allegory, which is either "an event in time which refers to another reality outside itself," that is, factual allegory, or a verbal statement without any "literal meaning or historical reference," but which can only be understood allegorically.[15] Bede's second bipartition refers to the nature of the allegorical meaning itself: this can be either "historical" or spiritual. In the case of historical meaning, the allegory has a concrete, historical event as its referent. Spiritual allegory, by contrast, conveys a transcendent or mystical meaning, and is in turn tripartite (typological, tropological, anagogical).

Bede's exposition of factual and verbal allegory was influential for centuries following.[16] Its most remarkable feature is that he places this hermeneutical nexus under the system of grammar, expanding the traditional limits of grammar to accommodate theological inquiry.[17]

Translation of *De arte metrica* reprinted from *The Art of Poetry and Rhetoric*, ed. and trans. Kendall, by permission; selection from *De schematibus et tropis* (opening of the treatise, first figures, and metaphor) translated from Kendall, ed., *CCSL* 123A, and (section on allegory) reprinted from *The Art of Poetry and Rhetoric*, ed. and trans. Kendall, both by permission.

---

[15] Kendall, introduction to Bede, *The Art of Poetry and Rhetoric*, 26–7.

[16] See Copeland, "Rhetoric and the Politics of the Literal Sense" and Strubel, " 'Allegoria in factis' et 'allegoria in verbis.' "

[17] Irvine, *The Making of Textual Culture*, 293–6.

From *De arte metrica*[18]

[The opening of the *De arte metrica*, the chapter on the letter (complete).]

I. *The Letter*

Anyone who wants to acquire a practical knowledge of poetic meters should first carefully learn the different (prosodic) values of the letters and syllables. The Latin alphabet consists of twenty-one letters, of which five, A, E, I, O, and U, are called vowels, and the rest, consonants. The consonants are divided into seven semivowels, F, L, M, N, R, S, and X, and nine mutes, B, C, D, G, H, K, P, Q, and T. However, on account of the Greek words which they routinely used, Latin-speaking peoples adopted a sixth vowel, Y, and a seventeenth consonant, Z, because they had no other way to write words like *typus* and *zelus* and others of this kind. Since their conversion to Christianity, they have also taken over the Greek letters which are found in the Bible, *eta*, *chi*, *rho*, and *omega* and *alpha*, although they have not admitted them into the order of the alphabet. To be specific, they have introduced *eta*, which the Greeks write as a double form,[19] just as we write H, on the authority of the name of Jesus, *chi* and *rho* on the authority of the name of Christ, and *omega* on the authority of the Lord's words "I am Alpha and Omega".[20] *Alpha* differs only in name; otherwise it is equivalent both in form and in value to our A. The Greek *rho* differs from our R not only in name but also in form. *Eta* and *omega* differ from our E and O in that they are always long. For all our Latin vowels are common—that is, they may be used both in short and in long syllables, just like the Greek A, I, and Y. But the Greek E and O[21] always remain short by nature.

And so we use twenty-seven letters in all—namely, eight vowels, A, E, I, O, U, *eta*, Y, and *omega*, and nineteen consonants. But the vowels I and U frequently take on the value of consonants, either when they are paired with each other: as *iumentum*, *vinum*; or when they are joined with other vowels: as *ianua*, *iecor*, *iocus*, and *vanitas*, *veritas*, *volatus*. Sometimes U precedes itself, as: *vultus*. It can also act as a consonant following a vowel, as when we pronounce the Latin word *avarus* or the Greek word *evangelium*.[22]

---

[18] Trans. Kendall, with slight adaptations to make the translation conform to the text in *CCSL*; see *CCSL* 123A: (chap. I) 82–5; (chap II) 86, lines 1–8; (chap. IV) 94–95.16; (chap. XV)127.1–16, 128.35–129.45; (chap. XXIV) 138–139.31.

[19] Namely ⊢ and ⊣.   [20] *Apocalypse* 1:8.   [21] *epsilon; omicron.*

[22] On *i* and *u*, see section on Donatus, p. 88.

It is a puzzle why Donatus said that U is considered neither a vowel nor a consonant when it is found between the consonant Q and another vowel, as: *quoniam, quidem*. Possibly he meant that it is then uttered so lightly that it can scarcely be perceived. The argument by which Pompeius and Sergius tried to explain Donatus' meaning does not seem to be a strong one. They say that U cannot be a consonant, because another consonant, that is Q, precedes it, and that it cannot be a vowel, because a vowel follows it, as: *quare, quomodo*. Therefore, they say, in such a case it is not a letter at all. Isn't it really? When we write *status*, should we really claim that T cannot be a consonant because the consonant S precedes it, and that it cannot be a vowel because a vowel follows it? Of course not. When we say *stratum*, R must be acknowledged to be a letter, although not only does a vowel follow it, but two consonants precede it, and T must be a consonant, even though another consonant both precedes and follows it.

Alone among the vowels, I has this special property: when it acts as a consonant and has another vowel in front of it within the same part of speech, it always makes that vowel long by position, even when it was short by nature, e.g. *māius, pēiurium*. For this reason, consonantal I is called a double consonant. Because it has the same property, the letter X is also called a double consonant, as: *axis*. In contrast, but still according to a definite rule, the four liquids, L, M, N, and R, in poetry often lose the usual power of consonants to lengthen syllables which are short by nature, although sometimes we find that they do lengthen them.

[From chapters on the syllable.]

II. *The Syllable*

A syllable is any combination of letters, or even the utterance of a single vowel, which is capable of containing morae, because every syllable is either short and takes one mora, which prosodists regard as indivisible, like the first syllable of *păter*, or it is long and takes two morae, like the first syllable of *māter*. For when *mater* is pronounced with a circumflex accent because of its long first syllable, the syllable MA takes twice as much time as the syllable PA when *pater* is pronounced with an acute accent.[23]

---

[23] Kendall comments on this passage: "According to classical grammatical theory, a disyllabic word received a circumflex accent on its penultimate syllable if the penultimate syllable contained a long vowel or a diphthong and the final syllable was short. Otherwise the penultimate syllable received an acute accent" (*The Art of Poetry and Rhetoric*, 43n.).

IV. Initial Syllables

What I have briefly said thus far about the different values of syllables for the most part can be readily discerned from looking at examples by anyone who has taken the trouble to learn the scansion of heroic verse. But I also urge the student who has not yet reached this point to examine in the meantime even more attentively the syllables of all words at the beginning of heroic verses. For every hexameter verse, which is made up of six feet, and every pentameter verse, which is made up of five feet, has a long first syllable, because it begins either with a spondee or with a dactyl. The former foot consists of two long syllables, like *dīcens*, while the latter consists of one long and two short syllables, like *dīcĭmus*. And therefore when you pick up a codex which contains hexameter or elegiac poetry, whatever page you open and examine, whatever verse you select and read, you will find without any doubt that the first syllable is long either by nature or by position, and obviously so, since it must be the beginning of a spondee or a dactyl.

> [Chapter IV continues with more advice for non-native speakers on how to recognize the quantities of syllables: e.g. compounds may reveal the quantity of the simplex. The selection that follows below, from chapter XV, comes from the second part of the treatise. This section deals with the different forms of quantitative Latin poetry, and considers the limitations of the rules of metrical theory.]

XV. Concerning the Fact that the Rules of the Prosodists are Often Broken Both by Authority and from Necessity[24]

Nevertheless we should keep in mind that the rules of prosody are sometimes rightfully disregarded both by those poets whom we consider authoritative and from necessity. They must be disregarded from necessity in those words which otherwise cannot be put into a line of verse, such as those which have four short syllables, like *Ĭtălĭă*, *băsĭlĭcă*, and *rĕlĭgĭŏ*, or those which have three initial short syllables, like *rĕlĭquĭae*, or those which have one short syllable between two long ones, like *vērĭtās* and *trīnĭtās*. Words like these can make neither an ordinary dactyl nor a spondee. This problem is especially common with certain proper names. For example:

---

[24] Sources of this chapter: Jerome, *Praefatio in librum Job*; Victorinus, *De ratione metrorum* (*The Art of Poetry and Rhetoric*, ed. and trans. Kendall, 133 n. 55).

Ītaliam sequimur fugientem et mergimur undis
We seek Italy which keeps receding and we are overwhelmed in the seas[25]

Here the poet has put the I, contrary to its nature, in the position of a long syllable, because he could not otherwise have referred to Italy, which he was going to have to name rather frequently, unless he were either to lengthen a syllable that was short by nature or to put a tribrach[26] in place of a dactyl.

[There follow more examples of the breach of rules by necessity. Then the author transitions to infractions on the strength of authority.]

The rules of the grammarians, moreover, are sometimes disregarded on the strength of authority.[27] So, for example, at the end of the poem which I mentioned above, Sedulius, after saying:

Gloria magna Patri, semper tibi gloria, Nate
Great glory be to the Father, glory be always to you, Son

added:

Cum sancto Spiritu gloria magna Patri
Great glory be to the Father with the Holy Spirit[28]

The first syllable of *spiritus* is long, and therefore the correct scansion of this last line is: CŪMSĀNC (spondee), TŌSPĪRĬ (antibacchius,[29] instead of dactyl). But the poet, in order to celebrate clearly the glory of the holy and undivided Trinity, has neglected the rule forbidding the placement of an antibacchius in elegiac verse.

[There follow more examples. In chapter XVI, Bede argues that there were certain differences between the *prisci poetae* and the *moderni*. These Christian poets of the fourth century and later tended to adhere to the rules even more precisely than their illustrious predecessors. The third, and shortest part of the treatise leaves quantitative poetry behind, and discusses rhythmical poetry (ch. XXIV), and finally the three different kinds of narrative organization within poetry (ch. XXV).]

---

[25] *Aeneid* 5.629; for *Ītaliam* as example, see sections on Donatus and Servius (p. 94; p. 131 with note 51).

[26] A tribrach is a sequence of three short syllables, as in the first three syllables of *Italiam* (*The Art of Poetry and Rhetoric*, ed. and trans. Kendall, 133, n. 57.).

[27] *Auctoritate*: if the poet who thus uses his poetic license is *indeed* found to be authoritative by later generations, this will be a case of authority granting special permission; if not, it will be considered a fault. But the author claims a certain authority for himself by ignoring a rule. As Kendall points out (135 n. 61), "in all the cases which follow, Sedulius could have used the words in question without violating the norms of dactylic verse."

[28] *Hymn.* 1.109–10.   [29] An antibacchius consists of two long syllables and one short one.

XXIV. Rhythmic Verse

This must suffice on the more important meters of which I have found fairly numerous examples in the works of established authors. There are, besides, a great many other meters, which anyone who wishes will find set forth with plain examples in the Book of a Hundred Meters.[30] Some meters are also found in that noted volume of the poet Porfirius, which when he sent it to the Emperor Constantine earned him release from exile. I have preferred not to deal with them because of their pagan nature.

Rhythmic verse resembles metrical verse. Rhythmic verse is a harmonious arrangement of words which is scanned, not by a quantitative system of meter, but by the number of syllables judged in accordance with the way they sound to the ear, as are the verses of the common poets.[31] Rhythm can certainly exist by itself without meter, but meter cannot exist without rhythm. This can be defined more clearly as follows: metrical verse is a quantitative system with a rhythmical beat,[32] while rhythmic verse has a rhythmical beat without a quantitative system.[33] However, you will commonly find measured quantities by chance in rhythmic verse, not because the regular artistic arrangement has been preserved, but from the influence of the sound and the rhythmical beat itself. The common poets inevitably do this awkwardly, and the learned poets skilfully. This is how that celebrated hymn was composed most beautifully in the likeness of iambic meter:[34]

> Eternal Lord King,
> Creator of all things,
> you who were before the worlds
> eternally the Son with the Father;

and quite a few other hymns by Ambrose. Similarly, they sing a hymn about Judgment Day—an abecedary[35]—in the form of trochaic meter:[36]

> The great day of the Lord
> will suddenly appear,

[30] Probably Servius' *De centum metris.* See Kendall, *The Art of Poetry and Rhetoric*, 161 n. 90.

[31] Kendall (*The Art of Poetry and Rhetoric*, 161 n. 92) rejects the possibility that "Bede is here referring to poets writing in their native Anglo-Saxon tongue," but assumes Bede is talking about "composers of crudely isosyllabic, non-quantitative Latin poems like many of those in the *Antiphonary of Bangor* and the Irish *Liber hymnorum*."

[32] *metrum est ratio cum modulatione*   [33] *rithmus modulatio sine ratione*

[34] *Rex aeterne domine* 1–4.

[35] Kendall (163 n. 94): "An abecedary is a poem in which successive stanzas begin with the successive letters of the alphabet. The author of this one is unknown."

[36] *Apparebit repentina* 1–4.

like a thief in the dark of night
seizing those not expecting it.

XXV. *The Three Genres of Poetry*

Since I have examined poetry and its meters in some detail, it is appropriate to observe in conclusion that there are three genres of poetry. There is the "active" or "imitative" genre, which the Greeks call *dramaticon* or *micticon*.[37] There is the "expository" genre, which the Greeks call *exegematicon* or *apangelticon*. There is the "common" or "mixed" genre, which the Greeks call *coenon* or *micton*. The dramatic or active is the genre in which the speakers are introduced without comment by the poet, as happens in tragedies and *fabulae* (for drama is called *fabula* in Latin). In this genre is written:[38]

Where are you off to, Moeris? Where the road goes, to town?

In our own Holy Scripture, this is the genre of the Song of Songs, in which is clearly found the voice of Christ alternating with that of the Church without comment by the poet. The narrative or expository genre is that in which the poet speaks in his own voice without introducing any other speakers, as happens in the whole of the first three books of the *Georgics* and the first part of the fourth, and also in the poems of Lucretius, and in other works similar to these. In Holy Scripture, the Proverbs of Solomon and Ecclesiastes are written in this genre. It is well known that they, like Psalms, were composed in their original language in meter. The common or mixed is the genre in which the poet both speaks in his own voice and introduces characters who speak. The *Iliad* and *Odyssey* of Homer and the *Aeneid* of Virgil are written in this genre, as is, in Holy Scripture, the story of the blessed Job, although in its original language the latter was not written entirely in poetry, but partly in rhetorical prose and partly in metrical or rhythmical verse.

I have taken pains to make these extracts from the works of the ancient authors for your benefit, beloved son and fellow deacon, Cuthbert, and what I found in scattered sources I myself collected over a long period of work and offered to you as a collection, in order that I might instruct you intelligently in the art of metrics, which is not unknown in the Bible, just as I endeavored to give you your first training in divine letters and ecclesiastical law. I thought it would not be inappropriate to add to it also a little work on the figures and manners of speech which the Greeks call *schemata* or *tropi*. I earnestly beg you, my

---

[37] "A corruption, found in Bede's sources, of *mimeticon*" (Kendall, *The Art of Poetry and Rhetoric*, 165 n. 96). Through the school grammar of the Latin empire, this theory of the three kinds of narration in poetry ultimately goes back to Plato, *Republic* 392D ff.

[38] Virgil, *Eclogues* 9.1.

beloved one, to devote your efforts especially to the reading of that Book in which we believe that we have eternal life.

FROM *DE SCHEMATIBUS ET TROPIS*[39]

On Figures

[Opening, and discussion of the first figure.]

Quite frequently one finds in Holy Scripture word order that has been figured differently from ordinary speech for the sake of embellishment. The grammarians, using a Greek term, call this *schema*, we rightly call it a "dressing,"[40] "form," or "figure," because through it discourse is so to speak dressed up and ornamented. One also finds troped language,[41] which occurs when a word has been transferred from its proper signification to a non proper similitude for the sake of necessity or embellishment.[42] The Greeks pride themselves on being the inventors of such figures or tropes. But you should know, my dearest son, and so should everyone wishing to read this, that Holy Scripture surpasses all other writings not just in authority, since it is divine, or in usefulness, since it leads to eternal life, but also in age and in its very style. Therefore I decided to collect examples from it in order to show that the masters of worldly eloquence cannot lay claim to any of these figures or tropes without there being an earlier example in Scripture.

There are many kinds of figures, but the most important are these: prolepsis, zeugma, hypozeuxis, syllepsis, anadiplosis, anaphora, epanalepsis, epizeuxis, paronomasia, schesis onomaton, paromoeon, homoeoteleuton, homoeoptoton, polyptoton, hirmos, polysyndeton, and dialyton.

1. *Prolepsis*, that is, anticipation or taking up in advance is the figure that occurs when those things which should follow are put first, as in Psalms:

> Fundamenta eius in montibus sanctis; diligit Dominus portas Sion.[43]
> [The foundations thereof are in *the holy mountains*: The Lord loveth the gates of Sion]

---

[39] Sections on figures and on metaphor translated from Kendall, ed., *De arte metrica et de schematibus et tropis*, *CCSL* 123A:142–4, 151–3. See also the first translation into English by Tannenhaus, "Bede's *De schematibus et tropis*— A Translation."

[40] *habitus*   [41] *tropica locutio*   [42] *Rhetorica ad Herennium* 4.14.21.   [43] Psalm 86:1–2.

He put the word "his"[44] first, and afterwards adds whose it is, namely (of) the Lord. And elsewhere:

> Diviserunt sibi vestimenta mea, et super vestem meam miserunt sortem[45]
> [They parted my garments among them, and upon my vesture they cast lots]

instead of "they will part" and "they will cast."[46] Ezechiel begins as follows without any introduction:

> Et factum est in tricesimo anno[47]
> [Now it came to pass in the thirtieth year]

He uses a conjunction [et] without putting anything in front of it, to which this could be connected.

On Tropes and on Metaphor

[Beginning of the section on tropes and discussion of metaphor.]

A trope is an expression transferred for reasons of ornamentation or necessity from its proper signification to one that is similar but not proper to it.[48] There are thirteen tropes, which may be called *modi* or *mores* "manners" in Latin:[49] metaphor, catachresis, metalepsis, metonomy, antonomasia, epitheton, synecdoche, onomatopoeia, periphrasis, hyperbaton, hyperbole, allegory, and homoeosis.

Metaphor is the transfer of words and things.[50] It is produced in four ways: from animate to animate; from inanimate to inanimate; from animate to inanimate; from inanimate to animate. An example of "from animate to animate" is: "Why have the Gentiles *roared*?"[51] and: "The Lord who delivered me out of the *paw* of the lion and out of the *paw* of the bear,"[52] and: "If I take *my wings* early in the morning."[53] For human beings, animals and birds are all animate. From inanimate to inanimate, e.g.: "Open thy *gates*, O Libanus";[54] and: "That pass through the *paths* of the sea."[55] For here a transfer takes place from a city to a mountain and from land to sea, and none of those items are animate. From animate to inanimate, e.g.: "The *head* [*vertex*] of Carmel is withered."[56] For human beings have heads,

---

[44] *eius*   [45] Psalm 21:19.

[46] This is an "anticipation" in a different sense. The text is read as a prediction, yet it is put in the past tense.

[47] Ezechiel 1:1.   [48] Donatus, *Ars maior* 3.6, *GL* 4:399.13.

[49] The Greek word *tropos* also means "manner."

[50] Donatus *Ars maior* 3.6, *GL* 4:399.17–30.   [51] Psalm 2:1.   [52] 1 Kings 137.

[53] Psalm 138:9.   [54] Zachariah 11:1.   [55] Psalm 8:9.   [56] Amos 1:2.

mountains do not. From inanimate to animate, e.g.: "I will take away the *stony* heart."[57] For a stone is not animate, but people are. This trope is also used in many ways to refer to God. Transfer from birds, e.g.: "Protect me under the shadow of thy *wings*."[58] Transfer from wild animals, e.g.: "The Lord will *roar* from Sion."[59] Transfer from parts of the human body, e.g.: "Who hath measured the waters in the *hollow of his hand*, and weighed the heavens with his *palm*?"[60] Transfer from the inner parts of the human body, e.g.: "I have found David the son of Jesse, a man according to my own *heart*."[61] Transfer from human emotions, e.g.: "Then shall he speak to them in his *anger*";[62] and: "I *regret* that I have made man,"[63] and: "I *have been jealous* for Sion with a great *jealousy*."[64] And innumerable similar cases. Transfer from insensible objects, e.g.: "Behold, I will *creak* over you,[65] as a wain creaketh that is laden with hay."[66] Of course, this trope is also most common in daily usage, as when we say that "the corn is *waving*," "the vines are *budding*,"[67] "youth is *blossoming*" and "gray hair is *milk-white*."[68]

On Allegory[69]

[Selection from on allegory.]

It is important to observe that allegory is sometimes factual, and sometimes purely verbal.[70] Factual allegory is found, for example, in: "It is written that Abraham had two sons: the one by a bondwoman, and the other by a free woman."[71] The women "are the two testaments," as the apostle Paul explains.[72] Purely verbal allegory is found in: "There shall come forth a rod out of the root of Jesse, and a flower shall rise up out of his root."[73]

---

[57] Ezechiel 11:19.   [58] Psalm 16:8.   [59] Amos 1:2; Joel 3:16.   [60] Isaiah 40:12.

[61] Acts 13:22.   [62] Psalm 2:5.   [63] Genesis 6:6. In Bede's text, *Penitet enim me fecisse hominem.*

[64] Zachariah 8:2.   [65] In Bede's text, *Ecce ego stridebo super vos.*   [66] Amos 2:13.

[67] *Vites gemmant*, literally, the vines are "gemming," producing little gems.

[68] These common examples are probably intended to illustrate the four types again, but the first two examples both represent the transfer of inanimate to animate; they are then followed by examples of the transfer of animate and inanimate to inanimate.

[69] Translation of this section on allegory reprinted from *The Art of Poetry and Rhetoric*, ed. and trans. Kendall, 201–7, with minor adaptations. See also text in *CCSL* 123A:164–9.

[70] Literally, "It sometimes happens 'through the facts/events,' sometimes 'through the words only,'" cf. Strubel, "'Allegoria in factis' et 'Allegoria in verbis.'"

[71] Galatians 4:22.

[72] Galatians 4:24. In this case, therefore, one fact or event allegorically represents another; this is what Kendall calls "historical allegory"—we have replaced this with "factual allegory" in order to prevent confusion with Bede's term "historical allegory" which refers not to the vehicle of the allegory, but to its tenor.

[73] Isaiah 11:1.

By this is meant that our Savior the Lord was to be born of the Virgin Mary from the race of David.[74] Sometimes one and the same event is signified both by factual and by verbal allegory. (The betrayal of Christ is signified) by factual allegory in: "They sold Joseph to the Ismaelites for twenty pieces of silver."[75] It is signified by verbal allegory in: "They weighed for my wages thirty pieces of silver."[76] Or, to give another example, the same idea is signified by factual allegory in: "Now David was ruddy and beautiful to behold, and Samuel anointed him in the midst of his brethren";[77] and by verbal allegory in: "My beloved is white and ruddy, chosen out of thousands."[78] Both signify mystically that "the Mediator of God and men"[79] was beautiful indeed in wisdom and virtue, but rosy from the shedding of his own blood, and that the same Mediator was anointed by God the Father "with the oil of gladness above his fellows."[80]

Moreover, whether allegory is verbal or factual, sometimes it refers figuratively to a historical event, sometimes it prefigures typologically (an event in the life of Christ or of the Church), sometimes it figuratively expresses a tropological, or moral principle, and sometimes it figuratively expresses an anagogical sense, that is, a sense leading the mind to higher things. History refers figuratively to history, when the creation of the first six or seven days is compared to the same number of ages of this world.[81] History is prefigured by verbal allegory, when the Patriarch Jacob's pronouncement: "Juda is a lion's whelp; to the prey, my son, you have gone up,"[82] etc., is understood to refer to the kingdom and victories of David.[83] Verbal allegory expresses a spiritual sense concerning Christ or the Church, when the same speech of the Patriarch is taken in faith to refer to the Lord's passion and resurrection.[84] Likewise, factual allegory conveys a tropological, that is, a moral lesson, when the ankle-length coat of many colors which the Patriarch Jacob made for his son Joseph[85] alludes to the grace of the various virtues which God the Father commanded us always to be clothed in to the end of our life and which he confers upon us.[86] Verbal allegory can signify the same idea of moral perfection, as in: "Let your loins be girt, and lamps burning."[87] Factual allegory can express an anagogical sense, that is, the sense leading the mind to higher things, as in: "Enoch, the seventh from Adam, was translated

---

[74] In this case, therefore, there never was such an "event" as the coming forth of a rod out of the root of Jesse: we are dealing with purely verbal allegory.

[75] Genesis 37:28.   [76] Zachariah 11:12.   [77] 1 Kings 16:12–13.   [78] Song of Songs 5:10.

[79] 1 Timothy 2:5.   [80] Psalm 44:8.

[81] This is a case of factual allegory (vehicle) of an historical sense (tenor).   [82] Genesis 49:9.

[83] This is a case of verbal allegory (vehicle) of an historical sense (tenor).

[84] Here begin the cases of spiritual interpretation of allegory: a verbal allegory (vehicle) of a spiritual, typological sense (tenor).

[85] Genesis 37:3; 23.

[86] A factual allegory (there really was a coat of many colors) here stands for a spiritual, tropological sense (tenor).

[87] Luke 12:35. A verbal allegory with spiritual, tropological sense.

from the earth."[88] This trope prefigures the Sabbath of the blessedness to come, which is reserved in the end of time for the elect after they have accomplished the good works of this world, which is completed in six ages. Verbal allegory points to the same joys of heavenly life, as in: "Wheresoever the body shall be, there shall the eagles also be gathered together,"[89] because where the Mediator of God and men is in the flesh, there surely souls are both now being raised to Heaven, and after the glory of the final resurrection has been accomplished, the bodies of the just will also be brought together there.[90]

Sometimes a single factual or verbal allegory will figuratively reveal a historical [literal] sense, a mystical sense concerning Christ or the Church,[91] a tropological sense, and an anagogical sense all at the same time. For example, the temple of the Lord in the literal historical sense is the house which Solomon built;[92] allegorically, it is the Lord's body, of which Christ said: "Destroy this temple, and in three days I will raise it up,"[93] or his Church, to whom the apostle Paul said: "For the temple of the Lord is holy, which you are";[94] tropologically, it is each of the faithful, to whom the Apostle said: "Know you not, that your bodies are the temple of the Holy Spirit, who is in you?";[95] anagogically, it is the joys of the heavenly mansion, for which the Psalmist sighed, when he said: "Blessed are they that dwell in your house, O Lord; they shall praise you for ever and ever."[96] Another example is the verse of the Psalmist: "Praise the Lord, O Jerusalem; praise your God, O Sion. Because he has strengthened the bolts of your gates, he has blessed your children within you."[97] This trope can rightly be taken as referring literally (in the historic sense) to the citizens of the earthly Jerusalem, allegorically to the Church of Christ, tropologically to each saved soul, and anagogically to the celestial homeland. I have said that it can be taken "allegorically" in reference to the Church, following the example of that learned commentator, Pope Gregory the Great, who, in his *Moralia*, specifically used the term "allegory" in connection with those verbal expressions and historical events which he interpreted figuratively as referring to Christ or the Church.[98]

---

[88] Jude 14; Hebrews 11:5. A factual allegory with spiritual, anagogical sense.   [89] Matthew 24:28.

[90] A verbal allegory with spiritual, anagogical sense.   [91] Paraphrasis for a typological sense.

[92] 3 Kings 6. The *house* of the Lord is a verbal allegory for what is literally/historically his temple. The temple of God then becomes a factual allegory for the three spiritual levels of meaning.

[93] John 2:19.   [94] 1 Corinthians 3:17.   [95] 1 Corinthians 3:16; 6:15; 19.

[96] Psalm 83:5.   [97] Psalm 147:12–13.

[98] Kendall, *The Art of Poetry and Rhetoric*, 207 n. 28: "That is, the term *allegory* is sometimes restricted to typological allegory: the interpretation of events (or prophetic sayings) of the Old Testament as figures for events of the New Testament." Gregory used "allegory" as the "proper term" for that.

ALCUIN, *ARS GRAMMATICA* AND *DISPUTATIO DE RHETORICA ET DE VIRTUTIBUS*, CA. 790–800

INTRODUCTION

Alcuin of York (ca. 731–804) is arguably the greatest pedagogue of the Carolingian Renaissance.[1] His work ranges from the *opera didascalica*, our main focus of interest in this section, to dogmatic theology, to pedagogy. He also wrote poetry. Alcuin spent almost fifteen years at the court of Charlemagne (782–796), as the leader of the "school of Albinus," his court nickname.[2] In this period, he designed Charlemagne's education policy, in which grammar, and textual culture in general, formed the basis for a thoroughly Christianized erudition (*eruditio* being a key term) in the spirit of Augustine, Cassiodorus, and Bede (whose student Egbert was Alcuin's teacher).[3] Politics, Christianity, and textual culture are integrated into a new pedagogical program.

Alcuin's *opera didascalica* consist of four works in question-and-answer form: *Ars grammatica*, *De orthographia*, *Ars rhetorica*, and *De dialectica*. The question-and-answer form had been traditional in grammar since Donatus' *Ars minor*, and for rhetoric there was an example in the *Ars* by Fortunatianus.[4] The *Ars grammatica* actually consists of two dialogues, one the *Ars* itself, the other, preceding it, a *Disputatio de vera philosophia* (Dialogue on the True Philosophy).[5] The content of these works is highly derivative, but the pedagogy is innovative, and the way in which the work of compilation has been

---

[1] For general studies of Alcuin, see e.g. Wallach, *Alcuin and Charlemagne*; Allott, *Alcuin of York: His Life and Letters*; Marenbon, *From the Circle of Alcuin to the School of Auxerre: Logic, Theology, and Philosophy in the Early Middle Ages*; and the collection of papers in Houwens and MacDonald, eds., *Alcuin of York: Scholar at the Carolingian Court*.

[2] His other nickname in literary play was Flaccus, after the poet Horace (Q. Horatius Flaccus), just as Charlemagne was called David after King David.

[3] See Irvine, *The Making of Textual Culture*, 313–33 for an analysis of Alcuin's work on grammar and its cultural context; and see ibid., 307 for Charlemagne's mandate *De litteris colendis* (ca. 790), which may have been written by Alcuin.

[4] See Matter, "Alcuin's Question-and-Answer Texts." On *De orthographia*, see Irvine, *The Making of Textual Culture*, 327–30.

[5] *Disputatio* is simply "dialogue" here; see *The Rhetoric of Alcuin and Charlemagne*, trans. Howell, 3.

executed gives a new ideological twist to traditional material. The content of the *Ars grammatica* is based on the framework of Donatus, supplemented with material from Priscian.[6] There is a merging of the disciplines of grammar and dialectic in the organization of the work, particularly in the refusal of the master to begin with *littera*.[7] He first wants to discuss the underlying notions of *vox* and the *modi* of any disputation.[8] The rhetoric is based on Cicero's *De inventione*, Julius Victor's *Ars rhetorica,* and possibly also the rhetorical treatises of Cassiodorus and Isidore.[9]

The new twist given to this traditional material is clear, both from the combination of the *Disputatio de vera philosophia* and *Ars grammatica,* and from the expansion of a "regular" *ars rhetorica* into the *Disputatio de rhetorica et de virtutibus* (Dialogue on Rhetoric and on Virtues). The *Disputatio de vera philosophia* sees the acquisition of the *artes liberales* as a means of achieving wisdom (*sapientia*), construed as insight into the correct reading of the Bible. Grammar, rhetoric, dialectic, arithmetic, geometry, music, and astrology are the steps leading up to his higher goal.[10] This *Disputatio*, serving as it does as an introduction to the *Ars grammatica*, replaces traditional introductory definitions of *ars, disciplina*, and *grammatica*, which would have provided a purely academic contextualization.[11] Similarly, the *Disputatio de rhetorica et de virtutibus* integrates politics, law, and morals, in a way consistent with the Ciceronian tradition. As one of the speakers, Charlemagne makes explicit the links between the doctrinal content of the work and his daily activities as a ruler. It is also Charlemagne himself who makes the connection to the section on (Christian) virtues that ends the work. The whole work has been viewed as a treatise on kingship or a *Fürstenspiegel*, and it certainly combines the characteristics of an ethical or political treatise with those of a rhetorical handbook.[12] But the political outlook

---

[6] On the sources of *De grammatica*, see Frey, *De Alcuini arte grammatica commentatio*, 1–7, and Engels, "Priscian in Alcuin's De orthographia." Vineis, "Grammatica e filosofia del linguaggio in Alcuino," argues that this integrative use of Priscian's *Institutiones* originates with Alcuin (404 n. 5).

[7] Irvine, *The Making of Textual Culture*, 321–5.   [8] Vineis, "Grammatica e filosofia," 424.

[9] Calboli Montefusco, "Un catechismo retorico dell' alto Medioevo," leaves open the question whether Alcuin had read Cicero's *De inventione* himself or simply worked with later handbooks and compendia, such as Cassiodorus on rhetoric. Since Alcuin seems to rely very heavily on *De inventione* for the section on invention and on Julius Victor for the rest, and since Julius Victor in turn relies on Cicero's *De oratore* and *Orator*, the end result is thoroughly Ciceronian: see *The Rhetoric of Alcuin and Charlemagne*, trans. Howell, 29–30. On the influence of Cassiodorus and Isidore, see ibid., 22.

[10] Cf. Augustine, *De doctrina christiana* 2.7.9 ff. for the *gradus* leading to *sapientia*.

[11] These introductory definitions can be found in the grammars of Charisius, Diomedes, Servius in Don., Pompeius, Isidore: see Irvine, *The Making of Textual Culture*, 318.

[12] On the text as *Fürstenspiegel*, see Wallach, *Alcuin and Charlemagne*, 29; as political treatise, see Irvine, *The Making of Textual Culture*, 325. For the presentation of Charlemagne as a Christian king, see also Murray, "The Idea of the Shepherd King," 12.

of the work should not overshadow the importance in itself of the rhetorical doctrine that it contains: here rhetorical theory is given new significance through its integration into a program of political education.

Considered from the perspective of pedagogy, the *De grammatica* and *Disputatio de rhetorica* offer interesting material for comparison.[13] In Donatus' question-and-answer text, there is an inherent ambiguity about the role assignment. Is it the student who asks for information and the master who imparts it? Or is the student supposed to have learned his lessons, and is the master now examining him, expecting *verbatim* repetition of the lesson? In *De grammatica* (ca. 798), the speakers are two boys, named Franco, age 14, and Saxo, who is 15 years old. As their names indicate, they represent non-native students of Latin, the one a Frank, the other a Saxon. At the same time, they are suggestive of the Saxon Alcuin and the Frank Charlemagne and his entourage. The younger boy, Franco, asks the questions and so clearly has less information, but at the same time, he constantly takes the initiative and in that way drives the progress of the lessons. The older boy provides the answers and refers to the master, the third character, whenever a topic goes beyond the elementary (e.g. metrical theory) or becomes more "philosophical."

The dialogue offers a window on common schoolroom scenarios in which the master wields the familiar instruments of coercion; but it also gives a perspective on an ideal schoolroom scenario in which the boys are deeply curious and eager to learn, and are only impeded when one student jealously keeps information from others. The boys organize their own lesson, including the breaks, and they play with the empowering grammatical information, using difficult adverbs when they have only just learned that part of speech, and using an interjection when asked to explain this phenomenon. The self-reflexive and playful elements in this dialogue illustrate the use of humor in teaching. The empowerment that comes with mastering the canonical literary texts that are the object of the art of grammar can be seen briefly in the episode in which the younger student manages two relevant quotations from Virgil, which are seamlessly inserted in the flow of the dialogue.[14]

In the *Disputatio de rhetorica et virtutibus* the genre is the same, but the pedagogical context is very different.[15] This time, the interlocutors are Charlemagne himself and Albinus (Alcuin), a situation which asks for great diplomacy on the teacher's part. Alcuin solves

---

[13] On Alcuin's pedagogy in his *ars grammatica*, see also Fortgens, "De paedagoog Alcuin."

[14] *PL* 101:885D (see translation below). In his poem of praise on York (*versus de patribus, regibus et sanctis euboricensis ecclesiae* [Verses on the fathers, kings, and saints of the church of York], Alcuin presents a list of grammatical and literary texts that formed the basis of his educational program. They include Probus, Phocas, Donatus, Priscian, Servius, Eutyches, Pompeius, Cominianus, Christian poets such as Sedulius and Juvencus, and the classical poets Virgil, Statius, and Lucan. See Irvine, *The Making of Textual Culture*, 315.

[15] For the *disputatio*, see Jaeger, *The Envy of Angels*, 30–5.

the problem by emphasizing the co-production of knowledge by questioner and answerer. One feature that sets this work apart from many pedagogical dialogues, including Alcuin's own *Ars grammatica,* is the mutual politeness and respect of the interlocutors, which is of course an aspect of the unusual power relations between teacher and student staged here. Even though Charles is not (yet) a theoretician, his state affairs ensure his expertise in rhetorical practice. This also means he is the kind of "student" who anticipates the next topic to be treated (see § 5 where he assumes there must be certain kinds of cases, and demands a demonstration). And it is never quite clear who is the "leader" in the discussion, the master who has all the information, or the student, who "leads" him on by his intelligent questions. Sometimes the master prompts the next question, but the royal student is seen to appropriate the information completely (see § 19). There is an explicit statement of the equal value of interrogating and teaching, which are in some ways similar (§ 35). Towards the end, the dialogue turns to the relation between rhetoric and Christian kingship.

From *Ars grammatica*

Translated from text in *PL* 101:849C–902B

[We begin with an excerpt from the *Disputatio de vera philosophia* (end of dialogue): the students are asking their master to help them reach true *sapientia*. Instruction in the disciplines of the seven liberal arts is necessary for this: they are the *gradus* ("steps") to wisdom.][16]

STUDENTS Give us your right hand, master, and lift us up from the ground of ignorance, and make us stand with you on the steps of wisdom, on which we know, on the basis of your moral dignity, and the truth of your words, that you have often stood. As we have heard, the most beautiful rationality of being has led you there from a very young age. And if it is allowed to lend our ears to the stories of the poets, what they say does not seem wrong to us, that reason is the banquet of the gods.[17] TEACHER With more truth, sons, you can say that reason is the food of angels, the jewel of the souls, than the banquet of the gods. STUDENTS However one should put it, we beg you to show us the first steps to wisdom, so that we may be able, if God so gives and you teach us, to reach the higher levels

---

[16] *PL* 101:853A–854A

[17] "The banquets of the gods" are too pagan to the master's taste, hence the Christian emendation.

from the lower ones. TEACHER We read the words of Solomon, through whom wisdom sings about itself [Proverbs 9,1]: "Wisdom has built her house; she has hewn her seven pillars." Although this sentence refers to divine wisdom, which built itself a home, that is, a body, in a virginal womb, this wisdom is also made firmer by the seven gifts of the Holy Spirit. And wisdom has illuminated the Church, that is: the house of God, by these same gifts. Wisdom is held up by the seven columns of the liberal arts. And there is no other road to a perfect science unless one is elevated by these seven columns or steps.[18]

STUDENTS Then finally divulge what you have promised, and in view of the fragility of our age start by feeding us soft milky food,[19] so that we may the more easily reach more solid foods when we are older. TEACHER With the help of divine grace that came before and will lead to completion, I will do what you have asked, and I will show to you the seven steps of philosophy, so that you may see them. If God so gives and life supports us, I will lead you, in proportion to my powers, to the higher levels of speculative science, when the time and your age permits it.

STUDENTS Lead us, lead us and settle us finally away from the nest of ignorance[20] on the branches of the wisdom that God gave to you. And may we be able to see some light of truth from there. Show us what you have so many times promised us, the seven stages of theoretical learning [*theorasticae disciplinae*]. TEACHER All right then, the steps you are asking for are the following—and may you always be so eager to learn as you are now curious to see: grammar, rhetoric, dialectic, arithmetic, geometry, music, and astrology. For on these steps philosophers have spent their free time and their work time. Under their consulate they have become more famous, under their monarchy more widely known, through them they have become praiseworthy in eternal memory. Through them the saints and doctors and defenders of our catholic faith have always proven themselves superior to all leaders of heresies in public debate. May your youth also run its daily course along these paths, dearest boys, until a more mature age and a firmer state of mind arrives at the summits of holy Scripture. In the meantime arm yourselves with these so that you may turn into absolutely invincible defenders of the true faith and upholders of truth.

[The text segues into the beginning of the *ars grammatica*. After the introduction, the students discuss the syllable, noun (including *genus, numerus, figura, casus*), pronoun (*genus, figura, numerus, casus*), verb (*modi, figura, coniugatio, numerus*), adverb (*figura*),

---

[18] Cf. Augustine, *De doctrina christiana* 2.7.9–11. On Alcuin's architectural image and its medieval influence, see d'Alverny, "La Sagesse et ses sept filles."

[19] *Nos mollioribus incipe lactare.* The notion that grammar is a kind of infant food is a commonplace.

[20] *De nidulo ignaviae*, cf. Fronto, *epistula ad Antoninum imperatorem* 1.1.2, M. Cornelii Frontonis *Epistulae*, ed. M. P. J. van den Hout (Leipzig: Teubner, 1988): *pullus noster Antoninus aliquo lenius tussit: quantum quisque in nidulo nostro jam sapit, tantum pro te precatur* (86).

participle, conjunction, preposition, and finally the interjection. The order of these topics derives from Donatus.][21]

SAXO, FRANCO:[22] STUDENTS; TEACHER

In the school of master Albinus there were two boys, one called Franco, the other Saxo, who had only recently broken their way into the thorny undergrowth of the denseness of grammar. Therefore they decided to pick out a few rules of the science of letters [*litteralis scientia*] in order to memorize them, in question and answer form [*per interrogationes et responsiones*].

Franco began and said to Saxo: "Hey, Saxo, you must answer me when I ask you questions, for you are the oldest. I am fourteen, you fifteen, I think." Saxo answered: "I'll do that. But on the condition that if something needs inquiring into in more depth, or must be explained on the basis of philosophy, I may ask the master."

To this the master said: "I like your plan, boys: and I will happily support your sharp-wittedness. Tell me first what you think is the best point at which to begin your discussion."

STUDENTS From where else, master, sir, than from the letter?

TEACHER Well judged, if you had not made mention of philosophy a little earlier. That means your discussion must certainly start from "sound/voice" [*vox*],[23] for the sake of which the letters were invented: or rather, before anything else we must ask, in what modes a discussion consists.[24]

STUDENTS And we ask you humbly, master, that this be explained by you. For we confess that we do not know in what modes a discussion consists.

TEACHER There are three things through which any conversation and discussion is produced, *res* [things], *intellectus* [understanding], *voces* [expression].[25] "Things" are what we perceive by our reasonable mind. "Understanding" is that through which we learn the things. "Expression" is that by which we proffer the things we have understood. For its sake, as I said, the letters were invented.

---

[21] *PL* 101:854B–856B

[22] We have chosen to render Franco and Saxo as personal names. Obviously, the words also mean "a Frank," "a Saxon."

[23] See note on terminology in section on Donatus, p. 87, note 29 above. For the master's refusal to start with *littera* and his remarks about *vox*, see Vineis, "Grammatica e filosofia," 424–5 and the introduction to this section. According to Irvine, Alcuin here "attempts a philosophical unification of the arts of discourse as constitutive of *sapientia*" (*The Making of Textual Culture*, 323).

[24] This is a form of power-play pedagogy: the question is formulated in such an obscure way that it is impossible for the students to produce the answer unless they have already been told.

[25] This notion comes from Boethius' commentary on Aristotle's *De interpretatione* I, ed. Meiser, 37.5–10. See Vineis, "Grammatica e filosofia," 424–5. See also Alcuin, *De dialectica*, *PL* 101:956B.

STUDENTS Since you have told us the modes of discussion, please explain the different kinds of voice.

TEACHER There are four different kinds of voice: articulate, inarticulate, literate, non-literate.[26] "Articulate voice" is expressed in combination and connection with meaning, e.g. *arma virumque cano* ["I sing of arms and the man": *Aeneid* 1.1] ... "Inarticulate" does not arise out of any meaning, for example, creaking or lowing.[27] "Literate voice" can be written; "illiterate voice" cannot. STUDENTS Why is it called *vox* ["voice"]? TEACHER From *vocare* ["to call"].[28] Well, here you have what you were asking for. Now start from the letter, boys.

FRANCO First tell me, Saxo, where does the name "letter" come from?

SAXO I think *littera*, ["letter"] is as it were *leg-iter-a* ["a reading-road"], because it provides a path for readers.[29]

FRANCO Give the definition as well. SAXO A letter is the smallest part of articulate voice.[30] STUDENTS Does the letter also have a second definition, master? TEACHER Yes, it does, but it means much the same. "The letter is indivisible":[31] for we divide sentences into parts of speech, the parts into syllables, the syllable into letters. But letters are indivisible.

STUDENTS Why are letters called "elements"?[32] TEACHER Because just as elements come together to form complete bodies, these stick together and form the sounds that can be written [*litteralis vox*].[33] FRANCO Colleague, give the division of the letters. SAXO[34] They are either vowels or consonants. Similarly, the consonants can be divided into semi-vowels and mutes. FRANCO Explain the various divisions. SAXO Vowels can be pronounced by themselves[35] and form a syllable by themselves. Consonants can neither be pronounced by themselves, nor form syllables by themselves.[36] STUDENTS Is there another reason, master, why they are divided? TEACHER Yes. Vowels are like souls, consonants like bodies. The soul moves both itself and the body. The body is immobile and devoid of soul. That is

---

[26] This whole section summarizes Priscian, *Institutiones* 1.1, *GL* 2:5.1ff. Priscian sets up a scheme whereby both criteria are needed in conjunction, so that some examples of *vox* are both articulate and literate, some are one but not the other or vice versa, and some are neither. See the section on Priscian, p. 173.

[27] *crepitus, mugitus*. The Migne text wrongly italicizes these terms, suggesting incorrectly that they are themselves the examples of the kind of *vox* intended. Reference is to the sounds that these words denote, cf. Priscian, *Institutiones grammaticae* 1.2, *GL* 2:6.1f. *aliae vero sunt inarticulatae et illiteratae quae nec scribi possunt nec intellegi, ut crepitus, mugitus.*

[28] Priscian, *Institutiones* 1.2, *GL* 2:6.4.　　[29] ibid. 1.3, *GL* 2:6.12.　　[30] ibid. 1.3, *GL* 2:6.6.

[31] ibid. 1.3, *GL* 2:6.10f. (offering an alternative definition): *possumus et sic definire: litera est vox quae scribi potest individua.*

[32] Cf. Priscian, *Institutiones* 1.4, *GL* 2:6.14ff.　　[33] ibid. 1.4, *GL* 2:6.15ff.

[34] For Saxo's answer, cf. Donatus, *Ars maior* 1.2, *GL* 4:367.9f., above p. 88.　　[35] Donatus, *Ars maior* 1.2, *GL* 4:367.11.

[36] Alcuin generalizes a remark that in Donatus refers to the mute consonants only (*Ars maior* 1.1, *GL* 4: 368.5f.): *mutae sunt quae nec per se proferuntur nec per se syllabam faciunt.*

how consonants are without vowels. For they can be written by themselves; but they cannot be pronounced or have a force [*potestas*] without vowels. FRANCO Where do the names "vowels" and "consonants" come from? SAXO *Vocales* ["vowels"] have that name because they complete a *vox* ["sound"] without any consonants clinging to it. *Consonantes* ["consonants"] have that name because they do not sound by themselves, but they sound together with [*con-sonant*] vowels.[37] FRANCO What is the difference between semi-vowels and mutes? SAXO Semi-vowels surpass mutes to the same extent that vowels surpass semi-vowels. For they begin with a vowel and end in themselves.[38] They sound with more euphony, and words end more frequently in semi-vowels than in mutes because of their euphony, i.e. their sonorous tone. Mutes begin with themselves and end in vowels[39]—they sound uglier. FRANCO I believe we read in Donatus[40] that letters have three accidents: name, form [*figura*], and force [*potestas*]. We do not need to speak about their names and forms,[41] but could you please say something about their force, and first about that of the vowels. SAXO The Latins have five vowels. For the Latins have adopted the letter *y* as the sixth vowel, because of the Greek names,[42] just like the consonant *z*. Vowels then form syllables even by themselves, as has been said. They can also form complete parts of speech by themselves: *a*, e.g.: "Ah! [*a*] may the harsh ice not cut my tender feet!";[43] *e*, e.g. "Thirsty he drank out of [*e*] a river"; *o*, e.g. "Oh [*o*], if only the victor over the Gauls had come back to the city!"; *i* can also be a verb: "Go [*i*], our jewel, go and have a better fate."[44] But *i* and *u* can go over into the force of consonants,[45] when they are being joined to other vowels at the beginning of a syllable, e.g. *janua, vates, jecur, veritas, Jonas, votum*. Or when they are put in front of each other, e.g. *Juno, virgo*. These letters themselves can also become "middle" letters,[46] when they have the sound of the Greek upsilon, when they are put after *u* instead of a consonant, before a *d*, or *m*, or *r*, or *t*, or *x*: *video, vim, virtus, vitium, vix*. *U* has the same sound, i.e. *y*, when put between *q* and another vowel, or after *g* and [before][47] another vowel in the same syllable, e.g. *quisque, pingue, lingua*. Sometimes *i* is used instead of two consonants, where it is put between two vowels, e.g. *Troja, Maja*. *U* is also sometimes taken instead of the double digamma, e.g. *cupĭi* [short *i*], *cupīvi* [long *i*]. Whenever *u* is used as a consonant, it must always be taken as a digamma.[48] FRANCO Are

---

[37] Cf. Isidore, *Etymologiae* 1.3.3.   [38] E.g. /r/, /m/, /n/, /l/ are voiced as "er," "em," "en," "el."

[39] E.g. "be" for /b/ etc., see section on Isidore, p. 238.   [40] Donatus, *Ars maior* 1.2, *GL* 4:368.14f., see p. 88 above.

[41] Note how the information is divided over the speakers. Beginners' material is for the boys. The master is called in when things get harder. See also the way in which Saxo breaks off the passage on the letters.

[42] I.e. in order to be able to spell Greek names.

[43] Virgil, *Eclogues* 10.49 (where the text reads *tibi* rather than *mihi* as in Alcuin).

[44] *Aeneid* 6.546.   [45] Cf. Donatus, *Ars maior* 1.2, *GL* 4:367.12ff, p. 88 above.

[46] Cf. Donatus, *Ars maior* 1.2, *GL* 4:367.14f.; Priscian, *Institutiones* 1.6, *GL* 2:7.15ff

[47] Not in the text (the MS has a page break): add <*ante*>   [48] I.e. a fricative /w/.

there any consonants with special force? SAXO Yes. In the first place because every single one of them has its own specific force [*potestas*], just like it has a name [*nomen*] and a form [*figura*].[49] Some of them are liquids, which have even lost their consonantal power [*vim*]. They also frequently change accents in prose. FRANCO Which ones are they? SAXO *L, R, M, N.* But *S* also has a remarkable force. *H* is also the sign of a rough breathing.[50] *X* and *Z* are double consonants. But I think that these theories belong to the fine details of metrical theory, and we have not had that yet. Therefore do not ask me any more about these, but let's hasten on to the syllables.

> [The students now discuss the syllable, giving things over to the master when they become harder; the master proceeds until the topic again becomes too technical (long and short syllables) and rather more relevant to metrical studies. The teacher therefore interrupts himself to suggest that they take up the parts of speech—but first there is another special request.][51]

TEACHER I will show you these things more fully, God willing, when dealing with metrical theory, boys ...

STUDENTS What would you prefer, master: should we follow the order of master Donatus and ask about "feet" and "accents"?[52]

TEACHER Of those, too, you will get a fuller understanding in that same detailed treatment of metrics. For feet and accents cannot be understood unless with the help of long and short syllables. You had better turn to the parts of speech.

STUDENTS If you please, master, explain to us first where the name "grammar" comes from, or what its function is.

TEACHER Grammar is the science of letters [*litteralis scientia*], and she is the guardian of correct speaking and writing. She is based on nature [*natura*], analogy [*ratio*], authority [*auctoritas*], and usage [*consuetudo*].[53]

STUDENTS In how many species is grammar divided?

---

[49] Cf. Priscian, *Institutiones* 1.6, *GL* 2:7.26.

[50] Cf. Donatus, *Ars maior* 1.2, *GL* 4:368.9f., p. 89 above on letters, see also Isidore I iv (above, pp. 237–40).

[51] *PL* 101, 857D–859D.

[52] As in Donatus, *Ars maior* 1.4, *GL* 4:369.16ff. (*de pedibus*), and 1.5, 371.1ff. (*de tonis*).

[53] These are the traditional "Kriterien der Sprachrichtigkeit": see in particular Siebenborn, *Die Lehre von der Sprachrichtigkeit und ihren Kriterien*, and e.g. Sluiter, *Ancient Grammar in Context*, 56ff. Cf. for the formulation in Alcuin's text e.g. Julius Romanus (incorporated in Charisius' *Ars grammatica*) (62.14.5, ed. Barwick): *constat ergo Latinus sermo natura analogia consuetudine auctoritate.* See edition by Schenkeveld, ed. and trans., *A Rhetorical Grammar: C. Iulius Romanus, Introduction to the liber de adverbio.* This fourfold division (with "nature") goes back to Varro (fragment 115 in Varro, *De lingua Latina*, ed. Goetz and Schoell; Diomedes, *GL* 1:439.15–17). The three main criteria are: *ratio* or *analogia*, the system of rules and regularities in language (a theoretical criterion)—if this criterion is used, a

TEACHER Twenty-six:[54] Voice/sound [*vox*], letters, syllables, parts [of speech], words [*dictiones*], sentences/discourse [*orationes*],[55] definitions, feet, prosody, punctuation marks [*positurae*], critical signs [*notae*], orthographies, analogies, etymologies, glosses, semantic distinctions [*differentiae*], barbarism, solecism, faults, metaplasm, schemata, tropes, prose, meters, fictions [*fabulae*], histories [*historiae*].

STUDENTS Give us just an idea of all of these items, master, before we embark on the discussion of the parts, by going through each single one of them.

TEACHER You have already had the voice, letter, and syllable just now.[56] A word [*dictio*] is the smallest part of constructed voice, having a full meaning.[57] A sentence [*oratio*] is the ordering of words, yielding a congruent and complete meaning [*sententia*]. It is called *oratio*, as if it were *oris ratio* ["the reason of the mouth"].[58] A definition [*definitio*] is a short sentence [*oratio*], enclosing each thing in its peculiar meaning, e.g. "man is a mortal rational animal, capable of laughter."[59] You should know that definition is valid for all disciplines and things. A foot [*pes*] is the combination of syllables and a fixed measure of time-units.[60] They are called "feet," because the meters walk on them. Prosody [*accentus*] is a certain law and rule to elevate and compress a syllable.[61] Punctuation marks [*positurae*] are points to distinguish meanings. Critical signs [*notae*] are certain marks, either to abbreviate words, or to express meanings; or they are used for a variety of reasons, such as the obelus [÷] in Holy Scripture, or the asterisk [*]. Orthography (*orthographia*) is correct writing, e.g. the preposition *ad* should get a *d*; [the conjunction *at* a *t*]. Analogy (*analogia*) is the comparison of what is similar, so that what is not certain may receive confirmation from what is. Etymology [*etymologia*][62] is the origin and explanation of words, e.g. *rex* ["king"] comes from *regere* ["to rule"], *homo* ["human being"] comes from *humus* ["soil"].

---

problematic case may be decided with reference to the language system; *consuetudo* or the (daily) usage of the educated, an empirical criterion (often used to sanction "irregular" usage); and the equally empirical "authority," the usage of the received authors, which may make a certain usage acceptable even if it does not lend itself to imitation.

[54] Cf. for this section (with slight variations) Isidore, *Etymologiae* 1.5.4, p. 241 above.

[55] With the familiar translation difficulty: in this hierarchical grammatical system, where each level uses the previous one as its point of departure, *oratio* is the level above the "words," i.e. the "sentences." But in rhetorical and dialectical contexts, it obviously refers to longer speech units.

[56] The teacher is skipping the parts of speech (*partes*), since that is going to be the job of the boys themselves.

[57] The first half of this definition is taken from Priscian, *Institutiones grammaticae* 2.14, *GL* 2:53.7.

[58] For the etymology, see Isidore, *Etymologiae* 1.5.3, p. 241 above. The etymology is a frequent one: see Victorinus, *Ars grammatica*, *GL* 6:192.3; Dositheus, *Ars grammatica*, *GL* 7:389.8; Charisius, *Ars grammatica*, ed. Barwick, 193.4; Cassiodorus, *Explanationes Psalmorum* 16.11.10.

[59] The definition is Aristotelian, cf. Cassiodorus *Institutiones* 2.3.14; Isidore, *Etymologiae* 2.19.1.

[60] *Pes est syllabarum compositio et temporum certa dimensio*. Cf. Donatus, *Ars maior* 1.4, *GL* 4:369.16 (with *dinumeratio* for *dimensio*).

[61] This refers to pronunciation on a higher or lower pitch.

[62] See the Etymology dossier (Part 2), pp. 339–66.

A gloss [*glossa*] is the paraphrase [*interpretatio*] of one verb or noun, e.g. *catus* ["clever"], i.e. *doctus* ["learned"].[63] A semantic distinction [*differentia*] is the distinction of two things with their translations, e.g.: we call [a ruler] *rex* ["king"], because he is modest; *tyrannus* ["tyrant"], because he is cruel. A barbarism is one part of speech with a mistake in it, e.g. the common proverb *malae arboris nodo malus cuneus quaerendus est* "it takes a bad hammer to deal with a bad piece of wood."[64] A solecism [*soloecismus*] is a sentence [*oratio*] which is wrongly construed. Faults [*vitia*] are things to guard against in speaking, and there are seven of them.[65] A metaplasm [*metaplasmus*] is metrical license, or a necessary change in regular speech. Schemata are ornaments of speech and the dressing up of thought.[66] A trope [*tropus*] is a word that has been transferred from its proper meaning to a likeness that is not proper to it for reasons of embellishment [*ornatus*] or necessity.[67] Prose is straight speech composed without meter and verse. Meters have that name because they are defined by fixed measures of feet. Stories [*fabulae*] are fictions for the sake of play or to convey a certain meaning. A history [*historia*] is the narrative of something that happened. Here you have short definitions of the individual species. Now turn to the parts.

STUDENTS We will do as you order. Yet, would you please first briefly explain to us the characteristics of the individual parts?[68]

TEACHER Your curiosity knows no limits and makes you wish to exceed the limits of a little handbook. It is characteristic of a noun to signify a substance or a quality or a quantity.[69] And it is characteristic of a pronoun to be put instead of a proper noun and to signify certain persons.[70] It is characteristic of a verb to signify an action or the undergoing

---

[63] I.e. the explication of one word by another word, here in the same language.

[64] Jerome, *Epistle* 69.5: "interim iuxta vulgare proverbium malo arboris nodo malus cuneus quaerendus est" (*Eusebii Hieronymi Epistulae* 1, ed. I. Hilberg, *CSEL* 54 [Vienna: Österreichische Akademie der Wissenschaften, 1996]: 686); "einen groben Keil auf einen groben Klotz setzen" (*Des heiligen Kirchenvaters Eusebius Hieronymus ausgewählte Briefe, aus dem Lateinischen übersetzt von L. Schade* [Munich: Kösel and Pustet, 1937], 360). The precise problem here is not altogether clear: the barbarism probably consists in the use of *malus* with *cuneus* (semantic) or the use of *malae* instead of *malo*.

[65] Another indication of the beginners' level of the boys: this is all they need to know at this stage, no further subdivision is worked out.

[66] *ornamenta eloquii et habitus, quibus sententiae vestiuntur*. Cf. the use of *habitus* in the opening of Bede, *De schematibus* (see above, section on Bede, p. 267).

[67] Donatus, *Ars maior* 3.6, *GL* 4:399.13., p. 97 above.

[68] In what follows, Alcuin adopts the following order for the parts of speech: noun, pronoun, verb, adverb, participle, conjunction, preposition (the definition of the interjection is omitted, but Alcuin does have it discussed, in last position). This is the Donatan order of the parts of speech. However, the definitions (introduced by the characteristic *proprium est*) are based on Priscian, whose order is different and based on his Greek models (noun, verb, participle, pronoun, adverb, preposition, conjunction [no interjection]).

[69] "Quantity" is added by Alcuin. See Priscian, *Institutiones* 2.18, *GL* 2:55.6f., p. 176 above. In this whole passage the formulation with *proprium est* is Priscianic.

[70] Priscian, *Institutiones* 2.18, *GL* 2:55.13f., p. 177 above.

of action or both with moods and tenses.[71] It is characteristic of an adverb[72] to be put with a verb, and not to have a complete meaning without it, e.g. "I read well." It is characteristic of a participle to have tenses and cases. That is why some call it a "casual verb" [*verbum casuale*, verb with cases]. It is characteristic of the conjunction[73] to be connected with all the parts, sometimes in preposition, sometimes in postposition, and to connect the parts. It is characteristic of the preposition always to be put before words with cases separately.[74]

On the Noun

FRANCO Come on, Saxo, let us start our discussion of the noun in proper order, and tell me first, what a noun is?

SAXO A noun[75] is a part of speech, according to the grammarians, which assigns to each body or thing a common or proper quality. It is called *nomen* ["name, noun"] as if it were a *notamen* ["a mark"],[76] since we mark individual substances or things with it: common substances or things, e.g. *homo* ["human being"], *disciplina* ["discipline"]; or proper ones, e.g. Vergil, arithmetic. However, Franco, let us ask the master for the philosophical definition of the noun.[77]

TEACHER The noun is a sound with arbitrary meaning, without tense, signifying something definite in the nominative case in conjunction with *is* or *is not*, e.g. "man is," "man is not." In the oblique cases, even if you add *is* or *is not*, it does not mean anything certain, unless you add what is or is not.[78] E.g. "Ø is <characteristic> of a man [genitive]" "Ø is not

---

[71] This is a short version of Priscian, *Institutiones* 2.18, GL 2:55.8f., p. 177 above.

[72] Priscian, *Institutiones* 2.20, GL 2:56.3f., p. 177 above.

[73] Priscian, *Institutiones* 2. 21, GL 2: 56.26f.; the actual definition in Priscian (2.21, GL 2:56.16f., p. 178 above) is slightly longer. Alcuin used the part following the definitions of conjunction and preposition, in which the difference between the two is outlined more clearly. On the basis of that passage he produces these definitions. GL 2:56.21ff.: *interest…hoc* [sc. between conjunction and preposition]…[l. 25ff.] *quod praepositio casualibus separata praeponitur semper, coniunctio vero omnibus potest dictionibus modo praeposita modo postposita coniungi.* ("The difference is that the preposition is always put before words with cases separately, while the conjunction may be connected with all the parts, sometimes in preposition, sometimes in postposition.")

[74] Priscian, *Institutiones* 2.21, GL 2:56.25f., p. 178 above; again, the actual definition in Priscian is longer (GL 2:56.12f., see previous note). "Separately" means "not forming a compound."

[75] Priscian, *Institutiones* 2.22, GL 2:56.28f. (slightly simplified).

[76] The etymology selects one of several possibilities offered by Priscian, *Institutiones* 2.22, GL 2:57.3; cf. also Isidore, *Etymologiae*, 1.7.1.

[77] For this overlapping between grammar and dialectic, see Vineis, "Grammatica e filosofia," 424–5.; Luhtala, "Priscian's Definitions are Obscure," 60. The philosophical (i.e. dialectical) definition comes from the Boethian translation of Aristotle's *De interpretatione*.

[78] *Nomen est vox significativa secundum placitum, sine tempore, definitum aliquid significans in nominativo,* cum *est* aut *non est.* Cf. Alcuin's *De dialectica* PL 101:973AB: *Nomen quid est? Vox significativa secundum placitum, sine*

<characteristic> of a man [genitive]." "Arbitrary," i.e. "according to the way different peoples put them together" is how names have been made, so that what you call *aurum* ["gold"] in Latin is called *khrusos* in Greek. The substance is one, but the names are different.

FRANCO How many accidents does the noun have?

SAXO Six, according to Donatus: quality, comparison, genus, number, figure, case. According to Priscian, there are five.[79] For he takes quality and comparison together and calls them "species," for all names belong to the proper [or "appellative"] species; and to the "principal" one or the "derivative" one. Proper, e.g. *Julius*. Appellative, e.g. *mons* ["mountain"]. "Principal," e.g. *Julius, mons*. Derivative, e.g. *Julianus, Montanus*. In that latter category [i.e. the derivatives] he also put the nouns in the grades of comparison.

FRANCO How many kinds of proper nouns are there?

SAXO Four: *praenomen* ["first name"], *nomen* ["name"], *cognomen* ["surname"], *agnomen* ["nickname"]. First names are names which are put before proper names for the sake of dignity or distinction, e.g. *Anicius* Boethius: he is called Anicius because of the nobility and freedom of his family. For the sake of distinction, e.g. *Lucius* Cornelius and *Publius* Cornelius. First names are written either with one single letter, or with two each or with three each. Single letters, e.g. M. = Marcus. With two letters, e.g. Cn. = Cneus. With three letters, e.g. Sex. = Sextus. A name is characteristic for any individual, e.g. Paulus. The surname is a common name for relatives [*cognationis*] or a family, e.g. Scipio. For that whole family [*cognatio*] was called by that name. A nickname is occasioned by some special event, e.g. Africanus, because he had conquered Africa.

> [The boys go on to discuss the appellative nouns (such as *homo* and *terra),* the grades of comparison and the diminutives. Saxo ends this part as follows, occasioning some play on the familiar themes of eagerness and jealousy, which at the same time represents mnemonic help for the difference between the easily confused Latin terms *invidus* and *avidus* (cf. the practice of *differentiae*).][80]

---

tempore, diffinitum aliquid significans, in nominativo casu, cum est aut non est, in obliquis casibus nihil, cuius nulla pars est significativa separata. The philosophical, i.e. dialectical, definition of the noun goes back to Boethius' translation of the Aristotelian definition in *De interpretatione*, see Aristoteles Latinus, *De interpretatione* ch. 2, 16a19–21 (ed. Minio-Paluello, 6, 4–6): *vox significativa secundum placitum sine tempore, cuius nulla pars est significiativa separata.* As Kneepkens has shown ("Some notes on Alcuin's *De Perihermeniis*, with an Edition of the Text," in Houwen and MacDonald, eds., *Alcuin of York, Scholar at the Carolingian Court*, 88–91), Alcuin also used Boethius' first commentary, which explains the slightly expanded and changed form of the definition found both here and in *De dialectica*. According to Kneepkens, "Boethius is speaking on the level of logic, that is about making an affirmation or a negation, whereas Alcuin deals with the semantics of the noun" (ibid., 91). Cf. also Alcuin, *De dialectica*, PL 101:973AB; Cassiodorus, *Institutiones* II.3.11; Isidore, *Etymologiae* 2.27.5. For the integration of dialectic and grammar, see Irvine, *The Making of Textual Culture*, 322–3.

[79] Donatus, *Ars maior*, 2.2, GL 4:373.4; Priscian, *Institutiones* 2.22, GL 2:57.8.   [80] *PL* 101:861D–862A.

SAXO Here you have plenty, I think, Franco, on the kinds of appellative nouns—although nobody can satisfy your eagerness.

FRANCO It is not so much that I am eager [*avidus*], but you are jealous [*invidus*]: you begrudge me any knowledge, unless I force you into explaining by my questions.

SAXO Ask what you want: I will not be slow to answer!

> [The boys continue with the accidents, in order, starting from gender, and then move on to the verb. In the discussion of the passive forms of the verb, Saxo introduces his answer to "explain to me the rules of the passive" by another reference to the status of his explanations as suitable for beginners, and then ends his quick overview of all the passive forms with the difficult infinitive of the future passive. This leads to more play on curiosity and envy, "use" and "mention," and an evocation of a familiar schoolroom scenario.][81]

SAXO I will explain them briefly; I don't want to be more expansive than is suitable for this children's school [*puerili ludo*] . . .

SAXO Here you have what you were asking for, Franco. But your curiosity *is causing that you will not be loved.*[82]

FRANCO Nor is your jealousy [*invidia*] *causing that you will be "gratefulled."*[83]

SAXO Careful! Don't let the man who wields the whip hear you. Continue with the rest.

> [The boys move on to the persons of the verb. From here on, their increasing self-confidence shows in the text. After Saxo has reeled off the conjugations of *sum fero edo volo*, Franco takes the opportunity to show off his knowledge of poetry. But his request for information about the adverb also betrays more knowledge than one would expect at this point.][84]

SAXO You're a hard taskmaster for me, Franco. Look what a burden you've imposed on me, leading me through rough and thorny terrain.[85] Finally let me take a breath for a while.

FRANCO I will, and with Virgil [*Eclogues* 9.65] "I will relieve you of this bundle" [*ego hoc te fasce levabo*].

SAXO Although you've relieved me of this one, I'm afraid you'll impose another.

---

[81] *PL* 101:881A–C.

[82] *sed tua curiositas te facit non amatum iri*, in which Saxo "uses in a sentence" the difficult infinitive passive future of the paradigmatic verb *amare*; in fact, this was the last form Saxo had just reeled off (*Et futurum in* iri, *ut* amatum iri).

[83] *gratum iri*, which is just as ungrammatical in Latin as the English translation above.

[84] *PL* 101:885D–886A   [85] "leading me" (*ducens*): note that the questioner drives the dialogue.

FRANCO Don't be afraid: "unrelenting hard work vanquishes everything" [*labor omnia vincit/improbus* (Virgil, *Georgics* 1.145)].

SAXO It does: so let us go the remaining part of the road.

On the Adverb

FRANCO Finally open your mouth, which you've kept shut for so long, Saxo, and explain to me the rules of the adverbs which so far have been closed to me.[86]

[The boys work their way through the doctrine of the adverb, which Saxo rounds off as follows (with another possible case of "use" and "mention").][87]

SAXO Demonstrative adverbs ... are also found in first position, e.g. *en, ecce* ["look"]. Look [*en*], Franco, this is enough about the adverb for you.

FRANCO Not enough: however, let us take a break at the hour [*ad horam*].

SAXO Yes, let's.

On the Participle

FRANCO Get up, Saxo.

SAXO What do you want, Franco?

FRANCO That you explain the rules for the participles to me.

SAXO I will.

[After discussion of the participle, conjunction, and preposition, only one part remains, and Saxo once again makes use of the "use" and "mention" strategy for humorous effect.][88]

FRANCO I am satisfied. But let us finish the little bit of distance that remains.

SAXO All right. Continue to ask questions as you've been doing [*more tuo*]: I will follow and answer.

---

[86] Note that this request contains three adverbs, one of which (*hucusque*) is very rare: **Tandem**, Saxo, **diu** obserata ora reclude, et **hucusque** clausas adverbiorum regulas enuclea mihi.

[87] *PL* 101:889A

[88] *PL* 101: 901A–902A. "Use" and "mention" is also noted by Matter, "Alcuin's Question-and-Answer Texts"; see also Ruff, "*Desipere in loco.*" Sluiter, "Persuasion, Pedagogy, Polemics," analyzes the way knowledge about this part of speech is co-produced by the two boys here.

On the Interjection

FRANCO What is an interjection?

SAXO Whoa!! Why are you asking about the interjection?[89] How many have you heard me utter with disordered sound [*incondita voce*], while I was lying in front of the master's feet?

FRANCO I've heard them and was afraid, and I understood there is emotion [of the soul] in the exclamation of the voice. Yet I think interjections have different meanings, as there are different movements of the soul.

SAXO Yes, you're right.

> [Saxo then sums up the interjections of joy, laughter, disgust, adhortation, mockery, pain, cursing, fear, admiration. The treatise ends with a brief remark on the uncertain accents of interjections.]

FROM *DISPUTATIO DE RHETORICA ET VIRTUTIBUS*

Translated from Halm, ed., *Rhetores latini minores*, by permission.

[Opening of the dialogue][90]

> Whoever wishes to get to know civil customs[91]
> please let him read these precepts, contained within this book.
> Its author is King Charles, amidst the concerns of the court,
> together with Albinus: the latter produced it, the former gave his approval.
> One work of both men, although from different motives:
> Charles is the father of the world, Albinus a poor inhabitant.
> Don't disparage this book, reader, for its moderate size:
> with its very moderate size, the bee does bring you honey.

KING CHARLES AND MASTER ALBINUS

1. CH. Since God has brought you to us once again, venerable master Albinus, I ask you for permission to put some questions to you on the precepts of rhetorical theory. For I

---

[89] *Heu! Quid interrogas de interiectione? Heu* is the standard example of the interjection.

[90] *Rhetores latini minores*, 525–9.

[91] The work opens with four distichs. Note in the first line the importance attached to *civiles . . . mores*, "civil, political usage," see *The Rhetoric of Alcuin and Charlemagne*, trans. Howell, 62 on the political value attributed by Alcuin to his work. Cf. *Rhetorica ad Herennium* 1.2.2.

remember that you said once that the power of this art totally resides in political questions. As you know very well, we are always engaged in such questions because of our state business and the concerns of the court. It seems absurd not to know the precepts of that art, in whose exercise we are necessarily involved on a daily basis. From the time when you offered me a few answers and thus put the doors of the arts of rhetoric ajar and partially opened the gates of subtle dialectic, you have made me most interested in these theories, especially since you have already given me an insightful introduction into the spaces of arithmetic and have illuminated me by the splendor of astrology. ALB. God has illuminated you, my lord King Charles, with all the light of wisdom, and he has adorned you with the clarity of science, so that you are not only capable of following closely the minds of your teachers, but can even quickly run in front of them on many topics. Although the spark of my small talent cannot add anything to the flame-vomiting light [*flammivomo . . . lumine*] of your wisdom, I will still answer promptly to your questions, so that nobody can criticize me for disobedience—I hope my answers will be as smart as they will be obedient.

2. CH. First reveal to me, master, the beginning of this art or study. ALB. I will do so based on the authority of the ancients.[92] For there was, they say, a time, when men were roaming over the fields everywhere, like animals, and they did not manage anything by rational thought, but most things by bodily strength. Nobody respected yet a sense of awe towards the divine, or duty towards men, but like a blind and wilful mistress desire abused the powers of the body to fulfill itself. In that day, a certain man, obviously great and wise, realized what a potential and how great an opportunity for the greatest things existed in the souls of human beings, if someone would be able to tease it out and make it better by teaching: according to some plan he drove the people who were dispersed over the fields and were hiding in forest shelters together in one place and assembled them, and he got them to do every individual useful and honorable thing. At first they were protesting against it because they were not used to it, but then they listened more attentively to his argument and his speech, and so from wild and fierce he made them mild and gentle. And it seems to me, my lord King, that no silent wisdom nor one at a loss for words could have achieved this, to make people abruptly turn away from what they are used to and bring them to different ways of life.

3. CH. Where does the name rhetoric come from? ALB. *Apo tou rhêtoreuein* [Greek: "from '(public) speaking'"], that is eloquent speech.[93] CH. What is its goal? ALB. The science of speaking well. CH. What issues is it involved in? ALB. In political questions, that is

---

[92] The following is based closely on *De inventione* I.2.2; cf. the commentary by Marius Victorinus, above, p. 104–24.
[93] Cf. Cassiodorus, *Institutiones* 2.2.1, above, p. 224.

questions based on learning that can be grasped by the natural talents of the mind. For just as it is natural for everyone to defend oneself and to hit the other, even without learning this through the use of arms and exercise, similarly it is natural for everyone to accuse others and purge oneself, even without having learned this through exercise. But one can use speech more usefully and readily if one has had some instruction in the field, and with some exercise in practice. It is natural for everyone to speak, but the man who speaks according to the rules of grammar far exceeds the rest. CH. Well spoken, master: our whole life also profits from study [*disciplinis*] and is strong by practice [*usu*]—so please open up to us the rules of this discipline of rhetoric. The day-to-day demands of our occupations force us already to practice them. First tell us how many parts this art has.

4. ALB. The art of rhetoric has five parts:[94] invention, arrangement, style, memorization, and delivery. *Invention* is the devising of arguments which are true or which resemble true arguments to make a case appear credible. *Arrangement* is the distribution in regular order of the arguments devised. *Style* is the use of suitable words adapted to the arguments. *Memory* is a lasting comprehension by the mind of the arguments and the language [in relation to invention]. *Delivery* is the harmonious adjustment of voice and gesture in keeping with the dignity of the arguments and the language. For the first thing is to find [*invenire*] what to say, then to arrange [*disponere*] what one has found, third, to express in words [*verbis explicare*] what one has arranged, fourth, to memorize [*memoria conprehendere*] what one has found, arranged, and clothed in words, and last but not least to deliver [*pronuntiare*] what one has memorized.

5. CH. If rhetoric is concerned with cases and political questions, it seems necessary to me that the cases themselves have certain kinds [*genera*]: I would like to know them and have them demonstrated with examples. ALB. The art of rhetoric is involved in three kinds, the demonstrative, deliberative, and judicial.[95] The demonstrative kind is divided into praise or blame of a particular person, e.g. it is said in *Genesis* about Cain and Abel [Genesis 4,4–5]: "and the Lord had respect to Abel and to his offerings, but to Cain and his offering he had no respect." The deliberative kind rests on persuasion and dissuasion, e.g. it is read in the book of Kings [Samuel 2,15; 31] how Achitophel gave the advice to ruin David, and how Chusai dissuaded him from that plan, so that he saved the king. The judicial kind is that which contains accusation and defense, e.g. we read in the Acts of the Apostles [Acts 24,1–9] how the Jews together with a certain public speaker named Tertullus accused Paul before the governor Felix, and how Paul defended himself before the same magistrate. For

---

[94] *De inventione*, 1.7.9.   [95] Cf. Boethius, *De differentiis topicis* 4 (*PL* 64:1207B), p. 195.

in law cases the question is often what is equitable, in demonstrations one understands what is honorable, in deliberations one considers what is honorable and useful.[96]

6. CH. How many circumstances does a case have? ALB. A full case has seven circumstances, person, deed, time, place, way, occasion, means. For the circumstance "person" one asks "who did it?"; for "deed" "what did he do?"; for "time" "when did he do it?"; for "place" "where did it happen?"; for "way" "how could it have happened?"; for "occasion" "why did he want to do it?"; for "means" "did he have at his disposal the possibilities to do it?". These circumstances can be used to make a case stronger or weaker. For in a controversy you will ask in vain what happened, if there is no person who did it; and again, you will show the person in vain, if the person did not do anything. Similarly,[97] such a thing could not have happened at such a time, or in such a place; it could not have happened in the way that you assert; he could not have wanted to do it for that reason; such a man did not have the means to have been able to do this.

7. CH. How many positions of controversies are there?[98] ALB. The positions of controversies, which the rhetoricians call the *status* of cases, i.e. where the question is situated and the first point of disagreement among the parties, are either rational or legal. CH. How many rational ones are there? ALB. Four,[99] the position taken on the deed [*facti*], its name [*nominis*], its quality, or the position of transference. CH. Give examples of the individual kinds. ALB. The first is the controversy over the deed itself, e.g. "you did it, I did not do it"; this first controversy, which is based on the deed, is called the "conjectural position," because it has to be explored by inference whether he did it or not. When the litigants agree on the deed, they often introduce a controversy of definition [*nominis*], since the prosecutor strives to make the charge worse by the name he attaches to it, and the defense strives to make it look smaller. For instance, if somebody has taken something sacred from a private house, has he committed a "theft" or a "sacrilege"? The defense wants it to be theft, because a thief just pays four times the value of the goods, but the prosecution wants it to be sacrilege, because the penalty for that is death. This position is called "definitional," for one needs to define rationally what is a thief and what a sacrilegious person, and then one should determine under which definition the case of someone taking away

[96] For the distinction between "equitable," "honorable," and "useful', see *De inventione* 1.9.12; 2.23.69; 2.53.159; 2.55.166.

[97] What follows is a list of possible forms the argument can take (topical arguments), based on the "circumstances"; cf. Boethius *De topicis differentiis* 4, above, pp. 191, 203–6.

[98] This is the transition to status theory. Alcuin actually uses the term *status* instead of *constitutio*, which may suggest that he is not using *De inventione* as his source here. Cf. *The Rhetoric of Alcuin and Charlemagne*, trans. Howell, 37. See further introduction to Part i, pp. 67–9 above.

[99] Known in Cicero as the *status coniecturalis, definitionis, qualitatis,* and *translationis*: see *De inventione* 1.8.10.

something sacred from a private house would come. However, if prosecution and defense agree on the fact and the name for it, then one should ask about its valuation, i.e. the quality of the deed: is it just or unjust? useful or useless? And this is called "the general position." For example: a Roman general was besieged by the enemy and could not escape in any way. He agreed with the enemy to surrender his arms. After having surrendered his arms, he led his army away safely. Some people accuse him of high treason. In this instance, the parties agree on what was done, and what to call it, but the quality of the deed comes under discussion in the following way: was it better to lose the soldiers or to come to this disgraceful situation? This position has several parts, which we will discuss later. In the fourth position, which we call the "translative" one,[100] it is asked whether the proper man is doing the thing [*rem facere*], or at the proper time, or in the proper way, or in the proper place, or with the proper adjuncts. For example, if Orestes is accused of having killed his mother Clytaemnestra:[101] it is not just for a son to have killed his mother, although she had killed his father Agamemnon, the king of the Greeks. In this case it should be asked through the translative status, if he had acted justly or not.

8. CH. Once one has found the status of a case,[102] how should one then consider the status? ALB. As soon as one has found the position of the case, one should consider whether the question of the case is simple or complex. A simple one contains a single point, as in the following question: "Shall we declare war against Corinth or not?" A complex subject arises from the joining of several points, for example, whether Carthage should be destroyed, or whether it should be given back to the Carthaginians, or whether a colony should be transplanted there.[103]

9. CH. Now give examples for the legal positions. ALB. As I have said already,[104] one must consider whether the controversy is based in argument or in a written document. A *controversy over a written document* originates in written law, e.g.: Law: "whoever abandons ship in a storm, loses everything; cargo and ship belong to the people who have remained on board ship." Two men were sailing on high seas, the one the owner of the ship, the other of the cargo. They took pity on a shipwrecked person floating in the sea, and took

---

[100] Alcuin seems to have misunderstood his sources here. The translative status looks into the proper procedures *of the law case* (i.e., which kind of court the case should be tried in), not of the deed under discussion. By changing the phrase *causam agere* into *rem facere*, Alcuin is forced uncomfortably to interpret the translative status as something resembling the *status qualitatis*. Cf. *The Rhetoric of Alcuin and Charlemagne*, trans. Howell, 31.

[101] This is normally the classic example of the *status qualitatis*, cf. *De inventione* I.13.18–I.14.19; *Rhetorica ad Herennium* I.10.17.

[102] Status theory is part of invention.   [103] Cf. *De inventione* I.12.17 and section on Cassiodorus, p. 225 above.

[104] This seems to be nowhere in our text; we also miss the list (and definitions) of the legal positions. This may be a reference to the basic division into *rationales* and *legales* at the beginning of section 7.

him on board their ship. A little later, they themselves were also tossed about very badly by a storm, so badly that the owner of the ship, who was also the helmsman, took refuge in a little boat, which had been tied to the ship and remained attached to it—from there he assisted the ship as much as he could. The owner of the cargo, on the other hand, threw himself into his own sword right there in the ship. The shipwrecked person, however, took the helm and steered the ship. When the storm had calmed down the ship reached port. The man who had thrown himself into his sword was only lightly wounded and recovered from his wounds. Every man of these three claimed, basing himself on written law, that the ship with its cargo was his. This is where a *question based on written texts* arises, who has title to the ship, with definitions added of what it is to abandon ship, and what it is to remain on board. Similarly, *ambiguity in written law* often causes questions, e.g.: "a prostitute may not have a crown; if she does, confiscation follows." Here there is ambiguity in the written text about whether the prostitute or the crown must become public property. Questions also frequently arise from a *conflict of law*, when on one issue one law says something different than another. Law: "whoever kills a tyrant, will ask whatever he wishes as a reward from the magistrate, and he will get it." Different law: "when a tyrant has been killed, the magistrate must also kill the five closest relatives of the tyrant." Alexander, tyrant in Thessalia, was killed at night by his wife, Thebe. As her reward she asked for the son which the tyrant had fathered with her. There are people who say the law demands that the boy be killed; there are those who say that he should be surrendered to his mother as her reward. The case comes to court. This is where one should consider what law has the greater use, which one is older, who were the legislators of each of the two. The *controversy of letter and spirit* occurs when one party uses the very words that were written, the other connects his argument to that which according to him the writer meant, e.g.: a law prohibits opening the gates at night. Someone opens the gates and admits his friends into the city to prevent them from being killed by the enemy, as would have happened had they remained outside. The prosecution concentrates on the literal text exclusively, the defense on the intention: the lawgiver had ordered that the gates be kept closed to the enemy, not to friends. Questions arise through *reasoning or legal definition*, when one party strives to interpret the text with one argument, the other with another, or if they try to establish the intention of the lawgiver in different ways.[105] In this way, as I said, questions arise based on written texts.

---

[105] This again seems to double the previous categories. In classical theory, cases are envisaged under this category in which by a process of analogical reasoning, deduction, or extrapolation, a law is made to cover cases not originally intended to be covered by it, and for which no separate law exists.

[After a further discussion of the details of status theory, a transition is made to new topics.][106]

16. (ALB.) Here you have the information on the positions of questions, the status of cases, the parts of the discipline: all of these you can recognize in daily practice shown by nature. CH. I will, if the creator of nature will help me. Yet I still have a question for you. ALB. Ask what you please, I will proceed where you lead me. CH. How many persons are usually involved in a law case? ALB. Four: the prosecution, the defense, the witnesses, the judge.

[The discussion of the persons involved in a case continues, and then turns (§ 19) to the material organization of a court case. This is followed by a revealing interchange between Charles and Albinus showing the complicated nature of their collaboration in this work (§ 20).][107]

19. CH. Now that you have discussed the persons involved in a case, tell me please where each of them is located. ALB. I will, although this has more to do with the dignity of their duties than with the precepts of the art. The judge is seated on the tribunal, while the case plays out in the middle before him when it deals with rewards and punishment, e.g. the defense or betrayal of someone's fatherland. The prosecution is on the left-hand side, the defense on the right. The witnesses are behind them. CH. Does every party have its own distinctive attire? ALB. Yes, they do: the judge should be armed with the sceptre of equity, the prosecutor with the dagger of malice, the defense with the shield of piety, the witnesses with the trumpet of truth. CH. Now that we have also found all these circumstances which are attendant on the case, what should we look for next, master? ALB. What else than the individual parts of the case as a whole?[108] CH. I would like to hear what they are, and how many. ALB. Well, there are six parts, by which an orator should structure his speech in a case: exordium, narration, partition, direct argument, refutation, conclusion.

20. CH. What is an exordium? ALB. The exordium is an utterance which suitably prepares the hearer's mind for the rest of the discourse. CH. How is this brought about? ALB. First, make sure you make your audience benevolent, alert, and curious. CH. According to me, this should be given the utmost care, to make the audience benevolent, alert, and curious. But what I would like to know is: how can this be brought about?

[After the discussion of exordium, narration, and partition, the discussion turns to the fourth part: proof (*confirmatio*). Again, the interaction between teacher and student, with emphasis on their respective areas of expertise (theory/practice) and roles in the production of the text, is noticeable.][109]

---

[106] *Rhetores latini minores,* 533.   [107] *Rhetores latini minores,* 534.
[108] Cf. Cassiodorus, *Institutiones* II.9.   [109] *Rhetores latini minores,* 536–7.

24. Now turn to the instructions about proof, master, which I feel are most necessary to all, so that everyone will know to prove his case. Even though he does so willingly, he will not do it with sufficient dignity unless his case can be conducted according to the rules [*praeceptis*] and practice [*usu*]. ALB. It is as you say, my lord King. For all argumentation has to do with the theory of proof. Yet, the forest of arguments is so large that it is hardly possible within this short dialogue of ours to open any of it. CH. Yet touch on more issues by means of a few; for often one key will open the many treasures within a treasury. ALB. I will do what I can. Proof is a form of argument by which you induce belief for your cause and add strength. This happens in two ways, on the basis of the persons or of the business in hand. We hold that the following are attributes of persons: name, nature, way of life, position [*fortuna*], habitus, emotion, interests, plans, deeds, what has happened to someone [*casus*], words.[110]

25. CH. I know you aim for brevity, but I still wish to hear this more fully.

[In the discussion of compelling and probable forms of argument, the dialogue first explicitly introduces the issue of the compatibility of rhetoric and Christianity.][111]

29. ALB. There are also forms of argument that work through induction or deduction, but those pertain more to philosophers. CH. Tell me about them anyway.

30. ALB. Induction is speech which proves something that is uncertain through something that is certain, and that leads somebody to assent against their will. CH. That seems strange, if it can make someone agree against his will. ALB. Just listen, maybe you will believe my example.[112] A certain philosopher struck up a conversation with a certain Xenophon and his wife, and he first started talking with the wife. "Tell me, please, wife of Xenophon, if the neighbor woman has better gold jewelry than you do, would you prefer hers or yours?" "Hers," she said. "What if she has more valuable clothes and other female attire than you do, would you prefer hers or yours?" "Hers, of course," she said. "Well," said he, "what if she has a better husband than you do, would you prefer hers or yours?" At that the woman blushed. Then the philosopher started talking with Xenophon. "Tell me, Xenophon," he said, "if your neighbor has a better horse than you do, would you prefer your horse or his?" "His," he said. "What if he had a better piece of land than you do, which piece of land would you prefer?" "That better one, of course," he said. "What if he has a better wife than you do, which one would you prefer?" And at this point, Xenophon himself also fell silent. Then the philosopher said: "Since neither of you has answered this one question which I had wanted an answer to, I will tell you what each of you is thinking. You, madam, wish to have the best husband, and you, too, Xenophon, want the

---

[110] Cf. *De inventione* 1.24.34 and Boethius, *De topicis differentiis* 4, above, p. 203.
[111] *Rhetores latini minores*, 540. For a biblical example, see also § 5.   [112] Cf. *De inventione* 1.31.51–2.

most desirable wife most of all. So, unless you achieve this that there is no better husband nor a more desirable wife on earth, you will definitely always desire most of all what you will think is the best, namely that you are the husband of the best possible wife, and that she is married to the best possible man." He proved a dubious proposition by indubitable things, because of the similarity in inductive argument. If someone would ask these things separately, he might not have got the concession. CH. That philosopher was no Christian. ALB. He was no Christian, but a rhetorician. CH. Why do we believe him? ALB. He has followed his art. CH. So? Must we also follow ours? ALB. Follow what you want, I will follow you in following.

[Albinus then proceeds to illustrate deductive (syllogistic) reasoning with an argument designed to prove that the world is governed by providence, not accident. This is again rounded off by a reference to the Christian context in which these teachings are received.][113]

(ALB.) This argument is effective against those who say that the world is driven by accident, not governed by a plan. CH. What can be more stupid than that view? ALB. The stupid have stupid ideas—but with Solomon we should answer him so that he will not think himself wise.

[After having finished the discussion of the parts of a speech, Albinus tries to steer the conversation in a different direction, but Charlemagne makes a different request first, and one that needs delicate handling by Albinus. The passage also contains another legitimation of the full authorship of both parties by stating that interrogating and teaching are basically two sides of the same coin. Note how this point is made while at the same time the fact that Charlemagne will allow himself to be questioned will in this case lead to his becoming the victim of a sophism.][114]

(34) (ALB.) Here you have your information about the first and greatest part of rhetoric, namely invention. Let us now go on to the other parts.

35. CH. Yes, let's, but tell me first, what is sophistic speech? ALB. If anyone else from the school of your palace had asked me that, maybe I would have shown him. CH. Why someone else and not me? Do you begrudge me the knowledge? ALB. I do not begrudge you anything, but I spare and honor you. CH. I do not see that it is an honor to me when you refuse what I ask you. ALB. May I ask you some questions? CH. Why not? For asking wise questions is teaching. And if the one who asks questions and the one who teaches are two different people, it is still the case that for both parties understanding springs from one

---

[113] *Rhetores latini minores*, 541.

[114] *Rhetores latini minores*, 543–4. On Alcuin's treatment of sophistical discourse and its possible sources, see Copeland, "Ancient Sophistic and Medieval Rhetoric," 266–8; see also Wallach, *Alcuin and Charlemagne*, 39.

source, namely that of wisdom. ALB. Indeed it does, even if the one who asks questions and the one who teaches are two different people. So you, who ask the questions, are not the same as I, who answers. CH. Not the same at all. ALB. What are you? CH. I am a man. ALB. Do you see how you can draw a conclusion about me? CH. How? ALB. By saying, if you and I are not the same, and I am a man, it follows that you are not also a man. CH. Yes, that does follow. ALB. How many syllables does *homo* "man" have? CH. Two. ALB. Are you two syllables then? CH. Not at all, but what are you driving at? ALB. That you get an idea of sophistic cunning, and see how you may be the object of conclusions. CH. I see, and I understand that my prior concessions, when I admitted that I was a *homo* ["man"] and that *homo* is two syllables, made me the object of the conclusion that I am these two syllables. I am astonished how stealthily you brought me, first, to the false conclusion about you, that you would not be a man, and then about myself, that I would be two syllables.

[At this point, Charlemagne follows Albinus' previous suggestion and starts asking about arrangement. Albinus devotes only a short answer to this topic. The next part is "style," and Charlemagne desires a somewhat more expansive treatment to which Albinus replies, again playing on the role division of the two speakers.][115]

ALB. I do not make up excuses, but will follow your questions, my lord King, even if with slow foot, yet never with slow will.

[After the discussion of style, memorization, and delivery, the two discuss the importance of regular practice and exercise, and then turn to the importance of morality—the last part of the dialogue is a discussion of the (Christian) virtues. We have excerpted the transition to this part.][116]

43. CH. I also see that it is necessary to begin to avoid in one's language at home what may be criticized by public convention. If one wishes to use decent language among strangers, one should not use indecent language at home, for decency is absolutely necessary in every part of one's life, especially in conversations. For the proof of almost anyone's character is his speech, unless you think differently, master. ALB. Impossible that I should think differently about this. This is why in daily conversation one should choose decent, clear, simple words, spoken clearly, with calm face and composed expression, without immoderate laughter or shouting. For there is a good way of speaking, like there is of walking, going mildly, without jumping, without delay, until everything is shining with the temperance of moderation, which is one of the four virtues which are like the roots out of which the other virtues sprout. Among them are nobility of mind, dignity of life, decency of character, and praise of discipline. CH. I understand that that philosophical

---

[115] *Rhetores latini minores*, 544.   [116] *Rhetores latini minores*, 547–8.

proverb should not only be applied to character, but also to words. ALB. Which one? CH. "Nothing in excess." ALB. Yes, and it is really necessary in everything, for whatever exceeds due measure is sinful. That is why the virtues are in an intermediate position.[117] I could have told your Venerable Authority more about them, if our discussion was not hastening towards its end, and if it would not seem superfluous to talk to you about virtues: for you are not only distinguished by knowledge of the virtues, but also by their practice.

44. CH. Yet I will not allow you to rest your pen and stop answering, master, before you expound to me the names and parts of the four virtues which you have called the roots of the other virtues. A little while ago we agreed that practicing speech is necessary: what topic can we better exercise speaking on than the excellence of the virtues, which can be of great use to both authors and readers? ALB. Of great use, indeed, my lord King, but I am caught in a dilemma: compressed brevity demands few words, yet the difficulty of the subject matter wishes for more. CH. Exercise moderation in either direction, and do not let either prolixity produce boredom, nor brevity ignorance. ALB. First we need to know that some things are so brilliant and noble, that they should not be aspired to because of any other advantage, but are to be loved and pursued because of their own dignity only. CH. These are the things I would very much like to get to know. ALB. They are: virtue, knowledge, truth, good love. CH. Isn't it especially the Christian religion which praises these? ALB. Yes, it praises and practices them. CH. What do the philosophers have to do with them? ALB. They understood them in their human nature and practiced them with the utmost effort. CH. What is the difference then between such a philosopher and Christians? ALB. Faith and baptism. CH. Continue anyway your philosophical definitions of the virtues and tell me first, what is virtue itself.

[The discussion now focuses on virtue and its four main distinctions, with subdivisions, and then turns to the Christian view of the virtues. The virtues are Christianized versions of those treated in Cicero's *De inventione* 2.53.159—2.59.178. The dialogue ends with the promise of heavenly rewards for the exercise of virtue and the pursuit of the love of God and one's neighbor. The book ends with emphasizing its range in that it has covered both pagan knowledge and the pursuit of virtue. Charlemagne obviously has the last word.][118]

CH. What is the right order of the soul? ALB. That it loves what is higher, namely God, and governs what is lower, namely the body, and that it nurtures and cherishes its fellow souls with love. When a soul has purged and unburdened itself by such sacrifices it will fly back

---

[117] Namely, between the vices that are on either end of each virtue as excess and deficiency: e.g. courage is intermediate between rashness and cowardice. This is Aristotelian doctrine, see e.g. *Nicomachean Ethics* 1106a26—b28.

[118] *Rhetores latini minores*, 550.

from this laborious and troublesome life to its rest, and it will enter the joys of its Lord. CH. You are talking about a great and truly happy man, master. ALB. May God make you great and truly happy, my lord King, and may he allow you to fly in the chariot drawn by these four virtues, which we talked about just now, high above this evil world on the double wings of love[119] to the summit of the heavenly kingdom. CH. May that happen, may that happen by the gift of divine grace. ALB. May this dialogue of ours, which started from the changeable ingenuity of political questions, end on this note of eternal stability, so that nobody may think we traversed such a long journey of discourse in vain. CH. Who would dare to say that our discussion was fruitless, if he is either a researcher who desires to know about honorable pagan arts, or a researcher of eminent virtues? For I have to confess that I was brought to these investigations by the love of knowledge, and I am grateful to you for not having refused what I asked; I commend your benevolence in answering, and I think that it will prove of use to students, as long as the taint of ill-will does not corrupt the reader.

[119] Namely for God and for one's neighbor [Matthew 22:37–40; 1 Timothy 1:5], the central criteria for biblical interpretation in Augustine's *De doctrina christiana* (see 1.26.27).

GLOSSES ON PRISCIAN BY REMIGIUS AND HIS FOLLOWERS (NINTH AND TENTH CENTURIES)

INTRODUCTION

Remigius (ca. 841–908) was one of the famous teachers at Auxerre.[1] He was active as a grammarian and biblical commentator, often putting his knowledge of grammar and pagan authors in the service of theology.[2] He is an advocate of concision, and often offers down-to-earth solutions. Remigius shows classicizing tendencies in his use of literary examples, which he mixes with examples taken from the Bible.[3] His grammatical sources are Donatus, Priscian, Servius/Sergius, Diomedes, Charisius, Probus, the anonymous *Ars Bernensis*, and Isidore.[4]

Remigius' work represents a characteristic development in Carolingian grammar, its pedagogical focus in approaching grammar.[5] His grammatical activity must have mostly taken place in the context of oral teaching.[6] The commentaries that we have are revisions of lectures in constant progress, hence the text was "unstable" from the very beginning, in keeping with the essentially "open" commentary genre.[7] Remigius' teaching method is the running commentary, a step-by-step explication and paraphrase of the text being studied—there is no fundamental difference in technique whether he is explaining Donatus or a psalm. We have his commentaries on the *Ars minor* and the *Ars maior* of Donatus, and

---

[1] Cf. Iogna-Prat et al., eds., *L'école carolingienne d'Auxerre de Murethach à Remi 830–908*, and especially the contribution by Jeudy, "L'oeuvre de Remi d'Auxerre." The book also contains a useful Clavis, a complete reference tool, to the works by Remigius (457ff.).

[2] On Remigius' commentary techniques and the relation between his scriptural and grammatical commentaries, see Kneepkens, *Het iudicium constructionis*, 1:7; Law, *The Insular Latin Grammarians*, 82.

[3] Irvine, *The Making of Textual Culture*, 89 and 463 (calling attention to this aspect of classicizing both in Remigius' sense of Latinity and in his appeal to textual authority); for literary examples adduced by Remigius, see, e.g., Huygens, ed., "Remigiana," 332–3.

[4] De Marco, ed., "Remigii inedita," 499–500.

[5] See the introduction to the selection from Alcuin, pp. 272–5.

[6] Jeudy, "L'oeuvre de Remi d'Auxerre," 380.

[7] See Robins, "The Authenticity of the *Technê*," 19–24, for the "open" character of teaching manuals.

on Priscian's *Partitiones duodecim versuum Aeneidos principalium* (Divisions of the Twelve First Lines of *Aeneid* Books 1–12)[8] and *Institutio de nomine pronomine verbo* (Instruction on the Noun, Pronoun, and Verb), from which we give excerpts here, the *Ars de nomine et verbo* by Phocas,[9] the *Ars de verbo* by Eutychius,[10] and Bede's *Ars metrica* and *De schematibus et tropis*. He wrote substantial commentaries on Martianus Capella's *De nuptiis Philologiae et Mercurii* and on Boethius' *De consolatione philosophiae* which were long influential for their literary content as well as pedagogical appeal.[11]

We excerpt the beginning of his commentary on the short treatise *De nomine pronomine verbo* (On the Noun, Pronoun and Verb), a practical beginners' grammar aimed mainly at teaching morphology.[12] In this commentary and the commentary on the *Ars minor* of Donatus, the teaching setting is obvious. The text begins with an elaborate exegetical rephrasing of the opening sentence, followed by a discussion of four prologue topics, and continues with an interesting mix of fragmentation, produced by dividing the texts into lemmata, and continuous argument. Remigius is arguing that the order of the declensions is in principle based on the order of the Latin vowels: his best argument seems to be that the first declension has a genitive in ae (this uses up a and e), so that with the second ending in i, at least the beginning of the series is entirely regular.

Considerations of logic and syntax may be primarily associated with the *Glosule* tradition and commentaries of the very early twelfth century,[13] yet it is important to realize that they originated earlier. Carolingian grammar is characterized by a new interest in syntax, and the interaction of grammatical and logical analysis of language. Priscian obviously fits both these interests.[14] Sedulius Scotus and John Scotus Eriugena wrote commentaries on his work in which interpretation was couched in philosophical terms.[15] The influence of philosophical considerations has also been detected in Remigius,[16] and,

---

[8] Along with Bede's *De arte metrica*, this was a standard work for teaching metrical theory.

[9] A grammarian of the fifth century AD.   [10] A student of Priscian.

[11] See *In Artem Donati minorem commentum*, ed. Fox. The commentary on Martianus is edited by Lutz, *Commentum in Martianum Capellam*; portions of the Remigian commentary on Boethius are edited in T. W. Machan, with A. J. Minnis, *Sources of the Boece* (Athens, GA: University of Georgia Press, 2005). See also Jeudy, "L'oeuvre de Remi d'Auxerre," for a survey of the manuscripts.

[12] *GL* 3:443–56; *Prisciani Caesariensis Opuscula*, ed. Passalacqua, vol. 2: *Institutio de nomine pronomine verbo. Partitiones duodecim versuum Aeneidos principalium*. See the introduction to the section on Priscian, p. 170.

[13] R. W. Hunt, "Studies on Priscian I," 21 (214). See within, sections on William of Conches, Petrus Helias, and Ralph of Beauvais, pp. 377, 384–9, 444–60, 511–17.

[14] See especially Luhtala, "Syntax and Dialectic in Carolingian commentaries on Priscian's *Institutiones grammaticae*."

[15] For the work on Priscian by Sedulius Scotus (ca. 850) and John Scotus Eriugena, see Luhtala, "A Priscian commentary attributed to Eriugena"; for Priscian in this period, see also Kneepkens, "The Priscianic Tradition," 240–1.

[16] Luhtala, "Syntax and Dialectic," 157–67.

in fact, the passage on the order of the declensions certainly betrays a concern for *ordo*, the logical coherence of the structure of grammar itself, which ideally reflects the natural rational order and the orderliness of language. This concern is often reflected in discussions of the order of the parts of speech, with Priscian's primacy of noun and verb taken to reflect a correct philosophical appreciation of the importance of substance and action. On the syntactic level, the importance of the categories of substance and action has as its correlate the inseparability of noun and verb, or "the inherence of the noun in the verb." We excerpt an anonymous gloss from the tenth century which offers "the most orderly presentation of what we have by now come to know about Carolingian syntactic theory":[17] it contains definitions of noun, verb, and pronoun, mentions the *proprium* of each part of speech, and pays particular attention to the philosophical and syntactic implications of the definition. Basically ignoring the formal characteristics of the parts of speech, the text concentrates on the "inherence of the substance in the verb" mentioned above.

Remigian commentaries translated from "Remigii inedita," ed. de Marco, and "Remigiana," ed. Huygens, reprinted by permission;[18] translation of the anonymous gloss on Priscian reprinted from Luhtala, "Syntax and Dialectic in Carolingian Commentaries" (with minor adaptations), by permission.

THE INTRODUCTION OF REMIGIUS' COMMENTARY

[The simple sentence commented on is: "Here begins the (Book of) Instruction by the grammarian Priscian of Caesarea."[19] The text shows a serious scholastic at work. Note how the same technique of exegetical paraphrase is transferable to different text genres, from biblical texts to grammatical textbooks.]

"Here begins" [*incipit*], that is "starts" [*inchoat*] or "takes its starting-point" [*initium sumit*], "the instruction" [*institutio*], that is "teaching" [*eruditio*] or "forming" [*formatio*]: from *statuo* ["to set up"] is made the compound *instituo* ["to instruct"], that is *erudio* ["to

---

[17] Luhtala, ibid. 166, who also suspects a link with the work of Sedulius Scotus.

[18] De Marco, ed., "Remigii inedita," 503–7, 517, from Paris, BN MS lat. 7581, fols. 47v–49v; Huygens, ed., "Remigiana," 331–2, 334, 340, from Leiden, Universiteitsbibliotheek MS BPL 67, fols. 214–218v (cf. the new edition of these texts by Huygens, *Serta Medievalia* [*CCCM* 171]: for the passages selected here, the text of the new edition is identical with the older edition). The text edited by Huygens gives a fuller version of the Remigian commentary, restoring the mythological, geographical, and related information absent in the versions studied by de Marco.

[19] Huygens, ed., "Remigiana," 331–2.

teach"]. It conjugates into the participle *institutus*, [gen.] *instituti* ["instructed"], and by adding an *o* one gets *institutio* ["instruction"]. Hence Quintilian's book is also called *Institutiones* ["Instructions"], in which he teaches how to instruct children. "(Of) Priscian" [*Prisciani*] is the proper name of the author of this book, "the grammarian" [*grammatici*] is the name of his profession. "Of Caesarea" [*Caesariensis*]: the word comes from Caesarea in the region of Cappadocia. There are three Caesareae,[20] called after the name of Caesar of course: one is in the region of Palestine, the second is Caesarea of Philippus, which Philippus himself built and called Caesarea Philippi by his own name and that of the Emperor, the third one is in Cappadocia, and it is after this one that he [Priscian] is called "of Caesarea": that is where he came from. And he taught there for a long time, but later, as some maintain, he was in Rome. Alternatively, John Scotus [Eriugena] says he is called Caesariensis because of his dignified position, i.e. "royal."[21]

At this point we have to ask four things, place, person, time, and reason for writing.[22] The place is Rome, the person is Priscian, the time is under the consulate of Julian, the reason for writing is the instruction of boys. For after his major work he composed this little book for the instruction of boys, dealing with these three parts of speech because rather difficult problems are encountered here, or because they undergo flection in cases and also in moods. He also introduces the participle because he assigns it an intermediate position between noun and verb: for it seems to have the form [*litteratura*] of a noun and the meaning of a verb.[23]

EXPOSITION ON PRISCIAN BY REMIGIUS[24]

BEGINNING [*INCIPIT*] OF THE INSTRUCTION OF THE GRAMMARIAN PRISCIAN ON THE NOUN, PRONOUN, AND VERB Perhaps someone may ask why Priscian decided to discuss the

---

[20] Cf. Bede, *Expositio actuum apostolorum et retractatio*, ed. M. L. W. Laistner, *CCSL* 121 (Turnhout: Brepols, 1983): 170.92–105.

[21] As it were "Caesar-like."

[22] These are four of the "circumstances" (*circumstantiae*) that Remigius uses in his commentary prologues: see within, introduction to Boethius' *De differentiis topicis*, p. 190–3.

[23] Priscian does indeed discuss some aspects of participle formation, e.g. *GL* 3:456 (= 39.13ff. ed. Passalacqua). The participle is generally explained as "taking part" (*parti-ceps*) in the properties of both noun and verb, cf. e.g. Donatus, *Ars minor* 6, *GL* 4:363.13f.: *participium quid est? pars orationis partem capiens nominis, partem verbi.*

[24] De Marco, ed., "Remigii inedita," 503–7, commentary on Priscian, *De nomine pronomine verbo, GL* 3:443.1ff.

declensions of nouns, pronouns, and verbs, although he knew that the matter had already been dealt with by many authors. The answer is that some of the old authors held different views on these topics, which some of them discussed briefly, others with too many words. As a result, the beginner could not find perfection there. We should also add this question, why he only discussed the noun and the parts mentioned above, but not the other parts of speech. The rejoinder to that is that he saw variety and ambiguity of declension in these parts rather than in the rest.

[at *GL* 3:443.3] ALL THE NOUNS THAT LATIN ELOQUENCE [*ELOQUENTIA*] MAKES USE OF ETC. This is a rightly asked question, why he said "that Latin eloquence makes use of," when he has already preceded this with "all the nouns." In this connection one should know that if he had said "the nouns that the Latin language [*lingua*] uses," it would have seemed as if he was including the words of one ending [*monoptota*].[25] By adding "eloquence," he excluded all words of one ending. For whenever there is deficiency, eloquence, i.e. copiousness of expression, is not to be found at all.[26]

[at 443.3] The text continues with: UNDERGO FLECTION IN FIVE DECLENSIONS If declension is an accident of the noun, then why is it not counted among its accidents by Donatus[27] and the other *auctores* of the art of grammar? Because one of their accidents encompasses it, namely case. And if declension falls within case, then why isn't the number of declensions equal to the number of cases, namely six? Because some count only five cases, not six, since nominative and vocative are considered one case.[28] Now if case and declension are taken together, is there a difference? Yes, it would seem to be as follows, that "case" is called the difference in form of the last syllable,[29] something occurring in all cases, while "declension" is the inflection of the inner meaning.[30]

---

[25] The *monoptota* are words that use one form for all cases, e.g. *nequam* "bad." According to Remigius, they have no place in a work on flexional morphology (although Priscian does mention the fact that the letters of the alphabet are indeclinable [*GL* 3:443.21; 6.14ff. ed. Passalacqua], see below).

[26] This text also appears in Thurot, *Notices et extraits*, 64; Huygens, ed., "Remigiana," 339 has another Remigian note on *eloquentia*: "*eloquentia* 'eloquence' is exuberant facility of speech, *eloquens* 'eloquent' is *bene loquens* 'speaking well,' hence *eloquentia* is ornamented speech. The difference between *eloquentia* and *elocutio* is that *elocutio* 'uttering' refers to only one word or one sentence, 'eloquence' has many sentences."

[27] De Marco ("Remigii inedita") refers to *Ars minor* 2, *GL* 4:355.6.

[28] De Marco ("Remigii inedita", 500) refers to Servius (Sergius), *Commentarius in artem Donati*, *GL* 4:433.12, noting that almost all of the ancient grammatical writers agree that although there are six cases, the cases are actually five in number in their theoretical impact, because the nominative is not strictly speaking a "case" but the base form. See e.g. Charisius, *Ars grammatica*, 195, ed. Barwick.

[29] De Marco refers to Diomedes in *GL* 1:301.34.

[30] De Marco refers to Varro, *De lingua latina* 10.77 (ed. Goetz-Schoell, 190.9).

[at 443.4] And the declensions ARE ORDERED ON THE BASIS OF THE ORDER OF THE VOWELS USED TO FORM THE GENITIVE Why did he say "according to the order of the vowels," when in fact they are not ordered according to the order of the vowels?[31] For in the first [declension] we do find an *a*, but already no *e* without consonant in the second, nor is any vowel at all found in the third.[32] Perhaps the endings of the genitive are not found at all,[33] since the genitive of the first [declension] is found not to end in *a*, that of the second does end, in *i*, but that of the third not in a vowel at all, but in a consonant. Has he then said "order" instead of "number"? Absolutely not! Would he have been incapable of saying "number" if he had wanted to? No, but[34]

[at 443.4] ON THE BASIS OF THE ORDER OF THE VOWELS USED TO FORM THE GENITIVE Say what vowels are found in the formation of the genitives.

[at 443.5] For in the first declension the genitive has two vowels, since it "has a genitive ending in the diphthong *ae*, e.g. *hic poeta huius poetae* ['the poet,' nominative, 'of the poet,' genitive"]

[at 443.6] In the second declension, the order is preserved as well: we find a genitive ending in *i*, e.g. *doctus docti*. In the third declension we see a repetition, although we cannot find a "pure"[35] *i* without a consonant here. Then we skip a letter.[36] In the fourth declension, the main order is preserved, although the ending is not always in "pure" *u*, but in *s*, e.g. *hoc genu, huius genu* ["the knee," nominative, "of the knee," genitive], *hic fluctus, huius fluctus* ["the river," nominative, "of the river," genitive]. In the fifth declension, the letter *i* is repeated again: *haec species, huius specie-i* ["the species," nominative, "of the species," genitive]. The number of declensions should also be considered now that we are dealing with declensions.[37] For some have wanted to maintain that there are more than five,

---

[31] Remigius voices an objection to Priscian here for which he will give complete arguments, but which he will refute from this point onwards: although it may seem Priscian is wrong and the order of the vowels does not correspond to that of the declensions, in fact this parallelism may be upheld.

[32] Because the third declension has the consonant stems.

[33] The text as printed in the edition seems confused The point is that the order of the vowels *a e i o u* is not adhered to in the formation of the genitive endings in the successive declensions, and in fact in only one case (the second declension) does the genitive end in one vowel (*i*); in the first, *a* is at least still part of the diphthong *ae*, in the third, there is an *i*, but the ending is *-is*, and therefore consonantal. This is the reading of de Marco: *nec aliqua etiam ex vocalibus. Sic nec in tertia forsitan terminatione<s> genitivorum minime inveniuntur* ("or in fact any of the vowels. Similarly, in the third (declension) the endings of the genitives maybe cannot be found at all"). We have tentatively emended to *nec aliqua etiam ex vocalibus in tertia. Forsitan terminatione<s> genitivorum minime inveniuntur* (reflected in the translation).

[34] Text intended to be read on; the Priscian quotation that follows is an integral part of Remigius' argument.

[35] A "pure" vowel is not followed by a consonant in the same syllable.   [36] I.e., no genitive ends in *o*.

[37] The text speaks of "the declension of numbers," rather than "the number of declensions."

dividing the first one into three parts: they count as the first kind the one with genitive in *ae*, like *Musa Musae*; the second with genitive in *as*, like: *familia familias*, the third with genitive in *ai*, the way we find it in the poets, e.g. *aula aulai*.[38]

So why haven't they received a [favorable] hearing? Because this is only found in a few nouns, and therefore the *auctores* have decided that they should be subsumed under one species.

Others have given their approval to a lower number of declensions:[39] they subsume what we call the fifth declension among the second and third ones, because of a certain similarity of cases, which it seems to have in certain endings. They coincide with the second in the genitive ending in -*i*, e.g. *Tydeus, Tydei*, and *species, specie-i*, and similarly in the genitive plural ending in -*rum*: *doctorum* and *dierum*; (they coincide) with the third (declension) in the dative singular ending in *i*, and in the accusative <and in the ablative> and in the rest of the plural cases, e.g.: *patri diei, patrem diem, patre die, hi patres* and *hi dies*. The findings in the other cases are similar.

Why then do we not follow them? In order to avoid confusion. For it would seem to be very confusing if these nouns were divided among two declensions, namely with some cases from the second, as we said, and some from the third.

[at 443.5] THE FIRST DECLENSION THEN, HAS A GENITIVE ENDING IN THE DIPHTHONG AE, E.G. HIC POETA HUIUS POETAE ["THE POET," NOMINATIVE, "OF THE POET," GENITIVE]. This also is a fitting question, why the *auctores* of the art of grammar have decided to distinguish the declensions through the genitive rather than the nominative. In this connection one should know that the nominative has countless and numerous endings.[40] Then, if not through the nominative, why not through the dative or the other cases? Because the genitive is closer to the nominative than the other cases, and signifies the possession of everything.[41]

[at 443.5] THE FIRST DECLENSION THEN, HAS A GENITIVE ENDING IN THE DIPHTHONG AE, E.G. HIC POETA HUIUS POETAE ["THE POET," NOMINATIVE], ["OF THE POET," GENITIVE]. *Igitur* ["then"] is a logical conjunction:[42] above he had said that there are five declensions, and therefore he adds "the first declension *then* etc." Why did he say "in the diphthong -*ae*"? In order to prevent the idea that the vowels are divided [over two syllables] in the

---

[38] De Marco refers to Charisius, 16. 22–7, ed. Barwick; Priscian, *Institutiones* 7.3, *GL* 2:284.21.
[39] De Marco refers to Charisius, 31.23–32.13, cf. 16. 1–4, ed. Barwick.
[40] De Marco refers to pseudo-Sergius, *Explanationum in artem Donati*, *GL* 4:496.33.
[41] De Marco refers to Isidore, *Etymologiae* 1.7.31.
[42] The *rationales* are one subdivision of the conjunctions, cf. Donatus, *Ars maior* 2.15, *GL* 4:389.

pronunciation.[43] For "diphthong" means "twofold sound."[44] Why then do they not render their sound separately, like the other vowels? Because the sound itself of the two vowels should be understood when they are being pronounced as one sound.[45]

[at 443.6; 447.27] THE SECOND [DECLENSION] IS THE ONE OF WHICH THE CASE MEN-TIONED ABOVE [I.E. THE GENITIVE] ENDS IN A LONG *Ī*, E.G. *HIC DOCTUS HUIUS DOCTĪ* ["LEARNED," NOMINATIVE, "OF THE LEARNED," GENITIVE]. When he has said "in -*i*," why did he add "long"? Lest it be thought short, as one may find in the adverbs.

[at 443.7; 448.12] THE THIRD [DECLENSION HAS A GENITIVE ENDING] IN SHORT *ĭs*, E.G. *hic pater huius patrĭs* ["THE FATHER," NOMINATIVE, "OF THE FATHER," GENITIVE]. Why does he say "in short -*ĭs*" when in fact one may find long -*īs*, e.g. *haec vis huius vīs* ["this force," nominative, "of this force," genitive]? Because this is considered an exception, and one noun does not break the rule.

[at 443.8; 448.26] THE FOURTH [IS THE DECLINATION HAVING THE CASE MENTIONED BEFORE ENDING] IN LONG -*ŪS*, E.G. *HIC SENATUS HUIUS SENATŪS* ["THE SENATE," NOM-INATIVE, "OF THE SENATE," GENITIVE]. Why did he say "in long -*ūs*"? Lest it be thought short, as it is in the nominative.

[at 443.9; 448.33] THE FIFTH [DECLENSION LETS THE AFOREMENTIONED CASE END] IN -*E-I* DIVIDED OVER TWO SYLLABLES, E.G. *HIC MERIDIES HUIUS MERIDIE-I* ["THE AFTERNOON," NOMINATIVE, "OF THE AFTERNOON," GENITIVE]. Why did he say "in -*e-i* divided over two syllables"? To prevent people from thinking they are joined, as is found in the second declension, e.g. *Protheus Prothei*. Why is that one put first whose genitive ends in the diphthong -*ae*, although it is not more important than the others? Because of the order of the vowels, which is being preserved there, as we have already said before. A second question is why the second (declension) is put before the third, although the third looks longer superficially: again because there the order of the vowels is preserved more than in the third, which does not have a genitive case that ends in a "pure" vowel, but in a consonant.

[at 443.10] Now, THE FIRST DECLENSION CAN HAVE TWO FINAL LETTERS, -*A* AND -*S*, BUT THREE ENDINGS, -*A*, -*AS*, AND LONG -*ĒS*, E.G. *HAEC SYLLAB-A HUIUS SYLLAB-AE* ["THE SYLLABLE," NOMINATIVE, "OF THE SYLLABLE," GENITIVE], and the other examples. What is the difference between "final" and "ending"? "Final" is only said of the (last) letter, but

---

[43] De Marco refers to pseudo-Probus, *De ultimis syllabis*, GL 4:219.25.

[44] De Marco refers to Isidore, *Etymologiae* 1.16.2.

[45] Cf. the opposite discussion of the genitive of the fifth declension below: in that case the ending *e-i* is divided over two syllables, and cannot therefore be considered a diphthong.

"ending" is the syllable that is produced by the two letters at the end of a certain word. Why did he say "in long -*ās* and -*ēs*"?[46] Lest they be thought short, like -*ă*, or in any case like these endings are found in the nouns of the third declension.[47]

[at 443.12] WORDS ENDING IN -*A*, WHETHER GREEK OR LATIN, THAT ARE MASCULINE, FEMININE, OR COMMON,[48] BELONG TO THE FIRST DECLENSION, E.G. *HIC CITHARISTA HUIUS CITHARISTAE* [GREEK WORD; MASCULINE: "THE LYRE-PLAYER," NOMINATIVE, "OF THE LYRE-PLAYER," GENITIVE] et cetera. In every rule we need to ask for three things: the ending, the gender, and the language.[49] In this rule Priscian has made an effort to show these three things: he showed the ending when he said "words ending in *a*," the language when he said "Greek or Latin," the gender when he said "masculine or feminine or common."

[at 443.16] EXCEPTIONS ARE [NINE[50] (ADJ.) NOUNS OF THREE ENDINGS] *UNA ULLA* [AND THE REST] WHICH FOLLOW THE DECLENSION OF PRONOUNS THAT HAVE A GENITIVE ENDING IN -*IUS*; JUST LIKE THE ONES THAT ARE COMPOUNDS: *ALI-QUA NE-QUA SI-QUA* ["SOMEONE," "LEST ONE," "IF ONE"]. Why does he say "just like the ones that are compounds," although nobody thinks of these as compound nouns? That is not what he means, but rather that, just as the ones that are compounds have the declension of pronouns with a genitive ending in -*ius*, so too do the above-mentioned nine nouns that are exceptions. *Ali-qua* is a compound of *alia* and *quis*; *nequa* is a compound of *ne* and *quis*. Then why don't we say *aliquae nequae siquae* ["someone," "lest one," "if one" (f. gen.)"]? Well, either because [*ali-*, *si-*, and *ne-*] can be considered [empty] syllabic additions,[51] or because no feminine noun is found in Latin with a nominative singular ending in *ae*. Or at least because, when nouns are formed through compounding, then the words <that go into the compound> are normally corrupted by each other.[52]

---

[46] Priscian's text gives the (correct) "in -*as* and long -*ēs*."

[47] Cf. Priscian, *GL* 3:446 K. (= 14.6f. ed. Passalacqua): "all Latin words in -*as* are of the third declension." Words in -*es* of the third declension, cf. e.g. ibid. (14.10f. ed. Passalacqua): "All nouns in short -*es* are of the third declension."

[48] I.e. either masculine or feminine in the same form.   [49] Cf. Remigius on 443.16.

[50] Remigius apparently also read *neutra*, which Keil has not adopted in his text. Accordingly, he has only eight exceptions.

[51] *I.e.* they are redundant additions to the headword *quis* and do not affect its declension (therefore the genitive is the normal -*cuius* also in the feminine). The words do not behave like feminine nouns in *a*. Cf. for *adiectio syllabica*, *syllabica epectasis*, Priscian, *Institutiones* 5.65, *GL* 2:182.15; *syllaba expletiva*, Priscian, *Partitiones duodecim versuum Aeneidos principalium*, *GL* 3:479.31f. (= 77.4–5 ed. Passalacqua).

[52] De Marco refers to Remigius, *In Artem Donati minorem commentum*, ed. Fox, 22.3; see Donatus, *Ars minor* 2, *GL* 4:355.21ff., p. 87 above: compounds are either formed through combining two complete words, or from one complete and one "corrupted" word, i.e. one or the other is affected by the word-forming process, or both are so affected.

Note that every exception should be similar to those words on which it forms an exception, and also to those to which it crosses over, a similarity in three ways: in ending, gender, and language, the very similarities these words[53] have with the ones discussed before, to which they form an exception. For the former end in -*a* and so do the latter; the gender [of the former] is feminine, and so is [the gender of the latter]; it is agreed that these are Latin, and so are those, although this is a difficult thing to find in all rules.[54]

[at 443.18; 446.8] NEUTER WORDS (ENDING) IN -*A* ARE GREEK AND BELONG TO THE THIRD DECLENSION and the rest up to where he says *poema* ["poem"], meaning *positio* ["position"], *emblema* ["emblem"], which means *abundantia* ["abundance"], *toreuma* ["embossed or carved relief"], which means *carmen navale* ["a poem about ships"].[55]

The reason he said "neuter words are Greek and belong to the third declension" is to prevent anyone from thinking that they belong to the first declension, because he had said before [443.12ff.]: "words ending in -*a*, whether Greek or Latin belong to the first declension."[56]

[at 443.21] THE NAMES OF THE LETTERS ARE INDECLINABLE BOTH IN GREEK etc. The reason why he is adding that the names of the letters are indeclinable is to prevent anyone from thinking that they are declinable, like the neuter words belonging to the third declension which he mentioned above.

[On this text, there is an alternative version from Leiden, Universiteitsbibliotheek MS BPL 67:[57]]

THE NAMES OF THE LETTERS ARE INDECLINABLE because they are the foundations of the arts: for a foundation should be unmovable. If it does move, it vacillates, i.e. it totters, straightaway. Alternatively, the reason why the letters are indeclinable, because they were invented by barbarians, who did not know how to decline them, namely the Phoenicians. That is why the titles, that is the headings of books are written in Phoenician (i.e.: red or minium) color.

[at 443.23][58] THE GREEK [NOUNS] THAT END IN -*AS* OR -*ES* HAVE A GENITIVE IN GREEK THAT ENDS IN THE DIPHTHONG -*OU* OR IN -*A*; IN LATIN [THEY BELONG] TO THE FIRST DECLENSION, E.G. LYSIAS etc.

---

[53] *Aliqua, siqua, nequa.*   [54] Cf. Remigius on 443.12.

[55] This passage with its absurd explanations for Greek words is often used to demonstrate the lack of knowledge of Greek among Remigius and his contemporaries, cf. de Marco, ed., "Remigii inedita," 502.

[56] Both in 443.12ff. and here Priscian had added to what genders the nouns in question should belong: masculine, feminine, and common in 443.12ff., neuters here.

[57] Huygens, ed., "Remigiana," 340.   [58] Text in de Marco, ed., "Remigii inedita," 506–7.

[at 443.27] TAKE NOTE THOUGH THAT IF ONE FINDS PROPER [NAMES] OF THE SAME FORM AS PATRONYMICS, that is appellative nouns ending in <-es>, that look like proper names by their form, or certainly if they are proper names, THE ANCIENTS TEND TO PRONOUNCE [THE ENDING] RATHER ACCORDING TO THE THIRD DECLENSION than according to the first, E.G. HIC THUCYDIDES HUIUS THUCYDID-IS ["THUCYDIDES," NOMINATIVE, "OF THUCYDIDES," GENITIVE], which is a proper name, etc.[59]

[at 444.2] THE AUCTORES DO THE SAME WITH FOREIGN NAMES OF THE SAME ENDING, E.G. TIGRANES HUIUS TIGRAN-IS ["TIGRANES," NOMINATIVE, "OF TIGRANES," GENITIVE], which is a proper name, etc.

[at 444.4] THERE ARE ALSO A COUPLE OF OTHER CASES OF Greek nouns IN WHICH ONE MAY FIND THAT THEY HAVE DONE THE SAME, i.e. to have pronounced them according to the third declension, with the authority of the ancients, as *hic Orontes huius Orontis* ["Orontes," nominative, "of Orontes," genitive].

[Remigius is an advocate of brevity, and there are many remarks on the lines of the following:[60]]

[at 445.24] NEUTER NOUNS ENDING IN EITHER SHORT OR LONG -US ARE OF THE THIRD declension, LIKE *IUS, IURIS* ["LAW"] et cetera. EXCEPTIONS ARE *PELAGUS, PELAGI* ["SEA"], WHICH IS GREEK, and the rest, which we have not judged it necessary to explain, because they are, according to our small understanding, free of difficulties.

[An example of the use of a classical author:[61]]

[at GL 3:445.27] *Vulgus* means a mixed throng of people. And in Virgil it is masculine: *ut ambiguas in vulgum spargere voces.*[62] For if it had been neuter, he would have said *in vulgus.*

[A final example, in which Remigius sorts out existing and sometimes fanciful explanations and opts for a more down-to-earth one:[63]]

---

[59] Priscian discusses those words here which look like patronymics, but are simply proper names. We read the following text (with some slight changes against the de Marco text): *Sciendum autem quod, si inveniuntur* nomina *propria formae patronymicorum,* id est in <-es> desinentia ap<p>ellativa, quae forma illorum propria vide<n>tur, vel certe si propria fuerint eadem, terminationem *veteres auctores* subauditur *magis proferunt secundum tertiam* quam secundum primam, *ut: hic Thucydides, huius Thucydidis,* quod proprium est, et cetera [where italics correspond to Priscian's text and roman font to Remigius' comments].

[60] De Marco, ed., "Remigii inedita," 510, and cf. 497 for Remigius' stated purpose to be as concise as possible. There are similar notes on other passages in Priscian's text (GL 3:446.19; 450.13).

[61] Text in Huygens, ed., "Remigiana," 334.   [62] *Aeneid* 2.98–9.

[63] Text in de Marco, ed., "Remigii inedita," 517.

[at *GL* 3:456.23] EVERY PAST PARTICIPLE HAS *S* OR *T* OR *X* BEFORE *-US*, *S* AS IN *LAESUS*, *T* AS IN *AMATUS*, *X* AS IN *AMPLEXUS*, etc. THE EXCEPTION IS *MORTUUS* ["DEAD"]. Why is *mortuus* an exception,[64] and why don't we say *mortus*, which would seem to be according to the rule? As some say, it is because of this: just like a man who dies stops being of this life, so this participle also, which is born from the verb signifying death, falls outside the rule of all participles. But it seems better [to say] that this happens on grounds of euphony, because *mortuus* sounds better than *mortus*.[65]

[An anonymous gloss from the tenth century:[66]]

GLOSSES ON CONSTRUCTION

It is proper to the noun to signify substance in itself, that is, to show and distinguish between proper and common quality. It is proper to the substance to act and to suffer.[67] It is proper to the verb to signify the action and suffering of the substance. It is from the nouns that the action or suffering in the verb can be known, since there is a nominative understood in the verb. For if the meaning of the nominative were not present in the verb, albeit understood and latently, the verb would not be able to signify the action and the suffering of the substance, which is contained in the noun. Therefore the verb can properly signify action and suffering principally and manifestly. But substance inheres in the verb, secondarily and latently, because of the force, hidden inside, of the nominative. It is proper to the pronoun to signify substance without a distinction of quality, as far as the mere word form is concerned, namely by demonstrating a substance or referring to one. With this capacity it fulfills the function of the noun joined to the verb. But it is because of the verb that the pronoun has got three definite persons, in order that it should indicate the person congruent with the verb that is joined to it; that it should show the substance which is acting or suffering in the verb, as a substitute for the noun, and that it should assign to the verb three definite persons, in a congruent order. It is because of the verb that the pronoun has this property to effect a distinction of persons in the verb, since verbs in themselves are neutral as to such a distinction.

---

[64] Cf. Isidore, *Etymologiae* 11.2.33; cf. on this passage de Marco, ed., "Remigii inedita," 501.

[65] De Marco refers to Probus, *GL* 4:126.16. Remigius may have been inspired by Priscian himself here, who had just explained the last set of exceptions from euphony (456.21ff.).

[66] Translation (with minor adaptations) from Luhtala, "Syntax and Dialectic in Carolingian Commentaries," 167, from Paris BN MS lat. 7501, fol. 186r.

[67] For the technical use of *actio* "action," and *passio* "passion," the suffering or undergoing of an action, expressing the meaning of a verb, see section on Priscian, p. 181 with n. 68, above.

PART 2
DOSSIERS ON THE ABLATIVE ABSOLUTE
AND ETYMOLOGY

INTRODUCTION

This Part presents a diachronic overview of two important themes in the theory and teaching of grammar. The first section of this Part focuses on a grammatical phenomenon, the so-called "ablative absolute," and the different intellectual contexts and concerns that shaped successive discussions of this construction, still considered "typically Latin" in modern grammars. As the range of texts on the ablative absolute from late antiquity to the late Middle Ages suggests, an apparent continuity in themes and terms may conceal a discontinuity in interests. The second section of this Part offers a broad and long view of the "habit" of etymology, which is rooted in grammatical thought and practice. Because etymology was such a basic tool of pedagogy and interpretation, its theoretical purpose was continually restated and refined across disciplinary contexts.

In late antique grammar the term "ablative absolute" was not yet in use, although the phenomenon itself was recognized. Its grammatical description was characterized by two main features: the use of Greek as a constant foil; and the framework of the parts of speech (words-and-accidents model), which makes it easier to classify instances of single ablatives than a "construction" consisting of two of them. But by the twelfth century, the construction of the ablative absolute came to be of interest to the other language disciplines as well. It took on rhetorical importance in the teaching of textual composition, especially in the art of letter-writing (the *ars dictaminis*). Here the active use of the ablative absolute (the term is now found for the first time) is promoted because it enables authors to increase the complexity and sophistication of their prose. To this end they should know how to transform (*commutatio*) simple sentences into complex ones. The descriptive framework used is that of Priscian, but the context and goal are new.

In the thirteenth century, commentary practice on Priscian reflects the contemporary philosophically inspired grammatical concern with the notion of *regimen*. The term "absolute" now specifically reflects the absence of *regimen*, but since there is some form of construction going on in the relationship between the two ablatives, the reconciliation between construction and its absence in one and the same grammatical phenomenon becomes an issue. Interest in this feature of grammar had other philosophical applications as well. Since Priscian had indicated that the semantic characteristic of these two ablatives was to signal a relationship of *consequentia* ("following") between the action of the participle and that of the (main) verb, the ablative absolute could also become the object of a battle of competence between grammarians and dialecticians. Siger of Courtrai solves this problem by delineating a clear difference between the work of the logician and the grammarian: grammatical correctness (and "following") is independent from questions of truth and falsity. In his work, we also encounter a new pedagogical environment for the topic, which is now treated as a *sophisma*, a school exercise. The Prologue to the Wycliffite Bible, from the end of the fourteenth century, sees the ablative absolute in yet a different light: there, the context is a theory of translation. The Priscianic commentators explained that the construction could be "resolved" into a subordinate clause introduced by a conjunction—for them, this was part of their analysis of the problem of being "construed" versus being "absolute." The Wycliffite writer keeps the notion of "resolution," but treats it as a recipe for translation.

In the second section of this Part we will turn to etymology. Throughout antiquity and the Middle Ages, etymology was a multifaceted tool for understanding the present. Etymology offers an explanation of why things have the name they have. It serves both heuristic and mnemonic functions, helping to discover and then remember the meaning of words in their relation to the world. For this reason it was also a persuasive pedagogical instrument. As a form of thought, interpretation, and argument, it had a long tradition of use before it was pressed into the service of the language disciplines. Grammar considered it one of its tasks, in rhetoric it was part of *inventio* and served *memoria*. Isidore promoted it to the organizing principle of his encyclopedia, and used this flexible and dynamic instrument of interpretation to permit him to comment on any aspect of what he happened to be discussing. In later grammatical treatises, "etymology" becomes the name of the section where most of the traditional parts of the *ars grammatica* belonged, notably all remarks about morphology. It also became a driving force behind lexicographical work, where it relates in different ways to the notions of translation and derivation (the exposition of words in terms of their "primitive" and "derived" forms). For medieval Latinity, etymology and its newer form, derivation, were revered as methods for in-depth analysis of language, enabling the interpreter to uncover what Osbern of Gloucester was to call the "deep secrets" of Latin.

The etymology dossier will demonstrate the different contexts in which one and the same intellectual tool was put to use. In this survey, the focus is less on subtle discontinuities than on the consistency of intellectual methods across various language disciplines and critical purposes across the Middle Ages.

THE ABLATIVE ABSOLUTE DOSSIER

INTRODUCTION

For the late antique Latin grammarians who depended in many ways on their Greek predecessors, the ablative case offers a particular challenge, because this case does not exist in Greek. The three earliest discussions of the ablative absolute presented here (none of which uses the term "ablative absolute") make constant reference to Greek grammar as a conceptual anchor-point, and actively use the model of the parts of speech. All three early grammarians presented here compare the use of the ablative absolute with the similar use of the genitive in Greek.[1] Sacerdos and Diomedes devote much attention to the *form* of the construction, the fact that two ablatives are combined. Sacerdos actually introduces a new term, "seventh case,"[2] for the *combination* of two ablatives, which means a step towards syntactic analysis. In placing his discussion between the regular account of the parts of speech and his treatment of barbarism (rather than making it part of his discussion of the noun) Sacerdos also reveals some unease about classification. Diomedes returns to a more morphology-based approach within the discussion of the noun. Priscian's whole attitude to grammar had been shaped by the influence of the philosophically inspired grammars by Apollonius Dyscolus and his son Herodian. This is why Priscian gives more attention to the *meaning* of the construction, which for him includes both combinatory ("syntactic") and semantic aspects. He uses the notions of *transitio* and *consequentia*, which would provide a point of departure for more philosophically inspired discussions that would follow later. Priscian's views are relevant for the analysis of (literary) texts, but he is also explicit in his instructions to language users: in these cases one must not use a genitive instead of an ablative.[3]

In the early Middle Ages, comparison with Greek recedes into the background. There is increasing emphasis on the active use of these constructions, and their discussion is now

---

[1] For more detailed introductions to the different grammarians excerpted here, see below.

[2] His usage remains exceptional. The term *septimus casus* otherwise came to be used for the ablative without preposition, or for an ablative not indicating separation or removal: Murru, "Les cas et la linguistique ancienne"; Murru, "À propos du *septimus casus*."

[3] *Institutiones* 18.30, *GL* 3:222.2f.

part of explicit instructions for textual production, that is, rhetorical handbooks. We find the first use of the term "ablative absolute" in the rhetorical manual of Alberic of Montecassino, where the construction is a means to achieve a higher degree of complexity in one's prose compositions. Rather than producing two paratactic sentences, an author may "transform" or "rewrite" using the ablative absolute to embed one sentence in the other and create a complex sentence.

In the twelfth and thirteenth centuries, we find the term "ablative absolute" again in interpretations of Priscian. The author of the gloss *Promisimus* (last quarter of the twelfth century) uses the term when commenting on Priscian's use of *transitio* and *consequentia*; here the term is a well-known entity. The *Promisimus* gloss notes an exception within Priscian himself on his own rule of "transition of person," and comments on the fact that *consequentia* cannot be taken in a strictly logical sense. It also uses Priscianic theory to interpret literary texts and texts from the Bible.

The introduction of the central notion of *regimen* and *regere* in the grammar of this period provokes some fresh interest in this use of the ablative, since it seems characterized precisely by its lack of *regimen*.[4] The term *absolutus* now refers directly to this characteristic, thus diverging from its ancient use.[5] This is how we see it used in Petrus Helias (ca. 1140–1150) and in the *Doctrinale* by Alexander of Villa Dei (1199).[6] Alexander's *Doctrinale* was in turn the object of commentary practice. The gloss *Admirantes* (thirteenth century) also worries about the relation between the term "absolute" and the presence of some form of construction.

Siger of Courtrai (Flanders) represents the modistic grammar of the fourteenth century, the new theoretical setting for his discussion of the ablative absolute. There are still concerns over *regimen*,[7] but the new context of the theory of the modes of signifying (*modi significandi*) is explicitly invoked and the discussion of "governing" operates at a metaphysical level: "governing" is seen as dependent on the relative value of what is governed and what governs. Siger also frames the whole discussion in terms of areas of competence of the grammarian and the logician: what is grammatical (*congruus*) need not be logically sound. This is again indicative of late medieval debates about the respective

---

[4] Golling, "Einleitung in die Geschichte der lateinischen Syntax," 29, discusses the term *regere, regimen*, which gained in popularity from the eighth century. It does not necessarily denote a relation of hierarchy or dependence, but can also be used for the mutual relationship in which every term is put in the proper case. Cf. Thurot, *Notices et Extraits*, 239–44.

[5] But remember that in antique grammar, it was not applied to this construction. In classical grammar, *absolutus* refers to the positive grade of the grades of comparison, or to the use of the pronoun when it is not opposed to a different pronoun.

[6] See the introduction to the sections on Petrus Helias, pp. 444–7, and on Alexander of Villa Dei, pp. 573–6.

[7] Siger is unusal among the *modistae* in his use of "regimen," which belongs to an earlier generation of grammarians. See Pinborg, ed., *Sigerus de Cortracio, Summa modorum significandi. Sophismata*, xxxiii.

domains of the language sciences that can also be seen, for example, in the commentary on the *Barbarismus* attributed to Robert Kilwardby.[8] In Siger's work, we also encounter a new pedagogical environment for the topic, which is now treated as a *sophisma*, a school exercise.

Finally, in the Prologue to the Wycliffite Bible,[9] we see how these questions move out of the schools. The author (or authors) of the Prologue recounts the practical problems of translation posed by the ablative absolute, and proposes a recipe for its resolution into English. According to the Prologue, the better way to translate the Bible is to render its sense ("sentence," Lat.: *sententia*), rather than give a word-for-word rendition.[10] Here the ablative absolute is put on a par with other participle constructions and relative sentences: all of these constructions can either be rendered by embedded constructions in English, in a word-for-word translation of the Latin that would potentially make the English hard to follow, or be "resolved" into paratactic constructions by the addition of a connector (e.g. "and"). Note that the concept of "resolution" was also operational in the gloss *Admirantes*, but there served the goal of explaining that the ablatives are, in fact, construed, although they are called "absolute." The goal in the Wycliffite Bible is a translation that produces clear English while staying as close as possible to the Latin. But clarity is paramount. This text is also an example of an attempt to explain linguistic phenomena of a foreign language (Latin) by "calques," literal transpositions, in the vernacular, as in "the maistir redinge, I stonde."

FIRST PERIOD: SACERDOS, DIOMEDES, PRISCIAN

[M. Plotius Sacerdos (third century AD) is the author of the oldest Latin imperial school grammar that has come down to us.[11] His discussion of the ablative absolute (under the title "on the seventh case") takes up an unusual position in his grammar, between the discussion of the parts of speech and the section on faults and errors (barbarism and solecism).[12] He does not regard the "seventh case" as a case of a noun, but as a construction of two ablatives.[13] These ablatives have the "meaning of genitives," that is,

---

[8] See [Kilwardby], commentary on the *Barbarismus*, within, pp. 724–34.

[9] For an introduction to the Wycliffite Bible, and more extracts from the Prologue, see within, pp. 845–53.

[10] Cf. Jerome's *Epistle 57*, in Bartelink, ed., *Hieronymus liber de optimo genere interpretandi (ep. 57)*. On the classical and early medieval background of these theories of translation, see Copeland, *Rhetoric, Hermeneutics, and Translation*, chapters 1 and 2.

[11] Cf. Jeep, *Zur Geschichte der Lehre von den Redetheilen bei den lateinischen Grammatikern*, 73ff.

[12] Discussion of this passage in Sluiter, "Seven grammarians on the Ablative Absolute," 381ff.

[13] This is a syntactic criterion, but in the ancient grammatical sense, where "syntax" is purely combinatory. This forces Sacerdos to enumerate all the different possible combinations of different parts of speech (he does not have concepts such as subject and predicate at his disposal).

Sacerdos uses the Greek genitive absolute as his point of reference. The unusual position of Sacerdos' discussion, and his use of his own name in an example,[14] suggest that Sacerdos may be original in his discussion of this construction.

The grammarian Diomedes (first half of the fourth century AD) belongs in a different group of Roman imperial grammars.[15] He too constantly refers to Greek and Greek grammar. His starting-point is that Greek and Latin are essentially the same, so that he only needs to indicate where the two diverge in order to showcase the *idiomata* of Latin.[16] Alternatively, he will point out where the Latin of his time diverges from older usage. For Diomedes, the ablative thus forms an interesting case, especially for those types of usage that cannot readily be filed under uses of the genitive or dative in Greek. His text is also of interest in that it offers confirmation for the special role played by Sacerdos in the tradition of the "ablative absolute."[17]

Priscian (fl. ca. 500)[18] has a short chapter *de casu* in his long discussion of the noun (which runs from halfway through book 2 to book 7).[19] He reports that Latin has six cases, and that not all words are declined through all of those, and then goes on to discuss and reject the view of "certain people" who claim that there is also a *septimus casus*.[20] He criticizes the argument that the presence or absence of a preposition should make the difference between ablative and *septimus casus*,[21] and points out inconsistencies in the position of his adversaries. Priscian does admit that the ablative has very different uses, one of which is its usage in place of a Greek genitive. It is here that we find a very "syntactic" description of our ablative absolute.[22] Priscian realizes that noun and participle in the ablative constitute, as it were, their own sentence, which combines with a noun and verb (in the "main" sentence). Priscian uses the term "transition of person" (*transitio personarum*) to indicate, as we would say it, that the subject of the participle and the subject of the main verb are not identical.[23] Semantically, this construction expresses *consequentia*, "following (temporal/logical) order." In the later commentary tradition on Priscian, it will be pointed out that even if this "following" is

---

[14] This suggestion is reinforced by the use of Sacerdos' name in an example by Diomedes, see below.

[15] Jeep, *Zur Geschichte der Lehre von den Redetheilen*, 56ff.; Diomedes belongs in the so-called "Charisius group." For division of ancient grammarians into a Donatus group, a Sacerdos group, and a Charisius-Diomedes group, see Barwick, *Remmius Palaemon und die römische Ars grammatica*.

[16] Cf. *GL* 1:311.3ff.

[17] Discussion of Diomedes' text on the ablative in Sluiter, "Seven Grammarians," 384ff.

[18] See introduction to section on Priscian, within, pp. 167–70.

[19] *Institutiones* 5.68–81, *GL* 2:183.20–191.16.   [20] *Institutiones* 5.78–81, *GL* 2:190.2–191 16.

[21] In this type of argumentation he follows his example, the Greek grammarian Apollonius Dyscolus (second century AD).

[22] *Institutiones* 5.80, *GL* 2:190.20–191.7.

[23] This is the normal case. Priscian also knows that there are exceptions, cf. *Institutiones* 17.18, *GL* 3:119.12ff., where he offers (119.17) the example *"me legente proficio" pro "lego et proficio"* (no transition of persons).

not logically correct, it can still lead to a grammatically acceptable sentence (see also Siger of Courtrai, below).]

Translations from Sacerdos, Diomedes, and Priscian's *Institutiones*, book 5 reprinted from Sluiter, "Seven Grammarians on the Ablative Absolute" (with minor adaptations), by permission; from Priscian's *Institutiones*, book 18 translated from *GL* 3:221–2, by permission.

From Sacerdos, Ars Grammatica[24]

On the seventh case

The seventh case originates when two ablatives are coupled together; it has the form of ablative cases, but the sense of genitives: for it does not indicate that anything should be removed [*auferre*, hence *ab-lativus*]. It comes about in eight ways: either from a participle and a noun, like *ducente dea* ["while the goddess is leading the way"], *volente deo* ["God willing"]; or from a noun and a participle, e.g. *oratore declamante* ["while the orator is giving a speech"], *Sacerdote docente* ["while Sacerdos is teaching"]; or from two participles, e.g. *docto exponente* ["while the learned man is explaining"]; or from two nouns, like *bono homine* ["?since the man is good"];[25] or from a pronoun and a noun, e.g. *me duce* ["under my guidance"]; or from a noun and a pronoun *,[26] e.g. *laetante me* ["to my joy"]. For no seventh case can come about from two pronouns. Some people think that connecting these cases produces the sense of a dative, and that that phenomenon is also called "seventh case," e.g. *et magno se corpore miscet* ["and he unites with the big body"], but they are wrong: in that passage, he [Virgil, *Aeneid* 6.727] has used an ablative instead of a dative in accordance with ancient usage, which one can do even without combining *two* ablatives, e.g. *haeret pede pes* "one foot is stuck to the other" [*Aeneid* 10.361] and *parce metu Cytherea* "do not fear, Cytherean one" [*Aeneid* 1.257]—instead of *pedi* and *metui* [both dative]. But note that a seventh case cannot come into being without two ablatives or without the meaning of a genitive.

---

[24] *GL* 6:447.13–28.   [25] Example of dubious Latinity.
[26] There follows a lacuna, which must have contained an example of the combination of noun and pronoun (e.g. *auctore me*); an announcement and an example of the combination of pronoun and participle; and an announcement of the combination of participle and pronoun, of which *laetante me*, with which our extant text continues, is the example. See Sluiter, "Seven Grammarians," 382 n. 4.

From Diomedes, Ars Grammatica[27]

Moreover, there are many things that the Romans usually express in the ablative case. For the freedom of use of this case is immense, and we use it very frequently instead of two cases, the genitive and the dative. For many things which the Greeks say in those cases, we express through the ablative, in nouns, pronouns, and participles. The following are instances of ablatives understood as genitives, in nouns: singular *Pompeio consule* ["in the consulate of Pompey"], plural *Pompeio et Crasso consulibus* ["in the consulate of Pompey and Crassus"], *duce patre* ["with father leading"], *ducibus patribus* ["with their fathers leading"], *varia victoria bellum* ["a war with victory now on one side, now on the other"], *homo mira eloquentia* ["a man of amazing eloquence"], *magnis viribus adulescens* ["a young man of great strength"], *bona forma mulier* ["a woman with a nice figure"], etc. [The ablative] in nouns and participles of the present tense as follows: *deo volente* ["God willing"] and *deis volentibus* ["the gods willing"], *te praesente, vobis praesentibus* ["in your (sg.) presence"; "in your [pl.] presence"], *cedente adversario vici, cedentibus adversariis vicimus* ["I won because my adversary withdrew"; "we won because our adversaries withdrew"], *audiente ipso praeceptore legi, audientibus ipsis praeceptoribus legimus* ["I read while the teacher himself was listening"; "we read while the teachers themselves were listening"], etc. Expressed by participles of the past tense, as follows: *peracto tempore, peractis temporibus* ["when the time had passed"; "when the times had passed"] *coepto bello* ["when the war had begun"], *his ita actis* ["when these things had been done like this"], *recitatis litteris* ["when the letter had been read"], etc. But in these past tenses [the participle in] the ablative is taken as a nominative and it is understood to signify an indefinite tense, which the Greeks call aorist,[28] and which we have in participles, e.g. singular: *audito hoc verbo respondit* ["having heard this word (lit.: this word having been heard), he answered"]; plural: *auditis his verbis responderunt* ["having heard these words, they answered"]; singular and plural: *auditis his verbis respondit* ["having heard these words, he answered"], *inventa veritate tacuit* ["having discovered the truth, he fell silent"], *peracta oratione sedit* ["having finished his speech, he sat down"], *viso fratre gavisus est* ["having seen his brother, he rejoiced"], and other cases like these.

Instead of a dative we use the ablative as follows, e.g. in the first declension of nouns, singular: *cura consumitur* ["he is consumed by worry"]; plural: *curis consumuntur* ["they are

---

[27] *GL* 1:316.35–318.22.
[28] Unlike Latin, Greek has an active participle of the aorist tense, which allows it to use the participle in the nominative when the participle has the same subject as the main clause. In Latin, which does not have an active participle of the perfect, the passive participle of the perfect is used in the ablative absolute construction.

consumed by worries"]; second declension: *studio te vinco* ["I surpass you in effort"]; third declension: *dolore victus est* ["he is conquered by grief"]; fourth declension: *aestu solutus est* ["he is wiped out by the heat"]; and with pronouns: *hoc tempore nihil habeo* ["right now I have nothing"]; *illis temporibus valuit haec lex* ["in those days this law was valid]," *hoc anno non vidi eum* ["this year I have not seen him"], *hac via* ["by this route"], *his rebus* ["through these things"], *hoc modo* ["in this way"] and cases like these.

So far about the ablative. But disagreement is voiced by those who also assume a seventh case, which resembles the ablative, but does not agree with it in its functioning. I am quite willing to add this different usage. The ablative case always takes prepositions and is used in one way, namely to indicate that something is removed [*ablatum*] from a person, a thing, or a place. The Greeks express this meaning in two different ways. It will be pointed out either by means of a genitive or by adverbs that are used to indicate "place" and are derived from a noun. Here is an example of the use of a genitive,[29] to indicate something removed from a person: *ab oratore accepi* ["I received it from the orator"]; to indicate something removed from a thing: *a libris Ciceronis intellectum est* ["it is understood from the books of Cicero"]. An example of the use of adverbs signifying the "place whence," when they demonstrate that something is removed from a place, e.g. *a Roma in Africam redit* ["he returned from Rome to Africa"] and *a Troia* [or: *ab Ilio*] *navigavit Aeneas* ["Aeneas sailed from Troy (or: from Ilium)"]. The Greeks express this through an adverb, like this: *Troiêthen, Iliothen* ["from Troy, from Ilium"]; and again *ab alto* ["from the deep"], Greek: *hupsothen* etc. etc.

The seventh case, however, is used when these prepositions, which go with the ablative case, have been left out; it is employed in four ways:

1. When the sense is that of "in" a person, a place, or a thing, e.g. *in Scipione militaris virtus enituit* ["in Scipio military virtue was shining"], *in monte Caucaso poenas luit Prometheus* ["on the Caucasus Prometheus underwent his punishment"], *in statua Ciceronis victoria coniuratorum inscribitur* ["on the statue of Cicero there is an inscription about his victory over the conspirators"]. This stylistic device is translated by a dative [in Greek] *en Skipiôni, en tôi Kaukasiôi orei, en tôi andrianti* ["in Scipio (dat.), on the Caucasus (dat.), on the statue (dat.)"]. This rule also holds good for nouns that have identical ablative and dative forms, e.g. *ab hoc Vergilio, huic Vergilio* ["Virgil (abl., dat.)"], and *ab hac securi, huic securi* ["axe (abl./dat.)"], *ab hoc suavi, huic suavi* ["smooth (abl./dat..)"].

2. When the combination of two ablatives is translated into Greek by a genitive, e.g. *ducente dea elapsus est Aeneas* ["under guidance of a goddess (while a goddess was guiding him) Aeneas escaped"], *incusante Cicerone Catilina convictus est* ["through the indictment of Cicero Catiline was convicted"], *studente sacerdote differentia inventa est* ["through the

---

[29] The example that follows is in Latin, but would translate into a Greek genitive.

efforts of the priest (note: Sacerdos can also be a proper name)[30] the different usage was discovered"], *hêgemoneuousês tês theou exôlisthen Aineias, katêgorountos Kikerônos elenkhthê Katilinas, spoudazontos hiereôs hê diaphora hêurethê* [translations the same; all Latin ablatives have been rendered by Greek genitives]. It also makes a big difference whether we say *ab hoc praesente accepi* ["I got it from him while he was there"], or *hoc praesente ab alio accepi* ["while he was there, I got it from someone else"]; the same goes for *ab oratore venio* ["I come from the orator"], and *oratore magistro utor* ["I have an orator for a teacher"].

3. When we take the following Greek constructions: *elpidi tou dunasthai* ["in the hope of power"], *prohairesei tou lêisteuein* ["from the desire to loot"], *skhêmati tou epibouleuein* ["through the plan to conspire"], and render them into Latin as follows: *spe posse, voluntate latrocinandi, consilio insidiandi* [same translations; all datives in Greek have been rendered by Latin ablatives].

4. When, as Scaurus reports, Latin lacks a certain word, as in the case of *ontos ousês ontôn ousôn* [the participles of the verb "to be" in gen. sing. m./n.; gen. sing. f.; gen. plur. m./n.; gen. plur. f.]. For we say *nullo timore hostium castra inrupit* ["without any fear (abl.) he burst into the enemy camp"], *nulla spe rerum potiundi vallo fossaque moenia circumdat* ["without any hope (abl.) of gaining power he surrounded the walls with ramparts and a trench"], *nullis custodibus palladium ereptum est* ["without there being any guards (abl.), the Palladium was stolen"], *nullis insidiis palam victus est hostis* ["without using any ambush (abl.) the enemy was beaten openly"]. In all these cases the Latin language is deficient, to be sure because two *nominal* ablatives have been coupled. As long as one of them is a participle, Latin is not deficient, but complete, as was explained above: *ducente dea elapsus est Aeneas* ["because a goddess was leading the way, Aeneas escaped"], and the other cases discussed under (2).

Priscian, Institutiones *5.78–81*[31]

The following also we must not omit, that according to some the ablative, when used without a preposition, is a "seventh case." This seems rather illogical. It is certainly not the case that the addition or omission of a preposition can change the (semantic) value of a case.

---

[30] Names used in examples are often indicative of the preceding tradition because grammarians have the habit of using their own names, but also of preserving examples once they have been coined. Here, the Latin example seems to indicate the fact that Sacerdos had been instrumental in establishing this Latin usage. However, the Greek translates as if there was no proper name in the Latin, but just the words for "priest" (*sacerdos*). But in a different text in the Charisius group to which Diomedes belongs, we do find a Greek translation (*spoudazontos Sakerdôtos*) that preserves the proper name. See Sluiter, "Seven Grammarians," 387 note 14.

[31] *GL* 2:190.2–191.16.

For the accusative can also take many prepositions, and yet it is not one case, when it has the prepositions, and another, when it is used without them. And who would doubt that all prepositions in Latin are either construed with the accusative or with the ablative? So if their addition or omission with the ablative should change its semantic value, their addition or omission with the accusative should also effect a change of case. Moreover, the ablative is usually employed without a preposition in comparisons. Yet, nobody claims that we are dealing with a "seventh case," but rather with an ablative, when I say *fortior Achilles Hectore* ["Achilles is stronger than Hector (abl.)"]. All authors of grammatical handbooks agree on this. They claim there are six cases, not seven. For Latin has one case more than Greek, not two. Therefore, it is a redundant exercise to add a seventh case which does not differ in a single noun in any respect from the sixth. One should be aware, however, that this case [i.e. the ablative] may be used at one time instead of a Greek genitive, at another instead of a Greek dative. Instead of a genitive, when the ablative is combined with prepositions or adverbs taking the ablative, e.g. *ex illo* ["out of there"], *de illo* ["away from there"], *ab illo* ["from there"], *pro illo* ["for him"], *coram illo* ["in his presence"], *cum illo* ["with him"], and with comparatives *fortior illo* ["stronger than him"]; further, when an ablative of one noun and a participle are combined with a verb and a nominative of a different noun,[32] with transition [*transitio*] of persons, e.g. *sole ascendente dies fit* ["when the sun rises, it becomes day"], and *Traiano bellante victi sunt Parthi* ["When Trajan was conducting the war, the Parthians were conquered"]. We use this construction, when we wish to show a certain order [*consequentia*] of things [*res*][33] expressed by the verb relative to the things [*res*] expressed by the participle. For what else does *Traiano bellante victi sunt Parthi* ["When Trajan was conducting the war, the Parthians were conquered"] mean, except that the victory followed on [was a consequence of] Trajan's expedition? And what does the sentence *sole ascendente factus est dies* ["when the sun rose, it became day"] mean, except that it becoming day followed on [was a consequence of] the rising of the sun?[34] Incidentally, one also finds nouns used instead of participles in these expressions, as Virgil writes in his seventh book: *non vobis rege Latino / divitis uber agri Troiaeve opulentia deerit* ["as long as Latinus is king, you will not lack the abundance of a rich field and Troy's riches"]; here, *rege Latino* [lit. "Latinus king (abl. noun)"] stands for *regnante Latino* ["while Latinus is king (abl. participle)"]. But even in these kinds of construction, a participle is mentally supplied,

---

[32] This case is similar to the Greek genitive absolute.

[33] *Res* is a pregnant term, translating Greek *prâgma*, and indicating the semantic (this includes "syntactic") content of a verb (or participle). The term is part of Priscian's Stoic heritage (through the mediation of the grammarian Apollonius Dyscolus). Cf. Long, "Language and Thought in Stoicism," 76; Nuchelmans, *Theories of the Proposition*, 49–50.

[34] It is particularly this latter example that would give rise to discussions about "logical" consequence. The standard example of a conditional in logic is "if it is light, it is day."

namely that of the verb "to be." The Greeks are accustomed to use infinitives, too, in this type of construction instead of a participle in the genitive, e.g. *en tôi basileuein Traianon anti tou basileuontos Traianou* ["'during the time of Trajan being king' (inf.) instead of 'while Trajan was king' (gen. abs.)"]. [The ablative] is also used instead of a Greek genitive, when we translate it by means of the participle *habens* ["having"], and an accusative, e.g. *pulchra forma mulier* ["a woman with a good figure"], i.e. *pulchram formam habens* ["having a good figure"], *magna altitudine domus* ["a house of great height"], i.e. *magnam altitudinem habens* ["having great height"]. The ablative also stands for the dative when it is connected with the preposition *in* ["in"], or *sub* ["under"], e.g. *in illo* ["in it"], *sub illo* ["under it"], and when we translate the ablative by itself by means of an accusative and the preposition *per* ["by (means of), through"], e.g. *vinco te manu* ["I conquer you by hand (abl.)"], i.e. *per manum* ["by means of my hand"], *video te lumine* ["I see you by the light (abl.)"], i.e. *per lumen* ["through the light"].

Priscian, Institutiones *18.30*[35]

Similarly, when signifying consequence [*consequentia*] they[36] use the genitive, but we only the ablative, e.g. [Greek] *emou horôntos ton paida etupsas*, that is: "while I am watching, you have hit the boy," which we express thus: *me vidente* [abl. abs.] *puerum cecidisti*; *Augusto imperatore* [abl. abs.] *Alexandria provincia facta est*, that is: "when Augustus was emperor" (Alexandria was made a province); *Bruto defensore* [abl. abs.] *liberata est tyranno respublica*, that is: "when Brutus was its defender" (the republic was liberated from a tyrant); *Sulla victore* [abl. abs.] *perierunt Romani* instead of "when Sulla was victorious" (the Romans perished). In this sense, as we have shown, it is not permitted to use the genitive instead of the ablative.

RHETORICAL INTERLUDE

[Alberic of Montecassino (fl. 1057–1088) is the author of *De dictamine*, a rhetorical manual on letter writing.[37] The discussion of the ablative absolute is part of his treatment of participle constructions (note that the discussion has now moved away

[35] Translated from *GL* 3:221.25–222.3.   [36] Sc. the Greeks.
[37] See also Scaglione, *Ars grammatica*, 131–9.

from the noun or its cases), which enable the student to increase the complexity of their prose. Alberic considers the introduction of a participle construction a way of rhetorically "transforming" (*commutatio*) straight parataxis or constructions with subordinated clauses introduced by a conjunction. He shows his dependence on Priscian by his use of the notion *sine retransitione* "without retransition," meaning that the participle does not "go back" to the subject of the main verb. Grammar is recontextualized in this text.]

Translation reprinted from Sluiter, "Seven Grammarians on the Ablative Absolute."

Alberic of Montecassino, De Dictamine, *Chapter 3*[38]

A transformation occurs into the nominative of the present participle, when verbs are being used in the same person, number, and tense, e.g. *ambulo et clamo* ["I walk and I yell"]: *ambulans clamo* ["I yell (while) walking"] and *clamans ambulo* ["I walk (while) yelling"]; *ambulamus et clamamus* ["we walk and we yell"]: *ambulantes clamamus* ["we yell (while) walking"] and *clamantes ambulamus* ["we walk (while) yelling"].

There is also a transformation into that case [viz. the nominative], when the imperfect past tense [i.e. the imperfect] in the indicative or subjunctive mode is construed with a perfect past tense [i.e. the perfect] in the same person, number, and mood, e.g.: *cum ad urbem tenderem* or *tendebam* ["when I went (subj. or ind.) to the city"], *occurri necessario* ["I ran into an acquaintance"]: *occurrens necessario ad urbem tendebam* ["running into an acquaintance I went to the city"], or *tendens ad urbem necessario occurri* ["(going) on my way to the city I ran into an acquaintance"].

The ablative absolute[39] of the present participle will occur when verb forms are used in the same tense, but different persons or number without retransition [*sine retransitione*], e.g.: *ego lego et tu canis* ["I am speaking and you are singing"]: *me legente tu canis* ["while I am speaking (abl. abs.) you are singing"], or *te canente ego lego* ["while you are singing (abl. abs.) I am speaking"]; *ego solus laboro et omnes laboris mercedem percipimus* ["I am doing the work by myself and we all share the reward for the work"]: *nobis omnibus laboris mercedem percipientibus ego solus laboro* ["while we all share the reward for the work (abl. abs.), I am

[38] *De dictamine*, in Rockinger, ed., *Briefsteller und Formelbücher*, 30f.
[39] This is the first time this *terminus technicus* is found (cf. Scaglione, *Ars grammatica*, 131–9). Its context does not suggest that Alberic is inventing the term here, since he uses it as a well-known entity.

doing the work by myself"], or *me laborante solo omnes mercedem laboris percipimus* ["while I am doing the work by myself (abl. abs.), we all share the reward for the work"].

The same case will also be used when the imperfect past tense [i.e. the imperfect] in the indicative or subjunctive is construed with a perfect past tense [i.e. the perfect] in a different person or number without retransition [*sine retransitione*], e.g. *cum precinebam* or *precinerem* ["when I was leading the singing (ind. or subj.)"], *tu succinuisti* ["you sang after me"]: *me precinente tu succinuisti* ["when I was leading the singing you sang after me"], or *te succinente ego precinebam* ["while you were singing after me, I was leading the singing"].

The corresponding case of the present participle will be used when there is a turning back [*reconversio*] through the nominative to an oblique case, either by means of the same noun, or a relative noun, or a relative pronoun.[40] By means of the same noun, as in: *Johannes diligit te, et tu diligis inimicos eius* ["John loves you and you love his enemies"]: *Johannes diligit te diligentem inimicos eius* ["John loves you (while you are) loving (acc. participle) his enemies"]. By means of a relative noun, as follows: *diligo Johannem qui diligit inimicos meos* ["I love John, who loves my enemies"]: *diligo Johannem diligentem inimicos meos* ["I love John (while he is) loving (acc. participle) my enemies"]. By means of a relative pronoun as follows: *ego diligo Johannem* ["I love John"]; *ipse* ["he"], or *is* ["he"], or *ille* ["he"] *diligit inimicos meos* ["loves my enemies"].

The corresponding case of the past participle will be used when there is a turning back [*reconversio*] through the accusative to another case. Either through the same noun, as follows: *ego amo Johannem, Johannem amat Petrus* ["I love John, Peter loves John"]: *ego amo Johannem a Petro amatum* ["I love John (who is) loved (acc. participle) by Peter"]. Or through the same pronoun, as follows: *ego misereor tui, te Johannes exodit* ["I feel sorry for you, John hates you"]: *ego misereor tui a Johanne exosi* ["I am sorry for you (who are) hated (gen. participle) by John"]. Or through [the same] relative pronoun, as follows: *ego misereor tui quem Johannes exodit*: *ego misereor tui a Johanne exosi* ["I am sorry for you whom John hates: I am sorry for you (who are) hated (gen. participle) by John"], or through a relative pronoun, as follows: *lego Virgilium, ipsum* or *eum* or *illum legis et tu* ["I read Virgil; you read him (*ipse/is/ille*) as well"]: *lego Virgilium lectum a te* ["I read Virgil (who is) read (acc. participle) by you"].

A transformation [*conversio*] into the ablative absolute of the past participle will take place when the verb governs an accusative, to which we do not turn back [*reconversio*] through an oblique case, e.g. *deserui seculum et ivi ad monasterium* ["I left the (secular)

---

[40] Judging from the examples, these categories do not correspond to ours. In the first instance, the repeated "noun" is the personal pronoun *te/tu*; the "relative noun" is what we call the relative pronoun *qui*; the "relative pronoun" is what we call an anaphorically used demonstrative (*ipse, is, ille*).

world behind and went into a monastery"]: *deserto seculo ivi ad monasterium* ["having left the (secular) world behind (abl. abs.), I went into a monastery"].

THE PRISCIANIC TRADITION: TWELFTH AND THIRTEENTH CENTURY

[Texts from the gloss *Promisimus* (last quarter of the twelfth century),[41] Petrus Helias, Alexander of Villa Dei's *Doctrinale* (1199), and the gloss *Admirantes* (thirteenth century) illustrate the reception of Priscianic theory, its application to the interpretation of (biblical) texts in the twelfth century, and its development in the period dominated by the notion of *regimen*.]

Texts translated from Hunt, "Studies on Priscian in the Twelfth Century II: The School of Ralph of Beauvais"; Petrus Helias, *Summa super Priscianum*, ed. Reilly; Thurot, *Notices et extraits*; Alexander of Villa Dei, *Doctrinale*, ed. Reichling, by permission.

School of Ralph of Beauvais: Gloss Promisimus *on Priscian,* Institutiones 5.80 *(GL 2:190.21)*[42]

WITH TRANSITION OF PERSONS [*cum transitione personarum*] this refers to the case where nominative and oblique case signify different persons, namely *sole* ["sun," abl.], and *dies* ["day," nom.].[43] Some people want to have it on the authority of these words that the ablative absolute [*ablativus absolutus*] can never be used without transition of persons, whence they reject the following type of construction: *me sedente ego disputo* ["while I am sitting (abl. abs.), I (nom.) am debating"]. But they have forgotten about the example which Priscian uses in the beginning of the *Books on Syntax* [*Institutiones* 17.19], where he says: *me legente proficio* ["while I am reading (abl. abs.) I (nom.) am making progress"].[44] So we say that his statement "with transition of persons" is not universally valid, but for the most part . . .

---

[41] See also the introduction to section on the school of Ralph of Beauvais, within, pp. 511–13.

[42] Text in Hunt, "Studies on Priscian in the Twelfth Century II: The School of Ralph of Beauvais," 74 (checked against the recent edition by Fredborg, "*Promisimus*: An Edition").

[43] The commentator is referring to the example *sole ascendente dies fit* "when the sun is rising it becomes day."

[44] *GL* 3:119.17.

BY THIS he shows what is the sense of such a construction, namely to indicate that the content [*rem*] of the ablative that is used absolutely is the cause of the content designated by the following sentence, e.g. *sole ascendente fit dies* ["because the sun is rising it becomes day"], i.e. the rising of the sun is the cause of it being day. Sometimes, however, we use such a construction simply to indicate contemporaneity rather than consequence, e.g. *Socrate legente pugnat Plato* ["while Socrates is reading (abl. abs.), Plato is fighting"]. For Socrates' reading is not the cause of Plato's fighting, but the one action happens at the same time as the other, as if it were *dum Socrates legit, Plato pugnat* ["while (temporal relator) Socrates is reading, Plato is fighting"].

School of Ralph of Beauvais: Gloss Promisimus *on Priscian,* Institutiones *6.1 (GL 2:194.11)*[45]

IF GOD GRANTS LIFE [*deo vitam praebente*] This ablative absolute can be explained in two ways, by means of the conjunction "if" [*si*] and a verb, as follows: "*if* God will have granted life"; or by a temporal adverb, as follows "*as long as* God grants life." For that is how we have to explain that verse in Lucan [4.815] "and to whom, when following the good [*recta sequenti*], the constitution owed more," that is "if he would follow the good." Many times participles like this, which should be explained like this, are used loosely [*dissolute*], so that no construction can be assigned to them, e.g. [Numbers 20,6] "that being satisfied [nom.] their [gen.] murmuring [nom.] may cease"[46] and elsewhere "In order that, placated [nom. sing.] by her intercessions, we may be saved by you [abl. sing.] from the impending perils."[47]

Petrus Helias on Priscian, Institutiones *18.15–16*[48]

We should not ask what part (of speech) requires those ablatives *sole* ["sun"] or *oriente* ["rising"], when one says *sole oriente dies fit* ["when the sun is rising, it becomes day"]. For

---

[45] Text in Hunt, "Studies on Priscian in the Twelfth Century II: The School of Ralph of Beauvais," 74f.

[46] *Satiati cesset murmuratio eorum.* In the Douai translation: "... that being satisfied, they may cease to murmur." *Satiati* (ptc. nom.) and *eorum* (gen.) have the same referent.

[47] Text of prayer *in sanctificatione beatae Mariae Virginis* (e.g. in Missale Praedicatorum, Venetiae 1504): *praesta ... ut ... eius intercessionibus a te de instantibus periculis eruamur.* The insertion of *placatus* between *intercessionibus* and *a te* makes the sentence ungrammatical.

[48] Text in *Summa super Priscianum*, ed. Reilly, 2:1022.65 ff; cf. Thurot, *Notices et extraits*, 247.

they are used absolutely [*absolute*] and are not governed by anything here. The same goes for other absolute constructions.

Alexander of Villa Dei, Doctrinale[49]

There are several ablatives without a word governing them [*rectore soluti*]: "the students must study, while the teacher is reading [*doctore legente,* abl. abs.]."

Gloss Admirantes[50]

THERE ARE ABLATIVES . . . as the Commentator says,[51] when ablatives are used absolutely, they are not deprived of all forms of construction, but they are arranged with each other[52] and are sufficiently determined by each other. The ablative of the participle is resolved into a verb and a congruent noun, e.g. *Sorte legente* ["while Socrates is reading" (abl. abs.)], i.e. *dum Sors legit* ["while Socrates is reading"].[53] So because of the nature of this verb "is reading" and this nominative *Sortes,* the construction is intransitive here, and its meaning is conveyed through ablatives which are used absolutely. This makes it clear that the ablatives in fact do have a construction among themselves, when they are used absolutely. Thus, they are said to be used absolutely because they are free of external dependency. . . . They are not construed . . . with the following verb, but are arranged to indicate discontinuity and coincidence in time.[54] In its own way, the expression "while [*dum*] the teacher is reading" etc. is similar, because the whole phrase "while the teacher is reading" does not express a complete meaning at all, nor does it allow the mind to rest until something else has followed . . . The problem is raised why it is used in the ablative rather than in another

---

[49]   Lines 1339–40, ed. Reichling. Cf. Priscian, *Institutiones* 18.30, *GL* 3:221.25–222.3.

[50]   Text in Thurot, *Notices et extraits,* 325–6. This is a thirteenth-century gloss on the *Doctrinale* by Alexander of Villa Dei (on whom see within, in Part 3, pp. 573–83).

[51]   Petrus Helias.

[52]   *Inter se comparantur:* this seems to indicate primarily that the ablative absolute is, in fact, construed, but internally. But the term *comparantur* also suggests some form of analogy with the ablativus comparationis, which is often discussed in the direct vicinity of the ablative absolute. So in Petrus Helias, *Summa super Priscianum,* ed. Reilly, 2:1022.65–1023.101.

[53]   Sors or Sortes is Socrates. The word may have arisen out of a compendiate abbreviation of the name, but then took on a life of its own in the scholastic period, as did Agellius for Aulus Gellius.

[54]   *Ratione suspensionis et concomitantie.* This is a subtle argument: the ablatives are construed with each other, but there is a break (*suspensio*) between the ablative absolute and the main clause—on the other hand, there is also a relationship of *concomitantia,* accompaniment, i.e. temporal coincidence, between the ablative absolute and the main clause.

case ... The reply must be that here the fact that one act accompanies [*concomitantia*] the other is indicated, since one act is the cause of the other, and the ablative expresses substance as the origin of action or passion. And therefore this construction should be in the ablative case. However, others hold a different opinion and say that the word *dum* ["while"] is understood here, which is synonymous to the word *cum*, which is a preposition taking the ablative case.[55] Since it represents that meaning, therefore, the participle is used in the ablative in these constructions, and not in a different case.

THE FOURTEENTH CENTURY: SIGER OF COURTRAI (D. 1341)

[Siger of Courtrai (Flanders) studied in Paris around 1300, and wrote most of his work in the first quarter of the fourteenth century.[56] He belongs with the *modistae*, but represents a moderate form, rather closer to traditional grammar than the other modists.[57] Among his grammatical works were a *Summa modorum significandi* and the *Sophismata*, the work that concerns us here. A *sophisma* is one of the medieval pedagogical genres and also became a generic term for a university-level exercise in logic. Its starting point is a proposition which "for some reason is odd or has odd consequences," but it may also arise from a phrase which forms the pretext to discuss any matter of interest.[58] In the case of Siger, this interest is mainly grammatical, but the *sophisma* with its back-and-forth of questions and reactions also offers the opportunity to expound the "logico-epistemological tenets presupposed in Siger's linguistic theory."[59] The *sophisma* "Magistro legente pueri proficiunt" is the new pedagogical locus for Siger's treatment of the ablative absolute. Like earlier thirteenth-century commentators on Priscian, Siger discusses the question of government (*regimen*), but he puts this discussion in the new context of the theory of the modes of signifying (*modi significandi*).[60] He also elevates the discussion to the metaphysical and philosophical level by explaining the nature of "governing" as being

[55] This is a fallacy, of course. *Cum* can either be a conjunction, and is then synonymous to *dum*, or a preposition—in which case it takes the ablative. This does not mean that *dum* should necessarily be replaced by an ablative construction.

[56] For his life, see Wallerand, ed., *Les oeuvres de Siger de Courtrai*, 1–8; Pinborg, ed., *Sigerus de Cortraco*, xi–xii.

[57] See Wallerand, ed., *Les oeuvres de Siger de Courtrai*, 34–60; Pinborg, ed., *Sigerus de Cortraco*, xiv.

[58] Pinborg, ed., *Sigerus de Cortraco*, xv, comparing the *Quaestiones quodlibetales*.

[59] Pinborg, ed., *Sigerus de Cortraco*, xv.

[60] For Siger's version of this theory, see Wallerand, ed., *Les oeuvres de Siger de Courtrai*, 34–60; Pinborg, ed., *Sigerus de Cortracio*, introduction. Siger is unusual in his retention of the older notion of *regimen* and makes no attempt to really integrate it into the system of modistic grammar; see Pinborg, ed., xxxiii.

dependent on the relative value of what is governed and what governs. And he frames the whole discussion in terms of areas of competence of the grammarian and the logician: what is grammatical (*congruus*) is not the same question as whether something is true or false. This concern about domains of expertise is characteristic of the teaching in the arts faculties of the universities.[61] In spite of the speculative nature of modist grammar, and its focus on understanding the universal features of language and its causes (rather than on teaching practical language use), the modists do regard themselves as grammarians, not logicians.[62] The structure of the *sophisma* is such that Siger's own view is saved for the last.]

Translated from Thurot, *Notices et extraits*, by permission.

Siger of Courtrai, Sophismata II[63]

WHILE THE MASTER IS READING [ABL. ABS.], THE BOYS ARE MAKING PROGRESS This is an academic problem [*sophisma*] about the question whether the ablative which is said to be construed absolutely is governed by anything.[64]

It would seem [*videtur*] not, since what is absolute, i.e. free from regimen, is not governed. And this is true of the ablative absolute, as is made clear by Petrus Helias. Therefore it is not governed.

Moreover [*praeterea*]: if this ablative is governed, it is either governed by "boys," or by "are making progress," or by the combination. But it is not governed by "boys," because no proportional *modus significandi* is found between "boys" and the ablative.[65] Nor is it governed by "are making progress"; nor by the whole combination, because a *modus significandi* should not be attributed to a sentence, but to a word or part of speech.

Moreover [*praeterea*]: something that is generally maintained is not completely false.[66] But it is generally maintained that the ablative is construed absolutely and without governing part [*regens*]. Therefore it is not governed.

---

[61] See introduction to the selection from the *Barbarismus* commentary (attributed to Kilwardby), within, pp. 724–5; cf. Rosier, "La grammaire dans le '*Guide de l'étudiant.*'"

[62] Cf. Pinborg, ed., *Sigerus de Cortraco*, xxi, and *Sophisma* I, 46–7.

[63] Text in Thurot, *Notices et extraits*, 318–25 (wrongly attributed to Siger of Brabant); cf. Pinborg, ed., *Sigerus de Cortraco*, 49–55; Wallerand, ed., *Les oeuvres de Siger de Courtrai*, 137–43.

[64] Notice how the problem of *regimen* is made central straightaway.

[65] Pinborg, ed., *Sigerus de Cotracto*, xxix: "Two words can only be combined when at least one *modus significandi* of one word is related to a *modus significandi* of the other word. Their relationships are of two kinds: the two words may have identical modes (. . . 'concord' in traditional grammar), or the mode of one word may be proportional to a mode of the other word (. . . 'government' in traditional grammar)."

[66] Aristotle, *Nicomachean Ethics* 10.2.1172b36; 7.13.1153b27.

Moreover [*praeterea*]: theoretical explanations of constructibles cannot be provided by logical entities.[67] But there does not seem to be anything in the ablative absolute that could provide a theoretical explanation for its construction with "the boys are making progress," unless that it is the antecedent, and the other part is the consequent.[68] But those are logical entities. Therefore, it is not governed in any way.

Moreover [*praeterea*]: that item is not governed in any way, to which no *modus significandi* can be attributed in any way. But no *modus significandi* can be attributed in any way to a sentence. Therefore it is not governed in any way. The major premise is obvious. The minor is explained because a *modus significandi* is a simple mental construct.[69] Therefore its object must also be simple. But a sentence is a composite. Therefore etc.

The opposite position [*oppositum*] is argued for thus: a construction is the combination of constructibles. Therefore wherever there is construction and proportional combination,[70] there one also has regimen. But in this sentence that is the case. Therefore, etc.

Moreover [*praeterea*]: everything that is worth less seems to be governed by what is worth more. Now in this sentence one can find something worth less and something worth more. Therefore one can find regimen here.

Moreover [*praeterea*] wherever one may find something that is more and something that is less noble, there one may find regimen. But that is the case in the present problem. Therefore one may find regimen there.

For a discussion of the question [*ad questionem dicendum*] three things are to be understood first. First: what is an ablative; second: what is "absolute"; third: what is "to govern"?

Ad 1 [*circa primum*]: we need to understand that the ablative is a *modus significandi*. Now there is an active and a passive *modus significandi*, an essential and an accidental one, an absolute and a relative one, as is clear from the academic problem [*sophisma*] "To love is a verb" [*Amo est verbum*].[71] In what way the *modi significandi* are the beginning of

---

[67] Mental constructs belong to the domain of the logician.

[68] Priscian also uses the term *consequentia*, but here that term is reserved for the logical domain and hence cannot function in a grammatical explanation of the relation between ablative absolute and main verb. Cf. *Institutiones* 5.80 (*GL* 2:190.23).

[69] *Ens rationis simplex*, cf. Pinborg, ed., *Sigerus de Cortracio*, xxviii.   [70] See above note 65.

[71] See Siger of Courtrai, *Sophismata* I, in Pinborg, ed., *Sigerus de Cortracio*, 41–9. For the different *modi significandi*, see also Pinborg, xxiii–xxvii; Bursill-Hall, *Speculative Grammars of the Middle Ages*. The active *modus significandi* refers to properties of words, the passive *modus significandi* to properties of the signified or conceived objects. The *modus significandi essentialis* determines the subsumption of a word under one of the parts of speech. The *modus significandi accidentalis* refers to the basic grammatical features, or, traditionally, the "accidents" of a word. The absolute mode does not take relations with other words into account, the relational mode implies that the word signifies in a construction with another word (Pinborg, xxix).

construction, and which ones are the beginning of construction [namely the relational ones], this is discussed in that academic problem "To love is a verb." Now the ablative is a *modus significandi*, because its form has the property that through that ablative it designates a *modus essendi* in reality. Its *modus significandi* is accidental, because it is added to a word when that is essentially already complete. And its *modus significandi* is relational, because it is joined to a word in comparisons—relational to the *modus significandi* of another word that is proportional to itself, as will appear below.[72] That *modus significandi* which is the ablative is contained within that accidental *modus significandi* which is "case." For "case" is an accidental, relational *modus significandi* that designates the property of a thing by which one constructible determines the dependence of another. However, under the *modus significandi* "case" come various species of *modi significandi*, which may be paraphrased by adding forms of *qui* to it: thus, the *modus significandi* of the nominative designates in the *modus* of "something" [*ut quod* (nom.)], the genitive of "of someone/ something" [*ut cuius*], the dative of "for someone/something" [*ut cui*], the accusative of "someone" [*ut quem* (acc.)], the vocative in the *modus* of alerting someone, and the ablative of "from someone/something" [*ut a quo*]. So the ablative is an accidental, relational *modus significandi* designating the *modus essendi* of a thing in the way of "from someone/something." And since the *modus essendi* "from someone" is said in many ways, therefore that *modus significandi*, the ablative, because it is in use for that *modus*, has many constructions, as is clear from Priscian in the second book of the *Minor*,[73] for if the cause is multiplied, so is the effect. This resolves the first item, namely what is an ablative.

Ad 2 [*circa secundum*]: we need to understand that "absolute" is used in four ways, as the Commentator[74] has it in commenting on the *Minor*: (1) "absolute" may mean "free from transition," and this is how the substantive and neuter verbs are called absolute by Priscian;[75] (2) "absolute" may mean "free from regimen," as in our problem, but it will appear below how this must be understood; (3) "absolute" may mean "free from contrast" [*a discretione*]; and this is how Priscian can say in the first book of the *Minor* that all oblique cases of the pronouns are "absolute" in Latin;[76] (4) "absolute" may mean "free

---

[72] A reference to the ablativus comparationis which, of course, *is* governed. "Proportional" refers to this relation of governing.

[73] The *Priscianus minor*, the common designation of books 17 and 18 of the *Institutiones*, on construction: here reference is to book 18.

[74] Petrus Helias.

[75] *Verba neutra* have active forms, but no corresponding passive, see e.g. *Institutiones* 8.7, *GL* 2:373.26–8; called "absolute," *Institutiones* 8.23, *GL* 2:389.16; 18.135, *GL* 3:270.10ff; the "substantive verb" is e.g. the verb "to be," e.g. *Institutiones* 17.35, *GL* 3:130.16–25.

[76] See *Institutiones* 17.18, *GL* 3:118.21f.

from determination by an adjective"—thus, substantives are sometimes called "absolute," when they are used to designate the essence, e.g. "man of peace"—or conversely "free from determination by a substantive," e.g. "one, two, three."[77] The way it is used here, "absolute" is a *modus significandi* attributed to a word in such a way that it is somehow free of regimen, as will appear below. This clarifies the second preliminary, namely "what is 'absolute,'" the way it is used here.

Ad 3 [*circa tertium*]: we need to understand that regimen in grammatical entities should be interpreted on the likeness of true "governing." According to the theory of the first book of the *Politics*, wherever there is a multitude the more worthy governs the less worthy.[78] So, as is clear from the eighth book of the *Physics*, and the twelfth book of the *Metaphysics*, in the genus of entities it is possible to reach some first most worthy and noble entity, which governs all entities, namely the first cause or God—this is clear from the book on Causes. Similarly, in the genus of bodies it is possible to reach some one simple body that is worthiest, which governs all other bodies according to some order of divine providence, namely the heavenly body—this is clear from the book *On the Heavens*. Similarly in the genus of animals, one can reach some one animal that is worthiest, which governs all animals, namely man. In the *Physics* it is written that we are the final end.[79] Similarly, within one and the same man, one can reach some one bodily part, which rules all the other members, namely the heart. That is why it is located in the middle, just like a king in his kingdom—this is clear from the book *On Life and Death*.[80] Similarly, in the genus of human virtues, it is possible to reach some one virtue, which governs all the others, namely the potential intellect, or, according to Averroes, the acquired intellect, as is clear from the effort of Avicenna and Algazel.[81] This then makes it clear that in every multitude one governing body [*regimen*] is found. If this directs the others to the right goal, it is called "right government" [*regimen rectum*]; if not, it is not called government, or it is not called right. Now, in parallel to this [*ad similitudinem*] is developed the notion of regimen among the parts of speech, and hence it is possible to reach a part of speech that is most worthy with respect to such a multitude, because it completes the multitude and the sentence. It rightfully governs all the other parts and is not governed by any other part— this is, of course, the verb. Therefore we say in grammar that some words govern but are not governed themselves, and this is how in any sentence, whether complete or incomplete, the more worthy always governs the less worthy. So in grammar, "to govern" is an act of reason [*actus rationis*] that is attributed to a word in as far as it rules one or more other

---

[77] The famous opening of Plato's *Timaeus*.   [78] Aristotle, *Politics,* I 5, 1254a17–1255a2.
[79] Thurot, *Notices et extraits*, 321 n. 2 refers to Aristotle, *Politics* I 8, 1256b16–17.
[80] Aristotle, *De vita et morte* III 469a24.   [81] Avicenna (980–1037); Algazel (Al-Ghazali) (1058–1111).

words in order to achieve the right goal of expressing mental concepts congruently and appropriately. However, the ancient grammarians claimed that "to govern" is to cause a word to be put in the right case, and they attributed regimen to cases: but for the abovementioned reason this should not happen. Thus they said that indeclinable words neither govern nor are governed, which is not true as appears from that other academic problem *o magister*.[82] But they claimed that appellatives both govern and are governed, as in "the hood of Socrates" [*capa Sortis*], and they are right: for every noun signifying its referent in the *modus* of possession rules a genitive case signifying its referent in the *modus* of the possessor—this appears from the second book of the *Minor*.[83] But they said that proper nouns are governed but do not govern themselves. This is not true, for a proper noun governs its adjective. Therefore it is clear now what it is "to govern."

In view of this [*his visis*][84] we should say that the ablative which is said to be used "absolutely," is governed, when we take "to govern" in its proper sense, the way it should be taken. Yet, speaking about regimen in a less proper sense, it is not governed by anything.

The explanation of the former point is that wherever there is construction, there we have a relationship [*proportio*] between many parts. Now, there is a construction between the ablatival signification of an antecedent and the consequent. This appears from Priscian in the second book of the *Minor*, where he calls such a construction of the ablative a construction of consequence.[85] Therefore there is also a relationship between many parts. Now we have said before that in every multitude one necessarily finds some regimen. In the construction discussed here that is the consequent, namely "the boys are making progress." Since what is more worthy and noble governs what is less worthy, and the consequent is more noble than the antecedent, therefore the relationship between consequent and antecedent, which is called "consequence," takes its name from the consequent. Thus that which takes the position of the consequent governs the ablative which takes the position of an antecedent. And as a universal rule the verb governs the rest, as we said before.

Now someone might object: "Everything that is more worthy and noble governs what is less worthy and less noble. But a noun is worthier than a verb, because substance is worthier than accident. This is clear because what is closer to being is worthier; but substance is of that kind; therefore etc. Further, what is more self-sufficient governs [*regit*] the other, because a king [*rex*] must be self-sufficient, as it says in the *Ethics*.[86] But a substantive is more self-sufficient; therefore etc." To this one should reply that although a

---

[82] Siger of Courtrai, *Sophismata* III, ed. Pinborg, *Sigerus de Cortracio*, pp. 55–66. Cf. on this *sophisma*, Rosier, "'*O Magister*...' Grammaticalité et intelligibilité selon un sophisme du XIIIe siècle."

[83] Priscian, *Institutiones* 18.9 *GL* 3:212.29–213.20.   [84] Notice that this is an ablative absolute.

[85] Priscian, *Institutiones* 18, *GL* 3:221ff; the concept of *consequentia* comes from *Institutiones* 5. 80, *GL* 2:190.23.

[86] Aristotle, *Nicomachean Ethics* 8.12, 1160b4.

noun considered by itself is more worthy and noble and more self-sufficient, yet in view of the whole construction the verb is more noble, because it is more closely related to the complete configuration [*forma*]. Now the configuration of a sentence is its composition, as is said in the seventh book of the *Metaphysics*.[87] The verb influences the composition more. Therefore etc.

Therefore it is clear that there is regimen between "while the master is reading" [abl. abs.] and "the boys are making progress" through the proportional *modi significandi*. For one thing signified in the *modus* of the consequent is related proportionally to another thing signified in the *modus significandi* of the ablative as an antecedent. This is clear, since their *modi essendi* are related proportionally, since the *modus essendi* "from someone" is related proportionally as a consequent to the *modus essendi* "from someone" as an antecedent. Now the *modus essendi* "from someone" [*ut a quo*] is the *modus essendi* of the ablative, as we've seen before. Therefore the *modi significandi* are related proportionally. This is what Priscian means, because everything that signifies its referent through the *modus consignificationis* of consequence, governs something that signifies its referent through the *modus* of the ablative as its antecedent.

Now someone might object: "That which properly fits the nominative does not fit the ablative; but the *modus essendi* of that about which something else is enunciated is the *modus significandi* of the nominative, and therefore not of the ablative." To this we must reply that the *modus essendi* of the nominative is the *modus essendi* "something" [*ut quid*], as was pointed out before. The *modus essendi* of that about which something else is enunciated is not proper to the nominative, but it is suitable to other cases, as I said, namely the accusative and the ablative. This therefore makes it clear that there is regimen between these.[88] Similarly there is right government between these through comparison [*per comparationem*] in order to achieve a right goal, to express correctly a mental concept. Someone has in mind that because of the words of the master, the listening boys are making progress; he wishes to express this mental concept of one act following [*consequentiae*] another without a conjunction; and he forms the expression "while the master is reading [abl. abs.], the boys are making progress." For that construction was invented for this purpose that something that expresses its content through the *modus* of an act follows on something that expresses its content similarly through the *modus* of an act, without a conjunction—this is clear from the first book of the *Minor*.[89] This therefore makes it clear that between these there is right government, and through what *modi significandi*: the *modus significandi* of an act by way of consequent, and the *modus significandi* of the

---

[87] Thurot, *ad loc.*, remarks that one could come to this conclusion on the basis of Aristotle's *Metaphysics* VIII 2, 1043a12ff, but *oratio* is not expressly mentioned there.

[88] Namely between "while the master is reading" and "the boys are making progress."

[89] Priscian, *Institutiones* 17.18, *GL* 3:119.15–17.

ablative by way of antecedent. Similarly, it is clear from what *modi essendi* these derive: the *modus essendi* "from someone" [*ut a quo*], namely from the antecedent; and the *modus essendi* of something acting as consequent. This then makes it clear how this construction differs from the other constructions of the ablative.

Now somebody might object: "In saying 'while someone is walking [abl. abs.], there was a flash of lightning' we use an ablative absolute, yet there is no antecedent or consequent, nor is the sentence demonstrative, as is said in the first book of the *Posterior Analytics*."[90] To this we must reply:[91] Given that there is no antecedent or consequent, as long as meaning is conveyed in the *modus* of consequent and antecedent, this suffices for this construction and for the grammarian who considers the *modi significandi*.[92] That is why the grammarian attributes different constructions to the same item under a different *modus significandi*, as is clear from "reading" [*lectio*, noun] and "to read" [*lego*, verb]. Now "to walk" is in no way the antecedent of lightning. Therefore, if the mind should indicate this by means of the sentence just quoted, the relation of consequence is not in order, yet the sentence is grammatical [*congruus*]. And because the ablative must signify in the *modus* of an antecedent, and one ablative cannot signify in the way an antecedent does, therefore there must be two ablatives—and that makes "the master [abl.] the boys are making progress" ungrammatical [*incongrua*]. And because the construction was invented to designate one act following on another one without a conjunction, therefore one ablative must signify in the *modus* of an act. And even if something is antecedent or consequent, if it is not signified through the abovementioned *modi significandi*, it does not suffice to create this construction. And because this construction is called a construction of consequence [*consequentie*], and the following conjunctions *si* ["if"], *dum* ["while"], and *quia* ["since"] signify their content through the *modus* of consequence, therefore this construction may be resolved with their help.[93]

This then resolves the first point [*primum*], namely how the ablative, which is said to be used absolutely, is governed, taking regimen in the proper sense of the word.

The explanation of the second point [*secundi*] is, of course, that, if one takes regimen in a less proper sense, the way the ancient grammarians did, it is said not to be governed, because according to them "to govern" is "to cause a word to be put in the right case"; and since in such a construction one word is not enough, but at the minimum one sentence, as said before, therefore they said that it is used absolutely, and is not governed.

---

[90] Aristotle, *Posterior Analytics*, I 4, 73b12ff.

[91] In what follows, Siger points at the important issue of what is and is not part of the grammarian's competence, cf. the introduction to this section and see the section on [Kilwardby], *Barbarismus* commentary, within, pp. 724–34.

[92] The *modi significandi* are thus part of the *consideratio*, the intellectual domain, of the grammarian. The same term is used in Kilwardby, see previous note.

[93] I.e. the participle construction can be paraphrased analytically with the help of these conjunctions.

This brings us to the arguments [*rationes*]:[94]

1. [*ad primam*,] when it is said: "Everything that is free [*absolutum*] from regimen, is not governed," this is true; and when it is said "such an ablative is of that kind," that is true—if one talks about regimen in a less proper sense of the word. Yet, talking about regimen in the proper sense, as is clear from the above, it is governed.

2. [*ad aliam*,] when it is said: "if that ablative is governed, then it would be either by 'boys', or by 'are making progress,' or by the combination, then we should say it is by the combination"; and when it is said "the combination is a sentence, and no *modus significandi* should be attributed to a sentence," that is false. To the contrary, one should rightly attribute a *modus significandi* to a sentence, qua sentence. For a conjunction is construed through its own *modus significandi* with sentences under the relative *modus significandi*, as is clear about *si* ["if"], *et* ["and"], *vel* ["or"] etc.

3. [*ad aliam*,] when it is said: "constructions should not be accounted for through logical entities," yes, that is true. Yet, if they are considered differently, this is entirely possible. For one and the same thing is rightly considered a principle of construction by the grammarians, but differently by a logician, as is clear when one only looks.

4. [*ad aliam*,] when it is said: "something that is generally maintained is not completely false," that is true, and from what has been said it is clear how it is true and false.

5. Finally [*ad ultimam rationem*]: when it is said: "that to which no *modus significandi* is rightly attributed is not governed," that is true; and when it is said: "no *modus significandi* is rightly attributed to a sentence, that is false, as is apparent from what has been said."

And this reveals the solution of the whole academic problem.

WYCLIFFITE BIBLE, PROLOGUE

Text from *The Holy Bible… made from the Latin Vulgate by John Wycliffe and his Followers*, 1, ed. Forshall and Madden, by permission.[95]

First it is to knowe, that the best translating is out of Latyn into English, to translate aftir the sentence, and not oneli aftir the wordis,[96] so that the sentence be as opin, either [*or*]

---

[94] Cf. the beginning of this text.

[95] Chapter 15, Forshall and Madden, eds., 1:57. In this section, the Wycliffite Bible text is given in the original, and translations follow in brackets.

[96] Discussion of the relative merits of "literal" or "word-for-word" translation versus translating the meaning or sense goes back to Cicero. Especially influential was Jerome's *Liber de optimo genere interpretandi* (*Epistle* 57), ed. Bartelink. See Copeland, *Rhetoric, Hermeneutics, and Translation*, chapters 1 and 2.

openere, in English as in Latyn, and go not fer fro [*far from*] the lettre [i.e. *the literal sense*]; and if the lettre mai not be suid [*followed*] in the translating, let the sentence [*sense*] euere be hool [*complete*] and open, for the wordis owen [*ought*] to serue to the entent [*intention*] and sentence, and ellis [*or else*] the wordis ben superflu either false. In translating into English, manie resolucions moun [*may*] make the sentence open, as an ablatif case absolute may be resoluid into these thre wordis, with couenable verbe, *the while, for, if*, as gramariens seyn; as thus, *the maistir redinge, I stonde*, mai be resoluid thus, *while the maistir redith, I stonde*, either *if the maistir redith*, etc. either *for the maistir*, etc.; and sumtyme it wolde acorde wel with the sentence to be resoluid into *whanne*, either into *aftirward*, thus, *whanne the maistir red, I stood*, either *aftir the maistir red, I stood*; and sumtyme it mai wel be resoluid into a verbe of the same tens, as othere ben in the same resoun, and into this word et, that is, and in English, as thus, *arescentibus hominibus prae timore*,[97] that is, *and men shulen wexe drie for drede*. Also a participle of a present tens, either preterit, of actif vois, eithir passif, mai be resoluid into a verbe of the same tens, and a coniunccioun copulatif, as thus, *dicens*, that is, *seiynge*, mai be resoluid thus, *and seith*, eithir *that seith*; and this wole, in manie placis, make the sentence open, where to Englisshe it after the word, wolde be derk and douteful. Also a relatif, which mai be resoluid into his antecedent with a coniunccioun copulatif, as thus, *which renneth, and he renneth*.

---

[97] Luke 21:26.

ETYMOLOGY DOSSIER

INTRODUCTION

Etymology is a central tool for any ancient and medieval thinker or writer. From classical antiquity onwards, we encounter frequent examples of etymologies of proper names or other words in literary texts.[1] Like genealogy, etymology is a way to ground thinking or interpretation in a tradition. The goal is not to establish historical origins, but to gain a grasp on the present. Not restricted to usage in literature, etymology is a form of thought, speech, and communication. With the development of the discipline of (Greek) grammar, it becomes one of the six canonical tasks of the grammarian, as e.g. in the opening section of our first western European grammar, the *Tekhnê grammatikê* attributed to Dionysius Thrax (second century BC). This task is defined as "the invention of etymology," which is at the same time a prefiguration of the later role of etymology in rhetoric.

In ancient grammar and lexicography, etymology is mainly used to get a better grip on the meaning of a word, because it helps one understand why the word should have that particular meaning, or, put in different words, why the thing has been given that particular name, especially in relation to other expressions in that language.[2] Many etymological formulas will typically feature causal language: a thing has a particular name, because x (*quod, quia*). The reason (*ratio*) or cause (*causa*) for a particular name is x. The relationship between the name or word whose etymology is in question and the explanation may take many forms—which is one of the main reasons why etymology has often come in for modern ridicule. The connection between word and etymology is primarily a semantic one, usually connected with similarity of some kind in form. Letters may be added, taken

---

[1] On ancient etymology, see especially Amsler, *Etymology and Grammatical Discourse in Late Antiquity and the Early Middle Ages*; Herbermann, "Antike Etymologie"; Sluiter, "The Greek Tradition." See further the studies collected in Buridant, ed., *L'étymologie de l'Antiquité à la Renaissance*, and Nifadopoulos, ed., *Etymologia: Studies in Ancient Etymology*. A very useful work of reference is Robert Maltby, *A Lexicon of Ancient Latin Etymologies*. On etymology as a "form of thought" ("Denkform") in the Middle Ages, see Curtius, *European Literature and the Latin Middle Ages*, 495–500.

[2] See Herbermann, "Antike Etymologie," 366.

away, their order may be inverted, or they may be changed into something else entirely.[3] Some syllabic etymologies compose the word in question out of parts of the words that form the explanation.[4] The semantic relationship can be of different kinds. The relationship *a contrario* has often been received very critically: these types of etymologies are based on opposites, as in the famous *lucus a non lucendo* ("a sacred grove [*lucus*] is called that because it is not light [*lucere*] there").[5] However, such cases can more profitably be related to the phenomenon of euphemism, where a favorable word is chosen to avert evil, as in the more common name of the Furies, the "Eumenides" ("Benevolent Ones").[6] Avoiding words of bad omen (which does suggest a semi-magical relation between name and thing) may then lead to *a contrario* usage. In any event, etymology is a highly flexible tool, with little formalized theory.[7]

Etymology has various intellectual functions. It serves a heuristic function: for example, in the case of obscure poetical words it may be a clue to meaning and orthography.[8] It also serves mnemonic purposes by turning words into epistemological archives.[9] The combination of these two turns etymology into a dynamic tool of interpretation and argumentation, which in the course of history subsumes large parts of the language disciplines. In grammar, as we will see, it becomes the locus for teaching morphology and lexicon. In rhetoric, it forms part of *inventio*, and in approaching literature it becomes an interpretive tool, which helps both to find a certain interpretation, to remember it, and to persuade others of its correctness. In dialectic, it is a way to look at the relation between signs and the world.

The most important classical texts on the topic are Plato's *Cratylus* (fourth century BC), Varro's *De lingua latina* (esp. books V–VII) (first century BC), and Augustine's *De dialectica* (fourth/fifth century AD). Plato's dialogue raises the question of whether the etymologies are to be taken seriously,

---

[3] For these four categories of change, see Usener, "Ein altes Lehrgebäude der Philologie," and Ax, "*Quadripertita ratio*: Bemerkungen zur Geschichte eines aktuellen Kategoriensystems (*adiectio-detractio-transmutatio-immutatio*)." They are also at work elsewhere: for example, they shape the systematic explanation for all forms of barbarism: see section on Donatus, above, pp. 93–4. Ultimately, they derive from Aristotelian physics, in which they exhaust the possibilities for change in matter.

[4] One of the examples from the texts below is *cadaver*, which is said to stand for *caro data vermibus* "flesh given over to the worms."

[5] Quintilian, *Institutio oratoria* 1.6.34; Augustine, *De dialectica* 6 (see below) and *De doctrina christiana* 3.29.41; Martianus Capella, *De nuptiis* 4.360. See also the section on *antiphrasis*, one of the species of "allegory" in Donatus, *Ars maior* 3:6, *GL* 4:402 (and see p. 98).

[6] Cf. Sluiter, "The Greek Tradition," 159.

[7] Augustine's *De dialectica* (see below) represents an unusually systematic treatment.

[8] On these two functions, see e.g. Maltby, "The Role of Etymologies in Servius and Donatus," 103–18.

[9] See Carruthers, "Inventional Mnemonics and the Ornaments of Style."

or whether they are meant humorously or as parody. In fact, this may be a false dilemma. Since both in its heuristic and mnemonic forms etymology is not about correct historical derivation, its ends may be equally well served by both. Humor may serve an ultimately serious purpose.[10] Ancient critics of arguments from etymology include Aristotle and Galen.

In this section we present texts by Augustine (*De dialectica*), Isidore of Seville (*Etymologiae*), Petrus Helias (*Summa super Priscianum*), Osbern of Gloucester (*Derivationes*), the gloss *Promisimus*, the gloss *Tria sunt*, Hugutio of Pisa (*Magnae derivationes*), and Joannes Balbus (*Catholicon*).

Augustine's *De dialectica* circulated widely in the Middle Ages and early Renaissance. It was used in the curricula of monastic and cathedral schools as well as universities, especially in the context of logic.[11] The treatise opens with a discussion of simple words, combined words, and simple and combined statements (propositions). In the section dealing with speaking (*loqui*) rather than with "making propositions" (*proloqui*), Augustine distinguishes the concepts of *verbum, dicibile, dictio*, and *res* (chapter 5):[12] *verbum* is a word (-form); *dicibile* is the semantic content of a word; *dictio* is the combination of verbum and *dicibile*, i.e. a word considered as a meaningful expression; *res* is "whatever remains beyond the three that have been mentioned" (the referent). Chapter 6, reproduced in its entirety here, is devoted to the origin of words.[13] It develops a double theory of etymology: names/words are either given on onomatopoetic principles, imitating and reproducing sounds; or they are based on (a) a relationship of similarity between form and content (sounds and things); (b) a relationship of similarity between things among themselves; (c) proximity; or (d) contrariety. It is widely assumed that this chapter mainly goes back to Varro, and it is sometimes listed as one of his "fragments." The last part of *De dialectica* 6 shows etymology in action, both as a constructive tool that uses the force of sounds as building blocks to get a grasp (both heuristically and mnemonically) on the meaning of words, and as an analytical tool that breaks a word into the smallest components that contribute to its meaning. To an ancient etymologist working in this

[10] See below on the etymology of *fenestra* (from Petrus Helias onwards). Whereas earlier etymologies had emphasized the fact that "windows" allow light into a room, Petrus Helias' suggestion treats it as an emergency exit (probably for bored students). That makes it a memorable (as well as funny) illustration of the use of syllabic etymology.

[11] The ascription to Augustine has been disputed. Jackson discusses this question and concludes that the ascription is authentic; see his introduction to Augustine, *De dialectica*, ed. Pinborg, trans. Jackson, 30. On its use in the Middle Ages, see ibid., 18ff.

[12] See Long, "Stoic Linguistics, Plato's *Cratylus*, and Augustine's *De dialectica*," 49–55, with discussion of the Stoic antecedents.

[13] See Allen, "The Stoics on the Origin of Language and the Foundations of Etymology."

Stoic tradition, such a "smallest component" would again be the sound of the "letter," and the associations it carries. After the chapter on the origin of words, Augustine takes up the effect of words, obscurity and ambiguity, and equivocation. Etymology is here fully integrated in a dialectical context.

Isidore of Seville (ca. 560–636) turned "etymologies" into the organizing principle of his sprawling presentation of the encyclopedic knowledge of his day.[14] In the first book of his *Etymologiae* or *Origines*, devoted to grammar, he reserved a separate chapter for "etymology" itself, in this case therefore a part of grammar. By linking etymology to the dynamic practice of *interpretatio* he not only made it a suitable instrument for any reading practice, including that of the Bible, but made it a vehicle for commenting on any aspect of a concept that catches the attention of the analyst. As a central intellectual tool, it could be used to ground all practical knowledge of the world.[15]

Etymology usually functions within the same language; that is, a Latin word, for example, is explained by means of a Latin etymology. At later points in its history, etymology might incorporate the procedures of translation (between languages), and derivation, where all word-forms deriving from the same base word are listed.[16] The latter concept may be considered a pedagogical device related to the teaching of Latin to non-native speakers. In many medieval grammars, the section devoted to *ethimologia* became the locus for discussions of morphology.[17] An excerpt from the *Summa super Priscianum* by Petrus Helias (ca. 1150) presented here shows a scholar in whose work *derivatio* comes up in connection with *ethimologia*; with the following texts in these selections the distinction between and connection of the two concepts becomes a constant and explicit issue.[18] When a distinction between *ethimologia* and *derivatio* is made, *derivatio* refers to "the method of creating etymologically related families of words, in which one is the principal, the others its derivatives," while *ethimologia* remains the discipline of the interpretation of words.[19]

Beginning in the late eleventh century, etymology comes to be closely linked to lexicography. Important texts in this respect are the *Elementarium* of Papias (ca. 1063),

---

[14] See introduction to section on Isidore of Seville, within, pp. 232–4.

[15] Cf. Bloch, *Etymologies and Genealogies*, 55.

[16] Hunt, "The 'Lost' Preface to the *Liber derivationum* of Osbern of Gloucester," 270. In all such cases, there are (late) ancient examples (e.g. Jerome's attention to Hebrew and Greek), but this approach is now systematized. Priscian himself also sometimes collects words with the same stem, and in that sense may have served as a source of inspiration for the practice.

[17] Law, "Linguistics in the Earlier Middle Ages," 191.

[18] Teeuwen, *The Vocabulary of Intellectual Life in the Middle Ages*, 266–7 credits Petrus Helias with the first explicit distinction between *derivatio* and etymology, referring to R. Klinck, *Die lateinische Etymologie des Mittelalters* (1970), 17ff. and Olga Weijers, *Lexicography in the Middle Ages* (1989), 147–8.

[19] Teeuwen, *The Vocabulary of Intellectual Life in the Middle Ages*, 266–7.

Osbern's *Derivationes* (third quarter of the twelfth century), the *Magnae derivationes* by Hugutio (Hugh) of Pisa (end of the twelfth century),[20] and the *Catholicon* by Joannes Balbus of Genoa (end of the thirteenth century). Strikingly, Osbern and Hugh adduce words from the vernacular to explain the Latin lemmata.[21]

Osbern's work comes between the commentary of Petrus Helias on Priscian's *Institutiones* and later glosses on Priscian. In this period there is a growing "vogue for *derivationes*," of which Osbern's work is a result.[22] Language is presented as a stream from which rivers and rivulets branch off. The metaphor of streaming and flowing, both for thought processes and for products of language, is prominent in Osbern's work as well as in that of Joannes Balbus (see below).

The gloss on Priscian known as the "*Promisimus* gloss" (last quarter of the twelfth century; so-called from its opening word) presents two views of etymology. In one *ethimologia, interpretatio, derivatio,* and *compositio* are distinguished, with increased prominence for *derivatio* and *compositio*. The alternative view presented by this glossator is that *ethimologia* and *derivatio* are the same.[23] The *Tria sunt* gloss on Priscian (similarly named for its *incipit*), which was composed slightly later, is also concerned with the relationship between etymology, translation, and derivation.

Hugutio of Pisa (ca. 1190) was bishop of Ferrara and a famous teacher of canonical law. In his *Magnae derivationes*, he deals with a Latin characterized by its bold use of neologisms, which Hugutio connects and groups in fanciful ways in order to make them qualify as *derivationes*. This is a way to turn what Hugutio calls the "natural poverty" of Latin into the flexibility of a modern language.[24] His enthusiastic use of Greek betrays a virtually complete lack of knowledge of that language.[25] Hugutio uses the grammatical and rhetorical tradition (Cicero, Priscian, Martianus Capella), as well as other classical authors (Virgil, Horace, Ovid, Plautus, Terence, Juvenal, Persius, Statius, Lucan, and the church fathers). He probably used Osbern of Gloucester directly.[26] He was very influential: for example, some of Dante's Italian words must be explained with the help of his lexicon.[27]

---

[20] Or *Thesaurus novus latinitatis*, cf. Marigo in Hugutio of Pisa, *Magnae derivationes*, ed. Marigo.

[21] Marigo, 99 n. 5, gives examples involving Italian, French, and German.

[22] Hunt, "The 'Lost' Preface," 273. On the alternative title *Panormia,* see Hunt, 269. Osbern himself refers to his work as "Derivations."

[23] See Hunt, "The 'Lost' Preface," 271f. See Joannes Balbus below.

[24] For the origins of the idea that Latin is naturally less rich than Greek, see Fögen, *Patrii sermonis egestas*. We have encountered this idea in Terentianus Maurus (Part 1, p. 79).

[25] Cf. Marigo in Hugutio of Pisa, *Magnae derivationes*, ed. Marigo, 100, 106f.; notice however the two etymologies of his own name at the end of the prologue (8).

[26] Hunt, "The 'Lost' Preface," 267, 1 and n. 1.   [27] Marigo, 107.

The *Catholicon* of Joannes Balbus (John of Genoa) dates from 1280. Any biographical information we have for Balbus comes from his own work (e.g. provenance from Genoa in the lemma with etymology of *ianua*). Balbus is mostly dependent on Papias and Hugutio, whom he cites regularly;[28] he also uses Eberhard of Béthune.[29] His grammatical sources include Priscian and Donatus, but also Isidore and the church fathers. The *Catholicon* is divided into five parts. The first four follow the division into four parts that replaced the structure of Donatus' *Ars maior* in the Middle Ages: *ortographia*, *prosodia*, *ethimologia*, *diasintastica* ("syntax"). However, the parts as listed in the "list of contents" do not quite correspond to these four. Rather, the first part deals with orthography and letters; the second with matters such as accidents and the syllable; the third part treats *de ethimologia* and the question *an translacio faciat derivacionem*, and goes on to list different kinds of nouns (e.g. adjectives, relatives, collectives, complexives, patronymica, etc.) followed by a section on the verb and the other parts of speech, and further sections on construction and regimen. Here *ethimologia* has become the heading for traditional grammatical teaching on the parts of speech. Part four is dedicated to barbarism, solecism, and figures. The fifth part returns to etymology with a lexicographical turn by adding an alphabetical word list (not just alphabetized according to first letters, but throughout), which gives etymologies for every entry. Joannes Balbus provides a good example of the way glossaries and grammatical works merge: the grammatical part deals in explanations of words, and the lexicon contains grammatical (morphological) rules.[30]

AUGUSTINE, *DE DIALECTICA*[31]

Chapter VI. The Origin of Words

Any word [*verbum*] whatsoever though not its sound [*sonus*]—since its sound belongs to the exercise of dialectic to dispute well about but does not belong to the science of dialectic, just as the speeches of Cicero belong to the exercise of rhetoric but rhetoric itself is not taught by means of those speeches—every word, I say, apart from its sound,

---

[28] Marigo, 100.

[29] On Joannes Balbus, see also Della Casa, "Les glossaires et les traités de grammaire du moyen âge," and on Joannes' sources, 43f. (with n. 43).

[30] Della Casa, "Les glossaires et les traités de grammaire du moyen âge," on Joannes Balbus especially 41ff.

[31] Translation reprinted (with minor adaptations) from Augustine, *De dialectica*, ed. Pinborg, trans. Jackson, by permission.

necessarily raises questions about four things: its origin [*originem suam*], force [*vim*], declension [*declinationem*], and arrangement [*ordinationem*].[32]

We ask about the origin of a word when we ask why it is called such and such; but in my opinion this is more a matter of curiosity than necessity. And I do not feel that I am bound to say this because it is the opinion of Cicero.[33] For who needs authority in such a clear matter? Even though it is a great help to explicate the origin of a word, it is useless to start on a task whose prosecution would go on indefinitely. For who is able to discover why anything is called what it is called? Discerning the origin of words is like the interpretation of dreams; it is a matter of each man's ingenuity. Let us take as an example *verbum* itself. One man thinks that *verba* are so called because, as it were, they *verberent* ["strike or reverberate on"] the ear; another man says no, they reverberate on the air. But what difference does this make to us? Their dispute is not great, for in either case the word is derived from *verberare*.[34] But a third man introduces a dispute. He says that we ought to speak what is true [*verum . . . loqui*][35] and that the judgment of nature finds a lie hateful; therefore *verbum* is named from *verum* ["true"]. And there is a fourth piece of cleverness, for there are those who agree that a *verbum* is named from *verum*, but think that attention should not be directed to the first syllable to the neglect of the second. For when we say *verbum*, they surmise, the first syllable signifies what is true, the second sound. And this latter they decide is *bum*. Thus Ennius calls the sound of hooves *bombum pedum*; and in Greek "to shout" is βοῆσαι [*boêsai*]. And Virgil says *reboant silvae* ["the woods resound"].[36] Therefore, *verbum* is derived, as it were, from *verum boare*, that is, from a sounding of what is true. If this be so, this word *verbum* certainly forbids us to lie when we produce a word. But I am afraid that those who say this are lying. Consequently it is up to you to judge whether you think *verbum* comes from *verberare* or from *verum* alone or from *verum*

---

[32] Augustine uses *declinatio* for "changes in both the inflection and the function of words" (*De dialectica*, 127 n. 2 [Jackson]). Three of these topics (*origo*, *declinatio*, and *ordinatio*) are the organizing principles of Varro's *De lingua latina*. In Varro, *declinatio* is grammatical inflection and other forms of word change. *Ordinatio* (the actual term used in Varro is *coniunctio*) is syntax. See Jackson's note 2, cited above, which also refers to Barwick, *Probleme der Stoischen Sprachlehre und Rhetorik*.

[33] Cicero, *De natura deorum* 3.24.61–3.

[34] Jackson prefers to render constructions like *a verberando* as "from *verberans*"; we have substituted the infinitive throughout. For the etymology from *verberare*, see e.g. Quintilian, *Institutio oratoria* 1.6.34; Priscian, *Institutiones* 8.1, GL 2:369.6; Isidore, *Etymologiae* 1.9.1 and *saepius*. Cf. Maltby, *Lexicon*, s.v. *verbum*.

[35] Note that this also seems to allude to the etymology of *etymologia* as *veri-loquium*. For the derivation of *verbum* from *veritas*, cf. Varro *apud* Donatus, commentary on Terence, *Andria* 952: *verbum dixit veram sententiam, nam verba a veritate dicta esse testis est Varro*.

[36] Virgil, *Georgics* 3.223. Cf. also the etymology of *vox*, where there is recourse to Greek *boaô*: see Priscian, *Institutiones* 1.1, GL 2:6.4–5.

boare or whether its origin is a matter of indifference so long as we understand what it signifies.

Nevertheless I do wish for you to consider for a little while this topic which we have indicated briefly, namely, the origin of words, so that we might not seem to neglect any part of the work we have begun. The Stoics, whom Cicero ridicules in this matter, as only Cicero can, think that there is no word whose definite origin cannot be explained. Because it would be easy to refute them by saying that this would be an infinite process, for by whichever words you interpret the origin of any one word, the origin of these words would in turn have to be sought, they assert that you must search until you arrive at some similarity of the sound of the word to the thing, as when we say "the clang of bronze," "the whinnying of horses," "the bleating of sheep," "the blare of trumpets," "the rattle of chains."[37] For you clearly see that these words sound like the things themselves which are signified by these words. But since there are things which do not make sounds, in these touch is the basis for similarity. If the things touch the sense smoothly or roughly, the smoothness or roughness of the letters will produce names for those things in accordance with how smoothly or roughly the letters touch the hearing. For example, *lene* ["smoothly"] itself has a smooth sound. Likewise, who does not by the name itself judge *asperitas* ["roughness"] to be rough? It is gentle to the ears when we say *voluptas* ["pleasure"]; it is harsh when we say *crux* ["cross"]. Thus the words are perceived in the way the things themselves affect us. Just as honey itself affects the taste pleasantly, so its name, *mel*, affects the hearing smoothly. *Acre* ["bitter"] is harsh in both ways. Just as the words *lana* ["wool"] and *vepres* ["brambles"] are heard, so the things themselves are felt. The Stoics believed that these cases where the impression made on the senses by the things is in harmony with the impression made on the senses by the sounds are, as it were, the cradle of words [*cunabula verborum*]. From this point they believed that the license for naming had proceeded to the similarity of things themselves to each other. For example, take the words *crux* ["cross"] and *crura* ["legs"].[38] A *crux* is so called because the harshness of the word itself agrees with the harshness of the pain which the cross produces. On the other hand, *crura* ["legs"] are so called not on account of the harshness of pain but because their length and hardness as compared with other members is more similar to the wood of the cross. Next we come to the transferred use [*abusionem*] of words, when a name is borrowed not from a similar thing but, as it were, from a nearby thing. For what similarity is there between the signification of *parvum* ["small"] and the signification of *minutum*

---

[37] I.e., analysis should go on until an onomatopoetic principle is found. This principle is then extended from sound to qualities that affect the other senses.

[38] Jackson (*De dialectica*, 128) notes that the similarity is particularly obvious in the singular: *crux* (cross) and *crus* (leg).

["diminished"], since something can be small which is not only in no way diminished, but has even grown somewhat?[39] Nevertheless we say *minutum* for *parvum* according to a certain proximity of signification. But this transferred use [*abusio*] of a name is within the discretion of the speaker, for he has the word *parvum* and need not use *minutum*. This bears more on what I now wish to show, namely, that when *piscina* ["fish-pond," "swimming pool"] is applied to baths, in which there are no fish and nothing like fish, the baths are, nevertheless, named from *pisces* ["fish"] because they contain water, in which fish live.[40] Thus the term is not applied by any similarity but is borrowed because of a certain proximity. But if someone should think that men are like fish because they swim and that the term *piscina* comes from this, it is foolish to oppose his theory, since neither explanation is incongruous with the thing and each is obscure.[41] It is fortunate that we can see by means of this one example the difference between the origin of a word drawn from proximity and the origin of a word derived from similarity. We can thus move on to contrariety. It is thought that a *lucus* ["sacred grove"] is so called because *minime luceat* ["it has little light"];[42] and *bellum* ["war"] because it is not *bella* ["pretty"]; and a *foedus* ["alliance"] has that name because the thing is not *foeda* ["dishonorable"].[43] But if, as many think, *foedus* is named from *foeditas porci* ["the filthiness of the pig"] then its origin is based on the proximity we were talking about, since that which is made is named from that by which it is made.[44] Proximity is a broad notion which can be divided into many aspects: (1) from influence, as in the present instance in which an alliance is made through the filthiness of the pig; (2) from effects, as *puteus* ["a well"] is named, it is believed, from its effect, *potatio* ["drinking"]; (3) from that which contains, as *urbs* ["city"] is named from the *orbis* ["circle"] which was by ancient custom plowed around the area after taking auspices at the place (Virgil mentions where "Aeneas laid out the city by plowing");[45] (4) from that which is contained, as it is affirmed that by changing a letter *horreum* ["granary"]

---

[39] Translation slightly adapted.

[40] For the relationship between *piscina* and *pisces*, cf. Augustine, *De doctrina christiana* 3.29.40 and Donatus, *Ars maior* 3.6, *GL* 4:400, on tropes, where it is an example of *abusio* or *catachresis*: a word is not used in a "literal" or "proper" sense, but on the other hand there simply is no more proper term to designate the thing (the word for "swimming pool" is always *piscina*).

[41] I.e., the truth of neither can be demonstrated.   [42] Cf. introductory note to this section.

[43] Translation slightly adapted to bring out the opposition between *nomen* and *res*.

[44] The explanation of the origin of *foedus* is deemed obscure by Jackson, *De dialectica*, trans., 128. However, the idea is clearly that through the *foeditas porci* (i.e. by means of a filthy pig), treaties are concluded: reference is to the customary sacrifice. Cf. Varro, *De re rustica* 2.4.9, where the Greek word for pig, ὗς, is derived from θύειν, "to sacrifice." Varro claims pigs were the oldest sacrificial animals. A trace of this is to be found in the fact *quod initiis Pacis f<o>edus cum feritur, porcus occiditur* "that at the beginning of Peace, when a treaty is concluded, a pig is sacrificed." Cf. Livy, *Ab urbe condita*, 1.24.7–9 for such a sacrifice.

[45] Virgil, *Aeneid* 5.755.

is named after *hordeum* ["barley"]; (5) or by transference [*abusionem*], as when we say *horreum* and yet it is *triticum* ["wheat"] that is preserved there;[46] (6) or the whole from a part, as when we call a *gladium* ["sword"] by the name *mucro* ["point" > "sword"], which is the terminating part of the sword;[47] (7) or the part from the whole, as when a *capillus* ["hair"] is named from *capitis pilus* ["hair of the head"]. Why continue?[48] Whatever else is added you will see that the origin of a word is contained either in the similarity of things and sounds, in the similarity of things themselves, in their proximity, or in their contrariety.[49]

We cannot pursue the origin of a word beyond a similarity of sound, and at times we are unable to do even this. For there are innumerable words for which there either is no origin that one could give an account of,[50] as I believe, or for which it is hidden, as the Stoics maintain.

But now consider for a moment the way in which the Stoics think they arrive at that cradle or root [*stirpem*] of words, or more precisely the seed [*sementum*] of words, beyond which they deny that the origin can be sought or that anything can be found even if someone wishes to search. No one denies that syllables in which the letter V functions as a consonant produce a dense and powerful kind of sound, for example, in the first syllable of the words *vafer* ["clever"], *velum* ["sail"], *vinum* ["wine"], *vomis* ["plough"], *vulnus* ["wound"].[51] Thus ordinary usage approves our removing this sound from certain words lest they oppress the ear. For this reason we say *amasti* ["you loved"] more readily than *amavisti* ["you loved"] and *abiit* ["he went away"], not *abivit* ["he went away"]. There are innumerable examples of this. Therefore when we say *vis* ["force"], the sound of the word is, as I said, in a way powerful, congruous with the thing signified. We can see that chains are called *vincula* from a proximity with that which they do,[52] that is, because they are *violenta* ["forcible"] and that a *vimen* ["withe"] is so called because by it something *vinciatur* ["is bound"]. Then, *vites* ["vines"] are so named because they seize the stakes which they press upon by entwining. On account of this Terence called a bent old man *vietum* ["withered"] by similarity.[53] Further, the ground which is winding and worn by the feet of travelers is called *via* ["road"]. If it is thought to be called *via* more because it is worn by the *vis* ["force"] of feet, then the origin of the word returns to the realm of

---

[46] Where the name of the storage facility seems to indicate a different kind of grain than is actually being stored there.

[47] The topic of the "origins" of words extends beyond what we would consider "etymological" in a stricter sense to encompass a notion of "part and whole" here.

[48] Translation adapted.   [49] Translation slightly adapted.   [50] Translation slightly adapted.

[51] In this section, Augustine first explains the development of several words on the basis of the properties of the sound V and the procedures of similarity and proximity. He then imagines a dialogue with someone who pursues the way back from the most complex word to the letter V. Translation slightly adapted to reflect this dialectical process.

[52] I.e., the first category distinguished above.   [53] Terence, *Eunuchus* IV 4.21.

proximity. But let us derive it from a likeness to a vine or a withe, that is, from its winding. So someone asks me: "why is a road called *via*?" I answer, from winding, because the ancients called what is wound or bent *vietus* ["withered"]. For this reason they called the woods of wheels which are encircled by iron *vieti*. The questioner pursues: "Why is something bent called *vietus*?" And to this I answer, from the similarity to *vites* ["vines"]. He insists and wants to know why a *vitis* has this name. I say that it is because it *vincit* ["binds"] that which it lays hold of. He inquires why *vincire* itself is called that. We say, from *vis*. He will ask "why is it called *vis*?" He will be told the reason is that the word, with its robust and powerful sound, is congruent with the thing that is signified. That ends his questions. It is useless to inquire about the number of ways in which the origin of words is varied by the alteration of utterances, for such an inquiry is long and it is not as crucial as these matters of which we have spoken.

ISIDORE OF SEVILLE, *ETYMOLOGIAE* (FROM BOOK 1, ON GRAMMAR)[54]

xxix. Etymology[55]

1. Etymology is the origin of words, when the meaning of a word or a name is established through interpretation.[56] Aristotle called this *symbolon*, Cicero *annotatio*

---

[54] Translated from *Isidori Hispalensis Episcopi Etymologiarum sive originum libri xx*, ed. Lindsay, by permission. For further information on Isidore's grammar, see the introduction to the section on Isidore, within, pp. 232–4.

[55] On this chapter, see Amsler, *Etymology and Grammatical Discourse*, 133–72; Fontaine, "Aux sources de la lexicographie médiévale," and "Cohérence et originalité de l'étymologie isidorienne"; Schweickard, "'*Etymologia est origo vocabularum*'"; Codoñer Merino "'Origines' o 'Etymologiae'?"; Valastro Canale, "Isidoro di Siviglia: la vis verbi come riflesso dell' omnipotenza divina,"149ff. The sources for this chapter are (ultimately) Aristotle and Cicero (*Topica* 35), Quintilian, *Institutio oratoria* 1.6.28, and Boethius' commentary on Cicero's *Topics*. Disciplinary influence comes from grammar (technical), rhetoric (use in argument), philosophy (epistemological connection of etymology), folk-linguistics, biblical exegesis, and pedagogy (in that etymology serves the purposes of clarification and memory).

[56] *Vis verbi vel nominis*: this could, of course, also be rendered: the meaning of a verb or a noun (cf. just below in the same section). For the more general translation, cf. Amsler, *Etymology and Grammatical Discourse*, 139f. *Interpretatio* is the dynamic moment which establishes the static *origo* in a process of *inventio*, Schweickard, "'*Etymologia est origo vocabularum*,'" 3; Valastro Canale, "Isidoro di Siviglia," 160. Schweickard's proposal to change *origo* into *originatio* in order to make both halves of the definition dynamic is unnecessary. The opening of *Etymologies*, book 10 seems to protect the traditional reading (cf. Magallon, review of Barney et al., *Etymologies*, *TMR* 07.05.30, 2007). Fontaine, "Aux sources de la lexicographie médiévale," 100–1 emphasizes the importance of the etymological *process* rather than the *results*.

["annotation"],[57] because it makes names and words for things *nota* "known" by giving an example. E.g. *flumen* ["river"] is called that from the word *fluere* ["to flow"] because it increases *fluendo* ["by flowing"].[58]

2. Knowledge of this fact often has a necessary use in interpreting. For once you have seen what the origin of a word is, you understand its meaning more quickly. The examination of anything is clearer once its etymology is known.[59] It is not the case however that all names have been imposed by the ancients according to nature; some have also been given arbitrarily, just as we too sometimes give names to our slaves and possessions just as we please.[60]

3. This explains why an etymology cannot be found for every name, since some things have acquired names not according to their quality, how they are by nature, but on account of a decision of the human will. The etymologies of names are either given on the basis of their cause, e.g. *reges* ["kings"] from *recte agere* ["acting correctly"], or on the basis of their origin, e.g. *homo* ["man"] because he is *ex humo* ["made of dirt"], or on the basis of the contrary, e.g. *lutum* ["mud"] from *lavare* ["to wash"], whereas mud is not clean, and *lucus* ["grove"] because it is darkened by shadows and hardly *luceat* ["shines"].[61]

4. Some are made by derivation of nouns, e.g. *prudens* "prudent" from *prudentia* "prudence"; some also because of the sounds [*ex vocibus*], such as "chattering" [*garrulus*]

---

[57] Cf. Cicero, *Topica* 8.35 (where the term used is *notatio*, not *annotatio*, from this passage the reference to Aristotle's *sumbolon* is also taken): *Multa enim ex notatione sumuntur. Ea est autem, cum ex vi nominis argumentum elicitur; quam Graeci* etumologian *appellant, id est verbum ex verbo veriloquium; nos autem novitatem verbi non satis apti fugientes genus hoc notationem appellamus quia sunt verba rerum notae. Itaque hoc idem Aristoteles* sumbolon *appellat, quod Latine est nota.* "Many things are taken from the etymology (*notatio*). Etymology is, when an argument is derived from the meaning of a word. The Greeks call it *etymologia*, the literal equivalent of which is *veriloquium* 'true speech.' However, we prefer to avoid the unusualness of a word which is not quite fitting, and call this kind *notatio* 'signing,' because words are the signs of things. That is why Aristotle calls this *symbolon* [cf. Aristotle, *De interpretatione* 16a; rendered very freely], which in Latin is *nota*." Isidore derives this passage from Quintilian, *Institutio oratoria* 1.6.28. The change of Ciceronian *notatio* into *annotatio* turns etymology into the central intellectual activity. Whereas *notatio* refers to the designating (or connoting) power of words, *annotatio* is a "commenting" procedure that allows any kind of observation to be subsumed under the practice of etymology (so Fontaine, "Aux sources de la lexicographie médiévale," 101; and Fontaine, *Isidore de Séville: genèse et originalité*, 186–7).

[58] Maltby, *Lexicon* s.v. offers parallels from Varro, *De lingua latina* 5.27 and Priscian, *Institutiones* 4.16, *GL* 2:126.7.

[59] In fact, this is the hermeneutic principle on which the *Etymologiae* was composed.

[60] The philosopher Diodorus Cronus tried to prove that even *sundesmoi* ("conjunctions," particles, and some adverbs) could have (lexical) meaning. He therefore gave his slaves the names of conjunctions. This is also an example of the arbitrary imposition of names. Cf. e.g. Ammonius on Aristotle, *De interpretatione*, ed. A. Busse, *CAG* IV.5:38,17–20; Simplicius on Aristotle, *Categories,* ed. K. Kalbfleisch, *CAG* VIII:27,18–21; Stephanus Alexandrinus on Aristotle, *De interpretatione*, ed. M. Hayduck, *CAG* XVIII.3:9,21–4.

[61] See the introductory note above, p. 340 for such etymologies *a contrario*.

from "loquacity" [*garrulitate*];[62] some originate from a Greek etymology and are made into Latin forms, e.g. *silva* ["wood"], *domus* ["house"].[63]

5. Other things have acquired their names from the names for places, cities, or rivers. Many are called whatever the language of different peoples calls them.[64] That means their origin can hardly be seen. For a great many names are foreign (*barbara*) and unknown to Latins and Greeks.

PETRUS HELIAS, *SUMMA SUPER PRISCIANUM* I 2[65]

Now, since it remains to give the etymology [*ethimologiam*] of this word *vox*, we will first briefly deal with the matter of what *ethimologia* is. *Ethimologia*, then, is the expounding of a word through either one or more other words which are better known,[66] in accordance with the characteristics of the thing designated [*secundum rei proprietatem*] and the similarity of the letters, e.g. *lapis* ["stone"] as if it were *ledens pedem* ["hurting the foot"],[67] *fenestra* ["window"] as if it were *ferens nos extra* ["taking us outside"].[68] For in

---

[62] The sentence is very imprecise, but reference here is to onomatopoetic formation, with both *garrulus* and *garrulitas* somehow being related to *graculus* "jackdaw," whose name is related to the noise it produces, as is clear from Isidore, *Etymologiae*, 10.114 and 12.7.45. In that latter passage, the etymology of *graculus* from "gregarious flight" is rejected (it was defended by Varro, *De lingua latina* 5.76): "*graculus* ['jackdaw'] . . . not, as some claim, because they fly in formation [*gregatim volent*]; for it is manifest that they get their name from their sound [*ex voce*]." Cf. also Quintilian, *Institutio oratoria* 1.6.37.

[63] Varro, *De lingua latina* 5.160, *domus Graecum*: "*domus* ['house'] is a Greek word"; Priscian, *Partitiones*, GL 3:505.32; Isidore, *Etymologiae* 9.4.3; 15.3.1 "the word *domus* ['house'] comes from a Greek name; for the Greeks call houses *dòmata*"; for *silva*, see Sextus Pompeius Festus, *De verborum significatu quae supersunt cum Pauli epitome*, ed. Lindsay, 290 (*hulas*); Isidore, 17.6.5 where it is derived not from Greek *hulê* "material, wood," but from Greek *xulon* "wood."

[64] A reference to loan words.

[65] Translated from *Summa super Priscianum*, ed. Reilly, 1:70.86–71.103, by permission; Cf. Thurot, *Notices et extraits*, 146f. (XXII 2); text in Hunt, "The 'Lost' Preface," 271, from Paris, Bibl. de l'Arsenal 711, fol. 2rb.

[66] Petrus Helias' view of etymology demonstrates both how the technique functions as part of *inventio* and as a pedagogical tool. He sees it as a clarificatory procedure, reminiscent of the technique of substituting something more familiar to explain something obscure. In the Greek rhetorical tradition, starting with Aristotle's *Topics* (e.g. 111a8), this technique was known as *metalêpsis*, and it was adopted by the grammarians (notably Apollonius Dyscolus) in order to ascertain the meaning of a word. Aristotle explicitly warns against using something *less* familiar (*Topics* 149a5ff.). The commentator Alexander of Aphrodisias (2nd cent. AD) subsumed the etymological procedure under this technique of substitution (*in Aristotelis Topica*, ed. M. Wallies, *CAG* II.2: 175.18). "Substitution" could also take the form of a definition. See on this topic Sluiter, *Ancient Grammar in Context*, 111–13, with n. 274.

[67] Cf. Isidore, *Etymologiae* 16.3.1 *lapis . . . dictus quod **laedat pedem***, an example of syllabic etymology.

[68] This etymology has no ancient pedigree, and given the unorthodox use of a window, it looks like an effective use of schoolboy humor for mnemonic purposes.

this case attention is paid to the character of the thing designated and to the similarity of the letters. *Ethimologia* is a compound word, from *ethimo*, which is translated "true" and *logos*, which means "speech," so that it is called *ethimologia* as in "true speech" [*veriloquium*]. For he who etymologizes assigns the true, that is, the first, origin of the word. It differs from *interpretatio*,[69] which is translation from one language into another. Etymology however mostly takes place within the same language.

The word *vox*, then, either comes *a vocando* ["from calling"], because etymology also sometimes follows derivation [*derivationem*], or *apo toy boo*, that is from the Greek verb *boo* ["to call"], with a change of the letter b into the consonant u, and of the o into x.[70] Note that *apo* is Greek for *ab* in Latin; *toy* is the article, and means the same as *hoc* ["the," "this"]. Hence *apo toy boo*, that is, from [*ab*] that [*hoc*] which is *boo*, which is translated "sound." Hence we find the compound *reboo*, *reboas*, *resono*, *-nas*, as in the hymn: Glory resounds [*reboat*] in the whole world.

OSBERN OF GLOUCESTER, DERIVATIONES[71]

Preface

Greetings to the venerable father Hamelinus,[72] through the grace of God abbot of Gloucester, from his devoted Osbern.

The book which they call *Derivations*, which you, too, dearly beloved Father, have frequently worked through in the service of learning in order to instruct those without much understanding, I started writing as a young man. But only as an old man did I put the last touch to it, though not because I spent so much time in constant work on this text. Good and bad fortune took turns in necessitating breaks from it, and I also devoted attention to other work in the meantime, when that was necessary.

Of course you know that as different people pursue different studies, so different people have different ways of approaching the advancement of this science, as long as they are all competent in deriving forms. Some follow the standard methods, but yet come up with

---

[69] Note that here a distinction is drawn between *interpretatio* and *ethimologia*, whereas in Isidore, *Etymologiae* 1.29 they formed part of the same technique.

[70] See Priscian, *Institutiones* 1.1, *GL* 2:6.4f. for this double etymology *a vocando*, and cf. Augustine, *De dialectica* 6, above.

[71] Translated from Hunt, "The 'Lost' Preface,", 275–7, by permission.

[72] Abbot of Gloucester, 1148–1179.

subtle and very rare words to teach to the young. Others definitely perceive more important things in their studies and seem to have a better grasp of this science; they extend themselves in manifold ways into the manifold channels of deriving.[73] It is a sound and very useful discipline, extremely conducive to the formation of the minds of beginners. The best ancient minds exerted themselves over its many lessons [*institutiones*]; it leads along certain steps upwards to the highest perfection in the knowledge of Latin [*latialis scientie*]. And just as it is impossible for anyone to be vigorous without art, or perfect without virtue, so it is hard to know the deep secrets of Latin without knowledge of this art.

Our forefathers acknowledged this, prominent because of their antiquity and eminent through the perfection of their wisdom. They show us the discipline of learning and the form of wisdom. For just as in building a tower the biggest stones are used as the foundation to shore up the whole weight, the rest of the construction progressing more openly and directly through this,[74] so they also established the art of this science as the first foundation of Latin instruction, so that it becomes easier to arrive at the top of the tower of Latinity once this science has been fully grasped in one's studies. They set the standard of such an excellent art and they were its mirror, they extolled it with the highest praise, and they gave over this science in many different ways to the common instruction of all.

However, most of our contemporaries, who think they are knowledgeable, are completely foolish and do not follow them at all. They imitate themselves rather than the authority of these great predecessors, and talk in an incomplete and imperfect way about this art. Confusing everything, they often lapse into error. Therefore, I decided to revise my *Derivations* anew and perfect it in accordance with the copiousness of all words. In this I did not just follow the ancients, who were the keys to them and helped me judge them, but also some moderns, who through their knowledge of this important science were influential in the progress of Latinity.

As far as we are concerned, the ancients are Donatus, Cornutus, Probus,[75] and Priscian, and the many others who took over from their learned predecessors the suitable inductions, natural origins, proper forms, and true analogies expressed in the regular way, and bequeathed them to the army of their successors.[76] The "moderns," so to speak, that is,

---

[73] *in multiplices se derivandi rivos multipliciter extendunt.* The verb *derivare*, "to derive" is itself derived from *rivus*, "river," and refers to diverting streams of water. The *derivatores* here "branch off" into all kinds of "channels of derivation." For the importance of the metaphor of the river, see below (Osbern on *amnis*, and Hugutio of Pisa.)

[74] "Openly" because the superstructure will be more visible than the foundation.

[75] Hunt, "The 'Lost' Preface," 274, warns us not to take these as the first-century AD African grammarian L. Annaeus Cornutus and the Syrian M. Valerius Probus, but the glossators on Persius and Juvenal, Lucan and Virgil, to whom these names are attached in the medieval manuscript tradition.

[76] For the notion of scholarship as military service, see also the beginning of Osbern's letter.

those who lived close to our own time in the recent past, and as it were a little while ago, are Servius in his commentary on Virgil,[77] Remigius in his commentary on Donatus, Isidore,[78] Rabanus in his book on Etymologies,[79] and John Scotus on Martianus.[80] There are others as well, the younger the brighter,[81] through whose learning the science has been perfected. In their time they made an enormous effort to instruct us, who are almost deprived of knowledge of Latin. These I emulate, and innumerable others too, whose names I have left out in order not to bore my reader. I imitate them as closely as possible and have excerpted from the books of each of them, which I have often reread and worked through, all the most useful things. I have also added everywhere the different derivations given by different authors, insofar as they had appropriate and sound views on this art. And I have presented to the reader whatever flowed forth out of my own ingenuity in such a way that in no way did I omit any good suggestions from others. I focused on this work's usefulness and necessity in consolidating those parts[82] which form the subtle usage [*tenues*] of the more serious scholars of our time, and of the less commonly read authorities among the authors and philosophers, including the authoritative usage of the divine books, and of those historiographers who often talk about these things, in the hope that when these words are read and dealt with more frequently, these authors will create a common usage of what was not usual to them at all, and that the book may be the more welcome and accepted to the degree that it truly blossoms with the attested usage of all authors [*auctores*].[83]

Let it not escape the reader that I had composed another book of *Derivations* as soon as I had left behind the whip of the schoolmaster and had joined a monastery, in order to correct those who were wrong in their explanations of words, and who were so confused that they made their understanding in all aspects incongruous and absurd. It was an outstanding work, prepared with the greatest care, but it was stolen from me by someone suffering from the pest of jealousy.[84] To prevent the charge of the competition that I had

---

[77] A surprising and unexplained entry under the *moderni*.   [78] Also hardly a "modernus."

[79] Rabanus Maurus (d. 856) wrote an encyclopedic work, *De naturis rerum*, almost completely dependent on the *Etymologiae* of Isidore of Seville.

[80] The commentary by John Scotus Eriugena on Martianus Capella did not circulate widely (Hunt, "The 'Lost' Preface," 274).

[81] Cf. Priscian's letter of dedication to the consul Julian, *GL* 2:1.7.

[82] I.e. in adducing attestations for those words (parts of speech).

[83] We thank Dr Christoph Pieper for helpful discussion of this passage. This sentence is a fine example of Osbern's lurid style.

[84] Osbern seems to be going one better than his example Priscian here, who merely complains that he had to publish his work more quickly than he would have liked because people were trying to steal it and pass it off as their own: see *Institutiones, GL* 2:2.16ff.

given my words to the wind and so that it would not seem I had started such a great and useful work for nothing, I started again with the same book and did not just restore it to a state of much greater perfection than it had before, but even doubled its size. I did this both because those closest to me who were aware of my most intimate thoughts urged this labor on me, and because I knew that this would be welcome and very necessary for those who keep consulting different volumes.

So I wrote two elegant treatises, each in alphabetical order. In the first I describe the origins, forms, compositions, and proper understanding of all words from which anything originates through derivation. In the second, I present separately, and clearly ordered, all the words that are considered more difficult, and I set out in how many ways they are used in Scripture. So anyone who entertains doubts about the nature of these words or has any hesitation about their meaning will have them ready and, so to speak, at hand in this work. However, if anyone who is quick of understanding and motivated to study finds many things in this work that he has never come across in reading or has never heard, let him not be surprised. Nor let him abhor whatever is offered here as frivolous or fictive, but let him remember that many things are worth narrating that were important to the ancients: they may be unknown to the lazy and the lax, but that does not mean they should be held cheap by reasonable people. For if I have read in school only some books by modern authors (themselves few and far between), and have not become familiar with the pursuits of the ancients, if I have not noticed the wisdom of philosophical doctrine, have not read either the contents of the divine books or the various histories or the manifold commentaries by many authors—what criterion do I have then, if I've never seen those, to reject what I don't know, and to think that because they are no part of my own active usage, they should not be used at all and must not be taken up by anyone else? No: it behooves a sound head and an alert mind to call everything that is not known back to mind and rehearse it in one's head. By going over it many times we will make it known to us, and whatever has lapsed from use through laziness will be worked over again and again in reading and hearing it, so that it is not just not new anymore, but even familiar, and we can give it back to ourselves to use.

Most sincere father, to your censure I have given over this work. Although it is the product of my labor over which I have exerted myself such a long time, it is up to your commendation, to whom it is given, for I have finally perfected it to honor you. I followed Martianus Capella in introducing grammar herself as a speaking character. Just as he speaks about the liberal arts and brings on the individual ones as individual characters speaking in their own voice, so I, too, in dealing with good Latin, for the greater part of the work have made mother Latinity herself hold forth from the depths of knowledge itself, as if from a greater authority.

s.v. Amnis[85]

Amnis, -is ["river"], that is, "water"; hence the diminutive *amniculus*, [gen.] *-li* ["rivulet"], and *amnicus, -a, -um* ["of a river"], and masculine *amnenses*, [gen.] *-is*, that is, "a villa situated close to a river."[86] And through composition feminine *interenna*, [gen.] *-ae*, that is, "a rope which often gets into water," as in fishing or on boats, and feminine *antenna*, [gen.] *-ae*, that is, the main rope on ships, which pulls the sail up, ["sail-yard"], and it is called *antenna* because it has the water "in front" [*ante*] of it. Hence Ovid in the *Tristia*: "no favorable wind carried my *antennas* ['sail-yards']."[87] From *amnis* the compound *amnicola*, [gen.] *-ae* [masculine: "river-dweller"] is formed.

GLOSSES ON PRISCIAN

From the Gloss Promisimus[88]

Some people point out the following difference between *ethimologia, interpretatio,* and *derivatio*: etymology is the expounding of a word through one or more others which are better known, in accordance with the characteristics of the things designated and the similarity of the letters,[89] e.g. *oratio* ["speech"] as if it were *oris ratio* ["oral account"],[90] *lapis* ["stone"], *ledens pedem* ["hurting the foot"],[91] *fenestra* ["window"] *ferens nos extra* ["taking us outside"],[92] *cadaver* ["cadaver"], *caro data vermibus* ["flesh given to the worms"],[93] *amicus* ["friend"], *animi custos* ["guardian of the soul"]. These people say that *amicus* is derived [*derivatur*] from the verb *amo* ["to love"] and gets its etymology from *animus* ["soul"] and *custos* ["guardian"].[94] *Interpretatio* is the explanation of one language through another,

---

[85] Text in Hunt, "The 'Lost' Preface," 270.

[86] Cf. Paulus in Festus, *De verborum significatione quae supersunt cum Pauli epitome*, ed. Müller, 17, where *amnenses* (plur. f.) is given for towns situated near a river.

[87] Ovid, *Tristia,* V 12.40, where the text actually has *dum* rather than *non* (*dum tulit antennas aura secunda meas*).

[88] Translated from Hunt, "The 'Lost' Preface," 271f.   [89] The definition of Petrus Helias, see above.

[90] A common etymology from the third century onwards, cf. e.g. Cassiodorus, *Expositio Psalmorum* 16.11.10; Isidore, *Etymologiae* 1.5.3; and cf. Maltby, *Lexicon,* s.v. *oratio.*

[91] Isidore, *Etymologiae,* 16.3.1.   [92] Syllabic etymology without classical pedigree, see on Petrus Helias above.

[93] This etymology is common in the later middle ages, see e.g. the gloss *Tria sunt* and Joannes Balbus below.

[94] The link between *amicus* and *amor*, e.g. Jerome, *Commentarium in Michaeam* 2.71.174; for the syllabic etymology, cf. Isidore, *Etymologiae* 10.4: *amicus per derivationem quasi animi custos.* Note that Isidore uses the term *derivatio.*

e.g. *antropos*, that is *homo* ["man"]. *Derivatio* is the bending [*detorsio*] of a word to resemble another one that was invented earlier.[95] *Compositio* is the joining together of more words to make one. They say that these four also proceed from. [*sic*][96] Etymology is sometimes produced with the help of a word which does not signify, e.g. *imago* ["image"] as if it were *imitago* ["imitage"],[97] sometimes with the help of one that does signify. M[aster] says that etymology is the same as derivation. Wherever there is etymology, there is derivation and he proves it through Strabus who says in his commentary on Genesis: "Just as *issa* comes from *is* in Hebrew, so does *virago* ['(manly) woman'] trace its etymology, i.e. its derivation, from *vir* ['man'] in Latin."[98] Etymology is so called from *ethimos*, "origin" [*origo*] and *logos*, "speech" [*sermo*].

From the Gloss Tria Sunt[99]

Lux a lucendo This is a simple similarity. *Apo* is translated *ab* ["from"] *toy* is *hoc* ["the"], *boo, -as* is *sono, -as* ["to sound"]. Hence the compound *reboo, -as*, which is *resono, -as* ["to resound"]. *Reboat in omni gloria mundo* ["His Glory resounds in the whole world"].[100] Yet it seems that the author has not assigned an etymology, but a derivation, when he says *vox a vocando* ["sound comes from calling"] or a translation [*interpretatio*] when he says "or *apo tou boo* ['from calling']."[101] For the difference between etymology and translation is this, that translation is the explanation of a word in a different language, whether the similarity of the words is preserved or not. However, as some say, etymology is the simple expounding of a word through one or more other words in accordance with the characteristics of the thing designated [*secundum rei proprietatem*] and the similarity of the letters.[102] The addition of "simple" is meant to exclude compounding or derivation, e.g. *fenestra* ["window"], *ferens nos extra* ["taking us outside"].[103] But in a wider sense etymology is taken like Isidore takes it, to include also the explanation through composition or through derivation

---

[95] *Detorsio*, so also Joannes Balbus (see below).   [96] *Dicunt autem ista quatuor esse excedentia et ex.*

[97] Cf. Paulus in Festus, *De verborum significatione quae supersunt cum Pauli epitome*, ed. Müller, 112: *imago ab imitatione*, and Augustine, *In epistolam Johannis* 4.9, *PL* 35:2010D, *imago in imitatione*.

[98] Jerome, *Hebraicae quaestiones in libro Geneseos*, ed. P. de Lagarde et al., *CCSL* 72 (Turnhout: Brepols, 1959), 5.1ff. (on Genesis 2,23) for the link between *is–issa* and *vir–virago*. For *virago* see also Isidore, *Differentiae* 2.80; *Etymologiae* 11.2.22.

[99] Translated from Hunt, "The 'Lost' Preface," 272.   [100] See Petrus Helias, above.

[101] For the two etymologies (without the distinction between etymology, derivation, interpretation/translation), Priscian, *Institutiones* 1.1, *GL* 2:6.4, and Augustine and Petrus Helias above.

[102] Definition from Petrus Helias, see above.

[103] For this syllabic etymology, see on Petrus Helias above (n. 68), and the gloss *Promisimus*.

or through a different language as long as the letters are similar. For sometimes it is done through composition, as *celebs* ["bachelor"], *celestium vitam ducens* ["leading the life of the heavenly ones"],[104] *cadaver* ["cadaver"], ***caro data vermibus*** ["flesh given to the worms"].[105] Sometimes it is done through derivation, either with affinity of both sound and meaning, or with affinity of sound but not of meaning, but through a likeness with the opposite, e.g. *dux* ["leader"] from *ducere* ["to lead"],[106] *lux* ["light"], from *lucere* ["giving light"]; sometimes through both, as *lapis* ["stone"], *ledens pedem* ["hurting the foot"],[107] *homo* ["man"] *ab humo* from *humus* ["dirt"].[108]

HUGUTIO OF PISA, *MAGNAE DERIVATIONES*[109]

Prologue

1. When through the devil-induced transgression of our first-created[110] the human race fell very far from its high dignity, and was much oppressed by a threefold trouble, namely poverty, vice, and ignorance, God offered us a threefold remedy for this threefold trouble, namely commodities, virtue, and knowledge [*scientia*]. For commodities remove the inconvenience of poverty, virtue the corruption of vice, and knowledge the blindness of ignorance.

2. Men approached Knowledge from a great distance, tore a small piece off her clothing, and believed she had been joined to them in marriage completely.[111] If at some point they possessed a certain part of her, they behaved like animals: thus not only did they not redeem the aforementioned triple misery through any kind of virtue, so that through the exercise of the honorable arts[112] they would finally manage to advance to the heavenly honor of their former dignified state, but they even tried to increase their misery from day to day.

---

[104] Cf. Quintilian, *Institutio oratoria* 1.6.36; Paulus in Festus, *De verborum significatione quae supersunt cum Pauli epitome*, ed. Müller, 44, *caelibem dictum existimant quod dignam caelo vitam agat*; Priscian, *Institutiones* 1.23, *GL* 2:18.10.

[105] Common, but not classical, etymology; see Gloss *Promisimus* above and Joannes Balbus below.

[106] Priscian can also be used as a starting point for the later *derivationes* that mostly serve pedagogical goals of structuring morphology. On *ducere/dux* etc., see *Institutiones* 8.63, *GL* 2:421.22–4.

[107] Isidore, *Etymologiae* 16.3.1.

[108] Quintilian, *Institutio oratoria* 1.6.34; Isidore, *Etymologiae* 1.29.3 (cf. 10.1; 11.1.4). Following this passage there is a longer quotation from Isidore, *Etymologiae* 1.29.

[109] Translated (with notes) from Marigo, "De Hugucionis Pisani 'Derivationum' latinitate earumque prologo," 101–6, by permission.

[110] Adam.

[111] Marigo compares Matthew 25:10. For marriage as a metaphor for the acquisition of knowledge, cf. also the title and opening allegory of Martianus Capella's *De nuptiis Philologiae et Mercurii*.

[112] *honestae artes*, i.e. *artes liberales*.

3. For they made no effort to polish irregularities off their teeth, or scrape off the eruptions on their stuttering tongues,[113] nor to stimulate the slowness of their mind or to attack the forgetfulness of their weak memory,[114] to refute negligence, punish bad language,[115] and repel filth and vice. No, they rather wallowed in the hog-pool of vices,[116] strove to amass money and be the slave of what they amassed, or to ignore all decent duties and gorge their hollow bodies on food. Learning, life, and death: for these people they should be considered the same.[117]

4. But we strove upwards, in order that we may not be patently convicted, if we buried the talent that God had granted us,[118] of secreting it away. We worked hard to expand what the favor of nature was not automatically giving us, by spreading the word, so that the totality of all flesh[119] might not completely allow that learning (however insignificant) to dissolve together with the body.[120]

5. So we decided to compose a work, with the favor of divine grace, in which mostly the different significations of words, the origins of derivations, the assigning of etymologies, and an expounding of translations [*interpretationum*][121] will be found. Latin is naturally poor[122] in these and is much constrained by a certain laziness of the teachers [of grammar].

6. And we will not try to achieve this only in order to acquire the glass-like fragility of empty fame [*cenodoxie*] but also in order that the common good of all serious students of literature may flourish because of it.

7. And let no one put it in his head that we are making the suggestive [*insinuatim*][123] promise of perfection in this work. Nothing among human inventions can be found to be polished to the last detail,[124] although we may rightfully seem capable of surpassing

---

[113] For these two activities of Grammar, see *De nuptiis Philologiae et Mercurii*, 3.226 (translated in section on Martianus Capella, above, p. 152).

[114] *Madide memorie*, cf. Priscian, *Institutiones* 6.47, *GL* 2:235.

[115] Marigo suggests reading *male dicta punire* rather than *maledicta*. We have followed this suggestion in translating.

[116] Cf. 2 Peter 2,22.   [117] Cf. Sallust, *Bellum Catilinae* 2 (*doctrinam* ["learning"] is the addition of Hugutio).

[118] Matthew 25,18ff.   [119] *Universe carnis generalitas*: i.e. all of humanity.

[120] Presumably primarily Hugutio's own; but the idea is also that *doctrina* must not depend on any individual living person being around.

[121] Namely of one word into another, i.e. synonymy, cf. *Rhetorica ad Herennium* 4.28.38. This is also used for translation between languages.

[122] The "natural poverty" of Latin (when compared with Greek) was a topos already in classical antiquity, cf. Fögen, *Patrii sermonis egestas*. See section on Terentianus Maurus, p. 79.

[123] Marigo, 105 note *ad loc.* rightly points out that Hugutio may be recalling the rhetorical precepts about two types of proems here, one of which is called the *insinuatio*. Cf. Cicero, *De inventione* 1.15.20.

[124] Cf. Priscian, *Institutiones*, preface, *GL* 2:2.13f., from the dedicatory letter of the *Institutiones* to the consul Julian: *nihil enim ex omni parte perfectum in humanis inventionibus esse posse credo.*

through a singular perfection others dealing with the same subject matter.[125] For here the little boy will find sweeter milk,[126] here the adult will eat more richly,[127] here the full-blown scholar [*perfectus*] will find more abundant delight, here the learned doctors [*gignosophiste*][128] of the trivium will make progress, and so will the teachers of the quadrivium, and so will the professors of law, and so will the researchers of theology, and so will the leaders of the church; here will be supplied whatever up to now has been passed over through a lack of knowledge, here will be polished away whatever mistakes have been in use since a long time.

8. If one were to ask who is to be called the author of this work, the answer must be: God. If one asks who was the instrument in producing this work, the answer must be: native from Pisa, by name of Ugutio [Hugutio], as it were *Eugetio*, that is *bona terra*,[129] not just for our contemporaries, but also for future generations, or Ugutio [Hugutio], as it were *Uigetio*, that is *virens terra*,[130] the "flourishing land" not just for himself, but also for others.

9. So with the help of the grace of the Holy Spirit, may the Dispenser of all goods deign to supply us richly [*auctim*] with an abundance of words: let us then take the beginning of what we have to say from the word "increase" [*augmentum*].

JOANNES BALBUS, *CATHOLICON*[131]

[fol. 1ra: from the opening of the work]

Ethymologia is so called from *ethymon*, which is "true" and *logos* "speech" [*sermo*]. Hence etymology, i.e. a discussion of the truth of all parts of speech, not considering construction [*absolute*].

[fol. 1ra: the contents of the fifth part of the work is described as follows]

---

[125] Marigo, 105 note *ad loc.* refers to earlier glossographers and lexicographers, in particular Isidore, Papias, and Osbern, and the books on derivations or glosses, as sources that Hugutio used.

[126] Cf. 1 Corinthians 3:1.   [127] Cf. Ecclesiasticus 15:3.

[128] Marigo, note 105: " 'gigno hec gymnia, -ae .i. exercitatio . . . et hic gymnosophistae .i. magister gymnasii,' unde Prudentius [*Hamartigenia* 404] in libro contra haereses: ostenditque suos vicatim gymnosophistas, Mai, *Thes.* VIII [*Osberni Panormia*] 'Gymnosophista, doctor'[Papias]. Quae auctoritates codicum omnium lectionem graeci sermonis inscitia corruptam esse ostendunt."

[129] First etymology of the name Hugutio, derived from *bona terra* (hiding Greek *eu* "good," *gê* "earth").

[130] Second etymology of the name Hugutio, derived from *virere* "to be green, strong," and *terra* (probably hiding the Greek *gê*).

[131] Translated from the Mainz 1460 edition (rpt. 1971).

In the fifth part we will deal with orthography, prosody, origin, and meaning of certain words, which are often found in the Bible and in the words of Saints and also of the poets. I will add these in alphabetical order.

[fols.17rb–18rb: to the beginning of the section on the adjective]

Ethimologia, as I said above at the beginning of this work, is so called from *ethimon*, which is "true" and *logos* "speech." Hence etymology, i.e. a discussion of the truth of all parts of speech, not considering construction. Under it are comprised the eight parts of speech and their accidents.[132] I will discuss a couple of these. And particularly on the noun, verb, and participle. First about the noun. At the end I will also add something on construction and regimen.

The noun, then, as Priscian says in the second book of his *Maior*,[133] is a part of speech that assigns a common or proper quality to each of the underlying (*subiecta*) bodies or things. The noun has six accidents: species,[134] quality, gender, number, form,[135] case...

[fol. 17va: Having raised the question whether *derivativa* should count as one of the species, Balbus continues]

In the first place I raise the question where these words "primitive" and "derivative" come from. I reply that these words are taken metaphorically [*transsumptive*]. For "primitive" is taken from a spring [*fons*] where water coming through hidden channels first [*primus*] appears. "Derivative" is taken from the stream [*rivus*] that flows forth [*de-*] from the spring itself. Hence just as a stream can be deduced from another stream, so one derivative originates from another. But spring and streams [*rivi*] flow down to produce a river [*flumen*]. And both primitives and derivatives produce speech [*oratio*],[136] which may be called a river [*flumen*]. For all rivers come out of the sea, and finally return to the sea. And the sea does not overflow [*redundat*]. Similarly, all sentences [*orationes*][137] take their origin from grammar, and they return to the same, and yet grammar is not redundant [*redundat*]. Because, just as a sentence takes its origin in the parts, and the parts in the syllables, in accordance with the material of sound, and the syllable takes its origin in the letters, so they may be resolved into the same. Nor can there be any redundance ("overflowing") in this sea. For nothing can be added to grammar in as far as the integrity of the art is concerned [*quantum ad integritatem artis*]. [The notion] to call grammar a "sea" [*pelagus*], we have from Priscian, who said in his

---

[132] I.e. *ethimologia* has become virtually synonymous with the core elements of the art of grammar.
[133] Priscian, *Institutiones* 2.22 (*GL* 2:56.29f.).
[134] Later in the text explained as "primitive" or "derivative"; within these groups there are more distinctions.
[135] Simplex or compound.   [136] Or: a sentence.   [137] Or: speeches.

prooemium: "Although in comparison with the sea of writings of Herodian, etc." Horace too speaks about this spring, when he says, "be sparing in the use of words derived from the Greek spring" [*greco fonte cadent parce detorta*].[138] The same author also speaks about the river of this art: "He will also acquire new words, which the fertile stream will have brought forth, vehement and liquid and most like a pure river."[139] For words too have "flow." And sometimes they are arid, depending on whether common usage accepts them or disapproves of them.

I also raise the question whether etymology is a species of derivation, as cadaver is as it were *ca*ro *da*ta *ver*mibus ["flesh given to the maggots"].[140] But it seems not, for if this were the case, every word could be called derivative, since every word is capable of being etymologized, as long as someone is willing to be creative. My reply is that etymology is not a species of derivation, but a quasi-species. For it alludes to the signification, extracting an argument from elsewhere by using letters or syllables.[141] For example, *bos* ["cow"] as if it were *b*onus *o*peratur *s*oli ["he is useful for the soil"]. And *mons* ["mountain"] as if it were *m*oles *o*pposita *n*ascenti *s*oli ["a mass of earth facing the rising sun"]. And *taurus* ["bull"] as if it were *t*uens *a*gmina *v*accarum *r*obore *v*irium *s*uarum ["protecting through the strength of his powers the herds of cows"]. And *deus* ["God"] as if it were *d*ans *e*ternam *v*itam *s*uis ["giving eternal life to His people"]. And *Roma* as if it were *r*adix *o*mnium *m*alorum *a*varicia ["greed is the root of all evil"]. And *homo* ["man"] as if it were *h*ominis *o*mnia *m*anu *o*mnipotentis ["everything belonging to man is [given] by the hand of the Almighty"], because the Almighty created everything for the sake of man. And *sincerus* ["sincere"] as if it were *sin*e *car*ie ["without corruption"], etc. And yet we should not say that they are derived or compounded from the words through which their etymologies are formed.

> [Balbus discusses whether compounds are "derived" from the constituents of the composition (he follows Priscian in answering in the affirmative), and whether *principalia* (like "whiteness") are derived from *sumpta* (like "white"). Again Balbus follows Priscian in this idea. He then proceeds to "derivation in meaning," 17[vb]]

---

[138] Reference is to Priscian, preface to *Institutiones*, GL 2:2.21f. (from the dedicatory letter of the *Institutiones* to the consul Julian); cf. also preface, GL 2:1.1f. (opening of the same letter): *omnis eloquentiae doctrinam et omne studiorum genus...a Graecorum fonte derivatum* "the teaching of all eloquence and every kind of study has been derived from the wellspring of the Greeks."

[139] Horace, *Epistle* 2.2.119f.: *adsciscet nova, quae genitor produxerit usus. / vehemens et liquidus puroque simillimus amni.* Joannes has a predilection for using Horace as a source of examples, cf. Della Casa, "Les glossaires et les traités de grammaire du moyen âge," 43.

[140] For this etymology, see above on the gloss *Promisimus* and *Tria sunt.*

[141] The form of etymology used here explains the meaning by considering words as (mnemonic) acronyms, that would make it easy to remember the name because it "stores" the meaning in a variety of creative ways.

Furthermore the question is raised whether there is such a thing as derivation in meaning only. Priscian says there is, for example, *semel* ["once"] from *unus* ["one"].[142] That seems rather strange, for along the same line of reasoning "mountain" could be derived from "high." Solution: I say that a true and proper derivation should bear the image of the sound [*vox*] and meaning [*significatio*] of its primitive word, just as a river recalls the water and the taste of its source. However, sometimes derivation is degenerate, just like a son of a father, because it only imitates its primitive form in its sound [*vox*], e.g. *fere* ["approximately"] from *ferus* ["savage"], and *sane* ["indeed"] from *sanus* ["healthy"]. For these adverbs come from these words, but are much removed from their meaning. Sometimes there is derivation in meaning only, and with this it is as with an adoptive son, as *semel* ["once"] from *unus* ["one"]. But "mountain" is not derived in the same way from "high." For the art of grammar requires that numeral adverbs derive from numeral nouns, as *ter* ["three times"], *quater* ["four times"], etc. But those cannot exist without their "principals," namely *unitas* ["unity"] and *binarium* ["doubleness"]. So once we had the nouns, we had to have the adverbs for the same numbers, and that is how *unus* adopted *semel* ["once"] and *duo* adopted *bis* ["twice"]. But the art of grammar only requires that a "principal" derive from its adjective, "height" from "high." Thus the derivation of "mountain" from "high" is not part of the art of grammar. So, just like there are natural and legitimate sons, and sons who are only natural, and sons who are only sons for the law, similarly there are three types of derivation: the derivation in sound and meaning is like the natural and legitimate son, born from legal marriage. Derivation in sound only can be called "bastard" [*spuria*], just like a son who is only a natural son is called a bastard. Derivation in meaning only may be called adoptive, just like a son for the law only, who is called an adoptive son.

> [After a short exploration of the relation between *formatio* (as of genitive from nominative or passive from active) and *derivatio* Balbus turns to the problem of antiphrasis.]

There is also doubt about that form of derivation that takes place *per anthifrasim*, i.e. through the contrary [*per contrarium*], e.g. *lucus a lucendo* ["a sacred grove" (*lucus*) from "being light" (*lucere*)],[143] *Parca* ["goddess of fate"] from *parcere* ["to spare"], *Libitina* ["goddess of funerals"] from *libere* ["to please"].[144] I say that this is a rational form of derivation because it occurs through sound and meaning. Just as there is a double goal in

---

[142] Cf. Priscian, *Institutiones* 15.37, *GL* 3:88.5ff., *et sciendum, quod omnia, quae ab aliis derivantur, illorum significationem vel qualitatem generalem seu specialem servant* (example 88.14f.: *ab uno semel profertur*).

[143] The classic phrase *lucus a non lucendo* has lost the negative here.

[144] If this example belongs in the category *per anthifrasim,* the goddess of funerals must be meant. In the classical tradition, it is the other name for Venus, Libitina (or Libentina), that we find etymologized (in which case, presumably, it is connected with *libere/libido* directly and not *per contrarium*), cf. Varro, *De lingua latina* 6.47.

nature, *consumens* ["consuming"] and *consummans* ["perfecting"] (*consumens* is the one that destroys; *consummans* is the one that perfects), so there ought to be a double goal in species.[145] So when a derivative imitates the meaning of its primitive positively, such a derivation is *consummativa* ["perfective"]. But when it imitates the meaning of its primitive through destruction, such a derivation is *consumptiva* ["destructive"], e.g. *libitina* ["goddess of funerals"], because it is not pleasing [*quia non libet*]. For it is certain that both ends obtain for any substance plus quality, like *consumens* ["consumer"] and *consummans* ["perfector"]. For it is finally destroyed, just as it is perfected.

About Translation

About translation a further question is whether it always creates derivation, as *theos* into *deus* ["god"], *patir* into *pater* ["father"], *matros* into *mater* ["mother"].[146] Some people say this is the case. According to them *ego tu sui* ["I, you, of himself"] are derivatives, because they are translated into Latin from the Greek, as Priscian says.[147] Further, according to them one and the same word is both primitive and derivative, like *etherem* or *ethera* ["aether" (acc.)] because the Greek accusative should be primitive and the Latin accusative should be derivative. But every Latin noun will be derivative when it can be declined in the Greek way and be derived from a Greek noun, e.g. Martinos, hence: Martinus, and Priamos, hence: Priamus. I reply to this that since the Latin has completely the same meaning as the Greek or Hebrew noun, there is no derivation, but only a certain bending [*detorsio*][148] of one language into another, for example, Jacob, hence: Jacobus; Joseph, hence: Josephus. So *deus* ["god"] is not derived from *theos* nor *pater* ["father"] from *patir*, nor *mater* ["mother"] from *matir*, for they are the same. They are not derived in meaning nor in their mode of signifying [*modus significandi*]: we shouldn't say that one is a different man when speaking Greek than when speaking Latin. Similarly, we shouldn't say that the Greeks have different gospels than the Latins, although they contain different words or pronunciations. However, if Latin derives from Greek or Hebrew by a subtle change in meaning in the mode of signifying so that they would not be the same, then if there is transfer into the Latin language, there is without any doubt derivation. For example *gigno* ["to create"] from *geos*, which is earth, and *olor, oloris* ["swan"] from *olon*,[149] which is "whole," because it is "wholly white."[150] And Paraclitus from

---

[145] I.e. a species can be "positive" or "negative," "affirming" or "eliminating."

[146] The first of each of these forms is intended to represent Greek (*theos, patêr, mêtêr*).

[147] Cf. Priscian, *Institutiones* 13.4, *GL* 3:2.30.   [148] Cf. gloss *Promisimus* above.   [149] Gr. *holon*.

[150] I.e. a swan is wholly white. "Whole" is (*h*)*olon* in Greek, so Latin *olor* "swan" derives from the Greek. Cf. Philargyrius, *Explanatio in Bucolica Vergilii*, ed. Hagen, *Appendix Serviana*, 9.36. For *olon* = *totum*, cf. Isidore, 12.7.18.

paraclisis, which is "consolation."[151] And Spirit from *pir*,[152] which is "fire." And thus one has to judge with circumspection. That is the opinion of Master Bene,[153] and he takes derivation in the strict and proper sense, and I follow him. If you will find something else below in the fifth part, know that I don't assert what it says there, but am rendering the opinion of Hugutio,[154] who takes derivation in a very wide sense.

[fol. 65ra]

With the help of God we have given information about the four main parts of this work. What remains is to speak about the fifth part, which is on orthography, prosody, signification, origin, and etymology of certain words which occur frequently in the Bible and in the words of saints and poets. In accordance with the poverty of our knowledge and the weakness of our brain let us explain a few matters for our own use and that of our friends. Other information will be given here about etymology beyond what was provided in the third part, as will be clear when we discuss it in its proper place.[155] In this fifth part I will proceed everywhere according to the order of the alphabet.

> [Balbus now offers an explanation of how a strict alphabetical order works, i.e. one that does not just look at the first letter, and then proceeds to the alphabetical part itself. As an example, we translate the entries related to *amnis*, namely *amnensis, amnicola, amniculus, amnicus, amnis* (fol. 74v).]

Amnensis, [gen.] *-nensis*. Of feminine gender. Any villa situated close to the river [*amnis*]. Comes from *amnis*.

Amnicola, [gen.] *-l(a)e*. Of common gender.[156] The penultimate syllable is short. *Colens amnem* ["living on the river"]. A compound from *amnis* and *colens*.

Amniculus, [gen.] *amniculi*. Diminutive, that is, little *amnis* ["river"]. Has a short penultimate syllable.

Amnicus [fem.] *-ca* [n.] *-cum*. The penultimate syllable is short; i.e. "of a river" [*fluvialis*]. Comes from *amnis*.

Amnis. From *amenus* [= *amoenus* "lovely"] is said *hic amnis* ["river, m."], *huius amnis* [gen.], i.e. "river" [*fluvius*]. Because of the loveliness [*amenitas* = *amoenitas*] of its banks. According to Hugutio,[157] Papias says the following: *Amnis* is river. Named from

---

[151] Paraclete, of the Holy Spirit (as intercessor).   [152] Gr. *pur*.

[153] The text has the compendium BN, which probably stands for Master Bene Florentinus (Bene da Firenze, fl. ca. 1218–1226), a grammarian and teacher of dictaminal rhetoric, who wrote a *summa dictaminis* and another dictaminal treatise called *Candelabrum* (ed. G. C. Alessio, *Bene Florentini Candelabrum* [Padova: In aedibus Antenoreis, 1983]). We thank Dr Olga Weijers and Prof. C. H. Kneepkens for discussion of this passage.

[154] Hugutio of Pisa, see above.   [155] See below, where the entry "ethimologia" is translated.

[156] I.e. may be either masculine or feminine, depending on context.

[157] Reference is to Hugutio of Pisa, see above.

am(o)enitas ["loveliness"] because it is surrounded by foliage. And the ablative ends in E and in I.

[fol. 155ra: the entry *Ethimologia* gives the following information]

Ethimologia: *ethimo* [Greek] is called *verum* ["true"] in Latin; *logos* is *sermo* ["speech"] or *ratio* ["reason"]. Hence *ethimologia*, as it were "true speech" [*veriloquium*]. By etymologizing this word, too, we proclaim its true origin. It is defined as follows: Etymology is the explanation of one word through either one or more other words that are better known, within the same language or in different ones, in accordance with the characteristics of the things designated and the similarity of the letters, e.g. *lapis* ["stone"], *l(a)edens pedem* ["hurting the foot"], *piger* ["lazy"], *pedibus (a)eger* ["sick in one's feet"]. Hence *ethimologicus*, [f.] -*ca*, [n.] -*cum*, figurative, either "pertaining to etymology", or "he who etymologizes." *Ethimologizo*, [2nd pers.] -*as*, to explain thus according to Hugutio.[158] Whether etymology makes derivations I discussed in the third part, near the beginning in my discussion of the species of the noun. You must also know that etymology is conceived differently when it is taken as one part of grammar. For grammar is divided into four parts, namely orthography, etymology, diasintastica [syntax], and prosody. In that case etymology is so called from *ethimon* ["true"] and *logos* ["speech"]. Hence "etymology," i.e., a discussion of the truth of all parts of speech, not considering construction [*absolute*]. That's how the third part of this book is conceived.

[in list of contents cxxxiiii]

The fifth part of this work deals with etymology [*ethimologia*], according to the correct order of the letters of the alphabet.

---

[158] Reference is to Hugutio of Pisa, see above.

PART 3
SCIENCES AND CURRICULA
OF LANGUAGE IN THE
TWELFTH CENTURY

INTRODUCTION

The twelfth century is the period of the first great systematic commentaries and encyclopedic overviews of the disciplines that go beyond simply describing the doctrine contained in each area and attempt to explain the intellectual and cognitive principles that justify the divisions of knowledge. This development is often ascribed to the resurgence of Aristotelian logic in the curricula, and much of it is certainly linked to the growing impact of Platonic and Aristotelian epistemological theory through the Arabic learned texts that were being translated into Latin in the great centers of southern Europe. This is also the period in which we see a flurry of revived interest in Platonic cosmology through studies of the *Timaeus*, and in the explanatory power of natural philosophy (i.e. "physics"). We may justly call this the age of the "big picture," that is, the big meta-scientific statement, as exemplified by the innovative scheme of the "extrinsic prologue" to commentaries on the arts, the model for which seems to have been the prologue by Thierry of Chartres to his commentaries on the Ciceronian rhetorical texts.

Among the key institutional contexts for these emergent interests was the success of the cathedral schools in or near many of the major commercial and administrative centers in northern France and along the Rhineland. To this we should add the energetic activity at Toledo, which was a nexus of Greek, Arabic, Hebrew, and Latin learning. All of these schools allowed for a concentration of academic talent, the quick dissemination of information and opinions among masters and between generations of scholars, and the circulation and copying of texts. These are not the only sites of activity: for example, Rupert of Deutz wrote his encyclopedic survey of the arts during the early years of his career when he was a monk in an abbey near Liège. But Rupert had had contact with some of the masters of northern France in the first years of the twelfth century, and was also the beneficiary of the Rhineland's own intellectual efflorescence.

What does this mean for grammar and rhetoric? In the case of studies devoted to grammar, we see a turn away from the explicative glosses on Priscian and Donatus of earlier periods in favor of continuous commentaries that can allow for sustained and critical analysis. The departure from marginal glosses to independent commentaries was not entirely new with the twelfth century: Sedulius Scotus' commentary on the opening books of Priscian's *Institutiones*, written in the ninth century, is a notable early example.

But from the last quarter of the eleventh century, scholars raised the stand-alone commentary to a new level of importance. These continuous, free-standing commentaries were keyed to the original text by short quotations (i.e. *lemmata*) of the passage to be explained, the quotations thus linking the exposition together. Such a free-standing commentary was easier to copy and transmit than a full text along with marginal glosses (although it presumes the availability of a full text).[1] The earliest of these was the *Glosule*, a systematic compilation of glosses on Priscian's *Institutiones* 1–16, reflecting a distinctive logical, theoretical approach to grammar.

The *Glosule* and the associated gloss collections were the sources—and more important the spurs—for the first major stand-alone commentary on Priscian's *Institutiones*, the commentary by William of Conches. William's views, in turn, were disseminated by his younger contemporary, Petrus Helias, who specialized in the teaching of grammar and rhetoric.[2] In its very form, Petrus' *Summa super Priscianum* (written about 1150) took grammatical study to a new conceptual level, because as a *summa* it organized its treatment of Priscian according to major topics and theoretical questions rather than following the text phrase by phrase, thereby helping to make Priscian's text more accessible for advanced study.[3] Petrus' *Summa* also had the effect of disentangling grammar from logic and establishing a strong grammatical terminology.[4] In doing this, it created a place in grammatical teaching for using literary examples that go beyond the citations found in Priscian's *Institutiones*. This is not to suggest that grammatical study was rigidly separated from dialectic, but rather that Petrus Helias recognized the different roles of the two arts and the specific uses of their respective terminologies. Yet Petrus Helias' *Summa* also lent its authority to the work of the thirteenth-century speculative grammarians, with whom the logical dimensions of grammar superseded literary interests and monopolized semantics and theoretical questions of syntax. Through the influence of the *Summa*, the great achievements of twelfth-century grammatical thought—including developing a more nuanced vocabulary for studying syntax and refining the notion of the "special properties" (*modi significandi*) of the parts of speech—were conveyed to the speculative grammarians or *modistae* of the next century.[5]

---

[1] On the mobility of the free-standing gloss-commentary, see Ward, "Medieval and Early Renaissance Study," 20.

[2] Fredborg, "The Dependence of Petrus Helias' *Summa super Priscianum* on William of Conches' *Glose super Priscianum*."

[3] See Gibson, "The Early Scholastic 'Glosule,'" 247; Reilly, ed., introduction to Petrus Helias, *Summa super Priscianum*, 1:16.

[4] Reilly, ed., introduction to Petrus Helias, *Summa super Priscianum*, 1:2, 20; Bursill-Hall, *Speculative Grammars of the Middle Ages*, 28–9; and see Reynolds, *Medieval Reading*, 25–6.

[5] For overviews, see Covington, *Syntactic Theory in the High Middle Ages: Modistic Models of Sentence Structure*; Pinborg, *Die Entwicklung der Sprachtheorie im Mittelalter*, 19–59; Rosier, *La grammaire spéculative des modistes*, 13–17.

Towards the later part of the twelfth century, Ralph of Beauvais (fl. ca. 1170), and the teachers and glossators associated with him, achieved a new, though not enduring, synthesis between logical and literary approaches to grammar. The teaching of these late masters developed in two directions: first, in relation to logic, greater refinements of syntactic theory;[6] and second, along literary lines, the generous use of examples from the classical authors to flesh out grammatical analysis and illustrate problems of morphology and syntax.[7] We can see the impact of this synthetic outlook in the teaching of Alexander Neckam, who had studied in Paris in the later years of the twelfth century. Alexander, writing around the turn of the century, insists upon the classical literary foundations of grammatical study, but at the same time he elevates grammar to the status of a logical inquiry. He claims that grammar is not only an art of correct speaking and writing, but also an art of understanding through attention to syntax and its principles of agreement. But even as Alexander was proclaiming a synthetic perspective, the gulf between the literary and logical domains of grammar was widening. The logical direction of grammatical study had been building on the philosophical and theological interests of twelfth-century thinkers, notably Abelard and Gilbert of Poitiers, and began to take hold in the arts faculty at the University of Paris. By the end of the thirteenth century, the purely logical-semantic interests of speculative grammar dominated in the arts faculties of Paris and Oxford. Grammatical study oriented to literary Latinity, on the other hand, became the property of the new introductory grammatical texts that ultimately replaced Priscian's *Institutiones* as teaching texts, the *Doctrinale* of Alexander of Villa Dei and the *Graecismus* of Eberhard of Béthune.[8] The object of refining a literary Latinity was also taken up by the new and highly successful genre of the *ars poetriae*, the great innovation of early thirteenth-century grammatical-rhetorical teaching.

Like grammar, rhetoric also saw the rise of a dedicated tradition of study during the twelfth century. It followed a formal pattern similar to that of grammatical study: this was the age of the great stand-alone commentaries designed to get to grips with the known primary texts of Roman antiquity. If grammatical study moved away from "uncritical" marginal glosses to the free-standing commentary on Priscian, so rhetorical study moved away from rehearsing the rhetorical compendia of late antiquity (for example the compendium by Fortunatianus, or the treatments of rhetoric by Martianus Capella and Isidore of Seville) to full critical and explanatory engagement with the key Ciceronian texts, the *De inventione* and the *Rhetorica ad Herennium*. This was the age of the great continuous commentaries on the Ciceronian texts. The long exposition of *De inventione* by Victorinus

---

[6] Hunt, "Studies on Priscian in the Twelfth Century. II: The School of Ralph of Beauvais," 70–6.
[7] Ibid., 67–70; Reynolds, *Medieval Reading*, 26.   [8] For the *Doctrinale* and *Graecismus*, see Part 4.

in the fourth century provided an important model for the rhetoric commentaries. The earliest continuous commentary on Ciceronian rhetoric from the Middle Ages is a short exposition of the *De inventione* by Lawrence of Amalfi, in a manuscript compiled in Italy in the middle of the eleventh century.[9] But the center of such rhetorical interests established itself in northern Europe, first in the Rhineland and then in northern France and the cathedral schools of Rheims, Laon, Chartres, and Paris. All together we have the records (many of them fragmentary) of some twenty different lecture series on the *De inventione* or *Ad Herennium* or both, surviving in about one hundred manuscripts.[10] Of these, a series of interrelated commentaries are by named masters. From the later eleventh century there are commentaries on both texts by a "Master Manegaldus."[11] But it was in the twelfth century that the commentaries began to proliferate. During the first decades of the twelfth century, a "Master Gulielmus" or "Willelmus," who was almost certainly William of Champeaux (one of Abelard's early teachers), commented on both the *De inventione* and the *Ad Herennium*, and incorporated references to the earlier Manegaldus commentaries.[12] The commentaries by Thierry of Chartres on both the Ciceronian texts were probably produced during the 1130s, and represent the mature phase of rhetorical study during this period. Thierry's commentaries reflect the influence of Manegaldus and especially William of Champeaux. During the following decade, Petrus Helias, Thierry's younger contemporary and famed teacher of rhetoric as well as grammar, also produced commentaries on both the Ciceronian texts which derive much of their approach from Thierry's work.[13] From the later years of the twelfth century there is an important commentary on the *Ad Herennium* by a "Master Alanus," which refers to the commentaries of both Thierry and Petrus Helias.[14] The *Rhetorica ad Herennium* came into its own as the key teaching text in the second half of the century: it proved to be a better introduction to the whole of the rhetorical art. But even very early in the century the

[9] Ward, "Medieval and Early Renaissance Study," 20–1.   [10] Ibid., 25–6, and list of commentaries, 70–5.
[11] The identity of this commentator remains unknown. Links with Manegald of Lautenbach, an important figure in the Investiture controversy, remain only tentative: see Dickey, "Some Commentaries on the *De inventione* and *Ad Herennium* of the Eleventh and Twelfth Centuries"; Ward, *Ciceronian Rhetoric in Treatise, Scholion, and Commentary*, 136; and against this, see Fredborg, "The Commentaries on Cicero's *De inventione* and *Rhetorica ad Herennium* by William of Champeaux," 15.
[12] See Fredborg, "The Commentaries on Cicero's *De inventione* and *Rhetorica ad Herennium*," who establishes the identification and prints many excerpts from this commentary; Dickey, "Some Commentaries on the *De inventione* and *Ad Herennium*," discusses and prints excerpts from this commentary, citing it by its incipit, *In primis*.
[13] See Fredborg, "Petrus Helias on Rhetoric."
[14] Possibly the work of Alan of Lille: see Fredborg, "Petrus Helias on Rhetoric," 31; *Alain de Lille: textes inédits*, ed. d'Alverny, 52–5; Ward, *Ciceronian Rhetoric*, 154n. On the significance of this commentary for the ascendancy of the *Ad Herennium* as the key classical teaching text, see Ward, *Ciceronian Rhetoric*, 154–67, and "Medieval and Early Renaissance Study," 50–4. A section of the commentary is translated in Cox and Ward, eds., *The Rhetoric of Cicero*, 413–27.

Ad Herennium had received substantial attention by William of Champeaux, and Rupert of Deutz is one of the earliest encyclopedists to use the *Ad Herennium* as his main source (possibly under the influence of a commentary related to those of Manegaldus or William of Champeaux).

What drove this energetic new interest in rhetoric and the Ciceronian renaissance that accompanied it? First of all, rhetoric, like grammar, was the beneficiary of new epistemological interests, new scientific inquiries into the essential nature of knowledge. These new epistemological interests called for a return to the original sources, the authoritative statements by the "inventors" of the arts. This is the optimistic theme sounded in Thierry's famous prologue to his anthology of the arts, the *Heptateuchon*: Thierry will not be satisfied with the distilled lore of compendia (that is, summaries), but seeks out the original words of the authors. In the case of rhetoric, this motive expresses itself as a desire to know the causes and origins of eloquence, whether the origins of eloquence lie in practice or in an ulterior set of principles, that is, art. Thierry pursues this question at length in his comments on Cicero's myth of the origins of rhetoric. Second, as John Ward has suggested, the turn to rhetoric may be seen in social-historical terms as part of a larger sensitivity with the workings of language in relation to the "flexibility" of truth in a highly charged intellectual and political environment. Eloquence (as John of Salisbury was to remind his contemporaries) was something to be prized on its own terms not only in the schools but in the professional spheres of civic and church bureaucracies. There was not only competition among individuals for professional success, but among political and ecclesiological ideas for claims to truth. The power of artistic persuasion was to be seen as a necessary advantage.[15] Third, the turn to the Ciceronian text for its own sake (as opposed to the always helpful compendia) is in keeping with the classicism of the twelfth century: just as grammarians came to prefer classical sources to illustrate points of grammar and to provide models for Latin composition, so the Ciceronian rhetorical texts were "re-canonized" as the authentic classical sources on eloquence. Alongside these motivations there was another major factor: that rhetoric, like grammar, could usefully be studied as an art auxiliary to logic. It was within this logical framework that Boethius had produced his authoritative (and much studied) account of rhetorical topics; and the attention given to topical invention in the twelfth-century commentaries on Cicero can suggest how the study of rhetoric benefited from the ascendancy of dialectic in the cathedral schools of northern Europe. Rhetorical topics could serve as a foil to dialectical topics, the particularity of rhetorical topics helping to clarify the generality of their dialectical counterparts.

---

[15] Ward, "Medieval and Early Renaissance Study," 37–41.

Ultimately, the dedicated study of rhetoric, like the dedicated study of grammar, was inseparable from a literary outlook, even if rhetoric, like grammar, was not always studied in recognizably literary terms. The force and the proliferation of the new rhetorical commentaries enlarged the ways that scholars and students thought about literary language and the construction of narrative.[16] It gave them the beginnings of a new vocabulary for literary genres; it helped to give more precise definitions to long-familiar classifications of narrative (the triad of history, argument, fable); it gave a more supple language for understanding tropes; it clarified the relationship between the truth-and-knowledge questions of dialectic and the plausibility-and-belief questions of rhetoric; and it worked alongside of grammar to render students more sensitive to the artifice of language. One measure of the literary interests behind the study of rhetoric in the twelfth century is that this is the period that sees an expanded interest in *elocutio* and the rhetorical colors (*colores rhetorici*). We see this in the proliferation of new handbooks devoted to the figures and tropes or *colores* which drew from *Rhetorica ad Herennium*, book 4 rather than from Donatus' *Barbarismus*. Among the earliest of these rhetorically based manuals of verbal ornaments or *colores* was Marbod of Rennes' *De ornamentis verborum,* a verse treatise composed around the end of the eleventh century which had a traceable influence through the twelfth century, notably in the teaching of Peter Riga (his anthology *Floridus aspectus* and its redactions) and an early work by Geoffrey of Vinsauf, the *Summa de coloribus rhetoricis* (Summa On the Rhetorical Colors).[17]

Beyond the foundational twelfth-century commentaries on grammar and rhetoric, it is important to see how these arts were integrated into epistemological systems, and to see their places in the great scientific and curricular surveys of the period. Many of the texts selected here reflect the twelfth-century interest in the systematic "big picture." Our earliest example here is the survey of the seven liberal arts by Rupert of Deutz in his vast encyclopedic history *De sancta trinitate et operibus eius* (On the Holy Trinity and Its Works) (1112–1116). This is extremely traditional in its overall monastic perspective on learning as subordinate to theology and in its standard classification of the sciences according to the scheme of the seven liberal arts. But Rupert's sources for his treatment of rhetoric are surprisingly modern, or perhaps even ahead of their time, for he draws primarily on the *Rhetorica ad Herennium*, well in advance of that work's ascendancy in the second half of the twelfth century. Other encyclopedic and survey texts reflect the innovations of specialized studies in the arts, showcasing these developments in consciously revisionist frameworks of knowledge. To this category would certainly belong

---

[16] Copeland, "The Ciceronian Rhetorical Tradition and Medieval Literary Theory," 259–64.
[17] See Camargo, "Latin Composition Textbooks," 270–3; Ward, "From Antiquity to the Renaissance," 45.

the *Heptateuchon* of Thierry of Chartres (a product of the 1140s), which proclaims the unity of the arts on a philosophical model of wisdom and its expression through language, and boasts of its unprecedented accomplishment of bringing the original writings of the founders of the disciplines together in one compilation. Accordingly, Thierry presents the major curricular writings of Donatus, Priscian, and Cicero as the primary representatives of grammar and rhetoric. Of a different but equally innovative order is Gundissalinus' major treatise, *De divisione philosophiae* (On the Division of Philosophy; written sometime after 1150), which works on various revisionist fronts and levels.[18] In its overall structure it is a response to Arab learning and the mediation of Greek philosophy, especially Aristotelian epistemology, through translations from Arabic. At the local levels of individual arts, Gundissalinus combines traditional sources with the most recent innovations of his scholarly contemporaries. His treatment of grammar reflects the newer work of Petrus Helias but also goes back to Priscian as well as to Al-Farabi's account of grammar; his account of rhetoric borrows wholesale from Thierry of Chartres' commentary on Cicero. Gundissalinus looks both to the newly available resources of the world of Arab learning and to the remarkable developments of the schools of northern France.

Not all twelfth-century surveys of knowledge follow in such a boldly revisionist outlook. Some present less innovative perspectives on the arts, subordinating specialist innovations to a larger purpose of defending traditional teaching methods or presenting a pedagogical overview. Yet such texts can also offer a highly synthetic perspective and affirm the centrality of grammar and rhetoric to larger learned and literary enterprises. Three texts from the second half of the century exemplify this. The *Metalogicon* by John of Salisbury (1159) is an important milestone in the history of grammatical thought, not just for its fervent defense of a curricular tradition that emphasized literary Latinity, but for its picture of a continuity of grammatical teaching over the decades of the first half of the century, from Bernard of Chartres to Petrus Helias. The *Anticlaudianus* of Alan of Lille, probably from the early 1180s, incorporates its coverage of the seven liberal arts into a cosmographical poem, exemplifying in its complete form the mastery of the grammatical and rhetorical traditions that constitute part of its teaching. And finally in Alexander Neckam's *Sacerdos ad altare* ("the priest [approaching] the altar," from the opening words of the text), from the turn of the century or the very early 1200s, we see the grammarian as polymath. Alexander surveys the reading list of an entire curriculum, from the alphabet to the canonical Latin poets, and from the theoretical knowledge of grammar and rhetoric to the newest professional skills of medicine and law, enfolding all this ideal breadth of

---

[18] For an overview, see Jolivet, "The Arabic Inheritance," 136–7.

knowledge in an introduction to Latin vocabulary. His work gives us a grand vision of grammar as a literary and intellectual building-block. As a curricular overview, Alexander's treatise sums up the intellectual system-building of the twelfth century, with its sense of a continually expanding canon of authoritative texts; in its marked emphasis on literary Latinity, it reflects the emergent pedagogy of the *ars poetriae* which would find its most important expression among the grammarians of the first half of the thirteenth century.

COMMENTARIES ON PRISCIAN, CA. 1080 TO CA. 1150: *GLOSULE, NOTE DUNELMENSES*, WILLIAM OF CONCHES

INTRODUCTION

Towards the end of the eleventh century, grammar masters teaching at the higher levels of the curriculum increasingly began to turn to the *Institutiones grammaticae* of Priscian to address philosophical questions about language.[1] Donatus' *Ars minor* remained a fixture in the elementary classroom, but attention to his *Ars maior* diminished in favor of the richer theoretical fields of Priscian's long work.[2] This shift in approach to grammar is dramatically reflected in a set of free-standing glosses on books 1–16 of the *Institutiones* which are found in a number of manuscripts, the earliest of which dates from about 1080. They are known as the *Glosule*, so named by R. W. Hunt, after the name given to them in one of the manuscripts. From about the same period there is a separate but related gloss on books 17–18 of the *Institutiones*. Another gloss of a slightly later date, known as the *Note dunelmenses* (after the *ex libris* of the late twelfth or early thirteenth century, which places the manuscript in Durham), is more fragmentary than the *Glosule*, but clearly connected with its teachings and institutional contexts.[3] Some groups of these glosses have been linked with William of Champeaux. These glosses were the seed beds for the more exhaustive and influential Priscian commentaries by William of Conches and Petrus Helias.

---

[1] For the antecedents of this tendency in Carolingian grammar, see Luhtala, "Syntax and Dialectic in Carolingian commentaries"; see also the introduction to the section on Remigius, above.

[2] Book 3 of the *Ars maior*, the *Barbarismus*, was to have a separate career as a source for grammatical and philosophical commentary on figures and tropes: see within, Part 5 and section on the commentary on the *Barbarismus* attributed to Robert Kilwardby, pp. 724–34.

[3] See Hunt, who first called attention to the *Glosule* in his "Studies on Priscian in the Eleventh and Twelfth Centuries. I: Petrus Helias and his Predecessors"; on the gloss on *Institutiones* 17–18, see Kneepkens, "Master Guido and his View on Government," and Kneepkens, "The Priscianic Tradition," 242. For introductions to the *Glosule*, see Gibson, "The Early Scholastic *Glosule* to Priscian, *Institutiones Grammaticae*: the Text and its Influence"; Gibson, "Milestones in the Study of Priscian, circa 800–circa 1200"; and Rosier-Catach, "The *Glosulae in Priscianum* and its Tradition."

Reporting the opinions of various early masters, these free-standing gloss compilations exhibit a clear orientation to understanding grammar in terms of logic. The contribution of the *Glosule* and the related commentaries was to focus on theoretical questions of grammar as set forth in Priscian's work. The *Glosule* set in motion an effort that was to build throughout the twelfth century: to harmonize grammatical concepts with contemporary interest in logic as received through the *logica vetus* (Aristotle's *Organon* and the commentaries of Porphyry and Boethius). Thus the *Glosule* and associated commentaries explore such issues as the purposes of the various parts of speech: what is "substantial" to a part of speech (e.g. to the verb or the noun) and what is "accidental" to it. The notion of grammar's *causa inventionis* (cause of invention) is a theme that will reappear in later commentators, notably Petrus Helias: the origin of grammar is equated with the origin of language and the imposition of names on things.[4] The glosses also raise issues that were important in dialectical analysis of predication, adding the notion of inherency to Priscian's discussions of the verb and its signification of action and passion, as well as attempting to distinguish the signification of the verb from that of the noun.[5] It is now recognized that the discussions represented in these glosses were the channels through which twelfth-century philosophers and theologians, such as Abelard, turned to grammatical analysis as their starting points.[6]

The *Glosule* and the related glosses inspired the first major commentary on the *Institutiones* by William of Conches (ca. 1090—ca.1154), remembered by John of Salisbury as "the most accomplished grammarian since Bernard of Chartres" (*Metalogicon* 1. 5).[7] At the end of his early treatise *Philosophia mundi*, William announces a treatise on grammar, setting out a scholarly program for this project. William explains his goals in approaching grammar: between the strong and weak points of Priscian and the earlier commentators working on this text, it is left for William to discuss the *causae inventionis* of the parts of speech and the accidents. The later version of William's commentary on Priscian was one of the key twelfth-century texts to introduce the use of the extrinsic and intrinsic prologue, that is, an introduction to the nature of the whole "art" under consideration before the commentator introduces the particular book to be expounded.[8]

---

[4] See Hunt, "Studies on Priscian I," 18–21 (211–14), and see especially texts I.1, II.1, and III.1 in this section, below.

[5] See below, text I.2. For earlier examples, see Luhtala, "Syntax and Dialectic."

[6] Rosier-Catach, "The *Glosulae in Priscianum*," 90–3.

[7] The most recent account of the life and writings of William of Conches is by Jeauneau in his edition of William's *Glosae super Platonem*, xix–xli; an older but useful account is in Gregory, *Anima mundi*, 1–40. For a summary of the controversy about William's role in teaching at the schools of Chartres and Paris, see Weijers, "The Chronology of John of Salisbury's Studies in France (*Metalogicon* II.10)."

[8] See within, pp. 407–8, introduction to Thierry of Chartres' Cicero commentaries.

William's exposition of Priscian is a phrase-by-phrase commentary. It survives in two versions, reflecting his teaching of Priscian over some years of his career, from about 1120 to about 1140. The commentary offers an extended discussion of the nature and function of grammar, and the "causes" or specific functions of the parts of speech, that is, why they were invented: in this, William drew on the *Glosule* and their consideration of the causes of word classes. William's commentary also continued an older tradition (and was then itself established as a precedent) for a theoretical analysis of syntax and the arrangement of the parts of speech according to natural order. This idea had been part of Latin syntactical theory since Priscian himself,[9] both in the form of the order of the parts of speech in grammatical analysis, and the order of the parts of speech in actual sentences.[10] The idea of a natural order in syntax was recognized as important for composing as well as understanding poetry and prose: the job of the author is to determine, according to grammatical science, when art demands deviation from natural order; the grammarian's job is to explain the sentences in which these choices are evident.[11] This anticipates the further development of the interest in syntax during the twelfth century.

I.1–5 and II.1–2. *Glosule* and *Note dunelmenses*, **translated from Hunt, "Studies on Priscian, I"**

III.1. William of Conches, *Philosophia mundi*, **translated from Thurot,** *Notices et Extraits*

III.2. William of Conches, Second Redaction to his commentary on Priscian's *Institutiones,* **Prologue and opening of the commentary. English translation from Minnis and Scott,** *Medieval Literary Theory*

III.3. William of Conches, from the Second Redaction of his commentary on *Institutiones.* **English translation from Reynolds,** *Medieval Reading*

(with permissions)

---

[9] In his views on the rational order of the parts of speech, Priscian goes back to Apollonius Dyscolus, and before him to the Stoa and the rhetorical tradition, represented e.g. by Dionysius of Halicarnassus. See the introduction to the section on Priscian above, pp. 167–70, and cf. de Jonge, *Between Grammar and Rhetoric: Dionysius of Halicarnassus on Language, Linguistics and Literature*, 251–328.

[10] Priscian, *Institutiones* 17.12, GL 3:115.20ff. (order of the the parts of speech in grammatical discourse; translated within); *Institutiones* 17.105, GL 3:164.16–20 (actual parts of speech in a sentence, with the addition of the term *naturaliter*; substance and person should naturally have priority over the act).

[11] Kneepkens, "*Ordo naturalis* and *ordo artificialis*," 63–6.

GLOSULE

I.1 On Priscian, Institutiones *Preface (GL 2:1.7)*[12]

We ought not to wonder if the younger grammarians are said to be more perceptive in their invention. For whereas the first inventor worked throughout his whole life to invent maybe four letters, a younger grammarian could learn those in a single day, and then for his part proceed to invent others. By the additions of later grammarians this art thus grew to perfection.

I.2 On Priscian, Institutiones *2.18 (GL 2:55.8)*[13]

We should consider how the verb is said to signify pure action and passion.[14] For if the verb is said to signify pure action and passion, its signification will be the same as that of the noun, because the nouns "action" and "passion" signify all actions and passions. We say therefore that it signifies neither action simply nor a person acting, but it signifies that action is *in* a person acting, as for example "[He] runs." But the noun, e.g. a "run," though it signifies an action, signifies it simply and does not say it is *in* something. We should not deny that since the verb signifies the inherence of both action and substance, it may be said to signify action and substance themselves in a certain way, but in a different way from the noun: for the noun signifies them considered simply, by themselves, but the verb signifies them in as far as they cohere.

I.3 On Priscian, Institutiones *2.18 (GL 2:55)*[15]

Someone may object that "white" seems to be a verb, since it signifies whiteness inhering in a body; but this will not hold, because, though "white" signifies whiteness inhering in a

---

[12]Chartres, Bibliothèque municipale, MS 209, f. 1va; Paris, Bibliothèque nationale, MS nouv. acq. lat. 1623, f. 1rb; Hunt, "Studies on Priscian I," 19 (212), n. 2.

[13] Chartres MS 209, f. 11vb and Paris, Bibliothèque nationale, MS nouv. acq. lat. 1623, f. 10va; Hunt, "Studies on Priscian I," 25 (218), n. 1. Hunt's paraphrase (24–5 [217–18]) has been slightly adapted and supplemented.

[14] "Passion" (*passio*), i.e. the condition of being acted upon, often expressed by the passive voice. For "action" and "passion," see above, section on Priscian, p. 181 n. 68.

[15] Chartres, Bibliothèque municipale, MS 209, f. 11vb and Paris, Bibliothèque nationale, MS nouv. acq. lat. 1623, f. 10va; Hunt, "Studies on Priscian I," 26 (19) n. 1. Hunt's paraphrase (25–6 [218–19]) adapted and supplemented.

body, it does not signify the inhering itself [*ipsum inherere*],[16] for "white" [*album*] signifies in one way, but "[it] is white" [*albet*] in another. For "white" signifies whiteness determined in such a way that it is affixed to something, but "[it] is white" signifies the actual inhering of whiteness in a substance. Against this it may reasonably be argued that if "[he] runs" signifies that running inheres in Socrates, it signifies either the actual inherence [*inherentiam*] of running in Socrates or something else. But to say that it signifies the inherence of running in Socrates is inconsistent, since inherence is a quality which is different from the signification "[he] runs." For according to this view all verbs would signify a quality. Again, if "[he] runs" signifies that running is in Socrates [as an equivalent to the common expression of "actually inhering"], then it is a proposition. For it signifies an understanding that is true or false. For he who says or understands that something is in something else, is correct or incorrect [*verus vel falsus est*]. We say therefore that it is to be understood that "[he] runs" signifies running [*cursio*] in as much as running inheres in something, and so of other verbs that every verb signifies action or passion as it inheres in substances. Nor do we say that in this respect the signification of derivatives [*sumpta*][17] differs from that of verbs. For just like "[he] runs" signifies running [*cursio*] in as much as running inheres in something, so does "white" signify whiteness [*albedo*] as it inheres in Socrates or someone else. So in what respect do derivatives differ from verbs? Well, in that verbs signify with moods and tenses, but derivatives do not.

I.4 After Comments on Priscian, Institutiones 8.37 (GL 2:403–4)[18]

On the verb substantive

It seems worth investigating whether, when every verb principally signifies action or passion, the substantive verbs,[19] which do not signify a definite action or passion, may be judged to be verbs. Let us present the various opinions of the masters on their meaning.

---

[16] "Inhering itself," here expressed by a verb in Latin, since that is the point of the distinction between the adjective and the verb.

[17] The translation suggested by Hunt, "Studies on Priscian I," 25 (218) n. 2, not referring to the Greek term. *Sumpta* are Aristotle's *parônuma*: terms that signify substances indirectly, derivatively, by referring to their accidental qualities. Whiteness is a quality. "White" describes a thing/substance by means of its quality, i.e. derivatively. Besides *sumpta* we also find *denominativa*. Note that grammarians also use that term very differently than the dialecticians to refer to a noun or name which is derived from another noun, cf. Priscian, *Institutiones* 4 (GL 2:117.1–140.24).

[18] Chartres, Bibliothèque municipale, MS 209, f. 37rb; Hunt, "Studies on Priscian I," 32–5 (225–8). We only translate the beginning of the passage: Hunt, 32 (225).

[19] For *verba substantiva*, see Priscian, *Institutiones* 7.51, GL 2:414.14f.

Some say that *sum* "to be" is neuter[20] and signifies action, but it does not signify any thing in a definite way that is contained under any of the ten categories (for it is an equivocal verb): they make the term "action" equivocal, and call "action" anything that is not passion, whether it be a quality or something else. So if "to be" does not signify one action, but many and various ones, they reasonably claim it is not one verb, but many. In the same way, *ens* "being" is not one noun, since it does not signify a substance or even substances with any one property, but is proven to be many things. No wonder that this is their judgment about "to be," when even the equivocal verb *amplector* ["to embrace/to be embraced"], which clearly *is* a verb,[21] is claimed to be not one verb (because it does not simply signify action or passion but both at the same time), but rather, it is claimed to be different verbs, because it appears in different constructions.

Others again do not completely dissent from the opinion mentioned above, but take it that whatever "to be" is, it signifies something like an action. But these actions are confused and indeterminate, when *sum* ["to be"] is proffered by itself, and even when it makes a simple statement about anything, as when I say "I am," "Socrates is." But if there is a third adjacent [*adiacens*], its action is made definite in that sentence, as when I say "Socrates is an animal." And they affirm that in this proposition the thing [*rem*] "animal" is signified by "is" as its action.[22] But since every verb, as stated before, signifies action or passion, not simply but as adjacents [*adiacentes*], if it be conceded that the thing "animal" is the action of the verb, then it is affirmed that in the aforementioned proposition it is the adjacent of Socrates—which is absurd.

I.5 A Note at the End of the Text, in a Contemporary Hand[23]

Opinions of various people on the verb substantive *sum* "to be"

Wido Lingonensis (Guy of Langres) said that this verb signifies action only in the case of God, as when we say "God is," but passion in all created things, as when we say "man is,"

---

[20] For *verba neutra* (which have active-looking forms, but no passives), see Priscian, *Institutiones* 7.7, *GL* 2:373.26–8.

[21] On *amplector*, which is a *verbum commune*, i.e. it can have active and passive meaning expressed through the same set of forms, see Priscian, *Institutiones* 8.15, *GL* 2:379.5–6.

[22] See Nuchelmans, "*Secundum/tertium adiacens*": *Vicissitudes of a Logical Distinction*: a "second adjacent" is *est*, in *Socrates est.* "Animal," in "Socrates is an animal" is called the "third adjacent."

[23] Chartres, Bibliothèque municipale, MS. 209 f. 86ᵛ; Hunt, "Studies in Priscian I," 31–2 (224–5) (appendix I). On this codicil, see ibid., 13 (206), and on the teachers whose views are mentioned, 13–15 (206–8).

"an ass is" etc. He seems to have derived this view from Macrobius,[24] who says that *stare* "to stand" signifies action and passion. When we say "the man stands," "stands" signifies action, because the man stands by his own effort; but when we say "the spear stands," there it signifies passion, because a spear cannot stand unless it has been fixed [in the ground] by somebody.

The archbishop Lanfrancus said that this verb *sum* ["to be"] only signifies action in substances, as in "man is," "an ass is," and similar cases; but passion in all accidental things, which do not exist by themselves, but through substances, as when we say "whiteness is" etc. And the same distinction that Master Wido makes between God and things created, Lanfrancus makes between substances and accidents. Master Ruobertus said that this verb does not have any substances, but rather that it signifies the substantial differences of any given thing of which the subject itself is predicated, and that these differences are the action of that verb, as when we say "man is": here "is" signifies rationality and mortality, and in other cases similarly. Master Garmundus said that the action of that verb is substances and accidents. When we say "man is an animal," "animal" is the action of that verb which functions as copula [*copulat*]; but when we say "this color is whiteness," "whiteness" is the act of that verb, and so on in similar cases.

Master Durandus of Anglia said that this verb both signifies action proper and passion proper. Literally he says: "*is*": this is not called a verb because it signifies action or passion, but it is indicative [*significativum*] of action and passion, that is, it is capable of signifying both. For in a certain place it signifies action properly, e.g. *Socrates est legens* ["Socrates is reading"]; in certain contexts it signifies passion properly, e.g. *liber est lectus* ["the book is read"], and thus it is a verb well and properly, because it is properly indicative of action or passion. And his view seems to be the best.

Note Dunelmenses

II.1 At Priscian, Institutiones 8.1[25]

For when the philosophers distinguished eight parts of speech, they considered that all parts of speech, that is all words, were comprised under eight different properties, of which

---

[24] Macrobius, *Commentum in somnium Scipionis* 2.15.14–15. Macrobius refers to Virgil, *Aeneid* 6.652 (not by name): *stant terrae defixae hastae*. In our text, the literary reference is reduced to a bare unpoetic minimum.

[25] Durham Cathedral Library MS C. IV. 29, f. 2rb,va and f. 22ra; Hunt, "Studies on Priscian I," 20 (213), n. 1, and 21 (214): Hunt's paraphrase slightly adapted.

one, for example, was to signify substance with quality; and they decided to designate this property with the word "noun." Thus they placed under "noun" all words that agreed principally [*principaliter*] in this property, and said that to signify substance with quality was substantial [*substantiale*] to these words. Whatever they assigned to them afterwards, that is besides this principal signification, they wished to be accidental. Hence it comes about that often the principal signification of one part is the accidental signification of another, which is not inconsistent. For when concerning any word we establish under which part of speech it is contained,[26] we always have recourse to its principal signification, in which it was principally placed by the *inventor*. Now although he cannot indicate this to us by telling us himself, he left us sure signs of his intention for each part of speech in certain accidental properties not interchangeable with others, by which they could be distinguished as if by a well-known face; and for some parts of speech these accidental properties are the only distinguishing marks, as in the case of the verb and participle . . . In grammar we call those features "substantial" to a word which it has from its invention.

II.2[27]

Although "reading" [*lectio*], "he reads" [*legit*], and "reader" [*lector*] signify the same thing, they do so in different ways. For—to put it in a simile—"reading" signifies reading as it were out of doors, "he reads" signifies the same coming indoors, i.e. as it is in motion, "reader" concerns the same staying at home and resting without regard to time. In a similar way do "whiteness," "is white," "white" signify the same, and so do other examples of this kind.[28]

---

[26] This refers to that central classroom activity, parsing (Greek *merismos*), of foremost interest to the late-antique word-and-accident grammar.

[27] Durham Cathedral Library MS C. IV. 29, f. 94vb; Hunt, "Studies on Priscian I," 26 (219), n. 4. Hunt's paraphrase (26) adapted and supplemented.

[28] Cf. John of Salisbury, *Metalogicon* 3.2, on the use of "whiteness," "is white," and "white" to illustrate the relation between nouns, verbs, and derivatives: "Bernard of Chartres says that 'whiteness' [*albedo*] signifies an uncorrupted virgin, '(she) is white' [*albet*] the same girl going into the bedroom, or lying on her pillow, 'white' [*album*] the same girl again, but corrupted. This is so because 'whiteness' from what it asserts signifies the quality itself, namely one kind of color, dazzling to the faculty of vision, simply and without any participation of a subject. 'It is white' principally signifies the same, even though it admits the participation of a person. For if you force out what the verb means as its substance, the quality of whiteness will come to mind, but you will find 'person' in the accidents of the verb. 'White' signifies the same quality, but infused and mixed with substance, and in some way already more corrupt" (our translation).

WILLIAM OF CONCHES

III.1 *From* Philosophia Mundi[29]

Since grammar takes priority in all learning, we have made it our topic to talk about it, for, although Priscian says enough at a later point, yet he gives obscure definitions and does not explain them,[30] and he omits the causes of invention of the different parts and of the different accidents within each part; and the earlier glossators [*antiqui glosulatores*][31] did a good job of expounding the thread of the argument and have mostly and on the whole also correctly given the exceptions to the rules, but they erred in expounding the accidents. So we have made it our topic to say what has not been said by them, to expound what they left obscure: in our work someone may look for the causes of invention of the items mentioned above, for exposition of Priscian's definitions, and from the earlier glosses he can mostly and on the whole take the continuous exposition of his argument and the exceptions to the rules. But since we have talked succinctly about what we set out to do above, that is, on the things that exist and are not visible, and on the things which exist and are visible, we will put an end to the length of this work, so that the soul of the reader may the more energetically move on to learning other things.

III.2 *From the Second Redaction of his Commentary on Priscian's* Institutiones: *Prologue and Beginning of the Commentary*[32]

Since we know on the authority of Priscian that in all things devised by man there can be nothing that is completely perfect,[33] it is not inappropriate if in our old age we revise something we wrote in our youth, but which is incomplete. For "knowledge flourishes among the aged, and wisdom among old men" [Job 12,12]. So, we have undertaken the

---

[29] Text translated from Thurot, *Notices et extraits*, 17–18. Cf. edition by Maurach, 116 (§59). On this passage, see Hunt, "Studies on Priscian I," 18 (211).

[30] Priscian's definitions show clear traces of philosophical provenance, but did not match the Aristotelian principles of his commentators. This fact in itself gave them the conceptual space to expound grammar through a strictly logical lens. See Luhtala, "'Priscian's definitions are obscure'"; Kneepkens, "The Priscianic Tradition," 242.

[31] *Antiqui* refers to earlier medieval scholars, not to ancient authorities, cf. Hunt, "Studies on Priscian I," 7 (200).

[32] Translation from Minnis and Scott, *Medieval Literary Theory and Criticism*, 130–4, with slight adaptations. Original text in Jeauneau, "Deux rédactions des gloses de Guillaume de Conches sur Priscien," 366–70.

[33] Priscian, Letter to Julian, *GL* 2:2.13–14.

task of correcting in our old age our glosses on orthography, which we wrote in an incomplete form in our youth. The reader must not look for the composition of a new work here, but rather the correction of an old one in terms of the addition of things omitted and the cutting-out of superfluous material.

But orthography belongs to the field of grammar, which no one doubts is one of the arts, and every art is either extrinsic [*extrinsecus*] or intrinsic [*intrinsecus*]. Priscian's exposition of the intrinsic aspect of the art of grammar is such that he does not discuss the extrinsic one. So let us briefly say something about the extrinsic aspect of the art before we begin our exposition. It belongs to the extrinsic features of the art to consider what the art itself is, its name, the reason for its name, the category [*genus*] within which it falls, what is its office or function, its end, subject matter, parts or divisions, what instrument it uses [to achieve its ends], who is its practitioner, who is its teacher, and what is the intention of the author.

The art of grammar, then, is a collection of precepts by which we are instructed in writing correctly and in pronouncing correctly that which is written. It is called an art [*ars*] because its precepts constrain [*artant*][34] the hands and tongues of men in a certain way so that they cannot either write or pronounce in any other way. It differs from knowledge [*scientia*]. For knowledge is that mental quality which makes the person in whom it resides a grammarian. There are as many forms of that knowledge as there are grammarians and each of these forms is called grammar. But among us, and among Latin writers, there is only one art.

The name [*nomen*] of this art is the art "of grammar," which is translated "of letters," for *gramma* is a letter. The Latins call this art the art "pertaining to letters" [*litteratoria*] or "of letters" [*litteralis*], but the Greeks call it the art "of grammar." But because the Greeks have precedence over the Latins, it is more frequently called the art of grammar than the art of letters. But since the object of its investigation is not only letters but also syllables and words, the question is asked, why is it called the art of grammar, that is, of letters, rather than the art of syllables or words or sentences? Some respond to this question as follows: "Only letters are dealt with in that art," and claim that letters are considered in four ways. For sometimes they are considered in their simple form, that is, without the addition of any other letters, and when this is the case they are called letters. Sometimes they are considered conjointly, but without sharing in the meaning of a syntactic structure [*consignificatio*], and then they are called words [*dictiones*]. And sometimes as signifying something which has full meaning and a fully expressed thought. Then they are called sentences. Thus, they are sentences, words, letters, and syllables, although considered differently in each case. Since, therefore, all those things with which one is concerned in

---

[34] For the etymological link between *ars* and *artare/artus*, see Isidore, *Etymologiae* 1.1.2, translated above, p. 234.

this art are letters, but not all of them are syllables or words, quite rightly the art is called "grammar," that is, the art "of letters," and not the art "of syllables" or "of words."

Others say that it is called [the art of] grammar not from the letters but from the words [*voces*] expressed by letters, because it excludes words not expressed by letters and deals only with words so expressed. The difference between a word expressed in letters and a word not so expressed will be explained subsequently.[35]

Others say that it was the habit of writers of antiquity to give their works titles from the subjects treated at the beginning of the book. For instance, the book of Genesis is so called not because the whole book deals with genesis, that is, creation, but because it deals with it at the beginning. Likewise, they call one book Leviticus, so to speak "the book of sacrifices," from the Levites who in olden times used to perform these sacrifices, not because the book deals with sacrifices throughout, but because it does so in its first section. And in another instance Moses calls a book the book of Deuteronomium, so to speak "concerning the second law" (for *deuter* is "second"; *nomen* is "law"), because that book deals in its first section with the second law. So that art is called "grammar," that is, "of letters," because in its initial part it deals with letters.

The category [*genus*] within which this art falls is that of eloquence. Three things are necessary for someone to be perfectly eloquent. [The first is] to know how to write correctly for the enlightenment of those who are not present and to make men's recollection [of the subject] more enduring, and to know how to pronounce correctly that which has been written, in order to enlighten those present. This grammar teaches. The second skill is to know how to define, divide up, and argue. This logic teaches. The third is to know how to persuade and dissuade. This rhetoric teaches. There are, then, three divisions of eloquence: grammar, dialectic, rhetoric. But some say that grammar is not a division of eloquence, because eloquence is not predicated of grammar.[36] For [they say] it is not true that grammar is eloquence, because, if grammar were a kind of eloquence someone could be called eloquent because of his knowledge of that science. But if someone knew grammar without rhetoric and dialectic he would never seem eloquent. But I, on the contrary, assert that, if someone were a grammarian without being a logician or an orator, he would be eloquent and yet would not seem eloquent. For, following common usage, we do not grant this attribute [i.e. of eloquence] except to the man who has facility in finding words and shines in the way he puts them together. Likewise, although arithmetic is a division of wisdom, if someone knew the nature of numbers without knowing anything else he would

---

[35] See the section on Priscian above, pp. 172–3 for the distinction between being articulate or not, and being "literate," i.e. susceptible to being written.

[36] I.e. he who is eloquent knows grammar, but the grammarian qua grammarian is not necessarily eloquent. So one cannot say "grammar is eloquence."

not be considered wise. So grammar is eloquence, though it is not perfect eloquence, and the grammarian is eloquent, though not perfectly so.

Alternatively, to remove all dispute, the category to which grammar belongs may be called logic applied through the medium of words [*logica sermocinalis*]. One form of logic is that which works through reason, the other that which works through words. So this name "logic" is applied equally to the two, a name which, in line with the use of *logos* among the Greeks, applies equally to speech [*sermo*] and to reasoning. Logic which works through words contains within its scope the *trivium*. But logic which works through reason embraces dialectic, rhetoric, and sophistic [*sophistica*], not grammar.

The function [*officium*] of this art is to write correctly, and to pronounce correctly what has been written. Its end [*finis*] is to know these things. Because we frequently speak of "writing correctly" and "pronouncing correctly what has been written," let us see what this means. To write is to represent, by means of visible symbols, something which is expressible [*pronunciabile*]. So, to write correctly is to arrange these visible symbols according to the precepts of this art. Correct pronunciation is speaking without the fault of barbarism and solecism. Barbarism is every fault which occurs in the parts of a word [*dictio*]. This happens sometimes in the substance of the word, when without any reason we remove a letter or syllable which has been in that word from the time when it was first thought of, or when we add things which ought not to be there. Sometimes the barbarism occurs in its accidental properties [*accidentia*], namely in its order [*ordo*], quantity [*tempus*], breathing [*spiritus*], accentuation [*accentus*], or writing [*scriptura*]. It happens in its order when we put a letter after another which ought to be put before it, or vice versa. It happens in the quantity when that which is normally long is cut short or that which is short is lengthened. It happens in the breathing when the rough is smoothed out and the smooth is pronounced roughly. It happens in terms of accent when the accent which ought to be acute is turned into a grave or circumflex and vice versa. It happens in writing, for instance if the noun *quae* is written without the diphthong or the conjunction *que* with a diphthong. Every such fault is called a barbarism, that is, the usage of barbarians. For barbarians, since they lack the rules of the art of grammar, err in many respects. Solecism is every fault which occurs in the putting together of words. It gets its name "solecism" from the city Soloe, of which the speech was corrupt because it lay on the border with barbarian lands. But the faults which are called barbarisms are called *metaplasmi* if they occur with reason [i.e. deliberately]. If solecisms occur with reason they are called *sc[h]emata* by the Greeks and "figures" by the Latins. Thus Isidore says: "A figure is a fault which occurs with reason."[37]

---

[37] *Etymologiae* 1.35.7, with *ratione* for *oratione*.

The subject matter [*materia*] of this art is threefold:[38] the letter, the syllable, and the word. Some add the sentence as a fourth, for they assert that Priscian deals with it in his book of constructions. But this seems to us not to be so for the following reason. When he shows what a letter is and what its properties are, and what letters may be put in front of which to constitute a syllable, the discussion is about the letter, not about the syllable. Again, when he shows what a syllable is, and what its properties are, and what syllables can be put in front of which to construct a word [*dictio*], the discussion is about the syllable, not the word. Likewise, when he shows what a word is, what its properties are, and which words may be put in front of which to construct a sentence, the discussion must be said to be about the word, not the sentence. Again, if he were dealing with the sentence, he would define it, as he defines his other subjects, and would divide it into its various kinds, and would explain what difficulties there were concerning it. But even if he defines it to clarify the nature of words, in the course of defining which he had mentioned the sentence, nevertheless he never divides it up, nor does he explain what difficulties there are concerning it. Again, it is the task of a grammarian to lead his pupil towards the construction of a sentence. But it is the task of a logician to define and divide a sentence. So, the subject matter of this art is threefold: the letter, the syllable, and the word.

Grammar has two parts [*partes*]: orthography, that is, correct writing (for *ort[h]os* is "correct"; *graphia* is "writing"), and correct pronunciation. This art has no separate subdivisions within itself. For we do not agree with those who say that Latin grammar and Greek grammar are separate divisions of this art. For one would have to make a similar concession in the case of the other arts, and [in that case] the arts would not be the same with us as with the Greeks.

The practitioner [*artifex*] of this art is the grammarian. A grammarian is he who knows how to write correctly and to pronounce correctly what has been written.

The author [*auctor*] is Priscian of Caesarea.

The author's intention [*intentio auctoris*] is to give the emperor Julian[39] definite rules about the third declension of nouns and the past tenses of verbs, and to correct all the faults of the Latin grammarians, and to add what they have omitted.

SINCE [I FIND THAT THE TEACHING OF] ALL ELOQUENCE [*GL* 2:1] Since many had written about the art of grammar before Priscian, he prefaces his work with a prologue in which he sets out the various reasons for his having written after others had written, lest this work, coming after the work of others, should appear superfluous. In this prologue he makes the

---

[38] Cf. Reynolds, *Medieval Reading*, 90–1.

[39] For this confusion between the consul Julian and the emperor Julian the Apostate, see the introduction to the section on Priscian, p. 170.

reader receptive to teaching, well disposed, and attentive.[40] He makes him receptive to teaching by setting out how he is going to conduct that discussion, and attentive by setting out his motives for engaging in it.

The first reason he alleges here is necessity. For that art had been imperfectly written about by all who had written about it, and had not been put right by any Latin author. So it was necessary that it should be put right by him.

Now let us expound the letter [of the text] . . .

III.3 On Natural Word Order, from the Second Redaction of his Commentary on Priscian, Institutiones (at 17.2, GL 3:108)[41]

All authors write in meter or in prose or in a mixture of the two. Even though the natural order of words is necessary, it can be changed by the law of meter. So, natural word order demands that the nominative is placed first in the phrase, that the verb follows, then the oblique case, that the adverb adheres to the verb and so on. But sometimes, this order can be changed by the beats[42] and feet of the meter, as here *Iram patet mihi* ["Anger he shows to me"]. Here, the accusative is put first, with the verb following. Moreover, it is necessary in the exposition [of a text] to rework the words into their natural word order, which cannot be done easily without a knowledge of construing [*sciencia construendi*]. But whoever composes in prose will similarly [to whoever writes in meter] diverge from natural word order, since there are words which sound bad after certain other words and good after others. Thus, those who compose by design and not by chance first work at this knowledge; then they examine closely the number of ways in which a meaning [*sentencia*] can be expressed. Afterwards, they employ the words which are more beautiful to express it, taking into consideration the order in which the words sound best when uttered. Whoever wants to know more about this, let him read the *Rhetoric* of Marcianus,[43] where he deals with the elegance of the phrase. [On the other hand], the knowledge of construing is necessary for the correct exposition of them [the *auctores*], so that the words might be reworked into their natural word order. Therefore, the knowledge of construing is necessary for the exposition of all the authors.

---

[40] "Receptive, well-disposed, attentive": these are the conventional rhetorical tasks of any proem, demonstrating that Priscian himself is an example of a grammarian who has full command of rhetoric (see discussion in this text, above).

[41] Text (from Paris, Bibliothèque nationale, fonds lat. MS 15130, f. 86ra) and translation (slightly adapted) from Reynolds, *Medieval Reading*, 114–15. See discussion in introductory note.

[42] *tempus*: length-unit, beat, measure.   [43] I.e. Martianus Capella.

RUPERT OF DEUTZ, *DE SANCTA TRINITATE ET OPERIBUS EIUS*, 1112–1116: GRAMMAR AND RHETORIC

INTRODUCTION

Rupert (ca. 1075–1129) spent most of his career in two monasteries, the Abbey of St. Lawrence, near Liège, and for the last eight years of his life the Abbey of Deutz, near Cologne, where he was abbot. He was an extraordinarily prolific writer: in addition to the massive *De sancta trinitate et operibus eius* (On the Holy Trinity and its Works) he wrote many other treatises and epistles, including an influential commentary on the Divine Office, a dialogue between a Christian and a Jew, and biblical commentaries.[1] *De sancta trinitate* develops an encyclopedic salvation history (running to approximately 2,000 pages in its modern edition by R. Haacke) through extended commentaries on the historical books of the Bible, and encompasses theological concerns up to the author's own time. It is divided thematically into three parts, the works of the Father (Genesis), the works of the Son (the remaining historical books of the Old Testament and the Evangelists), and the works of the Holy Spirit, which concerns the gifts of sanctification: wisdom, understanding, counsel, fortitude, knowledge, piety, and fear.[2]

It is in this last part of the whole, on the works of the Holy Spirit, that Rupert addresses the human sciences, seeking to bring the seven liberal arts under the aegis of the Trinity and its works, and discover their theological and ecclesiological value. The section on the sciences (chapter 40 of the whole, or book 7 of part 3, on the works of the Holy Spirit) represents a tiny fraction of the vast composition. Rupert has justly been viewed as a conservative thinker about the arts and the value of human knowledge, quietly absorbing secular learning and finding its application in the combating of theological error.[3]

---

[1] On Rupert's life and works, see van Engen, *Rupert of Deutz*, and Magrassi, *Teologia e storia nel pensiero di Ruperto di Deutz*.

[2] For detailed accounts of this work, see Leichtfried, *Trinitätstheologie als Geschichtstheologie*, and Gribomont and de Solms, *Rupert de Deutz: Les oeuvres du Saint-Esprit*. A good general account is in Evans, *The Language and Logic of the Bible: The Earlier Middle Ages*, 13–17.

[3] Evans, *Old Arts and New Theology*, 57–79; van Engen, *Rupert of Deutz*, 93.

Certainly his account of grammar shows him working within a framework set by earlier expositors who saw Scripture as the grammatical model *par excellence* (we may think in particular of Bede's *De schematibus et tropis*). His approach to rhetoric seems at first to be similarly traditional, although he devotes greater space to it than to any of the other arts. He demonstrates the superiority of Scripture over any secular (pagan) models of rhetoric, and fiercely defends Scripture's exemption from the merely technical rules of the rhetoricians, while at the same time noting the skill with which Scripture often deploys those very rules. Rupert stands at the beginning of a renaissance of rhetorical study in the twelfth century, which would culminate in the grand commentaries on the Ciceronian rhetorics by Thierry of Chartres, Petrus Helias, and others in the middle and later years of the century. Whether he had access to any of the earliest commentaries on the Ciceronian rhetorics, such as the gloss of "Master Manegaldus" of the late eleventh century (and probably of Rhineland provenance), cannot be known.[4] But his outlook on the art seems to have little in common with what was to characterize the interrelated tradition of Ciceronian commentaries, because his interest in rhetoric is exegetical rather than compositional, meditative and interpretive rather than professional and literary. In this conception he is a product of the monastic tradition and more closely linked with a figure like Cassiodorus than with his own contemporaries, the masters of the cathedral schools. Unlike the latter (for example, Thierry of Chartres), he was not interested in examining the inherent theoretical problems of the art or the differences among various authorities.[5]

However, if we look beyond the initial impression of a traditional approach, we find some unexpected features in Rupert's treatment of rhetoric. Most importantly, his chief source is the *Rhetorica ad Herennium*, rather than the *De inventione*. Rupert's prominent use of the *Ad Herennium* has been masked in Haacke's edition, which cites only the *De inventione* and Isidore's *Etymologiae* as sources and parallels for his presentation of rhetorical doctrine. But a closer look shows how much Rupert drew from the *Ad Herennium* for explanatory language about almost all the technical matters of rhetoric and for streamlined presentations of the elements of inventional theory. While the structure of Rupert's account is clearly modeled on the *De inventione*, because he confines himself to the subject of invention, his explanations are often taken verbatim from the more straightforward *Ad Herennium*.[6] The importance of this is worth underscoring because it shows that in his use of textual authority, if not in his scientific outlook, Rupert was decidedly a "modern." After a long period of some obscurity, the *Ad Herennium* had begun

---

[4] On these commentaries see the introduction to Part 3, above.   [5] See Evans, *Old Arts and New Theology*, 73.
[6] See also Fredborg, "Ciceronian Rhetoric and the Schools," 24 and 36n.

to come into its own as a textbook in the eleventh century, when it started to circulate with the *De inventione*, and was increasingly commented on throughout the twelfth century.[7] It is likely that Rupert had a manuscript containing both texts, and was thus an eager beneficiary of the explosive new interest in the arts of the trivium in the twelfth century. Certainly the evidence of the classical citations in Rupert's writings at large suggests that he had access to a good monastic library.[8]

Looking even more closely at the work on its own terms, one finds that Rupert's treatment of rhetoric in relation to Scripture is distinctive and even surprising, for all the quiet conservatism of his general approach to the arts. The originality of his exegetical application of rhetoric to Scripture is probably a measure of his isolation from a broader, "modern," scholarly conversation about the role and value of the trivium arts. He uses Scripture to illustrate the elements of rhetorical doctrine, but not with the idea of teaching how to use rhetoric; unlike Augustine's *De doctrina christiana*, Rupert's work does not present itself as a Christian appropriation of prescriptive rhetoric to guide future preachers. Rather, his purpose is to return us to the reading of Scripture itself, armed with a greater understanding of how skillfully Scripture perfects its discourse and purveys its message of salvation.[9] In showing us how to read Scripture rhetorically, he focuses on the forensic dimension of rhetorical theory. He is especially fascinated by what is known as "status theory," the technical system for determining the juridical status of an accusation (is the accusation flatly denied? is the deed admitted but hedged about by various legal questions that limit how the crime will be tried or change how the accused will plead?). Rupert shows a profound sensitivity to the intricacy of argumentation and judicial process, showing how these questions can illuminate not only the Bible's forensic structures but also its moral and theological underpinnings. For every legal concern broached in rhetorical theory, Rupert supplies a corresponding principle of faith. Thus, for example, he illustrates the juridical issue of *remotio criminis* (rejecting responsibility and shifting the blame to another) by the hapless and fatal attempts of Adam and Eve to shift the blame from themselves, Adam to Eve, Eve to the serpent. At every turn the forensic subtleties of classical rhetoric are infused with cosmic significance, and rhetorical theory becomes an exegetical lever for the proper apprehension of scriptural law and salvation history. We will not see the like of such a passionate exegetical approach to rhetoric again. The professionalization of rhetorical teaching would become the norm by the end of the twelfth

---

[7] See Ward, *Ciceronian Rhetoric in Treatise, Scholion and Commentary*, 90–100 (on the textual tradition of the *Ad Herennium*) and 134–67 (on the growth of commentaries on the text).

[8] See the articles by Silvestre, "Les citations et réminiscences classiques dans l'oeuvre de Rupert de Deutz," and "Rupert de Saint-Laurent et les auteurs classiques."

[9] See Ward, *Ciceronian Rhetoric*, 131.

century, and Rupert's attempts to harmonize scriptural principles of faith with the interior structures of forensic rhetoric seem to have no clear influence on rhetorical theory in later generations.

Translated from *De sancta trinitate et operibus eius*, ed. Haacke, *by permission.*

ON GRAMMAR

Grammar, that is, skill in speaking, comes first among the liberal arts and so also came first in Holy Scripture or the wisdom of God. Thus there is no doubt that the Hebrews received the primary forms of this art, that is the common letters that make up books—knowledge of which is as it were the childhood of the art of grammar—when they took the law of God from Moses.[10]

It is not my purpose here to distinguish and describe the divisions of the art of grammar, which are numbered by some at thirty—that is, the eight parts of speech, articulate sound, the letter, the syllable, (metrical) feet, accent, the punctuation mark, the critical sign, orthography and analogy, etymology, gloss, the near-synonym [*differentia*], barbarism, solecism, faults, metaplasm, schemes, tropes, prose, meters, fables [*fabulae*], and history[11]—although in fact these are contained and observable everywhere in Holy Scripture to such a degree that it does not even overlook *fabula*. The grammarians called them *fabulae* from *fari* ["speaking"], because they are not actual events, but only things made up in speaking [*loquendo fictae*]. *Fabulae* are used in order that through the fiction of a dialogue between dumb creatures, or even of inanimate things, we may discover a certain likeness to human life. The son of Jerubbaal, in the book of Judges, used such a device: "Hear me, ye men of Sichem, so may God hear you. The trees went to anoint a king over them: and they said to the olive tree: 'Reign thou over us.' And it answered: 'Can I leave my fatness, which both gods and men make use of, to come to be promoted among the trees?' And the trees said to the fig tree: 'Come thou and reign over us.' Etc."[12] And take this example from Chronicles, when Amaziah king of Judah sent to the king of Israel, saying: " 'Come, let us see one another.' But he sent back the messengers, saying: 'The thistle that is in Libanus sent to the cedar in Libanus, saying: Give thy daughter to my son to wife: and behold the beasts that were in the wood of Libanus passed by, and trod down the thistle.' "[13]

---

[10] Cf. Isidore, *Etymologiae* 1.2.1–1.3.5.   [11] Cf. Isidore, *Etymologiae* 1.5.4.   [12] Judges 9:7–11.
[13] 2 Chronicles 25:17–18.

Schemes, which is a Greek word, and which we (in Latin) rightly call "nature" [*habitus*], "forms," or "figures," because through them speech is in some way clothed and adorned,[14] may properly be found ready for discovery everywhere in Holy Scripture, as for example in the psalm: *Fundamenta eius in montibus sanctis, diligit Dominus portas Sion* ["His own buildings in the sacred hills, the Lord loves the gates of Sion"].[15] This figure is called *prolepsis*, that is, *praeoccupatio* or *praesumptio*, when those words which ought to follow are placed in front.[16] He placed the word *eius* [his] in front, saying *fundamenta eius* [his own building], subjoining to it afterwards whose it was, that is God's, *diligit Dominus* [the Lord loves]. This and other figures or kinds of schemes are found everywhere in Holy Scripture. Indeed the Greeks pride themselves greatly on having discovered figures and tropes; but since Holy Scripture is preeminent among all other writings, not only on account of its authority, because it is divine, or on account of its usefulness, because it leads to eternal life, but also on account of its antiquity, their pride is not only vain but also false.

Holy Scripture did not even ignore metrical lines, which are so called because they are determined by fixed measures [*mensurae*] and lengths of feet.[17] The psalms are made up of lyric feet, and virtually the whole book of blessed Job is comprised of hexameter verses flowing in swift measures of dactyl and spondee.

On Rhetoric

If anyone has ever, anywhere, set eyes clearly on rhetoric—the science of speaking well—so that he is capable of truly recognizing its face; and if that man then enters upon Scripture, of which we speak here, without either being half asleep or blinded by a cloud of malevolence, he is not wrong in saying that rhetoric is especially prominent there. Let us present some brief examples here of the first part of rhetoric, that is, invention. There are five parts of rhetoric: invention, arrangement, style, memory, and delivery.

With invention as our subject, let us assert from the start that the most excellent and truest invention is that of those true rhetoricians of whom we now speak, who, in writing Scripture, argued the cases of God before men, because what they "discovered" [*invenire*] or expressed eloquently [*eloqui*] or delivered in speeches [*pronuntiare*] they found [*invenire*], not in their own hearts and minds like speakers in forensic or civil exercises, but rather in the Holy Spirit, just as the apostle Peter said: "Understanding this first: that

---

[14] Cf. Isidore, *Etymologiae* 1.36.1.
[16] Cf. Isidore, *Etymologiae* 2.21.29.
[15] Psalm 86:1–2 (our translation for clarity).
[17] Cf. Isidore, *Etymologiae* 1.39.1.

no prophecy of Scripture is made by private interpretation. For prophecy came not by the will of man at any time: but the holy men of God spoke, inspired by the Holy Ghost."[18]

The rhetoricians say that invention is divided or located in six parts, which are exordium, statement of facts [*narratio*], partition [*divisio*], proof [*confirmatio*], refutation [*confutatio*], and conclusion.[19]

The exordium is the beginning of the discourse, through which the mind of the hearer or judge is disposed or prepared for listening.[20]

The statement of facts sets forth the events that have occurred or might have occurred.[21]

By means of the partition we make clear what matters are agreed upon and what are contested, and announce what points we intend to take up.[22]

Proof is the presentation of our arguments together with their corroboration.[23]

Refutation is the destruction of our adversaries' arguments.[24]

The conclusion (peroration) is the end of the discourse, formed in accordance with the principles of the art.[25]

The first of these parts, the exordium, is divided into two kinds, the introduction [*principium*] and the insinuation [*insinuatio*].[26] We use an introduction when straight away, in an overt way, we prepare the mind of the hearer to attend to our speech, that is, we make him attentive, receptive, and well disposed. We use an insinuation when, because of the nature of the case [*causa*], we see that the mind of the audience is hostile to our arguments, and through indirection and dissimulation we do everything to be able to reach the same favorable position in speaking [as there would be with introduction]. But on the other hand, if the case is really an honorable one, it will be acceptable either to use an introduction or not. Now what dishonorable case would the Holy Spirit, the author of Holy Scripture, take on, or wish for us to hear from him? By rights, then our author should not be criticized by those [pagan] orators, for it was permissible for Him either to

---

[18] 2 Peter 1:20–1.

[19] *Ad Herennium* 1.3.4 (where Rupert's wording is especially close to the *Ad Herennium*, as in this section on the parts of the oration, we follow the wording of Caplan's translation); cf. *De inventione* 1.14.19; Isidore, *Etymologiae* 2.7.1.

[20] *Ad Herennium* 1.3.4; cf. *De inventione* 1.15.20.

[21] *Ad Herennium* 1.3.4, cf. *De inventione* 1.20.28.

[22] *Ad Herennium* 1.3.4; cf. *De inventione* 1.22.31.

[23] *Ad Herennium* 1.3.4; cf. *De inventione* 1.24.34.

[24] *Ad Herennium* 1.3.4; cf. *De inventione* 1.42.78.

[25] *Ad Herennium* 1.3.4; cf. *De inventione* 1.52.98.

[26] *Ad Herennium* 1.4.6, where *principium* (translated by Caplan as "direct opening") is equated with *prooemium*; cf. *De inventione* 1.15.20.

use an introduction or not. Moses does not use an introduction, but begins directly with his statement of facts [*narratio*], saying "In the beginning God created heaven and earth";[27] nor do Joshua nor Judges nor Kings use an introduction, but they start straight away with the statement of facts. This is not by accident or for lack of skill, because where it was needed no one was better equipped than Moses to use an introduction, by which he was able to command the attention not only of men but of the heavens, and make the earth attentive and eager to listen, when he said: "Hear O ye heavens, the things I speak, let the earth give ear to the words of my mouth."[28] The patriarch Jacob also knew how to use an introduction to good effect, where he said: "Gather yourselves together, that I may tell you the things that shall befall you in the last days. Gather yourselves together, and hear, O ye sons of Jacob, hearken to Israel, your father."[29] This is clearly the introduction of a man who wishes to make his sons attentive, receptive, and well disposed to listen. Elsewhere, in the Laws and in the prophets, we find the same introduction serving the same purpose almost in every single chapter, namely: "And the Lord spoke to Moses, saying,"[30] or "Thus saith the Lord of hosts, saying."[31]

Furthermore, there is insinuation, the other species of exordium, which is said to be useful when the mind of the hearer is alienated or offended, or when he is tired of listening. Thus the woman of Tekoa used insinuation in the presence of King David, who in his heart was alienated from his son Absolom because of the dire quality of the case: "Alas I am a widow woman; for my husband is dead. And thy handmaid had two sons: and they quarrelled with each other in the field, and there was none to part them: and the one struck the other, and slew him. And behold the whole kindred rising against thy handmaid, saith: Deliver him that hath slain his brother, that we may kill him for the life of his brother, whom he slew, and that we may destroy the heir."[32] But why seek examples here and there when Wisdom incarnate saw fit to use this form [i.e. an introduction] with his own mouth? For he said: " 'Simon, I have somewhat to say to thee.' But he said, 'Master, say it.' 'A certain creditor had two debtors; one owed five hundred pence, and the other fifty. And whereas they had not wherewith to pay, he forgave them both. Which therefore of the two loveth him most?' "[33]

We find many examples of narration in Scripture with or without the aforesaid introduction, as the speaker chooses. Is not every narration in Holy Scripture brief and lucid? We believe, and certainly not mistakenly, that the most perfect narration of all secular authors is slack, redundant, and overly obscure in comparison with that of Holy

[27] Genesis 1:1.   [28] Deuteronomy 32:1.   [29] Genesis 49:1–2.   [30] Exodus 32:7.
[31] For example, Zechariah 6:12.   [32] 2 Samuel 14:5–7.   [33] Luke 7:40–2.

Scripture. So brief and lucid is it that it always delights the audience in a way that is wondrous and almost ineffable, and it always fascinates. No less surprisingly, its style is so simple that anyone would believe himself able to imitate it, and so profound that virtually no one would prove himself capable of matching its character [*modus*]. Here one would be entirely right to quote that famous verse by Flaccus: "whoever hopes for the same success, may sweat much and yet toil in vain when attempting the same";[34] and elsewhere: "[as he wrought his verse] he would oft scratch his head and gnaw his nails to the quick. Often must you turn your pencil to erase, if you hope to write something worth a second reading . . ."[35]

We could give many magnificent examples of how the Holy Spirit, the author of Scripture, makes use of partition; but one will suffice, taken from the same passage in Luke that we have cited above. Simon said to himself: "This man, if he were a prophet, would know surely who and what manner of woman this is that toucheth him, that she is a sinner."[36] Now it was agreed between Simon and the Lord that she was a sinner, wherefore the controversy lay in the fact that she had touched the Lord. For the Lord freely let himself be touched. Simon silently reproved this touch. In his response, the Lord made use of partition: for, passing over the fact that she was a sinner, he proceeded to defend the fact that she touched him. "Dost thou see this woman?" he said. "I entered into thy house: thou gavest me no water for my feet. But she with tears hath washed my feet; and with her hairs hath wiped them."[37]

Defense is made through proof and refutation: through proof of one's own side of the case, through refutation of the adversary's side. For examples of these things, we need go no further than this same chapter. Immediately producing three pairs of opposing arguments, Christ proves, on the one hand, the true justice of penitence, which comes from faith and love, and on the other hand he refutes false justice with chastisement. He says, "thou gavest me no water for my feet. But she with tears hath washed my feet; and with her hairs hath wiped them. Thou gavest me no kiss. But she, since she came in, hath not ceased to kiss my feet. My head with oil thou didst not anoint. But she with ointment hath anointed my feet."[38] Then immediately follows a fourth opposition; and with what mildness and restraint does it avoid increasing the envy of the man who had made the reproaches. For he says, "Wherefore, I say to thee: Many sins are forgiven her, because she hath loved much. But to whom less is forgiven, he loveth less."[39] It is as if he said, "You think that you have few sins to be forgiven, but you also love the less." The

---

[34] Horace, *Ars poetica* 240–3.   [35] Horace, *Satires* 1.10.71–3, trans. Fairclough.
[36] Luke 7:39.   [37] Luke 7:44.   [38] Luke 7:44–6.   [39] Luke 7:47.

sense of this is: "She who loves a great deal, will be forgiven many sins; but for you who love less, your sins are less to be forgiven."

He uses the conclusion, which is a skillful ending of a speech, no less wisely and justly than skillfully, when he says to the woman: "Thy faith hath made thee safe. Go in peace."[40]

In the proof and the refutation in particular, the rhetoricians think it is very important to use arguments, and they think it is very hard to polish what they have found, and to deliver it expeditiously.[41] Expeditious delivery, they say, ensures that we do not dwell longer than necessary on the same topics [*loci*], nor return to the same one several times, nor leave an argument undeveloped, nor pass incommodiously to the next one.

They say that the most complete and perfect form of argumentation is divided into five parts: the major premise [*propositio*], reasoning [*ratio*], proof of the reasoning [*rationis confirmatio*], embellishing of proofs [*exornatio*], and conclusion [*complexio*].[42] The spirit of God also did not neglect this form for his own purposes in Scripture, nor did he despise it. If you study this diligently, it shines forth there with no paucity of examples. Most of them are manifest enough, but I would like briefly to discuss some examples from places where this skill happens to be less obvious. An example of a premise [*propositio*] is that verse of Psalm 8: "O Lord, our Lord, how admirable is thy name in the whole earth!"[43] There the prophet shows in summary form what it is that he intends to prove. An example of reasoning [*ratio*] is what he connects to it in the next two verses: "For thy magnificence is elevated above the heavens. Out of the mouth of infants and of sucklings thou hast perfected praise, because of thy enemies, that thou mayst destroy the enemy and the avenger."[44] By means of these verses he demonstrates the truth of what he intended to prove, that is, he proves that the name of God is majestic, because Christ was elevated to glory and ascended to the heavens. And so from the mouth of the apostles, who were like infants, that is, "illiterate and ignorant men,"[45] he has perfected the praise of his evangelical preaching. The proof of the reasoning [*rationis confirmatio*] is what he adjoins to this: "For I will behold thy heavens, the works of thy fingers: the moon and the stars which thou hast founded."[46] This verse briefly proves the reasoning that he has set forth, that it is truly not a strange or incredible thing that God has perfected his praise in the mouth of babes: for indeed those who were babes or infants, who accepted the Holy Spirit, have become

[40] Luke 7:50. [41] This refers to invention and *pronunciatio* or delivery.

[42] Cf. *De inventione* 1.34.58–9, and especially 1.37.67: *propositio, approbatio, assumptio, assumptionis approbatio, complexio* (major premise, proof, minor premise, proof of minor premise, conclusion); Victorinus, *Explanationes*, 243, and Isidore, *Etymologiae* 9.1 on the rhetorical syllogism. Rupert's treatment is a simplified synthesis of classical and late antique theory.

[43] Psalm 8:2. [44] Psalm 8:2–3. [45] Acts 4:13. [46] Psalm 8:4.

the heavens, and in their faith the moon and the stars, that is, the Catholic church and all the elect, could be founded. The embellishing of proofs [*exornatio*] is what is contained in the following verses: "What is man, that thou art mindful of him? or the son of man, that thou visitest him? Thou hast made him a little less than the angels, thou hast crowned him with glory and honor: and hast set him over the works of thy hands. Thou hast subjected all things under his feet, all sheep and oxen: moreover, the beasts also of the fields. The birds of the air, and the fishes of the sea, that pass through the paths of the sea."[47] In these verses he has graced and embellished the case outstandingly with rich adornment of piety, admiring the greatness of the honor done to man, how God has so greatly redeemed man, who was so long cast out of eternal life because of the devil's envy. The conclusion is the first verse, repeated: "O Lord, our Lord, how admirable is thy name in the whole earth."[48] In concluding thus briefly, he gathers together the parts of the syllogistic argument.[49] This is a complete five-part argument of someone proving his case: for he proves that the name of God is wonderful throughout the earth. However, in the following psalm, from the verse where he says "Arise, O Lord God, let not man be strengthened," to the verse where he says "Arise, O Lord God, let they hand be exalted,"[50] if you look carefully, there is a complete, five-part argument of someone refuting a case. For he refutes the enemy, the "man of sin," "the son of perdition," as the apostle says, "Who . . . is lifted up above all that is called God, or that is worshipped."[51] It remains to consider where or whence arguments can be made more briefly, with one or two parts left out, that is, where we present the case succinctly so that it is easily held in the memory. The embellishing of proofs [*exornatio*] is to be omitted under these circumstances if the case seems insufficiently rich for amplification and embellishment. If however the case is both slight and humble, then both the embellishment and the summing up are omitted. This practice is found so commonly in our Scriptures that it would be superfluous to give any examples, especially when enough has been said about this topic and we are hastening on to our next subject.

Next, our orators and inventors of rhetoric admitted three kinds of causes: demonstrative, deliberative, and judicial.[52] For they frequently deal with the praise and blame of one or many (definite) persons, these being the parts of the demonstrative [epideictic] genre—for example, when God receives praise and the devil vituperation. Again, it is not in few places or rarely that they refer to persuasion or dissuasion, for these are the parts of the deliberative genre, for example, persuading us to do something good or dissuading us from doing something bad. Again, they often treat accusation and defense, which are the parts

---

[47] Psalm 8:5–9.   [48] Psalm 8:2.

[49] Cf. Victorinus, *Explanationes* 243, who distinguishes between "argument" and "argumentation," the latter signifying "syllogistic reasoning."

[50] Psalm 9:20–33.   [51] 2 Thessalonians 2:3–4.   [52] *De inventione* 2.4.12; Isidore, *Etymologiae* 2.4.1.

of the judicial genre, for example, accusing a criminal or defending a righteous person, as for example in the apostle, when one man is accused on account of a disobedience through which "many were made sinners," and one man is defended on account of obedience through which "many shall be made just."[53]

Those questions also which the ancient rhetoricians call constitutions [*status*], that is, the conjectural, the legal, and the juridical, no secular writer ever treated or was able to treat so justly or wisely as it is treated in sacred Scripture, of which we speak here.[54] Now it is a conjectural status when there is a controversy concerning a fact,[55] as in this way: A man has given to his neighbour an ass, an ox, a sheep, or any animal to keep, and by chance it died or was hurt or was raided by enemies, but no one saw this. How to determine what happened? "There shall be an oath between them, that he did not put forth his hand to his neighbour's goods: and the owner shall accept of the oath, and he shall not be compelled to make restitution."[56] And there are many similar examples of this. It is a legal status when some controversy arises from the letter of a text or from the meaning implicit in writings,[57] as in this example: the Jewish people believed that they were faithfully fulfilling the sacred law of Holy Scripture by offering burnt sacrifices and eating the flesh. But was this so? "Add your burnt offerings to your sacrifices, and eat ye the flesh. For I spoke not to your fathers, and I commanded them not, in the day that I brought them out of the land of Egypt, concerning the matter of burnt offerings and sacrifices. But this thing I commanded them, saying: Hearken to my voice, and I will be your God, and you shall be my people."[58] The apostle Paul, writing to the Hebrews concerning this regulation, affirms the words of Jeremiah. The apostle compares the intention of the author, God, with the mere

---

[53] Romans 5:19. In this passage Rupert merges the rhetorical system of accusation and defense with the Pauline comparison between Adam's transgression (the sin of a single man) and Christ's redemption (the just act of a single man). In Rupert's language, however, it is the transgression itself—*iniustitia*—that is "accused," i.e., "the disobedience of one man" by which "many were made sinners," as if the scriptural meaning is that there is a judicial case against disobedience itself. Rupert blends rhetorical theory with Pauline language on the understanding that Scripture deploys legal rhetoric, not just against one sinning individual, but also against the very category of sin as embodied in the first sinner.

[54] The term *constitutio* is the Latin equivalent of the Greek term *stasis*. In *De inventione* Cicero uses the term *constitutio*, as does the *Ad Herennium*; in later works Cicero uses the Latin term *status*. Literally, *stasis* (Greek) or *status* (Latin) means "position," i.e. the defense takes up a certain defensive "position" with regard to the accusations. The Latin terms *status* and *constitutio* are usually rendered in English as "status," "issue," or "constitution." In this section, Rupert draws mainly on *Ad Herennium* 1.11.18–1.15.25. Other sources are Isidore's *Etymologiae* 2.5, which is a rather compressed account of status theory based on Cassiodorus, and *De inventione*. Rupert has preferred the relatively streamlined system of *Ad Herennium* to the overly complex treatment in Isidore, which derives from Cassiodorus' *Institutiones* and the Hermagorean system given there. On status theory, see Boethius, *De topicis differentiis* (above, pp. 198–201) and introduction to Part I; and see Calboli Montefusco, *La dottrina degli 'status' nella retorica greca e romana*.

[55] *Ad Herennium* 1.11.18; Isidore, *Etymologies* 2.5.3.   [56] Exodus 22:9–12.

[57] This closely follows *Ad Herennium* 1.11.19; cf. Isidore, *Etymologiae* 2.5.9.   [58] Jeremiah 7:21–3.

letter of the text, on which the Jews rely; he prefers the intention to the letter, expounding the writer's intention most lucidly and plausibly.[59]

The status is juridical when there is agreement on the act, that is, the act itself is not denied, but there is dispute about the right or wrong of the act. Of this issue there are two types, one called "absolute," the other "assumptive."[60] In God's judgments, an absolute issue is damned entirely. Now it is called an absolute issue when the act, in and of itself, without drawing on any extrinsic considerations, is said to be right.[61] But nothing that was done rightly is ever disputed by God as if it was not done rightly. Therefore this type (of issue) [i.e. the kind of defense mounted on this type of issue] is worthy of damnation in his eyes and it does not merit indulgence, as in the following example: "And Samuel said: 'What meaneth then this bleating of the flocks, which soundeth in my ears, and the lowing of the herds, which I hear? . . . Why then didst thou not hearken to the voice of the Lord: but hast turned to the prey, and hast done evil in the eyes of the Lord?' And Saul said to Samuel: 'Yea, I have hearkened to the voice of the Lord, and have walked in the way by which the Lord sent me, and have brought Agag, the king of Amalec, and Amalec I have slain.'"[62]

The other type of juridical issue is assumptive, which, before God, is partly endorsed and partly damned. It has four subdivisions: concession (acknowledgement of the charge), rejection of the responsibility [*remotio criminis*], shifting of the question of guilt [*translatio criminis*], and comparison with the alternative course [*comparatio*].[63] Before God, concession or acknowledgement of the crime is not only endorsed, it is in fact almost the only kind, or the best kind, of assumptive issue. For concession is where the accused asks for forgiveness. Indeed, we all stand accused before God, and every path to our peace is

---

[59] See Hebrews 7:28; and see *Ad Herennium* 1.11.19 on controversy from letter and spirit (*scriptum et sententia*); Cicero, *De inventione* 2.40.116–2.48.143 on controversies arising from ambiguity about the author's intention behind a written legal document, which is treated in Cicero as the "literal sense"; and Augustine, *De doctrina christiana*, book 3 for a Pauline reassessment of "authorial intention" as that which constitutes the "spiritual" sense of the written text. See Copeland, "The Ciceronian Rhetorical Tradition and Medieval Literary Theory," 235–43; Eden, "The Rhetorical Tradition and Augustinian Hermeneutics in *De doctrina christiana*."

[60] *Ad Herennium* 1.14.24. According to *Ad Herennium*, the absolute issue is one in which the act is considered only inherently, on its own terms without extraneous matter. The issue is assumptive when the defense must draw on extraneous considerations, of which there are four subtypes: acknowledgement of the charge, rejection of the responsibility, shifting the question of guilt, and comparison with the alternative course.

[61] Ibid.

[62] 1 Samuel [1 Kings] 15:14, 19–20. God had ordered Saul to destroy all of the Amalekites, including their flocks and their king Agag. Saul instead takes the king prisoner and spares the best of the flocks for sacrifice. He defends himself as if his act was inherently right: but on the terms that Rupert lays out here, Saul's act was inherently wrong, without extraneous considerations, because it involved disobedience to the order to destroy all. Here no defense is to be mounted on the basis of the act itself: the absolute type of issue must be damnable because there is no room, within an act of disobedience against God's command, for arguments about rightness or wrongness.

[63] *Ad Herennium* 1.14.24; cf. *De inventione* 1.11.15.

this one.[64] He is the most righteous who concedes the most and who most asks for forgiveness, as it is written: "The just is first accuser of himself."[65]

There are two subtypes of concession: the plea for mercy [*deprecatio*] and the exculpation [*purgatio*].[66] The plea for mercy is used when the wrongdoer confesses that a wrong was committed with intent, and that he sinned, and then asks for mercy,[67] as in the example of David: "To thee only have I sinned, and have done evil before thee."[68] The exculpation is where the wrongdoer denies that he acted with intent, but [says] rather that he acted through ignorance, or fortune [*fortuna*] (which we should rather call accident [*eventus*]), or necessity.[69] This is an example of acting through ignorance: "And God came to Abimelech in a dream by night, and he said to him: 'Lo thou shalt die for the woman that thou has taken: for she hath a husband.' Now Abimelech had not touched her, and he said: 'Lord, wilt thou slay a nation that is ignorant and just?'"[70] Wrongdoing through chance or accident (which the ancients called "fortune") is exemplified here: "[While these things were a doing, when Moses sought for the buck goat, that had been offered for sin, he found it burnt.] And being angry with Eleazar and Ithamar, the sons of Aaron that were left, he said: Why did you not eat in the holy place the sacrifice for sin, which is most holy, and given to you, that you may bear the iniquity of the people, and may pray for them in the sight of the Lord. Especially, whereas none of the blood thereof hath been carried within the holy places: and you ought to have eaten it in the sanctuary, as was commanded me? Aaron answered: This day hath been offered the victim for sin, and the holocaust before the Lord: and to me what thou seest has happened. How could I eat it, or please the Lord in the ceremonies, having a sorrowful heart?"[71] Wrongdoing through necessity is exemplified in this way: "And when [Jephthah] saw her, he rent his garments, and said: 'Alas, my daughter, thou hast deceived me, and thou thyself art deceived: for I have opened my mouth to the Lord, and I can do no other thing.'"[72] For it was by necessity of a vow, because he had opened his mouth to God, saying: "If thou wilt deliver the children of Ammon into my hands, whosoever shall first come forth out of the doors of my house, and shall meet me, when I return in peace from the children of Ammon, the same will I offer a holocaust to the Lord."[73] It was by necessity of a vow, I say, that he who killed his daughter for a burnt offering is exculpated and excused, and he deserves to be included in the catalogue of saints, "who by faith conquered kingdoms."[74] Thus also David accepted and

---

[64] Cf. Proverbs 21:2.   [65] Proverbs 18:17; Vulgate: "Iustus prior est accusator sui."
[66] *Ad Herennium* 2.16.23; cf. *De inventione* 2.31.94.   [67] *Ad Herennium* 2.17.25; *De inventione* 2.34.04.
[68] Psalm 50 (51): 6 (4).   [69] Cf. *Ad Herennium* 2.16.23; *De inventione* 2.31.94.   [70] Genesis 20:3–5.
[71] Leviticus 10:16–19.   [72] Judges 11:35.   [73] Judges 11:30–1.
[74] I.e., the catalogue of exemplars of faith in the Epistle to Hebrews, chapter 11; Hebrews 11:33.

ate the holy bread given by Abimelech the priest,[75] and because he did this out of necessity, he is exculpated and excused, as God says to the Pharisees, "Have you not read what David did when he was hungry, and they that were with him: how he entered into the house of God, and did eat the loaves of proposition, which it was not lawful for him to eat, nor for them that were with him, but for the priests only?"[76] And just after this, "And if you knew what this meaneth: 'I will have mercy, and not sacrifice':[77] you would never have condemned the innocent."[78] Thus concession and its two parts, the plea for mercy and exculpation, are acceptable in the judgment of God.

Comparison with the alternative course of wrongdoing [*comparatio*][79] is exemplified in this way: As you said, Paul, "if you be circumcised, Christ shall profit you nothing";[80] so why did you circumcise Timothy?[81] Similarly, why is it, Paul, that you "took the men and, the next day being purified with them, entered into the temple, giving notice of the accomplishment of the days of purification, until an oblation should be offered for every one of them"?[82] Paul says, it was in order to escape the peril of a greater accusation, because the Jews had heard that I was teaching deviation from the law of Moses,[83] but this was false, for I am with the law of Moses in spirit and truth. However, this could not be demonstrated by reasoning with the Jews, and I could not demonstrate it without resorting to the appearance of wrongdoing.[84]

Shifting of the question of guilt [*translatio criminis*] and rejection of the responsibility [*remotio criminis*], which are the two remaining parts of the assumptive issue (which in turn was one of the two types of the juridical issue), are to be avoided by the wise everywhere in God's judgment, because in these lie both the origin and the increase of sin. Thus God said to Adam, "And who hath told thee that thou wast naked, but that thou hast eaten of the tree whereof I commanded thee that thou shouldst not eat?" And Adam: "'The woman,' he said, 'whom thou gavest me to be my companion, gave me of the tree and I did eat.'"[85] By saying this he wanted to shift the question of guilt [i.e. shift the accusation away from himself]. The issue is one of shifting the question of guilt "when we do not deny our act but plead that we were driven to it by the crimes of others."[86] Here is another example: "And the Lord God said to the woman, 'Why hast thou done this?' And

---

[75] 1 Kings (1 Samuel) 21:1–6.   [76] Matthew 12:3–4.   [77] Hosea 6:6.   [78] Matthew 12:7.
[79] *Ad Herennium* 1.15.25; *De inventione* 1.11.15.   [80] Galatians 5:2.   [81] See Acts 16:3.
[82] Acts 21:26.   [83] See Acts 21:21.
[84] That is, Paul observed Jewish purification rituals, which the early Christians had rejected.
[85] Genesis 3:11–12.
[86] *Ad Herennium* 1.15.25. The *Ad Herennium* exemplifies this by way of the case of Orestes, "when he defended himself by diverting the issue of guilt from himself to his mother"; Rupert's scriptural example of Adam is similarly grandly mythic.

she answered: 'The serpent deceived me, and I did eat.'"[87] By saying this surely she wanted, not to remove the accusation from herself, but rather the culpability, that is, the cause of the accusation. The issue is one of rejecting the responsibility [*remotio criminis*] "when we repudiate, not the act charged, but the responsibility, and either transfer it to another person or attribute it to some circumstance."[88] But to what kind of "person" [*persona*] did the woman transfer the accusation, if indeed it is to be dignified by being called a "person"? A snaky spirit, that is, the devil, or a ground creeper, a snake. To what kind of circumstance [*res*]? The deception by the snake.[89] Thus this transference does not exculpate her, but defiles her; it does not absolve her, but envelops her further.[90] For what was the promise of the deceitful snake? "And the serpent said to the woman: 'No, you shall not die the death. For God doth know that in what day soever you shall eat thereof, your eyes shall be opened: and you shall be as gods, knowing good and evil.'"[91] Let the woman say that the serpent not only urged her, but also showed her the reason why she should eat the fruit. Does she not make the accusation worse by such a rejection of it? Thus rightly will we say that shifting of responsibility and rejecting responsibility for the accusation should in no way be sought out in sacred Scripture, nor should issues of this sort be argued between man and God; and comparison with the alternative course of wrongdoing is barely acceptable. But concession, or acknowledgement of the crime, is always desirable between us and God, and especially the plea for mercy, which is the better of the two types of concession.

---

[87] Genesis 3:13.   [88] *Ad Herennium* 1.15.25.

[89] The terminology here, *persona* and *res*, continues to draw from the account in the *Ad Herennium* 1.15.25.

[90] Rupert considers *translatio criminis* (shifting responsibility) and *remotio criminis* (rejecting responsibility) to be essentially the same thing in terms of scriptural law, and uses the terms almost interchangeably, giving the example of Eve and the serpent to illustrate both.

[91] Genesis 3:4–5.

THIERRY OF CHARTRES, COMMENTARIES ON THE *DE INVENTIONE* AND *RHETORICA AD HERENNIUM*, CA. 1130–1140

INTRODUCTION

Thierry (born ca. 1095) was a native of Brittany, and was possibly the younger brother of Bernard of Chartres, who had been a master at the cathedral school and then chancellor in the 1120s. There are many contemporary testimonies to Thierry's influence and reputation as a teacher, but the outlines of his actual career are somewhat difficult to trace. His teaching career spans a period from the 1120s until at least the 1140s. He was chancellor of Chartres Cathedral from about 1142/3, and in the following decade retired to a Cistercian monastery where he died as a monk sometime after 1156. It is not known with certainty how much of his teaching career he spent at the cathedral school of Chartres before the 1140s, since there is also evidence to place him in Paris for some periods during those earlier years.[1] Like Bernard of Chartres, on the one hand, Thierry was known as a consummate and charismatic teacher of the language arts; on the other hand, like his contemporary William of Conches (who was also renowned for his grammatical expertise), Thierry was recognized for his philosophical and scientific investigations. Unlike William of Conches, however, Thierry did not produce a substantial original treatise on scientific or philosophical matters or on any of the arts. We know the innovative and systematic quality of his thought through his commentaries on Boethius' theological writings and on the Ciceronian rhetorics, his unfinished commentary on the six days of creation in the book of Genesis, and his encyclopedic anthology of primary texts on the seven liberal arts, the *Heptateuchon*.

---

[1] The best overview of the evidence for Thierry's teaching career is given by Fredborg in her edition of Thierry: *The Latin Rhetorical Commentaries by Thierry of Chartres*, 3–9. Detailed information can be found in Häring, "Chartres and Paris Revisited," 279–94; and Ward, "The Date of the Commentary on Cicero's *De inventione* by Thierry of Chartres," 238–47. See also Jeauneau, *L'Âge d'or des écoles de Chartres*, 65–72.

There are abundant witnesses to his standing as a teacher, scholar, and thinker. The disciples and former students who recorded their debts to him include some of the greatest figures of twelfth-century literary and scientific culture. Most famously, John of Salisbury lists him among the luminaries of the urban schools as "a most zealous investigator of the arts."[2] Others who cited him for his wit and innovative learning include Bernardus Silvestris, Hermann of Carinthia, Clarembaldus of Arras, and William of Tyre.[3]

A verse epitaph for him, copied during the second half of the twelfth century, begins "Here lies Thierry, worthy successor of Aristotle."[4] When placed against what we have of Thierry's own scholarly output, the epitaph gives a strikingly accurate picture of his intellectual interests and contributions to studies. It presents him both as supreme explicator of the mysteries of Platonic thought about cosmic creation, and innovative exponent of Aristotle's *Prior Analytics* and *Sophistical Refutations*—that is, what we would now see as the early wave of the *logica nova*.[5] The epitaph mentions his distinction as a teacher of Latinity [*lingua latina*] and his mastery of the explanatory power of the quadrivial arts. His commitment to the language arts is attested in his careful commentaries on the *De inventione* and *Ad Herennium*. His philosophical thought is represented in a series of commentaries on Boethius' *De trinitate* (On the Trinity), and in the hexaemeral commentary on Genesis, the *Tractatus de sex dierum operibus* (Treatise on the Works of the Six Days), which is his best-known scientific work.[6] In these works, his philosophical outlook can best be summed up as the exploration of the "seminal causes" of natural and divine truths through the theoretical or speculative sciences, that is, physics (physical or

---

[2] *Metalogicon* 1.5.

[3] See *Cosmographia*, ed. Dronke, 96; Burnett, "Arabic into Latin in Twelfth-Century Spain: the Works of Hermann of Carinthia," 112; Häring, *Life and Works of Clarembald of Arras*, 225–6; William of Tyre, *Historia rerum in partibus transmarinis gestarum*, ed. Huygens, chapter XIX.12. It is probably also our Thierry who appears in Abelard's autobiography as a "Terricus, schoolmaster," who intervened on Abelard's behalf at the Council of Soissons in 1121 (*Historia calamitatum*, ed. Monfrin, 88). There is also an anecdote about Abelard attending Thierry's lectures on mathematics: see Mews, "In Search of a Name and its Significance: A Twelfth-Century Anecdote about Thierry and Peter Abaelard." Other contemporary references to his sharp wit include the poem *Metamorphosis Goliae* (1142/3), ed. Huygens, "Mitteilungen aus Handschriften," lines 764–72, and see Wetherbee, *Platonism and Poetry in the Twelfth Century*, 127–34, and Benton, "Philology's Search for Abelard in the *Metamorphosis Goliae*." Thierry's fame is mentioned in Otto of Freising's biography of Frederick Barbarossa, *Gesta Frederici I imperatoris*, ed. Waitz, 68; and in the biography of Adalbert of Mainz by Anselm of Havelberg, ed. Jaffé, 589–92, where Thierry is described as "orator, rhetor, and lover of the arts of grammar and logic."

[4] Vernet, "Une épitaphe inédite de Thierry de Chartres."

[5] See Jacobi, "Logic (ii): the Later Twelfth Century," 236–7.

[6] In edition by Häring, ed., *Commentaries on Boethius by Thierry of Chartres and His School*, which includes an edition of the *Tractatus* on Genesis. See also Häring, "The Creation and Creator of the World," for a close study of the *Tractatus*; and for interpretations of the *Tractatus*, see Dronke, "Thierry of Chartres"; Lejbowicz, "Thierry de Chartres entre *expositio* et *tractatus*"; and Coleman, "Universal History *secundum physicam et ad litteram* in the Twelfth Century."

natural science), mathematics (which comprises the four disciplines of the quadrivium), and theology. His work is exemplary of the Platonist cosmology that has been associated with the "School of Chartres."[7]

The commentaries on the *De inventione* and *Rhetorica ad Herennium* record Thierry's teachings of these texts during the 1130s, either at Paris or Chartres, or perhaps both. Thierry's commentaries signal the mature phase of eleventh- and twelfth-century study of Ciceronian rhetoric. His commentaries represent the high water mark, with respect both to influence and innovation. The influence of Thierry's rhetorical teaching extends beyond commentaries and glosses on Ciceronian texts: his insights became a definitive reference for understanding the art of rhetoric. In the *De divisione philosophiae*, Gundissalinus used Thierry's "prologue to the art of rhetoric" in its entirety for his own account of the "extrinsic" aspects of the art. In about 1213, Ralph of Longchamps produced a commentary on Alan of Lille's *Anticlaudianus*, making extended and apparently grateful use of Thierry's *De inventione* commentary to elaborate Alan's abbreviated account of rhetoric.[8] The innovations of Thierry's commentaries on the Ciceronian texts can be summed up as an intelligent "refurbishment" of the rhetorical gloss of the preceding generations: he seeks out a systematic terminology for rhetorical concepts, imposes order and method on his explanations, strives for brevity and clarity, and gives pride of place to the oldest and most authoritative sources, the late antique commentaries of Victorinus and of the sixth-century grammarian Grillius, and Boethius' *De topicis differentiis*.[9]

Thierry's prologue to the art of rhetoric clearly exemplifies his methodological innovation. He applies a newly current analytical technique of twelfth-century scholarship, the *accessus ad artem* (introduction to the art), and builds into it a definitive statement of the "extrinsic art."[10] The headings of his prologue go back to the *De inventione* (1.4.5) and to Boethius' *De topicis differentiis*, book 4: these ten headings—the genus of the art, its definition, its subject matter, its function, its goal, its parts, its species, its instrument, its artificer, and why it is so called—enable the commentator to place the art in a larger epistemology, to recognize that the art is not an end in itself, but is part of a larger system of knowledge.[11]

---

[7] Among many studies, see Jeauneau, "Un représentant du platonisme au XIIe siècle: Maitre Thierry de Chartres," and "Mathématiques et trinité chez Thierry de Chartres"; Maccagnolo, *Rerum universitas*, 25–101; Rodrigues, "La conception de la philosophie chez Thierry de Chartres"; Speer, "The Discovery of Nature."

[8] *In Anticlaudianum Alani commentum*, ed. Sulowski.

[9] Ward, review of Fredborg, ed., *The Latin Rhetorical Commentaries by Thierry of Chartres*, 362. See also Fredborg, "Thierry of Chartres, Innovator or Traditionalist," and Fredborg's edition of Thierry, 13–14; cf. Ward, *Ciceronian Rhetoric*, 143.

[10] See Fredborg edition, 14–16, and Hunt, "The Introductions to the 'Artes' in the Twelfth Century," 86–93, 98 (rpt. 118–25, 130).

[11] Ward, "The Date of the Commentary on Cicero," 249–50.

As Thierry notes, these are the "extrinsic" topics that we should consider before we enter into the "intrinsic" concerns of particular precepts in Tully's books. The distinction between "extrinsic" and "intrinsic" knowledge of an art was in no way new with Thierry: he attributes it to the ancients, and in fact these terms are found in Victorinus' commentary, and the distinction was used by some of the commentators in the generations immediately before Thierry.[12] But it was Thierry's innovation to present this epistemological information systematically, by bringing the introductory topics concerning the art under the heading "extrinsic," and by defining each topic methodically and precisely.

Thierry's innovations were important to his own contemporaries. Gundissalinus was to assimilate this careful presentation of the "extrinsic" art to his own encyclopedic purposes, not only borrowing Thierry's analysis for the section on rhetoric, but also applying the principles of this artistic procedure for his overall exposition of the sciences. We find the same *accessus ad artem* in William of Conches' redactions to his commentary on Priscian's grammar, and the extrinsic and intrinsic prologue became a useful tool for distinguishing between theoretical precept and practical application of a discipline.[13]

Thierry's commentary embodies and sums up twelfth-century concerns to understand and articulate the nature of any discipline. That Thierry brought a rhetorical terminology of "topics" to bear upon his understanding of the nature of rhetoric should not disguise the fact that his efforts belong to a much broader scientific inquiry into the essence of knowledge, the primary causes of all phenomena, and the nature of causality itself. In the comments that he devotes to the mythological proem of the *De inventione* (1.1.2), Thierry unpacks the meaning of the concept of the "beginning" (*principium*) of rhetoric, turning to the language of contemporary natural sciences and Platonic cosmology in order to determine the difference among kinds of "beginning" or "origin" of the art that Cicero's text seems to have implied. Thierry's attention to the nature of the art of rhetoric is consistent with his other scientific and epistemological interests, and with the philosophical and scientific investigations of his contemporaries, colleagues, and disciples, notably Bernard of Chartres, William of Conches, Bernardus Silvestris, Hermann of Carinthia, and Adelard of Bath.[14]

Thierry's commentaries are also a turning point for clarification of Ciceronian rhetorical precept and for appreciating its application to all kinds of discursive skills. Thierry made

---

[12] Ward traces the history of the distinction between the "extrinsic art" and the "intrinsic art" from ancient writers to the Ciceronian commentators of the eleventh and twelfth centuries, including Thierry and his immediate predecessors; see "The Date of the Commentary on Cicero's *De inventione* by Thierry of Chartres," 247–61.

[13] See Copeland, "The Ciceronian Rhetorical Tradition and Medieval Literary Theory," 250–3, and Minnis et al., eds., *Medieval Literary Theory and Criticism*, 130–4.

[14] Ward notes the rise of rhetoric commentaries in parallel with the rise of commentaries on the Calcidian *Timaeus* during the twelfth century; see *Ciceronian Rhetoric*, 236.

an unusual effort to resolve the key doctrinal discrepancies between the *De inventione* and the *Rhetorica ad Herennium*.[15] His commentaries are close and quite literal, so as to clarify, for the benefit of the twelfth-century scholar, the textual structure and theoretical value of these archaic republican rhetorics. The commentaries are sensitive to the literary character, the language, and the formal and argumentative coherence of the Ciceronian texts. In the selection below, we have a good example of Thierry's method of using Cicero's text to teach the effectiveness of rhetorical forms: according to Thierry, Tully mounts his defense of rhetoric in the form of an argument from insinuation, as if the case for rhetoric is a "difficult" one, and follows the order of a "deliberative" oration in which we set out the various "parts" or subdivisions of our case and then examine them one by one. Here Cicero speaks both *de arte* and *ex arte* (about the art and from the art): according to Thierry, Cicero is teaching about rhetoric by exemplifying rhetorical precepts, just as the *Ad Herennium* advises when it describes its own procedure of illustrating the precepts that it teaches (4.3.6). One important index of Thierry's literary interests is the way that he devotes such generous attention to Cicero's proem, giving it a far greater proportion of space in his commentary than it actually occupies in Cicero's text. Cicero's proem is a repository of mythological and historical exemplification, a powerful argument on behalf of the moral, social, and intellectual value of rhetoric. Above all, the proem demonstrates the need to unite eloquence with wisdom, providing ancient authority for the epistemological vision that Thierry was to articulate a few years later in the prologue to the *Heptateuchon*, the unity of eloquence and understanding (trivium and quadrivium).

Such literary analysis of the structure and preceptive method of the Ciceronian rhetorics became a fixture of twelfth-century commentaries, and was taken up as a self-conscious pedagogical device in the arts of poetry in the following generations.[16] Thierry and his twelfth-century successors also established a set canon of literary references for illustrating rhetorical precept, so that the same authors—notably Virgil, Statius, Terence, Horace, and Sallust—are cited from one commentary to the next.[17] This may suggest the close affiliation between grammatical study of the authors and the study of rhetoric. Indeed, Thierry's actual teaching on Ciceronian precept finds its way directly into grammatical study: the particular group of literary illustrations that he assembles for teaching inventional topics derived from the attributes of the person was inserted, virtually unchanged, into the section on character description in the *Ars versificatoria* of Matthew of Vendôme.[18]

---

[15] Fredborg, "Thierry of Chartres, Innovator or Traditionalist," and Fredborg's edition, 20–6.

[16] See Fredborg, "Ciceronian Rhetoric and the Schools," 29–31.

[17] Ward, *Ciceronian Rhetoric*, 143; Fredborg, "Thierry of Chartres, Innovator or Traditionalist," 130.

[18] Thierry (Fredborg edn.), 132–3; *Ars versificatoria*, in Matthew of Vendôme, ed. Munari, *Mathei Vindocinensis opera*, 1: §§ 79–82; cf. *De inventione* 1.24.35.

Thierry's discussions of the genres of narration, the levels of style, and stylistic ornamentation give us a clear indication of how Ciceronian rhetoric began to be adapted to literary interests and the teaching of literary composition during the twelfth century. His treatment of narration and the threefold generic division into *historia, fabula*, and *argumentum* or realistic fiction (*De inventione* 1.19.27) joins a long tradition of medieval elaboration of these distinctions, which finds its apogee in the arts of poetry in the next century.[19] Thierry's explanation of the doctrine of the levels of style in *Ad Herennium*, book 4 shows an adherence to the precept of the classical text, in which the level of style is independent of subject matter: "the grand type of discourse is an arrangement of discourse from words that pertain to great and lofty matters, irrespective of whether the speech is about matters great or lowly." Later in the twelfth century, there was to be a decisive shift away from this "elocutionary" concept of style to a "material" concept, where the level of style is tied directly to the subject matter (i.e. different genres and their social and moral contents). But Thierry's commentary occupies a transitional place in this development: he introduces examples from Horace's poetic teaching about stylistic propriety to illustrate the rhetorical doctrine of levels of style and their corresponding "faults" (at *Ad Herennium* 4.10.15), thereby anticipating the combination of Ciceronian and Horatian doctrine that was to be an important feature of later poetic theories of style.[20] Thierry's commentary also seems to have links with a near-contemporary commentary on Horace's *Ars poetica*, the "Materia" commentary: in both texts we encounter the very same explanation of the terminology for levels of style.[21] Whether or not this was a case of direct borrowing from one commentary or the other, it is more important to recognize how the two kinds of teaching, of rhetoric and of poetry, were deeply interconnected. This is particularly clear in the treatment of the ornaments or figures of speech from *Ad Herennium*, book 4, from which we provide the passages on metaphor and allegory: in his treatment of allegory, Thierry also attempts to bring Christian theological understandings of spiritual meaning into line with grammatical and rhetorical teaching, much as we see in Bede's explanation of *allegoria* and in Thomas of Chobham's discussion of tropes.[22] Finally, as Fredborg has noted, the very conception of an "art" of poetics, treated as an independent theoretical entity, has much in common with the scientific approach to the "art" of rhetoric exemplified in Thierry's commentary, in which rhetoric merits its own "extrinsic" introduction

---

[19] See Part 4 below.   [20] See Fredborg, "Ciceronian Rhetoric and the Schools," 32 and n. 89.

[21] See the selection from the "Materia" commentary in Part 4 below, and see Thierry's commentary at *Ad Herennium* 4.8.11 (*styli, figurae, characteres*).

[22] See selection from Thomas of Chobham in Part 4 below.

(the *accessus ad artem*) as a theoretical system separate from its instantiation in the Ciceronian textbooks.[23]

Translated from *The Latin Rhetorical Commentaries by Thierry of Chartres*, ed. Fredborg, by permission. Many of the notes about sources in rhetorical doctrine are based on the editor's apparatus.

THE PROLOGUE TO PART ONE

As Petronius said, "we masters will be left behind in the schools unless we flatter the masses and lay traps for the ears."[24] But that is not my way. To be sure, by God, I have prostituted my wares to the multitude for the sake of the few. But I have also made good my intention to exclude the profane mob[25] and the wanton hodgepodge of the schools. Those who imitate intelligence but abhor study, and those who profess private study but know no teacher, and even the play actors of scholastic disputation armed for the battles of empty words, such have been followers of my camp; but let those who are detained by nothing but the aura of my name, so that they may fabricate the pretty fiction that Thierry is on their side, remain outside the palace. As Persius said, "granted, wrinkled Baucis has no meaner wisdom."[26] But now, lest the preface upon which this work rests overtake it by its own prolix argument, let us proceed to the beginning of the commentary.

PROLOGUE TO THE ART OF RHETORIC

There are ten points to consider about the art of rhetoric: what is the genus of this art, what is the art itself, what is its subject matter, what is its function, what is its goal, what are its parts, what are its species, what is its instrument, who is its practitioner, and why it is called rhetoric.[27]

 The ancient rhetoricians use the term "art" extrinsically [*artem extrinsecus vocant*] for the art of defining these things, dividing them, and demonstrating them by reasoning, because

---

[23] Fredborg, "Ciceronian Rhetoric and the Schools," 33.   [24] Cf. Petronius, *Satyricon* 3.

[25] Cf. Horace, *Odes* 3.1.1.

[26] Persius, *Satires* 4.20–1. The implication here (based on the satirical spirit of Perseus' lines) is that such false followers of Thierry have no higher self-understanding or knowledge of the arts than the old peasant woman Baucis (cf. Ovid, *Metamorphoses* 8.624–724), who markets her vegetables on the streets.

[27] *Genus, materia, officium, finis*: see *De inventione* 1.4.5–1.7.9; *partes, species, instrumentum, actor*: Boethius, *De topicis differentiis* 4, *PL* 64:1207a, 1211c.

it is outside and is reached before the precepts for practice, and thus must be known in advance.[28] They use the term "art" intrinsically [*intrinsecus*] for the actual art of eloquence, because the prior knowledge is introductory to this. However, we do not distinguish between "extrinsic" and "intrinsic" in the sense that they are two (separate) arts, but rather on the grounds that by these two modes one and the same art is taught.

Next, concerning the book of Tully that we are about to expound, two things are to be considered: what is the author's own intention [*intentio auctoris*] and what is the utility [*utilitas*] of the book. Each of these things is to be explained in the order we have set forth.

The genus [*genus*] of the art of rhetoric is the essential quality of this technical system [*artificium*] with respect to its outcome.[29] This is because this art is the greater part of civil science. Now, we call "civil reasoning" whatever the civil community either speaks or does according to reason. For example, we say: "there is a reason to do or say this or that." We also call "civil reasoning" [*civilis ratio*] the science of both speaking and acting according to reason, and this very reasoning is called civil science, of which a constitutive and most important part is called rhetoric. Now wisdom, that is, the comprehension of things according to their nature, and rhetoric comprise civil science.[30] Thus, unless one were both wise and eloquent, he could not be said to have mastery of civil science.

The greater part of civil science is called rhetoric, since it plays the greater role in civil affairs than wisdom, although, without wisdom, it would be of no use. Eloquence has the greatest virtue in the state, if it is joined to wisdom, as Tully shows in what follows.

Furthermore, according to Boethius the genus of the art of rhetoric is that it is itself a competence [*facultas*],[31] that is, making eloquent, which is the greater part of civil science.[32] One and the same science is called an art when it is embodied in the teacher, because he regulates [*artare*] the discipline according to rules,[33] and a competence [*facultas*] when it is embodied in the orator, because it makes him eloquent [*facundus*].

Rhetoric should not be called logic or part of logic, given that logic is concerned with the thesis alone, that is, only with general propositions, whereas rhetoric is concerned with the hypothesis alone, that is, only with particular propositions.[34]

---

[28]   On *antiqui rhetores* cf. Cicero, *De oratore* 1.42.188; Victorinus, *Explanationes* 170–1.

[29]   Victorinus defines genus as *qualitas*: see *Explanationes*, 171.17.

[30]   On the definition of wisdom as *conceptio rerum secundum earum naturam* see Victorinus, *Explanationes* 171.31.

[31]   *Facultas*; cf. Stump's note, *Boethius' De topicis differentiis*, trans. Stump, 97 n. 5.

[32]   Boethius, *De topicis differentiis*, 4, PL 64:1207a–b (*facultas*).

[33]   This is a pun that depends on a hidden etymology, *ars* from *artare*, that is, to constrain with rules (cf. William of Conches, p. 385 within, who gives the same etymology).

[34]   Thierry relies here on the Boethian tradition which clearly distinguishes rhetoric from logic on the basis of the kind of proposition each one treats. Compare, on this, Gundissalinus, within, p. 482, who reflects the Arabic reception of Aristotle's *Organon* and places rhetoric under logic: see *De divisione philosophiae*, 71–4. See also Isidore of Seville, who at least once accepts the classification of rhetoric as a part of logic (*De differentiis* 2.39.153, PL 83:94c).

According to the ancient rhetoricians, there are many and various definitions of the art of rhetoric. Certain authors define it this way: the art of rhetoric is the science of speaking well.[35] Others give this definition: rhetoric is the science of employing copious and consummate eloquence in cases related to private individuals and the state.[36] But others define it in the following way: rhetoric is the science of speaking in a manner suited to persuade in the cases at hand.[37] And philosophers define rhetoric in yet other ways, and anyone wishing to know about these should read Quintilian's *Institutio oratoria*.[38]

Now for the subject matter [*materia*] of the art. The subject matter of any kind of art is that which the artificer ought to treat according to the art. The subject matter of rhetoric thus is the hypothesis, which the Latins call a case [*causa*], since the orator must treat this according to rhetorical art.[39] The hypothesis or case is a matter which involves a verbal controversy entailed in what is to be said about a given word or action of a certain person; for example, there is a controversy about whether Orestes was within his right to kill his mother.

It is not that homicide or theft or adultery or anything of this sort is itself the subject matter of the art of rhetoric, but rather a controversial matter which can be shown to be true or false by probable arguments, as, for example, it is shown by probable arguments whether or not Orestes was within his right to kill his mother.

This is called a "case" [*causa*] because "to bring a case" [*causari*] is the term used to mean "to accuse someone of something and bring a lawsuit against him." Or it is called a case because the ancients said that "to bring a case" was to bring an action about something, so it is called a case in the sense of a legal action about something.

The hypothesis, that is, what is placed beneath [*suppositum*], is so called because it is subordinate to the thesis.[40] It is also called the question involved in the circumstances, that is, in certain specific persons, actions, causes, places, times, manners, and means, which are designated the "circumstances" in this memorable line: "who, what, where, by what means, why, in what way, when." But what a circumstance is exactly will be explained more clearly later on.[41]

Civil controversies customarily concern a matter of law before judges, and then these controversies are called judicial cases; or they concern interests among administrators of public or individual affairs, and then they are called deliberative cases; or they concern what is honorable among the people in assemblies, and then they are called demonstrative cases.[42]

---

[35] Quintilian, *Institutio oratoria* 2.15.38.   [36] Victorinus, *Explanationes*, 156.24.

[37] Cicero, *De inventione* 1.5.6; *De oratore* 1.31.138.   [38] Quintilian, *Institutio oratoria* 2.15.1–38.

[39] Victorinus, *Explanationes*, 213.42.

[40] For the Greek term "hypo-thesis" Thierry gives a Latin calque, *sub-positum* (*suppositum*).

[41] Cf. Boethius, *De topicis differentiis* 4, *PL* 64:1205d, 1212c–d; Victorinus, *Explanationes*, 207.

[42] Cf. Cicero, *De inventione* 1.5.7 (demonstrative or epideictic, deliberative, and judicial genres); Boethius, *De topicis differentiis* 4, *PL* 64:1207c–d; Victorinus, *Explanationes* 175.22.

These three matters, that is, justice, interest, and honor, are the objects [*fines*] of all (the kinds of) cases, that is, civil controversies, out of which every (special) case arises. These three kinds of case constitute the subject matter of the art of rhetoric.

The function [*officium*] of any art is what the practitioner must do according to the art. The task of the art of rhetoric is what the orator must do according to the art of rhetoric. This is to speak in a way suitable to persuasion, that is, to speak such things that are appropriate and sufficient to persuasion, although in fact an orator may not necessarily persuade. Whence Aristotle says in the first book of the *Topics*: an orator will not always persuade, but, if he has omitted none of the things relevant to this purpose, we consider him to have the wherewithal sufficient to the purpose.[43]

The goal [*finis*] of any art is what the practitioner aims to do with respect to the task of the art. The object of the art of rhetoric is what the orator aims to do with respect to its task. This is to persuade by means of speech, which is to persuade insofar as it depends on him as speaker, although the actual effect depends on the audience.[44] And the art always seeks after this object (i.e. persuading by means of speaking). But there is another object of the art which it does not always pursue, that is to persuade the hearers, as was shown above.

But the goal of the art is not the same as its utility, nor its task the same as its intention (since its utility is various and multiple), but the object of the art only that which we have just stated. Similarly the intention of the art, or of the orator, is to move hearers to believe him, but the task only that which we have just stated.

The parts [*partes*] of the art of rhetoric are those fitting elements that make an orator; and should even one of these elements be missing, we have no orator. They are called parts because they are similar to the parts of a whole: if they all come together, the whole exists, but if one part is missing, there is no whole.[45] These parts are five in number: invention, arrangement, delivery, memory, and style. If these five elements come together in some-one, an orator is made, but if one element is missing, we have no orator. And so, by comparison these elements are called parts when they form the tasks of the orator.[46]

The species [*species*] of the art of rhetoric are the genera of cases [*genera causarum*].[47] The genera of cases are the common [*generales*] qualities of cases according to their ends.

---

[43] Aristotle, *Topics* 3.101b5; the *Topics* were considered to be comprised of two parts, the *Topics* and the text also commonly known as the *Sophistical Refutations*.

[44] See Boethius, *De topicis differentiis* 4, *PL* 64:1208c.

[45] On "parts of a whole" (*partes integrales*), cf. Boethius, *De topicis differentiis* 4, *PL* 64:1207d and 1208a.

[46] In this explanation, Thierry is mapping a convention of scientific classification onto the existing structures of the art of rhetoric. Thus the category "parts of the art," which is a standard subject of scientific classification, is exemplified here in terms of the traditional division of rhetoric into five canons, invention, arrangement, style, delivery, and memory.

[47] Cf. Boethius, *De topicis differentiis* 4, *PL* 64:1207b, 1211b.

For the objects of cases are, as was stated above, justice or honor or utility. Thus every case admits such quality, since it is said to be either judicial or demonstrative or deliberative.

Such qualities of cases are therefore called common because each genus contains all the constituent parts. It is fitting that they are called genera of cases because all cases arise from the qualities of the aforesaid ends. The species of the art of rhetoric are called the genera of cases not because rhetoric will be predicated from them, but rather on analogy, because just as the whole genus is inherent in individual species, so all the parts of rhetoric are carried into effect in individual genera of cases.[48]

The instrument [*instrumentum*] of the art of rhetoric is the rhetorical oration, which consists of six parts: the exordium, the narration, the partition, and so forth.[49] The oration is said to be the instrument, because through it the orator acts, just as any practitioner treats his subject matter by means of an instrument.

The practitioner [*artifex*] in this art is the orator. The orator is a good man who is skilled in speaking, and who uses a copious and consummate eloquence in private and public cases.[50] The rhetor and the orator differ in this way: the rhetor is the teacher of the art, whereas the orator knows how to treat civil cases according to the art. And it often happens that neither are rhetors orators nor orators rhetors.

This art is called "rhetoric" from copious speaking: for "rhetoros" in Greek is called, in Latin, "copious speaking" [*copia loquendi*].[51] Whence this science is called "rhetoric" because it makes (its owner) eloquent [*eloquentem*].

PROLOGUE TO THE BOOK

Having treated those things that must be considered in regard to the whole art of rhetoric, now we turn to the topics to be addressed regarding this particular book by Tully. Tully's intention in this work is to teach just one part of the art of rhetoric, that is, invention. The utility of this book is the knowledge of how to invent a rhetorical oration.

---

[48] Cf. Boethius, *De topicis differentiis* 4, *PL* 64:1207b; and *De inventione* 1.9.12. The argument here (which seems to follow Boethius' discussion) is that the three "species" of rhetoric (judicial, deliberative, demonstrative or epideictic) are also referred to as its *genera* or "genres" because in each species/genre the whole *genus* of rhetoric is present, that is, rhetoric is complete in its judicial, deliberative, or demonstrative genre.

[49] On the instrument, cf. Boethius, *De topicis differentiis* 4, *PL* 64:1208b, 1211b.

[50] See Boethius, *De topicis differentiis* 4, *PL* 64:1208d, 1211b; "good man skilled in speaking" (*vir bonus dicendi peritus*): among many sources, see Quintilian, *Institutio oratoria* 12.1.1; "copious and consummate eloquence": see Victorinus, *Explanationes* 156.24.

[51] Cf. *De inventione* 1.1.1; Victorinus, *Explanationes* 157.6–11.

The First Part [of Thierry's Commentary] on the First Book [of the *De inventione*]

On Tully's Prologue:

De inventione 1.1.1

I have often seriously debated with myself whether men and communities have received more good or evil from oratory [*copia dicendi*] and a consuming devotion to eloquence[52] Tully wishes to persuade us that the art of rhetoric must be studied,[53] so that he both commends the art of rhetoric, in order to capture the attention of his readers, and defends it against Plato and Aristotle. Plato asserted that rhetoric was not an art, but is innate in men by nature,[54] whereas Aristotle asserted that rhetoric was an art, but a bad one, because truth is often impugned through it, and falsehood may take the place of truth in men's beliefs. Thus in this prologue, Tully finds it necessary to prove against Plato that rhetoric is an art, and against Aristotle that rhetoric is good. In doing this he renders his audience—who, on the authority of these philosophers, were hostile to rhetoric—well disposed towards the art.

Since he is about to challenge such philosophers, Tully uses a certain kind of prologue, which is called an "insinuation," as if he did not dare to contradict such authorities directly. The nature of the insinuation will be explained later.[55] He also uses the deliberative genre of case, dealing with a kind of case whose nature is said to be difficult. A difficult case occurs when we defend something towards which the audience feels hostility.[56] In accordance with the order of a deliberative case, Tully puts the parts [*partes*] of the deliberation itself first, then the examinations [*exsecutiones*] of the parts, and after that his opinion, namely what he thinks about either part, and finally the proof for his opinion about either part. With these four elements the prologue is complete.[57]

---

[52] The *lemmata* of the Ciceronian texts are based on the translations by Hubbell (*De inventione*) and Caplan (*Rhetorica ad Herennium*). Where emphasis or lexical and grammatical usages in the commentary demand, the translations have been modified. For the sake of context, we have given fuller quotations from the classical texts than the short keywords typical in the manuscripts of Thierry's commentary.

[53] Cf. Victorinus, *Explanationes* 155.19.

[54] Cf. Grillius, *Commentum in Ciceronis rhetorica*, ed. Jakob, 2–3.

[55] At 1.17.23–18.25 (Fredborg, ed., 114–17).   [56] *De inventione* 1.15.20, 1.17.23.

[57] Cf. Victorinus, *Explanationes*, 155.13–22; on the parts of a deliberative oration, see also *Ad Herennium* 3.4.7–3.5.9.

The parts of the deliberation, then, he puts as follows: I HAVE OFTEN SERIOUSLY DEBATED WITH MYSELF WHETHER MEN HAVE RECEIVED MORE GOOD OR EVIL FROM RHETORIC, not whether rhetoric is good or bad. In this passage Tully does not question the intrinsic nature of the art, but the quality it takes on from those who use it. It is well known to all that the art of rhetoric is good in itself; but it brings many bad things to men if bad people abuse it.

Since it is evident that the art is good in itself, noxious among evil men but useful among good men, since—as I say—this is so, Tully does not simply question whether it is good or bad—for this would introduce an ambiguity, whether one should deliberate about the nature of the art or about its effect—but rather he deliberates about its effect, whether it brings more good or more evil to men. If it brings more evil, then it is clearly a bad thing for men, whatever it may be in itself, and there should be no devotion to it, which is what Aristotle believed. But if it brings more good, then it should be deemed a good thing. "Good" and "evil" are equivocal terms, either for that which retains in itself the nature of either of these, or for that which produces a good or bad effect.

Tully says that he has OFTEN debated with himself, so that he emphasizes a frequency of thought, SERIOUSLY, to indicate assiduous attention, WITH [HIM]SELF, so as to indicate the deliberative genre. For one sometimes deliberates with oneself, sometimes with others.

Observing a proper order, he asked WHETHER IT HAS BROUGHT MORE GOOD OR EVIL,[58] since eloquence first helped and afterwards harmed *men*, that is individual affairs, and *communities*, that is public affairs. A republic is formed from these two elements.

ORATORY [*COPIA DICENDI*] AND A CONSUMMATE DEVOTION TO ELOQUENCE One of these, that is, oratory [*copia dicendi*], which is eloquence, is the effect of the art of rhetoric, because rhetoric makes eloquent men; the other is the cause of the art of rhetoric, because if one has devoted thorough study to eloquence, through this CONSUMMATE, that is, thorough, DEVOTION, he will be able to attain to the art of rhetoric. Thus Tully has rightly defined the art of rhetoric through its cause and its effect.

FOR WHEN I PONDER THE TROUBLES IN OUR COMMONWEALTH, AND RUN OVER IN MY MIND THE ANCIENT MISFORTUNES OF MIGHTY CITIES, I SEE THAT NO LITTLE PART OF THE DISASTERS WAS BROUGHT ABOUT BY MEN OF ELOQUENCE.

FOR WHEN I PONDER THE TROUBLES IN OUR COMMONWEALTH Here begins the examination of the parts [*partes*] of the deliberation. To examine the parts of the aforesaid deliberation is nothing other than to show how on the one hand advantages and on the other hand misfortunes have resulted from rhetoric, so that it may be asked which one has more commonly resulted from it.

---

[58] See Cicero's text: *bonine an mali plus attulerit.*

For this reason, Tully uses an insinuation; in order to disguise a defense, he first presents the part dealing with misfortunes,[59] saying FOR WHEN I PONDER THE TROUBLES, that is, the detriments, IN OUR COMMONWEALTH, which I saw before my eyes, and when I RUN OVER IN MY MIND, that is, I reflect upon the fame and historical memory of THE ANCIENT MISFORTUNES, that is, the calamities and destructions OF MIGHTY CITIES; when, I say, I PONDER this matter, as if present there, but that matter I RUN OVER IN MY MIND, as if removed from it, I SEE, that is, I understand, NO LITTLE PART OF THE DISASTERS to have been BROUGHT ABOUT BY MEN OF ELOQUENCE, that is, by those who have sufficient eloquence, but little or no wisdom.

In using the word TROUBLES, which usually means a lesser injury,[60] and ANCIENT MISFORTUNES, that is, not new, and NO LITTLE PART OF THE DISASTERS, in using these terms, I suggest, he sufficiently attenuates that side of the argument which seems to pertain to the censure of rhetoric. Moreover, he does not say that evil was brought about through the art of rhetoric, but through MEN OF ELOQUENCE, so that it is not to the art, but to someone abusing the art that he attributes guilt.

WHEN, ON THE OTHER HAND, I BEGIN TO SEARCH AGAIN IN THE RECORDS OF LITERATURE FOR EVENTS WHICH ARE REMOVED FROM OUR MEMORY BECAUSE OF THEIR ANTIQUITY, I FIND THAT MANY CITIES HAVE BEEN FOUNDED, THAT THE FLAMES OF A MULTITUDE OF WARS HAVE BEEN EXTINGUISHED, AND THAT THE STRONGEST ALLIANCES AND MOST SACRED FRIENDSHIPS HAVE BEEN FORMED NOT ONLY BY THE USE OF THE MIND'S REASON BUT ALSO MORE EASILY BY THE HELP OF ELOQUENCE Here he presents the part dealing with advantages: just as he had to attenuate the part about misfortunes when he was making a diligent defense of the art, so with the same diligence he augments the part about advantages, saying: WHEN I BEGIN TO SEARCH AGAIN, that is, when I propose to bring back to my memory, from THE RECORDS OF LITERATURE, that is, through annals or through histories, EVENTS WHICH ARE REMOVED FROM OUR MEMORY BECAUSE OF THEIR ANTIQUITY, that is, events that took place before our time and which have fallen away from common memory because of their great age: when (I say), I consider these things, I FIND that from ELOQUENCE, that is, from rhetoric, when it is joined to THE MIND'S reasoning, that is, to wisdom, these good things have come about, the foundation of cities and the other things that follow upon that, which I did not think it was necessary to describe in detail. For all these things mentioned frequently come about through the persuasiveness of rhetoric. Since he said that these things MORE EASILY come about through eloquence, we must understand that these two things, wisdom and eloquence, assist each other in proper persuasive arguments, and neither is of use without the other; but nevertheless to this purpose, the greater instrument is eloquence.

---

[59] Cf. Grillius, *Commentum*, ed. Jakob, 11.61.   [60] Cf. Grillius, *Commentum*, ed. Jakob, 12.75.

For my own part, after long thought, I have been led by reasoning [*RATIONES*] itself to hold this opinion first and foremost, that wisdom without eloquence does too little for the good of states, but that eloquence without wisdom is generally highly disadvantageous and is never helpful. Therefore if anyone neglects the most excellent (*RECTISSIMUS*) and most honorable study of reasoning and moral conduct [*STUDII RATIONIS ET OFFICI*], and devotes his whole energy to the practice of oratory, his civic life is nurtured into something useless to himself and harmful to the country; but the man who arms himself with . . . eloquence, not to be able to attack the welfare of his country but to fight for it, he, I think, will be a citizen most helpful and most devoted both to his own interests [*RATIONES*] and those of his community Having set forth the parts of the deliberation and examined them, at this point he presents his opinion, which is comprised of four propositions. The first three propositions he puts in front and proves them; with these points proved he brings in the fourth proposition, that there must be studious devotion to eloquence, at the end of the prologue. Of those propositions which he puts in front and proves, the first is THAT WISDOM WITHOUT ELOQUENCE DOES TOO LITTLE FOR THE GOOD OF STATES, that is for the assembling together of men so that they can live according to law, which is best accomplished by eloquence. The second proposition is that ELOQUENCE WITHOUT WISDOM IS GENERALLY HIGHLY DISADVANTAGEOUS and in truth NEVER HELPFUL. He says GENERALLY, because it is not the case that it is always or overwhelmingly harmful, even if it is frequently so; but where he said that REASON led him TO HOLD THIS opinion, there he was calling reason what are firm arguments by which he was led to this opinion.

THEREFORE IF ANYONE NEGLECTS THE MOST EXCELLENT AND MOST HONORABLE STUDY OF REASONING AND MORAL CONDUCT Having set forth two propositions, the first and the second, from these he infers: because eloquence without wisdom is highly disadvantageous, therefore if someone had studied only eloquence, that man would be USELESS TO HIMSELF AND HARMFUL TO THE COUNTRY, for he does not consider his own interests and he harms his country.

Moreover, study of REASONING AND MORAL CONDUCT is his name for the study of wisdom, which we call philosophy. Wisdom is perfect knowledge, either of reasoning, which pertains to speculative science and logic, or of MORAL CONDUCT, which pertains to ethics. The highest excellence pertains to reason,[61] and honor pertains to moral conduct,

---

[61] *Rectus, rectissimum*: in Cicero's text the word *rectissimus* has a strong connotation of virtue; Thierry, however, seems to read the term along more scientific lines, with a connotation of correctness and intellectual virtue.

which is the suitable behavior of each person in accordance with the custom of the country. The PRACTICE OF ORATORY is a definition of the study of eloquence.

BUT THE MAN WHO ARMS HIMSELF WITH ELOQUENCE With these words Tully presents the third proposition, and the sense of the words is this: BUT THE MAN WHO ARMS HIMSELF WITH ELOQUENCE, that is, he who is robust in wisdom, defends himself through eloquence as if by weapons, NOT TO ATTACK HIS COUNTRY, but TO BE ABLE to fight FOR it, that is, he is ready to defend his country through eloquence joined to wisdom; I say that HE is the one who SEEMS helpful TO HIS OWN INTERESTS, that is, to conduct his affairs, AND a friend to THE INTERESTS OF HIS COMMUNITY, that is, benevolent in the course of the affairs which pertain to the republic.

In this passage, "reason" [ratio] is called the course of affairs to be carried out. He put this well, that this person is useful to himself and his country, in contrast to what he said of the man who has only eloquence, namely that such a one is USELESS TO HIMSELF and HARMFUL TO HIS COUNTRY.

De inventione 1.1.2

MOREOVER, IF WE WISH TO CONSIDER THE BEGINNING [PRINCIPIUM] OF THIS THING WE CALL ELOQUENCE—WHETHER [ITS ULTIMATE CAUSE (INITIUM) DERIVES FROM][62] ART, STUDY [STUDIUM], PRACTICE [EXERCITATIO], OR NATURAL TALENT—WE SHALL FIND THAT IT AROSE FROM MOST HONORABLE CAUSES AND CONTINUED ON ITS WAY FROM THE BEST OF REASONS In this passage he begins to prove the propositions above in the reverse order from which he gave them above. For here he proves the last proposition first, then the second one, and lastly the first one.

In the first place, he shows that eloquence conjoined with wisdom is most beneficial, when he says IF WE WISH TO CONSIDER THE BEGINNING [PRINCIPIUM] of eloquence, that is, the start [inchoatio] of eloquence, WE SHALL FIND that the beginning [principium] AROSE FROM A MOST HONORABLE CAUSE, that is, that it had its start [inchoatio] in an honorable impulse of the soul, AND CONTINUED ON ITS WAY FROM THE BEST OF REASONS, that is, was

---

[62] A substantial minority of medieval manuscripts of the *De inventione* present this reading of the passage, in which the word *initium* appears in this clause: *Ac si volumus huius rei, qui vocatur eloquentia, sive artis* initium, *sive studii sive exercitationis cuiusdam sive facultatis ab natura profectae considerare principium . . .* See *De inventione*, ed. Stroebel, 2.14 and apparatus; this reading is not accepted as authentic in standard modern editions of the work. The appearance of the word *initium* alters the meaning of the text slightly, suggesting to some medieval commentators that Cicero was making a distinction between one kind of "beginning" (*initium*) and another kind of "beginning" of rhetoric (*principium*). Thierry's commentary clearly depends upon a text that contained both of these words (see text and note below). We find similar evidence in the earlier commentaries by Manegaldus and William of Champeaux: see the parallels noted by Dickey, "Some Commentaries on the *De inventione* and *Ad Herennium* of the Eleventh and Twelfth Centuries," 21. The copy of *De inventione* included in Thierry's *Heptateuchon* also contains the phrase *sive artis initium* (Chartres Bibl. municipale 497, fol. 192r).

accomplished in a most orderly way. Now a cause is an impulse of the soul towards doing something. And reason is an ordering of matters to be carried out arising from a cause, so that you understand what you must do or say at any given time.[63] Thus if one wishes to inquire about the start [*inchoatio*] of something, he must first consider the cause of that start [*inchoatio*].

Since Tully introduced the idea that the ultimate cause [*initium*] of eloquence was *either* from ART, *or* from STUDY, etc., I say that there was a certain doubt concerning the origin [*origo*] of eloquence, whether it is born from art, study [*studium*], practice [*exercitatio*], or natural faculty—that is from a natural ability. The difference between study and practice is this, that study is a determination of the soul to do something, whereas practice is a sustaining of the action undertaken.[64]

Thus we can see the meaning of the whole passage according to the order of its words: if, he says, we wish to consider the start [*inchoatio*] of eloquence, whose origin [*origo*] is either art or effort or something else, if (I say) we want to consider this, we shall find that this start [*inchoatio*] arose from the most honorable cause. This is the difference between ultimate cause [*initium*] and beginning [*principium*]: in this place, at least, an ultimate cause is said to be the origin [*origo*] of eloquence, from which it is born, which origin [*origo*] Tully presents somewhat doubtfully; but the start [*inchoatio*] of eloquence in terms of action is called a beginning [*principium*].[65]

---

[63] Victorinus, *Explanationes* 160.4–6.

[64] Cf. Victorinus, *Explanationes* 160.8. *Studium* can mean not only "study," but also effort, zeal, eagerness.

[65] The argument here can be understood as follows. Thierry's manuscript copy of the *De inventione* has the word *initium* as the immediate subject of the genitives *artis, studii*, etc. (see note 62 above). On this reading, Cicero seems to be saying that he is doubtful about the *initium* of eloquence, whether it derives from art, study, practice, or natural talent, although he is sure about the *principium* of eloquence, because he asserts that it arose from honorable causes. Thierry takes *initium* and *principium* to be different kinds of beginnings, one anterior to the other. *Initium* seems to refer to an ultimate source or essence of eloquence, that is, whether eloquence takes its essence from art, study, practice, or natural talent. Thierry aligns this ultimate source or essence with the term "origin" (*origo*). He takes *principium* here to signify a secondary beginning in action (the story of how rhetoric came to be used to civilize savage humans), and this secondary beginning he glosses with the term *inchoatio*. The vocabulary in his distinctions between the ultimate causes and the secondary causes of rhetoric derives from several related traditions: the language of hexaemeral exegesis (such as Thierry's own *Tractatus de sex dierum operibus*), in which commentators sought to determine the primary or underlying causes of God's creation of the universe; the language of Trinitarian commentary and debate (including Thierry's own commentaries on Boethius' *De trinitate*); twelfth-century natural science, which also dealt with "causes and the beginnings of causes of things" (see Adelard of Bath, *De eodem et diverso*, ed. Burnett, 17); and the terminology of the Calcidian translation of Plato's *Timaeus*, in which the Greek term *arkhê*, the ultimate or primary cause, is rendered with the Latin words *initium* and *origo*. There are also grammatical sources, e.g., Isidore of Seville, *Differentiae* 1.7: *Inter initium et principium. Initium est rerum a quo quid incipit, ut fundamenta domus, carina navis, principium autem verborum exordium est*, ed. Codoñer Merino, 90; cf. Probus, *GL* 4:203.22. Given the importance for a twelfth-century schoolman of determining such essences or ultimate causes, Cicero's apparent doubts about the *initium* of eloquence would have been perplexing and would require some explanation. On this passage, see also Copeland, "The History of Rhetoric and the *Longue Durée*."

De inventione 1.2.2

FOR THERE WAS A TIME WHEN MEN WANDERED AT LARGE IN THE FIELDS LIKE ANIMALS AND PRESERVED THEIR LIVES WITH WILD FARE; THEY DID NOTHING BY THE GUIDANCE OF REASON, BUT RELIED CHIEFLY ON PHYSICAL STRENGTH Wanting to show the causes from which eloquence arose, that is, its start [*inchoatio*] with respect to action, Tully at first briefly and properly described the bestial savagery of men, as it was at the beginning [*principium*] of the world, so that he may show how, through the joining of eloquence to wisdom for the first time—which was given its start on account of the savage condition of men—savagery was driven out, cities were built, and many other good things came about (as shown in the text). This makes readers well disposed to the art of rhetoric.

The sense of the words is this: There was a time at the beginning of the world when men were savage and lived in the manner of beasts, and did not practice any study of wisdom, but only their bodily strength, without any reason. At this time there was a certain man who was wise and eloquent, because he saw the divine soul and the reason latent in man. He recognized that because of this, man was open to persuasion; and so at that time, impelled by this cause, the wise man began to use eloquence and he drove out the savagery and brought men together to live by law, and he instructed the assembled people in the laws of living according to what is right. This passage shows the start [*inchoatio*] of the practice of eloquence and the cause for which it began to be practiced, and the order by which it was most fittingly put to work and made useful.

Now let us look closely at the text. WANDERED: this is to be without houses. PRESERVED THEIR LIVES: that is, sustained, WITH WILD FARE, that is, with raw meats and vegetation and the like, which wild beasts commonly enjoy. Or, WITH WILD FARE, because like wild beasts they did not plan beyond filling the belly each day.[66] He says CHIEFLY, because it was not for all things that THEY RELIED, that is, functioned, ON PHYSICAL STRENGTH. For they did not fulfill natural needs like drinking, eating, and the like, either BY PHYSICAL STRENGTH or by REASON.

THERE WAS AS YET NO REASONED SYSTEM DEVOTED TO RELIGIOUS WORSHIP NOR TO SOCIAL DUTY Here he says that they did not yet practice the study of wisdom, which is concerned with two kinds of matters, divine and human. What he called a "reasoned system" of RELIGIOUS WORSHIP is knowledge of divine matters, and this reasoning is called theoretical, that is, speculative science; but what he called a reasoned system of DUTY is the knowledge of human affairs, which is called ethics [*ethica*].

NO ONE HAD SEEN LEGITIMATE MARRIAGE NOR HAD ANYONE LOOKED UPON CHILDREN WHOM HE KNEW TO BE HIS OWN; NOR HAD THEY LEARNED THE ADVANTAGES OF AN

---

[66] Victorinus, *Explanationes* 160.33.

EQUITABLE CODE OF LAW He continues on the subject of things that pertain to ethics, because these are the matters with which the orator is most concerned. LEGITIMATE MARRIAGE is what he calls the joining of husband and wife according to law. Unrecognized CHILDREN whose fathers are unknown were unrecognized because there were no lawful marriages. He called justice a CODE OF LAW; the term he added, EQUITABLE, is a property of justice, because through this is distributed to each person what is his. He said NOR HAD THEY LEARNED, as if to say that no one had learned to know it from another person.

AND SO THROUGH THEIR IGNORANCE AND ERROR, DESIRE, A BLIND AND RASH MISTRESS OF THE SOUL, SATISFIED ITSELF BY MISUSING BODILY STRENGTH, WHICH IS A VERY DANGEROUS SERVANT This is the difference between error and ignorance: ignorance is not to know what you truly do not know, whereas error is if you believe yourself to know what you do not know.[67] Tully refers blindness back to ignorance, rashness back to error.

A VERY DANGEROUS SERVANT, ETC. He says that bodily strength is a servant of desire for self-satisfaction. This desire exercises a certain tyranny over the souls of men, once the use of reason has disappeared.[68] MISUSE means to use for a bad purpose.

AT THIS JUNCTURE A MAN—GREAT AND WISE I AM SURE—BECAME AWARE OF THE POWER LATENT IN MAN AND THE ADVANTAGES INHERENT IN HUMAN MINDS FOR GREAT ACHIEVEMENTS He points to the moment when the use of eloquence began. He calls the man great for his virtue, and wise on account of his discretion. He says that there is power [*materia*] latent in the human mind, which power is a potential of the mind itself, so that from being rude it may become virtuous or excellent or the opposite. He calls the mind's own facility for doing great things an ADVANTAGE for GREAT ACHIEVEMENTS, if the mind itself is drawn out by learning, that is, if it is stirred to action. There are many powers through which it is possible to accomplish something, whether this is easy or not. Both these facilities, power and advantage, were inherent in HUMAN MINDS, whence good things are achieved by natural means, but better things are achieved through learning.

MEN WERE SCATTERED IN THE FIELDS AND HIDDEN IN SYLVAN RETREATS WHEN HE COLLECTED AND ASSEMBLED THEM TOGETHER IN ACCORDANCE WITH A REASON, INTRODUCING THEM TO EVERY USEFUL AND HONORABLE OCCUPATION Above we spoke of the cause from which eloquence was born, and reason, that is the necessary ordering of doing something, from which eloquence was perfected.[69] Having considered the cause in the preceding passage, he now talks about reason, and thus he says HE COLLECTED THEM TOGETHER IN ACCORDANCE WITH A REASON. So that he might show the ordering of doing

---

[67] Grillius, *Commentum*, ed. Jakob, 19.91–3.   [68] Cf. Victorinus, *Explanationes* 161.9.

[69] *Perfecta*: note that in the passage that Thierry recalls here, 1.1.2, the term is actually *profectum* "continued on its way" or "advanced."

things, he said COLLECTED, as if to say they were reluctant, and then ASSEMBLED, as if to say that they were by now willing, and INTRODUCING, as if using introductions to show what is useful and honorable. To collect and assemble people is nothing other than to constitute a state.[70]

THOUGH THEY CRIED OUT AGAINST IT AT FIRST BECAUSE OF NOVELTY [INSOLENTIA], AND THEN WHEN THROUGH REASON AND SPEECH [ORATIO] THEY HAD LISTENED WITH GREATER ATTENTION, HE TRANSFORMED THEM FROM WILD SAVAGES INTO A KIND AND GENTLE FOLK By the word NOVELTY he means the desuetude of good study. He says THEY CRIED OUT, because they were unwilling when he first collected them; THEY LISTENED WITH GREATER ATTENTION, because afterwards they were willing to be assembled. He calls the wisdom [sapientia] and eloquence [eloquentia] of this man REASON [RATIO] and SPEECH [ORATIO]; or, according to Victorinus, reason [ratio] refers to a gravity of ideas, while speech [oratio] refers to the ornamentation of words.[71] He calls them WILD because they were rude, SAVAGES because they were raging. And he opposed WILD to KIND, SAVAGE to GENTLE.

De inventione 1.2.3

TO ME, AT LEAST, IT DOES NOT SEEM POSSIBLE THAT A MUTE AND VOICELESS WISDOM COULD HAVE TURNED MEN SUDDENLY FROM THEIR HABITS AND INTRODUCED THEM TO DIFFERENT PATTERNS OF LIFE He has proved that eloquence joined to wisdom is of great benefit to states, and now he proves another proposition, that wisdom without eloquence is of little help to the constitution and ruling of states. Thus in this passage he says that it seems to him that this turning of men could never have come about through a mute wisdom without resources, that is, which persuades without words, by example of good work, nor through a wisdom, that is, which in its persuasions uses words naturally, without art. For this was a turning away from habit, which is pleasant, and a sudden change, that is a transformation to a contrary pattern of life, that is to a different order of living.

CONSIDER ANOTHER POINT; AFTER CITIES HAD BEEN ESTABLISHED HOW COULD IT HAVE BEEN BROUGHT TO PASS THAT MEN SHOULD LEARN TO KEEP FAITH AND OBSERVE JUSTICE AND BECOME ACCUSTOMED TO OBEY OTHERS VOLUNTARILY AND BELIEVE NOT ONLY THAT THEY MUST WORK FOR THE COMMON GOOD BUT EVEN SACRIFICE LIFE ITSELF, UNLESS MEN HAD BEEN ABLE BY ELOQUENCE TO PERSUADE THEIR FELLOWS OF THE TRUTH OF WHAT THEY HAD DISCOVERED BY REASON? Above he said that through eloquence not only were cities FOUNDED, but also that WARS had been EXTINGUISHED, and ALLIANCES and FRIENDSHIPS had BEEN FORMED. After having spoken about the foundation of cities, he now adds details

---

[70] Cf. Victorinus, *Explanationes* 162.10–11.   [71] Victorinus, *Explanationes* 163.8.

that he passed over, saying: AFTER CITIES HAD BEEN ESTABLISHED, so that men kept faith and were just and obeyed each other and not only worked for the fatherland but, if necessary, would die for it; I say, it could not be that all these things came about unless wise men had persuaded them, through eloquence joined to wisdom, to do these things...

THIS WAS THE WAY IN WHICH AT FIRST ELOQUENCE CAME INTO BEING AND ADVANCED BY A GREATER DISTANCE, AND LIKEWISE AFTERWARD IN THE GREATEST UNDERTAKINGS OF PEACE AND WAR IT SERVED THE HIGHEST INTERESTS OF MANKIND He has proved these propositions, that eloquence joined to wisdom is of great benefit to states, and that wisdom without eloquence is of little help. Thus he briefly restates what was said above, and then moves to another proposition. He says that eloquence was born, that is, began, just as he has shown above; and he says that it advanced BY A GREATER DISTANCE, that is, progressed for the noblest of reasons, as he has shown so well. THE GREATEST UNDERTAKINGS OF PEACE AND WAR are what he calls those deeds that are accomplished through eloquence, as much in peace as in war. He calls the HIGHEST INTERESTS the ones that are also honorable.

BUT WHEN A CERTAIN AGREEABLENESS OF MANNER—A DEPRAVED IMITATION OF VIRTUE—ACQUIRED THE POWER OF ELOQUENCE UNACCOMPANIED BY ANY CONSIDERATION OF MORAL DUTY, THEN LOW CUNNING SUPPORTED BY TALENT GREW ACCUSTOMED TO CORRUPT CITIES AND UNDERMINE THE LIVES OF MEN Here he begins to prove the third proposition, that eloquence without wisdom is disadvantageous. He says that there were certain cunning men who, having acquired eloquence without wisdom, corrupted the cities and undermined the lives of men...

De inventione 1.3.4

LET ME NOW SET FORTH THE ORIGIN OF THIS EVIL ALSO, SINCE I HAVE EXPLAINED THE BEGINNING OF THE GOOD DONE BY ELOQUENCE, ETC. Just as in the preceding passages he shows that many good things arose and were brought to fulfillment through eloquence, so in this passage he shows the beginning of evil which comes about through an eloquence that is empty of wisdom.[72] He says that it seems to him that there was a time in which eloquent men who were also wise were occupied entirely with public affairs, and could not be involved in private lawsuits. Tully claims that since the wise men could not be involved in private suits, various cunning men, busying themselves in private affairs, acquired such garrulous facility that they could thwart the truth; emboldened by constant practice in speaking, they brought many injuries upon citizens and upon the friends of the wise.

---

[72] In this short summary of 1.3.4, Thierry gives an overview of Cicero's argument by simplifying the complex construction of Cicero's narrative, retelling it in plain and direct syntax and in a linear way. A comparison of Thierry's straightforward summary with Cicero's more convoluted presentation gives a good insight into the grammatical practice of *enarratio* which underlies Thierry's exposition of this text.

Because of these injuries, it was necessary for the better class of people to involve themselves in private suits in order to defend their friends. However, since they made so much noise, these garrulous talkers were seen by the mob as the equals or superiors of the wise men. Thus it came about that these windbags were chosen by the ignorant mob to govern the state. This meant that the republic was in the greatest peril, and deservedly so, and thus eloquence without wisdom brought great harm . . .

THESE EVENTS BROUGHT ELOQUENCE INTO SUCH ODIUM AND UNPOPULARITY THAT MEN OF THE GREATEST TALENT LEFT A LIFE OF STRIFE AND TUMULT FOR SOME QUIET PURSUIT Eloquence in the hands of evil men had as bad an effect on private affairs as on governance of the state . . . MEN OF THE GREATEST TALENT, such as Aristotle and Plato and their many followers . . . LEFT A LIFE OF STRIFE AND TUMULT . . . These men of great talent took themselves away from such a LIFE, that is from pursuit of this kind of life (of strife and tumult), in favor of other quieter pursuits, that is, to other arts which are free from this kind of strife . . .

FOR THIS REASON, I THINK, AT A LATER PERIOD THE OTHER WORTHY AND HONORABLE STUDIES WERE PROSECUTED VIGOROUSLY IN QUIET SECLUSION BY THE MEN OF HIGHEST VIRTUE AND WERE BROUGHT TO A BRILLIANT DEVELOPMENT, WHILE THIS STUDY OF ELOQUENCE WAS ABANDONED BY MOST OF THEM AND FELL INTO DISUSE AT A TIME WHEN IT NEEDED TO BE MAINTAINED MORE EARNESTLY AND EXTENDED WITH GREATER EFFORT Because the talented men deserted the study of eloquence, that is, rhetoric, and turned themselves to other arts, that is, the theoretical and practical sciences, so on this account, Tully said, it seemed that OTHER STUDIES, that is, other arts, WORTHY AND HONORABLE, WORTHY in so far as it applies to the practical sciences, HONORABLE in so far as it applied to the theoretical sciences, were PROSECUTED VIGOROUSLY IN QUIET SECLUSION . . . WHILE THIS, that is, the study of rhetoric, BY MOST OF THEM, as if he said not by all of them, WAS ABANDONED AND FELL INTO DISUSE, that is, became worthless . . .

We may ask whom Tully reprehends here, those whom he called (in the passage just quoted) "men of highest virtue" or others. I say that he reprehends others, the Greek authors in whom outrage overcame perseverance. Thus we see that he said MOST OF THEM that is, of the talented men, not of the virtuous men. For many people who are talented lack virtue.

De inventione 1.3.5

FOR THE MORE SHAMEFULLY A MOST HONEST AND WORTHY PROFESSION WAS ABUSED BY THE FOLLY AND AUDACITY OF DULL-WITTED AND UNPRINCIPLED MEN WITH THE DIREST CONSEQUENCES TO THE STATE, THE MORE EARNESTLY SHOULD THE BETTER CITIZENS HAVE PUT UP A RESISTANCE TO THEM He proves, by way of what is honest, what is useful, and what is easily accomplished, that they should have persevered in the study of the art of rhetoric... A MOST HONEST AND WORTHY PROFESSION. He calls the study of eloquence an honest and worthy thing: honest because it is honorable, and worthy because rectitude is revealed through eloquence. This is proof through what is honest... OF DULL-WITTED AND UNPRINCIPLED MEN Here he persuades through what is easily accomplished. For because the enemies were dull-witted, that is, stupid, and unprincipled, that is, lacking virtue, it was easy to resist them. WITH THE DIREST CONSEQUENCES TO THE STATE Here he persuades through utility. For since these evil men brought about such dire consequences, that is, great detriment, to the state, it was useful to resist them...

De inventione 1.4.5

THEREFORE, IN MY OPINION AT LEAST, MEN OUGHT NONE THE LESS TO DEVOTE THEM-SELVES TO THE STUDY OF ELOQUENCE ALTHOUGH SOME MISUSE IT BOTH IN PRIVATE AND IN PUBLIC AFFAIRS. AND THEY SHOULD STUDY IT THE MORE EARNESTLY IN ORDER THAT EVIL MEN MAY NOT OBTAIN GREAT POWER TO THE DETRIMENT OF THE COMMUNITY; ESPECIALLY SINCE THIS IS THE ONLY THING WHICH HAS A VERY CLOSE RELATION TO BOTH PRIVATE AND PUBLIC AFFAIRS Because it is honest, useful, and easily brought to effect, because great men have studied it, thus on account of evil men people should not LESS DEVOTE THEMSELVES TO THE STUDY OF ELOQUENCE. According to Victorinus, the fourth proposition is placed here, which is that one should devote oneself to eloquence, whence he urges wise men to study eloquence.[73] IN MY OPINION, that is, in my estimation. ALTHOUGH, that is, even if, IN PRIVATE AND PUBLIC AFFAIRS, that is in individual law suits and public cases, SOME MISUSE IT, that is they put it to perverse use. AND THEY SHOULD STUDY IT THE MORE EARNESTLY: in urging that eloquence is to be studied he argues from utility, from honor, and from what can be brought to effect; and from this point he begins to commend the art of rhetoric in order to make his readers attentive. He says that it should not be studied the less on account of evil men, but more earnestly, IN ORDER THAT EVIL MEN MAY NOT OBTAIN GREAT POWER, that is, that they may not be in the most powerful positions, for their power is detrimental to good men and pernicious to all, that is, destructive. This exhortation is made from utility: it is useful to repel evil. ESPECIALLY SINCE THIS IS THE ONLY THING WHICH HAS A VERY CLOSE RELATION TO BOTH PRIVATE AND PUBLIC AFFAIRS This exhort-ation is from utility and honor...

FURTHERMORE, I THINK THAT MEN, ALTHOUGH LOWER AND WEAKER THAN ANIMALS IN MANY RESPECTS, EXCEL THEM MOST BY HAVING THE POWER OF SPEECH. THEREFORE THAT MAN APPEARS TO ME TO HAVE WON A SPLENDID POSSESSION WHO EXCELS MEN THEMSELVES

---

[73] Victorinus, *Explanationes* 168.39–169.6.

IN THAT ABILITY BY WHICH MEN EXCEL BEASTS Through such a comparison the praise of rhetoric is augmented. ALTHOUGH, he says, men are LOWER IN MANY RESPECTS, that is, in relation to size, AND WEAKER than beasts in terms of strength, still in this men are MOST superior, BY HAVING THE POWER OF SPEECH, that is that they are born with an aptitude for speech. He says MOST, because they are also superior to beasts in intelligent skill. A SPLENDID POSSESSION: since it is a splendid thing for men to be superior to beasts in speech, therefore it is more splendid to excel other men in that very thing which comes out of rhetoric, so that one may surpass men in that very ability in which men themselves surpass beasts.

AND IF, AS IT HAPPENS, THIS ABILITY IN ELOQUENCE IS NOT BROUGHT ABOUT BY NATURE ALONE NOR BY PRACTICE, BUT IS ALSO ACQUIRED FROM SOME SYSTEMATIC INSTRUCTION, IT IS NOT OUT OF PLACE TO SEE WHAT THOSE SAY WHO HAVE LEFT US SOME PRECEPTS FOR THE STUDY OF ORATORY Up to this point, he has proved, against Aristotle, that rhetoric is good because of its effect, namely eloquence, which is good. From this point onwards he argues against Plato, who said that rhetoric was not art but nature.[74] So he says that if THIS, that is, eloquence, IS NOT BROUGHT ABOUT BY NATURE ALONE, that is, if it is not only possessed through natural talent. "Not only" is an important point, for eloquence has its beginning in nature, and is perfected by art. He said AS IT HAPPENS, because he wanted to argue temperately against Plato. NOR BY PRACTICE: some people claimed that eloquence is attained only by practice, without any art: those he refutes again. And the whole construction comes together as follows: eloquence IS BROUGHT ABOUT not only by nature or by practice, but ALSO IS ACQUIRED, that is, achieved, by art. He commends on the basis of what may be done. There should be study of eloquence because it can be grasped by art. If, I say, this is so, IT IS NOT OUT OF PLACE, that is, it is not beyond what is useful, TO SEE, that is, to understand, the PRECEPTS of the ancients about rhetoric. Tully brings these precepts together and presents them clearly.

De inventione 1.19.27

[On *narratio*]

THE NARRATION IS AN EXPOSITION OF EVENTS THAT HAVE OCCURRED OR ARE SUPPOSED TO HAVE OCCURRED ETC He defines the narration, and afterwards he briefly gives its division and clears away the other kinds of narration so that he may get to the kind of narration which is his concern, and last he gives instruction about how the orator's narration should be made. Thus he says that the narration is that part of the oration by which factual events, that is, civil matters [*civilia negotia*] or things contained in histories, are recounted, that is,

---

[74] Grillius, *Commentum*, ed. Jakob, 37.68–9.

clearly set forth; or by which deeds are recounted as if they were factual, that is, things that never happened, whether probable or not, but are asserted as if they happened, like the actions presented in comedies and stories [*fabulae*].[75]

THERE ARE THREE KINDS OF NARRATION, ETC. He divides narration into three species. The first of these explains THE CASE ITSELF [*IPSA CAUSA*], that is the matter about which there is a dispute [*controversia*], AND THE WHOLE REASON, that is, the whole cause of the issue, namely why there is a dispute, and this kind of narration is called oratorical [*oratoria*].

Another kind of narration is called a digression [*digressio*], that is, a narration of something extrinsic. This has four purposes: to bring incriminating charges against someone, for example, if someone accusing Ulysses of something should digress on the death of Palamedes;[76] or to express something through a comparison, as this in Virgil: "As a lion in the fields of Africa";[77] or so as to entertain our audiences, as in the description of the delights of Sicily in the *Verrines*, although this is not extraneous to proving the charge of adultery which the case was about, since sexual desire is more readily excited in a pleasant location; or in order to amplify the point that is already proved, as Tully in the *Verrines* amplifies when he says that Verres, who desired what he had not seen, was more avaricious than Eriphyla, who fell in love with gold that she had seen.[78] This kind of narration pertains to the case, even if not principally.

The third kind, which is for poets and historians, is completely unrelated to the case, although it gives delight and profit; and so he states that it is SOLELY FOR AMUSEMENT BUT AT THE SAME TIME PROVIDES VALUABLE TRAINING. IT IS SUBDIVIDED INTO TWO CLASSES, ETC. He passes briefly over the divisions of this kind of narration, so that he can return to his main purpose. Thus he says that this kind of narration is divided into two species. One of these serves the purpose of introducing a person so as to express the quality of his character; for example, in Terence, Micio introduces the character Demea, who uses words which reveal the rigor and austerity of his personal character.[79] The other species serves the purpose of producing an exposition of events or supposed events, either with characters represented or not. This may occur in a story [*fabula*], that is, something that is only fiction and which lacks plausibility and truth (like the flying dragons drawing Medea's chariot);[80] or in a history [*historia*], that is, a narration concerning events that are remote from our time, as in the case of this narration whose opening verse is "Appius decreed war on men of Carthage";[81] or it is

---

[75] Cf. Victorinus, *Explanationes* 201.22–3.

[76] The story of the enmity between Ulysses and Palamedes is recounted in Hyginus, *Fabulae* 95 and 105.

[77] *Aeneid* 12.4.   [78] *Verrine Orations* 2.4.18.39; cf. Victorinus, *Explanationes* 202.5–7.

[79] Terence, *Adelphoe* 60–4 and *De inventione* 1.19.27, where this example from Terence is offered as a form of *prosopopoeia*, representing an absent person speaking or acting.

[80] Cf. *De inventione* 1.19.27.   [81] Ennius, *Annales* 7.223, cited from *De inventione* 1.19.27.

the matter of a realistic fiction [*argumentum*], that is, a narration of something fictive yet plausible, as in Terence, "For after he had left the school of youth."[82] Here Terence seems to narrate in order that the quality of character may be expressed by introducing the person. Here, however, there is no person introduced whose own words may reveal the quality of his character; rather this is revealed through the words of another.

It happens that in a narration that is concerned with persons, actions are revealed, and so also the converse of this, but this is not by intention. Thus we must consider the differences among these species in terms of intention. For this reason Tully says that in a narration that is concerned WITH PERSONS, both events (that is, actions) and CONVERSATION AND MENTAL ATTITUDE are explained, that is, the quality of mind may be perceived from conversation attributed to the person himself in accordance with his character. But nevertheless, narration of this sort is concerned with a person, that is, with the marks of his character.

Let us note that these three names, "story," "history," and "realistic fiction," are properly names of the things that are narrated; but nevertheless we divide narration according to these names, whence Tully says HISTORY IS AN ACCOUNT OF ACTUAL OCCURRENCES, ETC. These can also be the names of narratives, but they are not used in this way here.[83]

THIS FORM OF NARRATION SHOULD POSSESS GREAT VIVACITY, ETC. He briefly indicates what the nature of a narration concerned with persons should be. What he calls "vivacity" [*festivitas*] is ornament. After this he shows the variety of materials from which ornament is constructed: for one person is serious, that is, severe like Demea, another is easygoing like Micio; likewise one person hopes to possess something, as Charinus desires Philumena, and another is afraid, like Pamphilus; and then one of them may suspect ill of the other, and they have conflicting desires, and the fathers conceal affection for their sons, and they fail to recognize their daughters, and the young men are stirred by tenderness for their mistresses;[84] and sometimes people have good luck, sometimes bad, and in either case unexpectedly, and everything is happily resolved at the end of the comedy:[85] in all these possibilities, I say, the variety of materials and the contrast of characters are made manifest. From such things is drawn embellishment [*ornatus*] of words as well as of ideas. He promises to return to such matters in a treatment of style.[86]

---

[82] Terence, *Andria* 51, cited from *De inventione* 1.19.27.

[83] Thierry makes a valuable distinction between the things referred to in the narrative and the modes of narration (the names of genres), that is, between content and form; on Thierry's formulation and its significance, see Mehtonen, *Old Concepts and New Poetics*, 56–60.

[84] The references to Charinus, Philumena, Pamphilus, fathers, daughters, mistresses, and sudden turns of events are to the characters and plot of Terence's *Andria*.

[85] Compare Thierry's commentary on *Rhetorica ad Herennium* 1.8.13 (on *narratio*), in Fredborg, ed., *The Latin Rhetorical Commentaries*, 235.

[86] Compare Dickey, "Some Commentaries on the *De inventione* and *Ad Herennium*," 23–4, on links between this passage in Thierry's commentary and a passage in the earlier *In primis* commentary (now known to be by

De inventione 1.20.28

Now it seems necessary to speak of that form of narration which contains an exposition of a case at law He quickly clears away those things which were not his main purpose, and now he teaches how the oratorical narration is constructed. It will be brief if it begins with what needs to be said And appropriately he says, "with what needs to be said." For one should not commence with the embryonic beginnings of the Trojan War,[87] and this is why he adds and is not carried back to the most remote events; if it does not include details when it is sufficient to have stated the substance of the story, etc. Likewise, brevity is maintained if the substance of the case, that is, what happened, is set forth without giving the other circumstances, that is, why, in what way, and so forth, which are not necessary. And if the narration is not carried farther than is needed, and if it does not digress to another story. Likewise, brevity is maintained by not proceeding beyond what is necessary, as Statius says: "and my raft has put into port."[88] And if it does not digress to another story, if no digression [*digressio*] is allowed. Above he said that digression is useful to the orator, but here he says it is inimical to brevity; however, he says that such digression that does not pertain in the least to the case is to be avoided. Brevity may be gained, etc. Likewise, brevity may be maintained if only those things are said from which other things may be understood, as when we say "he came from the villa," we understand that he had left for his villa previously. And if it does not begin all over again at the point at which it has just stopped It is as if someone were to say "I started out from the city, and having started out from the city I came to the villa."[89]

He teaches eight ways in which brevity can be maintained. The first and second of these pertain to the beginning of the narration, the third pertains to the end, and the others seem to pertain chiefly to the middle of the narration.[90] Many are deceived by an appearance of brevity so that they are prolix when they think they are brief The ninth point

---

William of Champeaux), which also gives an extended account of Terence's comedies. Cicero's text only faintly suggests the direction in which the anonymous commentator and Thierry lead at this point. The *De inventione* mentions various traits, emotions, and fortunes which can be used towards a vivacious character portrait: "severity, gentleness, hope, fear, suspicion, desire, dissimulation, delusion, pity, sudden change of fortune, unexpected disaster, sudden pleasure, a happy ending to the story." But both William of Champeaux and Thierry apply this enumeration to the plots and characters of Terence's *Adelphoe* and *Andria*, thus attaching the enumeration of character traits to a concrete literary context with which they might expect their readers to be familiar, given the ubiquity of Terence's comedies (along with the ancient and medieval commentaries on them) in grammatical curricula. On Terence in the medieval schools, see Munk Olsen, "Les poètes classiques dans les écoles au IXe siècle," and bibliography there; and Reeve and Rouse, "New Light on the Transmission of Donatus's *Commentum Terentii*."

[87] Cf. Horace, *Ars poetica* 147; Victorinus, *Explanationes* 204.26; *a gemino ovo* (from twin eggs), referring to the birth of Helen.

[88] *Thebaid* 12.809.   [89] Victorinus, *Explanationes* 205.19–20.   [90] Ibid., 204.27–8.

is a precept about avoiding false brevity. False brevity is when, although the things we say cannot be put in fewer words, yet some of these details are superfluous to the case; thus, however brief the speech appears to be, given its paucity of words, still it is prolix because of the superfluity of details. Tully gives an excellent example of this: "I WENT TO HIS HOUSE, I CALLED THE SLAVE. HE ANSWERED. I ASKED FOR HIS MASTER. HE SAID THAT HE WAS NOT AT HOME." HERE, ALTHOUGH SO MANY THINGS COULD NOT BE SAID MORE BRIEFLY, . . . IT IS MADE TOO LONG BY THE ABUNDANCE OF DETAILS

But since in this example the earlier points can be surmised from the conclusion it would seem that this precept is the same as the fifth precept (i.e. avoid digression); but this is not the case. In the earlier passage he teaches how to make true brevity, but here he teaches how to recognize false brevity. THEREFORE IN THIS SECTION OF THE SPEECH TOO, A FALSE BREVITY IS TO BE AVOIDED, AND ONE MUST REFRAIN NO LESS FROM AN EXCESS OF SUPERFLUOUS FACTS THAN FROM AN EXCESS OF WORDS Since there is length, that is, superfluity, in a multitude of things, such speech is to be avoided. He said, "one must refrain" [*supersedendum est*] as if to say we must "cease from" [*cessandum*] this kind of vice.

De inventione 1.20.29

IT WILL BE POSSIBLE TO MAKE THE NARRATION CLEAR, ETC. Having taught how a narration should be made brief, now he teaches how it should be made clear [*aperta*], that is, intelligible [*intellegibilis*], and so it will be if we observe the same order in narrating the matter as the order in which the events occurred. This should not be given just like a series of things, where the first thing that happened is listed first and then follows the next thing that happened, but rather according to a chronological narrative where, for example, we first mark out something that occurred on the first day, and afterwards we mark out the event of the succeeding day, and so forth: IF THE EVENTS ARE PRESENTED ONE AFTER ANOTHER AS THEY OCCURRED, AND THE ORDER OF EVENTS IN TIME IS PRESERVED SO THAT THE STORY IS TOLD AS IT WILL PROVE TO HAVE HAPPENED OR WILL SEEM POSSIBLE TO HAVE HAPPENED This is what he said above, THE NARRATION IS AN EXPOSITION OF EVENTS THAT HAVE OCCURRED OR ARE SUPPOSED TO HAVE OCCURRED.

ON THIS POINT CARE MUST BE TAKEN, ETC. Having taught what should be done so that the narration is made clear, now he teaches what must be avoided lest it be obscure. So he says NOT TO SAY ANYTHING IN A CONFUSED STYLE: narrating in a confused style is when one does not observe the order of events and their place in time; narrating in a CONTORTED STYLE is when, even while preserving the narrative order, one proceeds obliquely, that is, obscurely, from one point to the next, so that it is not obvious how one point derives from another. So Aristotle in his *Categories*: although beforehand he was speaking of the divisions of the differentiae, after passing cryptically to the constitutive elements, he added this, saying "so that the differentiae of the genus predicated will be differentiae of the subject also."[91] NOT TO SHIFT TO ANOTHER SUBJECT All these matters are treated in the precepts on brevity, so they need not be repeated here. FOR OFTEN A CASE IS MISUNDERSTOOD MORE FROM EXCESSIVE LENGTH OF THE NARRATION THAN FROM OBSCURITY He says that prolixity sometimes impedes understanding more than obscurity, that is, complexity of the narration. THE DICTION MUST ALSO BE CLEAR In the section on style he calls clear diction that which is customary and appropriate.[92]

De inventione 1.21.29

THE NARRATION WILL BE PLAUSIBLE, ETC. He teaches how a narration is made plausible [*probabilis*]. Those things which usually appear in reality are those things through which the appearance of truth, that is verisimilitude, is usually present in narration. These are eight in number, that is, the seven circumstances and an eighth, belief [*opinio*], without which the others are worth little.[93] For if one will have presented circumstances in the narration that are not believable to the audience, there is no plausibility.

The first of the circumstances is "who," that is, an attribute of the person, which Tully calls the "proper nature" [*dignitas*], that is, the quality of the person, when he says IF THE PROPER QUALITIES OF THE CHARACTER ARE MAINTAINED. For in narrating, the quality of the person is to be observed, as Horace teaches in his *Ars poetica*, where he says: "It will make a vast difference whether Davus be speaking or a hero," and elsewhere: "If you reprise the honoring of Achilles, let him be impatient," and so forth, following on from this.[94]

The second circumstance is "what," that is the summary of the facts or the threefold organization of the case, that is before the matter, in the matter, and after the matter. The third circumstance is "why," that is, the cause. He designates these two circumstances when he says IF THE REASONS FOR THEIR ACTIONS ARE PLAIN. IF THERE SEEMS TO HAVE BEEN ABILITY [*FACULTAS*] TO DO THE DEED This marks the fourth circumstance, that is "with what facilities," that is, abilities. After this are indicated the fifth and sixth circumstances, that is "place" and "time"; but because after "time" he adds OPPORTUNITY AND THE SPACE SUFFICIENT, he designated the quality of the time and the occasion. Concerning the seventh circumstance, "'manner," he is silent, because it does not occur in every

---

[91] *Categories* 1.1b21; *Aristoteles latinus* 1.1–5, *Categoriae*, ed. Minio-Paluello, 6. Compare William of Champeaux's commentary (*In primis*) on this curious invocation of Aristotle, in Dickey, "Some Commentaries on the *De inventione* and *Ad Herennium*," 24.

[92] In reference to *Rhetorica ad Herennium* 4.12.17 (treating the *Ad Herennium* as a complementary work to Cicero's *De inventione*).

[93] Cf. Victorinus, *Explanationes* 207.1.

[94] *Ars poetica* 114, 120; the translations of Horace's lines here reflect the versions cited in Thierry's text. Davus (a rude or boorish slave) is a stock character of ancient comedy.

narration.[95] A narration about a conjectural issue does not contain the manner of the action, because whether the action took place is completely in dispute.[96]

IF THE STORY FITS IN WITH THE NATURE OF THE ACTORS IN IT, THE HABITS OF ORDINARY PEOPLE AND THE BELIEFS OF THE AUDIENCE He says that the narration should accord with the beliefs of the audience, but this is achieved in three ways: according to the nature—that is, the customs—of the characters acting, those who are described as doing something, for example, when Terence says that courtesans are delicate and fastidious about food when in other people's houses, but at home "devour stale bread dipped in yesterday's soup";[97] or according to the common talk of people; or according to the beliefs of the audience.

De inventione 1.21.30

IN ADDITION TO OBSERVING THESE PRECEPTS, ONE MUST ALSO BE ON GUARD NOT TO INSERT A NARRATION WHEN IT WILL BE A HINDRANCE OR OF NO ADVANTAGE, ETC Having taught the principles to be observed in a narration, now he teaches that it is not necessary to make a narration in every case, when, that is, a narration either hinders the case or is of no use. Or if there is to be a narration, still it is not proper to place the narration in the same part of the speech all the time, but rather, sometimes before the argument, sometimes after the argument, sometimes elsewhere, but always in accordance with the needs of our case.

WHEN IT WILL BE A HINDRANCE, ETC. He exemplifies the individual circumstances that he has proposed. He says that when a narration is offensive [*quando ipsa offendit*], it should be mingled piecemeal among the arguments so that these may lessen its offense. OF NO ADVANTAGE, ETC. note the combination of words. For he says IT IS OF NO IMPORTANCE TO US TO TELL THE STORY AGAIN OR IN A DIFFERENT WAY, that is, it is not to our advantage. THE SPEAKER MUST BEND EVERYTHING TO THE ADVANTAGE OF HIS CASE . . . BY TOUCHING LIGHTLY ON THE ADVERSARY'S POINTS[98] AND BY TELLING HIS OWN SIDE OF THE STORY CAREFULLY AND CLEARLY Touching LIGHTLY [*leviter*] on things is mentioning them briefly, CAREFULLY [*diligenter*] is when nothing is omitted, and CLEARLY [*enodate*] is what is spoken plainly.

---

[95] Cf. Victorinus, *Explanationes* 207.25–30.

[96] This refers to the rhetorical theory of status, the four legal issues (conjectural, definitional, qualitative, and translative) which determine the juridical status of the case. See introduction to Part 1, and Boethius, *De topiciis differentiis* and Rupert of Deutz on rhetoric, above. For Thierry's understanding of the system in particular, see *De inventione* 1.8.10–1.14.19 and 2.4.14–2.39.115. Thierry notes that the "manner" or *modus* of an action would be irrelevant in a narration that is contesting whether the action indeed took place. Thierry's explanation of the circumstances of narration actually represents an overlay of the later rhetorical doctrine of the seven circumstances (as the basis of topics for invention) on Cicero's account of the precepts to be observed for plausibility in narration.

[97] Terence, *Eunuch* 939.

[98] The accepted reading of the passage is *quae dicenda erunt*, "those things which must be said." The lemmata in the manuscripts of Thierry's commentary follow a different reading of this phrase. See *De inventione*, ed. Stroebel, 28.6 note.

[From Thierry's Commentary on the *Rhetorica ad Herennium*]

Rhetorica ad Herennium 4.7.10–4.8.11

Concerning "types of discourse" or "manners [of speaking]"

I SHALL THEREFORE DIVIDE THE TEACHING OF STYLE [*ELOCUTIO*] INTO TWO PARTS. FIRST I SHALL STATE THE KINDS [*GENERA*] TO WHICH ORATORICAL STYLE [*ORATORIA ELOCUTIO*] SHOULD ALWAYS CONFINE ITSELF, THEN I SHALL SHOW WHAT QUALITIES STYLE SHOULD ALWAYS HAVE. THERE ARE, THEN, THREE KINDS [*GENERA*], CALLED TYPES [*FIGURAE*],[99] TO WHICH DISCOURSE, IF FAULTLESS, CONFINES ITSELF: THE FIRST WE CALL THE GRAND; THE SECOND, THE MIDDLE; THE THIRD, THE PLAIN. THEREFORE This introduces the subject. He teaches style [*elocutio*], the last part of the art of rhetoric, in this order: first, the three "types" [*figurae*] of discourse [*orationis*] with which all style [*elocutio*] is concerned, and then WHAT QUALITIES STYLE SHOULD ALWAYS HAVE. The ornamentation [*ornatus*] of speech, or ornamented diction, belongs to style. The KINDS of style are arrangements of words. The "type of discourse" [*figura orationis*] is an arrangement of words in the speech itself.[100] There are three types of discourse: grand, middle, and plain.

The grand [*gravis*] type of discourse is an arrangement of discourse from words that pertain to great and lofty matters, irrespective of whether the speech is about matters great or lowly.[101] This can be achieved, for example, by metaphor, using a lofty type of discourse when treating a lowly subject, applying words for great matters to trifling things by means of a kind of likeness. Virgil did this in the *Georgics*, when he spoke about bees, a lowly subject, and called their mothers kings: in this similitude, just as kings lead their troops, so

---

[99] The word *genera* (i.e. *genera dicendi*) in the *Ad Herennium,* signifying "kinds" or "categories" of style or discourse (what we commonly call "levels of style"), corresponds to the Greek word *kharaktêres* ["characters"]. On this terminology, see the edition of *Rhetorica ad Herennium* by Calboli, 287 n. 30.

[100] *Figura orationis*: this is not to be confused with "figure of speech"; rather, it is an extension of the *genera* of discourse. Thierry's commentary keeps close to the usage of the *Ad Herennium*. We have translated *figura orationis* as "type of discourse" to distinguish it from "figures of speech." The term *figura* as "figure of speech" comes into common use later, with Quintilian (*Institutio oratoria* 9.1, where it corresponds to Greek *skhêma*, Latin *schema*). The *Ad Herennium* uses the term *exornatio verborum* "embellishment of words" (4.13.18) to designate ornamented or figurative language, what we would call "figures of speech" (or the Greek term *skhêmata*, Latin *schemata*). See further Thierry's *explanation of* this terminology at 4.8.11 below, and notes to that section.

[101] Note that Thierry seems to adhere to an "elocutionary" model of style, in which level of style does not depend on subject matter, and can even override it by choice of vocabulary. See Fredborg edition, 27.

the mothers of bees lead their swarms.[102] Virgil introduced his handling of material in this manner with the following verses:

> I'll tell you the wondrous spectacle of a tiny state...
> [kings] and works and peoples and battles.[103]

Orators are said to write in the high manner [*stilus*] when they use this type of discourse, just as Virgil did in the *Georgics*, even though he was treating of small matters. In the *Aeneid*, where he presents great matters, such as the destruction of Troy and related subjects, he used the high manner as well.

The plain [*attenuata*] type is a composition of discourse out of the kinds of words that pertain to humble matters [*res humiles*] whatever kind of things we speak about. But note that it occasionally happens that matters of great importance are treated in humble language. Terence, who used the humble manner, used this type of discourse more elegantly than other authors.

The middle [*mediocris*] type of discourse takes its composition from words pertaining partly to great and partly to lowly matters. Writers of satires, such as Juvenal, use this kind of speech (*genus loquendi*):

> I feel like running away from here beyond the Sarmatians and the icy
> Ocean whenever those people...have the gall to talk about morality.[104]

Thus far he has used words that pertain to great matters. But following this he descends to the humble type, saying:

> [those people] who imitate the Curii but live like Bacchanals...[105]

Note that authors often vary the kinds of discourse [*genera orationis*] they use. Sometimes they descend from the grand to the middle, from the middle to the plain, and conversely they ascend, going back up the ladder in the same material. Style [*elocutio*] ought to have these elements: elegance, coherence, and excellence. Those elements which we deem to be in their appropriate place are called the parts or properties of style (*partes elocutionis*).

Rhetorica ad Herennium 4.8.11

THERE ARE, THEN, THREE KINDS [*GENERA*], CALLED TYPES [*FIGURAE*] Note that some call these genera "manners" [*stili*], others call them "types" [*figurae*], and others call them

---

[102] *Georgics* 4.21.   [103] Cf. *Georgics* 4.3, 5.   [104] Juvenal, *Satires* 2.1–2, trans. Braund.
[105] Ibid., 2.3, trans. Braund.

"characters."[106] But type [*figura*] properly refers to discourse [*oratio*], and *genus* to style [*elocutio*], whence we say a "type of discourse" [*figura orationis*] and a "kind of style" [*genus elocutionis*], the properties of which ought to inhere in all types [*figurae*].

Rhetorica ad Herennium 4.34.45

[On *translatio* (metaphor)]

METAPHOR [*TRANSLATIO*] IS the common transference of the meaning of a word for signifying something, because there is some likeness involved. The difference between *abusio* [i.e. catachresis] and metaphor is that in *abusio* an unusual transference of a word takes place, but in this case, the transference is commonplace. This transference is accomplished in many ways, which you should examine in this book. Note that something is placed BEFORE OUR EYES in the oration when something is expressed in words in such a way that it seems to be displayed in our presence.

METAPHOR IS USED FOR THE SAKE OF CREATING A VIVID MENTAL PICTURE, AS FOLLOWS: "THIS INSURRECTION AWOKE ITALY WITH SUDDEN TERROR." AWOKE, that is, aroused people at rest. Note that the likeness rests in the following: just as sleepers are aroused from their quiet by sudden clamor, so the insurrection of Hannibal awoke the Romans who were peacefully at rest.[107] Similarly you should note likenesses in the remaining examples of metaphor. FOR THE SAKE OF BREVITY, AS FOLLOWS: "THE RECENT ARRIVAL OF AN ARMY SUDDENLY EXTINGUISHED THE STATE." EXTINGUISHED PROPERLY APPLIES TO WATER. FOR THE SAKE OF AVOIDING OBSCENITY [*OBSCENITAS*], AS FOLLOWS: "WHOSE MOTHER DELIGHTS IN DAILY MARRIAGES." OBSCENITY, that is, turpitude. WHOSE MOTHER: by these words he really means to call the person he is speaking with a son of a harlot. This metaphor is made FOR THE SAKE OF AVOIDING OBSCENITY. FOR THE SAKE OF MAGNIFYING: . . . "AND GLUTTED HIS HORRIBLE CRUELTY." GLUTTED applies to food. FOR THE SAKE OF MINIMIZING, AS FOLLOWS: "HE BOASTS THAT HE WAS OF GREAT HELP BECAUSE, WHEN WE WERE IN DIFFICULTIES, HE LIGHTLY BREATHED A FAVORING BREATH." "To breathe" applies to the exhaling of breath; here HE BREATHED is put in place of "he labored." We breathe when we labor, and so one word is put in place of another . . .

---

[106] *Characteres*: Cicero, *Orator* 134, and Fortunatianus, *Ars rhetorica*, ed. Halm, *Rhetores latini minores*, 125; see the notes on the classical background of this terminology in Fortunatianus, *Ars rhetorica*, ed. Calboli Montefusco, 446–54. The phrase *figurae orationis* was originally introduced into medieval manuscripts of the *Rhetorica ad Herennium* as a marginal rubric, and appears in some form in all families of the manuscript tradition. See Taylor-Briggs, "Reading Between the Lines," 85. See also similar wording in the "Materia" commentary (below, Part 4, pp. 554–5).

[107] The application of this example to Hannibal's invasion is not specified in Cicero's text.

TRANSLATIO OUGHT TO BE MODEST, SO AS TO BE A TRANSITION WITH GOOD REASON TO A KINDRED THING, AND NOT SEEM AN INDISCRIMINATE, RECKLESS, AND PRECIPITATE [*CUPIDE*] LEAP TO AN UNLIKE THING He shows how we ought to construct a metaphor. MODEST [*PUDENS*], lest we transfer a word from obscene matters, taking it up WITH GOOD REASON, that is, not without cause, AND NOT SEEM INDISCRIMINATE, that is without discretion; Tully explains this, saying RECKLESS, ETC. PRECIPITATE [*CUPIDE*], that is, out of a desire [*cupiditas*] to make metaphors.

Rhetorica ad Herennium 4.34.46

[On *permutatio* (allegory)]

ALLEGORY [*PERMUTATIO*] IS A MANNER OF SPEECH DENOTING ONE THING BY THE LETTER OF THE WORDS, BUT ANOTHER BY THEIR MEANING *Permutatio* is the arrangement of words in their proper meaning, but through which meaning the signification of another thing emerges, as in this example: "It is written that Abraham had two sons: the one by a bondwoman, the other by a free woman."[108] By "Abraham," the one who wrote these verses intended, that is signified, God, and by "two sons," he signified the Jewish and gentile peoples.[109] *Permutatio* is called *allegoria* in Greek.

IT ASSUMES THREE ASPECTS: COMPARISON (*SIMILITUDO*), ARGUMENT (*ARGUMENTUM*), AND CONTRAST Comparison is a *collatio* that is made when many things are compared to many things, as in this example: "The seed is the word of God ... on the good ground are they who in good and perfect heart, hearing the word, keep it."[110] In Greek, *collatio* is *parabola*.[111] Argument is a speech in which one person or one thing is compared to just one thing.[112] Contrast is a form of speech in which contraries are ranged against contraries.

---

[108] Galatians 4:22; cf. Genesis 16:15; 21:2.

[109] See Bede, above, p. 269. As in Bede's attempt to extend a grammatical definition of the trope "allegory" to divine poetics, Thierry's treatment of allegory here attempts to reconcile a rhetorical definition of allegory, as a verbal figure, with a theurgic approach to *allegoria* as a way of understanding spiritual truths. The example used here suggests that Thierry's definition of allegory may derive from Bede.

[110] Luke 8:11; 8:15.

[111] *Collatio*, comparison or similitude. See *Ad Herennium* 4.46.59–4.49.62: comparison, exemplification, and simile form a common triad of figures of thought; cf. *De inventione* 1.3.49.

[112] Compare the definition given in the *Ad Herennium* at this site: "An allegory is presented in the form of argument when a similitude is drawn from a person or place or object in order to magnify or minimize, as if one should call Drusus a 'faded reflection of the Gracchi.'" In contrast, Thierry's definition seems to be interested in giving clear formal precepts for distinguishing between the types of *permutatio*-allegory, that is, how many elements are present in a type of allegory. The form of *argumentum* here is related to *argumentum* as realistic fiction (cf. *Ad Herennium* 1.8.13; *De inventione* 1.19.27), although this connection is not made obvious in Thierry's definition.

THIERRY OF CHARTRES, PROLOGUE TO THE *HEPTATEUCHON*; PROLOGUES TO DONATUS, CA. 1140

INTRODUCTION

The *Heptateuchon* of Thierry of Chartres is an encyclopedic project of unprecedented ambition. Thierry's *Heptateuchon,* deriving probably from the 1140s when he was chancellor at Chartres, was intended as an encyclopedic anthology of all of the curricular texts that would constitute the education of the ideal clerical intellectual. It is a vast compilation of over fifty textbooks of the liberal arts—namely the major works of Donatus and Priscian, the Ciceronian rhetorics, nearly all of Aristotle's *Organon* and the Porphyrian and Boethian sources in dialectic, and similarly important texts for each of the sciences of the quadrivium, including some texts on arithmetic, geometry, and astronomy newly translated from Arabic.[1] In contrast to previous collections, as Thierry proudly points out, the *Heptateuchon* consists of original source texts, not his "own writings," that is, his own summaries or expositions of the disciplines. The majority of the texts are presented in their entirety. The objective was to bring together these advanced curricular texts so that they might be read according to the order of the trivium and quadrivium. The term *Heptateuchon* is a clever play on the notion of a bible: combining the Greek term for the five books of Moses, "Pentateuch," with the Greek word for "seven," *hepta*, produces a new word to signify a "bible" of "seven liberal arts." Underpinning this enterprise is a synthesis of Neoplatonist philosophy, mathematical science, and theology. As in Martianus Capella's *De nuptiis Philologiae et Mercurii*, so here too, Thierry promises, wisdom and eloquence will be united to demonstrate the essential unity of all the arts.[2] "Wisdom" and "eloquence" are presented here, not as allegorized figures, but as instruments of philosophical inquiry: "wisdom" is

---

[1] The contents of the *Heptateuchon* are described by Evans, "The Uncompleted *Heptateuch* of Thierry of Chartres," and by Clerval, "L'enseignement des arts libéraux à Chartres et à Paris." On the quadrivial contents, see Burnett, "The Contents and Affiliation of the Scientific Manuscripts Written at, or Brought to, Chartres." See also the articles by Jeauneau cited in this section. There is a short account in Lemoine, *Théologie et platonisme au XIIe siècle*, 72–5.

[2] On the links with Martianus Capella, see Jeauneau, *L'Âge d'or*, 67–8.

intellectus, or understanding, and "eloquence" is *interpretatio*, or elegant expression of what has been understood. These two instruments are served, in turn, by the appropriate classes of knowledge: the understanding is illuminated by the mathematical arts of the quadrivium, while verbal expression of understanding is to be trained by the arts of the trivium. The uniting of wisdom and eloquence is also an echo of Cicero's famous theme in the opening of his *De inventione*, but Thierry has shifted the emphasis from politics to philosophy, to a Platonic search for abiding truths: "wisdom is the comprehension of the truth of existing things," a theme that he pursues in his glosses on Boethius' *De trinitate*.[3] Only the sciences of the quadrivium, that is, the theoretical or speculative knowledge of mathematics, can lead us to ontological truths, a knowledge of causes: as Thierry says in his *Tractatus de sex dierum operibus*, it is the four sciences of the quadrivium that lead men to a knowledge of God.[4] The order of the *Heptateuchon* is that of the seven liberal arts, the trivium and quadrivium; but its orientation is the Platonic division of the sciences into logic (language and reasoning), ethics, and speculative science, in which we ascend from the lowest to the highest orders of knowledge, the knowledge of being and of the causes of being.

Thierry's compilation is not finished; there are some gaps in the manuscripts where bridging introductions, or geometrical figures, or even chapter headings might have been inserted. Apart from the main prologue and some local prologues, the work has not been edited. The compilation took up two large codices, Chartres, Bibliothèque municipale, MSS 497 and 498. The original codices were destroyed by Allied bombing in 1944, along with most of the other medieval manuscripts of the library at Chartres. But the volumes of the *Heptateuchon* had earlier been microfilmed, and now the text can be consulted in photographic reproduction.

General prologue to the *Heptateuchon* and prologue to the *Ars minor* of Donatus translated from the text edited by Jeauneau, "Note sur l'École de Chartres"; prologue to Donatus' *Ars maior* translated from Jeauneau, "*Le Prologus in Eptatheucon* de Thierry de Chartres," by permission.

PROLOGUE TO THE *HEPTATEUCHON*

Here begins Thierry's Prologue to the *Heptateuchon*. Among the Latins, Marcus Varro was the first to assemble a volume of the seven liberal arts, which the Greeks call the

---

[3] For example, in the edition of Häring, ed., *Commentaries on Boethius*, 68.18.
[4] *Tractatus* §30, ed. Häring, *Commentaries on Boethius*.

"Heptateuchon," and after him Pliny and then Martianus Capella. But these were their own writings. We, however, have joined together, in orderly measure [*modulatio*], not our own writings, but rather the discoveries [*inventa*] of the most important authorities on the arts, in a book forming a single corpus [*in unum corpus voluminis*]; and we have joined the trivium to the quadrivium, as if in marital union, to propagate a noble race of philosophers. The ancient poets, the Greeks as much as the Romans, witness that Philology was joined to Mercury in a solemn wedding ceremony, by all the power of Hymen leading the way, and the great consent of Apollo and the Muses, and with the ministrations of these seven arts, as if nothing can be accomplished without them. And this was not unmerited. For there are two chief instruments of philosophical work: understanding [*intellectus*] and its expression in language [*interpretatio*]. The quadrivium illuminates the understanding, and the trivium enables the elegant, rational, and beautiful expression of understanding. Thus it is clear that the Heptateuchon constitutes a single, unified instrument of all philosophy. Philosophy is the love of wisdom, and wisdom is the integral comprehension of the truth of existing things, which no one can attain even in part unless he has loved wisdom. Thus no one is wise who is not a philosopher.

In this synod of the seven liberal arts, assembled for the education of humanity, Grammar comes forth into their midst, first among them all, a matron of severe countenance and bearing. She calls the boys together, she prescribes the rules of correct writing and correct speaking, she fittingly adopts [*transumere*] the idioms of languages,[5] and she sets forth the textual exposition of all the authors, as is her right. Whatever the authors have said is entrusted to her authority. The pupils revere, not argument, but rather the gray-haired authority of this matron.

> Now they say that she was born of a sacred union of the ancient gods
> The offspring of a father of the Nile banks and an Egyptian mother,
> When Osiris reigned in the city of Memphis.
> She was a long time in hiding; then when she was found
> She was raised by Atlantiades [Mercury], and she went forth among the Greek cities;
> And at last when she was aged she came to the descendants of Romulus.[6]

---

[5] This may refer generally to idiomatic usages among languages which are governed by grammar; or it may refer to translation between languages (i.e. she "transfers" the idioms of languages): see Jeauneau, "Le *Prologus*," 88: "[Grammatica] a le secret de traduire une langue dans une autre."

[6] Cf. Martianus Capella, *De nuptiis*, 3.223.

PROLOGUE TO DONATUS' *ARS MINOR*[7]

[Donatus flourished at the time of Constantinus and Constans and] Constantius, the sons of Constantine the Great.[8] He taught the art with admirable brevity, skillful completeness, and the most subtle teaching system. He published the first book [*Ars minor*] to initiate the boys in the mode of questions for learning and answers for instructing, in such a way that he brought together the whole art in chapters containing its essence, and with a minimum of examples leading inductively to universal rules. What others spun out with various and endless kinds of instruction, to the point of taxing their readers, and what they complicated through many errors and difficulties, he poured into the mouths of children like milk. Here the prologue ends.

PROLOGUE TO DONATUS' *ARS MAIOR*[9]

This is the second work [*secunda editio*][10] of Donatus, grammarian of the city of Rome, in which he addresses advanced students, and therefore starts from the elements of the art, but brings forward its doctrine to the very end. For he forms the basis of its doctrine [in the chapters] on voice [*vox*] and letters, on syllables and feet, on tones or accents and punctuation marks [*positurae*], then builds the theory of the parts of speech on that foundation, and finally concludes his *Art* with an artful ending which he calls "barbarism":[11] this ending enables him to provide people with the firmest grasp of combinations of elements that could not be understood from the rules of the accidents of the letter, the syllable, the word, or the sentence. This goes for barbarisms, solecisms, and deviations [*allotete*] or tropes, and other phenomena like them. There are two main

---

[7] The prologue to the *Ars minor* follows immediately upon the general prologue to the *Heptateuchon*, although it is separated from that by what was intended to be a decorated initial.

[8] The words in brackets are missing in the manuscript. The space for them was left blank, because the miniaturist would have filled in these words at the same time that a decorated initial was executed. But the lacuna can be filled in from the corresponding passage in Remigius of Auxerre's commentary on the *Ars minor*. [Note by Jeauneau.]

[9] The *Ars maior* follows in the manuscript after the *Ars minor* and another short treatise (of unknown authorship) that continues the *Ars minor*.

[10] I.e. the *Ars maior*, after the "first work" of the *Ars minor*.

[11] I.e. the *Barbarismus*, or book 3 of the *Ars maior*, so called in the Middle Ages because of its first word, "barbarism."

methods of teaching. One is in the form of a conversation, which accustoms beginners to ask questions of the teachers; this method the Greeks call *dialecticismus*. The other is positive instruction [*affirmatio*]. It asserts what should be remembered on the basis of long research, and those same Greeks call it *analecticismus*. Donatus, that excellent teacher, made use of the former method in his first work, but of the latter in this, his second work.

PETRUS HELIAS, *SUMMA SUPER PRISCIANUM*, CA. 1140–1150

INTRODUCTION

Petrus Helias was born around 1100 close to Poitiers; his *floruit* as a teacher and scholar was about 1140–1150.[1] He studied and taught in the school of Thierry of Chartres in Paris, and was the teacher of John of Salisbury. He wrote a commentary on Cicero's *De inventione* and may also have written one on the *Ad Herennium*,[2] and a commentary in hexameters on the Song of Songs. His rhetorical work is important, if only because he forms the bridge between Thierry of Chartres and Alan of Lille, who used his work.[3] Petrus Helias' major work is the *Summa super Priscianum*, a massive textbook on grammar based on the *Institutiones grammaticae* of Priscian. The main sources for this commentary were the *Glosule* associated with William of Champeaux, and the *Glose* by William of Conches.[4]

Petrus Helias' *Summa super Priscianum* is the earliest example of the *summa* as a pedagogical genre, and his work set the standard for this new form in the twelfth century.

---

[1] For the life of Petrus Helias, see Gibson, Introduction to "The *Summa* of Petrus Helias on Priscianus minor," ed. Tolson; Reilly, ed., introduction to Petrus Helias, *Summa super Priscianum* I:11–13; Fredborg, "The Dependence of Petrus Helias' *Summa super Priscianum* on William of Conches' *Glose super Priscianum*," 2–6. See further Kneepkens, "Peter Helias."

[2] For discussion, see Fredborg, "Petrus Helias on Rhetoric." She dates the commentary on *De inventione* to 1130–1139, earlier than the *Summa* (ibid., 34). The work stands in the tradition of Boethius and Victorinus, and among other things concerns itself with staking out the territory of rhetoric vis-à-vis dialectic and philosophy. Fredborg (ibid., 35) points out Petrus Helias' remarkable claim (based on medieval courtroom order) that it is the prosecution rather than the defendant who determines the *status* of the case. The commentary on *Ad Herennium* was apparently known to his contemporaries, but no such text is clearly ascribed to him in any manuscript. See Ward, "The Medieval and Early Renaissance Study," 33 n. and 74; Fredborg, "Rhetoric and Dialectic," 169.

[3] Fredborg, "Petrus Helias on Rhetoric," 32; see section on Alan of Lille, within.

[4] Reilly's view on the importance of "Stoic" sources should be rejected. The Stoic flavor of some of Petrus Helias' views is directly reducible to his use of Priscian. Priscian's "Stoicism" depends on that of his Greek example Apollonius Dyscolus, and even in that author there is no attempt to preserve the coherence of the philosophical positions of the Stoa, once these are made operational in the grammatical context. For the dependence of Petrus Helias on William of Conches (whose name is not mentioned in the *Summa*), see Fredborg, "The Dependence of Petrus' Helias *Summa super Priscianum* on William of Conches' *Glose super Priscianum*." For the *Glosule* tradition and for William of Conches, see introductions to section on William of Conches, pp. 377–8.

Around the middle of the twelfth century, the enrollment of ever larger numbers of students necessitated a different and less labor-intensive mode of teaching. The *Summa* is "a commentary complete in itself without recourse to the primary text," which allows the students to work through the material by themselves.[5] The tone is lively, and Petrus Helias spikes his work with humor and sarcasm, such as when he criticizes the view that "voice" is a body and suggests to his opponents that they might just as well defend the view that birds could fly between the antecedent and the consequent of a proposition.[6] He also adds appealing similes, for example, comparing speech to making a painting: one needs stable material to make a painting; by contrast, if one relied on words such as "categorical" to convey information about reality, that would be like painting on fast-streaming water.[7] Petrus Helias starts each part of his *Summa* by giving an overview of available views on the topic at hand, and then provides a commentary, not on the familiar basis of lemmata, but of concise and systematic renditions of Priscian's argument which are discussed in detail, setting out arguments against and for Petrus Helias' own positions.[8] Thus the *Summa* can be read, without having to consult either Priscian or any other predecessor, as a continuous exposition of grammar. The new genre became an instant success: it is the standard textbook form of the later twelfth century. Petrus Helias' own *Summa* was popular through the early fifteenth century.[9]

The period in which Petrus Helias works is characterized by the increasing convergence of grammar and logic. Literary examples are reduced to a minimum. However, Petrus Helias resists the appropriation of grammar by logic and stakes out a domain of competence for the grammarian separate from, if close to, that of the logician.[10] This by no means entails the reduction of grammar to a practical skill: it is a scientific activity in its own right.[11] This orientation is clear from the very opening of the work, which takes the form of the *accessus* made popular by Thierry of Chartres and William of Conches in the

---

[5] Reilly, ed., introduction to Petrus Helias, *Summa super Priscianum* 1:12.

[6] Petrus Helias, *Summa super Priscianum*, ed. Reilly, 1:66.14–16.   [7] Ibid., 2:833.33–834.45.

[8] Cf. Hunt "Studies on Priscian I," 5 (198): "an attempt to systematize the discussions on Priscian."

[9] Gibson, "Introduction: Petrus Helias," 163. Paradoxically, his influence was based on the mistaken identification of the summa *Absoluta cuiuslibet* by Petrus Hispanus non papa with the work of Petrus Helias (on which it is partly based). This was probably the most popular syntactical textbook (based on *Priscianus minor*) in the Middle Ages. See Kneepkens, *Iudicium constructionis*, 516–17; for the attribution to Petrus Hispanus non papa rather than to Petrus Helias, see Hunt, "*Absoluta*: The *Summa* of Petrus Hispanus on *Priscianus minor*."

[10] For the grammatical (rather than logical) inclinations of Petrus Helias, see Hunt, "Studies on Priscian I," 22–9 (215–22); Kneepkens, "Master Guido and his View on Government," 137. Fredborg, "The Dependence of Petrus Helias' *Summa super Priscianum* on William of Conches' *Glose super Priscianum*," 44, points out that Petrus Helias' position in this matter is largely derivative, in spite of his self-presentation. Nevertheless, Hunt's point that Petrus Helias resisted the infiltration of logic rather than promoted it still stands.

[11] Reilly, ed., introduction to Petrus Helias, *Summa super Priscianum*, 1:17.

1120s, and adopted by Gundissalinus.[12] It seems likely that for Petrus Helias, as for his contemporary Gilbert of Poitiers, grammar as an activity *sui generis*, not closely linked to the study of literature but also independent from the concerns of logic, may be a first step towards (speculative) theology.[13]

Petrus Helias holds the view that words (*verba*) signify a speaker's understanding (*intellectus*) about reality (*res*).[14] Points of interest in his commentary are, first, his argument that the "material" of grammar, *vox*, is not an "existing thing," but a fleeting activity of an animate being, the production of utterance. He also uses the notion of the "complexive noun," both in the section on the letter and in the section on the parts of speech, to indicate terms that can apply to a group or class, but also to each member of that class: in terms of logic, this may seem problematic, but in the (grammatical) description of language, it is a useful concept. Thirdly, in his discussion of the parts of speech, Petrus Helias pinpoints as their *causa inventionis* that human beings needed to be able to make it clear to each other what they wanted (*voluntatem*).[15] The *different* parts of speech are distinguished on the basis of their *modus significandi* "mode of signifying."[16] The concept is based on—or at least was connected to—a passing remark of Priscian, to the effect that "the parts of speech can only be distinguished from each other if we pay attention to the *proprietates significationum* [properties of meaning] of each of them."[17]

The early twelfth century is characterized by an expansive growth of interest in issues of syntax and the connection of grammar and logic, both inspired by the last two books (On Construction) of Priscian's *Institutiones grammaticae*.[18] Petrus Helias resists this conflation: he discusses the important notion of "congruence" and insists on a distinction

---

[12] Hunt traces the similarities between Petrus Helias and Gundissalinus to a common source, Thierry of Chartres; see "The Introductions to the 'Artes' in the Twelfth Century," 122 (90). More recently, Reilly has argued that in this work Petrus Helias was reacting to Gundissalinus; see his introduction to Petrus Helias, *Summa super Priscianum*, 1:30–2. For summary and discussion of these different views, see Fidora, *Die Wissenschaftstheorie*, 67–70. See sections on Thierry of Chartres (above), William of Conches (above), and Gundissalinus, within.

[13] We thank Professor C. H. Kneepkens for discussion of this issue. It is not clear that the commentary on the *Song of Songs* (which has not been edited) is authentic; if it is, there may be evidence for this connection there. For Gilbert of Poitiers, see Kneepkens, "Grammar and Semantics in the Twelfth Century"; Spruyt, "Gilbert of Poitiers on the Application of Language to the Transcendent and Sublunary Domains."

[14] See Fredborg, "The Dependence of Petrus Helias' *Summa super Priscianum* on William of Conches' *Glose super Priscianum*," 15–22 for discussion of this and of the terminology of *nominatio, suppositio,* and *significatio*.

[15] Petrus Helias, *Summa super Priscianum*, ed. Reilly, 1:177.51–4.

[16] The term is used relatively sparingly by Petrus Helias and William of Conches, cf. Fredborg, "The Dependence of Petrus' Helias *Summa super Priscianum* on William of Conches' *Glose super Priscianum*," 28–31.

[17] Priscian, *Institutiones grammaticae* 2.17, *GL* 2:55.4–5. See Kneepkens, "Linguistic description and analysis in the Late Middle Ages," 552.

[18] For antecedents of this movement, see Luhtala, "Syntax and dialectic in Carolingian commentaries," and the introduction to the section on Remigius, above. For a description, see the introduction to the section on William of Conches, above.

between "congruent in form" and "congruent in sense." The distinction allows him to explain several constructions that appear irregular, but that he finds to be in good grammatical order. He connects this discussion with recent views on words of primary and secondary imposition, i.e. words to describe reality and what happens in it, and words to talk about words (metalanguage). The sentence "Socrates has hypothetical shoes with categorical shoe-laces" is congruent in form (and in that sense "correct"), but there is no congruence in meaning, and hence no complete "construction."[19]

Another passage where recent insights are effectively connected to Priscian's text is the section on "government" [*regimen*],[20] a key notion of early medieval syntax. In a rather casual remark, Priscian uses the term *exigere* "to require," a concept not central to his own grammar. Used intransitively, Priscian says, a verb "requires" a nominative, used transitively it requires an accusative.[21] Petrus Helias follows William of Conches in replacing the term *exigere* with *regere*. In a careful discussion which again marks the fact that his interests are more grammatical and constructional than logical, Petrus Helias draws a distinction between *regere*, where a word "governs" another word in order to produce a complete construction, and *determinare* "to determine," where a word helps to disambiguate another word semantically, but is not necessary for forming a complete grammatical construction This relationship of *determinatio* is not the same as (syntactic) *regimen*. In cases where *determinatio* is operational it produces, instead of a complete construction, an "even completer" construction in which not only the problem of construction has been solved, but also any semantic or referential vagueness has been cleared away.[22] It is remarkable that for all his emphasis on construction, Petrus Helias almost completely neglects word order, a fixture of earlier grammars.[23] Petrus Helias holds a sophisticated view of government as a principle of syntactic completeness, judged from the listener's standpoint. His attempts to explain *regimen* primarily in purely constructional terms again testifies to the fact that Petrus Helias' orientation is more "grammatical" than "logical."[24]

---

[19] See Grondeux, *Le Graecismus d'Évrard de Béthune à travers ses gloses*, 31; Kneepkens, *Iudicium constructionis*, 54; Petrus Helias uses *constructio* in three ways (*Summa*, ed. Reilly, 2:900.79–90; Kneepkens, *Iudicium constructionis*, 57–8): in an "active" sense (as the activity of the listener or the reader), in a "passive" sense, as the relation between two words, and taken as *oratio constructa*, the construed sentence.

[20] See de Rijk, *Logica modernorum*, 2.1:517–19; Kneepkens, *Iudicium constructionis*, 547–51; Kneepkens, "Master Guido and his View on Government," 134–7 on Petrus Helias.

[21] Priscian, *Institutiones* 18.10, *GL* 3:213.7–10.

[22] Cf. Kneepkens, "Master Guido and his View on Government," 140.

[23] Kneepkens, "*Ordo naturalis* and *ordo artificialis*," 67, explains this by the fact that Petrus Helias must have taken Priscian's *ordinatio dictionum* and *constructio* "as equivalent terms and disconnects *ordinatio* and actual word order."

[24] Cf. Reynolds, "*Ad auctorum expositionem*: Syntactic Theory and Interpretative Practice in the Twelfth Century," 43, and see note 10 above.

Translated from Petrus Helias, *Summa super Priscianum*, ed. Reilly, by permission.

BOOKS 1–16

[In his prologue, Petrus Helias discusses the topics "what is grammar," "what is its genus," "what is its material," "what is its task (*officium*)," "what is its goal (*finis*)," "what are its parts (*partes*)," "what are its species," "what is its instrument," "who is its practitioner," "why is it called grammar," "what is the order of teaching and learning it."[25] Interestingly, Petrus Helias also mentions the possibility of a grammar of the vernacular (French).[26] We give the very end of the proem and the opening of the section on *vox*.[27]]

This is the order in which grammar should be taught: First we have to discuss the letter [*de littera*]; this section also contains the art of shorthand writing, which we have completely lost.[28] Then, we need to deal with the syllable [*de sillaba*]; this section will contain metrics which is very relevant to music.[29] In the third place, we have to discuss words [*de dictionibus*] and teach what their accidents are, according to which they must be construed. Finally, we must deal with the sentence [*oratio*], teaching how the words are construed in accordance with those accidents.

On Voice [De Voce][30]

Since voice is the material of this discipline, and also because Priscian uses the word "voice" in his description of the letter, the syllable, the word, and the sentence, therefore he starts with "voice," and his discussion is organized as follows: First he gives a twofold description of "voice." Then he divides voice into four kinds, in order to be able to separate the one at which he is directing his attention from the other kinds. Finally, he gives the etymology of the word "voice," the way grammarians do. But before we explain

---

[25] These are the topics of the "extrinsic" prologue; cf. Thierry of Chartres and William of Conches, above, pp. 377, 407–8.

[26] Ed. Reilly, 1:64.58–9.   [27] Ed. Reilly, 1:65.73–7.

[28] *Ars notaria*, cf. Gundissalinus, *De divisione*, ed. Baur, 53.12.

[29] *Ars metrica*, cf. Gundissalinus, *De divisione*, ed. Baur, 53.15–19.

[30] Ed. Reilly, 1:65.1–70.85. For the term *vox* (voice, sound, utterance, word-form), see section on Donatus, above, p. 87.

the descriptions given by Priscian, we have thought it necessary to set out the different opinions of different scholars on voice.

In his book "Attic Nights," Agellius[31] sets out two ancient views on "voice," one of the Stoics, the other of Plato. The Stoics said that voice is air [*aer*], and therefore a body [*corpus*]; most of our contemporaries also hold and affirm that, even to the point where most of them commit disgraceful mistakes in conceding that "voice" is white and black and foul-smelling, in accordance of course with the different qualities of air! They could just as easily concede that birds fly through hypothetical propositions. But I wish those completely misguided people would tell me, whether they sometimes fly between the antecedent and the consequent! This claim is completely frivolous in my eyes, and not suited to philosophical dogma. Plato also said that voice is a stroke of air, i.e. the striking of air. But this striking some of our contemporaries have called a passion[32] linked to a quality that can undergo something, others have called it an action, others again a quantity.

Thus, some people have claimed that voice is a substance [*substantia*], others that it is a quality, others a quantity, others an action, others have put it in a different category [*predicamentum*], but we reject all of these as false.

For we say that voice does not belong to the things [*res*] that exist, but to what is uttered.[33] Therefore we flatly deny that voice is either substance, or quality or anything else of the ten categories. For by means of those ten categories we divide the things that exist. But voice belongs to the things that are uttered, not to those that exist. For "things" [*res*] we call only those entities that are either substances or that are in substances as in their underlying entities [*in subiectis*]. However, voice is not a substance and does not inform substance either, therefore voice is not a thing, but it is uttered. And so it does not have to do with any category. For the categories follow nature. "Voice" does not propose anything in nature, because it is neither a substance, nor does it inform substance, as has been said frequently.

Voice is a sound [*sonus*] formed in air by natural instruments, it is not a substance or an accident, since it is not a thing, but it is uttered. And this description is fitting to "voice," when it is being used for "uttering by an animate being."[34] For sometimes voice is equated to sound in general. Hence this description "voice is the striking of air etc." is given through its cause, because voice is formed when the tongue strikes the air.

---

[31] Agellius was the common medieval name for A. (Aulus) Gellius, the second-century-AD collector of *faits divers* from antiquity. See Aulus Gellius, *Noctes atticae* 5.15.6–7.

[32] For 'passion' (*passio*) as 'being acted upon' see section on Priscian, p. 181 n. 68 above.

[33] See Reilly, ed., introduction, 1:32. Reilly (introduction, 1:20) argues that Petrus Helias' claim that *vox* is not among the things that "exist" only covers *vox* as the (human/animate) activity of uttering, not to *vox* as *sonus*; but that seems incorrect in view of *Summa* 1:67.34–5, translated just below.

[34] I.e. "voice" is the production of sound by an animate being, it is an activity.

Priscian sets out the following description: "voice is very fine air when it is struck."[35] Either we will say, therefore, that he agreed with the Stoics, and was clearly wrong in that respect—this means his definition consists of the genus and the substantial differences. For according to this view, air is the genus of voice. Or, if we wish to defend Priscian against [the charge of having committed] this error, we will say that this description is given through the cause, just like this one: Day is the sun when it shines over the earth, not because day is sun, but because the light of the sun is the cause of it being day. Therefore, too, voice is air when it is struck, not because voice is air, but because the striking of air is the cause of voice.

"Very fine" is being added because in thick air no voice can be formed—that is also why fish are called mute; alternatively, "very fine" is used in accordance with the ancients, because air in its natural state is fine, it is finer when it is drawn in, finest ["very fine"] when it is being filtered in the lungs, or, yet again, it becomes fine when drawn in, finer when filtered in the lungs, and finest ["very fine"] when it is let out through the arteries; it is, of course, this "letting out" in which voice is formed.

He also sets out a different description:[36] "voice is that which it is the property of ears to perceive," i.e. what it is the proper accident of ears to hear. "The property of ears" is well put, because an ear can also perceive something by touch, but the ear is not the instrument of touch, but rather of hearing.

"The former definition is taken from the substance,"[37] i.e. it is given through the cause, which confers as it were its own substance on voice. Alternatively, "is taken from the substance" means it is a "substantial definition" consisting of genus and differences, if Priscian has indeed followed the error of the Stoics. "But the second [definition is taken] from the concept, which the Greeks call *ennoia*, i.e. from the accidents."[38] It is good that he called the concepts [*notiones*] "accidents," since accidents occur to our senses first. Therefore, the accidents primarily underlie our cognition [*noticie*] according to the senses. For things having substance are better known according to nature, and accidents are better known according to the senses.[39] Through this reasoning he calls accidents "concept" [*notio*] because the accidents come to our knowledge first according to the senses. The addition "which the Greeks call *ennoia*" is good, because *en* is translated "in," and *nois* is "mind": knowledge [*cognitio*] of things is transferred from the senses to the mind, so that the mind, obviously, may distinguish of what kind [*qualis*] or how big [*quanta*] a thing is.

One kind of voice is "articulate" [*articulata*], another "inarticulate" [*inarticulata*].[40] Again, one kind of voice is "literate," another "illiterate." "Articulate voice" is the voice

---

[35] Priscian, *Institutiones* I.I, *GL* 2:5.I.   [36] Ibid. I.I, *GL* 2:5.I–2.   [37] Ibid.I.I, *GL* 2:5.2–4.
[38] Ibid.I.I, *GL* 2:5.2–4.   [39] I.e. through sense-perception.   [40] Priscian, *Institutiones* I.I, *GL* 2:5.5–9.

that is coupled with a certain meaning or co-signification. For *artare* is "to couple," and the diminutive *articulo, articulas* ["I articulate, you articulate"] is derived from it. "Inarticulate voice" is the one that is not linked to any meaning or co-signification. "Literate" is the voice that can be written with letters that have already been invented; "illiterate" is the one that cannot be written with letters that have already been invented.[41]

So if the difference "literate" is added to the difference "articulate,"[42] that species of voice will come into being which is "articulate and literate voice," e.g. *arma virumque cano* "I sing of weapons and the man."[43] Again, combine "illiterate" and "articulate" and you will get a different species of voice, namely the "articulate and illiterate," like the moaning of the sick. Again, let "literate" combine with "inarticulate," and you will get the third species of voice, namely the "literate and inarticulate" one, e.g. *coax*, which is the sound of frogs—in Sidonius[44] one finds the made-up verb *coaxo, coaxas* ["I croak, you croak"]. Similarly, *cra* is also inarticulate and literate voice—the sound made by ravens. If "illiterate" and "inarticulate" are combined, the fourth species of voice originates, the "inarticulate and illiterate" one, e.g. the lowing of cattle etc.[45]

On the Letter [De Littera]

[The text continues with the beginning of *De littera*.[46] This part is called *De Ortographia* in medieval grammar.[47]]

After this discussion of voice, Priscian deals with the letter in the following order. He gives a twofold description of the letter, then he etymologizes the name "letter." Thirdly, he sets out a fixed number of forms and shows that there are many more ways to pronounce them.[48] Fourth, and finally, he enumerates the accidents of the letter and pursues that topic until the end. Let us first therefore explain what the ancients thought about the letter; after that we will clarify what we think ourselves.

---

[41] I.e. with the conventional alphabet.

[42] For this paragraph, cf. Priscian, *Institutiones* 1.1–2, *GL* 2:5.9–6.2, pp. 172–3.

[43] *Aeneid* 1.1; the example comes from Priscian, as do all the others in this paragraph.

[44] Suetonius, *Augustus* 94.

[45] Petrus Helias next discusses the etymology of the word *vox* (1:70.86–71.103); this passage is translated in the etymology dossier, above, pp. 351–2.

[46] Ed. Reilly 1:72.1–73.32.

[47] In Priscian, this takes up *Institutiones* 1.3–2.13, *GL* 2:6.6–53.6; we only translate the beginning.

[48] I.e. there is a definite number of letter forms, but many more sounds can be covered by them.

The ancients, then, said that "letter" is said equivocally of the form and pronunciation, something we do not believe at all. For we say that the same letter is the form and the pronunciation which it represents. For "letter" is a complexive noun,[49] not an equivocal one. A complexive noun is a noun that is uttered in the singular, but fits many as well as every single one of those many. Just as this noun "man" is this part of speech, "noun," so every noun is this same part of speech, with the understanding that all nouns together are this part of speech, and every single noun is this same part of speech.[50] Therefore part of speech, as I just said, is said complexively of nouns. In the same way, therefore, "letter" is a complexive noun for both the writing and the pronunciation, as follows: this form *a* is a letter, and again this pronunciation *a* is that same letter. So the form and the pronunciation represented by that form are one letter: the form itself is the letter and the pronunciation is the same letter.

A "complexive" noun differs from a "collective" noun in that a collective noun fits more items at the same time and none of them individually, e.g. *populus* "people."[51] But a complexive noun fits more items in such a way that it fits all of them at the same time and every single one of them individually, as has been demonstrated above.

So we say that a letter is a simple pronunciation represented by a form. For neither is a pronunciation without a form a letter, nor a form without a pronunciation, but only the pronunciation which is represented by a form, as follows: form and pronunciation are together the same letter and each single one of them in itself, as I said before. So Priscian is dealing with "letters" everywhere in this chapter, but sometimes according to their form, sometimes according to their pronunciation. For some things he attributes to the letter because of its form, some because of its pronunciation.

On the Word

[From *De dictione*.[52] After a brief doxography of predecessors Petrus Helias states his own view on the parts of speech.]

---

[49]   This use of the notion of *nomen complexivum* is an innovation of Petrus Helias. See Reilly, ed., introduction, 1:32–3 and the introduction to this section.

[50]   I.e. a *nomen complexivum* can refer *both* to a whole class *and* to each individual element of that class. "Part of speech" can be used "complexively" of all nouns together, but also of every word that is itself a noun.

[51]   The group is "a people," but no member of the group can be called "a people." Cf. Priscian, *Institutiones* 2.31, *GL* 2:61.21–2: "a collective noun signifies a multitude in singular form, e.g. *populus* 'people,' *plebs* 'populace.'"

[52]   Ed. Reilly 1:181.23–182.54.

But we say that every word is a part of speech, with the understanding that this itself, namely, part of speech, is complexive. What a complexive noun is, we have said above when discussing the letter, and also the difference between a complexive and a collective noun. We said, then, that the complexive noun is uttered in the singular, i.e., with the addition of the pronoun that serves as an article, but fits many, both each individual one of them by itself and all together at the same time. This very thing that is a part of speech, i.e. a noun, and this [particular] noun *Socrates* or *teacher* is this same part, and thus every single noun accepted in itself can truthfully be called this same part, with the understanding *both* that all nouns taken together are this part of speech, the noun, *and* every single one of them taken by itself can truthfully be called this same part.

But somebody will object: "words are infinite in number. But every word is a part of speech. Therefore the parts of speech are infinite in number." This does not follow since many and infinite words are one and the same part of speech, in such a way, of course, that every single one of them taken by itself is that part.

Do you know why all nouns are said to be one and the same part of speech, with the understanding that every single one of them is that part? This is because this part of speech is distinguished from the others according to its manner of signifying [*modus significandi*].[53] For this manner of signifying, namely to signify substance with quality, makes it into a noun and causes it to be called one part of speech. Now, since it is on the basis of this manner of signifying, as we will demonstrate more amply a little later, that the noun has the characteristic of being one part of speech—all nouns have that manner of signifying as well as every single one of them taken by itself—this is the reason why every single noun is that part of speech.

Notice then that the appellative noun [*appellativum nomen*] is this part of speech, viz. a noun, and the proper noun is the same part. This does not mean, however, that the proper noun is appellative, nor that the proper noun and the appellative are the same, although they are the same part of speech. For to be the same part of speech does not mean to be the same, but rather it means "to have the same manner of signifying." This, then, is the way to explain that description "a part of speech is utterance [*vox*] indicating a mental concept," that is: utterance [*vox*] that was invented in order to signify something, or to co-signify.

---

[53] The concept of the *modus significandi* is based on Priscian, *Institutiones* 2.17, *GL* 2:55.4–5: "the parts of speech can only be distinguished from each other if we pay attention to the *proprietates significationum* ('properties of meanings') of each of them."

THE BOOK OF CONSTRUCTIONS

[Petrus Helias' commentary on Priscian's books 17 and 18 (*De constructione*, known as the *Minor*) was written before that on books 1–16. This is its beginning.[54]]

Now that we have to discuss construction we should see first what construction is, and in what order Priscian treats it. For in that same order we will also deal with it.[55]

Construction, then, is the congruent ordering of words.[56] "Congruent" should be taken to mean both in form [*voce*] and in sense [*sensu*].[57] The ordering of words is congruent in form [*voce*] when the forms are connected to each other in a congruent way in accordance with their accidents, so that a masculine will be coupled with a masculine, a feminine with a feminine, a neuter with a neuter, and a singular with a singular—for forms are connected among each other in the same accidents. E.g. *homo albus currit* ["(a) white man is running"]: the masculine is connected with the masculine and the singular with the singular. The ordering of words is congruent in sense when on the basis of words that are ordered as I just said the listener knows what reasonably to understand, whether it be true or false, as when one says "a man is running," or "Socrates is a stone." For although this proposition is false, yet the listener understands something by it.[58]

Note that sometimes the ordering of words is congruent in sense and not in form [*vox*], since the words are not connected congruently in accordance with their accidents. E.g., when I say "the crowd are rushing,"[59] the ordering is not congruent in form because "crowd" is singular, "are rushing" is plural, and the singular is not combined with the plural. Yet, this ordering is congruent in sense, since the listener knows what reasonably to understand from it. For "crowd" is a collective noun and signifies a plurality. It cannot be

---

[54] Ed. Reilly, 2:832–5.

[55] This general discussion of *constructio* seems to have been introduced here under the influence of the *accessus* scheme, cf. Kneepkens, *Iudicium constructionis*, 58.

[56] Kneepkens, *Iudicium constructionis*, 54 traces this definition back to the *Glosule* tradition, rather than to William of Conches. For the equation of "ordering" (*ordinatio*) and "construction" (*constructio*) in Petrus Helias, see note 23 above.

[57] Kneepkens, *Iudicium constructionis*, 54 points out that this is new in the twelfth century: there is not just a distinction between form and (logical) propositional content, but a grammatico-semantic level is introduced, where an utterance does not need to be true, but should be interpretable. In this passage, commenting on Priscian where he is most dependent on the antecedent Greek (Stoic-influenced) tradition with its rigid separation of a level of form and meaning, *vox*, referring to the sound aspect (i.e. the formal side) of words will be translated "form."

[58] See on this passage and its relation to Abelard, Reilly, ed., introduction to Petrus Helias, *Summa super Priscianum*, 1:27–8. Petrus Helias separates the notions of grammaticality (dependent on agreement in form and intelligibility) and truth/falsehood.

[59] *Turba ruunt*, Ovid, *Heroides* 1.88 and 12.143.

used unless about more people, and because of this plurality which is understood from it, this statement is understood correctly: "the crowd are rushing." Whenever the sense is congruent, although the form is not, we have a figure. Such a construction is accepted by the grammarians.

Sometimes, however, the ordering is congruent in form, but not in sense, because the words are connected to each other congruently according to their accidents, but they do not signify an understanding [*intellectus*], as when an adjective of secondary imposition is connected with a substantive of primary imposition,[60] e.g. "Socrates has hypothetical shoes with categorical shoe-laces": the words are connected congruently as far as the form [*vox*] goes, but the listener cannot reasonably understand anything from them. I will make this clear through a comparison.

Speech [*locutio*] is similar to a painting, for just as a painting represents and depicts a thing, in the same way speech, too, depicts an understanding [*intellectum*]. For speech-acts [*locutiones*] do not come into being unless to represent an understanding. So if you wish to do a painting on a torrential river, you will not be able to depict the thing, and you cannot represent it because the material eludes you.[61] Similarly, an adjective depicts a substantive in a certain way: when I say "white man," "white" depicts the man. And an adjective of secondary imposition also depicts a substantive, with the understanding that it does not have any signification in itself, but only when linked to a substantive. When I say "categorical" by itself, the listener does not understand anything. But if I say "a categorical proposition," a proposition is understood with a finite predicate and a subject. However, if it is connected with a substantive of primary imposition, for instance, "a categorical eye," the meaning of this adjective vanishes in connection with such a substantive, just as a painting vanishes in the stream.

Similarly, if I say "your shoe-laces are negative," the mind of the listener understands something incoherent and elusive. So we say that the listener does not reasonably have any understanding. For there is a discrepancy between those terms, so that the meaning of the one vanishes when the other appears, and such an ordering can never be accepted as a construction, according to Priscian.[62] "Every construction, which the Greeks call *sintasis*,[63]

---

[60] For primary and secondary imposition, see Pinborg, *Die Entwicklung der Sprachtheorie im Mittelalter*, 37–8; Kneepkens, "Linguistic description and analysis in the Late Middle Ages," 551. Primary imposition gives names to things, events, and qualities, secondary imposition produces metalanguage, i.e. language to talk about language (nominative, case, etc.).

[61] The notion of the vanity of "writing on water" is ancient. See e.g. Catullus, *Carmina* 70.3–4 *sed mulier cupido quod dicit amanti / in vento et rapida scribere oportet aqua* ("what a woman says to her eager lover / should be written in the wind and on fast-streaming water").

[62] Priscian, *Institutiones* 17.187, *GL* 3:201.11–12.   [63] I.e. *syntaxis*, "syntax."

should be brought back to understanding." There will be no construction unless it brings about a certain understanding in the listener.

The problem is raised whether this is a Latin uttering: "with a negative hood" [*habens cappam negativam*].[64] We need to divide this. It is a Latin uttering, i.e. it consists of Latin words: this is true. It is a Latin uttering, i.e. the person who speaks this way is speaking Latin: this is false. For one cannot say that somebody is speaking Latin, unless what he says generates some understanding in the listener.

Second problem: is it possible for a construction to come into being from a substantive noun of secondary imposition and an adjective of primary imposition, for instance, "the proposition is white"? This is a construction, since it generates some understanding in the mind of the listener. For an adjective of primary imposition does not derive its meaning from a substantive, but is capable of signifying something when uttered by itself. Therefore, it brings about some understanding irrespective of the substantive with which it is connected. For I understand from this sentence that the proposition is colored with whiteness—which is false.

[At the end of his commentary Petrus Helias adds a chapter on the newest concept in grammar, *regimen*.[65]]

Of all these constructions Priscian gives many examples, demonstrating the constructions of Latin in some cases, of Greek in others, and Attic ones in others again. And from this passage until the end of his work he only gives examples of Attic constructions, i.e. used by Athenians. Hence the following treatise is called "Atticism," i.e. "usage of the people of Attica"—therefore let this suffice about construction; we will just add some information on government [*regimen*] of words.

On Government [De Regimine] [66]

Where the grammarians of our day say that a word "governs" another word, Priscian says that a word "requires" another word, and what others call "government" [*regimen*], he himself, using a clearer term, calls "requiring" [*exigentia*].[67] However, I do not blame the

---

[64]   The example has a substantive of primary imposition and an adjective of secondary imposition.

[65]   Ed. Reilly, 2:1049.78–1057.67. In other Priscian commentaries, remarks on *regimen* are connected with the first section of Priscian's book 18; Petrus Helias turns it into an independent section (Kneepkens, *Iudicium constructionis*, 547).

[66]   Ed. Reilly, 2:1049.85–1051.32. See Kneepkens, "Master Guido and his View on Government," 134–7.

[67]   Priscian, *Institutiones* 18.10, *GL* 3:213.7–10.

term used by the grammarians of our own day, for "a word governs another word" is said metaphorically, and the metaphor is apt enough. For just as a general governs an army, so a verb governs a nominative which is construed with it.

Now it is a matter of doubt and a question by the old scholars what it is for a word to govern a word. Most people have claimed that for a word to govern a word is just for one word to adopt another in a construction to determine its own meaning.[68] So a verb is said to govern a nominative because the verb adopts the nominative in a construction with itself to determine what the verb means. For when I say "is running," I signify an action by means of the verb, but the action can only exist "in somebody." Therefore it is impossible to determine the meaning of that verb unless it is shown about whom it is said. So this verb adopts a nominative to determine its own meaning, when I say "Socrates is running." That is why the verb is said to govern the nominative.

But this explanation of what it is to "govern a word" seems a poor one. For if to govern a word is to join that word to oneself to determine one's own signification, then the nominative governs the verb. For when I say "Socrates," I have a thing about which there is speech [*sermo*]. But it is impossible for it to be spoken about, unless something is said about it: therefore in order to determine what this noun "Socrates" means, it is necessary to add a verb, as in "Socrates is running." Therefore the nominative governs the verb, which contradicts every rule in the grammatical textbook. On this line of reasoning, an oblique case would also govern the preposition, since it joins the preposition to itself in a construction in order to determine its own meaning. For a preposition determines the meaning of a noun. Therefore, the oblique case governs the preposition, which makes no sense. In the same way a substantive noun governs the adjective in construction.[69] For when I say "a white man is running," "white" is joined to the substantive "man" in order to determine its meaning: when it is joined to it, it determines and secures its meaning. Therefore in that case "man" governs the nominative "white," which contradicts Priscian, although some have dared assert that in that case the adjective is indeed governed by the substantive, saying that the nominative "man" is governed by the verb "is running." But "white" is governed by the nominative "man." Why? Because the substantive governs the adjective in order to determine its own meaning when the adjective is added to it. This, however, I have not found in any *auctor*. Therefore, for this reason and many others, I do

---

[68] Petrus Helias' solution will be based on a distinction between semantic clarification and disambiguation (*determinare*), and grammatical, purely constructional, government (*regere*). On *exigentia, regimen, determinatio*, see also Kneepkens, *Iudicium constructionis*, 550.

[69] Note that this is still part of a position that Petrus Helias rejects; his solution follows in *Summa*, ed. Reilly, 2:1053.70ff.

not want to say that to govern a word is to join it to oneself in a construction to determine one's own meaning.

[Petrus Helias now states his own view:]

But in order to be briefer and closer to the truth: for a word to govern another word is nothing else than to take it into a construction with itself to make the construction complete—*not*, however, to determine the meaning. That explains why a verb requires a nominative case, because in order to make a complete construction it takes a nominative into a construction with itself. When I say: "I am speaking," I indicate that the act of speaking is in somebody, and thus I signify that there is speech about somebody. The nominative signifies that about which there is speech, therefore the verb takes the nominative with it into a construction to complete a construction, since otherwise the construction will not be complete.

[Petrus Helias demonstrates how this works for the three persons. The verb in the third person requires a noun to create a perfect, i.e. complete construction. The argument is continued as follows:[70]]

However, the converse is not true, namely that a noun takes a verb into a construction with it, since a noun does not signify its thing [*rem*] as if something is predicated of it [*ut aliquid de ea dicitur*].[71] For it does not signify its thing [*rem*][72] by making it the subject [*supponendo*] of anything; it does not signify its thing as being made the subject [*ut supponitur*] of the content [*rem*] signified by the verb,[73] although it does signify the thing [*rem*] about which the content [*res*] of the verb is said. But it does not signify its thing for that purpose.[74] For when I say "Socrates," I do not immediately understand the thing as if the content of a verb is said about it. But when I say "reads," I designate content [*rem*] as if it is said about the referent [*res*] of a noun. So it is not the case that the nominative takes the

---

[70] Ed. Reilly, 2:1052.52–1053.86

[71] The noun signifies a "thing" (*res*), but not yet in its capacity of something that will be the subject of predication. The *res nominis* is its extra-linguistic referent.

[72] Reading (at 1052.54 Reilly) *non enim significat* instead of *nomen enim significat*, which is printed in the editions of Reilly and Tolson. *Non* is supported by MS Arsenal 711; MS Paris, BN lat. 15121 (oral communication from C. H. Kneepkens). *Non* is also the reading adopted by Thurot, *Notices et extraits*, 242; de Rijk, *Logica modernorum* 2.1: 517–19; Kneepkens, *Iudicium constructionis*, 114.

[73] The *res verbi* is the "particular meaning which each verb has, and by which it distinguishes itself from every other verb," the lexical meaning of the verb; Kneepkens, "Grammar and Semantics in the Twelfth Century: Petrus Helias and Gilbert de la Porrée on the Substantive Verb," 238. In Priscian, *res verbi* renders the Greek *prágma tou rhêmatos*, which refers to the semantic level of language description (as opposed to the formal—phonological and morphological—level of description). This bipartition went back to Stoic semantics through Apollonius Dyscolus.

[74] The noun is capable of functioning as the subject of a predicate, but its final cause is not to serve as a subject term.

verb into a construction, but the verb takes the nominative in order to complete the construction. Therefore, the verb governs the nominative case, but the nominative does not govern the verb.[75]

If somebody objects that in that case the preposition does not govern the oblique case because it does not take the oblique case into a construction, but, quite the reverse, the oblique case takes the preposition, I say that this is false, since the preposition does take the oblique case into a construction. For when I say: "I avert my eyes from him," "avert" signifies separation, which separation is signified by the preposition [*a*], since the preposition signifies separation but does not determine separation from what. Therefore, it necessarily takes the oblique case with it, so that it may clarify that separation. Hence the preposition must govern the oblique case.

However, in accordance with this it is obvious that the substantive does not govern the adjective. For when I say "A white man runs," "man" does not take "white" with it to form a complete construction [*ad perfectionem constructionis*], but to determine the signification, because the signification of this noun "man" is too vague. Therefore, it is determined by having that adjective joined to it, and the verb "runs" requires [*exigit*] the noun "white," since if we only said "[the] man runs," the utterance would be too vague. Therefore, for the greater perfection of the construction [*ad maiorem constructionis perfectionem*] it is necessary to add the adjective to the noun.[76]

Now the verb does not only govern the nominative, but also the oblique case. When a verb signifies an act which goes over to somebody else,[77] then the verb takes an oblique case into the construction: when I say "Socrates is reading," I show that the act goes over from Socrates, but the mind of the hearer is kept waiting for a thing [*res*] to be signified by an oblique case. For one always asks "what is he reading?" And thus this verb takes an accusative case with it to reach fuller completion of the construction [*ad maiorem constructionis perfectionem*], as in "Socrates is reading Virgil." Yet the construction will be complete if I say "Socrates is reading" without adding an oblique case, so that "is reading" is used absolutely, i.e. "is engaged in the act of reading."

---

[75] See for the interpretation of the term *supponere* Kneepkens, "*Suppositio* and *supponere* in Twelfth-Century Grammar," 331–5: Petrus Helias uses *supponere* as "to put (an extra-linguistic entity) as subject." The object of *supponere* is always a *res*, i.e. an extra-linguistic entity, the referent of a subject-term.

[76] I.e. Petrus Helias ultimately solves the conundrum by making a difference between governing and determining. The adjective is not (constructionally) "governed" by the substantive, but is (semantically) "required" by the verb, since it "determines" (semantically) the substantive. For the distinction between *ad perfectionem constructionis* and *ad maiorem constructionis perfectionem*, see Kneepkens, "Master Guido and his View on Government," 136–7.

[77] *Transeuntem*, hence "transitive." See Kneepkens, "Transitivity, Intransitivity and Related Concepts in Twelfth-Century Grammar: An Explorative Study"; Luhtala, "On the Concept of Transitivity," and "On the Origins of the Medieval Concept of Transitivity."

[One of the standard problems in the discussion of *regimen* is the accusative with infinitive. This is Petrus Helias' version:[78]]

In this way we have said what it is for a word to govern another word, and what the noun and the verb and the participle can govern, and the prepositions and some adverbs; they govern oblique cases in accordance with the nature of the word.

The ancients were not sure how this construction worked: *bonum est nos hic esse* "it is good that we are here." Here *nos* ["we"] is in the accusative case and the question is by what it is governed. Some maintain that *nos* is in the accusative case here and that it is not governed by anything. For just like the ablative is sometimes used absolutely, so too is the accusative. However, what an absolute accusative would be, I've never found in Priscian. But because Priscian looks into the differences between constructions and never sets out this construction of the accusative among them, therefore I cannot assent to those people. Others have said that this accusative *nos* is governed by the nominative *bonum* ["good"], in a construction like *dominus iste est bonus animam* ["that gentleman is good (nom.) in his soul (acc.)"]. Others again say that we should not ask by what *nos* is governed here, because in itself it is not governed by anything, on the contrary: this whole phrase *nos hic esse* ["that we are here"] is used instead of a single nominative, and that nominative is governed by the verb *est* ["is"]. Yet, *nos hic esse* ["that we are here"] is an incomplete sentence. So the words should be construed with each other one way or the other. Therefore, *nos* is construed with the verb *esse* ["to be"]. And therefore one must say that the infinitive governs the accusative, viz. in accordance with the rule that every infinitive, irrespective of the way its verb is construed, governs an accusative because of the meaning [*vis*] of the infinitive.

[78] Ed. Reilly, 2:1054.11–1055.29.

DOMINICUS GUNDISSALINUS, *DE DIVISIONE PHILOSOPHIAE*, CA. 1150–1160

INTRODUCTION

Dominicus Gundissalinus (Domingo Gundisalvo) may have been born very early in the twelfth century and died in the decade after 1181. He was Archdeacon of Segovia and then of Toledo. His scholarly career is attested from the 1150s onwards and may have continued up to his death possibly as late as ca. 1190. He played a central role in the transmission of Arabic and Hebrew philosophical works to Latin intellectual culture. Alone or in collaboration, Gundissalinus translated many Arabic philosophical texts, including Al-Farabi's *De scientiis*, Al-Kindi's *On the Intellect*, and Avicenna's *On the Soul*. More translations of various works cannot be securely attributed to Gundissalinus himself, but are associated with his circle of fellow scholars and translators at Toledo, and may have been undertaken at his initiative if not by him directly: these include logical, ethical, and scientific works by Al-Kindi, Al-Farabi, Avicenna, Ibn Gabirol (Avicebron), and Al-Ghazali (Algazel). Gundissalinus also wrote a number of independent treatises in which he drew substantially upon the translations: *De unitate* (On Unity); *De processione mundi* (On the Procession of the World); *De anima* (On the Soul); and the treatise *De divisione philosophiae* (On the Division of Philosophy).[1] In *De divisione philosophiae*, Gundissalinus is largely indebted to Al-Farabi's *De scientiis*, but he also draws from other texts in the Arabic philosophical and scientific tradition, and from older and contemporary Latin writings, including works by Augustine, Boethius,

---

[1] Among surveys of Gundissalinus' career and intellectual milieu, particularly valuable are Jolivet, "The Arabic Inheritance," 134–44; and Burnett, "Arabic into Latin: the Reception of Arabic Philosophy," 376–81, with a list of Arabic philosophical works translated into Latin, 391–400; see also the introduction to the edition of Gundissalinus' *De processione mundi* by Soto Bruna and del Real. The major study devoted to the philosophical and scientific thought of Gundissalinus is by Fidora, *Die Wissenschaftstheorie des Dominicus Gundissalinus*. See also the German translation of *De divisione philosophiae* (with Latin text, notes, and introduction) by Fidora and Werner, *Über die Einteilung der Philosophie*. We wish to thank Alexander Fidora for invaluable advice on Gundissalinus' text.

Isidore of Seville, Bede, and even Thierry of Chartres' commentary on Cicero's *De inventione*.[2] Gundissalinus also adopts the scheme of the *accessus* or introduction to the *artes* that had been current among French schoolmen at least since the 1120s, and that had been used famously by Thierry of Chartres and William of Conches. There are also parallels between Gundissalinus' treatment of the material and parts of grammar and the discussion of these questions in Petrus Helias' *Summa super Priscianum*.[3] Scholastic writers of the next century drew on Gundissalinus' treatise for their understandings of scientific classification and the nature and purpose of individual sciences.[4]

Gundissalinus' *De divisione philosophiae* is an important resource for understanding the reception and transformation of Arabic thought about the sciences in the Latin West, and it is particularly interesting for its complex treatment of the traditional components of the trivium and its scientific placement of poetics. Gundissalinus places the sciences under theoretical and practical. He considers grammar, poetics, and rhetoric together as the "sciences of eloquence," and places them under practical sciences, treating them also as civil sciences (a division of practical science). Grammar, rhetoric, poetics, and secular law represent the means of organizing communication, and thus constitute the point of departure for practical sciences. The place of poetics in civil science is justified because poetry delights and edifies, and in this way contributes to civil matters. In this scheme, as in other discussions, Gundissalinus explodes the traditional notion of the trivium, by placing logic outside of the "sciences of eloquence," and adjoining poetics to grammar and rhetoric. The insertion of poetics into "sciences of eloquence" shows the influence of Al-Farabi, who places poetics among the sciences of language. Gundissalinus' treatment of grammar is also significant: grammar is merely an instrument of philosophy, and preparatory to it, whereas logic is both an instrument and a part of philosophy. Gundissalinus juxtaposes and also tries to reconcile Arabic and Latin sources. We see this in his treatment of individual arts, notably in his discussion of the contents of grammar, where he attempts to harmonize Al-Farabi's ideas of grammar, based on Arabic usage, with traditional Latin grammars. Because of his work as a translator from Islamic philosophers, his conception of the "species" of the art of grammar—the individual languages in which the grammatical art resides—exceeds the traditional boundaries of the languages of

---

[2] See Fredborg's edition of Thierry of Chartres, *The Latin Rhetorical Commentaries by Thierry of Chartres*, 15–20; and see within, pp. 480–1.

[3] Hunt traces these similarities between Petrus Helias and Gundissalinus to a common source, Thierry of Chartres; see "The Introductions to the 'Artes' in the Twelfth Century," 122 (90). More recently, Reilly has argued for a direct relationship between Petrus Helias and Gundissalinus; see Petrus Helias, *Summa super Priscianum*, ed. Reilly, 1:30–2. For summary and discussion of these different views, see Fidora, *Die Wissenschaftstheorie*, 67–70.

[4] See the discussion of the scientific legacy of Gundissalinus by Baur in his edition of the text, 368–97. Specific instances of Gundissalinus' influence on thirteenth-century classifications of the *artes sermocinales* are noted in Marmo, "*Suspicio*," 148, 154, 159–63.

antiquity (Greek, Latin, Hebrew) to include the "modern" language of Arabic. He also brings Arabic and Latin (or classical Western) sources together in his general treatment of scientific categories. Thus he imports the Arabic tradition of dividing the parts of logic according to the books of Aristotle's *Organon*. The Arabs had received a tradition passed down by Syriac scholiasts in which the *Organon* was extended to include the *Rhetoric* and the *Poetics*, thus producing a system in which there were eight parts of logic, corresponding to eight "logical" works of Aristotle. In this system, the "parts" of logic represent techniques or functions rather than content or subject matter: the *Categories*, *De interpretatione*, *Prior Analytics*, and *Posterior Analytics* correspond to the purpose of demonstration; the *Topics* corresponds to probable demonstration; *On Sophistical Refutations* belongs to deceptive or false demonstration; the *Rhetoric* corresponds to persuasion; and the *Poetics* corresponds to imaginative representation. The presence of this logical scheme in Gundissalinus' treatise should not be seen as a contradiction to the other systems that he presents, but rather as another dimension of classification based on reasoning techniques rather than subject matter. But we should note also that grammar, which has no book associated with it in the Aristotelian *Organon*, is not accommodated to this scheme of the parts of logic: it is perhaps for this reason that Gundissalinus treats grammar as merely preparatory to logic.

Translated from Gundissalinus, *De divisione philosophiae*, ed. Baur, by permission.

FROM *DE DIVISIONE PHILOSOPHIAE*

Here begins the book about the division of philosophy into its parts and the subdivisions of those parts, according to the philosophers.

Prologue

Happy was the former age that brought forth so many wise men who, like the stars, illuminated the world's darkness. For with as many sciences as those wise men brought forth they bequeathed to us so many torches to illuminate the ignorance of our minds. But because now people are dedicated to worldly concerns, some are busy with the study of eloquence, others burn with ambition for temporal honor. Thus nearly all grow listless in the pursuit of wisdom, and like blind men they pay no attention to the light that is there. Thus for their sake we thought it worthwhile to give a brief account of what wisdom is and what parts it has, and to offer them a taste of what use and pleasure it contains in each of its parts, so that at least they might taste a concise summary of wisdom (which is abhorred by those who are miserably drunk on worldly vanity); and so that, attracted by a taste of a part, they might strive to claim the whole for themselves, knowing from tasting part of it that its sweetness is great.

We say, then, that since there is no one who does not desire one particular thing rather than another, and man does not want anything by nature except what he knows contributes to the advantage of flesh or spirit, from which he is directly composed, therefore man's desire is more forceful either for things of the flesh or of the spirit . . .

Things that are of the spirit are either harmful or vain or useful. Vices such as pride, avarice, vainglory, and the like are harmful. Secular honors and magical arts are vain. Useful things are virtues and legitimate sciences, and from these two the whole perfection of man is comprised. Neither virtue alone, without knowledge, nor knowledge alone, without virtue, produces the perfected man. Some legitimate sciences are divine; others are human.

Divine science [*divina scientia*] is so called because it is known to have been transmitted to men by God's authority, namely in the Old Testament and New Testament. Whence the words "God said" are found throughout the Old Testament, and in the New Testament, "Jesus said to his disciples."

Human science [*humana scientia*] is so called because it is proven that it was discovered through human reasoning, such as all the arts that are called liberal. Some of these clearly pertain to eloquence, others to wisdom. The arts that pertain to eloquence, that is, grammar, poetic, rhetoric, and human law, are all the ones that teach us to speak correctly or in embellished style. The arts that pertain to wisdom are all those that either illumine the soul of man to bring about knowledge of the truth or kindle it so that it loves the good. All of these are philosophical sciences. For this reason, since there is no science which is not some part of philosophy, at the outset these points must be considered: what is philosophy and why is it so called; then, what is its intention and its goal [*finis*]; then, what are its parts and the parts of those parts; and finally, what is to be observed about each one of these parts . . . [5]

[The section covering "what is philosophy," "why is it so called," and "what is its intention" has been omitted here. We resume at the section treating the "goal" of philosophy.]

It is clear that everything that exists either comes from our actions and our will or not from our actions, but from those of God or nature.[6] But because there is no science which

---

[5] On this distinction between divine and human science, see Fidora, *Die Wissenschaftstheorie*, 25–7.

[6] This paragraph derives from Al-Ghazali, *Philosophiae tractatus*, ed. Muckle, *Algazel's Metaphysics: A Mediaeval Translation*, 1–2 (the Latin translation, prepared by Gundissalinus and fellow Toledan scholars, of the *Maqasid al-falasifa* [The Meanings of the Philosophers] of Al-Ghazali [d. 1111]); and from Avicenna's *Logica* (the medieval Latin

does not have a subject that it treats, and there is nothing which does not derive from one of these two categories, therefore philosophy is primarily divided into two kinds: the first, by which we know the disposition of our actions; the second, by which we know everything else that exists. The first of these is the part of philosophy which has us know what ought to be done, and this is called "practical"; the other part has us know what ought to be understood, and this is called "theoretical." The latter is in the intellect, the former in effect; one consists only in mental cognition, the other in the performance of actions. Because philosophy was invented so that the soul might be perfected through it, and there are two ways by which the soul is perfected, knowledge and action, therefore philosophy, which is the ordering of the soul, is necessarily divided into knowledge and action, just as the soul is divided into the senses and reason. Action belongs to the sensible part of the soul, and speculation belongs to the rational part of the soul. But because the rational part of the soul is divided into cognition of divine things (which do not derive from our action) and cognition of human things (which result from our action), therefore the goal of philosophy is the perfection of the soul, not only that one may know what one should understand, but so that one may know what one should do, and do it. Now, the goal of speculation is to grasp the meaning of what is to be understood; the goal of practice is to grasp the meaning of what is to be done.

Thus the parts into which philosophy is first divided are theoretical and practical. Now it remains to consider what and how many are the parts of each of these main divisions of philosophy.[7] We said above that theoretical science is the cognition of those things which do not derive from our actions. According to some philosophers, those things which do not derive from our actions or our will are divided into two kinds: entities to which no motion ever occurs,[8] that is, God and the angels; and other entities to which motion does occur, such as identity, unity, multiplicity, and causality. But those entities to which motion occurs are also divided into two: those which can never exist without motion, such as human beings or a square;[9] and others which can exist without motion, such as unity and cause.

translation of Avicenna's *Isagoge* or introduction to the logical books of his *Shifa*): see *Avicenna, Opera philosophica*, fol. 2ra.

[7] This paragraph is based closely on Avicenna, *Logica*, fol. 2ra. On the classification of entities here, see Hugonnard-Roche, "La classification des sciences de Gundissalinus et l'influence d'Avicenne," 44–7. For discussion and English translation of the Arabic text of Avicenna, see Marmura, "Avicenna on the Division of the Sciences in the *Isagoge* of his *Shifa*."

[8] "Motion," for *motus*, here in the sense of change or alteration, especially material change. These ideas about what has or does not have motion, as relating to objects of study, derive ultimately from Aristotle's *Metaphysics*, book 6 (E), 1025–6, and from Boethius, *De trinitate* 2: see Boethius, *The Theological Tractates and the Consolation of Philosophy*, 8.

[9] A square cannot exist except as embodied in matter, just as a human being cannot exist except as embodied in flesh; cf. Aristotle's *Metaphysics*, book 7 (Z), 1036.

Furthermore, those entities which cannot exist without motion are also divided into two: those which can be understood without matter itself, although they cannot exist immaterially, such as a square, and others which can neither exist nor be understood immaterially, such as human beings. Those which can exist without motion, although motion may occur to them, can be considered in two ways: one, as they are in themselves without any matter; and two, as motion occurs to them. Considering them as motion occurs to them has two modes: either they are considered according to their proper matter and their proper motion, as when fire is said to be a single entity and the elements are said to be four, and warmth or cold is said to be a cause and the soul is said to be the origin of bodily movement although it can exist separately in itself. Or they are not considered according to their proper matter and proper motion, as when we understand the dispositions of those entities which are aggregation, division, multiplication, and so forth which accompany matter, although these do not occur to matter unless from matter and from a mixture of movement. These are attached to number but are either in the human intellect or exist in things that move, divide, separate, or combine. And when the intellect abstracts them in some way, then it is not necessary to assign them particular matter.

Of those things, then, which do not derive from our actions, some exist and are understood without motion and motion never occurs to them, such as God and the angels. Other things exist and are understood without motion, but motion does occur to them: such things are unity, cause, number, and the like. There are yet other things which, even though they do not exist without motion, are nevertheless understood apart from motion, such as a square. But there are still others which neither exist nor are understood without motion, such as human beings.

According to others the aforementioned division seems to be formed in another way, although the meaning is the same.[10] All things that are understood are, on the one hand, completely separate from matter and motion, and do not cohere in mutable or movable bodies, such as God and the angels, unity, cause and being caused, congruence and non-congruence, being and negation, and the like. Among these there are some that cannot possibly exist in matter, such as God and the angels; and there are some to which a material existence happens, even though it is not necessary for them to exist materially, such as unity and cause (that is, a body can be said to be one and a cause, and an angel can also be said to be a cause and one). And on the other hand there are some that exist entirely through matter and motion, such as a shape or a human being. But among the latter group there are some things which cannot exist nor can be understood to exist except in terms of

---

[10] The scheme in this paragraph closely follows Al-Ghazali; see *Algazel's Metaphysics*, ed. Muckle, 3, and Hugonnard-Roche, "La classification des sciences de Gundissalinus et l'influence d'Avicenne," 44–7.

their own proper matter, such as a man, a vegetable, an animal, the sky, the earth, a metal, and the rest of such corporeal species; and there are some which can be understood to exist without their own proper matter, such as a shape, a square, roundness, curvedness, and the like, which, even though they have no existence except in matter, do not depend for their existence on one given matter as opposed to another.

Thus according to all these divisions, theoretical philosophy necessarily has three parts:[11] speculation about those things which are not separate from their own matter either in their being or in the understanding of them; or speculation concerning those things which are separate from matter in the understanding of them but not in their being; or speculation about those things which are separate from matter in both being and the understanding of them. The first part of the division is called physics or natural science, which is first and least; the second is called mathematical science or *disciplinalis*,[12] which is in the middle; and the third is called theology or first science, or first philosophy, or metaphysics. With respect to this Boethius says that physics is non-abstract and has motion, mathematics is abstract and has motion, and theology is abstract and has no motion.[13] These three sciences are the only parts of theoretical philosophy, because other than these, there cannot be more kinds of things about which speculation is possible. Whence Aristotle says, there are three kinds of science: the first, natural, speculates about what is moved and subject to decay; the second, *disciplinalis*, speculates about what is moved and is not subject to decay; the third, divine, considers what neither moves nor is subject to decay.[14]

The general utility of this tripartite division of theoretical science is to know the dispositions of all things that exist, so that the form of all being may be delineated in our souls according to its order, just as visible form is delineated in a mirror.[15] A delineation of this kind in our soul is the perfection of the soul itself, because the soul's aptitude for

---

[11] Cf. *Algazel's Metaphysics*, ed. Muckle, 2–3.

[12] Medieval explanations of the term *disciplinalis* for mathematics point to the discipline and stringency of this study which tames arrogant hearts: see Gundissalinus, *De divisione philosophiae* 34, lines 18 ff.; Vincent of Beauvais, *Speculum doctrinale*, chapter 18. Gundissalinus (and after him, Vincent of Beauvais) attributes the usage to Arabic texts, which call it the "taming" science. Cf. the use of the term in the Latin translation of Al-Ghazali's *Metaphysics*, ed. Muckle, 2. See Weijers, "L'appellation des disciplines dans la classifications des sciences aux XIIe et XIIIe siècles," 47. In *De trinitate* 2, Boethius uses the adverb *disciplinaliter* to describe how the science of mathematics proceeds (i.e. "in a disciplined way").

[13] *De trinitate* 2; see Boethius, *The Theological Tractates and the Consolation of Philosophy*, 8.

[14] Cf. Aristotle, *Metaphysics*, book 6 (E) ch. 1 and book 11 (K) ch. 7. On Gundissalinus' reception of these ideas from Aristotle's *Metaphysics* and Boethius' *De trinitate* and their transmission in his milieu, see Burnett, "The Blend of Latin and Arabic Sources in the Metaphysics of Adelard of Bath, Hermann of Carinthia, and Gundisalvus"; and on Gundissalinus' particular indebtedness to Boethius for a methodology of the theoretical sciences, see Fidora, *Die Wissenschaftstheorie*, 38–76.

[15] Cf. *Algazel's Metaphysics*, ed. Muckle, 2.

receiving the image is the very property of the soul. Thus the delineation of the image is the soul's highest nobility at the present moment and the cause of happiness in the future.

But achieving future happiness requires not only the science of understanding whatever exists, but also the science of doing what is good. Therefore after theoretical science comes practical science, which is similarly divided into three parts.[16]

The first is the science of organizing one's communication with all people. This purpose requires grammar, poetics, rhetoric, and the science of secular law, under which is comprised the science of governing cities and the science of understanding the rights of citizenship, and which is called political science [*politica scientia*], and by Tully is called "civil reasoning" [*civilis ratio*].

The second is the science of ordering one's own home and family: this science teaches how a man is to live with his wife and his children and his servants and all his household. This science is called household management [*ordinacio familiaris*].

The third is the science by which a man learns how to order the proper conduct of his own self in terms of the honest virtue of his soul, that is, so that he is not corrupted and that there is a benefit to his moral behavior. This science is called ethics or morals. For every man lives either alone or with others, and if with others, then either with his household or with his fellow citizens. Thus practical philosophical science is by necessity divided into these three sciences, that is, into the science of ordering public interaction [*conversacio*] with one's fellow citizens, and the science of ordering private interaction with one's household, and the science of ordering individual dealings with oneself so that one may be in accord with oneself and not internally divided in any respect.

The general utility of this tripartite practical science is to know the nature of actions that are to be done, from which arises their usefulness to us in this world and hope of eternal life in the future is affirmed.[17] The truth of all these things is universally affirmed by speculative proof and by authority of divine law. But each one individually is also affirmed by divine law.[18]

In these six sciences is contained whatever can be known and should be done. And thus it is said that the intention of philosophy is to comprehend, as much as possible, whatever exists.

Its utility is the attainment of perfection of the human soul in order to achieve future happiness. The human soul cannot be perfected if not through knowledge of truth and love of goodness. In general the goal [*finis*] of the speculative sciences is knowledge of truth, and the goal of the practical sciences is love of the good. The former teach how the truth may be known about every thing; the latter teach how in every matter virtue is to be

---

[16] The following sections on practical science may be compared with *Algazel's Metaphysics*, ed. Muckle, 2, and with Avicenna, *Logica*, fol. 2ra–b. But the placement of the "sciences of eloquence"—grammar, poetics, rhetoric, and "civil law" or politics—is Gundissalinus' contribution; Avicenna and Al-Ghazali say nothing of these sciences of discourse.
[17] Cf. *Algazel's Metaphysics*, ed. Muckle, 2.   [18] Avicenna, *Logica*, fol. 2rb.

loved and brought to completion through action. By these two means, knowledge of truth and love of goodness, man is perfected and is made worthy of eternal happiness.

A truth is either known or unknown.[19] A known truth, for example, is that two are more than one, or every whole is greater than its parts, and the like. An unknown truth, for example, is that the world began, or that an angel is composed of matter and form, and similar things that need proof. Every single unknown truth becomes known only through something that is already known.

Logic alone is the science that teaches how to arrive at understanding of the unknown through what is known; this will be proved later on. This is why logic precedes all the parts of theoretical philosophy, and is necessary to them for getting at truth. But because logic does not signify truth except through a proposition, and every proposition consists of terms, but grammar is the science that prepares the terms by forming them and combining them, therefore grammar temporally precedes logic and all the other sciences, for at the very beginning, like a wet-nurse, it imparts the skill of speaking correctly.

Each science is either a part or an instrument of philosophy; or it is both part and instrument. Natural science is a part of philosophy, like mathematical science or divine science, as we said above. Grammar is just an instrument of philosophy.

But logic is both part and instrument. Grammar is an instrument of philosophy with respect to teaching, but not with respect to learning—for without words philosophy can be known, but it cannot be taught. Now logic, because it is useful for truth in itself and for what is to be discovered in the other sciences, is an instrument; but it is also a part, in that philosophy investigates the dispositions of its subject, much as it inquires about other matters.

[The text turns to an overview of the natural sciences and a close treatment of mathematics, then to an overview of divine science. At this point it introduces grammar, poetics, rhetoric—the *scientiae eloquentiae*—because these are the entry way into all of the other sciences, and "in temporal terms are prior to the sciences of wisdom."]

On Grammar

Grammar is the beginning of all the sciences, because it teaches the first elements of articulate speech by which every art is taught and learned, that is, speaking, explaining,

---

[19] "Known" and "unknown" (*notus, ignotus*): here in the sense, respectively, of self-evident and mysterious. These final paragraphs of Gundissalinus' prologue are loosely based on the logical tractate in the *Maqâsid al-falâsifah* of Al-Ghazali, from the Latin translation prepared by Gundissalinus in concert with another Toledan scholar. See Al-Ghazali, *Logica Algazelis*, ed. Lohr, 239–43.

questioning, and answering.[20] Let us see what it is necessary to consider first about this art.

The following questions are to be asked of grammar, just as of any of the other arts: what is it, what is its genus, what is its subject matter, what are its parts, what are its species, what is its function, what is its goal, what is its instrument, who is its practitioner, why is it so called, and in what order is it to be taught and learned.[21]

The ancients use the term "art" extrinsically [*artem extrinsecus vocant*] for the knowledge of defining these things, making distinctions, and verifying them with reasoning, because it is necessary to know this first on the outside, before the actual doctrine is to be taken up. They use it intrinsically [*intrinsecus*] for the actual doctrine of rules and precepts by which they instruct a man to proceed according to the art, for knowledge of which an understanding of those earlier matters is necessary.[22] But in distinguishing the art extrinsically and intrinsically, as it were, we are not saying that there are two arts, but rather that one and the same art is taught in these two ways—just as, for example, we regard one and the same house in one way when we consider its extrinsic form, that is, its height, material, and exterior walls, and in another way when, having gone inside the house and surveyed the household and all the furnishings, and settled down on the dining couches, we are sated with various courses of a meal. So indeed the teaching of those things which are called "extrinsic" does not instruct the practitioner to proceed according to the art, but rather to understand what it is necessary to know in advance of the art. For it would be a disgrace if someone, working at any kind of art, should not know what the art is, of what genus it is, what matter it has, and the other issues set out beforehand. Every art may be divided into theoretical and practical, because either it is achieved only in mental cognition—this is theoretical—or in the exercise of action—and this is practical. Truly, then, the extrinsic art seems to pertain to the theoretical, and the intrinsic art to the practical. For the extrinsic art does not teach action, but only knowledge; the intrinsic art

[20] From Al-Farabi(?), *De ortu scientiarum* (probably translated by Gundissalinus): Baeumker, ed., *Alfarabi: Über den Ursprung der Wissenschaften*, 22. The attribution of the treatise to Al-Farabi is not certain.

[21] Gundissalinus' headings are identical with those used by Petrus Helias; see *Summa super Priscianum*, ed. Reilly, 1:61; cf. William of Conches in the prologue to the second redaction of his commentary on Priscian; see Jeauneau, "Deux rédactions des gloses de Guillaume de Conches sur Priscien," 244; see within, pp. 385–8, 448. The ultimate model for these headings was the prologue to the Cicero commentary by Thierry of Chartres (see within, pp. 407–8, 411–15).

[22] This distinction between the extrinsic and intrinsic art (although without the helpful analogy to a house and its interior) is also present in William's prologue to his Priscian commentary. For this distinction William was likely indebted to Thierry of Chartres. Its ultimate source is in Victorinus' *Explanationes* on Cicero's *De inventione*, in Halm, *Rhetores latini minores*, 170. See Hunt, "The Introductions to the 'Artes'," 119–23 (87–91). See above, William of Conches, p. 385, and Thierry of Chartres, pp. 411–12.

teaches action and knowledge. When precepts relating to the art are taught to us, they give us action and knowledge . . . [23] First let us consider what grammar is.

Grammar is the art or skilled science of speaking correctly and writing correctly. It should be noted that "art," "knowledge," "doctrine," "discipline," and "faculty" are one and the same thing.[24] "Ars" and "doctrina" are used with respect to the "doctor," who binds us with his rules and precepts and constrains [*artat*] us to work according to the art. Thus "art" is so called from *artare* [constraining] and "doctrina" from *docere* [teaching].[25] The term "discipline" is used with respect to the *discipulus* (pupil), because discipline is learned [*discitur*]. But it is called "knowledge" when it is already being retained in the soul; for, as Aristotle says, all knowledge is in the soul.[26] But because all knowledge is first in the disposition for it, and afterwards in the habit [*habitus*] of it, so when knowledge is a habit of mind it is called a faculty, because it gives a man the faculty of working according to an art.

Grammar therefore is an art or a skillful—that is, expert—knowledge of speaking correctly and writing correctly: correctly, that is, without the errors of solecism and barbarism. A solecism is a faulty arrangement of words in speech, when, for example, words are not joined in speech according to their accidents: this happens when a case is not joined with a similar case, or a number with a similar number, or verb tense with verb tense, or person with person, and the like, as in *dominus venit ad domo sua*.[27] A barbarism is a faulty pronunciation of a letter or syllable in a word, that is, when we pronounce a long syllable as a short one, and the reverse.[28]

In order to avoid these faults, the science of language, which by nature is the first of all the sciences, is initially divided into two: that is, the science of considering and observing what every verbal expression signifies according to the people whose language it is, and the science of observing the rules of those expressions.[29] The former is the science of understanding what

---

[23] For the distinction between knowledge (extrinsic art) and action (both extrinsic and intrinsic arts), see Victorinus, *Explanationes*, 170–1.

[24] *ars* "art," *scientia* "knowledge," *doctrina* "doctrine," *disciplina* "discipline," *facultas* "faculty." The general ideas in this paragraph, and some of the derivations, are based on Isidore, *Etymologiae* 1.1, "On Discipline and Art"; cf. Martianus Capella, *De nuptiis*, 3.

[25] Cf. William of Conches, prologue to the commentary on Priscian, within, p. 385.

[26] Possibly *On the Soul* 3.4 (429a27); cf. *Generation of Animals* I.22 (730b15–16).

[27] Classical usage would be *venit domum* ("[going] home"), using the accusative case without preposition. Gundissalinus is exemplifying the wrong case with the prepositon *ad*. Petrus Helias uses a similar example of grammatical solecism: "if instead of *Dominus venit* one says *Dominum* [i.e. accusative case] *venit*," *Summa super Priscianum*, ed. Reilly, 2:844.

[28] For these definitions of solecism and barbarism, see Donatus, *Ars maior* 3.1–2; Isidore, *Etymologiae* 1.32–3. Gundissalinus abbreviates his treatment of these issues here, to return more fully to the same material later in the grammar section.

[29] Here and over the next nine paragraphs, Gundissalinus incorporates *verbatim* passages from his own loose translation or adaptation of Al-Farabi's *De scientiis*: Gundissalinus, *Domingo Gundisalvo: De scientiis*, ed. Alonso Alonso.

meaning individual words were created to express, the latter is the science of ordering individual expressions in discourse so as to signify concepts of the mind. The former is learned naturally by children just from hearing; the latter is learned by adults through doctrine and study. The former is acquired just from the habit of hearing; the latter is grasped from the rules of a master. The former varies among all people according to the diversity of languages; the latter is virtually the same among all people because of a similarity of rules. For in every art, whether practical or theoretical, whether a liberal art or a mechanical art, there are rules that in general cover all or most of those things that the art treats.[30] Indeed, the rules were devised for a purpose: so that with their help we might know whether we are perhaps committing some error in terms of the art, and that we might more easily grasp and observe the elements of the art. Individual instances do not constitute an art except when they are united by rules comprehended in the human soul according to a known order. The ancient Romans used to say that not only is every utterance [*oratio*] a rule of this sort, but every instrument through which one discerns whether one has gone astray in any art; for example, in the mechanical arts the plumb line and the compass, and similar instruments in other arts.[31]

Thus since rules for writing and speaking correctly are found exclusively in the art of grammar, therefore grammar is deservedly said to be the science of writing and speaking correctly.

... The genus of an art is its quality according to its effect. This art is of this particular quality: it is a science of letters, and its effect in those who study it is to render them lettered.[32] Other arts do not have this effect: rhetoric does not make a man lettered, but rather eloquent; and logic makes one fluent in argumentation; and the mathematical arts make men wise. Thus grammar alone has as its foremost effect to make the ones who study it literate with regard to correctness of speaking and writing.

The *De scientiis* begins with a short chapter on the "science of language," which contains some of the elements taught in the Latin tradition under "grammar" (although the term is not used in the Al-Farabian text); Gundissalinus' translation often substitutes terminology from the Latin tradition. The passage here is from *De scientiis*, ed. Alonso Alonso, 58.

[30] From this passage to the end of the paragraph, Gundissalinus incorporates his version of Al-Farabi, *De scientiis*, ed. Alonso Alonso, 60–1.

[31] Gundissalinus has taken this somewhat out of the Al-Farabian context. Al-Farabi's meaning is that the ancients originally meant by "rule" any instrument that would guard against error in the practice of an art, including tools and other aids for achieving precision (e.g. a compass, an arithmetical table, etc.), whereas the term now (in Al-Farabi's use) can extend to a comprehensive statement about an art. See Mahdi, "Science, Philosophy, and Religion in Al-Farabi's *Enumeration of the Sciences*," 118–19. The Latin translation of Al-Farabi's *De scientiis* by Gerard of Cremona, a contemporary of Gundissalinus who also worked in Toledo, is more literal than that of Gundissalinus, and makes this context clearer: see the edition (with German translation) of Gerard of Cremona's translation by Schupp, *Über die Wissenschaften/De scientiis*, 6–8.

[32] Cf. Martianus Capella, *De nuptiis*, 3.231.

The subject matter of any art is that which the practitioner ought to treat according to the art. The subject matter of this art is voice or the alphabetical elements.[33] The practitioner treats this by showing what happens to them when they are written or spoken, either on their own or in combination with other forms. If in combination, it is either in a syllable or a word or in a sentence [*oratio*].

Now we turn to the parts of the art. The parts of an art are described in terms of integral parts, which, when they come together in one entity, form an integral whole. In this respect the parts of an art are those things knowledge of which will render the man in whose mind they are collected perfected in that art. According to every people, the parts of grammar are seven, namely: the science of simple expressions, the science of discourse, the science of the rules governing simple expressions, the science of rules governing expressions when they are compounded in discourse, the science of rules governing correct writing, the science of rules governing correct reading,[34] and the science of rules for versification.[35]

The science of simple expressions teaches what each expression signifies, that is, either a genus or species or something else of this sort.[36] In every language some signifying expressions are simple, such as the words "man" and "animal," and others are compound, such as "man is an animal."[37]

Some simple expressions are proper, such as "Socrates" and "Plato," others are common, such as "man" and "animal." Some common expressions are nouns, some are verbs, and some are the other parts of speech. This division is not the same according to all peoples. But in whatever way the division occurs, certain properties belong to each word. To nouns belong the properties of masculine and feminine, plural and singular, and other such things; to verbs belong the properties of mood, tense, and other such things.[38]

The science of compound expressions concerns discourses, which, among a certain people, are used by orators or versifiers, those considered wise or eloquent.[39]

---

[33] *Elementum* as distinguished from *littera*: see Priscian, *Institutiones grammaticae* 1.4, *GL* 2:6.25f.; cf. however Isidore, *Etymologiae* 1.3.4: "But the Hebrews used twenty two letters (*elementa litterarum*) according to the books of the Old Testament."

[34] Manuscripts of *De divisione philosophiae* have the phrase *ad recte loquendum* "correct speaking," and Baur's edition has *loquendum*. But most manuscripts of Gundissalinus' version of Al-Farabi's *De scientiis* (from which Gundissalinus has taken this group of paragraphs) have the words *ad recte legendum*, "correct reading," an accurate rendering of the Al-Farabian text, which gives rules about writing and reading. "Correct reading" is more consistent with the following treatment of grammar, which is based on Gundissalinus' version of *De scientiis*.

[35] This sentence is from Gundissalinus' adaptation of Al-Farabi, *De scientiis*, ed. Alonso Alonso, 62. The literal translation by Gerard of Cremona makes this clearer. Expressions are simple (i.e. individual words) or compound (clauses and sentences): *dictiones simplices, dictiones compositae*, where for the latter Gundissalinus gives *orationes*, meaning speech or discourse in general. See Schupp's edition of Gerard of Cremona's translation, *Über die Wissenschaften/De scientiis*, 8–10.

[36] From Gundissalinus' adaptation of Al-Farabi, *De scientiis*, ed. Alonso Alonso, 63.

[37] Ibid., 61 etc.   [38] Ibid., 61–2.   [39] Ibid., 63.

The science concerning the rules of simple expressions first considers the pronunciation of letters and their number, and the vowels and non-vowels, and which letters are conjoined to which to form a syllable, and which syllables are conjoined to which to form a word, and words and their accidents.[40] The science of rules about expressions that are compounded teaches which word is combined with which in a sentence.[41] Some compounding of expression is formed to make a sentence such as "man is an animal";[42] other compounding is for augmenting or weakening or in some way altering the meaning of a word: to augment, as in *prepotens*; to weaken, as in *impotens*; to alter, as in *compotens*.[43] And the science of rules concerning correct writing teaches which letter ought to be written with which, and which letters do not go together: this is called orthography.[44] The science of the rules of correct reading[45] teaches the marks of punctuation, i.e. full stops, brief pauses, and medium pauses;[46] and it teaches grave, acute, and circumflex accents.[47] The science of the rules of versifying first teaches which syllables are short or long;[48] and then teaches about feet and caesurae; and then about various kinds of meter. The number and diversity of feet produces a variety of meters; and individual meters are called either by the name of the foot or the name of the inventor [of the meter].[49]

Therefore these are the parts of grammar, because they render anyone in whom they come together perfected in the science of the art of grammar. Those who say that letter,

---

[40] Ibid. Here Gundissalinus harmonizes grammatical rules found in his Arabic sources with standard Latin grammatical theory.

[41] Ibid., 64.

[42] Ibid., 61. This passage describes two forms of compounding, sentence construction and word formation.

[43] For similar examples of *potens*, see Priscian, *Institutiones* 5.60, *GL* 2:180.10ff. *Prepotens*: extremely powerful; *impotens*: weak, powerless; *compotens* (very rare): having power with someone or something, or having control over something. See *Firmini Verris dictionarius: Dictionnaire Latin-Français de Firmin le Ver*, eds. B. Merrilees and W. Edwards, *CCCM*, series *Lexica latina medii aevi* 1 (Turnhout: Brepols, 1994), at "compos"; and see *Thesaurus linguae latinae*, 3:2136, "compos" (esp. line 73) and 2143, "compotens."

[44] Gundissalinus' adaptation of Al-Farabi, *De scientiis*, ed. Alonso Alonso, 64.

[45] At this site, as above (see n. 34), manuscripts of *On the Division of Philosophy* have *scientia ... recte loquendi* ("science of correct speaking"); but Gundissalinus' version of Al-Farabi's work *De scientiis* (his source for this passage), has *recte legendi* "correct reading," which makes better sense in this context.

[46] *distinctiones, subdistinctiones, medias distinctiones*: as in Donatus, *Ars maior* 1.6 (period, colon, comma). This passage is from Gundissalinus' version of Al-Farabi's *De scientiis*. In his adaptation of Al-Farabi, Gundissalinus has substituted Latin grammatical concepts of clauses and punctuation for Al-Farabi's discussion of Arabic script and the rules for reading its diacritical marks. The literal translation by Gerard of Cremona renders this clearly: see the edition of Schupp, ed. and trans., *Über die Wissenschaften/De scientiis*, 18, and notes. See also the Spanish translation of Al-Farabi's Arabic text in González Palencia, ed., *Al-Farabi: Catálogo de las ciencias*, 11 (this edition also contains the Arabic text, along with the versions by Gerard of Cremona and Gundissalinus).

[47] *De scientiis*, ed. Alonso Alonso, 64.

[48] The Al-Farabian text actually deals with syllabic length under the previous heading, the rules of correct reading. Here, as in his own translation-adaptation of Al-Farabi's text, Gundissalinus moves material around from one heading to another.

[49] *De scientiis*, ed. Alonso Alonso, 64.

syllable, word, and sentence are the parts of the art of grammar are wrong: for these are parts of its subject matter, not of the art.[50]

The species of the art are those things in every instance of which the whole art is contained, just like species is to genus, for in every example of species the whole genus is found. Thus the species of the art of grammar are kinds of languages, such as Latin, Greek, Hebrew, Arabic, and the like, because in every one of these the whole of grammar, with all of its parts, is found.[51]

The function [*officium*] of any art is that which the practitioner ought to do according to the art. The function of this art is to write and speak correctly: correctly for the sake of banishing solecisms and barbarisms. To write is to order, in a suitable way, shapes [*figuras*] that can be enunciated so that actual enunciation may be based on them. To read is to adduce the enunciation from seeing the shapes [of the letters]. And note that a solecism can occur in speaking and in writing: for the one who says *dominum venit* enunciates incorrectly, just as the one who writes it in this way writes it incorrectly.[52] Similarly, a barbarism can occur in speaking and in writing: for someone who utters the penultimate syllable of this word, *dominus*, with a long accent enunciates it incorrectly, just as someone who puts a critical sign designating a long accent over that syllable writes it incorrectly. Writers have certain critical signs for shortening or lengthening syllables. Note that not everywhere is the solecism or the barbarism used in error. In the (canonical) authors they become schemes, i.e. figures. In this case, even though it may be a solecism or a barbarism, it is still not an error. Whence Isidore says, "a figure is an error that occurs for a reason."[53] But if no reason can be found for it, it is not a figure, but an error.

The goal of the art is what the practitioner strives for through the art's function, and indeed a goal is understood through function. The goal of this art is to write correctly and speak correctly.

The instrument of an art is the means through which the practitioner works in the subject matter of the art. Since this art has a double effect, in that it teaches to speak

[50] See Alonso, "Hugo de San Víctor, refutado por Domingo Gundisalvo hacia el 1170," 215, arguing that this criticism is directed at statements in Hugh's *Didascalicon* 2.29 (we thank Alexander Fidora for this reference).

[51] Cf. Petrus Helias, prologue to the *Summa super Priscianum*, ed. Reilly, 1:63–4: "The species of the art of grammar are the kinds of languages in which the art of grammar is treated and ordered [i.e. by rules] ... Thus grammar is ordered in the Greek language, and in Latin, Hebrew, and Chaldean. The species of this art can increase, that is, there can be more of them, for example if grammar is treated in the French language, which could happen, or in some other language in which it is not yet treated."

[52] Cf. Petrus Helias, *Summa super Priscianum*, 2:844, on the solecism *Dominum venit*, and Gundissalinus' earlier example of the solecism (above).

[53] Cf. *Etymologiae* 1.35.7.

correctly and write correctly, it has, accordingly, a double instrument. For there are nine natural instruments which form the instrument of speaking; by these voice is formed, and without them a locution would not sound forth externally. These are the two lips, upper and lower teeth, the tongue, the palate, the two parts of the windpipe, and the lungs.[54] These are called the nine muses by the poets, as if *mousa* from *mous*, which is water.[55] Muse [*Musa*] was the earliest name of harmony, and it was derived from "hydraulic" musical instruments; for "hydraulic" is so called from *ydor*, which means water.[56] The ancients used to place instruments in water; and through the ebbing movement of the water, the instruments would strike each other in a regular proportion, and would thus produce a harmonious sound. And because harmony was so much created in water, from water instruments, "muse" is so called from *moys*, which is water, and the name "muse" was carried over to the natural instruments from which voice is formed. For just as in the case of the water instruments, there was a certain proportion and harmony through which these natural instruments were brought into mutual concordance with each other to form voice. Whence grammar is called music, because these instruments (as mentioned) are necessary to form a letter in enunciation and in words and in the other things that grammar treats. Whence Priscian says that the grammarian possessed the art of both kinds of music.[57]

For writing, there are other instruments: hand, reed-pen, parchment, and ink. Where it is natural to speak, it is artificial to write, and so the instruments of the one are natural, and of the other, artificial.

The practitioner is one who treats the subject matter, through an instrument, according to the terms of the art. Here the practitioner is a grammarian, that is, one who is learned in letters [*litteratus*]. Note that a "literary man" [*litterator*] and "someone learned in letters"

---

[54] Cf. Martianus Capella, *De nuptiis*, 3.261.

[55] See Hugh of St. Victor, *Didascalicon* 2.8 : "The term 'Music' comes from *mou*, that is, water, because no euphony, that is, harmonious sound, can be made without moisture." Cf. the Third Vatican Mythographer in Bode, ed., *Scriptores rerum mythicarum latini tres*, 231: "Certainly *mous* in Greek means water, whence *Musa*, as it were, 'watery.' Air passing through the windpipe of the singer is sprinkled with moisture, for song can never be produced through the pipe of the throat without the help of moisture. According to Varro the Muses are Nymphs, and for Servius this is not without merit. For, he says, the sound of water produces music, as in *hydraulii*, that is, water organs." And cf. Isidore of Seville, *Etymologiae* 8.11.96: "Nymphs are said to be goddesses of water, so called from clouds (*nubibus*); water comes from clouds, hence the derivation. Nymphs are goddesses of water, as if *numina lympharum* (spirits of springs). The Muses are said to be nymphs, not undeservedly, for a motion of water produces music." Cf. Baur's note in his edition of Gundissalinus, 278, pointing to Greek derivations. On Greek, Latin, and biblical sources behind this etymology, see Swerdlow, " '*Musica dictur a moys, quod est aqua*.'"

[56] I.e., *hydraulus*, water organ; *ydor*, Greek *hydor* / *hudor*, water.

[57] *Utriusque possederit artem musice grammaticus.* Cf. Priscian, *Institutiones*, preface to Julian the Consul, *GL* 2:2.27–9: "[you] whose mind, I believe, is united as much with the spirit of Homer as of Virgil, both of whom possessed the art of music" (*quorum uterque arcem possederat musicae*).

[*litteratus*] differ. The literary man is one who, without any art, knows how to give an exposition of authors, even though he does not know what should be considered with regard to letter, syllable, word, and sentence; the man learned in letters is the one who knows all these things through his art.

Let us consider why it is called "grammar." Grammar takes its name from *grammaton*, which is "letter."[58] Certain authorities say that it takes its name from letters because it treats them. When they are challenged as to why, on the same principle, it is not named *syllabalis* after "syllable" or *dictionalis* after "word," because it treats them, the authorities respond that grammar is so called from its most worthy part, that is, from letters. Even though it treats of syllables, words, and sentences, it is preferable that it still be named for letters, because all these other entities consist of letters. Thus the letter is more worthy than all those entities. It is also said that it takes its name from letters only because it is the custom of authors to take their book titles from the beginnings of the books, as in the case of the Book of Genesis, which is named for its first part, even though the book does not deal throughout with generation.[59] We say, however, that grammar takes its name from letters as if from its effect, which is that it renders a man learned in letters.

The order of this science is this: because it is the science of correct speaking and correct writing, it should be learned before all the other sciences. The boy who is being educated should be nourished in its cradles for such a time until, having acquired skill in speaking and writing, he seems ready to be sent to learn the other sciences. In terms of the order in which this science must be taught and learned, treatment of the letter comes first, and with respect to the letter we must consider the following: what is a letter, how many are there, how are they written, what are they called, how are they pronounced. After this, the syllable is to be given similar attention: what is it, what is it made from, from how many letters is a syllable composed, and how should letters be arranged in order to constitute a syllable; then we treat the accidents of a syllable, its quantity and accent. Third, in presenting the word, we show what it is, what it is made from, how many syllables make up a word, and its forms and accents. Finally we turn to the sentence: what is it, how is it composed of words, and what are its forms, for some are intransitive, some are transitive, others are retransitive, and others are reciprocal.[60]

---

[58] Cf. Isidore of Seville, *Etymologiae* 1.5.1.

[59] The comparison with Genesis is also found in the prologue to the second redaction of William of Conches' gloss on Priscian, see within, p. 386.

[60] These constructions represent the kinds of predicates contained in the sentences. "Retransitive" and "reciprocal" are both forms of reflexive constructions. See Priscian, *Institutiones* 17.30 and 17.105–9, *GL* 3:127.12ff. and 164.16.ff. These are also explained at length by Petrus Helias, *Summa super Priscianum*, ed. Reilly, 2:897–900.

These, then, are the extrinsic matters about the art of grammar that ought to be considered.

On Poetics

With regard to the art of poetry too, we must consider these same questions: what is it, what is its genus, what is its subject matter, its species, its parts, its function, its goal, its instrument, its practitioner, why is it so called, and in what order should it be acquired.

What it is may be defined thus: Poetics [*De poetica*] is the science of composing metrical song [*carmina metrice*]. Meter [*metrum*] is speech [*oratio*] modulated by the marked alternation of quantities and feet [*temporum et pedum distincta varietate*]. Meter gets its name from *mensura* [measure], because it is divided by certain measurings or intervals of feet, nor does it stray beyond the quantities fixed by measuring. In Greek, *mensura* is *metrum*. Quantity [*tempus*] is observed in the lengthening or shortening[61] of the syllable; a foot is a kind of counting out of syllables and quantities.[62]

The genus of this art is that it is part of civil science, which is a part of eloquence. What delights or edifies, whether in terms of knowledge or of morals, plays no small part in civil matters.

The subject matter of this art falls into two categories: events that took place or fictions.[63] The narrative of an event that took place is history, in which those things that were done in past times are made manifest, as in "I sing of arms and the man who first from the shores of Troy came."[64] It is called "history" *apo tu istorio* ["from *istorio*"] in Greek, which means to see or to know.[65] Among the ancients, no one wrote a history unless he was present at the events and had witnessed those things that he wrote about. For we grasp events better with our eyes than when we gather them from hearsay.[66] One sort of fiction is something that could have happened: this is called a "realistic fiction,"[67] and an example of it is the parables of the Gospels. The other sort is something that could not have happened, and this is called

---

[61] Reading *correptio* for *corruptio* in Baur's base text: see apparatus, 54, line 9.

[62] Isidore of Seville, *Etymologiae* 1.39.1; Donatus, *Ars maior* 1.4, *GL* 4:369.17. In Cassiodorus, *Institutiones* 2.1.2, *tempus* is a prolongation of sound.

[63] This is the classic distinction between *res gesta* and *res ficta*.   [64] *Aeneid* 1.1

[65] Greek: *apo tou* (from the [word]) *historeô*, to inquire into something or record what one has learned.

[66] This section on *historia* comes nearly verbatim from Isidore of Seville, *Etymologiae* 1.41.1. Cf. Hugh of St. Victor, *De scripturis et scriptoribus sacris*, ch. 3 (*PL* 175:11D–12A). See within, Thomas of Chobham, p. 617.

[67] *Argumentum*: see section on John of Garland, within, p. 656.

story [*fabula*].[68] *Fabula* takes its name from *fari* ["to talk"], because it consists only of talk.[69] Some stories are devised to entertain; others are devised by the poets in order to edify. The kind that common people tell or that Terence composed are for entertainment. Of those that are for edification, some relate to natural things, others to human behavior. Examples of stories about natural things are that Vulcan is called crippled, because by nature fire is never straight up and down,[70] or that the three-form beast, with a lion's head, a serpent's tail, and a she-goat's body, represents the ages of man.[71] . . . Examples of stories that pertain to human behavior are the fables of Avianus or of Horace, where a mouse speaks to a mouse or a weasel to a fox.[72] These are called "apologues" [*apologi*], that is, discourses that fit a purpose. The whole story is devised to reveal human behavior, so that one gets to the intended point by means of fiction, but with a truthful meaning. These, therefore, constitute the subject matter of the art, because the poet treats these matters.

The species of the art are, just as in grammar, the kinds of languages, in each of which the whole of the art is practiced.

The parts of the art are the diverse kinds of meters. Some of these are given the names of feet, such as dactylic and iambic; others are named for the number of feet, such as hexameter and pentameter; others take their names from the inventors of the meter, such as sapphic and glyconic;[73] or it may take its name from the subject matter, such as the heroic and elegiac meters.[74]

The function of this art is to order words in discourse according to the number of feet and quantities, just as the law of meter requires.

The goal of the art is to delight with pleasantries or to edify with serious matters, in accordance with the famous verses:

> Poets aim either to benefit, or to amuse . . .
> He has won every vote who has blended profit and pleasure.[75]

The instrument of the art is the poem. A poem is a song composed in meter, created for pleasure or for a useful purpose. There are three genres of poems:[76] the active or imitative

---

[68] The distinction between *argumentum* and *fabula* is taken from Isidore of Seville, *Etymologiae* 1.44.5 (under genres of history).

[69] The section on *fabula* closely follows Isidore of Seville, *Etymologiae* 1.40.1–6.

[70] The word *claudus* means both crippled (hence applied to Vulcan) and wavering (hence, by transference, applied to fire).

[71] I.e., the chimaera: Lucretius, *De natura rerum* 5.903.   [72] Cf. Horace, *Epistles* 1.7.32.

[73] *gliconium*, from its inventor Glycon.

[74] This section summarizes Isidore of Seville, *Etymologiae* 1.39.5–9.   [75] Horace, *Ars poetica* 333, 343.

[76] This section is based closely on Bede, *De arte metrica*, ch. 25.

genre, the expository genre, and the common or mixed genre. The active is the genre in which the speakers are introduced without remarks by the poet, as in tragedy and comedy. Among our writings, the Song of Songs is written in this genre. Expository is the genre in which the poet himself speaks without the introduction of any speaking character, such as in all of the first three books of the *Georgics* as well as the beginning of the fourth book, and in our writings, the Proverbs of Solomon and Ecclesiastes, which, as is commonly known, were written in meter in their original language, just like the Psalter. Common or mixed is the genre in which the poet himself speaks and speaking characters are introduced, as in the writings of Homer and Virgil's *Aeneid*, and among our writings, the story of the blessed Job, although in its original language this was not written entirely in poetry, but partly in rhetorical, partly in metrical, and partly in rhythmical style.

The practitioner is the poet, who knows how to compose songs according to the art of poetry.

"Poetics" or "poetry" gets its name from "poem," that is, from its instrument, because the whole art is practiced through poems.

Poetics is to be learned after grammar. When grammar has taught how to compose syllables from letters, and words from syllables, and sentences from words according to their accidents, then poetry should show how to make feet from syllables, and from feet meters with due regard for quantities.

[The remainder of this very long section on poetics treats metrics, and in particular the understanding of syllabic quantity, drawing closely from Isidore of Seville, *Etymologiae*, book 1, Donatus, *Ars maior*, book 1, and especially Bede's *De arte metrica*.]

On Rhetoric

[Gundissalinus' extrinsic treatment of rhetoric is taken almost entirely, and nearly word for word, from Thierry of Chartres' extrinsic prologue to his commentaries on the Ciceronian rhetorics. In the case of rhetoric, as in that of poetics, Gundissalinus had to look beyond Al-Farabi and Avicenna for discussion of the art, because poetics and rhetoric did not figure extensively in the scientific classifications of the particular Arabic texts he was using. While Gundissalinus' treatment of grammar depends wholly on Al-Farabi's treatment of the "science of language," he must look elsewhere to fill out his conception of the *scientiae eloquentiae*, that is, grammar, poetics, rhetoric. Thus just as he turned to Isidore of Seville and Bede for authoritative discussions of poetics, he now turns to a Latin source for rhetoric, and one that was perhaps the most informative, concise, and authoritative extrinsic treatment of the art to date, Thierry's extrinsic prologue.

Gundissalinus needed to add almost nothing to Thierry's text. Gundissalinus' scheme of topics to be considered in each discussion of an art is virtually the same as Thierry's (definition, genus, material, parts, species, function, goal, instrument, practitioner, and why the art is so named), although Thierry considers these in a different order, requiring Gundissalinus to adjust the sequence of some of Thierry's paragraphs. Only one of Gundissalinus' usual topics, the order in which the art should be learned, is not covered by Thierry's prologue, and so for this last topic alone Gundissalinus provides his own text. The new material added by Gundissalinus is given below.]

. . . Rhetoric is to be learned after poetics; since grammar is first, and after grammar comes poetics, so certainly after poetics, and in consequent order, rhetoric is to be learned. For it is reasonable that someone who is first taught, through grammar, to speak correctly, should then learn through poetics how to give pleasure or profit to a listener; then when he knows, through the poetic art, how to delight or benefit, he should at once learn through rhetoric how he can persuade and move the listener. The one who delights has already moved his audience a little; but the one who persuades carries his audience away. Therefore it is natural that poetics comes after grammar and that rhetoric comes after poetics. For it is not enough to speak correctly unless one also strives to delight; and it is not enough to delight if one does not also utterly prevail upon the listener.[77]

On Logic

[In the scheme presented by Gundissalinus, logic is outside of the arts of discourse (the *scientiae eloquentiae*). Logic is both part and instrument of philosophy. Its place is between eloquence and the sciences of wisdom (the theoretical and practical sciences).[78] But as Gundissalinus carries over the thought of his Arabic sources, he also imports different systems of classification, depending on context. His treatment of logic is based largely on book 2 of Al-Farabi's *De scientiis* (in his own adaptation of the text), and from this he reiterates the notion that the parts of logic correspond to the books of Aristotle's *Organon*. Early scholiasts had associated Aristotle's *Rhetoric* and *Poetics* with the *Organon*, thus counting it as eight books instead of six. This traditional scheme, which modern scholars call the "context theory," is reflected and expounded in Al-Farabi's influential treatise, and thus finds its way into Latin writings, including Gundissalinus' text.[79] It was long an influential notion: we see it, for example, in

[77] Cf. the language in Augustine, *De doctrina christiana* 4.13.29.
[78] See *De divisione philosophiae*, ed. Baur, 81, lines 7–8.
[79] See Black, *Logic and Aristotle's Rhetoric and Poetics in Medieval Arabic Philosophy*, 1–102.

Aquinas' division of logic in the prologue to his commentary on the *Posterior Analytics* (within, pp. 789–91). Provided below is that section of Gundissalinus' treatment of Logic which presents this influential scheme (based directly on the corresponding passages in his version of Al-Farabi's *De scientiis*). Note therefore that in this scheme, two of Gundissalinus' "sciences of eloquence," rhetoric and poetics, become part of logic; as parts of logic, rhetoric and poetics would also have a claim to being both instruments and parts of philosophy.]

. . . After this we turn to the parts of this art. According to Al-Farabi there are eight parts of logic: *Categories*, *Peri hermeneias* [*On Interpretation*], *Prior Analytics*, *Posterior Analytics*, *Topics*, *Sophistical Refutations*, *Rhetoric*, *Poetics*. The names of books are given for the names of the sciences which are contained in them. Each of these parts has a property which is its purpose and means of proof, and a manner in which it works, and a use which comes from it. . . .

From the aforesaid eight parts there are five by which knowledge[80] is verified: demonstration, topics, sophistic, rhetoric, poetics.

The property of demonstration[81] is to give the most determinate knowledge—of which the contrary is impossible, and in which there exists no fallacy—about a question proposed either by oneself or by another.

The property of *Topics* is to produce belief about a doubtful issue using probable arguments that are either true or plausible.

The property of sophistic is to feign and dissimulate and to make what is not true appear to be true, and the reverse. Sophistic is the name of a certain power through which a man knows how to deceive someone else and lead him into error even though he may be of good character. The name "sophist" is from the Greek *sophos*, which is wisdom, and "estos,"[82] which is deception. Thus sophistic is called deceptive wisdom, and the sophist is called a wise deceiver. . . One whose power is sophistry is rightly called a sophist, and the action that proceeds from his particular power is the work of a sophist.

The property of rhetoric is to move the mind of the hearer through persuasive speech, and to incline the hearer to the purpose that the speaker wants, so that what he says is believed, and he produces in the hearer reasoning that is proximate to certitude.

It is the property of poetics to cause something beautiful or ugly, which does not exist, to be imagined through discourse, in such a way that the hearer believes it, and despises it

---

[80] Taking *scientia* for *sentencia*: see Baur's apparatus, 73, and Gundissalinus' version of Al-Farabi's *De scientiis*, ed. Alonso Alonso, 72, line 9.

[81] The demonstrative part of logic is linked with the *Posterior Analytics*; see Baur's edition, 71–2, and *De scientiis*, ed. Alonso Alonso, 80–3.

[82] No such Greek word exists.

or desires it; for even though we are certain that it is not real, nevertheless our minds are roused to abhor or desire what is pictured forth to us. For imagination sometimes works better in a man than knowledge or reasoning; often a man's knowledge or reasoning is contrary to what he imagines, and in that case he acts according to what he imagines and not what he knows or thinks. Thus it is said that a man's dung can seem like honey.

These, therefore, are the species of syllogism, syllogistic methods, and the species of locution that men use for determining truth in all matters. But these five syllogistic species may also be called by the following names: certain, probable [*putativa*], fallacious, persuasive [*sufficiens*], and imaginative.[83]

---

[83] Cf. Gonzalez Palencia's rendering in Spanish of the Al-Farabian source of this passage: *Al-Farabi: Catálogo de las ciencias*, 31.

JOHN OF SALISBURY, *METALOGICON*, 1159

INTRODUCTION

The career of John of Salisbury (ca. 1120–1180) is one of the best known of twelfth-century writers and public men.[1] His *Metalogicon* also gives one of the largest and clearest windows onto the educational world of northern France in the first half of the twelfth century. His famous account in *Metalogicon* 2.10 of the various masters under whom he studied during his formative years in France provides an invaluable "Who was Who" of the schools, even if its detail has also given rise to long debate about the locales and the sequence of his encounters with the particular teachers he mentions.

An even greater and more important debate that his writing has generated concerns the core issue of his *Metalogicon* (literally, "about the arts of verbal reasoning"), which he presents as a reply to the "Cornifician" attacks on the trivium. What was this attack, and who, if anyone, were the "Cornificians"? At a deeper level, what was the nature of the educational controversy or malaise that John was describing, and in what ways and for how long had it manifested itself? "Cornificius" is the name that John of Salisbury gives to an adversary of traditional education in the trivium (grammar, rhetoric, and here especially dialectic) or better yet, to an adversarial view of such education. As suggested by the various references in the text to a "sect" of Cornificians, "Cornificius" is a personification of an opinion shared by many that traditional attention to the trivium as an organic whole is obsolete and should give way to a more streamlined academic training for professional success in fields such as civic and church administration. The name "Cornificius" seems to be derived from some versions of the ancient lives of Virgil, where a Cornificius is mentioned as a critic and enemy of the great poet.[2] John presents his "Cornificius" as a detractor of all the great teachers of Paris and the cathedral schools beyond, and as one who cultivates the friendship of the Cistercians, Cluniacs, and Premonstratensians (see *Metalogicon* 1. 5), but beneath the pseudonym, no particular historical figure can be identified.[3] But the idea that the trivium, as a valuable study in itself, is under attack also appears in the writings

---

[1] A good summary of his career and works is by Brooke, "John of Salisbury and his World."
[2] Brugnoli and Stok, eds., *Vitae Vergilianae Antiquae*, III, 115, 228, 246, 266.
[3] See Liebeschütz, *Mediaeval Humanism in the Life and Writings of John of Salisbury*, 118 (Appendix IV).

of other twelfth-century teachers whom John mentions in the *Metalogicon*: Hugh of St. Victor, William of Conches, Robert of Melun, and Thierry of Chartres; John also refers to the subject in his *Policraticus* (7.9 and 12).[4] In the broadest terms, the "Cornifician movement" anticipates the greater professionalizing of studies in the later twelfth century, when law, medicine, and dialectic became the most popular studies as preparation for lucrative careers.[5] The long study of grammar, exemplified in John's vivid and nostalgic picture of the classroom of Bernard of Chartres, would have seemed otiose to some modern students. Similarly, such students would have felt that they could assimilate the principles of rhetoric quickly through the newer and more utilitarian practices of the *ars dictandi* or art of letter writing and prose composition. Bernard's careful and repetitive method of teaching a solid foundation in grammar was characteristic of the early cathedral schools, but newer generations of students (according to John) fail to appreciate its benefits. John gives an impassioned defense of the old masters and their traditional educational practice, an appreciation of a slow and meditative approach to studying the arts of the trivium, where one approaches dialectic only after gaining a solid understanding of language and eloquence. This is a theme crystallized in Thierry's prologue to his *Heptateuchon* and sounded among contemporary and later commentators.[6] John himself returned to this theme in his own *Entheticus*, written a few years after the *Metalogicon*.[7] The theme recurs in the thirteenth century, for example, in Henri d'Andeli's *Bataille des VII ars*, where the new generation of dialecticians reigns supreme over the older grammarians, and in Guido Faba's introduction to his *Rota nova*, in which he defends his own preference for literary study over law.[8]

John's main object is dialectic (books 2–4), but he prepares the case for the proper absorption of dialectic by considering grammar in all of its dimensions—as a system of rules, as proficiency in speech, and as path to eloquence. John's concerns (unlike those of his famous teachers William of Conches and Petrus Helias), do not lie with the deep linguistic questions of grammar, but rather with an appreciative proficiency that he sees being cast aside in favor of a new technocratic training. Above all, grammar for him is an "orthopraxis," a coordinated structure of language and understanding that sustains and reflects a moral order. In this his outlook has something in common with Alan of Lille's near-contemporary *De planctu Naturae* (The Plaint of Nature, ca. 1160–1165), which

---

[4] For *loci* see Ward, "Date of the Commentary on Cicero's *De inventione*," 222 n. 2. In dedicating his translation of Ptolemy's *Planisphere* to Thierry of Chartres, Hermann of Carinthia spoke of a "serious lack of Latinity" among his contemporaries, although such complaints about the debasement of learning can be merely conventional.

[5] "The Date of the Commentary," 223–8. See also Ward, "Educational Crisis."

[6] On the views, for example, of William of Conches, see Jeauneau, "Deux rédactions des gloses de Guillaume de Conches," 359–61.

[7] *Entheticus*, ed. and trans. van Laarhoven.   [8] For these texts, see within, Part 5.

develops this principle into an elaborate and at times arcane poetic conceit. John deals very little with technical rhetoric as separate from grammar and the argumentative methods of dialectic.[9] However, when he asks "Who are the most prosperous and wealthy among our fellow citizens? Who the most powerful and successful in all their enterprises? Is it not the eloquent?" (1.7), he articulates the essence of twelfth-century interest in rhetorical study, as a knowledge of the means of persuasion that has real application to civil affairs as well as, indeed, to questions of belief.[10] To have a grammatical (and dialectical) understanding of how language can represent truth and interpret cognition must also necessitate, in the public sphere, a mastery of persuasive argument and verbal style. John is claiming that the old, integrated methods of study help one to achieve greater influence and authority than the new methods that disdain the trivium.

In *Metalogicon* 1.17 John refers to a controversy about the classification of poetry in relation to the sciences of language, and insists that it belongs under grammar. His stridency here may be motivated in part by traditional dismissals of poetry altogether from the arts, such as, famously, by Hugh of St. Victor (see *Didascalicon* 3.4). But John focuses his attention so precisely on the relation of poetry to grammar or rhetoric that it seems that he might have in mind newer ideas about the independent status of poetry among the arts. The Arabic tradition that saw poetry as a separate division of logic was such a "new" idea, even though it was in fact very old. This idea was making its way into Western Europe, notably through Gundissalinus' use of Al-Farabi's writings. In his treatise *De divisione philosophiae*, Gundissalinus first places poetry as a separate entity among the "arts of eloquence," alongside of grammar and rhetoric, because like them it deals with linguistic representation. He then gives poetics a place under logic, along with rhetoric, according to the inherited terms of the "context theory," or the expansion of Aristotelian logic to include rhetoric and poetic.[11] While pedagogical thought was to maintain the traditional link between grammar and the teaching of poetry, seeing literature as the province of grammar (as John of Salisbury does), academic philosophy would take the other route, and treat poetry as a separate science, as one of the tools of logic.[12]

Translation reprinted from *The "Metalogicon" of John of Salisbury: A Twelfth-Century Defense of the Verbal and Logical Arts of the Trivium*, trans. McGarry, by permission.[13]

[9] In *Metalogicon* 2.10, John tells us that he first studied rhetoric under Thierry without understanding very much, but returned to it under Petrus Helias, from whom he learned more.

[10] Ward, "Medieval and Early Renaissance Study," 37–41.

[11] See Mehtonen, "Poetics, Narration, and Imitation," 300–2; and see Gundissalinus section above, pp. 468–9, 478–83.

[12] See Dahan, "Notes et textes sur la poétique au moyen âge."

[13] Notes from McGarrry's translation have been revised and updated. Edition used for reference: *Metalogicon libri IIII*, ed. Webb.

FROM *METALOGICON*, BOOK I

From Chapter 5. What Great Men That Tribe Dares Defame, and Why They Do This

Master Gilbert,[14] who was then chancellor at Chartres, and afterwards became the reverend Bishop of Poitiers, was wont to deride or deplore, I am not sure which, the insanity of his time. When he would observe the aforesaid individuals scurrying off to the above-mentioned studies, he used to predict that they would end up as bakers— the one occupation, which, according to him, usually received all those among his people who were unemployed and lacked any particular skill. For baking is an easy trade, subsidiary to the others, and especially suited to those who are more interested in bread than in skilled workmanship. Others, who were [real] lovers of letters,[15] set themselves to counteract the error. Among the latter were Master Thierry,[16] a very assiduous investigator of the arts; William of Conches, the most accomplished grammarian since Bernard of Chartres;[17] and the Peripatetic from Pallet,[18] who won such distinction in logic over all his contemporaries that it was thought that he alone really understood Aristotle. But not even all these [great scholars] were able to cope with the foolish ones. They themselves became [temporarily] insane while combating insanity, and for quite a time floundered in error while trying to correct it.[19] The fog, however, was soon dispelled. Thanks to the work and diligence of these masters, the arts regained their own, and were reinstated in their pristine seat of honor. Their popularity and good fame were even increased after their exile, as by the right of those who return home after having been held captive by the enemy. Cornificius begrudged the arts their good fortune. Jealously feeling it would be a disgrace for one

---

[14] Gilbert of Poitiers (Gilbert de la Porrée) (ca. 1075–1154), was chancellor at Chartres 1126–40.

[15] *litterarum*, letters or literature; McGarry translates this as "learning," but we have chosen to emphasize the literary or grammatical dimension of the term.

[16] Thierry of Chartres (see the introductions to the selections from Thierry's writings, within).

[17] On William of Conches, see the introduction to Part 3 and the selections from William's writings; on Bernard of Chartres, see the introduction and, below, chapter 24 from the *Metalogicon*.

[18] Peter Abelard.

[19] Ward's explanation of this passage is that the Cornifician outlook manifested itself as early as the 1130s through a notable "preoccupation with dialectic" among all the masters—even those remarkable men listed here—who were then teaching in Paris and Chartres. See "The Date of the Commentary on Cicero's *De inventione*," 224–9.

advanced in years to go to school, and for an old man to be shown up as but a boy in understanding, he set himself to carping on what he despaired of learning.

[The remainder of this chapter describes the "attacks" of Cornificius on many other academic leading lights from the early to the middle years of the twelfth century, including Anselm of Laon, Alberic of Rheims, William of Champeaux, Hugh of St. Victor, and Robert Pullen.]

Chapter 6. The Arguments On Which Cornificius Bases His Contention

In the judgment of Cornificius (if a false opinion may be called a judgment), there is no point in studying the rules of eloquence, which is a gift that is either conceded or denied to each individual by nature. Work and diligence are superfluous where nature has spontaneously and gratuitously bestowed eloquence, whereas they are futile and silly where she has refused to grant it. Generally the maxim that "A person can do just as much as nature allows" is accepted as an axiom.[20] Thus prudent and reliable historians are sure that Daedalus did not really fly, for nature had denied him wings, but say, rather, that he evaded the wrath of the tyrant by quickly departing aboard a ship.[21] The device of learning precepts in order to become eloquent fails to accomplish its object. Even the most diligent study of rules cannot possibly make one eloquent. The use of language and speech suffices for intercourse among fellow countrymen, whereas he who most assiduously employs his faculty of speech becomes most fluent. This is evident with the Greeks and Latins; the Gauls and Britons will also bear witness to it; nor is it otherwise among the Scythians and Arabs. Everywhere it is true that "Practice makes perfect," and "Persevering application surmounts all obstacles,"[22] for assiduous devotion to an art produces the master workman. Even though rules may be of some help in acquiring eloquence, still they involve more trouble than they are worth, and the return never compensates for the investment. The Greeks and Hebrews use their languages to advantage without bothering about rules; and the peoples of Gaul and Britain, as well as others, learn how to talk in their nurses' arms [long] before they receive instruction from doctors who occupy official chairs. The way

[20] *maximarum propositionum*, maximal propositions, first principles. Cf. Boethius, *In Ciceronis topica* (*PL* 64: 1051), trans. Stump, *In Ciceronis Topica*, 33: "We call the highest and maximal propositions those propositions that are universal and known and manifest to such an extent that they need no proof but rather themselves provide proof for things that are in doubt."

[21] Servius, *In Vergilii Aeneidos* 6:14 (ed. Thilo, 2:7).   [22] Virgil, *Georgics* 1.145.

one talks in manhood often smacks of the manner of speech of one's nurse.[23] Sometimes the [most] strenuous efforts of teachers cannot extricate one from habits imbibed at a tender age. How well and effectively do all the peoples speak in the languages they have been granted by divine providence! Did they first have to await the art of speech[24] or the rules of eloquence? Finally, [Cornificius argues,] what can eloquence and philosophy possibly have in common? The former relates to language, but the latter seeks after, investigates, and applies itself to learning the ways of wisdom, which it sometimes efficaciously apprehends by its study. Clearly the rules of eloquence confer neither wisdom nor love of wisdom. More often than otherwise, they are not even helpful for the acquisition of wisdom. Philosophy (or wisdom, its object) is concerned not with words, but with facts. From what has been said, [if we are to believe Cornificius,] it is evident that philosophy eliminates the rules of eloquence from its activities.

Chapter 7. **Praise of Eloquence**

The foolish flock of Cornificians caws away (in a language all their own), evidencing that they have contemned every rule of speech. For, as they themselves inform us, they cannot simultaneously take care to make sense and also to worry about the troublesome agreement of tenses and cases. We refrain from comment. The sect may still perceive the truth, even while it is lying, but this condition surely cannot endure. A man who is a liar in word and spirit will come to believe the falsehood he peddles. According to the Cornificians, "Rules of eloquence are superfluous, and the possession or lack of eloquence is dependent on nature." What could be farther from the truth? What is eloquence but the faculty of fittingly saying what the mind wishes to express?[25] As such, it brings to light and in a way publishes what would otherwise be hidden in the inner recesses of the heart.[26] Not everyone who speaks, nor even one who says what he wants to in some fashion, is eloquent. He alone is eloquent who fittingly and efficaciously expresses himself as he intends. This appropriate effectiveness postulates a faculty—so called from facility, to follow our wont of imitating the concern of the Stoics about the etymologies of words as a key to easier understanding of their meanings.[27] One who can with facility and adequacy verbally

[23] Cf. Quintilian, *Institutio oratoria* 1.1.4–5.

[24] *ars orationis*: McGarry translates this as "art of verbal expression."

[25] Translation modified; cf. *Metalogicon*, trans. McGarry, 26 n. 95.

[26] Translation modified; cf. *Metalogicon*, trans. McGarry, 26 n. 96.

[27] The translator's punctuation has been modified to capture more exactly the sense of John's aside on Stoic etymologizing. John's knowledge of the Stoic penchant for etymology or word derivation in their language theory

express his mental perceptions is eloquent. The faculty of doing this is appropriately called "eloquence." For myself, I am at a loss to see how anything could be more generally useful: more helpful in acquiring wealth, more reliable for winning favor, more suited for gaining fame, than is eloquence. Nothing, or at least hardly anything, is to be preferred to this [precious] gift of nature and grace. Virtue and wisdom, which perhaps, as Victorinus believes, differ in name rather than in substance, rank first among desiderata,[28] but eloquence comes second. Third is health, and after this, in fourth place, the good will of one's associates and an abundance of goods, to provide the material instruments of action. The moralist lists things to be desired in this order, and aptly epitomizes the sequence:

> What more could a fond nurse wish for her sweet charge,
> Than that he be wise and eloquent,
> And that friends, fame, health, good fare,
> And a never failing purse be his without stint?[29]

If man is superior to other living beings in dignity because of his powers of speech and reason, what is more universally efficacious and more likely to win distinction, than to surpass one's fellows, who possess the same human nature, and are members of the same human race, in those sole respects wherein man surpasses other beings? Moreover, while eloquence both illumines and adorns men of whatever age, it especially becomes the young. For youth is in a way to attract favor so that it may make good the potentialities of its natural talent. Who are the most prosperous and wealthy among our fellow citizens? Who the most powerful and successful in all their enterprises? Is it not the eloquent? As Cicero observes, "nothing is so unlikely that words cannot lend an air of probability; nothing is so repulsive and rude that speech cannot polish it and somehow render it attractive, as though it had been remade for the better."[30] He who despises such a great boon [as eloquence] is clearly in error; while he who appreciates, or rather pretends to appreciate it, without actually cultivating it, is grossly negligent and on the brink of insanity.

---

may be traced to his reading of Augustine's *De dialectica*, which he cites and quotes in *Metalogicon* 2.4 and 3.5. *De dialectica* ch. 6 treats the subject of word derivation with a great deal of dubiousness about the value of such an exercise, citing Cicero's ridiculing of the Stoics for the importance they place on this; see the selection from *De dialectica* within, pp. 344–9. On the importance of etymology in Stoic grammatical thought, see Frede, "Principles of Stoic Grammar," 68–75; Colish, *The Stoic Tradition*, 1:56–60, 329–30 and 2:181–98 (on Augustine), and references therein. Cf. Quintilian's interest in grammatical etymology (which John would likely also have noted): *Institutio oratoria* 1.6.28. John's knowledge of the Stoics more generally, and his impressions of them, both positive and negative, was derived from his intimate knowledge of Seneca's *Letters* and Cicero's *De officiis* as well as the *De oratore* (the latter being less commonly known), and even the *Paradoxa stoicorum*; see Jeauneau, "Jean de Salisbury et la lecture des philosophes," and Liebeschütz, *Mediaeval Humanism in the Life and Writings of John of Salisbury*, 74–90.

[28] See the opening of Victorinus' commentary on the *De inventione*, within, pp. 107–8.
[29] Horace, *Epistles* 1.4.8–11.   [30] Cicero, *Paradoxa stoicorum*, preface, 3.

[Chapter 8, *The necessity of helping nature by use and exercise*, continues refuting the Cornificians, rebutting their claims that eloquence comes naturally and study is useless. If the Cornificians were correct, they would be able to speak all languages spontaneously; moreover, many examples in history attest to the usefulness of study and discipline.]

Chapter 9. That One Who Attacks Logic is Trying to Rob Mankind of Eloquence

Who has ever, by nature's gift alone, and without study, had the privilege of being most eloquent in all tongues, or even in only one language? If it is good to be eloquent, surely it is better to be very eloquent. The degrees of comparison are not here in inverse ratio to the good proposed, as with "fluent" and "extremely fluent," where the positive term connotes wisdom and eloquence, but wisdom diminishes, and the flow of speech swells to a flood, in proportion as the comparison increases. So [at least] some grammarians have taught. Although some of the arts pertaining to and imparting the power of eloquence are natural, still that art [of eloquence] which is practically as we would want it cannot be known by nature since it is not natural. For it is not the same among all [peoples]. It is imprudent to expect of nature, without human assistance, that which is chiefly the work of man. While this [Cornician] sect does not condemn eloquence, which is necessary to everyone and approved by all, it holds that the arts which promise eloquence are useless. The Cornificians do not propose to make everyone mute, which would be impossible and inexpedient. Rather, they would do away with logic. The latter, according to them, is the fallacious profession of the verbose, which dissipates the natural talents of many persons, blocks the gateway to philosophical studies, and excludes both sense and success from all undertakings.

Chapter 10. What "Logic" Means, and How we should Endeavor to Acquire all Arts that are not Reprobate

Behold, the Cornificians disclose their objective, and advance to attack logic, although, of course, they are equally violent persecutors of all philosophical pursuits. They have to begin somewhere, and so they have singled out that branch of philosophy which is the most widely known and seems the most familiar to their heretical sect. First, bear with me while we define what "logic" is. "Logic" (in is broadest sense) is "the science of verbal expression and reasoning."[31] Sometimes [the term] "logic" is used with more restricted extension, and limited to rules of [argumentative] reasoning.[32] Whether logic teaches only the ways of reasoning, or embraces all rules relative to words, surely those who claim that it is useless are deluded. For either of these services may be proved by incontrovertible arguments to be very necessary. The twofold meaning of "logic" stems from its Greek etymology, for in the latter language *logos* means both "word" and "reason."[33] For the present let us concede to logic its widest meaning, according to which it includes all instruction relative to words, in which case it can never be convicted of futility. In this more general sense, there can be no doubt that all logic is both highly useful and necessary. If, as has been frequently observed (and as no one denies), the use of speech is so essential, the more concisely it [the use of speech] is taught, the more useful and certainly the more reliable will be the teaching. It is foolish to delay a long time, with much sweat and worry, over something that could otherwise be easily and quickly expedited. This is a fault common among careless persons who have no sense of the value of time. To safeguard against this mistake, the arts of doing all things that we are to do should be taken up and cultivated. Our devotion to the arts should be augmented by the reflection that the latter stem from nature, the best of all mothers, and attest their noble lineage by the facile and successful accomplishment of their objects. I would say, therefore, that the arts of doing things we are to do should be cultivated, with the exception of those [arts] whose purpose is evil, such as lot-reading and other mathematical methods of divination that are reprobate. Arts such as the latter, which are wrong,[34] should, by the decree of sound philosophers, be banished from human society. This matter, however, is discussed more at length in our *Policraticus*.[35]

> [Chapter 11, *The nature of art, the various kinds of innate abilities, and the fact that natural talents should be cultivated and developed by the arts*, defines "art" as an immanence of natural ability that is cultivated through study, memory, and reason. Chapter 12, *Why some arts are called "liberal,"* redefines "art" (with reference to the trivium and quadrivium) as that which delimits (Latin, *artare*) or as virtue (Greek *aretê*), and "liberal," according to common derivations, from *liber* (offspring) or from *libertas* (liberty, freedom).]

---

[31] *loquendi vel disserendi ratio*: McGarry's translation here reads: "the science of verbal expression and [argumentative] reasoning" (32). Cf. Boethius, *In Ciceronis topica*: *Cicero definivit diligentem disserendi rationem* "Cicero defined it [the science of reasoning, or logic] as a careful system of discourse" (*PL* 64:1045; Stump, trans., *In Ciceronis topica*, 25).

[32] Cf. Boethius, *In Ciceronis topica*, describing the various schools of definition: Plato, the Peripatetics, the Stoics, Cicero (*PL* 64:1045).

[33] Cf. Hugh of St. Victor, *Didascalicon* 1.12.

[34] *quae quoniam ab officiis alienae sunt*: literally, which are contrary to our duties.   [35] *Policraticus* 2.19.

Chapter 13. Whence Grammar Gets its Name

Among all the liberal arts, the first is logic, and specifically that part of logic which gives initial instruction about words. As has already been explained,[36] the word "logic" has a broad meaning, and is not restricted exclusively to the science of argumentative reasoning. [It includes] Grammar which is "the science of speaking and writing correctly—the starting point of all liberal studies."[37] Grammar is the cradle of all philosophy, and in a manner of speaking, the first nurse of the whole study of letters. It takes all of us as tender babes, newly born from nature's bosom. It nurses us in our infancy, and guides our every forward step in philosophy. With motherly care, it fosters and protects the philosopher from the start to the finish [of his pursuits].[38] It is called "grammar" from the basic elements of writing and speaking. *Grama* means a letter or line,[39] and grammar is "literal," since it teaches letters, that is, both the symbols which stand for simple sounds, and the elementary sounds represented by the symbols. It is also [in a way] linear. For in augmenting size, the length of lines is fundamental, and, as it were, the basic dimension of plane surfaces and solids. So also this branch, which teaches language,[40] is the first of the arts to assist those who are aspiring to increase in wisdom. For it introduces wisdom both through ears and eyes by its facilitation of verbal intercourse. Words admitted into our ears knock on and arouse our understanding. The latter (according to Augustine) is a sort of hand of the soul, able to grasp and to perceive.[41] Letters, that is, written symbols, in the first place represent sounds. And secondly they stand for things, which they conduct into the mind through the windows of the eyes. Frequently they even communicate, without emitting a sound, the utterances of those who are absent.[42] This art [of grammar] accordingly imparts the fundamental elements of language, and also trains our faculties of sight and hearing. One who is ignorant of it [grammar] cannot philosophize any easier than one who lacks sight and hearing from birth can become an eminent philosopher.

---

[36] See *Metalogicon* 1.10, above.

[37] *scientia recte loquendi scribendique, et origo omnium liberalium disciplinarium*: Isidore, *Etymologiae* 1.5.1 See section on Isidore, within, p. 240.

[38] The metaphors of nurse and cradle here constitute some of the basic imagery of grammar: see Gundissalinus, above, pp. 469, 477.

[39] For this part of John's treatment, see Isidore, *Etymologiae* 1.5.1, and Macrobius, *In somnium Scipionis* 1.5.7.

[40] *linguam erudit*: educates the tongue.

[41] The reference to Augustine may perhaps be traced to his *De natura et origine animae* (On the Nature and Origin of the Soul), book 4, ch. 18, where Augustine quotes his opponent, Vincentius Victor: "As you say, the hand of the soul (*manus animae*) contracts itself, nor is it amputated with the bodily hand," ed. Urba and Zycha, 408. Cf. (Pseudo) Aristotle, *Problemata* 30.5.955b25. See also Webb's note in the edition of the *Metalogicon*, 32.

[42] Cf. Isidore, *Etymologiae* 1.3.1.

Chapter 14. Although it is Not Natural, Grammar Imitates Nature

Since grammar is arbitrary and subject to man's discretion, it is evidently not a handiwork of nature. Although natural things are everywhere the same, grammar varies from people to people. However, we have already seen that nature is the mother of the arts.[43] While grammar has developed to some extent, and indeed mainly, as an invention of man, still it imitates nature,[44] from which it partly derives its origin. Furthermore, it tends, as far as possible, to conform to nature in all respects. Thus it has, at nature's bidding, limited the number of elementary vowel-sounds to five among all peoples, even though with many peoples the number of written symbols may be greater. At the same time, our friend Tenred,[45] a grammarian who has more real scientific knowledge than he has been given credit for, has demonstrated that the number of elementary sounds is even greater. According to him, if one carefully notes the differences of vowel sounds, one will observe that they are seven. Among the consonants, nature has likewise formed various semi-vowels and mutes, as well as simple and double consonants; whose differences cannot remain hidden from one who observes mouths modulating sounds according to the marvelous laws of nature, and carefully estimates the vocal quality of these sounds. The very application of names, and the use of various expressions, although such depends on the will of man, is in a way subject to nature, which it probably imitates at least to some modest extent.[46] In accordance with the divine plan, and in order to provide verbal intercourse in human society, man first of all named those things which lay before him, formed and fashioned by nature's hand out of the four elements or from matter and form, and so distinguished that they could be discerned by the sense of rational creatures and have their diversity designated by names as well as by properties. Hence it is that (as Boethius observes[47]) one entity is called "man," another "wood," a third "stone," names being, so to speak, stamped on all substances. Also, since there are numerous differences among given substances, some

---

[43] See *Metalogicon* 1.11 (omitted here).

[44] The thought is commonplace. One possible relevant locus for the notion of "art" here may be found in *Ad Herennium* 3.22.36, "let art imitate nature," and the gloss on this passage of the *Ad Herennium* by one of John's teachers, Thierry of Chartres: "Truly art ought to imitate nature, because the beginning of science is in nature, and from learning [*doctrina*], that is, from art, perfection comes" (Fredborg, ed., *The Latin Rhetorical Commentaries by Thierry of Chartres*, 309; at *Ad Herennium* 3.22.36).

[45] See Webb's edition of *Metalogicon*, xx–xxi and note on 33: Webb tentatively identifies this with Tenred of Dover. See also Webb, "Tenred of Dover."

[46] Cf. Abelard, *Dialectica*, ed. de Rijk, 576.34–7, and *Theologia christiana* 3 (*PL* 178:1245A).

[47] See Boethius' commentary on Aristotle's *De interpretatione*, first edition, ed. Meiser (*Commentarii in librum Aristotelis Peri hermeneias*), 1, 2.

quantitative and some qualitative, some accidental and some from things more intimately connected with them and pertaining to their essence, names to express such differences have been invented so that they can be added to substantive names [i.e. nouns]. These [i.e. adjectives] in a way depict the force and nature of nouns in the same way that the properties of substances indicate their differences. Just as accidents provide raiment and form for substances, so, with due proportion, adjectives perform a similar function for nouns. And that the devices of reason may cleave even more closely to nature, since the substance of a thing is not susceptible of greater or less intensity, a noun does not admit of degrees of comparison. Neither do words referring to substantial differences admit degrees of comparison, despite the fact that they are adjectival, since they denote substantial qualities. Nor do things added to substances in the category of quantity admit of degrees of comparison, inasmuch as a given quantity cannot become greater or less and yet remain itself.[48] In fine, just as accidents alone, though not all accidents, can be increased or diminished, so only adjectives denoting accidents, though not all such adjectives, can be compared. Upon reflection, one sees that this imitation of nature also maintains in other parts of speech, as well as in nouns. Since a substance presented to our senses or intellect cannot exist without some movement, whereby it undergoes temporal change by acting or being acted upon, verbs have been invented to denote the changes occurring in things acting or being acted upon in time. Also, since there is no movement independent of time, there cannot be a verb without designation of its tense.[49] Furthermore, as movement is not always uniform, but has, so to speak, several different shades, and action or being the recipient of action occurs in diverse places and ways, as well as at various times, adverbs have evolved for the purpose of expressing differences in motion, and serve the same function for verbs as adjectives do for nouns. Moreover, is not the fact that some verbs do not have certain tenses, as meditative and inchoative verbs lack a preterite,[50] since the deliberation concerning future action extends over some time and the things undertaken are not immediately accomplished, is not this a clear footprint of nature impressed on [the devices] of human reason?

[In chapters 15 and 16, John of Salisbury continues the argument that grammar imitates nature with the examples of adjectives of "secondary imposition" and "primary imposition," and the kinds of nouns they should modify. An adjective of "secondary

---

[48] Cf. Aristotle, *Categories* 6, 6a, 19–26.

[49] Boethius, *In librum Aristotelis Peri hermeneias* (ed. Meiser, pars prior), 1.3.

[50] Inchoative verbs denote a state of beginning, and in Latin are formed with the suffix *sc*: e.g. *senescere* "to grow old," from the noun *senex*, old man. Meditative verbs denote a state of desire for, or to do, something, as in *esurire* "to want to eat." According to Priscian (echoed by Petrus Helias), such verbs need not have a preterite form in use because they do not in themselves designate a fixed end point for the state of being. See Priscian, *Institutiones* 8.59, *GL* 2:418.25. John's sentence seems to follow Petrus Helias, *Summa super Priscianum*, ed. Reilly, 1:518.84. Cf. Donatus, *Ars minor, De verbo* (*GL* 4:359.11), and the elegant explanation in Remigius' commentary on the *Ars minor*, ed. Fox, 47.

imposition" is coined to describe, not a thing, but a concept or statement (e.g. the adjectives "categorical" or "patronymic"). Such adjectives make no sense when applied to nouns of primary imposition, as in a "patronymic horse" or a "categorical man." But it is possible sometimes to combine adjectives of primary imposition with nouns of secondary imposition (i.e. naming non-corporeal entities) as in such common transferred expressions as "rough speech" or "sweet name," where the adjectives normally refer to corporeal entities.][51]

Chapter 17. That Grammar also Imitates Nature in Poetry

Grammar also imitates nature in further respects. Thus the rules of poetry clearly reflect the ways of nature, and require anyone who wishes to become a master in this art to follow nature as his guide. [So the poet tells us:]

> Nature first adapts our soul to every
> Kind of fate: she delights us, arouses our wrath,
> Or overwhelms and tortures us with woe,
> After which she expresses these emotions employing the tongue as their interpreter.[52]

So true is this [principle] that a poet must never forsake the footsteps of nature. Rather, he should strain to cleave closely to nature in his bearing and gestures, as well as in his words:[53]

> . . . If you expect me to weep, then first
> You yourself must mourn . . .[54]

Likewise, if you want me to rejoice, you yourself must first be joyful. Otherwise,

> . . . If you speak your piece poorly,
> I will either drift off to sleep or will laugh at you.[55]

Consequently, we must take into account, not merely poetical feet and meters, but also age, place, and time, in addition to other circumstances, whose detailed enumeration does not suit our present purpose. Suffice it to say that all of these are products from nature's

---

[51] See within, Petrus Helias section, pp. 444–60.

[52] Horace, *Ars poetica* 108–111. On John's possible familiarity with contemporary Horace commentary, see Friis-Jensen, "Horace and the Early Writers of Arts of Poetry," 360–1, 382.

[53] Fredborg (see "Ciceronian Rhetoric and the Schools," 33) sees in this statement a moment of crossbreeding between the technical rhetoric of Cicero (bearing and gesture) and Horatian commentaries on words and decorum. This intermixture is the core of the material concept of style that is found in the "Materia" commentary on Horace's *Ars poetica*, written in the same period as John's *Metalogicon*. For the "Materia" commentary, see within, pp. 551–6.

[54] Horace, *Ars poetica* 102–3.   [55] *Ars poetica* 104–5.

workshop. Indeed, so closely does it cleave to the things of nature that several have denied that poetry is a subdivision of grammar, and would have it be a separate art. They maintain that poetry no more belongs to grammar than it does to rhetoric, although it is related to both, inasmuch as it has rules in common with each. Let those who wish argue this (for I will not extend the controversy). Begging leave of all, however, I venture to opine that poetry belongs to grammar, which is its mother and the nurse of its study. Although neither poetry nor grammar is entirely natural, and each owes most of its content to man, its author and inventor, nevertheless nature successfully asserts some authority in both. Either poetry will remain a part of grammar, or it will be dropped from the roll of liberal studies.

From Chapter 18. What Grammar Should Prescribe, and What it Should Forbid

[This chapter begins with discussions of solecisms, barbarisms, and metaplasms; the last, when used as figures, are permissible. It then turns to discussion of *schemata* and such "licensed" deviation from correctness.]

. . . There are thus three subjects which the grammarian should master: the grammatical art, grammatical errors, and figures [of speech]. Otherwise he will find it difficult to become secure in his art, to avoid mistakes, and to imitate the graceful style of the authors. If someone who is ignorant of the aforesaid [three] subjects writes or speaks correctly, he does so more through chance than as a result of scientific skill. The art [of grammar] is, as it were, a public highway, on which all have the right to journey, walk, and act, immune from criticism or molestation. To use faulty grammar always means that one is forsaking the proper thoroughfare. He who pursues such devious by-paths is likely either to end up at a precipice, or to become an easy target for the darts and jousts of those who may challenge what he says. The figure [of speech], however, occupies an intermediate position. Since it differs to some extent from both [regular grammar and grammatical error], it falls in neither category. All strive to conform to the [grammatical] art, since it is commanded, and to shun [grammatical] mistakes, since these are forbidden; but only some use figures, since the latter are [merely] permissible. Between errors, that is to say, barbarisms and solecisms, and the art [of grammar], which consists in normal good speech,[56] stand figures and *schemata*.[57] With the metaplasm, there is, for

---

[56] *que virtus eloquii est et norma*: literally, the excellence and norm of eloquence (or speech).
[57] Cf. Isidore, *Etymologiae*, 1.35.7.

sufficient reason, some modification of a word;[58] with the *schema*, for due cause, some deviation from the rules of construction.[59] According to Isidore, a figure is "an excusable departure from the rule."[60] License to use figures is reserved for authors and for those like them, namely, the very learned. Such have understood why [and how] to use certain expressions and not use others. According to Cicero, "by their great and divine good writings they have merited this privilege," which they still enjoy.[61] The authority of such persons is by no means slight, and if they have said or done something, this suffices to win praise for it, or [at least] to absolve it from stigma. One who has not proved himself deserving of imitation by such "great and good writings" will, however, vainly try to expropriate this privilege. The excellence of their other virtues has rightly made these faults of earlier authors sweet and delectable to posterity. Whence Augustine says, in the second book of his work *On Order*: "Poets have chosen to call the solecisms and barbarisms, whereby they express themselves, and to which they are addicted, *schemata* and *metaplasmos*, preferring to change their names rather than give up these evident faults. Rob poems of the latter, and we would keenly miss these delicious condiments. But when we transfer to scenes of informal conversation and forensic discussion, who will not banish this sort of diction, and bid it be off and hide itself in the theater? Furthermore, if anyone piles up very many such expressions together, we become nauseated by the consequent rancid, ill smelling, and putrid heap. Therefore the moderating principle of good order will neither allow *schemata* and metaplasms to be employed everywhere, nor suffer them to be absolutely banished. And when these expressions are mixed with ordinary ones, life and color are breathed into style that would otherwise be dull and commonplace."[62] So says Augustine. Thus we find that one whose authority we have been admonished to heed confirms the great necessity of a knowledge of these forms of speech, which are licitly used by the more learned, and are found practically throughout the length and breadth of literature. Consequently one must learn to discriminate between what is said literally, what is said figuratively, and what is said incorrectly, if one is ever easily and accurately to comprehend what he reads.

---

[58] Earlier in this chapter, John gives the definition of metaplasm as an irregularity or deformation in an individual word, hence a "figure." See Donatus, *Ars maior* 3.4, *GL* 4:395.28–9.

[59] *delictum in contextu verborum*: literally, defect in the connecting of words. John has previously defined *schemata*, along standard lines, as figures of words or sense that occur in the joining together of words. Cf. Donatus, *Ars maior* 3.5. *GL* 4:397–9 and the examples there.

[60] Cf. Isidore, *Etymologiae* 1.35.1 and 7. John's phrase is not an exact quotation from Isidore, but the idea is commonplace.

[61] Cicero, *De officiis* 1.41.148.   [62] Augustine, *De ordine* 2.4.13.

Chapter 19. That a Knowledge of Figures of Speech is Most Useful

Grammar also regulates the use of tropes, special forms of speech whereby, for sufficient cause, speech is used in a transferred sense that differs from its own proper meaning. Examples of tropes are found in metaphors, metonymy, synecdoche, and the like. An enumeration of all the various kinds of tropes would be too lengthy.[63] The employment of tropes, just as the use of *schemata*, is the exclusive privilege of the very learned. The rules governing tropes are also very strict, so that latitude in which they may be used is definitely limited. For the rules teach that we may not extend figures. One who is studiously imitating the authors by using metaphors and figures must take care to avoid crude figures that are hard to interpret. What is primarily desirable in language is lucid clarity and easy comprehensibility.[64] Therefore *schemata* should be used only out of necessity or for ornamentation. Speech was invented as a means of communicating mental concepts; and figures [of speech] are admitted so far as they compensate by their utility for whatever they lack in conformity to the [rules of the grammatical] art. It is especially necessary to understand those three things which are generally most to blame for blocking comprehension of meaning, namely *schemata* together with rhetorical tropes; sophisms which envelop the minds of listeners in a fog of fallacies; and the various considerations[65] which prompt the speaker or writer to say what he does, and which, when recognized, make straight the way for understanding. Indeed, as Hilary tells us, "What is said should be interpreted in the light of why it is said."[66] Otherwise, even in the canonical scriptures, the Fathers would be at odds, and the Evangelists themselves would be contradicting each other, if we were foolishly to judge only from the surface of their words, without considering their underlying purposes. Such procedure indicates a perverse disposition and disregard of one's own progress. Does not Solomon, in the same book, on the same page, and even in consecutive verses, declare: "Respond not to a fool according to his foolishness, lest you become like him"; and "Reply to the fool according to his foolishness, lest he be deluded into imagining he is wise."[67] One should learn the rules whereby one can determine what is right and what wrong in speech. One cannot

---

[63] Cf. Isidore, *Etymologiae* 1.37.1   [64] Quintilian, *Institutio oratoria* 1.6.41.

[65] *rationum diversitas*, literally, multitude of reasons.   [66] Hilary, *De trinitate* 4.14 (*PL* 10:107).

[67] Proverbs 26:4,5.

correct mistakes save by rule, and one cannot avoid pitfalls which one fails to recognize owing to one's failure to study. Among the rules of the arts, I do not believe that there are any more useful or more compendious than those which, in addition to taking note of the figures used by authors, clearly point out the merits and defects of their speech. It is a matter of [no small] wonder to me why our contemporaries have so neglected this part [of grammar], for it is very useful, and equally concise, and has been carefully treated by most writers on the art of grammar. Donatus,[68] Servius,[69] Priscian,[70] Isidore,[71] Cassiodorus,[72] our Bede,[73] and many others, have all discussed it, so that if one remains ignorant of it, this can only be attributed to negligence. Quintilian also teaches this part of the art.[74] In fact, he praises it so highly that he would say that, if one lacks it, it is doubtful whether he has the right to be called a grammarian, and certain that he cannot hope to become a master of the [grammatical] art. The meaning of words should be carefully analyzed, and one should diligently ascertain the precise force of each and every term, both in itself and in the given context, so that one may dispel the haze of sophistries that would otherwise obscure the truth. The considerations prompting the speaker may be surmised from the occasion, the kind of person he is, and the sort of listeners he has, as well as from the place, the time, and various other pertinent circumstances that must be taken into account by one who seriously seeks the truth.[75] If one applies himself to mastering the above-suggested means of overcoming the three obstacles to understanding, not only will he be agreeably surprised by his own increased proficiency in comprehending what he reads and hears, but he will also come to be admired and respected by others.

[Chapter 20. *With what the grammarian should concern himself.* In this short chapter, John treats metrical feet, accent, and clauses or *cola* (following Isidore of Seville, *Etymologiae* 1.17–20), and mentions the *ars memoriae* as taught in book 3.16–34 of the *Rhetorica ad Herennium*.]

[68] Donatus, *Ars maior* 3.1–6.

[69] Servius, *Commentarium in artem Donati*, GL 4:443–8.

[70] See Priscian, *Institutiones* 17.166–8, *GL* 3:192–3, where some figures of speech are treated under the general rubric of construction or syntax.

[71] Isidore of Seville, *Etymologiae* 1.37 and 2.21.   [72] Cassiodorus, *Institutiones* 2.1.2 (brief discussion).

[73] Bede, *De schematibus et tropis.*

[74] Such a compendious resource might be Quintilian's account of the virtues and vices of usage (barbarisms and solecisms) among the authors: see *Institutio oratoria* 1.5 and 8.6–9.3; for Quintilian on ill-prepared grammar teachers, see 1.5.7.

[75] Here John applies the rhetorical doctrine of circumstances to grammatical proficiency in properly interpreting a discourse. This suggests how he conceived the arts of the trivium as an integrated entity.

Chapter 21. By What Great Men Grammar has been Appreciated, and the Fact that Ignorance of This Art is as Much a Handicap in Philosophy as is Deafness and Dumbness

From what has been said, it is clear that [the function of] grammar is not narrowly confined to one subject. Rather, grammar prepares the mind to understand everything that can be taught in words. Consequently, everyone can appreciate how much all other studies depend on grammar. Some of our contemporaries apparently pride themselves on being able to babble along garrulously without benefit of this art. They regard it as useless, openly assail it, and glory in the fact that they have never studied it. But Marcus Tullius [Cicero] did not hate his son, of whom, as is evident in his letters, he insistently required the study of grammar.[76] And Gaius Caesar wrote books *On Analogy*, conscious that, without grammar, one cannot master philosophy (with which he was thoroughly familiar) or eloquence (in which he was most proficient).[77] Quintilian also praises this art to the point of declaring that we should continue the use of grammar and the love of reading "not merely during our school days, but to the very end of our life."[78] For grammar equips us both to receive and to impart knowledge. It modulates our accent, and regulates our very voice so that it is suited to all persons and matters. Poetry should be recited in one way; prose in another. The governing principle in pronunciation is at one time harmony, at another rhythm, at still another the sense. The law of harmony reigns in music. Caesar, while still a boy, with fine sarcasm remarked to a certain person, "If you're trying to read, you're singing, and if you're trying to sing, you're doing a miserable job."[79] In similar vein, Martianus, in *The Marriage of Philology and Mercury*, represents grammar as provided with a knife, a rod, and the ointment case carried by physicians.[80] She uses the knife to prune away grammatical errors, and to cleanse the tongues of infants as she instructs them. Nursing and feeding her charges, she conducts them on to the art of philosophy, thoroughly training them beforehand so that they will not babble in barbarisms or solecisms. Grammar employs her rod to punish offenders; while with the ointment of the propriety and utility which derive from her services, she mitigates the sufferings of her patients. Grammar also guides our hand to write correctly, and sharpens our vision so that it is not nonplussed by fine convolutions of letters, or by parchment crowded with intricate and elaborate script. It opens our ears, and accommodates them to all word sounds, including those that are deep or sharp. If, therefore, grammar is so useful, and the

---

[76] Quintilian, *Institutio oratoria* 1.7.34. [77] Ibid. [78] Ibid. 1.8.12. [79] Ibid. 1.8.2.
[80] *De nuptiis* 3.223.

key to everything written, as well as the mother and arbiter of all speech, who will [try to] exclude it from the threshold of philosophy, save one who thinks that philosophizing does not require an understanding of what has been said or written? Accordingly those who would banish or condemn grammar are in effect trying to pretend that the blind and deaf are more fit for philosophical studies than those who, by nature's gift, have received and still enjoy the vigor of all their senses.

[Chapter 22, *That Cornificius invokes the authority of Seneca to defend his erroneous contentions*, argues that detractors cannot take refuge under certain of Seneca's ambivalent remarks about the value of grammar. John of Salisbury's axiom is "Poetry is the cradle of philosophy," echoing twelfth-century Platonist ideas and language.[81]]

Chapter 23. The Chief Aids to Philosophical Inquiry and the Practice of Virtue; as Well as How Grammar is the Foundation of Both Philosophy and Virtue

The chief aids to philosophical inquiry and the practice of virtue are reading, learning,[82] meditation, and assiduous application.[83] Reading scrutinizes the written subject matter immediately before it. Learning likewise generally studies what is written, but also sometimes moves on to what is preserved in the archives of the memory and is not in the writing, or to those things that become evident when one understands the given subject. Meditation, however, reaches out farther to what is unknown, and often even rises to the incomprehensible by penetrating, not merely the apparent aspects, but even the hidden recesses of questions. The fourth is assiduous application. The latter, although it owes its form to previous cognition, and requires scientific knowledge, still smoothes the way for understanding, since, in itself, it constitutes "a good understanding for all who do it."[84] The heralds of the truth, it is written, "have proclaimed the works of God, and have understood His doings."[85] Scientific knowledge, by the nature of things, must precede the

---

[81] For example, William of Conches' commentaries on Macrobius' *In somnium Scipionis* speak of poetry as the cradle or nursery of philosophers; see Dronke, *Fabula: Explorations into the Uses of Myth in Medieval Platonism*, 17–18, 68 (2 a–b).

[82] Learning: *doctrina* (study, learning, grasping intellectual or doctrinal content). Cf. Hugh of St. Victor, *Didascalicon* 3.7–11, 5.7. On *doctrina* as a term in medieval usage, see Leclercq, "*Disciplina*"; Marrou, "'Doctrina' et 'disciplina'"; and Zeeman, *Piers Plowman and the Medieval Discourse of Desire*, 134–43.

[83] *assiduitas operis*, diligent application, action in accordance with knowledge and virtue.

[84] Psalm 110:10. The Psalm refers to practical "fear of the Lord," or observance of the divine commandments.

[85] Psalm 63:10.

practice and cultivation of virtue, which does not "run without knowing where it is going," and does not merely "beat the air" in its battle against vice.[86] Rather "it sees its goal, and the target at which it aims." It does not haphazardly chase ravens with a piece of pottery and a bit of mud.[87] But scientific knowledge is the product of reading, learning, and meditation. It is accordingly evident that grammar, which is the basis and root of scientific knowledge, implants, as it were, the seed [of virtue] in nature's furrow after grace has readied the ground. This seed, provided again that cooperating grace is present, increases in substance and strength until it becomes solid virtue, and it grows in manifold respects until it fructifies in good works, wherefore men are called and actually are "good." At the same time, it is grace alone which makes a man good. For grace brings about both the willing and the doing of good.[88] Furthermore, grace, more than anything else, imparts the faculty of writing and speaking correctly to those to whom it is given, and supplies them with the various arts. Grace should not be scorned when it generously offers itself to the needy, for if despised, it rightly departs, leaving the one who has spurned it no excuse for complaint.

Chapter 24. **Practical Observations on Reading and Lecturing, Together With [an Account of] The Method Employed by Bernard of Chartres and his Followers**

One who aspires to become a philosopher should therefore apply himself to reading, learning, and meditation, as well as the performance of good works, lest the Lord become angry and take away what he seems to possess.[89] The word "reading" is equivocal. It may refer either to the activity of teaching and being taught, or to the occupation of studying written things by oneself.[90] Consequently, the former, the intercommunication between teacher and learner, may be termed (to use Quintilian's word) the "lecture";[91] the latter, or the scrutiny by the student, the "reading,"[92] simply so called. On the authority of the same Quintilian, "the teacher of grammar should, in lecturing,[93] take care of such details as to have his students analyze verses into their parts of speech, and point out the nature of the metrical feet which are to be noted in poems. He should, furthermore, indicate and

---

[86] 1 Corinthians 9:26.   [87] Persius, *Satires* 3.60–1.   [88] Philippians 2:13.   [89] Matthew 25:29.
[90] The Latin words *lectio, legere* (a reading, to read) had greater semantic range in the Middle Ages than the modern English equivalents. A "reading" could be individual study of a book, but also a lecture or presentation to others of knowledge (this is preserved in some modern English usages, as in a "public reading").
[91] *praelectio*; cf. Quintilian, *Institutio oratoria* 2.5.4.   [92] *lectio.*   [93] *in praelegendo.*

condemn whatever is barbarous, incongruous, or otherwise against the rules of composition."[94] He should not, however, be overcritical of the poets, in whose case, because of the requirements of rhythm, so much is overlooked that their very faults are termed virtues. A departure from the rule that is excused by necessity is often praised as a virtue, when observance of the rule would be detrimental. The grammarian should also point out metaplasms, *schemata*,[95] and oratorical tropes, as well as various other forms of expression that may be present. He should further suggest the various possible ways of saying things, and impress them on the memory of his listeners by repeated reminders. Let him "shake out"[96] the authors, and, without exciting ridicule, despoil them of their feathers, which (crow fashion) they have borrowed from the several branches of learning in order to bedeck their works and make them more colorful.[97] One will more fully perceive and more lucidly explain the charming elegance of the authors in proportion to the breadth and thoroughness of his knowledge of various disciplines. The authors by *diacrisis*,[98] which we may translate as "vivid representation,"[99] or "graphic imagery,"[100] when they would take the crude materials of history, arguments,[101] narratives,[102] and other topics, would so copiously embellish them by the various branches of knowledge, in such charming style, with such pleasing ornament, that their finished masterpiece would seem to image all the arts. Grammar and Poetry are poured without stint over the length and breadth of their works. Across this field, as it is commonly called, Logic, which contributes plausibility by its proofs,[103] weaves the golden lightening of its reasons; while Rhetoric, where persuasion is in order, supplies the silvery luster of its resplendent eloquence. Following in the path of the foregoing, Mathematics rides [proudly] along on the four-wheel chariot of its Quadrivium, intermingling its fascinating demonstration in manifold variety. Physics,[104] which explores the secret depths of nature, also brings forth from her [copious] stores numerous lovely ornaments of diverse hue. Of all branches of learning, that which confers the

---

[94] *Institutio oratoria* 1.8.13. The following three sentences are also based loosely on Quintilian's program for reading the poets in the grammar school, *Institutio oratoria*, book 1.

[95] For translator's word "schematisms."   [96] *excutiat*, shake out, search, thoroughly examine or analyze.

[97] Cf. Horace, *Epistles* 1.3.18–20.

[98] *diacrisim*: perhaps from Greek *diakrisis*: separation, discernment, solution, interpretation; or perhaps from Greek *diatuposis*, vivid description; see Webb's note in the edition of *Metalogicon*, 54. Cf. Martianus Capella, *De nuptiis* 5.524; and Cassiodorus' *Expositio Psalmorum* 30.11, 90.1, 125.4.

[99] *illustratio*, illustration, illumination, vivid representation or description; cf. Quintilian, *Institutio oratoria* 6.2.32.

[100] *picturatio*.   [101] *argumentum*, realistic fiction: see above, General Introduction, pp. 37, 42–4.

[102] *fabula*, meaning myth, story, fiction, part of the triad of *historia-argumentum-fabula* (see note above).

[103] *colores probandi*, credible proofs (cf. "giving color," providing plausible background or story).

[104] For translator's term "physical philosophy": Latin *physica*, referring to a division of knowledge, usually in the threefold division of logic, ethics, and physics (which John has partly adapted here).

greatest beauty is Ethics, the most excellent part of philosophy, without which the latter would not even deserve its name. Carefully examine the works of Virgil or Lucan, and no matter what your philosophy, you will find therein its seed or seasoning. The fruit of the lecture on the authors is proportionate both to the capacity of the students and to the industrious diligence of the teacher.

Bernard of Chartres,[105] the greatest font of literary learning[106] in Gaul in recent times, used to teach grammar in the following way. He would point out, in reading the authors, what was simple and according to rule. On the other hand, he would explain grammatical figures, rhetorical embellishment, and sophistical quibbling, as well as the relation of given passages to other studies. He would do so, however, without trying to teach everything at one time. On the contrary, he would dispense his instruction to his hearers gradually, in a manner commensurate with their powers of assimilation. And since diction is lustrous either because the words are well chosen, and the adjectives and verbs admirably suited to the nouns with which they are used, or because of the employment of metaphors, whereby speech is transferred to some beyond-the-ordinary meaning for sufficient reason,[107] Bernard used to inculcate this in the minds of his hearers whenever he had the opportunity. In view of the fact that exercise both strengthens and sharpens our mind, Bernard would bend every effort to bring his students to imitate what they were hearing.[108] In some cases he would rely on exhortation, in others he would resort to punishment, such as flogging. Each student was daily required to recite part of what he had heard on the previous day. Some would recite more, others less. Each succeeding day thus became the discipline[109] of its predecessor. The evening exercise, known as the "declination,"[110] was so replete with grammatical instruction that if anyone were to take part in it for an entire year, provided he were not a dullard, he would become thoroughly familiar with the [correct] method of speaking and writing, and would not be at a loss to comprehend

---

[105] Bernard was subdeacon at the cathedral of Chartres in the first decade of the twelfth century until his death; he was appointed master probably by 1112 and remained so until at least 1119; in 1124 he was chancellor, and he died soon afterward. The best account of Bernard's life and the complex historiography around him is in Bernard of Chartres, ed. Dutton, *The Glosae super Platonem of Bernard of Chartres*, 21–45. John of Salisbury was taught by Bernard's pupils, Gilbert of Poitiers, William of Conches, and Richard the Bishop. A letter written possibly by Gilbert of Poitiers to Bernard contains the same effusive language about Bernard's teaching that John of Salisbury uses, suggesting perhaps that John derived his estimation of Bernard from Gilbert's reverent attitude; see Dutton, *Glosae*, 35. See also Häring, "Chartres and Paris Revisited"; Jeauneau, "*Nani gigantum humeris insidentes*: Essai d'interprétation de Bernard de Chartres"; and Keats-Rohan, "John of Salisbury and Education in Twelfth-Century Paris."

[106] *exundantissimus fons litterarum*, the greatest font of letters, or literary and grammatical learning.

[107] Metaphor, i.e. *translatio*, literally transference.

[108] I.e., this was an oral lecture, in which the students were hearing the authors read aloud to them.

[109] *discipulus*, literally, pupil.

[110] *declinatio*: probably an exercise in declension of nouns and inflections of verbs; also derivations of other parts of speech from the primary forms (e.g. adverbs derived from nouns or verbs).

expressions in general use. Since, however, it is not right to allow any school or day to be without religion, subject matter was presented to foster faith, to build up morals, and to inspire those present at this collation[111] to perform good works. This [evening] "declination," or philosophical collation, closed with the pious commendation of the souls of the departed to their Redeemer, by the devout recitation of the Sixth Penitential Psalm[112] and the Lord's Prayer. He [Bernard] would also explain the poets and orators who were to serve as models for the boys in their introductory exercises in imitating prose and poetry.[113] Pointing out how the diction of the authors was so skillfully connected,[114] and what they had to say was so elegantly concluded,[115] he would admonish his students to follow their example. And if, to embellish his work, someone had sewed on a patch of cloth filched from an external source,[116] Bernard, on discovering this, would rebuke him for his plagiary, but would generally refrain from punishing him. After he had reproved the student, if an unsuitable theme had invited this, he would, with modest indulgence, bid the boy to rise to real imitation of the [classical] authors, and would bring about that he who had imitated his predecessors would come to be deserving of imitation by his successors. He would also inculcate as fundamental, and impress on the minds of his listeners, what virtue exists in economy;[117] what things are to be commended by facts and what ones by choice of words,[118] where concise and, so to speak, frugal speech is in order, and where fuller, more copious expression is appropriate; as well as where speech is excessive, and wherein consists just measure in all cases. Bernard used also to admonish his students that stories and poems should be read thoroughly, and not as though the reader were being precipitated to flight by spurs. Wherefore he diligently and insistently demanded from each, as a daily debt, something committed to memory.[119] At the same time, he said that we should shun what is superfluous. According to him, the works of distinguished authors suffice. As a matter of fact, to study everything that everyone, no matter how insignificant, has ever

---

[111] For translator's "quasi-collation"; *collatio*: a conference or a meal. Cf. the Benedictine Rule (*Benedicti Regula monachorum*, ed. Woelfflin, 42).

[112] Psalm 129. Literally this was an "offering" of the psalm, *devota oblatio*.

[113] *praeexercitamina*, exercises; cf. Priscian's set of exercises by that name (based on the *Progymnasmata* of Hermogenes), *GL* 3:430–40.

[114] *iunctura dictionum*, connection of things said; cf. Quintilian, *Institutio oratoria* 9.4.32.

[115] *clausulae sermonum*, conclusions.   [116] Horace, *Ars poetica* 16; Matthew 9:16.

[117] Cf. Quintilian, *Institutio oratoria* 3.3.9, on *oeconomia* in matters relating to expression.

[118] "What is to be praised in beauty of content [*rerum*, things] and beauty of words": this restates one of the commonplaces of rhetorical teaching about style: cf. *Rhetorica ad Herennium* 4.13.18, on the difference between figure of diction (*exornatio verborum*) and figure of thought (*exornatio sententiarum*): "It is a figure of diction if the adornment is comprised in the fine polish of the language itself. A figure of thought derives a certain distinction from the idea [*in ipsis rebus*] not from the words."

[119] Cf. Quintilian, *Institutio oratoria* 1.1.36, recommending that children should memorize "the sayings of famous men and selected passages from the poets" as one of the exercises in elementary grammatical training.

said, is either to be excessively humble and cautious, or overly vain and ostentatious. It also deters and stifles minds that would better be freed to go on to other things. That which preempts the place of something that is better is, for this reason, disadvantageous, and does not deserve to be called "good." To examine and pore over everything that has been written, regardless of whether it is worth reading, is as pointless as to fritter away one's time with old wives' tales. As Augustine says in his book *On Order*, "Who is there who will bear that a man who has never heard that Daedalus flew should [therefore] be considered unlearned? And on the contrary, who will not agree that one who says that Daedalus did fly should be branded a liar; one who believes it, a fool; and one who questions [anyone] about it, impudent? I am wont to have profound pity for those of my associates who are accused of ignorance because they do not know the name of the mother of Euryalus, yet who dare not call those who ask such questions 'conceited and pedantic busy-bodies.' "[120] Augustine summarizes the matter aptly and with truth. The ancients correctly reckoned that to ignore certain things constituted one of the marks of a good grammarian. A further feature of Bernard's method was to have his disciples compose prose and poetry every day, and exercise their faculties in mutual conferences,[121] for nothing is more useful in introductory training than actually to accustom one's students to practice the art they are studying. Nothing serves better to foster the acquisition of eloquence and the attainment of knowledge than such conferences, which also have a salutary influence on practical conduct, provided that charity moderates enthusiasm, and that humility is not lost during progress in learning. A man cannot be the servant of both learning and carnal vice.[122] My own instructors in grammar, William of Conches[123] and Richard, who is known as "the Bishop,"[124] a good man both in life and in conversation, who now holds the office of archdeacon of Coutances, formerly used Bernard's method in training their disciples. But later, when popular opinion veered away from the truth, when men preferred to seem, rather than to be philosophers, and when professors of the arts were promising to impart the whole of philosophy in less than three or even two years, William and Richard were overwhelmed by the onslaught of the ignorant mob, and retired. Since then, less time and attention have been given to the study of grammar. As a result, we find

---

[120] Augustine, *De ordine*, ed. Green and Daur, 2.12.37. Euryalus: in *Aeneid* 9, the friend of Nisus who perishes in a raid.

[121] *collationes* (see above).   [122] Cf. Jerome, *Epistles* 125.11 (*PL* 22:1078).

[123] See the introduction to the selections from William of Conches, within. In book 2, ch. 10 of the *Metalogicon*, John mentions studying with William for three years, which must have been from 1138 to 1141, and most likely at Chartres.

[124] Richard the Bishop (Richard l'Evèque, Richard Episcopus) was archdeacon of Coutances (in Normandy) before 1171, when he became bishop of Avranches. He died in 1182.

men who profess all the arts, liberal and mechanical, but who are ignorant of this very first one [i.e. grammar], without which it is futile to attempt to go on to the others. But while other studies may also contribute to "letters," grammar alone has the unique privilege of making one lettered. Romulus,[125] in fact, refers to grammar as "letters," Varro[126] calls it "making lettered," and one who teaches or professes grammar is spoken of as "lettered." In times past, the teacher of grammar was styled a "teacher of letters." Thus Catullus says: "Silla, the 'teacher of letters,' gives thee a present."[127] Hence it is probable that anyone who spurns grammar, is not only not a "teacher of letters," but does not even deserve to be called "lettered."

Chapter 25. A Short Conclusion Concerning the Value of Grammar

Those who only yesterday were mere boys, being flogged by the rod, yet who today are masters, ensconced in the magisterial chair[128] and invested with the official stole, claim that those who praise grammar do so out of ignorance of other studies. Let such patiently heed the commendation of grammar found in the book, *On the Education of an Orator.*[129] If the latter is acceptable to them, then let them spare innocent grammarians. In the aforesaid work we find this statement: "Let no one despise the principles of grammar as of small account. Not that it is a great thing to distinguish between consonants and vowels, and subdivide the latter into semi-vowels and mutes. But, as one penetrates farther into this (so to speak) sanctuary, he becomes conscious of the great intricacy of grammatical questions. The latter are not only well calculated to sharpen the wits of boys, but also constitute fit subject matter to exercise the most profound erudition and scientific knowledge."[130] Quintilian also says: "Those who deride this art as petty and thin deserve even less toleration. For if grammar does not lay beforehand a firm foundation for the orator, the whole structure will collapse. Grammar is accordingly first among the liberal arts. Necessary for the young, gratifying to the old, and an agreeable solace in solitude, it alone, of all branches of learning, has more utility than show."[131]

---

[125] "Romulus," metonymy for Romans; see Martianus Capella, *De nuptiis* 3.229.

[126] Varro is cited in Augustine, *De ordine* 2.12.35 and Isidore of Seville, *Etymologiae* 1.3.1.

[127] John of Salisbury probably cites this from Martianus Capella, *De nuptiis*, 3. 229.

[128] *in cathedra*, literally the throne or chair of authority; modifying McGarry's translation slightly

[129] I.e., Quintilian's *Institutio oratoria.*

[130] *Institutio oratoria* 1.4.6.

[131] *Institutio oratoria* 1.4.5, to which John has added the sentence "Grammar is accordingly first among the liberal arts."

[Books 2–4 of the *Metalogicon* are concerned with logic and its method, dialectic, and a close account of the elements of the "old logic" and "new logic." From these books we give one short selection.]

From *Metalogicon*, Book 2

Chapter 9. That Dialectic is Ineffective When it is Divorced from Other Studies

It is a well known fact that "Eloquence without wisdom is futile."[132] Whence it is clear that eloquence derives its efficacy from wisdom. The utility of eloquence is, in fact, directly in proportion to the measure of wisdom a person may have attained. On the other hand, eloquence becomes positively harmful when it departs from wisdom. It is accordingly evident that dialectic, the highly efficient and ever-ready servant of eloquence, is useful to anyone in proportion to the degree of knowledge he possesses.[133] It is of greatest advantage to a person who knows much; and of least use to one who knows little. In the hand of a pygmy or dwarf, the sword of Hercules is worthless; but in the grasp of an Achilles or a Hector, it becomes a veritable thunderbolt, which levels everything in its way. So also, if it is bereft of the strength which is communicated by the other disciplines, dialectic is in a way maimed and practically helpless; but if it derives life and vigor from other studies, it can destroy all falsehood, and at least enables one to dispute with probability concerning all subjects. Dialectic, however is not great, if, as our contemporaries treat it, it remains forever engrossed in itself, walking round about and surveying itself, ransacking its own depths and secrets: limiting itself to things that are of no use whatsoever in a domestic or military, commercial or religious, civil or ecclesiastical way, and that are appropriate only in school. For in school and during youth, many things are permitted within certain limits, and for the time being, which are to be speedily sloughed off when one advances to a more serious study of philosophy. Indeed, when one has become intellectually or physically mature, the treatment of philosophy becomes more earnest. It not only divests itself of puerile expressions and speech that were permitted by indulgent concession, but even frequently discards all books. This is the lesson contained, beneath a veil of poetic fiction, in the Marriage of Mercury and Philology, contracted with the approval of all the gods, and useful for all men who observe it. According to this [fiction], Philology, on ascending

---

[132] Cicero, *De inventione* 1.1.1.   [133] Cicero, *Partitiones oratoriae* 23.78.

to the heavenly temples and attaining the freedom of a purer state, relieved herself of the numerous books with which she had been burdened.[134] It is easy for an artisan to talk about his art, but it is much more difficult to put the art into practice. What physician does not often discourse at length on elements, humors, complexions, maladies, and other things pertaining to medicine? But the patient who recovers as a result of hearing this jargon might just as well have been sickened by it. What moral philosopher does not fairly bubble over with laws of ethics, so long as these remain merely verbal? But it is a far different matter to exemplify these in his own life. Those who have manual skills find no difficulty in discussing their arts, but none of them can erect a building or fight a boxing match with as little exertion. The like holds true of other arts. It is a simple matter, indeed, to talk about definitions, arguments, genera, and the like; but it is a far more difficult feat to put the art [of dialectic] into effect by finding the aforesaid in each of the several branches of knowledge.[135] One who has the sad misfortune of being in want of the other disciplines, cannot possess the riches that are promised and provided by dialectic.

[134] Martianus Capella, *De nuptiis*, 2.136.
[135] *in singulis facultatibus*, literally, in particular faculties or inquiries. The meaning here is that it is easier to talk about dialectic than to apply its complex technical detail to other fields.

GRAMMATICAL COMMENTARIES FROM THE "SCHOOL" OF RALPH OF BEAUVAIS, CA. 1165–1175

INTRODUCTION

In the decades following the commentaries of William of Conches and Petrus Helias on Priscian's *Institutiones*, other masters continued to teach and gloss Priscian's work, and to refine approaches to grammatical theory, especially on syntax. One master whose influence we can trace through commentaries associated with his teaching is Ralph of Beauvais, who knew and used the work of William of Conches.[1] From a few contemporary testimonies to his teaching and influence, we know that Ralph was an Englishman who studied in France with Abelard and then taught at Beauvais;[2] that he continued to teach and study grammar well into his old age (the 1180s);[3] and that he was remembered well into the next century as a preeminent authority on grammar and literature.[4]

R. W. Hunt was able to reconstruct his influence through several channels: a gloss on Priscian, known as the *Promisimus* gloss, that names a number of masters, but Ralph with greatest frequency;[5] two other glosses that are closely related to the *Promisimus* gloss in their approach to grammatical teaching;[6] and Ralph's authorship of two works which have come down to us: a commentary on Donatus' *Ars minor* and a grammatical commentary on Ovid and Lucan known as the *Liber Tytan*, which is also quoted in the *Promisimus* gloss on Priscian.[7] From evidence in the *Promisimus* gloss it also seems that Ralph wrote a gloss on Priscian's *Institutiones*, but no copy of this has yet been identified.[8] The anonymous

---

[1] This suspicion of Hunt, "Studies on Priscian in the Twelfth Century II: The School of Ralph of Beauvais," 59 (orig., 21) is now confirmed by Fredborg, ed., "*Promisimus*: An Edition," 84.

[2] Helinand of Froidmont, *Chronicon*, PL 212:1035D.

[3] Peter of Blois, *Epistle* 6, PL 207:16–19; see Hunt, "Studies on Priscian in the Twelfth Century II," 50 (12) and note 3 for dating of this letter.

[4] Gerald of Wales, *Gemma ecclesiastica*, II.37 (written about 1197–9) and *Speculum ecclesiae*, preface (written about 1220): see Hunt, "Studies on Priscian II," 49 (11), n. 4.

[5] Hunt, "Studies on Priscian II," 49 (11).   [6] Ibid. 67–70, 77 (29–32, 39).   [7] Ibid. 50–3 (12–15).

[8] Ibid. 83 (45), and Kneepkens, ed., introduction to Ralph of Beauvais, *Glose super Donatum*, xi.

glosses reflect the kind of teaching for which Ralph was known and which can be seen in his surviving writings: the development of syntax and the reapplication of grammar to the study of the classical authors.[9]

The *Promisimus* gloss (so-called from its incipit, "we promised to hasten to the literal exposition . . ."), which survives in one manuscript, Oxford Bodleian Library, MS Laud lat. 67 (second half of the twelfth century), is a *reportatio*, a report by a student of a master's lectures. Its most likely period of composition is the 1170s.[10] The gloss extends to the eighth book of the *Institutiones grammaticae*. This gloss, like the two others that are related to it in the "circle" of Ralph of Beauvais' teachings, continues the work begun by Petrus Helias of systematizing grammatical theory. The glossators achieve this in part by refining some of Petrus Helias' own definitions. For example, where Petrus Helias had said that words were invented so that men might show their "will" (*voluntas*) to one another, one glossator takes a slightly different view, substituting the word "concept" (*intellectus*) for "will."[11] The *Promisimus* gloss develops this difference into a new understanding of the causes of the invention of words (see text 1, below). We also see a reaffirmation of syntax as the grammarian's concern (text 2, below), although the *Promisimus* "seems rather conservative, particularly in handling its technical terminology."[12] There are many instances in the gloss where Ralph of Beauvais is invoked by name, but the glossator does not hide his disagreement with him. Such critical independence in relation to the text and to contemporary authorities is one of the defining features of this generation of grammatical commentators.[13]

In his *Liber Tytan*, likely composed during the 1160s, around the same period as his gloss on Donatus,[14] Ralph of Beauvais collected grammatical notes on a number of verses from Ovid's *Metamorphoses* and Lucan's *Pharsalia*. These mostly served as exempla, pegs on which to hang grammatical explanations. They cannot have been intended for elementary language training, but were probably used to instruct students who already had a reasonable grasp of Latin and some elementary knowledge of logic. The level of the text is comparable to that of Alexander Neckam's *Corrogationes Promethei*, devised for students

---

[9] Cf. Reynolds, "*Ad auctorum expositionem*: syntactic theory and interpretative practice in the twelfth century," 32 and 48.

[10] The most recent edition of the *Promisimus* is Fredborg, "*Promisimus*. An Edition." The *Promisimus* is not complete: the beginning of the *accessus* is lacking, see Hunt, "Studies on Priscian in the Twelfth Century II," 43 (5), and Fredborg, "*Promisimus*: An Edition," 82.

[11] See Hunt, "Studies on Priscian II," 70 (32), n. 4, quoting from one of the associated commentaries, "Words are invented so that we might have a means of expressing our concepts (*intellectus*) and of showing them to others."

[12] Fredborg, "*Promisimus*: An Edition," 83.

[13] Apart from the texts translated here, another selection from the *Promisimus* gloss may be found in the ablative absolute dossier, above, pp. 326–7.

[14] For dating the Donatus gloss, see Kneepkens, ed., *Glose super Donatum*, xxiv. Since it is quoted in the *Promisimus* gloss, it has to have appeared somewhat earlier than the 1170s.

at an intermediate stage.[15] Ralph's interests here do not extend to logic or semantics, except insofar as such inquiries enabled him to explain grammatical incongruences to his students, as we see in the opening of the text.[16] The work is richly illustrated with classical and biblical quotations, and its structure is entirely determined by the order of the verses in the original work (the same structure principle that line-by-line commentaries would follow). As an illustration of the literary work for which Ralph of Beauvais was well known, and his particular interest in syntactic analysis, we translate the opening section of the work.

Translated from Hunt, "Studies on Priscian in the Twelfth Century II: The School of Ralph of Beauvais" (selections from *Promisimus* gloss), by permission, and Ralph of Beauvais, *Liber Tytan*, ed. Kneepkens, by permission.

1. PROMISIMUS GLOSS (LAUD LAT. 67, F. 21RA)[17]

(The Task of the Grammarian)

These two things, the confident allocation of (grammatical features under) rules[18] and the subtle investigation into the assessment of constructions and their solution make the perfect grammarian.

2. PROMISIMUS GLOSS (LAUD LAT. 67 F. 22RA)[19]

(Authorship and the Names of Masters)[20]

In the old days it was customary in Rome for people to plot against each other, and if somebody had seen the work of another, he would erase the name of the author from the

---

[15] Kneepkens, ed., in Ralph of Beauvais, *Liber Tytan*, xv–xvi; and see within, Alexander Neckam.

[16] Kneepkens, ed., *Liber Tytan*, xix.

[17] Hunt, "Studies on Priscian II," 75 (37). All texts of the *Promisimus* have also been checked against the Fredborg edition.

[18] I.e. every instance of discourse can be evaluated because there will be an applicable rule—the rules are exhaustive. Cf. Hunt, "Studies on Priscian II," 62 (24).

[19] Ibid. 78 (40).

[20] At *Institutiones grammaticae*, preface (*GL* 2:2.19), Priscian says that he had to publish the work quickly, lest one of his rivals attempt to steal credit for the work by substituting his own name under the title.

title, before the work was published, and substitute his own name. So Priscian says that fear of that happening forced him to publish his book more hurriedly.[21] In our times this also happens in the school of Master Peter Abelard. A book was written there with the title "Here begins work x of author x," but other people had inserted their names: the book of Master Alberic, or of Mananerius, or of Master Valetus, or of Master Garnerus the Grammarian—and none of the names was left in place.[22]

3. *Promisimus Gloss (Laud lat. 67 f. 24*[RA]*)*[23]

(On the Causes of the Invention of Words)

Note that in all conversation, that is in the speech of one man to another, three things are necessary, a thing supposed,[24] a concept (*intellectus*) and a word—a thing so that there may be discourse concerning it, a concept so that by it we may know the thing, and a word so that by it we may represent the concept.[25] And since there are many modes of understanding (*intellectus*), there had to be many different kinds of words [*oportuit multimodas esse voces*] and that is why the minutest particles of sound [*vocis*], which are called "elementary sounds," were invented: so that through their different variations different words might be constituted from them.

4. *Promisimus Gloss (Laud lat. 67 f. 46*[VA]*)*[26] (at *Institutiones* 2.15, on the Parts of Speech)

Some people say[27] that the set of all words that have the same mode of signifying [*modus significandi*] form the same part of speech, but they deny that any element from that set is a

---

21 For a similar story of academic piracy, see above, pp. 354–5, the excerpt from Osbern, *Derivationes*.

22 See Hunt, "Studies on Priscian II," 78–9 (40–1), for identification of these masters.

23 Hunt, "Studies on Priscian II," 48 (10), paraphrase at 70–1 (32–3), supplemented and slightly adapted.

24 For *suppositio*, see the section on Petrus Helias, above, and Kneepkens, "*Suppositio* and *supponere* in Twelfth-Century Grammar."

25 Hunt, "Studies on Priscian II," 71 (33) and note, refers to Boethius' second commentary on Aristotle, *De interpretatione*, ed. Meiser, 7: *vox per intellectuum medietatem subiectas intellectui res manifestat,* and points out that this view contains "the germ of the 'modi essendi, modi intellegendi, modi significandi,' which is the foundation of the later speculative grammar."

26 Hunt, "Studies on Priscian II," 83 (45).

27 Cf. Petrus Helias, *Summa super Priscianum*, ed. Reilly, 180.96ff. (reference owed to Fredborg, "*Promisimus*: An Edition," *ad loc.*).

part of speech, just as the collection of all people living at the same time under the same law form one people, but no one from that collection is a people.[28] Others say that both the set and any element from the set are one part of speech.[29] Master Ralph agrees with neither group, but our master agrees with the second one.

5. *PROMISIMUS* GLOSS (LAUD LAT. 67 F. 67RB–67VA)[30] (AT *INSTITUTIONES* 5.8, ON THE NAMES OF THE ELEMENTS)

Note that Master Ra[lph] of Be[auvais] says that the names of the elements, although they are proper to the elements, still are not proper names, because any name of an element serves to name anyone of a great number. For any element is just one of many utterings. But since all those utterings are the same element, although [the names of the elements] fit those utterings together [*communiter*], and although they are simply "common names," yet they must be called "proper to the elements," just as we say that the term "this name" is universal. For any of a multitude of words is "this name." That the name of an element is not a proper name becomes manifest when one finds "two short *i* (in the plural!) make one long."

FROM RALPH OF BEAUVAIS, *LIBER TYTAN* (OPENING SECTION)

NULLUS ADHUC MUNDO PREBEBAT LUMINA TYTAN (Ovid, *Metamorphoses* I 10):
NO TITAN YET GAVE LIGHT TO THE WORLD: Sometimes a universal sign[31] is connected with a noun [*nomen*] which has the form of an appellative (noun) but fits only one (referent). This yields no incongruity, as in Ovid's NO TITAN YET etc., because although this noun *Titan* fits only one (referent), yet it is naturally common to more. For it signifies substance and quality in a common way.[32]

---

[28] Cf. Victorinus on *De inventione* in Halm, *Rhetores latini minores* 158.12 (reference owed to Fredborg, "*Promisimus*. An Edition." *ad loc.*).

[29] Cf. Petrus Helias, *Summa*, ed. Reilly, 180.16–18. Cf. pp. 452–3 above.

[30] Hunt, "Studies on Priscian II," 85 (47). This text is not in the Fredborg edition.

[31] A word like "all" or "no." The problem here is the use of *nullus*, "no(one)": "no Titan" suggests there are more Titans, whereas reference is to the Sun exclusively (who is the son of the Titan Hyperion).

[32] There are more "Titans," so the word Titan may be considered a common noun, even though in the Ovidian phrase it refers exclusively to the Sun (and so functions almost as a proper name). The last sentence ("For it signifies substance and quality...") defines it as an appellative noun.

But when a universal sign is connected with a proper name [*nomen*], there is incongruity, as in Ovid's "you have already forgotten me; you know no Phyllis [*nullam... Phillida*], I think."[33] But in a proper name an appellative noun may be understood, to which a universal sign may be connected appropriately.[34] We can also say that in this expression NO TITAN YET ETC. "no" [*nullus*] is used instead of "not" [*non*], as in Lucan "no blood [*nullus sanguis*] once lapped up will ever tolerate that the thus polluted throat becomes tame again."[35] So too in Terence "<Chremes:>I am liberated today, Davus, through your work. <Davus> Oh no, you're not! [*ac nullus quidem*]":[36] *nullus* is used instead of *non*.

Similarly, one finds that although the word *nemo* ["no one"] has the force of the words *nullus homo* [no man],[37] it sometimes only retains the meaning of the word *nullus* "no," as in Virgil: "Turnus, what none of the gods [*divum... nemo*] would dare promise to someone praying for it."[38] Similarly in Terence "there is no man [*nemo homo*],"[39] i.e. there is "no one" [*nullus*].

When a word marking diversity is connected with an appellative noun that fits only one referent, there is incongruity, as in Lucan "kings lying under another sun [*alio... sole*],"[40] because the sign of diversity "other" [*alius*] when connected with a word requires that it fits different referents. But we should say that the noun "sun" [*sol*] is used instead of a noun or a phrase whose name does fit different referents, e.g. the noun "star" [*sidus*] or the phrase "part of the world" [*pars mundi*].

Moreover, note that when something is compared to (other) things by means of this word "other" [*alius*], for the phrase to be proper the compared items must be in agreement with respect to the word that is linked to the word "other" [*alius*]. That explains why "the man lives among *the other cows*" is not said with due agreement. Sometimes, however, what is being compared does not agree with its comparanda in the word that is used, but rather in the word that is understood within it, as in orthography "H is written among *the other letters*."[41] For H is no letter, so there is no

---

[33] Ovid, *Heroides* 2.105.

[34] I.e. if Phyllis does not refer to the individual Phyllis, but to "a(ny) woman like Phyllis."

[35] Lucan, *Pharsalia* 1.331–2.   [36] Terence, *Andria* 370.

[37] *Nemo* was commonly derived etymologically from *nullus homo*. See R. Maltby, *A Lexicon of Ancient Latin Etymologies*, s.v.

[38] Virgil, *Aeneid* 9.6. The argument is that "none (*nemo*) of the gods" would be an impossible conjunction if the force of *homo* was still felt in *nemo*.

[39] Terence, *Phormio* 808. Again, *nemo homo* would be a pleonasm if the force of *homo* within *nemo* was still felt.

[40] Cf. Virgil, *Georgics* 2.512; Horace, *Odes* 2.16.18–19.

[41] Priscian, *Institutiones* 1.16, *GL* 2:12.20–21, *h autem aspirationis est nota et nihil aliud habet literae nisi figuram et quod in versu scribitur inter alias literas*. Cf. *Tractatus Anagnini* V (*de V dictionum generibus*) in de Rijk, ed., *Logica modernorum* II 2:315.31–2 (reference from Ralph of Beauvais, ed. Kneepkens, *ad loc.*).

agreement, but in the noun "letter" we understand the noun "figure," which fits both H and the items among which it is written.[42]

Note also that the noun in which the compared items agree must fit them in the same meaning. That explains why this phrase is improper: "the animal that barks is a different [*alius*] dog from the sea monster."[43] Yet this phrase is found in Priscian, and many other examples come with it. Similarly, when a relative is referred to a noun used earlier, the noun must be repeated in the same meaning in which it was used earlier. Yet (the other usage) is found in Tully when he says "the *topos* is now derived from (the subject as a) whole, now from its parts."[44]

[42] I.e. the letters.

[43] Cf. *Tractatus Anagnini* V (*de V dictionum generibus*), in de Rijk, ed., *Logica modernorum* II.2:316.26 (reference from Kneepkens, ed., *ad loc.*).

[44] Cicero, *Topica* II 8.

ALAN OF LILLE, *ANTICLAUDIANUS*,
CA. 1182

INTRODUCTION

Like his now more famous *De planctu Naturae* (Plaint of Nature, composed in the 1160s), Alan of Lille's *Anticlaudianus* is a cosmological poem about knowledge and perfection, tracing the formation of an intellectual and ethical subject. In this, the *Anticlaudianus* takes its inspiration from the great cosmological writings of the twelfth century, among them the commentaries and philosophical works of Thierry of Chartres and William of Conches and, notably, the *Cosmographia* of Bernardus Silvestris.[1] But the *Anticlaudianus* bears special comparison with the *Cosmographia* for another reason: like that earlier work, it achieved the status of "literary masterpiece" in its own time. It was a work cited and read by the following generations because it demonstrates the skills that it teaches and conspicuously showcases grammatical teaching and rhetorical technique. When we look at its legacy through citations and literary influence, we find that it was often used and remembered for its poetic lessons and its illustration of grammatical and rhetorical knowledge, and not only for its philosophical content.[2] It was very likely the literary inspiration for the *Architrenius* by Jean de Hanville (1184), a virtuoso performance in Latin hexameters that is a social satire on the world of learning rather than, like the *Anticlaudianus*, a work of profound cosmological scope. It was adapted and simplified in both Latin and French in the thirteenth century.[3] Gervase of Melkley cites the *Anticlaudianus* in his *Ars versificaria* (Art of Versifying) (ca. 1215), presenting it as a difficult text compared with the works of Ovid, Bernardus

---

[1] For background, context, and analysis, see the introduction to the edition by Bossuat, *Anticlaudianus*; Raynaud de Lage, *Alain de Lille*, 43–102; d'Alverny, ed., *Alain de Lille*, 32–59; Evans, *Alan of Lille*, 133–65; Simpson, *Sciences and the Self in Medieval Poetry*, 1–133.

[2] Chaucer famously invokes its philosophical authority in the *House of Fame* (l. 986), in the course of the narrator's own cosmological quandary about whether to believe the heavenly visions now before his eyes as the eagle carries him aloft. See Simpson, *Sciences and the Self*, 21 n. 38, for other citations of the *Anticlaudianus* in English poetry.

[3] On the likely influence of Alan's work, see the edition of *Architenius* by Wetherbee, xxx–xxxii. Adam de la Bassée, *Ludus super Anticlaudianum*, ed. Bayart; for the French version by Ellebaut, see the edition by Creighton.

Silvestris, and others: it "teaches us more indirectly than directly," but it merits citation for exemplifying compositional technique. In his *Bataille des VII ars* (Battle of the Seven Liberal Arts), Henri d'Andeli places the *Anticlaudianus*, by title, among the allegorized figures who compose Grammar's army: that is, Alan's text as a whole stands for grammatical knowledge. Hugh of Trimberg cites the *Anticlaudianus* several times as a canonical example of rhetorical and literary mastery.[4] In the *Laborintus* (after 1215), Eberhard the German invokes Alan's survey of the arts in a list of classical and medieval authors who should be studied.[5] Jean de Meun used the vivid description of Fortune's house (7.405–8.14) for his own *descriptio* of Fortune in the *Roman de la Rose*.

Perhaps most remarkable is the commentary on the *Anticlaudianus* by Ralph of Long-champs (ca. 1212). Ralph treats the *Anticlaudianus*—with due respect for its philosophical and cosmological lore—as a compendium of the liberal arts. The commentary stops after the account of Arithmetic (beginning of book 4). In Ralph's treatment of the arts, his commentary on the teachings of rhetoric holds pride of place, longer than any of his expositions of the other arts. Ralph uses, as his own base text for an elaboration of rhetorical doctrine, the commentary on the *De inventione* and *Ad Herennium* by Thierry of Chartres. Working closely from Thierry's commentary, Ralph enlarges his exposition of Alan's 134 lines on rhetoric to develop a complete art of rhetoric, stripping away Alan's poetic integument and replacing it with a version of the "new" Ciceronian tradition of the twelfth century. Here the art of rhetoric is both the textual object of inquiry and the means of understanding that text.[6]

The *Anticlaudianus* had as great, if not even greater, influence on later generations as Alan's *De planctu Naturae*. Both texts survive in over one hundred manuscripts.[7] The figurative ambiguity, ingenious grammatical jokes, and playful indeterminacy about language theory that characterize the *De planctu Naturae* (which have ensured its appeal to modern audiences) give way, in the later *Anticlaudianus*, to a relatively straightforward pedagogical approach to grammar and exemplification of grammatical and rhetorical teaching. Moreover, his approach to grammar here is preeminently literary, as opposed to the speculative concerns of some of his earlier theological discussions of grammar.[8] Alan's treatment of the seven liberal

---

[4] For Gervase of Melkley and Hugh of Trimberg, see Part 4. For Henri d'Andeli, see Part 5.

[5] See Faral, ed., *Les arts poétiques*, 360 line 661.

[6] *In Anticlaudianum Alani commentum*, ed. Sulowski, 135–73. Ralph presents a full treatise on rhetoric, complete with extrinsic and intrinsic prologues, following the template laid down by Thierry of Chartres. See also Copeland, "The Ciceronian Rhetorical Tradition and Medieval Literary Theory," 257–9.

[7] For tables of manuscripts, see Raynaut de Lage, *Alain de Lille*, 182–6. See also Alan of Lille, *Anticlaudianus*, ed. Bossuat, 14–25 for manuscripts, and 43–6 for a survey of literary influence. There is also a late-medieval cycle of illustrations of the *Anticlaudianus*: see Mütherich, "Ein Illustrationszyklus zum *Anticlaudianus*."

[8] On Alan's *Regulae theologiae* (Theological Rules; probably from the 1160s) and its speculative and theological approach to grammar, see Kelly, *The Mirror of Grammar*, 44, 48, 74, 76, 99–101, 110, 180–96; and Evans, *Alan of Lille*, 64–80.

arts may owe its allegorical scheme to Martianus Capella, but it also has strong debts to the holistic vision so prized by the cathedral schools of the earlier twelfth century, summed up in Thierry's prologue to his *Heptateuchon* and reaffirmed in the *Metalogicon* of John of Salisbury. On the other hand, Alan's treatment of grammar and rhetoric bears comparison with the *ars poetriae*, the preceptive genre that took form in the same years that Alan probably composed his *Anticlaudianus*: Matthew of Vendôme's *Ars versificatoria*, the earliest work to combine grammatical and rhetorical teaching into one pedagogical art, dates from around 1175. On the basis of Alan's implementation of certain codified techniques of ornamentation, vocabulary, and style, Raynaud de Lage argued that Alan was the beneficiary (directly or indirectly) of the compositional teaching of Matthew of Vendôme, whose nearly contemporary *Ars* prescribes the techniques that are seen to such effect in Alan's poetry.[9] But if Alan derived his technique from the precepts of the great grammarian, his own work was to serve this preceptive function for later readers, because it seamlessly combines teaching *de arte* and *ex arte*, about the arts of language by means of the arts of language.

Translation reprinted from *Anticlaudianus; or the Good and Perfect Man*, trans. Sheridan, by permission.[10]

Plot Summary

Nature (God's vicar), wishing to correct the defects of her other creations, wishes to create a perfect being, man. ("Man" is not simply a generic term: we are witnessing the creation of a perfected masculinity as body and intellect.) In order to produce a perfect man, Nature consults with the Virtues, and it is decided that while they can produce a body on their own, God must create the soul. In the course of the consultation, Reason advises that Prudence must be the emissary to go to heaven and ask God for a soul. Prudence ultimately accepts the task, and Reason orders the Seven Liberal Arts to build a chariot to take Prudence to heaven. Books 2–4 describe the contribution of the Seven Liberal Arts in constructing the chariot part by part. When the chariot is completed, five horses (the five senses) are hitched to it and Prudence takes it to heaven. There, aided by the interventions of Theology and Faith, she is able to ask God for a soul for the "new man." God creates a soul from an exemplar made by "Nous." Prudence takes this back to earth, where she and the other Virtues, along with the Liberal Arts and Nobility and Fortune, succeed in

---

[9] Raynaud de Lage, *Alain de Lille*, 131–63, esp. 146, and 166.

[10] Many of the translator's notes have been used or adapted here. Edition used for reference: Bossuat, *Alain de Lille. Anticlaudianus.*

fashioning the perfect "new man." After a battle between the Virtues and the envious Vices, the "new man" is victorious and becomes ruler of the earth, along with the Virtues who decided to stay on earth in peace and harmony.

FROM BOOK 2

There are seven maidens,[11] cautious, prudent, beautiful, resembling one another: under seven countenances they reflect one countenance: one faith and one will guide those whom one face, one family, one age, one form, one power encompass. They come to Phronesis' aid and carry out her orders, ever ready to show fervour in her service. The gifts of Sophia lavish so many endowments on them that Prudence pours her entire self into them. She shares herself with them and builds up her treasure in them. Thus, though divided, she yet remains whole; though scattered, she is in the end concentrated; though diversified, she returns with high interest. Turning their faces towards her and towards the hidden depths of her mind, in her countenance as in a mirror, the band of sisters sees, considers, learns, notes, and is instructed in whatever parchments contain, the mind conceives, the tongue dares say, and it absorbs from this limitless wisdom whatever the artisan's hand, the painter's charm, the carpenter's skill, the tireless application of the sculptor can do. This band[12] paints like Zeuxis,[13] shapes like Milo,[14] speaks like Fabius,[15] perorates like Tullius, gives opinions like the Samian,[16] philosophizes like Plato, catechizes like Hermes,[17] makes distinctions like Socrates, draws conclusions like Zeno,[18] perseveres

---

[11] I.e. the Seven Liberal Arts.

[12] Many of the names in the following list are drawn from the fifth-century Christian writer Sidonius Apollinaris, *Epistles* 4.3.5–6. On other figures named by Alan who are not found in Sidonius, see Bossuat, "Quelques personnages cités par Alain de Lille," and the full notes in Sheridan's translation. William of Auxerre, the theological writer of the thirteenth century, is credited with a gloss on the *Anticlaudianus* in which he correctly identified most of the other ancient references.

[13] Greek painter, perhaps known to Alan from Cicero's citation in *De inventione* 2.1.1.

[14] Probably Myron (Athenian sculptor of the fifth century BC); on William of Auxerre's correct identification of this, see Bossuat, "Quelques personnages," 36.

[15] A reference to the tradition that Fabius Cunctator delivered Rome's ultimatum to Carthage in 218 BC, cited by Sidonius.

[16] Pythagoras, as cited in Sidonius; on William of Auxerre's identification of this, see Bossuat, "Quelques personnages," 36.

[17] I.e. Hermes Trismegistus or Hermes the Egyptian, the name associated with various mystical, astrological, or alchemical writings deriving from late antiquity, including the fragment *Asclepius*, which is in the form of a dialogue. On William of Auxerre's identification of this, see Bossuat, "Quelques personnages," 36.

[18] A reference to Zeno of Elea, the Presocratic philosopher.

like Brisso,[19] studies like Critias,[20] sees like Argus, corrects time discrepancies like Caesar, investigates the stars like Atlas, balances like Zethus,[21] deals with numbers like Crissipus,[22] measures like another Euclid, sings like Phoebus, plays the harp like Orpheus, draws circles like Perdix,[23] constructs citadels like Daedalus, forges like Cyclops, fashions arms like the Lemnian,[24] teaches like Seneca, flatters like Appius,[25] insists like Cato, inflames like Curio,[26] conceals like a second Perseus,[27] pretends like Crassus, disguises like a second Julius,[28] condenses like Soldius,[29] explains like Naso, blooms like Statius, composes like Maro, understands, explains, imitates, assumes, completes the capacities of Mercury, the rage of our own Demosthenes, the flow of Ovid, the flash of Lucan, the depth of Virgil, the sting of Satire, the refuge of Solon.

Minerva, then, seeing that the sisters are shining with the splendour of Sophia and with so many great gifts and endowments, arranges, charges, bids, commands, begs that each of these companions, accompanied by Sophia, should immediately, in body, mind and faithfulness, show zeal, sweat, pant, press on and see to it that the chariot races towards existence, the chariot in which Prudence could cross the extent of earth, the sea, the stars, the clouds, the heavens and passing the pole of the triple heavens,[30] investigate the secrets of Noys,[31] draw on her deep meaning and inquire into the will of the supreme master. Scarcely has she expressed her wish when her sisters show zeal and rivalry in fulfilling the desires of the mistress and they gird themselves for the task. Their heart is not in opposition to the work, nor their hands to their heart; rather the heart's desire sets the hand to work, the hand's work proclaims without what the heart holds dear within.

[19] Bryson the sophist, mentioned by Aristotle in several works, including *Sophistical Refutations* (171b16, 172a4) and *Posterior Analytics* (75b40). On William of Auxerre's acuity in identifying this reference, see Bossuat, "Quelques personnages," 37–9.

[20] One of the speakers in Plato's *Timaeus*; on William of Auxerre's correct identification, see Bossuat, "Quelques personnages," 37.

[21] A figure from ancient drama, mentioned in Cicero, Horace, and Hyginus, who weighed the merits of music and philosophy, cited by Sidonius.

[22] Chrysippus, a Stoic philosopher, cited by Sidonius.

[23] Nephew of Daedalus and inventor of the compass, cited by Sidonius; see Ovid, *Metamorphoses* 8.247.

[24] I.e. Vulcan.   [25] The consul Appius Claudius Caecus of the third century BC, cited by Sidonius.

[26] Enemy and later ally of Julius Caesar, cited by Sidonius.

[27] William of Auxerre identifies "Perseus" either with the mythological hero who, rendered invisible, was able to slay Medusa, or with the Roman satirist (i.e. Persius), who wrote veiled satire; see Bossuat, "Quelques personnages," 36.

[28] Crassus, the Roman financier and politician, ca. 105–53 BC; "second Julius," i.e. Julius Caesar. Alan's phrasing here, *Crassus simulans, ut Iulius alter / Dissimulans*, follows Sidonius' text closely.

[29] Possibly a reference to Alan's source for much of this list, Gaius Sollius Apollinaris Sidonius; see Bossuat, "Quelques personnages," 37 (taking "Sollius" for "Solidus"): see Ralph of Longchamps, *In Anticlaudianum*, ed. Sulowski, 107, line 34.

[30] Compare Bernardus Silvestris, *Cosmographia* 2.7.10–110 on the heavens.   [31] *Nous* or divine wisdom.

Thus the hand becomes the faithful interpreter of the heart and in its work lays the heart before us.

The first of these enthusiastically sets about having the pole produced, so that it may be the first part of the great work, the pole which is ahead of the axle and is a kind of preface, so to speak, to the coming chariot. This maiden, wakeful, enthusiastic, willing, attentive, energetic, delighting in her task, turns her attention to work. Her dress is not mean nor her face smeared nor her carriage ignoble nor her language unadorned nor her actions barbarous. Yet pallor draws on her face the lines of toil, but it is a modest pallor which does not obliterate the rosy-red glow of her face or the beauty of the snow-white skin, since the bloom of virginity is not deflowered in her nor does the cleft of Venus ruin her chastity. Her breasts, however, float in a deep flood of milk and give the appearance of the ravages that come from lost nulliparity.[32] While the child still sighs at the breasts of his nursing mother, this food feeds him and the one who cannot yet take solids is nourished by liquid. While at this milk-white age, he enjoys draughts of milk and, in one and the same draught, there are food and drink coming from milk alone. She increases the severity of one of her hands with a whip with which she punishes the faults which youth in its way absorbs. Thus by blows she makes the milk more bitter, by the milk she makes the blows more mild. In one and the same action she is father and mother. By the blows she makes up for a father, by the milk she fills the role of mother. Her other hand fulfills its function with a file; it clears the tartar from the teeth as she changes the teeth's boxwood tint to an ivory gleam and beautifies them by her whitening process. If, however, one tooth strays from the rest of the row, she cuts the outgrowth back to normal.[33] This maiden teaches infants to speak, looses tied tongues and shapes words in the proper mould. A white garment, woven from Egyptian papyrus, clothes her. She does not impair its beauty and its beauty does her no disservice. Raiment and beauty unite in a charming marriage and each pays its own homage to the other. On the garment the following are inscribed and show forth their description: the force, nature, power, order, matter, divisions, purpose, title and author, function, species, genus, tools and capacity of the art of grammar.[34] There authority is given to the art and rules hold sway, deficiencies suffer exile and know not how to merit pardon. Facing indefinite rejection at grammar's hands, defending itself on account of

---

[32] I.e. Grammar is a virgin who nevertheless gives the appearance of having given birth.

[33] Cf. Martianus Capella, *De nuptiis* 3.226.

[34] That is, an extrinsic prologue to the art of grammar as a whole, as found, for example, in the introductions of the commentaries on Priscian by William of Conches and Petrus Helias. The notion of an inscription on Grammar's garment recalls Boethius, *De consolatione*, where the symbols of practical and theoretical sciences are woven into the hem of Philosophy's garment (1 pr. 1). As is suggested at the end of the section on Grammar, the depiction of the extrinsic prologue on the garment encompasses the whole of the grammatical lesson.

sufficient reason,[35] figure sleeps outside the doors and craves indulgence.[36] Art admits her, answers her prayer for indulgence but does not cherish her in her bosom but does, however, support her. Here art teaches, reason shows, instruction proclaims why a letter is termed simple and indivisible, why a letter borrows for itself the name "element" or why a letter is usually called "element" by way of metaphor,[37] what formation represents the elements,[38] what names indicate them, what is their total number,[39] what is their right order,[40] what is their pronunciation[41] and what brings all these matters under a definite rule; why the other letters, deprived of even a weak sound, when seeking expression, are mute while the vowel rings clear and gives other letters the breath of expression; what is the explanation of, and what lies behind, the fact that H is not a letter,[42] though it affects a writing-shape, a name and a use, but has only the status of a cipher and maintaining its right to a shape, bears but the shadow of an element. Here was to be seen how in poetry a vowel in conflict with another vowel melts away and loses the honour of being sounded;[43] how in poetry a letter loses its natural strength and its force, banished for a time, languishes; how in poetry one letter claims for itself the force and rights of two, by making good the loss of its fellow-letter; how the same syllable takes on different tones;[44] a grave accent lowers it, an acute raises it, a circumflex rounds it. There could be seen there what the letter can successfully claim as its own;[45] what the syllable can claim;[46] what the word[47] keeps as its own special right; what the noun rightly claims as its own;[48] what the verb appropriates;[49] what the pronoun chooses for itself;[50] what the other parts of speech keep

[35] *propria racione*. The translation of the phrase has been modified to capture the distinct echo of standard grammatical teaching about the "figure": a deviation from rules, made for a good reason (i.e. on account of necessity, meter, or for embellishment). Donatus, *Ars maior* 3.6, *GL* 4:399.14; Isidore, *Etymologies* 1.35.7.

[36] The order of this whole translated sentence has been changed slightly to bring out Alan's demonstration of the figure (or, as in Donatus, *schema*) *prolepsis*, where the subject is placed after its modifiers.

[37] *Elementum* is used for a letter of the alphabet. Cf. Priscian, *Institutiones* 1.4, *GL* 2:6.23 ff. "By way of metaphor," *tropice*.

[38] Cf. Priscian, *Institutiones* 1.2, *GL* 2:6.23ff.: "a letter is the notation of an element and as it were a picture of literate sound, which may be recognized by the quality and quantity of the form of the lines" (see section on Priscian, within, p. 174).

[39] Donatus, *Ars maior*, 1.2, *GL* 4:368.12; Priscian, *Institutiones* 1.5, *GL* 2:7.6ff

[40] Priscian, *Institutiones* 1.50, *GL* 2:37.5ff.   [41] Priscian, *Institutiones* 1.5, *GL* 2:7.5ff.

[42] Priscian, *Institutiones* 1.8; 1.16; 1.47 (in) *GL* 2:8.22; 12.20; 13.9; 35.24.

[43] I.e., an elision in poetry.   [44] Donatus, *Ars maior* 1.5, *GL* 4:371.

[45] Donatus, *Ars maior* 1.2, *GL* 4:367–8.

[46] Donatus, *Ars maior* 1.3, *GL* 4:368.18; Priscian, *Institutiones* 2, *De syllaba*, *GL* 2:44–53.

[47] Priscian, *Institutiones* 2.14, *GL* 2:53.8ff.

[48] Donatus, *Ars maior* 2.2–10 (*De nomine*), *GL* 4:373–9; Priscian, *Institutiones* 2.22ff. (*De nomine*), *GL* 2:56.27ff (*De nomine*).

[49] Donatus, *Ars maior* 2.12 (*De verbo*), *GL* 4:381–5.

[50] Donatus, *Ars maior* 2.11, *GL* 4:379–81; Priscian, *Institutiones* 12.1–12 (*De pronomine*), *GL* 2:577–84.

as their special rights; what a noun strictly denotes and what outside implications it takes on;[51] what a verb denotes;[52] what a pronoun indicates;[53] since pronouns point to subjects discussed why do they disdain the aid of declension;[54] why is demonstration their only help and why does it take the place of declension in them.[55] There could be seen on what basis part governs part or is governed by it; why a noun, taking the place of something or portraying something else, performs the function of matter and adds the idea of form; why the voice of a verb is active; why, passive; why nouns enter into a friendly pact with verbs and the noun joined to the verb fulfills its pact; unless noun and verb agree, speech will be mute and silent and the statement cut short will not give complete sense; why a word, formed partly from a noun and partly from a verb, repays each what is owed it and noun and verb together give a meaning that neither could separately, when the word, holding a middle position, effects a union between them.[56] There could be seen why the other parts of speech respect these (noun and verb), submit to them and refuse not to serve them. This series of pictures painted successively drenches the eyes with delight and serve the mind a feast. A very talented painter had painted it or rather, one more powerful than any painter, and the painting proclaims his skill.

The aforementioned maiden, setting about her special task, does not tremble though fear of the burden, is not broken by the prospect of the toil. She exerts herself at her special work. The very refractory material is finally subdued and yields to her will. The tools spoken of before lie inactive and are idle for a time, the tools with which she refines boyhood years. Adopting the role of a craftsman, she uses a craftsman's tools; she overcomes the instability of her material[57] and forces it though unwilling to serve her purposes; she tames the inflexible wood and dresses it to the shape of a pole.

Here a cultural medium gives a place to the artificers of grammar and makes them live with a new birth and a fitting life. There Donatus, grammar's leader, advocate and

---

[51] I.e., the meanings a noun acquires beyond its literal use; cf. Priscian, *Institutiones* 2.25, *GL* 2:59. 4ff.

[52] Donatus, *Ars maior* 2.12, *GL* 4:381.14–15.

[53] Donatus, *Ars maior* 2.11, *GL* 4:379.23–4; Priscian, *Institutiones* 12.1, *GL* 2:577.1–2.

[54] Priscian (*Institutiones* 17.61, *GL* 3:144.21–5) says that pronouns have no real declension, because while *mei* is genitive, it cannot be said to be the genitive of *ego*.

[55] For Priscian (*Institutiones* 12.1 *GL* 2:577.14), the first and second personal pronouns are always demonstrative because "a person who is present is indicated." The other pronouns are demonstrative if the person or object is present and relative if they are not.

[56] I.e. the participle, which takes gender and case from the noun, tense and voice from the verb, and its number and figure (simple or compound) from both. See Donatus, *Ars maior* 2.14, *GL* 4:387.18–20.

[57] *materie fluxus*: a term familiar from the cosmological thought of twelfth-century philosophy, especially in the writings of Thierry of Chartres. See Häring, ed., *Commentaries on Boethius by Thierry of Chartres and his School*, 161.30; 270.41; 273.41; 275.96 and 17; 303.8; 525.50.

heir, teaches the rules of grammar, corrects mistakes, ennobles, exalts, enriches, defends, adorns grammar by scholarship, exhortation, zeal, reasoning, inflection.[58] He earns himself a special name so that he is not called grammarian but emphasis calls him *Mr. Grammar*, indicating the divinity under the name.[59] Our friend, Aristarchus, heaps offerings on the art of grammar, enlarges her treasures, increases her riches and measures his power in her. Dindimus gathers together the tattered shreds of grammar and assigns each to its proper place in the plan.[60] Our Apostate strings out tracts on grammar and, somewhat tiresome in style, is the victim of sluggish dreams. As he strays far and wide in his writings, he is thought to be drunk or quite insane or to be drowsy. He falters in his faith to prevent the reputation of its book from faltering and he sells his faith not to lose the sales from his book; his faith goes astray to prevent popular fame from straying away from him.[61]

This painting contains only those artificers whose reputation has blessed them with long-standing praise and the glory of whose work has not fallen from fame. It disdains to recognise base grammarians who rejoice in mere husks, whom the richness of the marrow within does not set apart: if they seek chippings from the outside, content with mere shells, they cannot taste the flavour of the nut.[62]

---

[58] "reasoning, inflection": *racione, figura*. This sentence exemplifies several *schemata*, notably *zeugma*, where the word "grammar" is the object of many verbs, and *hypozeuxis*, where each verb in turn has its corresponding dative of means ("ennobles . . . by scholarship, exalts . . . by exhortation," etc.). In addition, in the Latin verses, a word in one line is linked to the word in the same position in the next line, to achieve a symmetrical distribution or pattern: on this elaborate versification form, *singula singulis* (which can go across a line or line to line), used by Sidonius Apollinaris, see Eberhard the German, *Laborintus*, in Faral, ed., *Les arts poétiques*, 361–2, lines 669–704; and Raynaud de Lage, *Alain de Lille*, 157–8.

[59] "*Mr. Grammar*": *grammatica*; i.e. Donatus is grammar incarnate.

[60] Aristarchus (ca. 216–144 BC), Greek grammarian and textual critic, founder of a school at Alexandria, mentioned in Horace, *Ars poetica* 450; "Dindimus": Didymus (first century BC), Greek grammarian and textual critic, a member of the school founded by Aristarchus at Alexandria, mentioned in Priscian's *Institutiones*, *GL* 2:15.4 and 445.14, and *GL* 3:408.6 and 492.8.

[61] Priscian's *Institutiones* was dedicated to "Julian, consul and patrician," who commissioned the work. This is probably the source of the confusion about Priscian's book being received by the emperor Julian the Apostate. Priscian lived, not in the age of Julian (AD 361–363), but of Anastasius (491–518). The confusion is not new with Alan's pronouncement here, although the influence of the *Anticlaudianus* lent the misidentification further authority: see Hugh of Trimberg, within, p. 661. In his commentary on the *Anticlaudianus*, Ralph of Longchamps also continues the story of Priscian's apostasy: "Julian the Apostate told Priscian that his book would not be accepted, but rather destroyed, unless he (Priscian) renounced his faith, which he did even though he was a deacon" (ed. Sulowski, 120).

[62] Mockery of the pedantic, superficial grammarian is a *topos* of later Roman writings: see, e.g., Seneca, *Epistulae morales* 108; Aulus Gellius, *Noctes Atticae* 11.1.5; 15.9.6; 16.7.13.

FROM BOOK 3

No way inferior in refinement and appearance, taking second place to none among the arts, the third maiden[63] does not defraud the chariot of her service. She calls her mind into action; when it has answered the call, she fixes it on the projected work and directs her hand under the guidance of her mind. She applies those hands which give the finishing touch, brings the work of her sisters to perfection and adds embellishment to the thing just produced.[64] She raises to the superlative degree what on its production was in the positive degree and did not attain the glory of the upper limits but was restricted to a secondary position. It is no wonder that, in giving added embellishment to things previously produced, she perfects them and gives the charm of further refinement, since beauty and grace of form smile on her, because she outstrips her peers in many of the painter's skills and enfolds in her bosom the complete art of the painter.

Her locks reflecting the gloss of gold lie adorned with wondrous artistry: her hair falls down to cover her neck. Her countenance is steeped in radiant colour;[65] a brilliant red glow tints her face with roseate lustre but a foreign glitter haunts her face to some extent and tries to combine with the native hue.[66] Now a many-streamed flood of tears bedews her face; now the oft-changing smile of dawn makes it fair, as it chases away the tears of sorrow; now the maid adopts a countenance stern with a dignified inflexibility; now her eyes turn their gaze on high; now this high gaze is lowered; now turning her full keen glance to the side, she seeks the shade of digression.[67] In her right hand she bears a

---

[63] Rhetoric. The description of Rhetoric is preceded by the description of Logic.

[64] This commonplace about rhetoric, that it adds embellishment to an existing product, involves identifying the whole art with *elocutio* or style, which classical rhetoric treats last in the building of the text. See the introductory essay, "Figurative Language in Grammar and Rhetoric," above, pp. 28–38.

[65] Colors (*colores*) and coloring are frequently used to describe style in Rhetoric.

[66] "foreign glitter haunts her face" (*candor peregrinus inheret*), i.e. rhetoric was imported into Latinity from another culture, Greece; cf. Cicero, *De inventione* 1.5.7; Martianus Capella, *De nuptiis* 5:427–36; Isidore, *Etymologiae* 2.2. The phrase *candor peregrinus inheret*, describing the allegorical figure Rhetoric, is also found in the *De consolatione rationis* by the so-called Petrus Compostellanus, ed. Soto, 62, line 25. This work has not been conclusively dated, but was long thought to be from the middle of the twelfth century, leading Sheridan to assume that Alan of Lille borrowed this line (and other unusual language) from the text: see Sheridan, "The Seven Liberal Arts in Alan of Lille and Peter of Compostella." Opinion has shifted in favor of a mid-fourteenth-century date for the work: see Briesemeister, "The *Consolatio philosophiae* in Medieval Spain." On this argument, Petrus Compostellanus borrowed from Alan of Lille and other twelfth-century authors, including Bernardus Silvestris' *Cosmographia*. See the study by Gonzalez-Haba, *La obra De consolatione rationis de Petrus Compostellanus*.

[67] Alan summarizes the various facial expressions and gestures of the orator. The final reference is to *digressio*. In this the orator speaks of something only very vaguely connected with the case, e.g. reference to some other

trumpet, her left she decks with a horn and on it she gives the signal for the preliminary exercises of the war. A garment covers her: painted in various colours, it rejoices that it is overlaid with various hues. Here with the painter's aid gleams a picture of Rhetoric's power of colour and thus a picture adds colour to a picture. Here, as in a book, one reads:[68] what is the end in view; who is the orator; what are Rhetoric's species; what is its role; what is a lawsuit; what is arrangement; what is the special domain of Rhetoric; what is its special excellence; how at one time it thunders over us with threats, again flashes with the light of words, now pours forth prayers, now fills the ear with praise; what establishes the genera in Rhetoric; what the aim of Rhetoric is; to what terminal point it is making its way when it discusses the useful, decides what is just, confirms the right, designates the honourable; what are the parts of the art, by what arrangement they are connected; how at first the art discovers arguments, then arranges them, gets the fitting style, memorizes them, delivers them, so that in the regular scheme of arrangement, arrangement may make a fitting arrangement for itself; what and how many parts the orator's speech has and by what sequence they are knit together; how the exordium stirs the judge's mind, makes him prick his ears, sharpens his attention, conditions his heart so that the auditor becomes more attentive, more tractable, more kindly disposed and devotes his attention to what he hears; how the narrative is a brief exposition of the truth or of the falsehood lurking beneath the guise of truth; how the partition brings together in summary fashion all that is to follow, collecting together what is scattered, compressing what is prolix; how a statement favouring our side highlights the arguments, establishes them, sets them forth, structures them, draws inferences from them;[69] how a refutation is a blow to the opposite side, ruins them, weakens them, breaks them up, puts pressure on them;[70] in what way the peroration, rounding out the several parts, brings the speech to a close with a regular end and reins in the discourse; which deed or type of deed or alleged deed[71] does a point at issue look for when it is supported by several lines of argument,[72] which suit involves a dispute about a fact,[73] which a question of law,[74] what and how many kinds of issues are there, which issue is simple, which has a connection with something else and what are the constituents of this connection,[75] why this aspect intensifies the charges in the accusation, that calls for a

cases that might emphasize a point for himself. Cicero does not treat this as one of the proper divisions of the speech (*De inventione* 1.51.97).

[68] For the following list of topics, cf. the extrinsic prologue to the commentary on Cicero's rhetorical texts by Thierry of Chartres, above, pp. 411–15.

[69] A reference to *confirmatio*, the positive side of proof. Cf. Cicero, *De inventione* 1.31.143.

[70] *Refutatio*, the negative side of proof. Cf. *De inventione* 1.31.143.

[71] *De inventione* 2.17.52.   [72] Cicero, *Topica* 25.95; cf. Quintilian, *Institutio oratoria* 3.6.

[73] Cicero, *De inventione* 2.4.14.   [74] Cicero, *Topica* 25.95.

[75] *De inventione* 1.12.17; cf. Quintilian, *Institutio oratoria* 3.10.1.

change of court,[76] another rebuts, still another, weighing advantages and disadvantages, finds them equal;[77] how a case on either side gains strength when a law clashes with and opposes a kindred law[78] or the intent disagrees with and conflicts with the letter of the law[79] or an ambiguous sentence in the written law gives rise to a doubt[80] or when a word can be so defined that the undisputed definition removes the ambiguity[81] or when by a judicial point of place, person, time, the case itself is changed to another court[82] and will cause confusion elsewhere or if a claim, covered by no definite law, is being urged and obtains support by an argument from analogy;[83] in what way a person's character arms and strengthens the arguments, while arguments based on name, disposition, mode of life, fortune showing harassed face, habit, feeling, plan that miscarried, interests, accident, speeches, achievements, fail as they have only the appearance of strength;[84] what things have sequels, what does a question of act include, what are inseparable adjuncts of a deed or what, as circumstances demand, follows it in the normal course of events; what is the manner of performing the deed, what are the constituents of the deed, what is the place, time, occasion, motive, opportunity.[85]

One part of the garment has this representation of the art of Rhetoric, the other, however, shows the outlines of its artificers. There Marcus[86] makes Rhetoric a child adopted by him alone or rather fathers it: thus this art will rightly be called Cicero's daughter since Tullius begets her and the art tracing its origin to him may well be called Tullia.[87] There Ennodius bedecks his poems with many a flower and smoothes out all rough edges from his discourse.[88] Quintilian is here, cloaking fictitious cases with the appearance of real ones; he sets forth a new type of hypothetical lawsuit and forces us into the courts with no actual issue at stake. Symmachus, sparing of words, profound in mind, expansive in intellect, restricted in diction, rich in intelligence, somewhat poor in expression, happy in his fruit rather than his foliage, compresses richness of intellect by conciseness of language.[89] The discourses of Sidonius, in ceremonial dress, gleaming with many a star, flash forth and glitter with gems of colour and the painted peacock

---

[76] *De inventione* 2.19.57.   [77] *De inventione* 1.52.78; cf. *Institutio oratoria* 4.2.26.

[78] *De inventione* 2.49.144; *Institutio oratoria* 3.6.84, 3.7.7.

[79] *De inventione* 2.42.121; cf. *Institutio oratoria* 7.6.1.

[80] *De inventione* 2.40.116; cf. *Institutio oratoria* 7.10.1.   [81] *De inventione* 2.5.153; cf. *Institutio oratoria* 7.10.3.

[82] *De inventione* 2.19.57; cf. *Institutio oratoria* 3.6.46.   [83] *De inventione* 2.50.148; cf. *Institutio oratoria* 3.6.87.

[84] This refers to the attributes of the person; see *De inventione* 1.24.34.

[85] Attributes of the act; see *De inventione* 1.26.38.   [86] Marcus Tullius Cicero.

[87] Cicero's only daughter was called Tullia.

[88] Ennodius, bishop of Pavia, wrote model speeches in an ornate style that combined pagan and Christian elements. See the *Opusculum* VI, ed. Ritter von Hartel, 401–10.

[89] Symmachus, writer of the fourth century AD, representing here the plain style.

finds an echo in his words.[90] Now he exercises his delicate Muse on a slender reed; yet it is not an anaemic discourse bewailing its hunger. Now he holds a middle course, neither falling to the depths nor swelling to the heights; now he thunders, as he treats serious matters in high-sounding words; now in bombast he rumbles with loud, windy noise. Gay in this attire, the maiden does not refuse the aid of her art but rather her skill in production is given in abundance to the chariot's formation. She bespangles the pole with the beauty of gems and sets it in a class apart; she clothes it liberally in silver and the highest decoration is brought in to supplement the wooden material, which has less distinction and this decoration compensates for the wood's inferior status. An adoptive splendour hides wood's primeval origin from sight and removes every basis for complaint; the old age of wood disappears and thus it forgets its primeval origins.[91] A star-cluster of gems, then, gilds the pole; in fact its light restores true day and the actual day grows dull, for the natural light of day sinks down in admiration before an adoptive light so great. The maiden in like manner traces many a flower on the axle and with fresh blooms makes the steel grow young again. Though steel is usually rigid with the stiffness of cold and reminds one of deep Winter's frost, this steel knows no Winter, leaves behind its congenital cold, establishes its claim to the smiling joys of Spring and with its pattern of flowers sets before us a view of meadow. While the maiden thus enlivens the pole with gems and flowers, giving it the ultimate in ornament, the trumpet gives place to the painter's reed, the horn makes way for an engraver's burin and thus these two assume the rights of the other pair.

[90] Sidonius Apollinaris (see above, note 12) represents all three styles, the plain, the middle, and the grand.
[91] Bernardus Silvestris, *Cosmographia* 1.1.1–1.2.35.

ALEXANDER NECKAM, A LIST OF TEXTBOOKS (FROM *SACERDOS AD ALTARE*), CA. 1210

INTRODUCTION

The Englishman Alexander Neckam (1157–1217; also called Nequam)—schoolmaster at Dunstable and St. Albans, scholar and teacher at Paris, teacher in the Oxford schools, canon and finally abbot of the Augustinian abbey at Cirencester—brought his polymathic interests to his grammatical teaching at all levels. Neckam produced a remarkable array of writings, always witty, and often breathtaking in their range of subject matter and quality of learning.[1] His major encyclopedic works, the prose *De naturis rerum* (On the Nature of Things; ca. 1204) and the verse *Laus sapientiae divinae* (Praise of Sacred Wisdom; ca. 1213) sum up the information that he collected and purveyed, often in minute detail, across his many other writings.[2] One way by which we can know or surmise a great deal about his scholarly practices, his habits of working, are his grammatical commentaries, his reworkings of curricular authors, lexicographical works and vocabulary lists, and the list of textbooks translated below. Sometimes he incorporates various of these elements in one text, and some of his other writings contain cross-references to his grammatical works or borrowings from them. Neckam was a consummate grammar master, devising approaches for all levels of teaching, and recording his pedagogy in prose and verse.

Neckam's first major grammatical work was the *De nominibus utensilium* (On the Names of Useful Things), dating from sometime after 1177, during the general period when he is known to have been a schoolmaster at Dunstable and St. Albans (although it is also during this period, sometime between 1175 and 1182, that he would have been studying in Paris).[3] Whenever it was composed, it is a vivid testimony to the teaching of Latin at the

---

[1] R. W. Hunt, *The Schools and the Cloister: The Life and Writings of Alexander Nequam*, 1–31.

[2] *De naturis rerum, De laudibus divinae sapientiae*, ed. Wright; see also *Suppletio defectuum: A Supplement to the Laus sapientie divine*, ed. and trans. McDonough.

[3] For the text, see T. Hunt, *Teaching and Learning Latin in Thirteenth-Century England*, 1:177–90. For chronology, see R. W. Hunt, *The Schools and the Cloister*, 3–4.

simplest level and had wide success as a teaching text. It gives a lexicon of Latin words (some classical, some medieval) for everyday objects. It was often transmitted with similar works by Adam of Petit Pont (*De utensilibus*, from the middle of the twelfth century) and John of Garland (*Dictionarius*, from about 1220). In Neckam's text, as in these other related works, the lexicon is presented through descriptive prose rather than just a list of words. In thematic clusters Neckam's *De nominibus utensilium* covers such subjects as the kitchen, food, and cooking; storerooms and closets; going out on foot or horseback; the house and its rooms, furnishings, and features; and various other aspects of quotidian life, including the equipment of a scribe:

> Scriptor habeat rasorium sive novaculum ad radendum sordes pergameni vel membrane. Habeat etiam pumicem mordacem et planulam ad purgandum et equandum superficiem pergameni. Plumbum habeat et linulam, quibus lineatur pergamenum, margine circumquaque tam ex parte tergi quam ex parte carnis existente libera.
>
> A scribe should have a razor [*rasorium*] or a *novaculum* [razor] to scrape away the filth of the parchment or skin. He should have a rough pumice stone and a little plane for cleaning and levelling out the surface of the parchment. He should have a plumb and line with which the parchment may be lined, with a clear margin on every side, on the outer side as well as on the flesh side.[4]

Here we gain a precious insight into the relationship between grammatical thought and formal grammatical precept, on the one hand, and on the other hand, the practical implications of teaching Latin as an acquired but still living language. During the same period that he composed *De nominibus utensilium* he reworked two standard works of the elementary curriculum, the Aesopic fables (known through Latin versions) and the fables of Avianus.[5] In some cases, his renderings of the fables wear their origins or roles in classroom exercises very clearly. In his Avianus collection, Neckam presents the story of the Eagle and the Tortoise in three versions: *copiose* (thirty-two lines), *compendiose* (ten lines), and *succincte* (four lines), pointing to the exercises in amplifying and abbreviating a set text that had been practiced since antiquity, and that Geoffrey of Vinsauf illustrated with such piquancy in his three versions of the "Snow Child" story.[6]

The other two major grammatical writings date from the period when he was a canon of Cirencester, that is, from ca. 1197 through the first decade of the thirteenth century, the

---

[4] Hunt, *Teaching and Learning Latin*, 1:188.

[5] For Neckam's Aesop see Hervieux, ed., *Les Fabulistes latins*, 2:392–416; for his Avianus, see Hervieux, ed., *Les Fabulistes latins*, 3:462–7.

[6] See the section on Geoffrey of Vinsauf in Part 4 below.

same period when he wrote his encyclopedia, *De naturis rerum*. The earlier of these was the tremendously popular *Corrogationes Promethei*, a title whose meaning modern scholars have interpreted variously.[7] This work comprises two sections: first, a grammatical treatise and commentary on Donatus and Priscian; second, a set of literal glosses on selected passages of Scripture, generally aimed at explaining difficult words. In these glosses Neckam sometimes uses Anglo-Norman words as equivalents.[8] He clearly designates the *Corrogationes* as a work for beginners: "I propose to teach the least instructed," he says at the beginning, warning off from his treatise those who have attained the height of the art.[9] The immediate audience of beginners, the students who would have been the first beneficiaries of this school text, would presumably have been the young pupils of the abbey of Cirencester. Yet his prologue on grammar offers an important theoretical pronouncement on the definition of the art, indicating the increasing identification of grammar with logical study that we see in the northern French schools of the twelfth century. Like those grammatical thinkers, Neckam attempts to find in grammar an order that arises from nature, to give some grounding to its human-imposed rules. Construction (that is, the ordering of words in a way that is congruent or in agreement) has its basis in a natural order of intelligibility; a correct combining of such grammatical features as the nominative case with a personal verb makes sense to us because this is based in our understanding of agreement and non-agreement: "The nature of intelligible congruities naturally precedes agreement of (grammatical) expression . . . The regulation of construction follows the law of intelligibility."[10] With the notion of intelligibility at stake, Neckam advances an important argument about the definition of grammar itself:

> From these (examples), it is clear that grammar is an art of understanding. Those who say that grammar is the "art of correct writing and correct speaking" describe it inadequately. They omit what is foremost in the art. They ought to add: "and of

---

[7] Meyer, "Notice sur les *Corrogationes Promethei* d'Alexandre Neckam," taking *corrogationes* as *congregationes* (compilations), suggested "Travaux d'un homme condamné à l'oisiveté," because Prometheus was condemned to idleness when he was chained to the rock, and used the enforced leisure to study the heavens; thus Neckam's text is the product of some kind of enforced leisure. Hunt, *The Schools and the Cloister*, 36, interpreted the title to mean "Collections of an instructor in the rudiments," because medieval mythographers viewed Prometheus as a teacher imparting knowledge. There is no complete edition of this work, but Meyer, "Les *Corrogationes Promethei*," prints long extracts from one of the manuscripts.

[8] For the Anglo-Norman glosses, see Hunt, *Teaching and Learning Latin*, 1:235–46.

[9] Meyer, "Les *Corrogationes Promethei*," 658; in the *De naturis rerum* he describes the *Corrogationes* as a work aimed at instructing those who are unformed (ed. Wright, 16).

[10] Meyer, "Les *Corrogationes Promethei*," 650. Here Neckam is pursuing questions that were also key among the major grammarians of the twelfth century, including William of Conches and Petrus Helias. See Reilly, ed., introduction to Petrus Helias, *Summa super Priscianum* 1:38–41, and see also Petrus Helias' discussion of agreement in construction, 2:870–1.

correct understanding." But understanding what? It seems rather that dialectic ought to be called an art of understanding, without whose help no one, in truth, ought to be called one who understands perfectly... So dialectic alone, as the queen of the arts, will seem to be the art of understanding. But here it is necessary to distinguish among different properties of understanding. Dialectic applies to understanding true or false. But grammar applies to understanding agreement and non-agreement. Therefore either one can be said to be a science of understanding. Grammar has rules, dialectic has axioms, and rhetoric has commonplaces.[11]

For all that it purports to aim at rank beginners, the *Corrogationes Promethei* makes a profound claim for the intellectual scope of grammar. With the claim that it is an art of understanding, Neckam at once ennobles grammar and tries to bridge the widening gulf between the study of grammar as a literary art of language and the highly theoretical orientation of its study in the advanced schools.

The last of Neckam's major grammatical writings is the *Sacerdos ad altare*, named for its opening phrase, *Sacerdos ad altare accessurus* ("A priest who is about to approach the altar"). Its main text was written late in the first decade of the thirteenth century. It survives in only one known manuscript, Cambridge, Gonville and Caius College MS 385/605, a grammatical collection from the second half of the thirteenth century containing many works by John of Garland.[12] The text is accompanied by extensive grammatical, lexico-graphical, etymological, or literary and historical glosses clearly linked by lemmata to particular sections, and often quoting or referring to other works by Neckam. Some of the glosses use Anglo-Norman vocabulary. The *Sacerdos ad altare* was first identified and discussed by Charles Homer Haskins, who believed the gloss to have been composed by Neckam himself.[13] Neckam's authorship of these glosses (often quite vast in proportion to the text) has now been confirmed on the basis of a florilegium of Neckam's works dating from the mid-thirteenth century. The gloss is in a less polished state than the text, suggesting that Neckam may have continued working on this component up to the point when he became abbot in 1213.[14]

In many respects the *Sacerdos ad altare* is a text like the *Corrogationes Promethei* and the *De nominibus utensilium*: it describes and analyzes various aspects of priestly, monastic, eccle-

---

[11] Meyer, "Les *Corrogationes Promethei*," 660.

[12] For a description of the manuscript, see Jeudy, "Israël le grammairien et la tradition manuscrite du commentaire de Rémi d'Auxerre à *l'Ars minor* de Donat," 209–11.

[13] Haskins, "A List of Text Books from the Close of the Twelfth Century." Hunt also assumed the glosses were by Neckam (*The Schools and the Cloister*, 29).

[14] For the proof of Neckam's authorship of the glosses and further analysis of them, see McDonough, "Cambridge, University Library, Gg. 6. 42, Alexander Neckam and the *Sacerdos ad altare*." Hunt, *Teaching and Learning Latin*, 1:250–73, prints some of the glosses.

siastical, courtly, clerical, and even scribal life by accumulating information and vocabulary about them. Its audience would also have been students at the monastic school, but it operates at a more advanced level than the other works. The *Sacerdos ad altare* culminates in a broad curricular survey, itself encyclopedic in scope, that moves from the rudiments of grammar and the classical literary canon to the other elements of the trivium and quadrivium, and to medicine, canon law, and civil law, ending with the sacred knowledge of Scripture. Text and gloss together form a transitional work. The curricular survey looks back to those great themes of twelfth-century arts scholars, the unity of the sciences and the canon of classical authors; but it also has a more professional outlook, reflecting the range of scientific developments and specializations throughout the twelfth century, including medicine at the school of Salerno and civil law at Bologna. The treatment of grammar is both traditional and new: on the one hand, the text cites the old, standard works by Donatus and Priscian that had been the focus of energetic scholarly commentary during the twelfth century and that Neckam himself studied and perhaps taught in Paris; on the other hand, the gloss shows Neckam taking account of a new work, the *Doctrinale* of Alexander of Villa Dei, the comprehensive verse grammar completed in 1199 which was to grow in popularity to such a degree that it would come to supplant the old works on grammar.[15]

Suzanne Reynolds gives a close study of the first section of the *Sacerdos ad altare* as "an anthropology of reading, where there is a direct correlation between stage of life, reading ability and the kind of text that it is permissible to read."[16] The beauty of Neckam's curricular list is that it lays out quickly, almost in shorthand, an entire life's course of learning (reaching into more areas than it would be possible for one person to master completely), but at the same time indicates clearly the graduated stages at which the learner leaves one subject to approach the next. As a formal study, grammar is a more advanced subject than Latinity or learning to read. The basic text of Latinity is Donatus' *Ars minor*, which the boy will learn after he has the alphabet and other "rudiments." After this come the medieval standards from the *Liber catonianus* (Theodulus' *Ecloga* and the *Disticha Catonis*), and then the classical literary canon, graded more or less from poetry to prose (along the lines of the Roman grammatical curriculum, presented, for example, in Quintilian's *Institutio oratoria*), but also roughly by subject matter, from the great mythological, elegiac, and satiric writers to the moralists and historians, arriving finally at the great Seneca. The accomplished range of reference surely derives from *florilegia*. Whether he imagines the children covering all of these materials or is just setting out a list of suggested readings, it is clear that this reading is the foundation for a now advanced and rigorous entry into the

---

[15] See Hunt, *The Schools and the Cloister*, 30 n. 65. Neckam cites the *Doctrinale* by name four times in the gloss.
[16] Reynolds, *Medieval Reading*, 8.

trivium proper. Grammar, dialectic, and then rhetoric are elevated theoretical studies. Donatus' *Ars maior*, with its section on schemes and tropes, and Priscian's treatment of syntax (the *De constructione* or last two books of the *Institutiones grammaticae*), represent the deepest theoretical reach of grammatical study. The brevity of the entry on rhetoric is deceptive: in fact, Neckam is recommending a complete course in the Ciceronian "renaissance" of the twelfth century. Imperceptibly, the child has graduated to the highest levels of learning. The graduated ascent through the liberal arts is formulated explicitly: "Thus from the rules of grammar the student may pass to the greatest matters of dialectic, then to the commonplaces of rhetoric, and after to the complex arguments of arithmetic, and last to the axioms of music. Then he can pass to the theorems of geometry...At last, [he turns his] attention seriously to the secrets of astronomy." All the stages of this progress through the arts are required: only after this is there an elective element, so that if the student "wishes" to know medicine or law, Neckam will supply a foundational reading list. A deep knowledge of sacred Scripture is reserved for the mature mind.

Translated from Hunt, *Teaching and Learning Latin in Thirteenth-Century England*, by permission.

A student who is to be educated in the liberal arts should carry a wax tablet on which anything noteworthy may be written. Let him suffer the "palmer" or slap of the hand or the ferule by which a boy's hand is more lightly struck for minor offenses; let him yield to the rod when he has failed to do something that he ought. Without scourges and whips there is no means of correction. After he has learned the alphabet and has been instructed in other rudimentary matters suitable for children,[17] let him learn Donatus[18] and that useful compendium of moralities which common opinion attributes to Cato, and let him move on from the *Ecloga* of Theodulus[19] to the eclogues of the *Bucolics*,[20] but having read beforehand certain little books containing necessary instruction for youthful ignorance. Then let him read the satirists and historians, so that while he is young he may learn what kinds of actions are to be avoided and what noble actions of heroes he should seek to imitate. From the delightful *Thebaid* let him pass to the divine *Aeneid*; but let him not

---

[17] On this passage and instruction in such "rudiments," see Reynolds, *Medieval Reading*, 8–10.

[18] I.e. the *Ars minor*.

[19] On the importance of this ninth- or tenth-century poem in the elementary curriculum of the following centuries, see Green, "The Genesis of a Medieval Textbook: The Models and Sources of the *Ecloga Theoduli*." For further discussion of its place among the elementary readings of the *Liber catonianus* ("Cato book"), see Hunt, *Teaching and Learning Latin*, 1:59–79, and Reynolds, *Medieval Reading*, 7–16. An important commentary on the poem is ascribed in two manuscripts to Alexander Neckam, and his name is mentioned in a number of other copies of this commentary: see Quinn, "Ps-Theodolus," 389–90.

[20] Virgil's *Bucolics* (perhaps referring here to selections from them); the *Bucolics* are also mentioned below.

neglect the prophet born in Cordova who described not just civil wars but internecine conflict.[21] Let him take to heart the moral sayings of Juvenal and let him studiously shun disgrace[22] to the greatest extent of his nature. Let him read the *Satires* and *Epistles* of Horace, and the *Ars poetica* and the *Odes* and *Epodes*. Let him hear the "Elegies"[23] of Naso and the *Metamorphoses* of Ovid, but let him be especially familiar with the *Remedia amoris*. On the other hand it has pleased grown men that the song of love along with the satires[24] be taken out of adolescent hands, as if it was said to them: "Ye who cull flowers and low-growing strawberries, away from here, lads; a chill snake lurks in the grass."[25] Some people feel that the *Fasti* should not be read.[26] Men have found Statius' *Achilleid* to be a most profound work. The *Bucolics* and *Georgics* of Virgilius Maro are very useful. The works of Sallust, and Tully's *De oratore* and *Tusculanae disputationes* and *De amicitia* and *De senectute* and *De fato* are worthy of much commendation, along with the *Paradoxa stoicorum*. Some disapprove of the book called *De multitudine deorum*.[27] Tully's *De officiis* is most useful. Martial "Cocus"[28] and Petronius contain much that is of use, but also much that is offensive to the ears. Symmachus' brevity is admirable. I commend Solinus' *De mirabilibus mundi*,[29] and Sidonius, Suetonius, Quintus Curtius,[30] Pompeius Trogus,[31] Crisippus,[32] and Titus Livius, but you may also think it worthwhile for you to reread

---

[21] I.e. Lucan.

[22] Reading *flagitium* (from the gloss) for *flacium* in the text: see Hunt, *Teaching and Learning Latin*, 1: 269 n. 100.

[23] "Elegies," i.e. *Heroides*, although the title is more commonly *Epistulae*. See Hunt, *The Schools and the Cloister*, 48.

[24] "Song of love": *carmina amatoria*, presumably Ovid's *Amores*; "satires": presumably the *Ars amatoria*.

[25] *Eclogues* 3.92–3, trans. Fairclough.

[26] In his *Ecclesiale*, a calendar of the Christian year, Alexander of Villa Dei objected bitterly to the study of Ovid's *Fasti* (i.e. calendar), with its treatment of pagan religious observances, and singled out the school of Orleans for particular scorn because of the prominence given there to studies of Ovid (Arnulf of Orleans lectured on the *Fasti* and other works). The *Fasti* should be avoided in favor of a Christian calendar. See Alexander of Villa Dei, *Ecclesiale*, ed. Lind, line 55, deriding those who would read the falsehood "de fastis" (concerning the calendars/*Fasti*); and see the editor's introduction, 2 and explanatory notes, 105. Whether Neckam is referring directly to the *Ecclesiale* here is difficult to judge, because the composition of the *Ecclesiale* may postdate Neckam's work; but Neckam's reference to the *Fasti* shows his familiarity with contemporary debate.

[27] I.e. *De natura deorum*.

[28] On "Cocus" as a medieval epithet of Martial, see Huygens, ed., *Accessus ad auctores, Bernard d'Utrecht, Conrad d'Hirsau*, 62, note at line 110 of *Commentum in Theodolum*.

[29] Caius Julius Solinus (third century AD), *Collectanea rerum memorabilium*, ed. Mommsen. Neckam uses this source extensively in his own *De naturis rerum*. See also Hunt, *The Schools and the Cloister*, 120 n. 14, for identification with the Pseudo-Ovid, *De mirabilibus mundi* (eleventh century); and see M. R. James, "Ovidius *De mirabilibus mundi*," in E. C. Quiggin, ed., *Essays and Studies Presented to William Ridgeway* (Cambridge: Cambridge University Press, 1914), 286–98.

[30] Quintus Curtius Rufus (first or early second century AD), *Historia Alexandri Magni*, ed. Rolfe.

[31] The author of the lost "Philippic Histories," known through the epitome of Marcus Junianus Justinus.

[32] Haskins, "A List of Text Books," 373 n. 11, takes this as a name for Sallust.

Seneca's *Ad Lucilium* [*Epistulae morales*] and *De quaestionibus physicis*[33] and *De beneficiis*. It will not be useless to read his tragedy,[34] and his *Declamationes*.[35]

When he is about to give his attention to grammar, let him hear and read the *Barbarismus* of Donatus and the *Priscianus maior* with the *De constructione*,[36] . . . [*blank space in ms*] and let him carefully look over Remigius,[37] and Priscian, *De metris Terentii*,[38] the *De ponderibus*,[39] and the *Partitiones duodecim versum Aeneidos principalium*, and the *De accentibus* (although many reject the attribution of this last work to Priscian).[40]

Then when he desires to give serious attention to the liberal arts, let him hear the *De syllogismo categorico* published by Boethius, as well as his *Topica*[41] and *Liber de divisione*, Porphyry's *Isagoge*, Aristotle's *Categories*, *On Interpretation*, *Sophistical Refutations*, *Prior Analytics*, his *Apodoxim*,[42] and *Topics*, and Cicero's *Topica*, and Apuleius' book *On Interpretation*. Let him look carefully at the *Metaphysics* of Aristotle, and at his *Generation and Corruption* and the book *On the Soul*.[43] For teaching about rhetoric, let him first read Tully's

---

[33] I.e. *Quaestiones naturales*.

[34] *tragediam*: Hunt (*The Schools and the Cloister*, 490) suggests this may be a slip for *tragedias*. The whole corpus of Seneca's tragedies did not begin to be well known until later in the thirteenth century. On earlier circulation of the tragedies in extracts and as a corpus, see the articles by Rouse: "The *A* Text of Seneca's Tragedies in the Thirteenth Century" (on Neckam's knowledge see 113 and note 1), and "New Light on the Circulation of the A-Text of Seneca's Tragedies."

[35] The *Declamationes* (i.e. the *Controversiae* and *Suasoriae*) are the work of the Elder Seneca.

[36] I.e. the *Priscianus minor*.

[37] While no title for a work by Remigius is listed (and the name follows a blank space in the manuscript), the context calls for one of Remigius' well-known commentaries on the grammars of either Donatus (probably the *Ars maior* or the *Barbarismus*, since Donatus' *Ars minor* is not part of this advanced study of grammar) or Priscian (glosses on the *Partitiones XII versuum Aeneidos* and *Institutio de nomine pronomine verbo*). See Remigius of Auxerre, *Commentum in Martianum Capellam*, ed. Lutz, 1:12 for a list of the works on grammar; and see the articles by Jeudy: "La tradition manuscrite des *Partitiones* de Priscien," and "Un nouveau manuscrit du commentaire de Remi d'Auxerre à l'*Ars maior* de Donat." In the *Corrogationes Promethei*, Neckam takes some definitions from a commentary on Donatus, possibly that of Remigius, since he also cites Remigius there by name (Meyer, "Les *Corrogationes Promethei*," 662 and notes.)

[38] *GL* 3:418–29.

[39] *Carmen de ponderibus*, a work from late antiquity on weights and measures, often attributed to Priscian throughout the Middle Ages and the early Renaissance. See Raïos, *Recherches sur le Carmen de ponderibus et mensuris*, 27–8. Priscian's *De figuris numerorum* (*GL* 3:406–17) also contains a section *de ponderibus*.

[40] *GL* 3:519–28. The authenticity of the *De accentibus* had been questioned by Hugo of Pisa in his *De dubio accentu* (written before 1180), ed. Cremascoli, 71.

[41] I.e., *De differentiis topicis*.   [42] I.e. *Posterior Analytics*: see Haskins, "A List of Text Books," 373 n. 14.

[43] Hunt (*The Schools and the Cloister*, 68) notes that there is no evidence from his other writings that Alexander had used these three works. Haskins ("A List of Text Books," 373 n. 15) considers the possibility that these three works, which do not belong under a dialectic curriculum, may have been added by Neckam to his original list, when the works were still a novelty, but before the Paris proscription of 1210.

Rhetoric[44] and the *Ad Herennium*, and Tully's *De oratore* and Quintilian's *Cases* and Quintilian concerning the *Institutio Oratoria*.[45]

When he is to be informed about the institutes of arithmetic, let him read Boethius and Euclid.[46] Afterwards, let him read Boethius' *De musica*. Thus, from the rules of grammar the student may pass to the greatest matters of dialectic, then to the commonplaces of rhetoric, and after to the complex arguments [*aporismata*] of arithmetic, and last to the axioms of music. Then he can pass to the theorems of geometry, which Euclid set forth in artificial order. At last, when he is about to turn his attention seriously to the secrets of astronomy, let him approach the *Canons* of Ptolemy.[47] On the art which Ptolemy sets forth in full with the greatest subtlety, Alfraganus wrote a compendious introduction.[48]

Anyone who wants to plunge into the study of medicine,[49] in this way to serve the needs of the children of Adam, should pay attention to Johannicius.[50] He should study the *Aphorisms* as much as the *Prognostics* of Hippocrates, and the *Tegni* and *Pantegni* of Galen. Galen is the author, but the translator is Constantinus.[51] The student should read the

[44] I.e. *De inventione*

[45] What Neckam knows as Quintilian's *Causae* or "Cases" are in fact the *Declamationes* (i.e. *controversiae* or "cases") of the Pseudo-Quintilian, known from the major twelfth-century florilegia. On the *Florilegium Gallicum*, see Gagnér, *Florilegium Gallicum*, 121–3 for lists of texts excerpted in the major branches of the manuscripts; for studies see Hamacher, *Florilegium Gallicum: Prolegomena und Edition der Exzerpte von Petron bis Cicero*, and Burton, *Classical Poets in the Florilegium Gallicum*. It is from a version of this florilegium that Vincent of Beauvais derived his knowledge of the Pseudo-Quintilian *Causae*: see *De morali principis institutione*, ed. Schneider, xxxi n. 24. On the *Florilegium Angelicum*, see Rouse and Rouse, "The *Florilegium Angelicum*," esp. Appendix II. The *Declamationes* of the Pseudo-Quintilian are edited by Håkanson, *Declamationes XIX maiores Quintiliano falso ascriptae*. While Quintilian's *Institutio oratoria* circulated (although commonly in an incomplete form), it could also be known from florilegia, such as those above. See Munk Olsen, "Les classiques latins dans les florilèges médiévaux antérieurs au XIIIe siècle," and McGuinness, "Quintilian and Medieval Pedagogy." On Alexander's use of florilegia in general, see Hunt, *The Schools and the Cloister*, 44–50.

[46] The mention of Euclid is out of place here: see Haskins, "A List of Text Books," 374 n. 16.

[47] A revised and enlarged version of the *Almagest* tables.

[48] Al-Fargani (or Al-Farghani, in Latin known as Alfraganus), the ninth-century Persian astronomer. His *Elements*, a descriptive digest and explanation of Ptolemy's *Almagest*, was twice translated into Latin in twelfth-century Spain, by John of Spain (John of Seville) and then by Gerard of Cremona; from here its influence spread throughout medieval Europe.

[49] The texts listed in this section on medicine constitute an extended version of the corpus known as the *Articella,* the basic medical texts studied at Salerno, which achieved its greatest importance as a school of medicine in the twelfth century. For a survey of this tradition, see O'Boyle, *Thirteenth- and Fourteenth-Century Copies of the Ars Medicine*, i–xvi.

[50] *Johannicius*: the Latin name for Hunayn ibn Ishaq (d. 873), physician, philosopher, and theologian, active in Baghdad. See the valuable article on Hunayn by Anawati and Iskandar (*Dictionary of Scientific Biography*, 15). The Latin work known under the name "Johannicius" is the *Isagoge ad artem Galeni* (Introduction to Galen's Art), an adaptation, made by Constantine the African (or his circle), ca. 1080, of an introductory treatise on medicine by Hunayn. See Jacquart, "Aristotelian Thought in Salerno," 412–13.

[51] Constantine the African (fl. 1080), a Tunisian monk of Montecassino, was an important translator of Arabic and Greek medical texts. Among the works that he translated was a medical encyclopedia by Ali ibn al-Abbas al-Majusi,

Particulares dietae (Particular Diets) as well as the *Universales dietae* (Universal Diets) of Isaac and the *Liber urinarum* (Book of Urines),[52] and the *Viaticum* of Constantine,[53] along with the *Liber urinarum* and the *Liber pulsuum* (Book of Pulses),[54] and Dioscorides and Macer in which the natures of herbs are treated,[55] and the books of Alexander.[56]

The student to be instructed in ecclesiastical law should read Burchard,[57] the *Canons* or *Decretum* of Gratian,[58] and the *Decretals* of Ivo,[59] and the *Decretals* of Alexander III.[60]

One who desires expertise in civil law should first learn the *Institutes*, and one wishing to know the highpoints of law should hear the *Code* of Justinian, and each [of the parts called] *Digest* and the *Tres partes* and the *Infortiatum*.[61] One barely presumes to read the tenth book of the *Code*, and the eleventh and the twelfth, in view of their extraordinary difficulty.[62]

known in this translation as the *Pantegni* (*Universal Art*). Neckam mistakenly attributes the *Pantegni* to Galen. See Jacquart, "Aristotelian Thought in Salerno," 413–16; for studies on the *Pantegni*, see Burnett and Jacquart, eds., *Constantine the African and 'Alî ibn al-'Abbâs al-Magûsî*. *Tegni*: Galen's *Tekhnê* (*Art of Healing*), which was known in various Latin versions, one of which was produced (from an Arabic intermediary) by Gerard of Cremona.

[52]   These three works were the work of Isaac Judeus, translated by Constantine of Africa.

[53]   The *Viaticum*, translated by Constantine, was written by Ibn al-Jezzar, also known in the West by the name Isaac.

[54]   These two texts (along with the *Isagoge*, the *Aphorisms*, the *Prognostics*, and *Tegni*) formed the earliest grouping of the *Articella*. The *Book of Urines* was the work of the Byzantine physician Theophilos, and was translated from Greek around 1100; the *Book of Pulses*, in its Latin version attributed to Philaretus, was a Greek text that was well known in Byzantium and was also translated into Latin around 1100.

[55]   The *De materia medica* (*Peri hulês iatrikês*) of Dioscorides (first century AD) was the major ancient treatise on pharmacology, with a continuous history of influence. It was early translated into Latin, but was also abbreviated and interpolated. Neckam's citation of Dioscorides here along with Macer, as in his citation in his *De naturis rerum* (ed. Wright, 275), shows that he understands the work as an herbal treatise, a form of the *Herbarium Dioscoridis* mentioned by Cassiodorus (*Institutiones* 1.31). See Thorndike, *A History of Magic and Experimental Science*, 1:605–12. Macer Floridus is the putative author of the poem *De viribus herbarum*, written in the early twelfth century by the physician Odo of Meung.

[56]   Alexander of Tralles, Byzantine physician of the sixth century, whose *Therapeutica* was known to the West in a Latin (as well as Arabic) translation from at least the ninth century onwards. See Diels, *Die Handschriften der antiken Ärzte*, 11–13; Alexander of Tralles: Brunet, ed., *Oeuvres médicales d'Alexandre de Tralles*, 1:49; Langslow, *The Latin Alexander Trallianus*.

[57]   Burchard of Worms, ca. 965–1025, whose *Decretum* set the stage for the development of canon law in the following centuries

[58]   *Decretum* or *Concordia discordantium canonum*, written by Gratian ca. 1140, the authoritative text of canon law.

[59]   One of three canonical collections by Ivo of Chartres, composed around 1094.

[60]   Pope Alexander III (d. 1181).

[61]   For a historical explanation of this difficult passage, see Kantorowicz, "A Medieval Grammarian on the Sources of the Law," 39–44. Kantorowicz also prints (33–5) the long vocabulary gloss that corresponds to this text in the manuscript of the *Sacerdos ad altare*. The *Digest* had been divided, by conventions of study beginning in the eleventh century, into three parts: the *Digestum vetus*, the *Infortiatum* (including a subdivision, the *Tres partes*), and the *Digestum novum*; *vetus* and *novum* indicated place in the division ("first" and "last"), not "old" and "new." As the vocabulary gloss suggests, Neckam is pointing out—in the manner of a grammarian—that only two of the conventional parts of the *Digest* actually carry that name, but the student should read all the sections of the work.

[62]   The last three books of the *Code*, treating administrative law of the late Empire, were less comprehensible to medieval students. See Haskins, "A List of Text Books," 375 nn. 27 and 28.

A man of mature understanding who wants to hear the sacred page should hear the Old Testament as much as the New Testament. He should hear not only the Pentateuch, but the Heptateuch, that is, Genesis, Exodus, Leviticus, Numbers, Deuteronomy, Joshua, and Judges. Then let him hear Ruth and Kings and Chronicles (which the Hebrews call the Book of Days). Let him hear Ezra and Nehemiah and Tobias, Judith, and Esther. He will be happy if he comes upon the prophetic teachings contained in Ezekiel, Isaiah, Jeremiah, and Daniel, and in the book of the Twelve Prophets. Let the Book of Job shepherd the pious meditations of his heart. Let him approach Solomon's Book of Proverbs, Ecclesiastes, and Song of Songs. It will be as useful to hear the Book of Wisdom which is said to be by Philo as it will be to hear the book Ecclesiasticus which is attributed to Jesus the son of Sirach.[63] The Book of Maccabees will explain the battles of Judah and his brother Jonathan and Simon. How truly useful is the Book of Psalms no one can hope to explain faithfully in words. Someone desiring to know the New Testament should hear Matthew along with Mark, Luke, and John, the Epistles of Paul with the canonical epistles, the Acts of the Apostles, and the Apocalypse.

---

[63] See Isidore of Seville, *Etymologiae* 6.2.30–1.

PART 4
PEDAGOGIES OF GRAMMAR AND RHETORIC, CA. 1150–1280

INTRODUCTION

Beginning in the the second half of the twelfth century, several innovative kinds of instructional treatises emerged which drew upon the ancient grammatical and rhetorical traditions. New grammars updated the teaching of the art to accommodate contemporary intellectual and linguistic outlooks. In response to changing pedagogical needs in an expanding curriculum, new treatises on verse and prose composition combined the two dominant rhetorical traditions, Ciceronian oratory and Horace's poetic precept, bringing them under the capacious umbrella of grammatical instruction. The texts presented in this section exemplify various dimensions and stages in the pedagogical tradition of the arts of language: grammatical treatises; the *artes poetriae*, which draw on both grammatical and rhetorical precept; the early phase of the arts of preaching, in which we see the strong influence of grammatical thought about tropes and of rhetorical thought about argument and structure; the teaching about the literary canon, which came within the purview of the grammatical curriculum; and a late hybrid form of the arts of poetry and prose in which instruction in letter writing is incorporated into the grammatical framework of compositional theory.

To understand the context for the emergence of these various pedagogical initiatives, we must consider the expansion and diversification of grammatical teaching during the twelfth century. The preceding Part of this volume illustrates some key aspects of the philosophical study of grammar in the twelfth century. Commentaries on Priscian produced in the milieu of the northern cathedral schools went beyond the ancient text to seek out the causes of linguistic phenomena, notably the accidents of the parts of speech. Their interests were in the theoretical aspects of language, aimed at advanced students, rather than the practical training for which Donatus and Priscian had long been used. In this respect, the study of grammar followed a similar course to that of rhetoric, as we have seen: the commentaries by Thierry of Chartres and his contemporaries on the Ciceronian rhetorics paid close attention to the ancient texts in terms of various global philosophical orientations: the ethics of rhetoric, its relationship to dialectic, its status within a system and theory of knowledge, and the nature of an art itself.

But apart from such theoretical interests, there remained the practical orientation of grammatical teaching. This presented emerging concerns that could not be addressed adequately by the standard textbooks of late antiquity. Foremost here was the vastly changed historical context in which Latin grammar now had to be learned: students came to it from their own vernacular languages, and the Latin language itself had undergone change. Moreover, the need for comprehensive but more accessible grammars which could distill the precepts of Priscian's vast *Institutiones,* as well as develop teaching of the figures and tropes in Donatus' *Ars maior*, called for new kinds of grammatical texts. Two grammars produced at the turn of the twelfth century answered these needs with enormous success: the *Doctrinale* of Alexander of Villa Dei (1199) and the *Graecismus* of Eberhard of Béthune (traditionally dated 1212).[1] Both of these grammars were in verse, thus gaining them an immediate popularity in the schools, where their metrical form aided memorization of grammatical precept. Both works depended substantially upon Donatus and Priscian for their doctrine. Eberhard's *Graecismus* in particular represented an effort to counter recent philosophical approaches to Priscian's work in favor of a more down-to-earth approach to grammar. But both works also offered new materials for the study of grammar and modern approaches to the subject. The *Doctrinale* explicitly recognized that students would be learning Latin as a second language.[2] It also presented an updated approach to syntax, and it gave an extensive treatment of prosody and figures. Eberhard's *Graecismus* gave primary attention to etymology as well as to the figures and tropes, here pursuing an interest in the *ornamenta verborum* that had re-emerged with some vigor in the twelfth century.[3] In the thirteenth century, Henri d'Andeli was to name the *Graecismus* and the *Doctrinale* as "nephews" of Priscian, allies of grammar in the war against Parisian dialectic.[4] Such was the success of these texts that they came to rival Priscian's *Institutiones* as standard advanced grammars, studied in universities as well as in lower schools, and the object of continuous and sophisticated glossing through the later Middle Ages.

The new grammars, like their ancient sources, were normative and prescriptive, aimed at correctness of usage and reading, at comprehension, mastery, and application of rules. However, it was not the purpose of these grammars to teach about composition, that is, to give advice about how to compose whole texts. Of course, their attention to the figures and tropes, that is, to usage that departs from correctness in order to achieve a certain stylistic distinction, suggests their proximity to compositional teaching, that is, learning to apply

[1] For a general introduction to the twelfth-century pedagogical grammars, see Murphy, *Rhetoric in the Middle Ages*, 145–56, and "The Teaching of Latin as a Second Language in the Twelfth Century."

[2] For further discussion see Hunt, *Teaching and Learning Latin*, 1:433–7, and on the recognition of vernacular instruction in the *Doctrinale* see also Lusignan, *Parler vulgairement*, 38 (also cited in Hunt).

[3] See Grondeux, "Les figures dans le *Doctrinale* d'Alexandre de Villedieu et le *Graecismus* d'Évrard de Béthune," and Grondeux, *A la frontière entre grammaire et rhétorique*, 181–96; see also Camargo, "Latin Composition Textbooks."

[4] Lines 200–2 (see Part 5, within).

grammatical precept to the production of texts in order to exercise one's new facility in Latin. Nevertheless, the extension of grammatical "correctness" to the composition of a work or the creation of a style were not subjects explicitly addressed in the older traditional grammars or in their modern avatars. While it would have been understood that studying the rules of usage would lead to producing texts, the traditional grammatical textbooks did not pursue the subsidiary questions of how one develops a literary "style" or effectively deploys tropes and figures. Although their remit included the grammatical exposition of the canonical authors (*enarratio poetarum* or *auctorum*), the traditional grammars did not address how the pupil moves from this preliminary level of study to the next stage, compositional imitation of literary exemplars. This latter stage was certainly an important element of ancient grammatical teaching, as Quintilian indicates in his account of higher grammatical training in book 2 of the *Institutio oratoria*: Quintilian presents such grammatical composition as the pre-condition of advancement to the rhetorical program of instruction. From antiquity through the Middle Ages, the move from exposition to composition was the property of the grammarian's teaching. But the nature of the transition from one stage to the next was not fully articulated in grammatical textbooks.

Medieval grammar students were taught how to compose by imitating the examples from classical poetry which they also expounded for grammatical usage: in other words, composition was intimately connected with the central procedure of the grammatical classroom, *enarratio poetarum*. The tradition that spoke most immediately to the literary application of grammatical knowledge was that of Horace's *Ars poetica*. It is a prescriptive poetics, teaching and illustrating the principles of literary decorum and the faults of style, narrative coherence, generic consistency, and poetic license and its limitations. Importantly, it also teaches about the balance between imitating traditional materials and devising one's own subject matter. The *Ars poetica* had a long and unbroken history of commentary and of pedagogical importance. Late antique scholia were repeatedly copied along with the text throughout the Middle Ages. But some manuscripts, especially of the twelfth and thirteenth centuries, also attest to a persistent tradition of teachers providing their own glosses and commentaries on the text, going beyond the late antique glosses to link Horace's precepts to the circumstances of their own classroom teaching, and the compositional needs of their students.[5]

---

[5] Keller, ed., *Pseudacronis scholia in Horatium vetustiora*; Zechmeister, ed., *Scholia Vindobonensia ad Horatii artem poeticam*; and see the editions of Horace commentaries by Botschuyver, *Scholia in Horatium* (1935, 1939, 1942). See also Munk Olsen, *L'Étude des auteurs classiques latins*, 1:421–522. The tradition of glossing on Horace's poems is studied extensively in Reynolds, *Medieval Reading*. See also the notes in the selection from the "Materia" commentary, within, pp. 551–8.

An important example of such modern glossing on the *Ars poetica* is the mid-twelfth-century commentary known as the "Materia" commentary (from its opening phrase, *Materia huius auctoris*), from which we present a selection here. This commentary makes a significant contribution to the tradition of teaching composition as a part of grammatical training, because it develops Horace's advice about stylistic decorum and the corresponding faults of style into a simple, prescriptive list of six faults to avoid in composing poems. Its straightforward treatment of the six poetic faults may be the source for the very same prescriptive teaching found in the arts of poetry by Matthew of Vendôme, Geoffrey of Vinsauf, and John of Garland, as well as the *Summa de arte prosandi* (Summa on the Art of Prose) by Conrad of Mure (1276).

Horace's *Ars poetica* was never displaced from the grammatical curriculum, so foundational was its role. But it was the new genre of the arts of poetry that was most fully to answer the comprehensive needs of compositional training in the medieval grammar schools. This is the form that truly bridged descriptive treatises on language and prescriptive advice about how to generate a new text by imitating canonical models. The earliest of the arts of poetry was Matthew of Vendôme's *Ars versificatoria* (Art of Poetry or Versification), written ca. 1175. Within the following generations five more arts of poetry were written: Geoffrey of Vinsauf's *Poetria nova* (New Poetics, ca. 1208–1213) and *Documentum de modo et arte dictandi et versificandi* (Treatise on the Method and Art of Prose and Verse, before ca. 1213); Gervase of Melkley's *Ars versificaria* (Art of Versifying, ca. 1215–1216); John of Garland's *Parisiana poetria* ("Parisian" Poetics) (1231–1235); and Eberhard the German's *Laborintus* (written after ca. 1215, and probably in the second half of the thirteenth century). A later anonymous treatise (long thought to be a longer version of Geoffrey of Vinsauf's *Documentum*), known by its incipit as the *Tria sunt*, can be dated somewhere between 1256 and the end of the fourteenth century. We have presented excerpts from five of these texts here.[6]

The new genre of the *ars poetriae* advanced on the tradition of Horace's *Ars poetica* and its medieval glosses by showing how the teaching technique of *enarratio poetarum* could be turned to the purpose of generating texts. These new treatises brought a pragmatic grammar together with a pragmatic rhetoric, synthesizing the literary precept of Horace's *Ars poetica* with the rhetorical precept of Cicero's *De inventione* and the pseudo-Ciceronian *Rhetorica ad Herennium*. James J. Murphy has called them "preceptive grammars" because they are aimed at the future text.[7] They build on the long traditions of commentary

---

[6] For overviews of these works see Murphy, *Rhetoric in the Middle Ages*, 135–93, and Kelly, *The Arts of Poetry and Prose*.

[7] *Rhetoric in the Middle Ages*, 135; see also Kelly, "The Scope of the Treatment of Composition."

on ancient grammar, rhetoric, and poetic, but they stand as independent prescriptive treatises that adapt the older teachings to new purposes. The arts of poetry filled a need in the grammatical curriculum for a focused and consolidated approach to composition, a need which Horace's *Ars poetica*—for all of its sophisticated insight—could no longer fulfill by itself. The *Ars poetica* is elusive in its advice, it speaks to fellow poets rather than to students, and of course it assumes a native Latinity on the part of its Roman audience. The innovation of the medieval arts of poetry lay in the way that they combined three traditions: the formal and stylistic outlook of Horace's text; the more systematic Ciceronian teaching on composition and style; and the grammatical tradition of figures, tropes, and versification. The arts of poetry set out to grasp the literary text in its formal or structural entirety, just as the ancient rhetorics offered a theoretical grasp of the oratorical product, the speech and its argumentative structure, in its entirety. While much of their advice is aimed at composition from literary models, they encompass much more than imitation: they chart the progress from an interpretive stance—what is poetry? what is poetic signification? how does one form an understanding of a text?—to a generative stance, encompassing the conceptual process of invention and the inner formal logic of the text which the writer will bring into being.[8]

The arts of poetry also exemplify the kinds of judgments involved in assembling a group of texts as canonical models: in addition to the overwhelming force of tradition in which certain texts have long been accorded canonical status, there are pragmatic judgments about the illustrative value of certain texts for students who will be attempting to produce similar formal effects. In their generous quotations from canonical authors, the writers of the arts of poetry indicate the practical as well as artistic considerations that grammar teachers brought to their classroom use of certain model texts. It is thus that Matthew of Vendôme can elevate a modern text like Bernardus Silvestris' *Cosmographia* to the status of "masterpiece," because it contains so many exemplary passages.[9] Thus the arts of poetry show us with great exactness the process by which linguistic understanding and literary appreciation were to be applied to the enterprise of textual production.

So successful was the synthetic genre of the medieval *ars poetriae* (sometimes combined with an art of prose) that its exemplars reached audiences far beyond the elementary grammar schools. Indeed all of these works may have been intended for diverse levels of instruction. Even the earliest of the arts, Matthew of Vendôme's *Ars versificatoria*, assumes a fair degree of knowledge on the part of its readers. Geoffrey of Vinsauf's *Poetria nova* had

---

[8] Not all of the arts of poetry give equal attention to all these matters: where Matthew of Vendôme, Geoffrey of Vinsauf, John of Garland, and the anonymous author of the *Tria sunt* deal with structure as well as style, Gervase of Melkley and Eberhard the German focus on figures, tropes, and verse forms.

[9] See Kelly, *The Arts of Poetry and Prose*, 57–64.

a vast circulation throughout the academic circles of Europe, acquiring its own tradition of commentaries and glosses. It even achieved the status of an independent statement about literature, constituting a modern theoretical authority on poetic production and interpretation, as we see in Chaucer's famous citation of the text in *Troilus and Criseyde* (1.1065–9). John of Garland's *Parisiana poetria* and the anonymous *Tria sunt* were produced in the environs of universities, where they contributed to supplementary instruction in grammar and rhetoric, as well as composition in epistolary prose. These latter two works are more comprehensive than the earlier arts of poetry and prose, and may have been intended for advanced students.

During the period that saw the rise of the arts of poetry and prose, two other compositional art forms also emerged: the *ars dictaminis* or art of letter writing, and the art of preaching. The treatises of Gervase of Melkley and John of Garland reflect the interrelatedness of these pedagogical developments, as they also incorporate advice on letter writing in their treatises. But the arts of letter writing and the arts of preaching, as independent treatises, represent technical instruction in highly specialized forms of composition. In their most typical and developed phases, these two arts do not overtly address the broader theoretical principles of textual interpretation and composition that derive from grammatical and rhetorical teaching. For this reason, the specialized arts of letter writing and preaching lie outside the main parameters of this volume.

But two texts in this Part illustrate the underlying connections between these specialized arts and the literary traditions of grammar and rhetoric. Thomas of Chobham's *Summa de arte praedicandi* (Summa of the Art of Preaching) is one of the earliest formal arts of preaching. It was written during the same period as the Fourth Lateran Council of 1215, which made annual confession compulsory and which thus also created the need for a systematic approach to preaching which could be widely disseminated and imitated. The interest that Thomas' *Summa* holds for us is that its orientation is still close to that of a broad-based pedagogy in grammar and rhetoric. Its preceptive treatment of poetic language draws from the same grammatical sources that informed the arts of poetry, and like the arts of poetry, it shows how one progresses from interpretive mastery of poetic devices and literary genres to compositional mastery of them. Also like the arts of poetry, it treats the conceptual and formal composition of a work along the architectonic lines of classical rhetoric.

The treatise *Tria sunt*, written by an anonymous author sometime after 1256 and before 1400, is an unusually comprehensive treatise on prose and verse that draws on Geoffrey of Vinsauf's *Documentum de arte dictandi et versificandi* and *Poetria nova* as well as on other arts of poetry and prose. It follows the pattern of those earlier arts of poetry and prose that devote a section to the art of letter writing. But its treatment of this material reflects the orientation, not of a narrow technographic tradition, but of a broad grammatical pedagogy of composition in which the literary text is seen as a product of formal and conceptual amplification. The discussion of how to generate a letter is a synthesis of grammatical attention to words and syntax, and rhetorical systems of topical invention, specifically probable arguments, conjectural proof, and the attributes of persons and actions. In this respect, then, the teaching of letter writing is enfolded into the larger literary and instructive purposes of the treatise.

Hugh of Trimberg's *Registrum multorum auctorum* (Register of Many Authors) should be seen in the light of the development of the arts of poetry, with their emphasis on "masterpieces" to be imitated. It is also to be seen as an extension of twelfth-century notions of a complete curriculum in which the classical authors induct students into grammar and are read for their moral or historical content: its dependence upon the twelfth-century curricular collection of Conrad of Hirsau certainly argues for it to be read as an outgrowth of this tradition. But its perspective is enlarged by the preceptive grammars, because it is a comprehensive introduction to a schoolroom literary culture in which modern authors have joined the ancients in an expanded canon of valuable literary models. Among those modern authors whose writings Hugh of Trimberg presents for study and imitation are the most influential of the preceptive grammarians themselves, Matthew of Vendôme, Geoffrey of Vinsauf, and John of Garland.

PROLOGUES TO TWELFTH-CENTURY SCHOOL COMMENTARIES ON HORACE'S *ARS POETICA*, CA. 1150

INTRODUCTION

These two anonymous texts are prologues to commentaries on Horace's *Ars poetica*, and represent a high point in the medieval reception of Horace's text.[1] The first text presented here has come to be known as the "Materia" commentary from its opening word. This commentary is important to our understanding of the immediate backgrounds of the medieval arts of poetry. The commentary was very likely composed in France and has been dated to the years after 1125 and before 1175. It may be the source of much of the compositional and stylistic doctrine in the arts of poetry by Matthew of Vendôme, Geoffrey of Vinsauf, and John of Garland, as well as the theory of style in the later art of prose by Conrad of Mure (1276). The arts of poetry clearly follow in the preceptive tradition of Horace's *Ars poetica*, but the "Materia" commentary reveals the chain of reception of Horace's doctrine in the twelfth century that led to the influential compositional theory in Matthew's *Ars versificatoria* (ca. 1175), Geoffrey's *Documentum de modo et arte dictandi et versificandi* (ca. 1215) and its later anonymous expansion, the so-called *Tria sunt* (or "Longer Documentum") and John's *Parisiana poetria* (1231–1235). The most recent editor of the "Materia" commentary, Karsten Friis-Jensen, has called it the "missing link" between Horace's "old poetics" and the new arts of poetry, which often borrow word for word from the commentary (see notes to the text). The "Materia" commentary gives the Horatian doctrine of poetic unity and self-consistency a distinctively medieval cast: it reinterprets Horace's compositional precepts in light of the stylistic teaching of the *Rhetorica ad Herennium*, which was achieving a new popularity during the twelfth century. The prologue to this commentary, containing the doctrine of the six faults of poetic

---

[1] On the tradition of Horace scholia and commentary, see the introduction to Part 4, above. On the "Materia" commentary see Friis-Jensen, "Horace and the Early Writers of Arts of Poetry." For a comparative study of several medieval commentaries, including the "Materia" commentary, see K. M. Fredborg, "*Difficile est proprie communia dicere*"; and see also Copeland, *Rhetoric, Hermeneutics, and Translation*, 151–78.

composition and their corresponding virtues, also circulated as an independent text, indicating the particular value that medieval teachers attached to this systematic treatment of a core poetic precept. The doctrine of the "six rules" is the most prominent feature of this commentary, and probably originated with it. The "Materia" commentary is one of the earliest texts—and perhaps the most influential—to develop the distinctively medieval transformation of the doctrine of the three levels of style. In the *Rhetorica ad Herennium*, the doctrine of the low, middle, and high styles simply represents distinctions among verbal styles. But there was a growing tendency to associate the three styles with levels of subject matter and especially social status (characters of low, middle, or exalted position). The "Materia" commentary presents this newer dimension of the doctrine of style as if it is already a current and well-developed notion, and its influence in this area can be seen in Geoffrey of Vinsauf's *Documentum* and especially in the highly elaborated theory of style and subject matter in John of Garland's *Parisiana poetria*.

The second text presented here is a prologue to a copy of the *Ars poetica* in a manuscript that contains all the the works of Horace. It offers some valuable insights into the use of Horace's work for the teaching of composition in the period just preceding the emergence of the full-scale medieval arts of poetry at the end of the twelfth century. It brings a learned or scientific vocabulary to the treatment of Horace's preceptive work: it notes that because the *Ars poetica* is itself in verse, it both teaches about the art of poetry (*de arte*) and proceeds from the art (*ex arte*). It also assigns Horace's work to logic (rather than, as might be expected for a poetic work, to ethics), explaining that Horace's instruction concerns verbal composition and not morals. In other words, for this commentator, Horace's work clearly pertains to the verbal arts of the trivium.[2]

ANONYMOUS (FROM THE "MATERIA" COMMENTARY): GLOSSES ON HORACE'S POETICS: INTRODUCTION

Translated from "The *Ars Poetica* in Twelfth-Century France: The Horace of Matthew of Vendôme, Geoffrey of Vinsauf, and John of Garland," ed. Friis-Jensen, by permission.

---

[2] By contrast, for example, the twelfth-century introduction to the *Ars poetica* printed by Huygens (*Accessus ad auctores*, 50–1) makes a double assignment: to ethics, because it treats the behaviors suitable to a poet, or to logic, because it teaches correct and embellished speech and introduces us to the practices of correct writers.

The material [*materia*] of the author in this work is the art of poetry. His intention is to give precepts concerning the art of poetry. The cause of this intention is twofold: one is general and one is specific. The general cause is that he might instruct any erring poets in the art of poetry. The particular cause, that is, the personal purpose, is so that he might instruct the Pisones, at whose request he undertook this work. The Pisones were the noble sons of Piso; seeing the writings of others censured, and fearing that the same would happen to their own verses, they asked Horace, the best teacher of the art of poetry, to instruct them in writing. Bowing to their request, he sought to give instruction in the art of poetry. One of them wrote comedy, the other wrote satire, and since he undertook this work on their behalf, he gave some specific precepts about comedy, and some specific precepts about satire. But so that he might give more universal advice, he provided general precepts that pertain to any poets. The precepts are given in two ways, first in showing which faults are to be avoided, and second which virtues are to be sought out. Thus he first teaches what is to be avoided, and with the errors of style purged, he then adds the rules and precepts of the art of poetry. For as he says in his Epistles, "Unless the vessel is clean, whatever you pour in turns sour."[3]

There are six faults to be avoided in poetic composition; not that there are not others, but these are the chief ones.[4]

The first of these is the incongruous placing of the parts [*partium incongrua positio*].[5] The parts of a work are the beginning, the middle, and the end. Parts are placed incongruously when the beginning is discordant with the middle, and the middle is discordant with the end.[6] Horace censures this by likening it to a picture, where he says: "If a painter chose to join a human head to the neck of a horse."[7] For congruent placing of the parts is when the beginning accords with the middle, and the middle accords with the end.

The second fault is incongruent digression [*incongrua orationis digressio*]. One digresses by abandoning the course of one's speech for something else which does not

---

[3] *Epistles* 1.2.54.

[4] Cf. *Tria sunt-Documentum*, § 1, as transcribed by Friis-Jensen; all references to the *Tria sunt* (i.e. the treatise once thought to be Geoffrey of Vinsauf's expansion of the *Documentum de modo et arte dictandi et versificandi*) are to the paragraph numbers in the transcription by Friis-Jensen, "The *Ars Poetica* in Twelfth-Century France," appendix, 385–8. See also John of Garland, *Parisiana poetria*, within, pp. 626–9.

[5] Cf. Matthew of Vendôme, *Ars versificatoria*, ed. Faral, *Les arts poétiques*, 1.37; Geoffrey of Vinsauf, *Documentum de modo et arte dictandi et versificandi* (hereafter *Documentum*), ed. Faral, *Les arts poétiques*, 2.3.154–5; *Tria sunt-Documentum*, § 2; Conrad of Mure, *Summa de arte prosandi*, ed. Kronbichler, 100. See also John of Garland, *Parisiana poetria*, within, p. 627.

[6] Cf. *Ars poetica* 152; Matthew of Vendôme, *Ars versificatoria*, ed. Faral, 1.31; Alan of Lille, *Anticlaudianus* 1.422.

[7] *Ars poetica* 1.

pertain to the matter.[8] Horace condemns this fault where he says: "Works with noble beginning and grand promises often have one or two purple patches so stitched on as to glitter far and wide."[9] However, there can also be a congruent digression, when one strays from the theme for a useful purpose, digressing to another topic to the advantage of the argument. This was the method that Cicero followed in the *Verrines*. He had begun to accuse Verres of committing adultery in Sicily, but then, straying from the course of his speech, he began to describe the charms of that land, speaking of the lovely springs, most beautiful trees, and verdant meadows there, all to the advantage of his argument, namely that it would be likely that Verres had committed adultery in such delightful surroundings.[10] This is also what Virgil does at the beginning of the *Aeneid*: after he had said that Aeneas, carrying his father and his gods, "was much buffeted on land and sea," and "had endured much in war,"[11] it would seem unbelievable that a man of such piety should be afflicted with such perils; therefore, straying from his subject, he digresses and inquires the cause of the gods' anger, saying: "Tell me, O Muse, the cause; wherein thwarted in will or wherefore angered, did the Queen of heaven drive a man, of goodness so wondrous, to traverse so many perils, to face so many toils."[12] Great indeed should be the anger of the god if it shows no consideration for piety. You will be able to recognize this method as a whole in the digressions of other authors.

The third fault is obscure brevity [*brevitas obscura*], which happens when one wants to speak concisely, but does not make clear the things that he ought to say.[13] Horace criticizes this where he says "Striving to be brief, I become obscure."[14] But there is also an appropriate form of brevity that explains clearly and does not produce obscurity.

The fourth fault is incongruous variation in style [*incongrua stili mutatio*].[15] There are three manners of speaking, which some call styles, others call types [*figurae*], and others call characters: the simple or low style, the middle style, and the grand style [*humilis*

---

[8] Cf. Matthew of Vendôme, *Ars Versificatoria*, ed. Faral, 2.35; Geoffrey of Vinsauf, *Documentum*, ed. Faral, 2.3.256; *Tria sunt-Documentum*, § 3; Conrad of Mure, *Summa de arte prosandi*, ed. Kronbichler, 101. See also John of Garland, *Parisiana poetria*, within, p. 627.

[9] *Ars poetica* 14–16.

[10] Cicero, *Verrines* 2.5.80, 2.4.118; cf. Matthew of Vendôme, *Ars versificatoria*, ed. Faral, 1.110.

[11] *Aeneid* 1.3, 5.   [12] *Aeneid* 1.8–11.

[13] Geoffrey of Vinsauf, *Documentum*, ed. Faral, 2.3.152; *Tria sunt-Documentum*, § 4; Conrad of Mure, *Summa de arte prosandi*, ed. Kronbichler, 101. See also John of Garland, *Parisiana poetria*, within, p. 627.

[14] *Ars poetica* 25–6. Gervase of Melkley also develops this Horatian theme in his prologue, although he is not using the formulaic system of the six faults of style.

[15] Geoffrey of Vinsauf, *Documentum*, ed. Faral, 2.3.145, 151, 157; *Tria sunt-Documentum*, §§ 5–8; Conrad of Mure, *Summa de arte prosandi*, 101. See also John of Garland, *Parisiana poetria*, within, p. 628.

stilus, mediocris et altus].[16] The low style is when someone uses simple or humble words about people of low station, as in comedy. The middle style is when we treat people of middle status in words of a middle type, as in satire. The grand style is when we treat people of high status in grand words, as in tragedy. But each of these styles has its own corresponding fault which is very close to it. The middle style has the fault of drifting and of being loose [*fluctuans et dissolutum*]. Someone pushing a middle style too hard falls into drifting and looseness: although he still has ideas, he levels them out too much and he does not sufficiently link them together; thus the ideas are disconnected and loose.[17] Horace criticizes this where he says: "Aiming at smoothness, I fail in force and fire."[18] The high style has the fault of being turgid or inflated [*turgidum et inflatum*].[19] Someone striving for the high style falls into turgid or inflated style when he uses rough metaphors or bombastic words, as in the following: "The sea so vastly violent must still be navigated by us,"[20] and this, "Of Priam's fate and famous war I'll sing."[21] Horace censures this when he says "promising grandeur, it is (in fact) bombastic."[22] The simple style has the fault of being arid and bloodless [*aridum et exsangue*].[23] Pushing the simple style too hard, one will lapse into aridity and bloodlessness when one composes one's words without the force of ideas, as in the speech of children. Horace criticizes this where he says that one who is "overcautious and fearful of the gale, creeps along the ground."[24] Here, however, we can point to no corresponding virtue, as we did for the other faults.[25]

---

[16] Cf. *Ad Herennium* 4.8.11: *Sunt igitur tria genera, quae genera nos figuras appellamus, in quibus omnis oratio non vitiosa consumitur.* Note that the *Ad Herennium* author uses the word *figura*, but not in a sense equivalent to the English "figure of speech," for which the *Ad Herennium* author uses the term *exornatio* (e.g. at 4.13.18: *exornatio verborum, exornatio sententiarum*). *Figura* meaning "figure of speech" came into common use with Quintilian, *Institutio oratoria* 9. 1. Compare the wording in this passage with the commentary of Thierry of Chartres at *Ad Herennium* 4.8.11 (pp. 436–7, above).

[17] Cf. *Ad Herennium* 4.11.16; Matthew of Vendôme, *Ars versificatoria*, ed. Faral, 1.31; Geoffrey of Vinsauf, *Documentum*, ed. Faral, 2.3.149. See also John of Garland, *Parisiana poetria*, within, p. 628.

[18] *Ars poetica* 26–7.   [19] Cf. *Ad Herennium* 4.10.15.

[20] *Pelagus quantitatis* [*sic*] *procellosum nobis utcumque enavigandum est.* This may be a line composed for a classroom exercise to illustrate the grammatical as well as stylistic dangers of bombast.

[21] *Ars poetica* 137.   [22] *Ars poetica* 27.   [23] Cf. *Ad Herennium* 4.11.16.   [24] *Ars poetica* 28.

[25] On the doctrine of the levels of style set forth here, see Friis-Jensen, "Horace and the Early Writers of Arts of Poetry," 375–8. For the distinction between verbal and material (or social) conceptions of levels of style, see Quadlbauer, *Die antike Theorie der genera dicendi im lateinischen Mittelalter*, 34–9, and Kelly, *The Arts of Poetry and Prose*, 71–8. Faral finds the earliest move towards a material application of style in a Horace commentary that predates the eleventh century: see *Les arts poétiques*, 86–8. The material or social component of the theory is most elaborated in John of Garland, *Parisiana poetria*, within, pp. 625, 628. In the commentary by Thierry of Chartres on *Rhetorica ad Herennium* 4.8.11 (Part 3 above), level of style is a question of "words that pertain" to lofty, middling, or base subjects, but it does not depend on the nature of the subject matter itself.

The fifth fault is the incongruous variation of material [*incongrua materie variatio*], which happens when one's subject matter is left aside and something else is introduced, but is found clashing, either by clumsy variation or by a discordant mode of exposition.[26] Horace criticizes this where he talks about the one "who tries to vary a single subject in monstrous fashion."[27] There is an acceptable form of varying the material, when a subject matter is left aside in favor of something else which embellishes it and which avoids clashes, as we see in Virgil, when he leaves aside his subject matter and invents the story of how Aeneas came to Dido. But with such skill does he interpose this material that someone reading Virgil assumes that this was taken from history. And it is only appropriate to poets to vary their material, since they intersperse history with fiction. Whence they are called poets, that is, makers. For *poire* means "to make."[28] And this is the difference between variation of material and digression of speech: to vary the material is appropriate to poets only, but to digress from the speech is appropriate both to poets and historians.

The sixth fault is an incongruous incompleteness of the work [*incongrua operis imperfectio*], which happens when someone begins to write, but either from ignorance or negligence does not bring what was started to a close.[29] Horace criticizes this by an extended comparison with a bronze-founder, where he says, "Near the Aemilian School . . . there is a craftsman who in bronze will mold nails and imitate waving locks, but is unhappy in the total result, because he cannot represent a whole figure."[30] There is a certain permissible incompleteness of the work, not to be condemned, when someone has begun to write something, but, interrupted by illness, or exile, or death, does not complete it, as in the unfinished states of the *Aeneid* and the *Achilleid*.

The utility of this work is the science of poetic composition, that is, making good verses. The title is "Here begins the book of Poetics of Horace," or "Here begins Horace's book on the Art of Poetry," which means the same thing. The meaning is: "Here begin the precepts on the Art of Poetry." For *poio, pois* is "I make, you make."[31] Whence *poesis* or *poetria*, i.e. a creation [*fictio*] or anything made [*figmentum*], and the poet is one who makes [*fictor*].

With these preliminary matters concluded, let us move to the literal exposition.

---

[26] Cf. Geoffrey of Vinsauf, *Documentum* 2.3.161; *Tria sunt-Documentum*, §§ 9–11; Conrad of Mure, *Summa de arte prosandi*, 102. See also John of Garland, *Parisiana poetria*, within, p. 629.

[27] *Ars poetica* 29.   [28] *poire*: a corrupt form of Greek *poiein*, and cf. below.

[29] Geoffrey of Vinsauf, *Documentum* 2.3.162; *Tria sunt-Documentum* § 12; Conrad of Mure, *Summa de arte prosandi*, 102. See also John of Garland, *Parisiana poetria*, within, p. 629.

[30] *Ars poetica* 32.   [31] *poio, pois*, corrupt forms of Greek *poiô, poieis*.

ANONYMOUS: PROLOGUE TO HORACE'S *ARS POETICA*

Translated from Friis-Jensen, "*Horatius liricus et ethicus.* Two Twelfth-Century School Texts on Horace's Poems," 137, by permission.

Here begins the "Book of Poetics," i.e. that deals with instructing poets to compose their poems well. Alternatively it is the "book of poesis," that is, fiction [*fictio*]: for he teaches how to fabricate [*fingere*] fittingly—the ancients said *poio, pois*, whence we have *poesis* and *poeta*, one who makes fictions. This is also called the *Ars Poetica*, wherein precepts are given for the art of writing poetry. Writing *about* the art is to teach precepts about it. Working *from* the art is to follow the teacher's precepts.[32] The poem itself [i.e. Horace's "Art of Poetry"] contains the matter which it treats, by giving precepts through which it impresses upon us the art of composing poetry well. It is called a poem because it is composed in meter, and either some parts of it or everything in it is fiction, but the kind of fiction that is judged to be very much like the truth in the opinion of men. Or, all those people who are instructed in this work are its material. The work proceeds by giving general precepts, that is, rules that are as suitable to comedies as to other poems. Or it gives precepts proper to comedies, to which it pays special attention. In strict terms Horace intended principally to instruct Piso, the elder son of the Piso family, in writing comedies, which at that time were handled badly, as much on account of the baseness of material as on account of the vulgarity of language. Or we may say that both of the Piso sons are instructed here, the elder in writing comedies, and the younger in writing tragedies, for their efforts focused on these forms. One may infer this from the fact that this book dwells more on the materials, meters, and properties of these forms than those of other kinds of poetry. This book belongs under logic, because here poets are instructed, not about the shaping of morals, but about the arrangement of words for composing poems. Note that he sets out his precepts in two ways: either he simply teaches what is to be done; or first he censures what seemed to be badly done by certain writers, either in choice of language or material, and then he teaches the precepts. He uses this latter approach at the beginning of the poem. First he censures those who do not observe unity of the material, with the initial criticism of painters who do not observe the principle of unity in their pictures. He usefully compares the painter to the writer. Just as a painter ought to imitate nature either as it really is or as it is in the opinion of men—for example, if he were to paint a centaur, even

---

[32] This is the commonplace principle of writing *de arte*, that is, teaching or speaking about the art, and *ex arte*, that is, according to the principles of the art. See above, Thierry of Chartres, pp. 409, 416–20.

though it never existed, he should still represent it as half man and half horse according to men's fabled image of it, and he should not join together a human head, an ass's neck, a lion's chest, and other different things, which arrangement no human opinion recognizes—so a poet, even though he may represent fictitious things, ought not to stray out of keeping with human opinion. Sounding similar themes at the start, Horace says, "If a painter chose," etc.

MATTHEW OF VENDÔME,
ARS VERSIFICATORIA, CA. 1175

INTRODUCTION

Matthew of Vendôme was born probably before 1130. Details of his biography are known from passages in one of his verse letters (*Epistulae* 1.3). He says that he studied at Tours, where he was taught by Bernardus Silvestris. He also studied at Orleans, where he became a master, teaching in the literary or grammatical curriculum there. He later studied in Paris and then returned to Tours.[1] In addition to the *Ars versificatoria* (Art of Poetry or Versification), he also wrote a number of poetic works: *Tobias, Pyramus and Thisbe, Milo,* and the *Epistulae.*[2]

The *Ars versificatoria* was composed about 1175, and is the earliest of the "new" arts of poetry. The *Ars* divides its matter into four uneven parts:[3] (1) inner meaning, which includes advice on beginning a poem, on decorum and the incongruities of style to be avoided, and most importantly on composing descriptions (the longest part of the treatise, nearly half its length); (2) elegance of diction; (3) *schemata,* tropes, and colors of rhetoric; (4) treatment of the material. Matthew's main theoretical authority is Horace's *Ars poetica*; after that, he depends extensively on Cicero's *De inventione*, especially for his treatment of the attributes of the person and the act, from which he develops his precepts for description. He derives his theory of style and the faults of style by combining the advice in *Rhetorica ad Herennium* book 4 and Horace's *Ars poetica*. In bringing these two sources together, he shows much in common with the "Materia" commentary, which is probably his source. Matthew makes liberal and continuous use of classical examples to illustrate nearly every precept. This feature also places Matthew's text in the same tradition of grammatical literary study that would culminate, a century later, in Hugh of Trimberg's register of canonical authors (in fact, Hugh cites Matthew's own *Tobias* as a canonical text).

---

[1] On Matthew's life and writings, see Harbert, "Matthew of Vendôme."
[2] Ed. Munari, *Mathei Vindocinensis opera* 2.
[3] See within, pp. 569–70, for Matthew's account of the thematic divisions of his treatise.

Douglas Kelly has argued that Matthew's treatise, like Eberhard the German's *Laborintus*, is silent on invention because the material to be treated will already have been chosen for the student: the student will be imitating a source rather than devising his own subject matter.[4] This evidence suggests that Matthew's text is directed to students at a more elementary level, for whom this treatise offers an introduction to compositional exercise. But it is also important to note that it is through the theoretical framework of invention that Matthew approaches the practice of poetic imitation: thus his advice on developing description is based mainly on the inventional system of the attributes of the person and the action; he echoes the definition of invention in the *Rhetorica ad Herennium* when he says that description should consist of "true things or verisimilitudes"; and he cites Horace's famous line from the *Ars poetica* (119) "Either follow tradition or invent [*finge*] things that are self-consistent." Since the treatise is at all points concerned with approaches to style, its divisions do not correspond precisely with the divisions of rhetoric into invention, style, and arrangement. But the first and longest part, on the development of descriptions, explains how the "inner ideas" of the poem, which are understood or grasped through the topics of invention (the person and the act), take on literary form; this section, therefore, may have the strongest claims to being the "inventional" part of the treatise.

Translation reprinted from "Matthew of Vendôme: Introductory Treatise on the Art of Poetry," trans. Gallo, by permission.[5]

FROM PART 1: IDEAS

[Beginning a poem, decorum and stylistic defects, and description]

Since our present concern is with the introduction of verses, we ought to present some kind of description of a verse. Verse is a metrical discourse proceeding succinctly member by member,[6] decorated with the pleasing marriage of words and with the

---

⁴ Kelly, "The Scope of the Treatment of Composition."

⁵ Edition used for references: Munari, ed., *Mathei Vindocinensis Opera*, 3. The text is also edited in Faral, *Les arts poétiques*, 109–93. There are two other published English translations: *Ars versificatoria: The Art of the Versemaker*, trans. Parr, and *The Art of Versification*, trans. Galyon. Translations of classical sources in this text are by Gallo.

⁶ *clausulatim progrediens.*

flowers of ideas, and containing neither too little nor too much. For it is not the piling up of expressions, the counting of feet, the recognition of measure that make a verse, but rather the elegant joining of words, and the expression of the characteristics and the observed quality of a thing.

An accidental quality[7] is one attributed to a certain substance and pertaining to good, evil, or the indifferent; for example, to evil, in

Laertes, an old man[8]

since, as Horace says, "Many troubles surround an old man";[9] to good, in

Telemachus, a child[10]

since "youth rejoices in frivolity";[11] to the indifferent, in

The white swan sings at the banks of the Maeander[12]

since being white or black signifies neither good nor evil . . .

> [Matthew now turns to the methods of beginning a poem: zeugma (yoking several clauses together with one subject or verb); hypozeuxis (the opposite of zeugma, each individual clause has its own verb); metonymy; or a proverb (*communis sententia*). He offers many examples of each, but especially of proverbs. He then continues:]

In opening with zeugma or hypozeuxis, three defective styles associated with opening and developing the subject matter are especially to be avoided, according to the authority of Horace: namely, the styles which are loose and disjointed, turgid and inflated, dry and feeble.[13]

Anyone pursuing the mean among words may arrive at overly decorated words, or may sink to words that are too artless and everyday. In the latter case he incurs the fault of a loose and disjointed style, that is, one lacking connection among parts, so that the beginning is discordant with the middle, and the middle with the end.[14] Horace condemns this error, when he says, "In seeking smoothness, force and strength are lost."[15]

The second fault occurs when anyone employing unnecessary verbal ornamentation and decorated discourse comes up with an empty mist, since apparently no conclusion could possibly correspond to the grandeur of the opening. Horace condemns this fault

---

[7] I.e. an epithet. [8] Ovid, *Heroides* 1.98. [9] *Ars poetica* 169.
[10] Ovid, *Heroides* 1.98. [11] Maximian, *Elegies* 1.105. [12] Ovid, *Heroides* 7.2.
[13] *fluctuans et dissolutum, turgidum et inflatum, aridum et exsangue.* Cf. "Materia" commentary, p. 555, and see Horace, *Ars poetica* 14–31; these errors are also discussed in *Ad Herennium* 4.10.15–4.11.16.
[14] Cf. *Ars poetica* 152, and cf. "Materia" commentary, above, p. 555. [15] *Ars poetica* 26.

when he says, "Promising loftiness, he becomes turgid."[16] Elsewhere, he gives [an] example of the turgid and inflated opening of the "cyclical writer":[17]

I will sing the fortune of Priam and the famous war[18]

and at once convicts him of a presumptuous opening, when he says

What has this maker of promises to say worthy of such pompous language? The mountains will labor, a laughable mouse will be born.[19]

The third fault, the dry and feeble style, occurs when, employing an excessively low style, we omit every flower of speech and elegance of thought.[20] Horace condemns this fault, taking his metaphor from the sailor who

overly cautious and afraid of the storm crawls along the shore.[21]

Compatibility of ornament and a certain restraint in language must be observed, "lest in your imitation you leap into a narrow place whence shame, or the exigencies of the work, will bar return."[22] Rather, observe the characteristics of persons and let the development of the subject matter "be preserved to the end, just as it proceeded from the beginning, and remain consistent within itself,"[23] so that no excess or lack may be found in the development.

There are other faults which Horace, in the opening of the *Art of Poetry*, teaches us to avoid, but which—to eschew prolixity, the enemy of memory—I here pass over, commending the diligence of the student to further inquiry into the discipline of poetry.[24]

[After briefly treating inconsistencies of grammar and syntax, Matthew moves to one of his main topics in the treatise, description.]

In description we ought to observe both the characteristics of persons and the diversity of those characteristics. We must observe the characteristics of condition, age, office, sex, place, and the others named by Cicero as the attributes of persons.[25] Horace recognizes this diversity of characteristics when he says:

It makes a great difference whether it is Davus or a hero who speaks [diversity of condition]; a mature old man, or one yet aglow with flowering youth [diversity of age]; a high-ranking lady or a busy nurse [diversity of condition among women]; a wandering merchant, or the cultivator of a fertile field [diversity of office]; a Colchian or an Assyrian [diversity of nation]; a son of Thebes or of Argos [diversity of city].[26]

---

[16] *Ars poetica* 27.   [17] *Ars poetica* 136, and cf. "Materia" commentary, above, p. 555.
[18] *Ars poetica* 137.   [19] *Ars poetica* 138–9.   [20] Cf. "Materia" commentary, above, p. 555.
[21] *Ars poetica* 28.   [22] *Ars poetica* 134–5.   [23] *Ars poetica* 126–8.
[24] cf. "Materia" commentary, above, p. 554–6.   [25] *De inventione* 1.24–5.   [26] *Ars poetica* 114–18.

Horace explains why we should thus distinguish characteristics, when he says

> We will dwell always on the characteristics joined and suited to the age, lest by chance we assign the part of an old man to a youth, or that of a man to a boy.[27]

However, any person ought to be designated by that epithet[28] which overshadows all the others and from which he receives the clearest mark of his renown, in accordance with this example in Horace:

> If perhaps you bring again to the stage the honored Achilles, let him be hasty, easily provoked, pitiless, fierce; let him deny laws were made for him, let him adjudge everything to arms.[29]

The character of words ought to conform to the facial expression of the persons speaking and to their inner fortune; for "somber words suit the sad face; threatening words, the angry; jesting words, the light-hearted; words of sober import, the serious."[30] Horace adds the reason why we must observe such appropriateness of words: "If the words do not correspond to the fortunes of the speaker, all the Romans will laugh in derision."[31] But this seems to have special reference to the manner of recitation.

Hence the descriptions we set down must be different for a pastor of the church, an emperor; a girl, an old woman; a matron, a concubine or a waiting-woman; boy or young man, old man; freedman, slave; and thus must we represent in description the variations of other characteristics, which Horace calls the shadings of the work.[32]

To make the point clear, since example aids understanding, I will supply descriptions of certain persons under the condition that no detractor taunt me with abuse if many blemishes occur in the following verses... Whence it must be understood that nothing in the following descriptions is set down as a model, but only by way of example...

[In the passages that follow, Matthew sets forth versified examples of descriptions based on attributes of the person. On the model of epideictic oratory, these are divided into categories of praise and blame: in praise of a pope, of Caesar, and of Ulysses; blame of Davus the slave (a stock character of Roman comedy); praise of Marcia (for virtue) and Helen (for beauty); blame of Beroe (for ugliness). These descriptions offer a close relationship between speaking about the rules of the art (speaking *de arte*) and using the rules of the art (speaking *ex arte*). After providing these examples, he offers further advice about description through attributes: the student must understand that the authors whom they are imitating use specific names to stand for general types (i.e. Caesar's attributes could pertain to another man of his stature); the inverse

---

[27] *Ars poetica* 176–8.   [28] Cf. Isidore of Seville, *Etymologiae* 1.37.12.   [29] *Ars poetica* 120–2.

[30] *Ars poetica* 105–7.   [31] *Ars poetica* 112–13.   [32] Cf. *Ars poetica* 86.

of this must also be appreciated (i.e. some of Caesar's attributes are his alone); an excellent description will combine many attributes; some attributes should be stressed, others deemphasized. All this is in the interest of achieving verisimilitude, a likeness to truth.]

And since the chief pursuit of the poetic faculty lies in skill in description, on this point my advice is to cultivate accuracy in descriptive expression, so that true things or verisimilitudes[33] may be uttered, in accordance with this passage from Horace:

Either follow tradition or invent things that are self-consistent.[34]

...It must be noted that description of any person can take two forms, external or internal. Description is external[35] when the grace of the members (that is, the outer man) is described, and internal[36] when the characteristics of the inner man (reason, constancy, patience, probity, harshness, pride, lust, and the other characteristics of the inner man, that is, the soul) are expressed for the purposes of praise or blame.

It must also be noted that the description of a person ought to be informed chiefly by his office, sex, quality, rank, condition, age, appearance. In order that diversity among words may not confuse the student, let us accept "rhetorical decoration of the work," "characteristics," "epithets," and "personal attributes"[37] as meaning the same thing. And since the properties of any person consist of his personal attributes, for the sake of greater clarity I will run through them briefly and succinctly in order that the diligent student may be able in his verses to assign with greater clarity commonplaces or arguments to actions and to persons in accordance with their attributes.

The words "argument" or "commonplace from name or nature" must be understood otherwise here than in the discipline of logic.[38] Here, to form an argument or to draw a commonplace from name or nature is nothing other than, through the interpretation of a name and through natural characteristics, to prove or disprove something about a person, to affirm that something belongs to him or to deny it.

---

[33] *ut vera dicantur vel veri similia*; cf. *Ad Herennium* I.2.3: *Inventio est excogitatio rerum verarum aut verisimilium, quae causam probabilem reddant* ("Invention is the devising of matter, true or plausible, that would make the case convincing." Note how Matthew echoes the classical definition of invention in his treatment of description, linking it with the well-known passage from the *Ars poetica* on imitating sources or devising new material.

[34] *Ars poetica* 119. In medieval commentaries on Horace, this line was sometimes read in the light of line 125, *Difficile est...*, to mean that while it is harder to make commonplaces your own, it is also more laudable to treat well-worn material in a new way. See Copeland, *Rhetoric, Hermeneutics, and Translation in the Middle Ages*, 170–3.

[35] *superficialis.*   [36] *intrinseca.*   [37] *colores operum; proprietates; epitheta; personae attributa.*

[38] *Argumentum* and *locus* (i.e. topic or "place" of invention, a term which serves both for dialectic and rhetoric).

There are eleven attributes of persons: name, nature, way of life, fortune, acquired disposition, pursuit, feeling, deliberation, accident, deeds, speeches[39] ...

[Matthew proceeds to discuss each of these, illustrating his definitions with passages drawn mainly from classical authors and scripture. The structure of rhetorical invention out of topics (attributes of the person and the act) or circumstances is here transferred to the central work of poetic composition, description of character and event. After detailed exemplification of each of the attributes of person, Matthew takes up Cicero's next category, attributes of the action.]

We now discuss the attributes of action, which is a deed or word through which some man or woman is brought to the bar of justice as guilty.

There are nine attributes of action: summary of the action; motive of the action; circumstances before the act, during the act, and after the act; facilities for the act; quality of the act; time; place ...

[Each of these attributes of the action is defined more closely and illustrated with examples from classical authors. The attribute of place occasions a special exemplification, an *ekphrasis* composed by Matthew himself, to illustrate the composition of a topography, here a natural paradise populated by different birds and replete with every possible charm. The description is lengthy in order to afford the student a panoply of examples, for "that building is more solid which is supported by a diversity of columns."]

... Attributes of action as well as of person are contained in this little verse:

Who, what, where, with what aid, why, how, when.[40]

Who contains the eleven attributes of person; *what* contains the summary of the action and the threefold execution, that is, before, during, and after the action; *where* contains place; *with what aid*, the facility of acting; *why*, the motive of the action; *how*, the manner or quality; *when*, the time.

Lest the teacher seem to depart from traditional theory, we observe that zeugma, hypozeuxis, and the other colors and schemes can be pointed out almost everywhere in the above descriptions. In what follows we shall speak more clearly concerning these colors

---

[39] Cicero, *De inventione* 1.24.34.

[40] This tag line is derived from the seven "circumstances" outlined in Boethius' *De topicis differentiis*, see above, p. 193. See also Victorinus, *Explanationes*, in Halm, *Rhetores latini minores*, 220. But the transmission of these terms, especially as questions, also owes something to early medieval commentaries on the classical authors. Beginning in the ninth century, the question format became a convention in the *accessus ad auctores*. See Hunt, "The Introductions to the 'Artes' in the Twelfth Century," and Remigius of Auxerre, *Commentum in Martianum Capellam*, ed. Lutz, 1:65. See also Walther, ed., *Initia carminum ac versuum Medii Aevi*, no. 16103.

and schemes. And so in the above verses the careful attention of the student ought to consider the manner of speaking rather than the content of the speech, so that those examples may be understood to take their place in this work because of the beauty of what is set forth and not because of the importance of what must be set forth . . .

FROM PART 2: ELEGANCE OF DICTION

Since in the above section of this little work our course of studies dwelled somewhat on the method of describing, now that we are about to go on to the three kinds of elegance in versifying, in order to allure the audience I thought it proper first to present a fanciful vision of the preceding night, so that with the help of a pleasant narrative, receptivity may abound, attention revive, good will overflow, the desire to listen be renewed, the disadvantage of weariness be averted, and desire for instruction somewhat increase . . .

> [The author describes a vision in which he saw a beautiful natural setting including eight rhymed lines depicting the ministrations of Genius and the glories of spring. Lady Philosophy roams this place along with her handmaidens, who are the arts. Among these last are the poetic genres Tragedy, Satire, Comedy, and Elegy.]

> I heard Elegy expound the threefold grace of the poetic discipline:

> > There are three things which have savor in a poem: polished words, ornament of expression, and inner sweetness.[41]

Verse draws its grace from the beauty of the inner meaning, or from the outer decoration of words, or from the manner of expression. It draws grace from the beauty of the inner meaning as in Horace:

> > It is something to progress so far, if we can go no further.[42]

and in Lucan:

> > The sin which many commit goes unpunished.[43]

---

[41] *verba polita, dicendique color, interiorque favus.* Matthew repeats this line in part 3 of the *Ars* (see below). Munari's edition gives various possible analogues and parallels: see in Matthew of Vendôme, Munari, ed., *Mathei Vindocinensis Opera*, 1:137 (note at 2.9). Matthew's line is cited as an example of "numerical apothegms" by Curtius, *European Literature and the Latin Middle Ages*, 511.

[42] *Epistles* 1.1.32.   [43] *Pharsalia* 5.260.

In these examples the verse possesses no grace in its outer ornament, for the words used are commonplace; nor in the quality of the expression, since we can point out neither figures nor tropes[44] in these examples. The grace rather resides in the general *sententia* which is given to be understood in each example, so that the beauty of the words may be understood to redound from their very meaning.

Poetic grace is drawn from the outer decoration of words when the verse derives beauty from the charm of the words and thus wins to its side an amiable audience, as in Lucan:

Every magistrate was concealed under the dress of the common people.[45]

Statius:

Day came forth from Ocean and freed the world from the embrace of damp shades.[46]

Indeed the poet ought to be well practiced in this matter, lest lack of decoration cause an unpolished heap of words to seem to go a-begging in the verse. To make comparison with material things, just as no one can weave a pleasing garment from goats' wool and worn-out rags (since a little ferment ruins the whole mass), likewise in verse if the verbal material is graceful, that grace will redound to the very subject embodied in that material. Unadorned verses testify to the ignorance or carelessness of the poet. Indeed, just as in the making of a material object the whole shines with more elegant beauty from the incorporation of some pearl or mosaic work, so [it is] also with certain words which as it were play the role of pearls, for the whole line will be adorned from their artful use.[47] In comradely manner, their manifold ornament imparts the benefit of its beauty to the other words and, as it were, sociably lends them the charm of its grace . . .

[At this point Matthew inserts lists of words and word forms that are particularly useful for ornamentation: adjectives ending in *-alis, -osus, -atus, -ivus,* and *-aris,* and adjectives in their comparative form and other elegant adjectives; and verbs that are especially decorative. He adds some advice about understanding the meaning or connotation of words so that the student will not join words (e.g. a subject and modifier) with contradictory meanings. He also recommends that the unskilled student avoid leonine verses in favor of elegiacs, and rules that certain consignificative words (*porro, autem, quoque* [moreover, however, also]) should not be used in poetry.]

---

[44] *schemata; tropi.*   [45] *Pharsalia* 2.18–19.   [46] *Achilleid* 2.1–2.
[47] Punctuation slightly emended.

From Part 3: Schemes, Tropes, and Colors of Rhetoric

It now remains to discuss the third member of the above division,[48] that is, the quality or manner of expression. Many verses draw their beauty from the manner of expression rather than from the matter of what is expressed, as is clear in this example:

> Tu dominus, tu vir, tu mihi frater eras.[49]

It is not adornment of meaning nor external grace of the words that bestows elegance upon this verse, but rather the manner of expression. "Three things have savor in a poem: polished words, adornment of expression, and inner sweetness."[50] The above example contains three figures.[51] The first is zeugma constructed from the end, for three parts of the sentence depend on "were" in the last part. Again, the example contains a rhetorical color,[52] namely repetition, for the pronoun "you" is thrice repeated. Dialyton or asyndeton may also be pointed out in the same example, since the several parts of the sentence are represented separately and distinctly, without copulative conjunctions. Just as, in material things, the material of a statue is crude and stamped with no value until the zealous polishing of the craftsman makes it more pleasing, so too in a poem is the verbal material crude and inelegant until decorated by the artful setting of some *schemata*, tropes, or rhetorical colors. Since *schemata*, tropes, and rhetorical colors are contained under this third part of the above division, we shall explain those which pertain to the poetic faculty, and we shall proceed first with the *schemata*.[53]

[The *schemata* (called by Isidore of Seville *figurae*[54]) that are most suitable to poetry are defined and illustrated: these are zeugma, hypozeuxis, anaphora, epanalepsis, anadiplosis, epizeuxis, paronomasia, paranomoeon, schesisonomaton, homoeoteleuton, polyptoton, polysyndeton, and dialyton or asyndeton.]

[The Greek *tropus* means "manner of speaking." Tropes are made for the adornment of the discourse and are unrelated to the beauty of the meaning. They are thirteen in

---

[48] See above, Elegy's exposition of the threefold grace of poetry: polished words, ornament of expression, and inner sweetness.

[49] "You were my master, you my husband, you my brother": Ovid, *Heroides* 3.52.   [50] See note 41 above.

[51] *Schemata.*   [52] *Color rhetoricus*; translated by Gallo as "rhetorical ornament."

[53] The following sections on *schemata*, tropes, and colors of rhetoric are derived to a large extent from Donatus' *Ars maior*, book 3 (the *Barbarismus*), and from Isidore of Seville, *Etymologiae* 1.36–7.

[54] It is Matthew who calls attention to Isidore's terminology (*skhêma* being the Greek term for *figura*).

number, but the ones most important for the poet are metaphor, antitheton, metonymy, synecdoche, periphrasis, epitheton, climax, allegory, and enigma.[55]]

[The colors of rhetoric are dealt with quickly. Certain colors of rhetoric are similar to certain *schemata* and tropes: antitheton and contentio; anaphora and duplicatio; paranomasia and annominatio; epanalepsis and repetitio; schesisonomaton and membrum orationis or articulus; dialyton and dissolutum; polysyndeton and conjunctum; metalepsis and climax or gradatio. The colors are repetitio, conversio, complexio, traductio, contentio, exclamatio, ratiocinatio, sententia, contrarium, membrum orationis or articulus, similiter cadens, similiter desinens, commixtio, annominatio, subjectio, gradatio, diffinitio, transitio, correctio, occupatio,[56] disjunctio, conjunctum, adjunctum, conduplicatio, commutatio, dubitatio, dissolutio, praecisio, conclusio.]

... [I]n order fully to demonstrate the adequacy of the presentation [of this treatise] in relation to the three parts of the above division, we have discoursed above on the first part, namely the norms for judging significance in the attributes of action and person. The second part, verbal ornament, was clearly explained in the examples of adjectives, according to their various endings. The third part, or manner of expression, was discussed in the schemes and tropes.

But perhaps some unskilled person will presume to caw, saying that in the above division the same thing is accounted as part of itself, since the first, second, and third parts are all concerned with the ornament of poetry. To him we must answer that the first, second, and third parts indeed do concern the ornament of verse, but in a threefold manner; for although there is uniformity in the purpose of my treatment [*causa tractandi*], diversity is discerned in the method of my treatise [*modus tractatus*]. For the first part discusses the ornament of the inner meaning; the second, verbal ornament; the third, the manner of expression. Hence, some orderly plan can be pointed out in these three parts. Indeed, just as in the above division meanings come first, then words follow, and finally the manner of expression is added, likewise in the exercise of the poetic faculty a mental image of the perception comes first; utterance, which expounds the meaning, follows; and

---

[55] Matthew's definitions of the tropes, and the examples he gives, usually follow those in Isidore of Seville, whose definitions in turn are based on Donatus, *Barbarismus*. On his use of the two authorities, see in Matthew of Vendôme, Munari, ed., *Mathei Vindocinensis Opera* 3:28–9. For example, the definition of metaphor in Matthew's treatise, taken from Isidore, is also virtually that of Donatus (see within, p. 97): "*metaphora* is a transference appropriated from some word. This trope is divided into four parts: it is most often made from animate to animate, from inanimate to inanimate, from animate to inanimate, from inanimate to animate." Similarly, Matthew's definition of allegory, taken directly from Isidore's definition, is derived from Donatus' definition: "Allegory is 'speaking otherwise' [*alienum eloquium*; cf. Isidore, *alieniloquium*], when the sense differs from the signification of the words."

[56] *Rhetorica ad Herennium* 4.27.37, *occultatio*.

finally, arrangement ensues in the nature of the treatment. The first is the conception of the meaning, next is the invention of words, and finally we have the nature of the subject matter or the disposition of the treatment.

FROM PART 4: TREATMENT OF MATERIAL (*MATERIA EXSECUTA, MATERIA ILLIBATA*)

We now discuss the treatment of the material,[57] in which certain ill-taught persons are often wont to go off the track and basely to deviate from the path of instruction, who in school exercises paraphrase the fables of the poets word for word,[58] as though they proposed to make a metrical commentary on the authors. But since the unlearned who transgress ought to be pardoned, and perhaps have been perverted by perverse teachers, they must be advised in the treatment of their material to strive to imitate wonted events, so that they utter truths or verisimilitudes.[59] Nor should anyone propose to "render word for word, like a *fidus interpres.*"[60]

Indeed, there are certain expressions which, as though condemned, ought to be omitted from the course of the work, for if they are handled that entire portion of the work will be deprived of value[61] rather than draw therefrom any spark of beauty; and this, with the authority of Homer. Whence Horace says of Homer, "What he despairs of making shine in his treatment he omits."[62] Hence what is not fully expressed [in the source] must be filled in, what is awkward must be improved, and what is superfluous must be entirely done away with.

Further, material which anyone may wish to work upon either is virgin ground or has first been treated by another poet.[63] If it has already been treated, you must proceed according to the general tenor of the poetic story, with this consideration, that you must omit certain appurtenances not essential to the principal subject; that is, their comparison, poetic licenses, figurative constructions, and the measure of quantities and syllables are not to be admitted...

---

[57] *exsecutio materiae.*   [58] *fabulas circinantes poeticas verbum verbo sigillatim exprimunt.*

[59] *Ad Herennium* 1.2.3; *Ars poetica* 119–20, 338; *De inventione* 1.19.27.

[60] Cf. Horace, *Ars poetica* 133–4. We have left the term *fidus interpres* untranslated, because its meaning is ambiguous: depending on context it can mean "faithful interpreter" or "faithful translator."

[61] Cf. Geoffrey of Vinsauf, *Poetria nova* 66–7.   [62] *Ars poetica* 149–50.

[63] *aut erit illibata, aut ab aliquo poeta primitus exsecuta.*

[Two sections follow: on excision of digressions and superfluities of meter, figures, and words (i.e. the doctrine of abbreviation) and on expanding that which is not fully expressed (amplification).]

Thus far we have discussed material already handled by others, that is, poetic fables, the kinds of things that naked Garamantes plow over in school exercises in versification.[64] We now discuss material not previously handled,[65] in the treatment of which we must above all seek after custom, so that with the help of words we may express actions according to their usual natures. Our purpose is that the expressive treatment of the material may inform the object materially, that is to say, that what we hear may correspond to the customary nature of the object.

The treatment will concern the attributes either of a person or of an action. If it concerns the attributes of a person, let the description express such a person as is preconceived by the content[66] of an imagined description or expectation, so that what first resided in our invention[67] may then be brought forth with the aid of expression. For example,

> Choose [a girl] to whom you may say, "You alone please me."[68]

and just as she pleased you, so let her be depicted in your treatment. All of the preceding has reference to praise.

Likewise for blame, she must be depicted deformed in such a way as can be expected to repel your—and everyone's—regard.

If that treatment concerns the attributes of an action, it must proceed inferentially according to the common way of thinking and the authority of custom. However, in the attributes of action more than in the attributes of person, you must employ a restrained brevity of discourse, so that the matter may be concisely set forth—unless the beauty of the meaning is a consideration, as in the writings of the authors, and in metaphors, epithets, and so on. Indeed, since as Boethius says, contraries go by contrary rule, just as we must omit what is displeasing to handle, so likewise we must fully unfold the beauty of meaning.

Many things yet remain to be said about the treatment of material; but since our course longs for its goal, lest tedium creep in let us discuss the variation of material (which indeed

---

[64] *Hucusque de materia pertractata, scilicet de fabulis poeticis, quas nudi Garamantes arant in scolastico versificandi exercitio* (translation slightly modified). "Garamantes" = "barbarians" (i.e. rude school boys); cf. Isidore of Seville, *Etymologiae* 14.5.13; *Aeneid* 4.198; Lucan, *Pharsalia* 9.5.2.

[65] *materia illibata.*   [66] *argumentum.*

[67] This is Gallo's term to translate *ingenium*; it is not properly the rhetorical canon of invention, although this section makes use of the elements of topical invention.

[68] Ovid, *Ars amatoria* 1.41.

pertains to the treatment). We may vary the material in two ways—by changing the words and *sententiae*[69] (but retaining the equivalent meaning); or by changing the words and not the *sententiae*...

[Following this, Matthew gives specific advice about variation of words and *sententiae*, and then about correction and the roles of teacher and student in removing blemishes from the work. The treatise ends with advice about how to conclude a poem.]

---

[69] Gallo translates this as "sentences" rather than "meanings," because of the following phrase, "retaining the equivalent meaning [*sensus*]."

ALEXANDER OF VILLA DEI, *DOCTRINALE*, 1199

INTRODUCTION

Alexander of Villa Dei studied in Paris. He wrote one of the two most popular teaching grammars in use in the thirteenth century, the *Doctrinale*, composed in 1199.[1] The book was intended for the grammatical education of the young relatives of the Bishop of Dol. The work thus predates the *Graecismus* by Eberhard of Béthune (1212), discussed in the next section.[2] Alexander is also the author of the *Alphabetum maius*, an encyclopedic work in prose with information for church functionaries about grammar, the church calendar, and canonical law. The *Doctrinale* presents itself as based to a large extent on this longer work. Alexander also wrote an *Alphabetum minus*, a primer, apparently also ordered alphabetically, to take the place of, or to supplement, Donatus' *Ars minor* as a manual for beginners.[3] The introduction of the *Doctrinale* makes reference to these other works (lines 26 ff.).

After the proem, the *Doctrinale* is divided into twelve parts or chapters:[4]

1. declinatio (lines 29–363)
2. heteroclita (lines 364–457)
3. comparatio (lines 458–98)
4. gender of nouns (lines 499–693)

---

[1] For the date, see the edition by Reichling, xxiv, xxxvii. Apart from Reichling's excellent introduction, the following works contain useful general introductions: Neudecker, *Das Doctrinale des Alexander de Villa-Dei*; Golling, "Einleitung in die Geschichte der lateinischen Syntax," 29–37 (on Alexander of Villa Dei); Manitius, *Geschichte der lateinischen Literatur des Mittelalters*, 3:756–61. See also the modern Spanish translation with introduction and notes by Gutiérrez Galindo, *El Doctrinal: Una gramática latina del Renacimiento del siglo XII*.

[2] For discussion of the date of the *Graecismus*, see the selection from this work below, p. 585, and Reichling's edition of Alexander of Villa Dei, lxxi ff. (who also defends the dating of 1212). The *Graecismus* thus used the *Doctrinale* rather than vice versa (Reichling, lxxix ff.; Manitius, *Geschichte der lateinischen Literatur*, 759).

[3] Reichling, ed., xxiv ff., esp. xxxi, xxxiii on the *Alphabetum maius*, xxxv on the *Alphabetum minus*; Reichling rejects the view (later revived as a possibility by Neudecker, *Das Doctrinale des Alexander de Villa-Dei*, 6; and see Law, "Why Write a Verse Grammar," 60) that the *Alphabetum minus* is actually identical to Donatus, and that the *Alphabetum maius* is Priscian. He concludes that both are by Alexander himself.

[4] Cf. Reichling, ed., lxxi ff.

5. perfect and supine (lines 694–949)
6. defective and anomalous verbs (lines 950–1047)
7. forms of the verb (lines 1048–73)
8. regimen (lines 1074–1368)
9. construction (lines 1369–1549)
10. quantities (lines 1550–2281)
11. accents (lines 2282–2360)
12. figures (lines 2361–2645, divided into figures of construction and diction; metaplasms; *schemata*; and tropes).

From the fourteenth century onwards, the twelve chapters were divided into three major parts: "Etymology" (chapters 1–7), based mostly on the first sixteen books of Priscian,[5] "syntax"(chapters 8–9), somewhat less directly based on Priscian's books 17 and 18, and a third part, consisting of the chapters 10–12, in which Alexander is most independent. These last chapters treat, among other things, the metrical properties of syllables.[6] The "etymological" part omits numerals, regular conjugations, adverbs, conjunctions, and prepositions. There is no theory of tenses and moods in the "syntax." All of this indicates that the *Doctrinale* was apparently intended for students who had already mastered Donatus' *Ars minor* and Alexander's own *Alphabetum minus*.[7] It replaces Priscian for more advanced students, and is mostly interested in exceptions to the grammatical rules.

The *Doctrinale* itself is a manual in leonine verses.[8] Like the *Graecismus*, it is a didactic poem,[9] consisting of short, simple, and memorable verses suitable for rehearsing something already explained at greater length. This form is especially suited for material that does not lend itself to a naturally structured presentation; indeed, to a large extent the *Doctrinale* consists of lists which can use the mnemonic support of the verse form.[10] It is impossible to envisage students independently studying the book. Alexander himself refers to the pedagogical use he has in mind, in which a teacher will explain the materials in the vernacular (Proem line 9). But teachers would need help as well: almost immediately, the

---

[5] See the introduction to the etymology dossier (Part 2, above) for the fact that "morphology" is now comprised under the heading "etymology."

[6] Reichling, ed., lxxviii.   [7] Reichling, ed., lxxiii.

[8] These were quite modern when Alexander used them: they were an invention of the poet Leonius (d. 1187). Alexander does not use rhyme as systematically as some: if there is rhyme at all, it is usually only at the end of the verse, not also in the middle (Reichling, ed., lxxiv).

[9] Reichling ed., lxxiv would like to distinguish "didactic" poetry from "technical" poetry, and assign the *Doctrinale* to the latter category, but this seems unnecessary in light of the study by Law (see following note).

[10] Cf. Law, "Why Write a Verse Grammar," 60, pointing out that the *Doctrinale* is not a full-scale, logically structured grammar, but "covers only those topics which did *not* lend themselves to organisation *per divisionem*."

Doctrinale became the object of a rich commentary practice, including glosses in both Latin and vernacular.[11]

The commentaries that accompanied the work in the thirteenth to fifteenth century offered a reading of the text that was thoroughly philosophical. Although the text of the *Doctrinale* itself still bore some traces of the philosophical ideas underlying the work of Priscian,[12] large parts of the text had been reduced to simple lists minus much of the ideological baggage pertaining to the logical, reasonable nature of language and its relationship to reality. The *Doctrinale* had a literary goal in that it prepared for the reading of the Vulgate,[13] while also taking exception to certain standard authors of the medieval schoolroom canon, such as the obscene Maximianus.[14] But the tendency to provide a philosophical framework for a grammatical treatise was far more marked in Priscian's text than in Alexander's *Doctrinale*. Whatever philosophical possibilities were offered by Alexander's grammar were expanded into full-fledged Aristotelian readings in the following centuries, when interest in logic was in the ascendant.[15] One example of such a reading is provided by the anonymous gloss referred to by its incipit as the *Admirantes* gloss (mid-thirteenth century), which can be associated with the *Barbarismus* commentary attributed to Kilwardby.[16] One indication that Alexander's text should not be identified with the readings of his commentators is provided by John of Garland, who was very critical of the work, precisely because it was not Priscianic enough. In all likelihood, John wrote a telling revision of the *Doctrinale*,[17] which he began by reinserting Priscian's discussion of *vox*, the unmissable beginning of a philosophically oriented grammar, into the *Doctrinale* from which Alexander himself had omitted it.

The *Doctrinale* (like the *Graecismus*) was used for over 300 years as part of the compulsory curriculum in many European universities. That it became an object of

---

[11] Cf. Reichling, ed., lx–lxx. For the *Doctrinale's* incomprehensibility without a commentary, see Heath, "Logical Grammar, Grammatical Logic," 13. For vernacular glosses on the *Doctrinale* (French and English) see Hunt, *Teaching and Learning Latin*, 1:84–94.

[12] Heath, "Logical Grammar, Grammatical Logic," 12, assumes a basically philosophical foundation for Alexander's grammar on the basis of Alexander's discussion of the "genitive of cause and effect," but in fact that passage is exceptional. Normally, Alexander cuts back on philosophical content in favor of excerpting, fact-finding, and listing activities.

[13] Cf. Heath, "Logical Grammar, Grammatical Logic," 12.

[14] Orme, *Medieval Schools: From Roman Britain to Renaissance England*, 100 sees Alexander's remarks about Maximianus as a symptom of a new tendency to prefer more moral or Christian-oriented literature in the thirteenth century.

[15] This is the main point of Heath, "Logical Grammar, Grammatical Logic."

[16] Cf. Thurot, *Notices et extraits*, 33, and Rosier-Catach, "Modisme, pré-modisme, proto-modisme," 73; see also Rosier, "La grammaire dans le '*Guide de l'étudiant*,'" 255–60.

[17] Cf. Colker, "New Evidence that John of Garland Revised the *Doctrinale* of Alexander de Villa Dei." See also Reichling, ed., lv for the addition of the part on *vox*.

mockery to the humanists is surely an irony of history: the humanists were dissatisfied with the philosophical (logical) reading imposed on it by later commentators, a reading which had been fully projected back onto Alexander's own text. This reading conflicted with the humanists' renewed interest in literature as opposed to the logical properties of language itself.[18] Under these conditions, the *Doctrinale* fell out of use.[19] But one testimony to its former glory is that it was one of the earliest books to be printed.[20]

We translate the prooemium, followed by the beginning of chapter 1 (the nominal endings of the first declension); then the regimen of the genitive, some remarks on construction, and the end of the poem.

Translated from *Das Doctrinale des Alexander de Villa-Dei*, ed. Reichling, by permission.

PROOEMIUM[21]

> I am getting ready to write a *Doctrinale* ["book of instruction"] for newer students[22]
> and will adopt many works of my teachers.
> Instead of the nonsense of Maximianus[23] boys will read
> those things which the ancients did not want to make accessible to their dear fellows.
> 5   May the Grace of the nurturing Spirit be present to this work.
> May it help me to complete something that may be of use.
> If the boys should be unable to pay full attention to it at first,
> let him then at least pay attention, who fulfills the tasks of a teacher,

[18] Alexander's offer of his own text instead of Maximianus on the students' reading list is an example of the equivalence of scholarly and literary language as the object of linguistic analysis: the grammarian does not confine himself to the analysis of literary texts, but analyses language more in general. See Heath, "Logical Grammar," 46.

[19] Cf. G. Müller and E. Neuenschwander, "Alexander de Villa Dei," in *Lexikon des Mittelalters* 1980 (1977¹), 381. See in particular the pertinent analysis of this process in Heath, "Logical Grammar, Grammatical Logic," 21, 28.

[20] Cf. Zedler, *Der älteste Buchdruck und das frühholländische Doktrinale des Alexander de Villa Dei*; Gaselee, *The "Costerian" Doctrinale of Alexander de Villa Dei*.

[21] Lines 1–28.

[22] *Clericulis...novellis.* "Schüler aus Kloster- u. Domschulen," Neudecker, *Das Doctrinale des Alexander de Villa-Dei*, 30 n. 299.

[23] An obscene elegist working in the sixth century, also mentioned in line 25; cf. Reichling, ed., xx and xxxvii for the notion that Alexander is here offering himself as a replacement for Maximianus on the reading list; Thurot, *Notices et Extraits*, 112 with n. 3. The *Elegiae* of Maximianus often circulated in verse anthologies. Eberhard thinks reading him is useful. Cf. J. A. Fabricius, *Bibliotheca Latina mediae et infimae aetatis*. t. II. Florence, 1858, s.v. Eberhardus 487. Maximianus' *Elegiae* formed part of the standard elementary reader of the grammar curriculum (the so-called *Liber catonianus* or "Cato-book"): see Woods and Copeland, "Classroom and Confession," and Hunt, *Teaching and Learning Latin*, 1:59–79.

who reads it to the boys, and will disclose it to them in the language of the laity;[24]
10   then for the most part it will be plain to the boys as well.

Words [*voces*], which you must give different forms in different cases,
I will first of all teach you to decline, in as easy a way as I can.
The place next to them is taken by the heteroclitic nouns.[25]
And "comparison" [*collatio*] in its three grades is dealt with after those.
15   I will indicate which word is to be combined with which article.[26]
And then I will follow Peter[27] on the past tenses and the supine verb-forms.
Defective verbs come after these topics, and irregular ones.
Subsequently, I will pick out the fourfold forms of verbs.[28]
And then, to the best of my ability, I will disclose the regimen [*regimen*] of words.
20   How a construction is to be put together, I will add to this.
After that it will be explained, what syllables have what length.
Then I will teach what the various rules are for the accents.
And finally I will teach the grammatical figures to the best of my ability.
Although this doctrine is not really general enough,[29]
25   yet it will be more useful than the nonsense of Maximianus.[30]
What I teach here will be read after the Smaller Alphabet,
and the Greater Alphabet will be read afterwards;[31] it will follow these writings of mine.
This book is almost completely an extract from that one.

CHAPTER I

[The first chapter deals with the endings of the nouns of the first declension, a topic
we know from Priscian's On the Noun, Pronoun, and Verb.[32]]

---

[24] I.e. the vernacular.

[25] I.e. nouns which form their nominative from a different stem than the other cases.

[26] Latin does not have articles (the part of speech). According to the grammarians, one function of the article is to indicate grammatical gender. The Latin grammarians use the forms of the demonstrative pronoun *hic, haec, hoc* to this same end—and call them "articles" when they do so.

[27] I.e. Peter Riga, cf. Neudecker, *Das Doctrinale*, 30 n. 302.

[28] Reference is to chapter 7. The four forms are inceptive/inchoative, meditative (verbs expressing a wish), and frequentative (the latter divided into two), cf. Priscian, *Institutiones* 8.72, *GL* 2:427.10 ff.

[29] *quamvis haec non sit doctrina satis generalis*. This phrase may refer to the fact that Alexander's grammatical observations do not attain the level of philosophical abstraction that Priscian does (i.e. he deals with the "specifics" of grammatical doctrine, not with the philosophical framework). See further the introduction to this section.

[30] See above, on Proem line 3.

[31] For the "Smaller Alphabet" and "Greater Alphabet," see introduction to this section.

[32] Immediately following on the first passage translated here; lines 29–45.

The first declension gives -*as* -*es* -*a* to the nominatives

30   and some Hebrew proper names are written with -*am*,
yielding the diphthong -*ae* for the genitives and datives.
The fourth case preserves -*am*; yet we do find -*en* or -*an*,
when the nominative ends in -*es* or in -*as*, or when a Greek nominative gives -*a*.
The nominative in -*a* of a Greek word causes -*an* in the fourth to be shortened.

35   The fifth case will end in -*a*, however after -*es* one finds -*e*.
The sixth case has -*a*, but [words with nominative in] -*es* you must sometimes give
      [a sixth case] in -*e*.
The -*am* of the nominative you will repeat in the fifth case, and add the sixth.[33]
In the first case plural and in the fifth it is fitting for -*ae* to be put.
And the second case has -*arum*, unless there is syncope.

40   The third or the sixth have -*is*, but there are exceptions:
when a masculine word ends in -*us*, and the feminine in -*a* without there being a neuter,
(the ending) -*abus* will be connected to the feminine forms, e.g. *dominabus* ["ladies,"
      dat./abl.],
in order to distinguish the gender; you may add *animae* ["souls," plur.] to this group.[34]
You will connect -*as* with the plural accusatives.

45   With these verses you now know the first declension.

ON *REGIMEN*

[The next passage is from the chapters on regimen and deals with the congruence between nominative and verb, especially when the subject term is compound; and the beginning of the discussion of the regimen of the genitive (1074–1147): the genitive in part–whole relationships.]

The order of my work commands that at this place the regimen[35] of words be
      disclosed.

1075   Intransitivity usually makes a nominative suppositive to a verb.[36]
But you must understand that this goes for personal verbs.

[33] In other words: the Hebrew words in -*am* have -*ae* in gen. and dat., but -*am* again in acc., abl., and voc. According to Priscian, *Institutiones* 5.11, *GL* 2:148.7, and Charisius, 151.15, ed. Barwick, such words are indeclinable, or *monoptota*: they look the same in all six cases.

[34] Referring to the dat./abl. *animabus*.

[35] Golling, "Einleitung in die Geschichte der lateinischen Syntax," 29, discusses the term *regere*, *regimen*, which gained in popularity from the eighth century. It does not necessarily denote a relation of hierarchy or dependence, but can also be used for the mutual relationship in which every term is put in the proper case. Cf. Thurot, *Notices et Extraits*, 239–44.

[36] *Supponere* expresses both "preposition," i.e. that these nouns/subjects are supposed naturally to precede the verb, and the "subject relationship." Cf. Kneepkens, "*Suppositio*' and *Supponere* in Twelfth-Century Grammar."

A verb of "calling" frequently will require that a nominative be apposed to it,[37]
as does the verb substantive, or one that retains the force of such verbs.[38]
The copula should connect similar cases

1080   when they refer to the same person.
From the force of the person, the copula governs the first nominative.
The nominative that follows is governed by the nature of the verb.
When creating apposition (*apponens*), you will connect two substantives with
    each other
in a similar case-form, and the gender may vary.

1085   Then it will be fitting for those substantives to refer to the same thing,
and the more common one should go first in these cases,
for example, the man, Sortes;[39] the animal, a she-goat, and similar cases.
In general, every nominative will be regarded as being of the third person,
but make an exception for four pronouns.

1090   These pronouns call nominatives to the first or second person,
I, a pauper [*ego pauper*], am playing, while you, a rich person [*tu dives*], are studying;
we talk in safety [*nos tuti*], while you are silent in fear {*vos timidi*}.[40]
Syllepsis [*conceptio*] connects persons, genders, numbers.[41]
Persons that are dissimilar are connected by syllepsis,

1095   and the syllepsis will be created through "and" which is put in the middle.
If it is preposed, no syllepsis will come into being.
A sylleptic form [*concipiens*] wants to retain a verb similar to itself.[42]
The first person takes up the other two, but not vice versa.
Apply syllepsis and give a third person to the middle one, but do not reverse.[43]

1100   Among third persons the one that is put first takes up (*concipit*) the rest.
Thus: *ego tuque damus* ["I and you (we) give"]; "I, you and our brother [we] ask";
"you and your brother [you] give," "the master and the slave [they] pray."
Syllepsis may take place when "with" is used, but never when "or" is used:
"you with me [we] must justly stick to justice."

---

[37] *Apponere* can denote both postposition with regard to the verb and a predicative semantic relationship.

[38] Substantive verbs are e.g. *sum, fio, existo*; vocative verbs: *appellor, dicor*; verbs that behave similarly: *sedeo, incedo, baptizor, ordinor* (i.e. there too a following nominative will be predicative (Reichling, ed., *ad loc.*)

[39] Sortes is Socrates.

[40] I.e. the nominatives *pauper, dives, tuti, timidi* refer to first and second persons in their respective sentences because of the use of the personal pronouns. See Priscian, *Institutiones* 18.4, *GL* 3.211.6–11.

[41] For *conceptio*, see Priscian, *Institutiones* 17.141, *GL* 3:178.18; cf. 17.155, *GL* 3:183.21 ff.

[42] Cf. Thurot, *Notices et Extraits*, 258–9: *conceptio* or syllepsis is the "taking together" of different persons (genders, numbers) with respect to one action or passion: the first person "takes up" the second (*ego et tu ambulamus*) etc. The sylleptic form (in the example: the first person) "wins."

[43] This means that the second person is the *concipiens* when coupled with a third: *tu fraterque datis*: so the third falls under the scope of the second (middle) person.

1105 Similarly: "I with Peter [we] enjoy being in charge."
But syllepsis will not occur in the fifth case,[44]
if a fifth case is lacking: "You, Peter [voc.], and your people [you, plur.]
   must ask";
and "with your friends, you [plur.] must pray, priest of Dionysus."
Between third persons no syllepsis occurs,

1110 but they are connected by "and" or "with,"
and neither is taken up (*concipitur*) (by the other): "the master and his slave
   (they) pray";
"Peter with Paul [they] reign with the King on high."
Most people though are convinced that between
third persons syllepsis can occur.

1115 As there is syllepsis of persons, there will also be syllepsis of genders.
Syllepsis of gender concerns adjectives: the masculine
takes up the feminine and the neuter, and do not reverse this:
"He and his wife are joined [ptc. m. plur.] in bed, but separated [ptc. m. plur]
   in the mind";
"Dear [m. plur.] to the Lord are a virgin[45] joined [*iuncti*, m. plur.] with [*cum*] a
   virgin."

1120 "The ox [m.] and the ass [n.] are tied up [m. plur.] at the manger."
You will see that neuters are as it were taken up by feminines:
"The laws [f.] and plebiscites [n.] are forced through [f.plur.] by coercion."[46]
And you will often do this also with distributives:
Say: "Each [m.] is lying face down," when talking about Peter and Helena.

1125 Prolepsis disconnects the regimen which had first put things together:[47]
"They [m.plur.] fear, one of them [m.sing.] the lords and another [m.sing.] the
   masters."
Or one redirects what one has said, by adopting something on the outside:
"they are hurrying [3 plur.], and [so am] I"; "you are playing (2 sing.) and so is he
   while sitting down."
You will also sometimes find a nominative without a governing word.[48]

1130 the word *ecce* "look" usually gives you a fourth or a nominative case.
There is regimen of oblique cases, a topic you make an effort to grasp.
First I will discuss the regimen which occurs through nouns, then
the one which occurs through verbs, and finally, the one through the others.

---

44 The fifth case is the vocative. Cf. Priscian, *Institutiones* 17.195, *GL* 3:203.28 ff.

45 The first instance of *virgo* is masculine here, since the reference is to sexual abstinence in either sex.

46 Lucan, *Pharsalia* 1.176, as in Priscian, *Institutiones* 17.158, *GL* 3:185.21 (see Reichling, *ad. loc.*).

47 Cf. Priscian, *Institutiones* 17.28, *GL* 3:125.14–17.   48 *Regente solutum*: i.e. a nominative absolute.

You should mind the examples, which will make you see these things clearly.

1135 Connect a noun signifying possession with the genitive.[49]

If you can say truthfully: "this is my thing,"

without adding anything, then you have a case of pure possession.[50]

Let the following serve you as examples: "the king's horse," "the duke's court."

If you need an addition, it is not pure possession.

1140 This will be divided into several kinds.

"Part" and "proper characteristic" govern the genitive and are governed by it,[51]

if only you pay due attention to praise and criticism on either side:

"a strong man's right hand is stronger than the beauty of a woman."

"a man of strong right hand," "a woman of admirable beauty,"

1145 "a strong-headed [gen.] man," "a woman of ugly appearance."[52]

What once was a part should be counted among the [gen. of] part.

You will say that *tunc temporis* ["at that time" (gen.)] belongs with
[the gen. of] parts.

FROM CHAPTER 9

[Chapter 9 deals with (in-)transitivity, construction, and natural word order; the following selection is the beginning of this chapter (1369–96)[53]]

After what we said before this is the right place for construction.

1370 Construction is divided into two kinds: subjoined to it
must be transitivity and intransitivity.

When the parts of which the full construction consists

---

[49] On the possessive genitive, cf. Priscian, *Institutiones* 18.9, *GL* 3:213.3 ff.

[50] Reichling, ed., *ad loc.* gives the gloss, which explains that when you point out your neighbor, you cannot simply say "he is mine," without adding "my neighbor, my friend."

[51] Priscian *Institutiones* 18.12–13, *GL* 3:214.5–14.

[52] The part–whole relationship can be expressed by a genitive in two directions: "the right hand of the man"; "a man 'of a strong right hand,' " i.e. characterized by having a strong right hand. The so-called *genitivus qualitatis* can be used for positive and negative characteristics: "a woman 'of great beauty,' " or "of great ugliness."

[53] Alexander splits verbal constructions into transitive and intransitive ones, and then subdivides the transitive ones into "simple" and "retransitive" ones, and the intransitive category into "simple" and "reciprocal" ones, cf. Golling, "Einleitung in die Geschichte der lateinischen Syntax," 33. On transitive and intransitive constructions and their subdivisions, see Priscian, *Institutiones* 12.12, *GL* 2:584.2–9; 13.23, *GL* 3:15.6–24; 14.14, *GL* 3:32.23–5. Priscian distinguished four types, intransitive, transitive, reciprocal, and retransitive. Intransitive involves only one person, transitive the "transition" from one person or thing to another, reciprocal means one acts on oneself ("Ajax killed himself"), and retransitive means that an action directed at another person "reverts" to oneself (*GL* 2:584.2–9). Cf. Thurot, *Notices et Extraits*, 230–3. From Petrus Helias the relationship between a noun and an accompanying genitive is discussed in these same terms of "transitivity" (Thurot, 231). It is possible that Alexander resists this notion (see note on lines 1387 ff.).

signify various things, let that construction be a transitive one.
One and the same judgment takes places as it were by marking different things.[54]

1375   Transitive constructions should be divided into two members; they are
its kinds: the one which is transitive simply, and the one that is retransitive.
You must pick out intransitivity by what was said before,
and you will distinguish two kinds; simple
and reciprocal intransitivity split it in the same way.[55]

1380   Look, this material must be taught to you by examples:
"he vanquishes his friend," or "Tullius asks Marcus."[56]
"Cicero persuades Marcus, because he (Marcus) loves him (Cicero)."[57]
Tullius is Marcus; the cow is a lion;[58] "the she-goat is a cow,"[59]
"he controls himself," "I love myself, you yourself, we love ourselves,"

1385   "they unite themselves," "you love yourselves."[60]
Note the transition of the action and the persons.
When there is no transition of action, and no undergoing of action
is inflicted on anyone, the full construction is never transitive:
"the son of Alphaeus[61] and Mary (mother) of Jacobus[62] are resting."[63]

1390   Construe as follows:[64] if it is there, begin with the vocative case;
then put the nominative; after that you will place the personal
verb—put this in first position, if the other elements are lacking.[65]
The third and fourth case often follow on this,
or you will add adverbs to the verb. Add the second

1395   case to its governor [rector]. The prepositive word[66]
must precede the fourth or sixth case, which it governs.

---

[54] *Iudicium fit idem tanquam diversa notando.* Different persons play a role and are indicated by different grammatical forms, but together one proposition is expressed. Neudecker, *Das Doctrinale*, 32 n. 327, notes *ad loc. Marcus et Tullius iudicio tanquam diversa notant*, comparing line 1381, but this remains unclear.

[55] Namely, the same way in which transitivity was split.   [56] Simple transitive.

[57] A retransitive construction.   [58] Cf. Isaiah 11:7.

[59] Simple intransitive. For the example, cf. Augustine, *De civitate Dei* 16.24, where both a she-goat and a cow are taken to refer to the *plebs* (in different states).

[60] Reciprocal intransitive.   [61] I.e. Jacobus minor.

[62] Cf. Isidore, *Etymologies* 7.9.15 *Maria uxor Alphaei* (this is Mary the sister of Mary, mother of Jesus).

[63] This is the interpretation of Neudecker, *Das Doctrinale*, 32 n. 331: *Jacobus minor et mater eius quiescunt.* Thus, Neudecker takes *quiescunt* as part of the example sentence. An alternative interpretation is to take *quiescunt* as "are (constructions) at rest." In that case the examples are the nouns + genitives "Jacobus son of Alphaeus" and "Mary mother of Jacobus." "Being at rest" would then be part of the metalinguistic vocabulary and indicate that there is no undergoing or exerting of action here: therefore the construction of noun plus genitive is not "transitive." Reichling, ed., *ad loc.* claims that the verb is only used to fill out the meter, but that does not seem right.

[64] Priscian, *Institutiones* 17.105, *GL* 3:164.16 ff.

[65] I.e. if there is no vocative or nominative in the sentence, you should start with the verbum finitum.

[66] *Vox praepositiva*: circumlocution for "preposition."

ON CONSTRUCTION

[From the discussion of exceptional constructions, the remarks on the verb substantive (1433) and those on the congruence of adjective and substantive (1434–41).]

The verb substantive you often look for outside (the text).[67]
It will be fitting to get to know the nature of the mobile and the fixed:[68]

1435 The adjective goes with the word(-form) or with the meaning.[69]
There is an adjective of gender only,[70] and it will change
its case and number, e.g.: "here comes one of the sisters";
"he is the good one among the brothers," or "one of the brothers."
When a verb is put between nominatives of different numbers,

1440 it is assimilated to either at will:
"the prayers to the highest father is the practice of the just."[71]

THE CONCLUSION

[The end of the *Doctrinale* (2640–5).]

2640 I think nothing has been asserted that cannot be maintained,
and I have signaled many things that you should not imitate.[72]
The *Book of Instruction* [*Doctrinale*] I have completed with the help of God's virtue.
I bring thanks to you, God the Father, and to you, Christ,
God son of God, and to you, God nurturing Breath:

2645 these three persons I believe to be equally divine.

---

[67] I.e. the verb "to be" is often not expressed in the text and should be mentally supplied.

[68] I.e. of the adjective and the substantive, which "naturally" should agree.

[69] Cf. Thurot, *Notices et Extraits*, 107. Reichling, ed., explains with the glossator that an *adiectivum vocis* is e.g. *omnis*, *nullus*; and an *adiectivum significati* is e.g. *magister* or *sartor*. So too Golling, "Einleitung in die Geschichte der lateinischen Syntax," 34.

[70] In constructions like *una sororum* "one of the sisters," the adjective *una* is congruent with the substantive in gender only.

[71] *Sermones summi patris est meditatio iusti*: in this kind of construction the verb "to be" can be either in the singular or the plural since it connects a singular and a plural (or vice versa).

[72] Reichling quotes the glossator who connects these two verses with the three parts of grammar: a preceptive part (*praeceptiva*), referred to here in line 2640, a permissive part (*permissiva*), referred to here by *pluraque signavi*, meaning notable uses of the *auctores* have been flagged, which are not to be condemned in their texts. The third part is the prohibitive one (*prohibitiva*), which does not permit certain usages to be taken over by the students—here: *quae non debes imitari*.

EBERHARD OF BÉTHUNE, *GRAECISMUS*, 1212

INTRODUCTION

Like the *Doctrinale* of Alexander of Villa Dei, the *Graecismus* by Eberhard of Béthune[1] (in Flanders) is a grammar composed in verse. Together with the *Doctrinale*, which it often accompanied in manuscripts, it came to replace Priscian in grammatical teaching, at various levels of the curriculum, from the thirteenth century onwards.[2] The metrical form of both texts gave them a mnemotechnical advantage over Priscian's *Institutiones*, which was regarded as too cumbersome and expansive. The *Graecismus* complements the *Doctrinale* in many ways, and like the *Doctrinale* it is not a complete grammar. As its introduction states, it has a primarily lexical interest in *differentiae* (words that need to be distinguished from each other). It uses the system of the parts of speech to bring some order into the unwieldy mass of these terms, but does not have a logical structure *per divisionem*. That lack of natural structure is what makes the verse form useful.[3] In its theoretical outlook, the *Graecismus* is slightly reactionary, in that it rejects metalinguistic reflection and advocates a return to the study of Latin words and their meanings in the tradition of Donatus, rather than more philosophically oriented theories of primary and secondary imposition.[4] With its grammatical teachings on the figures and tropes, the *Graecismus* is also closely linked with the contemporary genre of the *ars poetriae*, and indeed shares some source material with the poetic arts.[5]

The fortunes of the *Graecismus* resemble those of the *Doctrinale* in another way: it too was subjected to glosses, some of them elementary in their orientation (teaching aids), and

---

[1] Eberhard uses his own name in his work at various points, e.g. XXVII 19 and 25, see below, in the best grammatical tradition. Also e.g. in XXV 10 ff., cf. edition by Wrobel, vii.

[2] Cf. Bursill-Hall, "Teaching Grammars of the Middle Ages," 12–15.

[3] Law, "Why Write a Verse Grammar," 61–2.

[4] Cf. Grondeux, *Le Graecismus d'Évrard de Béthune à travers ses gloses*, 29. Ultimately, the attempts by Eberhard to stop the didactic success of Priscian were in vain; see Grondeux, *Le Graecismus*, 34.

[5] The section on the colors of rhetoric has as its source the *De ornamentis verborum* of Marbod of Rennes, the source also of Geoffrey of Vinsauf's *Summa de coloribus rhetoricis*.

some also in the vernacular.[6] It also attracted a rich tradition of university-level commentary which projected several generations of philosophical interests back onto the text (a development that parallels the reception of the *Doctrinale* in the medieval university). The prominence that Eberhard gives to the "figures" or forms of metaplasm, *schemata* (i.e. the "figures of speech"), the tropes, and other grammatical deviations, as well as to the "forms" of the "colors of rhetoric," would certainly account for the popularity of the treatise in elementary or intermediate grammatical studies. But the presentation of these matters also proved irresistible to university-level commentators, who used the treatise as an occasion to expound their interests in the logic and semantics of figurative language.[7] Thus it was that the *Graecismus*, along with the *Doctrinale*, had an important second life as a text studied and commented on in university milieus.

The date of the work is almost universally accepted as 1212.[8] The title of the work is really appropriate only to chapter VIII, in which Greek words are discussed. The chapter makes it clear that the author does not know much Greek, but it nevertheless earned him the title of *Graecista*. Eberhard himself probably composed chapters IX–XXVII, which fit the announcements made in the prooemium, and basically follow the system of the parts of speech based on Donatus.[9] However, the *dispositio* following the prooemium only takes chapters I–VIII into account.[10] Chapters I–VIII themselves are an amalgamation of other sources.[11] On the basis of this information and a colophon in one of the manuscripts,

---

[6] Hunt, *Teaching and Learning Latin*, 1:94–8.

[7] On this tradition of commentary, see Grondeux, *Le Graecismus d'Évrard de Béthune*, and Grondeux, "Terminologie des figures dans le Doctrinale d'Alexandre de Villedieu et le Graecismus d'Évrard de Béthune." See also the introduction to Part 5, within. For an example of scholastic interests in figures, see the selection from the "Kilwardby" commentary on the *Barbarismus* (Part 5, within).

[8] A distich deriving from the fifteenth century (appearing as a marginal scholion in a seventeenth-century printed edition of a work by Henry of Ghent) gives a date for the *Graecismus*, but the ambiguous formulation of the distich allows both 1124 and 1212 as the date. The earlier date is impossible, given the clear evidence that Eberhard drew on the commentary by Petrus Helias on Priscian, and the absence of any record of the text before the thirteenth century. For a clear account of the evidence for dating the *Graecismus* and the problematic status of the distich itself, see Williams, "The *De differentiis et derivationibus grecorum* attributed to William of Corbeil." Cf. Grondeux, *Le Graecismus d'Évrard de Béthune*, 10 with n. 16.

[9] This is clear from Eberhard's programmatic statements, but especially from the order of the parts of speech, which is that of Donatus (noun, pronoun, verb), not that of Priscian.

[10] The discrepancy between announcement and actual structure was noted by Thurot, *Notices et Extraits*, 100. He explains this as the result of adaptations to the text made in the course of its use as a school-text (ibid., 101). This possibility cannot be excluded, since school texts are a notoriously "open" genre, i.e. even though the text is regularly adapted, it will still be handed down under the authoritative name of its original author. Cf. Robins, "The authenticity of the *Technê*: the *status quaestionis*," esp. 22 ff.

[11] Cf. Lohmeyer, "Ebrard von Béthune. Eine Untersuchung über den Verfasser des Graecismus und Laborintus," 417 ff., esp. 419. The first part contains chapters on figures (metaplasm, *schemata*, tropes) (I), barbarism and solecism (II), rhetorical colors (III), metrical feet (IV), changing of letters (V), monosyllabic nouns (VI), names of Muses and pagans (VII), names deriving from the Greek (VIII); cf. Grondeux, *Le Graecismus d'Évrard de Béthune*, 19 ff.

Lohmeyer and Manitius have surmised that the work was published as a whole by Eberhard's friends after his death and that this explains these inconsistencies.[12]

The work must have appealed to students by its use of humor, sometimes misogynistic, as in XIII 10–11 translated below, sometimes in the form of a typical grammarian's joke, as in XIV 3 where the genitive of the name of Priscian is "split" into Prisci and ani (a "tmesis," with rather interesting consequences for the meaning of the verse and the author's attitude to Priscian).[13]

The best known of the other works which can be safely attributed to Eberhard of Béthune is the *Antiheresis* (ca. 1210), a treatise against the Cathars and Waldensians. The *Laborintus* of Eberhard the German, dating most likely from the second half of the thirteenth century, was formerly wrongly attributed to Eberhard of Béthune.[14]

We translate the highly rhetorical prose proem, followed by I 1–42 (on figures); XIII 1–21 (on adjective nouns, with emphasis on the distinction of near-synonyms); XIV 1–30 (on the pronoun), and a short section from the final chapter on diasyntastica (XXVII 11–27), which follows the chapters on the parts of speech.

Translated from *Eberhardi Bethuniensis Graecismus*, ed. Wrobel, by permission.

PROOEMIUM[15]

Disgracefully blinded by a cloud of ignorance, some ignoramuses give expression to their asinine stupidity by imagining Chimaera-like statues[16] and dreaming up something

---

[12] Lohmeyer, "Ebrard von Béthune," 427; Manitius, *Geschichte der lateinischen Literatur des Mittelalters*, 3:747–51. Colophon in MS Helmstedt 587 (s. XV) f. 140: *quidam dicunt nostrum Ebreardum fuisse preventum morte antequam istum librum composuit ad finem, qui adhuc plures regulas grammaticales addidisset si diutius supervixisset. Ergo quidam socii . . . ob reverentiam magistri Ebrardi habent librum [quem] duobus versibus concluserunt et sunt isti: Explicit Ebrardi Grecismus nomine Christi etc.* (Manitius, *Geschichte der lateinischen Literatur* 3:747) ("Some people say that our Eberhard died before he had finished this book. Had he lived longer, he would have added many more grammatical rules. So some of his companions out of respect for master Eberhard finished the book with the following two verses: Here ends the Grecismus of Eberhard, in the name of Christ etc.").

[13] See note *ad loc.* and Sluiter, "Persuasion, Pedagogy, Polemics." On Eberhard's sense of humor, see also Hauréau, "Eberhardi Bethuniensis Graecismus" (review of the Wrobel edition), 60 quoting from chapter VIII *choerus est porcus; ne dicas: "choere, eleison"*: "choiros is (Greek for) pig; don't say 'pig, have mercy'" (making a rather *risqué* joke on the similarity in sound between *choere eleison*, and *kyrie eleison*).

[14] Lohmeyer, "Ebrard von Béthune," 414. On the ascription of the *Laborintus* see further Thurot, "Document relatif à l'histoire de la poésie latine au moyen-âge," 260; Faral, ed., *Les arts poétiques*, 38–9.

[15] The proem is translated into French in Grondeux, *Le Graecismus d'Évrard de Béthune*, 29 f.

[16] The Chimaera is a hybrid creature, part lion, part dragon, and part goat. The grammarians criticized here have no idea of how a normal sentence is formed in a congruent and fitting way, because they are diverted by irrelevant

inconceivable: they make incongruent connections between completely dissimilar words in an unlawful matrimony and a completely incoherent conjunction, and that is why I thought they needed help and advice.[17] For they are implanting horse's hair on to a human head,[18] attribute feathers to fish and scales to birds, offer a categorical hood and a white syllogism[19] and thus they are fishing for boars and lions in the waters, using dogs, and they are hunting for pike and salmon in the woods, using hunting-nets. Now when I noticed that most people err in such a way (and nevertheless are unaware of their mistakes), in order that I may check their erroneous opinions by the file of correction, not the odium of reproach, I took courage to undertake this burdensome job, insofar as the poverty of my poor little talent is capable of sustaining it. Thus, I made it my topic to serve everyone's interest by setting out clearly the meanings of words, and the differences between meanings,[20] namely in what respects words fit together and in which ones they differ from each other. Now the mixing of words, and the entangling of the mixing, and the confusion of the entangling creates boredom and mistakes both for beginners and advanced students.[21] That is why I decided to follow the order of Donatus in dealing with everything that is confusing because of the differences of place and multiple meanings: I will sharpen my pen and discuss the noun first, then the pronoun, and the rest in order.

On the figures of metaplasm. On the figures of the schema. On the figures of the trope. On the figures of barbarism and soloecism. On rhetorical colors. On metrical feet. On the interchange of letters. On monosyllabic nouns, of what gender they are. On the names of the Muses and the pagans. On the names originating from the Greek in alphabetical order.[22]

---

philosophical considerations. Grondeux points out that we know of nobody who defends the view contested by Eberhard here (*Le Graecismus d'Évrard de Béthune*, 30 n. 70). Whenever the odd combinations he criticizes are mentioned, it is also to criticize them or declare their impossibility.

[17] There is an echo here of the prose introduction to the *Disticha Catonis* (A. Baehrens, ed., *Poetae latini minores* 3 [Leipzig: Teubner, 1881], 214); cf. Lohmayer, "Ebrard von Béthune," 424 n. 2.

[18] This recalls Horace's warning against incongruous composition, *Ars poetica* 1 ff.

[19] The "categorical hood" is considered congruent, but not "proper" by Thomas of Erfurt. See Grondeux, *Le Graecismus d'Évrard de Béthune*, 34, referring to Rosier, " 'O Magister...' Grammaticalité et intelligibilité selon un sophisme du XIIIᵉ siècle," 10 with note 23. On the incongruous construction of "adjectives of secondary imposition," such as "hypothetical" or "categorical" with "nouns of primary imposition," such as "hood," see the section on Petrus Helias, above. Cf. Grondeux, *Le Graecismus d'Évrard de Béthune*, 32 f.

[20] This is where Eberhard states his main goal of elucidating *differentiae*, ordered according to their parts of speech.

[21] *Rudes* and *provecti* respectively.   [22] For this incomplete table of contents, see introductory note.

CHAPTER I (I 1–42)

On Figures

On the figures of metaplasm

Literally, *meta* is Greek for *trans*, *plasma* Greek for *formatio*,
hence *metaplasmus* must be called *transformatio* ["transformation"].
When something is added or detracted for some reason
or transposed, e.g. a letter, syllable, or (metrical) length,

5   then that means there comes into being a figure truly and properly speaking,
which is said to subsume many figures.
Prothesis[23] adds something in front, *auferesis* cuts it back.
Syncopa removes something from the middle, which *epenthesis* adds.
Apocope takes away the end, which is added by *paragoge*.

10   *Systole* shortens a long vowel, *diastole* lengthens one:[24]
what nature orders should be long, *systole* shortens,
extasis on the other hand lengthens what should be taken short.
Ellipsis kills an *m*, *synalimpha* eliminates a vowel.[25]
The missing of one word is called *eclipsis*.

15   But *aposiopesis* is an incomplete sentence.
Pleonasmos is the adoption of a redundant word.
If you say *fieri* ["to become, to happen"] instead of *firi* ["to become, to happen"],[26]
    you have a case of *diaeresis*,
if you say *tibicen*, on the other hand, you have a case of *synaeresis*.[27]
Hac Arethusa tenus ["thus Arethusa"][28] one may say and produce a *temesis*[29]

20   When one word embraces two one has a case of *synthesis* ["composition"].
Double a syllable, word, or sentence:

---

[23] For the following series of figures (*prothesis, epenthesis, paragoge, aphaeresis, syncope, apocope, ectasis, systole, diaeresis*), cf. Donatus, *Ars maior* 3.4, *GL* 4:396.1 ff.

[24] *Diastole* divides a diphthong or long vowel over two syllables.

[25] I.e. synaloephe.

[26] *Firi* would have looked like a more regular form when compared to 3rd pers. *fit*.

[27] Instead of *tibii-cen* (from *tibia* "flute" and *canere* "to sing/play"): flute-player.

[28] Ovid, *Metamorphoses* 5.642.

[29] Tmesis "separation": *hac . . . tenus* for *hactenus* "so far; thus."

Tune duos, meme, leleges: this is *epidiasis*.[30]

If you say *Teucre* instead of *Teucer*, there is *metathesis*.[31]

Antithesis occurs if a syllable has its order reversed.[32]

25 Say *Transtra per et remos*: you will have *anastropha*[33]

"She raised and bore," this is a *hysteron proteron*.

Paralange of *prothesis* may also occur, when you

say: "Symeon took him in his arms."[34]

Epibasis is produced by the repetition of different words [*voces*],

30 if these words embrace the same sense.

Metabole is content [*res*] which is repeated in various forms:

"If fate preserves the man, if he enjoys ethereal air

and does not repose with the cruel shades."[35]

Epimone is a sentence which is repeated often,[36]

35 this is clear in verses with a refrain:[37]

"Cede, day, from the sky, since the girl does not know how to yield."[38]

"Impious Deianira, why do you hesitate to die?"[39]

The redoubling of one word is *epizeuxis*.

Say "give the winds to the boat," and you will have an *hypallage*.[40]

---

[30] The examples correspond chiastically to the description: a sentence is "doubled" in Juvenal VI 641–2 *tune duos una, saevissima vipera, cena? / tune duos?* "Did you (kill) two with one meal, you vicious viper? Did you (kill) two?". A word is doubled in *Aeneid* 9.427 *me, me, adsum qui feci, in me convertite ferrum*. A syllable is doubled in *Leleges* (either the medieval *lelex*, lawyer [see Du Cange, s.v.], or cf. *Aeneid* 8.725; Ovid, *Metamorphoses* 9.645; Pliny, *Natural History* 4.27). *Epidiasis* must be derived from Greek *duo*, but does not occur elsewhere. Donatus, *Ars maior* 3.5, GL 4:398.12 ff. uses *epizeuxis* and gives *Aeneid* 9.427 as an example (see above, *me me*).

[31] Cf. Donatus, *Ars maior* 3.4, GL 4:397.3.

[32] Usually, *antithesis* refers to the use of one letter for another, as *olli* for *illi*, e.g. Donatus, *Ars maior* 3.4, GL 4:397.1; Isidore, *Etymologiae* 1.35.6.

[33] *Aeneid* 5.663: "across the rowing benches and oars": *per* "belongs" before *transtra*.

[34] *Symeon accepit in ulnas*, Luke 2:25 (*et ipse accepit eum in ulnas*). This refers to *parallage*, or interchanging of prepositions (*prothesis*) (in this case of *in* for *inter*), cf. Cassiodorus, *Expositio Psalmorum*, ed. Adriaen, in Psalm 58:254 *Quae figura dicitur prothesios parallage, cum altera propositio pro altera ponitur*. Cassiodorus' Psalm commentary is an important source for chapters I and II of the *Graecismus*.

[35] *Aeneid* 1.546 f.: the content, repeated three times, is "if he is not dead."

[36] Cassiodorus, *Expositio Psalmorum*, e.g. in Psalm 71:58; Psalm 95:53; Psalm 143:55: *quae figura Graece dicitur epimone, Latine repetitio crebra sententiae*.

[37] On the use of refrains, cf. Cassiodorus, *Expositio Psalmorum*, in Psalm 106:40 *quod genus carminis a magistris saecularibus intercalare vocitatur, ubi adeo repetitio crebra geminatur, ut necessaria commonitio frequenti repetitione dulcescat*.

[38] *Ecloga Theoduli* (tenth century), lines 296 and 312.

[39] This line is repeated as a refrain four times in Ovid, *Heroides* 9.146, 152, 158, 164.

[40] *Aeneid* 3.60 in the form *dare classibus Austros*. Example discussed, e.g. Isidore, *Etymologiae* 1.36.22: *hypallage, quotienscumque per contraria verba intelliguntur, ut: dare classibus Austros, cum ventis naves demus, non navibus ventos*.

40   "The city (acc.) which I am founding is yours" is an *antitosis*.[41]
     If you use one number instead of the other, it will be *exallage*
     as in saying "the ships are filled with the armed soldier."[42]

CHAPTER XIII (1–21)

On Adjective Nouns[43]

Aeternus ["eternal"] is truly without a beginning and without an end
Perpetuus ["perpetual"] has a beginning, but will lack an ending,
   you can call a soul *perpetua*, and you can call it *perennis* ["perennial"], *per annos* ["through
      the years"],
But whatever you wish to call *sempiternus* ["sempiternal"], you may call it so correctly,
5   and yet, eternal and sempiternal are cotemporal.[44]
   A wound is called *illatum* ["inflicted"], a sore *innatum* ["innate"],
   The head-word of the first is *infero*, of the second *innascor*.
   A rumor is something *credibilis* ["credible"], *credula* ["credulous"] is a woman who is
      quick to believe.
   This is also the difference between *incredibilis* ["incredible"], and *incredula*
      ["incredulous"].
10   There are three words which equally form a substantive about women:
   dustria curia iuria, at least when preceded by *in*.[45]
   Wine is *bibile* ["drinkable"], to be *bibulus* ["drinking, absorbing moisture"] you may
      freely attribute to sand.
   Bibulus ["drinking"] signifies the act, *bibilis* ["drinkable"] makes something suitable for
      drinking.

---

[41]   *Antiptosis*: using one case instead of another. Reference is to *Aeneid* 1.572, cf. Cassiodorus, *Expositio Psalmorum*, in Psalm 34:295 *Quae figura dicitur antiptosis quando casus pro casu ponitur.*

[42]   *Aeneid* 2.18 (on the Trojan horse, rather than a ship); cf. Cassiodorus, *Expositio Psalmorum*, in Psalm 82:79; Isidore, *Etymologiae* 1.36.6 (under the term *syllempsis*: *pro multis, unus*, with this same example).

[43]   This chapter displays a semantic interest in the distinction between similar words. This promotes correct usage. A number of the words discussed here also feature in Isidore's *Differentiae* (*sempiternus/perpetuus*; *vulnus/ulcus*; *orbus/caecus*).

[44]   The differences between *aeternum*, *perpetuus*, *perennis*, and *sempiternus* are discussed here. Calling a soul "eternal" (*aeternus*), would contradict the dogma that the soul only comes into being with birth. However, there apparently is no such restriction on calling a soul *sempiterna*, although *aeternus* and *sempiternus* are strictly speaking synonyms, and denote the same extension of time forward and backward. For *anima sempiterna* cf. e.g. Augustine, *Soliloquia* 887.27.

[45]   *quae pariter substantivant muliebre*: they form feminine substantives, but also substantives that characterize women: *industria* "industry," *incuria* "carelessness," *iniuria* "injustice."

If someone is violently deprived of vision, he is called *orbus* ["blinded"]

15 Someone *caecus* ["blind"] has useless instruments of vision.

Abortivus ["born prematurely, aborted"] is someone who is pulled from the womb after cutting it open,[46]

postumus ["posthumous"] is somebody born after the death of his father.

Call someone *lepidus* ["witty"] because of his words and *facetus* ["humorous"] because of his deeds.[47]

Your clothes make you *pulcher* ["beautiful"], nature makes you *decorus* ["seemly"].

20 Time will be called *angustus* ["constrained, brief"], but a place is called *artus* ["constrained, narrow"].[48]

Let *ango* ["to press together"] be the headword of the former, *arceo* ["to enclose"] of the latter.

CHAPTER XIV (1–30)

On Pronouns

Following the first footsteps of our Donatus

I will now, having discussed the noun, speak about the pronoun

Not that I have anything against the words of Priscianus[49]

but because in this work I want to instruct *minores*.[50]

5 Well then, for the pronouns we find a double reason

why they are invented;[51] the first of these is necessary for you,

---

[46] Cf. Isidore, *Etymologiae* 10.20 *abortivus, eo quod non oriatur, sed aboriatur et excidat.*

[47] The distinction is probably based on a false etymology deriving *facetus* from *facta.*

[48] *Angustus* can be said of temporal and local constraints. The opposition between *angustus* and *artus* is a bit artificial.

[49] *Non quia sim prisci dictis contrarius ani*: The phenomenon of "tmesis" or "splitting" of constituents is part of the Latin poetical tradition from its beginnings, in imitation of the Homeric practice. However, it often has interesting semantic side-effects, also right from the beginning as in the famous verse, long attributed to Ennius (*Annals* 609, ed. J. Vahlen, *Ennianae poesis reliquiae* [Leipzig: Teubner, 1903]) *saxo cere comminuit brum*, where the skull (*cerebrum*) that was shattered by a rock is neatly split in two by the word for "shattering," creating an impressive sound-effect that imitates the process described in the last word of the verse. In this case, Eberhard claims that he has no problems with Priscian, but the tmesis also allows the verse to be translated as "not that I have anything against the words of the old ass-hole," which rather undermines its more innocuous meaning. John of Garland replies in kind when he writes on the *Graecismus* (*Morale scolarium*, ch. xiv, ed. Paetow, 11.359–60): *Mendax* Graecismus *est Grecis philosophis mus / quando latinismus est turget mons velut ismus*. See also Hunt, *Teaching and Learning Latin*, 1:92. Cf. Horace, *Ars poetica* 139. For this analysis see Sluiter, "Persuasion, Pedagogy, Polemics."

[50] Traditionally, Donatus was the beginners' manual.

[51] The *causa inventionis* is the topos where the *raison d'être* is discussed.

the other is a convenience. For with regard to the plural or singular pronouns
of the first or second person
those were invented for us out of necessity,
10   like *ego tu* ["I, you"] with their cases; however the ones
which belong to the other person,[52] those I think
were invented for convenience's sake, for example *iste* ["that (man), he"] or *ille* ["that (man), he"].
For pronouns mark the fact that the discourse continues to be
about the same thing, which is not true of the noun.
15   And referring to the same thing may be a certain *raison d'être*,
Deixis [pointing out] or distinguishing are also *raisons d'être*.[53]
For although nouns also point out something or refer,
they do so in an unclear way, while pronouns do it with certainty.
Now and then, though, nouns also demonstrate with certainty.
20   But really a noun will signify essence [*usia (ousia)*] to you,
and a pronoun signifies to you *hypostasis* itself
and makes you understand what substance is in an absolute way.[54]

CHAPTER XXVII (11–27)

On Syntax (diasyntastica)

You must say that an adjective is matched with a substantive
in whichever case and that it is made to agree with it.
About substantives the rule will be the following for you:
The rule has it that if it comes before the verb, you take it
15   in the nominative, for I say that it gives the person to the verb.
If it follows the verb, this is the rule I will give you: every
appellative verb or substantive verb or any other one like these
has similar cases within itself:
E.g. *vocor Ebrardus* ["I am called Eberhard (nom.)"],[55] or "I am good [nom.],"
    "I walk straight [nom.],"

---

[52] Namely, the third.

[53] So three functions are distinguished for pronouns: reference (anaphora), pointing out (deixis), and distinguishing (contrastive use).

[54] A more traditional distinction is between articles/pronouns indicating hypostasis or *ousia*, and the noun indicating "quality," cf. de Jonge, "Natura artis magistra."

[55] Note the use of the name of the author. See Lohmeyer, "Ebrard von Béthune," 416.

20   and *quam* ["than"] governs the nominative, if you join a comparative to it.
     But if a genitive is construed with a noun,
     this will be a possessive construction, or a distributive one,
     or one *par excellence* or a comparative one,
     or a natural attribute or maybe a consecutive one:
25   Examples: "the book of Eberhard [*Eberhardi*]" is correct, and "one of them [*eorum*]"
     "heavens of heavens [*caelorum*]," you say, and "first of his fellows [*sociorum*]"
     "worthy of praise [*laudis*]", you say, and "ages of ages [*saeculorum*]."

GEOFFREY OF VINSAUF,
POETRIA NOVA, CA. 1208–1213

INTRODUCTION

The *Poetria nova*, a two-thousand-line poem in hexameters, was the most influential of all the medieval *artes poetriae*. It survives in over two hundred manuscripts from the thirteenth to the seventeenth centuries, and became a standard textbook of rhetorical composition for the later Middle Ages and even into the seventeenth century, reaching into many parts of Europe. According to Marjorie Curry Woods, who has studied the manuscript tradition of this work in detail, about half of the manuscripts contain marginal commentaries and other interpretive materials, and some of the commentaries were copied independently of the text.[1] One early version of the commentaries on the *Poetria nova* was edited and translated by Woods.[2] The *Poetria nova* lent itself to teaching at all levels, from grammatical and literary instruction to professional training, because it contains so many different kinds of materials, including a dedication to Pope Innocent III, important set texts such as the laments on the death of Richard I, and a wealth of quotations from classical and "modern" authors, and because it both teaches and illustrates the whole process of composition.[3] Some commentaries stress literary appreciation of the work and in the nature of their glossing are more closely associated with elementary instruction; other commentaries focus on theoretical aspects of the art of rhetoric, and can be linked with advanced and university-level instruction in rhetoric (among these is a commentary by the Prague rhetorician Nicholas Dybinus). There is also a group of

---

[1] For an overview of these commentaries see Woods, *Classroom Commentaries*, chapter 1, "Why was the *Poetria nova* so Popular?"

[2] Woods, ed. and trans., *An Early Commentary on the Poetria nova of Geoffrey of Vinsauf*. See the introduction to Woods' edition, xix–lii, for detailed information about commentaries and glosses on the *Poetria nova*. Excerpts from the commentary edited by Woods have been incorporated into the notes to the selections from the *Poetria nova* below.

[3] See the articles by Woods, "A Medieval Rhetoric Goes to School—and to the University"; "An Unfashionable Rhetoric in the Fifteenth Century"; and "Classical Examples and References in Medieval Lectures on Poetic Composition."

pre-humanist commentaries from fourteenth-century Italy.[4] The *Poetria nova* was cited
and used, not only by other rhetoricians following in the tradition of preceptive grammar,
but by writers of treatises on *dictamen* and prose, scholastic thinkers and historians
(Vincent of Beauvais, Nicholas Trevet), and poets, including of course Chaucer's famous
apostrophe to "Galfridus" in the *Nun's Priest's Tale* and his quotation of the *Poetria nova* in
Troilus and Criseyde.[5]

Because manuscripts of the *Poetria nova* commonly attribute the poem to a "Galfridus
Anglicus," it is generally assumed that Geoffrey of Vinsauf was English. Of his life little else
is known with certainty.[6] The other writings that can be attributed to him with certainty are
the prose *Documentum de modo et arte dictandi et versificandi*, which is a treatise on both
verse- and prose-writing, and the *Summa de coloribus rhetoricis*.[7] The long treatise now
known by its incipit as the *Tria sunt* was once thought to be Geoffrey of Vinsauf's expansion
of his own *Documentum*, but it is now recognized to be the work of a later, anonymous
writer who made extended use of the *Documentum* as well as of other texts.[8]

The title *Poetria nova* consciously alludes to Horace's *Ars poetica*: this is a new poetics
which draws much of its teaching from Horace's "old" poetics. The term *nova* may also
refer to the *Rhetorica ad Herennium* (Geoffrey's other principal source), which was often
known during the Middle Ages as the *Rhetorica nova* or "new rhetoric" (Cicero's *De
inventione* being known as the *Rhetorica vetus* or "old rhetoric"). In the preceptive tradition
of the *Ad Herennium*, the *Poetria nova* covers all five of the canons of rhetoric, from the
teaching of invention as conceptual planning (the archetype), to disposition or arrangement through the natural and artificial orders of narration, and then to style, as both a
material function (amplification and abbreviation of the matter devised) and a verbal
(elocutionary) function (stylistic ornaments), and finally to advice about memory and
delivery.[9] The historical importance and cultural influence of the *Poetria nova* are due in

---

[4] Woods, "A Medieval Rhetoric Goes to School."

[5] See Kelly, *Arts of Poetry and Prose*, 116–19, and Kelly, "Theory of Composition in Medieval Narrative Poetry and
Geoffrey of Vinsauf's *Poetria nova*"; see also Camargo, ed., *Medieval Rhetorics of Prose Composition*, 98, 137.

[6] On a possibly autobiographical poem, see Richardson, "The Schools of Northampton in the Twelfth
Century," and Faral, *Les arts poétiques*, 16–18.

[7] The *Documentum* is edited in Faral, *Les arts poétiques*, 262–320; it is translated by Parr, *Instruction in the Method
and Art of Speaking and Versifying*. Excerpts of the *Summa de coloribus rhetoricis* (along with a summary) are given in
Faral, 321–7.

[8] See *Tria sunt* selection within, pp. 670–81, and references there. On relations with Geoffrey of Vinsauf's work,
see Camargo, "*Tria sunt*: The Long and the Short of Geoffrey of Vinsauf's *Documentum*."

[9] On topical invention in Geoffrey and Vinsauf and the other writers of arts of poetry, see Kelly, "La spécialité
dans l'invention des topiques," and Kelly, "The Scope of the Treatment of Composition in the Twelfth- and
Thirteenth-Century Arts of Poetry." See also the account of invention, disposition, and material style in Kelly, *The
Arts of Poetry and Prose*, 64–78.

large part to its synthetic comprehension of the theoretical and formal aspects of classical rhetorical teaching: the conceptual and architectonic dimensions of poetic narration as a whole along with the teaching of stylistic embellishment.[10] In its elaborate treatment of the doctrine of *transumptio*, Geoffrey defines a generalized "method" for approaching semantic conversion or transference, Here *transumptio* is the genus or methodological heading which subsumes the individual tropes of metaphor, allegory, antonomasia, and onomatopoeia.[11] In terms of its treatment of the figures, the *Poetria nova* positions poetic composition in relation to dialectical teaching about syllogistic method. In its attempts to isolate the functions of individual parts of speech to understand the roles they can play in altering stylistic effect, the work situates itself in both the preceptive and theoretical traditions of grammar.

Translation reprinted from *The Poetria nova and its Sources in Early Rhetorical Doctrine*, **trans. Gallo, by permission.**[12]

ON THE ART IN GENERAL

If anyone is to lay the foundation of a house,[13] his impetuous hand does not leap into action: the inner design of the heart measures out the work beforehand, the inner man determines the stages ahead of time in a certain order; and the hand of the heart, rather than the bodily hand, forms the whole in advance, so that the work exists first as a mental model rather than as a tangible thing.[14] In this mirror let poetry itself see what law must be

---

[10] On this see also Tilliette, *Des mots à la parole: une lecture de la Poetria nova de Geoffroy de Vinsauf.*

[11] See below, pp. 602–6.

[12] Edition in Faral, *Les arts poétiques*, 194–262 (Gallo also reprints Faral's edition, upon which his translation is based). Gallo's division of the text and headings have not been incorporated. Gallo lays his translation out as (irregular) verse lines (not followed here). Other translations of the *Poetria nova* are: Nims, *Poetria nova of Geoffrey of Vinsauf*, and Baltzell-Kopp, *The New Poetics (Poetria nova).*

[13] The mid-thirteenth-century commentary on the *Poetria nova* edited by Woods (which the editor designates as the *In principio huius libri* Type A Commentary) notes of this passage: "This section is assigned first to invention [*assignatur inventioni*] and second to the Narration" (p. 17). As this commentator points out in his *accessus* (pp. 3–5), the *Poetria nova* is laid out as the five parts of rhetoric and as the six parts of an oration; this section, on discovery of material, pertains both to invention and to that part of the oration, *narratio*, that sets forth information. While Geoffrey of Vinsauf did not use the term *inventio* to describe the subject matter of this section, his earliest commentators recognized the inventional doctrine contained therein, and recognized the resonance of this section with the treatments of invention in Cicero and Horace.

[14] This image is reprised most famously in Chaucer's *Troilus and Criseyde* 1.1065–9, where Chaucer clearly draws on the language of the *Poetria nova*. But the likening of the writer's task to that of an architect or builder is

given to poets. Let not your hand be too swift to grasp the pen, nor your tongue too eager to utter the word. Allow neither to be ruled by the hands of fortune but, in order that the work have better fortune, let a discreet mind, walking before the deed, suspend the offices of both hand and tongue, and ponder the theme for a while. Let the inner compasses of the mind lay out the entire range of the material. Let a certain order predetermine from what point the pen should start on its course, and where the outermost limits shall be fixed. Prudently ponder the entire work within the breast, and let it be in the breast before it is in the mouth.

When, in the recesses of the mind, order has arranged the matter, let the art of poetry come to clothe the matter[15] with words. However, when it comes to assist, let it make itself fit for the service of the mistress.[16] Let it beware lest its head with shaggy hair, its body with tattered garments, or the least little detail displease. Do not let polishing one part of the work mar it elsewhere, for if part of the work sits poorly anywhere, the whole sequence will contract shame therefrom.[17] A small taint spoils the whole apple. One blemish can ruin the entire face. Therefore consider the material cautiously, lest it fear disgrace.

Let the beginning of the poem, like a pleasant servant, introduce the matter. Let the middle, like a diligent host, prepare a dignified entertainment.[18] Let the end, like a herald of the completed course, send it away with honor. Let each part in its own way adorn the poem, lest it fail anywhere or suffer any eclipse.

---

traditional: Luke 14:28–30; Quintilian, *Institutio oratoria* 7 pref.l; Boethius, *De consolatione philosophiae* 4 prosa 6. See also Abelard's use of the image in his *De interpretatione* glosses (see above, General Introduction, pp. 25–6); and compare the use of the image in Hugh of St. Victor, *Didascalicon* 6.4. See de Jonge, *Between Grammar and Rhetoric*, ch. 4 on text as architecture; and see Carruthers, "The Poet as Master-Builder."

[15] *rem digesserit ordo*

[16] The *In principio huius libri* Type A commentary says here: "Up to this point he has treated the invention of the material, but here he treats its verbal adornment [*de ornatu eius*] so that it may be put into the medium of words . . . Just as the human body is adorned with clothes, so rude matter is adorned with words. POETRY he names the maid and its subject he calls the mistress, since just as a maid dresses her mistress, so poetry clothes its subject in suitable words" (Woods, ed., *An Early Commentary*, 19).

[17] Cf. *In principio* commentary: "Here he notes three considerations that have to be attended to in poetic art, namely that the beginning, middle, and end suit each other" (Woods, ed., *An Early Commentary*, 19). The pronouncement at this point in the *Poetria nova* serves as a transition from invention and style or expression to the doctrine of arrangement. The caution here is related to the first of the six vices discussed in the "Materia" commentary on Horace's *Ars poetica* (see within), incongruous placing of the parts.

[18] "prepare a dignified entertainment": *hospitium sollemne paret*. In the *In principio* commentary, this phrase is taken slightly differently, as "prepare hospitality" or even "prepare accommodation," as suggested in the comment on these lines: "LET THE MIDDLE, namely of the work, PREPARE A PLACE TO STAY [translating *hospitium*], in which it will remain for a long time; indeed the subject is developed at greater length throughout the MIDDLE of the work, for the MIDDLE comprises everything between the beginning and the end" (Woods, ed., *An Early Commentary*, 21).

Lest my pen neglect to reveal what order I will follow, the next series of remarks will deal with the question of order. The order having been determined, it is the first task to decide within what limits the order of development ought to run.[19]

The next task is to decide by what balance to adjust the weights of the discourse, so that the sentence will balance evenly; third, that your vocabulary be polished and not rude.

Finally, take care that your voice,[20] adorned with the double savor of feature and gesture, and modestly restrained, enter the ears of your listeners and nourish their hearing.

Order can take a double road: at times it advances through the by-paths of art;[21] at times it follows the path of nature.[22] We follow the straight path when words and events follow the same course, when the discourse does not depart from the natural order.[23] The work runs in by-paths if a more apt order places what comes last first, or puts the first last. Neither transposition of order should cause impropriety, but rather each part should take the other's place fittingly, without strife, yielding to the other freely and pleasantly. Expert art inverts matters so as not to pervert them; it displaces material so as to place it better thereby. This order, though reversed, is more pleasant[24] and by far better than the straightforward order. The latter is sterile, but the former fertile, from its marvelous source sending out more branches from the parent trunk, changing one branch into many, a single into several, one into eight. In regard to this art perhaps the air seems foggy, the path rough, the doors closed, the matter knotty. The following words shall be the cure for this disease: look upon them and you will find the light by which to purge the darkness, the feet with which to traverse the rough path, the key to open the doors, the fingers to untie the knots. Behold, the way lies open! Guide the reins of the mind by my explanation of the way.

---

[19] Geoffrey puns on the word and concept of "order" (*ordo*), used four times in four lines: in pointing to the orderly arrangement of his treatise, which proceeds according to a plan, he is also demonstrating the principle of order or arrangement of narrative which his treatise will teach.

[20] *vox*

[21] The *In principio* commentary takes a slightly different reading of this: "THE ORDER STRUGGLES (translating *nititur*), that is, labors, ON THE PATH, that is, on the narrow way, namely on the path that is subtle and known to few, just as the path of Artificial Order is subtle and known to few" (Woods, ed., *An Early Commentary*, 23).

[22] On natural and artificial order, cf. *Ars poetica* 42–5, 148–50; Quintilian, *Institutio oratoria* 7.10.11–12.

[23] Cf. the *In principio* commentary on these lines (*Linea stratae / Est ibi dux, ubi res et verba sequuntur eumdem / Cursum*): "IS THE LEADER [*est dux*]. Thus it leads the writer THERE [*ibi*] in that arrangement WHERE THE THING that is being treated AND THE WORDS by which things are described FOLLOW THE SAME SEQUENCE . . ." (Woods, ed., *An Early Commentary*, 23). The commentary places emphasis on the student responding to dispositional cues in the material.

[24] *civilior*. This might also be translated as "more elegant," "more urbane": cf. the *In principio* commentary on this line: "that order, ALTHOUGH IT PUTS LAST THINGS FIRST [*quamvis preposterus*], that is, places first the later events,

The part which comes first in order awaits outside of the door of the work; but let the ending enter first, a fitting precursor, and let it preempt the seat, like a more worthy guest, or almost like the host himself. Nature has placed the ending last, but the veneration of art defers to it and, lifting up the lowly, raises it on high.

The high point of the work does not radiate only from the very end, but has a double glory: the end of the work and the middle. Art can draw a pleasant beginning out of either. It plays about almost like a magician, and brings it about that the last becomes first, the future the present, the oblique direct, the remote near; thus rustic matters become polished, old becomes new, public private, black white, and vile precious.

If you should wish the opening to send forth a greater light, without disturbing the natural order of the theme, let the sentiment you begin with not sink to any particular statement but rather raise its head to a general pronouncement. With this new grace it is unwilling to think of the details at hand, but almost disdainfully refuses to remain in its bosom. Let it stand above the given subject; pondering thereon but saying nothing, let it gaze with brow uplifted. This method is triple, coming from a triple root; namely the first, middle, and final parts of a theme. From their trunks it arises like a shoot, and thus is engendered by a triform mother; but it remains in the dark and, when called, refuses to hearken. It is not wont to come forth at the pleasure of the mind; it is, so to speak, proud in nature: it does not offer itself willingly, or to everyone. It comes unwillingly, unless perhaps it is forced to come.

Thus do proverbs illustrate a work. Not less aptly can examples appear at the head of a work; the same splendor comes alike from each, and the ornament in both is the same: beauty alone links proverbs and examples.

Art has created other approaches but has preferred these two. They have more gravity. The others are younger and of a rather tender age; these are the more mature. In the art and application of these two approaches we can see that the road is more narrow, the use more apt, and the art more great.

Thus, by careful investigation, three branches of the opening are discovered: by the end, by the middle, and by proverbs. The fourth is by example, which, like the opening by proverbs, grows into three branches. And style takes pride in these eight branches...

is on the contrary the method of very sophisticated, distinguished writers [*civiliorum, honestiorum*], for the citizens of cities are distinguished and thoughtful, while rustics are stupid [*rustici autem stulti*]. Whence 'urbane' [*urbanus*] is often said for 'distinguished' and 'rustic' for 'stupid'; whence the phrase 'rustic Corydon,' that is, a stupid man" (Woods, ed., *An Early Commentary*, 25).

On Amplification and Abbreviation

The art taught above develops the opening in various ways;[25] now a further progress summons you. Direct your path and further course with this method leading the way. Your way is twofold: either wide or strait, a rivulet or a stream; you will either proceed more leisurely, or quickly jump over it; check off an item briefly, or treat it in a lengthy discourse. The passage through each way is not without labor; if you wish to be guided well, commit yourself to a sure guide. Ponder what is written below: it will lead your pen and will teach what must be taught concerning both methods. The principle of the matter is, like wax, hard to the touch at first. If, with sedulous care, your talent sets it afire, it will quickly grow soft under the warmth of your genius and, totally manageable, will follow wherever the hand leads. The hand of the inner man will lead to Amplification or Abbreviation. . . .

[The section on Amplification contains some well known illustrative examples, including Geoffrey's two laments on King Richard I, cited by Chaucer in the *Nun's Priest's Tale*, VII.3347–54. Amplification is achieved by eight methods: repetition or refining (*interpretatio*), periphrasis (*circumlocutio*), comparison (*collatio*), apostrophe (*exclamatio*), *prosopopoeia* (personification), digression, description, and opposition.]

On Abbreviation

If you wish to be brief, refrain from the above methods, which make for effusion; let a summary of the material be compressed into a modest range, which you can condense thus: Let Emphasis[26] reduce many expressions to a few; let Comma[27] constrain scattered material in a brief discourse; the Ablative Absolute has a certain conciseness; do not say the same thing twice; the discretion of the wise man observes what is said through what is left

---

[25] The *In principio* commentary offers an interesting view of the placement of this instruction on abbreviating and amplifying in the *Poetria nova*: "And it seems that this section, in which he teaches about a mode of expression that the poet ought to have at his command, should be assigned to the Style section, when he treats the Figures of Words and Thoughts just as Cicero did in the fourth book of the *Rhetorica ad Herennium* where he treats Style. And consequently he dwells upon this part of rhetoric for rather a long time" (Woods, ed., *An Early Commentary*, 39). Of the eight devices of amplification given here (*interpretatio*, periphrasis, *collatio*, apostrophe, *prosopopoeia*, *digressio*, *descriptio*, and opposition), six are treated in book 4 of the *Ad Herennium* under style.

[26] *emphasis*

[27] *Articulus* (also "phrase") is defined in *Rhetorica ad Herennium* 4.19.26: "when single words are set apart by pauses in staccato speech, as follows: 'By your vigour, voice, looks you have terrified your adversaries.'"

unsaid. Do not let conjunctions tie the clauses together, but let them proceed unbound. Or let the hand of the craftsman gather many clauses into one, so that through the perception of the mind, many can be seen in one . . . Hence let run together, but aptly, Emphasis, Comma, Ablative Absolute, a cunning hint at one [unspoken] statement to be found in the rest; removal of the conjunctions among clauses; the sense of many clauses fused into one; no repetition of the same expression.[28] . . .

Here is a mirror of the subject: the entire matter shines out from it:

> The husband being long absent to increase his holdings, his adulterous wife gives birth to a boy. When he returns long after, she pretends it was conceived of snow. Mutual deception. He cautiously restrains himself. He carries it away, sells it; he pays back her deception, telling her similar nonsense, that the sun has melted the boy.[29]

If you want brevity to be shorter yet, first of all eliminate all sententiousness.[30] Do not give thought to the verbs; rather, with the stylus of the heart, write down the nouns which express the essence of the theme. This done, work along the artificer's lines: heat the iron of your subject in the fire of your breast, then place the iron on the anvil of effort. Let the hammer of genius soften it, and let frequent blows strike the most essential words from the unformed mass. Then let the bellows of reason melt the words together, after having added all auxiliary words, so nouns to verbs and verbs to nouns are joined together.[31] Thus will a brief work shine forth; it expresses nothing more or less than is fitting. This latter kind of brevity is more pointed. The following brief passage will serve as an example:

> The child which the adulterous mother feigned was conceived of snow the father sold, similarly pretending that the sun had melted it.
> Because his wife pretended the son she bore was engendered of snow, the husband sold it and similarly pretended it had been melted by the sun.[32]

---

[28] The advice on abbreviation violates one of its own rules, to some pedagogical effect, by overtly repeating itself.

[29] The story of the Snow-Child was often used to illustrate amplification and abbreviation: see Gallo, *The Poetria nova and its Sources*, 195 n. 136 and references there. This particular abbreviated version contains the devices of ablative absolute, intimation, comma and asyndeton (omission of conjunctions), and fusion of statements.

[30] *sententia*

[31] Translation slightly adapted in favor of a more literal grammatical terminology. In the *Documentum de modo et arte dictandi et versificandi* 2.2.43, Geoffrey of Vinsauf makes this grammatical procedure even clearer: we choose the nouns which express the essence of the subject, and then it will be easy to adapt verbs to the nouns. In the Snow-Child story the essential nouns are "wife," "husband," "boy," "sun," and "snow," out of which the story can be told in two hexameter lines (ed. Faral, *Les arts poétiques*, 279–80).

[32] Each of these versions consists of two hexameter lines, each consisting of a high proportion of nouns and pronouns (or past participles used as substantives), very few active verbs, and a minimum of other parts of speech (prepositions, conjunctions).

ON STYLISTIC ORNAMENT

Whether short or long, let the discourse always be decorated within and without; but choose among ornaments[33] with discretion. First examine the soul of the word[34] and then its face, whose outward show alone you should not trust. Unless the inner ornament conforms to the outer requirement, the relationship between the two is worthless. Painting only the face of an expression results in a vile picture, a falsified thing, a faked form, a whitewashed wall, a verbal hypocrite which pretends to be something when it is nothing. Its form covers up its deformity; it vaunts itself outwardly but has no inner substance. This is the kind of picture which pleases at a distance, but displeases close up. Therefore remember not to be overhasty, but be like Argus in choosing your words: with an acute eye look over the words of the subject set out before you. If the sentiment be sincere, its sincerity will protect it. Do not let unworthy words do it dishonor, but, that all may be guided by rule, let a noble sentiment be graced by a noble expression, lest a well-born matron blush to be dressed in shabby garments. In order that the matter may adopt costly garments, if the words are old, be a physician and rejuvenate them. Do not always allow a word to reside in its usual place; such residence does not suit it; let it avoid its proper place and wander elsewhere, to find a pleasing seat in another's ground: let it be a new sojourner there and please by its novelty. If you prepare this remedy you will rejuvenate the face of the word.

This method teaches how to "transume" words.[35] If it is a man about whom I speak, I will speak in terms of something similar to this subject. When I see what is its proper

---

[33] *colores*

[34] *mens verbi*. Cf. the *In principio* commentary: "He says that those making metaphorical transpositions [*transumentes*, from *transumptio*, transposition; see following note] ought to utilize similitude and that the transference [*translatio*] ought to be made from one thing to another that seems transferable because of a certain similitude. And if a Transposition is made where there is no similarity, it does not adorn the expression but rather muddles it. And this is EXAMINE THE MIND, that is, the interior meaning, OF A WORD, namely of the one transposed" (Woods, ed., *An Early Commentary*, 67).

[35] *modus transsumere verba*. The Latin term used throughout the *Poetria nova* is *transumptio* (and its verb form *transumere*), encountered here, as in other texts, in its common medieval spelling: *transsumptio* (and *transsumere*). Gallo translates this as "metaphor," more or less following Faral's understanding of it as the equivalent of metaphor. But the term goes back to Quintilian, who gives it as the Latin equivalent of the Greek *metalepsis* (*Institutio oratoria* 8.6.37). The term *metalepsis* is found in Donatus' *Ars maior* 3 (*Barbarismus*), and it is from Donatus that Bede uses *metalepsis* in *De schematibus et tropis*. *Metalepsis/transumptio* has a much broader application than simply metaphor: it signifies a method of transference of the meanings of words which is common to various individual species of tropes. On this term in its classical and medieval uses, especially in the *Poetria nova*, but also in the other *artes poetriae* and in philosophical and logical texts, see Purcell, "*Transsumptio*: A Rhetorical Doctrine of the Thirteenth

garment in a similar case, I will draw upon it and make a new garment from the old. An example: the word properly applied to gold is *red-yellow*; to milk, *white*; to the rose, *deep red*; to honey, *sweet flowing*; to flames, *red*; to the body, *snow-white*. Therefore say, *teeth like snow, lips of flame, taste honey-sweet, rosy face, milk-white forehead, golden hair.* They fit each other well: teeth, snow; lips, flame; taste, honey; face, rose; forehead, milk; hair, gold. And, since very similar connection shines forth in these cases, if your subject is not a man, twist the reins of the mind back to human attributes. Make apt transumptive use of a word which is used literally to express a similar relationship. Assume you wish to say this:

> Springtime adorns the land; the first flowers shoot up; the time grows pleasant; storms cease; the sea is calm; there is motion without uproar; valleys lie low; mountains tower erect.[36]

Ask yourself what words describing human attributes might properly be applied: adorning, *you paint*; the beginning of birth, *you are born*; pleasant speech, *you allure*; ceasing all activity, *you sleep*; motionless, *you stand fixed*; lying low, *you recline*; shooting into the air, *you arise*. Hence the words will have savor if you say:

> Springtime paints the ground with flowers; birds are born; the quiet season allures; the calming storms sleep; the ocean stands still as if immobile; the low valleys lie; the erect mountains rise up.

When you transume your literal material, it is more pleasing, because it derives from what is your own.[37] Such a transumptive use of words serves you like a mirror, for you can see yourself in it, and recognize your own sheep in a strange countryside. . . .

Thus will you place words excellently; words so placed will be comprehensible to the eye of the mind. To place words with diligence is a troublesome thing. This manner of speaking is easy and hard; it is hard to find the expression, but once found, the expression should be easy to understand. Thus contraries mix; but they pledge peace, and enemies become friends. Herein is a certain commingling. Let not the expression be easy, mean, or unpleasant: it draws its grace and value from its gravity. But lest this gravity be turgid or opaque, let simplicity illuminate it and repress any bombast. Let the

---

Century." On the place of the notion of semantic transfer in logic and grammar, see Rosier-Catach, "*Prata rident.*" How Geoffrey came to know the term is not clear, whether he found it directly in Quintilian or in other sources. In the commentary on Donatus' *Ars maior* by the ninth-century scholar and poet Sedulius Scotus, Donatus' Greek term *metalêpsis* is clearly glossed with its Latin equivalent, *transumptio* (see edition of Löfstedt, 373.10; 379.59). Given the complex history and theoretical value of the term, we have decided to modify Gallo's translations of it in favor of more literal renderings.

[36] Geoffrey's Latin at this point is no less free from "submerged" metaphor than the translation, e.g. *primos exsurgere flores*, "the first flowers shoot up." But it is not especially ornamented language.

[37] Gallo does not translate this sentence (lines 801–2) directly. The translations by Baltzell-Kopp and Nims follow the original, but are also at variance with each other, differing on how to translate *tuum proprium*.

one quality restrain the other. Thus speak, joining gravity and simplicity. Do not let the one detract from the other but, mutually suited, let them enjoy the same seat. Let their concordant discord compose the strife.

That the transumption of the verb may be more polished, let not the verb come with one noun as its only companion; give it an adjective which will fully assist the verb and clear away the clouds from it, if there be any. If not, let it throw light abundantly on and through the verb. Thus it is not sufficiently clear if I say *The laws are pliable* or *The laws are rigid*, for the transumption of the verb is as it were hidden under a cloud. And since the verb so placed remains in darkness, the adjective helps and illuminates it. Rather say, *The dispensing laws are pliable; the strict laws are unbending.* The adjective clarifies the verb: strictness extorts rigor and rigidity, and kind dispensation tempers and softens the law. But what if a transumed verb shines of itself? Nonetheless, aid it with an adjective from whose splendor its own will double. It is sufficiently graceful to say, *The earth drank moisture more than was proper, and the rainstorm gave it out at random.* However, you would speak much better and more aptly if you were to say, *The drunken earth drank more water than proper and the prodigal rain dispensed it at random*; for, like vines of ivy, verb and adjective join together and bind each other as if to allow of no separation, but vow a pact of unity and remain harmonious companions. Such discernment imparts polish to a word from which the dress has been removed.

Yet a better word-picture surpasses this ornament when the noun conflicts with the verb: they are outwardly at odds, but inwardly there is love and accordance of meaning. An example: *By pouring forth his wealth, the bountiful man got it back again. The hand is never tired unless it is at rest.* And again: *Devout silence cries out before the face of God.* The same process occurs elsewhere: when lovers join battle in alternate reproaches, peace between souls grows from the strife between tongues: love is hidden in this hate. Thus also here: the meanings agree inwardly, so it is permitted for them to seem to be outward enemies. There is discord in their meanings, but the significance of the words puts all strife at rest.

A transumed word can shine with another light, when the word deployed is used metaphorically and literally, as in this sequence: *The old experience of Rome armed tongues with laws and bodies with weapons, so that tongues and bodies were at the same time fit for combat.*[38] This short expression is more pleasant: *Faith arms them in heart, weapons in body.*

---

[38] I.e. "to arm" taken in its common (literal) sense of equipping with weapons of war, and in a transferred or metaphorical sense of equipping the tongue with verbal weapons.

Thus should the verb be transumed, and thus an adjective, and thus a noun.[39] But the verb can be transumed in several ways: by corresponding with what precedes or what follows it, or with both at once.[40] . . . Similarly, an adjective can be used metaphorically in three ways. By reason of the noun to which it is joined . . . Or by reason of the complement . . . Or from both at once.

Now we discuss the transumption of the noun. If it is a common noun, its transumption decorates the words thus:[41]

> The uproar [*fragor*] of the people stirs up the city.

. . . If it is a proper noun, it is applied metaphorically to the subject for purposes of praise or blame, like a cognomen;[42] praise, such as *That Paris*, or blame, such as *That Thersites*. Or it is applied metaphorically because of a certain point of similarity:

> That ship's pilot is our Tiphis; that rustic cart-driver is our Automedon.[43]

. . . Thus a simple change makes a metaphor[44] of a single word. At times there can be several such changes, as in this verbal schema: *The shepherds plunder the sheep*.[45] Here you transfer two nouns, shepherd and sheep: *shepherd* to the prelates and *sheep* to their subjects. Further, an entire statement can be metaphorical and not merely a part of it, as we can see here:

> He plows the sand, scrubs the color from bricks, beats the air.[46]

These are the ways in which transumption can adorn words.

Transume in the above-mentioned ways; however, be restrained and neither bombastic nor turgid. Two things are mixed here: onus and honor—the onus of transferring a word properly, and honor for having succeeded.

---

[39] Gallo's translation slightly modified, following other readings of this passage. Cf. the *In principio* commentary: "He turns from generalized teaching to specialized application. Above he taught how similitude can be evoked by a transposed word, either noun or verb. Here he teaches how just a verb, then a noun, and then an adjective may be transposed" (Woods, ed., *An Early Commentary*, 69).

[40] The *In principio* commentary links this section with the discussion of figures of diction (or verbal ornaments) and of metaphor (*translatio*) in *Rhetorica ad Herennium* 4.31.42 and 4.34.45.

[41] An example of *nominatio* or *onomatopoeia*; cf. *Rhetorica ad Herennium* 4.31.42.

[42] *Pronominatio* or *antonomasia*; cf. *Ad Herennium* 4.31.42.

[43] Typhus: pilot of the Argo; Automedon: Achilles' charioteer.

[44] *sic transfert*. On metaphor (*translatio*) in Geoffrey of Vinsauf, see Nims, "*Translatio*: Difficult Statement in Medieval Poetic Theory."

[45] An example of *permutatio* or *allegoria* (Greek word) in its narrow rhetorical sense; cf. *Rhetorica ad Herennium* 4.34.46.

[46] These are *permutationes* for "he works in vain."

When a sentence appears decorated with such ornament, it is sweet to the delighted ear and a new enjoyment inwardly stimulates the mind.

Transfero, permuto, pronomino, nomino: these form from themselves "verbal expressions" which are the names of the figures of diction, all of which come under the heading of *transumptio*.[47] Acquire that food and that drink: this food satisfies, this drink inebriates the ears.

---

[47] Modifying Gallo's translation in favor of a more literal reading. Cf. the explanation of the derivations of the names of figures given in the *In principio* commentary: "from the verb *transfero* is formed *translatio* [i.e. "transference," whence the Latin term for "metaphor"] . . . From the verb *permuto* . . . is formed *permutatio* [i.e. "allegory"] . . . From the verb *pronomino* "to name in place of" is formed *pronominatio* [i.e. *antonomasia*]. . . . From the verb *nomino* . . . is formed *nominatio* [i.e. *onomatopoeia*] . . . (Woods, ed., *An Early Commentary*, 79–81).

GERVASE OF MELKLEY, *ARS VERSIFICARIA*, CA. 1215–1216

INTRODUCTION

Gervase of Melkley was born ca. 1185, and died sometime after 1220. He identifies his own name (Melkley) as English,[1] and makes reference throughout his work to English figures, leading Faral to conclude that he was himself English and lived in England (London).[2] Gervase locates his treatise in a tradition of poetic arts, citing as forebears Matthew of Vendôme and Geoffrey of Vinsauf, as well as Bernardus Silvestris, whose *Cosmographia* he cites frequently and which he may have regarded as an exemplary "art of poetry" because of the wealth of poetic devices which it illustrates.[3] The *Ars versificaria* (Art of Versifying) deals primarily with style, although there is a small section on developing argument. It is divided into three sections of uneven length: a very long section on rules common to any kind of discourse, a short section on rules pertaining to verse composition, and a short section on rules pertaining to prose composition; to the last of these in all three manuscripts is appended a very short *ars dictaminis*.

But the first and longest section, on rules pertaining to any kind of discourse, is itself broken down into several parts which articulate Gervase's unusual theoretical framework for classifying figures and tropes. Gervase groups these under the headings of identity (*identitas*), in which there is no change in the word's meaning, similitude or likeness (*similitudo*), in which meaning is transferred according to principles of resemblance among things, and contrariety (*contrarietas*), which concerns those tropes which can be seen as reasoning through contraries, of which the two species are allegory (contradiction in meaning) and enthymeme (contradiction in word and meaning, a form of reasoning treated here as a species of embellishment).[4] Gervase's organization is a conceptual variation on the classification of figures and tropes inherited from the *Rhetorica ad Herennium*, Donatus' *Barbarismus*, and Geoffrey of Vinsauf's *Poetria nova*, which distinguish between figures of speech and figures of thought, or figures and tropes, or difficult and easy ornament (tropes and colors). In Gervase's model,

---

[1] See the dedication of his *Ars versificaria*, below, and note.   [2] Faral, *Les arts poétiques*, 34–7.
[3] Kelly, *The Arts of Poetry and Prose*, 57–64.
[4] See Camargo, "A Twelfth-Century Treatise on 'Dictamen' and Metaphor." *Flores rhetorici*, a twelfth-century dictaminal treatise from Tours, may be the ultimate source of Gervase's theoretical framework.

the distinction among stylistic devices rests on topics derived from dialectic: arguments from sameness, likeness, or antithesis. Through this structure he achieves a functional rather than simply descriptive account of figures, allowing a student to see the progressively complex logical structures on which figures and tropes are built.[5] But underlying this innovative structure are the basic divisions between figures of speech and figures of thought.

In the first section on common rules, following the three divisions of figures and tropes, there are three further short chapters: on proverbs, stylistic elegance, and the embellishment of arguments through topics.

Gervase's range of literary and learned reference is considerable, taking in both ancients and moderns, and crossing many genres. This underscores the place of compositional teaching within a larger curriculum based on *enarratio poetarum* (exposition of the poets). Among his many references, however, are frequent citations of an anonymous poem on Pyramus and Thisbe. This is preserved in one of the manuscripts (Glasgow, Hunterian Museum MS V. 8. 14; formally MS 511) that also contain Gervase's treatise, the rhetorical arts by Matthew of Vendôme and Geoffrey of Vinsauf, and many other works, including a series of Latin poems illustrating rhetorical devices.[6] It is possible that the Pyramus and Thisbe poem is by Gervase himself, written at some point in his career to illustrate the same principles of composition and argumentation that he was to treat in his teaching.[7]

Translated from *Ars poetica*,[8] ed., Gräbener, by permission of the publishers.

DEDICATION AND PROLOGUE

To his dear Johannus Albus, more teacher than comrade, his Gervase of the "milky meadow" [*de Saltu Lacteo*, i.e. Melkley][9] offers this work with greetings.

---

[5] For detailed analysis of the structure of the work, see Purcell, "*Identitas, Similitudo,* and *Contrarietas* in Gervasius of Melkley's *Ars poetica*."

[6] The poems are edited by Harbert, *A Thirteenth-Century Anthology of Rhetorical Poems.* See also Faral, "Le Manuscrit 511 du Hunterian Museum de Glasgow." The Pyramus and Thisbe poem is printed in Faral, *Les arts poétiques,* 331–5.

[7] See the articles by Glendenning, "Pyramus and Thisbe in the Medieval Classroom," and "Eros, Agape, and Rhetoric around 1200."

[8] Gräbener's edition also includes a substantial analysis of the work. Faral presents a summary of the treatise, *Les arts poétiques,* 328–30. The complete work has also been translated, with valuable notes and discussion, by Giles, "Gervais of Melkley's Treatise on the Art of Versifying and the Method of Composing in Prose: Translation and Commentary."

[9] In the treatise, under the explanation of *transmutatio* Gervase uses his own name as an example of achieving this device by way of translation: "In this way, sometimes, for the sake of ornament, we change a name itself by translation. For example, 'Melkley' is composed of two whole words in English, and is translated literally as *lactis*

A request from our betters is armed and most kindred to a command. This is why, when the authority of your request had ordered me to explain to you the business of the art of versifying, I submitted, bold and rash, to your command, although I had never tried my hand at such a difficult project before. Faith and obedience urge that neither the graciousness of the request nor the importance of the command be despised.

Matthew of Vendôme has written fully about this art, Geoffrey of Vinsauf even more amply, and Bernardus Silvestris, who is a parrot in prose and a nightingale in verse, most copiously. One ought to be nervous about taking up a task which has occupied such great men. It would be more prudent for me to keep silent than to undertake such a work or to have promised it. However, I prefer to be faithful rather than fearful, obedient rather than prudent.

Thus I undertake this promised work. That it would not seem worthless next to what others have written, I have resolved to proceed in a way that is brief and comprehensive, and easy to understand. But since it is most difficult to present things at once briefly and clearly, I preferred to be verbose but understandable, even though difficulty supposedly gives books prestige. Thus the teaching of this little book will be selective in general matters, whereas for particular questions there will be a certain redundancy of expression, so that a verbosity that they can understand may be helpful to the beginners.[10] This is a rudimentary little book. We refer the advanced students to the authors mentioned above. However, we advise that they should not despise Donatus' *Barbarismus* nor Horace's *Ars poetica*, nor Cicero's *Rhetorics*.

We arrive at knowledge of something in two ways: directly and indirectly. For example, four classes of things comprehend the nature of speech: some involve prohibition [*prohibitio*], some involve license [*permissio*], some involve rule [*preceptum*], and some involve advice [*consilium*]. The class of prohibitions consists of faults [*vitia*], and the class of licenses consists of figures [*figurae*], both of which Donatus treats, giving rules in grammar, and advice in rhetoric. Therefore if we understand what a fault is and what a figure is in terms of the rules of grammar, then what constitutes advice will be apparent more readily by indirect means. This is true in the case of grammar, where we point out rules to be observed, and in the case of rhetoric, where we point out what belongs to graceful style. Priscian and Cicero instruct us directly; Donatus instructs us indirectly by pointing out improper usages.

In teaching this art it is necessary for us to explain faults as much as elegance of expression [*elegantiae*]. But you have considered the judgment of Ovid on faults, as related in Seneca's

---

saltus ['meadow of milk']. For the sake of ornament, where one was going to say 'Melkley,' one can say *lactis saltus* or *saltus lacteus* ['milky meadow']" (ed. Gräbener, 79).

[10] In Glasgow, Hunterian Museum MS V.8.14 (formerly MS 511), a marginal note refers to *Ars poetica* 25: "Striving to be brief, I become obscure." Cf. Augustine, *Enarrationes in Psalmos* 138: "Let us speak at greater length: better for the grammarians to criticize us than for the people not to understand us" (*PL* 37:1796; noted in Gräbener edition, xxx).

Controversiae.[11] Ovid was asked by some of his friends to expunge three lines of his verse; in return he asked if he could save three lines over which they would have no claims. In private the friends wrote down the lines they would condemn, while he wrote down the lines he would save. On both writing tablets the same verses were found, of which the first was: "Half-bull man and half-man bull,"[12] in which we see redundancy of expression [*perissologia*], that is, the fault of superfluity. It is clear that this man of highest genius did not lack the judgment to rein in the license of his verse, but the will. When asked why he would not suppress these lines, he said that a face is all the more handsome for some mole on it.

From these words of Ovid we could almost conclude that it is a fault to be without fault. Certainly it is well-nigh impossible to run on at some length even in prose without a mistake. Whatever is most easily pointed out will deservedly be most difficult to avoid. I will point out faults of style, not so that all faults are eliminated from all poems whatsoever, but so that they can be eliminated in part, one at a time, in accordance with each writer's ability.

It is also necessary to explain the particular beauty and forms of elegance that pertain to rhetoric, although these are better understood through constant use and practice than through precept. Indeed, the elegance of rhetorical beauty is infinite, and every day the inventiveness of modern people finds new ones.

Master John of Hanville, the breasts of whose art suckled my rude infancy, invented many elegant phrasings, and taught more of them to his pupils. He used most of them in his little book on the wandering philosopher, which he called *Architrenius.*[13] Careful study of his little book alone will suffice to inform a young mind. The same may be said of Claudian, Darius Phrygius, and Bernardus Silvestris, and also of the ancients, that is, Lucan, Statius, and Virgil. You may also learn much from Ovid's little books. But the *Anticlaudianus* teaches us more indirectly than directly.

In the art of rhetoric, natural genius will take precedence over instruction, if practice is in attendance. Indeed, rhetorical practice, most akin to a natural activity, comes spontaneously to an acute mind even without knowledge of theory. I know of one who, before he knew anything of the attributes of the person and the act, before he had even studied rhetoric, when he had to relate how Pasiphae constructed a brass cow and locked herself into it, since this was an abomination and odious to hear, used the device of *insinuatio* [i.e. subtle approach]:

> Say, what does a lover abhor? A lover who is a woman, what does she abhor?
> Pray now, if the lover is a woman and noble? Nothing.[14]

---

[11] *Controversiae* 2.2.12.   [12] *Ars amatoria* 2.24.   [13] Written ca. 1184. John of Hanville died ca. 1200.
[14] On the device of *insinuatio*, see above, Rupert of Deutz, p. 395. The source of these lines is not known. Glendenning has proposed that throughout his treatise, Gervase used verses he himself wrote as a student, recalling

The term *insinuatio* is not used here, but the principle of the thing was not concealed from the eyes of one naturally acute. While not yet knowing the terms of those topics of invention, he nevertheless used a threefold argument: from affection, when he said "a lover," from nature, when he said "a woman," from fortune, when he said "noble." For I attribute nobility, at least in our times, more to fortune than to nature. This writer did not yet know what it was to invent an argument from contraries, yet he produced this :

> It is a crime for a ruler to know nothing of crime, and this is the only thing royal power fears, namely to be fearful of what is not allowed.[15]

Thus one needs to take care that the theory of this art be set forth in brief for eager minds; the art may be elaborated in practice by reading thoroughly the works of others as well as by composing one's own verses. In reading the authors, a little bit suffices for pointing out solecisms or obvious faults, or rhetorical topics and colors [*loci rhetorici et colores*].

It should be noted that some rules are common to all kinds of discourse, while some are specific to meter and others to prose. Let us turn first to those rules that are common to all kinds of discourse.

FROM PART 1: RULES COMMON TO ANY KIND OF DISCOURSE

In common speech, once any subject matter has been determined, short clauses [*minutae clausulae*] immediately present themselves to the speaker. Thus a clause is a discourse, either complete or incomplete, provided that it brings about complete understanding, either through itself or through something implied. There is a threefold locus for the composition of clauses: either from sameness, from similarity, or from a contrary.[16] If "identity" [*identitas*], "similitude" [*similitudo*], and "contrariety" [*contrarietas*] are entrusted to exercise and knowledge, they produce the beauty of eloquence.

---

their illustrative value and inserting them into his own didactic work; see "Pyramus and Thisbe in the Medieval Classroom," 60. These may be verses from Gervase's own notebooks. In Oxford, Balliol College MS 263, a note in the margin at this point explains the Pasiphae story: "Pasiphae, the daughter of Phoebus was enclosed in a brass cow, and coupling with a bull conceived the minotaur" (Gräbener edition, 4).

[15] Source unknown. See note above.

[16] These are "topics" for the construction of dialectical arguments which were also imported into rhetoric. On arguments from sameness (or inherence), see Cicero, *Topica* 2.8; on arguments from similitude, *Topica* 10.41; on arguments from contraries, *Topica* 11.47–9, and for the rhetorical figure "reasoning by contraries," *Rhetorica ad Herennium* 4.18.25–6. On other possible sources, see Gräbener edition, xxxvii–xxxviii.

IDENTITY

Identity is a discourse presented in an absolute sense in which no transference or contrariety of meaning is presented. Some identity is unadorned or "rough" [*rudis*], some is "refined" [*polita*].

Unadorned identity is made up of a simple subject and predicate. Whatever is added either disfigures or decorates the clause. Of unadorned identities, some are rough, some are rougher, and some are roughest.

Rough identity is made solely from grammatical rules, and lacks figures as much as fault or color. Rougher identity is what involves some improper usage which does not decorate the speech, but which is excused by some necessity or law, whether of euphony, or meter, or rhythm, or rhetoric. Here the "figure" is introduced, many species of which are described by Donatus.[17] Roughest identity is what involves an inexcusable fault, and with this we have the barbarism or solecism....

Identity is refined [*politur*] by means of two kinds of rhetorical device, colors and arguments. Arguments are pleasing to the mind, and colors are pleasing to the ears. Colors find favor with the senses, arguments with the faculty of reasoning.

Faults, figures, and colors are clothed in a certain similar appearance, and in many cases match each other on even terms, while in many cases they go beyond the rule in a similar way or fall short of it. For example, Donatus says that a barbarism is made by a substitution of a letter, as in *olli* for *illi* ["those"].[18] Then he says the same thing later when treating metaplasm: "Antithesis is the substitution of a letter for a letter, as in *olli* for *illi*."[19] In the colors, this device is called *notatio* (distinguishing mark) as in *precones* [heralds] for *predones* [thieves].[20]

In this group it is easily possible that a fault goes unnoticed under the shade of a virtue. And therefore it is very difficult to differentiate these with the greatest precision. Compare the fact that the humors of men are differentiated by skilled musicians. They believe they

---

[17] Under "figure" here Gervase seems to classify all those deviations that are necessitated for reasons of meter or euphony, but which are not specifically decorative: cf. Donatus' list of metaplasms (which can be made for meter or ornament), *Ars maior* 3.4, *GL* 4:395–7.

[18] *GL* 4:392.16.   [19] *GL* 4:397.1.

[20] There may be two senses of *notatio* in operation here. One is the term in its meaning of "etymology": see Cicero, *Topica* 8.35, and see within, Isidore of Seville, p. 350. The other meaning of *notatio* is a figure of thought which changes meaning and gives "color" to a passage; Geoffrey of Vinsauf lists it under figures of thought (within the section on *colores*), as does the *Rhetorica ad Herennium* 4.44.63. The example here is a play on a familiar stereotype of heralds or messengers, that they are mercenary: thus *precones predones*, i.e. messengers are thieves (cf. Martial 5. 56).

will please choleric humors with one type of pitch, sanguine humors with another, phlegmatics with yet another, and melancholics with a fourth. Some people delight in soft sounds, others in harsh. Those who delight in soft sounds judge harsh sounds to be faults. We should not wonder, therefore, if among the colors and figures we find some that occur more frequently, and others that occur more rarely. Indeed, even though the *Architrenius* contains metaphors of the greatest difficulty occurring with the greatest frequency, still I have heard a very discerning man call the book faulty simply because no verse contained a fault! So it seems probable that what one man calls a fault, another man calls a figure and another man a color. So we leave it to the industry of the practitioner to distinguish these, since no art of due mixture has been invented yet.

[Most of the attention in this section is given to "refined identity," which involves the traditional figures of diction or rhetorical colors, that is, those devices that do not change the meaning, but ornament the language. In the next section, on "similitude," Gervase treats various forms of transference of meaning according to some kind of equivalence: by "adaptation" of words (*assumptio*), including catachresis, by transformation (*transumptio*), including metaphor, or by other forms of likeness.[21] In the next subsection, on "contrariety," he treats allegory (*allegoria*) and its subspecies, and enthymeme and its subspecies. He derives his definition of enthymeme, "reasoning by contraries," from Cicero's *Topica* 55. The last three sections of part 1 treat proverbs, elegance, and arguments. The treatment of arguments is scarcely about invention and mainly about finding stylistic devices from familiarity with the rhetorical topics of attributes of the person and the action. At the end of the section on arguments, before passing on to rules specific to versifying, Gervase states that he will not deal with the following subjects: artificial and natural order of narration; the philosophical mode of proceeding;[22] and the three levels of style—grand, humble, and middle. Thus he clarifies the parameters of his treatise: directing his efforts to younger pupils, he deals with style at the level of word and grammatical clause, rather than at the structural level of plot and stylistic register.]

---

[21] On the broader history of the term *transumptio*, from the earliest commentaries on Aristotle's *Sophistical Refutations*, see Rosier-Catach, "*Prata rident*," 155. On *transumptio* in the poetic arts, see Purcell, "*Transsumptio*: A Rhetorical Doctrine of the Thirteenth Century."

[22] This may be related to the idea, expressed in Bernardus Silvestris' commentary on the *Aeneid*, that while a poetic narrative may follow the artificial order of narration, its philosophical level of meaning observes a "natural" or linear order of argument. Thus Bernardus' philosophical explication of Virgil's *Aeneid* takes book 1 as the beginning of the philosophical argument and proceeds according to the order of the books rather than according to the complex temporal pattern of the narrative.

THOMAS OF CHOBHAM, *SUMMA DE ARTE PRAEDICANDI*, CA. 1220

INTRODUCTION

Thomas of Chobham (sometimes known as Thomas of Salisbury) was born around the middle of the twelfth century, and went to Paris to study arts and theology around 1178.[1] It is no doubt here that he gained his impressive familiarity with Ciceronian rhetoric as well as classical and late antique literary authors. He also came under the influence of two Parisian theology masters, Peter of Poitiers and Peter the Chanter. His treatment of allegory in the *Summa de arte praedicandi* (Summa of the Art of Preaching) is particularly indebted to the *Allegoriae super tabernaculum Moysi* of Peter of Poitiers; and his major work, the *Summa confessorum* (Guide to Confessors) (written ca. 1215), which was widely circulated, relies extensively on the writings of Peter the Chanter. Thomas of Chobham spent most of his career in England as subdean of Salisbury Cathedral, a position he held from about 1208 until his death ca. 1233. But he also returned to Paris at intervals, including the period from 1222 to 1228, when he taught theology.[2] The *Summa de arte praedicandi* most likely dates from the early part of this decade.

This is one of the first examples of the new genre of *ars praedicandi*, which developed through the later thirteenth century and reached its height in the fourteenth century. Thomas' *Summa* represents an early moment in the genre's formation, before the instructive approach of *artes praedicandi* became standardized and specialist, a stage at which the

---

[1] For more detailed biographical accounts see Thomas of Chobham, *Summa confessorum*, ed. Broomfield, xxviii–xxxviii; Baldwin, *Masters, Princes, and Merchants*, 1:34–6; and Morenzoni, *Des écoles aux paroisses: Thomas de Chobham et la promotion de la prédication*, 13–24.

[2] For Thomas' inception sermon, see his *Sermones*, ed. Morenzoni, no. 8. In one of his long poems, John of Garland mentions a Thomas of Salisbury as one of the masters active in Paris during the 1220s who may be Thomas of Chobham, and in one manuscript of the poem, London BL MS Cotton Claudius A.x., the name "Thomas of Salisbury" is glossed in another hand as "Thomas: de Chabeham": see *Summa confessorum*, ed. Broomfield, xxxii and note 88; Baldwin, *Masters, Princes, and Merchants*, 1:35; Morenzoni, *Des écoles aux paroisses*, 19; and see John of Garland, *Epithalamium Beate Virginis Marie*, ed. Saiani, book 10, line 478. While neither the mention of a Thomas of Salisbury in the poem nor the gloss is conclusive proof of a connection with John of Garland, the internal evidence of the *Summa de arte praedicandi* does indicate Thomas' strong familiarity with the recent pedagogical traditions in rhetoric and grammar that are represented in John's *Parisiana poetria*.

genre could still reflect the influence of twelfth- and early-thirteenth-century intellectual currents in rhetoric and grammar, and especially the renewed interest in the broad themes of Ciceronian rhetoric.[3] Thus his confident claim: "the teaching of the orator is very much necessary to the office of the preacher." Thomas' *Summa* demonstrates how the production of sermons could be conceived in terms at once theological and literary. A sermon should combine an exegetical command of scriptural text and meaning with the preceptive advice about language, style, and composition delivered in the *artes poetriae* and rhetorical commentaries of the previous decades (which no doubt formed the basis of Thomas' own early education). While he does not directly quote or mention contemporary grammarians or rhetorical writers (and his citations throughout the bulk of his treatise are overwhelmingly from Christian authors, both ancient and recent), he is manifestly interested in the poetic precepts about language and style which are found in the earlier *artes poetriae* and reach their fullest expression in John of Garland's *Parisiana poetria*: the absorption of Horatian dicta about style into Ciceronian teaching about rhetorical composition and form; the three levels of style (especially in their "material" application to the three social orders); the faults of style; the use of Donatus on tropes and similitudes; and even the genres of *historia*, *argumentum*, and *fabula*. At the same time, his treatment of the rhetoric of Scripture, his intention to identify the rhetorical devices that are latent in scriptural discourse, places him firmly in the tradition of Cassiodorus, Bede, and Rupert of Deutz. Like Bede, he finds grammatical figures and tropes in Scripture. Moreover, like Bede (and like the twelfth-century master Peter of Poitiers), Thomas of Chobham seeks to articulate a valid distinction between allegory as a trope, to be understood in the terms of grammar and rhetoric as a figurative device, and allegory as a kind of spiritual meaning that is beyond language and pertains to the significance with which the things of Scripture are divinely endowed. And like Rupert of Deutz (and more distantly, Cassiodorus), he discovers the essence of rhetoric, its argumentative forms and devices, in scriptural discourse: thus Scripture is not just the subject for the Christian preacher, but the formal pattern and exemplary model of a system of persuasive speech. Where classical rhetoric would have used the speeches of famous orators to exemplify individual precepts, Thomas of Chobham uses Scripture to illustrate rhetorical devices such as insinuation and the division of the speech into its parts (the latter is also used as the basic principle for the division of the sermon). Finally, behind Thomas of Chobham's immediate objectives to refine a pedagogy of preaching lies the synthesis of grammar, rhetoric, and hermeneutics

---

[3] On the twelfth-century rhetorical interests that lie behind the preceptive form of the *ars praedicandi*, see Jennings, " 'Non ex virgine': The Rise of the Thematic Sermon Manual"; on the developments of the *ars praedicandi* in the first decades of the thirteenth century and the role of Thomas of Chobham, see Murphy, *Rhetoric in the Middle Ages*, 310–31, and Morenzoni, *Des écoles aux paroisses*, 200–32.

that leads from the vitality of twelfth-century exegesis back to the powerful legacy of Augustine.[4]

Translated from Thomas of Chobham, *Summa de arte praedicandi*, ed. Morenzoni, by permission.

FROM THE PROLOGUE

Concerning the Mode of Signifying in Theology [De modo significandi in theologia]

In order that the seed of the word of God may be rightly planted in the human heart, let us consider what is read in the book of Kings, that Elijah went up to heaven in a chariot of fire.[5] The chariot is holy preaching, by which the faithful soul, as if on four wheels, is transported to heaven. The first wheel is history, the second is tropology, the third is allegory, and the fourth is anagogy. In this number of ways the letter of sacred Scripture, by which preaching is to be summoned forth, is expounded. And four virtues of the soul are subject to these four modes of understanding, each according to its own distinction: sense, reason, intellect, and wisdom [*sensus, ratio, intellectus et sapientia*]. By the senses, that is sight and hearing, we direct our attention to the historical level. By reason we comprehend tropology, that is, the moral sense of Scripture. By intellect, we turn our attention to the allegorical level, that is, a transferred level of signification concerning the church and the members of the church. By wisdom, we consider the anagogical level, that is, supernal love for God and for celestial things. Thus the historical level is common to philosophy and theology; but the sacred page reserves especially for itself the tropological, anagogical, and allegorical levels.

There are two kinds of understanding: first according to the signification of words [*secundum significationem vocum*], and the other according to the signification of things [*secundum significationem rerum*]. For, as Aristotle says in *On Interpretation*, "words are symbols of mental impressions," that is, what is understood in the intellect, for we communicate our understanding through words.[6] But again, through the signification

---

[4] On the influence of twelfth-century exegesis on Thomas of Chobham, see Evans, "Thomas of Chobham on Preaching and Exegesis."

[5] 4 Kings (= 2 Kings) 2:11.

[6] *Voces sunt note earum que sunt in anima passionum.* Thomas is quoting from Boethius' translation of Aristotle's text. See Boethius, *In librum Aristotelis Peri hermeneias, pars prior*, ed. Meiser, § 1 (*PL* 64:297A).

of things we comprehend something, as in seeing the sign of a hoop we understand that wine is for sale, and in seeing ashes we understand there has been a fire.[7]

Philosophers and theologians both study the signification of words. But only theology considers the signification of things.[8]

The signification of words is threefold: story [*fabula*], realistic fiction [*argumentum*], history [*hystoria*].[9] Story is what contains neither truth nor probabilities, and according to Macrobius, the philosophical treatise eliminates this kind of fiction from its sacred precincts;[10] no less does theology reject it, just as the apostle said to Timothy: "avoid old wives' tales."[11] Realistic fiction is a narration of things which, even if they did not happen, nevertheless might have happened.[12] Philosophy did not reject this genus of signification, nor does theology take exception to it: in parables [*in parabolis*], for the purpose of our instruction, it often recounts events which might have taken place, even though they did not. For this reason it is called an *argumentum* ["narrative"], that is, a "bright invention" [*argutum inventum*].[13] History is the true explanation of deeds. It is so called from "*hysteron*," which is "to see," or from "*hysteron*," which is a deed, because it recounts things seen or done.[14] This form is commonly attributed to both philosophers and theologians; but it is twofold. Some history is called "analogy" [*analogia*],[15] other history is called "metaphor" [*metaphora*]. Proper speech or proper reason [*rectus sermo vel recta ratio*] is called analogy, that is, when an event is described according to the literal meaning of the words [*secundum propriam significationem vocum*], as for example, Hannibal did battle with the Romans and defeated them. Metaphorical history is when something else is demonstrated through non-proper signification of words [*per inpropriam significationem vocum*], as for example, "a thistle sent to a cedar tree,"[16] that is, the lowly to the high. And again, in the phrase "in the beginning God created heaven and earth"[17] the noun "beginning"

---

[7] The hoop as sign of a tavern, signifying the sale of wine, was used in discussions of signs and things, for example, Peter of Poitiers, *Sententiae, PL* 211:1071 A: "sometimes . . . a thing and a sign are together, for example, the hoop and tavern." See Rosier, *La Parole comme acte*, 95–122 on the background to the interest in visual symbols as forms of conventional signs. For the commonplace of ashes and fire, see Augustine, *De doctrina christiana* 1.2.1.

[8] Cf. Hugh of St. Victor, *Didascalicon* 5. 3; Hugh of St. Victor, *De sacramentis, PL* 176:185AB; Robert of Melun, *Sententie* I, ed. Martin: 170.

[9] *Rhetorica ad Herennium* 1.8.12–13; *De inventione* 1.19.27. Cf. Peter of Poitiers, *Allegorie super tabernaculum Moysi*, ed. Moore and Corbett, 100, on which the following discussion largely depends. See within, John of Garland, pp. 643, 655–6; and see General Introduction, pp. 42–4.

[10] *Commentum in somnium Scipionis* 1.2   [11] 1 Timothy 4:7.

[12] Cf. Isidore of Seville, *Etymologiae* 1.44.5.   [13] *Etymologiae* 6.18.16.

[14] *Etymologiae* 1.41.1. Cf. Hugh of St. Victor, *De scripturis et scriptoribus sacris*, ch. 3 (*PL* 175:11D–12A): " 'History' is so called from the Greek word *historeo*, which means 'I see and I tell.' This is because among the ancients it was not permitted to write history unless one had witnessed it."

[15] Here meaning where words correspond to the thing directly.   [16] 4 Kings 14:9; 2 Chronicles 25:18.

[17] Genesis 1:1.

is transumed [*transsumitur*] for the purpose of signifying the son of God, and by the noun "heaven" the angels are understood figuratively and transumptively [*inproprie et transsumptive*],[18] and similarly by the noun "earth," other creatures are understood.[19] This non-proper signification has various names. It is known as "trope" [*tropus*], that is, a turning [*conversus*], as "tropology" [*tropologia*] that is, a turned speech [*conversus sermo*], as "metonymy" [*methonomia*], that is, that is, a transumption, and as "metaphor" [*metaphora*], that is, a transformation [*transformatio*], because everywhere that speech is turned, transumed, or transformed from proper to non-proper signification, this is known as metaphor.[20]

Grammar and dialectic deal with analogy, because these arts govern words in their proper significations, in the meanings they are instituted to signify. The art of rhetoric deals with metaphor, because rhetoric teaches how to transform words from their proper significations to non-proper meanings by various colors [*colores*].[21]

Now we must consider how theology treats the significations of things. The way in which one thing can signify other things is threefold. That which pertains to instructing and shaping morals and discouraging vices is called tropology [*tropologia*], that is, moral instruction. And here, tropology is understood in a different way than we saw earlier, when we spoke about transumption of a historical narration. In the present case, the tropological level is where night signifies sin and day signifies virtue, because through sin the soul is obscured just as it is illuminated through virtue.

Here is the next way in which a thing signifies a thing. It is when by one thing we understand that something pertains to the Church as it performs its function in the present time, either according to its head, that is, Christ, or according to its members, or when something is understood about the assembly of the wicked or its members. And then this is called allegory [*allegoria*], as if we were to say a "different [alien] subject": "subject" is called "gore" [in Greek], whence according to some, a proposition is said to be "categorical," because something is set forth concerning a subject.[22] Allegory thus changes the subject, as when it is said, "arise, my love, my beautiful one, and come":[23] here Christ

---

[18] On *transumptio* (*transsumptio*) or metalepsis (rhetorical term), see above, Geoffrey of Vinsauf, p. 602 and note. On theological uses of the term, where it is often interchangeable with the term *translatio* (metaphor), see Rosier-Catach, "*Prata rident*," Dahan, "Saint Thomas d'Aquin et la métaphore," and Constable, "Medieval Latin Metaphors."

[19] Cf. Peter of Poitiers, *Allegorie super tabernaculum Moysi*, ed. Moore and Corbett, 101.

[20] Cf. Donatus, *Ars maior* 3.6, GL 4:399.17.   [21] I.e. the "colors" of rhetoric.

[22] Thomas is deriving an etymology for "alle-gory" out of the words ***alienum*** and "gore," taken to mean a subject. For "allegory" meaning "other subject," he gives the parallel of "category," which he takes to mean "the subject about which one predicates." More generally this discussion derives from Boethius' second commentary on Aristotle's *De interpretatione*. See Boethius, *In librum Aristotelis Peri hermeneias, pars posterior*, ed. Meiser, [book 4] ch. 10 (*PL* 64:521A).

[23] Song of Songs 2:13.

speaks to the Church, and so the subject is there changed, because by a fleshly spouse we understand a spiritual spouse, that is the Church. And so in this context the term "allegory" is taken strictly, because sometimes it is understood generally so that it encompasses tropology and allegory and anagogy [*anagoge*].

Further, sometimes through one thing another thing is signified, through which we understand something concerning the Church triumphant, that is, celestial things, such as God and the angels and the saints in glory. And this signification is called anagogy, that is, leading on high, because such understanding leads to supernal things. Whence the *Isagoge* is known as an "introduction," a "leading in."[24]

From these remarks it is clear that not every signification of things is an allegory. If, in common usage or natural understanding, through one thing we understand something else, that does not make it an allegory; for example, when in common practice the sign of a hoop means that wine is for sale, that is not an allegorical signification. Whence we define allegory in the following way: it is allegory when, by something said, something else is understood,[25] pertaining, through hidden inspiration or the teaching of the sacred page, to morals or to the Church militant or to the Church triumphant.[26] So it is not allegory unless we take what is said or written, not according to the meaning that the word signifies, but rather according to the meaning that the signified thing produces.[27] Thus when it says "the lion of the tribe of Judah hath prevailed"[28] this word "lion" signifies the animal according to its proper signification, and the thing signified, that is, the animal itself, signifies to me the fortitude through which I understand Christ. And to signify a thing in such a way is what we call allegory.

It must be pointed out, however, that when I understand the meaning of a word, my understanding of something other than that meaning must be in accordance with what God has inspired or what sacred Scripture has taught. If by lion I were to understand a strong horse, that would not be allegory, because God did not inspire this signification nor did sacred Scripture teach it.

---

[24] See Isidore, *Etymologiae* 2.25.1. Thomas' point here is that "anagogy" and the title of Porphyry's work *Isagoge* are built on the same root (in fact, the Greek *agô* "to lead," although Thomas probably did not know the exact principles of Greek grammar on which the etymological link is based), the equivalent of the Latin *duco* ("lead"), so that "anagogy" is a *sursum ductio* (leading on high) and *isagoga* is an *introductio* (leading into).

[25] For this first part of the definition of allegory, cf. Donatus *Ars maior* 3.6; Isidore, *Etymologiae* 1.37.22.

[26] Thus allegory is defined as a trope in grammatical terms, and as a theological principle. Note also that, as in Thomas' usage here, the term "allegory" can be used for the whole process of the signification of things, and for the particular level of signification within that larger process.

[27] That is, this is a dynamic of things, not words. Compare Augustine, *Enarrationes in Psalmos* 103.1.13. On this see Evans, "Thomas of Chobham on Preaching and Exegesis," 169.

[28] Apocalypse 5:5.

This fourfold signification, that is, historical, allegorical, tropological, and anagogical, may be comprehended in one noun, for example, Jerusalem. At the historical level the name Jerusalem signifies the place; tropologically it signifies the soul; allegorically, the Church militant; and anagogically, the Church triumphant.

Let us note that in the sacred page one thing signifies another in multiple ways: through the interpretation of a name, through the quality of a thing, and similarly through quantity, condition [*habitus*], action, deed, and number; and especially through cause, manner [*modus*], place, and time.[29]

Through the interpretation of a name: for example, by the name David, which is interpreted as "beautiful in appearance, or of strong hands,"[30] Christ is signified, who is "beautiful above the sons of men," "on whom the angels desire to look,"[31] who by the power of his hand overcame the devil.

Through quality: for example, through Rachel, who was beautiful, the contemplative life is signified; through Leah, who was bleary-eyed and ugly, the active life is signified.[32]

Through quantity something is signified allegorically: as through a quadrangle the stability of the four cardinal virtues is signified.

Through condition: for example, the angel sitting at the sepulcher wore "garments white as snow," and "his countenance was as lightning."[33] By the white vestments is signified the first coming of Christ, which was benign and gentle; through red is signified the second coming which is terrible in its judgment.[34]

Through action: when Stephen saw "Jesus standing on the right hand of God,"[35] it is signified that Christ is always ready to assist his soldiers.[36]

Through deed allegory is studied, as through this instance: David slew Goliath, by which is signified that Christ vanquished the devil.[37]

---

[29] Compare this list of the multiple ways in which one thing can signify another with the Ciceronian attributes of persons and actions, given as the rules for the section of the oration known as "proof" (*confirmatio*), and the topics considered under "performance of the action." The attributes of persons are: name, nature, manner of life, fortune, habit, feeling, interests, purposes, achievements, accidents, and speeches made; the topics under "performance of the act" are: place, time, occasion, manner, and facilities. See *De inventione* 1.24.34–1.27.41. This is the core of the *circumstantiae* of topical invention; cf. Boethius, *De topicis differentiis*, book 4.

[30] Jerome, *Liber interpretationis hebraicum nominum,* ed. Lagarde: 103, 135.

[31] Psalm 44:3, and 1 Peter 1:12.

[32] Cf. Genesis 29:16–17; and cf., among many sources, Gregory, *Moralia in Job* 6.37, ed. Adriaen, 330.

[33] Matthew 17:2; 28:3.

[34] Cf. *Glossa ordinaria*, PL 114:177C; cf. Nicholas of Lyre, *Bibliae iampridem renovatae partes sex cum glossa ordinaria*, V, f. 87r.

[35] Acts 7:55.

[36] Cf. *Glossa interlinear*, *Bibliae iampridem renovatae partes sex cum glossa ordinaria*, VI, f. 178v.

[37] 1 Samuel (1 Kings) 17:50.

Through number: when Abraham "saw three and adored one,"[38] it is signified that God is a trinity and is one.

Through cause: by the example that Jacob served seven years for Rachel,[39] it is signified that the cause of our serving ought to be eternal beatitude.

Through manner: for example, when Heli lightly rebuked the wickedness of his sons,[40] it is signified that prelates who do not correct their subordinates as is fitting are to be punished severely.

Through place: for example, when God "stood in a plain place" when he preached,[41] it is signified by this that a sermon ought to be open and ample, not obscure.

Through time: when it was said "it was the feast of dedication, and it was winter,"[42] by this it was signified that the chill of infidelity was at that time in man.[43] And often, also, through daytime, prosperity is understood; and through nighttime, adversity.[44]

And it is a general principle that every property of each thing, whatever it is, which can be suitably applied either to the soul for the purpose of morals, or to the Church in the present time in its head and its members, or to God and celestial things, can become an allegory.

Among these, however, there are three that are most especially necessary to the preacher: first, that he know the meanings of vocabulary, for which Jerome and Remigius have provided instruction; second, that he know the properties and proportions of numbers, because in the sacred page allegories most often develop from numbers; and third, that he know the nature of animals and of other things, because there is nothing that can better move the hearts of listeners than correctly assigning the properties of animals and of other things about which one may preach, because similitudes of things [*similitudines rerum*], like novelties, move the soul more easily and pleasantly.[45] Thus if I will have said: "a mouse in a satchel, a fire within, and a serpent in the bosom repay their hosts poorly,"[46] this moves the listeners more than if I had said: "there is an evil man among us." Similarly, if I say "he that touches pitch shall be defiled with it,"[47] I move the mind of a man more than if I were to say: "whoever associates with an evil man will be corrupted by him."

---

[38] "Tres vidit et unum adoravit," *Glossa ordinaria*, at Genesis 18:2–3, *PL* 113:125D; cf. *Bibliae iampridem renovatae partes sex cum glossa ordinaria*, I, f. 69v.

[39] Genesis 29:18.   [40] 1 Samuel 2:22–24.   [41] Luke 6:17.   [42] John 10:22.

[43] Cf. Augustine, *In Iohannis evangelium*, ed. Willems, 413 (and *PL* 35:1741).

[44] Gregory, *Moralia in Job* 2.9, ed. Adriaen, 271.

[45] On the application of natural lore to sermons, see Thorndike, "The Properties of Things of Nature Adapted to Sermons." On the adaptation of "similitude" to the needs of preaching, see d'Avray, *The Preaching of the Friars*, 229–34. On Thomas' own use of similitudes in his sermons, see Spatz, "Imagery in University Inception Sermons."

[46] See Walther, ed., *Proverbia sententiaeque latinitatis medii aevi*, 5: no. 15778: *Mus, serpens, ignis reddunt male sepe benignis*; cf. no. 11401.

[47] Sirach (Ecclesiasticus) 13:1.

There is a certain vocabulary by which the modes of signifying in the sacred page are comprehended: as when we say that this thing is understood "mystically" or "typologically," or that thing is "parabolical" or "enigmatic."

A "mystery" [*misterium*] is a kind of secret signification; a "type" [*typus*] is like a figurative signification. For a type is called a figure. Thus mystery and type generally comprise these three species: tropology, allegory, and anagogy. Whence whatever is said tropologically or allegorically or anagogically can be called a mystical or typological expression.

But parable [*parabola*], *paradigma*,[48] and enigma [*enigma*] are modes of signifying common to theology and philosophy, that is, in theological and in secular writings. The philosophers, however, distinguish four kinds of similitude: *ycos*, *paradigma*, parable, and enigma.[49] All of these are approached through similitudes.

Ycos is a likeness of an inanimate thing to an inanimate thing. *Paradigma* is a likeness of a person to a person. Parable is a likeness of a fact to a fact. Enigma is the obscure meaning of an obscure similitude.[50]

In this way alone does the enigma differ from the previous three kinds of similitude: that it has a more obscure likeness and meaning than the others. This is shown in the following verse: "*ycos* is inanimate; parable compares facts to facts; but *paradigma* compares persons." On these terms, enigma is usually called an "obscure parable." However, the

---

[48] Traditionally equated with *exemplum*, example; cf. *Ad Herennium* 4.49.62. However, Thomas of Chobham's treatment of it is particular in its application to persons.

[49] The grouping of the terms given here, *ycos*, *paradigma*, parable (*parabola*), and enigma, can be traced to Donatus, *Ars maior* 3.6, GL 4:402.22 ff. The term *ycos* (which appears in both extant manuscripts of Thomas' *Summa*) is most likely a confusion of Donatus' trope *icon* (i.e. Greek *eikôn*, image) with the Aristotelian term *eikos*. In the *Prior Analytics* (70a) the term *eikos* means a probability or accepted premise (as distinct from a sign [*semeion*], which is a demonstrative premise). In one recension of Boethius' translation of the *Prior Analytics*, the Greek term *eikos* is preserved in the Latin text (rendered as *ikos*); but in another recension of Boethius' translation, the term is translated into the Latin *verisimile* (verisimilitude, probability; cf. rhetorical "plausible arguments," *veri similia*, in *De inventione* 1.7.9 and *Ad Herennium* 1.2.3); see *Aristoteles latinus* 3.1–4, *Analytica priora*, ed. Minio-Paluello, 137 line 10, 189 line 18. Thus the Greek term *eikos* comes into later medieval usage (rendered *ikos*, *icos*, *ycos*) as an equivalent for *verisimile*, meaning "probability" or "likeness to truth." John of Salisbury uses *icos* in *Metalogicon* 4.5 in a discussion of the *Prior Analytics*. But in Thomas' *Summa*, the term *ycos* occurs in a discussion of tropes which is clearly derived from Donatus, *Ars maior* 3.6, where Donatus presents the trope *homoeosis* and its three subtypes, *icon*, *parabola* (parable), and *paradigma*. *Homoeosis* is the illustration of something less known through its likeness (*similitudo*) to something better known: *icon* is a comparison among persons or things that pertain to persons; *parabola* is a comparison of things that are dissimilar in kind; *paradigma* is the setting forth of an encouraging or discouraging example. The association of the philosophical term *eikos-ycos* with its Latin equivalent *verisimile*, and of the trope *icon* with the general idea of *similitudo* may have led to the confusion of terminology, *ycos* for *icon*, in the text of Thomas' *Summa*, here and also in chapter 7, 2.1.1.

[50] Isidore of Seville takes up Donatus' triad *icon*, *parabola*, and *paradigma* (see *Etymologiae* 1.37.31–5) and equates them with the triad *imago*, *comparatio*, and *exemplum* of Cicero's *De inventione* 1.30.47–9. In Donatus' *Ars maior* 3.6, *aenigma* is a trope in which there is "an obscure meaning through an obscure similitude of things." But the definitions that Thomas gives of *ycos*, *paradigma*, and parable seem to derive from Donatus' definition of metaphor (*Ars maior* 3.6): animate to animate, inanimate to inanimate, animate to inanimate, inanimate to animate (see above, Donatus, p. 97).

names *ycos* and *paradigma* are not found in the sacred page. But the words "parable" and "enigma" are often found there.

Augustine described the parable in this way: parable is a likeness of things when, through the introduction of a likeness of things, what is said about certain things is understood to be about other things, as exemplified in Psalm 77: "attend."[51] Thus Augustine seems to mean that parables are open, and that it is clear that they are hidden.[52] Thus it is said in Matthew: "to you it is given to know the mysteries of the kingdom of heaven," "but to the rest in parables,"[53] that is, to the rest the mysteries remain hidden. But parables, on their own terms, are obscure; however, when they are applied to the things that are understood through them, they become open.

Concerning enigma, the Apostle speaks to the Corinthians, saying: "we see now through a glass darkly [*enigmate*],"[54] and on the same point Augustine says that the enigma is an obscure similitude of things, giving this example: "a mother bore me, and soon the same woman is born from me."[55] He says that whoever does not know about the modes of signification in discourse does not understand this passage.[56]

FROM CHAPTER 7. CONCERNING THE ART OF PREACHING

Now that we have explained the matters that the preacher must, of necessity, consider, we should finally proceed to the art of preaching. This is twofold: the oration or preacher's sermon considered in relation to its parts, and the actual matter of the sermon, the ideas it contains and the persons to whom it is to be preached. This is what we should know about the parts of the sermon: as a rule, the parts of the sermon are divided up in the same way as the parts of a discourse in rhetoric or poetics.

The parts of poetic discourses are divided up one way according to poets and another way according to comic writers. The comic writers divide their comedies into three parts: the argument, the act, and the scene [*argumentum, actus, et cenas*]. The argument in a

---

[51] I.e. "pay attention" or "take note"; Psalm 77:1.

[52] Augustine, *Enarrationes in Psalmos* 77, ed. Dekkers and Fraipont, 1066. Augustine describes *parabola* here in this way: "*Parabola* displays a similitude of something . . . and note that in parables, what are called similitudes of things are compared with such things that we act on. But propositions, which in Greek are called *problemata*, are questions that involve something to be solved by disputation. Who would read parables and propositions hastily? Who would not pay attention, with vigilant mind, while hearing these things, so that he might achieve the fruit of them by understanding?"

[53] Matthew 13:11 and Luke 8:10.   [54] 1 Corinthians 13:12.

[55] This quotation and the definition of enigma actually come from Donatus, *Ars maior* 3.6 (see note 49 above). Cf. the enigmas of the Pseudo-Symphosius (fourth or fifth century AD), in de Marco and Glorie, eds., *Variae collectiones aenigmatum Merovingicae aetatis*, 723.

[56] This refers to Augustine's discussion of 1 Corinthians 13:12 in *De trinitate* 15.9.16.

comedy is a brief summation of everything to be said in the whole comedy that follows. It is called "argument" as a kind of "bright invention/adroit plan," [*argutum inventum*][57] because it is a very clever thing [*argutia*] to summarize in brief the whole matter of what is to come.[58] And on this model, Saint Jerome laid out prefatory arguments at the beginning of certain letters of Paul and of certain other books. According to the comic writers, there are five acts in any comedy. Whence Horace said: "Let no play be either shorter or longer than five acts, if when once seen it hopes to be called for and brought back to the stage."[59] "Act" is the word for the bringing forth of characters to be involved in any part of the matter proposed. Any act has many scenes, that is, a frequent bringing forth of characters [*personae*] on stage from the wings. And there cannot be more persons in one scene than four. Whence Horace: "nor let a fourth actor essay to speak."[60] Sometimes in a scene one person may be introduced, sometimes two, sometimes three, and sometimes four. And then the fourth person ought not to speak, unless just a little bit.

Poets divide their poems into three parts, that is, the proposition, the invocation, and the narration [*propositio, invocatio, narratio*]. The poet first proposes what he wants to deal with; second he invokes the help of the gods so that he can follow through to his narration. And in this preachers often imitate poets: first they propose the theme that they want to treat, then they make their invocation by asking their hearers to pour out prayers on their behalf to God that the sermon may be fruitful for them [the listeners]; and when this is done, they expound the theme earlier proposed, as if in the form of a narration. It was the custom among the ancients, even among philosophers, that they never took up their work without invoking divine aid. Whence we read in Plato:

> Well then, Timaeus, you should begin once you have invoked divine aid, as is the custom.

And Timaeus responds:

> In truth, Socrates, it is customary, and something of a duty, for all who are about to undertake great or small things to pray for divine assistance, and the more so should we, who are about to present a discourse on the nature and substance of the universe, invoke divine aid, unless clearly we are seized by some wild fury or unstoppable insanity. Thus in my prayers be it understood above all that our words be pleasing to God, and also logically coherent to us, and may we set forth this matter in an intelligible way, so that you can follow it easily.[61]

So if a gentile philosopher so thoughtfully and attentively asks that the things he will say should be pleasing to God and self-consistent, and that his arguments be coherent and

---

[57] *argumentum* and *argutum inventum*; see above, Prologue. [58] Cf. Isidore, *Etymologiae* 6.8.16.
[59] Horace, *Ars poetica* 189–90. [60] *Ars poetica* 192.
[61] *Timaeus* 1.27.14–24; *Plato latinus* 4, *Timaeus a Calcidio translatus*, ed. Waszink, 20.

useful to hearers, how much more so should we, who preach the divine word. This has particular force when the Lord said in the gospel of John, chapter 15, "without me you can do nothing,"[62] and again in Matthew, chapter 5, "seek ye therefore first the kingdom of God."[63] And indeed in all the epistles of Paul there is an opening salutation, which is in place of a prayer. In a salutation one prays for the well-being of the auditor or reader, that it may come about through what is to be said or done thereafter.

It is a general rule in the church that, in every undertaking, each person prepare himself with prayer. Thus we are not allowed to eat without a prayer beforehand. And thus it is written in the gospel of Mark, chapter 9, "I do believe, Lord: help my unbelief."[64] And again Augustine says, "Lord, give what you command and command what you will"[65] For it would be great presumption and arrogance if someone, as if relying upon their own power, did not invoke the help of God. Whence it is ever to be said, as in the prophet Isaiah 26, "thou hast wrought all our works for us."[66]

Orators divide up their speeches in other ways. The kind of division that rhetoric gives is more appropriate to the preacher in his preaching than the aforesaid poetic divisions of discourse. Rhetoric is the art of speaking in an orderly fashion with the aim of persuading.[67] Similarly, the whole intention of the preacher ought to be to persuade men to value what is honorable and useful for them, and to dissuade them from doing what is dishonest and harmful. And thus the object that the preacher and orator have in view is more or less the same. And therefore the teaching of the orator is very much necessary to the office of the preacher.

1. Concerning the Parts of the Oration According to the Art of Rhetoric

Rhetoric divides the office of the orator both according to the parts of the oration and according to the parts of the art. These are the parts of the oration: the first the exordium, which is also called the prooemium or the prologue or the preface;[68] the second part is the narration; the third part is the division; the fourth part is the proof [*confirmatio*]; the fifth part is the refutation [*confutatio*]; and the last part is the conclusion or epilogue.[69] The orator sets an exordium out front at the beginning of his speech, as a preparation for what is to be said next. The exordium captures good will, ensures attention, and prepares the

---

[62] John 15:5.   [63] The correct reference is to Matthew 6:33.   [64] Mark 9:23.
[65] Augustine, *Confessions* 10, chapters 29 and 37.   [66] Isaiah 26:12–13.   [67] Cicero, *De inventione* 1.5.6.
[68] Cf. *Ad Herennium* 1.3.4; *De inventione* 1.14.19; for *praefatio* see Isidore of Seville, *Etymologies*, 6.8.9–10.
[69] Cf. *De inventione* 1.14.19 and *Ad Herennium* 1.3.4: exordium, narration (statement of facts), division (*partitio* or *divisio*), confirmation (proof), refutation, conclusion.

audience's receptiveness to teaching. So ought the preacher, so far as he can and insofar as it is in his power, see to it that his auditors are of good will towards him. This is quite difficult, as the philosopher says.[70] Sometimes auditors are unwilling to hear a sermon: when they are being dissuaded from things that please them very much and being urged towards things that displease them intensely. And then eloquence must be of greatest power when it must soothe unwilling ears. Thus in Isaiah chapter 30 it is read that when the children of Israel heard Isaiah dissuading them from their vices, they said to him: "speak unto us pleasant things, see errors for us."[71] And again, in Wisdom chapter 2, concerning such matters it is read: "Let us therefore lie in wait for the just . . . because he is contrary to our doings, and upbraideth us with transgressions of the law, and divulgeth against us the sins of our way of life."[72] And again in 3 Kings: "is there not here some prophet of the Lord, that we may inquire by him [of the Lord]? . . . but I hate him [nor do I hear him willingly, for he always prophesies evil to me]."[73] Whence in rhetoric as in preaching, it is not always possible to capture the good will of the audience by direct means; at times it must be done obliquely.[74]

When these rules for the prooemium are observed this is known as a beginning [*principium*], which is the same thing as a prologue, that is, a "proto-sermon," or an initial discourse before the principal matter. This is called a "prooemium," because the beginning is, as it were, half of the whole discourse, *hemi* being another term for "half."[75] It is also called a "preface," although this term is not used in rhetoric. It is called "preface" because it belongs to the things that we "say" [*famur*], that is, "speak" before the main topic. "Insinuation," however, is also called "epode," an oblique manner of speaking: when all points which, at other times, are commonly treated directly in the prologue, are covered indirectly and obliquely at the beginning of the sermon. Thus it is read that when Saint Stephen had to preach to the Jews, he began by speaking to his persecutors as if he were afraid of them: "Ye men, brethren, and fathers, hear," as in Acts chapter 7.[76] How softly and mildly he procured their eagerness so that he might commend the Savior to them. He began with flattery so that he would be heard at length, and because he was accused of speaking against the Lord and the Law, he gave an exposition of the Law itself, so that he would be a preacher of that very Law he was accused of desecrating. The passage

---

[70] Cf. *De inventione* 1.15.21. [71] Isaiah 30:10. [72] Wisdom 2:12.

[73] Cf. 3 Kings (= 1 Kings) 22:7–8.

[74] The reference is to the device of insinuation. See Cicero's discussion of *insinuatio*, the kind of exordium to be used in difficult or scandalous cases (*admirabilis genus*) or in the ambiguous, doubtful, or contemptible (*humilis*) case; see *De inventione* 1.15.21; and see Rupert of Deutz, above, pp. 395–6.

[75] Thomas derives "prooemium" (*proe[h]emium*) from [*h*]*emi*, or a "half" that goes before the whole discourse.

[76] Acts 7:2, and *Glossa ordinaria*, PL 114:440D; cf. *Bibliae iampridem renovatae partes sex cum glossa ordinaria*, VI, f. 175v.

in the Law that he expounded is in these words of Genesis: "The God of glory appeared to our father Abraham, when he was in Mesopotamia."[77] Again, it is read in the legend of Saint Matthew the apostle, that when the tyrant Hyrtacus desired to marry Efigenia the virgin who had taken the veil for God, he asked Saint Matthew, whose counsel he enjoyed, to sway the virgin's mind to consent to the tyrant. Saint Matthew asked if he might assemble all the people, so that all might hear his sermon about the excellence of matrimony. Hyrtacus believed that the apostle was going to comply with his request, so he had the whole multitude assembled. Standing in the middle of the crowd, Matthew began, in an extraordinary way, to praise matrimony, so that he almost seemed to prefer marriage to virginity. In this way he inclined the minds of Hyrtacus and all the others to hear him willingly. However, at the end he said that every virgin consecrated to God was a spouse of Christ, and he proved that anyone dissolving such matrimony would be an adulterer: when the people had assented to this argument, Hyrtacus was silenced.[78] But if the apostle had said this right away, at the beginning of his sermon, he would not have had the people's good will towards him, nor Hyrtacus' permission to preach at length. It is read that Saint James the Apostle used a similar insinuation when the Jews brought him out so that he might preach against the faith of Jesus Christ. Going up to the temple, he began his sermon concerning faith in the one God, and then, when he had won over the Jews, at last he began to preach the faith of Jesus Christ.[79] And sacred Scripture is full of such examples of insinuation.

That we should capture good will in our prooemia or prologues and that we should make our audience receptive to teaching is shown by Saint Jerome in all the prologues with which he usually prefaced the individual books of the Bible that he translated.

Rhetorical teaching shows quite clearly how we ought to make an audience attentive [*attentus*] and teachable [*docile*]. And there is small benefit to any sermon if the hearers are not well disposed to the preacher who preaches it. For if they are not attentive to the lesson that he teaches, and if they are not docile, that is, well instructed and well prepared, how can they reliably retain what they hear? All of these concerns are found in the sacred page. Whence even in the Lord's prayer God puts in front a brief "securing of good will," saying, as in Matthew 6, "Our father who art in heaven."[80] Moses and David, when they dared not beseech God on behalf of the people who had sinned so greatly, spoke the words: "Remember Abraham, Isaac, and Jacob, thy servants."[81]

---

[77] Correct reference is to the passage in Acts 7:2.

[78] *Acta sanctorum*, collected and edited by Joannes Bollandus et al., *Septembris* VI (Antwerp, 1757): 223–4.

[79] "Passio Sancti Jacobi apostoli prima die mensis maii," *Analecta Bollandiana*, ed. Société des Bollandistes 8 (1889): 136–7.

[80] Matthew 6:9. Cf. Thomas of Chobham, *Summa confessorum*, ed. Broomfield, 265.

[81] Exodus 32:13; Deuteronomy 9:27.

The preacher can secure good will [*captare benevolentiam*] by means of his own character by showing, without arrogance, that he is humble and obedient, and that he desires the well being of those to whom he preaches. He can also secure good will by invoking the character of those he preaches against, showing that they are disobedient to God and that they love injustice. He can also capture good will by what he preaches about, if he shows the honesty and utility of it. And he can also capture good will through the character of the audience, just as Saint Paul does in many places, when he says: "I give thanks to God for you," and other things in this vein.[82] A preacher should always make his listeners attentive as much as he can by presenting the kinds of things that they hear willingly about the promise of eternal salvation, and mixing this with terrible things about the punishments of hell. Moses does this at the end of Deuteronomy when he shows what rewards are in store for those observing the laws and what punishments for those disregarding them. The preacher must also make his auditors receptive to teaching, that is, he should not put them off with verbiage or too long a sermon, or by propounding things that are irrelevant or self-contradictory. For in this way a preacher may render his audience unreceptive, that is, where they are not readily able to understand what they hear. Sacred Scripture is full of examples of such things. A preacher will never be able to preach well if he does not know how to present a prooemium to his sermon, whether from practice or from skilled technique. Some preachers call their prologue a "protheme" [*prothema*], because it is a theme before the theme; that is, before they pursue the principal theme, they present and expound a kind of brief theme in order to secure good will, prepare the attention of the hearers, and make them receptive to teaching. The protheme should always be appropriate to the principal theme. For if what is presented is irrelevant and contradictory, the exordium is ruined. Thus if one wants the sermon to be about chastity, and presents a protheme about mercy towards the poor, the protheme is irrelevant.

The second part of the rhetorical oration is the narration. This is when the lawyer narrates the order of events in his case. Such narrations often occur in sermons, as when something that was done is recounted in order to clarify matters that are in the theme. The exposition of the theme is often set in place of the narration of rhetoric. When narrations are made either through a digression or an example, the preacher must be sure that his narration is brief, lucid, and plausible.[83] For if it should be long or obscure or less plausible, the narration will not be pleasing to the auditors, and the sermon will be to

---

[82] Cf. Romans 1:7–8; 1 Corinthians 1:3; 2 Corinthians 1:3. On means of securing good will, see *De inventione* 1.16.22; *Ad Herennium* 1.5.8.

[83] *Ad Herennium* 1.9.14; *De inventione* 1.20.28.

no avail. However, sometimes stories [*fabulae*] are mixed in with the sermon, not for the sake of fictional events themselves, but for the sake of the significations which may be understood through the stories, just as I described at the beginning of this treatise. The holy writers also mix such fables into their narratives. Thus it is read in Judges that all the trees came to the olive tree, the fig tree, and the vine to choose themselves a king, but none of these were willing to be king; so they went to the thorn bush, and chose him as their king, and with this they were all destroyed.[84]

The third part of the rhetorical oration is division. This is where the speaker, after his narration, distinguishes between what he has asserted in his case and what his opponent has asserted.[85] Such division occurs often in sermons, for it is especially necessary there. The preacher makes some kind of division into various parts, and next takes up a particular part. A distinction of this sort illuminates the minds of the listeners. Solomon often made such distinctions, as when he said: "Three things are hard to me, and the fourth I am utterly ignorant of. The way of an eagle in the air, the way of a serpent upon a rock, the way of a ship in the midst of the sea, and the way of a man in youth."[86] And God himself distinguished eight beatitudes in Matthew 5, and chapter 8 of Isaiah divides the gifts of the Holy Spirit into seven.[87] And we find this in many other places.

The fourth and fifth parts of the rhetorical oration are proof and refutation.[88] This is when the arguments put forward by the speaker are proved, and the opponent's arguments are refuted. Proof and refutation often occur in sermons, because the preacher often proves something that pertains to true faith or good morals, either through reasons, or examples, or holy authorities; and he strives to refute the false opinion of heretics. In such matters it is necessary to know arguments as well as probable or necessary reasons, whether these be of logic or rhetoric, and many holy authorities by which truth is proved and falsity is refuted. For the hearts of listeners cannot be moved to accept the preacher's intentions if not through reasons that are valid and effective. Those who are ignorant of reasoning never preach well. All the arts were created that they may serve sacred Scripture, for they are handmaidens to theology. Thus Jerome asserted that whatever is said in the physical sciences, the ethical sciences, or the logical sciences may be found in Isaiah.[89] And again, in Deuteronomy 20 it is written: "When thou hast besieged a city a long time . . . thou shalt not cut down the trees that may be eaten of"[90]; and here the *Glossa* calls the trees "physics,

---

[84] Judges 9: 8–15.

[85] *De inventione* I.22.31; *Ad Herennium* I.10.17. The terms *divisio* and *partitio* were used rather interchangeably to denote this part of the speech; but in his commentary on *De inventione*, Victorinus introduced a further refinement: "partition is the arrangement of the whole case according to its parts; division is the placing of elements within the partition," in Halm, ed., *Rhetores latini minores*, 208. See Murphy, *Rhetoric in the Middle Ages*, 315.

[86] Proverbs 30:18.   [87] Matthew 5:4–11; Isaiah 11:2–3.   [88] *De inventione* I.34.34 and I.52.78.

[89] Jerome, *Commentarii in Isaiam*, ed. Adriaen, 1–2 (prologue).   [90] Deuteronomy 20:19.

ethics, and logic, from which there is much value."[91] Whoever turns the arts to uses other than service to sacred Scripture does a great injury to theology, because he denies it its handmaidens. Thus at that place in Isaiah 44, "The carpenter hath stretched out his rule, he hath formed it with a plane, etc.," the *Glossa* says: "in the art of dialectic, it is as if with a carpenter's ax, drill, file, and plane they form their own god, and hammer it with mallets, and adorn it with the charm of rhetorical speech, those people 'whose God is their belly, and whose glory is in their shame,'" as in Philippians 4.[92] For indeed the sacred page has its own special topics, beyond the topics of dialectic and rhetoric, for praising God and disparaging sin. Thus we find in the psalm, "Sing ye to the Lord a new canticle: let his praise be in the church of the saints," and in many other places too.[93]

The last part of the rhetorical oration is the conclusion or the epilogue. This is when the things that were said are briefly recapitulated so that they are the better commended to memory.[94] Discerning preachers often use an epilogue, because this appeals strongly to hearers who are simple and less experienced, and because they more effectively retain what they heard before. Preachers add at the end of their sermon a certain element which is not found in rhetorical teaching, namely a prayer to God that the hearers may reach the kingdom of heaven through the preaching they have heard and through their works. This is joined to the end of the sermon, just as there is a prefatory prayer at the beginning of the sermon.

The parts of the oration in rhetoric, no matter how well they are ordered, cannot be put to good and discerning use without reference to the parts of the art of rhetoric as a whole. Thus one must know how to apply the elements of the whole art to the parts of the oration.

2. *Concerning the Parts of the Art of Rhetoric*

The parts of the art of rhetoric are invention, disposition, style, memory, and delivery. All of these have a place in preaching. It is necessary for the preacher to know how to discover everything required in each part of the sermon. Second, he must be well prepared to order and arrange what has been discovered. Whatever valid reasonings he has discovered, these will not help him, or barely help him, unless he knows how to bring them together. It is the same with an army: even if someone has strong soldiers, these are of no use unless the lines

---

[91] Interlinear gloss, *Bibliae iampridem renovatae partes sex cum glossa ordinaria*, I, f. 354r.

[92] Isaiah 44:13, and *Glossa ordinaria*, *PL* 113:1287B, and *Bibliae iampridem renovatae partes sex cum glossa ordinaria*, IV, f. 77v. For the verse in question, see Philippians 3:19.

[93] Psalm 149:1.   [94] *De inventione* 1.52.98, *Ad Herennium* 1.3.4.

of battle are well ordered. Third, when the preacher has successfully discovered those things that are to be said, and has determined correctly what will be put into which position, this preparation will be of little use to him unless he has good style, that is, embellishment of words and ideas as the matter requires [*ornatus verborum et sententiarum*]. For one should pay attention to embellishment not just of words but also of ideas. A sermon should be embellished in its words and its ideas, lest it appear base through speech that is too cheap and shabby. Thus we read that the prophets and the apostles have used nearly every ornament of word and idea in their writings. After the preacher has discovered and embellished what is to be said, he will need memory so that he may retain what he has discovered, arranged, and embellished. Although Tully devoted artful teaching to this, the skill of memory is achieved better through practice and application.[95] The last component of the art is delivery. It is very important that the preacher modulate his voice so that it is not loud and aggressive, but on the other hand, not too effeminate. Similarly, it is necessary to control his facial expression, so that he does not dart and twist his glance here and there, and so that he does not gesture wildly and excessively. For all of these characteristics make a preacher look contemptible, and if he himself is disdained, his sermon will also be disdained. There is more to be said about the elements of the art of rhetoric, and we will begin with how the preacher should discover what is necessary for his sermon.

2.1. Concerning invention

After this we must consider what kind of material is to be invented for each part of the sermon, and with what artful technique the preacher may find what is necessary. As the philosopher[96] says, "invention is the discovery of true or seemingly true arguments to render one's cause plausible."[97] He calls arguments that are necessary "true," and arguments that are plausible "seemingly true." One should know that the means of invention are different in the exordium, the narration, and all the other parts of the discourse. Every discovery must have its origin in three things: virtue, usefulness, and justice. No preacher ought to preach what is not virtuous, just, or useful. Whence the philosophers say that there are three kinds of cases: demonstrative, deliberative, and judicial.[98] The demonstrative case has virtue as its objective; the deliberative case has usefulness; and the judicial is directed to justice. The preacher ought to persuade his audience towards these things, that

---

[95] The reference here is to the section on memory in *Ad Herennium* 3.16.28–3.24.40.

[96] In this and the following sections, Thomas uses "the philosopher" to refer to Cicero.

[97] *De inventione* 1.7.9.

[98] That is, the three genres of rhetoric: see *Ad Herennium* 1.2.2. Thomas uses the word "philosophi" to refer to the ancient rhetorical theorists.

is, virtue, usefulness, and justice, and away from their contraries, that is, the sinful, the useless, and the unjust.

[Following this paragraph is a very long section in which Thomas describes in detail the method of invention to be used in each of the five parts of the sermon: exordium, narration, division, proof, and refutation. Thus in Thomas' treatise, as in *De inventione*, *Rhetorica ad Herennium*, the late antique rhetorical compendia, and the medieval commentaries on Ciceronian rhetoric, the great weight of emphasis falls on the first canon of rhetoric, invention. Thomas' exposition thus also follows the basic structure of the *De inventione* book 1, which discusses how each part of the oration is to be formed out of the kinds of arguments that are specific to its purpose.]

2.2. Concerning memory

The philosopher also treats the art of memory. This greatly helps the work of preachers, because the hearers can securely retain what they hear.[99] For if the sermon is diffuse, confusing, and disconnected so that no part coheres with the others, the audience will not retain anything. The sermon will be useless and fruitless if the hearers carry away nothing from it. This is why the philosopher provides teaching about this, that the oration should be connected and joined in its various parts so that the parts seem to cohere naturally with each other.[100] And he offers this image: if we see the head of a man coming forward, we should naturally understand that there is also a torso, hands, feet, and other members.[101] A sermon should also be ordered in this way, because upon hearing the "head," that is, the theme of the sermon, the auditor should immediately understand what parts the preacher attaches to it: he should know what parts of the sermon he is listening to now, and what parts he should anticipate. Thus he will hold in his memory what he is going to hear, and at the end of the sermon he will hold in his memory the means for retaining the things that have been said, since he understands that they are coherent with each other so that they cannot be separated.[102] The sermon that puts its parts together inconsistently is faulty. Thus says the poet: " . . . the middle is not discordant with the beginning, nor the end with the middle."[103] And the poet also says: "If a painter chose to join a human head to the neck of a horse . . ."[104] And again, "That was a wine-jar, when the moulding began: why . . . does it turn out a pitcher?"[105]

---

[99] Note that in this treatment of the rhetorical canon of memory, the technique is directed to enabling the audience to remember what has been said, rather than to the speaker's own skill at remembering what he wanted to say.

[100] Cf. *De inventione* 1.14.19.

[101] Cf. *De inventione* 1.18.26: "nec . . . aliquod membrum annexum orationi."

[102] Cf. *De inventione* 2.12.39.   [103] Horace, *Ars poetica* 152.   [104] Horace, *Ars poetica* 1–2.

[105] Horace, *Ars poetica* 21–2.

So that sermon whose parts are not coherent is completely vacuous, if for no other reason at least, because it undermines memory. The philosopher says that whoever proposes an argument and supports it appropriately is not to be criticized;[106] similarly, anyone who proposes a theme and follows out the parts of that theme in an appropriate way, and does not wander into extrinsic and irrelevant matters, ought to be praised. Even though one theme may be richer material for preaching a good sermon, and another theme less so, we ought not to blame the one who proposes a lesser theme, as long as he follows through on all those elements that pertain to it. The poets reprehend this fault in many ways, for example: "Works . . . often have one or two purple patches so stitched on as to glitter far and wide."[107] And elsewhere: "lest, if some day perchance the flock of birds come to reclaim their plumage, the poor crow, stripped of his stolen colors, awake laughter."[108] To make a sermon in this way is not to preach but to assemble bits and pieces. It is as if someone wanted to make a stone house, and went about collecting wood and reeds.

Prolixity of speech does great damage to the art of memory. The mind of the listener, burdened with many details, does not easily retain what comes after. As the philosopher said, "whatever you pour into a full vessel runs out."[109] Moreover, an unreasonable length of time greatly impedes the art of memory. If time pressures for other business distract the hearers, they cannot give their attention to a sermon for any extended period. Thus in such a case one should abbreviate the sermon, or invent such arguments as will detain even these unwilling auditors, for instance, if what is presented is so agreeable to them that they will rejoice in being detained and in hearing such matters. This is accomplished in two ways, as the poet says, through great profit or pleasure. The poet says: "Poets aim either to benefit or to amuse."[110] If the preacher is prepared to do neither of these things, it is better to postpone preaching the sermon than to preach a useless sermon.

2.3. Concerning arrangement

The philosopher also counts the art of arrangement among the parts of the art of rhetoric; for as he says, this is most necessary. He gives this similitude: if someone has strong soldiers in his army, they will avail him little or nothing unless they are well arranged and ordered by their squadrons and battle lines. Thus also should a preacher order and arrange his argument and his reasoning in his sermon so that they are effective, not only through their inherent power, but also through the way that they are organized. He should position his stronger reasonings and authorities at the beginning of the sermon so as to persuade and

---

[106] Perhaps *Ad Herennium* 2.27.43.   [107] Horace, *Ars poetica* 15–16.
[108] Horace, *Epistles* 1.3.18–19, trans. Fairclough.   [109] Source unknown; possibly proverbial.
[110] *Ars poetica* 333.

dissuade as he intends, then his weaker reasonings in the middle, and then at the end of the sermon, his very strongest reasonings. For if the auditors hear reasons that are probable, necessary, or greatly moving at the start of the sermon, they will believe more readily and they will pay attention to what follows. However, if the preacher starts off tepidly and ineffectively, it is easy for the audience to dismiss the sermon. Along the same lines, if the strongest reasoning is brought in at the end, it will adhere more firmly in their hearts, and as it were compel them to believe and do what was preached to them. This is treated in Canticles chapter 6, for not only the church, but even sacred Scripture is "terrible as an army set in array."[111] In preaching there should be not only a wall, but a bulwark, as in Isaiah 26: "A saviour, a wall and a bulwark shall be set therein."[112] Also in Numbers 24: "How beautiful are thy tabernacles, O Jacob, and thy tents, O Israel! As woody valleys, as watered gardens . . ."[113] Soldiers are often hidden in a wooded valley so that they unexpectedly make a stronger attack on the enemy. Just as certain arguments derive their force and excellence from the topic on which they depend, as in argumentative passages that draw a topic from genus or species or something else, and certain arguments derive their effectiveness only from the arrangement and combination of terms, not from any capacity that there may be among their terms, so in preaching, certain parts of the sermon derive their effectiveness from the very excellence of the authority that is introduced, which by itself suffices for proof; but other parts of the sermon derive their persuasive power from conjoining one authority or reason with another, so that where either element on its own would be weak, they are forceful when brought together. Thus the poet says, "but things that are useless on their own are powerful in numbers."[114] Thus for each instance the preacher must consider that if he should bring in a weak reason on behalf of any matter, he should have one or two other reasons to supplement it; for what are weak reasons on their own are strong when joined together. Thus when the Lord wished to defend his disciples who were plucking ears of corn on the sabbath, the argument that they were hungry was a weak one; so he added a stronger argument, that he himself was the God of the sabbath, and thus he could give them license to pluck corn on the sabbath.[115] Similarly, when the Jews reproached the Lord because he healed on the sabbath, he provided the reason that the woman whom he healed was possessed by Satan, and thus it was necessary and in God's power that she be released on the sabbath.[116] And when the Jews did not find this reason sufficient, he immediately added another, saying: "Which of you shall have an ass or an ox fall into a pit, and will not immediately draw him out, on the sabbath day?"[117] This is how one reason is made stronger by another.

---

[111] Song of Songs 6:3.   [112] Isaiah 26:1.   [113] Numbers 24:5–6.   [114] Ovid, *Remedia amoris*, 420.
[115] Matthew 12:1–4, Mark 2:23–8, Luke 6:1–5.   [116] Luke 13:10–17.   [117] Luke 14:5.

2.4. Concerning style

The philosopher also considers style as a part of the art of rhetoric; he calls it embellishment of speech [*ornatus loquendi*].[118] For eloquence, that is, embellished speech, is most
necessary to preaching. Thus it is written in Acts 2: "[the Apostles] began to speak with
divers tongues, according as the Holy Ghost gave them to speak."[119] Eloquence is to speak
ornately. But on the other hand, we find in Luke 12 and Matthew 10: "take no thought how
or what to speak: for it shall be given you in that hour what to speak,"[120] as if to say we
should not care about verbal ornament but about true meaning. But yet the saints affirm
that flowers of the philosophers[121] are found in gentile writings which are not native to the
sacred page. Whence, as Jerome says, Isaiah is written out by *cola* and *commata* [i.e. lines
and short periods]. In fact, these are colors of rhetoric, which in rhetorical doctrine are
called *membrum* [i.e. brief clause] and *articulus* [i.e. staccato phrasing].[122]

It should be noted that there are two kinds of ornament in rhetoric, figures of thought and
figures of speech.[123] Whoever would like to know about such embellishments should have
recourse to the art of rhetoric. But it is also to be noted that the sacred page does not readily
admit all the colors or figures of thought. Whence we read in Proverbs: "He that followeth
after words only, shall have nothing. But he that possesseth a mind, loveth his own soul."[124]
Such are those who have prurient ears, or whom nothing pleases unless it has a sweet sound.
Whence says Jerome: as often as I take more delight in what is sung than what is said, that is,
as often as I delight more in sound than in sense, so often do I confess to have sinned
gravely.[125] There are two kinds of rhetorical colors which are to be rejected in preaching,
similiter cadens [*homoeopototon*] and *similiter desinens* [*homoeoteleuton*]. *Similiter cadens* is

---

[118] *De inventione* 1.7.9; *Ad Herennium* 1.2.3 and 4.12.18.   [119] Acts 2:4.

[120] Matthew 10:19; Luke 12:11.   [121] I.e. ornaments of rhetoric.

[122] Jerome, Preface to Isaiah, *PL* 28:771. In this preface, Jerome describes how he has borrowed, from manuscripts of Demosthenes and Cicero, the practice of dividing a text into lines and short periods to make it easier to
follow, and thus he presents his translation of the prophetic books of the Bible in similar form. In describing his
experiments with page and text layout, Jerome suggests that this is a practice not previously applied to sacred books.
Thus the *cola* and *commata*, or "lines" and "periods," are associated with gentile writings, and according to Jerome
are not native to sacred Scripture. See Cassiodorus' remarks on Jerome's textual divisions at *Institutiones* 1.9, and in
An Introduction to Divine and Human Readings, trans. Jones, 72 and note. Thomas of Chobham has made a
connection between the *cola* and *commata* of textual layout that Jerome says he found in the gentile "philosophers"
(i.e. Jerome's references to Cicero and Demosthenes), and the "colon" or clause (*membrum*) and the "comma" or
phrase (*articulus*) of rhetorical figures of diction: see *Ad Herennium* 4.19.26. The Greek and Latin terminology are
found in Isidore's *Etymologiae* 2.18. Seeing the Latin equivalents for the Greek in Isidore's book on rhetoric may have
sparked the connection that Thomas makes between Jerome's discussion of textual layout and figures of diction.
Thus the "flowers of the philosophers found in gentile writings" are the figures of diction *membrum* and *articulus*,
that is, short pithy clauses strung together and words set apart by pauses.

[123] Translating *ornatus sententiarum* and *ornatus sermonum*.   [124] Proverbs 19:7–8.

[125] This sentence is actually derived from Augustine, *Confessions* 10.33, not from Jerome.

when a similar case ending is repeated several times, for example: *homo est indigens virtutis, habundans felicitatis*;[126] or *diligentia conparat divitias, negligentia corrumpit animum, et tamen cum ita vivat neminem [prae] se ducit hominem.*[127] *Similiter desinens* is the rhetorical figure in which more words have a similar ending, that is, either through consonants or through rhythm, as in *turpiter audes facere, nequiter studes dicere.*[128] Although the former color is sometimes acceptable, the latter color, *similiter desinens*, is laughable in a sermon.

But yet we should note that the sacred page has its own and singular mode of speaking which the preacher ought to observe if he can, in every way. Thus we find in 2 Peter, where the Gloss says: " 'for prophecy came not by the will of man at any time,' but the holy men spoke by inspiration of the Holy Spirit: pay attention to prophetic speech, for it comes from God; for it may be proved through this that prophecy is not written with the words and manner of speaking that men speak in their language and in which secular writings are composed. And thus the prophet speaks not by his own will or that of his auditors, but by the will of the Holy Spirit, who speaks through these words."[129]

Nevertheless, there is a certain stylistic ornament that is common to all writing, which the philosophers divide into three parts: the grand style, the middle style, and the humble style.[130] With respect to these styles, it is important that the preacher, like others, command words that are appropriate to the matter of which he speaks. The grand or high style, as a kind of dignified expression, is used in treating lofty matters or persons of great importance; the middle style is used when treating persons or things of middling importance; and the humble expression is used when the speech makes reference to low persons and matters.[131] Whence it is a fault of style to use magniloquent speech when treating matters of least importance; and similarly it is a fault to use simple language when speaking of lofty persons or things.[132] Thus, when the apostle spoke of God's word, which

---

[126] "The man is lacking in virtue but abounds in good fortune." This sentence is based on the example given in *Ad Herennium* 4.20.28.

[127] "Through diligence he acquires riches, but through negligence he corrupts his soul. And yet, living so, he counts no one any one before himself." Quoting *Ad Herennium* 4.20.28.

[128] "You dare to act dishonorably, you strive to talk despicably." Quoting *Ad Herennium* 4.20.28. The definition of *similiter desinens* given in the *Ad Herennium* differs slightly from Thomas of Chobham's defintion: "*Similiter desinens*" occurs when the word endings are similar, although the words are indeclinable (4.20.28): that is, the sound effect of *similiter desinens* depends, not on the similar sounds of Latin case endings, but on the similar sounds of indeclinable words such as adverbs (e.g. "turpiter," "nequiter").

[129] *Glossa ordinaria PL* 114:691B, at 2 Peter 1:21. Cf. *Bibliae iampridem renovatae partes sex cum glossa ordinaria*, VI, f. 224v.

[130] Cf. *Ad Herennium* 4.8.11 and Augustine, *De doctrina christiana* 4.12.27 (or 4.74) and 4.17.34–4.18.35 (or 4.96–7).

[131] Thomas' treatment of the three levels of style derives from the medieval tradition of "material" or social application of styles, not from Augustine's discussion. See the notes to the "Materia" commentary and to John of Garland's *Parisiana poetria*, pp. 555, 645.

[132] Cf. the doctrine of the faults of style in the "Materia" commentary and the *Parisiana poetria*, pp. 651–4.

is a great and lofty thing, he used grandiloquent language, saying at Hebrews chapter 4, "for the word of God is living and effectual, and more piercing than any two-edged sword; and reaching unto the division of the soul and the spirit."[133] Similarly, when his subject was the rejection of temporal goods, which are of middling and humble status, he used the appropriate language, saying in Philippians chapter 3, "[I have suffered the loss of all things,] and count them but as dung, that I may gain Christ."[134] And you find this rule observed throughout the entire sacred page.

2.5. Concerning delivery

The philosopher considers delivery the remaining part of the art of rhetoric. This is quite necessary to the preacher, as mentioned above. For "delivery is the graceful regulation of voice, countenance, and gesture."[135] It is a disgrace when the preacher conducts himself improperly in his voice, countenance, and gesture. Thus was the high priest reproached in Matthew 26, because he rose up in the tribunal and said furiously to Jesus: "Answerest thou nothing to the things which these witness against thee?"[136] The Gloss says on this passage, "he is angry because he does not find the pretext for a false accusation; with a disgraceful gesture of his body he displays the turpitude of his mind."[137] As a judge he ought to have sat peacefully, and calmly judged and asked questions.

The preacher ought to adjust his voice to the matter about which he is speaking. If he is speaking about God's threats or the execration of turpitude, he should have a grave voice. If he is talking about mercy or about things that pertain to mercy, he ought to soften his voice somewhat. If he is talking about terrifying things he should make his voice tremble like one who is afraid.

It is most important to moderate countenance and gesture, that is, one should not have flaming eyes or wandering hands like a fighter or a pantomime jester. Thus it is read in Ecclesiasticus 19: "the attire of the body, and the laughter of the teeth, and the gait of the man, shew what he is."[138] And in Isaiah 3: "Because the daughters of Sion . . . have walked with stretched out necks and with wanton glances of their eyes, and . . . with their feet . . . moved in a set pace."[139] And again in Amos 6: "Woe to you that are wealthy in Sion . . . that go in with state into the house of Israel."[140] The poet derides such manner of delivery when he says: "[he] throws aside his bombast and his sesquipedalian words";[141] or again, "Mountains will labour and a ridiculous mouse will come forth";[142] and again, "What will

---

[133] Hebrews 4:12.   [134] Philippians 3:8.   [135] *Ad Herennium* 1.2.3.   [136] Matthew 26:62.

[137] Cf. interlinear gloss, *Bibliae iampridem renovatae partes sex cum glossa ordinaria*, V, f. 81v, at Matthew 26:62.

[138] Ecclesiasticus (Sirach) 19:27.   [139] Isaiah 3:16.   [140] Amos 6:1.   [141] Horace, *Ars poetica* 97.

[142] *Ars poetica* 139.

this boaster produce in keeping with such mouthing?"[143] And again in Isaiah 16: "We have heard of the pride of Moab, he is exceeding proud . . . and his indignation is more than his strength."[144] Whence let us take note of what we read about David in 1 Kings chapter 21, that before King Achis he affected madness, that is, by certain bodily gestures he played the fool. Thus it is patently clear that those who use such gesticulations in preaching will be considered fools, and will seem to be actors rather than preachers.

3. Concerning the epilogue

The philosopher places the epilogue, that is, the conclusion or recapitulation, at the end of the oration.[145] This is important for the preacher. Nothing is more useful to solidifying the memory than to repeat briefly what was said in the sermon. The recapitulation should be brief so that it seems not so much a recollection of what was said as a confirmation of it. Everything that was said should not be repeated, but only the main issues, that is, those things that the preacher recognizes have most moved the hearts of the hearers, namely, the most valid and efficacious arguments and the most essential authorities. The preacher can end his sermon in two ways, by repeating the most valid reasons that he has set forth and drawing a conclusion about his proposition from them, so that the auditors understand fully and effectively that he has proved what he intended to prove. And the other reason to add a conclusion is so as to better imprint the memory with what was said. For otherwise the auditors would go away empty and without purpose if they did not remember what they heard.

However, it must be noted, as was said above, that every sermon ought to be ended and concluded with a prayer, just as the blessed Paul concluded his Epistles in prayer. Thus in prayer we conclude our little treatise.

---

[143] *Ars poetica* 138.   [144] Isaiah 16:6.
[145] *De inventione* 1.52.98; Victorinus, *Explanationes* at 2.52, in Halm, ed., 256; *Ad Herennium* 2.30.47.

JOHN OF GARLAND, *PARISIANA POETRIA*, CA. 1231–1235

INTRODUCTION

John of Garland (ca. 1185–ca. 1272) was born in England but spent his career as a teacher of grammar (and the grammatical curriculum) in France. He studied at Oxford around 1210–1213, and then went to Paris, where he taught for most of his life; for three years (1229–1231), during the dispersion of the University of Paris, he was Master of Grammar at the new University of Toulouse.[1] He was a prolific writer. Apart from the preceptive *Parisiana poetria*, he produced wordbooks and grammars;[2] in this vein he also wrote an influential commentary on the *Doctrinale* of Alexander of Villa Dei, and was probably the author of an equally influential commentary on the *Graecismus* which initiated a long tradition of lexicographical and philosophical glosses on that work.[3] Beyond these grammatical works he wrote musical theory; a versified pedagogical guide called *Morale scolarium*; the *Integumenta Ovidii*, which is a moralized Ovid commentary in verse; a philosophical allegory known as *Epithalamium Beatae Virginis Marie*, as well as other poems on the Virgin; and other religious poems.[4] To these writings we should also add the many original compositions that he produced to illustrate points of doctrine in the *Parisiana poetria* itself: a pastoral allegory; a life of St. Denis; a crusade poem; a short comic poem; a short narrative "tragedy"; many letters illustrating petition, praise, exhortation, legal

---

[1] For a complete biographical account, see John of Garland, *Morale scolarium*, ed. Paetow, introduction.

[2] See Bursill-Hall, "Johannes de Garlandia—Forgotten Grammarian and the Manuscript Tradition"; John of Garland, *Compendium gramatice*, ed. Haye.

[3] See Grondeux, *Le Graecismus d'Évrard de Béthune à travers ses gloses*, 71–6.

[4] For accounts and summaries of these works, see *Morale scolarium*, ed. Paetow, introduction, and Rigg, *A History of Anglo-Latin Literature*, 163–76. Since the publication of Rigg's book, new editions of some of these works have appeared, including: *L'Ars lectoria ecclesie de Jean de Garlande: une grammaire versifiée du XIIIe siècle et ses gloses*, ed. Marguin-Hamon; *Carmen de misteriis ecclesie*, ed. Könsgen; *Epithalamium Beate Virginis Marie*, ed. Saiani. On the musical works, see Waite, "Johannes de Garlandia, Poet and Musician." For earlier editions of the works, see notes to Rigg, *Anglo-Latin Literature*, and Lawler's edition of *Parisiana poetria*, xii n. 3. His religious and preceptive grammatical writings circulated with vernacular glosses (in English and Anglo-Norman): see Hunt, *Teaching and Learning Latin*, 1:36–8, 136–51, and 2:125–73.

procedures, and the structure of prose-writing itself; and various pieces designed to exemplify genres, rhetorical colors, and poetic meters.

The *Parisiana poetria* is the consummate product of the grammatical and rhetorical curricula. John of Garland is known to have taught at more advanced levels than the earlier preceptive grammarians, including at the university, and the exhaustiveness and sophisticated ambition of the *Parisiana poetria* are in keeping with such advanced instruction. The work develops the preceptive advice of the earlier *artes poetriae* to comprehend all kinds of written composition; but it also extends the theoretical scope of its ancient and medieval sources to attempt a synthetic picture of verbal style, literary form, and genres.

The work has some of the trappings of an "academic" or university text: it has a prologue in which it locates the place of its teaching among the sciences; it gives a division of the treatise; and it proceeds to a division of the subject matter. It attempts to cover all the canons of rhetoric. It treats first of invention in chapter one, using the Ciceronian-Boethian scheme of the circumstances to organize what had become a distinctly medieval tradition of literary and even bureaucratic subject matter; it also uses inherited precept concerning amplification and abbreviation through figures of speech. To invention it adds a further component, "selection" (*ars eligendi*, chapter 2). The art of memory is repositioned to serve under the heading of "selection," and we see that this *ars memoriae* is in fact a very textualized system. Arrangement (*ordinatio*) and style are distributed through the central sections of the work: arrangement through chapters 3 (beginning; natural and artificial order) and 4 (the arrangement of letters, using the classical scheme of the parts of the oration); style through chapters 5 (style and genres) and 6 (embellishment). Delivery receives token mention in passing. Chapter 7 gives many model texts and an *ars rhythmica*.

The *Parisiana poetria* uses the system of the "vices" or faults of style as an occasion to set forth a more comprehensive theory of style, represented in the figure of the "Wheel of Virgil." This figure is John of Garland's innovation. In this scheme, the three works of Virgil, the *Eclogues*, *Georgics*, and *Aeneid*, are used as the anchoring "authorities" for differentiating literary character types, subject matters and settings, and levels of style. While the contents of this scheme are to some extent traditional, John of Garland's treatment has turned the straightforward teaching of the "Materia" commentary on stylistic incongruity into a strong prescriptive reading of Virgilian style.

Translation reprinted from *The Parisiana poetria of John of Garland*, **ed. and trans. Lawler, by permission.**[5]

---

[5] Translations of classical sources are those in Lawler's text.

INTRODUCTORY SUMMARY (*ACCESSUS*)

Five things about this short work should be examined at the start: the subject matter, the author's purpose, its usefulness for its audience, what field of knowledge it belongs to, the method.[6] The subject matter is the art of writing letters, of quantitative verse,[7] and of rhymed syllabic verse;[8] but behind these three lie five others, which are: the art of invention, of selection, of memory, of arrangement, and of embellishment. The author's purpose is to publish a manual of style. Its usefulness is that it imparts a technique for treating any subject whatever in prose, quantitative verse, or rhymed syllabic verse. This book belongs to three particular fields of knowledge: Grammar, since it teaches how to speak properly; Rhetoric, since it teaches how to speak elegantly; and Ethics, since it teaches or instills a sense of what is right, and from this according to Cicero every virtue springs.[9] This is the approach: the author teaches how to invent, according to the categories of invention, words, that is substantives, adjectives, and verbs used both literally and metaphorically, in any kind of composition, whether it be a legal or academic letter, or an elegiac poem, or a comedy, or a tragedy, or a satire, or a history. For he deals sometimes with the art of prose, sometimes with that of poetry, back and forth from one to the other; sometimes with rhymed syllabic verse, but this toward the end; and at the very end he deals in a special way with quantitative verse, where nineteen poems, each in a different meter, are created in imitation of Horace, who assembled nineteen different meters in his odes, to one or another of which any other metrical poem or hymn is reducible. Thus he treats now of this matter, now of that, in part and by turns; for there are

---

[6] These five topics of inquiry, *materia, intentio auctoris, utilitas, cui parti philosophiae supponitur,* and *modus agendi* (along with the two more topics, title and author, which John adds below), are standard components of the form of the *accessus ad auctores* (introduction to the authors) that was most commonly used in the twelfth century, for secular as well as sacred writings, the form that Hunt called the "Type C" *accessus.* See Hunt, "The Introductions to the 'Artes' in the Twelfth Century"; Quain, "The Medieval *Accessus ad auctores*"; and Minnis, *Medieval Theory of Authorship,* chapters 1 and 2. It is notable that John equips his own work with an *accessus,* which was usually reserved for works of ancient or at least canonical authority.

[7] *metricandi*   [8] *rithmicandi*

[9] The *accessus* topic *cui parti philosophiae supponitur* (to what branch of philosophy/knowledge it belongs) is here given a threefold answer. Obviously the text belongs to the disciplines of grammar and rhetoric, because of its double instruction. That John also places the *Parisiana poetria* under ethics can be explained in two ways. First, the science of "ethics" was something of a default category for twelfth-century commentators on classical literary texts: to claim that a poem by a pagan author was useful for moral edification, no matter how scurrilous the content, was an acceptable justification for the reading, teaching, and enjoyment of pagan poetry. By this mechanism John of Garland associates his own didactic work, with its classicizing content, with the literary culture of twelfth-century schools. Second, classical theory made strong links between rhetoric and virtue, wisdom, and practical morality : see, notably, Cicero, *De inventione* 1.1.2, and the commentary on this by Victorinus (within, pp. 113–21). The intersection of ethics and practical morality lies behind the understanding of rhetoric (in its Ciceronian guise) as civil science; see the prologue to Thierry of Chartres' commentaries on Cicero (within, p. 412).

some who might cut the art of prose out of the book for its own sake, and others who might cut out the art of quantitative verse, or of rhymed syllabic verse, or of poetry in general, as they wish, and thus the poor book would be torn up into rags. As it is, you must take all or nothing.

The verses placed at the beginning contain three things: the motive of the work,[10] its usefulness, and a foretaste of it. The motive, as distinct from the cause, is to increase study at Paris, whose instruments ought consequently to be increased, namely books. This book is said to be composed from this motive, in the lines beginning "The glory of Paris"; its usefulness is explained in the lines beginning "Let the tender lambs"; a foretaste of the work and its method are suggested in the lines beginning "Some people's long treatises." The final question is the title; here it is : "Here begins the '*Parisiana Poetria*' of Master John of Garland, the Englishman, on the Art of Prose, Quantitative Verse, and Rhymed Syllabic Verse." The title is taken from the first word of the book.

Here begins the Treatise on Poetry of Master John the Englishman on the Art of Prose, Quantitative Verse, and Rhymed Syllabic Verse.

FROM CHAPTER 1

Prologue

> The glory of Paris diffuses splendor, the body of scholars grows, the fountain gushes forth Apollonian waters. The pasture is flourishing, the flock grows, the shepherd is busy; the pasture because it is in constant use, the flock through study, the shepherd because he loves the flock. Let the tender lambs snatch up the new food of the elementary course; let the shepherd watch over them, let him tread the sheepfold. Why are you scornful, you who are seeking greater things? We have often seen the foot stumble in the plain. Lest the foot find no foothold, art's straight-edge provides a bridge; put your foot back on that bridge. Some people's long treatises pour forth seas; the art of composition is here channeled in a short stream. The art of quantitative verse is joined to that of prose, the art of rhymed syllabic verse to that of quantitative verse: this one little book contains three.

The principal chapters. This treatise will have seven sections. First to be given will be the theory of invention; then a lesson on the method of selecting material; after that on arrangement, how to put the material in order; then on the parts of a letter; after that, on avoiding vices in any kind of writing. Then comes a careful treatise on rhetorical embellishment, covering both quantitative verse and prose, and including figures to

---

[10] *occasio operis*

shorten or lengthen material,[11] as the writer chooses. In the seventh and last part are appended examples of legal and academic letters, of elegant compositions in both quantitative and rhymed verse, and of various meters.

Definition and division of prose. Anyone who presents an art ought to define his terms, make distinctions, and include examples. What then is prose? Prose is pithy and elegant discourse, not in meter but divided by regular rhythms of *clausulae*. It comes from *pros*, which is "to," as it were "a discourse to others"; or from *prosopa*, which is "person," as it were "personal," that is, "popular"; or as Isidore says from *prosum* [i.e. *prorsum*], which is "led forward," as it were "discourse led forward."[12]

Example of a letter in prose

> Maurice, by the grace of God Archbishop of Rouen; to the venerable Master G., his beloved son in Christ from Reims, diligent in the pulpits of Theology at Paris: greeting, and may he achieve the eternal life which he is investigating in his studies.

> Laudable are the rewards which are bestowed on prudent men for long and fruitful labors, and which at length are possessed in flourishing old age. We recall that your prudence and praiseworthy faithfulness in the service of God had expected a benefice promised by us. But the opportunity has not yet offered itself to us by which we might confer on you a suitable benefice and so call you from school pulpits to a don's chair. Still, there is vacant in our church a living worth sixty Parisian pounds to someone residing in the church. And so we beg Your Discretion to come and see our church with the bearer of this letter, if Your Discretion should condescend to accept so small a benefice.

Furthermore, one type of prose is technigraphic, from *techne*, "art," and *graphos*, "writing,"[13] which Aristotle and others who publish manuals use. Another is *historialis*,[14] used by

---

[11] *de coloribus abbreviantibus et ampliantibus.*

[12] *Prosa.* This definition seems to be John's own, and rather a definition of *dictamen* in its broad sense of stylized prose than of prose itself. [Compare the definition of *dictamen* in its narrow sense of a letter in stylized prose, ch. 5 (below)]. It is too narrow to cover all the species of prose listed in the passage below. *Prosopa*: i.e. *prosopon* (singular; Greek word). *Prosos* (*prorsus*) is the correct etymology, although it is a contraction of *proversus*, not *productus* [Lawler's note]. See Isidore of Seville, *Etymologiae* 1.38.

[13] *Tegnigraphia*, actually *tekhnê*, "art," and *graph-* "writing."

[14] *ystorialis*: Lawler translates this as "narrative." We have left the original word in the text, because in John of Garland's usage, as well as in the *Tria sunt*, its meaning is ambiguous. *Historia* is part of the triad of terms, *historia*, *argumentum*, and *fabula*, associated with the part of the oration known as the *narratio* (narration): see *De inventione* 1.19.27. All of these provide accounts of events, but with diminishing degrees of truthfulness. According to Cicero, *historia* relates actual occurrences that are remote in time from the present age. At chapter 5.303–72 (see selection below), John offers a more calibrated account of the literary-generic branches of *historia*, *argumentum*, and *fabula*. The fact that *historia* is used here to designate a kind of prose-writing which is employed by churchmen, writers of tragedies and comedies, and philosophers, may perhaps be explained by its early and fundamental association with oratory. On this view, tragedy and comedy do not necessarily signify poetic (or indeed dramatic) genres, but rather kinds of narrative of events; but cf. John's further discussion of comedy and tragedy, both as levels of style and poetic (or

the Church and by writers of tragedies and comedies sometimes, and by various other *philosophi*.[15] Another is *dictamen*, which is employed by universities and courts, and whose various species will appear later on. Another is *rhythmus*, which we use in the "proses" or sequences of the liturgy. But note that the rhythmic is a species of music, as Boethius says in his *Art of Music*: "The art of music embraces three general areas: one such area deals with instruments, a second area with making songs; the third is theory, which assesses those instrumental works and songs ... And a musician is a man who has the skill to assess, by his systematic knowledge and by careful thought coupled with a 'feel' for music, meters, rhythms, and all varieties of songs ... and lyric poetry."[16] *Rhythmus* will be dealt with at the end of this treatise.

Definition and division of meter. The next step is to define meter. Meter is a certain series of uniform feet, divided into verses, and so called from *metros*, which is "measure." A foot is a certain length of syllables and quantities. A verse is a regular grouping of these feet. And so one meter is spondaic, another dactylic, another iambic, another trochaic, another choriambic; and there are other kinds, found in the odes of Horace, and which Boethius and Martianus use as well as Horace. These sometimes take their names from the inventor, sometimes from the feet: from the inventor, as the Asclepiad, from Asclepius its inventor; from the feet, as the iambic. Albinovanus even put together a "Book of a Hundred Meters,"[17] but since people today take pleasure in what is brief and practical, let us stick to what is necessary for us.

On invention. As Horace says of invention and selection of material in his *Art of Poetry*, we must first invent before selecting from what is invented, and first select before arranging what is selected. Here are his words:

> You who write, take material equal to your talents, and consider at length what your shoulders can bear and what they will refuse; neither facility nor lucid order will desert the man who chooses a subject within this power. [lines 38–41]

The explanation of these lines will appear later.[18] First, therefore, let us treat of the art of invention, before the other parts I mentioned.

---

narrative) genres, in ch. 4, ll. 416–83. The use of *historia* by churchmen may refer to hagiography or sacred narratives; philosophers also use subgenres of narrative in their didactic writings. See the note in Lawler edition, 228; and see Mehtonen, *Old Concepts and New Poetics*, especially 13, 35, 74. Cf. the distinctions among these terms in Isidore of Seville, *Etymologiae* 1.44.5 (on the genre of *historia*).

[15] *philosophi*: Lawler translates as "learned men."

[16] Boethius, *De institutione musica*, ed. G. Friedlein (Leipzig: Teubner, 1867), 1:34.

[17] The only *Centimetrum*, or "Book of a Hundred Meters," is by Servius. The attribution to an (unknown) Albinovanus may be the product of a confusion with a Celsus Albinovanus addressed in Horace, *Epistles* 1.3 and 1.8. See Lawler's note on this, 228–9. The manuscripts vary in their readings of this name.

[18] This will be the main matter of chapter 2, on selection of material.

On the art of inventing and what invention means. To invent is to come into knowledge of an unknown thing through the agency of one's own reason. Here is what Cicero says in the *Second Rhetoric*: "Invention is thinking up things that are true or at least realistic to make your case plausible."[19]

On its species. Under invention there are five species: where, what, what kind, how, and why.[20]

The first species: where to invent. "Where" has three sources: character, examples, and etymologies of words and the explanations that go with them ...[21]

Three kinds of characters and the three types of men. Three kinds of characters ought to be considered here, according to the three types of men, which are courtiers, city dwellers, and peasants. Courtiers are those who dwell in or frequent courts, such as the Holy Father, cardinals, legates, archbishops, bishops, and their subordinates, such as archdeacons, deans, officials, masters, scholars; also emperors, kings, marquises, and dukes. City dwellers are count, provost, and the whole range of people who live in the city. Peasants are those who live in the country, such as hunters, farmers, vine dressers, fowlers. According to these three types of men, Virgil invented a triple style, which will be dealt with later.[22]

The second species: what is invented. By the word "what" is meant what is to be invented; in practical affairs, and letters in particular, it means such things as seditions, murders, wars, thefts, plunderings, simonies, presentations, friendships, petitions, and the activities of ecclesiastical personages.

Subdivision: what may be invented as to persons. What to invent pertains to persons, examples, and etymologies. With persons there is always a pair of alternatives; as with kings: to rule the kingdom well, or to tear the kingdom to pieces like a tyrant; with prelates: to pursue divine contemplation, or to idle about in secular affairs; with city

---

[19] *Rhetorica ad Herennium* 1.2.3.

[20] These topics are derived ultimately from the seven circumstances that provide the topics for invention, most clearly seen in Boethius' list: who, what, where, when, why, how, and by what means (*De topicis differentiis* 4; see above, p. 203). John has dropped the topics "who," "when," and "by what means," and has introduced a new term, "what kind." For discussion of the role of the circumstantial scheme in the *Parisiana poetria* see Lawler's note, 229–30, and Copeland, *Rhetoric, Hermeneutics, and Translation*, 160–6.

[21] Here John of Garland offers an example of invention of subject matter and style from character, in the form of a letter to Simon Langton, Archdeacon of Canterbury, in which John of Garland appeals to the Archdeacon's friendship and generosity on behalf of the bearer of the letter, a cleric who has been struck with illness and needs admission to a leper hospital by the Archdeacon's intercession. The model letter illustrates how "subject matter and style are invented from the character of a sick man and from the characters of friends."

[22] Three types of men: for the connection between three levels of style and three social types, see also the "Materia" commentary (above, p. 555). See Lawler's note, 230–1. See also Curtius, *European Literature and the Latin Middle Ages*, 201 n., 232. On the distinction between elocutionary and material (or social) conceptions of levels of style, see Quadlbauer, *Die antike Theorie der genera dicendi*, especially 34–9, and Kelly, *The Arts of Poetry and Prose*, 71–8.

dwellers: to carry on the business of the city, to strengthen the republic, or to squander it; with peasants, it means sweating over rural duties, or giving up.

What is invented in examples. Let us consider what is invented in examples. An example is a saying or deed of some authoritative person that is worthy of imitation. Here, then, are invented sayings and deeds, authorities, and proverbs. But if no proverb is available to us, we should employ the following device.

On the art of inventing proverbs. We should consider whether we wish to praise or blame, the character of the sender, the character of the recipient, and the matter at issue; then, by applying to each of these three the double criterion, that is, praise or blame, right or wrong, we should be able to furnish ourselves with proverbs by putting in similitudes and comparisons. What follows will make this clearer.

Definition of a proverb. A proverb is a brief statement [*sententia*], moral in purpose, setting forth what is good or what is bad in an important matter.[23]

Proverbs. Some proverbs are taken from natural things, as when similitudes are drawn from plants, stones, animate or inanimate things. Other proverbs are taken from moral truths, when verses or aphorisms are cited from classical authors, as "A man is either the slave or the master of his money."[24] Proverbs are seldom taken from rational philosophy, but axioms often, as "Everything that is round can spin"; "Any whole is greater than its part." Proverbs can be invented from praise, from blame, from similitude, from the nature of the subject at issue, and from the character of the persons involved. . . .

"What kind" is the third species. "What kind" raises the question of the quality of the subject matter invented; for, as Cicero says, "There are two kinds of causes, honorable and disreputable";[25] thus there is honorable subject matter and disreputable subject matter. In honorable subject matter use plain sentences and words that put the case in the open. Disguising disreputable subject matter calls for subtlety, as Cicero says.[26] That means touching on the issue with various circumlocutions, which will keep the disreputable subject from showing through. For example, if a priest should accuse or blame an adulteress, he might say, "This tender woman enters a strange bed and has the pleasure

---

[23] As the examples show, by "proverb" [*proverbium*] John does not mean a popular maxim but a brief general statement invented by the author of a letter to suit his purpose, by serving as a kind of major premise on which he can construct the argument of his letter. Even when the sentiment is proverbial, as is frequently enough true, the expression is always that of the *dictator*, never of the folk. [Lawler's note] Cf. the role of the maxim as one kind of commonplace in Aristotle's *Rhetoric* 2.21.

[24] Horace, *Epistles* 1.10.47.

[25] *Est genus cause honestum et turpe.* Cf. *Rhetorica ad Herennium* 1.3.5: there are actually four kinds of causes, honorable, discreditable [*turpe*], doubtful, and petty [*humile*].

[26] Cf. *Rhetorica ad Herennium* 1.4.6.

of daily nuptials."[27] But in praise of a woman, he might say, "In voluntary chastity she imitates the rigid Sabines."[28]

To what end one invents. Since "to what end" is mentioned above, let us notice in passing that this denotes the inventor's purpose, which is of course to promote what is both useful and right, and even though he intends to accuse or condemn, that purpose is still good in itself.

The fifth species, which is divided into seven subspecies and parts. In considering the meaning of "how," we should note seven figures by which the subject matter is embellished and amplified. They are: Paronomasia, Transplacement, Repetition, Climax, Synonymy, Definition, and Dialogue.... [29]

[John of Garland defines and illustrates each of these *colores* by means of which one can embellish and amplify the matter that has been invented. These are not figures of thought or tropes, but rather figures of speech. From this section he proceeds to short discussions of the art of inventing nouns (through words that are "cognate" with the subject), adjectives ("invented" through various topics: effect, outcome, dress, place, family, size, quality), and verbs, including verbs used "transumptively."]

A way of inventing subject matter. Here is a device that is useful in certain kinds of writing; students particularly who aim to amplify and vary their subject matter may observe it. I mean they should not overlook the four principal causes—the efficient cause, and so on—of any subject proposed to them. Thus, suppose one of them is treating of his book. He might praise it or criticize it through the efficient cause, that is, through the writer; through the material cause, that is, through the parchment or the ink; through the formal cause, as through the layout of the book or the size of the letters; or through the final cause, by considering for what purpose the book was made, namely, that in it and through it the ignorant may be made more knowledgeable.[30]

---

[27] Cf. *Rhetorica ad Herennium* 4.34.45, on metaphor as a way of avoiding obscenity.

[28] Cf. Juvenal, *Satires* 10.299.

[29] *Annominatio, traductio, repeticio, gradatio, interpretatio, diffinicio, sermocinatio.* Compare the list of devices of amplification in Geoffrey of Vinsauf's *Poetria nova*: *interpretatio*, periphrasis, *collatio*, apostrophe [*exclamatio*], *prosopopoeia, digressio, descriptio.*

[30] The Aristotelian paradigm of the four causes—efficient, material, formal, and final—was most commonly a conceptual apparatus for philosophical inquiry. It came into general academic use with the assimilation of Aristotle's *Physics* and *Metaphysics* in various Latin translations from the later twelfth century and onwards (see *Physics* 198a–b; *Metaphysics* 983a); by the middle of the thirteenth century it was used widely as a form of *accessus ad auctores*. John of Garland's use of it here, as a device of amplification under invention of material, is unusual. He appears to adapt it to the purposes of literary analysis and production: analysis of "any subject proposed" to a student, and production of the student's own text through the device of amplifying the given material. This might be seen as a conceptual rather than a formal device of amplification (hence its placement under invention); compare John's formal treatments of amplification, below. On the impact of logic on the *artes poetriae* in general, see Kelly, *The Arts of Poetry and Prose*, 53–4.

FROM CHAPTER 2

The art of selection. The next subject after Invention of subject matter is the Selection of subject matter. Cicero puts Arrangement after Invention, then Style, then the Art of Memory, and last Delivery; but poets and writers of *dictamen* will find it useful to have the Art of Selection after Invention.[31]

On the principal of selection. Note then that we should select subject matter from a threefold principle; because it offers to us what is either entertaining, or attractive, or profitable; the entertaining appeals to the mind, by reason of a certain pleasantness; the attractive appeals to the eye, by reason of its beauty; the profitable appeals by reason of its utility.

What should be selected. Again, we should select both the brief and the prolix, what is light, and what is plain: the brief, for official business; the prolix, for treatises of poets; the light, for ease in writing; the plain, for ease in understanding. But should difficult matter be unavoidable, we select things that will make it smooth, not knotty . . .[32]

On the art of remembering. But since it is called Selection, as it were a drawing aside of a few things from a large number, we should select what we are going to say with the support of the Art of Remembering, which is essential for poets organizing their material. So, following Cicero, we should put aside in our minds some vacant spot, in a place which is neither too hazy nor too bright, because these qualities are inimical to memory and selection. This vacant spot is to be imagined as separated into three main sections and columns. The first section or column is subdivided into three parts, for courtiers, city dwellers, and peasants, with their arms and their respective implements, their concerns and their duties. If any word falls from the mouth of the teacher which means anything which pertains to any one of the three kinds of persons mentioned, there it will be, for later inventing and selecting. The second part or column should be imagined as containing, in separate compartments, examples and sayings and facts from the authors, and the

---

[31] None of John's predecessors include Selection (*ars eligendi*) among the parts of rhetoric; to them, invention is itself a selective process. John's division is based on *Ars poetica* 38–41, as his comment on that passage (chapter 1 above) indicates. He has virtually expanded Horace's single word *lecta* into a whole chapter. But the material he presents has little to do with Horace's dictum; that merely provides him with the name of the chapter, and its key verb. The actual material is drawn from Geoffrey of Vinsauf's *Documentum de modo et arte dictandi et versificandi*, and there is nothing in the processes described to distinguish them from invention—we might substitute *invenire* for *eligere* throughout. [Lawler's note]

[32] John will consider first complex embellishment [*difficilis ornatus*] (lines 44–86) and later simple embellishment [*facilis ornatus*] (lines 147–265), in which he distills the doctrine in Geoffrey of Vinsauf's *Documentum de modo et arte dictandi et versificandi*; Faral, ed., *Les arts poétiques*, 284–303.

teachers from whom we heard them, and the books in which we have read them. If memory should fail us on some point, we must then call to mind the time, be it vivid or hazy, when we learned it, the place in which, the teacher from whom, his dress, his gestures, the books in which we studied it, the page—was it white or dark?—the position on the page and the colors of the letters; because all these will lead to the things that we want to remember and select. In the third column let us imagine to be written all kinds of languages, sounds, and voices of the various living creatures, etymologies, explanations of words, distinctions between words, all in alphabetical order; and with a ready mind let each consider what word fits his own language. But since we do not know every language, nor have heard every word, we resort to those which we have heard; and when the teacher makes a philological or etymological explanation of any word, let us gather it into that third column, along with some natural phenomenon that may symbolize the word in question; and by means of its symbol we shall be able to memorize it and later select it for our own use.[33]

It should be noted that Virgil's Wheel,[34] which we have in front of us, also contains an arrangement of three columns; here the three styles are arranged inside a circle along a series of concentric circumferences.

The first column contains comparisons, similitudes, and names of things appropriate to the low style; the second to the middle; the third to the high. To express in one style a sentiment which is only to be found in the next is clearly a departure from the proper style; we should select for any given style only words invented in that style . . .[35]

---

[33] The memory system presented here is a somewhat confused reading of the *ars memoriae* in *Rhetorica ad Herennium* 3.16.28–3.24.40 (and cf. Quintilian, *Institutio oratoria* 11.2.1–51). The "vacant spot" recommended by the *Ad Herennium* (the *regio derelicta* of 3.19.31) is here a geometric diagram or in fact an open manuscript page rather than a real place to be imagined (in the *Ad Herennium*, an empty hall or similar space); see Lawler's note, 237–8. The divisions of the diagram that John imagines correspond, more or less, with the three sources of invention adduced in chapter 1, line 91 (see above): character, example, and etymology. The column on character, with its social types (courtiers, city dwellers, peasants) is loosely related to the Wheel of Virgil and its social types (see below). The second column, with examples and texts, enjoins the student to remember the material layout of the book from which he learned; similar theories about the mnemonic power of the material text are part of the lore of monastic biblical studies: see e.g. Hugh of St. Victor, *De tribus maximis circumstantiis gestorum*, ed. Green. The column on etymology, which includes grammar, *vox*, *differentiae*, and *littera*, seems to be related to the subgenre of *derivatio* and etymology in grammatical study (see above, Etymology dossier, Part 2). Carruthers analyzes John of Garland's substitution of columns on a manuscript page for the architectural columns of the *Ad Herennium*, and suggests that John's material on linguistic and animal sounds derives from medieval alphabetical handbooks and the mnemonic devices contained in bestiaries: see *The Book of Memory*, 123–30. On the *ars memoria* in the *Ad Herennium*, see also Caplan, "Memoria: Treasure-House of Eloquence."

[34] On the tradition behind John of Garland's Wheel of Virgil, see Laugesen, "La roue de Virgile: un page de la théorie littéraire du Moyen Age." See also Faral, ed., *Les arts poétiques*, 86–9; Kelly, *Arts of Poetry and Prose*, 71–8; Kelly, "La Spécialité dans l'invention des topiques," 108–13; and Quadlbauer, *Die antike Theorie*, 113–25.

[35] On three levels of style, see also the "Materia" commentary (above, p. 555).

From Lawler, ed. and trans., *The Parisiana poetria of John of Garland*

FROM CHAPTER 3 (OPENING SECTION)

On the art of beginning. The next subject after Invention and Selection of subject matter is how to begin and arrange it.[36] Any subject has three aspects: beginning, middle, and end (or commencement, development, and conclusion of the work, and similar labels).[37] These parts should be put straight first of all in the mind, because a word must be in the mind before it may be in the mouth.[38] If the subject embraces several issues, arrange the greater issue first: then turn to other issues with phrases such as "besides all that," "furthermore," "we add to the aforesaid," "we subjoin." In poetry, we can launch the subject with either the natural or the artificial beginning. The natural beginning is when a story is told in the order in which it takes place.[39]

On the artificial beginning and its eight types. The artificial beginning is when we start in the middle of the subject or at the end; we can do it in eight ways, and so this beginning has eight branches. The first branch or first type is when the artificial beginning is drawn

---

[36] The doctrine of this chapter accords with Geoffrey of Vinsauf's *Documentum* (Faral, *Les arts poétiques*, 265–71). [Lawler's note] "beginning," *inchoatio*.

[37] "development": *progressus*. Cf. Geoffrey of Vinsauf, *Poetria nova*, line 204, and the opening sentence of the *Documentum*: *Tria sunt circa quae cujuslibet operis versatur artificium: principium, progressus, consummatio* (Faral, *Les arts poétiques*, 265). [Lawler's note]

[38] Cf. *Poetria nova* (within, p. 597): "Prudently ponder the entire work within the breast, and let it be in the breast before it is in the mouth." [Lawler's note]

[39] "when a story is told": *quando res narratur*. The word *narratur* here is significant, for the whole doctrine clearly applies only to narrative poetry. Geoffrey states clearly that he is speaking only of narrative (*Poetria nova*, lines 4–5). [Lawler's note]

either from the middle of the subject or from the end, without a proverb and without an example. The beginning is sometimes made with a proverb, which may concern the head of the subject, or the middle, or the end. Again, it is sometimes made with an example, which may concern the beginning of the subject, or the middle, or the end; and there you have the eight types.[40] Let us subjoin models from the life story of Saint Denis. The beginning of the subject is his study in Athens; the middle is his preaching in Gaul; the end is his beheading for the Lord. . . .

[The rest of this short chapter illustrates, as promised, the types of artificial beginnings by recasting the narrative of the life of St. Denis according to the principle to be demonstrated.]

[Chapter 4 continues the discussion of arrangement, applying it now to letters: how to begin them, and recognizing their various parts. Then its takes up the six parts of a classical oration, illustrating these by application to a poem (one of those written by John of Garland for this treatise) exhorting its audience to join the Crusade.[41] After this it treats amplification and abbreviation, drawing much of its doctrine from Geoffrey of Vinsauf's *Poetria nova*, applying the principles to letters as well as poems. The last type of amplification involves levels of style and the style appropriate to subject matter: and this leads in turn to a discussion of comedy (the low style) and to a short treatise on comedies and tragedies (classified under *historia*: see *Parisiana poetria* ch. 1 [above] and ch. 5 [below]). Finally this chapter treats the "parts" of various kinds of documents. The heterogeneous mix of subject matter in this part of the treatise seems to be a result of John of Garland's ambitions to combine the teachings of classical rhetoric with Geoffrey of Vinsauf's "modern" poetics, and to bring verse and prose genres together under one common program of instruction.[42]]

.

FROM CHAPTER 5

On the six vices peculiar to verse.[43] I have charted out the parts for both a poem and a letter fully enough; the next subject is the vices to avoid both in verse and in prose. Let me speak first of the vices to avoid in verse.

---

[40] The eight types or branches should be seen as three different groups of branches: without a proverb or example: two "branches," (i.e. from the end and the middle); with a proverb: three branches (head, middle, end); with an example: three branches (beginning, middle, end).

[41] On this poem in relation to such themes in other works of John of Garland, see Paetow, "The Crusading Ardor of John of Garland."

[42] See Lawler's note, 242.   [43] See above, "Materia" commentary, pp. 553–6.

There are, then, six vices to avoid in a poem. The first is incongruous arrangement of parts; the second, incongruous digression from the subject; the third, obscure brevity; the fourth, incongruous variation of styles; the fifth, incongruous variation of subject matter; the sixth, an awkward ending.

The first vice to avoid in verse. The ideal is a consistent arrangement of parts, from which a writer deviates when he appropriates bits and pieces from another subject, as when someone writing a comedy, all of whose elements should be suited to light entertainment, shifts to elements of tragedy, which are made up of serious characters and sentiments suited to them. Avoid this by holding strictly to similar elements; Horace says of this vice in his *Art of Poetry*:

> Serpents are paired with birds, lambs with tigers. (13)

Serpents mean lowly men, birds lofty men; tigers fierce men, lambs gentle men, between whom there will never be any fitness.

The second vice. An incongruous digression from the subject deviates from the ideal. For ideally there are only two excuses to digress from the subject, namely, to explain a difficulty, and to move the minds of one's audience and to instruct them in hard matters. But it becomes an incongruous digression when a description or comparison or similitude is put forward, for the sake of moving, when it should not be done, of which vice Horace says:

> A purple patch or two is sewn on, and sticks out all over.[44]

This vice is to be avoided whenever, for either of two reasons—the reasons given above—a digression is made either to what is itself part of the subject matter, as when a place or a castle or the like is described, or to what is not part of the subject matter, but is aptly fitted to it, such as a comparison.

The third vice to avoid. Here the ideal is to speak briefly as circumstances permit; but this sometimes declines into a vice, when brevity leads to obscurity. To do away with that vice, choose words that make the matter plain. For example: Jupiter is a guest in the home of Lycaon, who has killed a hostage in order that he might place human flesh on Jove's table; when Jupiter found out, he changed Lycaon into a wolf and set fire to his house. Choose words of this sort: "Jupiter," "guest," "hostage," "the Arcadian," "wolf," "is changed," "is burnt." When the list is complete, turn it into poetry, thus:

> Jupiter is a guest; as food for him, a hostage falls; the Arcadian is changed; he is a wolf, and his house is burnt.[45]

---

[44] *Ars poetica* 15–16.
[45] This example of abbreviated narration is similar to the illustrations of *abbreviatio* in Geoffrey of Vinsauf's *Poetria nova*, lines 695–741 (ed. Gallo), in which ever-briefer versions of the Snow-Child story are given.

The fourth vice, and the three styles. There are, again, three styles, corresponding to the three estates of men. The low style suits the pastoral life; the middle style, farmers; the high style, eminent personages, who are set over shepherds and farmers. Shepherds find riches in animals; farmers accumulate them by cultivating the earth; but princes possess them by giving them away to inferiors. Virgil composed three works to correspond to these three types, the *Eclogues*, the *Georgics*, and the *Aeneid*. High matter can be lowered, in imitation of Virgil, who calls Caesar—or himself—Tityrus and Rome a beech; and low matter can be exalted, as when in a treatment of a high subject women's distaffs are called the "spears of peace." Here is an example of the high style:

> Charles, the shield of the Church and the column of peace, tames arms with arms and the fierce with ferocity.

In this style, nouns should be chosen which signify things placed in the top row; in the middle style, things placed in the middle row; in the low style, things placed in the bottom row.[46]

On avoiding the vices associated with the several styles.[47] The high style has two vices associated with it, bombast and inflation: bombast is a function of words, inflation of ideas. Here is an example:

> That most supernal peak of wars, the warrioress Rolandina, was the hand and club of peace.

The middle style has two vices associated with it, fluctuation and looseness: fluctuation is a function of words or diction, looseness of ideas. For since the middle style is a compromise between extremes, that is, between the high and the low, sometimes a poet fluctuates in diction and is loose in ideas. Here is an ideal example of the middle style:

> Charles was the guardian of the Church, the protection of the people, a cultivator of justice, a lover of peace.

The following exemplifies the vices to which this style is liable:

> The king is the staff of the army and a smooth lover to his wife; he bids his men be brave.

---

[46] The "rows" (*ordines*) in question refer to the Wheel of Virgil, above. The idea is that one should not move between appropriate styles, so one must stay within the boundary of a given style (i.e. if using the high style, one should keep to soldiers, horses, and swords and not stray over to farmers, cows, and plows, which are the matter—and thus nouns—of the *ordo* or row of the middle style). (Cf. Lawler's note.)

[47] The terms in this section—bombast and inflation, fluctuation and looseness, and aridity and bloodlessness—are based on the vices of style in *Rhetorica ad Herennium* 4.10.15–4.11.16 (swollen and inflated; slack and drifting; dry and bloodless).

The following lines are an ideal example of the low style:

> The shepherd carries his club over his shoulder; he uses it to beat the priest his wife has been playing with.

The two vices associated with this style are aridity and bloodlessness: aridity refers to ideas that are not juicy and tasty; bloodlessness refers to words whose surface is not purpled, as here:

> The peasant draws the club from his shoulder, and in three strokes removes that shorn sheep's testicles; he has a happy supper.

Notice, by the way, that "style" is used metaphorically. For a style is the middle section of a column, on which rests the epistyle, and whose lower section is called the base. "Style," then, in this sense is "the poetic quality" or an "uprightness" preserved throughout the body of the matter. Sometimes style means the poem itself. Style means the office of a poet, as in the *Anticlaudianus*:

> I beg the style[48] of an author and the trappings of a poet.
>
> (Prologue 1)

Finally, style means the pen we write with.

The fifth vice. The fifth vice of a poem, as I said above, is called incongruous variation of the subject matter. The ideal here is to vary the subject matter in order to forestall revulsion and avoid monotony; for monotony is the mother of satiety, which in turn produces boredom in the audience. To forestall that, vary the subject matter. In an amusing piece, bring in amusing things.... In a grave subject, bring in grave things.... But a poet falls into vice if he tries to describe a grave subject by means of amusing and comic details, or an amusing subject by means of grave details.... And note that a digression is made in order to amplify the subject matter; variation of subject matter [is made] in order to avoid monotony.

The sixth vice and the various kinds of endings. The sixth vice is an awkward ending, which means a conclusion inappropriate to its work; to avoid it, the ending or conclusion should be derived sometimes from the body of the matter, by way of recapitulation of what has gone before, which is appropriate for orators and preachers; sometimes purely from the poet's pleasure.... [The ending can be made with an example that contains a similitude, as at the end of Horace's *Ars poetica*, or taken from a proverb.] Letters on legal matters are brought to a conclusion as often as possible with these words: "so that," "lest," "since." "So that" introduces a good; "lest" dissuades from an evil; "since" introduces the reason for what has preceded....

[48] *stilus*

[Following this John gives a model letter of a student to his friend; details vices in meter (involving sounds of letters and syllables, or the adding or removal of letters and syllables); from this he turns to vices in letters (epistles). Then he offers some definitions of generic terms.]

Definition of dictamen. Dictamen is a letter marked off by *clausulae* and embellished by figures of words and sentences. An epistle is defined as follows: an epistle is a letter[49] directed to a certain person, laying bare the mind of the sender, sometimes containing a salutation, sometimes not. . . .

On the kinds of narration.[50] But since the narration is common to both prose and poetry, I should mention the various kinds of narration and the various poetic genres. Note, then, that the genus "discourse"[51] is threefold. The first kind is dramatic or deictic, that is, imitative or interrogative; the second is exegetical or apangeltic, that is, expository, which some call hermeneutic, that is, interpretive; the third is mictic or koinon, that is, mixed or common, also called didactic, that is, instructive.[52] Whoever speaks uses one or another of these three. Under the second falls the narration that Cicero divides as follows:[53] there is a kind of narration that is alien to, and remote from, legal causes, and it is twofold. One kind is rooted in plot, the other in character. That rooted in plot has three species, or parts, namely Fable, History, and Realistic Fiction.[54]

On Fable. A Fable contains events that are untrue, and do not pretend to be true; it follows that avoiding vice in fabulous narratives means lying with probability, as it says in the *Art of Poetry*:

> Either follow tradition or make up a consistent story. (119)

On History. A History reports an event which has taken place long before the memory of our age; whoever deals in it, to escape vice, should include, in order, proposition,

---

[49] *libellus*   [50] *narratio*   [51] *sermo*

[52] The classification here is ultimately derived from Diomedes, *Ars grammatica, GL* 1:482; cf. Bede, *De arte metrica* xxv (above p. 266). See Curtius, *European Literature and the Latin Middle Ages*, 440–1; Salmon, "The Three Voices of Poetry in Medieval literary Theory." The title of William of Conches' *Dragmaticon* (or *Dragmaticon philosophiae*), meaning a dialogue, is also derived from this terminology (*poema dramaticon*): see Ronca and Curr in *William of Conches: A Dialogue on Natural Philosophy (Dragmaticon philosophiae)*, trans. Ronca and Curr, xx–xxiii. Cf. the terminology in an anonymous twelfth-century introduction to Ovid's *Epistles* in Huygens, ed., *Accessus ad auctores*, 32; Minnis et al., *Medieval Literary Theory*, 23. The terminology is also found in Petrus Helias; see *Summa super Priscianum*, ed. Reilly, 1:158. "Apangeltic": from Greek, *apangeltikos*, recitative or narrative; "mictic": from Greek, *miktos*, mixed. See within, also Gundissalinus, above, pp. 479–80.

[53] *Rhetorica ad Herennium* 1.8.12.

[54] The *Tria sunt* offers a closely related list of genres and their subdivisions: see Lawler, Appendix 2, 330–2. The formal complexity of the genre scheme *historia-argumentum-fabula* in the *Parisiana poetria* and in the *Tria sunt* represents an entirely medieval development and elaboration of the early Ciceronian scheme (see above, note 14), a

invocation, and narration; then he should use the rhetorical figure called Transition, a figure whereby the mind of the listener, with the aid of the preceding narration, understands what is to come. (It is otherwise called the Epilogue, whence "to epilogue," which means to join what is still to be said to what has been said.)

On Realistic Fiction.[55] A Realistic Fiction is a fictitious event which nevertheless could have happened, as is the case in comedies. And no invocation should be made in a comedy, except for an insoluble complication in the plot, as Horace says:

> Let no god intervene, unless a knot develop that deserves such a deliverer.
>
> <div align="right">(<i>Ars poetica</i> 191–2)</div>

That is, a god should not be called on unless an insoluble complication develops.

[Further subdivisions of "historical narrative" offer brief definitions of epithalamium, epicedium, epitaph, apotheosis, bucolic, georgic, lyric, epode, secular song or hymn, invective, reprimand or satire, tragedy, elegiac, and comedy.[56]]

---

development of poetics away from the governing structure of rhetoric, ultimately forming a category of analysis— an *ars poetica* or "science" of poetic narrative—virtually independent of rhetorical doctrine. For extensive and detailed analysis, see Mehtonen, *Old Concepts and New Poetics*, especially 32–8, 72–80, and the Appendix, which prints a chart of definitions of the triad terms from antiquity through the twelfth and thirteenth centuries. On the context of John's treatment of *historia*, see Mehtonen, 73–9; on the context of *argumentum*, 107–10; on *fabula*, 130–1.

[55] *argumentum*
[56] On John of Garland's treatment of the genres, see Mehtonen, *Old Concepts and New Poetics*, 34–7.

HUGH OF TRIMBERG, *REGISTRUM MULTORUM AUCTORUM*, 1280

INTRODUCTION

Hugh of Trimberg was born about 1230, and died about 1313. He became master of the monastic school of St. Gangolf in Bamberg. He wrote didactic and moral works in German and in Latin. Of the Latin works his most important is the school text *Registrum multorum auctorum* (Register of Many Authors), in rhythmic verse (the so-called "Goliardic" lines), with rhyme. He tells us that this work derives from his years of reading and lecturing in the school. A prominent feature of this work is its unusual structure which is at once moral and pedagogical. It presents divisions among "greater" and "lesser" ethical authors according to their curricular role: the advanced students will read the *maiores*, the beginners will read the *minores*. In the middle are the theological authors, who will be read by the intermediate students: that is, when students have a good grasp of Latin, they are given the Christian poets of the traditional curriculum. In terms of ethics, they can learn as much from the "lesser" authors as from the "greater" ones, the difference being that the greater authors can inspire, while the lesser authors simply teach and the middle authors impart religious doctrine. The pedagogical calibration of curricular authors is not new with Hugh: we see it in such curricular lists as Alexander Neckam's *Sacerdos ad altare*. But Hugh's innovation is to overlay the distinctions of pedagogical level onto the canon, so that each level of the school has its own distinct "ethical" reading list.

Within this innovative structure we find the core group of texts that traditionally were read together in medieval classrooms as the *Liber catonianus* or "Cato-book": the core usually consisted of six works, the *Disticha Catonis,* the *Ecloga* of Theodulus, the *Fabulae* of Avianus, the *Elegiae* of Maximianus, the *Achilleid* of Statius, and the *De raptu Proserpinae* of Claudian.[1] These works or authors all play a role in the reading program of Hugh's *Registrum*; but they have been dispersed throughout the larger ethical-pedagogical system, so that their traditional linkage as elementary "gateway" works to the literary canon has been broken up and the works have been recombined in a new system of "ethical" levels of instruction. Only the

---

[1] See Woods and Copeland, "Classroom and Confession," 380–5, and the excellent survey of the curriculum by Gillespie, "From the twelfth century to c. 1450," 150–60.

Disticha Catonis, the *Fabulae* of Avianus, and the *Elegiae* of Maximianus remain together at the end, serving the most elementary level of "minor" or lesser ethical works.

It is also noteworthy that he seeks to incorporate many modern writers into these divisions, as well as seeking out Latin poets of German origin. Thus his divisions fall into "greater" ethical authors, ancient and modern, theological (intermediate) authors, ancient and modern, and "lesser" ethical authors, ancient and modern. Hugh exhibits a very strong sense of the historical distance between ancient and modern, and acknowledges as well that some of the ancient writers (in the category of the *minores*) must necessarily yield their place to the greater relevance or attractiveness of the modern poets. The purpose of the text seems to be to equip students (or their teachers) with a handy list of titles and incipits, an anthology for reference purposes and future recognition of the works, rather than for interpretive illumination. The matter covered is quite remarkable in its range and learning. While he often relies closely on Conrad of Hirsau's *Dialogus super auctores* for summary information about ancient authors, his treatments of modern authors represent his own judgments about how they should constitute a modern extension of the curricular canon. Thus the work offers a synthetic critical reception of twelfth- and thirteenth-century verse authors, a medieval literary history of medieval Latin poetry which shows an interest in the formal characteristics of contemporary writing. The work also demonstrates how the poetic arts such as the *Poetria nova* of Geoffrey of Vinsauf and the *Parisiana poetria* of John of Garland could be assimilated to a literary curriculum as "masterpieces" in their own right.

Translated from *Das "Registrum multorum auctorum" des Hugo von Trimberg*, ed. Langosch, by permission.

PROLOGUE

[lines 1–65]

For the instruction of schoolboys, the least of authors, Hugh by name, has made this handy compilation. Wishing to be helpful to all schoolboys, he has listed the titles of every author along with the first verses of each work. He has studied these for a long time, reading them frequently, because he has kept a school for the instruction of children. He passes over questions about the matter and order of books, putting aside what may cause boredom. He concerns himself with those who are eager to learn the authors perfectly, so that they may take on greater work and further exertions. A commonplace thing leaves only nausea and contempt; but whatever is bought dearly is treasured with care.

Let beginners now learn the incipits of the ethical authors, so that with practice they can grasp the ethical content of the texts, and by repeated study the fruit of proverbs may be harvested with the scent of their flowers. Or, if someone should happen on a whole collection of books, he will already know the titles of those very authors!

If one is ignorant of the parts of a subject, he is ignorant of the whole. Thus this Register is provided for school children, so that the young can learn these childish things first, that they may then desire to apply themselves to finer things. On high waves the simple lamb floats, where the huge elephant is swallowed up.

I do not spurn anyone's science, as long as it is good; but through my experience of life and deep cogitation in my own mind I conclude that every ancient study perishes with the ascendancy of modern interests. In former times, among the ancients, the authors were read: many clever youths achieved honor for this, and the very young learned excellent character models. But nowadays, everyone seeks labyrinthine labors.

So many are the ways of dialectic! what a tempest, how it transforms appearance, what training it takes! One might well scratch his head and ask, "With what knot can I keep hold of this Protean shape shifter?"[2] I do not disdain the study of dialectic, nor the glory of those skilled in the law, when I summon you to the exercise of ethics. Everyone is passionate about their own studies.[3]

But the one who cannot achieve perfection as an arts scholar,[4] or who cannot, for want of resources, become a lawyer, can at least strive to be an expert on the authors! In this way he will be a Latinist of some repute.

Let him know the rules of grammar, in which, with careful study, he can achieve proficiency. May he then, therefore, be of use to the ranks of inexperienced boys, without thinking himself better than the learned doctors.

Certain men glory too much in their science; among their fellows they caw like crows. Since they think very highly of themselves, they go about all swollen up with bombastic speech and gestures.

Those who apply themselves to high and subtle things are swallowing a camel while straining out a gnat.[5] Roaring loudly while they are ignorant of the least things, they vaunt themselves while not knowing who they are.

But now let us return to the subject of literary composition, lest our digressions offend the reader. And if perchance there is some digressive matter here, let it not be disparaged

---

[2] Horace, *Epistles* 1.1.90.   [3] Cf. Ovid, *Ex Ponto*, 1.5.35.

[4] I.e., as a dialectician: dialectic reigns supreme in conceptions of the arts and in their institutionalized form, university arts faculties.

[5] Matthew 23:24.

by my discerning colleagues, but rather, to better effect, amended courteously, without looking for unnecessary difficulty. May the divine spirit aid and instruct us. Amen.

THE REGISTER OF MANY AUTHORS

Here Begins the Register of Many Authors

[First part of the first division: "Advanced ethical readings"; lines 66–103c]

We read in the ancient chronicles of the Romans that their first Caesar was Julius, called "Caesar" from "hewing down" [*caedo*] his enemies, and that he was born in the month of July. After him the Roman leaders were called Caesars, imitating the first Caesar in their manly deeds. After the aforesaid Caesar, a noble Roman called Octavian succeeded to the imperial throne, the son of the noble senator Octavius and Atia, the sister of Julius Caesar.[6] This ruler so augmented Roman glory that the Roman people called him "Augustus"; after him the Roman Caesars were called "Augustus," "augmenting" the republic in imitation of him. He was the second Caesar and the first Augustus, powerful, truthful, prudent, liberal, and graceful, from whom the month of August was named, since he was born in that month. His power grew so much that he received riches from the corners of the earth. It was during his reign that God was made flesh, and a condition of unaccustomed peace was brought about again.

This conscientious ruler gave support to poets and philosophers. He gave them food, drink, and clothes, and enriched them with gifts. Through them he increased Rome's glory, and established its long lasting fame through the publication of literature. Thus he extended the fame of his own name, so that his own praise flew throughout the regions of the world.

He is said to have ruled for fifty-six years and to have brought innumerable people under his reign. During his time Virgil and Horace—in whose poetry the world delights—flourished at Rome, and along with them, Ovid, Sallust, and eloquent Tully produced their writings.[7]

We give precedence to the works of the most learned poet, whom Donatus praises brilliantly in his *Ars maior* and *Ars minor*, saying that this poet will be worthy of praise in song. Thus begins the *Bucolics* of Publius Virgilius Maro:

---

[6] Cf. Suetonius, *De vita Caesarum* 2.4. Octavian's mother Atia was not the sister of Caesar, but rather Caesar's niece, the daughter of Caesar's sister Julia.

[7] Hugh appears to accept the dating of the reign of Augustus from 43 BC (rather than the more usual 27 BC) to AD 14, i.e. he starts counting from the second Triumvirate; his sources are Jerome's *Chronicle*, and perhaps Cassiodorus and Vincent of Beauvais. See note in Langosch at line 94.

> Tityrus, here you loll, your slim reed-pipe serenading
> The woodland spirit beneath a spread of sheltering beech . . .[8]

[Hugh's procedure throughout the Register is, as here, to introduce a group of poets, and then to introduce each poet individually, followed by quotations of the incipits of the works. In this section (lines 103–77) he gives the incipits of Virgil's *Bucolics, Georgics,* and *Aeneid* (along with a work on Virgil spuriously attributed to Ovid, and a poem called the *Moretum* spuriously attributed to Virgil), Horace's *Ars poetica, Satires,* and *Epistles,* Ovid's *Heroides, Amores, Ars amatoria, Remedia amoris, Fasti, Metamorphoses, Tristia, Ex Ponto,* and *Ibis,* followed by introductions to the Silver Latin writers Juvenal, Perseus, Seneca Lucan, and Statius, with incipits of Juvenal's *Satires,* Perseus' *Satires,* the prologue of Lucan's *Pharsalia* along with the beginning of the work itself, and the incipit of Statius' *Thebaid.* Hugh also gives the beginning of the *Ilias latina* ("Homerus Minor"). Because of the focus on poetry, Hugh does not give incipits of prose works, although he mentions prose writers in his introductions.]

[Lines 178–379]

By right, a place among the metrical poets should be assigned to Priscian the grammarian, unless one denies the truth. Priscian became an apostate so that the emperor Julian would receive his book, *Priscianus maior,* for which he bargained away the comeliness of his faith.[9] But he wrote the book of the *Periegesis* in meter, when he still held to the Catholic faith. The book is called the *Periegesis* because it sets forth a description of the world.[10] The noble Alan of Lille, in his *Anticlaudianus,* says that Priscian strayed into apostasy out of confusion, and that he was insane and prolix in his writings.[11] Conversely, he utters manifold praises of Donatus as the true and tested grammarian.[12] If Donatus is to be credited with the whole art of grammar, Alan has withdrawn all but criticism from Priscian. Donatus the heretic, from whom the Donatists in Africa got their name, is not, dear reader, the same person. Our Donatus was a famous grammarian, the teacher of

---

[8] Translation by C. Day Lewis, *The Eclogues, Georgics, and Aeneid of Virgil* (Oxford: Oxford University Press, 1963).

[9] Priscian's *Institutiones* were dedicated to "Julian, consul and patrician," who commissioned the work. This is probably the source of the confusion about Priscian's book being received by the emperor Julian the Apostate. Priscian lived, not in the age of Julian (AD 361–363), but of Anastasius (491–518). Conrad of Hirsau also mentions Julian the Apostate in connection with Priscian.

[10] "Periegesis": from the Greek for "geographical description." Priscian's text is a translation of the work by the Greek author known as Dionysius Periegetes (second century AD?), based in turn on the teachings of the Hellenistic scholar Eratosthenes (d. ca. 194 BC), a celebrated polymath of Alexandria.

[11] *Anticlaudianus* 2.500–6. Alan refers to "our Apostate" in a discussion of grammarians, and some medieval glosses identify Priscian as the target of Alan's remarks. See above, p. 526 and note 61.

[12] *Anticlaudianus* 2.490–5.

Jerome, renowned throughout Rome, as Jerome clearly witnesses: you can read about it in his *De viris illustribus*.[13]

The great Aristotle laid down only two parts of speech capable of producing completeness; but Donatus added six *syncategoremata* [i.e. co-predicators], with which he wholly perfected speech. But Aristotle's parts of speech, the noun and the verb, would produce bitter problems for speakers, if the six supplementary parts did not clarify the sense and give students the confidence to speak. Thus where Aristotle more narrowly set forth the intrinsic nature of speech, Donatus taught more expansively the extrinsic character. He alone drained the rivers of grammar completely, and he put it all in one great book. But his successor, Priscian, revised this, and with garrulous chatter he dilated on it without improving it, so that his own work is read everywhere and the golden books of Donatus are neglected. This is what I will say of Donatus, even though he has no place among the metrical poets. I draw the line here.

Priscian would be more worthy of praise if he had stayed Christian, as he was before. As his life is despicable, so his teaching is sullied. For what the tongue speaks is spoiled by the angry heart. Someone may say that many pagans wrote many books of great renown and subtlety which are not condemned on account of the fact that their authors are non-believers. In truth such books are still used often by Christians. Such books may well be accommodated, as when they they are put to use in various ways in holy writings. If these pagans did not learn the Catholic faith, they yet persisted with great strength in their own faith, and they abound with such great virtue in their writing, because they very often wrote in a theological tenor. But if they had plainly known the Catholic faith, I believe that they would have adhered to it to the end. It is better to be ignorant of the Catholic faith than to waver in heresy after coming into knowledge of the faith. But lest the life of Priscian detract from his art, let the pearl rise up shining forth from the privy, and let his art, since it is useful, be commended, although its author is condemned with the other heretics. Honey sometimes trickles from a filthy vessel, because from one vessel one may drink, anoint, or bathe, on different occasions. Thus let readers give their forbearance to Priscian, so that he may have a place among the most learned authors.

Here begins the *Periegesis* of Priscian the Grammarian:

> Begetter of Nature, who contains the whole world,
> O king of heaven, creator of earth and water

---

[13] It is the Donatus of the Donatist schism in the fourth-century church who is mentioned in Jerome's *De viris illustribus* (93), not the grammarian Aelius Donatus. But Jerome mentions the grammarian Donatus in his *Apologia adversus libros Rufini*, PL 23:429A and his *Commentarius in Ecclesiasten*, PL 23:1071A.

> In which you gave the world to mortals,
> Grant me matter to produce a worthy song.[14]

After Priscian and Donatus the *Graecismus* follows, which we know observes the order of Donatus' book.[15] Here is the beginning of the prologue of the *Graecismus* of Eberhard of Béthune:

> Disgracefully blinded by a cloud of ignorance, some ignoramuses give expression to their asinine stupidity...

Here is the beginning of the *Graecismus* of Eberhard:

> Literally, *meta* is Greek for *trans*, *plasma* Greek for *formatio*,
> hence *metaplasmus* must be called *transformatio* ["transformation"].[16]

Not inappropriately, the *Doctrinale* follows the *Graecismus*, which is a fairly well-known text among grammarians. Here begins the *Doctrinale* of Alexander of Villa Dei:

> I am getting ready to write a *Doctrinale* ["book of instruction"] for newer students
> and will adopt many works of my teachers...[17]

After this comes the *De consolatione philosophiae* of Boethius, who is esteemed and honored among all peoples. He lived in the time of the king Theodoric, adversary of good men, enemy of law. Boethius translated certain books from Greek into Latin, and in one of the books that he wrote, *De trinitate*, he followed the example of Saint Augustine. In the prime of his life he also wrote the *Topics*, and he commented on many books of Aristotle, and thus he expanded his renown. Here begins Boethius' *De consolatione*:

> I who once wrote songs with youthful zeal
> am driven in tears, alas, to take up melancholy modes.

In order after Boethius comes Claudian, for he was also a Roman poet. He lived during the reign of Florentinus.[18] He wrote his books in an improvisatory style. He eagerly desired to record the deeds of Florentinus, and so he exercised his ingenuity in these matters. Here begins the prologue of Claudian's *De raptu Proserpinae*:

> He who first made a ship and clave therewith the deep, troubling the waters with roughly hewn oars...

---

[14] Text in Baehrens, ed., *Poetae latini minores*, 5: 275–312.

[15] See note at line 247 in Langosch's edition. Eberhard of Béthune says that he has followed the order of Donatus' *Ars*: see above, Eberhard of Béthune, Prooemium.

[16] See above, Eberhard of Béthune.   [17] See above, Alexander of Villa Dei.

[18] Claudian (ca. 370–404) was court poet under the emperor Honorius and his regent Stilicho. The Florentinus mentioned here was prefect of Rome from 395 to 397; Claudian dedicated book 2 of *De raptu Proserpinae* to him. See *Der Neue Pauly* (Stuttgart: J. B. Metzler, 1998), "Florentinus" [1].

Here begins Claudian's narrative:

> Once on a time the lord of Erebus blazed forth in swelling anger, threatening war upon the gods, because he alone was unwed...[19]

Claudian is followed by Macer, who versified the properties of herbs in the interests of human well-being.[20] Galen and Hippocrates also wrote about medicine, but they did not garland songs with meter, and for this reason they (and others like them) are excluded from the present work; their works in prose do not support inclusion.

This is the beginning of Macer's poem:

> We are going to treat the powers of herbs in a poem.
> Artemis gave her name to the mother of all herbs...

Sallust, Tully, Terence, and many of the ancients are not in common use among moderns. Although they taught just like the "ethical authors," they are not numbered among the poets.

Here Begins the Second Part of the First Division

Since basic information about the earlier authors—who they were, what they wrote—is now known, let me quickly redirect my pen to the incipits of the writings of certain authors who almost lived to see our modern times. Among these there were four especially who bedewed clerical learning with the nectar of beautiful language. There is the distinguished Alan of Lille, the sincere Matthew of Vendôme, the uncommon Geoffrey of Vinsauf, and Walter of Châtillon as well. These writers extolled the ancient poets in their writings; for they forged the purest songs. That Alan of Lille was a mellifluous author is witnessed in that most noble book, the *Anticlaudianus*. Alanus also composed the *Floridus aspectus* and a not insignificant book concerning the complaint of Nature.[21] Anyone who

[19] Translation by M. Platnauer, *Claudian*, vol. 2, Loeb Classical Library (London: Heinemann; Cambridge, Mass.: Harvard University Press, 1922), lines 1–2, 32–3.

[20] The hexameter poem *De viribus herbarum*, among the most popular medieval works on plants and their medicinal powers, was universally attributed to "Macer Floridus" or Macer (the ancient poet Aemilius Macer, d. 16 BC). It was composed in the early twelfth century by the physician Odo of Meung. See the facsimile edition and modern Spanish translation by P. Cabello de la Torre, *Macer Floridus* (León: Universidad de León and Cátedra de San Isidoro, 1990). The work was also translated into vernacular languages.

[21] Hugh attributes the *Floridus aspectus* to Alan of Lille, but the work is by Peter Riga (ca. 1140–1209), canon of Rheims. Peter Riga is the author of a larger and better known text, the *Aurora*, an interpretative summary of the Bible in Latin verse (which Hugh mentions, and ascribes correctly to Peter Riga, at line 416 of the *Registrum*). The *Floridus aspectus* was often confused and mixed in anthologies with short poems by others, including Marbod of

reads and understands these books will approve of them and will exalt Alan with fitting praise. Matthew of Vendôme versified the book of Tobit in metaphor; and Geoffrey of Vinsauf, in figures of rhetoric, wrote the *Poetria nova* for writers, and that he might win over the pope and appease the king of England through the book. For this very king, so it is said, killed Thomas the archbishop of Canterbury without fearing the sword of civil justice, nor spiritual judgment, nor the punishment of Hell. Walter of Châtillon versified the deeds of Alexander, mixing in extra material into the order of his narrative.[22] Dreaming in a trance, he brought in the Old Testament, making a wondrous prodigy.[23] Alan of Lille complained about this rather bitterly, saying that Walter wrote tattered verses.[24] But who among humans, either among the ancients or in our own times, was completely without a wart? Thus let Walter take his place in order with the other three poets just mentioned, and let my pen jump forward, leaving these behind. Here begins the prologue of Alan's *Floridus aspectus*:

> It is a rare thing to find a rich man who is humble.

Here begins the narrative of the *Floridus aspectus*:

> Olympus pours dewy nectar over the earth;
> Springs of honey sprinkle all the soil.
> The glittering rose of the saints,
> from the fields of paradise
> Fallen into the womb of a virgin,
> lay quiet there.[25]

Rennes and Hildebert of Tours. See studies by Fierville, "Notice et extraits des manuscrits de la bibliothèque de Saint-Omer, nos. 115 et 710" (with a partial edition); Boutemy, "Recherches sur le *Floridus aspectus* de Pierre la Rigge"; Camargo, "Latin Composition Textbooks and *Ad Herennium* Glossing." The "not insignificant book" referred to is Alan of Lille's *De Planctu Naturae*.

[22] Walter of Châtillon (ca. 1135–1202/3) studied at Paris and Rheims, and taught at Laon and Châtillon-sur-Marne. He also held a canonry at Rheims, where he was long in the service of William of the White Hands, archbishop of Rheims 1176–1201. It was to Archbishop William that Walter dedicated his epic poem on the life and deeds of Alexander the Great, the *Alexandreis*, in 5,464 hexameter verses, written between 1178 and 1182. The poem was extraordinarily successful, becoming a standard text in grammar schools. See *Alexandreis*, ed. Colker, and the studies by Cary, *The Medieval Alexander*, and Harich, *Alexander Epicus: Studien zur Alexandreis Walters von Châtillon*.

[23] This refers to the wondrous events of book 10 of the *Alexandreis*, in which Nature goes to the underworld to free Leviathan (the Old Testament). This is the "extra material" that Walter mixed into his metrical life of Alexander. See Meter, *Walter of Chatillon's Alexandreis Book 10: A Commentary*.

[24] Alan of Lille, *Anticlaudianus* 1.166–70; Alan criticizes Walter for using Alan's own *De Planctu Naturae* for book 10 of the *Alexandreis*, commenting that Walter produces at best tired verses in imitation of his own poetry. But Alan's criticism is anomalous; the medieval reception of Walter's poem was overwhelmingly positive, as witnessed in the many Latin and vernacular imitations of it.

[25] *PL* 171:1381A, 1382A.

Here begins Alan's *Anticlaudianus*:

> The pen of the author and the ornaments of the poet I beg,
> lest Clio, my Muse, depressed by indolence, wane in power...[26]

Here begins Alan's *De planctu Naturae*:

> I turn from laughter to tears, from joy to grief,
> from merriment to lament, from jests to wailing...[27]

Here begins the *Tobias* of Matthew of Vendôme:

> From an old field the seeds of virtue, the little shoots of morals, the ample crop of justice sprouts forth.[28]

Here begins the *Poetria nova* of Geoffrey of Vinsauf:

> Pope, marvel of the world, if I were to call you "Pope Nocent" I would be
> giving you a headless name; but if I add the prefix...[29]

Here begins the summary of the first book of Walter's *Alexandreis*:

> The first book describes how Alexander is imbued with Aristotle's holy nectar and confers
> distinction upon him by sceptre and arms...[30]

Before the course of the narrative is begun, a certain name must be revealed to inexperienced students. This name is assembled, letter by letter, at the opening of each book of the poem, and this can escape the notice of many readers who aspire to great things and overlook small things which they consider too meager. However, this is not something cheap and meager in which a subtle mind can have no profit: even if it should be a small point, whatever arises out of this material is apt for application. Consider nothing too small![31]

Now let us return our attention to the poem, lest the as yet unexplained name disappear from our sight! The name is that of the director and archbishop of Rheims, Guillermus [William], famous in this life, who, while he lived, gave favor to Walter of Châtillon by

---

[26] Ed. Bossuat; translation by Sheridan.

[27] Ed. Häring; translation by Sheridan.

[28] Ed. Munari, *Mathei Vindocinensis Opera* 2. Matthew's *Tobias*, a metrical paraphrase of the book of Tobit (now usually considered part of the apocrypha of the Hebrew bible), was written probably around 1187 (it cites Walter of Châtillon's *Alexandreis*, completed in 1182).

[29] Ed. Faral, *Les arts poétiques*; translation by Gallo, *The Poetria nova and its Sources*. The passage quoted is the opening invocation to Pope Innocent III, hence the play on the name "Innocent."

[30] Translation from Pritchard, *Alexandreis*. See also the verse translation by Townsend, *The Alexandreis of Walter of Châtillon: A Twelfth-Century Epic*.

[31] Compare Hugh of St. Victor, *Didascalicon* 6.3: "Do not look down upon these least things."

word and by deed. Walter gave Guillermus' name everlasting fame, because it is distributed across the books of the poem, linked by capital letters at the start of each book.[32] Here begins the *Alexandreis* of Walter:

> Great deeds [O muse, recount] of the Macedonian leader known throughout the world, how generously he dispersed his wealth, and with what soldiers he conquered Porus [and Darius].

Following these four poems, not by accident, is a certain poetical treatise by John of Garland, in which a clear method of composing poems is presented. This text is called the *Parisiana poetria*. Various kinds of meters and prose rhythms are also presented there, along with examples. Here begins the *Parisiana poetria* of John of Garland:

> The glory of Paris diffuses splendor, the body of scholars grows, the fountain gushes forth Apollonian waters . . . Why are you scornful, you who are seeking greater things? We have often seen the foot stumble in the plain, etc.[33]

Here Begins the Second Division of this Work

[intermediate "ethical" readings]

Every wise man reaching towards what is true must by necessity love God from his very heart. Man, who is ashes, does not cease to seek after God, who is the beginning and end of all things. A certain path leads to knowledge of him, which theology illuminates under manifold figures. Theology is the queen of all the sciences, to whom every discipline is rightly subject. The science of theology comprises diverse prose writers, but also as many metrical authors, and among these we should reckon Sedulius preeminent: indeed he deserves pride of place. He recounted the deeds of the savior in verse, and for this he earned his worthier position. Juvencus comes after him, and Prosper, Arator, Prudentius, Amarcius, and Peter Riga.

In the order of this treatise, the more advanced authors are placed first, so that the lesser ethical authors come at the end. Readers can be inspired by the greater ethical authors, and have blessed joy from the authors who come in the middle.[34] So the theological[35] authors

---

[32] The poem is designed as an acrostichon: the first line of each of the ten books of the poem begins with a letter of the name of Walter's patron, G-U-I-L-L-E-L-M-U-S.

[33] Translation by Lawler, *Parisiana poetria*; see within, John of Garland, p. 642. Hugh of Trimberg adds an extra line which is not found in the extant manuscripts of the text. See note at line 333 in Langosch's edition.

[34] These distinctions relate to pedagogical level: the first division of the treatise covers those authors read in the higher schools, and the second and third divisions treat authors read in the middle and lower schools respectively. The Christian authors are in the second section, because this order corresponds to the curricula of the middle schools, where mostly Christian authors would be read by the intermediate students.

[35] See Langosch's note, 223 (for line 354).

are placed in between, for it is written: the blessed hold to the mean. Because the lesser ethical authors come last of all, they teach the great men of this world that if they seek constant praise and honor, it is because they always believe themselves to be lesser than all.

[In the first part of this second section, Hugo covers ancient and "modern" Christian authors, using the same procedures as before, introducing information about each author and his works, and quoting incipits from the poems. Five ancient Christian authors are covered: Sedulius, Juvencus, Arator, Prosper, and Prudentius; and various medieval authors and works: Peter Riga, Bernard of Clairvaux (to whom some poems are incorrectly attributed), Sextus Amarcius, Theodulus, "Kalphurnius" (actually Hildebert of Tours), Warnerius of Basel, Master Adam (versifier of Raymond of Pennafort's *Summa de penitentia*), Godfrey of Viterbo, and several anonymous poems. In the second part of the second section, Hugo briefly treats seven saints' lives: John the Evangelist, Eustachius, Mauritius, Agnes, Mary of Egypt, Benedict, and Killian.]

Here Begins the Third and Last Division of this Work

[Elementary ethical readings: first part, ancient authors; lines 541–50]

Since there is nothing that is completely perfect in any part of human invention, whatever is overlooked in the present work should be courteously corrected by reliable friends when it is recited, lest the strivers grind it and break it up with spiteful teeth; small things befit small folk![36] It is difficult to give a finite or unambiguous rule about things that are infinite. Therefore this work is directed toward the unlearned, so that when they have progressed they may supply what is missing. . . .

[Lines 563–88]

Cato, the expositor of virtues, the regulator of morals, must take pride of place in the order of lesser authors. Who Cato was is much debated. It is recognized that there were many Catos at Rome at different times, such as Cato of Utica, whom the menacing sword of Julius Caesar drove into Africa, and Cato the Censor, and Cato "Rigidus,"[37] but none of these imparted these precepts to his son. According to Jerome, Cato was most eloquent, and according to Tully he was most wise; he is said to have written this book about morals, under the conceit of addressing his own son, for the instruction of children.[38] And

---

[36] Cf. Micah 3:5; Horace, *Epodes* 5.47; Horace, *Epistles* 1.7.44.

[37] An epithet for one of the Catos used in Boethius, *De consolatione philosophiae* 2m.7.16; cf. Alan of Lille, *Anticlaudianus* 6.230.

[38] Cf. Conrad of Hirsau, *Dialogus super auctores*, ed. Huygens, 82–3 (lines 328–50).

although he may belong among the minor authors, he is still placed among the order of the ancient writers. Step by step he is followed by Aesop, Avianus, the *Geta* and *Phisiologus*, Maximianus, and many others from the group of minor authors who are currently studied by boys. However, although they are quite old, they have justly yielded to the major authors and given pride of place over to them. So let them make a cursory appearance for the sake of the young boys. It is useless for more learned pupils to read such familiar things. Since it is difficult to show, one by one, who the authors were, what they wrote, at what time, and why, let the reader be content with the titles found here, and what he does not find here let him seek out in commentaries.[39]

[In the first section of the third division, he treats Cato, Aesop, Avianus, Maximianus, the *Pamphilus* (ca. 1100, but thought to be an ancient text), the pseudo-Ovidian comedy *De nuncio sagaci* (*Ovidius puellarum*), the *Geta*, *Facetus*, *Phisiologus*, and various other minor medieval poems thought to have been written in antiquity. In the second section of this division he introduces modern "supplements" to the "lesser" ethical authors of antiquity: two poems by Magister Henry of Würzburg,[40] a poem he calls *Catonis supplementum* (which Hugo introduces with a lament on the laziness of modern grammar students), a *Novus Facetus* by Reinerus Alemannicus, a *Novus Cato* by Martinus Lanquinus (in rhyme), a "new" Aesop (untraced), a poem called *De lino et ove* from the eleventh century, and various other poems from the twelfth and thirteenth centuries, including a life of Hildegund of Schönau.]

[39] Presumably because the antiquity of these authors, and their lesser status, make it difficult to identify them, as opposed to the wealth of information about the "major" authors, both ancient and modern.

[40] See H. Grauert, ed., *Magister Heinrich der Poet in Würzburg und die römische Kurie* (Munich: Königlich Bayerischen Akademie der Wissenschaften, 1912).

TRIA SUNT (AFTER 1256, BEFORE 1400)

INTRODUCTION[1]

The treatise known by its incipit *Tria sunt* ("There are three things...") is among the latest and the most comprehensive of the medieval Latin arts of poetry and prose. It survives in more than a dozen fifteenth-century English manuscripts, many of them produced in Oxford, where it was an important textbook for teachers of rhetorical composition. Judging from the works that accompany it in the manuscripts, the *Tria sunt* was used primarily within the advanced grammar courses offered under the supervision of the university's arts faculty. It was popular among the Benedictine monks whose numbers at Oxford increased dramatically in the course of the fourteenth century and could well have been written by one of them.

In all the extant manuscripts, the work is divided into sixteen chapters of varying length, dealing with the beginnings and endings of compositions, amplification and abbreviation of the subject matter, stylistic ornamentation and vices of style, attributes of persons and actions, and varieties of poetry and prose. Large stretches of the *Tria sunt* are quoted directly or paraphrased only slightly from other arts of poetry and prose, most extensively from Matthew of Vendôme's *Ars versificatoria*, Geoffrey of Vinsauf's *Documentum de modo et arte dictandi et versificandi* (before ca. 1213) and *Poetria nova*, and Gervase of Melkley's *Ars versificaria*. So extensive are the borrowings from Geoffrey of Vinsauf that many scholars regard the *Tria sunt* as Geoffrey's longer version of his *Documentum*. However, the *Tria sunt* quotes Hermannus Alemannus' 1256 translation of the *Middle Commentary* by Averroes on Aristotle's *Poetics*, which creates chronological problems for the attribution to Geoffrey. The treatise could have been composed any time between the second half of the thirteenth century and around 1400, when the first surviving copies were made.

Besides other arts of poetry and prose, the compiler of *Tria sunt* draws extensively on Latin poetry from antiquity through the early thirteenth century. His debt is especially great to Horace's *Ars poetica* and to twelfth-century commentary on that poem. Indeed, he explicitly measures his achievement against that of Horace, concluding the *Tria sunt* with

---

[1] Introduction by Martin Camargo.

the statement that "In this book is contained virtually everything useful that Horace provides in his *Poetics*" (chapter 16).[2]

The excerpt translated below comprises the final pages of *Tria sunt*, chapter 3: "On the Eight Ways of Extending the Subject Matter." The first part of the excerpt, up to the section on letter writing, is borrowed, with only minimal changes, from Geoffrey of Vinsauf's *Documentum de modo et arte dictandi et versificandi* 2.2.60–70.[3] In concluding the chapter with specific advice on writing letters, the *Tria sunt* resembles other arts of poetry and prose. Gervase of Melkley ends his *Ars versificaria* with a chapter on letter writing, for example, and John of Garland inserts epistolographic precepts and model letters at several points in his *Parisiana poetria*. Where the *Tria sunt* contrasts with Gervase's treatise, the *Parisiana poetria,* and most *artes dictandi* or letter-writing textbooks, is in casting letter writing as a special variety of amplification. While it was common for letter-writing textbooks to incorporate the lore of figures and other methods of stylistic ornamentation from the arts of poetry and prose, especially from the works of Geoffrey of Vinsauf, the *Tria sunt* is unusual in reversing the hierarchy, making letter writing an aspect of preceptive grammar. In this as in other regards, the *Tria sunt*'s brief treatment of letters is at the opposite extreme from the more conventionally schematic approach to letter writing of Oxford "business teachers" such as Thomas Sampson and William Kingsmill, whose courses on letter writing competed with the general composition courses of the university-sanctioned grammar masters. The overriding concern of their textbooks was with the parts of a letter, a topic to which the *Tria sunt* devotes but a single, short paragraph.

No printed edition of the *Tria sunt* exists, though select passages appear in the handful of scholarly studies published on it since Noel Denholm-Young first noted its existence in 1934.[4] Among the published excerpts is Martin Camargo's preliminary edition of the section on letter writing.[5]

Translation of this excerpt by Martin Camargo, from his critical edition and translation of the *Tria sunt*, in preparation.[6]

---

[2] Geoffrey of Vinsauf makes a similar statement in his *Documentum de modo et arte dictandi et versificandi* 2.3.162, ed. Faral, *Les arts poétiques*, 317.

[3] Ed. Faral, 282–4.

[4] For more details, including bibliography and lists of manuscripts, see Camargo, "*Tria sunt*: The Long and the Short of Geoffrey of Vinsauf's *Documentum de modo et arte dictandi et versificandi*."

[5] Camargo, "Toward a Comprehensive Art of Written Discourse: Geoffrey of Vinsauf and the *Ars Dictaminis*" (Latin text on 186–92).

[6] Translations of classical sources are Camargo's own.

[HOW TO CREATE AN EXTENDED COMPOSITION FROM THE BRIEFEST SUBJECT MATTER]

Thus we see how one should proceed with regard to a very brief subject matter, namely, that one verb is extended into three components—beginning, middle, and end—and thus eight artificial beginnings are derived and their continuations are fitted to them.[7]

Also worth adding is another general precept for those who are composing, when they do not know how to treat or discover [*invenire*][8] the subject matter, showing how the meaning of a single verb ought to be enough for them. Just as from a little spark they can kindle a great fire, so therefore may the sequence of a composition be drawn out from a single verb. A certain proverb [*proverbium*] should be found, in one part of which the meaning of the single verb that is designated to stand for the subject matter may be placed and in the other part the meaning of another verb may be placed. Afterwards, let the statement of facts be made from the one part of the proverb and let the conclusion be fashioned from the other. And in this way the three sentences [*clausulae*] of the composition may be derived, the first comprising the proverb, the second the statement of facts, and the third the conclusion. But since this quantity is meager, we can draw out the middle sentence, that is, the sentence containing the statement of facts, and strengthen it with arguments, on the one hand, and confirmations of arguments, on the other, and so extend the composition [*dictamen*] infinitely.

This teaching will be clarified through a rough example so that it may be understood better. Notice how this verb "I teach" is put forward as the subject matter. Now the sequence of the composition may be derived from this verb, thus: "Whoever knows ought to teach. I know. For this reason I teach." In this sequence the proverb "Whoever knows etc." is placed first, in one part of which is placed the verb of "teaching" when one says "ought to teach" and in the other the verb of "knowing" when one says "Whoever knows." For this reason the verb from which the proverb is derived always should be in the second part of the proverb and the verb from which the statement of facts is drawn out should be

---

[7] The eight artificial beginnings and their continuations are the subjects of *Tria sunt*, chapters 1 and 2, respectively. The eight artificial options are to begin with (1) the middle or (2) the end of the subject matter; with a proverb related to the (3) beginning, (4) middle, or (5) end of the subject matter; or with an exemplum related to the (6) beginning, (7) middle, or (8) end of the subject matter. This portion of the *Tria sunt* derives from the opening sections of Geoffrey of Vinsauf's *Documentum de modo et arte dictandi et versificandi*, ed. Faral, 266–71. As used here, the term "proverb" designates any sentential expression or concise statement of a general truth, including one created for the purpose at hand, and not necessarily a traditional saying. Similarly, "exemplum" does not designate a brief narrative but rather an illustrative image, as instanced in the letter of invective, below.

[8] The Latin verb *invenire* has been translated throughout as "discover," in preference to "find," which deemphasizes the creative aspect of rhetorical invention, and "invent," which overemphasizes it.

in the first part of the same proverb. Later follows the statement of facts, which is taken from the first part of the proverb. The verb of "knowing" is placed in this statement of facts when one says "I know." Third and last is the conclusion, which is taken from the second part of the proverb, in which the verb of "teaching" is placed when one adds the following: "for this reason I teach."

If we wish to extend this sequence more, we should take the sentence containing the statement of facts, namely, "I know," and confirm it with arguments and confirmations of arguments. Here are some arguments that can be used to confirm that "I know": "Because for a considerable time I have diligently sought knowledge and done so among the experts." Here is a confirmation of the argument: "Truly among the experts, because I have been among the Parisians, where knowledge of the trivium flowers; among the Toledans, where knowledge of the quadrivium; among the Salernitans, where knowledge of physicians; and among the Bolognese, where knowledge of the laws and decretals flowers."⁹ And so a great stream grows from a little one.

So now that we have a rough example of the composition to be fashioned, let us render this roughness into a shape. The proverb "Whoever knows ought to teach" may be extended by means of more refined words, thus: "The one into whose mind the streams of knowledge have flowed should not refuse a drink to those who thirst, but those streams should be dispersed abroad and he should distribute those waters even unto the highways." The statement of facts "I know" may be expressed more ornately, thus: "I have indeed drawn up the floods of knowledge, with which I have watered the dryness of the mind, which I have refreshed in them when it was burning with thirst." Here is an elaborated argument for "I know": "Nor is it strange if knowledge reveals to me its secrets, she whose intimate acquaintance I have earned with service over so long a time and extorted with numerous reproaches, as it were through violence of mind. For I put together a span of twenty years dwelling in the haunts of her familiars, where study consumed me entirely and the candle-lit toil of the nights continued in daytime labors, and this labor always found me burning, seldom catching my breath, never unoccupied in idleness. I attended eagerly to the instruction of distinguished experts and did so in the appropriate places that were allotted to a particular branch of knowledge. For I served at Paris in the science of the trivial arts, at Toledo I was a contemplator of the quadrivial arts, at Salerno I investigated the principles of medicine, and at Bologna, finally, I was taught the science of the laws and decretals. My mind came to quench its thirst from these springs, which, though they may

⁹ All of these associations were well established by the late twelfth century. Among the arts of the trivium, dialectic dominated at Paris. Toledo was a center for the transmission of Greek and Arabic scientific learning to Christian Europe. Salerno's association with medicine was especially ancient. Bologna's fame as the preeminent center of legal studies dates from at least the first half of the twelfth century.

derive their sweetness from another source, nonetheless offer sweet waters indeed for the drinking." Observe the conclusion, namely, "for this reason I teach": "Therefore, this which I have I distribute and the waters that I have gathered from all quarters I—an attentive cupbearer—give the thirsty mind to drink."

Thus we find in the aforesaid example how prolixity is created from brevity. In the same place we can also see how a rough sentiment can be made shapely with certain embellishments and how a facile sentiment is given weight through the difficulties of its words. However, a subsequent chapter will make plain the art of embellishing what is rough and giving weight to what is facile.[10]

On the Technique of Composing Letters [*Epistolas*]

But because an art of extending the subject matter is needful to those who are composing letters, let us append also another technique that is particular to letters. To one paying close attention, this technique will seem neither to differ entirely from the foregoing technique for amplifying nor to agree entirely with it. Here is the technique. First, let us pay close attention to three things: the nature of the subject matter, the nature of the persons, and the reason that moves one to write. Next, either in association with the beginning or in association with the middle, we should find an appropriate proverb or exemplum [*exemplum*], which should be put before the other parts of the letter. This proverb or exemplum ought to be the sort in which two verbs, or one verb and one participle, are situated. Furthermore, from the first verb of the proverb or exemplum one should discover the statement of facts, which is to be proved by means of reasons, probable arguments and effects of arguments, and certain conjectural proofs that work to the advantage of the case. The places from which conjectural proofs are taken will be shown later, when we speak about the attributes of persons and actions.[11]

In the statement of facts, moreover, let this hierarchy be observed, namely, that insofar as topics maintain themselves in greater generality they should claim for themselves priority in order, so that the more general come first and the less general follow. Similarly, after the proverb or exemplum, a special sentiment clarifying the proverb or exemplum should be turned in another direction, so that it may both serve what has been set forth

---

[10] The reference is probably to *Tria sunt*, chapter 9: "On the Art of Discovering Ornate Words."

[11] The attributes are discussed briefly, below, and then in greater detail in chapter 12: "On the Attributes of Persons and Actions." The attributes of persons and actions are treated by Cicero, in *De inventione* 1.24.34–1.28.43, and 2.9.28–2.14.46.

already and prepare the way for the main business. Afterwards, the request and conclusion should be discovered from the meaning of the second verb or participle.

And thus the four parts of a letter are obtained—the exordium, that is, the proverb or exemplum; the statement of facts; the request; and the conclusion—before which, if it pleases, we may put the greeting, in which good will is secured. This greeting constitutes a fifth part of a letter, although it pleases our contemporaries to omit the greeting and write it on the back of the letter. Moreover, there is not always need for all five of these parts.[12]

We also ought to see to it that throughout the entire epistle we employ the concise and pithy fullness of enthymemes, as well as brief sentences [*clausulae*], and that we preserve the weightiness of the sentiment as much as we are able. And that sentiment is weighty which readily moves the hearer. To insure that the sentiment is weighty, that is, persuasive, one should always discover the sort of sentiment that corresponds fittingly to the nature of the subject matter. So, if the subject matter be humorous, we should discover humorous sentiments, which with their humorousness may move the hearer to laughter; if it be serious, let us discover serious sentiments, which with their seriousness may move the hearer to piety or, if it be fitting, to weeping. And let the words do what they are by right obliged to do.[13] Horace teaches this in the *Old Poetics*,[14] thus:

> It's not enough for poems to be beautiful; they should be sweet and drive the spirit of the hearer wherever they will. As human faces smile on those who smile, so they weep at those who weep: if you wish me to weep, first you must feel pain yourself; then your misfortunes will harm me.[15]

And the same Horace, in the same work, later shows how the songs of a writer move the hearer with their sweetness, namely, by assigning its proper characteristics to each thing

---

[12] Most treatments of the *ars dictaminis* or art of letter writing are devoted almost exclusively to the parts of a letter, a topic sketched in this paragraph. While the five-part schema (*salutatio, exordium, narratio, petitio, conclusio*) is the most common, it is not unusual to encounter schemas that specify more or fewer parts or distinguish between essential and non-essential parts. The practice allegedly favored by the author's contemporaries, known as "endorsing," is to write the greeting on the back (*dorsum*) of a letter, after it has been folded and sealed or sewn up for sending, rather than as part of the text of the letter proper. Emphasis on "proverbs," both as the second part of a letter and as the source of a letter's underlying structure, is characteristic of letter-writing manuals written in France during the second half of the twelfth century. For another good example, see Camargo, "A Twelfth-Century Treatise on 'Dictamen' and Metaphor." John of Garland's very brief remarks on beginning a letter with a proverb containing two verbs probably derive from the same source as the more detailed instructions in the *Tria sunt*. See John of Garland: Lawler, ed. and trans., *The Parisiana Poetria of John of Garland*, 58–9.

[13] Geoffrey of Vinsauf, *Poetria nova* 1064, ed. Faral, 230.

[14] In using the title *Antiqua poetria* for the *Ars poetica*, the compiler of *Tria sunt* implicitly acknowledges his familiarity with the usual title for Geoffrey of Vinsauf's most famous work, *Poetria nova* or the *New Poetics*. He cites the *Poetria nova* frequently in *Tria sunt* but always by the title *Liber versuum* or *The Book of Verses*.

[15] *Ars poetica* 99–103.

regarding which we strive to speak persuasively. Horace calls these characteristics "colors of works" [*colores operum*], because with their weightiness they decorate and color any work whatsoever. But Tully says that they are "attributes of persons and actions,"[16] because they openly assign to persons and actions their properties, concerning which we must speak in more detail in a separate chapter.[17] Whence Horace says:

> If I am unable and don't know how to preserve the delineated changes and the colors of works, why am I hailed as poet?[18]

The meaning is "Why should I usurp for myself the name of poet if I do not know the colors of works?" (that is, the characteristics of the things that I wish to treat), as if he were to say "I am not worthy to be hailed as a poet." In proof of which point, more or less throughout his book, Horace calls for the observing of characteristics.

And because, according to Aristotle in his *Poetics*, "every poetic utterance rests on praise and blame [*laude . . . et vituperio*]"[19] and praise and blame mostly concern the characters of men, therefore in his book Horace portrays only the characteristics of men. But because the characteristics of men are discovered mostly from the attribute that is called nature, therefore Horace especially showed the characteristics that are taken from nature. The characteristics taken from nature, according to Tully, are divided in three, namely, into those things that are taken from the body, those that are from the soul, and those that are from externals.[20] However, those that belong to the body and soul are better known to the understanding, and for that reason Horace portrays the characteristics that are taken from externals. These are examined from six places, namely, from condition, as whether one is master or slave; from age, as a youth or an old man; from sex, as a man or a woman (and likewise where condition is examined); from profession, that is, position, as soldier or merchant; from race, as English or German; and from fatherland, as Roman or Athenian.

Horace lists these characteristics thus:

> It will make a great difference whether Davus speaks or a hero, whether a ripe old man or one still burning in his flowering youth, whether a potent matron or a busy nurse, whether a wandering merchant or the tiller of a little green field, a Colchian or an Assyrian, one raised in Thebes or in Argos.[21]

For when he says "Davus or a hero," the place from condition is cited; when he says "whether a ripe old man or one still burning in his flowering youth," the place from age is

---

[16] Cicero, *De inventione* 1.24.34.   [17] The reference is to *Tria sunt*, chapter 12.

[18] *Ars poetica* 86–7.

[19] Hermannus Alemannus, translation of Averroes' "Middle Commentary" on Aristotle's *Poetics* (1256), chapter 1, ed. Minio-Paluello, *De arte poetica, cum Averrois expositione*, 41.

[20] *Rhetorica ad Herennium* 3.6.10.   [21] *Ars poetica* 114–18.

cited; when he says "whether a potent matron or a busy nurse," the place from sex; when he says "whether a wandering merchant or the tiller of a little green field," the place from profession; when he says "Colchian or Assyrian," the place from race; and when he says "raised in Thebes or in Argos," the place from fatherland.

Moreover, since among these characteristics the poet is more concerned to distinguish among the characteristics of years, therefore he displays the characteristics of each age, speaking thus:

> You should notice the customs of each age, and provide what is fitting to the changing natures and years.[22]

And a little later the same Horace adds the reason why such discrimination among characteristics should be made, saying:

> Lest perchance the parts of old age be assigned to a youth and to a boy those of a grown man, we shall always linger on what is connected and suited to the age.[23]

And because in letters it is always fitting to assign their proper characteristics to things and persons, one should know that every sort of person ought to be named by that epithet [*epitheto*] in which he is allotted the greatest proof of his reputation and that which dominates in him beyond all others, according to this statement of Horace:

> Writer, if perchance you bring back honored Achilles, let him be energetic, irascible, inexorable, harsh. Let Medea be fierce and unconquered, Ino tearful, Ixion faithless, Io wandering, Orestes sad.[24]

Similarly, in commending or censuring any person it is fitting to assign many subsets of characteristics, for it is not possible to name any person adequately with one or two or even a few epithets. Because just as it profits little to have a single rose stifled by many thorns and one daisy pressed down by many reeds, so for commendation it does not suffice to assign any person one or a few virtues, lest perchance a richer abundance of vices hinder the praise. Therefore, for purposes of approbation, one ought to be labeled with many epithets, so that where individual ones do not avail, many may assist.[25]

Moreover, there are certain epithets that should be restricted when applied to certain persons, and there are others that should be expanded when applied to most persons, and

---

[22] *Ars poetica* 156–7.

[23] *Ars poetica* 176–8. Cf. Matthew of Vendôme, *Ars versificatoria* 1.43, ed. Munari, *Mathei Vindocinensis Opera*, 3: *Ars versificatoria*, 61.

[24] *Ars poetica* 120–1, 123–4. Cf. Matthew of Vendôme, *Ars versificatoria* 1.44 (ed. Munari, 62), who cites *Ars poetica* 120–2.

[25] Matthew of Vendôme, *Ars versificatoria* 1.63 (ed. Munari, 90).

there are also some that can be assigned to all persons in common. For example, in a pastor of the church constancy of faith, the eager desire for virtue, undiminished devoutness, and delight in piety should be expanded. In justice, however, he ought to be restricted, lest through the rigor of justice the churchman seem to turn into a tyrant. For his epithet, that is, the one proper to him, is "to spare the submissive and punish the proud." Conversely, in an emperor, a king, or a prince, rigor of justice should be assigned in abundance, since lukewarmness of piety is only a little to his detriment. And similarly, the remaining characteristics should be observed in a diverse fashion when applied to diverse persons, so that

Individuals all keep their place fittingly assigned to them.[26]

But every sort of person also should be described in such a way that the description causes the maximum support of belief to be extended and so that what is true or plausible is said about this person, according to the statement of Horace:

Either follow the reputation or invent what is consistent with itself.[27]

For we can invent and discover whatever we please so long as the consistency and simplicity of the subject matter is preserved. A simple subject matter is one into which no vice is enfolded, so that "simple" may be understood as "without fold,"[28] namely without vices. This is evident in Horace, thus:

Finally, whatever it is, only let it be simple and one.[29]

Now we can discover the subject matter, with this precaution. In accordance with the nature of the subject matter or the reason that drives us to write, we should think up a proverb or exemplum, which should be placed at the very head of the subject matter in a certain artful sequence of words. Then we should discover causes, reasons, demonstrations [*causas, rationes, evidentias*], and arguments for the advantage of our case, that is, in support of our purpose, and we should incorporate these always by putting the more general first, as was said before. For invention is the devising of probable arguments for the advantage of our case,[30] that is, for making persuasive that which we have in mind. And "an argument is reasoning that provides proof, by which one thing is inferred through another," as Quintilian says in *Institutio Oratoria*.[31]

---

[26] *Ars poetica* 92. Matthew of Vendôme, *Ars versificatoria* 1.64–6, 70 (ed. Munari, 91, 93), with variant readings.

[27] *Ars poetica* 119. Cf. Matthew of Vendôme, *Ars versificatoria* 1.73 (ed. Munari, 94).

[28] The derivation is clearer in Latin: the adjective *simplex* (with oblique forms *simplic-*) is analyzed as a compound of *sine* ("without") and *plica* ("a fold"). The same gloss to the same Horatian line appears, in a different context, in Geoffrey of Vinsauf's *Documentum de modo et arte dictandi et versificandi* 2.3.157–8 (ed. Faral, 315).

[29] *Ars poetica* 23.   [30] *De inventione* 1.7.9; *Rhetorica ad Herennium* 1.2.3.

[31] *Institutio oratoria* 5.10.11.

But so that the teaching that we have already provided may grow bright with the clarity of an example, let the following subject matter come among us by way of example. A certain ignoramus, when he had come to our hostel for the purpose of lodging there, having heard about the praiseworthy reputation of certain of our companions and seeing that no one applied the title of praise to him, falsely set himself above everyone else in three things, namely, the incomes from his properties, his understanding of the laws, and his practice of legal cases. However, since truth utterly contradicted his boastful display, once the truth had been recognized, he left the hostel in shame. We, however, entreated by our companions to send him a letter about this subject matter that he would not understand readily unless instructed by some other knowledgeable person, wrote an invective so that in this way his dullness would be clear. From the reason that drove us to write or from the business itself we took this exemplum, by way of imitating the technique that we provided earlier: "The painted surface of a wall, when the picture grows old through length of time, proclaims the baseness of the material that lies beneath it." From this exemplum, after the greeting has been put in front, a letter adorned with the flowery garments of the colors follows in these words:

> To A. of B. the greeting with which he deserved to be greeted. The hypocrisy of a gilded wall, as the pride of its gilding grows old, honest irony, the common exposer of lying pride, through the lie of its honesty exposes by lying honestly. By the same service of exposure, the feigned hyperbole of a tongue that takes pride in a pride of the superlative degree by covering over a poverty of the positive degree, by the true marvel of ironic exposure, as it becomes positive degenerates superlatively. Truly, how the wealthy abundance of your incomes had endowed you, how exceptional knowledge of the laws had instructed you, how subtle practice of legal cases had put you ahead of all others the common irony of a specific denunciation speaks by mocking in a genuine piece of writing. Don't you cast yourself down by raising yourself up in this way? Don't you make yourself foolish by being wise in this way? Don't you grow dumb by speaking in this way? Don't the people proclaim: "Let the deed overcome the word; boasting lessens renown"? Wherefore, once you have banned any hypocrisy of gilded pomposity whatsoever, you should hasten to assist the departure of an arrogant tongue, lest rumor lend the belief of the listening people to an ironic exposure.

In this letter one sees the artificial elaboration [*artificialis . . . prosecutio*] of the subject matter, which is a cloudy vapor in the beginning, clearly made plain by the light of exposition through the sentences that follow. For those who are composing artificially, as we have said often, place at the beginning of their subject matter an appropriate proverb or exemplum containing obscurely what chiefly is intended. And because the purpose lies hidden beneath a certain obscurity, the sentences that follow should be the sort that are able to elucidate the mist of obscurity with the open exposition of their light, according to what Horace says in praise of Homer, thus:

Not smoke from lightning, but from smoke he intends to give light, so that he then may produce lovely marvels, Antiphates and Scylla and with Cyclops, Charybdis.[32]

The meaning is: Homer does not intend to provide a flashing beginning and an obscure continuation in his book that he composed about the return of Ulysses from Troy, but from a misty and obscure beginning he intends to provide a clear continuation. Similarly, in this letter the exemplum, "The hypocrisy of a gilded etc.," is a kind of origin for the sentences that follow, containing their intention obscurely, and therefore it is arranged to be more difficult and more obscure than the others. In it is placed one verb ("exposes") and one participle ("gilded"). And because the participle in this exemplum is placed before the verb, the statement of facts is discovered from the meaning of the participle through a comparison, namely, "By the same service of exposure etc." Then follows the argument of the statement of facts, thus: "Truly, how etc." Then the confirmation of the argument, thus: "Don't you in this way etc." Then follows the request, "Wherefore etc.," which is discovered from the second verb of the exemplum, namely, from the verb "exposes." Then the conclusion, thus: "lest of the listening etc." And this is a part of the petition and is discovered from the same verb. However, we will show later the colors with which a letter is embellished.[33]

But because in the foregoing letter the words seem too decorated [*phalerata*], we will supply still another letter, plainer [*magis planam*] in words but weightier in meaning, whose subject matter is this. A certain Arthur by name, since he had presumed to plot an ambush and hostile villainies against his kinsman the king of England, when jailed at last by the same king, dispatched this letter, in which he moves the king to mercy:[34]

> To his most reverend lord John, by God's grace king of England, Arthur, his captive still, asks that you gather pity from so many misfortunes of your nephew. Clemency ought to temper royal rages, and princely mercy punishes less than what is deserved. I have deserved, I confess, I have deserved the punishment that I suffer. Indeed, after the days of my father, after the life of my grandfather, after the times of my uncles, in you only was I going to have the assurance of kinship and friendship. But against so great a friend I shamelessly presumed to plot warlike follies and hostile ambushes, deceived to be sure by hostile advice. I could not be mindful of my uncle, of my father—I could not even be mindful of my own blood. Now, however, I give thanks to heavenly mercy, which has

[32] *Ars poetica* 143–5.

[33] The reference is to *Tria sunt*, chapter 5: "On the Ten Varieties of Transumption that Constitute Difficult Ornamentation" and especially to chapter 7: "On Easy Ornamentation and on Determination, which is the Principal Seasoning of Style, and on the Colors of Words and Thoughts."

[34] This (fictional) letter is based on historical events: Arthur of Brittany was captured and imprisoned by his uncle King John of England in 1202 and perished under mysterious circumstances in 1203.

granted me both to recognize what I am and to repent my deluded stupidity. So may God restore me to your friendship or at least provide me softer chains. I would not wish that I, completely exempt, should not have felt this prison, which has restored me to my uncle and freed me from the French seducer. Your discretion knows that the punishments that I have endured to this point I have deserved, to be sure; but spare one who confesses. If the punishments inflicted on me seem to you not yet sufficient and equal to my deserts, consider what you would have done to your nephew, what you can do to your captive. Because if neither kinship nor your compassion for my suffering does, at least let grace move your pity. To a truly noble mind the power of punishing suffices for mercy.

Observe in this letter that the weightiness of the sentiment is maintained in accordance with what the nature of the subject matter requires. Moreover, this weightiness is discovered from the sorts of places by which the hearer's spirit may be moved to mercy.

Thus, sufficient instruction has been provided in extending the subject matter and composing letters artfully.

PART 5
PROFESSIONAL, CIVIC, AND SCHOLASTIC APPROACHES TO THE LANGUAGE ARTS, CA. 1225–CA. 1272

INTRODUCTION

In the university curricula of the thirteenth century, and in the professionalized environments of the Italian schools, the study of grammar and rhetoric took on a very different cast from the twelfth-century ideal of an integrated curriculum. The teachers associated with the northern cathedral schools of the twelfth century remind us that the language arts have a practical, cultural purpose, to produce elegant and correct expression and rational argumentation. These ideas were enshrined in such masterpieces of literary Latinity as Alan of Lille's *De planctu Naturae* and *Anticlaudianus* and Bernardus Silvestris' *Cosmographia*. This fundamentally literary and cultural idea of the language arts was also the engine driving the distinctively bellettristic form that these studies achieved, the *artes poetriae*, which emerged in the late twelfth century and flowered in the first decades of the thirteenth century. While their sphere of influence was largely the grammar school, the *artes poetriae* could also aspire to a higher and more comprehensive level of compositional instruction and literary knowledge, as in the case of the *Poetria nova* of Geoffrey of Vinsauf, the *Parisiana poetria* of John of Garland, and the anonymous *Tria sunt*.

By comparison with the scholarly institutions of the twelfth century, the world of the thirteenth century is one of specialization. Within each university, the individual faculties defined themselves through sharp disciplinary distinctions, most famously, for example, the faculties of arts and theology at Paris. Between different universities there were also marked disciplinary emphases. Further distinctions were observed within particular faculties: in the prestigious faculty of arts at Paris, the masters asserted a firm division between theoretical knowledge and practical application, and studies gave priority to the former;[1] and again in the arts faculty at Paris, logic was indisputably the dominant subject, and other disciplines, notably grammar, were subsumed within the interests of logic. The Italian universities and schools developed along different lines from their northern European counterparts, and at least in the case of Bologna seem to have achieved their institutional status at slightly earlier dates, but the specializing character is just as evident there. At the University of Bologna, law was the dominant study, and studies of grammar and rhetoric, while consistent, were subordinate to law.[2] But early on, Bologna was also a center for numerous *studia* where

---

[1] Ebbesen and Rosier-Catach, "Le *trivium* à la Faculté des arts," 97–9.
[2] Rashdall, *The Universities of Europe in the Middle Ages*, 1:142–253.

masters taught the professional art of letter writing, the *ars dictaminis*, which fed directly into legal practice and civic bureaucracy. During the late eleventh century through the twelfth century, the *ars dictaminis* had developed—among Italian and then French teachers—as a specialized rhetorical art that often substituted its own system of precepts for study of a broader rhetorical curriculum that included the classic Ciceronian texts.

Studies of grammar and rhetoric in their traditional forms did not disappear under the pressure of philosophical or professional specialization, although they were certainly often eclipsed by other, more powerful curricular factors, or reconceived to serve the newer, dominant interests. More importantly, however, the process of such intellectual and curricular focus, whether towards theoretical or professional ends, brought with it some remarkable reflections on the state of knowledge and some profound transformations in the content of that knowledge. Here we present key examples of these changing outlooks: the expression of a literary dimension in Bolognese dictaminal rhetoric; the conflict between traditional bellettristic grammar and the new logic in the French schools; the role and representation of the language arts in grammatical commentary and scientific classification; the entry of Ciceronian rhetoric into the vernacular civic sphere, where it was applied both to oral discourse and written composition; and the impact of the appearance of Aristotle's *Rhetoric* in the second half of the thirteenth century.

Dictamen and its Literary Links

Like the *artes poetriae* and *artes praedicandi*, the *ars dictaminis,* or art of letter writing, was a distinctively medieval development of rhetorical teaching that served new cultural and thus pedagogical needs. The *ars dictaminis* had its origins in the urban centers of Italy, where students and young professionals needed targeted compositional skills for serving in the bureaucracies of the church, the cities, the courts, and the legal systems, all of which depended on formal letters and documents. The term *dictamen* referred, most broadly, to "composition," whether prose or metrical or rhythmical.[3] In this larger sense, *dictamen* could refer to the study of written composition, including both verse and prose, grounded in classical literary authority and rhetorical theory.[4] But with reference to the *ars dictaminis*, *dictamen* had a much narrower meaning related to composing prose letters. To the extent that the *dictatores* (i.e. teachers and practitioners of the *ars dictaminis*) classified their field, they placed it with rhetoric; but they more often claimed that it was autonomous of other language arts.[5] Its history tends to justify this latter claim. In its earliest phase, beginning with Alberic of

---

[3] Camargo, *Ars dictaminis*, 17.   [4] Ward, "Rhetorical Theory and the Rise and Decline of Dictamen."
[5] Camargo, *Ars dictaminis*, 19.

Montecassino in the eleventh century, it was intended as an addition to the other language sciences, that is, part of a broad, traditional curriculum. But quickly the art separated itself from other teachings and developed a streamlined character with a particular practical application, substituting for, rather than supplementing, traditional rhetoric. However, in practice the *ars dictaminis* also had strong affiliations with grammar: in France and England, it was usually taught by grammarians.[6] Moreover, the more comprehensive of the *artes dictaminis* incorporate material on grammar that is relevant to prose style, for example, about the grammatical concerns of natural and artificial order, that is, "natural" grammatical word order, as opposed to metrical or euphonic deviations, which are the product of artifice.[7]

By the early twelfth century, Bologna had been established as a center of dictaminal teaching. Here the teaching of the art was standardized around the five-part letter, consisting of salutation, exordium or securing good will (*captatio benevolentiae*), narration, petition, and conclusion (a form that descends from the Ciceronian system of the six-part oration). In response to the professional needs associated with law studies at Bologna, the manuals of letter writing were very practical and narrow in their teaching, with little reference to classical rhetorical theory. During the twelfth century, a French tradition of dictaminal teaching also emerged, closer in its conception to grammatical and rhetorical doctrine, prizing a more eloquent and literary prose style. This newer tradition in turn was exported back to Bologna, where a second generation of *dictatores* established their fame as teachers. Among these were Boncompagno da Signa (1165–1240), Bene da Firenze (fl. 1220s), and Guido Faba (ca. 1190—ca. 1240).

In the Italian cities, *dictamen* seems also to have formed part of the secondary grammar curriculum, substituting for classical rhetoric. Even by the thirteenth century, when the *ars dictaminis* became a more advanced subject appropriate to university-level teaching, it was also represented in the syllabus of the Florentine grammar schools, where it was the conduit for instruction in prose composition.[8] But as a specialized subject for the advanced professional schools, the *ars dictaminis* developed so much of its own "modern" momentum that no less an authority than Boncompagno da Signa could boast that he had never lectured on Cicero and owed nothing to others' rhetorical precept.[9] Even the traditional canon of classical authors seems to have played a lesser role in the curricula of thirteenth-century Italian grammar schools.[10]

It is into this environment that Guido Faba projects his "reformist" claims, in his *Rota nova* (ca. 1225), to have reunited the "purple science of *dictamen*" with the Latin eloquence

---

6 Ibid., 19, 31–3.
7 Thurot, *Notices et Extraits*, 46; cited in Kneepkens, "*Ordo naturalis* and *ordo artificialis*," 68, and see also 81.
8 Black, *Humanism and Education in Medieval and Renaissance Italy*, 69, 338.
9 *Palma*, prologue, see Sutter, ed., *Aus Leben und Schriften des Magisters Boncompagno*, 105–6.
10 Black, *Humanism and Education*, 192, 198, based on evidence from Florentine schools.

of Cicero. Guido clearly identifies his own early training with the aims of *dictamen* in its largest sense, that is, the study of classical authors imparting a general mastery of literary style rather than simply narrow epistolary proficiency. The grand style and cosmic allegory of his autobiographical preface are meant to embody the aims of an idealized literary curriculum which teaches the refining—almost purifying—and persuasive powers of ornamental prose. Later in the century Brunetto Latini would also attempt to forge links between *dictamen*, classical literary culture, and a course of study that leads to mastery of style. The core issue in Brunetto's *Rettorica* (ca. 1260), the role of Ciceronian rhetoric in the public, vernacular sphere, will be treated separately, below. Here it is important to point out that Brunetto's understanding of rhetorical discourse is at once formed by the Italian practice of the *ars dictaminis*, which he maps onto Cicero's *De inventione*, and constrained by that very practice, because he seeks to accommodate all forms of written expression, from letters to love poetry, under the larger, more comprehensive rhetorical rubric of argument or "dispute."

The Changing Fortunes of Grammatical Study in the Northern Universities

In the arts faculty at the University of Paris, and similarly at the University of Oxford, the grammatical texts studied were basically the same as those studied in cathedral schools of the twelfth century. The Paris statutes of 1215, the earliest record of the Parisian curriculum for the degree in arts, prescribe that Priscian's "two books," *Priscianus maior* (*Institutiones* books 1–16) and *minor* (books 17–18), or at least one of them, be heard regularly (*ordinarie*) as a course of lectures.[11] The Paris statutes of 1255 are even more specific: the *Priscianus minor* and *maior*, and Donatus' *Barbarismus* and the pseudo-Priscianic *De accentibus*.[12] Similarly, the Oxford arts faculty statutes of 1268 declare that "before determination" Priscian's *De constructionibus* (i.e. the *Priscianus minor*) must have been heard twice, and the *Barbarismus* once. Those "determining on behalf of others" also had to hear the *Priscianus maior* once.[13] But the university scholars' approach to these texts marks a significant difference with the earlier period. They did not use them to teach Latin, to teach how to compose, or to expound literary texts. It was assumed that the students would already know Latin, having mastered the language through the widely used versified grammars, the *Doctrinale* of Alexander of Villa Dei and the *Graecismus* of Eberhard of

---

[11] Denifle and Chatelain, *Chartularium*, 1:78.   [12] Ibid., 1:278.
[13] Fletcher, "The Faculty of Arts," 376, 383; Gibson, ed., *Statuta antiqua universitatis Oxoniensis*, 25–6.

Béthune. The study of the ancient grammatical texts, whether Priscian's works or the *Barbarismus* of Donatus, was a theoretical enterprise. The subject of grammar was part of a course on logic, and the ancient grammars served as an entry into the study of linguistics and semantics, not as an occasion for considering the particular character of the Latin language. Language was thus to be the object of logical analysis, because logic and semantics were closely linked. Grammatical study served also to standardize a scientific discourse of Latin required by the new philosophy.[14] The Paris statutes of 1255 make these developments very obvious: here the *Priscianus maior* and *minor* are grouped with Aristotle's *Topics*, *Sophistical Refutations*, and *Prior* and *Posterior Analytics*.

Among university scholars, the scientific status of grammar became an important object of inquiry. The thought of Robert Kilwardby (in his *De ortu scientiarum* and his commentary on the *Priscianus minor*) offers a striking example of this trend during the first half of the century. The Aristotelian standard for a scientific discipline required that the knowledge in question be concerned with necessary facts proved by necessary premises. To make the study of language, in all of its irregularities and human particularities, fit this model, Kilwardby employed two arguments: first, that the notion of "science" was relative and that grammar could constitute an inferior but still valid form of scientific knowledge; and second, that the singular matters of grammar ultimately instantiate abstract, universal principles, that is, the essentials of grammatical function.[15] We also see these debates reflected in the various scientific classifications adopted by Vincent of Beauvais in the *Speculum doctrinale* (ca. 1260), where he incorporates some of the most current thought about the epistemological status of the language sciences, while also preserving much older models of scientific classification. The theoretical, philosophical interest in grammar was to culminate in the emergence of the approach known as modistic or speculative grammar in the last decades of the century, which entailed the study of semantics in terms of "modes" of signification and the changes of meaning brought about by grammatical features, reflecting an abstract extra-linguistic reality. The *modistae* sought to raise grammar to the status of a fully theoretical science which could explain the nature of language and its means of reflecting reality, whose explanatory structure is founded on universals and applicable to all languages. The *modistae* grounded their analysis of language in ontological and psychological principles, defining linguistic components and the rules of syntax in terms of the "mode of signifying" based on an ontological "mode of being" and a rational "mode of understanding."[16]

---

[14] Kneepkens, "*Ordo naturalis* and *ordo artificialis*," 81–2, and overview in Weijers, *Le maniement du savoir*, 131–9.

[15] Sirridge, "Robert Kilwardby as 'Scientific Grammarian.'"

[16] Rosier, *La parole comme acte*, 11; for greater detail see Rosier, *La grammaire spéculative des modistes*; J. Pinborg, "Speculative Grammar"; Covington, *Syntactic Theory in the High Middle Ages*, 19–21; *Grammatica speculativa of Thomas of Erfurt*, ed. Bursill-Hall, introduction.

The beginnings of the theoretical approaches that characterize university grammatical studies can already be seen in twelfth-century grammatical commentaries. Here too the authoritative textbooks are points of departure for philosophical speculation about the deep structure of language, semantics and syntax, and even the possibility of a universal grammar. William of Conches and Petrus Helias represent major turning points in the development of a *Sprachlogik*, a grammar that attended not just to describing grammatical forms but to speculating about their causes. By the late twelfth century there was a strong dialectical turn in grammatical thought, especially around the theoretical problem of syntax.[17] We see more evidence of the strong scientific interest in grammar in Alexander Neckam's insistence on grammar as a genuinely philosophical and logical subject. But twelfth-century commentators also preserved a robust interest in the literary and textual application of grammatical knowledge, quoting the classical *auctores* as examples of Latin usage. Petrus Helias uses the *auctores* liberally. William of Conches represents the study of syntax in terms of its value for literary analysis and composition: in his commentary on Priscian, he says that the purpose of the grammarian's exposition is to "reduce" artificial word order, as found in "metrical and prose authors," to natural order, and that the authors themselves must first learn grammatical science so that their word order will reflect "art" and not just chance.[18]

By contrast, the *auctores* play a diminished role in university grammatical writings in general, and are never mentioned among the speculative grammarians.[19] The break with earlier traditions was not abrupt: some authors continued to reiterate older outlooks. For example, a thirteenth-century prologue to a commentary on Priscian's *Institutiones* by a Master Arnoldus divides the extrinsic final cause (the purpose or goal) of grammar into two: that which is *propinqua* (immediate) is the exposition of the authors; that which is *remota* (ultimate) is the discipline of philosophy and the beatitude of the rational soul.[20] In his *De ortu scientiarum* Robert Kilwardby can still acknowledge that prose composition and poetics are subordinate branches of grammar, for which he cites the authority of Gundissalinus.[21] Of course there are contexts in which the *auctores* necessarily make an appearance, notably in commentaries on Donatus' *Barbarismus*, a text which makes liberal use of illustrative literary quotations, which the commentator must also reproduce and explain. Thus, for example, the commentary on the *Barbarismus* attributed to Kilwardby

[17] Fredborg, "Speculative Grammar"; Fredborg, "Universal Grammar According to Some Twelfth-Century Grammarians."

[18] Quoted from Paris BN MS, lat. 15130, f. 86, in Kneepkens, "*Ordo naturalis*," 64–5.

[19] See Biard, "Rapport de la Table ronde: les disciplines du trivium," 178 (discussant: I. Rosier).

[20] Kneepkens, "The Priscianic Tradition," 250. The Pseudo-Boethian *De disciplina scholarium*, probably composed in the 1230s, also recommends classical authors to students: ed. Weijers, 95–6.

[21] *De ortu scientiarum*, ed. Judy, § 491.

would have to deal with the literary quotations in Donatus' text. But despite such vestiges or reflections of the older tradition, university scholars were not primarily interested in appreciation or study of the classical authors. The distinctly literary orientation that we see at the end of the twelfth century, in the work of Ralph of Beauvais and his school, had no afterlife in the dominant university cultures of the thirteenth century.[22]

Traditional pedagogical grammar, including study of the authors, was certainly part of the larger environment of universities. In Paris, elementary and secondary grammar continued to be taught in the cathedral schools and the *petites écoles*, and by the early fourteenth century there was also a well-organized system of preparatory teaching for younger boys among the Parisian colleges.[23] In Oxford and later Cambridge, grammar schools established on the peripheries of the universities provided preparatory academic or pre-vocational instruction in Latin, and within the universities there were also faculties of grammar (in Oxford, overseen by the faculty of arts, and in Cambridge, under direct diocesan control) whose purpose was to produce licensed grammar masters.[24] Religious houses in the university milieux also came to serve this function.[25] Here it is important to recognize that the materials used in secondary Latin instruction and in university study could overlap, even to the extent of following similar approaches: the *Doctrinale*, which became a standard teaching text for secondary instruction and also penetrated into some university studies, is notable for its theoretical attention to syntax and its interest in the ontological foundations of linguistic form. The sophisticated *Admirantes* gloss on the *Doctrinale* is the product of a university milieu, and indeed has many passages almost identical with the commentary on the *Barbarismus* which has been attributed to Kilwardby.[26]

We must distinguish between what university scholars knew (for they would have read some of the *auctores* during their elementary and secondary training) and what they mention in their works, that is, what was considered important to them at the tertiary level for the purposes of theoretical study. It is what they mention that matters for the link between grammatical thought and literary culture, and this is a link that was weakened and ultimately severed by the logical cast of scholastic grammatical theory. Hence our volume does not attempt to represent the course of scholastic grammatical thought throughout the thirteenth century, because the developments in this field become part of the history of

---

[22] Kneepkens, "Priscianic Tradition," 250–1.

[23] See Gabriel, *Garlandia: Studies in the History of the Mediaeval University*, 97–124.

[24] Leader, *A History of the University of Cambridge*, 1:114–16; R. W. Hunt, "Oxford Grammar Masters in the Middle Ages."

[25] For example, on grammar instruction by the Benedictines in later medieval Oxford, see Camargo, "*Tria sunt.*"

[26] Rosier, "La grammaire dans le '*Guide de l'étudiant*,'" 256, 260.

logic, a "rational philosophy" branching off and away from the practice and theory of literary language. This does not mean that speculative grammar has no traceable impact on literary culture, but rather that its impact on literary culture is not *qua* grammar, but *qua* logic.[27]

But there are fascinating moments at which this emerging division between logical and literary concerns is registered, both from within and outside of the scholastic milieu. We have included two selections that address this from alternate perspectives, the commentary on the *Barbarismus* (after 1250?) which has been known under the name of Robert Kilwardby (now considered a doubtful attribution), and Henri d'Andeli's *Bataille des VII ars* (Battle of the Seven Arts) (ca. 1230). The commentary on the *Barbarismus* reflects the academic state of affairs that Henri d'Andeli criticized so severely. What did the *Barbarismus* offer to philosophical inquiry? Figures and tropes were a perfect test case for semantics and for violations of the natural rules of grammar that govern words. From the early twelfth century onwards there was a tradition of logical commentary on the semantics of figures of grammatical construction (deviations from the rules of syntax) and figures of speech or tropes; the latter served to demonstrate forms of transference of sense in logical terms. Commentaries on Aristotle's *Sophistical Refutations* also used tropes as examples of equivocation in meaning, that is, as a fallacy of speech.[28] On this plane the interests of grammar and logic were intertwined. Grammar is meant to provide a guide to correct expression so that logic can assess the truth content of the statement; but logic also provides the demonstrative method that is required for every science.[29] The analysis of deviation from canonical usage, and the situations that permit such deviation (for example, if a trope or figure of speech affords greater clarity than simple or direct expression) was a field in which grammatical-linguistic and logical enquiry intersected significantly.[30] Of course rhetorical theory also had a deep and continuous interest in the transfer of sense that a trope produces, and rhetorical analysis of tropes (as in commentaries on the fourth book of the *Rhetorica ad Herennium*) has much in common with the logical notion of the transference of sense from its proper meaning to another meaning, in a new context.[31]

---

[27] Speculative grammar was to have some role in reshaping some of the technical vocabulary of later medieval grammars, and its emphasis on the universality of Latin was to enable later efforts to consider vernacular grammars under the rubrics of Latin usage. See the introduction to Part 6, below.

[28] See Rosier-Catach, "*Prata rident*," 164–7.

[29] Ebbesen and Rosier-Catach, "Le *trivium* à la Faculté des arts," 115.   [30] Rosier, *La parole comme acte*, 35.

[31] Rosier, "*Prata rident*," 161, citing also Camargo, "A Twelfth-Century Treatise on *Dictamen* and Metaphor," 189; the treatise *Flores rhetorici* gives an explanation of metaphorical usage, the movement from a proper meaning to another meaning in a different context.

Henri d'Andeli's *Bataille des VII ars* gives us an outsider's perspective on the direction that grammatical study was taking in Paris. Its criticism of the intellectual currents of the academy is straightforward. But even though it hits with the blunt tool of satire, it is a remarkable document, an eyewitness record of the rift between the old grammatical curriculum, represented by the belletristic school of Orleans, and the new logical studies at Paris which were absorbing grammar into their orbit. In the *Bataille*, the "knights" Priscian and Donatus ride with the Orleanist army of Grammar against the Parisian army of Logic. Of course this only tells part of the story, since the works of Priscian and Donatus had also become the linguistic manuals for the logic curriculum, and thus were studied as closely as ever before; and indeed Henri acknowledges some of this crossover when he fingers the *Barbarismus* as a traitor to the cause of Grammar, owing to its newer value as a basis for logical study of language.[32] But the greater story that Henri seeks to tell is of the loss of the literary and (as he sees it) the communicative dimensions from grammatical logic, and the devaluing of literary studies in relation to the rising prestige of logic. That literary study has no role in a university arts curriculum focused on Aristotelian models of science is a given which Henri hardly needs to explain.

CICERONIAN AND ARISTOTELIAN RHETORIC

The extent of Ciceronian rhetorical teaching in the northern universities, and how, if at all, it was taught throughout the thirteenth century, remains a matter of debate. The statutes of the arts faculty at Paris from 1215 and 1255, and the Oxford arts statutes of 1268, offer at best ambiguous evidence which has been much studied and interpreted in both positive and negative lights. The statutes of 1215 mention "rhetorical [matters]" (*rhetoricas*) among those subjects which masters may lecture on during feast days, that is, what is not part of the regular lecture course: these are "[matters or books pertaining to] philosophers, rhetorical [matters], quadrivial [matters], the *Barbarismus*, the *Ethics* (if they wish), and the fourth book of the *Topics* [i.e. Boethius' *De topicis differentiis*]."[33] While the Paris regulations of 1255 give valuable details of the arts curriculum, they were imposed to ensure that masters did not curtail their lectures on certain important texts. They mention a rhetorical text only by way of exception: among the books of the Old Logic—Porphyry's *Isagoge*, Aristotle's *Categories* and *De interpretatione*, and the *Divisions* and *De topicis differentiis* of Boethius—only the fourth book of Boethius' *De topicis differentiis*, on rhetorical topics,

---

[32] For example, see the collection of grammatical sophisms from the second half of the thirteenth century edited by Grondeux and Rosier-Catach, *La Sophistria de Robertus Anglicus*; and see also Rosier, *La parole comme acte*, 316–19.

[33] Denifle and Chatelain, *Chartularium*, 1:78.

is exempted from regulation about adequate lecture time to be spent on it.[34] There is no clear-cut conclusion about the study of rhetoric to be drawn from the Paris statutes: in the words of John Ward, who has comprehensively studied the evidence for the teaching of rhetoric, we can infer only that "rhetoric was not a 'sensitive' lecturing subject: it was neither banned, nor 'required,' nor subject to graduation-oriented pressure and abbreviation."[35] The Oxford statutes of 1268, the earliest official accounts of that arts curriculum, are similarly exiguous. The statutes require students incepting to have heard all the books of the Old Logic twice, except for the books of Boethius, which they need have heard only once; and of these, the students are not required to have heard the fourth book of *De topicis differentiis*.[36]

The evidence beyond the statutes is also mixed. From the northern universities, there are no new commentaries on the Ciceronian works that might indicate continuity with the twelfth century in rhetorical study; while commentaries abound for grammatical and logical writings, rhetoric is a very small part of what is found in manuscripts.[37] This may be compared to what is found in Italy, where the late thirteenth century saw a significant upsurge of new glosses and commentaries on the *Rhetorica ad Herennium* (probably conditioned by dictaminal teaching), which continued through the fourteenth and fifteenth centuries.[38] In contrast, the northern schools yield a number of commentaries on Boethius' *De topicis differentiis*, where rhetoric is treated in a strongly dialectical guise.[39] Robert Kilwardby's *De ortu scientiarum* exemplifies some of the key features of the scholastic orientation. Boethius' *De topicis differentiis* provides the framework for Kilwardby's disciplinary explanation: rhetoric is inferior to and dependent on dialectic, because its topics are particular where dialectical topics are universal (§§ 473, 613); and in dialectic the judgment is contained in the art and the disputative process, but in rhetoric the judgment is provided by a third party (the judge who is persuaded or not), so the resolution lies outside the art (§§ 618, 619). Rhetoric lies at the low end of the curriculum, after the higher or more necessary studies of grammar, logic, and the speculative sciences (§§ 639–41). Rhetoric is valuable, however, because it supplies a knowledge of style and delivery to "civil ethics"; and it has a special role for helping students, because style and proper delivery make a teacher's lecture more accessible and enable the students to learn everything they are taught (§ 647).[40]

---

[34] Ibid., 1:278.

[35] Ward, "Rhetoric in the Faculty of Arts at the Universities of Paris and Oxford in the Middle Ages," 182.

[36] Gibson, ed., *Statuta antiqua*, 26.

[37] Ward, "Rhetoric in the Faculty of Arts at the Universities of Paris and Oxford," 206–12; and see the remarks of Ebbesen in Biard, "Rapport de la Table ronde: Les disciplines du trivium," 177.

[38] Ward, *Ciceronian Rhetoric*, 202–10.

[39] Fredborg, "The Scholastic Teaching of Rhetoric in the Middle Ages," 95–6, and n. 28.

[40] Kilwardby, *De ortu scientiarum*. See Fredborg, "Scholastic Teaching," 96–7.

On the other hand, some evidence for the study of rhetoric in the faculties of arts does emerge from various sources. The examination manual from about 1240, preserved in Barcelona MS Ripoll 109 and now known as the *Guide de l'étudiant*, treats rhetoric (and the *Ad Herennium*) briefly under *philosophia rationalis*, along with grammar and logic (to which it gives much greater attention).[41] Moreover, among the various instructional "introductions" to philosophy produced as review guides by Parisian masters in the middle of the century, the anonymous *Accessus philosophorum VII artium liberalium* (ca. 1230–1240) contains an extensive summary of the *Ad Herennium*, which its modern editor believes to be the fullest among any such expositions from the Parisian arts faculty.[42] Oxford sources also yield up some intriguing evidence. A group of epideictic orations from the late thirteenth and early fourteenth centuries, commending new arts graduates, led their modern editor, Osmund Lewry, to conclude that there was more rhetoric studied at Oxford than the statutory records about required subjects for lectures indicate. The speeches draw on a range of classical authors, including the *Ad Herennium* and the letters of Seneca for *sententiae*; one from the late thirteenth century even cites Aristotle's *Rhetoric*.[43] The range of classical citation, and more important, the very practice of composing formal epideictic speeches, may suggest that rhetorical study formed part of what Ward dubs an "option pool" of non-core subjects which could be recognized for their theoretical value (e.g. extrinsic comparisons of dialectic and rhetoric), but which could also find an outlet in such "applied" situations as public eloquence.[44] But whether we weigh the conflicting evidence in the most negative terms to conclude that traditional rhetorical study had no place in the curricula of the leading northern universities, or in more positive terms to envision the teaching of rhetorical theory as an option outside the highly regulated curricular core of logic,[45] it is clear that we will not find a renaissance of Ciceronian rhetoric in the centers of learning north of the Alps during the thirteenth century.

That great advance is rather to be found in the emergence of a vernacular Ciceronianism in the Italian culture of the 1260s. This event takes place outside of the academy, and seeks to unite the practical knowledge—what we might call the "market knowledge"—of the dictaminal teaching in the schools with a growing civic imperative to negotiate conflict in

---

[41] Lafleur and Carrier, eds., Le *"Guide de l'étudiant,"* 77–9. See also the detailed outline of the contents of the *Guide* in Lafleur and Carrier, eds., *L'enseignement de la philosophie*, xiv–xvii.

[42] Lafleur, ed., *Quatre introductions*, 237–44; and see Lafleur and Carrier, "Les *Accessus philosophorum*, le recueil *Primo queritur utrum philosophia* et l'origine parisienne du *"Guide de l'étudiant"* du ms. Ripoll 109," 595.

[43] Lewry, "Rhetoric at Paris and Oxford in the Mid-Thirteenth Century," 61. On epideictic oratory, see Lewry, "Four Graduation Speeches from Oxford Manuscripts."

[44] Ward, "Rhetoric in the Faculty of Arts at the Universities of Paris and Oxford," 175, 193–5.

[45] Ibid., 208.

public assemblies.[46] Brunetto sees Ciceronian rhetoric as relevant to any kind of vernacular writing. While he observes the traditional Ciceronian definition of rhetoric ("copious and consummate eloquence in public and private cases"),[47] he goes beyond to formulate a more comprehensive definition: a discourse that turns on a dispute (*tencione*). He derives this from Cicero's exposition of status theory, seeing in that a theoretical model that can apply to all forms of expression: written and oral; dictaminal, poetic, or political; private correspondence between friends and lovers; public correspondence about affairs of state. The radical originality of his program is underscored—paradoxically—by the archaic academic resources he must rely on: an early twelfth-century commentary from the school of William of Champeaux, as well as the commentary by Victorinus. In other words, he had no contemporary theoretical models to enlist in his approach to Cicero. The rise of a quasi-autonomous dictaminal rhetoric in Italy had effectively halted new developments in Ciceronian studies; one indication of this is Boncompagno da Signa's contemptuous dismissal of Cicero's relevance to the "new" Italian rhetoric. Brunetto's vernacularization represents the first wave of an Italian Ciceronian revival which would also be manifested in vigorous new interest in the *Rhetorica ad Herennium*.

But the greatest advance in the field of rhetoric occurs beyond the frontiers of Ciceronianism, and redraws the boundaries of rhetorical theory itself. This is the appearance of Aristotle's *Rhetoric* in the Latin West. There were a number of important stages preparatory to the definitive entry of Aristotle's *Rhetoric* in the late thirteenth century. Arab scholars had known the *Rhetoric* in an Arabic translation from as early as the eighth century. The Arab tradition of Aristotelian scholarship, with its important notion of an extended *Organon*, had made rhetoric, along with poetics, into a type of logic, focusing on its scientific method rather than its subject matter: its syllogistic method was the enthymeme, producing belief rather than certitude, and persuading and moving the mind of the hearer rather than offering demonstration. On this model, rhetoric was not simply a lesser or defective version of dialectic (as in Boethius' *De topicis differentiis*), but a legitimate science with its own method. In the twelfth century, as we have seen, Gundissalinus, Gerard of Cremona, and other Christian Latin scholars mediated Arabic Aristotelianism to the West through translations and synthetic compilations of Arab philosophy. Gundissalinus' treatise *De divisione philosophiae* was instrumental in purveying the scheme of the enlarged *Organon* to Western thinkers. We see the influence of the extended *Organon* reflected in various ways (and to varying degrees) during the thirteenth century, notably in Albertus Magnus' treatises on logic (1250–1255), and in Aquinas' classification of logic in the preface to his commentary on the *Posterior Analytics* (included in this volume).

---

[46] Cox, "Ciceronian Rhetoric in Italy, 1260–1350."   [47] See within, p. 758.

The notion of rhetoric as a kind of logic with a distinctive method of instructing and persuading whetted the appetite, or indeed created a need, for a text that could constitute a real "science" of rhetoric.[48]

Encounters with Arab scholarship had also begun to prepare the ground for the central Aristotelian idea that rhetoric should be linked with the field of ethics broadly defined, rather than limited to the specific matter of civil affairs. Robert Grosseteste (died 1253), in his treatise on the liberal arts, declares that the office of rhetoric is to use the topical methods of dialectic and produce arguments so that it may best fulfill its aim, which is to move the emotions—to excite or restrain, to arouse or to calm. He goes on to suggest that rhetorical ornament is the instrument of moral science (*moralis scientia*), because rhetoric moves desire and anger in the appropriate directions.[49] Roger Bacon, writing his *Moralis philosophia* (part 7 of his *Opus maius*) around 1267, similarly presents rhetoric in the service of moral teaching. The practical intellect, which is a more noble thing than the speculative intellect, needs a suitably forceful kind of teaching: it is rhetoric that can provide the strong suasion that will move the practical intellect to act on what is right. According to Bacon, Ciceronian theory is not sufficient to teach this ethical dimension of rhetoric, because it is too involved in forensic oratory.[50] In many respects, then, scholars were ready for the appearance of a true "science" of rhetoric.

Three different Latin translations of Aristotle's *Rhetoric* were produced in the thirteenth century. The translation of Hermannus Alemannus, from the Arabic version, was made in 1256. At the same time that he produced his translation of the *Rhetoric*, Hermannus also translated a commentary on the *Rhetoric* by Al-Farabi, known from its Latin title as the *Didascalia*, which reflects the nature of Arab theoretical interest in the logic and psychology of persuasion. Within the same period as Hermannus' translation, another translation of the *Rhetoric* appeared, this time directly from the Greek, the so-called Anonymous Vetus translation. Neither the translation by Hermannus nor the Anonymous Vetus version had significant circulation or audiences at the time of their composition. The third translation of the *Rhetoric* was executed a little before 1269 by William of Moerbeke (ca. 1215–ca. 1286), the Flemish Dominican who translated and revised much of the Aristotelian corpus.[51] The Moerbeke translation of the *Rhetoric* had a powerful and

---

[48] See Dahan, "L'entrée de la *Rhétorique* d'Aristote dans le monde latin entre 1240 et 1270," 66–80, for a brief survey of some of models of classification before and after the impact of Arab philosophy.

[49] Grosseteste, *De artibus liberalibus*, 2.1–5; 4.29–33. See Dahan, "L'entrée de la *Rhétorique*," 72.

[50] Bacon, *Moralis philosophia*, 251. See Marmo, "Suspicio," 164–5 for discussion and further references; and see Rosier-Catach, "Roger Bacon, Al-Farabi et Augustin."

[51] On the two translations from the Greek, see Schneider, *Die mittelalterlichen griechisch-lateinischen Übersetzungen der aristotelischen Rhetorik*. Both the Anonymous Vetus and the Moerbeke translations are edited by Schneider, *Aristoteles latinus* 31.1–2.

immediate impact and a very large circulation, surviving complete in 101 manuscripts and in three early modern printings.

The appearance of a close, authoritative translation of the *Rhetoric* from the Greek text was a significant event. Although the ground had been laid for the reception of Aristotle's work, understanding the text on its own terms required a shift in conceptual field. There was almost no scholarly tradition on Aristotle's treatment of rhetoric that could prepare students for the actual character of the text, embedded as it is in Athenian legal practice and political thought, as well as in a vast Greek literary culture (much of which is lost to us today as well). The distance between Aristotelian thought and Ciceronian-Boethian conceptions of rhetoric may not seem so very great to modern readers, who have the benefit of a relatively complete history of rhetorical practices from the Greek Sophists of the fifth century BC to Greek and Latin oratory of late antiquity, and who can therefore see how Roman rhetoric came to assimilate and absorb many of the elements of Greek rhetorical culture. To students in the thirteenth century, however, Aristotle's *Rhetoric* would have made a surprising contrast with the familiar Roman authors. Aristotle's text is less practical and prescriptive than the *De inventione* and *Rhetorica ad Herennium*; it is more a theoretical and descriptive pronouncement on the state of the art, its method, disciplinary relations, and social functions. Moreover, little in the rather technical Ciceronian and Boethian rhetorics would have prepared medieval readers for Aristotle's emphasis on the cognitive, ethical, and fluid psychological aspects of rhetoric (although these ideas had been foreshadowed in Arab scholarship). Indeed, Aristotle's *Rhetoric* found a context for reception that was very different from that of the Ciceronian-Boethian rhetorical tradition. This can be seen from the fact that the *Rhetoric* in William of Moerbeke's translation circulated in manuscript mainly with Aristotle's *Ethics* and *Politics*.[52] Despite the importance accorded to Aristotle's opening gambit ("Rhetoric is a counterpart of dialectic"), it seems that the *Rhetoric* was contextualized as a work that pertained to ethics. The placing of rhetoric under logic may have claimed some attention at a theoretical level, but it did not reflect the actual kind of interest that drew students and scholars to Aristotle's text.[53]

Almost as soon as the Moerbeke translation was available, the first and most influential commentary on the *Rhetoric* appeared: Giles of Rome's vast exposition (ca. 1272), which sought to make the work understandable in terms of established frameworks of Aristotelian science, especially logic and the dialectical method on the one hand, and ethics and politics on the other hand. Aristotle's text shifted and broadened the definition of rhetoric

---

[52] See Murphy, *Rhetoric in the Middle Ages*, 100, and for further manuscript evidence, Briggs, "Aristotle's *Rhetoric*."

[53] Marmo, "*Suspicio*," 170 and n. 97.

to encompass its relation to human affairs, ethics, the emotions, and the psychology of persuasion. Giles' commentary was pivotal in articulating this new perception of rhetoric. Giles' commentary, and his own *De regimine principum* (Regimen [Guide] for Princes), which derived much of its thought from the *Rhetoric*, also helped to establish a new link between rhetoric and literary culture, as mediums designed for the ethical instruction and persuasion of a broad public. Moreover, Giles drew from the tradition of Arab thought about the *Rhetoric*, which he knew mainly through the *Didascalia* of Al-Farabi (as translated by Hermannus Alemannus). Thus Giles brought the earliest phases of the text's medieval reception back into play. The force of the *Didascalia,* now re-established as an authoritative source in its own right, was still being felt in fourteenth-century commentaries on the *Rhetoric*. The Parisian master Jean of Jandun (d. 1328) depended on it extensively in his *Quaestiones* on Aristotle's *Rhetoric*, and Jean Buridan echoes some of its themes in his *Quaestiones* on the *Rhetoric* (probably 1350s).[54]

It is clear that Aristotle's *Rhetoric* penetrated university studies and milieus to various extents. It was a new addition to the Aristotelian corpus, it was widely copied, and a number of well-known as well as anonymous masters devoted commentaries to it. The statutes of the Oxford arts faculty of 1431 mention the *Rhetoric* along with the *Ad Herennium*, book 4 of Boethius' *De topicis differentiis*, Ovid's *Metamorphoses*, and Virgil's poetry as readings for a course of study in rhetoric.[55] However little or much the *Rhetoric* constituted part of a course of study in any of the universities before the early modern period, its effects came to be felt through its association with ethics and politics, and through the scope that it gave to the role of the emotions in a theory of discourse.

---

[54] For studies and further references, see Beltran, "Les *Questions* sur la *Rhétorique* d'Aristote de Jean de Jandun"; Biard, "Science et rhétorique dans les *Questions sur la rhétorique* de Jean Buridan"; Fredborg, "Buridan's *Questiones super Rhetoricam Aristotelis*"; Marmo, "Carattere dell'oratore et recitazione nel commento di Giovanni di Jandun al terzo libro della Retorica."

[55] Gibson, ed., *Statuta antiqua*, 234. The statute has been subjected to many interpretations: see Ward, "Rhetoric in the Faculty of Arts," 183–6 for summary and references; the most skeptical view of the relation between the statute and actual teaching is that of Fletcher, "Developments in the Faculty of Arts 1370–1520," 323–4.

GUIDO FABA, PREFACE TO THE *ROTA NOVA*, CA. 1225

INTRODUCTION

About the year 1225, Guido Faba (ca. 1190–ca. 1245), master of rhetoric and *dictamen* at Bologna, composed a dictaminal treatise, the *Rota nova* (New Wheel), for which he wrote a preface describing his life and especially his academic and professional career up to that point. This work consists of the preface and two doctrinal sections, *Ala prima* (First Wing), which is practical advice on the faults to be avoided in letter-writing, and *Ala secunda de regulis* (Second Wing concerning Rules), which is a more general treatise of *dictamen*. This second part briefly covers the definitions of *dictamen* and the letter, the salutation and the essential parts of a letter (according to Guido these are the exordium, *narratio*, and petition), punctuation (clauses), prose rhythm (the *cursus*), and syllabification. It also includes a string of examples of salutations, and ends with some general advice about signaling the divisions between parts of the letter and about brevity. The *Rota nova* and its preface survive together in only two manuscripts, both of the thirteenth century: Oxford, New College MS 255, in which the text is accompanied by three miniatures illustrating some of the verbal images in the preface and the treatise, and which also contains collections of model letters by Guido that elaborate the teaching of the *Rota nova* treatise; and Paris BN MS 7420B.[1]

The *Rota nova* would probably have represented a version of Guido's courses at Bologna, an early record of his teaching. Some years later, about 1229, he produced a greatly expanded version of his teaching, the *Summa dictaminis*, which had a wide and influential circulation, surviving in whole or in part in over ninety manuscripts.[2] The later

---

[1] There are two further manuscripts containing parts of the *Rota nova*. See Pini, "La tradizione manoscritta," 313–14. See also Campbell, "The Perfection of *Ars Dictaminis* in Guido Faba," who regards the *Rota nova* and supporting texts in the New College Oxford manuscript as one extended work. The texts of New College Oxford MS 255 have now been edited by Campbell and Pini, *Magistri Guidonis Fabe Rota nova*; the editors treat the entire contents as parts of the *Rota nova*. The contents are also described in Denholm-Young, "The Cursus in England," 94–5.

[2] *Guidonis Fabe Summa dictaminis*, ed. Gaudenzi. The manuscripts are listed in Pini, "La tradizione manoscritta," 315–40.

Summa dictaminis (Summa of Dictaminal Precepts) has been called "the definitive statement of the Bolognese school"; it found its way into libraries across late medieval Europe.[3] The doctrinal matter of the *Rota nova* coincides largely with that of the *Summa dictaminis*, and the overlap is often word for word. But the *Summa* includes more doctrinal theory about the parts of the letter, prose style, and the *cursus*, as well as stylistic questions of grammar, a list of rhetorical colors, a list of biblical proverbs that can be used as *sententiae* in the exordium, a set of exercises, and a quick foray into the *ars notaria*, that is, the method of drawing up legal documents. Clearly the doctrinal matter of the *Rota nova* was a preliminary attempt to bring together some essential practical teachings of the sort that Guido's lectures would develop at greater length, and that he was to expound more comprehensively in the *Summa dictaminis*, which achieved such international success. For the *Summa dictaminis* he abandoned the autobiographical preface of the *Rota nova* and gave an impersonal, if equally florid and bombastic, advertisement for his teaching.[4]

In his preface to the *Rota nova*, Guido establishes a sharp distinction between the narrow expertise of the notarial profession and the broad literary training of *dictamen* or the art of prose writing, which could include more than the *ars dictaminis*. The study entailed under the broad definition of *dictamen* might include not only prose composition and rhetorical theory, but the classical *auctores*, read as exemplars of style, as in the grammatical curriculum.[5] But alongside of this, the more narrowly focused *ars dictaminis*, which had attained the status of a quasi-autonomous discipline, served the epistolary needs of clerks, scribes, jurists, and notaries. Guido boasts of his own education in *litterae*, that is, a broad-based grammatical study, and decries what he sees as the professional narrowness and autonomy of *dictamen* understood solely in terms of the specialized concerns of the *ars dictaminis*. In view of this, he claims to have accomplished something remarkable (although such boasts of unparalleled originality are common among the Bolognese *dictatores*): he has reunited Latin eloquence with the "purple science of *dictamen*," that is, he has suffused the study of the dictaminal art with a traditional culture of humane letters.[6] Thus his "renovation" of the "crumbling buildings" of Saint Michael's chapel is an allegorical expression for his overhauling of the *curriculum* used in the grammar school that was held in Saint Michael's chapel. Whether his students there were from the notarial

---

[3] Faulhaber, "The *Summa dictaminis* of Guido Faba," 87, and see 86n.

[4] See Copeland, "Medieval Intellectual Biography: the Case of Guido Faba."

[5] Ward, "Rhetorical Theory and the Rise and Decline of Dictamen in the Middle Ages and Early Renaissance."

[6] That Guido's accomplishment is not so unparalleled in dictaminal teaching of the same period is witnessed, for example, in Bene da Firenze's *Candelabrum* (ca. 1220–6), which covers all five of the parts of classical rhetoric. See Camargo, *Ars dictaminis*, 19.

profession or more widely representative cannot be known.[7] But the range of teaching that could be brought under such a dictaminal curriculum may be glimpsed from the contents of the later *Summa dictaminis,* which has a more expansive reach than the briefer *Rota nova.*

Through Guido's own literary example in the preface to the *Rota nova,* students will see how Latin eloquence indeed suffuses the dictaminal art. The prologue is a tour de force of veiled meaning and highly ornamented style. Guido represents it as a "holy letter," a missive proclaiming the divine authority that backs his rhetorical mission. It shares this "cosmic tenor" with other public and ecclesiastical documents such as proclamations and papal bulls that were also directed to all Christian people, and that were composed according to the same rules for dictaminal eloquence that Guido's rhetorical treatise supplies.[8] Some of the allegories depend upon contemporary knowledge, and we owe the decoding of these mysteries to the remarkable detective work of Ernst Kantorowicz. Guido tells us that he abandoned his literary studies to descend to the "blacksmith's art." "Blacksmith's workshops" or "smithies" was slang in Bologna for the lawcourts: Guido's progress from studying dictaminal rhetoric to learning the law would have been a typical career path for an able student. But Guido develops the "similitude" of the smithy to full allegorical dimensions with his details about injuries that he sustained from pieces of burning metal that flew off the forge—injuries that left him lame, nearly blind, and nearly mute. The allegory opens into hagiography with the representation of these "injuries" as "miracles" sent to recall him to his proper vocations of literary study and teaching. His turn to the notarial profession, another very common career path for any student adept at both law and rhetoric, is also allegorized as being handed to the "solace of the tanners"— that is, going into the parchment business. Finally, his revitalization of a grammar school curriculum is presented as elevation to priestly office in the chapel of Saint Michael.

In addition to the *Summa dictaminis,* Guido's other major works include the *Dictamina rhetorica,* which is an important collection of model letters that often circulated with the *Summa dictaminis* or in collections of Guido's works; collections of *exordia,* including two, the *Summa de vitiis et virtutibus* (*exordia* organized around the vices and virtues) and the *Gemma purpurea,* which incorporate Italian vernacular translations of the Latin models; and two collections of model speeches, the *Arenge* and the *Parlamenta et Epistole,* the latter of which was designed both for letters and speeches, and was written in both Latin and Italian.[9]

---

[7] Ward "Rhetorical Theory and the Rise and Decline of Dictamen in the Middle Ages and Early Renaissance," 193.

[8] Kantorowicz, "An 'Autobiography' of Guido Faba," 262; Saiani, "La figura di Guido Faba nel prologo."

[9] A. Gaudenzi, "Sulla cronologia delle opere dei dettatori bolognesi da Boncompagno a Bene di Lucca," *Bullettino dell'Instituto Storico Italiano* 14 (1895): 85–161. The *Dictamina rhetorica* were edited by Gaudenzi, *Il propugnatore* n.s. 5 (1892), part 1: 86–129, part 2: 58–109. For editions and partial editions of Guido's other works, see the entries in Pini, "La tradizione manoscritta."

Translated from the text (based on Oxford, New College MS 255) in Kantorowicz, "An 'Autobiography' of Guido Faba," appendix, by permission of the publishers.

HERE BEGINS THE *ROTA NOVA* OF MASTER GUIDO FABA
[PROLOGUE]

Let the heavens rejoice and the earth exult, let the sea be moved and the fullness thereof,[10] and let all rational creatures glory, because the strength of God is affirmed and the divine magnificence reveals itself in commanding that the present day, on which this holy letter is written, be cherished in venerable memory by Christian people.[11] Watching over Latin eloquence, which was abandoned by the purple science of *dictamen*, the Celestial Piety, in her holy royal chamber on high, mercifully agreed to listen to the prayers of her suppliant servants. Just as she made Saint Peter her keeper of the keys, conferring upon him the power to bind and unbind,[12] so she also wanted to elevate the city of Bologna (which truly should be called *bona omnia* ["good in all things"][13]) in the profession of Rhetoric, just as in other fields it had undertaken the foundation. And thus it was the will of the divine council on high that Bologna be mother and mistress of the sciences on earth, from which, as from a summit or fountainhead, every single living being receives light and teaching, nor will any power be able to deprive it of dignity so conferred upon it from Heaven by divine auspices until the end of time. This privilege was confirmed by the signatures of the angels, and the whole army of the celestial host consented to it. Let masters and students transfer—if they can—to pursue studies someplace else, knowing that there they won't be able to teach or be taught, but will go astray like sheep unless they return to the sheepfold, trying to kick against the goad of the Lord, which is hard when they presume to devalue the gifts of the Holy Spirit.[14] Let the whole world be silent, and let Tullian skill and the

---

[10] Psalm 95:11.

[11] In Oxford, New College MS 255 (fol. 7r) there is a round miniature in the middle of the text, among the opening words "Letenti celi et exultet terra," depicting the sun, moon, and stars in a blue firmament, giving visual expression to the cosmic significance of Guido's "holy letter."

[12] See Kantorowicz, "An Autobiography," 263 note: "The power of binding and loosing (Matthew 16:19) refers, in [Guido's] *Gemma purpurea*, to Guido himself, not to Bologna."

[13] The pun *Bononia-bona omnia* was commonplace. See Kantorowicz, "An Autobiography," 263n.

[14] Acts 9:5; 26:14. The reference to students transferring their studies has a historical basis: in 1225–6, the emperor Frederick II attempted to close down the University of Bologna (as part of a general ban on Bologna) and invited students and masters to relocate to the new university at Naples; but the citizens of Bologna resisted the imperial order. See Kantorowicz, "An Autobiography," 264. See also Saiani, "La figura di Guido Faba nel prologo," 495–500, which considers Guido's prologue as a direct response to Frederick's order.

eloquence of Cicero speak,[15] and let the queen of the south come from the ends of the earth to hear the wisdom of Solomon[16] who, filled with manifold strength though he bears the beautiful image of a man,[17] speaks words so mellifluous and decorous that they exceed the beauty and splendor of gems, words adorned with pure gold and lovely flowers. Of this man it is rightly said and sung that even in his mother's womb the Lord beautified and filled him with the dew of sweetness,[18] desiring that he take precedence in mastery of prose style over the sons of men and give profit to them. Therefore Bologna, happy and beautiful creation beyond measure, lofty in your merit and virtue, may you indeed rejoice, and with you may all your citizens sing praises to the heavens, because from you was born this man,[19] who dispels the ignorance of the ancients and modern confusion, and cleanses both with his letters.

This Guido, so named from the cradle, acquired the name Faba [the Bean] during his childhood from the effect of the thing.[20] The malice of the adversary of old began to envy Guido's future wisdom and the service he would perform for humanity, to such an extent that Guido had to abandon his literary studies [*litterae*] in which he had achieved great proficiency, and descend to learning, in addition, the blacksmith's art.[21] In this he had advanced for two years when he was recalled by three miracles from God. First, a piece of raw iron, burning hot from the forge, escaped and, by order of the Thunderer, sprang up and flew about, and turning suddenly it landed on the ground and with this it splattered and wounded his bare foot, and so burnt it that from then on he was lame. Next, when a

---

[15] Guido separates "Tullius" from "Cicero" and bestows different attributes on each name; this is a figure of amplification, a form of *distributio*.

[16] Matthew 12:42.   [17] Isaiah 44:13.

[18] Cf. Luke 1:15: *et Spiritu sancto replebitur adhuc ex utero matris suae.*

[19] Cf. Micha 5:2; Matthew 2:6; *homo ille* refers to Guido Faba himself. See Kantorowicz, "An Autobiography," 265.

[20] *Ab effectu rei*: a specific form of etymology, "from the effect of the thing," i.e. the thing denoted by the word, e.g. *lapis* from the fact that a stone "hurts the foot" (*a laedendo pedem*, cf. Isidore, *Etymologiae* 16.3.1). For this type, see e.g. Augustine, *De dialectica* 6 (on *puteus* "well," and *potatio* "drinking"), Isidore, *Etymologiae* 16.7.12 (*causa nominis de effectu*), and Aquinas, *Quaestiones disputatae de veritate* 4.1 ad 8 (*nomen . . . imponi . . . ex parte rei . . . sicut lapis imponitur ab effectu*) (*Opera omnia*, 22.1 [Rome: Leonine Edition, 1970]: 121). Kantorowicz, "An Autobiography," 265–6, suspects a link with the expression *dicere fabas* (to engage in jokes and trifles, cf. Du Cange, *Glossarium*, 3:102), suggesting that he gained his nickname because of the renown of his antics. A further possibility, taking *ab effectu rei* as implying the appearance or size of a bean, is offered by Saiani, who translates: "da ragazzo per il suo aspetto ricevette il soprannome di Fava" ("La figura di Guido Faba," 513). One could also tentatively think of actual beans and their gastric effects (e.g. Cicero, *De divinatione* 1.62), referred to here in the most discretely academic (hence humorous) way possible. For nicknames deriving from such considerations, see V. Allen, *On Farting: Language and Laughter in the Middle Ages* (New York: Palgrave, 2007), 125–9 and 168–77 (etymologies and names relating to expressions for flatulence).

[21] "Blacksmiths' workshops" (*fabriles officinae*) was slang for the law schools of Bologna. Guido's description of descending to study the "blacksmith's art" seems to be a figure of speech for his turn from literary studies (*litterae*) to the professional schools of law. Kantorowicz, "An Autobiography," 267–8; Saiani, "La figura di Guido Faba," 476n.

second time he was heating the same piece of iron and was striking it over an anvil with a heavy hammer, a burning scale [*squama*] from it entered the pupil of his eye,[22] which damaged the eyesight of this overworked laborer. And why linger over our words? The third injury he suffered from that burning coal was a wound to his tongue. And so now afflicted with threefold suffering, he recognized the revelation of a mystery, and recovering himself and weeping, he humbly protested before all that with these three signs the Holy Trinity was calling him back from this labor.[23] Thus scourged and sorry, he swiftly returned to his former studies which he had wrongly put aside, upon which the masters as well as the students of Bologna rejoiced, saying: "The sheep who was lost is found, and he who was dead is come to life again."[24]

Now while he studied painstakingly day and night, his body grew thin. Skin and bones took counsel, and in league with anxiety of spirit and a macerated mind, decided together that for the sake of gaining some flesh he should leave the study of letters and be handed over to the solace of the tanners;[25] that is, he escaped a known evil through dog filth, by which the skins are prepared—which afterwards are stretched by the teeth—and through puncturing of the skins with an awl. So at length turning to the art of the notary, he deserved to be called "master of masters" in either court.[26] But because he was oppressed in no small way by the constrictions of such work, as much on account of fatigue as of the enmities he accumulated because he would not bend to right or to left, he turned to refuge with God, dwelling for two years as the scribe of the bishop of Bologna.

But because the courts provide not for the salvation of souls, but rather for worldly comforts, and not wanting to dwell in carnal deceits, squabbles, and lies, he recalled his

---

[22] Cf. Acts 9:18: *ceciderunt ab oculis eius tamquam squamae.*

[23] The three wounds are perhaps inversions of Christ's healing miracles on the Sea of Galilee. the implication would be that Rhetoric (into whose embrace Guido was recalled) can also heal the lame, blind and dumb. See Kantorowicz, "An Autobiography," 269.

[24] Cf. Luke 15:24.

[25] Kantorowicz finds a parallel image in a manual of chess written by Jacopo da Cessole around the year 1300, in which all people involved in working with skins (*qui circa pellem operantur*), from wool-weavers and tailors to barbers, skinners, curriers, and tanners, as well as notaries, are grouped together. "Because the notaries concerned themselves with parchment, they were placed among the tanners and all the others whose occupation was the preparing of skins." In Guido's text, being handed over to the "solace of the tanners" indicates that he went to work as a notary (as he goes on to say), dealing in the material as well as compositional aspects of the art, from preparing the parchment skin with "dog filth," stretching it with the teeth, and puncturing it with an awl, to writing on its surface. Moving from the law courts to the notarial profession was standard practice. See Kantorowicz, "An Autobiography," 270–1.

[26] I.e. both civil and canon law, because his notarial skills gave him proficiency in either. Kantorowicz, "An Autobiography," 271 and note.

pristine freedom, and as it pleased the Creator of all things, took on the care of the Chapel of Saint Michael, where he was happily promoted to sacerdotal office.[27] There he renovated the church itself along with the crumbling houses, and having borne with patience the many persecutions and scandals of the neighbors whose faction the clerics of the city covertly supported,[28] he had a new temple constructed in honor of the Archangel Michael by whose precepts and rules he has written this account. It deserves to be called "The New Wheel," because, just as the status of anyone goes through many changes with the advent of something new, so through the aforesaid mutation Guido ascended from a lower to a higher position. And sitting enthroned in the seat of the wheel, he holds in his right hand two wings, which he received from the archangel.[29] In one of these wings the vices of all letter writing are cut away, and in the other wing are contained the rules which constitute the knowledge of *dictamen* and of the ornate style,[30] lest without these wings (for neither can birds fly without feathers) certain ones make haste to fly; for those who hurry towards what is forbidden fall to the ground helplessly.

[27] The question of whether Guido actually became a priest is difficult to determine. He often calls himself *capellanus* or *sacerdos* of St. Michael's, but also calls himself "Master Guido of St. Michael's of Bologna." This may be a figurative office. In Bologna, classes might be held in chapels or churches. That teaching of *dictamen* was conducted in available rather than purpose-built spaces is suggested by Boncompagno da Signa, whose *Rhetorica novissima* describes an ideal "house of scholarly instruction," only to remark that such a dedicated structure does not yet exist; see Sutter, *Aus Leben und Schriften des Magisters Boncompagno*, 40 and note. Documents indicate that several "chapels of St. Michael" in Bologna were connected with the study of grammar and rhetoric. The "care of the Chapel of St. Michael" may thus be understood in terms of a *studium* or house of study under the auspices of the Chapel; the name of the chapel would stand for the "throne" or professorship of grammar and *dictamen* that he mentions at the end of the prologue; and the "sacerdotal office" could therefore be understood in terms of scholarly duty rather than formal ordination as a priest. See Kantorowicz, "An Autobiography," 272–4.

[28] By "renovating the church itself along with the crumbling houses" we may understand that Guido reorganized a (supposedly) neglected study of *dictamen* or rhetorical study, and by "the many persecutions and scandals," that he found himself in competition with other masters. See Kantorowicz, "An Autobiography," 274.

[29] In Oxford, New College MS 255 (fol. 1r), the apotheosis of Guido as *magister* is depicted in a detailed image. It shows a wheel, with a master (Guido himself) enthroned at the top; around the circumference of the wheel are three figures, one ascending, one falling, and one cast off below the wheel. From the other side of the image frame, an angel is bringing the *magister* a wing, because this picture stands at the head of the section *Ala prima* ("First wing"), with which the faults of letter writing will be cut away. (Because of early misbinding, the foliation of the manuscript is out of sequence with the order of the text. The preface of the *Rota nova* is bound in as fol. 7, while *Ala prima*, which should follow the preface, is at fol. 1r.)

[30] In New College MS 255 (fol. 2v), the initial "P" of the section *Ala secunda* (beginning *Properate sicientes ad fontem* "Make haste, you who thirst, to the fountain") is decorated with a complex image showing Guido *magister* holding a wing (in his left hand, over his right shoulder), representing the "Second wing, concerning rules." With his other hand the *magister* points to a fountain (i.e. the fountain of eloquence, Guido's treatise) from which two youths are drinking out of large chalices.

HENRI D'ANDELI, *BATAILLE DES VII ARS*, CA. 1230

INTRODUCTION

Henri d'Andeli's *Bataille des VII ars* (Battle of the Seven Arts) was most likely composed around 1230; its language is the French of the Isle de France.[1] The poem presents grammatical study as it was known at the school of Orleans, at its height in the twelfth century and lasting for some decades into the thirteenth century. The cathedral school of Orleans was famous for what we would call *belles lettres*: grammar as both language and literature, rhetoric, and an ornate, literary approach to the *ars dictaminis*. Long before its formal recognition as a university in 1306, the school of Orleans was renowned for its classical commentators, teachers of *dictamen*, and Latin poets, among them Hugh Primas. It was a stronghold of the classical literary tradition, and in Rashdall's words, it "seems to have escaped almost wholly the dialectical frenzy of the age: here, and here almost alone after the decline of Chartres, there lingered down to at least the middle of the thirteenth century the classical traditions of the age of Bernard [of Chartres] and John of Salisbury."[2] Richard Rouse has made a strong case for Orleans as the site at which two of the most influential classical *florilegia*, the *Florilegium angelicum* (a dictaminal collection) and the *Florilegium gallicum*, were compiled during the twelfth century. This provides new grounds to connect the medieval *topos* of Orleans as a center of classical studies with the witness of a textual tradition.[3]

Comparisons between Orleans as a bellettristic stronghold and Paris as a center of logical study became commonplaces early on.[4] Writing in the last quarter of the twelfth century, Matthew of Vendôme can claim that "Paris boasts logic, Orleans the *auctores*."[5]

---

[1] See *Les Dits d'Henri d'Andeli*, ed. Corbellari, 19, 32.

[2] *The Universities of Europe in the Middle Ages*, 2: 141–2.

[3] Rouse, "Florilegia and Latin Classical Authors in Twelfth- and Thirteenth-Century Orléans." Rouse notes that no medieval booklist or catalogue for any of the libraries of twelfth-century Orleans survives: "Orléans's books were dispersed without trace" (132). This research is an important contribution to the reconstruction of the role of Orleans in the transmission and dissemination of classical texts.

[4] Many of these contemporary testimonies are collected in *Arnulfi Aurelianensis: Glosule super Lucanum*, ed. Marti, xv–xvii.

[5] *Epistulae*, Prologue, lines 33–4, ed. Munari, *Mathei Vindocinensis Opera*, 2:76.

Geoffrey of Vinsauf carries forward the distinction in his *Poetria nova*: "In the area of disease, Salerno cures the sick with healing power; in legal cases, Bologna arms the defenceless with laws; in the arts, Paris dispenses the bread with which she feeds the strong. Orleans educates infants in the cradle with the milk of authors."[6] John of Garland also apostrophized Orleans as a bastion of classicism: "Aid me, illustrious poets, whom golden renown matches with gold, you whom the city of Orleans attracts from all the regions of the world, you, the glory of the fountain of Hippocrene. God has chosen you to sustain the edifice of eloquence shaken to its very foundation; for the Latin language is decaying, the green fields of the authors are withering, and the jealous blast of Boreas has blighted the flowery meadows."[7]

In the *Bataille des VII ars*, the grammatical tradition of Orleans is set against the dominance of Aristotelian logical studies at the University of Paris, and the poem takes an almost elegiac perspective on the decline of *belles lettres* in the face of the leviathan of Paris and its narrowly specialized arts faculty. The poem is also pitiless in its scorn for what it sees as a kind of "technocracy" of logic that produces highly trained students who have not mastered the groundwork of grammar, the function of speaking correctly. Towards the end of the poem, a possible truce between the forces of Grammar and Logic ends in failure when Logic's messenger, one of her pupils, cannot relay her message of peace because he has not learned to express himself clearly and to the point (372–97). In his satirical polemic against what he views as a technocratic distortion of learning, Henri d'Andeli revisits and distills themes that were sounded by John of Salisbury some seventy years earlier, although the world of learning represented in Henri's poem is far more polarized than even John might have imagined. Yet history seems to have provided greater continuity for the transmission of the Orleanist classical curriculum than Henri's poem envisages. Even though Orleans did not survive as a center of bellettristic study, the *Florilegium angelicum* and *Florilegium gallicum* were taken up and absorbed by mendicant and monastic communities during the thirteenth century and assimilated in their preaching compendia. Vincent of Beauvais uses the *Florilegium gallicum* in his widely used *Speculum historiale*, thus ensuring the survival of this classical lore among clerical and ultimately lay audiences.[8]

Orleans' other great distinction had been as a center for the study of civil and canon law, especially as an alternative to Paris during the first decades of the thirteenth century, and by

[6] Trans. Gallo, *The Poetria Nova and its Sources*, 69. "Arts" here is best taken to signify the work of the arts faculty of Paris, and thus connotes the logical study that was its primary interest.

[7] *L'Ars lectoria ecclesie de Jean de Garlande*, ed. Marguin-Hamon, lines 1516–23. Translation quoted from Henri d'Andeli, *Battle of the Seven Arts*, trans. Paetow, 18. John goes on to praise Paris as nurturer of philosophy and theology, but unlike his contemporary Henri d'Andeli, he does not set Paris against Orleans.

[8] Rouse, "Florilegia and Latin Classical Authors," 156–60.

mid-century its fame as a school of *belles lettres* was to dwindle in favor of its preeminence in law.[9] Yet Henri d'Andeli seems not to have foreseen this shift in its reputation: at the close of the poem, he predicts that the study of grammar at Orleans will rise again in thirty years. He makes no reference to the importance of, or legal context for, the study of dictaminal rhetoric at Orleans. Rather, he reserves his distaste for the "Lombard" notaries from northern Italian regions who came to Paris during the thirteenth century and prospered there by drawing up legal documents (lines 68–74). As we have seen in the example of Guido Faba's autobiographical preface to his *Rota nova*, the *ars dictaminis*, which was initially conceived as a branch of rhetoric, also became a specialized professional study of notarial rhetoric, at some points quite distinct from the broader study of rhetoric. It is the notaries' narrow but lucrative professional competence that Henri links, metonymically, with the *ars rhetorica*, presenting the "Lombard knights" as the army of a personified Rhetoric. They are presented here as lying, deceiving lawyers whose chicanery robs innocent people of their inheritances; but this view is also informed by the long tradition that sees rhetoric in general, and especially the rhetoric of the law courts, as an art of deception.

The *Bataille* is a virtual encyclopedia of classical and classicizing literary culture as it would have been known to an early-thirteenth-century clerk. But unlike Alexander Neckam's list of authors compiled in the early thirteenth century, or Hugh of Trimberg's *Registrum multorum auctorum* written a few years after the *Bataille*, Henri d'Andeli presents grammatical poetic study as advanced fare, as a serious form of intellectual activity which is being edged out by the hard professionalism of the Parisian dialecticians. His array of authors does not include examples of prose writers; by contrast, in Neckam's list the prose authors generally constitute a more sophisticated stage of Latin literary study, and Hugh of Trimberg passes over the prose writers because the poets comprise the preferred matter of elementary grammar-school instruction. But Henri d'Andeli's poem suggests that at Orleans the poetic tradition was elevated to the highest and most prestigious level of study.

Translation reprinted from *The Battle of the Seven Arts*, ed. and trans. Paetow, by permission.

THE BATTLE OF THE SEVEN ARTS

Paris and Orleans are at odds.
It is a great loss and a great sorrow

---

[9] Feenstra, "L'école de droit d'Orléans au treizième siècle et son rayonnement dans l'Europe médiévale"; Guenée, *Bibliographie de l'histoire des universités françaises*, 296.

That the two do not agree.
Do you know the reason for the discord?
5   It is because they differ about learning;
For Logic, who is always wrangling,
Calls the authors authorlings[10]
And the students of Orleans mere grammar-boys.
Each, she says, is well worth four Homers,
10   For they drink huge bumpers
And are so skillful at versifying
That about a single leaf of a fig-tree
They will compose you fifty verses.
But they retort that verily
15   They call Dialectic,
In evil spite, a cock-a-doodle-doo.[11]
As for those of Paris, the clerks of Plato,[12]
They do not think them worth a button.
However, Logic has the students,
20   Whereas Grammar is reduced in numbers.
Grammar is much wrought up;
And has raised her banner
Outside of Orleans, in the midst of the grain-fields;
There she assembled her army.[13]
25   Homer and old Claudian,
Donatus, Persius, Priscian,

---

[10] "Claime les autors autorians": the "autors" must be taken to refer to the *auctores* of the grammar curriculum, for which Orleans was famous, and for which the personified Logic of Paris expresses contempt.

[11] According to Paetow, *quiqueliquique* is a derisive term of uncertain meaning, perhaps an imitative word to designate the crowing of a cock, like the modern Spanish word *quiquiriqui*. Here it may suggest the loquaciousness or pomposity of the logicians.

[12] "Clerks of Plato" implies the Parisians' allegiance to philosophy or logic in general, not curricular study of Plato's works. See Paetow's note, 38; and cf. John of Garland's invocation of Plato along with Aristotle and Galen to characterize Parisian scholarship: *Ars lectoria ecclesie*, ed. Marguin-Hamon, lines 1528–31.

[13] Grammar's army will consist of the following divisions: (1) Grammarians: Priscian, Donatus, Martianus Capella, and the medieval authors Alexander of Villa Dei and Eberhard of Béthune; (2) standard readings from the elementary curriculum: Cato, Avianus, and Theodulus, and Orthography personified; (3) classical authors: Homer (the Homeric poems were not directly known in the medieval West), Claudian, Persius, Juvenal, Horace, Virgil, Lucan, Statius, Terence, Ovid, Seneca, and Martial; (4) early Christian poets: Sedulius, Prosper, Prudentius, and Arator; (5) medieval Latin poets: Jean of Hanville, Matthew of Vendôme, Walter of Châtillon, Peter Riga, Alan of Lille, Hugh Primas, Bernardus Silvestris, "Pamphilus," and Gautier (?); (6) various unknown poets of Orleans: Jean de St. Morisse, Odo, Garniers, and Balsamon. This array of authors would represent the kind of literary study for which Orleans was famous. See Paetow's note, 39.

Those good author knights
And those good squires who serve them,[14]
All set out with Grammar
30 When she went forth from her bookcase.
The knights of Orleans set out
Who were men-at-arms of the authors:
Master John of Saint Morisse,
Who knows his authors as well as one could wish,
35 Odo, Garnier and Balsamon,[15]
Who had inscribed a salmon
On his shield, between two dace,
With a hot pepper volant,
Blacker than charcoal,
40 A relish for the royal fish of the Loire
And for drinking the wines of Orleans
Which grow without the aid of fertilizers.
Then without jest or laughter,
They marched toward Paris.
45 Dame Logic heard of it;
She cried out full of wrath:
"Alas! I lost my support
When Raoul de Builli died."[16]
She marshalled her forces near Tournai[17]
50 Under Sir Pierre de Courtenai,
A very learned logician.[18]

[14] The knights are Homer, Claudian, and Persius; the squires are Donatus and Priscian.

[15] These were either contemporaries of Henri d'Andeli or older poets. See Paetow's note, 40 (at line 35); *Oeuvres de Henri d'Andeli, trouvère normand du XIIIe siècle*, ed. Héron, 138–43; and *Les Dits d'Henri d'Andeli*, ed. Corbellari, 107 (at lines 33–5).

[16] Corbellari (109n.) suggests that this Raoul de Builli may be a Raoul Ardent, from Beaulieu (d. ca. 1215), who was a master at the University of Paris; see Glorieux, *Répertoire des maîtres en théologie*, 1:234 (number 102).

[17] Tournai: according to Héron (ed., *Oeuvres de Henri d'Andeli*, 143), this refers to a house which the bishop of Tournai had near the wall of Philip Augustus on the ancient rue Bordet or Bordelle, which ended near the abbey of Sainte Geneviève. The army of Logic is thus drawn up on the hill of Sainte Geneviève in Paris ready to march out towards Orleans. Logic's army comprises: (1) the trivium and quadrivium, along with various masters of Paris, and with special reference to Rhetoric (represented by the Lombards), Arithmetic, Geometry, Astronomy, and Music; (2) Necromancy and Astrology; (3) Logic and Philosophy, represented by Aristotle's numerous books, along with Plato, Socrates, Porphyry, Boethius, Macrobius, and Gilbert of Poitiers; (4) Theology (supported by Augustine, Ambrose, Jerome, Gregory, Bede, and Isidore), who leaves the fight early; (5) Canon and civil law (the Authentics, Code, and Digest); (6) Medicine and chirurgy (represented by Hippocrates, Galen, and physicians of Paris). See Paetow, 41n.

[18] Héron (ed., *Oeuvres de Henri d'Andeli*, 144) identifies this Pierre de Courtenai as a canon of Paris.

There was master John the rustic,[19]
And Pointlasne, he of Gamaches,[20]
Master Nicholas with the prominent buttocks.[21]

55 These three put the trivium and quadrivium
In a tub on a large cart;[22]
The bedels drew the cart.
Robert the Dwarf in great derision
Pricked them all with a goad;

60 He pokes old Cheron in the bag.
Then they all set out.
There was many a pavilion of silk
On Montlhéry near Linas;[23]
There they gave one another cruel blows.

65 Civil Law rode gorgeously
And Canon Law rode haughtily
Ahead of all the other arts.
There was many a Lombard knight,
Marshalled by Rhetoric.[24]

70 Darts they have of feathered tongues
To pierce the hearts of foolish people
Who come to attack their stronghold;
For they snatch up many a heritage
With the lances of their eloquence.

[19] John the rustic (Jehans li pages): Paetow (41n.) identifies this figure with a Jean Pagus, a regent master (of arts) before 1229. See Glorieux, *Répertoire des maîtres en théologie*, 1:328–9 (number 147), and Corbellari (ed., *Les Dits d'Henri d'Andeli*), 109n. The term "pagus" designates rustic or peasant.

[20] Paetow (41–2n.) points to the famous thirteenth-century Parisian family bearing the name Pointlasne (Pungensasinum). Corbellari (109n.) prefers to identify the figure here with Guillaume Pungensasinum, possibly an older member of the family active around 1226. See Glorieux, *Répertoire des maîtres en théologie*, 1:82 (number 10, biographical note).

[21] This identification remains uncertain: see Paetow, 42n. (linking him tentatively with a Nicholas de Pondearche cited in a university document of 1248), and Corbellari, 109n. (who doubts this identification).

[22] The trivium and quadrivium have here become mere figures of speech, not to be taken as actual references to the Parisian curriculum at the time, since studies at Paris were much more specialized than this nomenclature might suggest; moreover, the battle is being waged between two components of the trivium, Grammar and Logic. See Paetow, 42n.; and on the notion and reality of the trivium in the Parisian curriculum, see Ebbesen and Rosier-Catach, "Le *trivium* à la Faculté des arts."

[23] Montlhéry ("Mont-le heri," meaning a difficult ascent), on the road to Orleans near Paris, had a fortified castle whose tower was still standing at the time this poem was written: the tower plays a role later in the poem (lines 307–9, 413). Linas is a small village south of Montlhéry. See Paetow, 42n., and Corbellari, 110n.

[24] A reference to the notaries from northern Italy who came to Paris during the thirteenth century. See the introduction to this text above.

75   Augustine, Ambrose, Gregory,
      Jerome, Bede, and Isidore,
      They quoted to Divinity as authorities
      So that she might avoid all this vanity.[25]
      Madam Exalted Science,

80   Who did not care a fig about their dispute,
      Left the arts to fight it out together.
      Methinks she went to Paris
      To drink the wines of her cellar,
      According to the advice of the chancellor,[26]

85   In whom she had the greatest confidence
      For he was the best clerk in the Isle de France;
      But in one trifle he considered her foolish,
      That when she holds disputations in his schools
      She abandons strict theological questions

90   And trumpets philosophy.
      As for the arts students, they care for naught
      Except to read the books of nature;[27]
      While the grammarians perverse
      Have for their part forsaken Claudian and Persius,

95   Two very good old books,
      The best belonging to the grammarians;
      All are in opposition
      To good antiquity.
      Medicine, Hippocrates, Galen,

100   And those bold chirurgeons,[28]
      He of the Rue Neuve, Robert,

[25] The French reads:
    Augustin . . . Ysidoire,
    Distrent à la Divinité
    Qu'ele eschivast lor vanité
The meaning here is that the science of Theology ("Madam Exalted Science") is far above all secular learning, and can keep a distance from squabbles among the secular arts.

[26] The chancellor is Philippe de Grève, chancellor of Paris 1218–36. See Paetow, 44n., and Corbellari, 110n. Henri also wrote a lament on the death of Philippe de Grève (ed. Corbellari, *Les Dits*).

[27] "Books of nature" refers to the Aristotelian texts on natural philosophy, including *Physics*, *Metaphysics*, *On the Heavens*, *On Generation and Corruption*, and other lesser treatises. The *Metaphysics* and natural philosophy are mentioned in the prohibitions of 1210 and 1215 (Denifle and Chatelain, *Chartularium*, 1:70, 78). These books would not have come back into universal use until 1229–31, the years of the dispersion and return of the University of Paris. See Paetow, 44–5n.

[28] The forerunners of modern-day surgeons, held in some contempt for their bloody work binding wounds, mending bones, and pulling teeth.

And he of Glatigny, Hubert,[29]
And master Peter the Lombard
Who tricks Paris with his arts,[30]
105   And Gerald, another devil,
And master Henry of Venables,
And Raoul of the Charité,
Little Bridge and their vanity,[31]
They all would turn to money making
110   If they saw in it no danger.
Villainous Chirurgy
Was seated near a bloody cemetery.
She loved discord much better
Than bringing about nice concord.
115   She carried boxes and ointments,
And a great plenty of instruments
To draw arrows from paunches.
It did not take her long to patch up
The bellies she saw pierced:
120   However, she is a science.
But she has such bold hands
That she spares no one
From whom she may be able to get money.
I would have had much respect for them
125   If they had cured my eyes;
But they dupe many people,
While with the copper and silver
Which they receive for their poisons
They build them fine houses in Paris.
130   From Toledo came and from Naples,[32]
She who knew the carnage of battles,

[29] The first of these may possibly be identified with Robert de Douai, physician to Saint Louis or Queen Marguerite. The second remains unidentified. Corbellari, 111n.

[30] A Peter Lombard (not the author of the *Sentences*) was physician to Louis IX, before becoming canon and subdeacon of Chartres.

[31] For possible identifications of these figures, see Paetow, 46nn., and Corbellari, 111nn. The "Petit Pont" or Little Bridge, leading from the Isle de la Cité to the left bank of the Seine, was known for its masters of logic who had established schools in the buildings on the bridge. The reference to it in this context is mysterious, because it was not associated with physicians.

[32] Toledo, as a center for the translation of Arabic scientific texts, became popularly associated with a subgroup of such texts, those on the arts of magic and divination. See Burnett, *Magic and Divination in the Middle Ages*,

At midnight, Necromancy,
Who clearly told them their evil destiny:
That everyone should arm his head,
135   Which destiny she had divined in the sword.
At a cross-road she made a fire,
Near a circle, at twilight.
There she had sacrificed two cats
And two stray pigeons
140   In the name of the malign deity
To search out the truth.
The daughter of Madame Astronomy,
Who was an accomplice in their evil deeds,
Told them very well that the battle
145   Would occur tomorrow without fail.
Arithmetic sat in the shade,
Where she says, where she figures,
That ten and two and one make thirteen,
And three more make sixteen;
150   Four and three and nine to boot
Again make sixteen in their way;
Thirteen and twenty-seven make forty,
And three times twenty by themselves make sixty;
Five twenties make hundred, and ten hundreds a thousand.
155   Does counting involve anything further? No.
One can easily count a thousand thousands
In the foregoing manner
From the number which increases and diminishes,
And which in counting goes from one to hundred.
160   The dame makes from this her tale.
That usurer, prince, and count
Today love the counteress better
Than the chanting of high mass.
Arithmetic then mounted
165   Her horse and proceeded to count
All the knights of the army;

especially chapter 4, "The Translating Activity in Medieval Spain." Naples was also a crossroads for the transmission of new scientific lore; its university had recently been founded (in 1224). The daughter of Madame Astronomy (line 142) is Astrology.

And she had at her side
Her companion Geometry
Who there again showed her skill.
170 In a spot between the combatants
She described a small circle,
And said that within a thousand feet of ground
This war would be brought to a close.
Madame Music, she of the little bells
175 And her clerks full of songs
Carried fiddles and viols,
Psalteries and small flutes;
From the sound of the first *fa*
They ascended to *cc sol fa*.
180 The sweet tones diatessaron
Diapente, diapason,[33]
Are struck in various combinations.
In groups of four and three,
Through the army they went singing,
185 They go enchanting them with their song.
These do not engage in battle;
But Donatus without delay
Dealt Plato such a blow
On the chin with a feathered verse
190 That he frightened him thoroughly;
And Sir Plato in great wrath
Struck back at him so hard with a sophism
Upon his shield, in the midst of a rhyme,
That he made him tumble in the mud
195 And completely covered him with blood.
Aristotle strikes Priscian
Our noble ancient authority
That he made him drop to the ground;
He wanted to trample him under his horse,
200 But Priscian had two nephews
Who were very handsome and brave,
Sir Graecismus and the Doctrinale;

---

[33] The intervals of a fourth, a fifth, and an octave, respectively.

They crippled him his horse,
And rendered the animal three-legged.
205   Aristotle, who was unhorsed,
Made Grammar tumble backwards.
Then pricked forward master Persius,
Sir Juvenal and Sir Horace,
Virgil, Lucan, and Statius,
210   And Sedulius, Propertius,[34] Prudentius,
Arator, Homer, and Terence:
All smote Aristotle,
Who stood firm as a castle on a hill.
Priscian with his two nephews
215   Tried to beat out his eyes,
When Sophistical Refutations and the two Logics,[35]
On Interpretation and the Topics,
The books of nature, Ethics,
Madam Necromancy, Medicine,[36]
220   And Sir Boethius and Sir Macrobius[37]
Dressed in a caitiff garb,
And Porphyry,[38] came on a run
To bring aid to Aristotle.
The Lombards of dame Rhetoric
225   Rode hard after Dialectic,
Although they did not love her,
For they were but little acquainted with her;
But they wounded many an honest man
For the booty which they won there.

[34] In his note on this line (50, line 210), Paetow identifies the poet, called in the French text "Propre," as Prosper of Aquitaine (fifth century), thus making a group of four late antique Christian poets; but in his text he gives the name as "Propertius," leading to confusion with the Augustan poet.

[35] The "two Logics" most likely refers to the *Prior* and *Posterior Analytics*, which, with the *Sophistical Refutations* and the *Topics*, comprised the *logica nova*.

[36] The French term here is *Fisique*, which can mean "medicine" (as in line 99), but which may also be taken to refer to Aristotle's *Physics*. See Corbellari, 114n.

[37] The works by Boethius indicated here would be his contributions to logic (*De topicis differentiis*, *De divisione*, and his commentaries on Porphyry and Aristotle); Macrobius is placed in the army of Logic because his *Commentum in somnium Scipionis* would be read as a contribution to philosophy and cosmology, although the prologue contains highly influential material on literary theory (the *fabula* or fabulous narration) and on dreams.

[38] A reference to Porphyry's *Isagoge* or introduction to the *Categories* of Aristotle, a basic textbook of logic.

230   The Categories and the Six Principles,[39]
       Two good buyers of tripe,
       Pricked after Sir Barbarismus
       Who rode the fiftieth of the troop.
       He was liege man of Grammar

235   One of the best men of her book case;
       But he favored this war
       Because he held land from Logic.[40]
       By treason he was alienated
       Because he was a native of Poitou.

240   These bad, spiteful people
       Attacked Grammar, their mother.
       Ah! if you had seen them there throwing lances
       To disembowel these good authors,
       Shaking heads and beating hands,

245   And loosening the reins on tongues!
       A thousand arrows flew at one time,
       Worse than those made of willow or aspen,
       For there is more venom in words
       Than in a hundred thousand silly sticks.

250   The authors defended themselves
       And struck them great wounds,
       With penknives and styluses,[41]
       Long fables and lies.
       Their castle would have been defensible enough

255   If it had not been so stocked with fables;
       For they palm off their nonsense
       As truth, by means of fine phrases.

[39] The *Six Principles* are the *Liber sex principiorum* of Gilbert of Poitiers. After about 1200 this text formed a supplement to Aristotle's *Categories*.

[40] While the *Barbarismus* would traditionally be classed with grammatical texts, its treatment of figures and tropes was also used, from the later twelfth century, as a point of departure for literature on sophisms and questions on grammatical logic. Thus Henri d'Andeli places it in the army of Logic as a traitor to Grammar. See the *Summa sophisticorum elenchorum*, in de Rijk, *Logica modernorum*, 1:404–10 (on solecism and barbarism). See the selection in this volume from the commentary on the *Barbarismus* attributed to Kilwardby. See also Ebbesen and Rosier-Catach, "Le *trivium* à la Faculté des arts," 116 and Rosier-Catach, "*Prata rident*."

[41] This may be an echo of the "death by stylus" story that survives in many forms, from Livy's *Ab urbe condita* 5.27 to Prudentius' *Peristephanon* 9 to William of Malmesbury's fictive account, in the *Gesta regum Anglorum* and the *Gesta pontificum Anglorum*, of the death of John Scotus Eriugena. In all these stories, pupils attack their grammar master with the instruments of grammatical practice, the styluses. See Bieler, "Vindicta scholarium: Beiträge zur Geschichte eines Motivs."

Grammar strikes one of their disciples
In the body with a participle
260   Which felled him to the ground,
Then to him said: "Now go and learn something."
Then she stretched five more of them on the sod
At the point of her adverb;
But Sir Socrates made her hide,
265   For she could not answer all his questions.
She turned towards those of Orleans,
Who for a long time have exalted her.
From the depths of a valley
They brought forth her horse
270   Which was being held by Orthography,
The foundation of learning;
Then back with her authors
Dame Grammar retreated.
Ah! if you had seen the logicians
275   How they slew the authorlings
And caused such havoc
Among those fine constructions!
The sophists despised them
Because they did not understand each other;
280   For there was so much contention among them
That the one knew little of what the other said.
One knight, On Interpretation,
Killed my lord Architrenius,[42]
One of the barons of Normandy;
285   After that he also slew Tobit.[43]
Four of them he killed in one onset.
Both the *Gesta ducis Macedum*[44]
And the versified Bible[45]
He then cut to pieces with a huge battle-ax.
290   But when against the Patronymics
Advanced the family of the Topics,[46]

---

[42] The *Architrenius* by Jean of Hanville.   [43] The *Tobias* of Matthew of Vendôme.

[44] The reference is to the *Alexandreis* of Walter of Châtillon, whose first line begins "Gesta ducis Macedum totum digesta per orbem."

[45] The *Aurora* of Peter Riga.

[46] "Family of the Topics" probably refers to the grouping of texts about dialectical topics by Aristotle, Cicero, and Boethius, all of which were used in the university curricula. The "Patronymics" may be a reference to the section *De patronymicis* in book 2 of Priscian's *Institutiones* (*GL* 2:62–8).

They failed to force their way through,
So strong are the Patronymics.
Sirs *Juste* and *Praeterea*
295   For this reason killed
The good *Ego mei vel mis*,
Who was their great enemy,
Because they did not know whence he came
Nor how he was declined.[47]
300   When Logic had shown her prowess,
She returned with great joy
To her standard, to her banner;
Then the army withdrew.
Astronomy and Rhetoric
305   Advised Dialectic,
That, before night-fall,
They had better enter Montlhéry.
The dames, who were very wise,
Entered Montlhéry,
310   And they did it not from fear,
But rather simply from the desire
To possess the castle;
And by this they made it known
That they love lofty things,
315   Whereas Grammar loves the fountains.
The authors were much troubled
When they assembled,
So they awaited the rear guard,
Which two knights were bringing up,
320   Primat of Orleans and Ovid.[48]
They brought to their aid,
With great impetuosity, ten thousand verses,
Inscribed on their banner,
Which Ovid wove with his hands

---

[47] Here Henri d'Andeli personifies certain common expressions of logical disputation, *juste* (justly) and *praeterea* (moreover), opposing them to a grammatical lesson in personal pronouns.

[48] The poet known as Hugh Primas was born at Orleans about 1093/4, and died about 1160. Along with the "Archpoet," Hugh Primas is the best-known of the so-called Goliardic poets. See edition by McDonough, *The Oxford Poems of Hugh Primas and the Arundel Lyrics*; and *Hugh Primas and the Archpoet*, trans. F. Adcock.

325   In the exile where he was in want:
       Martial and Martianus Capella,
       Seneca and Anticlaudian,[49]
       And Sir Bernard Silvester
       Who knew all the languages
330   Of the sciences and the arts;[50]
       He did not come as a mere squire,
       But he brought so large a band
       That the whole place was full of them.
       The Achilleis of Statius,
335   Strong in chest and back,
       Bore before him the stakes.
       There was the wise Cato,[51]
       Avianus and Pamphilus;[52]
       Sir Theodulus carried there
340   A banner bipartite;
       In it was woven with great skill
       Sir Pseustis with pierced shield
       Vanquished by Alithia,
       Who was pictured on the other half.[53]
345   Like leopards, this whole crowd
       Followed the banner;
       So nimble they are and so quick
       They almost flew,
       They almost captured
350   Among the stakes, dame Logic,
       Astronomy, and Rhetoric.
       But they are lodged so high up

[49] I.e., the *Anticlaudianus* by Alan of Lille.

[50] Bernardus Silvestris (called in French, as in Henri d'Andeli's text, "Bernardins li sauvages"), whose *Cosmographia* was viewed as a "masterpiece" work by later generations of grammarians. See above, Gervase of Melkley, pp. 609–10.

[51] I.e. the *Disticha Catonis*.

[52] Avianus, author of the *Fabulae* in Latin elegiac meter. "Pamphilus," the *Pamphilus de arte amandi*, popular in the grammar curriculum (ed. Becker, *Pamphilus: Prolegomena zum Pamphilus (de amore) und kritische Textausgabe*); Elliott, trans., *Seven Medieval Latin Comedies*. On the schoolroom uses of the *Pamphilus*, see Woods, "Rape and the Pedagogical Rhetoric of Sexual Violence."

[53] I.e. the scenario of the popular poem *Ecloga Theodoli*, which presents a contest between Pseustis (derived from Greek, "lies," championing pagan deeds) and Alithia (derived from Greek, "truth," on the side of biblical history), judged by Fronesis, who proclaims Alithia the victor.

That they strike them with their whips
And with their tongues the air and the wind.
355   They often fatten their scholars on it,
Whence they themselves are altogether weak.
The dames have tiresome tongues;
Logic strikes in her hand so much
That she has torn her gown into shreds.
360   She makes us a knife without a blade,
Who wears a sleeve without the gown.
We see from the looks of her arms,
That on her body she has no substance.
Rhetoric goes to her aid,
365   She who earns money by pleading.
The Authentics, the Code, and Digest,[54]
Make her hot potions for her head;
For she has so many quack lawyers,
Who of their tongues make clappers
370   To get the goods of the common herd,
That all the country is full of them.
One of the pupils of dame Logic
Was sent to Grammar;
He bore letters to make peace.
375   Now I simply cannot refrain from telling this,
That when he arrived at his destination
He did not know the sense
Of the presents nor the preterits;
And that there where he had been brought up,
380   He had dwelt on them but little.
He had not learned thoroughly
Irregular conjugations,
Which are most difficult to inflect,
Adverbs and parts of speech,
385   Articles and declensions,
Genders and nominatives,
Supines and imperatives,
Cases, figures, formations,
Singulars, plurals, a thousand terms;

[54] The Authentics, Code, and Digest are parts of the *Corpus iuris civilis* originally compiled at the command of the Emperor Justinian. "Authentics" became the common name for the the *Novellae constitutiones*.

390 For in the court of Grammar are more corners
Than in all of Logic's prattlings.
The boy did not know how to come to the point,
And came back in shame.
But Logic comforted him,
395 Carried him to her high tower,
And tried to make him fly
Before he was able to walk.
Astronomy, who soars high,
Has retained neither retreat nor school,
400 Neither in the city nor in the country;
In truth, she would have been entirely lost
Had it not been for brave master Gautier,
Who out of little makes his living,
The Englishman who holds disputations on the Little Bridge,
405 Who hides himself in poverty.[55]
Grammar withdrew
Into Egypt, where she was born.[56]
But Logic is now in vogue,
Every boy runs her course
410 Ere he has passed his fifteenth year;
Logic is now for children!
Logic is in a very bad situation
In the tower on Montlhéry;
There she practices her art;
415 But Grammar opposes her
With her authors and authorlings
Sententious and frivolous.
Echo answered in the tower
To the great blows given all around,
420 For there they all hurl their rhymes.
She defends herself with sophisms;
Often she makes them fall back
And they in turn hurl at her their verses,
So that the air is thick with them.

[55] Paetow (58n.) points out that the manuscripts are corrupt at this point, that some lines are missing in one and jumbled in the other, and that Gautier or Walter the Englishman who holds disputations on the Petit Pont has nothing to do with Astronomy. The Petit Pont was famous for logicians, not astronomers (see line 108 above). Paetow identifies this Gautier as a "master of arts in Paris who was partial to the poets of Orléans," perhaps an Englishman like John of Garland or even the fabulist Walter the Englishman.

[56] See Martianus Capella, Part 1 above, for the myth that Grammar was born in Egypt.

425 She defends herself with unsolvable questions,
With true and with false solutions.
The authorlings put in a great rage
All those assembled there
And so eager to get away,
430 Because, in truth, they will never raise the siege
Until the day that they surrender;
And if they [the besieged] fall into their hands,
They will drive them from better to worse.
All for naught they make their siege,
435 For Astronomy upon their tents,
From above, hurled her lightning;
All their pavilions she reduced to ashes;
And the authorlings fled,
And deserted Grammar.
440 The courtly Sir Versifier
Fled away between Orleans and Blois.
Henceforth he does not dare to go abroad in France
Since he has no acquaintance there;
For students of arts and of canon law
445 No longer care for their jurisdiction.
The Bretons and the Germans
Still do his bidding to some extent;
But if the Lombards got hold of him,
They (in a trice) would strangle him.
450 Sirs, the times are given to emptiness;
Soon they will go entirely to naught,
For thirty years this will continue,
Until a new generation will arise,
Who will go back to Grammar,
455 Just as it was the fashion
When Henri d'Andeli was born,
Who gives it us as his opinion
That one should destroy the glib student
Who cannot construe his lesson;
460 For in every science that master is an apprentice
Who has not mastered his parts of speech.

Here ends the Battle of the Seven Arts.

COMMENTARY ON THE *BARBARISMUS* (ATTRIBUTED TO ROBERT KILWARDBY),

CA. 1250

INTRODUCTION

This commentary on Donatus' *Barbarismus* was attributed by its editor (in 1984) to the English philosopher and theologian Robert Kilwardby (ca. 1215–1279). The attribution has since been questioned on the grounds that its content seems to place it closer to works written after the phase of Kilwardby's career when he was producing his known writings on grammar and logic.[1] Kilwardby studied in Paris from about 1231 and taught there as regent master of arts. During his tenure at Paris he wrote a commentary on the *Priscianus minor* (his authorship of this commentary has not been doubted). About 1245 he joined the Dominican order and went to Oxford, where he began to study theology, becoming a regent master there in 1256. His important treatise on the sciences, *De ortu scientiarum* (On the Rise [or Origin] of the Sciences), dates from his Oxford period. If Kilwardby were the author of the commentary on the *Barbarismus*, it would likely have been written sometime before 1245.

The commentary on the *Barbarismus* gives us an insight into the extent and limits of a philosophical approach to language. It has something in common with the outlook of modistic grammarians, who were interested in the universal principles that could be posited of all grammatical expression. The parts of the *quaestiones* translated here speak to concerns about the division between the disciplines of grammar and rhetoric. What are their respective domains or fields of study or specialization (the specific *consideratio* of each)? Here the commentary draws a boundary between what it views as the strictly linguistic concerns of the grammarian and the emotional concerns of the rhetorician. Grammar is a rational discipline, looking at the problems of tropes and ornamentation from a theoretical perspective. The grammarian is interested in speech in itself, for its own sake. The rhetorician, on the other hand, is interested in the practical application of verbal

---

[1] Grondeux, "Turba ruunt," 190; Rosier, "La grammaire dans le '*Guide de l'étudiant*,'" pointing out that it is closely linked with the *Admirantes* gloss. The question is also examined at greater length in Rosier, "O Magister."

ornaments for purposes of persuasion, and in that sense rhetoric is an "irrational" art, or appeals to the irrational parts of "virtue."[2] The rhetorician is thus interested in the instrumental value of figurative language, to persuade a judge. Thus from a general epistemological perspective, the spheres to which each discipline pertains are as distinct as possible: grammar pertains wholly to reason, rhetoric to emotions. These arguments resonate with other roughly contemporary accounts of the language sciences found in university introductions to philosophy.[3]

What modern students of poetics might see as an opportunity to bring language and emotion together, to give a philosophical and cognitive basis for the aesthetic power of figurative language, has no role here: the commentator pursues an analysis of the purely semantic operations of figures. This is striking in the discussion of allegory (given here), in which the commentary specifies the operations of that trope by the effect that this "transference of meaning" has grammatically and semantically on other words (parts of speech) in the sentence. This interest in semantics certainly has implications for theories about the power of literary language, because the commentator speaks of primary and secondary understanding, that is, how we pass from understanding or construing a word used in a trope to understanding the meaning that lies behind it. But such semantic arguments had already been assimilated to literary culture, as we see in Geoffrey of Vinsauf's sophisticated treatment of *transumptio* as a logical-semantic category.[4] Geoffrey's treatment of it has its own background in twelfth-century logic, rhetoric, and grammar.[5] Thus the poetic theory of the late twelfth and early thirteenth centuries had already arrived at this conceptual ground through earlier routes, and had already given a literary application to it. By contrast, the interests of this commentator on the *Barbarismus* remain at a relatively abstract semantic level.

Translated from *In Donati Artem Maiorem III*, ed. Schmuecker.

SELECTION I[6]

[In this section, the commentator discusses Donatus on metaplasm: metaplasm is a legitimate deviation from normal usage, permitted by meter, embellishment, or necessity.

---

[2] See Ebbesen and Rosier-Catach, "Le *trivium* à la faculté des arts," 116.

[3] On the treatise *Ut ait Tullius*, see Dahan, "Une introduction à l'étude de la philosophie: *Ut ait Tullius*," 52–3.

[4] See Geoffrey of Vinsauf, above, pp. 596, 602–6.   [5] See Rosier, "*Prata rident*," 155 and note.

[6] ed. Schmuecker, 103–5, lines 116–22, 142–69.

From considering the definition of metaplasm as a whole, the commentator poses a "doubt" about which discipline, grammar or rhetoric, should treat verbal embellishment.]

Next there is some doubt about his use of [the word] "embellishment" [*ornatus*],[7] for the following reason: embellishment regularly consists, as Tully says,[8] in the coloring [*coloribus*] of words [*vocum*] and meanings [*sententiarum*], but "coloring" is to be studied by the rhetorician, and therefore embellishment [*ornatus*] belongs to the study of the rhetorician as well. But what is to be studied by one specialist [*artificis*], is not to be studied by a different one. Therefore, since embellishment is to be studied by the rhetorician, it is not to be studied by the grammarian. Thus a grammarian cannot appropriately put forward the claim that embellishment is a ground for excuse.

[The commentator now turns to Donatus' phrase "or (because of) necessity" (*GL* 4:395.29).[9] The first objection is that meter and embellishment can also be regarded as forms of necessity. The second objection is that deviations in accent, breathing, and the like, are better described under "embellishment." Here is the commentator's solution:]

To the second objection we may reply that embellishment or plainness can be achieved in two ways: one to be studied by the grammarian, the other by the rhetorician.[10] For we should know that discourse [*sermo*] is used and studied in two ways: the first relates to how discourse is ordered for the sole purpose of understanding what is uttered correctly; it is ordered in this way to move rational virtue to understanding. Such discourse is to be studied by the grammarian. In the second way, discourse is studied not just in its goal of producing correct understanding, but in addition in the way it provokes irrational, i.e. irascible and concupiscent, virtue [*virtus*] in somebody else,[11] for example, a judge.[12] In this case it is to be studied by the rhetorician. Similarly, embellishment or plainness can be studied in two ways, depending, obviously, on whether it is embellishment of the former type of discourse or the latter. If it is studied in discourse to see how discourse is ordered for the sole purpose of bringing about understanding of the utterance, i.e. of affecting rational virtue (so that embellishment contributes to correct understanding and plainness to incorrect understanding, or to impede understanding), in that case it is to be studied by

---

[7] *Ars maior* 3.4, *GL* 4:395.29.

[8] No direct source. Cf. Cicero *De oratore*, 3.25.95–100, 3.52.199; *Brutus* 87, 298.

[9] *Necessitatisve causa*: in our section on Donatus, we follow the standard editions in omitting this phrase (transmitted by some of the manuscripts which Kilwardby clearly had in his text).

[10] See also *In Donati artem*, ed. Schmuecker, 137 lines 54 ff. (on *ornatus causa*) translated below.

[11] I.e. other than the speaker.

[12] The three types of virtue (rational, irascible, and concupiscent) owe a debt to Plato's tripartite soul (*logikon*, *thumos*, *epithumêtikon*) in the *Republic*. Grammar speaks to the rational part of the soul, rhetoric appeals to its irrational side (anger and desire). The terms *concupiscens* and *irascibilis* are both common medieval philosophical terms for these tendencies of the emotions.

the grammarian, and in that sense embellishment can be put forward as a ground for excusing impropriety. However, if embellishment or plainness is studied in actual discourse to see how discourse is ordered to provoke irascible virtue in a judge so that he marks out the opposing party, and to cause concupiscent virtue so that he feels sorry for one's own party, then it is to be studied by the rhetorician and not by the grammarian. Thus embellishment is studied differently by the grammarian and the rhetorician, and that is not unfitting.

There is also another distinguishing feature of the grammarian's way of looking at discourse, namely its indifference to content [*res*]. When one looks at embellishment and plainness of language in this way, it is to be studied by the grammarian, and that is how it is used here. Rhetoric, on the other hand, properly speaking is about discourse in its relation with civic affairs [*res*], as Tully has it,[13] and when embellishment or plainness occur in such discourse and in so far as they are like this, then they are to be studied by the rhetorician. This is not how embellishment is used here.

SELECTION II[14]

[This is the beginning of the commentary on the section "on tropes." The treatment is systematic. First the commentator explains the position of the topic that he will now discuss in the larger structure of Donatus' work. Then he gives the structure of the chapter at hand in a sustained binary fashion: Donatus' whole chapter consists of definition and division of the trope; the division in turn consists of division and discussion of the subdivisions. The last part is the *pars specialis*. The commentary is structured as a series of *quaestiones* or *dubitationes*, which are treated in order. In this chapter, too, concerns arise over the respective domains of the language disciplines, in this case the borderline between dialectic and grammar, as well as that between grammar and rhetoric.[15]]

On Tropes

A TROPE IS A WORD TRANSFERRED ETC.[16] Impropriety either arises because of a word-form [*vox*] or because of what is understood by a word-form. If [it arises] because of a word-form,

---

[13] See e.g. *Rhetorica ad Herennium* 1.2.2.   [14] Ed. Schmuecker, 136–9, lines 1–134.

[15] Cf. above on the division grammar/rhetoric, and see Ebbesen and Rosier-Catach, "Le *trivium* à la faculté des arts," 116.

[16] *Ars maior* 3.6, GL 4:399.13.

it occurs either in a word by itself, and in that case it is a barbarism, and it may be excused as a metaplasm; or it occurs in a word in context, and then it is a fault [*vitium*] closely related to a barbarism, and this happens in two ways, namely in letters or syllables immediately following each other (this yields e.g. obscenity [*cacenphaton*]) in which case it may be excused as metaplasm, e.g. ecthlipsis and synaloephe; or it happens through letters or syllables in the middle of a word, e.g. in obscenity [*cacenphaton*][17] and it may be excused as a figure of speech [*schema locutionis*]. But if impropriety arises in what is understood through a word-form, then this is either through the modes of signifying— and then it is a solecism and may be excused as a figure of construction—or it is because of the meaning, and then it is a fault closely related to solecism. This can happen in two ways, namely either without transfer of meaning (then it may be excused as a figure of speech, as was made clear above),[18] or with transfer of meaning (then it may be excused as a trope).

After having discussed figures [*schema*], the author here deals with tropes. This chapter is divided into two parts. In the first he gives the definition of a trope, in the second its divisions, where he says "THE KINDS OF TROPE ARE ETC."[19] This latter part is divided in two, the first dividing the trope, the second discussing the subdivisions, when he says "METAPHOR IS THE TRANSFER ETC."[20] This last part is divided in as many sections as there are divisions. It is clear where each of them starts.

The special part is sufficiently summarized if one looks at the text and the following specifications (this also applies elsewhere).

As to the trope, the first uncertainty regards its definition. And that also goes for each of its species.

As to the definition, the first uncertainty regards this part: "A WORD TRANSFERRED" [*dictio translata*],[21] for the following reason: a property or an accident of a word, is not [the same as] a word, but a trope is a property of a word, thus it is not a word, and therefore it is not "A WORD TRANSFERRED."

Further, a trope sometimes originates in the transfer of a sentence just as of a word, thus it does not characterize every trope in general to say "A WORD TRANSFERRED." Therefore that definition is impoverished and "A TROPE IS A WORD TRANSFERRED"[22] is not convertible.[23]

---

[17] *Cacenphaton* ("obscenity") can occur either at the point of (ignored) word division as in "cum navibus" (*Aeneid* 1.193, in a phrase that is in fact perfectly innocent) where one could hear a form of *cunn-* (female pudenda), or within a word, e.g. *arrige* in *arrige aures Pamphile* (Terence, *Andria* 933), "prick up your ears, Pamphilus," Donatus *Ars maior* 3.2, GL 4:395.1 f. Quintilian puts the blame for *cacenphaton* squarely on the shoulders of annoying readers: *Institutio oratoria* 8.3.45–7.

[18] Discussed in the previous section of Donatus' *Ars maior* (GL 4:397.5 ff.) and in the section *de schematibus* of *In Donati Artem*, ed. Schmuecker,117.1 ff.

[19] *Ars maior* 3.6, GL 4:399.14. [20] Ibid., GL 4:399.17.

[21] Ibid., GL 4:399.13. [22] Ibid.

[23] I.e. every "word transferred" may be a trope, but not every trope is a "word transferred."

The next question concerns this part: "FROM ITS PROPER SIGNIFICATION TO AN IMPROPER."[24]

It seems that all signification is proper and none improper. Tully says in the *Rhetoric* that proper words are those words that signify what is intended to be signified through them, or what can be signified through them.[25] Therefore it is clear that a word signifies properly, when it signifies what can be signified through it. But everything else that *is* signified through a word, *can be* signified through it. Therefore a word signifies properly whatever it signifies. Thus all signification is proper and none improper.

Further "transfer" or trope is an impropriety occurring in dialectical discourse and concerning it, hence the trope is to be studied by the dialectician and thus not by the grammarian. That the trope occurs in dialectical discourse, I can demonstrate as follows: Aristotle says in the beginning of *Topics* book II, that dialectical discourse is affected by two errors or faults, namely lying and transgressions against given usage.[26] This latter fault arises from obscure and improper change of meaning [*translocutio*], and a "trope" is the same as "change of meaning" [*translocutio*]. Therefore a trope is an impropriety occurring in dialectical discourse.

The next question arises from the fact that he says "FOR THE SAKE OF EMBELLISHMENT."[27] Whatever is for the sake of embellishment is to be studied by the rhetorician. Thus, if the trope is [used] for the sake of embellishment, it will fall to the discipline of the rhetorician and not to that of the grammarian. Alternatively, if it is to be studied by the grammarian, the claim that the trope exists for the sake of embellishment is inappropriate.[28]

The next question arises from the fact that he says "ACCORDING TO A LIKENESS" [SECUNDUM SIMILITUDINEM].[29] For it seems that not every trope originates in a likeness. Sometimes a trope is produced when one half of a pair of opposites is transferred to signify the other. Yet neither of the opposites is similar to the other, therefore this type of trope does not originate in a likeness. Therefore it seems that the definition of trope is not convertible.

---

[24] *GL* 4:399.13. Throughout this passage, the commentator reads a slightly different text. The standard edition of Donatus has *tropus est dictio translata a propria significatione ad non propriam similitudinem ornatus necessitatisve causa* (*GL* 4:399.13 f.).

[25] *Rhetorica ad Herennium* 4.12.17.   [26] Aristotle, *Topics* 2.109a20–30.

[27] *GL* 4:399.14.

[28] Cf. *In Donati artem*, 104–5, lines 142–69, translated above. The text here reads *male ponitur ipsum* [sc. the trope] *esse causam ornatus*. Although we have translated as if the Latin read *causa* (ablative, to be construed with genitive), it seems that the commentator takes *causa ornatus* as "the cause of embellishment," as befits his Aristotelian interest in causation. See also 104, line 156, *et sic ponitur ornatus causa excusandi improprietatem* ("in that sense embellishment can be put forward as a ground for excusing impropriety"), where the collocation of *ornatus causa* (which cannot be construed together in this phrase) suggests that the commentator is trying to explain the phrase.

[29] Cf. *GL* 4:399.14.

The first objection[30] may be met in the same way as when we dealt with the definition of barbarism.[31] The trope is defined as something bad, and in the definition of something bad it is not unfitting that the subject is predicated causally. For example, if we say, "day is the sun shining over the earth," in this definition that which is the efficient cause of it being day forms the predicate. Hence it is not unfitting that a cause is predicated of its effect in a causal predication. Similarly, it is not unfitting that when an impropriety is defined, the subject receives this kind of predicate.[32]

Further we must say that the trope can be studied in two ways: one, in so far as it is a fault which does not regard the subject in which it is located; this is not how it is defined here. In this sense, it is not the word [*dictio*] that is transferred, but its property, and this is how this objection proceeds. The other way to take it, is that it does regard that in which it is located, just as barbarism was used above. Just as "straight" is a property in so far as it regards something, and can and should rightly be defined by its subject, which it regards, so Donatus says that it is A WORD TRANSFERRED etc., just as "straight" is defined in so far as it regards a line, as if it ought to be defined through "line."[33]

The second objection may be met by saying that "word" in the definition of "trope" is used to refer both to words in context and to a word by itself. Therefore this definition encompasses both the trope in single words and the trope in connected discourse. As to the following objection, "if the trope is a WORD TRANSFERRED etc., then it is either a noun or a verb etc.,"[34] that objection is not valid. . . .

To the third objection we may say that there is a twofold signifying potential in a word, one that is owed to it according to the rules for a word used by itself, and one that is owed to it according to the rules for a word used in context to express its proper meaning. Tully is speaking about the latter, when he says that words have their proper meaning when they signify what is intended to be signified through them, or what can be signified through them.[35] For example, the noun "man" [*homo*] signifies "man" from its imposition,[36] and

---

[30] "A trope is not a word, but a property of a word" (136, lines 29 ff.).

[31] The definition of barbarism is *barbarismus est una pars orationis vitiosa in communi sermone* ("barbarism is one faulty part of speech in common discourse"). To this definition the commentator had equally objected that strictly speaking, barbarism is the fault, not the part of speech (*In Donati Artem*, 19, lines 552 ff.); see also the discussion of how to define something "bad," 17, lines 491 ff.

[32] The commentator's discussion of the definition of barbarism had focused on the Aristotelian notion (*Topics* 6.147b20 ff.) that the definition of a lack or of something negative should contain the positive element. In the definition of "barbarism" the term *pars orationis* is taken to be such an implicitly positive term, since it connotes the normative use of language. Similarly, in this definition of "trope," *dictio* is supposed to fulfill that function.

[33] I.e. a definition could start with "'straight' is a line that . . ."

[34] Cf. in the discussion of the definition of barbarism, *In Donati Artem*, 19, lines 543 ff.; 20, lines 578 ff.

[35] *Rhetorica ad Herennium* 4.12.17.

[36] I.e. the "instituting" or "imposing" of the name or term.

through signifying "man" it signifies soul and body and all such things. All these things can be signified properly through this noun "man," when the word is construed to express its proper signification, namely the meaning "man." Thus, it is used properly and without figured speech, the meaning of the word will not be repeated, and there will be no change of meaning [*translocutio*]. But not all words signify like that, as is obvious in words used in context. For a word is coined/given [*imponitur*] in order to signify something, and not to signify its opposite. Obviously, a word is construed to express its proper meaning; however it can also signify its opposite by somehow considering the single word itself by itself, without taking into account its original imposition. In such cases, then, a word may be considered in itself when used by itself, and not after or in as far as it has been coined [*imposita*] to signify. In this way, it may signify its opposite, because words are arbitrary. When one looks at it like this, a word properly signifies the opposite of its meaning. But if one considers a word in accordance with the way it was given [*imposita*] to signify and in a construction to bring out its proper meaning, then it properly signifies the opposite.[37]

So the answer to these arguments is as follows: when words are said to signify in accordance with what Tully said, that proper words signify etc., then one should answer that this should be understood as signification according to the rules for words used in context to express their proper meaning. Then when he says, "but everything that is signified by a word, may be signified by another word," we should answer that this premise is true according to the rules for words used by themselves. Hence, the major and minor premise are not true in the same way. Therefore, the fallacy is obvious.

To the fourth objection we may say that the trope may well have to be studied by the dialectician and the grammarian in different ways, and this is not unfitting. For we should know that the trope is to be studied by the grammarian because it signifies in a better way what is intended to be signified. Therefore, it is permitted to use the trope in grammar. But it should be studied by the logician as something that needs to be avoided, because it is a fault when it occurs in dialectical discourse.

To the fifth objection we may say that the trope occurs FOR THE SAKE OF EMBELLISHMENT in different ways: solely for the purpose of signifying in a better way—this is how it should be studied by the grammarian; or in order to signify and to provoke the concupiscent or irascible virtue in a judge—and this is how it should be studied by the rhetorician.

There is another distinction: a trope created for the sake of embellishment should be studied by the grammarian in order to have him distinguish between "simple" impropriety and "justifiable" impropriety (or impropriety "for a reason"). But it should be studied by the rhetorician in so far as it is for the sake of persuasion.

---

[37] Namely "the opposite of the opposite," i.e. it has its proper meaning.

To the sixth and last objection we may say that although one half of a pair of opposites is dissimilar from the other in that aspect that is opposed, it may yet be similar to the other in some other way. For opposites are in agreement in that they have an opposite relationship, and maybe in some other respects. Because of such an aspect in which they agree there could be a transfer of the one to signify the other, and that creates a trope in accordance with some similarity. Hence it is established that the definition of trope is true.

<h1 style="text-align:center">SELECTION III[38]</h1>

ALLEGORY IS ETC.[39] Here the author gives examples of allegory, and this part is divided into two. The first gives the definition, the second the division, where he says THERE ARE MANY KINDS OF ALLEGORY ETC.[40] This latter part is divided into two: the first gives the division, the second discusses the different kinds, where he says IRONY IS A TROPE ETC.[41] And this last part is divided in as many sections as there are different kinds of allegory; he offers discussion of every type separately. Where the different parts begin is clear in and of itself.

There is uncertainty about the definition of allegory. First of all, when he says, ALLEGORY IS A TROPE AFFECTING THE SIGNIFICATION OF A WORD,[42] for it seems that this definition is impossible. For what is signified by a word is said by it, and nothing else is. Therefore it is impossible that something else is signified by a word than is said by it. (Donatus: "Something else is signified than said").[43]

To this we may reply that "to signify" is here used for primary, principal, and proper signification;[44] it refers to the first and proper understanding. "To be said" is used here for non-primary, secondary, and improper signification; it refers to an improper and trans-ferred understanding. Hence, allegory is called a trope affecting the signification, affecting the primary and proper understanding. THAN SAID, i.e. affecting the secondary and improper understanding.[45]

We should know that primary understanding is achieved through a word without transfer; secondary understanding is mediated by transfer. But then it would seem that every trope is an allegory according to what we've said already and according to the

---

[38] *In Donati artem*, ed. Schmuecker, 163–5, lines 1072–1147.

[39] *Ars maior* 3.6, *GL* 4:401.26.   [40] Ibid., *GL* 4:401.28.   [41] Ibid., *GL* 4:401.30.

[42] Ibid., *GL* 4:401.26. The commentator's transmitted text has *allegoria est tropus quoad significationem dictionis*; the standard text of Donatus has *allegoria est tropus, quo aliud significatur quam dicitur*.

[43] Ibid., *GL* 4:401.26.

[44] This note seems to contradict the passage in Donatus, where "what is said" seems primary, and "what is signified" the result of transfer. However, the proper understanding of the allegory does depend on the signification rather than on "what is said."

[45] *quam dicitur* (at 401.26) forms a new lemma for the commentary, hence we have printed "than said" in small capitals.

definition of trope: A TROPE IS EVERY TRANSFER FROM A PROPER SIGNIFICATION TO AN IMPROPER ONE;[46] thus, there is transfer in every trope, but whenever there is transfer SOMETHING ELSE IS SIGNIFIED THAN SAID, because in every transfer the proper signification is signified and is called "transferred," i.e. it is intended to be signified, and so it seems that every trope is an allegory.

To this we should reply that transfer happens in different ways, depending on whether it is through allegory or the other tropes that one thing is signified and another is understood. This is obvious from the following: in an allegory, one thing is signified and another is being said. I mean that, for most people and primarily, in discourse (this may not work for antiphrasis),[47] one thing will be the possible or probable meaning, without parts of speech being transposed that are not connected with what is signified in a transferred way through the discourse; also, allegory does not make this one thing manifest through an overtly expressed similarity.[48] Through what I call "one thing is signified and another is being said in discourse," allegory differs from all tropes in which there is transfer in a word; through what I call "possible or probable," it is separated from hyperbole.[49] Through what I call "without parts of speech being transposed," it differs from hyperbaton.[50] Through what I call "not connected etc.," it differs from periphrasis, in which that which circumscribes and that which is circumscribed are connected. Through what I call "making manifest that other thing through an overtly expressed similarity," it is separated from "comparison" [*homoeosis*].[51] This proves that through allegory one thing is signified and another understood in a different way than through any other trope, and hence not every trope is subsumed under it. And we should know that the other tropes should be separated from one another by the same method, since all come into being from transfer and

---

[46] *GL* 4:399.13.

[47] *Antiphrasis* is a subspecies of allegory consisting in just one word, as opposed to *oratio*, discourse (Donatus, *Ars maior* 402.3 *antiphrasis est unius verbi ironia*).

[48] The complexity of this sentence is necessary to the commentator's argument. He wants to encompass in one comprehensive sentence everything that distinguishes allegory from the other tropes, and to exclude everything that allegory is not. That the commentator realizes the complexity of this statement is clear from the way that he then goes on to divide the long sentence into small units and comment on each one. The translation in the following four sentences revises Schmuecker's punctuation of this passage. After his detailed definition of "allegory," the commentator explains how the different parts of his definition set allegory apart from the other tropes. The text should read (l.1108 ff.): *per hoc quod dico 'significatur unum et aliud dicitur in oratione' differt allegoria ab omnibus tropis, in quibus est translatio in dictione; per hoc quod dico 'possibile vel probabile' separatur ab hyperbole; per hoc quod dico 'sine transpositione partium' differt ab hyperbaton; per hoc quod dico 'non coniunctum etc.' differt a periphrasi, in qua oratione circumloquens et circumlocutum simul coniunguntur; per hoc quod dico 'non manifestans aliud illud per similitudinem expressam' [significatur] separatur ab homoeosi.*

[49] Hyperbole is defined as defying belief, Donatus, *Ars maior* 3.6, *GL* 4:401.24 f. *dictio fidem excedens*.

[50] Ibid., *GL* 4:401.4 *hyperbaton est transcensio quaedam verborum ordinem turbans*.

[51] *Homoeosis* is explicit comparison, allegory is implied comparison, cf. ibid., 402.21 ff.

through positing their characteristic differences. This will become clear below, when we will discuss how many tropes there are and what number distinguishes them sufficiently.

Another question is what fault is excused by allegory, and why.

The answer to this is that in part it excuses *acyrologia* and in part *cacosyntheton*. *Acyrologia*, because it regards improper complex speech, *cacosyntheton*, because it originates from the bad construction of words, as will become clear in detail through the examples. The reason why this transfer can be made, is that one thing is understood within another through some similarity, either simply, or through stylistic means [*cum modo loquendi*], as will be clear from the examples. The reason why it is appropriate for the transfer to be made is the embellishment of something, or the expression of a thought for the sake of praising or blaming, as will be clear below.

Next there is a specific question about the first example that Donatus gives: AND NOW IT IS TIME TO FREE THE STEAMING NECKS OF THE HORSES,[52] meaning TO FINISH THE POEM.[53] The question is what similarity there is here, why this transfer can be made, and why it was appropriate for it to be made.

The answer is that horses that are tired by hard labor have steam coming off their necks, and when they are that tired, they must finish their work. Similarly, when someone has studied hard, he is tired from his study and must finish his intellectual work to take some rest. And because of this similarity in both cases we have found the reason why one can be transferred to signify the other. The reason why this transfer was appropriate is the expression of the thought [*sententia*], namely to have it signify that he was tired out by enormous exertion. For when horses have steam coming off their necks, they are utterly exhausted, and he wanted to convey that he had utterly exerted himself on a poem that was now finished. That is why it was necessary for him to use that transfer.

Further, embellishment or style [*modus loquendi*] can also be the cause: for what one intends to say is signified in a more beautiful and delightful way through transferred speech than through proper speech. It is clear, then, from the example just discussed, that this figure is an excuse for *acyrologia*,[54] since complex speech is used improperly to signify complex speech.[55]

---

[52] *GL* 4:401.27; Virgil, *Georgics*, 2.542.   [53] *GL* 4:401.28.

[54] *Acyrologia* is the imprecise use of language, the failure to use the proper term. If perpetrated on purpose for special effect, it turns into "allegory."

[55] *Dictio complexa*: i.e. this figure of speech does not affect the individual word out of context, but constructions and sentences.

HERMANNUS ALEMANNUS, AL-FARABI'S *DIDASCALIA* ON ARISTOTLE'S *RHETORIC*, 1256

INTRODUCTION

Hermannus Alemannus was active in Toledo from about 1240 to 1265, where he was part of the circle of Arabic–Latin translators who constituted the great second phase of this scholarly interchange. To modern literary historians he is best known as the translator of Averroes' *Middle Commentary* on Aristotle's *Poetics*. Even though very few manuscripts of it survive, Hermannus' version of the *Poetics* seems to have had some circulation: for example, it is cited in the rhetorical treatise *Tria sunt* and by Matthias of Linköping.[1] However, his translation of the Averroistic *Poetics* was only part of a larger Aristotelian project undertaken at the same time. Hermannus also made two remarkable attempts to usher Aristotle's *Rhetoric* into the Latin West, by translating the *Rhetoric* from an Arabic version of the text, and by translating the prefatory section of the "Great Commentary" on the *Rhetoric* (the *Sharh Kitâb al-khatâbah li-Aristûtalîs*) by Al-Farabi (fl. 950), which in Latin was called the *Didascalia in Rethoricam Aristotelis ex glosa Alpharabi*. The interdependence of Hermannus' prologues to all three works—*Poetics*, *Rhetoric*, and *Didascalia*—makes it clear that they were part of the same effort and were finished at about the same time, in 1256 (the date he gave for his translation of the *Poetics*).[2] Hermannus' two rhetorical translations had even less direct visibility than his *Poetics*: the *Rhetoric* survives in three manuscripts, and the *Didascalia* in one. Yet among the few scholars who knew or read his rhetorical translations were some very influential figures. Roger Bacon excoriated Hermannus' translations, while at the same time recommending further knowledge of Aristotle's *Rhetoric* and the Al-Farabian commentary on it, i.e. the *Didascalia*.[3] More

---

[1] For the *Tria sunt*, see Part 4 above; Matthias of Linköping, *Testa Nucis and Poetria*, ed. and trans. Bergh, 9–13, 55, 69.

[2] Boggess, "Hermannus Alemannus' Rhetorical Translations," 247–9.

[3] Bacon, *Moralis philosophia*, ed. Massa, 267. Here Bacon also reports how Hermannus admitted to him that he did not know logic, hence his difficulties translating. See also *Moralis philosophia* 251, and Bacon, *Opus maius*, ed. Bridges, 1:30–1, 71, 100. Bacon may not have read either Hermannus' *Rhetoric* or the *Didascalia*, deriving his ideas

important for future generations, Giles of Rome consulted Hermannus' Arabic–Latin version of the *Rhetoric* and the *Didascalia* when, around 1272, he produced his own vast commentary on William of Moerbeke's translation of the *Rhetoric* from the Greek text. It was through Giles' use of Hermannus' translations that Al-Farabian ideas about the nature and object of rhetoric properly entered and influenced Western thought. While general Al-Farabian themes, notably the placement of rhetoric and poetics among the logical arts of the *Organon*, had been known since the twelfth century, it was Giles in the thirteenth century who promulgated some of the richest and most profound observations about the cognitive nature of rhetorical persuasion and rhetoric's application to social and moral particulars. For this knowledge, Giles was indebted to the translations of Hermannus, especially the *Didascalia*, as in turn were the fourteenth-century commentators on the *Rhetoric*, Jean of Jandun and Jean Buridan.[4]

Only one of possibly several medieval Arabic translations of the *Rhetoric* is extant, and this, dating possibly from as early as the eighth century, survives in a unique manuscript. But this is believed to be the translation that served Al-Farabi, Avicenna (980–1037), and Averroes (1126–98) in their commentaries on the *Rhetoric*, and the Arabic version that Hermannus Alemannus used for his Latin translation.[5] The Arabic tradition of commentary on Aristotle's text was very rich, even allowing for the fact that the art of rhetoric would have been seen to occupy a decidedly secondary position within logic and learning. Medieval Arab bibliographers preserve the titles of many commentaries that do not survive. But for Al-Farabi, Avicenna, and Averroes each, we have two surviving works dedicated to commenting on the *Rhetoric*.[6] Hermannus availed himself of all three learned authorities when producing his translation of the *Rhetoric*, citing their names and incorporating their glosses to such an extent that it was long thought that he had simply translated a commentary by Averroes on the *Rhetoric*.[7] The views of these Arab commentators on the

about the science of rhetoric from Al-Farabi's *De scientiis* (as translated closely by Gerard of Cremona). See Rosier-Catach, "Roger Bacon, al-Farabi et Augustin," 107.

[4] See the introduction to Part 5, above, for further references.

[5] Aouad, "La *Rhétorique*. Tradition syriaque et arabe," 457–60; Aouad's introduction to Averroes, *Commentaire moyen à la Rhétorique d'Aristote*, 1:1–2. The extant Arabic version is edited by Lyons, *Aristotle's Ars Rhetorica*; on the dating, see 1:i, and on the relation between Hermannus' version and this Arabic translation, see's 1:xvi–xxiii. On Hermannus' use of different copies of this translation, see the introduction to the *Didascalia* by Grignaschi in Al-Farabi, *Deux ouvrages*, 134–7; and see Bottin, *Contributi della tradizione greco-latina e arabo-latina al testo della Retorica di Aristotele*, 75–85.

[6] For titles of lost works, and for editions of surviving works, see Aouad, "La *Rhétorique*," 460–72. On Al-Farabi, see below.

[7] Boggess, "Hermannus Alemannus' Rhetorical Translations," summarizes the tradition of erroneous identification and presents a correct analysis of the nature of Hermannus' translation. There is no critical edition yet of

Rhetoric thus found their way, sometimes in partial or indirect form, into the Latin scholarly world.

But a more extensive portion of Al-Farabi's work on the *Rhetoric* had an influential afterlife in the West, through Hermannus' *Didascalia*. The state of the surviving Al-Farabian commentaries on the *Rhetoric* is complex and merits attention in some detail here in order to contextualize the contribution of Hermannus. We have, in whole or in part, two commentaries by Al-Farabi dedicated to the *Rhetoric*. The *Kitâb al-khatâbah* (Book of Rhetoric) is an exposition of *Rhetoric* book 1, chapter 2 in terms of rhetoric's relation to logic and religious conviction.[8] The second work was known, until recently, only in its Latin form as the *Didascalia*. This is Hermannus' translation of the opening section of Al-Farabi's "Great Commentary." Hermannus translated Al-Farabi's prologue and the beginning of the commentary proper, i.e. the opening lines of the *Rhetoric* (1354a1–4) and Al-Farabi's gloss on these lines. Hermannus announces this clearly in his own prologue: he has translated as much of the gloss as introduces the *Rhetoric*.[9] The entire Al-Farabian original was a voluminous commentary that extended to book 3, chapter 9 of Aristotle's text. The original work in its full form was also known to both Avicenna and Averroes. Hermannus' *Didascalia*, in its turn, was abridged by Lancellotus de Zerlis in the fifteenth century and was printed in Venice in 1481 as the *Declaratio compendiosa Alfarabii super Rhetoricorum libris Aristotelis*, in an edition containing the Moerbeke translation of the *Rhetoric* and Hermannus' translation of the Averroistic *Poetics*. The *Declaratio compendiosa* is a "conflated extract" of the *Didascalia* which supplied a table of contents to the *Rhetoric* in the printed edition.[10] The *Declaratio* was printed again in the Venice 1515 edition of Giles of Rome's commentary on the *Rhetoric*, to which it also served as contents list and preface.

Hermannus' translation of the *Rhetoric*, although some passages are printed by Schneider as an appendix in the *Rhetoric* volume of the *Aristoteles latinus*, and by Boggess in his article.

   [8] Ed. Langhade, with French translation, in Al-Farabi, *Deux ouvrages*. Contrary to Langhade's view, Aouad regards the treatise that we have as a complete work, not a truncation of a larger commentary: see "Les fondements de la *Rhétorique* d'Aristote reconsidérés par Farabi," 134n. For analysis of the work, see also Butterworth, "The Rhetorician and his Relationship to the Community."

   [9] See Grignaschi's introduction in Al-Farabi, *Deux ouvrages*, 2: *Didascalia*, 125–33, 136, 146; Boggess, "Hermannus Alemannus' Rhetorical Translations," 245–7; Aouad, "La Rhétorique," 464–5. Portions of the Arabic original of the "Great Commentary" have now been identified by Aouad as incorporated in a treatise on logic by Ibn Ridwan (d. 1061 or 1068): see "La doctrine rhétorique d'Ibn Ridwan et la *Didascalia in Rhetoricam Aristotelis ex glosa Alpharabii*."

   [10] Boggess, "Hermannus Alemannus' Rhetorical Translations," 235; see also Grignaschi in Al-Farabi, *Deux ouvrages*, 2: *Didascalia*, 142–3.

Hermannus' *Didascalia* has long been viewed as a difficult and even puzzling text.[11] It survives in only one manuscript, which contains various lapses and errors. More importantly, however, Hermannus himself was often unsure of the subject matter, and turned to Al-Farabi's commentary to elucidate the teaching of the *Rhetoric*. Hermannus' struggles with the material are reflected in the ambiguity of some of his terms and formulations, and the absence of a complete Arabic original has made it difficult in some cases to determine what words or phrases Hermannus was trying to translate. Hermannus was quite explicit about the difficulties of understanding the *Rhetoric* itself. In the prologue to his Latin translation of the Arabic *Rhetoric*, he anticipates negative reviews:

> Let no one wonder at the difficulty of [this] translation or be contemptuous of its rough quality, for the translation from Greek into Arabic is a very difficult and rough text. This is why Al-Farabi, who first tried to draw out some meaning from the *Rhetoric*, abandoned his glossing, passing over many examples in the Greek text on account of their obscurity. And for this reason he left many ambiguities. Avicenna and Averroes believed this was why he did not take his gloss all the way to the end of the work [i.e. the "Great Commentary" of Al-Farabi stops in the middle of book 3] . . . And nowadays these two books [i.e. the *Rhetoric* and *Poetics*] are so neglected among Arabs that I could hardly find one person willing to expend the effort to study them carefully with me.[12]

Hermannus was sensitive to the historical importance of bringing both the *Rhetoric* and the *Poetics* to a Latin readership whose understanding of these arts was formed by Roman traditions. Here again the prologue to his translation of the *Rhetoric* is extremely informative. He brings these works to Latin audiences who, he says, have a particular zeal for logic:

> So now [with these two works] they may have the full complement of logical matter according to Aristotle's thought. No one who has studied the works of the famous Arabs, namely Al-Farabi, Avicenna, and Averroes, as well as some others, would doubt that these two books belong to logic. Indeed, this will appear with greater clarity from the text itself. Nor can these works be dispensed with, as someone might think, because of the *Rhetorica* of Marcus Tullius Cicero or the *Ars poetica* of Horace. For, by contrast, Tully considered rhetoric a part of civil science, and discussed it especially from this angle. And Horace

---

[11] For example, F. W. Zimmerman, review of Al-Farabi, *Deux ouvrages*, in *Cahiers de civilisation médiévale* 17 (1974):264, "Les traductions de Hermann n'ont pas connu un très grand succès. La chose n'a rien de surprenant pour qui a tenté de lire les *Didascalia*!"

[12] Translated from the text as reproduced in Boggess, "Hermannus Alemannus' Rhetorical Translations," 250.

treated poetics just insofar as it pertains to grammar. Nevertheless, the works of these men are of no small use for understanding the present works.[13]

Here Hermannus announces, with remarkable historical self-consciousness, the impact of the extended *Organon* on traditional conceptions of the trivium. While the idea that rhetoric and poetics were part of logic was no longer new, the Latin world would only know the full implications of that idea when the texts of the *Rhetoric* and *Poetics* were linguistically accessible. Rhetoric and poetics will now also be understood as parts of a logical enterprise, where they will constitute further methods of proof. Hermannus is marking the emergence of a scholastic, professional interest in rhetoric and poetics that disengaged them from their traditional contexts in language pedagogy and redefined them as kinds of proof that deal in lower degrees of certitude and complex cognitive mechanisms. In this new field, Hermannus says, Cicero and Horace will no longer be the complete story, because they do not treat rhetoric and poetics from the perspective of logic. Hermannus' own translations of Aristotle, especially of the *Rhetoric*, may not have had the immediate impact that he seems to promise here; but he accurately forecasts a much larger intellectual development in higher academic circles, where the study of rhetoric would come to be attached to Aristotelian logic and ethics.

The *Didascalia* is a distillation of the principles of rhetoric by way of a preface to an extended commentary on the source text. Al-Farabi synthesizes his understanding of Aristotle's theory of rhetoric with his own larger scientific interest in logic. The major Al-Farabian themes that emerge here are that rhetoric is a part of logic that uses the enthymeme and example as its main devices; that, unlike demonstration, persuasive speech produces belief without certitude; that rhetoric is persuasion about particular matters (but its methods are not appropriate to the particular matters of other sciences), and that rhetoric's moral utility is civic governance, especially the propounding of religious law. But it is often the way that Al-Farabi understands and expounds a specific issue in the *Rhetoric* that provides the richest insight into the intellectual conditions for the reception of this text. This is the case, for example, with his discussion of epideictic rhetoric (§ 25), where the classical treatment of ceremonial oratory (praise and blame) is filtered through Arabic traditions of public, ceremonial poetry appropriate to certain occasions (e.g. mourning) and subject matters (praise of the dead, exhortation or praise of the living). The account of the sciences in relation to Plato's cave and the process of enlightenment (§ 38) is startling as a literary explication of a philosophical system. As this passage demonstrates, Al-Farabi's placement of the *Rhetoric* and the *Poetics* with the

---

[13] Ibid.

logical works of the *Organon* does not demote them to merely instrumental functions, but rather elevates them to an important ethical status. When they are used for religious and political communication with mass audiences, they serve to modify philosophical understanding according to the capacities of ordinary people. The philosopher must ascend from the shadows of understanding to the highest method of demonstrative proof, as taught in the *Posterior Analytics*, but he must then descend through the remaining, lower, logical arts and thereby learn to communicate with mass audiences who respond willingly to rhetorical enthymeme and example, and to poetic representation.[14] While Al-Farabi's commentary is mainly given over to explaining the forms of reasoning entailed in the *Rhetoric* and to treating it as a branch of logic, the ethical and aesthetic applications of rhetoric are never distant from his interests. The fascination with the processes of cognition and kinds of conviction involved in dialectical and rhetorical proof allows him to situate the *Rhetoric* among the central concerns of the *Organon*, but also prompts him to analyze the psychology of belief and the sensory, emotional, and formal appeals of oratory. These are the themes that prepared the grounds for the full impact of the *Rhetoric* in its reappearance in the Latin West under the authoritative aegis of William of Moerbeke's translation and Giles' commentary.

Translated from *Didascalia in Rethoricam Aristotelis ex glosa Alpharabi*, ed. Grignaschi, in *Deux ouvrages inédits sur la réthorique*, ed. Langhade and Grignaschi, by permission.[15]

HERE BEGINS THE *DIDASCALIA* ON ARISTOTLE'S *RHETORIC* FROM THE GLOSSES OF AL-FARABI

Prooemium. Since every new and unfamiliar text arouses fear and anxiety in readers where there is a suspicion of difficulty, it seemed to me, Hermannus Alemannus, a good thing to translate as much[16] of the gloss of Al-Farabi as prefaces Aristotle's book of rhetoric, which I have recently translated from the Arabic language into Latin, along with those theoretical issues he treats in determining what rhetoric is and how it differs from the faculty of

---

[14]   Black, *Logic and Aristotle's Rhetoric and Poetics in Medieval Arabic Philosophy*, 6, 116–7.
[15]   We have found very useful the close readings of passages from the *Didascalia* in Aouad, "La doctrine rhétorique d'Ibn Ridwan et la *Didascalia in Rhetoricam Aristotelis ex glosa Alpharabii*."
[16]   Reading *in quantum* as in the transcription of this passage in Boggess, "Hermannus Alemannus' Rhetorical Translations," 249 (appendix 1).

oratory,[17] how many are the parts of Aristotle's book, how many tractates there are in each part of the book, and how many chapters there are in each tractate; and other[18] considerations that seem to pertain to the method of introductions. With these matters in hand, the approach to this book will be more familiar...

§ 1. Al-Farabi said: We propose to explicate what Aristotle treated in his book which he called the book of rhetoric. Certainly the utility that this book contains applies most to the matters that Aristotle set forth in his other books of logic, and its necessity there is the more keen. Rhetoric is counted among the noble and celebrated arts, and it is an excellent instrument for governance of states [*regimina civitatum*],[19] and necessary for ordering religious laws [*in legum directione*].[20] The majority of men, those who follow the common walk of life, involve themselves more readily in the actions of this faculty than in the actions of the other arts and faculties which precede rhetoric in the science of logic.[21] Of the majority of men, we would find hardly anyone who uses a demonstrative or a dialectical argument, or who argues from topics or even from sophistical reasoning, except in the sense that he communicates these things using rhetoric. And the wisest among the majority of men, and those who are accepted among them, aspire more to knowledge of what this art contains than to those matters that the other parts of logic contain, and they try harder to grasp the definition of oratorical art and to investigate what it is. Such efforts are not unique to the wise and industrious of one particular people: they are found among the wise of every nation who have any kind of access to thought and consultation.

---

[17] On the distinction between the terms "rhetoric" and "oratory" in Hermannus' *Didascalia*, see Grignaschi's edition, 152–3 n. 11. The editor notes that it is not possible to determine precisely what Arabic term stands behind the Latin word *oratoria* in Hermannus' text, because the Latin word occurs in various contexts, sometimes appearing to be interchangeable with *oratio* (a speech or oration). But in general, *oratoria*, like *oratio*, represents some component part (or parts) of the art of rhetoric, or an instance (not always perfect or complete) of the art.

[18] Reading *cetera* as in the transcription in Boggess, "Hermannus Alemannus' Rhetorical Translations," 249.

[19] See Grignaschi edition, 150 n. 2. This point is explained in more detail at a later point in the *Didascalia* (§ 31), where it is said that rhetoric is an instrument of governance and of propounding civil law to the multitude. This point is developed in Averroes' *Middle Commentary* on Aristotle's *Rhetoric*: see *Commentaire moyen à la Rhétorique d'Aristote*, ed. and trans. Aouad, 2:8: "La rhétorique a deux utilités. L'une des deux est qu'elle incite les citoyens aux actions excellentes." Hermannus' translation of the *Rhetoric* from its Arabic version incorporates this passage from Averroes' *Middle Commentary*: see *Aristoteles latinus* 31.1–2, *Rhetorica*, ed. Schneider, 339. Cf. Aristotle, *Rhetoric*, 1355a.

[20] On the understanding of this as "religious laws," see Grignaschi edition, 150 n. 3, which refers to Al-Farabian and Averroistic theses that religious legislators will use the methods of rhetoric to address the multitude. See Alfarabi, *Philosophy of Plato and Aristotle*, trans. Mahdi, 62, § 26: "Then he [Plato] investigated the method of instruction: how it is conducted by two methods—the method of rhetoric and another method he called *dialectic*; and how both of these methods can be employed in conversation and in speaking and employed in writing." A similar idea is found also in Al-Farabi, *The Canons of Poetry*, in Cantorino, trans., *Arabic Poetics in the Golden Age*, 113: "Epic and Rhetoric are kinds of poetry in which premises of political and religious law are described."

[21] Cf. Aristotle's *Rhetoric* 1354a.

§ 2. Let us begin our exposition of this book with those considerations that it is customary to put in the prologues of glosses.[22] These are eight in number: 1) the purpose of the book, 2) the fittingness of the book's title to its intention, 3) the parts of the book, 4) the utility which is in the book, 5) the comparative relation of the book,[23] 6) its place within the science studied in the book,[24] 7) the mode of teaching by which it is presented, 8) and who the author himself was.[25] First we will consider what is the purpose of the oratorical art and what is the purpose of rhetoric, and in what way the title is appropriate to this book, and what is the sum of knowledge that Aristotle brought together in it. After this[26] we will speculate about the definitions ventured by the majority of those ancients who were learned in the art of oratory, and we will compare these to what Aristotle clearly said about these very matters, so that the extent of that which most have attained concerning this definition may be clear to us. And then it will be made clear to us how the definitions of oratory given by the majority are defective.[27] And the defect that results from these definitions is revealed as the reason why this art and this faculty have not been fully investigated. When someone defines it, either in terms that do not comprehend all the parts, or in terms in which not all its parts but only certain parts of it are set forth, then—through such definitions from the parts of oratory and the parts of rhetoric—a man comprehends only those parts which are evident (in the definitions). Therefore it is necessary to have a definition in which all the parts of the art, and everything which the art comprises and through which it is complete, are explained, and in this way its whole essence and its parts may be fully understood.

[22] These eight topics derive from the Aristotelian commentators of Greek late antiquity. See Grignaschi's edition, 128–30; and see *Al-Farabi's Commentary and Short Treatise on Aristotle's De interpretatione*, trans. Zimmerman, xci–xciii and 1–9.

[23] I.e. in relation to other books of Aristotle's logic, which represent branches of logical science; "comparative relation," translating *proportio sive comparatio*, by which Hermannus Alemannus translates an Arabic term relating to a branch of philosophy. See Grignaschi's edition, 152 n. 7.

[24] See Grignaschi's edition, 152 n. 8: the Arabic term translated is equivalent to the Greek *taxis*. See also *Al-Farabi's Commentary and Short Treatise on Aristotle's De interpretatione*, xci n. 2.

[25] In Al-Farabi's usage and the late antique commentators, this represents a question of the authenticity of the work. See Grignaschi's edition, 128 and 152 n. 10.

[26] *post hoc*. Aouad and Rashed ("L'exégèse de la *Rhétorique* d'Aristote," 79) suggest that Hermannus may have incorrectly rendered the Arabic phrase meaning "along with this," since the question of defective definitions of rhetoric is not actually considered after the treatment of rhetoric's purpose, but rather in the course of that treatment.

[27] The defective definitions held by the majority of those among the ancients who were familiar with rhetoric are set forth in §§ 14–15: according to Al-Farabi, they are that rhetoric is equivalent to dialectic; or that it differs from poetic only in terms of meter or quantity (it is prose without meter); it is the means for discovering or acquiring eloquence or for choosing what is just; or it is a long duration that does not weary (*longitudo non tediosa*) or a brevity that is not irksome. These defective definitions do not derive from Aristotle (cf. *Rhetoric* 1354a–1355a), but from Arabic traditions: see Aouad and Rashed, "L'exégèse de la *Rhétorique* d'Aristote," 85–8.

To clarify this, we will start from a somewhat more general level, noting that knowledge is of two kinds, as has often been stated: one is an image in the mind of a non-compounded thing, and the other is assertion [*assertio*] or conviction [*creditio*] regarding the combination of things that are compounded.[28]

One kind of conviction or belief [*credulitas*] is based on certitude, and another kind is close to certitude, and another is based on persuasion. The conviction based on certitude is something about which one believes that it is thus, without any contrary, because it is not possible for it to be any other way. The conviction which does not belong to certitude falls into two remaining species. There is that which one believes to be thus, without any contrary, and that could be otherwise, i.e. that it is possible that it could have a contrary. The kind that is close to certitude involves something about which the contrary is not considered, or is allowed only with difficulty, for in fact it has a contrary. The conviction based on persuasion is something about which the soul is at rest. In this case the soul falls into assent [*assensus*] about something, since it is without a contrary; yet its contrary could exist along with it. The soul admits this easily, unless it is that the soul inclines more to one contrary than to the other. But this inclination is extreme relative to the inclination to the other contrary, whether the inclinations of the soul are many or few, strong or weak.[29] Generally speaking, there will be belief on the terms of persuasion, that is, "sufficient," when there is an inclination of the mind to one or the other of these contraries and if the inclination is moderate, as long as there is, in the mind, a certain excess towards one contrary relative to the other.

[. . .]

> [The sections of the exposition omitted here cover the following topics: § 3 two sources of conviction: *propositiones primae* (certitude without syllogism) and syllogisms (knowledge through demonstration, as in *Posterior Analytics*); §§ 4–8, non-artistic (atechnical) proofs; §§ 9–10, premises of persuasive discourse; §§ 11–12, conclusions and their use.]

§ 13. Now that we have set forth these matters, we have to consider what, according to Aristotle, is the purpose of oratory or eloquence. Concerning eloquence or rhetoric, it appears to everyone that its action [*actus*] is a certain discourse; but its action is not just any kind of discourse produced by any kind of person. Now it is appropriate for all or most people to speak; but one would not say that they are orators or rhetors. For a person would

---

[28] The distinction between knowledge of things that are non-compounded (*incomplexae*) and compounded (*complexae*) (i.e. knowledge that is either intuitive or discursive), goes back to Aristotelian discussions of predication. A simple or non-compounded term is something either known or unknown, but when terms are compounded in a proposition, the compounding is either true or false. See, *Categories* 1a 16 (and *passim*), and *Metaphysics* 9.10 (1051a34–1052a11).

[29] Cf. Aouad, "La doctrine rhétorique d'Ibn Ridwan," 225.

not seem, to most people, to be a rhetor unless he has the power for a certain definite kind of discourse, not any kind of discourse. In the same way, it appears to all people that rhetoric is a certain power and disposition [*habitus*] through which a certain discourse comes about. However, they do not make a further determination about the nature of this discourse than that it is a proper, graceful, and excellent discourse. The discourse which is called rhetoric does not achieve this propriety and grace except through definite dispositions [*dispositiones*] and conditions. And it appears that the use of rhetoric comes about by means of some definite purpose and aim. And the propriety and goodness or excellence of this usage exist when it is produced according to those dispositions through which its purpose is achieved. But in this, rhetoric is no different from the art of poetry, nor from a scientific faculty, nor from sophistical power. For any of these is a disposition [*habitus*] through which discourse that is proper and excellent comes about.

[. . .]

> [The sections of exposition omitted here cover the following topics: §§ 14–16, rhetoric and its object (continuing from § 13); § 17, three sorts of auditors; §§ 18–19, the means of influencing the auditors; §§ 20–22, subsidiary methods of rhetoric (emotional pleas, facial expressions, manner of declaiming, ethos or ethical proof); § 23, "incomplete rhetoric" or "necessary rhetoric," that is, discourse that achieves the persuasive aim without subsidiary methods.]

§ 24. Rhetoric that is complete is a disposition [*habitus*] through which discourse is formed according to all the means that bring about persuasion more completely, more efficiently, and more quickly in relation to each element of particular or singular things.[30] And these particular, singular things are the subjects of the conclusions of rhetorical syllogisms [*subjecta conclusionum*].[31] And sometimes these are individual matters concerning men and sometimes individual matters concerning certain other things. [Indeed, praise and blame, the proper and the improper, the beautiful and the ugly. . . [32]] As a rule, the individual matter about which such things as good will or hostility can be elicited is sometimes a certain individual matter pertaining to a man, sometimes a certain individual matter pertaining to other things. In one instance a horse is praised, in another instance a man.[33] However, in his book Aristotle says that the subjects of the conclusions of

[30] Aristotle, *Rhetoric* 1355b: "Let rhetoric be defined as an ability, in each particular case, to see the available means of persuasion."

[31] For reading of this as referring to rhetorical syllogisms, see Grignaschi edition, 187 n. 1.

[32] There is a lacuna in the text at this point. The context suggests that these are matters about which it is possible to argue only in terms of particulars. Cf. Aristotle, *Rhetoric* 1359a ("the good or the evil or the honorable or the shameful or the just or the unjust") and 1366a.

[33] Cf. *Rhetoric* 1366a.

rhetorical speeches are particulars concerning men and no other things. In fact, he does not speak about praise and blame except as these pertain to a human subject. And generally, [his] discussion [*sermo*] concerns the species of oratorical discourse (such as are considered in these books). Nor indeed is there discussion of these [species] if not in preparation for persuading about something concerning human beings, for affirming something about the same matter. It happens that such reasonings from the topics of argumentation [*ex modis sermocinatium*]—of which [Aristotle] makes mention—are used to establish belief [*credulitas*] about other living beings besides man, such as a horse or other domestic and untamed creatures; and from there to other things concerning plants or trees and places and cities and regions inhabited and uninhabited; and from there to other forms, such as in the waters or the stars or the clouds or the like.[34] However, the use of the faculty of rhetoric and its material is really more proper to human affairs [*in hominibus*]. Orations on matters that are not about man are of little profit and limited use. They may be found useful as a way of speaking about a man. For example, if someone wanted to praise a man or someone great, and he praised his horse or his house or his estates or other visible attributes, his intention would be to praise him by exalting and commending things that belong to him. When, however, the faculty of rhetoric, and orations which are based on rhetoric's material, are directed to human affairs, they are of very great use; and on that account, since Aristotle intended that the rhetor seek out this art for its proper utility, he maintained that the subjects from which orations proceed are individual matters pertaining to men, and no other things.[35] Since these rhetorical methods, by which one is directed to human affairs, comprehend matters which are not used for subjects other than human affairs, [Aristotle] maintained that what is in his book is directed only to human affairs.[36]

§ 25. Since this is the case, rhetorical argumentation (which is considered in this book) is completed by means of five things: the speaker; the one who is spoken about; the one to whom persuasion is directed; the adversary; and the judge. For example, in the case of praise [*laudatio*]: praise is completed through the one who praises; through the thing praised; through those who are to be persuaded, so that they believe this matter to be as praiseworthy as the speaker has claimed; through the adversary, who is put there to oppose

---

[34] Cf. *Rhetoric* 1366a: "But since it often happens . . . that not only a man or a god is praised but inanimate objects and any random one of the other animals, propositions on these subjects must be grasped in the same way."

[35] According to the editor, there is a mark indicating that the scribe corrected or completed this passage in the margin, but the marginal text disappeared in the process of binding (Grignaschi edition, 188 n. 2).

[36] Grignaschi (188 n. 3) explains this passage as follows: since in the domain of human affairs rhetoric makes use of forms of persuasion which have no application to other subjects, Aristotle had to define the art exclusively in terms of human affairs.

what the speaker proposes;[37] and through the judge, who is appointed to produce an opinion based on what is laid before him.[38] It can happen that the one whom the speech concerns, and the one to whom persuasion is directed, and the adversary are one and the same man. This happens mostly in condemnation [*vituperatio*] and complaint [*querimonia*]. Since man is the subject of this art, Aristotle posited three species of rhetorical argumentation: the genus of the deliberative case, of the judicial case, and of the demonstrative case. He posited that the deliberative genre involves permission or prohibition, and into this genus enter questions of laws and prohibitions, restrictions and rules and severe interdictions, and so forth. The judicial genre entails accusation, defense, and objection [*recusatio*]. The demonstrative entails praise and blame. Thus the primary genres of orations, which are spoken about some man or about something pertaining to the man, are these three and no others. And oratorical discourses [*orationes sermocinales*] that are profitable to men approach or ascend to these three and no others. The subject of praise is sometimes one who is living, sometimes one who is dead. Nor should it escape your notice that praise of a man is not always plaint [*planctus*] or [elegiac] lamentation [*lamentatio*].[39] But lamentations are part of poetics, not rhetoric. Moreover, some have thought that there is no difference between praise and lamentation on account of someone's bad fortune, except that praise of the dead is lamentation. But it is not as they have thought. A lamentation is nothing but a speech that elicits, or intends to elicit, someone's emotion and sorrow. It is meant to arouse sorrow, wretchedness, and tearful woe in the soul and strong emotion for someone—a man of upright and noble character—who has suffered calamity and affliction through no fault of his own.[40] When praise enters into lamentation, it is only when the hearer knows that the man who is oppressed by such calamity has not merited this, because he is virtuous, and so it arouses sympathy for his destruction and misery (since he was said to be of such virtue). And you will draw an example of this from

[37] This represents a misunderstanding by Al-Farabi, repeated elsewhere in his writings and also by later Arab commentators, about the audiences of orations. Aristotle speaks of two kinds of audiences (*Rhetoric* 1358b), spectators and judges (either those making political judgments or forensic judgments) and although this was rendered correctly in the Arabic version of the *Rhetoric*, Al-Farabi assumed that there were three kinds of auditors: the spectators, the judge, and a group whose role was to dispute or test the arguments of the orator. This misconception arose from Aristotle's reference to auditors who decide on a speaker's skill. See edition of the *Didascalia* by Grignaschi, 176–7 n. 9; and see Al-Farabi, *Kitâb al-khatâbah*, ed. Langhade, *Deux ouvrages*, fols. 257a–b (French translation, 64–8).

[38] See Al-Farabi, *Kitâb al-khatâbah*, ed. Langhade, *Deux ouvrages*, fols. 257a–b (French translation, 66–8), on whether the judge can make his own determination or is held to the arguments brought by the opposing parties.

[39] Aouad and Rashed, "L'exégèse," 96, translate *lamentatio* as "elegie," indicating that Hermannus' term renders an Arabic term for a poetic genre.

[40] Here, as in various other points throughout, the *Didascalia* evidences the close relation between rhetoric and poetics in the Arabic reception of Aristotle. Cf. Al-Farabi, *The Canons of Poetry*, in Cantorino, *Arabic Poetics in the Golden Age*, 113.

the [elegiac] laments, composed about the ancients and the calamities which befell them, adjoining the narratives of their histories. Those who first set about praising ancestors and exalting them, though the ancestors be dead, still do not show themselves weeping over them and lamenting them and composing [elegiac] songs of lamentation; neither do those who would praise the ancient fathers of certain peoples or their friends, eminent in virtues, who have just died, show themselves weeping over them. Rather, they undertake praises of the living, comparing their virtues to the merits of the dead. This is a mode of praising the dead which occurs in both rhetoric and poetry. But lamentation is [a form of] poetry.[41] Thus when it is used in rhetoric, it is used in emotional speeches on account of an argument which is made stronger through the use of these rhetorical devices. In this way, the living are sometimes accused and sometimes defended, and the dead are defended. A deliberative case pertains only to the living, because it arises as something proper to the living.

§ 26. Praise and commendation go with nobility and virtues. Blame [*vituperatio*] goes with the ignoble and vices or faults. The deliberative type of oration treats advantage and injury, providing instruction about what is advantageous and prohibition against injury and harm. A complaint arises from an unlawful act committed by a wrong-doer. On the other hand, a defense for this would show that the person did not do harm or that he had a right to do it. Advantage and injury, virtues and vices, and justice and wrong-doing are all entailed in the moral sciences, in politics, or in civil justice. And since (as was said earlier) rhetorical discourse is not complete except through orations that appeal to emotions and morals, and through those things that affirm the virtue of the speaker, it follows (from what was explained here, and earlier) that the propositions of rhetorical orations be drawn from matters that arise from moral science and the science of governing a state. It is obvious that orations appealing to the emotions are made from propositions pertaining to moral and civil matters. Similarly, orations in which the virtue of the speaker is affirmed are taken from propositions pertaining to moral matters. From this we posit that the art of rhetoric is meant to serve the useful advantage of man; it will be valuable because it is man's means for building up or taking away justice or injustice, what is useful or what is useless, what is noble and proper or what is ignoble and wrong. Therefore all the propositions through which these things are built up or taken away will rightly be moral and civil.

---

[41] Avicenna also treats lamentation as a poetic genre, as an extension of poetic praise in tragedy: see *Avicenna's Commentary on the Poetics of Aristotle*, trans. Dahiyat, 73: "The same was also done in Tragedy, i.e., the praise meant for a living or dead person . . . If he died, they would add to the length of the poem or to its tone certain notes portraying elegy and lamentation."

§ 27. Rhetoric arises from three modes: one is "necessary" rhetoric [*necessaria*];[42] the second is complete rhetoric [*completa*], when the discourse is concerned with human matters and things outside of human matters; and the third is [complete rhetoric] concerned with human matters [*ad homines*] alone. It does not follow that necessary rhetoric has to be about morals, except when it is being used in moral matters. But even so, necessary rhetoric is common to all particular subjects, apart from the fact that one or another of those things through which it becomes complete is moral matter. As to complete rhetoric brought to bear on all things singular, it is necessary that some of its parts be moral matters. For it is perfected or completed through confluence of the excellence of the speaker and the alteration of the hearer through emotions and morals. And if the speech through which one intends to induce conviction is persuasive about things other than human beings, it does not, therefore, necessarily follow that its propositions leading to conviction be moral propositions, nor its conclusions be about moral matters. When, however, complete rhetoric is directed to the utility of human beings, it follows that the propositions of its orations be moral matters, whether this involves orations inducing conviction, or emotions, or morals, or confirming the excellence of the speaker. But rhetorical method is used in all things, such that even in the sciences there is a certain rhetorical method used, [i.e.] necessary rhetoric.[43] Of course, since necessary rhetoric can be transferred to one science, it is possible to use it in every science. But the power to use this method is not rhetoric; rather, discourses formed according to rhetorical method are separated from rhetoric by this power and used for other matters whose method is that such discourses are used in them.[44] And such is what you see presented in the many books of Galen the physician, and oftentimes in his expositions of scientific matters. For example: the non-pulsating veins have their "beginning" or "origin" in the liver, because from among these veins the one that is closest to the liver is thicker, and in proportion to its distance from the liver the more aggregated it is and narrow it becomes; or, the excellence that guides the heart makes its home in the brain, because a king always lives in the highest place in the city; or, man understands by means of his brain, because people say of someone whom they

---

[42] See Aouad, "La doctrine rhétorique d'Ibn Ridwan," 231: "necessary rhetoric" (or "incomplete rhetoric") is that which has the minimum of elements needed to comprise a "rhetorical" speech: argument (something to be established) and proof, or purpose and verification, i.e. proof through discourse, without any extraneous procedures such as exordium, epilogue, or narration. "Complete rhetoric" makes use of all the devices interior and extraneous to rhetorical speech.

[43] For this sentence, Grignaschi (192 n. 2), suggests: "necessary rhetoric," which first sets out a thesis and then its demonstration by means of enthymemes, is even used in the sciences (of which practice Al-Farabi disapproves).

[44] According to Grignaschi (192 n. 5), this could be interpreted to mean that the use of necessary rhetoric in the sciences does not result from rhetorical power, but rather from a different power, just as discourses that demonstrate scientific problems do not involve rhetoric.

see to be defective in understanding that he is brainless; and courage and cowardice reside in the heart, because men say of a coward that he has no heart. All things of this sort are discourses or reasonings according to the method of rhetoric, used in the sciences and in matters whose nature is that these reasonings be used in them.[45] Discourses that deal in emotions, morals, and confirming the excellence of the speaker do not belong in the sciences at all, nor ought they to be used in them. They introduce error, and you will find all these discourses in the books of Galen. This relates to the means by which, in many of his books, he confirms or proves his own excellences. He strengthens or intensifies them by pointing to the honor and the reverence shown to him by men who have experienced his equity and justice, and then by boasting about himself and deprecating other physicians. All of these entail the confirmation of his excellences or his valor. The moral discourses which one uses are exemplified in words of his like these: "I do not speak this way except to someone whose mind is not corrupted through false opinions and sophistical deceptions"; and "this discourse is not used except for someone among the young who is assisted by divine support, whose intellect God on high has made firm and studious endeavors God has directed," and similar discourses.

[. . .]

> [The sections of exposition that are omitted here cover the following topics: § 28, rhetoric and the art of oratory (treating narration); §§ 29–31, speeches and written discourses, and the role of the rhetorician in the city; §§ 32–3, the faculties and kinds of knowledge necessary for the rhetorician; §§ 34–5, rhetoric as a part of logic; § 36, enthymemes and examples as the key devices of rhetoric.]

§ 37. Since what is in this book is a part of logic, we must speak about its ordering in relation to the other parts of logic; and since it is a different species of syllogism, it is clear that its order will be after the book in which the syllogism is treated in absolute terms, that is, the book of the *Prior Analytics*. Then we must consider its order in relation to those books which come after the above-mentioned book, that is, the *Prior Analytics*. Thus we say that, since it is clear that sophistical matters enter into the sum of the parts of the art of oratory, the order of this book will be after the book of *Sophistics*. It has also been shown that the parts of sophistic and its canons cannot be understood without previous knowledge of the parts and canons of the art of dialectic. Therefore it will be necessary for this

---

[45] For this last clause, Grignaschi (193 n. 1) suggests: "used in the sciences and in arguments which, by their nature, constitute the matter of discursive (oratorical) demonstrations." Aouad, "La doctrine rhétorique d'Ibn Ridwan," 229, notes that these are all examples of the intervention of "necessary rhetoric" (i.e. the form of rhetoric reduced to its most basic elements) in the sciences. These might be seen as illustrations of reasoning through enthymeme and example.

book to come after the *Topics* and *Sophistics*; and we have already shown in the first book of the *Topics* that it does not necessarily follow that this book comes after the book of *Demonstration*.[46] This is the order of the books according to the necessity of mastering them. According to what is fitting concerning the order of the parts of logic, this book will come after the book of *Demonstration* and the *Topics* and the book of *Sophistics* and before the book of *Poetics*; and it is thought that Aristotle placed the book [the *Rhetoric*] according to this ordering. And it seems that the reason for this kind of ordering of these books is that the art of logic is, in the first place, a preparation so that one may profit from it in study of the sciences; and in the second place, it is a preparation so that the greatest number of people may profit from it. It is already clear that the book of *Syllogisms*[47] must necessarily precede the other books and parts of logic. There are five other parts, of which three are instructive for the speculative sciences and two are directed to the use of the majority of people. The three that are directed to the speculative sciences are the book of *Demonstration* and the *Topics* and the *Sophistics*; and the two that are directed to the profit of the majority are the *Rhetoric* and the *Poetics*. Therefore if this art is, in the first place, an orientation to the sciences, then those three books must go before these two, so that in one's reading one encounters those three before the other two, in order that one has quick access to the primary purpose of logic. Of those three books, it is clear that the book of *Demonstration* is in a primary sense, and on its own account, directed to study of the sciences. Therefore a reading of it must precede a reading of the other two [i.e. the *Topics* and *Sophistics*]. Through dialectic one exercises the capacity for demonstration and is prepared for the principles of science; it enables the discovery of demonstrative reasoning in the sciences. Thus in a secondary sense it is preparatory to the sciences. The book of the canons of *Sophistics* is not in itself preparatory to the sciences, either in a primary or a secondary sense, but accidentally. And for this reason the book of *Sophistics* should come after the book of the *Topics*. With regard to the *Rhetoric* and the *Poetics*, the art which is of more general use and of benefit to more people and is needed more should come first. The art of oratory or rhetoric is of more general use to more people than poetics, and their need for it is greater than for poetics. Thus the book of *Rhetoric* should precede the book of *Poetics*. This is the order of these books according to their usefulness.

---

[46] I.e. the *Posterior Analytics*. The reference is to a commentary (no longer extant) by Al-Farabi on book 1 of the *Topics* which argued that the *Topics* does not necessarily come after the *Posterior Analytics* in the *Organon*. The order of knowledge represented by the books of the *Organon* was a recurring theme in Al-Farabi's thought and writings. See Grignaschi edition, 211 n. 1. "This book" (*liber iste*) in this sentence seems to refer to the *Topics*, and not to the *Rhetoric* (as in the previous sentences and following sentences).

[47] I.e. the *Prior Analytics*.

§ 38. But one may entertain the question of whether poetics ought to precede rhetoric on account of the exigencies of teaching. In many instances we see that the use of poetics occurs in rhetoric in terms of [metrical] quantity, as discussed in the second book of the *Rhetoric*.[48] On this account one could say that the book of *Poetics* ought to precede the book of *Rhetoric* doctrinally, because rhetoric needs poetics, but poetics does not need rhetoric. But since this need does not pertain to essential elements, and there are many reasons for the priority of rhetoric, rhetoric precedes poetic. And the example of the cave which Plato set forth in his book *The Republic*, showing how a man goes out from the cave and then returns to it, is consistent with Aristotle's ordering of the parts of the art of logic. He began with general notions,[49] that is, those which pertain to most things, and then he did not cease proceeding by degrees and gradually until he ascended to the most perfect of the sciences. Then he began to descend from this gradually until he arrived finally at the lowest, and least, and most base of the sciences. What is in the book of *Demonstration* is the most complete of the sciences and at the highest level; and what is in the book of *Poetics* is the most imperfect of them and the lowest in relation to the most perfect science. And this is similar to the picture of the sciences that Plato presented in the aforementioned example of the shadow in the cave. For a man who lives in the cave does not recognize himself or those who are with him by seeing them directly, but rather by seeing a shadow of each of them. And if one compares the knowledge by which the majority of people know themselves to the knowledge possessed by the wise, it will be just like the operation of one who did not see himself or any of those with him in a dark place, save but afterwards the sun appeared overhead and each of them cast a shadow and a shade, which he perceived with his sight—and then he knew himself and the comrades who were with him by recognizing the shadows and the shades that they cast—in comparison with someone who sees himself and his comrades with proper sight, not by means of their shadows and shades. And the book of the *Topics* is more proportionate to demonstrative science. After this comes the book of *Sophistics* and the book of *Rhetoric*. Thus Aristotle began with the book of *Categories*, that is, with knowledge that is most commonplace and general. Afterwards, he proceeded to the book *On Interpretation*, and there he affirmed propositions from a higher order of knowledge than what is in the book of *Praedicamenta* [i.e. *Categories*]. And it is the same with the propositions he set forth in the book of the *Prior Analytics*. He presented the fourth book [i.e. the *Posterior Analytics*] as that which is the most complete among the sciences. Then he descended gradually from this until, as we said, he came to that which is the most base

---

[48] The reference should properly be to book 3 of Aristotle's *Rhetoric*, which treats such formal matters. This may be a scribal error: see Aouad, "La doctrine rhétorique d'Ibn Ridwan," 210 n. 85.

[49] *sententiis summatis* (Grignaschi's emendation); Boggess ("Alfarabi and the *Rhetoric*," 89) retains the manuscript reading of *sentenciis minimis* ("lowest opinions").

among them, that is, *Poetics*. This method, which Aristotle followed in the tradition of logic, is probably what Plato intended in the example just cited.[50]

[The remaining sections of the *Didascalia* are as follows: §§ 39–56, a summary of the contents of the *Rhetoric*; § 57, the method that Aristotle uses in the *Rhetoric*; § 58, the opening passage of the *Rhetoric* and Al-Farabi's commentary on it, i.e. the opening exposition of Al-Farabi's "Great Commentary," the long preface to which has been translated by Hermannus as the *Didascalia*.]

[50] The *Categories*, *De interpretatione*, and *Prior Analytics* are thus preparatory for the most perfect science, the *Posterior Analytics*. The account of this passage by Boggess, "Alfarabi and the Rhetoric: The Cave Revisited," is extremely informative:

For Alfarabi, therefore, the philosopher must leave the shadows of the cave by progressing through the *Categories*, the *Peri hermeneias* and the *Prior Analytics*...to the *Posterior Analytics*, the *perfectissima scientiarum*....He must then re-enter the realm of fallacy...and gradually descend through the *Topics*, the *Sophistici Elenchi* and the *Rhetoric* to the *Poetics*, the most imperfect logical science...He must develop an appreciation for, and presumably the ability to use, five types of reasoning: the demonstrative, where all the premisses are true; the disputative, where the premisses are mostly true; the sophistic, where the premisses are mostly false; the rhetorical, where the premisses are equally true and false; and the poetical, where all the premisses are false. The *Rhetoric*, in this view, is no more a "productive" science than the *Topics* or the *Sophistici Elenchi*; it is rather the philosopher's tool for reasoning with those whose vision is limited to the deceptive shadows of the Platonic cave (90).

BRUNETTO LATINI, *RETTORICA*,
CA. 1260

INTRODUCTION

The mid thirteenth century saw the beginnings of a remarkable departure from long medieval traditions of rhetorical study: the turning of Cicero's own texts into vernacular languages, and the directing of Ciceronian precept to non-learned audiences. The first and most important phase of this movement was Italian, with two key exemplars: Brunetto Latini's *Rettorica*, his translation and exposition of the *De inventione* (completed only to 1.17.24), which he undertook in or about 1260 while he was living in France, in exile from Florence; and the *Fiore di rettorica* (Flower of Rhetoric) of Bono Giamboni, an abridged translation of the *Rhetorica ad Herennium*, also begun in the 1260s, and later revised and expanded by the author (and redacted at least twice again by later revisers).[1] The move to vernacularize the Ciceronian texts for lay audiences did not end with the thirteenth century and was not restricted to Italian translators, although the trend was strongest and most continuous in Italy.[2] Brunetto himself made a synthesis of the *De inventione* in book 3 of his *Trésor*, the grand encyclopedic work that he wrote in French, also during the 1260s during his exile (and which was almost immediately translated into Italian as the *Tesoro*).[3] In 1282, Jean d'Antioche made a French translation of both the *De inventione* and the *Ad Herennium* (surviving only in one manuscript);[4] in the early fifteenth century the *Ad Herennium* was translated into Spanish.[5] The Italian tradition of translating the Ciceronian rhetorics—with special attention to the *Ad Herennium*—continued well into the fifteenth century, when it began to be overtaken by newer Humanist interests in rhetoric and the ascendancy of Quintilian's *Institutio oratoria* as the ultimate classical authority on eloquence.

---

[1] *Fiore di Rettorica*, ed. Speroni.
[2] Cox, "Ciceronian Rhetoric in Late Medieval Italy," 136–43, for a list of Italian translations from the thirteenth to the fifteenth centuries.
[3] Brunetto Latini, *Li livres dou Trésor*, ed. Carmody.
[4] Delisle, "Notice sur la Rhétorique de Cicéron, traduite par Maitre Jean d'Antioche."
[5] See Monfrin, "Humanisme et traductions au moyen âge," 188.

Brunetto Latini's *Rettorica* is not only the earliest of medieval vernacularizations of Ciceronian rhetoric, but is also, certainly, the most ambitious in motive and sophisticated in composition. This motive has to be understood, first of all, in cultural terms. The *Rettorica* represents the first wave of a "Ciceronian revival" in thirteenth-century Italian rhetorical culture, a new interest in classical doctrine alongside what had become the primary modern form of the art in the Italian cities, *dictamen*. The *ars dictaminis* was a practical knowledge geared to the needs of Italian communal society: while it served in the orbits of law and politics, it did not attempt to provide a nuanced theory of argumentation or deliberation. Where Ciceronian rhetoric focuses, through the theory of invention, on the complex construction of an argument or dispute about a point of law, *dictamen* was for the most part a stylistic art, with a focus on *elocutio* and ornamentation of prose. Mid-thirteenth-century Italian audiences seem to have embraced the classical texts because of the very character of Ciceronian theory as an adversarial art, a theory of negotiating conflict. Virginia Cox has shown how this art would have had immediate relevance to adversarial deliberative debate within the councils and assemblies of the Italian communes, a practice that was gaining increasing importance in Italian political life.[6] This is the dimension of classical theory that Brunetto chooses to stress in his commentary on the *De inventione*, especially in relation to Cicero's dense discussion of status theory or the legal controversies that define a case (*De inventione* 1.8.10–1.14.19). Brunetto extends the parameters of the rhetorical "issue" or dispute to propose that all communication involves dispute (*tencione*), whether in courts of law or beyond, whether in expression of different viewpoints in public debate or the exchange of ideas, petitions, and responses in private letters or even in love poetry.[7] As Brunetto presents it, the adversarial art of Ciceronian rhetoric applies to all aspects of civic and private life, in written discourse as well as in oral debate, in councils, embassies, and private matters, as well as in courts of law.[8]

In the commentary, Brunetto attempts to link Ciceronian teaching about legal and political speech with the contemporary practice of writing on any topic. In the Italian

---

[6] Cox, "Ciceronian Rhetoric in Italy, 1260–1350," 256–9; and "Ciceronian Rhetoric in Late Medieval Italy," 117. See also Milner, "Communication, Consensus, and Conflict." It is to this cultural dossier of disputative practice that Brunetto's translations of some of Cicero's orations belongs. See Brunetto Latini, *Le tre orazioni di M. T. Cicerone dette dinanzi a Cesare … volgarizzate da Brunetto Latini*, ed. Rezzi.

[7] See section [76] below, pp. 774–9. On adversarial rhetoric and the culture of poetic debate, see Steinberg, *Accounting for Dante*, 70–3, 101.

[8] Witt ("Brunetto Latini and the Italian Tradition of *Ars Dictaminis*," 12–15) sees the discussion of dispute and the widening of its scope to this implicit *tencione* as a vestige of classical theory that puts Brunetto in a dilemma, because he must ultimately recognize that not all letters are contentious in nature. But Cox ("Ciceronian Rhetoric in Italy, 1260–1350," 268–9) sees this as a sign that Cicero could be revived as a model for handling all matters of political and social interaction.

communes, the ubiquity of notarial documents in legal and political life, and the fundamental role of *dictamen* in education, would make it both crucial and inevitable that Brunetto should extend Ciceronian theory to the practice of writing. Thus for Brunetto, rhetoric is not easily confined to the three genres (deliberative, judicial, epideictic) but, as he ultimately admits, should be able to take any matter for its subject. He also acknowledges the difference between oratory and the written text, but insists on the applicability to written compositions of a rhetoric designed for oral discourse. Here he goes further than the earlier commentary tradition by reflecting on the difference between a speech (where the audience is present) and writing (where the audience is absent), even as he tries to show the common ground of the two modes. He attempts to bring the formal properties of the speech (its six-part structure) into some explicit relationship with the formal properties of the epistle (its five-part structure). Dictaminal teaching had long recognized Ciceronian precept on the parts of the speech that had corresponding parts in the letter, that is, the exordium, narration, and conclusion; but the relevance of Ciceronian doctrine on form and structure was limited.[9] Brunetto, however, is bound to the Ciceronian text because he is translating and expounding it, and therefore finds himself having to explain where Ciceronian precept overlaps with dictaminal teaching, and where the contemporary and the classical diverge from one another absolutely. But his comments on grammatical teaching of correct usage and on the importance of grammar as a whole provide perhaps the deepest foundation for the commonality of the arts of speaking and writing.

Brunetto went beyond translating Cicero's text to establish an assertive, independent voice for what he calls "the expositor" [*lo sponitore*], which is the persona that Brunetto himself inhabits with varying degrees of self-reference. The proportion of text devoted to the exposition far exceeds the translation of Cicero (and perhaps the prospect of continuing at such length explains why he left off the work barely one-third of the way through book 1 of *De inventione*). The expositor is a lively presence, in constant dialogue with the Ciceronian text as he affirms its relevance to contemporary civic circumstances and to the literary culture of *dictamen*. The expositor also serves to fix and stabilize a perspective on "true" and "correct" rhetoric, to anticipate the possibility of misinterpreting Cicero's words, and to counteract the threat of false rhetoric and political injustice that always pervades the world of this commentary, written while Brunetto was himself a political exile. Exile (along with false accusation) is a theme that recurs in the expositor's passages.[10]

---

[9] Alessio, "The Rhetorical Juvenilia of Cicero and the *Artes Dictandi*."

[10] See Milner, "Exile, Rhetoric, and the Limits of Civic Republican Discourse," 172–5.

The discourse of the expositor leads us to another spectacular dimension of the *Rettorica*, its compositional complexity. Gian Carlo Alessio has shown that Brunetto made extensive use of a twelfth-century Latin gloss on the *De inventione* contained in Oxford, Bodleian Library MS Canon. Class. Lat. 201.[11] This gloss, called the *Ars rhetorice* from its incipit, is today no more than a fragment of its original length. It is a commentary based on the northern French cathedral school tradition, closely related to the most archaic of those, the commentary by William of Champeaux, from the early decades of the twelfth century, which was superseded by the commentaries of Thierry of Chartres, Petrus Helias, and other anonymous commentators of the second half of the twelfth century. The anonymous commentary in the Bodleian manuscript seems to have been written or redacted by an Italian or at least someone working in Italy (perhaps Milan). Comparison of the expositor's sections of the *Rettorica* and the gloss *Ars rhetorice* reveals that Brunetto used the commentary, not only for its doctrinal explanations (often translating these *ad verbum*), but also for its learned classical and late classical references to Lucan, Victorinus, and Boethius. Brunetto's use of this commentary links the world of thirteenth-century *volgare* Ciceronianism with the academic world of the twelfth-century northern French cathedral schools. Brunetto's final product combines an energetic civic reception of Ciceronian rhetoric with the literary classicism and philosophical-scientific outlook of an academic culture that was certainly, by his time, old-fashioned. What this may suggest is that the "Ciceronian revival" of mid-thirteenth-century Italy had to find its initial interpretive models in much older material, because the dominant dictaminal art had moved so far away from Ciceronian rhetoric that the *De inventione* and *Ad Herennium* occupied a very marginal role in Italian rhetorical study.[12]

In bringing together these starkly contrasting worlds, Brunetto also provides a sharper perspective on the nature of the archaic commentary tradition. This can best be seen where he moves away from his twelfth-century source: his proposal that all communication is disputative, his explicit pronouncements about the differences between Cicero's theory of (oral) speech-making and contemporary written rhetoric, and his attempts, nevertheless, to accommodate contemporary practice to the central pillars of Ciceronian rhetorical theory, all throw into relief the overwhelmingly academic and scientific character of earlier school commentaries. Where twelfth-century schoolmen (and their thirteenth-century descendants, such as Vincent of Beauvais or Robert Kilwardby) were content to repeat the formula that rhetoric is the art of speaking well in civic matters, Brunetto is keen to

---

[11] Alessio, "Brunetto Latini e Cicerone (e i dettatori)."   [12] See Ward, *Ciceronian Rhetoric*, 24–5.

determine exactly what those civic matters are, what kinds of social groups they involve, how civic rhetoric can extend into private affairs, how the dynamic of contention is created in different contexts, and how skill in speaking is continuous with—or crucially different from—effective writing. If twelfth-century teachers presented rhetoric as a mastery of the tools of language in preparation for a career of speaking and writing (as in John of Salisbury's passionate defense of the trivium), they did not articulate what must have been the puzzling limitations of Ciceronian speech-rhetoric for their own highly literary cultures. Brunetto assays this challenge, in order to claim a practical as well as moral relevance for Ciceronian rhetoric.[13]

Translation by Justin Steinberg from Brunetto Latini, *La Rettorica*, ed. Maggini, by permission.[14]

LA RETTORICA

*Here begin the teachings of rhetoric, translated into the vernacular by Ser Brunetto Latini of Florence from the books of Tullius and many philosophers. Where there is bold lettering [*la lettera grossa*], this is the text of Tullius, and where there is fine lettering [*la lettera sottile*], these are the words of the expositor.[15] The prologue begins.*

[De Inventione 1.1.1]

1. I have frequently wondered to myself if copious speech and the study of eloquence have done more good than harm to men and cities. For, when I consider the damage to our commune[16] and call to mind the ancient misfortunes of the great cities, I see that a not insignificant amount of harm was caused by men speaking without wisdom.

---

[13] On Brunetto's aim of cultivating moral judgment among his vernacular audience, see Gehl, "Preachers, Teachers, and Translators," 312–20.

[14] We have followed the format and numbering of Maggini's divisions of the text.

[15] This indication of "bold" (or large) and "fine" (or small) lettering seems to correspond to Brunetto's own intentions: see Brunetto's comment at *De inventione* 1.1.1 § 12 below (p. 760). But this visual distinction between the "text of Tullius" and the "words of the expositor" is not carried out in all of the manuscripts, and we have not used it here. See Maggini, ed., *La rettorica*, introduction, xxi–xxvii, esp. xxiii.

[16] Brunetto often uses the term *comune* for the Latin *civitas*, and we have given its English equivalent in order to preserve the political and historical resonances of Brunetto's text.

The Expositor Speaks Here [*Qui parla lo sponitore*]

1. Rhetoric is a twofold science [*scienzia di due maniere*]. The first part teaches how to speak, which Tullius treats in his book. The second part teaches letter writing [*dittare*], which, since Tullius does not treat it directly, the expositor will discuss in the course of the book, where appropriate. 2. Rhetoric is taught in two ways, as other sciences, namely, from within and without [*di fuori e dentro*].[17] In other words: it is taught from without by demonstrating what rhetoric is and what its genus is, as well as its subject matter, function, parts, proper instrument, goal, and artificer. Boethius proceeded in this way in the fourth book of the *Topics*.[18] It is taught from within by demonstrating what to do with the [subject] matter of speaking and letter writing, that is, how one ought to construct the exordium and the narration and the other parts of a speech or an epistle [*epistola*] (that is, a written letter). And Tullius treats both of these parts in his book. 3. But since he does not demonstrate what rhetoric is or who is its artificer [*artefice*], the expositor would like to speak about each of these in the interest of greater clarity.

4. Rhetoric is a science of speaking well, where we learn how to speak and write letters ornately. It could also be defined in a different way: rhetoric is a science of speaking well about the case that is proposed, that (science) through which we know how to speak ornately about a given question. An even fuller definition is this: rhetoric is the science of using copious and consummate eloquence [*piena e perfetta eloquenzia*] in public and private cases, that is, a science through which we know how to speak copiously and consummately in public and private questions. And certainly he who makes his speaking embellished [*adorne*] and full of good ideas will speak copiously and consummately. Public questions are those that treat the affairs of a city or community of people. Private questions deal with the affairs of a specific individual. However, it is the expositor's intention that this discussion pertain as much to writing letters [*dittare*] as to speech, since someone might know how to write well who does not possess the courage or knowledge to speak in front of people. However, he who knows how to speak well knows how to write letters well.

5. Having said what rhetoric is, now we will say who is its artificer [*artefice*]. I say that there are two. On the one hand, there is the rhetor [*rector*] and on the other hand the orator [*orator*]. For instance: the rhetor is the one who teaches this science according to the rules and precepts of the art. The orator has learned this art well so that he uses it to speak or write about given questions, as is the case with many good speakers and writers, such as

---

[17] I.e. the "intrinsic" art and the "extrinsic" art.   [18] I.e. *De topicis differentiis*, book 4.

Pier della Vigna, who was minister to the emperor of Rome, Frederick II, and ruled him and the empire completely.[19] Thus Victorinus says that the orator, that is the speaker, is a good man most skilled in speaking, who uses a copious and consummate eloquence in public and private cases.[20]

6. The expositor has said what rhetoric is and who is its artificer, that is, who puts it to work by either teaching or speaking. Now he wants to talk about the author, that is, the composer of this book, what was his intention in this book, what it treats, the reason it was written, and the utility, and the title of this book.

7. The author of this book is "duplex" [*doppio*]:[21] the first, who created this book of rhetoric from all of the teachings of the philosophers who came before him and from the inexhaustible fount of his own intelligence, was Marcus Tullis Cicero, the wisest of the Romans. The second author is Brunetto Latini, citizen of Florence, who put all of his study and understanding into expounding and illustrating what Tullius had said. This person who expounds and makes the book of Tullius understandable—through his own words and those of the philosophers and teachers that came before him—is called the expositor in this book. And in terms of the art (of rhetoric), this is all the more necessary for what was left out of the book of Tullius, as the attentive reader will understand shortly.[22]

8. His [i.e. Brunetto's] intention in this work was to give instruction to one for whose love he set himself to produce this treatise about speaking ornately about any given question.

9. And, following the form of Tullius' book, he treats all five of the general parts of rhetoric. For instance: *Inventio*, that is, the finding of what is necessary to present regarding the given material. The other four parts are found in the second book that Tullius wrote to his friend Herennius. He [i.e. the expositor] will give an account of these as appropriate.

10. The reason behind this book's creation is the following: Brunetto Latini, on account of the war between the two parties of Florence, was exiled from his homeland when his Guelph party, which sided with the Pope and the Church of Rome, was kicked out and exiled from the land. Then he went to France to take care of his affairs, where he

---

[19] Pier della Vigna (1190–1249) achieved vast influence over the emperor and the chancellery, which proved ruinous for him. See the treatment of him by Dante, *Inferno* 13.55–78, 93–108.

[20] Victorinus, *Explanationes* 156.25 (above, p. 108); 177.25–6.

[21] Brunetto invokes the scholastic notion of a twofold author, the *duplex causa efficiens* (double efficient cause). See Minnis, *Medieval Theory of Authorship*, 79–80, 102.

[22] The reference ("what was left out") is to the dictaminal art, which is not part of Cicero's treatise, but which *dictatores* such as Brunetto regard as a fundamental element of rhetorical teaching.

encountered a wealthy, elegant, and wise friend who was from his city and his party. Because this friend honored him and helped him, he was wont to call him his "port" as is evident in many parts of this book. This friend was a naturally good speaker who desired to know about what wise men had said about rhetoric. For his love, Brunetto Latini, who was an expert in letters and well studied in rhetoric, undertook to compose this work. He placed Tullius' text first for greater force and then joined to this the necessary knowledge of his own and of others.

11. The utility of this book is very great since anyone who understands well what the book and the art commands will know how to speak completely about a given question.

12. The title of this book, as appears in the beginning, is thus: *Here begins the teachings of rhetoric, translated into the vernacular from the books of Tullius and many philosophers.* The effect of the work clearly demonstrates that the title is good and perfect, because Tullius' book is translated into the vernacular [*volgare*] without error and set forth in bold letters [*grossa lettera*] to indicate greater dignity. Then the sayings of many philosophers and the knowledge of the expositor follow in fine letters [*lettera sottile*]. And at this point we depart from this material and return to explaining the text.

13. In this part the expositor says that Tullius, who wanted rhetoric to be loved and held dear, which was not at all the case at this time, in very wise fashion set forth his prologue in which he purged what seemed to him the gravest problems. As Boethius says in his commentary on the *Topics*, whoever writes about any subject matter must first purge it of what seems to him to be a difficulty.[23] In this manner Tullius purged three grave issues. First, he lays out the evils that stem from copiousness of speech; then he gives the opinion of Plato, and next the opinion of Aristotle. The opinion of Plato was that rhetoric is not an art, but a natural talent, since he saw many good speakers who were talented by nature and not through teaching of the art. The opinion of Aristotle was that rhetoric is an art, but a bad one, since it seemed that eloquence had created more harm than good to groups and individuals.[24] 14. Tullius purges these three grave issues by proceeding in the following manner. In the first place he says that he has frequently wondered about what effect [*effetto*] comes from eloquence. In the second part he demonstrates the good and the bad that come from it and whether it creates more good than bad. In the third part, he talks about three things: first he talks about what seems to him the part of wisdom, then he talks about what seems to him the part of eloquence, and then he talks about what seems to him wisdom and eloquence when they are conjoined. In the fourth part, he sets out the proofs

---

[23] Possibly *In Ciceronis topica*, *PL* 64:1045 (suggested by Alessio, "Brunetto Latini e Cicerone," 134 n. 3).

[24] Brunetto's references here are indebted to the *Ars rhetorice* commentary; see Alessio, "Brunetto Latini e Cicerone," 134–5, and cf. Thierry of Chartres above, p. 416.

[*le pruove*] about these three articles and concludes that we should study rhetoric, citing various arguments about honesty, utility, the possible, and the necessary. In the fifth part Tullius demonstrates what he will treat in this book and how.[25]

15. And since Tullius in his opening statement had spoken about how often he had thought much about the good and the bad that has occurred, he turns immediately to the bad, since men typically remember a new evil more than many past benefits. In this way, Tullius, seeming not to remember the old benefits, pretends to blame this science in order to more assuredly praise and defend it. 16. And through his own words that are written in the text above we can understand this clearly, in the very words where he talks about the evils that come from eloquence, which cannot be hidden, and in the very words where he defends it, by reducing and minimizing its harm. For where he says "damage" it sounds like the sort of superficial harm that people don't care about. And where he says "to our commune" ["*del nostro comune*"] he also reduces the harm since people care more about their own personal injury than that of the commune. And for "our commune" I mean Rome since Tullius was a new citizen of Rome without great eminence; but through his judgment and sense he rose through the ranks, to the point where all of Rome waited on his word. This was in the time of Catiline, Pompey, and Julius Caesar, and for the good of the homeland he was against Catiline. And in the war between Pompey and Julius Caesar he sided with Pompey like all the wise men who loved the Roman state. And perhaps he calls it "our commune" because Rome was the head of the world and commune of every man. 17. And where he says "the ancient misfortunes" he similarly reduces the harm done [by eloquence], since we care little about old injuries. And where he says "great cities" he also reduces the harm, since, as the good poet Lucan says, it is not granted to the greatest things that they endure for a long time.[26] And another says that great things are destroyed by their own weight.[27] And in this way it doesn't seem that eloquence is the reason for the evil that besets great cities. And where he says that much damage has resulted from men speaking copiously "without wisdom," he clearly defends rhetoric and reduces its harm by saying that the evil comes from speakers who lack judgment. And he does not say that the evil comes from eloquence, as Victorinus says: "The word *eloquentia* sounds good, and the bad does not spring from good."[28] 18. To defend while pretending to blame and to accuse while seeming to praise is a good example of a rhetorical color. And this mode of speaking is called *insinuatio*, which the book will discuss in its place. And here the account departs

[25] Cf. the breakdown of the "parts" of the "argument" in Cicero's prologue in Victorinus' *Explanationes*, ed. Halm, 155, and the commentary of Thierry of Chartres.

[26] Lucan, *Pharsalia* 70–1: *invida fatorum series, summisque negatum / stare diu.*

[27] Lucan, *Pharsalia* 71: *nimioque graves sub pondere lapsus.*

[28] Cf. Victorinus, *Explanationes* 157.6–12; above, p. 109.

from the first part of the prologue in which Tullius spoke about his thoughts and talked about past evils, and returns to the second part in which he demonstrates the good which has occurred through eloquence.

Tullius [De inventione 1.1.1]

2. Yet when I set about examining in ancient writings the records of past events which, because of their age, are remote from our memory, I find that eloquence conjoined with the use of reason,[29] that is, wisdom, has been more easily able to prevail and prepare for founding cities [*cittadi*], extinguishing many wars, creating the strongest alliances, and establishing sacred friendships.

The Expositor

1. After Tullius divides the evils that come from eloquence, he divides in this part the benefits, and on balance he considers more benefits than evils because he is more intent on praise. And note that he says "eloquence conjoined [*congiunta*] with wisdom" because wisdom provides the will to do good and eloquence permits its realization. 2. The other words that are in the text, that is, "for founding cities, extinguishing many wars etc." were well placed there, because men first assembled together so as to live by one reason and by good behavior, and to increase possessions. Then when they became rich, envy rose among them and through envy wars and battles. Then the wise speakers extinguished the battles and then men made alliances in which they worked and dealt commercially with each other. And with these alliances they began to create stable friendships through eloquence and wisdom. 3. But in order to better explain what these words mean and to further illustrate this work, it is important to define city, ally, friend, wisdom, and eloquence, because the expositor does not want to neglect even one word without applying all of his understanding.

4. What is a city [*cittade*]? A city is an association of persons created for living under rule of reason.[30] People simply living together within the physical walls of a town are not considered citizens unless they are living together under the rule of reason.

[29] Brunetto's term *ragione d'animo* directly renders Cicero's *animi ratio*.
[30] Cf. Victorinus, *Explanationes* 158.11–12; above, p. 110.

5. What is an ally [*compagno*]? An ally is someone who through some agreement joins another in some action. Victorinus says that if these alliances are strong, then through eloquence they become strongest.[31]

6. What is a friend? A friend is that person who through a similar life joins another in just and faithful love.[32] In other words: in order for persons to be friends they have to share a similar life and manners; and therefore he [Victorinus] says "through a similar life"; and he says "just love," because the friendship cannot be based on licentiousness or unclean deeds. And he says "faithful love" because it must not be dependent on acquisition or utility alone but on constant virtue. And thus it is very clear that true friendship does not consist of utility or delight but steers away from delight and the slightest utility.

7. What is wisdom? Wisdom is understanding the truth of things as they are.

8. What is eloquence? Eloquence is knowing how to speak in ornate words furnished with good ideas.

Tullius [De inventione 1.1.1]

3. And so after having thought long about it, reason itself has led me to this most firm opinion: wisdom without eloquence is of little use for cities, and eloquence without wisdom is often very harmful and never useful. Because of which, if anyone thus neglects the most upright and honorable studies of reason and duty, and devotes his whole energy only to the practice of speaking, as a citizen he is useless to himself and dangerous to his city and country. But he who arms himself with eloquence not to make war against the good of the country, but to fight for it, this, it seems to me, is an invaluable man and citizen, most devoted to his own and the public interests.

The Expositor

1. After the first two parts of his prologue, Tullius begins the third part in which he says three things. First he speaks about his notions of wisdom, up to the part where he says "Because of which." Then he begins the second part, in which he speaks of his notions of eloquence, up to the section where he says, "But he who arms himself." And from here he begins the third part, in which he presents what seems to him to be the joining of one together with the other.

---

[31] Cf. Victorinus, *Explanationes* 158.24–6.   [32] Victorinus, *Explanationes* 158.31–2; above, p. 111.

2. Whence Victorinus says: If we want to accomplish anything speedily in cities, wisdom needs to be joined with eloquence, since wisdom is always slow.[33] This is evident in any wise man who is not a speaker. If we were to ask advice of him, he would not be as quick in giving it as if he were a good speaker. But if he were both wise and eloquent, he would make what he wanted to say immediately credible. 3. Regarding what Tullius says about those who neglect the studies of "reason" and "duty," I take "reason" to refer to wisdom and "duty" to indicate the virtues, that is, valor and justice and the other virtues that have the office of bringing it about that we are discreet and just and well mannered. 4. If someone departs from wisdom and the virtues and strives only to speak well, with the result that he is not sincere about what he is saying, only harm can come to him and his country. For he does not know how to treat his own affairs and those of the commune in the appropriate time, place, and order. 5. Therefore he who arms himself with eloquence is useful to himself and to his country. For arms, I understand eloquence and for wisdom I understand force. Because just as with arms we defend ourselves against enemies and with force we sustain arms, in the same fashion through eloquence we defend our case against the adversary and through wisdom we abstain from saying what could bring us harm. And this part completes the third part of Tullius' prologue. 6. Now the treatise moves on to the fourth part of the prologue, in order to demonstrate what is said below, and to conclude that we must study rhetoric in such a way as to possess both eloquence and wisdom. On this topic Tullius provides many necessary and likely arguments, some of which are advantageous, others honorable. Here then the text of Tullius in bold letters followed by fine letters according to the form of the book.

Tullius [De inventione 1.1.2–1.2.2]

4. Therefore if we want to consider the origin of eloquence, whether man derives it from art or study or use or nature, we will find that it was born from honorable motives and continued along from the best of reasons. There was a time when everywhere men roamed the fields like beasts and led their lives in a savage way. Almost everything they did was accomplished by bodily force, not through the use of reason. In addition, in that time sacred religion and human duty [*officio*] were not revered. No man had seen legitimate marriage, no man had recognized children as his own. They had not considered the advantages of maintaining reason and equality. Thus through error and ignorance,

---

[33] Cf. *Explanationes* 159.1–4; above, p. III.

greed—that blind, mad, and reckless lord of the mind—in order to accomplish its deeds, misused bodily force with the help of miserable followers.

The Expositor

1. In this fourth part of the prologue, Tullius wants to demonstrate that eloquence arose and continued out of honorable motives and the best of reasons. He says that at one time men were coarse and ignorant like beasts. And man, according to philosophers and confirmed by Sacred Scripture, is composed of body and rational soul. This soul, through reason, has complete knowledge of things. 2. Thus says Victorinus: If the force of wine is diminished by the properties of the container holding it, in the same way the force of the soul is changed by the properties of the body joined to it.[34] Therefore, if that body is poorly disposed or has a complexion of bad humors, the soul, weighed down by the body, loses knowledge of things so that it can barely discern good from bad. In the past, many souls were weighted down by their bodies and so men were false and undiscerning and did not know God or themselves.[35] They exploited their bodily strengths in killing one another, in taking things by force and by thievery, and in evil licentiousness, not recognizing their own children or taking lawful wives. 3. But all the while Nature, that is, that divine disposition [*disposizione*], had not distributed bestialness in all men equally. There were some wise and eloquent men who, seeing that men were capable of reason, were wont to speak to them so as to bring them divine knowledge, that is to say, to love God and one's neighbor, as the expositor will discuss in the appropriate place.[36] Thus Tullius says in the above text that the origin of eloquence was from honorable motives and the most upright reasons, that is, for loving God and one's neighbor, without which humankind would not have endured. 4. And where the text says that men wandered in the fields I understand that they did not have homes or a set place but went here and there like beasts. 5. And where he says that they were living like animals I understand that they were eating raw meat, uncooked herbs, and other foods appropriate for animals.[37] 6. And where he says "almost everything they did was accomplished by bodily force and not through the use of reason" I understand that he says "almost" because not everything they were doing was through force, but some things were accomplished through reason and judgment, such as speaking,

---

[34] *Explanationes* 161.12–15; above, p. 114.
[35] *Explanationes* 161.15–20; above, pp. 114; cf. 155.31–2, 160.15–23; above, pp. 107, 113.
[36] Cf. *Explanationes* 160.21, 161.16–18; above, pp. 13–14.
[37] Brunetto borrows these details from the *Ars rhetorice* commentary: Alessio, "Brunetto Latini," 140.

desiring, and other things that come from the mind.[38] 7. And where he says that sacred religion was not revered I understand that they did not know that God existed. 8. And where he speaks of human office I understand that they did not know how to live according to good customs and were not acquainted with prudence, justice, or the other virtues. 9. And where he says that they did not maintain reason, I take "reason" in the sense of justice, which the law books define as a perpetual and firm will of the mind which gives everyone his due. 10. And where he says "equality" I understand that aspect of reason which allots equal punishment for the great and the small based on equivalent deeds. 11. And where he says "greed" I understand that vice which is the opposite of temperance; and this vice leads us to desire something we shouldn't want, and forces a corrupt rule in our minds, which does not allow us to refrain from bad actions. 12. And where he says "ignorance" I understand the inability to distinguish between useful and useless. He calls greed blind for this reason, because it does not know benefits from harm. 13. And where he says "reckless folly" I understand that reckless fools are mad and quick to do what they should not do. 14. And where he says "misused bodily strength" I understand misuse to mean to use in an evil fashion. Thus Victorinus says that bodily strength is a gift from God to use in doing honest and useful things, but these men were doing exactly the opposite.[39] 15. The expositor has examined in Tullius' text the reasons for which eloquence began to appear. Now he will say in what fashion it appears and how it continued.

Tullius [De inventione 1.2.2]

5. In that time there was a great and wise man who recognized the potential and what opportunity for great things there was in the minds of men if they could be directed and improved by instruction. He thus compelled and gathered together into one place those men who were at that time scattered in the fields and dispersed in the hidden woodlands. He taught them to know what was honest and useful. If at first these things seemed difficult because fallen into disuse,[40] they were soon desirous to listen through force of reason and beautiful speech. In this way he turned their beastliness and cruelty into humility and gentleness.

---

[38] Brunetto's *quasi*, meaning "almost," and his gloss on that term, are suggested by the *Ars rhetorice* gloss on Cicero's phrase *pleraque ... administrabant*: "But he said *pleraque* because they did not do everything by means of physical strength." See Alessio, "Brunetto Latini," 140–1.

[39] Cf. *Explanationes* 161.21–34; above, pp. 114–15. Brunetto actually derives this idea from the *Ars rhetorice* gloss: see Alessio, "Brunetto Latini," 141–2.

[40] Cf. Thierry of Chartres, who glosses the Latin term *insolentia* as *desuetudo* (disuse), above, p. 424.

The Expositor

1. In this part, Tullius wants to demonstrate whence and how eloquence originated and in what things. And the theme is as follows: in that time in which people were living so wretchedly, there was a man great through eloquence and wise through wisdom, who recognized that potential that man has in himself by nature, that is, reason, through which man can understand and reason, [and who recognized] the opportunity for accomplishing great things, such as maintaining peace and loving God and one's neighbor, constructing cities, castles, and homes, and establishing good customs, and observing justice and living in an orderly fashion. They only needed someone who could direct them, that is, lead them away from their bestial life and improve them through commandments, namely, through teaching and laws and statutes that might rein them in. 2. And here a question arises. Someone could say "How could they improve themselves seeing that they were not good?" I respond that the reasoning power of their soul was naturally good. Hence they could improve in the manner described.[41] 3. Then this wise man compelled them—and he says "compelled" them because they did not want to gather—and gathered—and he says "gathered" because then they wanted to meet. In fact, the wise man did so much by his judgment and eloquence—laying out fine arguments, underlining the usefulness of his proposals, and all the while providing excellent suppers and lunches and other pleasures from his own pocket—that they gathered and consented to hear out his words. And he taught them about useful things, saying "Live well together, help each other, and you will be safer and stronger. Build cities and villages." And he taught them about honor, saying "The small honors the great, the son fears the father" etc. 4. At first, for these men who had been living like animals, the idea of living according to reason and order seemed like dire admonishments, for they were naturally free and did not desire to be placed under any rule. Yet after hearing the fine speech of the wise man and considering with reason that a wide, free license to act harmfully brought grave destruction and danger to the human race, they listened and took care to understand him. And in this way the wise man drew them from their beastliness and cruelty (and he says "beastliness" because they were living like beasts and he says "cruelty" because father and son did not know each other, and on the contrary were killing one other) and rendered them humble and gentle, that is, desirous of reason and virtues and averse to evil. 5. After having said who originated

---

[41] See Victorinus, *Explanationes* 160.17–20, above, p. 114, cited in the *Ars rhetorice* gloss. See Alessio, "Brunetto Latini," 142.

eloquence and among whom and how, Tullius will say how it was not possible to accomplish these things without eloquence.

Tullius [De inventione 1.2.3]

6. It seems to me accordingly that mute wisdom, impoverished of words, would not have been able to accomplish as much, that suddenly men left behind an ancient, long-standing habit and were informed about diverse patterns of life.

The Expositor

1. In this part Tullius speaks of the faculty without which the wise man could not have accomplished what he did. And he calls "mute wisdom" the wisdom of those who teach not by words but by deeds, such as hermits. And he says "impoverished of words" to indicate those that do not know how to adorn their wise judgment with beautiful words and fullness of ideas in order to persuade others about their opinion. And from this we can understand that wisdom has little force if it is not joined with eloquence and we can know that great wisdom conjoined with eloquence is above all things. 2. And where it says "suddenly" I understand that the wise man would have been able to accomplish these feats through wisdom, but not so swiftly or immediately as he did through eloquence with wisdom. And where he says "about diverse patterns of life" I understand that one became a knight, another a clerk, and so on with the other professions.[42]

Tullius [De inventione 1.2.3]

7. In this way, after the cities and villages were built, men learned how to keep faith, maintain justice, obey one another through their own will, and not only endure pain and hardship for the common good but even be willing to die for it. This would not have been possible to accomplish unless men had been able to demonstrate and persuade through words, that is eloquence, what they thought of and discovered though wisdom. 8. And certainly those who had the power and force over many others would never have suffered

[42] Brunetto takes these details from the *Ars rhetorice* commentary: see Alessio, "Brunetto Latini," 143.

themselves to become the equals of those whom they could rule if they hadn't been moved by wise judgment and elegant speech, especially considering that the earlier customs were agreeable to them and through long use had acquired the semblance and function of a natural right. From which it seems to me that in this way eloquence first arose in ancient times and then continued, eventually reaching the highest interests of men in the events of peace and war.

The Expositor

1. In this part Tullius speaks of what wisdom was able to do in the company of eloquence, which it would not have been able to do alone. And the theme is the following. As mentioned above, after being instructed on doing good and loving each other, men gathered together and built cities and villages. After the cities were built they learned how to keep faith. 2. By keeping faith I understand those who do not trick others and who do not want fighting or discord within the city. And when fighting or discord does break out, they try to make peace. And faith, as a wise man says, is the hope of that which is promised. And the law says that faith is that which one promises and the other awaits. But Tullius himself says in another book, *De officiis*,[43] that faith is steadfastness in justice, truth in speech, and stability in promises. And this virtue is called loyalty. 3. And in this way Tullius supremely praises eloquence conjoined with wisdom, without which great things would never have been accomplished. And he says that they did much in war or peace. I understand this to mean that all the affairs of the commune and of private persons exist in two states, either in peace or war. In both one and the other, our rhetoric is required in the end, because without her they could not continue.

Tullius [De inventione 1.2.3–1.3.4]

9. But then men followed the power of eloquence unaccompanied by consideration of duty. Having learned copiousness of speech, they grew accustomed to exploiting their talents in the service of deception. And it followed that cities were ruined and men became infected with that pollution. And since we have spoken about the origin of benefits, now we will speak about the origins of harm.

[43] *De officiis* 1.7.23.

The Expositor

1. Since Tullius has spoken above about the benefits stemming from eloquence, in this part he speaks of the harm that comes when it is unaccompanied by wisdom. But since his intention is more to praise it, he places the blame for harm on those who misuse rhetoric and not on rhetoric itself. 2. And the theme is as follows:[44] there existed some mad men lacking in all discretion who noticed how others had risen in great honor and status because of the beautiful oratory they used following the rules of this art. So these men devoted themselves only to speech and neglected the study of wisdom, gaining such copiousness of speech that, through excess of words unseasoned by judgment, they began to bring sedition and destruction to cities and communes and to corrupt the lives of men. And this happened because they had the semblance of wisdom, of which in fact they were completely stripped and empty. 3. And Victorinus says that eloquence by itself is called "the appearance" [*"la vista"*] because it makes it seem that there is wisdom present in those in whom it does not dwell.[45] And in order to acquire honor and advantages in the commonwealth, these people speak without any true sense of what is good, and in this way agitate cities and exploit the populace for perverse usages. 4. And then Tullius says: Since we have recounted the origin of good, that is the benefits that have come from eloquence, it is appropriate that we take account of the origin of the harm that followed from it . . .

[Brunetto continues his close exposition of the text until he reaches *De inventione* 1.5.6 (section 17 in Maggini's numbering), containing Cicero's statement of the classification of rhetoric as a part of political science. Here Brunetto departs from Cicero's text to give an extensive account of scientific classification. For the most part, his account here is also independent of the *Ars rhetorice* commentary. His treatment of the sciences is based on Aristotelian systems as well as on more current (including newer curricular) models. In order to approach Cicero's classification of rhetoric under political science, Brunetto introduces scientific classification, beginning with the largest epistemological categories and narrowing gradually to particular sciences. His schemes follow this order: Philosophy (practical, logical, theoretical sciences); Logic (dialectical reasoning, "epideictic" [i.e. demonstrative reasoning],[46] sophistical reasoning); Theoretical (theology, physics, mathematics); Mathematics (the quadrivium); Practical (ethics,

---

[44] The *Ars rhetorice* (on which Brunetto bases the following passage) cites Victorinus as a source (Alessio, "Brunetto Latini," 144): see *Explanationes* 166.9–31; above, pp. 121–2.

[45] Cf. *Explanationes* 165.32–44; above, p. 121.

[46] Brunetto's term is *efidica*, perhaps a confusion with the Greek *apodeixis* (demonstration or showing forth), or perhaps a confusion with the demonstrative genre of rhetoric, "epideictic."

economics, politics); Politics (actions, speech); Speech (grammar, dialectic, rhetoric). Of these we translate the section on speech, that is, his account of the trivium.]

[Section 17]

18. . . . That part [of political science] that is constituted through speech is the science that concerns itself exclusively with language: and this consists of three sciences, which are grammar, dialectic, and rhetoric, as we see in this tree:

in speech

grammar   dialectic   rhetoric

19. And to indicate that this is true, the expositor explains that grammar is the entry into and the foundation of the liberal arts. It teaches how to speak correctly and to write correctly, that is, using appropriate words without barbarism or solecism. For without grammar, it is not possible for anyone to speak or to write well. The second science, namely dialectic, demonstrates the truth of the statement through arguments that make the statement trustworthy. Indeed, it is necessary for anyone who wants to speak and write well to demonstrate reasoning, so that his words may have such validity that the audience believes him and trusts what he says. The third science is rhetoric, which discovers and embellishes the words in proportion to the material, so that the audience is appeased and willing to believe, and is gratified and is moved to want what the speaker says. 20. Thus the three sciences are needed for speaking and writing (for without them there is nothing): grammar enables the good speaker and writer to speak and write correctly, so that through his words he is understood; and dialectic enables him to prove his statements and demonstrate his reasoning; and rhetoric enables him to set out and embellish his speech so that the audience believes and is gratified and does what he wants. 21. Now the expositor says that the part of civil science [*civile scienza*]—that is, governance of the city—which is constituted through speech is divided into two parts: that which involves dispute and that which does not involve dispute. Something involving dispute entails questioning and answering, as in dialectic, rhetoric, and law. Something that does not involve dispute also entails questioning and answering; however, this is not in the way of contention, but rather of giving instruction and good example to the people, as we find in the words of the poets, who have set down in writing the ancient histories, great battles, and other events that inspire us to live well.

On the Material [De inventione 1.5.7]

19. We call material that in which the entire art of rhetoric and the knowledge produced from it dwells. Just as we say that diseases and injuries are the material of the doctor, since all medicine deals with these things, in the same way we call material those things with which the art and knowledge of rhetoric are concerned. Some have found more subject matters for this art, others less. Gorgias of Leontini, who was almost the earliest rhetor, believed that a speaker could speak very well about anything. He seems thus to have allowed the art of rhetoric to encompass a vast, limitless material. But Aristotle, who gave many improvements and adornments to this art, thought that the office of the speaker is concerned with three classes of things, namely, the demonstrative, the deliberative, and the judicial.

The Expositor[47]

1. In this part Tullius says that the material of rhetoric was the reason why the precepts [*comandamenti*] of this art were considered and discovered, and the reason for which we learn the science created by these precepts.[48] For the same reasons the precepts of medicine and the remedies for sicknesses and injuries were discovered. And in short this is the material about which it is appropriate to speak and for which this art was invented—so as to teach how to speak well as required by the material, and in order to persuade the listener. 2. Yet there is a disagreement among wise men regarding the material of rhetoric. Many claimed that the material encompassed anything about which we could speak. However, if this were true, the art of rhetoric would be limitless, and this cannot be the case. Gorgias of Leontini, an ancient rhetor, was of this opinion, and in calling him ancient Tullius indicates that he is not to be believed. 3. Aristotle, on the other hand, who merits great credence—since he gave many improvements and adornments to this art by writing a book about invention and another about speech[49]—says that rhetoric concerns three kinds

---

[47] With his return to the close exposition of Cicero's text (at 1.5.6 on the *officium* of rhetoric, or section 18 in Maggini's numbering), Brunetto also resumes his dependence on the *Ars rhetorice* commentary. With some important exceptions, the exposition of section 19 (*De inventione* 1.5.7) is also dependent on the commentary.

[48] There are several parallels between this section and the outline of rhetoric in Brunetto's *Livres dou Tresor*, ed. Carmody, 319–22. See Alessio, "Brunetto Latini," 151 nn.

[49] The reference to Aristotle's "rhetorics" (precepts on invention and precepts on style) is taken from the *Ars rhetorice* commentary; see Alessio, "Brunetto Latini," 151. Neither the commentator nor Brunetto would have known Aristotle's *Rhetoric* directly.

of things and each kind is general with respect to its parts. These are demonstrative, deliberative, and judicial, as evident in this diagram:[50]

And Tullius is in agreement with this opinion, and the entire art of rhetoric concerns these three kinds of things. 4. But at this point certain teachers could very well suggest a division between speaking [*dire*] and letter writing [*dittare*], since it seems that the material of letter writing is so general that it is possible to write an epistle [*epistola*], that is, a letter, about almost anything. But rhetorical speech is limited to the aforementioned three kinds of things, since Tullius assigns all of rhetoric to verbal questions [*quistione di parole*].[51] And I understand a question to indicate a speech in which many statements employed could be supported by either side, that is, they could argue either for or against through attributes—properties of the action or person. 5. And here is an example of such a statement that will be proposed in this way: "Should Marcus Tullius Cicero be banished into exile for having sent, in front of the populace, many Romans to their death in the time when the commune was in peril?" This proposal has two parts, one affirmative, another negative. The affirmative is as follows: "Cicero should be banished because he committed such a deed." The negative is as follows: "He should not be banished since recalling his name alone indicates a good thing and banishment and exile indicate a bad thing, and it is not credible that a good man would do something worthy of banishment or exile." 6. We have already discussed what is the material of this art and Tullius affirms the opinion of Aristotle. And since he affirms it, each one of those three kinds [i.e. the three genres] will be properly discussed by him and by the expositor. In this way, the one for whom this book was written will be able to understand the material, the motive [*movimento*], and the nature of rhetoric. But let him carefully examine what is said in this part of the treatise and understand what it contains, because otherwise he will not be able to understand what follows.

[Brunetto's translation and commentary has worked through the dense section on status theory (the conjectural, definitional, qualitative, and translative issues or controversies), up through 1.14.19 (Maggini's section 76), and has now reached the point at which Cicero introduces the six parts of the speech. At this point the expositor steps back from the text

[50] Literally, "little circles," that is, a diagram consisting of linked circles with the key terms inside them.
[51] The two previous sentences of § 4, which introduce the problem of letter writing as a "new" division of rhetoric which is not limited to the three classical genres, are Brunetto's independent contribution.

to explain the relevance of Ciceronian rhetoric to contemporary civic society and its modes of communication, and to try to reconcile modern precepts about *dictamen* with classical teaching about the six parts of a speech.]

[76.] *The Expositor Explains Everything that has been Said Before*

2. And regarding this point, before he goes any further, the expositor would like to beseech his "port," for whose love the present book was composed (and not without great hardship of spirit), that his understanding be clear, his wits quick, and his memory tenacious in order to comprehend what has been said before and what will follow. In doing so, he will become, as he desires, a perfect letter-writer and noble speaker, for the science of which this book is a lantern and fountain. 3. And since this book has dealt above with controversies and has taught how to speak about things in dispute and to know cases and questions, and by way of examples has spoken often of accused and accuser, an unsophisticated reader might perhaps believe that Tullius was only speaking about disputes that happen in court. 4. However, the expositor knows that his friend is armed with great discernment and understands and sees the true intention of the book. While trials are of interest specifically for lawyers, rhetoric teaches how to speak about a given case, which need not only be part of a trial or between accuser and accused. Rather it can occur in other situations, such as knowing how to speak in diplomatic missions or in assemblies of lords or of the commons or in knowing how to compose a well-written letter. 5. And if Tullius says that the parts of speeches consist of the issue [i.e. *constitutio*], the question, the excuse or reason [i.e. *ratio*], the judgment [i.e. *iudicatio*], and the supporting argument [i.e. *firmamentum*],[52] an attentive reader needs to keep in mind that everyday people speak of various subject matters and often it happens that one states his opinion and another the contrary, so that they fall into dispute. And one censures and the other defends so that the one who censures is called the accuser and the one who defends is called the accused, and what they argue about is called the case. 6. From which, if one censures and the other denies, the only question that can arise between them is to know if what was denied was really done or said. However, when one censures and the other defends, then a legal case arises between them and is drawn up [*ordinata*]. And this is the issue from which the question arises, namely, if the defense is right or not. Then each party argues in an attempt to bolster his words or weaken the other's, as discussed above in the treatise regarding the question, excuse or reason, judgment, and supporting argument. 7. Thus

[52] *De inventione* 1.13.18.

let no one believe, as suggested in earlier examples, that Orestes was accused in court of the death of his mother. Rather, people argued about it amongst themselves, with one saying that he (Orestes) had done neither good nor right—and this one is called the accuser—and the other speaking in defense of Orestes, claiming that he had done what was good and right—and, according to the terminology of this book, this one is called the accused.

On councilmen [*consiglieri*]

8. In similar fashion it often occurs among councils of lords or of the commons [*comunanze*] that when they are assembled to consider some event, that is, some case, which is proposed before them, one side will see it one way, and the other side will see it another way. In this manner the issue of the case is framed, that is the dispute between them from which arises the question of whether or not the matter is to be considered. This is what Tullius calls the question. 9. And therefore the one, after having stated and recommended his view, immediately sets out the reason for which his counsel is good and right. And this is what Tullius calls the reason. 10. And after he has set out the cause and the reason, he works to demonstrate how any contrary counsel would be bad or not right. In this way, he weakens the side that opposes his counsel. This is what Tullius calls the judgment. 11. And when he has weakened the opposite side, he gathers the firmest arguments and strongest reasons he can find to weaken the other side and confirm his reasoning, and Tullius calls this the supporting argument. 12. And clearly these four parts—namely, question, reason, judgment, and supporting argument—can all be found in one of the speakers, as mentioned above. Or his speech could contain only one of these parts, the question, if he states his opinion and does not give another reason why. Or it could contain two parts, if he states his opinion and gives his reason why. Or it could contain three parts, if he states his opinion, states the reason why, and weakens the other side. And it could have all four parts as demonstrated above. 13. This is the speech of the first speaker. And after he has given his counsel and finished his speech, immediately another councilman rises up and says the exact opposite of what was just heard. In this way the issue is framed, that is, the case under way, and the dispute begins. And the question arises from the divergence in their statements, which are various, and as to whether the first speaker has counseled well. Then he (the second councilman) demonstrates why his counsel is better. Then he weakens the speech and counsel of the one who spoke before him. And then he reconfirms his counsel through the strongest arguments that he can find. Hence the aforementioned four parts can be in the speech of the first speaker or in the speech of the second or in both. 14. In the same way it often happens that two people send each other letters—whether in Latin, in prose, in verse, in the [Tuscan] vernacular, or in other languages—in which they argue and thus enter into a dispute [*tencione*]. Likewise a lover may cry for mercy to his

lady, speaking many words and providing reasons, while she defends herself in her own speech, bolstering her reasons and weakening those of the beseecher. In these and in many other examples we can clearly see that the rhetoric of Tullius is not just teaching how to speak in litigation or in courts of law, although no one can become a good or perfect lawyer unless they speak according to the art of rhetoric.

15. Yet certainly it is true that the teaching of this book has for the most part dealt with those situations where persons find themselves in dispute or in contention, where one is arguing against the other. And one might object that many times we send a letter to someone in which it does not appear that we are in dispute with them. Such is the case, for example, when one is in love and writes *canzoni* and poetry about his lady where there is no dispute [*tencione*] between them. In this light, one could criticize the book and blame Tullius and the expositor himself for not providing instruction in these matters, and especially on how to write letters, which are a more common practice and more often necessary to more people than orations and public speaking. 16. However, if one were to truly consider the structure of a letter or a *canzone*, it would be clear that whoever writes or sends it desires that the recipient does something for him. And this can be accomplished by entreating or asking or commanding or threatening or comforting or counseling. And in these same ways the recipient can deny the request or defend himself with any excuse. But the one who sends the letter furnishes it with ornate words, richness of ideas, and strong arguments, as he believes necessary to move the mind of the recipient so that the request will not be denied and so that, if there are any excuses, he can weaken or completely break them down. There exists therefore an implicit dispute [*tencione*] between them, and this is true with almost all letters and love poems [*canzoni d'amore*] where we have either an implicit or explicit dispute. If this were not the case, as Tullius makes clear at the beginning of the book, it would not be rhetoric. 17. However, whether or not there is a dispute involved, Tullius himself, in the text before us, strives to give instruction on speaking and writing according to the rules of rhetoric. Where it appears that Tullius provides instruction only about speaking in matters of dispute, the expositor will apply his little talent to explaining so much, and so comprehensibly, that his friend will be able to understand how it applies to both kinds of material. 18. And it is here that Tullius begins his treatment of the parts of a speech or of a written letter, about which he has not yet said anything. There are six parts, as we see in this scheme:

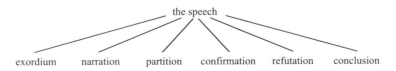

the speech

exordium   narration   partition   confirmation   refutation   conclusion

Tullius certainly shows that these six parts are to be found in the speech and in the epistle, especially where there is a dispute involved, as is clear from what the expositor has just said; and as was pointed out in another part of this book, Tullius limits rhetoric to cases which involve controversy or dispute. And he makes absolutely clear that words which are not spoken in a dispute between two parties are not rhetorical in form or art. 19. But since the epistle, that is, the written letter, is often neither a dispute nor a controversy, but is rather a presentation which one person sends to another, in which the mind speaks, and he who is silent and in a distant land is heard, he requests and receives good will. Thence good will grows and love flourishes.[53] There are many matters one puts into writing that one would hesitate or not know how to say verbally face to face. The expositor will give some opinions of wise men, as well as his own, about the part of rhetoric to which letter-writing belongs, as promised at the beginning of this book. 20. He says that *dictamen* is a correct and ornate treatment of every matter, appropriately adapted to that matter. This is the definition of *dictamen*, and it is necessary to understand every word of this definition. Note, therefore, that he says "correct treatment," because the words that are set down in a written letter must be put correctly: noun must agree with verb, and there must be agreement of masculine or feminine, of singular or plural, of first, second, and third person, and the other rules that are taught in grammar, to which the expositor gave some brief attention earlier in this book. This correctness of treatment is required in all parts of rhetoric, both spoken and written. 21. And he says "ornate treatment" [*ornato trattamento*] because every epistle must be furnished with gracious and pleasing words, and full of good ideas. Moreover, this embellishment is required in all parts of rhetoric, as was said above in the text of Tullius. 22. And he says "treatment of every matter," because, as Boethius says, every matter proposed for speech can be the material of the letter writer.[54] In this, [*dictamen*] differentiates itself from the opinion of Tullius, who says that the matter of the speaker is found only in three things, which are the classes of demonstrative, deliberative, and judicial rhetoric. And he says "appropriately adapted to that matter," because it is necessary that the letter writer adjust his words in accordance with his subject matter. The letter writer might very well use correct and ornate words, but they would be valueless were they not adapted to the material. 23. Thus the letter writer is differentiated from what Tullius says. And thus from these two kinds of matter, that is speaking and writing, and from the instruction about one and the other, the expositor's friend will be

---

[53] Cf. Bene da Firenze, *Candelabrum*, 5.18.2 (Alessio, "Brunetto Latini," 164).

[54] Boethius, *De topicis differentiis*, *PL* 64:1207 C; see above, p. 195. Boethius is referring to the material of the art of classical oratory, not to letter writing.

able to choose the correct path. And on account of this distinction, it is necessary to differentiate the parts of the letter from those of the speech, which, as Tullius has stated, are six...

25. From the foregoing discussion [a brief summary of the six parts of the speech], someone might assume that these very six parts could be appropriate to an epistle, whatever the letter happens to be about. However, whatever the subject matter may be, the epistle properly shares only three of these six parts with the speech: the exordium, the narration, and the conclusion. The other three, that is, the partition, the confirmation, and the refutation, can easily be left out as having no place in the epistle. Above all else, the epistle has five parts, of which one, the salutation, finds no counterpart in the speech. Another part, the petition, although it was not mentioned by Tullius among the parts of the speech, might and ought to have had such a place [in the speech]; it would hardly seem that the speech could do without a petition. Now, the epistle has five parts: the salutation, exordium, narration, petition, and conclusion, as we see in this scheme:

26. And if someone should ask why Tullius left out the salutation and did not treat it in his book, the expositor can certainly provide a good answer for this, in the following way. It is surely the case that in his book Tullius treats speeches that are delivered in the presence of an audience, so that it is not necessary to give the name of the one who speaks or the one who listens. But in the case of an epistle, it is necessary to give the name of the sender and the recipient, for otherwise one will not know the identity of the one or the other. With respect to this, the salutation seems to have the function of the exordium; inevitably, then, whoever greets the other person through the salutation of a letter seems already to have begun his exordium. Tullius treated the exordium as a whole, not wishing to divide it from the salutation nor to develop an extended account of the salutation, because he considered rhetoric to be limited completely to speaking and to disputing matters of controversy.[55] 27. For this reason, there have been some people who said that the salutation was not a part of the epistle, but was a title exterior to the text. I say that the salutation is the doorway of the epistle, that which illuminates,

---

[55] For this sentence, cf. Bene da Firenze, *Candelabrum* 3.55.7–8 (Alessio, "Brunetto Latini," 164).

in an orderly fashion, the names and the merits of the person addressed, and the affection of the sender.

[The "expositor" continues on the topic of the salutation (relying extensively at times on the *Candelabrum* of Bene da Firenze) for more than seventy lines in the edition, before returning to *De inventione* 1.14.19, the opening of Cicero's discussion of the exordium. The translation and commentary leave off at 1.17.24, and thus Brunetto's treatment of the relationship between *dictamen* and classical rhetoric does not extend beyond matters relating to the exordium.]

VINCENT OF BEAUVAIS, *SPECULUM DOCTRINALE*, CA. 1260

INTRODUCTION

The *Speculum maius* ("Greater Mirror") of Vincent of Beauvais was the "book of books," a vast encyclopedia composed for the use of the Dominican order, to bring together all sufficient knowledge to educate the friars for their careers of preaching and teaching. In its second and final form, which appeared about 1260, it consisted of three parts, *Naturale*, *Doctrinale*, and *Historiale*, the *Doctrinale* having been most recently added, and the other two parts having been revised considerably since their appearance in an earlier version of the 1240s.[1] The scope and orientation of the final three-part version reflects the re-establishment of Aristotelian natural philosophy and metaphysics, as well as Arab science, in the Parisian curriculum during the 1240s, under the authority of the Dominican master Albertus Magnus.

The *Speculum doctrinale* is a compendium of all of the sciences, intended (like the other parts of the *Speculum maius*) to substitute for the contents of a well-equipped library in those Dominican houses without means to provide one for their own members.[2] At the start of the *Doctrinale*, Vincent introduces the sciences through histories of the spiritual and moral purposes for which they were instituted (echoing his account of their role in human history in the *Speculum historiale*, book 1), and then (chapter 13) giving various definitions of philosophy that range from traditional late-antique authorities to more recent (mainly twelfth-century) sources. After this he surveys different classification schemes (chapters 14–18), striving, through his eclecticism, for an exhaustive completeness. The divisions of the sciences that he presents derive partly from traditional and familiar sources of the twelfth century and earlier: Hugh of St. Victor (theoretical, practical, mechanical, logical) and Isidore of Seville (logic, ethics, physics), as well as the Al-Farabian schemes that had achieved currency through the translations and adaptations of

---

[1] On the development of the two versions of the *Speculum maius*, see Paulmier-Foucart and Duchenne, *Vincent de Beauvais et le Grand Miroir du monde*, 12–14 and references there. A fourth section, the *Morale*, printed with the Douai edition of 1624, has long been recognized as apocryphal.

[2] On its value for the libraries of Dominican houses, see Tugwell, "Humbert of Romans, 'Compilator.'"

Gundissalinus (upon whose work Vincent depends regularly without citing his name, referring always to "Alpharabius"). But Vincent also offers two newer contributions to scientific classification, although by the time the *Doctrinale* was finished and ready to circulate, even these two "modern" schemes would have been decades old, and unrepresentative of the very latest academic thought at the University of Paris.

The first of these newer schemes (chapter 16) is by Michael Scot, who was active in the Toledo circle of scholars and translators between ca. 1200 and 1220, and is known both as a translator of Aristotle's *De animalibus*, and works by Avicenna and Averroes on the natural sciences, and also as the author of the *Liber introductorius*, an introduction to astrology in three books. This passage in Vincent's *Doctrinale* is the only record (perhaps fragmentary) of a work by Michael Scot on the division of the sciences.[3] It shows some clear links with the classification scheme of Gundissalinus, including the placement of the language sciences under civil science, which in turn is treated as a branch of practical science. While the language sciences play a relatively minor role here, the text is valuable for showing how this particular classification, familiar from Gundissalinus, could have an independent afterlife through Vincent's influential appropriation of Michael Scot's version of it. A form of this classification can also be seen in Brunetto Latini's *Rettorica* (also written around 1260): for Brunetto, politics is divided into actions and words, and under words he treats the language sciences of the trivium. However, Michael Scot adds another dimension to Gundissalinus' classification by expressly identifying civil science with "honorable citizens," separating it from the "vulgar" arts that pertain to the "common people."

The second of the "modern" classifications in Vincent's survey (chapter 18) may represent the teaching of a Parisian master, perhaps 1230–1240.[4] This offers a newer classification, one which would become common in scholastic thought, treating the *artes sermocinales* under theoretical sciences, where they constitute the "rational" branch.[5] The link between *ars rationalis* and *ars sermocinalis* (rational and linguistic art) is familiar from Hugh of St. Victor (*Didascalicon* 1.11, *logica rationalis*, and *logica sermocinalis*). But Hugh places the language sciences in the division of "logic," not as part of the theoretical sciences. In the scheme of this thirteenth-century master, the justification for seeing language sciences as a branch of theoretical science is that language is partly natural (like the traditional theoretical sciences, the study of things—physics, mathematics, metaphysics—that are not the result of human effort). Language is the product of natural instruments—presumably the voice and the organs of

---

[3] On the generation of this work and its possible place in the career of Michael Scot, see Burnett, "Vincent of Beauvais, Michael Scot, and the New Aristotle."

[4] Paulmier-Foucart and Duchenne, *Vincent de Beauvais*, 231.

[5] See Ebbesen and Rosier-Catach, "Le trivium à la Faculté des arts," 99.

speech. But as this master points out, the significative function of language is imposed and perfected by humans. This offers a newer combination and application of traditional strands of thought: language begins with natural instruments but proceeds to the humanly instituted imposition of meaning. For example, Petrus Helias considers the first of these notions in the prologue to his commentary on Priscian.[6] Robert Kilwardby, writing his *De ortu scientiarum* around 1250, makes a case similar to that of this anonymous master in terms of the double character of grammar: grammatical signification, he says, is founded partly on natural "reasons" and partly on human institutions.[7] But this does not invite a sideways (or upward) move for the language sciences into the theoretical sciences.[8] There is, however, a striking similarity between the master quoted by Vincent of Beauvais and the work of an anonymous Parisian master, the *Accessus philosophorum VII artium liberalium*, which has been dated to the years between 1230 and 1240. This master describes "speculative science as in some way natural, and in some way rational or linguistic [*sermocinalis*]."[9] This presentation was taken up ten years later (ca. 1250) by another Parisian master, Arnulf of Provence, who borrowed the wording of the *Accessus philosophorum* for his own introduction to the liberal arts.[10] Whether Vincent's source for this modern intervention is some version of a *reportatio* connected with the anonymous master who wrote the *Accessus philosophorum* remains unknown, but it is clear that he was combining the authority of traditional sources with newer perspectives. The classification here anticipates the realization of grammar as a theoretical inquiry by the *modistae* of later in the century, who sought for the universal—and thus scientifically consistent—features of language in the semantics of the parts of speech.[11]

The accounts that Vincent dedicates to grammar and rhetoric in the *Doctrinale* reflect the fullness of the commentary tradition of previous centuries. Before embarking on the subject of grammar (which will occupy book 2 of the *Doctrinale*) he gives a vocabulary list drawn from Papias' *Elementarium* (Rudiments of Instruction, eleventh century) "and other books." His treatment of grammar is notable especially for its generous reference to Petrus Helias' commentary on Priscian, along with the traditional

---

[6] *Summa super Priscianum*, ed. Reilly, 1:64.   [7] *De ortu scientiarum*, ed. Judy, § 638.

[8] Kilwardby is clear that speculative sciences precede practical and *sermocinale* (§ 631).

[9] Lafleur, ed., *Quatre introductions à la philosophie au XIIIe siècle*, 182.35–6.

[10] Arnulf of Provence, *Divisio scientiarum*, in Lafleur, ed., *Quatre introductions*, 321.280–1. One other classification scheme, an anonymous introduction to philosophy from about 1250, known from its incipit as "Ut ait Tullius," divides the theoretical sciences into those that deal with things (mathematical, natural, divine sciences) and those that deal with signs, under which are placed the language arts of the trivium. See Dahan, "Une introduction à l'étude de la philosophie: *Ut ait Tullius*."

[11] Pinborg, "Speculative Grammar," 255–6. On Vincent's classification (linking it to Gundissalinus) see also Covington, "*Scientia sermocinalis:* Grammar in Medieval Classifications of the Sciences."

sources (Donatus, Priscian, Isidore of Seville). His treatment of rhetoric in book 3 uses Boethius (book 4 of *De topicis differentiis*) as a general theoretical model, and the Ciceronian rhetorics (with additional references to *De oratore*), as well as some nuggets of Quintilian. Perhaps most interesting about the scientific construction of rhetoric in book 2 is that Vincent places poetics, as an independent art, *after* rhetoric, not after grammar. This placement of poetics following on rhetoric seems to reflect the influence of Al-Farabi's *De scientiis* as mediated through the work of Gundissalinus.

Vincent's sources, and his outlook, are largely conservative and traditional, which is to be expected of an encyclopedic compendium. His treatment of rhetoric captures a moment in the middle of the thirteenth century before the impact of Aristotle's *Rhetoric* came to be felt. His treatment of grammar reflects the great theoretical advances of the twelfth century (in Petrus Helias' Priscian commentary), and presents a linguistic, non-literary orientation of grammatical study, although not yet the highly theoretical, logical-semantic approach that would come to dominate in the second half of the thirteenth century. Although he adopts various scientific classifications, some of which were newly fashionable, his internal treatments of rhetoric and grammar stay close to older sources.

Translated from the Douai edition of 1624.

SPECULUM DOCTRINALE

16.[12] Michael Scot. Philosophy is divided into theoretical and practical. For, according to Aristotle, everything that exists either does not come from our work and our will, such as the intelligences, the elements, the heavens, and ultimately all natural things—and the science of these things is called theoretical, because its purpose is speculation; or it comes from our work and our will, such as laws and institutions, armies and warfare, and ultimately everything that is devised by art—and the science of these things is called practical, because its purpose is activity. Whence, elsewhere, it is said that there are two things through which the soul is perfected, knowledge (*scientia*) and activity.

Theoretical science is divided into three parts, that is, natural, mathematical, and divine. The first of these, namely natural science, considers what is subject to movement and corruption; the second, namely mathematical science, considers what is moved but is not subject to corruption; the third, namely the divine, what puts into motion but is

---

[12] Note: the text of the Douai 1624 edition is corrected against the edition of this section by Burnett, "Vincent of Beauvais, Michael Scot, and the New Aristotle." On Michael Scot, see headnote above.

neither moved nor corrupted. Practical science is divided into two parts, namely civil science and vulgar science. Know that the civil part is the science of language,[13] moral contemplation, and other sciences that pertain to honorable citizens; know that the vulgar science is sewing, metal-working, and other arts that pertain to the common people of mean status. Thus one can understand that there are three grades of sciences: some are noble, that is theoretical sciences; some are civil; and some are vulgar.

Or again, the practical part of philosophy is divided into three parts. The first is that which was invented by way of likeness to nature and which pertains to natural things, such as medicine, agriculture, and alchemy; and also the science which is concerned with the properties of things, called necromancy, and the science concerned with the significations of things, which is called the science of judgments [i.e. judicial astrology]; also the science of optics, the science of navigation, and many other sciences which bear a relationship to that part of theoretical philosophy which is called natural science and pertain to its practical dimension.[14] The second part was invented for its likeness to doctrine [i.e. mathematics], such as business, carpentry, metal-working, masonry, weaving, sewing, and many others of this sort, which are related to mathematics,[15] as if to its practical side. The third part is that which was invented for its likeness to divine things, and pertains to the divine, such as moral science, which has four parts, namely, how the city should be governed, how a man should interact with other citizens, how he should behave with his household, and how he ought to regulate the manner of his own life; and also the science of divine law, which comprises two parts, one, how we ought to believe, and the other, how we ought to act. And finally, all the sciences encourage us to piety and virtue, for all the sciences—civil as much as vulgar—relate to the divine, and are like its practical dimension. [...]

Magistralis

18. The Author. As Aristotle says at the beginning of book 2 of the *Physics*, we are, in a sense, the goal of all things.[16] Thus, since the nature of all things which are ordained to an end is brought to completion in that end, so in man the nature of anything that has a cause is understood to be as much corruptible, on account of the nature of the body, as incorruptible, on account of the nature of the soul. Wherefore, since the whole of

---

[13] See above, Gundissalinus, *De divisione philosophiae*, p. 468.
[14] Cf. [Al-Farabi], *De ortu scientiarum*, ed. Baeumker, 20.23–8.
[15] Douai edition, *ad mechanicam*.
[16] See *Physics* 194a35.

philosophy exists for the knowledge of things and their nature, philosophy was divided by the ancients into the mechanical and the liberal.

Mechanical science fights against the infirmities of the body. It is so called from what it effects, because the part to which it corresponds and which it serves is *mecha*, in Greek, which in Latin is *servitus* [servitude].[17] This is divided according to the various functions of the mechanical art, such as metal working, tanning, etc. Or, according to another viewpoint, the mechanical arts are so called because in Antiquity slaves and subordinates applied themselves to these matters because they were not permitted to study the liberal arts. Liberal philosophy strengthens the infirmities of the soul, which is the noble part [of humans], and free by law, which is clear on account of its coming into being through creation by the most noble agent, that is, the First Agent. Or, according to another viewpoint, this part of philosophy is called liberal because it liberates those who study it from worldly cares. Or because free men [*liberi*], not slaves, were permitted to study it.

Liberal philosophy is divided into theoretical and practical. The practical is moral philosophy, and this is so called from the effects it brings about, because it consists in acting, not in speculating, just as Aristotle said, that it is not by means of contemplation that we become good in some measure.[18] Thus mechanical and moral sciences are concerned with actions, but the mechanical entail activities of the body, while the moral entail activities of the soul. The ancients traditionally divided moral science into monastic, economic, and political, a division representing the various conditions of being, among which divisions one rules himself, or his household, or the whole city.

Theoretical science is divided into natural and rational. The natural part studies things that are determined, not by us, but by nature. The rational part, or arts of discourse [*sermocinalis*], considers those things that take their start from nature but are perfected by us. Such is language, which has its beginning from nature, because it uses natural instruments. But the perfection of language is that it signifies something, for it was made for this purpose. This value it takes from us, not from nature, because such and such a signification is imposed by us upon language. What is commonly called natural science is divided into the mathematical, the metaphysical, and what is properly called the natural. Things that are entailed in what is commonly called natural science are, on the one hand, abstracted from motion and matter according to being and according to essence; and this is the concern of metaphysics, or first philosophy, called "metaphysics" from *meta*, which is *trans* [beyond], and *physis*, which is *natura* [nature], because it "transcends" what we should properly call natural things. Or, [the things so entailed]

---

[17] This is a false etymology.
[18] Cf. Paulmier-Foucart and Duchenne, *Vincent de Beauvais et le Grand Miroir du monde*, 236.

are abstracted from matter according to essence but combined with it according to being; and this is the concern of mathematics, which is so called from *mathesis*, which is abstraction, and *icos*, which is science, as if to say "a science of abstract things."[19] Or [these things so entailed] deal with motion and matter according to both being and essence, and this is the concern of natural science properly speaking.

[19] Also a false etymology; see note 17 above.

THOMAS AQUINAS, PREFACE TO HIS *EXPOSITIO* OF ARISTOTLE'S *POSTERIOR ANALYTICS*, 1270

INTRODUCTION

Aquinas' commentary on Aristotle's *Posterior Analytics* was written about 1270. His preface to the commentary represents a culmination of twelfth- and thirteenth-century thought about the division of logic in response to the continued diffusion of Arabic Aristotelianism. It shows a thorough absorption and confident application of the extended *Organon*, that is, an *Organon* which includes rhetoric and poetics under the classification of logic. It also decisively separates logic as a whole from the trivium: here, logic is a "general discipline of thought," a *rationalis scientia* whose domain has been radically enlarged and reconceived.[1] For Aquinas, logic is not simply acts of reasoning or argumentation, but the intellect's very cognitive activity, the *ens rationis* ("being of reason"), an entity existing in the reason and a mental construct by which we conceive and speak about things.[2]

Building on what had become the convention of divisions of logic according to the Greco-Arabic tradition of the extended *Organon*, Aquinas treats rhetoric and poetics as forms of reasoning that produce less reliable kinds of knowledge. His scheme is more nuanced than those of his predecessors. Logic, or intellectual operations, can be divided into three groups: intellect that understands indivisible or non-compounded entities, which is dealt with in Aristotle's *Categories*; intellect that combines and divides entities, and therefore has to distinguish between true and false propositions, which is taught in *De interpretatione*; and reasoning by syllogisms. This last group is represented by the remaining six texts of the (extended) *Organon*, and has three subdivisions. The first, called "judicative," involves judgments that are made with certitude, which is the concern of the *Prior Analytics*, on the syllogism, and the *Posterior Analytics*, on the demonstrative syllogism. The second subdivision is called "inventive" in the sense of "discovery," and involves reasoning with varying degrees of certitude: relatively secure "belief" or "opinion" (*fides vel opinio*),

---

[1] Marmo, "*Suspicio*," 167.
[2] On this term, see Schmidt, *The Domain of Logic According to Saint Thomas Aquinas*, 52n., 45–6.

represented by the *Topics*, which treats the dialectical syllogism in the strict sense; reasoning that arrives at "a certain suspicion" (*suspicio*) in favor of one side, based on inclination rather than a high degree of certainty, which is the subject of the *Rhetoric*; and inclination to one side or the other by virtue of a mere "estimation" (*estimatio*), a kind of approximation of belief about something that is produced by poetic similitudes, which is covered in the *Poetics*. The third of these subdivisions is "sophistic," as treated in the *Sophistical Refutations*, about which Aquinas says nothing more here. Aquinas' teacher, Albertus Magnus, had used the terms *opinio*, *fides* (belief), *estimatio*, and *suspicio* as synonyms for the outcome of reasoning as taught by the art of logic. But Aquinas treats these terms as if they represent different degrees of certainty, from the strongest (opinion or belief), to an intermediate compromise (*suspicio*), to the very weakest kind of knowledge, *estimatio*.[3] The association of *estimatio* with the lowest grade of knowledge may have been suggested to Aquinas by one of William of Moerbeke's word choices in the translation of the *Rhetoric* (completed in the same period, about 1270), where *estimatio* signifies the mere "inkling" of truth that we derive from the effects of narrative, whether in rhetoric or in poetry (3.16; 1417b).[4] The distinction between "suspicion" and "estimation" enabled Aquinas to place poetry beneath rhetoric, not simply in terms of their respective objects (rhetorical persuasion, poetic representation), but in terms of their cognitive operations. Thus for Aquinas, rhetoric and poetics are lesser arts because they produce a lower grade of cognition than the syllogistic reasoning of the *Topics* or the *Analytics*.

Rhetoric, along with poetics, has become part of the "general discipline of thought" that is Aquinas' expansion of logic. Here rhetoric and poetics are no longer part of the toolbox of the language sciences, or even of an art of logic whose object is speech (as the trivium was often treated in scholastic thought),[5] but instead are incorporated into a descriptive system of cognitive procedures that pertain to different acts of reason. If Al-Farabi had elevated rhetoric, along with poetics, to philosophical status, Aquinas abstracts it even further. It was towards this state of intellectual affairs that Hermannus Alemannus had pointed with such prescience. But further and more comprehensive engagements with Aristotle's *Rhetoric* also gave rise to reassessments of rhetoric's place within the logical sciences. Giles of Rome, taking the whole of Aristotle's *Rhetoric* as his subject, responded to Aquinas' claims about rhetoric. Giles brackets poetics (and grammar)

---

[3] Marmo, "*Suspicio*," 168–9; Albertus Magnus, *De antecedentibus*, ed. Blarer, 206.

[4] Marmo, "*Suspicio*," 168; Gauthier, ed., *S. Thomae de Aquino Expositio libri Posteriorum*, 7, note at line III in apparatus. As Gauthier and Marmo note, the term *suspicio* also has a history of uses, either for a general form of unreliable reasoning, or specifically linked with rhetoric, as in Robert Kilwardby's *De ortu scientiarum*, where the "knowledge" yielded by dialectic is compared with the mere "belief or suspicion" produced by rhetoric (ed. Judy, 209, § 614).

[5] See Marmo, "*Suspicio*," 151–2.

out of his discussion, and focuses directly on what distinguishes rhetorical from dialectical assent. In contradistinction to Aquinas, Giles would claim that rhetoric is not "subaltern" to (*subalternatur*),[6] or weaker than, dialectic, but represents a different kind of assent altogether. For Giles, rhetoric is a form of assent governed by a movement of the will in relation to particular matters or events, while dialectic represents the intellect moving itself.[7] Giles was to move rhetoric farther apart from dialectic: while he still saw it primarily as an art of logic, he understood it as so closely bound up with the material particulars of ethics that its operations could not be subalternated to those of dialectic.

Translated from *S. Thomae de Aquino, Expositio libri posteriorum*, ed. Gauthier.

Preface

As Aristotle says at the beginning of the *Metaphysics*, humankind lives by art and reasonings.[8] In so saying, the Philosopher seems to touch on a certain property of human beings which differentiates them from the other animals. Other animals are led to their actions by a certain natural instinct; but man is directed in his actions by a judgment of reason. Thus it is that various arts serve the accomplishment of human actions fittingly and systematically. For an art seems to be nothing other than a certain order of reasoning whereby a human act fulfills its necessary purpose through well-defined means. Reason is not only able to direct the acts of the inferior parts: indeed, it is the director of its own act. It is a property of the intellect that it reflects on itself, for the intellect understands itself and similarly the reason is able to reason about its own act. Just as the art of building or metal-working was devised because reason applied reasoning to manual acts, enabling humans to perform such acts readily and systematically, so by the same reasoning it is necessary to have an art that directs the act of reason itself, through which humans can proceed in this very act of reasoning in an easy and systematic way, without error. This art is logic, that is, the science of reason. It is not the science of reason simply because it proceeds by reason, for this is common to all the arts, but because it concerns the act of reasoning itself as the matter that is proper to it. Thus it seems to be the art of arts, because it directs us in the act of reasoning from which all arts proceed.

---

[6] See p. 806 n. 35 below on "subaltern," etc.   [7] Marmo, "*Suspicio*," 188.
[8] *Metaphysics* 980b27.

Therefore one should understand the parts of logic in terms of the diversity of acts of reason. There are three acts of the reason. The first two of these are of reason understood as intellect. The first act of intellect is understanding of indivisible or non-compounded things, according to which it conceives what a thing is. Some call this operation the informing of the intellect or representation through the intellect. The teaching that Aristotle gives in the *Categories* pertains to this operation of reason.[9] The second operation of intellect is the combining or dividing of powers of understanding, in which true and false are now introduced; Aristotle's teaching in *On Interpretation* is devoted to this act of reason.[10] The third act of reason is of reasoning understood in its proper sense, that is, to reason back and forth from one thing to another, so that by what is known one may arrive at a knowledge of what is unknown; the remaining books of Aristotle's logic are devoted to this act of reason.[11]

It should be noted that acts of reason are similar to some degree to acts of nature, whence art imitates nature insofar as it can. We find a threefold diversity in acts of nature: in some, nature acts from necessity, so that it cannot fail; in some acts, nature is usually effective; however sometimes it can fail in its act. In these latter cases there must be a twofold act: one which happens most of the time, as when a perfect animal is generated from a seed; and one which happens when nature lacks something befitting it, as when a monster is generated from a seed because some principal element is corrupted. This threefold diversity is found in acts of reason. There is one process of reasoning that brings on necessity, in which no failure of truth is possible, and through the process of this sort of reasoning the certainty of knowledge [*scientia*] is produced. There is another process of reasoning which in most cases results in truth, without, however, carrying necessity. There is a third process of reasoning in which reasoning falls short of truth because of a defect of some principle which should have been observed in reasoning.

The part of logic which serves the first process is called the judicative part, because it gives judgment with the certitude of knowledge. And because a secure judgment concerning effects[12] cannot be made without resolving or analyzing [*resolvendo*] them into first principles, this part of logic is called analytic, that is, *resolutoria*. The certitude of judgment which is to be had from an analytic is either from the form of the syllogism itself—and this is the subject of the *Prior Analytics*, which treats the simple syllogism—or from the matter with the form, because the propositions are taken for themselves and as necessary—and this is the concern of the *Posterior Analytics*, which treats the demonstrative syllogism.

---

[9] *Categories* 1a20–2a10.   [10] *De interpretatione* 16a10–18.

[11] As will be clear from Aquinas' exposition below, these books are the *Prior* and *Posterior Analytics*, *Topics*, *Sophistical Refutations*, *Rhetoric*, and *Poetics*.

[12] I.e. the effects of causes, as in the products of efficient causes.

Another part of logic, which is called inventive, serves the second process of reasoning. For invention [i.e. discovery] does not always come with certitude, whence a certain judgment is required about those things discovered, in order to have certitude. As in the case of those natural processes that achieve their purpose most of the time, a certain degree [*gradus*] is reached, because the stronger the force of nature the more rarely does it fail in its purpose, so also in that process of reasoning which does not come with absolute certitude, a certain degree is reached accordingly as the process more or less approaches perfect certitude. For even though this process of reasoning does not produce knowledge, still at various times it produces belief or opinion on account of the probability of the propositions from which it proceeds, because reason inclines completely to one part of the contradiction, but there is still misgiving about the other side. To this subject pertain the *Topics* or dialectics, for the dialectical syllogism is formed from probable premises, which is Aristotle's concern in the *Topics*. At times, however, belief or opinion does not fully arise, but rather there is a certain suspicion [*suspicio*], because reason does not completely incline to one part of the contradiction, even though it inclines more to one side than to the other. To this the *Rhetoric* pertains. At other times only an estimation [*estimatio*] inclines to one part of the contradiction, on account of some representation, in the way that a man may conceive disgust at a certain food if it is represented to him under similitude of something disgusting; to this the *Poetics* pertains, for it is the poet's function to lead us to virtue through a fitting representation. All of these pertain to rational philosophy, for it is the function of reason to lead from one thing to another.

The third process of reasoning is served by the part of logic which is called sophistic, which Aristotle treats in the *Sophistical Refutations*.

GILES OF ROME, COMMENTARY ON ARISTOTLE'S *RHETORIC*, CA. 1272

INTRODUCTION

Giles of Rome or Aegidius Romanus (ca. 1243/7–1316) was a prolific writer on philosophy, theology, and political thought, an important commentator on many of Aristotle's works, and a polemicist in contemporary ecclesiastical politics. A member of the Augustinian order, he studied at Paris in the 1260s, and perhaps with Aquinas himself from 1269 to 1272. After leaving Paris in the wake of the condemnations of 1277, he returned there in 1285 to become a regent master in theology. In 1295 he was named Archbishop of Bourges, and died at Avignon. The work for which he was best known was his *De regimine principum* [Regimen [Guide] for Princes], perhaps the most influential example of the "mirror for princes" genre in the Middle Ages, surviving in nearly three hundred copies of the Latin text as well as many copies of vernacular translations, among them John Trevisa's English version.

Giles' vast commentary on Aristotle's *Rhetoric* has justifiably been called a work of "extraordinary theoretical penetration, creativity, and scientific mastery."[1] It achieved immediate success and remained an influential resource for many generations afterwards: it had the advantage of being timely (it was produced soon after the Moerbeke translation was finished), it was comprehensive in its coverage of the whole text, and it provided a very strong *divisio textus*, that is, a conceptual and structural overview of Aristotle's treatise.[2] It survives in whole or in part in twenty-eight manuscripts and was also printed five times between the late fifteenth century and the middle of the sixteenth century.[3]

---

[1] Staico, "Retorica e politica in Egidio Romano," 9.

[2] Marmo, "L'utilizzazione delle traduzioni latine della *Retorica* nel commento di Egidio Romano (1272–1273)," 111–15; Briggs, "Aristotle's *Rhetoric* in the Later Medieval Universities," 247. For dating of the commentary and its place in Giles' career, see Donati, "Studi per una cronologia delle opere di Egidio Romano 1," 32–5.

[3] Briggs, "Aristotle's *Rhetoric* in the Later Medieval Universities"; Staico, "Retorica e politica in Egidio Romano," 2. For the printed versions, see Lohr, "Medieval Latin Aristotle Commentaries: Authors A–F," 334–5, which also gives a census of the twenty-two manuscripts known to Lohr at that time.

To appreciate how ambitious Giles' undertaking was, we must consider the almost complete unfamiliarity of the Latin West with Aristotle's text before the Moerbeke translation. This was despite the existence of the two mid-century Latin translations, the Anonymous Vetus and the translation by Hermannus Alemannus, as well as Hermannus' translation of Al-Farabi's *Didascalia*. In his dedicatory epistle to an unknown addressee who must have requested the commentary, Giles describes the difficulties he encountered in this task: the text was hard to understand, not just because it was translated from Greek but also because of Aristotle's terse style; there is a multiplicity of examples or copies of the text (*multiplicitas exemplorum*); and there are few aids to interpreting it. While such excuses may themselves be commonplaces of the commentary tradition on Aristotle's writings,[4] they still pertain directly to Giles' own situation. In addition to all the general difficulties of historical interpretation of the text, there was the acute problem of language, of finding properly nuanced Latin equivalents for a Greek terminology that remains a subject of debate even for modern scholars: these include such crucial terms as *antistrophos* (usually translated in English as "counterpart"), *pistis* ("belief," "proof," "means of persuasion"), and *êthos* ("character"). These words were rendered differently in the three Latin translations of the thirteenth century, and in some cases we see Giles having recourse to the vocabulary of the older translations in order to get greater purchase on a term.[5] Giles also exploited the available Arabic interpretive tradition in order to develop a coherent theoretical understanding of Aristotle's scientific method in this work.

In his commentary, Giles shows no interest in the Ciceronian–Boethian tradition and does not try to reconcile Aristotle's work with the more familiar rhetorical frameworks. There are two closely related reasons for this. First, Aristotle says that rhetoric is like dialectic in so far as it does not have its own subject matter, but is applicable to a variety of questions. Second, Aristotle allies rhetoric with ethics. The combination of these new perspectives represented something very different from the standard Ciceronian definition of rhetoric as the "art of speaking well in civic affairs." The older definition involves fixing rhetoric to a determinate subject matter. But Aristotle's linking of it with ethics identified, to medieval readers, a broader, less determinate field of application for rhetoric's distinct method. In the words of Osmund Lewry, now "rhetoric is a dialectic applied to moral affairs."[6] As Giles' commentary puts it, "rhetoric is about those things are are applicable to morals" and "the instruments of rhetoric are the example and the enthymeme" (see below, at 1359a22). Not long after he finished the commentary on the *Rhetoric*, in his short treatise

---

[4] As suggested by O'Donnell, "The Commentary of Giles of Rome on the *Rhetoric* of Aristotle," 142.

[5] The evidence of Giles' use of the Anonymus Vetus and the Hermannus translations is traced in Marmo, "L'utilizzazione delle traduzioni latine."

[6] Lewry, "Rhetoric at Paris and Oxford," 56.

on the difference between rhetoric, ethics, and politics, Giles did consider the Ciceronian definition of rhetoric as a civil science. But in this treatise he uses it as a foil to the Aristotelian conception of rhetoric as an art that, like dialectic, has no determinate subject matter. Here Giles sides with Aristotle over Cicero: rhetoric is not a branch of politics (narrowly construed), but rather is closer to dialectic because it "brings a consideration of common principles [i.e. what dialectic teaches us to examine] to moral affairs."[7]

The new conception of rhetoric, what Charles Briggs has described as a shift of interest from the language sciences and eloquence to ethics and social relations,[8] also opened the way to a new understanding of the relationship between literature and rhetoric. Giles' commentary gives less original attention to the question of eloquence than to questions of ethics and the passions. But ironically, the long-term effect of the association between rhetoric and ethics was to pull rhetoric back into the circle of literature. Rhetoric could now be seen, not simply as eloquence lent to various subject matters, but as eloquence imbued with an ethical and persuasive purpose. Rhetoric, linked with politics and moral discourse, attains a broader definition than that of "speaking well in civil affairs."

Where do we see these effects? First of all, and most influentially, we see them in Giles of Rome's own *De regimine principum*, which found its way into many literary contexts from the early fourteenth century onwards. The literary notion of the moral *exemplum*, which achieved such wide expression in vernacular poetry, had its preeminent theoretical articulation in the conjunction of ethics, rhetoric, and poetics in the *De regimine*.[9] In the well-known opening chapter in which he refers directly to the *Rhetoric* (and to the *Ethics* and the *Politics*) Giles gives cogent expression to the notion that rhetoric is a moral discourse because its literary devices of figuration and broad, affective exemplification, can serve moral instruction (here cited from John Trevisa's Middle English translation):

> Thanne it is to wetyng that in al moral mater, that is to saye mater touchyng mannys maner, the maner of processe, as the philosofer seith, is figural, that is to say by liknes, rude and boystous [i.e. *broad*]. For in suche mater it nedeth to passe by fygures and liknes . . . al the peple is in som wise [*way*] lurner and scoler [*learner and student*] of this art, bot fewe ben scharp of wit; therfore it is iseid [in *Rhetoric* book 3], that the more peple is, the lasse and the further is the wit [*the larger the population, the less and more remote is their understanding*]. Than [*as opposed to*] the scoler of moral mater, that is to

---

[7] *De differentia rhetoricae, ethicae et politicae*, ed. Bruni, 7. The political-academic context of the treatise, in which Giles positions the interests of the arts and theology faculties (the study of moral philosophy) against the claims of the powerful jurists (professional training in legal rhetoric), is examined in detail by Staico, "Rhetorica e politica in Egidio Romano," 62–75.

[8] See Briggs, "Aristotle's *Rhetoric* in the Later Medieval Universities," 250–3.

[9] See Briggs, *Giles of Rome's De regimine principum*; Coleman, *A History of Political Thought*, 61–71. On the literary exemplum in Giles, see Scanlon, *Narrative, Authority, and Power*, 105–18.

saye of high and derke [*arcane*] mater, it [i.e. *the people*] is symple and boystous, as it is ischewed [*shown*] [in *Rhetoric* book 1]. Thanne for nought al the poeple may comprehende sotil [*subtle*] thinges, the processe in moral mater mote [*must*] be boistous and by liknes of figuris.[10]

This is an explicitly moral, as opposed to theological or indeed grammatical, justification for the use of figurative language. Among vernacular texts where we can see the more particular literary effects of rhetoric defined through ethics, we can cite Dante's *Convivio*, Gower's *Confessio amantis*, and Lydgate's *Fall of Princes*. In book 2 of the *Convivio*, Dante identifies rhetoric with the third heaven, the realm of love governed by Venus (2.13). Dante is describing an eloquence whose enticing sweetness will charm and induct readers into a love for the higher and much sweeter pleasures of philosophy. Although Dante refers to Cicero and Boethius as the models of a philosophy imbued with rhetorical power (2.15), his understanding of rhetoric is not the older definition of speaking well in civil matters, but rather an inclusive "literary ethics" of philosophical instruction through an eloquent vernacular (2.12).[11] Book 7 of Gower's *Confessio amantis* is a scientific encyclopedia in which "rhetoric" has been elevated to the status of a governing category of knowledge which encompasses ethics, politics, and public discourse. Although Gower owes much to Brunetto Latini's *Trésor* for this restructuring of epistemology, the impact of Giles' *De regimine principum* and its Aristotelian rhetoric is clearly visible in the thematic underpinnings of his argument. In his discussion of rhetoric in book 6 of the *Fall of Princes*, Lydgate's references are Ciceronian, but in terms of the applications of eloquence, the outlook is that of a moral and instructional discourse. Rhetorical ornament, "sugared language and virtuous dalliance," is the instrument of moral instruction, a suasion directed at what philosophers would call the "practical intellect," which requires forceful pressure to act on what is right. For Lydgate, rhetoric finds its public purpose in moving the emotions of rulers and ordering the social relations of the populace.[12]

Giles' commentary on Aristotle's *Rhetoric* makes other significant advances. Giles refines the scholastic understanding of the difference between dialectic and rhetoric: dialectic produces assent through the intellect operating on itself and by itself, but rhetoric

---

[10] John Trevisa, *The Governance of Kings and Princes*, ed. Fowler, Briggs, and Remley, 6–7. On this passage see Coleman, "Some Relations between the Study of Aristotle's *Rhetoric*, *Ethics*, and *Politics*," 147–8.

[11] *Convivio*, ed. Ageno. Dante also refers to Aristotle's *Rhetoric* in the *Epistle to Can Grande* (§ 18), citing *Rhetoric* 1414b20, on the likeness of the prooemium in oratory, the prologue in poetry, and the prelude in flute-playing, though Dante's source for this may be the commentary by Pace of Ferrara on Geoffrey of Vinsauf's *Poetria nova*: see Woods, *Classroom Commentaries*, chapter 3.

[12] For Gower and Lydgate, see Part 6 below.

produces assent through an action of will or appetite on the intellect. In this re-evaluation as well, the ethical dimension of rhetoric is clearly visible. These distinctions enable him to lay out a clear, five-point program for the social, psychological, methodological, and material differences between dialectic and rhetoric (at 1354a1). Giles also gives elaborate attention to Aristotle's discussion of the emotions in book 2, developing a highly codified philosophical approach to them: "there are four things to be determined: so that we may have some familiarity with the following treatise which deals with the passions (i.e. book 2 of the *Rhetoric*), first we must consider what is a passion; second, the number of the passions; third, their order; and fourth, in what way the passions stand in opposition to each other."[13] But the philosophical orientation of this discussion does not lead Giles to expand theoretically on a connection between the emotions and the composing of affective speeches. Nor, in the *De regimine principum*, does his interest extend to the *practice* of composition.[14] For modern students of rhetoric and persuasive discourse, Aristotle's *Rhetoric* is canonical for its dynamic distinctions among the kinds of proof: proof through the character projected by the speaker in the speech (ethos), proof through emotional appeal (pathos); and proof through the "logos" or argumentation of the speech itself. It is a fascinating feature of Giles' commentary that these questions are not extensively debated and analyzed, but accepted *prima facie*, while other claims in Aristotle's text receive what may seem to us disproportionate attention. Giles' commentary, like Al-Farabi's *Didascalia* on the *Rhetoric*, is a witness to the imaginative stretch that was required to make Aristotle's treatise comprehensible to a new audience that had no access to the cultural context of the work. That Giles should give such lengthy attention to the scientific method and the relation between dialectic and rhetoric is not surprising, given the importance of Aristotelian logic in university arts faculties. But these questions led in turn to deep probing of the psychological structures of cognition, knowledge, and belief. Through this Giles gained an understanding of Aristotle's fundamental insight about the relation between rhetoric and ethics, and delivered a profound and influential interpretation of the *Rhetoric*.

Translated from *Aegidius Romanus, Commentaria in Rhetoricam Aristotelis*, Venice, 1515.[15]

---

[13] Fol. 49ra, at 1378a15.

[14] On Giles' lack of interest in *Rhetoric* book 3 when he writes the *De regimine*, see Briggs, "Aristotle's *Rhetoric* in the Later Medieval Universities," 248. For full discussions of Giles' codification and analysis of the emotions, see O'Donnell, "The Commentary of Giles of Rome," 149–56; Marmo, "*Hoc autem etsi potest tollerari*..."

[15] We wish to thank Charles Briggs and D. Vance Smith for their invaluable advice on Giles' text and its context.

The Commentary

[1354a 1 (fol. 1^{ra-b} in Venice 1515 edition)]

Rhetoric is the counterpart [*assecutiva*] of dialectic.[16]

... Let us note that rhetoric is part of dialectic or part of logic, as the Philosopher suggests in the first book of the *Rhetoric*. Logic is so called from "logos": the Greek word "logos" is translated in Latin as discourse [*sermo*] or reasoning [*ratio*].[17] Thus it is a logical discourse or a science of reasoning...

The first point to be investigated is: since all sciences are in some way rational in that they each proceed through a process of reasoning, in what way is logic to be distinguished from other rational sciences, given the extent to which reasoning is present in every art that proceeds through reasoning...

On this first point: if we can set aside grammar as a matter of convention [*ad libitum*],[18] and poetics which depends upon accounts of deeds and representations, we can say that rhetoric differs from the other ratiocinative sciences in that it does not proceed through reasoning in the same way as they do. For our present purposes there are three kinds of reasoning to consider: probable reasoning, persuasive reasoning, and demonstrative reasoning. Probable reasoning pertains to dialectic, persuasive reasoning pertains to rhetoric, and demonstrative reasoning pertains to the other sciences. We can establish the differences among these kinds of reasoning according to the differences that are generated from them. Opinion [*opinio*] is generated through probable reasoning. Belief [*fides*] or assent [*credulitas*] is generated through persuasions.[19] Knowledge is produced through demonstrative reasoning. And thus we may easily see how belief or assent differs from opinion

---

[16] The passages incorporated from William of Moerbeke's Latin translation of the *Rhetoric* are from the edition by Schneider. Translations of the Moerbeke Latin text are based on the now standard English translation from Aristotle's Greek by Kennedy, *Aristotle on Rhetoric: A Theory of Civic Discourse*, but are modified to reflect the Moerbeke Latin terminology and interpretation of Aristotle's meaning.

[17] The term *ratio* is used throughout the commentary, where it means reasoning, the faculty of reasoning, or in more technical senses, logical reasoning.

[18] See Marmo, "*Suspicio*," 187 and note.

[19] The terms *fides* and *credulitas* are used throughout Giles' commentary as approximations of the word *pistis* (proof, means of persuasion, judicial proof; but also trust, confidence) in the original Greek text. The Moerbeke translation uses the term *persuasio*, but also the term *fides*. The term *pistis* has such a range of meaning that it is not surprising that there are various ways of rendering it in Latin. Moreover, *credulitas* and *fides* are the usual Latin terms used to translate the Arabic word *tasdiq*, which means assent, judgment, conviction, or belief. *Tasdiq* could be used to translate the Greek *pistis* in Arabic texts. The term *credulitas* is used by Hermannus Alemannus in his Latin

and knowledge. How rhetorical reasonings differ from dialectical and demonstrative reasonings will be transparently clear.

It is not very difficult to see how belief differs from knowledge [*scientia*]. But it is more difficult to see how belief differs from opinion, when neither one offers perfect understanding.

Some have said that assent or belief differs from opinion with respect to certitude, because we adhere with greater certainty to those things about which we opine than to those things that we believe; belief of this sort, and especially the belief generated by rhetoric, ought to be called a certain kind of suspicion.[20] Al-Farabi, in the introductions that he wrote about the *Rhetoric*, argued that rhetorical persuasion concerns particular things; wherefore we can say that since opinion is formed about universal matters, opinion differs from belief just as anything formed in respect of particulars differs from what should be formed from universals.[21] But these differences either do not seem to be true, or they do not attain the status of a radical difference. For it can happen that someone adheres more firmly to something that he believes than to something about which he has an opinion. Or on the other hand, there can be a kind of opinion about particular matters. We are of the opinion that the sun is greater than the whole earth even though the senses judge it to be the diameter of one foot...

Thus we may see how belief, which a rhetor means to produce, differs from knowledge and opinion. It should be understood that some things belong to the power of the soul [*potentia animae*] taken in itself, and others belong to one power only in relation to another, so that "willing" [*velle*] belongs to the will [*voluntas*] considered on its own terms, but "choosing" [*eligere*] belongs to the will as the will depends upon reason. For choice itself is not an end [*finis*], but rather the choosing of things that are ordered to an end; and since it belongs to reason to be able to put things in order, choosing cannot belong to the

rendering of Al-Farabi's *Didascalia in Rethoricam Aristotelis*. On the Arabic term and its Latin equivalents, see Black, *Logic and Aristotle's Rhetoric and Poetics in Medieval Arabic Philosophy*, 73 n. 63. Giles may have taken the term *credulitas* from the *Didascalia* of Al-Farabi, or even from Hermannus' translation of the Arabic text of Aristotle's *Rhetoric*: see Dahan, "L'entrée de la *Rhétorique*," 84–5 (which gives all three Latin versions of the text at 1355a3–9.) See also Marmo, "*Suspicio*," 187–8: "[Giles'] terminology is dependent on Arabo-Latin sources." Given that Giles is depending on Arabic sources for his terms and is using these terms to analyze cognitive habits, we have (unless otherwise noted) translated *fides* literally as "belief" and *credulitas* as "assent." Where Giles follows the Moerbeke text in using *persuasio* in the technical sense of a means of persuasion, we have rendered that literally as "persuasion."

[20] Marmo, "Suspicio," 188, recognizes this as a reference to Aquinas' commentary on the *Posterior Analytics*. The Venice 1515 edition omits some phrasing that makes the reference to Aquinas' commentary clear.

[21] This is a reference to the *Didascalia* § 24, on rhetoric and particulars (included in the *Didascalia* section above). The idea that opinion (formed through the dialectical syllogism) is stronger than belief (formed through rhetorical persuasion) would be familiar from Al-Farabi's *De scientiis*; see the translation of Gerard of Cremon, ed. Schupp 48–50. See the edition of Al-Farabi by Langhade and Grignaschi, eds., *Deux ouvrages*, 141 n.

will unless the will is dependent on reason. Thus Aristotle writes in book 6 of the *Ethics* that choice is either intellective appetite or appetitive intellect [*appetitus intellectivus, vel intellectus appetitivus*], and just as it proceeds from the will, so it is, when exercised, also of the intellect.[22] An act of the speculative intellect seems to belong to the intellect alone. An act of the practical intellect seems to belong to the intellect more as intellect is ordered to the appetite. Thus (for example), what makes us lie initially is malice, and this is not connected with speculative understanding. It belongs more to practical cognition, since it is about particular matters, not universals, that we are emotionally aroused through passions and malice. And as it is in actions so it is in assent [*assensus*], that sometimes the intellect assents through its own motion, and sometimes through a motion of the will, or sometimes it assents to propositions to which it is apt to assent according to its own nature; and sometimes when it assents to certain things, there is an assent that is ordered to the appetite. Moreover, if we properly direct our attention to this, we have the difference between knowledge, probability, and persuasion. For the assent of credulity [*assensus credulitatis*] through persuasive reasonings belongs to the intellect when it is by nature apt to be moved by appetite. An assent of knowledge or opinion, that is, to assent through demonstrative or probable reasonings, belongs to the intellect as it is by its nature apt to be moved by its own motion[23] ... And because the assent that the rhetorician means to produce belongs to the intellect as it is apt to be moved by the will, persuasion does not happen without an act of the intellect that is moved by the will. But because there is no persuasion in rhetorical matter unless it comes about in such a way that the intellect has been able to be moved by appetite ... belief differs from opinion with respect to certitude, because there is not so much certitude in rhetorical assent; for this is a certain kind of suspicion [*suspicatio*].

Let us lay out the difference between opinion and belief, or between dialectic and rhetoric, in very precise terms. As we have seen, the intellect assents to the persuasions of rhetoric as it is apt to be moved by the appetite; it believes the probable arguments of dialectic as it is moved according to its own movement. It follows that there is a fivefold difference between rhetoric and dialectic. First, the rhetorician descends more into moral matter, and the dialectician into speculative matter. Second, it behooves the rhetorician, but not the dialectician, to consider the passions. Third, the audience and judge of rhetorical discourse is simple and unsophisticated, whereas the audience of dialectical

---

[22] 1139b4.

[23] I.e. dialectical reasoning produces assent based on the intellect being moved by its own nature; rhetorical persuasion produces assent based on intellect being moved by appetite. On this idea, see Marmo, "*Suspicio*," 188; Green, "Aristotelian Rhetoric, Dialectic, and the Traditions of *Antistrophos*," 13–15, and Robert, "Rhetoric and Dialectic According to the First Latin Commentary."

discourse ought to be clever and subtle. Fourth, the instruments of rhetoric are the enthymeme and the example; the instruments of dialectic are the syllogism and induction. Fifth, as mentioned above, rhetorical persuasion is more concerned with particular matters, while dialectical proof is concerned more with universal matters. We can also give a sixth difference, which is that even though both dialectic and rhetoric use topics of argument, the two arts do not understand topics in the same way...[24]

[1355b36 (6ᵛᵃ)]

> Of persuasions [*persuasiones*], some are inartistic [or "atechnical": *inartificiales*] and some are artistic [or "technical": *artificiales*]. I call "inartistic" those that are not provided by us but are preexisting, as for example witnesses, information obtained by force, charters, and other things like this; "artistic" are those that it is possible to produce through a method and through us. Whence one must use the former and invent the latter.

He treats persuasions, with which rhetoric is concerned. He proceeds in two ways. First he divides such persuasions, saying that there are non-artistic and artistic persuasions. Second he states the components of the divisions, where he says "non-artistic persuasions are etc." He does two things here: the first as stated above; second, he subdivides artistic persuasions. Non-artistic persuasions are those that are not provided through our own efforts, but which exist beforehand, or which we use as if they existed already. Such persuasions are oaths, witnesses, information obtained by force, that is, by torture, charters, and other such things that we do not invent, but which we presume are already invented. Such non-artistic persuasions are mentioned in comparison with the rhetorical art; for the discursive art is such that the persuasions of the art should come about only through speeches and discourses [*orationes et sermones*].[25] And so he adds: artistic persuasions are those which it is possible to produce through a method, that is, through rhetoric, and through us, inasmuch as we have the said art. And thus, as stated, some persuasions are artistic, and

---

[24] Following this (fol. 2ʳᵃ), Giles lays out further discussions about the *assecutiva*: *assequi* means to be both equal and different. Rhetoric can be seen as an imitation of dialectic, sharing with it three features, subject (acts of reasoning), method, scope. Rhetoric is also deficient compared to dialectic in terms of certainty, instruments (enthymeme vs. syllogism), and relationship to the intellect. Here he also refers to the Hermannus translation of the Arabic version, which says that rhetoric corresponds to [*convertitur*] the art of topics. Al-Farabi explained this *conversio* as a kind of "adequation" and "equivalence." See Marmo, "*Suspicio*," 189–90, and "L'utilizzazione delle traduzioni latine,"126.

[25] Giles' pairing of these terms may show the influence of the translation by Hermannus Alemannus of Al-Farabi's *Didascalia*. Since we do not have the Arabic original of that text, we cannot be sure what words Hermannus was translating.

some persuasions are non-artistic, and these non-artistic persuasions or means of persuasion [*persuasibilia*] are to be used, whereas the other kind, that is, artistic means of persuasion, must be invented. Then he says:

[*1356a1 (6vb)*]

> Of those proofs/beliefs [*fides*] that are provided through rhetorical speech, there are three species: those which are in the character of the speaker [*in more loquentis*], those that are in disposing the listener in some way, and those that are in the speech itself through what it shows or seems to show.

In this section he subdivides artistic persuasions. He does two things. First he posits a threefold division. Second, he shows that rhetoric must consider all such persuasions. The second part is where he says "Since persuasions" [*Quoniam autem persuasiones* (1356a21)]. Regarding the first matter he does two things: first, he posits the said division; second, he lays out the elements of the division. This second part is where he says "It is produced through character" [*per morem* (1356a5)]. First he says "of those beliefs" [*earum fidierum (sic)*], that is, of those assents [*credulitatum*]: *fidierum* is the genitive plural of *fides*. Of such assents or beliefs [*credulitatum vel fidierum*] that are brought about through a speech, that is, through artistic means of producing belief, there are three species. There are those that are in the character[26] of the speaker, that is, a certain kind of belief is effected by the speaker, if he shows himself to be accommodating and restrained or of good moral character. The next one is the way in which the listener is to be disposed, that is, a certain kind of belief [*fides*] and assent [*credulitas*] is produced by putting the listener into a suitable state of mind through emotional discourse. The third kind of assent is effected through the thing itself, that is, when we invent persuasions and enthymemes through appropriate speeches and discourses. Through this he shows that the enthymemes so invented will be effective if they are apparently true or the speaker seems to prove his point.

So there are these three modes of artistic persuasion and no more, for every persuasion comes about through speech, because rhetoric is a discursive art. A speech in itself stands in relation only to three things: to the speaker, through whom it exists, to the listener, for

---

[26] The Greek term *êthos* has been translated by William of Moerbeke as *mos*, and by the Anonymous Vetus Translator as *consuetudo*. The term *êthos* carries these primary meanings, but it also carries a meaning close to that of *persona* or delineation of character, which the Latin terms do not quite convey. Cf., however, Aristotle's use of *êthos* in the *Nicomachean Ethics,* where it often means "moral character," especially in opposition to *dianoia* or intellect (see e.g. 1139a1).

whom it exists, and to the case in point, for which it exists. Thus belief is effected on the part of the speaker, and this is the first kind of belief, which is effected through character; or on the part of the listener, and this is the second kind of belief, which is effected through the emotions; and on the part of the case, and this is the third kind of belief, which is effected through reasonings and enthymemes. Then he says:

[1356a5 (6ᵛᵇ)]

It is produced through character when the speech is spoken in such a way that it makes the speaker worthy of belief. We believe men of good character to a greater extent and more quickly, in all subjects in general, and absolutely where there is no certitude, but opinion is divided on either side.

He states the elements of the division and does three things: first he states that willingness to believe (mentioned above) is effected on the part of the speaker; second on the part of the listener; third on the part of the speech itself. The second point is where he says "Through the listeners" [1356a14]; the third point is where he says "Through speeches" [1356a19]. Regarding the first issue, he does two things: first he lays out his intention, and second he states the case (where he says "This should . . . be effected" [1356a9]). First he says that willingness to believe is brought about through character when the speech is spoken in such a way that it makes the speaker worthy of belief. For if someone can show himself through his actions and words to be of good character, he demonstrates that he is worthy of belief. For in general, in all matters, we believe a man of good character more quickly than others, especially in ambiguous cases where there is no certitude, but opinion is divided on either side. Then we absolutely believe men of good character.

[1356a9 (6ᵛᵇ–7ʳᵃ)]

This should come about, not through the speech, but rather because the speaker is already considered to be a certain kind of person.[27] Thus it is not as if the speaker's good character in this art contributes nothing to persuadibility, as some of those who transmit

---

[27] *Oportet autem et hoc accidere non per orationem, sed propter preopinari qualem quendam esse dicentem.* Note that the Moerbeke translation seems to reverse Aristotle's meaning here: where Aristotle is clear that the effect of ethos must be produced through the art of the speech itself, and not through preconceptions of the speaker's character, the translation states that ethos should not be revealed through the speech, but through what is already thought about

the art of oratory posit, but rather we should say that character is the principal tool of belief.

He states the case, that is that willingness to believe should not be effected through the speech, but through opinion about the character of the speaker. Wherefore we see that a man who is equally emotionally affected will believe the reasonings and words proffered by a decent man; but he will not believe them when they are proffered by an unjust man.[28] When the very same speech is made, our willingness to believe does not come from the speech, but from the speaker whom we believe to be of a certain character, that is, the one whom we believe to be worthy and good. Thus it is not as some who transmit[29] oratorical arts say or posit, that is, assume or imagine, when they say that in the art of persuasion good character contributes nothing to the ability to persuade. This is false, and in fact one should say that good character or worthiness is the principal tool of belief. It is as if he says that in the act of speaking itself, belief relies more on enthymemes and reasonings; however, good character should have the principal force in generating belief on the part of the audience. Then he says:

[1356a14 (7ʳᵃ)]

It is produced through the listeners [*auditores*] when they have been led to feel emotion through the speech. For we do not render judgment equally when we are happy or sad, full of love or hate. We say that it is only this that those who have written arts of oratory have attempted to consider. These matters will be explained in detail in book 2, when we speak of the passions.

---

the speaker. But the Anonymous Vetus Translator was hesitantly correct in his translation (ed. Schneider, 9–10). Commentary on the Greek text recognizes various possible readings which could slightly affect the emphasis in Aristotle's meaning, but is uniform in accepting the general principle here, that judgment of the speaker's character should not depend on preconceptions, but on the speech itself. See Grimaldi, *Aristotle, Rhetoric 1: A Commentary*, 42; and Cope and Sandys, eds., *The Rhetoric of Aristotle*, 29 n., pointing out that Aristotle's meaning runs against the later current of the Ciceronian–Quintilianic tradition, in which the notion of *auctoritas* "expresses the influence of character upon opinion, in general." The Roman rhetorical tradition of the speaker's moral *auctoritas* would have been more familiar (and comprehensible) to William of Moerbeke and to Giles of Rome as well. On Giles' treatment of ethos in later sections of the *Rhetoric*, see Marmo, "Carattere dell'oratore e recitazione," 18–20.

[28] The argument seems to be that where emotion (of the audience) and arguments or reasoning (of the case) are equal, the decision depends on the speaker alone: the man who will be believed is the one with the better character, which is (according to Giles' commentary based on the Moerbeke translation) not produced through words.

[29] Edition: *credentes*; emended to *tradentes*.

He states that belief is effected on the part of the listeners, and he does four things. First he says that belief is produced through the listeners when they are led to feel emotion through the speech (given that they are susceptible to emotion). Second, he states the case: because we do not render judgment equally when we are happy or sad, full of love or hate, we judge diversely according to diverse passions. Third he adds that it is only this form of belief that those who have written arts of oratory have attempted to consider. . . . Fourth, concerning these passions, he adds that the genus of the passions will be explained in detail in book 2, because there we speak of the passions. The parts of this section are clear on a literal reading. Then he says:

[1356a19 (7ra)]

We have belief through rhetorical speeches when we show something to be true or apparently true through probable arguments about particular cases.

He states the third kind of belief, which is brought about through the speech itself, because belief produced through the speech is said to be proper to the speech itself. Such belief comes about when we demonstrate a truth or an apparent truth from probable arguments concerning the particular case. And it is said to be true on account of true reasonings; and apparently true on account of sophistical reasonings. He says true or apparently true, because it is the function of the rhetor to form a syllogism from either side of the argument, if the opposing side of the argument is probable and apparently true. Then he says:

[1356a21 (7^{ra-b})]

Since persuasions come about through these means, it is clear that the one who commands these three things is one who can form syllogisms, can understand (moral) character and virtues, and, third, can understand the emotions (what each of the emotions is, what is its quality, and from what things it comes into being and in what way).

In this section he shows that the function of the rhetor is to consider all methods for producing belief. He does two things. First, as was just given. Second, from what has gone before he concludes that rhetoric is a certain kind of dialectic applicable to civil matters. The second point is where he says "Thus it falls to rhetoric" [1356a25].

His reasoning is thus. Insofar as it pertains to rhetoric to persuade, since persuasions come about through these methods, method belongs to the one who can form syllogisms.

It is for rhetoric to grasp these three means, that is, to be able to consider the three methods of producing belief. And thus he adds that it can consider [moral] character insofar as it pertains to credibility [*credulitas*] on the part of the speaker, and that it can consider virtues in so far as it pertains to belief on the part of the speech. "Virtue" is understood here not in its proper sense: by "virtues" he means topics and rhetorical enthymemes in which the excellence of rhetoric principally consists.[30]

Third, it pertains to rhetoric to consider the emotions [*passiones*], what each of the passions is and what is its quality; that is, in what way it may put a man into a certain emotional state, and through what means this comes about; that is, what causes each passion has, and what way it comes about through its causes. Then he says:

[1356a25 (7rb–8ra)]

Whence it falls to rhetoric, as if by its nature at birth, to be a certain part of dialectic and of moral [i.e. ethical] concerns which justly is called politics. On account of this, rhetoric assumes the outward appearance of politics, and (so do) those who pretend to a knowledge of it [cf. the Moerbeke text: *et contrafacti huius*[31]], whether from lack of learning, or whether from boastfulness, or whether from other human causes. Rhetoric is part of dialectic and resembles it, just as we said at the beginning. Neither is a science that is concerned with any determinate subject; rather they are powers for producing arguments. Now we have said just enough about their potential and their relationship with each other.

From what was said before, he concludes that rhetoric is a kind of dialectic applicable to civic affairs, and he does three things. First he concludes, from the foregoing, that it falls to rhetoric, as if by its nature, to be a certain part of dialectic, and that its business is what concerns morals: this concern is justly called politics. From what has been said it follows that the Philosopher thinks that rhetoric is a part of dialectic applicable to civil morals, as he says. Now since it has been said that rhetoric is principally about persuasions, persuasion designates an act of reason about a matter out of which powerful passions can arise so as to

---

[30] Giles' explanation here seems to have misrepresented the text, because he discusses "virtue" as the second of three things that a speaker needs to command, and defines "virtue" as the excellence of the syllogistic tools at the speaker's disposal. But the Moerbeke text is straightforward: first the speaker must have the ability to syllogize, second he must understand character and virtue, and third, he must understand the emotions.

[31] See note 33 below.

mislead the intellect into believing what is said. Rhetoric is a particular kind of ratiocinative art, a particular kind of dialectic; it is an act of reason about particular things.

Note that the particular things to which rhetorical reasonings are applied are civil affairs, and so it is that rhetoric concerns morals and political affairs, on account of which it follows that rhetoric assumes the outward appearance or figure of politics.[32]

But because some would deny that rhetoric is a part of dialectic, he adds that there is a contrary position, that is, contrary to the fact or declaration that rhetoric is part of dialectic, and he says that this is on account of diverse causes: one cause may be that people say this for lack of learning, because they are ignorant of logic; another cause may be boastfulness, that is pride, because those who possess a knowledge of rhetoric are inflated and proud and do not want to concede that rhetoric is part of dialectic, lest on this account the dialecticians gain more prestige than they do.[33] Other reasons why they deny that rhetoric is part of dialectic may include various human causes: for example, civic power, or money, because such things may be more forthcoming if they deny that rhetoric is part of dialectic.

Third, he concludes by saying that rhetoric is a certain part of dialectic, as is clear from what has now been said, and that it is similar to dialectic, as we stated at the beginning: I refer to what was said in the opening section.[34] There it was noted that neither of these sciences is of any determinate genus, because neither dialectic nor rhetoric are sciences in the sense of having a determinate subject; rather they are certain powers for producing reasoning; that is, they are certain ratiocinative powers through which we can make arguments and prevail over adversaries in oratory and in speaking. Now we have said just enough about the potential of these arts and their relationship with each other. The second point (as above) begins where he says *et contra facti huiusmodi* [*sic*]. The third point is where he says "it is a certain part of dialectic."

To understand what has been said, three points need to be made. First, we must establish whether rhetoric is of a determinate genus or whether persuasions can be formed from every given subject. Second, we must determine whether rhetoric is subaltern to [*subalternetur*] dialectic.[35] Third, given that rhetoric is a certain ratiocinative power about

---

[32] "Outward appearance": in the Greek text the word is *skhêma*; in the Moerbeke translation and Giles' usage, the word is the Latin equivalent, *figura*.

[33] Giles has not grasped Aristotle's meaning in this passage, probably confused by the Moerbeke translation: the Greek *kai hoi antipoioumenoi* ("as well as those who lay a false claim to her") is rendered in the Moerbeke text by the ambiguous phrase *et contrafacti huius*. Giles reads this as meaning that there is a contrary position: some deny the claim that rhetoric is a part of dialectic, either because of ignorance or pride. The Anonymous Vetus translation reads *et qui contradicunt hanc* (ed. Schneider, 10).

[34] 1354a1.

[35] The English terms "is subaltern," "subalternates," and "subalternation" are terms from logic, and are used here to translate the technical terms from medieval logic that Giles uses: *subalternatur, subalternare, subalternatio*. These terms are not exactly identical with the English terms "subordinate" (noun, adjective, and verb) and

civil affairs, and that it is ordered in relation to dialectic and politics, and given that it is called a part of dialectic, we will have to consider whether it can also be called a part of politics.

Let us note regarding the first point: what is true of moral virtues is also true of the sciences, especially rhetoric and dialectic. In speaking of virtues we recognize that they are of a twofold material: one is proximate and one is remote. For example, in magnanimity, the immediate matter seems to be honor; the remote matter seems to be that with which all virtues are concerned.[36] Now every matter from which honor can arise is in some way a matter of magnanimity, and because honor can arise from the moral arts and from their subject matter, magnanimity is in some way concerned with all virtues. Thus the Philosopher thinks that magnanimity produces greatness in all the virtues.[37] Just as we can divide the matter of temperance and fortitude into two, that is, the emotions themselves and the things from which these emotions arise, so in the same way dialectic and rhetoric have acts of reasoning as their proximate material, and they take as their remote material the things to which the acts of this reasoning are applicable.

On this understanding we can state that dialectic and rhetoric are not of a determinate genus. For if we want to say that their materials are the acts of reason with which they are directly involved, such acts are not of any determinate genus, because "reasoning" itself cannot constitute a good delimitation of subject matter, since reasoning always applies to one thing or another, depending on what it is about. If we want to say that diverse matters are the things to which reasoning is applicable, then it is still true that these are not of a determinate genus. But if rhetoric is more applicable to particular matters, or indeed to political affairs, or to those things from which passions can arise, and dialectic has a different application, then on this account one can say that rhetoric is concerned with matters of a determinate genus. It does not just look to persuade about matters that arise from a generality, for such matters may not be persuasive about things that arise from any particular, either about action and emotion or about other categories [of things]. This is not the case with geometry, which is limited in scope to the genus of continuous quantity, nor with arithmetic, which is limited to the genus of differentiated quantity, nor with the other arts. In this way the Philosopher seems to maintain the indeterminacy of genus in

"subordination." In the usage of modern as well as medieval logic, "subalternation" describes the relationship between a general proposition and its corresponding particular proposition: the relationship is one of order (the pattern of inference) as well as dependency. Given the technical nature of Giles' discussion, and also since the terminology is still used in modern logic, we have preserved the terminology here with literal translations.

[36] Cf. *Nicomachean Ethics* 1123b–1125a.

[37] Cf. *Rhetoric* 1362b; cf. also a similar remark in *Eudemian Ethics* 1232a30 (from a chapter of the text not included in the medieval selection known as *De bona fortuna*).

rhetoric, because it can consider persuasions about any given contingent. On the other hand we can say, if we want, that while the use of rhetorical reasoning seems to be proper to political matters, nevertheless its use can be adapted to the materials of other sciences. Whence Al-Farabi, in his introduction to the *Rhetoric*, said: what is appropriate to persuasive discourses is used in the sciences, although the use of them in the sciences is not a scientific use.[38] But the rhetorical method occurs in non-rhetorical subjects, because the subject matter of rhetoric proper unto itself is the method of persuading about certain questions. These are particulars.

The second thing to be established is whether rhetoric is subaltern to dialectic. Let us note that subalternation can be understood in two ways.

In general, any superior thing subalternates an inferior thing to itself. From this perspective, metaphysics, which is supreme among the sciences, subalternates all the other sciences to itself; and on this understanding of subalternation, rhetoric is subaltern to dialectic. For in whatever class of things, that which approaches the highest and supreme entity excels the others which do not approach that entity, just as the first philosophy excels all the other particular sciences because it considers God, who is the highest entity. Thus, just as in categorizing things we designate one thing the best, the first cause, which is the focus of the highest of the sciences of realities,[39] so in categorizing forms of reasoning we designate one thing the best, the syllogism, whose purpose is to resolve bitter disputations and contradict the forceful arguments of an opponent, which is the focus of dialectic. Thus it follows that among the rational sciences dialectic is superior; indeed, on the terms of what has been laid out above, dialectic is more supreme among the rational sciences than metaphysics among the sciences of realities.[40] For if such excellence is achieved out of the highest good, the more the highest good is approached the more valuable is the excellence achieved; thus dialectic more essentially treats the highest form of reasoning than metaphysics treats the highest being, because the syllogism is more the main point of dialectic than God is the main point of the first philosophy.[41] Thus with respect to this measurement we must differentiate in the sense that dialectic is the more excellent among the sciences of reasoning, or that it is more superior to rhetoric than

---

[38] See above, *Didascalia*, p. 748.

[39] "Sciences of realities" (*scientiae realium*): studies of entities and beings that do not proceed from human intellect, including metaphysical realities, and which would exist even without the perception or existence of the intellect.

[40] That is, because without the tools of dialectic, we would not be able to evaluate the claims of other sciences, including metaphysics.

[41] I.e. dialectic has a greater power to explain and treat the syllogism than metaphysics has to treat the divine entity, which lies ultimately beyond the power of any human scientific explanation. Thus dialectic is more commensurate with its particular subject, the syllogism, than metaphysics with its subject, God.

metaphysics to the other sciences. Therefore, in terms of what was said above about subalternation, rhetoric is subaltern to dialectic.

But if we want to understand subalternation in a strict sense, as the Philosopher establishes the terms for it in the first chapter of the *Posterior Analytics* on the subalternation of the sciences,[42] we cannot maintain subalternation among the said sciences, because two ways of understanding can be posited.

The first is based on a principle of order, which is prerequisite to establishing the relationship between a subalternating and subaltern science.

The second is based on an unequivocal way of proceeding. We ought to conceive that subalternation invokes a certain order which is demonstrated from the name itself, that something is *under another* thing, and is ordered in relation to another; on this basis it is said to be subalternate. Therefore where things are not ordered in relation to each other, no subalternation can exist between them. It is necessary that a subalternating science, around which the subalternate science revolves, be considered for itself. On this account we do not say that sophistic is subaltern to dialectic, because the sophism, which the sophist treats for its own sake, is treated by the dialectician only by accident, in that this is a distortion of his proper art. So we ought not to say that rhetoric is subaltern to dialectic, because the enthymeme, which is treated in rhetoric for its own sake, is treated in dialectic only in an accidental way, that is, as a deficiency of the syllogism which dialectic treats for its own sake.

We can show in terms of property that rhetoric is not subaltern to dialectic.[43] If optics and geometry did not have the same mode of proceeding and demonstration, that is, both using lines and triangles, one would not be subordinate to the other. Naturally, if that field of study that pertains to the eye did not proceed through reflection of light and through pyramids made up of angles that are incidentally equal to the angles of reflection, as optics proceeds, then optics would not be subaltern to geometry.[44] Because the mode of proceeding in rhetoric is different from the mode of proceeding in dialectic, and is applicable to different material, it is not possible to assert a relationship of subalternation between them. Moreover, just as a method of knowing is generated through logical

---

[42]   71a1–10; see above, Aquinas' preface to the *Posterior Analytics*.

[43]   Property (*proprium*) is one of the categories treated in Aristotle's *Topics*. See the discussion of relative property (e.g. it is the property of a man, in relation to a horse, to be a biped) and essential property (e.g. man is a mortal being capable of receiving knowledge) in *Topics*, book 5 (128b–129a).

[44]   In other words, geometry has already established principles that are validly adapted to optics, and so optics derives its principles from geometry, as a lower science is derived from a higher science. See O'Donnell, "The Commentary of Giles of Rome," 146. The argument according to property here is that the relationship of subalternation between geometry and optics does not hold for dialectic and rhetoric, since rhetoric does not derive its mode of proceeding from dialectic.

reasoning which is not generated through the reasoning of the arts and the sciences of reality (which generate concrete knowledge), so that dialectic does not subalternate the sciences of reality to itself, nor the converse, so it is also the case that because rhetorical reasoning produces belief, which is not produced through dialectic (which produces opinion), dialectic does not subalternate rhetoric[45] to itself, nor the converse.

The third thing to be established is: although rhetorical reasonings are applicable to political affairs as something like rhetoric's proper material, still rhetoric should be called a certain kind of dialectic rather than a certain kind of politics. Now, as we have seen, rhetoric turns directly on acts of reasoning. However, civil matters are, as it were, the remote material of rhetoric, because an inculcated disposition [*habitus*] takes its form from what it is immediately concerned with. In this way the rhetor will be more a creator of reasonings than of realities, because he is more immediately involved in reasonings than in real matters. So he is more dialectician than statesman. In that rhetoric considers reasonings it would have more in common with dialectic, but in terms of the thing to which these reasonings are applied, that is, in terms of civil affairs, rhetoric would be a matter of moral behavior.

Let us note: particular events, from which emotions [*passiones*] arise, are said to be the proper matter of rhetoric when compared with universal political issues in which the emotions of love and hate have no role; but when compared with acts of reasoning, or persuasions, such particular events are in effect matter extraneous to rhetoric. Thus we can distinguish a threefold matter of rhetoric: matter that is proper to it in every way, i.e. acts of reason; matter that is extraneous to it in every way, i.e. universal matters; and matter that it takes for itself in a middling way, i.e. particular events are in effect its proper material, although not so much as acts of reasoning.

[1359a22 (14vb–15ra)]

It is clear that it would be necessary also to have propositions about the great and the small and the greater and the lesser, both generally and specifically; for example, [about] what is the greater or lesser good or injustice or justice, and similarly about other qualities. The subjects about which it is necessary to frame propositions have [now] been stated.

[Only one section, from the first part of the commentary on this passage, is provided here]

---

[45] Edition: *reales scientias*

[Since Aristotle has said that] rhetoric is a kind of dialectic, rhetoric is therefore a certain kind of disputative science [*disputativa scientia*]. So we ought to think that dialectic is purely disputative or ratiocinative [*ratiocinativa*]. For since to reason is an act of reasoning, that science which is purely about acts of reasoning should be called ratiocinative in a pure sense. And because dialectic is this kind of thing in a pure sense, it is ratiocinative. Whence it is the case that the syllogism and induction, which are kinds of reasoning, are purely the instruments of dialectic, especially the syllogism, which is most purely reasoning. Rhetoric, however, does not deal with acts of reason as understood purely and absolutely, but rather concerns things as they are applicable to individual facts. Thus the Philosopher says, "it falls to rhetoric, as if by its nature at birth, to be a certain part of dialectic and of moral concerns" [1356a25]. In the same way, geometry concerns lines in a pure sense; perspective, however, is not about lines understood in an absolute sense, but rather about visible lines. And in the same way, while arithmetic is about numbers in a pure sense, music is not about numbers purely speaking, but is applicable to sounds. So dialectic is about reasoning or acts of reason in a pure sense, but rhetoric is about those things that are applicable to morals. Thus it is correct to say that "it falls to rhetoric, as if by its nature at birth, to be a certain part of dialectic" applicable to "moral concerns." And thus it is that the instruments of rhetoric are the example and the enthymeme.

PART 6

RECEPTIONS OF THE TRADITIONS

THE LANGUAGE ARTS
AND POETICS IN THE LATER
MIDDLE AGES,
CA. 1369–CA. 1475

INTRODUCTION

With the ascendancy of vernacular learning and literary culture in the later Middle Ages, the traditions of grammatical and rhetorical teaching were diffused among new audiences and activated in new spheres. The texts featured in this section represent aspects of the diffusion of grammatical and rhetorical theory in Latin teaching and especially in English vernacular writing. We can bring these texts into perspective by approaching them through related developments in the language arts where old frameworks came to accommodate new critical interests and cultural values.

Of course, as the arts developed in new directions, there was also considerable continuity with older practices and outlooks, especially where the teaching of Latin language and composition were concerned. Thus we see the continued popularity of key ancient and medieval preceptive works: for grammar, Donatus (especially the *Ars minor*) and to some extent Priscian's *Institutiones*, along with the *Doctrinale* of Alexander of Villa Dei and the *Graecismus* of Eberhard of Béthune; and for the teaching of compositional rhetoric, the overwhelming presence of the *Poetria nova* of Geoffrey of Vinsauf, as well as the *Summa dictaminis* of Guido Faba. Some trends that had emerged more recently, in the thirteenth century, were also still in place or recognizable in the following centuries. The study of grammar at universities remained largely bound up with logic, as speculative grammar reached its highpoint during the first decades of the fourteenth century. The place of rhetoric in formal study at northern universities remains difficult to trace, although there is strong evidence from manuscripts and glosses that the *Poetria nova* and related works, such as the *Tria sunt*, were used in university settings; we will see that this is also the case with Nicolaus Dybinus' treatise on the colors of rhetoric.

But late medieval grammatical teaching also reached beyond traditional pedagogies in a number of important ways. One fascinating development was that grammar masters outside the universities began to infuse their teaching with contemporary philosophical interests. We see this, for example, in the grammar of the late-fourteenth-century Cremonese teacher Folchino dei Borfoni. Folchino's rich grammatical compendium, the *Cremonina*, draws on standard grammatical authorities (Priscian, Petrus Helias, Alexander of Villa Dei, Eberhard of Béthune). But for his presentation of syntax Folchino turns to the thought of the *modistae*, borrowing terminology and concepts from the speculative grammarian Martin of Dacia, whose *De modis significandi* (ca. 1270) established some of the basic formulations of modistic grammar. Folchino introduces modistic concepts in his definitions of the verb and participle as "modes of becoming," in his application of modistic terms for subject and predicate (*suppositum* and *appositum*), and in his adoption of the modistic notions of modes of being (i.e. what exists outside of language), understanding, and signifying (that is, the ways that grammatical forms denote the modes of being and understanding).[1] Yet this is an intermediate textbook intended for upper level, pre-university students, a prose *summa* typical of the Italian schools, with their orientation towards a practical Latinity.[2] As Folchino's treatise suggests, the speculative theory that defined university culture could penetrate the environment of the lower schools, as grammar masters imported their own intellectual interests into their classrooms.

The reception of Eberhard's *Graecismus* also shows how grammar masters might enlarge the scope of traditional pedagogical grammar to incorporate a high level of theoretical explanation. Anne Grondeux has traced an extensive, multi-layered tradition of glossing on the *Graecismus* extending from the middle of the thirteenth century through the fifteenth century. This tradition begins with lexicographical glossing, but later comes to incorporate more advanced thought, from the intentionalist grammatical theory of Kilwardby to the speculative grammars of the late thirteenth century. The teaching of the *Graecismus* is at times thoroughly revamped to reflect these academic developments. The later strata of glosses often use a scholastic style of prologue, presenting grammar within an introduction to philosophy, a genre clearly associated with university studies.[3] Yet the provenance of most of these manuscripts indicates non-university milieux, and the masters whose names are associated with the most rarified level of glosses are teachers who made their careers outside of the universities, as grammar masters of cathedral schools.[4] The authors and revisers of the glosses were the beneficiaries of university study, among them young graduates of the arts faculty who became grammar teachers and introduced into their own lectures the ideas that they had encountered at the University of Paris and elsewhere.[5] The boundaries between grammar for Latin pedagogy and grammar as a theoretical field thus became increasingly porous, as the glosses were copied and revised over two centuries.

Another mark of the extension of grammatical pedagogy into non-traditional arenas is the increasing use of vernacular languages as the medium of instruction. Of course this is not new with the later Middle Ages, as we see vernacular glosses in Latin teaching texts,

---

[1] DeSantis, introduction to edition of Folchino dei Borfoni, 53–8, 63–6, 77–8.
[2] Ibid., 71–3; Black, *Humanism and Education*, 87.
[3] Grondeux, *Le Graecismus d'Évrard de Béthune à travers ses gloses*, 58–122.
[4] Ibid., 86–7, 456.   [5] Ibid., iv–v, 457.

and even wholesale vernacular translations and versions of grammatical texts, from the early Carolingian period onwards, in Old High German, Old English, and other languages.[6] The vernacularization of Latin pedagogy was a practice in evidence throughout the Middle Ages. But with the ascendancy of literary vernaculars in the later Middle Ages, the expansion of vernacular grammatical teaching was inevitable, and we see a proliferation of vernacular translations and adaptations of elementary Latin grammars. This brought with it some new developments in the orientation of grammatical thought. One of these is the application of the metalanguage of Latin grammar to the grammatical structure of the vernaculars themselves, so that the vernacular is not only an access to Latin, but is itself revealed through the window of Latin grammar.[7] We see this, for example, in a related group of French translations of Donatus' *Ars minor*, in manuscripts primarily of the fourteenth and fifteenth centuries. These are not only texts for teaching Latin, but also "reflect a shadow analysis of French itself."[8] Throughout the treatises, French is the reference language for understanding the parts of speech, to the point where French words substitute for Latin examples of nouns and participles. By implication, French is analyzed according to the metalanguage designed for Latin, a conceptual framework that persists into fifteenth-century treatises devoted to the teaching of French itself.[9]

We find very nearly the same principles at work in Middle English grammatical treatises of the fifteenth century, during which period the innovation of using English to teach Latin gained enormous momentum, with more than thirty original English treatises on various aspects of Latin grammar known to us. The well-known testimony of John Trevisa (writing in 1385) about the mid-fourteenth-century grammar masters John of Cornwall and Richard Pencrych, indicates that using the Anglo-French vernacular to teach Latin grammar was an established practice which was slowly giving way to the use of English as the language of instruction.[10] The fifteenth-century treatises give English

---

[6] See the useful survey in Ising, *Die Herausbildung der Grammatik der Volkssprachen*, 21–34.

[7] For an extended treatment of this in relation to French, see Lusignan, *Parler vulgairement: les intellectuels et la langue française aux XIIIe et XIVe siècles.*

[8] Merrilees, "Teaching Latin in French: Adaptations of Donatus' *Ars minor*," 91. See also Merrilees, "*L'Art mineur* français et le curriculum grammatical." See the full study with editions by Timelli, *Traductions françaises de l'Ars minor de Donat au moyen âge (XIIIe–XVe siècles).*

[9] Merrilees, "Teaching Latin in French," 92–3. The application of a Latin metalanguage to teach a vernacular has earlier precedents, such as the Provençal *Donatz* of Uc Faidit, written about 1240 for Italian noblemen: see *The Donatz Proensals of Uc Faidit*, ed. J. H. Marshall (London: Oxford University Press, 1969).

[10] For Trevisa's remarks see *Polychronicon Ranulphi Higden*, ed. C. Babington, Rolls Series 41 (London: 1865–6), 2:158. See Bland, ed., *The Teaching of Grammar in Late Medieval England: An Edition, with Commentary, of Oxford, Lincoln College MS Lat. 130*, 88–96 and references there; Thomson, ed., *An Edition of the Middle English Grammatical Texts*, xi–xvi; and Miner, *The Grammar Schools of Medieval England*, 134–73.

examples of the categories and accidents of Latin grammar; the more elementary treatises simply define parts of speech and accidents through English alone, and the more advanced treatises on syntax not only give English examples, but analyze them on their own terms.[11] It has been suggested that the modistic view of Latin as a universal grammar provided the conceptual justification for applying the metalanguage of Latin grammar to English usage.[12] The study of Latin syntax was also aided by translation between Latin and the vernacular, either the translation of vernacular *themata* into Latin, or the translation of *latinitates* into the vernacular: in such translation exercises, the conventions of vernacular syntax are revealed through the analysis of Latin construction.[13]

But alongside the use of the vernacular to teach Latin, we also find the imposition of Latin linguistic categories on vernacular languages, that is, explicitly directing Latin grammatical principles to analysis of the vernacular. Dante's *De vulgari eloquentia* is an early and distinctive literary application of Latin grammar to the analysis of vernacular languages. In book 2, chapter 6, Dante takes up the principle of congruence or agreement among words and phrases. He considers the stylistic effects of different kinds of congruence in Latin before extending the principle to poetic lines in Provençal, French, and Italian which exemplify an ideal of "elevated" construction. The analysis of vernacular "rules" through Latin grammatical categories finds its expression, much later, in English contexts. It is the theoretical engine behind the extraordinary reflections on language and the problems of translation that are found in the General Prologue to the Wycliffite Bible, where the author considers the differences between Latin and English syntax, and pauses over the challenges of rendering the ablative absolute in English.[14] The late fifteenth-century Middle English treatise on the seven liberal arts (excerpted below) also depends on Latin categories for its treatment of grammar, deriving much of its terminology from Martianus Capella's chapter on grammar. But while its source is the most conservative authority on grammar, its main focus is pronunciation, with a distinct flavor of vernacular usage.

As in the teaching of grammar, so in the teaching of rhetoric there are significant continuities with earlier periods, but also new combinations of teachings, and certain more pronounced emphases within that teaching. The teaching of rhetoric through poetic

---

[11] Most of these are edited in Thomson, ed., *An Edition of the Middle English Grammatical Texts*. See also Bland, *The Teaching of Grammar in Late Medieval England*, esp. 145 and 164 (on the passive voice in English).

[12] Thomson, ed., *An Edition of the Middle English Grammatical Texts*, xvii.

[13] On the use of vernacular *themata* in fourteenth-century Italian grammar instruction, see Black, "The Vernacular and the Teaching of Latin in Thirteenth- and Fourteenth-Century Italy," 729. On *latinitates* accompanied by distorted English translations highlighting the differences between word order in Latin and in English, see Meech, "John Drury and his English Writings."

[14] See above, Part 2, Ablative Absolute dossier, pp. 337–8.

composition is reflected in the ever-expanding popularity of the *Poetria nova* throughout Europe, and the augmentation and proliferation of glosses on Geoffrey's work, representing all levels of instruction, from elementary studies to university-level teaching.[15] The teaching of prose composition continued to depend on dictaminal rhetorics, both in the ornate grammatical tradition of the French *dictatores* and the more practical plain style that looked back to the early Italian origins of the art; the strands of both traditions can be seen, notably, in the teaching of prose at Oxford in the later Middle Ages.[16]

One new development was the re-emergence of the *Rhetorica ad Herennium* as a text that was studied and glossed but that also figured as a primary resource for independent rhetorical treatises and compendia. The revival of the *Ad Herennium* is largely a product of teaching in the Italian cities, although many of the major European centers are also represented in this group of texts.[17] That many of these texts are of Italian origin and contain dictaminal matter may suggest that the *Ad Herennium* was increasingly found useful for the teaching of composition. Another dimension of the revival of the *Ad Herennium* was an intensified interest in the teaching of the colors of rhetoric, which expresses itself in heightened attention to the discussion of figures in book 4 of the work. According to Martin Camargo, the contents of glosses on book 4 in a number of manuscripts may indicate that the *Ad Herennium* was applied to the teaching of verse composition in particular: glosses that incorporate matter from the *Poetria nova* or from Marbod of Rennes' *De ornamentis verborum* (of the early twelfth century), suggest how the treatment of figures and tropes in book 4 could become a progressively more specialized component of compositional teaching, spawning new independent treatises that returned to older medieval sources but that also influenced new readings of the original Ciceronian text.[18]

As we see in the remarkable treatise on the colors by the fourteenth-century Central European teacher Nicolaus Dybinus (excerpted below), the study of the colors became a focus of highly theoretical attention in its own right. Study of the figures and tropes is certainly continuous with older medieval rhetorical practice, but the quality of theoretical interest, as seen in Dybinus' treatise, points to a greater pedagogical urgency to classify and quantify the colors. This theoretical interest in the colors as an independent field of compositional and language study recalls the centrality of the *Barbarismus* in university-level philosophical approaches to grammar, where the figures are studied as examples of linguistic and thus logical distortion. In this context, it is not surprising that the English

---

[15] See Woods, *Classroom Commentaries: Teaching the Poetria nova Across Medieval and Renaissance Europe*.
[16] Camargo, ed., *Medieval Rhetorics of Prose Composition: Five English Artes dictandi and Their Tradition*, 1–34.
[17] Ward, *Ciceronian Rhetoric*, 192–8. These texts remain for the most part unedited.
[18] Camargo, "Latin Composition Textbooks and *Ad Herennium* Glossing," 276–7.

poet Lydgate, writing in the middle decades of the fifteenth century, understands rhetoric almost exclusively in terms of the beauty and persuasive charm of the *exorna-tiones verborum*. Seen on these terms, his treatment of rhetoric in the *Fall of Princes* (excerpted below) may reflect some of the deeper aspects of rhetorical thought and teaching in the later Middle Ages rather than a reduction of rhetoric to "merely" the ornaments of style.

Brunetto Latini's Tuscan translation of the *De inventione* and his account of rhetoric in his French *Trésor* (both from the 1260s) represent the first wave of vernacularizations of classical rhetoric. This is a practice that continued in full force in Italy through the fifteenth century. But it was also inevitable that the rise of learned writing in the vernaculars would bring with it, as one of its auxiliary effects, new occasions for the diffusion of rhetorical teaching in the vernacular, whether through direct translations of Latin encyclopedic works (for example, the medieval Catalan translation of Isidore's *Etymologiae*[19]) or through literary syntheses of academic learning. The Middle English selections here represent both these avenues. The fifteenth-century treatise on the liberal arts adapts and to some extent translates Grosseteste's survey of the arts, *De artibus liberalibus*, from which the English text derives its association of rhetoric with music. Beginning in the late fourteenth century, English writers also began to treat Ciceronian rhetoric as a component of larger encyclopedic or historical projects. Gower's *Confessio amantis*, from the end of the fourteenth century, devotes its seventh book to an encyclopedic survey of all the sciences, and elevates rhetoric to the status of a whole epistemological category. Here Gower couches the presentation of the art of rhetoric in an account of Ciceronian practice in the celebrated speeches against Catiline. Lydgate's *Fall of Princes* is a historical project derived, ultimately, from Boccaccio's *De casibus illustrium virorum*, and his scientific presentation of rhetoric is occasioned by the narrative of Cicero's life. The effect of Aristotle's *Rhetoric* can also be seen in this vernacular tradition, as the newer Aristotelian model of rhetoric as a form of ethics, that is, knowing the political will and the psychological capacities of an audience, are grafted onto the older Ciceronian model of rhetoric as speaking well in civic affairs. Even without direct contact with Aristotle's *Rhetoric*, vernacular authors felt the impact of that work through the ubiquitous influence of Giles of Rome's *De regimine principum*. Thus even where the Ciceronian model is invoked, the ground has shifted. Beyond Gower's scientific elevation of rhetoric and Lydgate's defense of it as the greatest tool of statecraft lies the apotheosis of rhetoric in

---

[19] Ed. J. Gonzales Cuenca, *Las Etimologias de San Isidoro Romanceadas*, 2 vols. (Salamanca: Universidad de Salamanca, 1983).

Stephen Hawes' encyclopedic *Pastime of Pleasure* (printed 1509), which represents a last outgrowth of medieval learning.[20]

A further avenue for the emergence of a vernacular Ciceronianism is religious teaching, not only through the vernacular sermon literature that would rely upon the *ars praedicandi*, but through vernacular exposition of the language and meaning, the literal and spiritual senses, of the Bible itself. In the General Prologue to the Wycliffite Bible (see excerpts below), the impact and presence of the *De inventione* and the *Ad Herennium* are pervasive, but never recognized as such: Ciceronian legal thought about the letter and spirit of the law manifests itself there in the guise of Augustine's theological teaching in his *De doctrina christiana*, from which the General Prologue translates large segments into English. Thus there is a double tradition of ancient rhetoric, classical and early Christian, that finds its way into the vernacular.

[20] Another example of late medieval poetic didacticism about eloquence and ethics is the collection of set pieces by the Burgundian poet Georges Chastellain, composed in the early 1460s and known by its modern title *Les douze dames de rhétorique*. Here twelve allegorical ladies represent the faculties of *Science* (knowledge), *Eloquence*, *Profundité*, *Gravité de sens*, *Studiosité*, *Richesse de sens*, *Memoire*, *Noble Nature*, *Clere Invention*, *Precieuse Possession*, *Discretion*, and *Perseverance*. In many of the manuscripts (e.g. Cambridge University Library MS Nn. III. 2) these speeches are accompanied by exquisite miniatures. See Brown, "A Late Medieval Cultural Artifact."

NICOLAUS DYBINUS, *DECLARACIO ORACIONIS DE BEATA DOROTHEA*, CA. 1369

INTRODUCTION

Nicolaus Dybinus (or Tibinus) is the best-known representative of the Latin rhetorical and more broadly grammatical culture of Central Europe during the period of Charles IV (1316–1378), king of Bohemia and Holy Roman Emperor. Dybinus moved in the trilingual milieu of Latin, German, and Czech: he or his works can be associated with Dresden as well as with the universities of Prague and Vienna. We have only one secure date and place in Dybinus' biography: there is a notice of him as school master (*rector parvulorum*) at the Kreuzschule in Dresden in 1369.[1] His period of activity seems to extend from about 1369 to his death about 1387. But though we have only meager details of his biography, the range and character of his writings indicate a career of teaching rhetoric, grammar, and poetics at a relatively advanced theoretical level. He made commentaries on texts by medieval authorities: Geoffrey of Vinsauf's *Poetria nova*, Eberhard the German's *Laborintus*, and the *Doctrinale* of Alexander of Villa Dei.[2] He also composed dictaminal treatises (the *Viaticus dictandi* and the *Sporta florum rethoricalium*), a collection of model letters and poetic *exempla* (the *Correctoria*), and a treatise on poetic rhythm.[3] Along with these works he produced a monumental treatise on the colors of rhetoric, the *Declaracio oracionis de beata Dorothea*. This range of disciplinary genres (rhetoric, grammar, poetics) and sub-genres (dictaminal rhetoric, rhetorical poetics, poetic rhythms) suggests a comprehensive and synthetic approach both in terms of language theory and pedagogical application.

---

[1] Szklenar, "Hinweis auf Magister Nicolaus de Dybin, Kreuzschulrektor in Dresden im Jahre 1369," and Szklenar, *Magister Nicolaus de Dybin*, 63–79.

[2] A portion of the *Poetria nova* commentary is printed by Jaffe, "Des Witwers Verlangen nach Rat," 19–27; on the commentary on the *Laborintus*, see Szklenar, "Nicolaus de Dybin commentatore del 'Laborintus.'"

[3] Only the last of these, the treatise on rhythm, has been edited, in Mari, *I trattati medievali di ritmica latina*, 95–115. See Bourgain, "Le vocabulaire technique de la poésie rythmique." For an overview of Dybinus' writings, see Szklenar, "Magister Nicolaus de Dybin als Lehrer der Rhetorik" and Szklenar, *Magister Nicolaus de Dybin*, 80–203.

The *Declaracio oracionis de beata Dorothea* (Exposition of the Prayer on the Blessed Dorothea) is a systematic account of the *colores rhetoricales* as these are exemplified in a Latin poem that Dybinus wrote for the purpose, the *Oracio de beata Dorothea*, which consists of 330 lines in rhymed stanzas. The *Declaracio* was an influential work, surviving (in various versions, lengths, and forms of presentation) in nineteen known manuscripts.[4] Despite the formal variations that the treatise underwent throughout its manuscript transmission (reflecting its continuous classroom use), the theoretical structure of the *Declaracio* remains constant. All the colors of rhetoric are placed under the genus *transumptio*. This term has a long history in dialectic, theology, linguistic logic, and of course rhetoric, as in Geoffrey of Vinsauf's elevation of *transumptio* to a governing category of trope, a usage picked up by Gervase of Melkley and Eberhard the German.[5] In Dybinus' system, *transumptio* is then divided into eleven species: these are the traditional grouping of the tropes. Below these categories are the most specialized *colores*: thirty-six *colores verborum* (figures of speech) and twenty-one *colores sententiarum* (figures of thought), representing the lowest level of *color* under *transumptio*.

Through this theoretical framework, the distinction between genus (*transumptio*), species, and subspecies, Dybinus has attempted to map a scholastic outlook onto a traditional listing of figures and tropes. *Transumptio*, he tells us, is the most general category: it is "the color of all colors or the most general color of all."[6] The scheme may not work perfectly as a classification system, because it is tenuous to claim that figures of speech and figures of thought are truly "subalternated" to the first level of species. They are certainly more localized or particularized *colores*, but they are not dependent, as logical subcategories, on the tropes or the first level of species. But this does not seem to worry Dybinus. Rather, he is interested in finding a way to keep a mass of disparate information attached to a memorable literary example. The poem is devised to exemplify these levels of *color* in sequence, from the broadest to the most particular. The *Declaracio* examines the poem in detail, section by section and line by line, to point out the workings of the various *colores*. In his *Viaticus*, Dybinus describes the *Declaracio* as a detailed and comprehensive guide: "anyone who wants to know about the *colores* will find there [in the *Declaracio*] a full set of descriptions, nuances, exemplifications, model sentences, differentiations, and definitions of all the colors, presented according to the principles of the teachers of the science of rhetoric."[7]

---

[4] Nicolaus Dybinus: Jaffe, ed., *Nicolaus Dybinus' Declaracio oracionis de beata Dorothea*, 28–37, 271–90; Szklenar, *Magister Nicolaus de Dybin*, 119–26.

[5] See the selection from Geoffrey of Vinsauf, above.

[6] Jaffe, ed., *Nicolaus Dybinus' Declaracio*, 126, lines 19–20.

[7] Quoted in Jaffe, ed., *Nicolaus Dybinus' Declaracio*, 31.

Both external manuscript and internal thematic evidence suggest a university or scholastic milieu for this treatise and its teaching. Two of the manuscripts containing the *Declaracio*, Prague University Library MS XII. B. 12 and Munich Staatsbibliothek Clm. 19869, can be associated with university environments, either directly through the codex itself or through models from which the surviving manuscript was copied.[8] Most interestingly, the Prague manuscript contains a copy of Dybinus' commentary on the *Poetria nova* described by the copyist as *reportata Prage*, that is, transcribed from a lecture, and dated 1375, indicating that other works by Dybinus in the same compilation were being used in the University of Prague.[9] The internal thematic evidence is also powerful. The version of the *Declaracio* in Munich Staatsbibliothek Clm. 19876 (on which the translation below is based), from a fifteenth-century manuscript, uses the prologue format typical of Aristotelian science at universities from the thirteenth century onwards, the four "causes" of the text: efficient (the author), material (subject matter), final (purpose), and formal (structure).[10] Even more important is the continuity of Dybinus' own conceptual organization, his classification of the *colores* according to the scientific scheme of genus and species, and the minute and systematic division of each of the categories into its parts.

Dybinus positions himself among a procession of authorities, ancient and modern. In the *Declaracio* he cites Cicero and Horace frequently and invokes Aristotle. But he also draws by name upon a variety of "modern" authorities representing different aspects of the teaching of the language sciences: Geoffrey of Vinsauf, Eberhard of Béthune's *Graecismus*, Guido Faba's *Summa dictaminis*, Eberhard the German's *Laborintus*. He cites Geoffrey of Vinsauf to send his readers to an authority on abbreviation and amplification, an aspect of composition that Dybinus does not intend to pursue in this treatise. He uses Guido Faba along with ancient authorities to ground his rules about *transumptio*. A generation or so after his death, Dybinus in turn was to be counted among the *moderni* who valued rhetoric on its own terms as a theoretical science rather than as a mere instrument of law and politics. In the 1420s, another German teacher, a Magister Nicolaus, wrote a *Tractatulus rethorice* in which he listed Dybinus along with Guido Faba, Eberhard the German, Geoffrey of Vinsauf, and two other "modern" German masters, Nicolaus of Swidnitz and Heinrich of Mügeln. These teachers, says Magister Nicolaus, opened the study of rhetoric to its most scientific and speculative dimensions.[11]

---

[8] Jaffe, ed., *Nicolaus Dybinus' Declaracio*, 38–41, 46–8, 72, 281, 287–9.

[9] Woods, "A Medieval Rhetoric Goes to School—and to the University."

[10] Not all versions of the *Declaracio* use the same *accessus* format: for instance, the version in Prague University Library XII. B. 12, which is contemporary with Dybinus' own period of activity, uses a looser *accessus* form (see Jaffe, ed., *Nicolaus Dybinus' Declaracio*, 214–15). The differences among the versions reflect changing pedagogical circumstances and environments over time.

[11] See Jaffe, ed., *Nicolaus Dybinus' Declaracio*, 79–83.

The version of the *Declaracio* in Munich Staatsbibliothek Clm. 19876, from which the selection below is translated, has an elaborate commendation of rhetoric that involves comparison with the golden-robed queen of Psalm 44. The noble distinctions of rhetoric—its dignity, courtliness, benign radiance—are likened to those of a queen. As Samuel Jaffe, the editor of this text, notes, Dybinus employs the traditional figure of raiment "to express the operation of form upon matter," that is, the notion of rhetoric as adornment of matter that has already been given, discovered, or achieved.[12] Rhetoric enriches and elevates, embellishes the material and enhances the social standing of those who practice it. This certainly echoes such promises of rhetoric's riches as we see in Guido Faba's *Summa dictaminis*, which invites students who "wish to discover the gifts of wisdom" to enter the "garden of Master Guido" where beautiful rewards await.[13] But Dybinus does not attach rhetoric to a specific professional function or any individual purpose. Mastery of eloquence is not linked to the legal-bureaucratic profession of *dictamen*. He does not invoke the Ciceronian formula of "speaking well in civic matters" (which had long outgrown its value as a living definition), nor does he teach Latin composition in the narrow sense of the grammar curriculum. Rather, rhetoric is presented as a learned discourse that brings moral, social, or indeed political-historical advantage. Rhetoric is inherently genteel and virtuous; it is a symbol of nobility and therefore of magnanimity; it brings delight, recreation, and even spiritual remedy, but it is also the political tool of appeasement and mediation. These are the traditional roles of a queen, in literary representation as well as in history. It is just this role of eloquent mediator, appeaser of a king's anger, that Chaucer has Queen Alceste play in the *Prologue* to the *Legend of Good Women* (ca. 1385). And it was as persuasive intercessor that the historical queen Anne of Bohemia, daughter of the Emperor Charles and beloved wife of England's Richard II, was remembered after her death.[14] In his *Declaracio*, Dybinus can be said to register an important late-medieval understanding of rhetoric as a moral power independent of any immediate functional or professional purpose, an ennobling attribute that is nevertheless attainable by all who strive for this valuable knowledge.

Text of the Munich Staatsbibliothek Clm. 19876 text, translated from *Nicolaus Dybinus' Declaracio oracionis de beata Dorothea*, ed. Jaffe, by permission.[15]

---

[12] Ibid., 55–6.   [13] Prologue to the *Summa dictaminis*, ed. Gaudenzi, 287–8.

[14] On this queenly function for Alceste and the political role of Anne of Bohemia, see Wallace, *Chaucerian Polity*, 337–77, esp. 357–70.

[15] All annotations are ours.

DECLARACIO ORACIONIS DE BEATA DOROTHEA (EXPOSITION OF THE PRAYER ON THE BLESSED DOROTHEA)

Oracio de Beata Dorothea[16]

A mundi felle prepolita
castitatis margarita
dorothea es quesita
et inuenta in hac vita
salutis per negociantem

Aurea dum stirpe nata
clam baptismoque mundata
iubare diuo sis vmbrata
nec squalore post fedata
sic fide reddit te constantem

Prayer on the blessed Dorothea

Cleansed from the bile of the secular world
you, the pearl of chastity,
you, Dorothea, are being sought
and found in this life
through Him who brings deliverance.

Born from a golden stock
secretly purified by baptism
you are shaded[17] by divine radiance
nor were you defiled afterwards by squalor
so baptism has made you constant in faith.

Astitit regina a dextris tuis in vestitu deaurato circumdata varietate.[18] The words of this theme in the Psalter pertain intimately to the science of rhetoric, expounded in the following way: it is as if it exclaims to those who possess the science: O possessor of the art, Rhetoric, the queen of all the arts stands, i.e. is placed, at your right hand, in gilded clothing, i.e. decked out in courteous eloquence. Now that this statement has been expounded in this way, the science of rhetoric may be explained in two ways: first, she is commended as worthy of nobility; second, she is benign in her courteousness. The first is suggested when it says: *astitit regina*, "the queen stood"; the second is suggested when it says *in vestitu deaurato*, "in gilded clothing."

The first is shown through comparison of the noble science to a queen, to whom it is rightfully compared, by reason of many comparisons with a queen that are stored and subtly discovered in rhetoric itself.

First, a real queen administers to the honor of the king; second, she drives away his anger [*ira*] and melancholy [*dolor*]; third, with her decorous face she is a source of delight for him; fourth, she is an example of the virtues and good character of her family; fifth, she takes away her family's poverty [*paupertas*] and shame [*pudor*].

The first of these functions lies in the purity of her life, founded on justice; the second lies in the truth of her words born from play; the third lies in the chastity of her body

---

[16] We give the first two strophes of the poem.

[17] "Shaded," i.e. "illuminated," by the *transumptio* from contraries, see *Declaracio*, ed. Jaffe, 123.33 translated below, and 126.6, where *umbrata* is paraphrased as *illustrata*.

[18] Psalm 44:10: "The queen stood on thy right hand, in gilded clothing; surrounded with variety."

refined by her dress; the fourth lies in good deeds [*in gesti bonitate*] vigorously supported; the fifth consists in giving generous gifts with a gentle hand. Given that clearly the science of rhetoric possesses all these liberal qualities with full power (the qualities on account of which you think a real queen deserves to claim the name of queen, because of the reign of virtue), rhetoric strives to claim the name for itself; for it is the helper of the honor of the king and of any worker [*artifex*], in that it consists in the purity of her life, founded on justice. Whence the philosopher says in the first [book] of his *Rhetoric* that rhetoric teaches to persuade about what is just and to know the truth, while equally conferring honor on those who possess it.[19] Thus the first of these principles is shown.

Second, the science of rhetoric is also said to drive away anger and melancholy, and this function lies in the truth of her words born from play. For rhetoric teaches to speak ornately, mixing jokes with earnest. Whence Aristotle said, it is not enough for one to just be able to speak, but to speak well and ornately.[20] Concerning this, Tully says in the first book of his Rhetoric[21] (here speaking about rhetoric): "I found the one whom I sought," comforting the spirit,[22] teaching eloquence.[23] Whence Boethius says in his *De consolatione philosophiae* that Rhetoric teaches how to make sweet and mellifluous speeches, but also to be silent at the appropriate time and occasion.[24] This the philosopher especially commended, because rhetoric was a quality of those great men, Socrates, Solon, and Xenocrates, who knew, because of rhetoric, both the best kind of speaking and of being quiet. Socrates was once at a council of princes, and hearing some useless talk, he did not want to speak; but the prince was irritated and asked him why he kept quiet. Socrates said: "I have often regretted that I spoke, but never that I was silent." At another time, Solon [was][25] asked why he was quiet as if he were a fool or a mute. Then he answered, "To talk a lot is the business of fools."[26] Xenocrates was asked why he stopped speaking, whether he had some speech

---

[19] Cf. Aristotle, *Rhetoric* 1373b–1374b; cf. *De inventione* 1.2.3.   [20] Cf. Aristotle, *Rhetoric* 1403b15.

[21] I.e., Cicero's *De inventione*, which was considered Cicero's first book of rhetoric; *Rhetorica ad Herennium* was considered his "second" book of rhetoric.

[22] Text: *amicum*; emended to the reading (*animum*) in Päsdorffer, *Tractatus de modo dictandi*: see following note.

[23] *Hanc inveni quam quesivi, [animum] certificans, eloqui docens*. This tag (not found in Cicero) is repeated in later treatises influenced by Dybinus: Konrad Päsdorffer's *Tractatus de modo dictandi* and an anonymous *Ars dictandi*; in these texts the quotation is attributed to Aristotle. See Jaffe, ed., *Nicolaus Dybinus' Declaracio*, 61–2.

[24] Cf. *De consolatione* 2, pr. 3: "*Speciosa quidem ista sunt,*" inquam, "*oblitaque Rhetoricae ac Musicae melle dulcedinis; tum tantum, cum audiuntur oblectant. Sed miseris malorum altior sensus. Itaque cum haec auribus insonare desierint, insitus animum maeror praegravat*. Notker Labeo's commentary on the *Consolatio* includes, at this point, a long digression, *Quid sit rhetorica*, which summarizes the art and its principles, especially status theory and the relevance to the "present status" in Boethius' text (Notker the German, ed. Serht and Starck, *Notkers des Deutschen Werke* 1/1.2, 73–81).

[25] Text emended from *interrogavit* to *interrogatus est*; see the following note.

[26] For Socrates and Solon, cf. Pseudo-Walter Burley, *Liber de vita et moribus philosophorum*, ed. H. Knust (Tübingen: Bibliothek des literarischen Vereins in Stuttgart, 1886), 20. The context in Pseudo-Burley calls for the

defect. He said, "Nature allotted me one mouth and I have two ears, on account of which it is more useful to me to listen than to speak."[27] When philosophers and rhetoricians gave responses like these, the anger [*ira*] and melancholy [*dolor*] of princes was assuaged, and rhetoric made the philosophers themselves the beloved counselors of princes. Thus we can see how rhetoric drives away anger and melancholy, which was the second function.

Thirdly, the science of rhetoric is a source of delight, which Tully discusses in the first book of his Rhetoric. Only rhetoric gladdens the hearer and leads the violent spirit to delight.[28] Indeed, anyone is pleased on hearing a beautiful and ornate speech. Thus it is shown that the science of rhetoric is a source of delight, which was the third function.

Fourthly, she is said to be an example of the virtues and good character of her family, which consists in good deeds [*gestuum bonitas*] vigorously supported. According to Aristotle (as mentioned above), rhetoric teaches how to live properly and to be persuasive about matters of justice, there are examples of *auctores* discovered in the goodness of their deeds. Whence Seneca, in *Copia verborum*:[29] "whoever wishes to follow prudence should live well in accordance with reason." Thus the science of rhetoric is a worthy example of the virtues and good character of her own family and of the other sciences.[30] Without her, the information of grammar vanishes, disputation of logic grows tepid, the argument of natural and moral philosophy diminishes, the modulation of music grows silent, arithmetical calculation is vitiated with error, the measurement of geometry falls apart, the prognostication of astronomy is eaten away by doubt. Thus she is the worthy exemplar and embellishment of all the sciences, which was the fourth function.

Fifth, rhetoric takes away poverty [*pauperies*] and shame [*pudor*], which power consists in giving generous gifts with gentle hand. Whence Horace: "Among all teachings, the epistle holds pride of place."[31] By the epistle he implies rhetoric, taking the part for the whole. Not only does it conceal secret things, it also searches out absent things. He adds the following: Thus radiating and bestowing all worthiness, raising the pauper from the dust, she leads the

---

emendation of the text of Dybinus above. The stories of Socrates and Solon given by Dybinus are found in Pseudo-Burley as one story about Solon; see 122 for related stories about Socrates. On the revised attribution to Burley, see M. Grignaschi, "Lo pseudo Walter Burley e il 'Liber de vita et moribus philosophorum,'" *Medioevo*, 16 (1990): 131–90.

[27] Cf. Pseudo-Burley, *Liber de vita et moribus*, 264.   [28] Cf. *De inventione* 1.2.2.

[29] *De copia verborum*, one of several treatises often ascribed in medieval manuscripts to Seneca; see B. Munk Olson, "The Cistercians and Classical Culture," *CIMAGL* 47 (1984): 64–102 (at 76). For this line see Martin of Braga, *Formula honestae vitae*, PL 72:23C.

[30] Just as a queen demonstrates the virtues of the whole royal family, so rhetoric demonstrates the virtues of all rhetoricians and orators, but also of all other sciences.

[31] *Inter omnia dogmata epistola tenet principatum.* See notes 33 and 34 below. This phrase, with the attribution to Horace, is also repeated in Päsdorffer's *Tractatus de modo dictandi* and the anonymous *Ars dictandi*: see Jaffe, ed., *Nicolaus Dybinus' Declaracio*, 61–2 and notes. Cf. P. O. Kristeller, *Iter Italicum: A Finding List of Uncatalogued Or Incompletely Catalogued Humanistic MSS of the Renaissance in Italian and Other Libraries* (Leiden: Brill, 1998), 522.

poor man to the council of kings, she elevates the lowly.[32] Behold how the science of rhetoric takes away poverty and shame, which was the fifth and last function to be demonstrated. On account of those things which any queen should maintain within herself and which are also found and demonstrated in rhetoric itself, rhetoric wished to claim the worthy name of queen, of which she was worthy, for herself, in order that the words of the scriptural theme given above may be applied to herself (i.e. rhetoric): *Astitit regina*.

Concerning the second, that rhetoric is benign in her courteousness, this is made clear through the words of Horace in the *ars dictandi*, where he says that eloquence, which is part of the science of rhetoric, is benign in courteousness; this was touched on in the second phrase of the psalter theme, with the words "in gilded clothing."[33] Gold clothing makes a man pleasing and comely. According to what Horace says in the aforementioned work it is not beauty that makes the man pleasing so much as eloquence, as in the clear example he supplies: "Ulysses was not comely but he was eloquent,"[34] and eloquence more than good looks brought him love. From which it is inferred that fluency makes a man pleasing or agreeable to others. For Tully in the first book of his Rhetoric, eloquence is the discovery [*excogitatio*] of suitable words.[35]

Now rhetoric, eloquence, and color are different from one another, just as superior and inferior differ. Rhetoric is called the science of embellishing ideas or words, whether voiced expressly or understood, or not. Whence a rhetor, whether he practices or not, is said to possess the science of rhetoric.[36] But eloquence is understood to be an art in the sense of a conceptual or mental power, not yet expressed in words [or: sounds]. But color or coloration or embellishment (for now, I leave the synonyms), is when words, brought together appropriately in the voice and expressed in sound, are decorated through the necessary rhetorical colors.[37] Then it would be called coloration or color, even if such

---

[32]   These phrases are commonplaces of dictaminal texts; see Wieruszowski, *Politics and Culture in Medieval Spain and Italy*, 372 n. 6: "these phrases from Luke 1:53 and Psalm cxiii:7 are varied accordingly in the masters' letters and discourses exalting science."

[33]   This specific idea does not appear to be in Horace. See note below.

[34]   Ovid, *Ars amatoria* 2.123. This passage, with the incorrect attribution to Horace of a line from Ovid and the untraceable reference to Horace, has apparently undergone some confusion in the process of transmission. The confusion (perhaps beginning at the point of Dybinus' own lectures) is compounded by the problematic attributions to Horace in the previous paragraph. The *ars dictandi* attributed to Horace may be some kind of reference to the *Ars poetica*; perhaps the tag in the previous paragraph, *inter omnia dogmata epistola tenet principatum*, refers to the connection between letter-writing and eloquence itself, although it is difficult to attach this idea to any specific teaching of Horace.

[35]   Cf. *De inventione* 1.7.9.   [36]   Cf. Aristotle, *Rhetoric* 1355b.

[37]   The distinction thus drawn between rhetoric, eloquence, and color can be reformulated as follows: eloquence is only the potentiality of rhetoric, not yet expressed in actual words or sounds; *colores* are only the realization of rhetoric (no conceptual element, all execution); rhetoric embraces both potentiality and realization within the one term.

words are written or were composed to be written down. Thus, wherever there is color there is rhetoric and eloquence; but the converse of this does not hold.

Rhetoric applies as the common term to both genus and species, that is, in eloquence as well as in embellishment. What exactly a color [i.e. embellishment] is will be considered later.

I urge all men, failing [*degentes*] and needy, to come (as it were) to the copiously rich treasury of rhetoric. Rhetoric is the embellisher of all sciences, the uplifter of the failing [*degencium*], the dispenser of riches, the counselor of all who have gone wrong, the lover of wisdom, and bestower of the dignity of lovers on those who suffer [for love]. Since the handing on of this science or noble queen by the rhetoricians and authors, that is, Aristotle, Tully, and Horace in his "Old Poetics" and Geoffrey in his "New Poetics" is so prolix that it makes weary students afraid to study rhetoric, I dared, though quite young, to undertake the composition of this prayer,[38] as much as the maturing of reason was able to support, including in it brief and lucid embellishing of all the rhetorical colors, according to the descriptions and elaborations [*ornationes*] handed down in the various books by these same authors, making it as clear and easy as I could [*quanto facilius et clarius*], affirming myself to be the follower and pupil—though the least important—of various masters and rhetors, and with the compiling of this prayer or composition providing nourishment by conveying the authors' milk food to the young and tender. Having had a sweet taste of this brief thing, with this food may the young happily devour a banquet of the harder rhetoricians.

> [At this point Dybinus gives a "scholastic" introduction to his work. These are: the "material cause" or subject matter, a rhetorical exposition of the poem, and an exposition of its theological themes; the "efficient cause" or author, and here Dybinus steps aside modestly to say that we should not be concerned with the efficient cause, because it is more important to consider what is said than who is speaking; a "*duplex* final cause" or double purpose, which is information for the young who want to study rhetoric, and fulfillment of the petitions made in this prayer; and the "formal cause" or formal construction of the work, which in turn is divided into the "form of the treatise," that is, the exposition of the poem according to the division of its parts, and the "form of the treatment," that is, the "rhythmical" or metrical style of the work.]

A MUNDI FELLE PREPOLITA CASTITA[TIS] ["cleansed from the bile of the secular world"]

Tully, in the first book of his Rhetoric, and Guido in his *Summa,* distinguish style [*elocutio*] from "color." According to them, style is the thinking out of appropriate words

---

[38] *Oracio,* with double meaning as "oration" and "prayer."

and ideas.[39] This appropriateness consists in two things: first, in the amplifying [*prolongacio*] of curial matter,[40] and second, in the subtle abbreviation of it. Those wanting to know more about these issues should hasten eagerly to Geoffrey's *Poetria*.[41] Our present consideration is only about the color of words and ideas. Thus color, according to Tully, is a way of speaking pleasingly, achieved through the particular arrangement of what is graceful.[42] That is, color is achieved or brought about when we speak properly about any matter, deriving this from the special nature of the matter about which we speak, a matter which we have closely observed.

Moreover, we should note that, insofar as color falls under the province of rhetoric, it positions itself, so to speak, as a genus of the broadest kind (*genus generalissimum*). The genus that is subaltern to it [*genus subalternum*], its first species, will be *transumptio*, which further subalternates to itself [*sibi subalternat*] other modes and species, with respect to which the colors of words and ideas constitute (as it were) the most particular kinds of species (*species specialissime*). And so the prayer or composition that we are presently studying is divided into three principal parts in accordance with the fact that there are three colors or ornaments. In the first part the point is the color of *transumptio* in general and its modes; in the second part the point is the species that are subalternated to it; in the third part, the most particular species.[43] The second part begins where it says *Virgo felix ad me mea*; the third part begins where it says *Iuua virgo pellens ancta*.[44] This is the division according to rhetoric. Theologically this prayer can be divided into various parts according to the many petitions and commendations that are offered and given to this virgin, Dorothea full of glory. First she is commended with respect to her birth and noble parentage, second for the dignity of the place of her birth, third for the constancy of her faith, fourth for the purity of her life of faith, fifth for her martyr's sufferings. But since we have given an exposition of this sort in the proem, let us pass over this course of argument for now. The first part of the division that has been made, containing the color of *transumptio* and of its general modes, remains undivided, where it is said: O blessed Dorothea, you are the pearl of chastity, cleansed of the depravity of this world sought by

---

[39] *De inventione* 1.7.9; and cf. Guido Faba, *Summa dictaminis*, ed. Gaudenzi, §§ 103–4.

[40] I.e. writing concerned with administration, especially of the law courts.

[41] I.e. Geoffrey of Vinsauf, *Poetria nova*, famous for its elaborate and helpful discussion of the methods of abbreviation and amplification.

[42] Cf. *Ad Herennium* 4.11.16.

[43] The eleven tropes (*species transumpcionis*) are: *abusio, denominatio, intellectio, nominatio, perversio, permutatio, pronominatio, superlatio, traieccio, translacio, transgressio*. Subalternated to these are the lowest species of colors, which consist of thirty-six figures of speech and twenty-one figures of thought.

[44] Lines 11 and 33 of the poem, respectively. *ancta* is paraphrased later in the commentary as *tribulaciones* "tribulations."

Him who brings and loves deliverance; and you are found in the purity of your life, born from noble family lineage; and you are illuminated by the light of the holy spirit, while you are purified by the rivulet of secret baptism, which baptism made you constant in faith, so that afterwards you stood immaculate and free from the thousands of sins.

Following the letter of the text it is first necessary to know that the whole literal text takes its ornament from the Gospel of Luke.[45] In this parable the kingdom of heaven is likened to the man who seeks fine pearls. The blessed virgin Dorothea is worthy of comparison with a pearl. The pearl is guardian [*administrativa*] of chastity, and this glorious virgin maintained that chastity in an exemplary way. The pearl is a comfort of the infirm heart that removes its weakness. From it a medicine is prepared, "diamargariton," which takes away certain passions of the heart.[46] So the blessed virgin Dorothea [removes] the faintness of the heart that is downcast in its faith, as is made clear in many instances: by her teaching about faith she comforted the weak and removed their weakness. And likewise the pearl chases away poverty, because her nobility is more noble than purest gold, or she is likened in this way: the blessed Dorothea drives away and lifts the poverty of many, a pearl that was sought by Christ who brings deliverance through blessed predestination and that was found in the crown of eternity.

Let it be noted, moreover, how the [first] color of *transumptio* and some of its modes are touched on throughout the whole literal text. In Tully, *transumptio* is described in this way: *transumptio* is adapting a word for one thing to the topic at hand in accordance with a certain similarity.[47] Here is Guido's definition: *transumptio* is a transference of one word or expression, on account of a certain likeness, from its proper signification to another signification. Guido gives the example "the field [laughs]."[48] Example from Horace: "the visage grows rosy," i.e. the face reddens.[49]

It should also be noted that, according to Guido, *transumptio* has many modes. One mode occurs whenever a human, in his own person or through some property of his, and an irrational thing, whether animate or inanimate, partake together of the same accident or quality. From this a *transumptio* can be made from an inanimate or irrational thing to

---

[45] The correct reference is Matthew 13:45.

[46] A remedy made by apothecaries for curing, among other diseases, leprosy: see L. Demaitre, "The Relevance of Futility: Jordanus de Turre (fl. 1313–1335) on the Treatment of Leprosy," *Bulletin of the History of Medicine* 70 (1996): 25–61 (at 49 and n. 112).

[47] Cf. *Rhetorica ad Herennium* 4.45.59 (on *similitudo)* and 4.34.45 (on metaphor).

[48] Cf. Guido Faba, *Summa dictaminis*, ed. Gaudenzi, § 143: Translatio *est de una re ad aliam ex quadam idonea similitudine alterius verbi iam inventi traductio, ut "prata rident," idest "floret."* (*Prata rident* was a commonplace example of *transumptio*. See Rosier-Catach, "*Prata rident*.")

[49] *Vultus rosescit*. Perhaps this example attributed to Horace is a misquotation of *Odes* 2.11.10: *neque uno luna rubens nitet vultu*.

the human himself. And so there can be two modes of *transumptio*. An example of an irrational and animate thing applied to a human is when a man and an ass are linked in terms of stubbornness or stupidity or laziness. So if I say of a man that he is stubborn and ignorant, I say this by making a *transumptio* in this way: that man has an asinine mind. Or this man brays like an ass, if I am speaking about someone singing badly. And this is the first mode of *transumptio*.

The second mode of *transumptio* is when an irrational and inanimate thing is linked with a human in terms of some quality or property or accident, which accident should be "transumed" [*debet transumi*] to a person. Tully's rule if there is one accidental quality shared by two different things, is that the accidental quality should be inseparable from one, but separable from the other. Thus if someone should want to make a *transumptio* of that accident, let him do so based on this, as for example, a man and a rose are linked in rosy redness, which is inseparably innate to the rose but separable from the man. So if someone should want to make a *transumptio* of that accident, the accident that is inseparable from this rose should be attributed to the man through such a *transumptio*, as when speaking of a handsome man: his face has a rosy hue. And just as I speak of a rose, so likewise I speak about anything, for example: that girl has a glowing face, crystalline eyes, snowy teeth, rosy lips, deep red cheeks, a milky brow, and so forth.[50]

For such a mode of *transumptio* and for whatever other modes, I provide a rule that applies to all modes of *transumptio*, which is that the substantive expression which is to be transumed in this way should always be changed into an adjectival term, for example: gold into golden.

The third mode of *transumptio* is when any property, accident, or activity which is human is attributed, conversely, to an irrational thing or something that is simply inanimate. This mode will work in two ways. (I) The first is when a human activity is attributed to an irrational thing, for example, that a lion is noble or proud, for nobility or pride is not properly innate to anything irrational, but to man. But it is attributed to the lion for the sake of a similitude or a *transumptio*. (II) The second form of this occurs when, according to a similitude, what belongs to a rational thing is attributed to something that is simply inanimate. This is accomplished in a threefold way, along the lines of three kinds of human activity. (i) There is a certain kind of human activity which belongs only to the body and not to the mind, and this can be transferred to something inanimate, such as to sleep, and so forth. Thus, in saying "the sea is asleep," we are saying, by means of *transumptio*, that the sea is asleep because there are no storms on it. (ii) There are other

---

[50] I.e. adjectives derived from fire, crystal, snow, rose, purper-fish/purper-snail (from which *purpurea*, i.e. "purple" or "deep red," is derived), milk.

activities that belong only to humans, in this case of the mind, and not the body. And these may sometimes be attributed transumptively to inanimate things. So we say "the field laughs," to mean it flowers, "the flower rejoices" or "makes cheer," "the sea looks upon its depths" when there are no winds on it. Whence "to laugh," "to rejoice," "to look upon," are mental, not bodily, activities. (iii) There are other human activities which belong equally well to the body as to the mind, such as to feel or to see. With these we make a *transumptio* to inanimate things, as when we say "water feeling icy weather congeals hard or freezes."

Another mode of *transumptio* is whenever opposites are transumed mutually, as in "silence clamors," "the shadows illuminate," "clarity is darkened."[51] But since this mode coincides with the color known as *contentio* [antithesis], this will be considered in more detail later. It is, likewise, a general mode of *transumptio* and just like the foregoing, when any expression, whether a noun or a verb, is transumed to another signification.

---

[51] Represented in the poem above, *Oracio de beata Dorothea*, by line 8: *iubare divo sis umbrata*.

JOHN GOWER,
CONFESSIO AMANTIS, 1386–1390

INTRODUCTION

Gower's *Confessio amantis* was composed between 1386 and 1390, and revised during the early 1390s. It uses the frame fiction of an elderly lover who confesses his sins to Genius, the "priest of love." The seven deadly sins provide the thematic structure of most of the work: seven of the eight books of the poem are each devoted to a different sin. Within the fictive frame of the lover's confession about each of these sins, Gower presents a series of tales, drawn from classical and medieval sources, intended to exemplify the various sins. But book 7 departs from this pattern, and presents instead a scientific encyclopedia, using the traditional frame of the "education of Alexander," in which Aristotle teaches the young Alexander the Great all that a king should know in order to govern wisely and well. Gower's survey of knowledge is thorough in its coverage, although not as vast or detailed as the encyclopedic sources and world histories on which he relies, which include the *Secretum secretorum* (also a model for the "education of Alexander" theme), Godfrey of Viterbo's *Pantheon*, Brunetto Latini's *Trésor*, Giles of Rome's *De regimine principum*, and Ranulph Higden's *Polychronicon*. In the course of his scientific survey, Gower also replicates the pattern of the other books of the *Confessio amantis* by using illustrative tales drawn from classical poetry and history, ancient and medieval mythographers, and the Bible.

In keeping with the conventions of encyclopedic surveys, Gower imposes a classification of knowledge on his material. But his classification is unusual in its epistemological divisions. It resembles the Aristotelian division of sciences into theoretical, practical, and productive. But the actual divisions that Gower gives are "theoretical," "rhetorical," and "practical." Here Gower has elevated rhetoric from the status of an individual science to that of a governing epistemological category. The category of rhetoric encompasses the trivium, that is, all the arts that pertain to speech. Behind Gower's unusual division lies the influence of Brunetto's *Trésor* (written in the 1260s). In the three books of the *Trésor*, Brunetto had treated the theoretical and practical sciences: in book 1 he treated *theoretica*, in book 2 he considered *practica* as ethics, and in book 3, *practica* as politics. In this last book he devoted the greatest attention to rhetoric as the highest science of civic government or politics, drawing on Cicero's *De inventione* 1.5.6, where rhetoric is presented as a branch of politics. In Brunetto's treatment, rhetoric and politics together constitute a virtual division of knowledge that forms the subject matter of book 3.[1]

It becomes clear how Gower derived his epistemological division of theoretical, rhetorical, and practical. From the implicit scheme in the *Trésor* of theoretical, practical, and rhetorical-political sciences, he elaborated a system in which "rhetoric," comprising all the language arts, forms the crucial bridge leading from theoretical knowledge (theology, mathematics, and natural history) to practical knowledge (ethics, economics, politics). In the *Confessio amantis*, the category of rhetoric represents the power of the word, which, according to Gower, is the strongest instrument in human affairs. The "word above alle erthli thinges / Is vertuous in his doinges" (1547–8), and it is "the science / Appropred to the reverence / Of wordes that ben resonable" (1523–5). As the connection between theoretical knowledge, which concerns immutable principles, and practical knowledge, which considers the contingent matters of human society, "rhetoric" is the category of knowledge that converts theory into practice. All the language arts are subsumed by "rhetoric," because effective speech, or the powerful word, is the final product of all language study.

Within this category, Gower's treatments of grammar and logic are perfunctory. He dedicates two lines to grammar, noting that its role is to ensure that speech is congruent or correct according to the grammatical rules of agreement. Logic also receives an abbreviated account centering on the theme of distinguishing true from false propositions.[2] The bulk of Gower's attention is reserved for the individual science of rhetoric or eloquence. As the *Confessio amantis* as a whole positions itself in a vernacular literary and political culture (a book in "oure englissh," for "Engelondes sake," Prologue 22–4), so it is significant that here eloquence takes pride of place among the language arts. This inverts the standard emphases in Latin accounts of the trivium intended for university audiences where grammar and linguistic logic take priority. Where university texts focus on theoretical aspects of language, Gower's vernacular encyclopedia looks towards the practical, persuasive, and literary uses of language in the public sphere.[3]

On these terms, it follows that Gower should refrain from giving a theoretical discussion of rhetoric. Instead he presents narrative *exempla*, derived ultimately from classical

---

[1] See Copeland, *Rhetoric, Hermeneutics, and Translation*, 208–9.

[2] Brunetto's treatments of grammar and logic in book 1 of the *Trésor* are similarly brief. See *Trésor* 1.4, ed. Carmody, 20–1.

[3] See Copeland, "Lydgate, Hawes, and the Science of Rhetoric."

rhetorical lore (Ulysses' deceptions, the judgments of the Roman Senate about the fate of the traitor Catiline), that illustrate the power of eloquence for better and for worse. Gower's *exempla* work here to give visible, historical shape to theory, and to demonstrate a fundamental link between rhetoric and ethics. Eloquence itself is an art that pertains to ethics, but rhetoric is also the instrument of ethical exemplification that allows the greatest number of people to learn about ethics. Thus in both its subject matter and in its mechanics, rhetoric is an ethical art. These two correlative principles reflect the impact of the new Aristotelian model of rhetoric as a form of ethics, a teaching that was most clearly expressed in Giles of Rome's influential treatise *De regimine principum*, which John Trevisa translated into English in the late fourteenth century. Giles had defended the literary devices of rhetoric as necessary to teaching a broad public through figurative speech or poetic exemplification, and thus had established the ethical value of rhetoric in practical terms. Gower's explicit discussion of ethics comes in the following section of book 7, under the category of "practical science"; but these themes are anticipated in his treatment of the ethical dimensions of rhetoric.

Text from *The Complete Works of John Gower*, ed. Macaulay, by permission.

CONFESSIO AMANTIS

I Genius the prest of love,		[*priest*]
Mi Sone, as thou hast preid above		[*prayed*]
That I the Scole schal declare		[*school*]
Of Aristotle and ek the fare		[*also the condition*]
Of Alisandre, hou he was tauht,		[*how*] [*taught*]
I am somdel therof destrauht;		[*somewhat*] [*uneasy*]
For it is noght to the matiere		[*matter*]
Of love, why we sitten heiere		[*sit*] [*here*]
To schryve, so as Venus bad.		[*to hear in confession*] [*commanded*]
Bot natheles, for it is glad,	10	[*since it is welcome*]
So as thou seist, for thin aprise		[*as you say*] [*for your instruction*]
To hiere of suche thinges wise,		[*to hear*]
Wherof thou myht the time lisse,		[*relieve*]
So as I can, I schal the wisse:		[*guide*]
For wisdom is at every throwe		
Above alle other thing to knowe		

In loves cause and elleswhere.
Forthi, my Sone, unto thin Ere,   [*wherefore*] [*ear*]
Though it be noght in the registre
Of Venus, yit of that Calistre[4]   20
And Aristotle whylom write   [*what Callisthenes and Aristotle
                                                                        formerly wrote*]

To Alisandre, thou schalt wite.   [*know*]
   Bot for the lores ben diverse,   [*since the teachings are diverse*]
I thenke ferst to the reherce   [*I think I will first recount to you*]
The nature of Philosophie,
Which Aristotle of his clergie,   [*learning*]
Wys and expert in the sciences,   [*wise*]
Declareth thilke intelligences   [*these provinces of knowledge*]
As of thre pointz in principal.   [*three*]
   Wherof the ferste in special   30   [*foremost*]
Is Theorique, which is grounded
On him which al the world hath founded,
Which comprehendeth all the lore.   [*embraces all learning*]
   And forto loken overmore,
Next of sciences the seconde
Is Rethorique, whos faconde   [*eloquence*]
Above all othre is eloquent:
To telle a tale in juggement
So wel can noman speke as he.
   The laste science of the thre   40
It is Practique, whos office
The vertu tryeth fro the vice,   [*separates*]
And techeth upon goode thewes   [*by reason of good habits*]
To fle the compaignie of schrewes,   [*flee the company of scoundrels*]
Which stant in disposicion
Of mannes free eleccion.   [*which is in one's power of free choice*]
Practique enformeth ek the reule,   [*also provides the rule*]
Hou that a worthi king schall reule
His Realme bothe in were and pes.   [*war and peace*]

---

[4] Callisthenes (d. 327 BC), nephew of Aristotle, author of the *Deeds of Alexander* covering events of Alexander's reign to 330. The reference here is to the pseudo-historical Alexander-romances or "Pseudo-Callisthenes," popularly but falsely attributed to Callisthenes. Many variations of these narratives circulated and were translated into vernacular languages in the Middle Ages. For the Greek text see W. Kroll, ed., *Historia Alexandri Magni* (Berlin: Weidmann, 1926); trans. R. Stoneman, *The Greek Alexander Romance* (London: Penguin, 1991).

Lo, thus danz Aristotiles   50   [*master, "don" (title for a teacher)*]
These thre sciences hath divided
And the nature also decided,
Wherof that ech of hem schal serve.   [*of which each of them shall serve*]
   The ferste, which is the conserve   [*preserver*]
And kepere of the remnant,   [*the rest, the others*]
As that which is most sufficant
And chief of the Philosophie,
If I therof schal specefie
So as the Philosophre tolde,
Nou herkne, and kep that thou it holde.   60

Prima creatorem dat scire sciencia summum:
   Qui caput agnoscit, sufficit illud ei.
Plura viros quandoque iuuat nescire, set
                 illud
   Quod videt expediens, sobrius ille sapit.[5]

   Of Theorique principal
The Philosophre in special
The propretees hath determined,   [*properties*]
As thilke which is enlumined   [*as that which is illuminated*]
Of wisdom and of hih prudence   [*high*]
Above alle othre in his science:
And stant departed upon thre,   [*is divided into three*]
The ferste of which in his degre   [*first*] [*its*]
Is cleped in Philosophie   [*called*]
The science of Theologie,   70
That other named is Phisique,   [*next*]
The thridde is said Mathematique.   [*third is called*]

[Gower's text goes on to describe the three theoretical sciences: theology (occupying the place assigned to metaphysics in Aristotle's scheme), which enables distinctions between creator and created, eternal and temporal, and which stands above all the other sciences; physics, or knowledge of the physical and natural world; and mathematics, which is comprised of the elements of the quadrivium (arithmetic, music, geometry, astronomy), and which in its totality constitutes the science of measurement. Gower's discussion of

---

[5] The first science teaches us to know the highest creator:
    whoever knows the source, that suffices for him.
Sometimes it is good for men to be ignorant of more things,
    but a sensible person understands what he sees as expedient.

astronomy is preceded by an extended account of the four elements, the four humors and the human soul, and the division of the earth into continents and seas, and then takes up the subjects of astronomy proper: the planets, the signs of the zodiac, the stars, and the authors of astronomical science.]

Compositi pulcra sermonis verba placere
  Principio poterunt, veraque fine placent.
Herba, lapis, sermo, tria sunt virtute repleta,
  Vis tamen ex verbi pondere plura facit.[6]

   Above alle erthli creatures
The hihe makere of natures
The word to man hath yove alone,   *[has given words to mankind alone]*
So that the speche of his persone,[7]   1510
Or forto lese or forto winne,   *[either to lose or to win]*
The hertes thoght which is withinne   *[heart's]*
Mai schewe, what it wolde mene;   *[he may show]* *[intend, mean]*
And that is noghwhere elles sene
Of kinde with non other beste.   *[of nature, naturally]* *[no other creature]*
So scholde he be the more honeste,
To whom god yaf so gret a yifte,   *[to whom God gave so great a gift]*
And loke wel that he ne schifte   *[take care that]* *[turn]*
His wordes to no wicked us;   *[use, purpose]*
For word the techer of vertus   1520   *[language]*; *[teacher of virtue]*
Is cleped in Philosophie.   *[called]*
Wherof touchende this partie,   *[concerning this part]*
Is Rethorique the science
Appropred to the reverence   *[dedicated to]*
Of wordes that ben resonable:
And for this art schal be vailable   *[serviceable]*
With goodli wordes forto like,
It hath Gramaire, it hath Logiqe,
That serven bothe unto the speche.

---

[6] The beautiful words of a well-composed speech
      can give pleasure at first, but in the end it is truth that should please.
   Herb, precious stone, speech: these three are powerful;
      yet the power from the weight of the word accomplishes more.

[7] Gower's Latin marginal note: *Hic tractat de secunda parte Philosophie, cuius nomen Rethorica facundos efficit. Loquitur eciam de eiusdem duabus speciebus, scilicet Grammatica et Logica, quarum doctrina Rethor sua verba perornat.* ["Here he treats the second part of Philosophy, called Rhetoric, which makes eloquent speakers. He speaks also of its two species, Grammar and Logic, by whose teaching the rhetor graces his words."]

Gramaire ferste hath forto teche   1530
To speke upon congruite: [*correct grammatical agreement*]
Logique hath eke in his degre   [*also*] [*its*]
Betwen the trouthe and the falshode
The pleine wordes forto schode,   [*separate, divide*]
So that nothing schal go beside,   [*be unaccounted for*]
That he the riht ne schal decide,   [*i.e. so that one will decide the right thing*]
Wherof full many a gret debat   [*debate, argument*]
Reformed is to good astat,   [*restored*] [*condition, state*]
And pes sustiened up alofte
With esy wordes and with softe,   1540
Wher strengthe scholde lete it falle.
The Philosophre amonges alle
Forthi commendeth this science,
Which hath the reule of eloquence.
   In Ston and gras vertu ther is,
Bot yit the bokes tellen this,   [*books*]
That word above alle erthli thinges
Is vertuous in his doinges,
Wher so it be to evele or goode.
For if the wordes semen goode   1550 [*seem*]
And ben wel spoke at mannes Ere,   [*ear*]
Whan that ther is no trouthe there,   [*truth*]
Thei don fulofte gret deceipte;   [*commit*] [*very often*] [*deception*]
For whan the word to the conceipte   [*conception, thought*]
Descordeth in so double a wise,   [*is discordant in a duplicitous way*]
Such Rethorique is to despise
In every place, and forto drede.   [*and thus to fear*]
For of Uluxes[8] thus I rede,   [*Ulysses*]
As in the bok of Troie is founde,
His eloquence and his facounde   1560 [*fluency, facility*]
Of goodly wordes whiche he tolde,
Hath mad that Anthenor him solde   [*Antenor*]
The toun, which he with tresoun wan.   [*town*] [*won*]
Word hath beguiled many a man;
With word the wilde beste is daunted,
With word the Serpent is enchaunted,

---

[8] Ulysses, condemned by Virgil as the epitome of the deceitful orator, enters later Western literature as the archetype of the false rhetorician, as realized by Dante in *Inferno* 26.

Of word among the men of Armes
Ben woundes heeled with the charmes,   [*i.e. words are like charms that heal wounds*]
Wher lacketh other medicine;
Word hath under his discipline   1570
Of Sorcerie the karectes.   [*charm, conjuration*]
The wordes ben of sondri sectes,   [*various kinds*]
Of evele and eke of goode also;
The wordes maken frend of fo,   [*make a friend of a foe*]
And fo of frend, and pes of were,
And werre of pes, and out of herre   [*off the hinges, out of order*]
The word this worldes cause entriketh   [*entangles the business of the world*]
And reconsileth whan him liketh.   [*and reconciles when it wants to*]
The word under the coupe of hevene   [*vault*]
Set every thing or odde or evene;   1580   [*at evens or at odds*]
With word the hihe god is plesed,
With word the wordes ben appesed,   [*are appeased*]
The softe word the loude stilleth;
Wher lacketh good, the word fulfilleth,
To make amendes for the wrong;
Whan wordes medlen with the song,
It doth plesance wel the more.
    Bot forto loke upon the lore
Hou Tullius his Rethorique
Componeth, ther a man mai pike   1590   [*arranges, puts together*] [*may choose*]
Hou that he schal hise wordes sette,
Hou he schal lose, hou he schal knette,   [*set free*] [*bind together*]
And in what wise he schal pronounce
His tale plein withoute frounce.[9]   [*obstruction*]
Wherof ensample if thou wolt seche   [*an example of which*] [*seek*]
Tak hiede and red whilom the speche   [*take heed and read*]
Of Julius and Cithero,[10]   [*Cicero*]

---

[9] Gower's marginal note: *Nota de Eloquencia Iulii in causa Cateline contra Cillenum et alios tunc vrbis Rome Conciues.* ["Note: the eloquence of Julius, in the case of Catiline, against Cillenus (i.e. Silanus) and others who were then fellow citizens of the city of Rome."]

[10] Macaulay's note on this passage: "The discussion in the Roman Senate on the fate of the accomplices of Catiline is here taken as a model of rhetorical treatment . . . [I]t is borrowed from the *Trésor*, where Latini, after laying down the rules of rhetoric, illustrates them . . . by a report and analysis of the speeches in this debate, as they are given by Sallust. The 'Cillenus' mentioned below is D. Junius Silanus, who as consul-designate gave his opinion first . . . Gower did not identify Tullius with Cicero, though Latini actually says 'Marcus Tullius Cicero, cils meismes qui enseigne l'art de rectorique, estoit adonques consule de Rome'" (*The Complete Works of John Gower* 3: 526). The ultimate source of this material is Cicero's Fourth Catiline oration.

Which consul was of Rome tho,
Of Catoun eke and of Cillene,   [*also of Cato and Silanus*]
Behold the wordes hem betwene,   1600
Whan the tresoun of Cateline   [*Catiline*]
Descoevered was, and the covine   [*conspiracy*]
Of hem that were of his assent   [*of those in league with him*]
Was knowe and spoke in parlement,
And axed hou and in what wise   [*asked*] [*way*]
Men scholde don hem to juise.   [*bring them to judgment*]
Cillenus ferst his tale tolde,
To trouthe and as he was beholde,
The comun profit forto save,
He seide hou tresoun scholde have   1610
A cruel deth; and thus thei spieke,
The Consul both and Catoun eke,   [*both the Consul and Cato*]
And seiden that for such a wrong
Ther mai no peine be to strong.   [*there may be no punishment
                                                          too great*]

Bot Julius with wordes wise
His tale tolde al otherwise,
As he which wolde her deth respite   [*one who would spare them from death*]
And fondeth hou he mihte excite
The jugges thurgh his eloquence
Fro deth to torne the sentence   1620
And sette here hertes to pite.
Nou tolden thei, nou tolde he;   [*now they spoke, now he spoke*]
Thei spieken plein after the lawe,
Bot he the wordes of his sawe   [*speech*]
Coloureth in an other weie
Spekende, and thus between the tweie,   [*two*]
To trete upon this juggement,
Made ech of hem his Argument.
Wherof the tales forto hiere,
Ther mai a man the Scole liere   1630   [*learn the teaching*]
Of Rethoriqes eloquences,
Which is the secounde of sciences
Touchende to Philosophie;   [*concerning*]
Wherof a man schal justifie
His wordes in disputeisoun,

And knette upon conclusioun   [*bring together*]
His Argument in such a forme,
Which mai the pleine trouthe enforme
And the soubtil cautele abate,   [*undo the subtle trick*]
Which every trewman schal debate.   1640

Practica quemque statum pars tercia
                Philosophie
  Ad regimen recte ducit in orbe vie:
Set quanto maior Rex est, tanto magis ipsum
  Hec scola concernit, qua sua regna regat.[11]

The ferste, which is Theorique,
And the secounde Rethorique,
Sciences of Philosophie,
I have hem told as in partie,
So as the Philosophre it tolde
To Alisandre: and nou I wolde
Telle of the thridde what it is,
The which Practique cleped is.
  Practique stant upon thre thinges
Toward the governance of kinges;   1650
Wherof the ferst Etique is named,   [*Ethics*]
The whos science stant proclamed   [*which science is dedicated*]
To teche of vertu thilke reule   [*this rule*]
Hou that a king himself schal reule
Of his moral condicion
With worthi diposicion
Of good livinge in his persone,
Which is the chief of his corone.   [*dominion*]
It makth a king also to lerne
Hou he his bodi schal governe,   1660
Hou he schal wake, hou he schal slepe,
Hou that he schal his hele kepe   [*health*]
In mete, in drinke, in clothinge eke:
Ther is no wisdom forto seke

[11] Practica, the third part of Philosophy,
    leads every estate in the world to the rule of an honest life;
  but the greater the King, so much the more
    does this doctrine concern him, in order that
      he may rule his kingdom through it

As for the reule of his persone,
The which that this science al one
Ne techeth as be weie of kinde,
That ther is nothing left behinde.
    That other point which to Practique
Belongeth is Iconomique,   1670   [*Economics*]
Which techeth thilke honestete
Thurgh which a king in his degre
His wif and child schal reule and guie,   [*guide*]
So forth with al the companie
Which in his houshold schal abyde,
And his astat on every syde
In such manere forto lede,
That he his houshold ne mislede.
    Practique hath yit the thridde aprise,   [*teaching*]
Which techeth hou and in what wise   1680
Thurgh hih pourveied ordinance
A king schal sette in governance
His Realme, and that is Policie   [*Politics, art of government*]
Which longeth unto Regalie   [*Royalty, royal status*]
In time of werre, in time of pes,
To worschipe and to good encress   [*honor*] [*advancement*]
Of clerk, of kniht and of Marchant,
And so forth of the remenant   [*rest*]
Of al the comun poeple aboute,
Withinne Burgh and ek withoute,   1690   [*town*]
Of hem that ben Artificiers,   [*artisans*]
Whiche usen craftes and mestiers   [*occupations*]
Whos Art is cleped Mechanique.   [*Mechanical art*]
And though thei ben noght alle like,
Yit natheles, hou so it falle,
O lawe mot governe hem alle,
Or that thei lese or that thei winne,
After thastat that thei ben inne.   [*according to the estate*]
   Lo, thus this worthi younge king   [*i.e. Alexander the Great*]
Was fulli tauht of every thing,   1700
Which mihte yive entendement   [*give understanding*]
Of good reule and good regiment   [*government*]
To such a worthi Prince as he.

GENERAL PROLOGUE OF THE WYCLIFFITE BIBLE, CA. 1395–1399

INTRODUCTION

The English Wycliffite or Lollard heresy originated in the late fourteenth century, with the teachings of the Oxford theology master John Wyclif (d. 1384). From an academic circle at Oxford, the heretical movement spread into lay communities. The earlier circles of Wycliffite scholars and preachers produced a great many writings in Latin and English. One of the signature themes of Wycliffite teaching was the capacity and entitlement of lay readers to interpret Scripture themselves, without clerical mediation and mystification. To this end, Wycliffite scholars during the 1380s and 1390s had undertaken a program of vernacular Bible translation, Bible commentary, and vernacular sermon cycles of unprecedented ambition; this is in addition to the many vernacular polemical pieces, theological and political tractates, interrogation narratives, and anti-clerical satires that make up the Lollard "literary" canon. But the translation of the whole Bible into Middle English was undoubtedly the central and monumental achievement of the movement. The translation was achieved in two more-or-less distinct versions, the first a very literal rendering of the Latin, and the second a more idiomatic translation which strives for greater elegance and power in English prose. The Wycliffite Bible translations were collective efforts, and the names of those involved in it cannot be known with any certainty. In part or whole, the Wycliffite Bible survives in over 250 manuscripts. Readers of the vernacular Bible ranged across social classes, from noble sympathizers with Wycliffite ideas to learned laity, and to the artisanal communities in towns across England, where the Lollard heresy established strong footholds during the fifteenth century. Laypersons sometimes commissioned a copy of one portion of the Wycliffite Bible, which may account for the many manuscripts that contain only one section of the Bible.

The General Prologue of the Wycliffite Bible was almost certainly written during or after production of the Later Version of the Wycliffite translation of the Bible, that is, sometime in the later 1390s.[1] It exists only in eleven copies.[2] But while the General

---

[1] Hudson, *The Premature Reformation*, 243–7.   [2] Ibid., 231, 238.

Prologue was not as widely disseminated as the Wycliffite Bible itself, it constitutes a central theoretical statement about the most important vernacularizing project of the Lollard movement. The structure of the General Prologue reveals a great deal about its purpose. The first eleven chapters introduce the books of the Old Testament. The last four chapters present a series of hermeneutical and compositional precepts: the model of the fourfold interpretation of Scripture (using the ancient Alexandrian terminology that was familiar to late medieval theologians and that had been most influentially explained in Nicholas of Lyre's prologue to his literal postilla on the Bible, ca. 1333); explanations of figurative speech in Scripture and how to read it properly; the seven rules of Tyconius, taken from Augustine's account in *De doctrina christiana*;[3] the degrees of spiritual preparation for reading Scripture and the rule of charity; polemics against the enemies of the Lollards and especially against corruption at Oxford and against university learning; a theory of the primacy of the literal sense of Scripture, based on Lyre's prologue to his literal postilla; a second account of the seven rules of Tyconius, this time drawn from Lyre's prologue; an attempt to reconcile the apparent contradictions of Scripture by considering how literal readings in one place can explain seeming inconsistencies elsewhere; a theory of translation advocating an open sense that is not clouded by an overly literal (word for word) translation practice; precepts about grammatical equivalency in translation and the problems for English idiom posed by Latin grammatical usage;[4] a polemic on the right to Scripture in English, based on historical precedent in Britain and on the availability of Scriptures in other European vernaculars; and finally a brief return to practical problems of translation and linguistic equivalency, based on Augustine's discussions of translation from Greek to Latin in book 2 of *De doctrina christiana*.

The General Prologue occupies an important position in another historical tradition: the vernacularization of classical rhetoric. It is, in fact, a remarkable repository of Ciceronian thought in a medieval vernacular. This is a paradox, and one of which the author of the General Prologue could hardly have been aware. There is surely no evidence that the author intended to incorporate Ciceronian thought, and the Wycliffite outlook would have been singularly inhospitable to Ciceronian rhetorical theory. Wycliffite thought actively resisted rhetoric as a distorting force in language. Earlier theorists, such as Bede, Rupert of Deutz, and Thomas of Chobham, recognized the presence of figurative language or rhetorical indirection in Scripture and had been willing to separate its localized force from the profound and pervasive *intended* meaning of Scripture; this line

---

[3] On the reception of the rules of Tyconius see Bright, *The Book of Rules of Tyconius: Its Purpose and Inner Logic*, 16–18. For an edition of the rules see Burkitt, ed., *The Book of Rules of Tyconius*.

[4] The passage from the General Prologue on the ablative absolute is included in this volume in the Ablative Absolute Dossier, above, pp. 337–8.

of thought culminated in Aquinas' remarkable determination about "parabolic" language in Scripture in the opening articles of his *Summa theologica*. But Wyclif's thought moved in the opposite direction; he was suspicious of readings of Scripture that dwelt on the tension between words and "inner" truth, or that (in his mind) saw human eloquence on a continuum with divine eloquence, which rather should be understood as its own mysterious category.[5] How then did Ciceronian thought enter the General Prologue to the Wycliffite Bible?

Its route was not direct. Ciceronian rhetoric enters Wycliffite hermeneutical thought through Augustine's *De doctrina christiana*. Ciceronian rhetoric was a profound, but unacknowledged, influence on Augustine's hermeneutical thought. In books 2 and 3 of the *De doctrina christiana*, Augustine elaborated a dialectic between spirit and letter which he developed, not only out of Pauline doctrine, but also out of Ciceronian rhetoric.[6] Cicero's *De inventione* develops a distinction between the letter or apparent meaning of a legal document or a law and the intention that lies behind it (*De inventione* 1.13.17, 2.40.116–2.48.143; cf. *Ad Herennium* 1.11.19). Moreover, one might need to read the text for its figurative language, which would also entail a non-literal interpretation. Here a stylistic analysis can illuminate the spirit or intention behind the letter, as well as resolve discrepancies between the intention and what is actually stated. Augustine successfully synthesized the legal-rhetorical doctrine of Cicero with the Pauline doctrine of spirit and letter. It is these most Ciceronian sections of the *De doctrina christiana* that are appropriated in the General Prologue of the Wycliffite Bible, where Augustine is cited as an authority in matters of negotiating the practical and spiritual distinctions between literal and figurative reading.[7] The General Prologue takes on a considerable amount of the *De doctrina christiana,* especially continuous readings from book 3 chapter 5 to the end of book 3, and some matter from the beginning and the end of book 2. Chapter 12 of the Prologue shows an impressive attempt to collate the arguments of *De doctrina christiana* book 3 on ambiguous figurative signs; and chapter 13 deals (in somewhat less detail) with book 2 of Augustine's text, on the spiritual preparation needed for approaching the unknown signs of Scripture. Thus Ciceronian rhetoric stands behind much of the hermeneutical thought of Augustine that is taken on by the Wycliffite author.

[5] See Copeland, "Rhetoric and the Politics of the Literal Sense in Medieval Literary Theory: Aquinas, Wyclif, and the Lollards."

[6] See Eden, "The Rhetorical Tradition and Augustinian Hermeneutics in *De doctrina christiana*."

[7] For further discussion, see Copeland, "Wycliffite Ciceronianism? The General Prologue to the Wycliffite Bible and Augustine's *De doctrina christiana*."

Text from *The Holy Bible...made from the Latin Vulgate by John Wycliffe and his Followers*, ed. Forshall and Madden, by permission. Middle English characters have been replaced by their modern English equivalents.

FROM CHAPTER 12

But it is to wite [*to be known*], that holy scripture hath iiij. vndirstondingis; literal, allegorik, moral, and anagogik....Also holy scripture hath many figuratif spechis [*speeches, i.e. examples of figurative language*], and as Austyn [*Augustine*] seith in the iij. book of Cristen Teching, that autouris of hooly scripture vsiden moo [*used more*] figuris, that is, mo fyguratif spechis, than grammariens moun gesse [*may imagine*], that reden not tho [*who do not read the*] figuris in holy scripture.[8] It is to be war [*aware*] in the bigynnyng that we take not to the lettre a figuratif speche, for thanne, as Poul [*Paul*] seith, the lettre sleeth but the spirit, that is, goostly [*ghostly, spiritual*] vndirstonding, qwykeneth [*gives life*]; for whanne [*when*] a thing which is seid figuratifly is taken so as if it be seid propirly, me vndirstondith fleschly [*carnally*]; and noon is clepid [*nothing is called*] more couenably [*appropriately*] the deth of soule, than whanne vndirstonding, that passith beestis [*surpasses that of beasts*], is maad soget [*made subject*] to the fleisch in suyinge the lettre [*following the letter*].[9] What euer thing in Goddis word may not be referrid propirly to oneste [*honesty*] of vertues neither [*nor*] to the treuthe of feith, it is figuratyf speche. Onestee of vertues perteyneth [*concerns, i.e. means*] to loue God and the [*your*] neighebore; treuthe of feith perteyneth to knowe God and the neighebore.[10] Hooly scripture comaundith no thing no but charite, it blamith no thing no but coueitise; and in that manere it enfoormeth [*informs, teaches*] the vertues either [*or*] goode condiscouns of men. Holy scripture affermith no thing no but cristen feith bi thingis passid, present, and to comynge [i.e. *future*], and alle these thingis perteynen to nursche charite [*nourish charity*], and make it strong, and to ouercome and quenche coueitise.[11] Also it is figuratijf speche, where the wordis maken allegorie, ether a derk lycnesse [*or a dark likeness*],[12] either parable and it is fyguratyf speche in i. c. of Jeremye, "to day I have ordeyned thee on folkis and rewmys [*realms*], that thou draw up bi the roote, and distroie, and bylde, and plaunte;"[13] that is, that thou drawe out elde synnes

---

[8] *De doctrina christiana* 3.29.40.

[9] Ibid. 3.5.9; and cf. Wyclif, *De veritate sacrae scripturae*, ed. Buddensieg, 1:150.

[10] *De doctrina christiana* 3.10.14.   [11] Ibid. 3.10.15.

[12] I.e. *aenigma*: the English writer gives a periphrasis for the unfamiliar rhetorical term.

[13] *De doctrina christiana* 3.11.17 and 3.29.40; Jeremiah 1:10.

[*root out old sins*], and distroie circumstaunces either causis of thoo [*or causes of them*], and bylde [*build up*] vertues, and plaunte goode werkis and customys [*plant good works and customs*]. Alle thingis in holy scripture, that seemyn to vnwijse men to be ful of wickidnesse agens [*against*] a man himself, either agens his neighbore, ben [*be, are*] figuratyf spechis, and the preuytees [*secrets*], either goostly vndirstondinges, schulden be sought out of vs, to the feeding either keping of charite.[14] Such a reule [*rule*] schal be kept in figuratif spechis, that so longe it be turned in mynde bi diligent consideracoun, til the expownyng [*expounding*] either vndirstonding be brought to the rewme [*kingdom*] of charite; if eny speche of scripture sounneth propirly [*literally expresses*] charite, it owith not to be gessid [*ought not to be considered*] a figuratijf speche;[15] and forbeedith wickidnesse, either comaundith profyt either good doynge, it is no figuratyf speche;[16] if it seemith to comaunde cruelte, either wickidnesse, either to forbede prophit [*forbid what is beneficial*], either good doinge, it is a figuratijf speche. Crist seith, "if ye eten not the flesch of mannis sone and drinke not his blood, ye schulen not have lijf in you."[17] This speche semith to comaunde wickidnesse either cruelte, therfore it is a figuratif speche, and comaundith men to comune with Cristis passioun, and to kepe in mynde sweetly and profitably, that Cristis flesch was woundid and crucified for vs. Also whanne hooly scripture seith, "if thin enemy hungrith, feede thou hym, if he thurstith, yeue [*give*] thou drinke to him," it comaundith benefice, either good doinge; whanne it seith, "thou schalt gadere togidere coolis [*coals*] on his heed,"[18] it seemith that wickidnesse of yuel [*evil*] wille is comaundid. This is seid bi figuratijf speche, that thou vndirstonde, that the coolys of fijer [*fire*] ben brennynge weylyngis [*are burning sighs*], either moornyngis [*lamentations*] of penaunce, bi whiche the pride of hym is mad hool [*whole*], which sorwith [*who sorrows*], that he was enemy of a man that helpith and releuith [*who helps and relieves*] his wrecchidnesse.[19] Also the same word either the same thing in scripture is taken sumtyme in good, and sumtyme in yuel, as a lyoun [*lion*] singnefieth sumtyme Crist, and in another place it singnefieth the deuyl.[20] Also sour dough [*i.e. leavening*] is set sumtyme in yuel, where Crist seith, "be ye war of the sour dough of Farisees, which is ypocrisie;"[21] sour dough is sett also in good, whanne Crist seith, "the rewme of heuenes is lyk sour dough," etc.[22] And whanne not oo [*one*] thing aloone but tweyne, either mo [*or more*], ben feelid [*are sensed*], either vndirstonden, bi the same wordis of scripture,

---

[14] Ibid. 3.12.18.   [15] Ibid. 3.15.23.

[16] Ibid. 3.16.24; cf. Wyclif, *De veritate sacrae scripturae*, 1:200.

[17] John 6:54.   [18] Proverbs 25:21, 22; Romans 12:20.

[19] *De doctrina christiana* 3.16.24 (from the sentence beginning "Crist seith, 'if ye eten not the flesch of mannis sone . . .'" to this point in the text).

[20] Ibid. 3.15.36.   [21] Matthew 16:11.   [22] Luke 13:20–1; *De doctrina christiana* 3.25.35.

though that it is hid, that he vndirstond that wroot [*even if what the writer of the passage meant remains hidden*], it is no perel [*there is no danger*], if it may be preuyd [*proved, ascertained*] bi other placis of hooly scripture, that ech of tho thingis acordith with treuthe. And in hap [*perchance*] the autour of scripture seith thilk sentense in the same wordis which we wolen vndirstonde [*sees this meaning in the same words we desire to understand*]; and certys the Spirit of God, that wroughte these thingis bi the autour of scripture, bifore sigh withoute doute [*certainly foresaw*], that thilke sentense schulde come to the redere [*reader*], either to the herere [*hearer*], yhe, the Holy Goost purueyde [*provided, ordained*], that thilke sentence, for [*since*] it is groundid on trewthe, schulde come to the redere, either to the herere, for whi [*for indeed*] what myghte be purueyed of God largiliere and plentyuousliere [*what might be provided more generously and abun- dantly by God*] in Goddis spechis [*i.e. divine eloquence*], than that the same wordis be vndirstonden in manye maners, whiche maners, either [*other*] wordis of God, that ben not of lesse autorite, maken to be preued [*give proof of*].²³ Austin in iij. book of Cristen Teching seith al this and myche more, in the bigynnyng therof. Also he whos herte is ful of charite conprehendith, withouten eny errour, the manyfoold abundaunce and largest teching of Goddis scripturis, for whi Poul seith, "the fulnesse of lawe is charite," and in another place, "the ende of lawe," that is, the perfeccioun, either filling [*or fulfillment*], of the lawe, "is charite of clene herte, and of good conscience, and of feith not feyned," and Jhesu Crist seith, "thou schalt loue thi Lord God of al thin herte, and of al thi soule, and of al thi mynde, and thi neighebore as thi self, for in these twey comaundementis hangith al the lawe and prophetis."²⁴ And as the roote of alle yuels is coueitise, so the roote of alle goodis is charitee. Charite, bi which we louen God and the neighebore, holdith sykirly [*securely*] al the greetnesse and largnesse of Goddis spechis.²⁵ Therefore if it is not leisir [i.e. *if there is not leisure*] to seeke alle holy scriptures, to expounne alle the wlappingis [*subtle wrappings*] of wordis, to perse [*get inside*] alle the preuytes [*secrets*] of scripturis, holde thou charite, where alle thingis hangen, so thou schalt holde that that thou lernydist there; also thou schalt holde that that thou lernedist not, for if thou knowist charite, thou knowist sum thing wheronne also that hangith that in hap thou knowist not; and in that that thou vndirstondist in scripturis, charite is opin, and in that that thou vndirstondist not, charite is hid, therfore he that hooldith charite in vertues, either in goode condiscouns, hooldith bothe that that is opyn and that that is hid in Goddis wordis. Austyn seith al this and myche more in a sermoun of the preysing of charite . . .²⁶

---

²³ *De doctrina christiana* 3.27.38.   ²⁴ Romans 13:10; Timothy 1:5; Matthew 22:37–40.
²⁵ Cf. *De doctrina christiana* 3.10.16; 3.12.18.   ²⁶ Sermon 350, *PL* 39:1534–5. Cf. *De doctrina christiana* 3.12.18.

Also no thing may seme to be wijsere, no thing of more eloquence, than is hooly scripture, and the autours therof, that weren enspijrid of God. And thei oughten not to speke in other manere than thei diden, and the prophetis, and moost [*especially*] Amos, weren ful eloquent, and seint Poul waas ful eloquent in his pistlis [*epistles*]. Also the autouris of hooly scripture spaken derkly [*enigmatically*], that the preuyteis therof ben hid from vnfeithful men, and goode men ben exercisid, either ocupied, and that in expounnynge hooly scripture thei haue a newe grace, diuerse [*different*] fro the first autouris. Austin, in the bigynnyng of the iiij. book of Cristen Teching.²⁷ Also, as in the litle richessis of Jewis, whiche thei baren awey from Egipt, weren in comparisoun of richessis which thei hadden aftirward in Jerusalem, in the tyme of Salomon, so greet is the prophitable kunnynge [*useful learning*] of filosoferis bookis, if it is comparisouned to the kunnynge of hooly scripturis; for whi what euer thing a man lernith withouten hooly writ, if the thing lerned is veyn, it is dampned [*condemned*] in holy writ, if it is prophitable, it is foundid there. And whanne a man fyndith theere alle thingis which he lernyde profitably in other place, he schal fynde myche more plenteuously tho thingis in hooly scripture, which he lernede neuere in other place, but ben lerned oonly in the wondirful highnesse and in the wondirful meeknesse of hooly scripturis. Austin seith this in the ende of ij. book of Cristen Teching.²⁸ Also hooly scripture conteyneth al prophitable treuthe, and alle othere sciencis preuyly in the vertue of wittis, either vndirstondingis, as wynes ben conteyned in grapis, as ripe corn is conteyned in the seed, as bowis [*boughs*] ben conteyned in the rootis, and as trees ben conteyned in the kernels. Grostede, in a sermoun *Premonitus a venerabili patre*.²⁹ Also hooly scripture wlatith sofymys [*hates sophisms*], and seith, he that spekith sofisticaly, either bi sofymys, schal be hatful, and he schal be defraudid in ech thing, as the wijse man seith in xxxvij. c. of Ecclesiastici.³⁰ If filosoferis, and moost the disciplis of Plato, seiden eny treuthis, and prophitable to oure feith, not oonly tho treuthis owen not to be dred [*feared*], but also tho schulen be calengid [*taken back*] into oure vs [*use*], eithir profijt, fro hem, as fro vniust [*unjust*] possessouris. And as Jewis token, bi autorite of God, the gold, and syluer, and clothis of Egipcyans, so cristene men owen to take the trewe seyingis of filosoueris, for to worschippe oo [*one*] God, and of techingis of vertues, whiche treuthis the filosoueris founden not, but diggeden out of the metals of Goddis puruyaunce [*providence*], which is sched [*revealed*] euery where. So dide Ciprian, the swettest doctour and moost blessid martir, so diden Lactancius, Victorinus, and Illarie [*Hilary*], and Greekis withoute noumbre. Austin in ij. book of Cristen Teching.³¹ Bi these

²⁷ Ibid. 4.6.9; cf. Wyclif, *De veritate sacrae scripturae* 1.5.   ²⁸ Ibid. 2.42.63.
²⁹ See Thomson, *The Writings of Robert Grosseteste*, 173 (sermon no. 19).   ³⁰ Ecclesiasticus 37:23.
³¹ *De doctrina christiana* 2.40.60.

reulis of Austin³² and bi iiij. vndirstondinges of hooly scripture,³³ and bi wijs knowing of figuratijf spechis, with good lyuynge and meeknesse, and stodyinge of the bible, symple men moun sumdel [*to some extent*] vndirstonde the text of holy writ, and edefie [*edify*] myche hemself and other men…

FROM CHAPTER 13

Also holy scripture is betere knowen bi licnesses and bi derknessis; it doth awey anoyes [*weariness, discomfort*], and we owe to thenke and bileeue, that the thing that is writen in holy scripture, yhe, though it be hid, either not knowen, is betere and trewere than that we moun vndirstonde be vsself;³⁴ and worschipfully and heelfully [*in a salutary way*] the Holy Goost mesuride so holy scripturis, that in opyn placis he settide remedie to oure hungir, and in derk placis he wipte awey anoies; for almost no thing is seyn in tho derknessis, which thing is not founden seid ful pleynly in other placis.³⁵ Therefore bifore alle thingis it is nedeful, that a man be conuertid bi Goddis drede [*fear of God*], and be mylde bi pite [*meek through piety*], either cristen religioun; and that he agensie [*contradict, gainsay*] not hooly scripture, wher it be vnderstonden, though it smyte eny synnes of oure, whether it be not vndirstonden, as if we moun vndirstonde betere, either comaunde, either teche betere.³⁶ Be the yifte [*gift*] of drede and of pitee, me comith to degre of kunnyng, for whi ech fructuous [*productively studious*] man of hooly scripturis exercisith himself in this thing, and to fynde noon other thing in tho, than for to loue God for God himself, and for to loue his neighebore for God. Thane thilke drede, bi which he thenkith on Goddis dom [*judgment*], and thilke pite, bi which he must nedis bileeue and yeue stide [*yield*] to autorite of holy bookis, conpellith hym to beweyle hymself, for whi this kunnyng of good hope makith a man not to auaunce himself, but biweile himself; and bi this affeccioun, either good wille, he geetith with besy preieris the coumfort of Goddis help, that he be not broken bi dispeir; and he bigynneth to be in the fourthe degre of goostly strengthe, in whiche he hungrith and thirstith rightfulnesse; thanne in the v. degree, that is, in the counceyl of mercy, he purgith the soule, that makith noise and vnrestfulnesse of coueitise of erthly thingis; and thanne he dispisith filthis of soule, and louith God and neigheboris, yhe enemyes; bi this he stighith [*climbs*] to the vj. degre, where he purgith the iye of soule [*the spiritual sight*], bi which iye God may be seyn, as myche as he may be seyn of hem [*as

³² I.e. the seven rules of Tyconius, given in *De doctrina christiana* 3.30–7 (and quoted in an earlier part of chapter 12).

³³ I.e. the fourfold system mentioned at the beginning of the chapter.

³⁴ Cf. *De doctrina christiana* 2.6.7.   ³⁵ Ibid. 2.6.8.   ³⁶ Ibid. 2.7.9.

much as he may be seen by those] that dighen [*die*] to this world, as myche as they mowen [*to the best of their ability*]; for in so myche thei seen God in her [*their*] soule, thourgh feith and loue, hou myche thei dighen to this world; and in as myche as thei leuyn to [*live in*] this world, thei seen not God; and in this degre, wherinne a man dighith to the world, he neither preferrith, neither makith euene himself, neither his neighebore, with the treuthe of hooly writ [i.e. *he does not value himself or his neighbor over the truth of holy Scripture, nor does he give either one equal value to that truth*]; therfor this hooly man schal be so symple and clene of herte, that neither for pleasaunce of men he be drawe awey fro treuthe, nether be cause to eschewe eny harmys of himself [*nor in order to avoid any misfortunes*], that ben contrarie [*unfavorable*] to this lijf, such a chiild stighith to verey wisdom, which is the laste and the vij., which he vsith in pees and in reste. Seint Austyn seith al this in the bygynnyng of the ij. book of Cristen Teching.[37]

---

[37] Ibid. 2.7.10–11. This passage on the degrees of spiritual ascent in preparation for proper reading of Scripture may reflect the influence of Victorinus' commentary on Cicero's *De inventione*, which treats the ascendance through the arts to spiritual purity; see Victorinus, above, pp. 107–8.

JOHN LYDGATE,
FALL OF PRINCES, 1431–1439

INTRODUCTION

Lydgate's *Fall of Princes* is based on Laurent de Premierfait's *Des cas des nobles hommes et femmes*, a translation completed in 1409 of Boccaccio's influential *De casibus illustrium virorum*, which narrates the falls of distinguished persons in biblical, classical, and modern history. Lydgate wrote his vast work between 1431 and 1438/9 as edifying instruction for his noble patron Humphrey, Duke of Gloucester.

The account of rhetoric from book 6, presented here, is not part of a survey of the liberal arts integrated into a larger narrative, such as we find in Gower's *Confessio amantis* or Alan of Lille's *Anticlaudianus*. Rather it derives, via Laurent's version, from an excursus on rhetoric that Boccaccio appended to his account of Cicero's life and death. In Boccaccio's work, the logic for this excursus was to give an encomium of Cicero through a vehement defense of rhetoric against its detractors who are too ignorant to appreciate the virtues and social benefits of the art. Laurent de Premierfait, and Lydgate after him, elaborate this excursus and make it also an occasion for an intrinsic account of rhetoric, that is, its internal doctrine. This is a natural extension of Cicero's life into his teaching, and the rhetorical doctrine summarized is a general synthesis of the *De inventione* or the *Rhetorica ad Herennium*. But while much of Lydgate's matter on rhetoric is taken from his French source, some important detail is Lydgate's own, especially where he compresses his source and substitutes one potent illustration or verbal image for the longer explanations in the French text. Beyond Laurent's text (and Boccaccio's), Lydgate's work forges a link in the political sphere between rhetorical persuasion and the sweet power of poetry to instruct. In this way Lydgate connects the roles of orator and poet. Thus Lydgate's account, although not entirely original, represents a valuable vernacular statement about the capacities of rhetoric as a political art form.

Lydgate's text sums up and restates certain Ciceronian themes that medieval readers knew through the *De inventione*: rhetoric produces and cultivates civilized society (*De inventione* 1.2.2); and the distinctive attribute of speech makes humans inherently superior to animals (1.4.5). The elaboration of these themes extends back beyond Lydgate's sources through the long chain of commentaries on the *De inventione* that includes Brunetto's *Rettorica* and *Trésor*, the twelfth-century commentators, and ultimately Victorinus' Neoplatonist exposition. The Ciceronian theme that rhetoric produces civilized order and nurtures polity is, of course, a foundation myth: in the *De inventione* 1.2.2, Cicero tells the story of how an eloquent wise man took control of a savage people and persuaded them to erect social institutions and abide by laws. The story itself is not present in Lydgate's version, but the force of the myth is there as a theme that Lydgate develops beyond his immediate sources: prudent speech or eloquence enables religious preachers to teach people and discipline them, making them productive and obedient:

> Langage techeth men to plaunte vyne,
> Enfourmeth folk to worshepe hooli cherche,
> The artificeer treuli for to werche.

> (6.3421–3)

In the Ciceronian myth, eloquence serves the public interests of the republic. Lydgate changes the direction of this political myth. On his interpretation, the role of rhetoric is to provide moral and practical instruction, ordering the social relations of the populace and, even more important, moving or containing the emotions of rulers. For Lydgate, the orator's key role is not persuading a public or guiding a state, but serving, appeasing, and instructing a prince.

Lydgate takes some of his understanding of the ideal relation between orator (or rhetorician) and prince from Laurent de Premierfait, who speaks of managing the wrath of princes. Thus rhetorical ornament, the "sugared language and virtuous dalliance" that "appeased the terrible vengeance of tyrants" (6.3467–70), is the good and necessary instrument of moral advice. But early on in the *Fall of Princes*, in the Prologue, Lydgate has already recast the political foundation myth of rhetoric into something else, a political myth in which poets play the roles of orators and serve their princes accordingly. He gives a story of how poets first schooled their princes, and the greatest of these "poets" is none other than Tullius Cicero:

> And these poetis I make off mencioun,
> Were bi old tyme had in gret deynte,
> With kyngis, pryncis in euery regioun,
> Gretli preferrid afftir ther degre;
> For lordis hadde plesance for to see,
> To studie a-mong, and to caste ther lookis
> At goode leiser vpon wise bookis.

> For in the tyme off Cesar Iulius,
> Whan the tryumphe he wan in Rome toun,
> He entre wolde the scoole off Tullius
> And heere his lecture off gret affeccioun;
> And natwithstandyng his conquest & renoun,
> Vnto bookis he gaff gret attendaunce
> And hadde in stories ioie and gret pleasunce.
>
> (Prologue, 358–71)

As Lydgate goes on to suggest, Duke Humphrey is to the poet Lydgate as Caesar was to the poet-orator Tully, a mighty prince who seeks instruction from books and, by implication, from Lydgate's own "lectures," that is, the present book which Lydgate has translated at Duke Humphrey's command (Prologue, 372–434). Through such disciplined study, Duke Humphrey takes control over the vice of sloth (Prologue, 399), that is, his carnal nature. It is the role of the poet-orator now to help the prince manage his passions by offering moral instruction sweetened with eloquence. Lydgate has shifted rhetoric's political sphere from republic to monarchy, and transformed the persuasive orator into the advice-giving poet.

Reprinted from Lydgate, *Fall of Princes*, ed. Bergin, by permission. Middle English characters have been replaced by their modern English equivalents.

FROM BOOK 6

§ *A Chapitle ageyn [Ianglers and] diffamers of Rethorique*

Bochas compleynyng in his studie allone		
The deth of Tullie and the woful fall,		
Gruchching in herte made a pitous mone,		[*complaining, grumbling*]
The folk rebukyng in especial,	3280	
Which of nature be boistous & rurall,		[*ignorant*] [*rude*]
And hardi been (for thei no kunnyng haue)		[*eager*]
Craft of rethorik to hyndren and depraue.		
Clerkis olde dide gretli magnefie	3284	
This noble science, that wer expert & wis,		

Callid it part of philosophie,
And saide also in ther prudent auys,   [*opinion*]
Ther be thre partes, as tresours of gret pris,   3288
Compiled in bookis & of old prouided,
Into which philosophie is deuyded.

The firste of hem callid is morall,
Which directeth a man to goode thewes;   3292   [*conduct, moral character*]
And the secounde, callid naturall,
Tellith the kynde of goode men & shrewes;   [*nature*] [*rogues, wicked persons*]
And the thridde, raciounal, weel shewes   [*shows*]
What men shal uoide & what thing vndirfonge, 3296   [*avoid; undertake*]
And to that parti rethorik doth longe.   [*part; belong*]

Bi Tullius, as auctours determyne,
Of his persone rehersyng in substaunce,
Translatid was fro Greek into Latyne   3300
Crafft of rethorik; and for the habundaunce   [*abundance*]
Of elloquence stuffed with plesaunce,
All oratours remembrid, hym to-fore
Was ther non lik, nor aftir hym yit bore.   3304

Bochas also seith in his writingis
And preueth weel be resoun in sentence,
To an oratour longeth foure thingis: [*belongs*]
First naturel wit, practik with science,   3308
Vertuous lyff, cheef ground of elloquence,
Of port and maner that he be tretable;   [*affable in bearing and manner*]
Thes menys had, myn auctour halt hym able.   [*means, conditions; holds*]

In his writyng and in his scriptures   3312
Bochas weel preueth, if mut needis been,   [*demonstrates; if need be*]
How that of riht ther longe fyue armures   [*five "armors" belong*]
To eueri notable rethoricien,
Set heer in ordre, who that list hem seen,   3316   [*as anyone may see*]
Which he callith, rehersyng in sentence,
The fyue baneeres longyng to elloquence.   [*five banners*]

The firste off hem callid Inuencioun,
Bi which a man doth in his herte fynde   3320
A sikir grounde foundid on resoun,   [*secure*]
With circumstaunces, that nouht be left behynde,

Fro poynt to poynt enprentid in his mynde   [impressed]
Touchyng the mateer, the substaunce & the grete,   3324   [major part]
Of which he caste notabli tentrete.   [intends] [to deal with]

Another armure, in ordre the secounde,
Of riht is callid Disposioun[1]
As of a mateer whan the ground is founde,   3328
That eueri thyng bi iust dyuysioun   [proper division (of parts)]
Be void of al foreyn digressioun,
So disposid touchyng tyme & space,
Fro superfluite keepe his dewe place.   3332

The tridde armure namyd in sentence
Is Ellocucioun, with woordes many or fewe,
Materes conceyued bi iust conuenyence,
Disposid in ordre couenably to shewe,—   3336   [to show aptly]
Lik a keruer that first doth tymbir hewe,   [wood-carver] [timber]
Squier & compas cast fetures & visage,   [square and compass]
With keruyng tool makth [up] a fair image.[2]

Pronunciacioun is the fourth armure,   3340
Necessarie to eueri oratour,
In such caas whan craft onto nature
Iioyned is bi dilligent labour   [joined]
With execucioun, and that ther be fauour   3344
In declaryng, with eueri circumstaunce,
Folwyng the mateer in cheer & contenaunce.

An heuy mateer requereth an heuy cheer;
To a glad mateer longeth weel gladnesse;   3348   [gladness aptly belongs]
Men in pronouncyng mut folwe the mateer,—
Old oratours kan bern herof witnesse,—
A furious compleynt vttrid in distresse: [uttered]
This was the maner, as poetis do descryue,   3352
In his tragedies whan Senec was alyue.[3]

The fiffte armure callid Remembraunce,
With quik memorie be prouidence to see,   [by prudence]
So auisili to grose up in substaunce   3356   [carefully to assemble in its substance]

---

[1] Sic.   [2] Lines 3337–9 have no parallel in Lydgate's source.
[3] Lines 3352–3 have no parallel in Lydgate's source.

Hooli his mateeris, that nouht forgetyn be,   [*the whole of his matter*]
Liste foryetilnesse dirke nat the liberte   [*lest forgetfulness not obscure*]
Of cleer report, ech thing hadde in mynde,
That in pronouncyng nothing be left behynde.   3360

Afforn prouided, so that foryetilnesse   [*provided, arranged in advance*]
Be non hyndrere to inuencioun,
And in proceedyng no foreyn reklesnesse   [*extraneous negligence*]
Trouble nat the ordre of disposicioun.   3364
And for tacomplisshe al up with resoun,   [*to accomplish*]
That pronouncyng be cleere remembraunce
Be weel fauoured with cheer & contenaunce.

Thes saide thynges be inli necessarie   3368   [*very*]
To euery prudent notable oratour,
Nat to hasti nor ouer long to tarie,
But to conveie his processe be mesour;   [*present his discourse deliberately*]
In cheer accordyng stant al the fauour: 3372
For in pronouncyng, who lakketh cheer or face,
Of Tullius scoole stant ferr out of grace.⁴   [*far out of favor*]

Al erthli beestis be muet of nature,   [*mute*]
Sauf onli man, which haueth auauntage   3376
Bi a prerogatiff aboue ech creature
To vttre his conceit onli be langage.   [*express his meaning*]
The soule be grace repressith al outrage,
Namli whan resoun hath the souereynte   3380   [*sovereignty*]
To bridle passiouns of sensualite.

Kynde onto man hath youen elloquence,   [*given*]
A thyng couenabale in especiall   [*convenient*]
Whan that it is conveied bi prudence,   3384
To talke of mateeris that be natural
And secrees hid aboue celestial,–
Doth entrete of sunne, moone & sterris
Thynfluent poweer doun sent of pes & werris.   3388

God of al this hath graunted knowleching
Onli to man bi wisdam and resoun,
And thoruh langage youe to hym shewying,

---

⁴ Lines 3355–74 have no parallel in Lydgate's source.

Outward to make declaracioun   3392
Of the heuenli cours & sondri mocioun,   *[heavenly course]* *[sundry move-ment]*

Diuers chaunges, &, pleynli to diffyne,
The reuolucioun of the speeris nyne.   *[nine spheres]*

Men bi langage shewe out ther ententis,   3396
The naturall meeuyng & mutaciouns,
Accord & discord of the foure elementis,
Kyndli variaunce of foure complecciouns,
The generacioun & the corupciouns   3400
of erthli thynges, contrarie ech to other,
Corrupcioun of oon engendryng to another.

This the poweer & the precellence   *[excellence]*
Youe vnto man, which is resonable,   3404
That bi langage and bi elloquence
A man is tauht in vertu to be stable,—
Of soule eternal, of bodi corumpable,
Tauht with his tunge whil he is alyue   3408
Of his defautis how he shal hym shryue.   *[how he shall confess his sins]*

Bochas eek tellith, touchyng rethorik,
Ther been too maneres: oon is of nature,   *[two kinds]*
Lernyd in youthe, which doth oon speke lik   3412
As he heereth & lerneth bi scripture;—
Crafft of rethorik youe to no creature
Sauff to man, which bi gret dilligence
Be studie kometh to crafft of elloquence.   3416

Crafft of langage and of prudent speche
Causeth prechours bi spiritual doctryne
Vertuousli the peeple for to teche,
How thei shal lyue bi moral disciplyne.   3420
Langage techeth men to plaunte vyne,
Enfourmeth folk to worshepe hooli cherche,
The artificeer treuli for to werche.[5]   *[the practitioner]* *[to work]*

Yit ther be summe that pleynli preche and teche,   3424
Haue of langage this oppynyoun:

[5] Lines 3417–23 have no parallel in Lydgate's source.

God hath nat most reward onto speche,
But to the herte & to thaffeccioun;
Best can guerdone the inward entencioun   3428   [*reward*]
Of eueri man, nat after the visage,
But lik the menyng of ther inward corage.

To vttre langage is great dyuersite
Whan that men shewe theffect of ther menyng,   3432
Be it of ioie or off aduersite,
Cheer for taccord therwith in vtteryng,   [*to accord*]
Now debonaire, sumwhile rebukyng,
And in rehersyng, lik cheer alwei tapplie,   3436   [*declaring*] [*to apply*]
Be it of rudnesse, be it of curteisie.

Of discrecioun sette a difference
In his pronouncyng to perce or vndirmyne,   [*to touch deeply*] [*to influence*]
To drawe the iuge vnto his sentence   3440
Or to his purpos to make hym to enclyne,
Seen wher he be malencolik or benigne,–
Or his mateer be vttrid or vnclosid,
Considre afforn how that he is disposid.   3444

Peised al this thyng, the rethoricien,   [*having weighed all this*]
With other thynges which appertene of riht
To crafft of speche, he mut conueye & seen   [*convey and express*]
Mateeris of substaunce & mateeris that be liht,   3448
Dispose hymsilf tentretyn euery wiht   [*to address every person*]
Lik to purpos & fyn of his mateere,   [*purpose and end*]
As for the tyme rethorik doth requeere.

As bexaumple, myn auctour doth record,   3452
Men sette at werre, in herte ferr assonder,
The rethoricien to make hem for taccord   [*to accord*]
Mut seeke weies & menys heer & yonder,   [*ways and means*]
Of old rancour tappese the boistous thonder,   3456   [*to appease*]
Be wise exaumplis & prouerbis pertynent
Tenduce the parties to been of oon assent.   [*to induce*]

A man also that stant in heuynesse,
Disespeired and disconsolat,   3460
The rethoricien mut don his besynesse,
The ground considred & felt of his estat,

The cause serchid whi he stant desolat,   [*searched*]
Which to reffourme be dilligent labour   3464
Is the trewe offis of eueri oratour.   [*office*]

Of rethoriciens whilom that wer old
The sugrid langage & vertuous daliaunce
Be goode exaumples & prouerbes that thei tolde,   3468
Woordes pesible enbelisshed with plesaunce,
Appesid of tirauntes the rigerous vengaunce,
Sette aside ther furious sentence
Bi vertu onli of prudent elloquence.   3472

And in contrarie, pleynli to conclude,
Men seen alday bi cleer experience
Folk vnauised, & hasti foolis rude,
And braynles peeple, of wilful necligence,   3476
Because thei wern bareyn of elloquence,
Vttringe ther speche as nakid folk & bare,
For lak of rethorik ther mateer to declare.

Bi cleer exaumple, as purpil, who takth heede,   3480
Longeth to kynges, in stori men may fynde,   [*belongs*]
With clothes of gold & riche velwet weede
Fret with rubies and othir stonis Ynde,
Saphirs, emeraudis, perlis of ther kynde,–   3484
As alle thes thynges aproprid been of riht,
Plesaunt obiectis to a mannys siht,

So the langage of rethoriciens
Is a glad obiect to mannys audience,   3488
With song mellodious of musiciens,
Which doth gret counfort to euery hih presence.
Bexaumple as Amphioun, with song & elloquence
Bilte the wallis of Thebes the cite,   3492
He hadde of rethorik so gret subtilite.[6]

---

[6] Lydgate adds the allusion to Amphion, who built the walls of Thebes by playing his lyre and luring the stones to come forward. In his *Siege of Thebes* (written 1421/2), Lydgate features the Amphion myth prominently (189–315), using it to illustrate the importance of eloquence for a good ruler who should work by persuasion rather than coercion. See P. Clogan, "Lydgate and the *Roman Antique*," *Florilegium* 11 (1992): 7–21 [13–17], and D. Battles, *The Medieval Tradition of Thebes* (New York and London: Routledge, 2004), 152–8. In the *Siege of Thebes*, Lydgate cites Boccaccio as his source about Amphion (see *De genealogia deorum gentilium* 5.30), but there

In his langage ther was so gret plesaunce,
Fyndyng therbi so inli gret proffit,   [*very*]
That al the contre kam to his obeissaunce,   3496   [*country*]
To heere hym speke thei hadde so gret delit;
The peeple enviroun hadde such an appetit
In his persone, in pes & in bataille:
Heer men may seen what rethorik doth auaille!   3500

may be other sources as well. In his account of Ciceronian rhetoric in the *Trésor*, Brunetto Latini invokes the Amphion story to explain the Ciceronian myth of the civilizing power of rhetoric (Brunetto, ed. Carmody, 3.1.2–8).

A MIDDLE ENGLISH TREATISE ON THE SEVEN LIBERAL ARTS, CA. 1475

INTRODUCTION

This English treatise on the seven liberal arts survives in a manuscript written in the last quarter of the fifteenth century, Cambridge, Trinity College MS R. 14.52. The hand of the manuscript is that of the scribe of two copies each of the *Canterbury Tales* and Hoccleve's *Regiment of Princes*, as well as of minor works of Chaucer and Lydgate, who has been identified as a London scribe of the reign of Edward IV.[1] The manuscript is an important example of English vernacular scientific writing. It contains English versions of pseudo-Galenic treatises and many other medical writings, an herbal, and tracts on mathematics and astronomy. This compilation represents a high-water mark for the rendering of scientific and medical writings in English.[2] The treatise on the seven liberal arts is included with the material on astronomy; in its extant form, the liberal arts treatise gives most space over to geometry, with some additional, specialized texts on geometry embedded within that section.

The treatise on the seven liberal arts is based in large part on the *De artibus liberalibus* by Robert Grosseteste (1168–1253), bishop of Lincoln. Its composition seems to have gone through several stages or recensions (either in Latin or in English) before achieving the form in which it survives. The treatise draws on other traditional sources for the trivium and quadrivium, in addition to Grosseteste's work. For the section on grammar, these other sources include Martianus Capella, Priscian, and a Remigian commentary on Donatus. The rhetoric section refers to Quintilian's *Institutio oratoria*, which was achieving prominence in humanist studies on the Continent after its rediscovery in the early part of the fifteenth century. But the treatment of rhetoric here also derives much of its information from either Cicero's *De inventione* or Isidore's *Etymologiae*. The prologue to the treatise is based on Grosseteste's prologue.[3]

---

[1] Mooney, "The Scribe"; Mooney, "A Middle English Text on the Seven Liberal Arts," 1027.
[2] Voigts, "What's the Word: Bilingualism in Late-Medieval England."
[3] We present here only the prologue and the sections on the trivium.

The audience for whom the liberal arts treatise was actually destined cannot be known with certainty. To some extent, the audience of the manuscript as a whole can be deduced from other work that is associated with this London scribe. The surviving manuscripts in his hand represent the works of the best-known secular English poets, that is, Chaucer, Lydgate, and Hoccleve. These survivals indicate that the clientele who were able to commission such full-length manuscripts desired works written in English rather than in Latin.[4] In addition to their literary tastes, they had a broad interest in scientific writings, and the knowledge and confidence to commission such learned compilations, but they were readers of English rather than of Latin. Thus this is a prosperous readership, laying claim to what had traditionally been Latinate learning.[5] However, the exact group into which the commissioning readership of this scientific manuscript would fall, whether trained professionals or merchants, is more difficult to determine. It is known, however, that during the second half of the fifteenth century the manuscript was for a time owned by a member of the household of a wealthy London draper and mayor.[6] But even if the intended, commissioning audience was not the same as its eventual readership, it is clear that the treatise on the seven liberal arts would be a particularly attractive text for powerful mercantile audiences, because it contains some details that would resonate with their social ambitions. In addition to the seven standard liberal arts, the treatise mentions "another seven" that are not to be considered "special sciences," but rather "vsual or comune craftis and hand werkis the whiche bien daily vsed and exercised of comune artificers and werkmen" (ordinary or common crafts and handiwork which are daily used and practiced by common practitioners and workmen). These seven correspond to what encyclopedic tradition had classified as the seven "mechanical" or "productive" sciences.[7] The treatise lists agriculture, hunting, "physic" or medical knowledge, weaving, theatre, weaponry, and navigation (including commerce and shipping). Beyond this, the treatise links some of these useful arts with contemporary trades: it lists fishmongers, butchers, tanners, brewers, tailors, hosiers, drapers, fullers, shearmen, and skinners.[8] Most importantly, the treatise draws a sharp distinction between such practical craft knowledges and the intellectual

[4] Mooney, "A Middle English Text on the Seven Liberal Arts," 1036–7.

[5] Barron, "The Expansion of Education in Fifteenth-Century London," 240–5; Doyle, "English Books in and out of Court"; Meale, "Patrons, Buyers, and Owners: Book Production and Social Status."

[6] See M. L. Kekewich et al., eds., *The Politics of Fifteenth-Century London: John Vale's Book* (Gloucester: Alan Sutton, 1995), 108.

[7] See, for example, Hugh of St. Victor, *Didascalicon* 2.20–7.

[8] A few lines later, reference is also made to mercers and grocers, but the full sense of this is obscured by some loss of text at a page break in the manuscript (Mooney, ed., "A Middle English Text on the Seven Liberal Arts," 1035–6, 1052). Mercers and grocers were represented by powerful and prestigious London guilds which sponsored education and counted important city officials among their membership. See A. F. Sutton, *The Mercers of London: Trade, Goods, and People, 1130–1578* (Aldershot: Ashgate, 2005), 161–72.

scope of the liberal arts: "And these seven are not properly called sciences or true knowledges," but represent rather "a kind of knowledge of a thing"; therefore, they are "instruments and ministers to philosophy and to the seven liberal and special sciences."[9] In subordinating the practical knowledge of such contemporary crafts to the philosophical reasoning of the liberal arts, the treatise associates its intended audience with the prestige of an arts education. It represents its intended (or potential) readers as elite possessors of scientific understanding that distinguishes them from the non-scientific communities of the artisanal classes.[10]

Thus in terms of its ultimate reception, this text can represent a moment of arrival: the arts find a London mercantile home in the vernacular, and even the specifically Latin literacy associated with grammar and rhetoric has been converted into an equivalent English-language prestige value. The audience for this text appreciated the time-honored (if also rather old-fashioned) scheme of the seven liberal arts, and the use of Grosseteste's *De artibus liberalibus* lends authority to this vernacular compendium. But even in its relatively conservative treatment of the trivium, it has a number of distinctive features. Most prominently, its treatment of phonetics in the grammar chapter may reflect vernacular pronunciation more than standard Latin usage in the fifteenth century. Most of its coverage of grammar focuses on phonetics, but the elaborate description of how the sounds are formed according to the shapes assumed by the mouth, palate, and throat have no parallels in Priscian or Martianus Capella. The description of *r* as with a "tremelyng folowyng afterward" may indicate English vernacular pronunciation of *r* (with a trill). Thus the text not only conveys scientific knowledge in the vernacular, but reflects back upon its vernacular context. Second, the author of the treatise wears his classical learning with particular pride, foregrounding the traditional authoritative sources (for example, Priscian in the grammar chapter), but also newly prestigious sources, notably Quintilian in the chapter on rhetoric. This last also exemplifies a tendency towards a bellettristic, latinate showcasing among English books produced for the London merchant class of the fifteenth century.[11] The knowledge presented in this text is not only valuable in itself, but it is also a sign of the cultural aspirations of a powerful vernacular audience which lays claim to a learned style.

Text from "A Middle English Text on the Seven Liberal Arts," ed. Mooney, by permission. Middle English characters have been replaced by their modern equivalents.

---

[9] Mooney, ed., "A Middle English Text on the Seven Liberal Arts," 1051–2.

[10] Lindenbaum, "Literate Londoners and Liturgical Change: Sarum Books in City Parishes after 1414."

[11] S. Lindenbaum, "At Whittington's Deathbed: London Merchants and Poets in a Reaction to Artisan Writing," unpublished paper.

Glorious and mervailaus God in al his werkis the verray craft of wisdam of the fader of hevene, whiche in the bigynnyng beyng bifore al creatures, as witnessith scripture, made al creatures of nought, and man after the image and symilitude of the holi Trynite, puttyng hym in so high and grete dignite indowed hym with so grete giftes both in body and in soule, and in so myrry and pleasaunt place of paradice that he myght nat wele have be put in a more jocunde place but if he shuld atteyne to the veray sight of the godhed, so that the body was hole [*whole*] and nat corrupt and greved nat [*did not trouble*] the soule, for the lawe of the flessh was nat contrarye to the lawe of the soule but his outward and inward wittis obeied to reason, reason to his wil, and his wil to God alone. This was cald [*called*] the state of our rightwisnes: and in figure to kene [*proclaim, acknowledge*] therof, man is made of right stature in body that he shuld be also in his soule. But oure first fader thus put in so grete grace whan he was in honour and worship vndirstode it nat, and disobeyeng the comaundement of his maker, had a grevous falle both in werkis [*works*] of the soule and of his body, so that the light of his vnderstandyng was made derke bi ignoraunce, and his desire in wil and affeccioun cam nat to a due terme [*appropriate end*] or ellis passed without mesure his due terme and ende, and also the moevyng power of his body was made fieble and vnparfite [*feeble and imperfect*] thurgh the corrupcioun of the clog of his flesh. Wherfor the Lord of all vertu and God of al connyng [*understanding, learning*] *the veray wisdom of the fader*[12] consideryng the fowl [*foul*] fall both in orignal and actual synne ordeyned remedie whan plener and ful tyme cam, as Seynt Paul seith and *cut out of his passioun vij pilers that*[13] is to say vij sacramentis wasshyng awey bi theym both orignal venyal and actual vnclennes [*sin, uncleanness*]. And bifore this tyme he cut out of the grete tresour of his wisdam other vij pilers as the vij special sciences to helpe man to directe hym in his werkis and to purge al errours, ffor that is thoffice [*the function*] of the vij liberal sciences, as Lincoln[14] saith, to rectifie a mannes operaciouns and to deduce [*lead*] hem from errour to perfeccioun; the werkis that bien in mannes power, they bien in the knowlache of his reason and vndirstondyng or in affecioun and desire of his wil or in bodily moevynges [*motions*] or in bodily desires. Mannes soule considrith ij thynges; ffirst the thynges that he considerith bi his reason he knyttith to guyder [*gathers together*] or dividith and sundrith after their propirte [*nature, properties*] and offrith hem to the wil, that he may cheese [*choose*] and pursue suche thynges as bien convenient [*suitable, appropriate*], or flee and eschewe theym that bien noyous [*harmful, offensive*], and

---

[12] Underlined in the manuscript.   [13] Underlined.
[14] "Lincoln": Robert Grosseteste, bishop of Lincoln from 1235.

disconuenyent.[15] As for our vndirstandyng Gramer enformyth hym with congruyte [*correct agreement*] in spekyng, in writyng, and due pronunciacioun; Logik shewith without errour wherwith he is enformed; and than folowith Rethorik persuadyng what thynge mannes wil shuld mesurably flee or desire;[16] and so thiese iij sciences rectifie the vndirstandyng of mannes soule and bryng it to perfeccioun as it shalbe saide afterward. Furthermore if we bi our moevyng intende any other thyng be side [*beside, apart from*] our moevyng than we divide thingis joyned toguyder or ellis conteigne thynges divide [*i.e. divided*] or assigne to gyve order and situacioun or ellis we make figures and discripciouns or take mesuris of height playne and deepe thynges with suche other many, in the whiche Arsmetrike and Geometry maken direccioun.[17] And if we attende to rectificacioun of our moevyng and nat to thynges that bien made bi bodily moevyng, therfor is Musike specialy ordayned. But yit in thiese thynges we may soone erre, if wee knowe not the situacioun and order of the parties of the world. Also nat al our werkis be ordured but if thei bien mesured bi certyne space and tyme, for Astronomy is necessarie that techith to discerne and knowe the situacioun of the worde with distynccioun of tymes, bi the moevyng of hevene and cours of sterres [*stars*].

Gramer

First the office of Gramer is to enforme our soule with vndirstondyng and with due writyng and thynges vndirstondyng duely to pronounce with congruyte as it is declared in the iiij parties [*four parts*] of Gramer. For the first part that is cald Ortographic informyth in rect and congrue [*proper and correct*] writynge, and it is taught of Prescian in his more volume from the bigynnyng vnto that part wher he saith a letter is the last part of mannes

---

[15] "vij pilers as the vij special sciences to helpe man to directe hym in his werkis and to purge al errours, ffor that is thoffice of the vij liberal sciences, as Lincoln saith ... noyous and disconuenyent," cf. Grosseteste, *De artibus liberalibus*, ed. Baur, I (lines 8–18) and 57. The notion of the arts as remedies for sin is traditional (cf. Vincent of Beauvais, *Speculum doctrinale* book 1, chapter 9). The more general idea of the arts as the path to perfection is an ancient one (cf. Victorinus, *Explanationes*, above, pp. 107–8), and it is found among Carolingian commentators. See Verdier, "L' iconographie des arts libéraux dans l'art du moyen âge jusqu'à la fin du quinzième siècle," 309, on Eriugena. Alcuin, *De grammatica* (*PL* 101:853; and see Alcuin selection above, p. 276), expresses the notion of the sciences as "seven pillars" or columns that support the house of Wisdom, imagery that Grosseteste echoes. See D'Alverny, "La Sagesse et ses sept filles."

[16] Cf. Grosseteste, *De artibus liberalibus*, ed. Baur, I, lines 19–21.

[17] Cf. Grosseteste, *De artibus liberalibus*, ed. Baur, 4, lines 10–14.

voice.[18] But for more cliere knowlache of this part we shuln [*should*] vndirstonde the nature of our lettris, and firste of the v [*five*] vowels the whiche han divers placis and dyvers maners [*diverse places and means*] of their generacioun [*formation*]. The placis, as Remygius saith, been v: the lunges, the throte, the palate, the teeth, and the lippis;[19] the maner of generacioun is in this forme, for generaly whan any substancial voice is caused sumtyme of openyng is more in the mowth outward than withyn toward the lunges and than it is like a triangle whos foote is in the mowth, and the poynt in the throte, and this is the generacioun of the first letter a, and therfor it is in figure like a triangle; or ellis [*else*] it is contrarie wise and than is v caused,[20] and his figure is turned and hath contrarie situacioun. Somtyme the throte is opened equaly on every part, and so is I caused and therfor it hath a Rect [*straight*] and egal [*equal*] figure. The generacioun of o is in rounde openyng of the mowth, so that the tunge and the lippis bowe theym silf in their myddis; but e is gendrid [*formed*] in the inward of the throte and the mowth so that the mowth drawith to roundenesse more than the throte, and therfor his figure is half cercle like a bowe with a part of a strynge in the over ende. And for bicause that the place of the complete generacioun of the letter a is bifore the place of e, the place of e bifore i, and i bifore o, and the generacioun of o is bifore the generacioun of v [*"u"*], therfore thiese vowels be so ordeyned a e i o v.[21] Furthermore the consonauntis bien divided, for sum be semy-vowels [*semi-vowels*] and sum mutis [*mutes*]; a semy vowell hath the sowne [*sound*] of a vowel bifore, but a mvte afterward. The semy vowels bien vj [*six*], and thei bien gendred thurgh touchyng of the tung to on [*one*] of the palatis of the mowth. And if it touche the over palate with streyneng out of the tunge so that the pointe of the tunge towchith the palat so

---

[18] The phrase "more volume" indicates books 1–16 of Priscian's *Institutiones* (or *Priscianus maior*); "that part wher he saith a letter is the last part of mannes voice": cf. 1.3, *GL* 2:6.7, *Littera est pars minima vocis compositae*. The word "last" ("the last part of mannes voice") may be a scribal error for "least" (translating the Latin word *minima*); see Mooney, ed., "A Middle English Text on the Seven Liberal Arts," 1039 n. This is also the beginning of Donatus' *Ars maior*, the section *De littera* (*GL* 4:367.5), on which the author of this treatise may have to some extent depended.

[19] This section on the five "places" from which speech emanates—lungs, throat, palate, teeth, and lips—was possibly suggested by Martianus Capella's chapter on grammar in the *De nuptiis Philologiae et Mercurii*. The reference to Remigius ("as Remygius saith") is probably to a recension of one of the commentaries on Donatus' *Ars maior* attributed to him. See Holtz, *Donat et la tradition de l'enseignement grammatical*, 440–1, 481 and n. 107. See also *Commentum Einsidlense in Donati Artem maiorem* (ed. Hagen) in *GL* 8:219–66. The treatment of the letters, their formation, and phonology reflects some of the teachings of Donatus, Priscian, and Martianus Capella.

[20] "v," i.e. the vowel "u."

[21] "The cavity of the mouth, viewed from the side, is an isosceles triangle whose pointed angle is in the throat for production of the letter A, so the letter is shaped like an isosceles triangle. At the opposite extreme, the angle is reversed, with its pointed angle at the opening of the mouth, for production of the letter V [U], so the shape of that letter is like an upside-down A. In the middle between these two, the letter I [the long vowel i: pronounced as in "see"] is generated when neither end of the mouth is wider, so the shape of the letter is a straight line. The other two vowels are also described in relation to this schema" (Mooney, ed., "A Middle English Text on the Seven Liberal Arts," 1039 n.). On shapes of the letters, cf. Isidore of Seville above, p. 240.

is l causid, but if the tunge be more bowed and in maner with a tremelyng [*trill, vibration*] folowyng afterward than is r gendred.²² And if the tung be in party [*part*] streyned right and in part bowid so that the sowne goth nat oute completely bi the mowth but bi the nosethrillis [*nostrils*] so is n caused. And if the tunge touche the lower palate twies so is x. And if it touche but oones [*once*] with an hissyng sowne than is s gendred, for the sides of the tunge bien joyned to the sides of the palate. And if it touche the outward part with coniunccioun of the inward part of the lippis so is m caused. But the mvtis han iij placis of their generacioun: the lippis with both rowes of the teeth. If it be thurgh touchyng of the lippis, so that the nether [*lower*] smyte vpon the over lippe so is ff, and if this touchyng be more outward so is b, or ellis al without the mowth and so is p. And if the tunge touche the over egge [*edge*] of the teeth moche with so is d caused, or ellis it touchith the same place more withoute [*outside*] neere the teeth and than is t gendred. But if the tung touche the lower egge of the teeth with grete openyng of the mowth so is k, or with litel openyng and than is q, or ellis it is in a meane bitwixt both and so is c. And if the midpoynt of the tunge touche the nether teeth with a maner liftyng vp of the after part and depressioun of the part bi fore [*i.e. the front*] of the tung so is g. And for bi cause that a smoth [*smooth*] place and holl [*wholly*] moist and hote [*hot*] is a goode place for sowne, therfor the consonauntis that bien gendred in suche placis bien cald [*called*] semy vowels, for they sowne wele, but the place of teeth ne is nat playne ne hote [*is neither… nor*] but cald [*cold*] for thei bien made of erthly grosse matier. Also the place of the outward part of the lippis is cold for it is withoute [*outside of*] the mowth in the aire, therfor the consonauntis that bien gendred in theise placis bien cald mvtis, for their fieble [*feeble*] sown & cetera. Gramer also enformeth mannes soule with triewe vndirstandyng of euery part of reasoun bi hym silf bi the secunde part that is cald Ethymologye gyven and taught of Precian in thend [*the end, last part*] of the grete volume.²³ We bien also informed bi gramer in congruite and construccioun of partis of reason to guyder [*together*] bi the third part that is cald Diasintastik gevyn of Prescian in the lasse booke.²⁴

---

²² The "tremelyng" or vibration in pronunciation of the letter r is unique to this text. This indicates that the phonology of Middle English is used as a reference here. See Mooney, ed., "A Middle English Text on the Seven Liberal Arts," 1032.

²³ It is not clear to what part of Priscian's "great volume" (the *Institutiones* 1–16, i.e. the *Priscianus maior*) the author is referring. Priscian deals with *derivatio* in book 2 of the *Institutiones* (*GL* 2:56–68). Perhaps this author also has in mind Priscian's *Partitiones duodecim versuum Aeneidos principalium*, the word-by-word commentary on the opening line of each of the twelve books of the *Aeneid*, which uses *derivatio* as one of its explanatory methods.

²⁴ The reference here is to books 17–18 of Priscian's *Institutiones* (*Priscianus minor*), on syntax (*De constructione*, *GL* 3:106–377). The Greek-derived term *diasynthetica* (syntax) is attested among English Latin authors from the twelfth century onwards, including John of Salisbury, Pseudo-Grosseteste, Richard de Bury, Fortescue. See Latham and Howlett, eds., *Dictionary of Medieval Latin from British Sources*, Fascicule 1, A–L.

Also gramer enformyth a mannes soule with a grete and a due pronunciacioun bi the fourth part cald Prosodie.[25]

Logik

The office of Logik is to discerne and discusse that is formed and vndirstanden bi Gramer bi wey of argument and reason techyng [*teaching*] the forme of resownyng [*reasoning*] in every faculte. And so, as Boice saith, an argument is cald [*called*] a reason of a thyng that is doutful [to] make it certitude and feith of thyng that is douted, but many thynges maken feith, as our sight of thynges that we see, but it is no reason and son [*sound*] argument.[26] And it hath iiij kyndes vnder hym, Induccioun, Exsample, Emtymene [*enthymeme*] and a Silogisme. Induccioun is when an vniversal proposicioun is proeved bi al his [*its*] singuliers. Exsample is whan a thyng is proevid bi another like to hym [*it*]. Emtyme is a short Silogisme includyng only on premisse and oon [*one ... one*] conclusioun. But a Silogisme is an argument the which hath ij premysses and proposicions bifore the conclusioun, the whiche premisses grauntid muste nedely folowe the conclusioun bith the saide premysses. Logik is divided in to iij partis, Diffynicioun, Particioun, and Collectioun. Of Diffynicioun and his partis is treatid in old logik, as in Porphiries predicamentis & cetera.[27] Of Particioun treatith Boes in his divisiouns.[28] But Colleccioun is treatid in dyvers wises in the newe logik, for a disputacioun sumtyme procedith in triewe and necessarie argument the whiche is cald a demonstracioun.[29] And that may nat be but in a Silogisme wher both premisses and the conclusioun bien necessarie proposiciouns. Sumtyme the argument is made in probable proposiciouns the whiche have non evidens, and seme to be triewe to the more partie of wise men, and it is cald a topical reason, as Aristotil shewith in his topikes.[30] Sumtyme the proposiciouns be fals [*false*] in the argument, and semyth to have a diewe [*proper*] forme of a Silogisme, and it hath nat in deede. And this argument longeth [*belongs*]

---

[25] Cf., for example, Donatus, *Ars maior* 1.4, *De pedibus, GL* 4:369–70.

[26] Boethius, *De topicis differentiis*, book 1 (*PL* 64:1180C–1181B); trans. Stump, *Boethius' De topicis differentiis* 39.

[27] Porphyry's *Isagoge*, the basic introduction to Aristotles *Categories* and the teaching of "predicables." The "old logic" (a term that came into use in the twelfth century) comprised Porphyry's *Isagoge*, along with Aristotle's *Categories* and *De interpretatione*.

[28] Boethius, *Liber de divisione, PL* 64:875–92.

[29] The "new logic," which transformed the curriculum beginning in the twelfth century, included the *Prior* and *Posterior Analytics*, *Topics*, and *Sophistical Refutations*. The theory of demonstration is laid out in the *Posterior Analytics*: its function is to demonstrate, by means of the *differentia*, the property of a species.

[30] Aristotle, *Topics* 1.1 (100a30–b20). The text known was the translation of Boethius.

to the Sophister, whos spices and braunches [*species and sub-species*] bien declared in the Elynkes.[31]

Retorik

And in asmoche as thoffice of every craft and konnyng [*knowledge*] is that the artificer owith [*ought*] to do after [*to proceed according to*] his craft, thoffice of an oratour that he owith to do be [*by*] Rethorik is to say wele [*speak well*], as Quyntilian saith,[32] that is to say suche thynges the whiche bien convenient and sufficient to persuade;[33] wheither he persuade or nat, so as he do as longith [*does what pertains/belongs*] to the craft, for as the philosopher saith, an oratour shal nat alwey persuade ne a phisician shal at al tymes make a man [*i.e., heal a person*] though he do as his craft wil, for the whiche he is cald an oratour.[34] And so he intendith principaly to excite and awake theym that [*those who*] bien slugges [*lazy people*] and sleepers, to gyve audacite to fereful and tymerous, and to make theym that bien cruel and boistous,[35] and therfor Rethorik is cald Mercuries rod, with whos end he makith slepers to awake, and with that other end, wakyng men to sleepe. This is the harpe of Orphe, with whos melodie stones and trees bien divided, and a love day is made bitwixt the wulf and the lamb, the dogge and the hare, the calf and the lioun, whan thei here the sweete of this harp.[36] This harp and instrument of the oratour hath vj strynges, that is to say vj partis of the oracioun, as the begynnyng or Introduccioun, Narracioun, Particioun, Confirmacioun, Reprehensioun

---

[31] "Sophister": one who makes sophisms or sophistical arguments. "Elynkes": Aristotle's *De sophisticis elenchis* (*On Sophistical Refutations*), the last book of his logic or *Organon*, translated by Boethius.

[32] *Institutio oratoria* 2.15.38: *rhetoricen esse bene dicendi scientiam*. This definition is so commonplace that the author of this tract need not have taken it directly from Quintilian.

[33] *Institutio oratoria* 2.15.13, paraphrasing Aristotle, *rhetorice est vis inveniendi omnia in oratione persuasibilia* (trans. William of Moerbeke, ed. Schneider) and cf. 2.15.16. See Aristotle, *Rhetoric*, 1355b25.

[34] "the philosopher": Aristotle, whose *Rhetoric* (1355b) is paraphrased here. The same example, illustrating the gap between office (or purpose) and result, is given in Quintilian, *Institutio oratoria* 2.17.23–5 ("The speaker certainly aims to win; but when he has spoken well, even if he does not win, he has fulfilled the demands of his art . . . likewise a doctor seeks his patient's health, but if the force of the disease . . . or some other event, prevents this aim being achieved, he will not cease to be a doctor"), and in Cicero, *De inventione* 1.5.6.

[35] Loosely translating Grosseteste, *De artibus liberalibus*, ed. Baur, 2, lines 3–5: *Estque in eius potestate, affectum animosque torpentes excitare, effrenos modificare, timidos animare, truces mitigare*. The last phrase in the Middle English, "and to make theym that bien cruel and boistous," corresponds with the Latin *effrenos modificare . . . truces mitigare* (to restrain the unruly, to soften the savage); the Middle English phrase seems to be incomplete at this point.

[36] Grosseteste, *De artibus liberalibus*, ed. Baur, 2.3–7: "This is Mercury's rod: with one end of it he gives sleep to the watchful, and with the other end, vigilance to the sleeping. This is the harp of Orpheus, whose melody makes

and Conclusioun.[37] The introduccioun is cald the bigynnyng, wher the juge or the soule of the auditour is inclyned to take or gyve attendans [*attention*] to swiche [*such*] thynges as shalbe saide afterward.[38] Narracioun is a cliere exposicioun of thinges don and in like forme as they bien don[;][39] bi divisioun or Particioun we open and shewe that is [*what is*] accordyng to the processe [*case or legal proceeding*] and wherfor is contrauersie and striff. And also we declare and expowne of what thynges we take our accioun.[40] Confirmacioun is opposicioun of our argument with auctorite.[41] Reprehensioun is a dissolvyng and a ful avoidaunce of contrary reasons.[42] Conclusioun is a crafti end of the oracioun and of the holl processe bifore.[43]

---

rocks and trees follow after it, and with its sweet sound causes peace between the wolf and the lamb, the dog and the hare, and the calf and the lion." Grosseteste seems to be combining several traditions here. The power to arouse or calm emotions was long associated with both eloquence and music. Macrobius' *Commentum in somnium Scipionis* 2.3.8–10, on the power of music to excite or control emotions, may be one source for Grosseteste's passage. Similar imagery, including a citation of Orpheus, appears in Quintilian's treatment of music as a study necessary to the orator: "Everyone knows that music . . . was not only so much studied in ancient times but also so much venerated that Orpheus and Linus . . . were regarded both as musicians and as prophets and wise men. . . . the former, because admiration of him calmed even rude and savage minds, has been believed by later ages to have drawn not only the animals but the rocks and stones after him" (*Institutio oratoria* 1.10.9–10). The rod of Mercury, derived from *Aeneid* 4.242–4, may have been suggested by Macrobius in the *Commentum in somnium Scipionis* or possibly even the *Saturnalia* 1.17.22. The notion introduced here that eloquence, like Mercury's wand, can induce sleep and wakefulness, is unusual, and may be a distant echo of associations between rhetoric and magic. See Ward, "Magic and Rhetoric From Antiquity to the Renaissance." But the mythography of Orpheus' lyre, its power to enchant the rocks and forests and to make peace among beasts (the wolf and the lamb, the hare and the dog), is typically associated with music, as in Martianus Capella's *Marriage of Philology and Mercury* 9.907, on the art of music. The elision of rhetoric with music, in Grosseteste's treatise and in the Middle English text based on it, seems to derive from a chain of sources.

[37] *De inventione* 1.14.19; Isidore, *Etymologiae* 2.7.1.   [38] *De inventione* 1.15.20.   [39] Ibid. 1.20.28.
[40] Ibid. 1.22.31.   [41] Ibid. 1.24.34.   [42] Ibid. 1.42.78.   [43] Ibid. 1.52.98.

SELECT BIBLIOGRAPHIES

1. Primary Sources

Medieval authors are cited by their first names (e.g. Hugh of St. Victor, William of Conches), except for those who are conventionally cited by surname (e.g., Aquinas, Thomas; Abelard, Peter). Anonymous works and collections of writings by multiple authors are listed by the names of their modern editors.

Abelard, Peter. *Dialectica*. Ed. L. M. de Rijk. 2nd edn. (Assen: Van Gorcum, 1970).

—— *Historia calamitatum*. Ed. J. Monfrin. 3rd edn. (Paris: Vrin, 1967).

—— *Theologia christiana*. PL 178:1113–1330.

—— *Peter Abaelards philosophische Schriften*, 1.3: *Die Glossen zu Peri hermeneias*. Ed. B. Geyer. Beiträge zur Geschichte der Philosophie des Mittelalters, 21/3 (Münster: Aschendorff, 1927).

Adam de la Bassée. *Ludus super Anticlaudianum*. Ed. P. Bayart (Lille: G. Frères, 1930).

Adelard of Bath. *De eodem et diverso*. In C. Burnett, ed. and trans., *Adelard of Bath, Conversations with his Nephew* (Cambridge: Cambridge University Press, 1998).

Aegidius Romanus. See Giles of Rome.

Alan of Lille. *Anticlaudianus*. Ed. R. Bossuat (Paris: Vrin, 1955).

—— *Anticlaudianus; or the Good and Perfect Man*. Trans. J. J. Sheridan (Toronto: Pontifical Institute of Mediaeval Studies, 1973).

—— *De planctu Naturae*. Ed. N. Häring, *Studi medievali* (3rd ser.) 19 (1978): 797–879.

—— *Plaint of Nature*. Trans. J. J. Sheridan (Toronto: Pontifical Institute of Mediaeval Studies, 1980).

—— M. T. d'Alverny, ed. *Alain de Lille: Textes inédits* (Paris: Vrin, 1965).

Albertus Magnus. *De antecedentibus ad logicam*. Ed. J. Blarer. *Teoresi: Rivista di cultura filosofica* 9 (1954): 177–233.

Alcuin. *De grammatica*. PL 101:849C–902B.

—— *Disputatio de rhetorica et virtutibus*. In Halm, ed., *Rhetores latini minores*, 525–50.

—— *The Rhetoric of Alcuin and Charlemagne*. Trans. W. S. Howell (Princeton: Princeton University Press, 1941).

Alexander of Hales, OM. *Summa theologica*. 4 vols. Ed. B. Klumper (Florence, 1924–1948).

Alexander of Tralles. *Oeuvres médicales d'Alexandre de Tralles*. Ed. F. L. E. Brunet. 4 vols. (Paris: Librairie orientaliste Paul Geuthner, 1933–7).

Alexander of Villa Dei. *Das Doctrinale des Alexander de Villa-Dei: kritisch-exegetische Ausgabe.* Ed. D. Reichling (New York: Burt Franklin reprint, 1974; originally published 1845).

—— *El Doctrinal: Una gramática latina del Renacimiento del siglo XII.* Trans. M. A. Gutiérrez Galindo (Madrid: Akal, 1993).

—— *Ecclesiale.* Ed. and trans. L. R. Lind (Lawrence: University of Kansas Press, 1958).

Al-Farabi. *The Attainment of Happiness.* In M. Mahdi, trans., *Philosophy of Plato and Aristotle,* rev. ed. (Ithaca: Cornell University Press, 2001).

—— *The Canons of Poetry.* See Cantorino, *Arabic Poetics in the Golden Age.*

—— *Commentary and Short Treatise on Aristotle's "De interpretatione."* Trans. F. W. Zimmerman (London: British Academy and Oxford University Press, 1981).

—— *Al-farabi: Deux ouvrages inédits sur la réthorique.* Ed. J. Langhade and M. Grignaschi, (Beirut: Dar el-Mashreq, 1971).

—— (?). *De ortu scientiarum.* C. Baeumker, ed. *Alfarabi: Über den Ursprung der Wissenschaften (De ortu scientiarum).* Beiträge zur Geschichte der Philosophie des Mittelalters 19.3 (Münster: Aschendorff, 1916).

—— *Philosophy of Plato and Aristotle.* Trans. M. Mahdi, revised edn. with foreword by C. E. Butterworth and T. L. Pangle (Ithaca: Cornell University Press, 2001).

—— *De scientiis.* A. Gonzáles Palencia, ed. *Al-Farabi: Catálogo de las ciencias,* 2nd edn. (Madrid: Consejo Superior de Investigaciones Científicas, 1953).

Al-Ghazali. C. H. Lohr, ed. "*Logica Algazelis*: Introduction and Critical Text." *Traditio* 21 (1965): 223–90.

—— *Philosophiae tractatus.* J. T. Muckle, ed. *Algazel's Metaphysics: A Mediaeval Translation* (Toronto: Institute of Mediaeval Studies, 1933).

Anselm of Havelberg. *Vita Adalberti.* Ed. P. Jaffe. *Bibliotheca rerum germanicarum,* 3 (Berlin, 1866).

Apollonius Dyscolus. *Apollonii Dyscoli quae supersunt, GG* II (II i, *Scripta minora: De pronominibus, De adverbio, de coniunctionibus,* ed. R. Schneider; II ii, *De constructione,* ed. G. Uhlig; II iii, *Fragmenta,* ed. R. Schneider).

—— *Apollonius Dyscole: De la Construction (syntaxe).* Ed. and trans. J. Lallot. 2 vols. (Paris: Vrin, 1997).

—— *Apollonius Dyscole: Traité des Conjonctions.* Ed. and trans. C. Dalimier (Paris: Vrin, 2001).

Aquinas, Thomas. *Expositio super librum Boethii de Trinitate.* Ed. Bruno Decker (Leiden: Brill, 1955).

—— *S. Thomae de Aquino, Expositio libri posteriorum.* Ed. R.-A. Gauthier (Rome: Comissio Leonina/Paris: Vrin, 1989).

—— A. Maurer, trans., *The Division and Methods of the Sciences: Saint Thomas Aquinas* (Toronto: Pontifical Institute of Mediaeval Studies, 1963).

Aristotle. J. Barnes, ed. *The Complete Works of Aristotle: The Revised Oxford Translation*. 2 vols. (Princeton: Princeton University Press, 1984).

—— L. Minio-Paluello, ed. *Aristoteles latinus*, 3.1–4: *Analytica priora* (Bruges-Pars, Desclée de Brouwer, 1962).

—— —— ed. *Aristoteles Latinus*, 33: *De arte poetica, cum Averrois expositione*. 2nd edn. (Brussels: Desclée de Brouwer, 1968).

—— —— ed. *Aristoteles latinus*, 1.1–5: *Categoriae* (Bruges-Paris: Desclée de Brouwer, 1961).

—— —— and G. Verbeke, eds. *Aristoteles Latinus*, 2.1–2: *De interpretatione, vel Periermenias. Translatio Boethii, specimina translationum recentiorum. Translatio Guillelmi de Moerbeka* (Bruges : Desclée de Brouwer, 1965).

—— B. Schneider, ed. *Aristoteles Latinus*, 31.1–2: *Rhetorica*: *Translatio Anonyma sive Vetus et Translatio Guillelmi de Moerbeka* (Leiden: Brill, 1978).

—— *Aristotle's Ars Rhetorica*: *The Arabic Version*. Ed. M. C. Lyons. 2 vols. (Cambridge: Pembroke Arabic Texts (Pembroke College), 1982).

—— *The Rhetoric of Aristotle with a Commentary*, vol. 1. Ed. E. M. Cope and J. E. Sandys. (Cambridge: Cambridge University Press, 1877).

—— *Rhetoric*. G. A. Kennedy, trans., *Aristotle on Rhetoric: A Theory of Civic Discourse* (New York and Oxford: Oxford University Press, 1991).

—— H. Arens, ed. and trans. *Aristotle's Theory of Language and its Tradition: Texts from 500 to 1750* (Amsterdam and Philadelphia: John Benjamins, 1984).

Arnobius Afer. *Adversus nationes libri VII*. Ed. C. Marchesi. 2nd edn. (*Corpus scriptorum latinorum paravianum*. Aug. Taurinorum 1953).

Arnulfi Aurelianensis: Glosule super Lucanum. Ed. B. Marti (Rome: American Academy in Rome, 1958).

Augustine. *De civitate Dei*. Ed. B. Dombert and A. Kalb. 2 vols. *CCSL* 47–8 (Turnhout: Brepols, 1955).

—— *De dialectica*. Ed. J. Pinborg. Trans. B. D. Jackson (Dordrecht; Boston: D. Reidel, 1975).

—— *De doctrina christiana*. Ed. J. Martin. *CCSL* 32 (Turnhout: Brepols, 1962).

—— *Enarrationes in Psalmos*. Ed. E. Dekkers and J. Fraipont. *CCSL* 39 (Turnhout: Brepols, 1956).

—— *In Iohannis evangelium*. Ed. D. R. Willems. *CCSL* 36 (Turnhout: Brepols, 1954).

—— *De natura et origine animae*. In C. F. Urba and J. Zycha, eds. *Opera* 8.1. *CSEL* 60 (Vienna: Tempsky; Leipzig: Freytag, 1913).

—— *De ordine*. In W. M. Green and K.-D. Daur, eds. *Aurelii Augustini opera*, vol. 2. *CCSL* 29 (Turnhout: Brepols, 1970).

Averroes. *Commentaire moyen à la Rhétorique d' Aristote*. Ed. M. Aouad. 3 vols. (Paris: Vrin, 2002).

Avicenna. I. M. Dahiyat, trans. *Avicenna's Commentary on the Poetics of Aristotle: A Critical Study with an Annotated Translation of the Text* (Leiden: Brill, 1974).

—— *Avicenna (Ibn Sina,† 1037), Opera philosophica* (Venice, 1508; rpt. Louvain: Édition de la bibliothèque S. J., 1961).

Bacon, Roger. *Moralis philosophia*. Ed. E. Massa (Zurich: Thesaurus Mundi, 1953).

—— *Opus maius*. Ed. J. H. Bridges (Oxford: Clarendon, 1900).

Baehrens, E., ed. *Poetae latini minores*, vol. 5 (Leipzig: Teubner, 1883).

Balbus, Joannes. *Catholicon*. (Mainz, 1460; rpt. Westmead, England: Gregg International Publishers Limited, 1971).

Becker, F. G., ed. *Pamphilus: Prolegomena zum Pamphilus (de amore) und kritische Textausgabe*. Beihefte zum "Mittellateinischen Jahrbuch" 9 (Ratingen: A. Henn Verlag, 1972).

Bede. *De arte metrica et de schematibus et tropis*. Ed. C. B. Kendall. In *Bedae Venerabilis opera: Opera didascalica*, ed. C. W. Jones. *CCSL* 123A (Turnhout: Brepols, 1975).

—— *Libri II De arte metrica et de schematibus et tropis: The Art of Poetry and Rhetoric*. Ed. and trans. C. B. Kendall (Saarbrücken: AQ-Verlag, 1991).

—— "Bede's *De schematibus et tropis—A Translation*." Trans. G. H. Tannenhaus. *Quarterly Journal of Speech* 48 (1962): 237–53.

Benedicti Regula monachorum. Ed. E. Woelfflin (Leipzig: Teubner, 1895).

Bernard of Chartres. *The Glosae super Platonem of Bernard of Chartres*. Ed. P. E. Dutton. (Toronto: Pontifical Institute of Mediaeval Studies, 1991).

Bernard of Utrecht. *Commentum in Theodolum*: see Huygens, *Accessus ad auctores*.

Bernardus Silvestris. *Cosmographia*. Ed. P. Dronke (Leiden: Brill, 1978).

—— *The Cosmographia of Bernardus Silvestris*. Trans. W. Wetherbee. (New York: Columbia University Press, 1973).

—— *The Commentary on Martianus Capella's De Nuptiis Philologiae et Mercurii Attributed to Bernardus Silvestris*. Ed. H. J. Westra (Toronto: Pontifical Institute of Mediaeval Studies, 1986).

Bland, C., ed. *The Teaching of Grammar in Late Medieval England: An Edition, with Commentary, of Oxford, Lincoln College MS Lat. 130* (East Lansing: Colleagues Press, 1991).

Bode, G. H., ed. *Scriptores rerum mythicarum latini tres* (Cellis, 1834).

Boethius. *In Ciceronis topica*. Ed. E. Stump (Ithaca: Cornell University Press, 1988).

—— *Commentarii in librum Aristotelis Peri hermeneias I–II*. Ed. K. Meiser (Leipzig: Teubner, 1877–80).

—— *The Theological Tractates and the Consolation of Philosophy*. Ed. and trans. H. F. Stewart, E. K. Rand, and S. J. Tester. Loeb Classical Library (Cambridge, Mass.: Harvard University Press, 1973).

—— *De topicis differentiis*. PL 64:1173C–1216D.

—— *Boethius's De topicis differentiis*. Trans. E. Stump (Ithaca: Cornell University Press, 1978).

(Boethius). Pseudo-Boethius, see Weijers, ed.

Bono Giamboni. *Fiore di Rettorica*. Ed. G. Speroni (Pavia: University of Pavia, 1994).

Botschuyver, H. J., ed. *Scholia in Horatium codicum parisinorum latinorum 7972, 7974, 7971* (Amsterdam: Bottenburg, 1935).

—— ed. *Scholia in Horatium codicum parisinorum latinorum 10310 et 7973* (Amsterdam: Bottenburg, 1939).

—— ed. *Scholia in Horatium in codicibus parisinis latinis 17897 et 8223* (Amsterdam: Bottenburg, 1942).

Braulio of Saragossa. *La Renotatio librorum Domini Isidori de Braulio de Zaragoza*. Ed. and trans. J. C Martin (Logrono: Fundación San Millán de la Cogolla 2002).

Brunetto Latini. *Li livres dou Tresor*. Ed. F. J. Carmody (Berkeley and Los Angeles: University of California Press, 1948).

—— *La Rettorica*. Ed. F. Maggini (Florence: Felice le Monnier, 1968).

—— *Le tre orazioni di M. T. Cicerone dette dinanzi a Cesare . . . volgarizzate da Brunetto Latini*. Ed. L. M. Rezzi (Milan: Fanfani, 1832).

Camargo, M., ed. *Medieval Rhetorics of Prose Composition: Five English Artes dictandi and Their Tradition* (Binghamton, New York: Medieval and Renaissance Texts and Studies, 1995).

Cantorino, V., trans. *Arabic Poetics in the Golden Age* (Leiden: Brill, 1975).

Cassiodorus. *Expositio Psalmorum*. Ed. M. Adriaen. *CCSL* 97–8 (Turnhout: Brepols, 1958).

—— *Explanation of the Psalms*. Trans. P. G. Walsh. 3 vols. (New York; Mahwah, New Jersey: Paulist Press, 1990–1).

—— *Cassiodori Senatoris Institutiones*. Ed. R. A. B. Mynors (Oxford: Clarendon Press 1937).

—— *An Introduction to Divine and Human Readings*. Trans. L. W. Jones (New York: Columbia University Press, 1946).

Charland, Th.-M., ed. *Artes praedicandi. Contribution à l'histoire de la rhétorique au moyen âge* (Paris: Vrin; Ottawa: Institut d'études médiévales, 1936).

Charisius. *Flavii Sosipatri Charisii artis grammaticae libri V*. Ed. K. Barwick (Leipzig: Teubner, 1925; rpt. 1964).

Cicero. *Brutus, Orator*. Trans. G. L. Hendrickson and H. M. Hubbell. Loeb Classical Library (Cambridge, Mass.: Harvard University Press; London: Heinemann, 1971).

—— *De inventione*. Ed. E. Stroebel (Leipzig: Teubner, 1915).

—— *De inventione, De optimo genere oratorum, Topica*. Trans. H. M. Hubbell. Loeb Classical Library (Cambridge, Mass.: Harvard University Press; London: Heineman, 1949; rpt. 1976).

—— *Paradoxa stoicorum*. Ed. A. G. Lee (London: MacMillan, 1953).

—— *Partitiones oratoriae*. Ed. R. Giomini (Rome: Herder, 1996).

[Cicero]. *Rhetorica ad Herennium*. Ed. G. Calboli (Bologna: Pàtron, 1969).

—— *Rhetorica ad Herennium*. Ed. and trans. H. Caplan. Loeb Classical Library. (Cambridge, Mass: Harvard University Press; London: Heinemann, 1954; rpt. 1977).

Conrad of Hirsau. *Dialogus super auctores*. See Huygens, *Accessus ad auctores*.

Conrad of Mure. *Konrad von Mure. Summa de arte prosandi*. Ed. W. Kronbichler (Zürich: Fretz und Wasmuth, 1968).

Dante Alighieri. *Convivio*. Ed. F. B. Ageno. 2 vols. (Florence: Casa Editrice Le Lettere, 1995).

Denifle H. and E. Chatelain, eds. *Chartularium Universitatis Parisiensis*. 4 vols. (Brussels: Culture et civilisation, 1964; orig. publ. Paris, 1889–1897).

Disticha Catonis. Ed. M. Boas and H. J. Botschuyver. (Amsterdam: North Holland Publishing Co., 1952).

Donatus, Aelius. *Ars minor, Ars maior*. GL 4:353–402. See also Holtz, *Donat et la tradition de l'enseignement* (secondary sources bibliography).

Donatus, Tiberius Claudius. *Interpretationes Vergilianae*, vol. 1. Ed. H. Georges. (Leipzig: Teubner, 1905; rpt. 1969).

Dybinus, Nicolaus. *Nicolaus Dybinus' Declaracio oracionis de beata Dorothea: Studies and Documents in the History of Late Medieval Rhetoric*. Ed. S. P. Jaffe. (Wiesbaden: Franz Steiner, 1974).

Eberhard of Béthune. *Graecismus*. Ed. J. Wrobel. *Corpus grammaticorum medii aevi*, vol. 1 (Breslau: G. Koebner, 1887).

Ellebaut. *Anticlaudien: A Thirteenth-Century French Adaptation of the Anticlaudianus of Alain de Lille*. Ed. A. J. Creighton (Washington, D.C.: The Catholic University of America Press, 1944).

Elliott, A. G., trans. *Seven Medieval Latin Comedies* (New York: Garland Publishing, 1984).

Ennodius. *Opusculum*, vol 6: *Ambrosio et Beato*. Ed. W. A. Ritter von Hartel. *CSEL* 6 (Vienna: Tempsky, 1882).

Eriugena, John Scotus. "*Eriugena in Priscianum*." Eds. P. E. Dutton and A. Luhtala. *Mediaeval Studies* 56 (1994): 153–63.

—— *Johannis Scotti annotationes in Marcianum*. Ed. C. Lutz (Cambridge, Mass.: Medieval Academy of America, 1939).

Faral, E., ed. *Les arts poétiques du XIIe et du XIIIe siècle* (Paris: Champion, 1924).

Festus, Sextus Pompeius. *De verborum significatione quae supersunt cum Pauli epitome*. Ed. C. O. Müller (Leipzig: Weidmann, 1839).

—— *De verborum significatu quae supersunt cum Pauli epitome*. Ed. W. M. Lindsay (Leipzig: Teubner, 1913).

Folchino dei Borfoni. *Folchini de Borfonibus Cremonina*. Ed. C. DeSantis. *CCCM* 201 (Turnhout: Brepols, 2003).

Fortunatianus. *Ars rhetorica*. Ed. L. Calboli Montefusco (Bologna: Pàtron, 1979). See also Halm, ed., *Rhetores latini minores*, 79–134.

Fredborg, K. M., ed. "*Promisimus*: An Edition." *CIMAGL* 70 (1999): 81–228.

Friis-Jensen, K., ed. "The *Ars Poetica* in Twelfth-Century France: The Horace of Matthew of Vendôme, Geoffrey of Vinsauf, and John of Garland." *CIMAGL* 60 (1990): 319–88.

—— ed. "*Horatius liricus et ethicus*. Two Twelfth-Century School Texts on Horace's Poems." *CIMAGL* 57 (1988): 81–147.

Fulbert of Chartres. *The Letters and Poems of Fulbert of Chartres*. Ed. and trans. F. Behrends (Oxford: Clarendon, 1976).

Funaioli, H., ed. *Grammaticae romanae fragmenta* (Leipzig: Teubner, 1907).

Geoffrey of Vinsauf. *Poetria nova*. In Faral, ed., *Les arts poétiques du XIIe et du XIIIe siècle*, 194–262.

——— *Documentum de modo et arte dictandi et versificandi: Instruction in the Method and Art of Speaking and Versifying*. Trans. R. Parr. (Milwaukee: Marquette University Press, 1968).

——— *Poetria nova of Geoffrey of Vinsauf*. Trans. M. F. Nims. (Toronto: Pontifical Institute of Mediaeval Studies, 1967).

——— *The Poetria nova and its Sources in Early Rhetorical Doctrine*. Trans. E. Gallo. (The Hague; Paris: Mouton, 1971).

——— *The New Poetics (Poetria nova)*. Trans. J. Baltzell Kopp. In Murphy, ed. *Three Medieval Rhetorical Arts*, 27–108.

Gerard of Cremona. *De scientiis*. F. Schupp, ed. and trans. *Über die Wissenschaften/De scientiis: Nach der lateinischen Übersetzung Gerhards von Cremona* (Hamburg: Meiner, 2005).

Gervase of Melkley. *Ars poetica*. Ed. H.-J. Gräbener. Forschungen zur romanischen Philologie 17 (Münster: Aschendorff, 1965).

——— C. Y. Giles, trans. "Gervais of Melkley's Treatise on the Art of Versifying and the Method of Composing in Prose: Translation and Commentary." Ph.D. Diss. Rutgers University, 1973.

Gibson, S., ed. *Statuta antiqua universitatis Oxoniensis* (Oxford: Clarendon, 1931).

Giles of Rome (Aegidius Romanus). *Commentaria in Rhetoricam Aristotelis* (Venice, 1515; rpt. Frankfurt: Minerva, 1968).

——— "The *De differentia rhetoricae, ethicae et politicae* of Aegidius Romanus." Ed. G. Bruni. *The New Scholasticism* 6 (1932): 1–18.

Gower, John. *The Complete Works of John Gower*. Ed. G. C. Macaulay. 4 vols. (Oxford: Clarendon, 1899–1902).

Gregory. *Moralia in Job*. Ed. M. Adriaen. *CCSL* 143 (Turnhout: Brepols, 1979).

Grillius. *Commentum in Ciceronis rhetorica*. Ed. R. Jakob (Munich and Leipzig: Teubner/Saur, 2002).

Grondeux, A., and I. Rosier-Catach, eds. *La Sophistria de Robertus Anglicus* (Paris: Vrin, 2006).

Grosseteste, Robert. *De artibus liberalibus*. In L. Baur, ed., *Die philosophischen Werke des Robert Grosseteste, Bischofs von Lincoln* (Münster: Aschendorff, 1912).

Guido Faba. *Magistri Guidonis Fabe Rota nova*. Ed. A. P. Campbell and V. Pini (Bologna: Istituto per la storia dell'Università di Bologna, 2000).

——— *Guidonis Fabe Summa dictaminis*. Ed. A. Gaudenzi. *Il Propugnatore* n.s. 3.1–2 (1890): 287–338; 345–93.

Gundissalinus, Dominicus. *De divisione philosophiae*. Ed. L. Baur. Beiträge zur Geschichte der Philosophie des Mittelalters, 4.2–3 (Münster: Aschendorff, 1903).

—— *De divisione philosophiae: Über die Einteilung der Philosophie.* Trans. A. Fidora and D. Werner (Freiburg : Herder, 2007).

—— *De processione mundi.* Ed. and trans. M. J. Soto Bruna and C. A. del Real (Pamplona: EUNSA, 1999).

—— *Domingo Gundisalvo: De scientiis.* Ed. M. Alonso Alonso (Madrid and Granada: Escuelas de Estudios Arabes de Madrid y Granada, 1954).

—— [*De scientiis* of Al-Farabi] *Über die Wissenschaften: die Version des Dominicus Gundissalinus.* Ed. and trans. J. H. J. Schneider (Freiburg im Breisgau: Herder, 2006).

Halm, C., ed. *Rhetores latini minores* (Leipzig: Teubner, 1863; rpt. Dubuque, Iowa: Brown Reprint Library, 1964).

Harbert, B., ed. *A Thirteenth-Century Anthology of Rhetorical Poems* (Toronto: Pontifical Institute of Mediaeval Studies, 1975).

Henri d'Andeli. *The Battle of the Seven Arts: A French Poem by Henri d'Andeli, Trouvère of the Thirteenth Century.* Ed. and trans. L. J. Paetow. (Berkeley: University of California Press, 1914).

—— *Les Dits d'Henri d'Andeli.* Ed. A. Corbellari (Paris: Champion, 2003).

—— *Oeuvres de Henri d'Andeli, trouvère Normand du XIIIe siècle.* Ed. A. Héron (Rouen: Cagniard, 1880).

Hermannus Alemannus. *Averrois expositio poeticae* [Averroes' Middle Commentary on Aristotle's *Poetics*]. In Minio-Paluello, *Aristoteles latinus*, 33: *De arte poetica* (see under Aristotle).

Hervieux, L. ed. *Les Fabulistes latins*, 2: *Phèdre et ses anciens imitateurs*, 2nd edn. (Paris: Firmin-Didot, 1894).

—— ed. *Les Fabulistes latins*, 3: *Avianus et ses anciens imitateurs* (Paris: Firmin-Didot, 1894).

Horace. *Opera.* Ed. S. Borzsak (Leipzig: Teubner, 1984).

—— *Satires, Epistles, and Ars poetica.* Trans. H. R. Fairclough (Cambridge, Mass.: Harvard University Press; London: Heinemann, 1926; rpt. 1978).

Hugh of St. Victor. *Didascalicon.* Ed. C. H. Buttimer (Washington, D.C.: Catholic University Press, 1939).

—— *The Didascalicon of Hugh of St. Victor: A Medieval Guide to the Arts.* Trans. J. Taylor. (New York: Columbia University Press, 1961).

—— *De tribus maximus circumstantiis gestorum.* Ed. W. M. Green. *Speculum* 18 (1943): 484–93.

Hugh of Trimberg. *Das "Registrum multorum auctorum" des Hugo von Trimberg.* Ed. K. Langosch. Germanische Studien 235 (Berlin: Emil Ebering, 1942).

Hugh Primas. C. J. McDonough, ed. *The Oxford Poems of Hugh Primas and the Arundel Lyrics* (Toronto: Pontifical Institute of Mediaeval Studies, 1984).

—— F. Adcock, ed. and trans. *Hugh Primas and the Archpoet* (Cambridge: Cambridge University Press, 1994).

Hugo of Pisa. *De dubio accentu, Agiographia, Expositio de symbolo apostolorum.* Ed. G. Cremascoli (Spoleto: Centro Italiano di studi sull'alto medioevo, 1978).

Hugutio (Hugh) of Pisa. *Magnae derivationes.* Ed. A. Marigo, "De Hugucionis Pisani 'Derivationum' latinitate earumque prologo." *Archivum Romanicum: Nuova rivista di filologia romanza* 11 (1927): 98–107.

Hülser, K. *Die Fragmente zur Dialektik der Stoiker: neue Sammlung der Texte mit deutscher Übersetzung und Kommentaren.* 4 vols (Stuttgart, 1987–1988).

Huygens, R. B. C., ed. *Accessus ad auctores: Bernard d'Utrecht, Conrad d'Hirsau* (Leiden: Brill, 1970).

Isidore of Seville. *Differentiae. Isidoro de Sevilla, Diferencias, Libro I.* Ed. and trans. C. Codoñer Merino. (Paris: Les Belles Lettres 1992).

—— *Isidori Hispalensis Episcopi Etymologiarum sive originum libri xx.* Ed. W. M. Lindsay. 2 vols. (Oxford: Clarendon, 1911).

—— *Etymologies Book II: Rhetoric.* Ed. and trans. P. K. Marshall. (Paris: Les Belles Lettres, 1983).

—— *The Etymologies of Isidore of Seville.* Trans. S. A. Barney, W. J. Lewis, J. A. Beach, O. Berghof, with M. Hall (Cambridge: Cambridge University Press, 2006).

Jean de Hanville. *Architrenius.* Ed. and trans. W. Wetherbee (Cambridge: Cambridge University Press, 1994).

Jerome. *Commentarii in Isaiam.* Ed. M. Adriaen. *CCSL* 73 (Turnhout: Brepols, 1963).

—— *Hebraicae quaestiones in libro Geneseos, Liber interpretationis Hebraicorum nominum, Commentarioli in Psalmos, Commentarius in Ecclesiasten.* Ed. P. de Lagarde. *CCSL* 72 (Turnhout: Brepols, 1959).

—— G. J. M. Bartelink, ed. *Hieronymus liber de optimo genere interpretandi (ep. 57): Ein Kommentar* (Leiden: Brill 1980).

John of Garland. *L'Ars lectoria ecclesie de Jean de Garlande: Une grammaire versifiée du XIIIe siècle et ses gloses.* Ed. E. Marguin-Hamon (Turnhout: Brepols, 2003).

—— *Johannes de Garlandia: Carmen de misteriis ecclesie.* Ed. E. Könsgen (Leiden: Brill, 2004).

—— *Johannes de Garlandia: Compendium gramatice.* Ed. T. Haye (Cologne: Böhlau, 1995).

—— *Epithalamium Beate Virginis Marie.* Ed. A. Saiani (Florence: Olschki, 1995).

—— *Morale scolarium of John of Garland.* Ed. L. J. Paetow (Berkeley: University of California Press, 1927).

—— *The Parisiana poetria of John of Garland.* Ed. and trans. T. Lawler. (New Haven and London: Yale University Press, 1974).

John of Salisbury. *Entheticus maior and minor.* Ed. and trans. J. van Laarhoven. 3 vols. (Leiden: Brill, 1987).

—— *Metalogicon.* Ed. C. C. I. Webb (Oxford: Clarendon, 1929).

—— *The Metalogicon of John of Salisbury: A Twelfth-Century Defense of the Verbal and Logical Arts of the Trivium.* Trans. D. D. McGarry. (Berkeley: University of California Press, 1955).

—— *Policraticus.* Ed. C. C. I. Webb. 2 vols. (Oxford: Clarendon, 1909).

Keller, O., ed. *Pseudacronis scholia in Horatium vetustiora*. 2 vols. (Leipzig: Teubner, 1902–1904).

Kilwardby, Robert. *In Donati Artem Maiorem III*. Ed. L. Schmuecker (Brixen: Weger 1984).

—— *De ortu scientiarum*. Ed. A. G. Judy (Toronto: Pontifical Institute of Mediaeval Studies; London: British Academy, 1976).

—— *On Time and Imagination: De tempore, De spiritu fantastico*. Part 1, ed. P. Osmund Lewry. Part 2, trans. A. Broadie (Oxford: Oxford University Press, 1987–1993).

Lactantius. *Institutions divines*. Ed. P. Monat et al. 6 vols. Sources chrétiennes (Paris: Éditions du Cerf, 1973–2007).

Lafleur, C., ed. *Quatre introductions à la philosophie au XIIIe siècle* (Montreal: Institut d'études médiévales; Paris: Vrin, 1988).

—— and J. Carrier, eds. *Le "Guide de l'étudiant" d'un maître anonyme de la Faculté des arts de Paris au XIIIe siècle* (Quebec: Laboratoire de philosophie ancienne et médiévale de la Faculté de philosophie de l'Université Laval, 1992).

Latini, Brunetto. See Brunetto Latini.

Lydgate, John. *Fall of Princes*. Ed. H. Bergin. 4 vols. Early English Text Society, extra series 121–4 (London: Oxford University Press, 1924–7).

Macrobius. *Opera*. Ed. J. Willis. 2 vols. (Leipzig: Teubner, 1970).

Marco, M. de, and Fr. Glorie, eds. *Variae collectiones aenigmatum Merovingicae aetatis; De dubiis nominibus*. CCSL 133–133A (Turnhout: Brepols, 1968).

Mari, G. *I trattati medievali di ritmica latina* (Bologna: Forni, 1899; orig. publ. Milan: Bibliotheca musica Bononiensis, 1899).

Marie de France. *Lais*. Ed. A. Ewert (Oxford: Blackwell, 1944).

Martianus Capella. *De nuptiis Philologiae et Mercurii*. Ed. J. Willis (Leipzig: Teubner, 1983).

—— *Martianus Capella and the Seven Liberal Arts*, 2: *The Marriage of Philology and Mercury*. Trans. W. H. Stahl and R. Johnson with E. L. Burge (New York: Columbia University Press, 1977).

Martin of Laon (?). Dunchad. *Glossae in Martianum*. Ed. C. Lutz (Lancaster, PA.: American Philological Association, 1944).

Matthew of Vendôme. *Ars versificatoria*. In Faral, ed., *Les arts poétiques du XIIe et du XIIIe siècle*, 106–93.

—— *Ars versificatoria*: *The Art of the Versemaker*. Trans. R. Parr. (Milwaukee, Wis.: Marquette University Press, 1981).

—— *Mathei Vindocinensis opera*. Ed. F. Munari. 3 vols. (Rome: Edizioni di Storia e Letteratura, 1977–1988).

—— "Matthew of Vendôme: Introductory Treatise on the Art of Poetry." Trans. E. Gallo. *Proceedings of the American Philosophical Society* 118 (1974): 51–92.

—— *The Art of Versification*. Trans. A. E. Galyon. (Ames: Iowa State University Press, 1980).

Matthias of Linköping. *Magister Mathias Lincopensis, Testa Nucis and Poetria*. Ed. and trans. B. Bergh. Samlingar utgivna av Svenska Fornskriftsällskapet, ser. 2, vol. IX:2 (Arlöv: Berlings, 1996).

Metamorphosis Goliae. Ed. R. B. C. Huygens. "Mitteilungen aus Handschriften." *Studi Medievali* (ser. 3) 3.2 (1962): 747–72.

Minnis, A. J., and B. Scott, eds., with D. Wallace, *Medieval Literary Theory and Criticism, c.1100–c.1375: The Commentary Tradition* (Oxford: Clarendon, 1988).

Mooney, L., ed. "A Middle English Text on the Seven Liberal Arts." *Speculum* 68 (1993): 1027–52.

Murphy, J. J., ed. *Three Medieval Rhetorical Arts* (Berkeley and Los Angeles: University of California Press, 1971).

Neckam, Alexander. *Commentum super Martianum*. Ed. C. J. McDonough (Florence: SISMEL Edizioni del Galluzzo, 2006).

—— *De naturis rerum, De laudibus divinae sapientiae*. Ed. T. Wright. Rolls Series (London: Longman, 1863).

—— *Sacerdos ad altare*. In T. Hunt, *Teaching and Learning Latin in Thirteenth-Century England* (Cambridge: D. S. Brewer, 1991), 1:269–72.

—— *Suppletio defectuum, Book 1. Alexander Neckam on Plants, Birds, and Animals: A Supplement to the Laus sapientie divine*. Ed. and trans. C. J. McDonough. (Florence: SISMEL edizioni del Galluzzo, 1999).

Nicholas of Lyre. *Bibliae iampridem renovatae partes sex cum glossa ordinaria et expositione N. de Lyra* (Basel, 1501).

Notker the German. *Notkers des Deutschen Werke* I/1.2. Ed. E. H. Sehrt and T. Starck. Altdeutsche Textbibliothek 32 (Halle: Max Niemeyer, 1933).

Otto of Freising. *Gesta Frederici I imperatoris*. Ed. G. Waitz (Hannover and Leipzig: Hahn, 1912).

Palaemon (Pseudo). *Ps. Remmii Palaemonis Regulae*. Ed. M. Rosellini (Hildesheim: Olms 2001).

Persius. *Satires*. S. M. Braund, trans. *Juvenal and Persius*. Loeb Classical Library (Cambridge, Mass.: Harvard University Press, 2004).

Peter of Poitiers. *Allegoriae super tabernaculum Moysi*. Ed. P. S. Moore and J. A. Corbett (Notre Dame: University of Notre Dame Publications in Mediaeval Studies, 1938).

Petrus Compostellanus. *De consolatione rationis*. Ed. P. B. Soto. Beiträge zur Geschichte der Philosophie und Theologie des Mittelalters 8 (Münster: Aschendorff, 1912).

Petrus Helias. "The *Summa* of Petrus Helias on Priscianus minor." Ed. J. E. Tolson. Introduction by M. Gibson. *CIMAGL* 27–28 (1978).

—— *Summa super Priscianum*. Ed. L. Reilly. 2 vols. (Toronto: Pontifical Institute of Mediaeval Studies, 1993).

Plato. J. H. Waszink, ed. *Plato latinus*, 4: *Timaeus a Calcidio translatus* (London and Leiden: Warburg Institute and Brill, 1962).

Priscian. *Institutiones grammaticae. GL* 2–3.

—— *Prisciani Caesariensis opuscula*. Ed. M. Passalacqua. 2 vols. (Rome : Edizioni di Storia e Letteratura, 1987–1999).

Promisimus gloss. See Fredborg, ed.

Quintilian. *Institutio oratoria*. Trans. H. E. Butler. 4 vols. Loeb Classical Library (Cambridge, Mass.: Harvard University Press; London: Heinemann, 1920).

—— (Ps.). *Declamationes XIX maiores Quintiliano falso ascriptae*. Ed. L. Håkanson (Stuttgart: Teubner, 1982).

Ralph of Beauvais. *Glose super Donatum*. Ed. C. H. Kneepkens (Nijmegen: Ingenium, 1982).

—— *Liber Tytan*. Ed. C. H. Kneepkens (Nijmegen: Ingenium, 1991).

Ralph of Longchamps. *In Anticlaudianum Alani commentum*. Ed. J. Sulowski (Wroclaw: Wydawnictwo Polskiej Akademii Nauk, 1972).

Remigius of Auxerre. *In Artem Donati minorem commentum*. Ed. W. Fox (Leipzig: Teubner, 1902).

—— *Commentum in Martianum Capellam*. Ed. C. Lutz. 2 vols. (Leiden: Brill, 1962–1965).

—— M. de. Marco, ed. "Remigii inedita." *Aevum* 26 (1952): 495–517.

—— R. B. C. Huygens, ed. "Remigiana." *Aevum* 28 (1954): 330–44.

—— R. B. C. Huygens, ed. *Serta Mediaevalia: Textus varii saeculorum X–XIII*. CCCM 171 (Turnhout: Brepols 2000).

Robert of Melun. *Oeuvres de Robert de Melun*, vol. 3: *Sententie*, Part I. Ed. R. M. Martin, (Louvain: Spicilegium Sacrum Lovaniense, 1947).

Rockinger, L., ed. *Briefsteller und Formelbücher des elften bis vierzehnten Jahrhunderts*. 2 vols. (New York: B. Franklin, 1961; orig. publ. Munich, 1863–1864).

Romanus, C. Julius. D. M. Schenkeveld, ed. and trans. *A Rhetorical Grammar: C. Iulius Romanus: Introduction to the Liber de adverbio (as incorporated in Charisius' Ars grammatica II 13)* (Leiden: Brill, 2004).

Rufus, Quintus Curtius. *Historia Alexandri Magni*. Ed. and trans. J. C. Rolfe. Loeb Classical Library (Cambridge, Mass.: Harvard University Press, 1946).

Rupert of Deutz. *De sancta trinitate et operibus eius*. Ed. H. Haacke. CCCM 21–4 (Turnhout: Brepols, 1971–1972).

Scholia in Horatium. See Botschuyver, H.

Sedulius Scotus. *In Donati Artem minorem; In Priscianum; In Eutychem*. Ed. B. Löfstedt, CCCM 40 C (Turnhout: Brepols, 1977).

Servius. *Servii grammatici qui feruntur in Vergilii carmina commentarii*. Ed. G. Thilo and H. Hagen. 3 vols. (Leipzig: Teubner, 1881–1887).

Sidonius Apollinaris. *Epistles*. Ed. and trans. W. B. Anderson. Loeb Classical Library. (Cambridge, Mass.: Harvard University Press; London: Heinemann, 1964).

Siger de Courtrai. G. Wallerand, ed. *Les philosophes Belges*, 8: *Les oeuvres de Siger de Courtrai* (Louvain: Institut supérieur de philosophie de l'Université, 1913).

Siger de Courtrai. *Sigerus de Cortraco: Summa modorum significandi: sophismata*. Ed. G. Wallerand and J. Pinborg. (Amsterdam: John Benjamins, 1977).

Solinus, Caius Julius. *Collectanea rerum memorabilium*. Ed. T. Mommsen (Berlin: Weidmann, 1895; rpt. 1958).

Terentianus Maurus. *De litteris, de syllabis, de metris*. Ed. C. Cignolo. 2 vols. *Collectanea grammatica latina* 6.2.1–2 (Hildesheim: Olms-Weidmann, 2002).

—— *De syllabis*. Ed. and trans. J.-W. Beck (Göttingen: Vandenhoeck & Ruprecht, 1992.)

Thierry of Chartres. K. M. Fredborg, ed. *The Latin Rhetorical Commentaries by Thierry of Chartres*. (Toronto: Pontifical Institute of Mediaeval Studies, 1988).

—— N. Häring, ed. *Commentaries on Boethius by Thierry of Chartres and His School*. (Toronto: Pontifical Institute of Mediaeval Studies, 1971).

Thomas of Chobham. *Sermones*. Ed. F. Morenzoni. *CCCM* 82 A (Turnhout: Brepols, 1993).

—— *Summa de arte praedicandi*. Ed. F. Morenzoni, *CCCM* 82 (Turnhout: Brepols, 1988).

—— *Summa confessorum*. Ed. F. Broomfield (Louvain and Paris: Nauwelaerts, 1968).

Thomas of Erfurt. *Grammatica speculativa of Thomas of Erfurt*. Ed. and trans. G. L. Bursill-Hall (London: Longman, 1972).

Thomson, D., ed. *An Edition of the Middle English Grammatical Texts* (New York and London: Garland, 1984).

Timelli, M. *Traductions françaises de l'Ars minor de Donat au moyen âge (XIIIe–XVe siècles)* (Florence: La Nuova Italia Editrice, 1996).

Trevisa, John. *The Governance of Kings and Princes*. Ed. D. C. Fowler, C. F. Briggs, and P. G. Remley (New York and London: Garland, 1997).

Tyconius. *The Book of Rules of Tyconius*. Ed. F. C. Burkitt. (Cambridge: Cambridge University Press, 1894).

Varro. *De lingua latina quae supersunt*. Ed. G. Goetz and F. Schoell (Leipzig: Teubner, 1910).

Victorinus. *Ars grammatica*. Ed. I. Mariotti (Florence: Felice le Monnier, 1967).

—— *Explanationes in Ciceronis rhetoricam*. In Halm, ed., *Rhetores latini minores*, 153–304.

—— *Explanationes in Ciceronis rhetoricam*. Ed. A. Ippolito. *CCSL* 132 (Turnhout: Brepols, 2006).

Vincent of Beauvais (Vincentius Bellovacensis). *Speculum maius*. 4 vols. (Douai, 1624; rpt. Graz: Akademische Druck, 1964–1965).

—— *De morali principis institutione*. Ed. R. J. Schneider. *CCCM* 137 (Turnhout: Brepols, 1995).

Virgil. *Eclogues, Georgics, Aeneid I–VI*. Ed. and trans. H. R. Fairclough. Loeb Classical Library, rev. edn. (Cambridge, Mass.: Harvard University Press, 1999).

—— Brugnoli, G. and F. Stok, eds. *Vitae Vergilianae Antiquae* (Rome: Istituto poligrafico, 1997).

—— Hardie, C., ed. *Vitae Vergilianae Antiquae*. 2nd edn. (Oxford: Clarendon, 1963).

Virgilius Maro. *Virgilio Marone grammatico, Epitomi ed Epistole*. Ed. G. Polara, with Italian translation by L. Caruso and G. Polara (Naples: Liguori 1979).

—— *Virgilius Maro grammaticus: Opera omnia*. Ed. B. Löfstedt (Munich: Saur; Leipzig: Teubner, 2003).

Vitae Vergilianae. See under Virgil.

Walter of Châtillon. *Alexandreis*. Ed. M. Colker (Padua: Antenore, 1978).

—— *Alexandreis*. Trans. R. T. Pritchard (Toronto: Pontifical Institute of Mediaeval Studies, 1986).

—— *The Alexandreis of Walter of Châtillon: A Twelfth-Century Epic*. Trans. D. Townsend. (Philadelphia: University of Pennsylvania Press, 1996).

Walther, H., ed. *Initia carminum ac versuum Medii Aevi posterioris Latinorum*. Carmina medii aevi posterioris latina 1 (Göttingen: Vandenhoeck and Ruprecht, 1959).

—— ed. *Proverbia sententiaeque latinitatis medii aevi*, vol. 5. Carmina medii aevi posterioris latina 2 (Göttingen: Vendenhoeck and Ruprecht, 1964).

Weijers, O., ed. Pseudo-Boethius, *De disciplina scholarium*. Leiden: Brill, 1976.

Westra, H. J., ed. with C. Vester. *The Berlin Commentary on Martianus Capella's De Nuptiis Philologiae et Mercurii*, vol. 1 (Leiden: Brill, 1994).

—— and T. Kupke, eds., with B. Garstad. *The Berlin Commentary on Martianus Capella's De Nuptiis Philologiae et Mercurii*, vol. 2 (Leiden: Brill, 1998).

William of Conches. *Glosae super Platonem*. Ed. E. Jeauneau. *CCCM* 203 (Turnhout: Brepols, 2006).

—— *Philosophia*. Ed. G. Maurach (Pretoria: University of South Africa, 1980).

—— *William of Conches: A Dialogue on Natural Philosophy (Dragmaticon philosophiae)*. Trans. I. Ronca and M. Curr. (Notre Dame: University of Notre Dame Press, 1997).

William of Tyre. *Historia rerum in partibus transmarinis gestarum*. Ed. R. B. C. Huygens. *CCCM* 63–63A (Turnhout: Brepols, 1986).

Woods, M. C., ed. and trans. *An Early Commentary on the Poetria nova of Geoffrey of Vinsauf* (New York and London: Garland, 1985).

Wyclif. *The Holy Bible, containing the old and new testaments with the apocryphal books in the earliest English versions made from the Latin vulgate by John Wycliffe and his followers*. 4 vols. Eds. J. Forshall and F. Madden (Oxford: Oxford University Press, 1850; rpt. New York: AMS Press, 1982).

Wyclif, John. *De veritate sacrae scripturae*. Ed. R. Buddensieg. 3 vols. (London: Wyclif Society, 1905–1907).

Ysagoge in theologiam. Ed. A. Landgraf. *Écrits théologiques de l'École d'Abélard* (Louvain: Spicilegium sacrum Lovaniense, 1934).

Zechmeister, J., ed. *Scholia Vindobonensia ad Horatii artem poeticam* (Vienna, 1877).

Ziolkowski, J. M., and M. C. J. Putnam, eds. *The Virgilian Tradition: The First Fifteen Hundred Years* (New Haven and London: Yale University Press, 2008).

2. SECONDARY SOURCES

Alessio, G. "Brunetto Latini e Cicerone (e i dettatori)." *Italia medioevale e humanistica* 22 (1979): 123–69.

—— "The Rhetorical Juvenilia of Cicero and the *Artes Dictandi*." In Cox and Ward, eds., *The Rhetoric of Cicero* (2006): 335–64.

Allen, J. "The Stoics on the Origin of Language and the Foundations of Etymology." In Frede and Inwood, eds., *Language and Learning: Philosophy of Language in the Hellenistic Age* (2005): 14–35.

Allot, S. *Alcuin of York: His Life and Letters* (York: William Sessions, 1974).

Alonso, M. "Hugo de San Víctor, refutado por Domingo Gundisalvo hacia el 1170." *Estudios eclesiásticos* 21 (1947): 209–16.

Alverny, M.-Th. d'. "La Sagesse et ses sept filles: recherches sur les allégories de la philosophie et des arts libéraux du IXe au XIIe siècle." *Mélanges dédiés à la mémoire de Félix Grat* 1 (Paris: En dépôt chez Mme Pecqueur-Grat, 1946): 245–78.

Amsler, M. *Etymology and Grammatical Discourse in Late Antiquity and the Early Middle Ages* (Amsterdam and Philadelphia: John Benjamins, 1989).

Anawati, G. C., and A. Z. Iskandar. "Hunayn ibn Ishaq." In *Dictionary of Scientific Biography*, 15 [Supplement 1] (New York: Scribner, 1978): 230–49.

Aouad, M. "La doctrine rhétorique d'Ibn Ridwan et la *Didascalia in Rhetoricam Aristotelis ex glosa Alpharabii*." *Arabic Sciences and Philosophy* 7 (1997): 163–245, and 8 (1998): 131–60.

—— "La *Rhétorique*. Tradition syriaque et arabe." In R. Goulet, ed., *Dictionnaire des philosophes antiques* (Paris: CNRS, 1989): 1:455–72.

—— "Les fondements de la *Rhétorique* d'Aristote reconsidérés par Farabi, ou le concept de point de vue immédiat et commun." *Arabic Sciences and Philosophy* 2 (1992): 133–80.

—— and M. Rashed, "L'exégèse de la *Rhétorique* d'Aristote: recherches sur quelques commentateurs grecs, arabes et byzantins. Première partie." *Medioevo: Rivista di storia della filosofia medievale* 23 (1997): 43–189.

Arts libéraux et philosophie au moyen âge (Montréal: Institut d'études médiévales; Paris: Vrin, 1969).

Astell, A. W. "Cassiodorus's *Commentary on the Psalms* as an *Ars rhetorica*." *Rhetorica* 17 (1999): 37–75.

Auroux, S., et al., eds. *History of Linguistics 1999: Selected Papers from the Eighth International Conference on the History of the Language Sciences* (Amsterdam: John Benjamins, 2003).

Ax, W. *Laut, Stimme und Sprache: Studien zu drei Grundbegriffen der antiken Sprachtheorie* (Göttingen: Vandenhoeck and Ruprecht, 1986).

—— "*Quadripertita ratio*. Bemerkungen zur Geschichte eines aktuellen Kategoriensystems (Adiectio-Detractio-Transmutatio-Immutatio)." *HL* 13 (1986): 191–214.

—— "Zum *de voce*-Kapitel der Römischen Grammatik, eine Antwort auf Dirk M. Schenkeveld und Wilfried Stroh." In Swiggers and Wouters, eds. *Grammatical Theory and Philosophy of Language in Antiquity* (2002): 121–41.

Bacherler, M. "Cassiodors Dichterkenntnisse und Dichterzitate." *Bayerische Blätter für das Gymnasial-Schulwesen* 59 (1923): 215–19.

Backes, H. *Die Hochzeit Merkurs und der Philologie: Studien zu Notkers Martian-Übersetzung* (Sigmaringen: Thorbecke, 1982).

Baldwin, J. W. *Masters, Princes, and Merchants: The Social Views of Peter the Chanter and his Circle*, 2 vols. (Princeton: Princeton University Press, 1970).

Baratin, M. *La naissance de la syntaxe à Rome* (Paris: Éditions de Minuit, 1989).

—— "Priscian." In Stammerjohann et al., eds., *Lexicon grammaticorum* (1996): 756–9.

—— and F. Desbordes, "La 'troisième partie' de l'*ars grammatica*." *HL* 13 (1986): 215–40.

—— and A. Garcea, eds. *Autour du De Adverbio de Priscien*, special issue of *Histoire, Épistémologie, Langage* 27.2 (2005).

Barron, C. "The Expansion of Education in Fifteenth-Century London." In J. Blair and B. Golding, eds., *The Cloister and the World: Essays on Medieval History in Honour of Barbara Harvey* (Oxford, 1995): 219–45.

Barwick, K. *Probleme der stoischen Sprachlehre und Rhetorik* (Berlin: Akademie-Verlag, 1957).

—— *Remmius Palaemon und die römische Ars grammatica* (Leipzig: Dieterich, 1922).

Baswell, C. *Virgil in Medieval England : Figuring the Aeneid from the Twelfth Century to Chaucer* (Cambridge: Cambridge University Press, 1995).

Beck, J.-W. "Terentianus Maurus *non paenitendus inter ceteros artis metricae auctor*." In W. Haase, ed., *Aufstieg und Niedergang der römischen Welt*, II 34.4 (Berlin/New York: De Gruyter, 1998): 3208–68.

—— *Zur Zuverlässigkeit der bedeutendsten lateinischen Grammatik. Die* ars des Aelius Donatus. *Abhandlungen d. Geistes- und Sozialwissenschaftlichen Klasse. Akademie der Wissenschaften und der Literatur Mainz* (Stuttgart: Franz Steiner Verlag, 1996).

Beltran, E. "Les *Questions* sur la *Rhétorique* d'Aristote de Jean de Jandun." In Dahan and Rosier-Catach, eds., *La Rhétorique d'Aristote* (1998): 153–67.

Bennett, B. S. "The Significance of the *Rhetorimachia* of Anselm de Besate to the History of Rhetoric." *Rhetorica* 5 (1987): 231–50.

Benton, J. F. "Philology's Search for Abelard in the *Metamorphosis Goliae*." *Speculum* 50 (1975): 199–217.

Bergner, K. *Der Sapientia-Begriff im Kommentar des Marius Victorinus zu Ciceros Jugendwerk De Inventione* (Frankfurt: Peter Lang, 1994).

Biard, J. "Rapport de la Table ronde: les disciplines du trivium." In Weijers and Holtz, eds., *L'enseignement des disciplines à la Faculté des arts* (1997): 173–82.

—— "Science et rhétorique dans les *Questions sur la Rhétorique* de Jean Buridan." In Dahan and Rosier-Catach, eds., *La Rhétorique d'Aristote* (1998): 135–52.

Bieler, L. "*Vindicta scholarium*: Beiträge zur Geschichte eines Motivs." In R. Muth et al., eds., *Serta Philologica Aenipontana*. Innsbrucker Beiträge zur Kulturwissenschaft 7–8 (Innsbruck: Felizian Rauch, 1962): 83–5.

Black, D. L. "The 'Imaginative Syllogism' in Arabic Philosophy: A Medieval Contribution to the Philosophical Study of Metaphor." *MS* 51 (1989): 241–67.

—— *Logic and Aristotle's Rhetoric and Poetics in Medieval Arabic Philosophy* (Leiden: Brill, 1990).

—— "Tradition and Transformations in the Medieval Approach to Rhetoric and Related Linguistic Arts." In Lafleur and Carrier, eds., *L'enseignement de la philosophie au XIIIe siècle* (1997): 233–54.

Black, R. *Humanism and Education in Medieval and Renaissance Italy: Tradition and Innovation in Latin Schools from the Twelfth to the Fifteenth Century* (Cambridge: Cambridge University Press, 2001).

—— "The Vernacular and the Teaching of Latin in Thirteenth- and Fourteenth-Century Italy." *StM*, ser. 3, 37/2 (1996): 703–51.

Blank, D. L. *Ancient Philosophy and Grammar: The Syntax of Apollonius Dyscolus* (Chico: Scholars Press [American Philological Association], 1982).

Bloch, R. H. *Etymologies and Genealogies: A Literary Anthropology of the French Middle Ages* (Chicago and London: University of Chicago Press, 1983).

Boggess, W. "Alfarabi and the *Rhetoric*: The Cave Revisited." *Phronesis* 15 (1970): 86–90.

—— "Hermannus Alemannus' Rhetorical Translations." *Viator* 2 (1971): 227–50.

Bossuat, R. "Quelques personnes cités par Alain de Lille." In *Mélanges d'histoire du moyen âge dédiés à la mémoire de Louis Halphen* (Paris: Presses Universitaires de France, 1951): 33–42.

Bottin, L. *Contributi della tradizione greco-latina e arabo-latina al testo della Retorica di Aristotele* (Padova: Antenore, 1977).

Bourgain, P. "Le vocabulaire technique de la poésie rythmique." *ALMA* 51 (1992–3): 139–93.

Boutemy, A. "Recherches sur le *Floridus aspectus* de Pierre la Rigge." *Moyen âge* 54 (1948): 89–112, continued in *Latomus* 8 (1949): 159–68; 283–301; 451–81.

Briesemeister, D. "The *Consolatio philosophiae* in Medieval Spain." *Journal of the Warburg and Courtauld Institutes* 53 (1990): 61–70.

Briggs, C. F. "Aristotle's *Rhetoric* in the Later Medieval Universities: A Reassessment." *Rhetorica* 25 (2007): 243–68.

—— *Giles of Rome's De regimine principum: Reading and Writing Politics at Court and University, c. 1275–c. 1525* (Cambridge: Cambridge University Press, 1999).

Bright, P. *The Book of Rules of Tyconius: Its Purpose and Inner Logic* (Notre Dame: University of Notre Dame Press, 1988).

Brooke, C. "John of Salisbury and his World." In Wilks, ed., *The World of John of Salisbury* (1984): 1–20.

Brown, C. J. "A Late Medieval Cultural Artifact: *The Twelve Ladies of Rhetoric (Les Douze Dames de Rhétorique)*." *Allegorica* 16 (1995): 73–105.

Brown, G. H. *Bede the Venerable* (Boston: Twayne, 1987).

Buridant, C., ed. *L'étymologie de l'Antiquité à la Renaissance. Lexique* 14 (1998).

Burnett, C. F. "Arabic into Latin in Twelfth-Century Spain: The Works of Hermann of Carinthia." *Mittelateinisches Jahrbuch* 13 (1978): 100–34.

—— "Arabic into Latin: The Reception of Arabic Philosophy into Western Europe." In P. Adamson and R. Taylor, eds., *The Cambridge Companion to Arabic Philosophy* (Cambridge: Cambridge University Press, 2004): 370–404.

—— "The Blend of Latin and Arabic Sources in the Metaphysics of Adelard of Bath, Hermann of Carinthia, and Gundisalvus." In Lutz-Bachmann et al., eds., *Metaphysics in the Twelfth Century* (2004): 41–65.

—— "The Contents and Affiliation of the Scientific Manuscripts Written at, or Brought to, Chartres in the Time of John of Salisbury." In Wilks, ed., *The World of John of Salisbury* (1984): 127–60.

—— *Magic and Divination in the Middle Ages: Texts and Techniques in the Islamic and Christian Worlds* (Aldershot: Variorum, 1996).

—— "Vincent of Beauvais, Michael Scot, and the New Aristotle." In Lusignan and Paulmier-Foucart, eds., *Lector et compilator: Vincent de Beauvais* (1997): 189–213.

—— and D. Jacquart, eds. *Constantine the African and ʿAlî ibn al-ʿAbbâs al-Magûsî: The Pantegni and Related Texts* (Leiden: Brill, 1994).

Bursill-Hall, G. "Johannes de Garlandia—Forgotten Grammarian and the Manuscript Tradition." *HL* 3 (1976): 155–77.

—— *Speculative Grammars of the Middle Ages* (The Hague: Mouton, 1971).

—— "Teaching Grammars of the Middle Ages." *HL* 4 (1977): 1–29.

Burton, R. *Classical Poets in the Florilegium Gallicum* (Frankfurt and Bern: P. Lang, 1983).

Butterworth, C. E. "The Rhetorician and his Relationship to the Community: Three Accounts of Aristotle's *Rhetoric*." In M. E. Marmura, ed., *Islamic Theology and Philosophy: Studies in Honor of George F. Hourani* (Albany: SUNY Press, 1984): 111–36.

Calboli, G. "The *Schemata lexeos*: A Grammatical and Rhetorical Tool." *Rhetorica* 22 (2004): 241–56.

Calboli Montefusco, L. *La dottrina degli 'status' nella retorica greca e romana* (Bologna: Università degli studi di Bologna, 1984).

—— "Un catechismo retorico dell' alto Medioevo: la *Disputatio de rhetorica et de virtutibus* di Alcuino." In M. S. Clentano, ed., *Ars—Techne: Il manuale tecnico nelle civiltà greca e romana*. Collana del Dipartimento di Scienze dell' Antichità Sez. filologica 2 (Chieti: Edizioni dell'Orso, 2003): 127–44.

Camargo, M. *Ars dictaminis, Ars dictandi*. Typologie des sources du moyen âge occidental 60 (Turnhout: Brepols, 1991).

Camargo, M. "Latin Composition Textbooks and *Ad Herennium* Glossing: The Missing Link?" In Cox and Ward, eds., *The Rhetoric of Cicero* (2006): 267–88.

—— "Toward a Comprehensive Art of Written Discourse: Geoffrey of Vinsauf and the *Ars Dictaminis*." *Rhetorica* 6 (1988): 167–94.

—— "*Tria sunt*: The Long and the Short of Geoffrey of Vinsauf's *Documentum de modo et arte dictandi et versificandi*." *Speculum* 74 (1999): 935–55.

—— "A Twelfth-Century Treatise on 'Dictamen' and Metaphor." *Traditio* 47 (1992): 161–213.

Cameron, A. *Christianity and the Rhetoric of Empire: The Development of Christian Discourse* (Berkeley: University of California Press, 1991).

—— "Martianus and his First Editor." *CP* 81 (1986): 320–7.

Campbell, A. P. "The Perfection of *Ars Dictaminis* in Guido Faba." *Revue de l'Université d'Ottawa* 39 (1969): 314–21.

Caplan, H. "Memoria: Treasure-House of Eloquence." In *Of Eloquence* (1970): 196–246.

—— *Of Eloquence: Studies in Ancient and Medieval Rhetoric*, ed. A. King and H. North (Ithaca: Cornell University Press, 1970)

Carruthers, M. *The Book of Memory* (Cambridge: Cambridge University Press, 1990).

—— *The Craft of Thought* (Cambridge: Cambridge University Press, 1998).

—— "Inventional Mnemonics and the Ornaments of Style: The Case of Etymology." *Connotations* 2 (1992): 103–14.

—— "The Poet as Master-Builder: Composition and Locational Memory in the Middle Ages." *New Literary History* 24 (1993): 881–904.

—— "Rhetorical *Memoria* in Commentary and Practice." In Cox and Ward, eds., *The Rhetoric of Cicero* (2006): 209–38.

Cary, G. *The Medieval Alexander* (Cambridge: Cambridge University Press, 1956).

Catto, J., ed. *The History of the University of Oxford*, vol. 1: *The Early Oxford Schools* (Oxford: Clarendon, 1984).

—— and R. Evans, eds., *The History of the University of Oxford*, vol. 2: *Late Medieval Oxford* (Oxford: Clarendon, 1992).

Chance, J. *Medieval Mythography*, vol. 2: *From the School of Chartres to the Court of Avignon, 1177–1350* (Gainsville: University of Florida Press, 2000).

Chevallier, R., ed. *Colloque sur la rhétorique: Calliope I* (Paris: Les Belles Lettres, 1979).

Chinca, M. *History, Fiction, Verisimilitude: Studies in the Poetics of Gottfried's Tristan* (London: Modern Humanities Research Association, 1993).

Clerval, J. A. "L'enseignement des arts libéraux à Chartres et à Paris dans la première moitié du XIIe siècle d'après l'*Heptateucon* de Thierry de Chartres." *Congrès scientifique international des catholiques tenu à Paris du 8 au 13 Avril, 1888,* vol. 2 (Paris, 1888): 277–96.

Clogan, P. M. *The Medieval Achilleid of Statius* (Leiden: Brill, 1968).

Codoñer Merino, C. "Differentia y etymologia, dos modos de aproximación a la realidad, II." In *De Tertullien aux Mozarabes: mélanges offerts à Jacques Fontaine*, vol. 2: *Antiquité tardive et christianisme ancien (VIe–IXe siècles)* (Paris: Institut d'Études Augustiniennes, 1992): 19–30.

—— "'Origines' o 'Etymologiae'?" *Helmantica* 45 (1994): 511–27.

Coleman, J. *A History of Political Thought from the Middle Ages to the Renaissance* (Oxford: Blackwell, 2000).

—— "Some Relations between the Study of Aristotle's *Rhetoric*, *Ethics*, and *Politics* in Late Thirteenth- and Early Fourteenth-Century University Arts Courses and the Justification of Contemporary Civic Activities (Italy and France)." In J. Canning and O. G. Oexle, eds., *Political Thought and the Realities of Power in the Middle Ages* (Göttingen: Vandenhoeck and Ruprecht, 1998): 127–57.

—— "Universal History *secundum physicam et ad litteram* in the Twelfth Century." In J.-P. Genet, ed., *L' Historiographie médiévale en Europe* (Paris: CNRS, 1991): 263–75.

Colish, M. *The Stoic Tradition from Antiquity to the Early Middle Ages*. 2 vols. (Leiden: Brill, 1985).

Colker, M. L. "New Evidence that John of Garland Revised the *Doctrinale* of Alexander de Villa Dei." *Scriptorium* 28 (1974): 68–71.

Conley, T. *Rhetoric in the European Tradition* (New York and London: Longman, 1990).

Constable, G. "Medieval Latin Metaphors." *Viator* 38.2 (2007): 1–20.

Contreni, J. J. "John Scottus, Martin Hiberniensis, the Liberal Arts, and Teaching." In M. W. Herren, ed., *Insular Latin Studies: Papers on Latin Texts and Manuscripts of the British Isles: 550–1066* (Toronto: Pontifical Institute of Mediaeval Studies, 1981): 23–44.

Copeland, R. "Ancient Sophistic and Medieval Rhetoric." In Lanham, ed., *Latin Grammar and Rhetoric* (2002): 258–83.

—— "The Ciceronian Rhetorical Tradition and Medieval Literary Theory." In Cox and Ward, eds., *The Rhetoric of Cicero* (2006): 239–65.

—— ed. *Criticism and Dissent in the Middle Ages* (Cambridge: Cambridge University Press, 1996).

—— "The History of Rhetoric and the *Longue Durée*: Ciceronian Myth and its Medieval Afterlives." *Journal of English and Germanic Philology* 106 (2007): 176–202.

—— "Lydgate, Hawes, and the Science of Rhetoric in the Late Middle Ages." *Modern Language Quarterly* 53 (1992): 57–82.

—— "Medieval Intellectual Biography: The Case of Guido Faba." In A. Galloway and R. Yeager, eds., *Through a Classical Eye: Transcultural and Transhistorical Visions in Medieval English, Italian, and Latin Literature in Honour of Winthrop Wetherbee* (Toronto: University of Toronto Press, 2009): 109–24.

—— *Pedagogy, Intellectuals, and Dissent in the Later Middle Ages: Lollardy and Ideas of Learning* (Cambridge: Cambridge University Press, 2001).

Copeland, R. *Rhetoric, Hermeneutics, and Translation in the Middle Ages: Vernacular Traditions and Academic Texts* (Cambridge: Cambridge University Press, 1991).

—— "Rhetoric and the Politics of the Literal Sense in Medieval Literary Theory: Aquinas, Wyclif, and the Lollards." In M. Hyde and W. Jost, eds., *Rhetoric and Hermeneutics in Our Time* (New Haven: Yale University Press, 1997): 335–57.

—— "Wycliffite Ciceronianism? The General Prologue to the Wycliffite Bible and Augustine's *De doctrina christiana*." In Mews et al., eds., *Rhetoric and Renewal in the Latin West* (2003): 185–200.

Coronati, L. "La dottrina del tetrametro trocaico in Bede." *Romanobarbarica* 6 (1981–2): 53–62.

Cousin, J. *Études sur Quintilien*, vol. 1 (Paris: Librairie Boivin, 1936).

Covington, M. A. "*Scientia sermocinalis*: Grammar in Medieval Classifications of the Sciences." In McLelland and Linn, eds., *Flores Grammaticae: Essays in Memory of Vivien Law* (2005): 49–54.

—— *Syntactic Theory in the High Middle Ages: Modistic Models of Sentence Structure* (Cambridge: Cambridge University Press, 1984).

Cox, V. "Ciceronian Rhetoric in Italy, 1260–1350." *Rhetorica* 17 (1999): 239–88.

—— "Ciceronian Rhetoric in Late Medieval Italy." In Cox and Ward, eds., *The Rhetoric of Cicero* (2006): 109–43.

—— and J. O. Ward, eds. *The Rhetoric of Cicero in its Medieval and Renaissance Commentary Tradition* (Leiden: Brill, 2006).

Curtius, E. R. *European Literature and the Latin Middle Ages*, trans. W. R. Trask (New York: Bollingen Series-Pantheon, 1953).

Dahan, G. "L'entrée de la *Rhétorique* d'Aristote dans le monde latin entre 1240 et 1270." In Dahan and Rosier-Catach, eds., *La Rhétorique d'Aristote* (1998): 64–86.

—— "Les classifications du savoir aux XIIe et XIIIe siècles." *L'Enseignement philosophique* 40 (1990): 5–27.

—— "Notes et textes sur la poétique au moyen âge." *AHDLMA* 47 (1980): 171–239.

—— "Origène et Jean Cassien dans un *Liber de philosophia Salomonis*." *AHDLMA* 52 (1985): 135–62.

—— "Saint Thomas d'Aquin et la métaphore. Rhétorique et herméneutique." *Medioevo* 18 (1992): 85–117.

—— "Une introduction à l'étude de la philosophie: *Ut ait Tullius*." In Lafleur and Carrier, eds. *L'enseignement de la philosophie* (1997): 3–58.

—— and I. Rosier-Catach, eds. *La Rhétorique d'Aristote: Traditions et commentaires de l'antiquité au XVIIe siècle* (Paris: Vrin, 1998).

Daintree, D. "The Virgil Commentary of Aelius Donatus: Black Hole or *éminence grise*?" *Greece and Rome* 37 (1990): 65–79.

Davis, C. T. "Brunetto Latini and Dante." *StM* 3rd ser. 8 (1967): 421–50.

D'Avray, D. *The Preaching of the Friars: Sermons Diffused from Paris before 1300* (Oxford: Clarendon, 1985).

Delhaye, P. "*Grammatica* et *ethica* au XIIe siècle." *RTAM* 25 (1958): 59–110.

Delisle, L. "Notice sur la Rhétorique de Cicéron, traduite par Maitre Jean d'Antioche, MS 590 du Musée Condé." *Notices et extraits des manuscrits de la Bibliothèque Nationale* 36 (1899): 207–65.

Della Casa, A. "Les glossaires et les traités de grammaire du moyen âge." In Lefèvre, ed. *La lexicographie du latin médiéval* (1981): 35–46.

Demats, P. *Fabula: Trois études de mythographie antique et médiévale* (Geneva: Droz, 1973).

Denholm-Young, N. "The Cursus in England." In *Oxford Essays in Medieval History Presented to Herbert Edward Salter* (Oxford: Clarendon, 1934): 68–103.

Denyer, N. *Language, Thought, and Falsehood in Ancient Greek Philosophy* (London: Routledge, 1991).

Dickey, M. "Some Commentaries on the *De inventione* and *Ad Herennium* of the Eleventh and Twelfth Centuries." *MRS* 6 (1968): 1–41.

Diels, H. *Die Handschriften der antiken Ärzte* (Berlin: Akademie der Wissenschaften, 1906).

Dietz, D. B. "*Historia* in the Commentary of Servius." *TAPA* 125 (1995): 61–97.

Dinkova-Bruun, G. "Peter Riga's *Aurora* and its Gloss from Salzburg, Stiftsbibliothek Sankt Peter, Ms. a.VII.6." In G. R. Wieland et al., eds., *Insignis Sophiae arcator: Medieval Latin Studies in Honour of Michael W. Herren on his 65th Birthday* (Turnhout: Brepols, 2006): 237–60.

Donati, S. "Studi per una cronologia delle opere di Egidio Romano 1: Le opere prima del 1285—I commenti aristotelici." *Documenti e studi sulla tradizione filosofica medievale* 1 (1990): 1–111.

Doyle, A. I. "English Books in and out of Court." In V. J. Scattergood and J. W. Sherborne, eds., *English Court Culture in the Later Middle Ages* (London: Duckworth, 1983): 162–81.

Dronke, P. *Fabula: Explorations into the Uses of Myth in Medieval Platonism* (Leiden: Brill, 1974).

—— ed. *A History of Twelfth-Century Western Philosophy* (Cambridge: Cambridge University Press, 1988).

—— "Thierry of Chartres." In Dronke, ed. *A History of Twelfth-Century Western Philosophy* (1988): 358–85.

—— "William of Conches' Commentary on Martianus Capella." In *Études de civilisation médiévale (IXe-XIIe siècles): Mélanges offerts à Edmond-René Labande* (Poitiers: C.É.S.C.M., 1974): 223–35.

Ebbesen, S., ed., *Sprachtheorien in Spätantike und Mittelalter* (Tübingen: Gunter Narr, 1995).

—— and I. Rosier-Catach. "Le *trivium* à la Faculté des arts." In Weijers and Holtz, eds., *L'enseignement des disciplines* (1997): 97–128.

Eden, K. *Poetic and Legal Fiction in the Aristotelian Tradition* (Princeton: Princeton University Press, 1986).

Dronke, P. "The Rhetorical Tradition and Augustinian Hermeneutics in *De doctrina christiana*." *Rhetorica* 8 (1990): 45–63.

Edwards, R. R. "Poetic Invention and the Medieval *Causae*." *MS* 55 (1993): 183–217.

Engels, L. J. "Priscian in Alcuin's *De orthographia*." In Houwen and MacDonald, eds., *Alcuin of York, Scholar at the Carolingian Court* (1998): 113–42.

Engen, J. van., ed. *Learning Institutionalized: Teaching in the Medieval University* (Notre Dame: University of Notre Dame Press, 2000).

—— *Rupert of Deutz* (Berkeley: University of California Press, 1983).

Evans, G. R. *Alan of Lille: The Frontiers of Theology in the Later Twelfth Century* (Cambridge: Cambridge University Press, 1983).

—— *The Language and Logic of the Bible: The Earlier Middle Ages* (Cambridge: Cambridge University Press, 1984).

—— *Old Arts and New Theology: The Beginnings of Theology as an Academic Discipline* (Cambridge: Cambridge University Press, 1980)

—— "Thomas of Chobham on Preaching and Exegesis." *RTAM* 52 (1985): 159–70.

—— "The Uncompleted *Heptateuch* of Thierry of Chartres." *History of Universities* 3 (1983): 1–13.

Faral, E. "Le Manuscrit 511 du Hunterian Museum de Glasgow." *StM* n.s. 9 (1936): 18–121.

—— *Les arts poétiques*, see primary sources.

Faulhaber, C. B. "The *Summa dictaminis* of Guido Faba." In Murphy, ed., *Medieval Eloquence* (1978): 85–111.

Feenstra, R. "L'école de droit d'Orléans au treizième siècle et son rayonnement dans l'Europe médiévale." *Revue d'histoire des facultés de droit et de la science juridique* 13 (1992): 23–42.

Fidora, A. *Die Wissenschaftstheorie des Dominicus Gundissalinus: Voraussetzungen und Konsequenzen des zweiten Anfangs der aristotelischen Philosophie im 12. Jahrhundert* (Berlin: Akademie, 2003).

Fierville, C. "Notices et extraits des manuscrits de la bibliothèque de Saint-Omer, nos. 115 et 710." *Notices et extraits des manuscrits de la Bibliothèque Nationale et autres bibliothèques* 31.1 (1884): 49–156.

Fletcher, J. M. "Developments in the Faculty of Arts 1370–1520." In Catto and Evans, eds., *The History of the University of Oxford*, 2 (1992): 315–45.

—— "The Faculty of Arts." In Catto, ed., *The History of the University of Oxford*, 1 (1984): 369–99.

Fleteren, F. van. "St. Augustine, Neoplatonism, and the Liberal Arts: The Background to *De doctrina christiana*." In D. W. H. Arnold and P. Bright, eds., *De doctrina christiana: A Classic of Western Culture* (Notre Dame: Notre Dame University Press, 1995): 14–24.

Flobert, P. "La théorie du solécisme dans l'Antiquité: de la logique à la syntaxe." *Revue de Philologie* 60 (1986): 173–81.

Fögen, T. Patrii sermonis egestas: *Einstellungen lateinischer Autoren zu ihrer Muttersprache. Ein Beitrag zum Sprachbewusstsein in der Römischen Antike* (Munich: Saur, 2000).

Fontaine, J. "Aux sources de la lexicographie médiévale: Isidore de Séville, médiateur de l'étymologie antique." In Lefèvre, ed., *La lexicographie du latin médiéval* (1981): 97–103.

—— "Cohérence et originalité de l'étymologie isidorienne." In F. Rodriguez and J. Iturriaga, eds., *Homenaje a Eleuterio Elorduy* (Bilbao: Universidad de Deusto, 1978): 113–44.

—— *Isidore de Séville et la culture classique dans l'Espagne wisigothique.* 2nd edn. (Paris: Études augustiniennes, 1983).

—— *Isidore de Séville: genèse et originalité de la culture hispanique au temps des Wisigoths* (Turnhout: Brepols, 2000).

Forhan, K. L. *The Political Theory of Christine de Pizan* (Aldershot: Ashgate, 2002).

Fortgens, H. W. "De paedagoog Alcuin en zijn ars grammatica." *Tijdschrift voor Geschiedenis* 60 (1947): 57–65.

Fowler, D. "The Virgil Commentary of Servius." In C. Martindale, ed., *The Cambridge Companion to Virgil* (Cambridge: Cambridge University Press, 1997): 73–87.

Franklin, C. V. "Grammar and Exegesis: Bede's *Liber de schematibus et tropis*." In Lanham, ed., *Latin Grammar and Rhetoric* (2002): 63–91.

Fredborg, K. M. "Abelard on Rhetoric." In Mews et al., eds., *Rhetoric and Renewal in the Latin West* (2003): 55–80.

—— "Buridan's *Questiones super Rhetoricam Aristotelis*." In J. Pinborg, ed., *The Logic of Buridan* (Copenhagen: Museum Tusculanum, 1976): 47–59.

—— "Ciceronian Rhetoric and the Schools." In van Engen, ed., *Learning Institutionalized* (2000): 21–41.

—— "The Commentaries on Cicero's *De inventione* and *Rhetorica ad Herennium* by William of Champeaux." *CIMAGL* 17 (1976): 1–39.

—— "The Dependence of Petrus Helias' *Summa super Priscianum* on William of Conches' *Glose super Priscianum*." *CIMAGL* 11 (1973): 1–57.

—— "*Difficile est proprie communia dicere* (Horats, A.P. 128): Horatsfortolkningens bidrag til middelalderens poetik." *Museum Tusculanum* 40–43 (1980): 583–97.

—— "Petrus Helias on Rhetoric." *CIMAGL* 13 (1974): 31–41.

—— "The *Promisimus*." In S. Ebbesen and R. L. Friedman, eds., *Medieval Analyses in Language and Cognition* (Copenhagen: Royal Danish Academy of the Sciences; C. A. Reitzels Forlag, 1999): 191–206.

—— "Rhetoric and Dialectic." In Cox and Ward, eds., *The Rhetoric of Cicero* (2006): 165–92.

—— "The Scholastic Teaching of Rhetoric in the Middle Ages." *CIMAGL* 55 (1987): 85–105.

—— "Speculative Grammar." In Dronke, ed., *A History of Twelfth-Century Western Philosophy* (1988): 177–95.

—— "Thierry of Chartres, Innovator or Traditionalist." *Ciceroniana* n.s. 9 (2000): 121–32.

Fredborg, K. M. "The Unity of the Trivium." In Ebbesen, ed., *Sprachtheorien in Spätantike und Mittelalter* (1995): 325–38.

—— "Universal Grammar According to Some Twelfth-Century Grammarians." *HL* 7 (1980): 69–84.

Frede, D., and B. Inwood, eds. *Language and Learning: Philosophy of Language in the Hellenistic Age* (Cambridge: Cambridge University Press, 2005).

Frede, M. "Principles of Stoic Grammar." In J. M. Rist, *The Stoics* (Berkeley and Los Angeles: University of California Press, 1978): 27–75.

Frey, J. *De Alcuini arte grammatica commentatio* [= Jahresbericht über das königliche Gymnasium zu Münster] (Münster, 1886).

Friis-Jensen, K. "Horace and the Early Writers of Arts of Poetry." In Ebbesen, ed., *Sprachtheorien in Spätantike und Mittelalter* (1995): 360–401.

Gabriel, A. L. *Garlandia: Studies in the History of the Mediaeval University* (Notre Dame: University of Notre Dame; Frankfurt: Knecht, 1969).

Gagnér, A. *Florilegium Gallicum: Untersuchungen und Texte zur Geschichte der mittellateinischen Florilegienliteratur* (Lund: H. Ohlssons, 1936).

Gaselee, S. *The "Costerian" Doctrinale of Alexander de Villa Dei* (Cambridge: Cambridge University Press, 1938).

Gasti, F. "Isidore e la tradizione grammaticale." In *Discentibus obvius: omaggio degli allievi a Domenico Magnino* (Como: New Press 1997): 31–51.

Gehl, P. F. *A Moral Art: Grammar, Society, and Culture in Trecento Florence* (Ithaca: Cornell University Press, 1993).

—— "Preachers, Teachers, and Translators: The Social Meaning of Language Study in Trecento Tuscany." *Viator* 25 (1994): 289–323.

Gibson, M. "The Early Scholastic *Glosule* to Priscian, *Institutiones grammaticae*: The Text and its Influence." *StM* 3rd ser. 20 (1979): 235–54.

—— "Introduction: Petrus Helias." In J. E. Tolson, ed., "The *Summa* of Petrus Helias on *Priscianus minor*" (2nd volume of edition). *CIMAGL* 28 (1978): 159–66.

—— "Milestones in the Study of Priscian, circa 800–circa 1200." *Viator* 23 (1992): 17–33.

—— "Priscian, *Institutiones grammaticae*: a Handlist of Manuscripts." *Scriptorium* 26 (1972): 105–24.

Gillespie, V. "From the Twelfth Century to c. 1450." In Minnis and Johnson, eds., *The Cambridge History of Literary Criticism*, vol. 2: *The Middle Ages* (2005): 145–235.

Gioseffi, M. "Ut sit integra locutio: esegesi e grammatica in Tiberio Claudio Donato." In F. Gasti, ed., *Grammatica e grammatici latini: Teoria ed esegesi* (Como-Pavia: Ibis 2003): 139–59.

Glauch, S. *Die Martianus-Capella Bearbeitung Notkers des Deutschen*. 2 vols. (Tübingen: Max Niemeyer, 2000).

Glauche, G. *Schullektüre im Mittelalter: Entstehung und Wandlungen des Lektürekanons bis 1200 nach den Quellen dargestellt* (Munich: Arbeo-Gesellschaft, 1970).

Glendenning, R. "Eros, Agape, and Rhetoric around 1200: Gervase of Melkley's *Ars poetica* and Gottfried von Strassburg's *Tristan*," *Speculum* 67 (1992): 892–925.

—— "Pyramus and Thisbe in the Medieval Classroom." *Speculum* 61 (1986): 51–78.

Glorieux. P. *Répertoire des maîtres en théologie de Paris au XIIIe siècle*. 2 vols. (Paris: Vrin, 1933).

Glück, M. *Priscians Partitiones und ihre Stellung in der spätantiken Schule* (Hildesheim: G. Olms, 1967).

Gneuss, H. "The Study of Language in Anglo-Saxon England." In D. Scraggs, ed., *Textual and Material Culture in Anglo-Saxon England* (Cambridge: D. S. Brewer, 2003): 75–105.

Gnoza, J. S. "Finding an Orator in the Poet: The *Interpretationes Vergilianae* of Tiberius Claudius Donatus." Unpublished Dissertation, Harvard University, 2005.

Golling, J. "Einleitung in die Geschichte der lateinischen Syntax." In G. Landgraf et al., eds., *Historische Grammatik der lateinischen Sprache*, vol. 3 (Leipzig: Teubner, 1903): 1–87.

Gonzalez-Haba, M. *La obra De consolatione rationis de Petrus Compostellanus* (Munich: Bayerische Akademie der Wissenschaften, 1975).

Grabmann, M. *Die Geschichte der scholastischen Methode*. 2 vols. (Freiburg im Breisgau: Herder, 1911).

Grebe, S. *Martianus Capella 'De nuptiis Philologiae et Mercurii': Darstellung der sieben freien Künste und ihrer Beziehungen zueinander* (Stuttgart-Leipzig: Teubner, 1999).

Green, L. D. "Aristotelian Rhetoric, Dialectic, and the Traditions of *Antistrophos*." *Rhetorica* 8 (1990): 5–27.

Green, R. P. H. "The Genesis of a Medieval Textbook: The Models and Sources of the *Ecloga Theoduli*." *Viator* 13 (1980): 49–106.

Gregory, T. *Anima mundi: La filosofia di Guglielmo di Conches e la Scuola di Chartres* (Florence: Sansoni, 1955).

Gribomont, J., and E. de Solms, *Rupert de Deutz: Les oeuvres du Saint-Esprit (De Trinitate, Pars III)*. 2 vols. *Sources chrétiennes* 131 and 165 (Paris: Cerf, 1967, 1970).

Griffiths, J., and D. Pearsall, eds. *Book Production and Publishing in Britain, 1375–1475* (Cambridge: Cambridge University Press, 1989).

Grimaldi, W. M. A. *Aristotle, Rhetoric 1: A Commentary* (New York: Fordham University Press, 1980).

Grondeux, A. *À la frontière entre grammaire et rhétorique: Les figures "extravagantes" dans la tradition occidentale* (Turnhout: Brepols, 2009).

—— *Le Graecismus d'Évrard de Béthune à travers ses gloses: Entre grammaire positive et grammaire spéculative du XIIIe au XVe siècle* (Turnhout: Brepols, 2000).

—— "Les Figures dans le *Doctrinale* d'Alexandre de Villedieu et le *Graecismus* d'Évrard de Béthune—étude comparative." In Auroux et al., eds., *History of Linguistics 1999*, 31–46.

—— "Terminologie des figures dans le *Doctrinale* d'Alexandre de Villedieu et le *Graecismus* d'Évrard de Béthune." In B. Colombat and M. Savelli, eds., *Métalangage et terminologie linguistique* (Louvain : Peeters, 2001): 315–30.

Grondeux, A. "*Turba ruunt* (Ov. HER. 1, 88?): histoire d'un exemple grammatical." *ALMA* 61 (2003): 175–222.

Guenée, S. *Bibliographie de l'histoire des universités françaises des origines à la Révolution*, vol. 2 (Paris: Picard, 1978).

Hadot, I. *Arts libéraux et philosophie dans la pensée antique*, 2nd edn. (Paris: Vrin, 2005).

Hadot, P. "Les divisions des parties de la philosophie dans l'Antiquité." *Museum Helveticum* 36 (1979): 201–23.

—— *Marius Victorinus: Recherches sur sa vie et ses oeuvres* (Paris: Études Augustiniennes, 1971).

Hamacher, J. *Florilegium Gallicum: Prolegomena und Edition der Exzerpte von Petron bis Cicero, De oratore* (Bern: H. Lang; Frankfurt: P. Lang, 1975).

Harbert, B. "Matthew of Vendôme." *Medium Aevum* 44 (1975): 225–37.

Harder, M. A., R. F. Regtuit, and G. C. Wakker, eds. *Genre in Hellenistic Poetry* (Groningen: Egbert Forster, 1998).

Hardison, O. B. "The Place of Averroes' Commentary on the *Poetics* in the History of Medieval Criticism." *Medieval and Renaissance Studies* 4 (1968): 57–81.

Harich, H. *Alexander Epicus: Studien zur Alexandreis Walters von Châtillon* (Graz: Technische Universität Graz, 1987).

Häring, N. "Chartres and Paris Revisited." In J. R. O'Donnell, ed., *Essays in Honour of Anton Charles Pegis* (Toronto: Pontifical Institute of Mediaeval Studies, 1974): 268–329.

—— "The Creation and Creator of the World According to Thierry of Chartres and Clarenbaldus of Arras." *AHDLMA* 22 (1955): 137–216.

—— *Life and Works of Clarembald of Arras* (Toronto: Pontifical Institute of Mediaeval Studies, 1965).

Haskins, C. H. "A List of Text Books from the Close of the Twelfth Century." In C. H. Haskins, *Studies in the History of Mediaeval Science* (Cambridge, Mass.: Harvard University Press, 1924): 356–76 (orig. publ. *Harvard Studies in Classical Philology* 20 [1909]: 75–94).

Hauréau, B. "Eberhardi Bethuniensis Graecismus." *Journal des Savants* (1889): 57–62.

Heath, T. "Logical Grammar, Grammatical Logic, and Humanism in Three German Universities." *Studies in the Renaissance* 18 (1971): 9–64.

Herbermann, C.-P. "Antike Etymologie." In P. Schmitter, ed., *Sprachtheorien der abenländischen Antike* (Tübingen: Narr, 1991): 353–76.

Herren, M. "*Bigero sermone clefabo:* Notes on the Life of Vergilius Maro Grammaticus." *Classica et Mediaevalia* 31 (1970): 253–7.

—— "Some New Light on the Life of Vergilius Maro Grammaticus." *Proceedings of the Royal Irish Academy* 79 C 2 (1979): 27–71.

Hexter, R. J. *Ovid and Medieval Schooling: Studies in Medieval School Commentaries on Ovid's Ars amatoria, Epistulae ex Ponto, and Epistulae Heroidum* (Munich: Arbeo-Gesellschaft, 1986).

Holtz, L. "Aelius Donatus." In W. Ax, ed., *Lateinische Lehrer Europas: fünfzehn Portraits von Varro bis Erasmus von Rotterdam* (Cologne and Vienna: Böhlau, 2005): 109–31.

—— "À l'école de Donat, de Saint Augustin à Bède." *Latomus* 36 (1977): 522–38.

—— *Donat et la tradition de l'enseignement grammatical: Étude sur l'Ars Donati et sa diffusion (IVe–IXe siècle) et édition critique* (Paris: CNRS, 1981).

—— "Grammairiens et rhéteurs romains en concurrence pour l'enseignement des figures de rhétorique." In Chevallier, ed., *Colloque sur la rhétorique* (1979): 207–20.

—— "Le Parisinus latinus 7530, synthèse cassinienne des arts libéraux." *StM*, 3rd ser. 16 (1975): 97–152.

Horsfall, N. "Virgil: His Life and Times." In N. Horsfall, ed., *A Companion to the Study of Virgil* (Leiden: Brill, 1995): 1–25.

Houwen, L. A. J. R., and A. A. MacDonald, eds., *Alcuin of York, Scholar at the Carolingian Court* (Groningen: Egbert Forsten 1998).

Hudson, A. *The Premature Reformation: Wycliffite Texts and Lollard History* (Oxford: Clarendon, 1988).

Hugonnard-Roche, H. "La classification des sciences de Gundissalinus et l'influence d'Avicenne." In J. Jolivet and R. Roshed, eds., *Études sur Avicenne* (Paris: Les Belles Lettres, 1984): 41–75.

Hunt, R. W. "*Absoluta*. The *Summa* of Petrus Hispanus on *Priscianus minor*." *HL* 2 (1975): 1–22.

—— *The History of Grammar in the Middle Ages: Collected Papers (1941–1975)*. Ed. G. L. Bursill-Hall (Amsterdam: John Benjamins, 1980).

—— "The Introductions to the 'Artes' in the Twelfth Century." In Hunt, *The History of Grammar in the Middle Ages: Collected Papers*, 117–44 (orig. published in *Studia Mediaevalia in honorem R. J. Martin* [Bruges: De Tempel, 1948]: 85–112).

—— "The 'Lost' Preface to the *Liber Derivationum* of Osbern of Gloucester." *MRS* 4 (1958): 267–82.

—— "Oxford Grammar Masters in the Middle Ages." In Hunt, *The History of Grammar in the Middle Ages: Collected Papers*, 167–97.

—— *The Schools and the Cloister: The Life and Writings of Alexander Nequam (1157–1217)*. Ed. and revised by M. Gibson (Oxford: Clarendon, 1984).

—— "Studies on Priscian in the Eleventh and Twelfth Centuries, I: Petrus Helias and his Predecessors." In Hunt, *The History of Grammar in the Middle Ages: Collected Papers,* 1–38 (orig. publ. *MRS* 1. 2 [1941–3]: 194–231).

—— "Studies on Priscian in the Twelfth Century, II: The School of Ralph of Beauvais." In Hunt, *The History of Grammar in the Middle Ages: Collected Papers*, 39–94 (orig. publ. *MRS* 2.1 [1950]: 1–56).

Hunt, T. "Aristotle, Dialectic, and Courtly Literature." *Viator* 10 (1979): 95–129.

—— *Teaching and Learning Latin in Thirteenth-Century England*. 3 vols (Cambridge: D. S. Brewer, 1991).

Ildefonse, F. *La naissance de la grammaire dans l'Antiquité grecque* (Paris: Vrin, 1997).

Iogna-Prat, D. C. Jeudy, G. Lobrichon, eds. *L'école carolingienne d'Auxerre de Murethach à Remi 830–908* (Paris: Beauchesne, 1991).

Irvine, M. *The Making of Textual Culture: Grammatica and Literary Theory, 350–1100* (Cambridge: Cambridge University Press, 1994)

—— "Medieval Grammatical Theory and Chaucer's *House of Fame*." *Speculum* 60 (1985): 850–76.

Ising, E. *Die Herausbildung der Grammatik der Volkssprachen in Mittel-und Osteuropa* (Berlin: Akademie-Verlag, 1970)

Jackson, B. D. "The Theory of Signs in St. Augustine's *De doctrina christiana*." *Revue des études augustiniennes* 15 (1969): 9–49.

Jacobi, K. "Logic (ii): The Later Twelfth Century." In Dronke, *A History of Twelfth-Century Western Philosophy* (1988): 227–51.

Jacquart, D. "Aristotelian Thought in Salerno." In Dronke, ed., *A History of Twelfth-Century Western Philosophy* (1988): 407–28.

Jaeger, C. S. *The Envy of Angels: Cathedral Schools and Social Ideals in Medieval Europe, 950–1200* (Philadelphia: University of Pennsylvania Press, 1994).

Jaffe, S. "Antiquity and Innovation in Notker's *Nova rhetorica*: The Doctrine of Invention." *Rhetorica* 3 (1985): 165–81.

—— "Commentary as Exposition: The *Declaracio oracionis de beata Dorothea* of Nicolaus Dybinus." *Studies in Medieval and Renaissance Teaching* 6 (1998): 34–47.

—— "Des Witwers Verlangen nach Rat: Ironie und Struktureinheit im *Ackermann aus Böhmen*." *Daphnis: Zeitschrift für mittlere deutsche Literatur* 7 (1978): 1–53.

Jeauneau, E. "Deux rédactions des gloses de Guillaume de Conches sur Priscien." In Jeauneau, *Lectio philosophorum*, 333–70 (orig. publ. in *RTAM* 27 [1960]: 212–47).

—— "Jean de Salisbury et la lecture des philosophes." In Wilks, ed., *The World of John of Salisbury* (1984): 77–108 (orig. publ. in *Revue des études augustiniennes* 29 [1983]: 145–74).

—— *L'Âge d'or des écoles de Chartres* (Chartres: Houvet, 1995).

—— *"Lectio philosophorum": Recherches sur l'École de Chartres* (Amsterdam: Hakkert, 1973).

—— "Le *Prologus in Eptatheucon* de Thierry de Chartres." In Jeauneau, *"Lectio philosophorum,"* 87–91 (orig. publ. *MS* 16 [1954]: 171–5).

—— "Mathématiques et trinité chez Thierry de Chartres." In Jeauneau, *"Lectio philosophorum,"* 93–9 (orig. publ. in *Miscellanea mediaevalia: Veröffentlichungen des Thomas-Instituts an der Universität Köln*, 2: *Die Metaphysik im Mittelalter* [Berlin: De Gruyter, 1963]: 289–95).

—— "*Nani gigantum humeris insidentes*: Essai d'interprétation de Bernard de Chartres." In Jeauneau, *"Lectio philosophorum,"* 51–73 (orig. publ. in *Vivarium* 5 [1967]: 79–99).

—— "Note sur l'École de Chartres." In Jeaneau, *"Lectio philosophorum,"* 5–49 (orig. publ. in *Studi Medievali* [Series 3a] 5 [1964]: 821–65).

—— "Un représentant du platonisme au XIIe siècle: Maître Thierry de Chartres." In Jeauneau, *"Lectio philosophorum,"* 77–86; (orig. publ. in *Mémoires de la Société archéologique d'Eure-et-Loir* 20 [1954–7]: 1–12).

Jeep, L. *Zur Geschichte der Lehre von den Redetheilen bei den lateinischen Grammatikern* (Leipzig: Teubner, 1893).

Jennings, M. "'Non ex virgine': The Rise of the Thematic Sermon Manual." *Collegium Medievale* 1/2 (1992): 27–44.

Jeudy, C. "Israël le grammairien et la tradition manuscrite du commentaire de Rémi d'Auxerre à *l'Ars minor* de Donat." *StM*, 3rd ser. 18 (1977): 185–248.

—— "La tradition manuscrite des *Partitiones* de Priscien et la version longue du commentaire de Rémi d'Auxerre." *RHT* 1 (1971): 123–43.

—— "L'*Institutio de nomine pronomine et verbo*." *RHT* 2 (1972): 73–144.

—— "L'oeuvre de Rémi d'Auxerre." In Iogna-Prat et al., eds., *L'école carolingienne d'Auxerre de Murethach à Rémi 830–908* (1991): 373–96.

—— "Un nouveau manuscrit du commentaire de Rémi d'Auxerre à l'*Ars maior* de Donat." In M. H. King and W. M. Stevens, eds., *Saints, Scholars, and Heroes: Studies in Medieval Culture in Honour of C. W. Jones,* 2 vols. (Collegeville, Minn.: Hill Monastic Library, 1979), 2:113–26.

Jolivet, J. "The Arabic Inheritance." In Dronke, ed., *A History of Twelfth-Century Western Philosophy* (1988): 113–48.

—— and A. de Libera, eds. *Gilbert de Poitiers et ses contemporains: Aux origines de la Logica modernorum* (Naples: Bibliopolis, 1987).

Jones, J. W., Jr. "Allegorical Interpretation in Servius." *Classical Journal* 56 (1961): 217–26.

Jonge, C. de. *Between Grammar and Rhetoric: Dionysius of Halicarnassus on Language, Linguistics and Literature* (Leiden: Brill, 2008).

—— "*Natura artis magistra*. Ancient rhetoricians, grammarians, and philosophers on natural word order." In T. van den Wouden and Hans Broekhuis, eds., *Linguistics in the Netherlands* (Amsterdam and Philadelphia: John Benjamins, 2001): 159–66.

Kantorowicz, E. "An 'Autobiography' of Guido Faba." *MRS* 1.2 (1941–1943): 253–80.

Kantorowicz, H. "A Medieval Grammarian on the Sources of the Law." *Tijdschrift voor Rechtsgeschiedenis* 15 (1937): 25–47.

Kardaun, M., and J. Spruyt, eds. *The Winged Chariot: Collected Essays on Plato and Platonism in Honour of L. M. de Rijk.* (Leiden: Brill, 2000).

Kaster, R. "The Grammarian's Authority." *CP* 75 (1980): 216–41.

—— *Guardians of Language: The Grammarian and Society in Late Antiquity* (Berkeley and Los Angeles: University of California Press, 1988).

—— "Notes on 'Primary' and 'Secondary' Schools in Late Antiquity." *TAPA* 113 (1983): 323–46.

Keats-Rohan, K. S. B. "John of Salisbury and Education in Twelfth-Century Paris, from the Account of his *Metalogicon*." *History of Universities* 6 (1986): 1–45.

Kelley, D. R., ed. *History and the Disciplines: The Reclassification of Knowledge in Early Modern Europe* (Rochester, N.Y., 1997).

Kelly, D. *The Arts of Poetry and Prose*. Typologie des sources du moyen âge occidental 59 (Turnhout: Brepols, 1991).

—— "La Spécialité dans l'invention des topiques." In L. Brind'Amour and E. Vance, eds., *Archéologie du signe* (Toronto: Pontifical Institute of Mediaeval Studies, 1983): 101–25.

—— *Medieval Imagination: Rhetoric and the Poetry of Courtly Love* (Madison: University of Wisconsin Press, 1978).

—— "The Scope of Medieval Instruction in the Art of Poetry and Prose: Recent Developments in Documentation and Interpretation." *Studies in Medieval and Renaissance Teaching* 6 (1998): 49–68.

—— "The Scope of the Treatment of Composition in the Twelfth- and Thirteenth-Century Arts of Poetry." *Speculum* 41 (1966): 261–78.

—— "Theory of Composition in Medieval Narrative Poetry and Geoffrey of Vinsauf's *Poetria nova*." *MS* 31 (1969): 117–48.

Kelly, H. A. "Aristotle-Averroes-Alemannus on Tragedy: The Influence of the *Poetics* on the Middle Ages." *Viator* 10 (1979): 161–209.

Kelly, L. G. *The Mirror of Grammar: Theology, Philosophy, and the Modistae* (Amsterdam and Philadelphia: John Benjamins, 2002).

Kennedy, G. A. *Classical Rhetoric and its Christian and Secular Traditions from Ancient to Modern Times*, 2nd edn. (Chapel Hill: University of North Carolina Press, 1999).

Klopsch, P. *Einführung in die Dichtungslehren des lateinischen Mittelalters* (Darmstadt: Wissenschaftliche Buchgesellschaft, 1980).

Knapp, E. *The Bureaucratic Muse: Thomas Hoccleve and the Literature of Late Medieval England* (University Park, PA.: Pennsylvania State University Press, 2001).

Knappe, G. "The Rhetorical Aspect of Grammar Teaching in Anglo-Saxon England." *Rhetorica* 17 (1999): 1–35.

—— *Traditionen der klassischen Rhetorik im angelsächsischen England* (Heidelberg: C. Winter, 1996).

Kneepkens, C. H. "Grammar and Semantics in the Twelfth Century: Petrus Helias and Gilbert de la Porrée on the Substantive Verb." In Kardaun and Spruyt, eds., *The Winged Chariot* (2000): 237–76.

—— *Het iudicium constructionis: Het leerstuk van de "constructio" in de 2ᵉhelft van de 12ᵉeeuw*, vol. 1: *een verkennende en inleidende studie* (Nijmegen: Ingenium Publishers, 1987).

—— "Linguistic Description and Analysis in the Late Middle Ages." In S. Auroux, K. Koerner, H.-J. Niederehe, and K. Versteegh, eds., *History of the Language Sciences: Geschichte der Sprachwissenschaften. Histoire des sciences du langage* (Berlin and New York: Walter de Gruyter, 2000): 551–60.

—— "Master Guido and his View on Government: On Twelfth-Century Linguistic Thought." *Vivarium* 16 (1978): 108–41.

—— "'Mulier quae damnavit, salvavit': A Note on the Early Development of the *Relatio simplex*." *Vivarium* 14 (1976): 1–25.

—— "*Ordo naturalis* and *ordo artificialis*: A Note on the Terminology of Thirteenth-Century University Grammar." In Weijers, ed., *Vocabulary of Teaching and Research* (1995): 59–82.

—— "Peter Helias." In J. J. E. Gracia and T. B. Noone, eds., *A Companion to Philosophy in the Middle Ages* (Oxford: Blackwell 2003): 512–13.

—— "The Priscianic Tradition." In Ebbesen, ed., *Sprachtheorien in Spätantike und Mittelalter* (1995): 239–64.

—— "The *Relatio simplex* in the Grammatical Tracts of the Late Twelfth and Early Thirteenth Century." *Vivarium* 15 (1977): 1–30.

—— "Some Notes on Alcuin's *De Perihermeniis*, with an Edition of the Text." In Houwen and MacDonald, eds. *Alcuin of York, Scholar at the Carolingian Court* (1998): 81–112.

—— "*Suppositio* and *Supponere* in Twelfth-Century Grammar." In Jolivet and Libera, eds., *Gilbert de Poitiers et ses contemporains* (1987): 325–51.

—— "Transitivity, Intransitivity and Related Concepts in Twelfth-Century Grammar: An Explorative Study." In G. L. Bursill-Hall, S. Ebbesen, and K. Koerner, *De ortu grammaticae: Studies in Medieval Grammar and Linguistic Theory in Memory of Jan Pinborg* (Amsterdam: John Benjamins, 1990): 161–89.

Kretzmann, N. "Aristotle on Spoken Sound Significant by Convention." In J. Corcoran, ed., *Ancient Logic and its Modern Interpretations* (Dordrecht: D. Reidel, 1974): 3–21.

—— A. Kenny, J. Pinborg, and E. Stump, eds. *The Cambridge History of Later Medieval Philosophy: From the Rediscovery of Aristotle to the Disintegration of Scholasticism, 1100–1600* (Cambridge: Cambridge University Press, 1982).

Kristeller, P. O., ed. *Catalogus translationum et commentariorum*, 8 vols. (Washington, D.C.: Catholic University of America Press, 1960–2003).

Lafleur, C., and J. Carrier. "Les *Accessus philosophorum*, le recueil *Primo queritur utrum philosophia* et l'origine parisienne du 'Guide de l'étudiant' du ms. Ripoll 109." In Lafleur and Carrier, eds., *L'enseignement de la philosophie* (1997): 589–642.

—— —— eds. *L'enseignement de la philosophie au XIIIe siècle: Autour du "Guide de l'étudiant" du ms. Ripoll 109* (Turnhout: Brepols, 1997).

Langslow, D. R. *The Latin Alexander Trallianus: The Text and Transmission of a Late Latin Medical Book* (London: Society for the Promotion of Roman Studies, 2006).

Lanham, C. D., ed. *Latin Grammar and Rhetoric: From Classical Theory to Medieval Practice* (London and New York: Continuum, 2002).

Latham, R. E., D. R. Howlett et al., eds. *Dictionary of Medieval Latin from British Sources* (Oxford: Oxford University Press, 1975–).

Laugesen, A. T. "La roue de Virgile: un page de la théorie littéraire du Moyen Âge." *Classica et Mediaevalia* 22 (1962): 248–73.

Law, V. *Grammar and Grammarians in the Early Middle Ages* (London and New York: Longman, 1997)

—— *The History of Linguistics in Europe: From Plato to 1600* (Cambridge: Cambridge University Press, 2003).

—— *The Insular Latin Grammarians* (Woodbridge, Suffolk: Boydell Press, 1982).

—— "Linguistics in the Earlier Middle Ages: The Insular and Carolingian Grammarians." *Transactions of the Philological Society* 83 (1985): 171–93.

—— "Memory and the Structure of Grammars in Antiquity and the Middle Ages." In M. de Nonno, P. de Paolis, and L. Holtz, eds., *Manuscripts and Tradition of Grammatical Texts from Antiquity to the Renaissance*, vol. 1 (Cassino: Università degli Studi di Cassino 2000): 9–57.

—— "The Mnemonic Structure of Ancient Grammatical Doctrine." In P. Swiggers and A. Wouters, eds., *Ancient Grammar: Content and Context* (Leuven and Paris: Peeters, 1996): 37–52.

—— "Why Write a Verse Grammar." *The Journal of Medieval Latin* 9 (1999): 46–76.

—— *Wisdom, Authority, and Grammar in the Seventh Century: Decoding Virigilius Maro Grammaticus* (Cambridge: Cambridge University Press, 1995).

—— ed. *History of Linguistic Thought in the Early Middle Ages* (Amsterdam and Philadelphia: Benjamins, 1993).

—— and W. Hüllen, eds. *Linguists and Their Diversions*. The Henry Sweet Society Studies in the History of Linguistics 2 (Münster: Nodus, 1996).

Leader, D. *A History of the University of Cambridge*, vol. 1: *The University to 1546* (Cambridge: Cambridge University Press, 1988).

Leclercq, J. "*Disciplina.*" In M. Viller, C. Baumgartner, et al., eds., *Dictionnaire de spiritualité*, vol. 3 (Paris: Beauchesne, 1957): 1291–1302.

Lefèvre, Y., ed. *La lexicographie du latin médiéval et ses rapports avec les recherches actuelles sur la civilisation du moyen-âge* (Paris: CNRS, 1981)

Leff, M. C. "Boethius' *De differentiis topicis,* Book IV." In Murphy, ed., *Medieval Eloquence* (1978): 3–24.

—— "The Topics of Argumentative Invention in Latin Rhetorical Theory from Cicero to Boethius." *Rhetorica* 1 (1983): 23–44.

Lehmann, P. *Die Parodie im Mittelalter.* 2nd edn. (Stuttgart: Hiersemann, 1963).

Leichtfried, A. *Trinitätstheologie als Geschichtstheologie: "De sancta Trinitate et operibus eius" Ruperts von Deutz* (Würzburg: Echter, 2002).

Lejbowicz, M. "Thierry de Chartres entre *expositio* et *tractatus.*" In *Aristote, l'École de Chartres et la cathédrale: Actes du Colloque Européen des 5 et 6 juillet 1997* (Chartres: Association des Amis du Centre Médiéval Européen de Chartres, 1997): 81–99.

Lemoine, F. *Martianus Capella: A Literary Re-evaluation* (Munich: Arbeo-Gesellschaft, 1972).

Lemoine, M. *Théologie et platonisme au XIIe siècle* (Paris: Cerf, 1998)

Leonardi, C. "I codici di Marziano Capella." *Aevum* 33 (1959): 443–89; 34 (1960): 1–99, 411–524.

—— "Raterio e Marziano Capella." *Italia medioevale e umanistica* 2 (1959): 73–102.

Lewry, P. O. "Four Graduation Speeches from Oxford Manuscripts (c. 1270–1310)." *MS* 44 (1982): 138–80.

—— "Rhetoric at Paris and Oxford in the Mid Thirteenth Century." *Rhetorica* 1 (1983): 45–63.

Libera, A. de, and I. Rosier, "La pensée linguistique médiévale." in S. Auroux, ed., *Histoire des idées linguistiques* 2 (Liège: Mardaga, 1992): 115–86.

Liebeschütz, H. *Mediaeval Humanism in the Life and Writings of John of Salisbury* (London: Warburg Institute, 1950).

Lindenbaum, S. "Literate Londoners and Liturgical Change: Sarum Books in City Parishes after 1414." In M. Davies and A. Prescott, eds., *London and the Kingdom in the Later Middle Ages: Essays in Honour of Caroline Barron*. Proceedings of the 2004 Harlaxton Symposium (Donington: Shaun Tyas, 2008): 384–99.

Lockett, L. "The Composition and Transmission of a Fifteenth-Century Latin Retrograde Sequence Text from Deventer." *Tijdschrift van de Koninklijke Vereniging voor Nederlandse Muziekgeschiedenis* 53 (2003): 105–50.

Lohmeyer, K. "Ebrard von Béthune. Eine Untersuchung über den Verfasser des Graecismus und Laborintus." *Romanische Forschungen* 11.2 (1901): 412–30.

Lohr, C. H. "Medieval Latin Aristotle Commentaries." *Traditio* 23 (1967): 313–413; *Traditio* 24 (1968): 149–245; continued in volumes 26 (1970), 27 (1971), 28 (1972), 29 (1973), 30 (1974).

Long, A. A. "Language and Thought in Stoicism." In A. A. Long, ed., *Problems in Stoicism* (London: Athlone Press, 1971): 75–113.

—— "Stoic Linguistics, Plato's *Cratylus*, and Augustine's *De dialectica*." In Frede and Inwood, eds. *Language and Learning: Philosophy of Language in the Hellenistic Age* (2005): 36–55.

Luhtala, A. "Early Medieval Commentary on Priscian's *Institutiones grammaticae*." *CIMAGL* 71 (2000): 115–88.

—— *Grammar and Philosophy in Late Antiquity: A Study of Priscian's Sources* (Amsterdam and Philadelphia: John Benjamins, 2005).

—— "Linguistics and Theology in the Early Medieval West." In S. Auroux et al., eds., *History of the Language Sciences* (Berlin-New York: De Gruyter, 2000): 510–25.

—— "On the Concept of Transitivity in Greek and Latin Grammars." In G. Calboli, ed., *Papers on Grammar* 3 (Bologna: CLUEB, 1990): 19–56.

—— "On definitions in ancient grammar." In Swiggers and Wouters, eds., *Grammatical Theory and Philosophy of Language in Antiquity* (2002): 257–85.

—— "On the Origins of the Medieval Concept of Transitivity." In A. Ahlqvist, ed., *Diversions of Galway* (Amsterdam and New York: John Benjamins, 1992): 39–48.

Luhtala, A. "A Priscian Commentary Attributed to Eriugena." In Auroux et al., eds., *History of Linguistics 1999* (2003): 19–30.

—— "'Priscian's Definitions are Obscure': Carolingian Commentators on the *Institutiones grammaticae*." In Law and Hüllen, eds., *Linguists and Their Diversions* (1996): 53–78.

—— "Syntax and Dialectic in Carolingian Commentaries on Priscian's *Institutiones grammaticae*." In Law, ed., *History of Linguistic Thought in the Early Middle Ages* (1993): 145–91.

Luscombe, D. E. "Peter Abelard." In Dronke, ed., *A History of Twelfth-Century Western Philosophy* (1988): 279–307.

Lusignan, S. *Parler vulgairement: les intellectuels et la langue française aux XIIIe et XIVe siècles* (Paris: Vrin; Montréal: Presses de l'Université de Montréal, 1986).

—— and M. Paulmier-Foucart, eds. *Lector et compilator: Vincent de Beauvais, frère prêcheur, un intellectuel et son milieu au XIIIe siècle* (Nancy and Montreal: ARTEM CNRS/Université de Nancy 2; Université de Montreal, 1997).

Lutz, C. "One Form of *Accessus* in Remigius' Works." *Latomus* 19 (1960): 774–80.

—— "Remigius's Ideas on the Classification of the Seven Liberal Arts." *Traditio* 12 (1959): 63–86.

—— "Remigius' Ideas on the Origin of the Seven Liberal Arts." *Medievalia et Humanistica* 10 (1956): 32–49.

Lutz-Bachmann, M., A. Fidora, and A. Niederberger, eds. *Metaphysics in the Twelfth Century: On the Relationship among Philosophy, Science, and Theology* (Turnhout: Brepols, 2004).

Maccagnolo, E. *Rerum universitas: Saggio sulla filosofia di Teodorico di Chartres* (Florence: Felice le Monnier, 1976).

Magallon, A.-I. *La tradicion gramatical de differentia y etymologia hasta Isidoro de Sevilla* (Zaragoza: Universidad de Zaragoza, 1996).

Magrassi, M. *Teologia e storia nel pensiero di Ruperto di Deutz*. Studia Urbaniana 2 (Rome: Apud Pontificiam Universitatem Urbanianam de Propaganda Fide, 1959).

Mahdi, M. "Science, Philosophy, and Religion in Al-Farabi's *Enumeration of the Sciences*." In J. E. Murdoch and E. D. Sylla, eds., *The Cultural Context of Medieval Learning* (Dordrecht and Boston: D. Reidel, 1975): 113–47.

Maltby, R. *A Lexicon of Ancient Latin Etymologies* (Leeds: Cairns, 1991).

—— "The Role of Etymologies in Servius and Donatus." In Nifadopoulos, ed., *Etymologia: Studies in Ancient Etymology* (2003): 103–18.

Manitius, M. *Geschichte der lateinischen Literatur des Mittelalters*, 3 vols. (Munich: C. H. Beck, 1911–31; rpt.1974).

Mansfeld, J. *Prolegomena: Questions to be Settled Before the Study of an Author, or a Text* (Leiden: Brill, 1994).

Marenbon, J. *From the Circle of Alcuin to the School of Auxerre: Logic, Theology, and Philosophy in the Early Middle Ages* (Cambridge: Cambridge University Press, 1981).

Marmo, C. "Carattere dell'oratore e recitazione nel commento di Giovanni di Jandun al terzo libro della *Retorica*." In L. Bianchi, ed., *Filosofia e teologia nel Trecento* (Louvain-la-Neuve: F.I.D.E.M., 1994): 17–31.

—— "*Hoc autem etsi potest tollerari*...Egidio Romano e Tommaso d'Aquino sulle passioni dell' anima." *Documenti e studi sulla tradizione filosofica medievale* 2.1 (1991): 281–315.

—— "L'utilizzazione delle traduzioni latine della *Retorica* nel commento di Egidio Romano (1272–1273)." In Dahan and Rosier-Catach, *La Rhétorique d'Aristote* (1998): 111–34.

—— "*Suspicio*: A Key Word in the Significance of Aristotle's *Rhetoric* in Thirteenth-Century Scholasticism." *CIMAGL* 60 (1990): 145–98.

Marmura, M. E. "Avicenna on the Division of the Sciences in the *Isagoge* of his *Shifa*." *Journal for the History of Arabic Science* (Aleppo) 4 (1980): 239–51.

Marrou, H.-I. "'Doctrina' et 'disciplina' dans la langue des Pères de l'Église." *Bulletin du Cange (ALMA)* 19 (1934): 3–23.

Marshall, P. K. "Tiberius Claudius Donatus on Virgil *Aeneid* 6.1–157." *Manuscripta* 37 (1993): 3–20.

Martin, J. *Antike Rhetorik: Technik und Methode* (Munich: Beck, 1974).

Matter, E. A. "Alcuin's question-and-answer texts." *Rivista di storia della filosofia* 45 (1990): 645–56.

McDonough, C. J. "Cambridge, University Library, Gg. 6. 42, Alexander Neckam and the *Sacerdos ad altare*." *StM* ser. 3, 46 (2005): 783–809.

McGuinness, L. "Quintilian and Medieval Pedagogy: The Twelfth-Century Witness Stuttgart, Württembergische Landesbibliothek, Theol. octavo 68." *ALMA* 57 (1999): 191–259.

McKeon, R. "Rhetoric in the Middle Ages." *Speculum* 17 (1942): 1–32.

McLelland, N., and A. R. Linn, eds. *Flores Grammaticae: Essays in Memory of Vivien Law*. Henry Sweet Society Studies in the History of Linguistics 10. (Münster: Nodus, 2005).

Meale, C. "Patrons, Buyers, and Owners: Book Production and Social Status." In Griffiths and Pearsall, eds., *Book Production and Publishing in Britain, 1375–1475* (1989): 201–38.

Meech, S. "John Drury and his English Writings." *Speculum* 9 (1934): 70–83.

Mehtonen, P. *Old Concepts and New Poetics: Historia, Argumentum, and Fabula in the Twelfth- and Early Thirteenth-Century Latin Poetics of Fiction* (Helsinki: Finnish Society of Sciences and Letters, 1996).

—— "Poetics, Narration, and Imitation: Rhetoric as *Ars aplicabilis*." In Cox and Ward, eds., *The Rhetoric of Cicero* (2006): 287–310.

Meijering, R. *Literary and Rhetorical Theories in Greek Scholia* (Groningen: Forsten, 1987).

Merrilees, B. "L'*Art mineur* français et le curriculum grammatical." *Histoire, Épistémologie, Langage* 12/2 (1990): 15–29.

—— "Teaching Latin in French: Adaptations of Donatus' *Ars minor*." *Fifteenth-Century Studies* 12 (1987): 87–98.

Meter, G. *Walter of Châtillon's Alexandreis Book 10: A Commentary* (Frankfurt: Peter Lang, 1991).

Mews, C. J. "In Search of a Name and its Significance: A Twelfth-Century Anecdote about Thierry and Peter Abaelard." *Traditio* 44 (1988): 171–200.

—— et al., eds. *Rhetoric and Renewal in the Latin West 1100–1540: Essays in Honour of John O. Ward* (Turnhout: Brepols, 2003).

Meyer, P. "Notice sur les *Corrogationes Promethei* d'Alexandre Neckam." *Notices et extraits des manuscrits de la Bibliothèque Nationale* 35.2 (1896): 641–82 (reprinted separately, Paris: Klincksieck, 1897).

Milner, S. "Communication, Consensus, and Conflict: Rhetorical precepts, the *Ars concionandi*, and Social Ordering in Late Medieval Italy." In Cox and Ward, eds., *The Rhetoric of Cicero* (2006): 365–408.

—— "Exile, Rhetoric, and the Limits of Civic Republican Discourse." In S. Milner, ed., *At the Margins: Minority Groups in Premodern Italy* (Minneapolis: University of Minnesota Press, 2005): 162–91.

Miner, J. N. *The Grammar Schools of Medieval England: A. F. Leach in Historical Perspective* (Montreal and Kingston: McGill-Queen's University Press, 1990).

Minnis, A. J. *Medieval Theory of Authorship: Scholastic Literary Attitudes in the Later Middle Ages* (London: Scholar Press, 1984).

—— and I. Johnson, eds. *The Cambridge History of Literary Criticism*, vol. 2: *The Middle Ages* (Cambridge: Cambridge University Press, 2005).

Monfrin, J. "Humanisme et traductions au moyen âge." *Journal des savants* 148 (1963): 161–90.

Mooney, L. "The Scribe." In Tavormina, ed., *Sex, Ageing, and Death in a Medieval Medical Compendium* (2006): 55–64.

Moos, P. von. "*Poeta* und *historicus* im Mittelalter. Zum Mimesis-Problem am Beispiel einiger Urteile über Lucan." *Beiträge zur Geschichte der deutschen Sprache und Literatur* 98 (1976): 93–130.

Morenzoni, F. *Des écoles aux paroisses: Thomas de Chobham et la promotion de la prédication au début du XIIIe siècle* (Paris: Institut d'Études Augustiniennes).

Moretti, G. "Il manuale e l'allegoria: La personificazione allegorica delle arti liberali come tradizione del genere manualistico." In Maria Silvana Celentano, ed., *Ars-Techne*, vol. 1: *Il manuale tecnico nelle civiltà greca e romana*. Collana del Dipartimento di Scienze dell' Antichità Sez. filologica 2 (Chieti: Edizioni dell'Orso, 2003): 159–86.

Morse, R. *Truth and Convention in the Middle Ages* (Cambridge: Cambridge University Press, 1991).

Müller, H. E., *Die Prinzipien der stoischen Grammatik*. Dissertation masch. Rostock, 1943.

Munk Olsen, B. "Les classiques latins dans les florilèges médiévaux antérieurs au XIIIe siècle." *RHT* 9 (1979): 47–121; 10 (1980): 123–72.

—— "Les poètes classiques dans les écoles au IXe siècle." In B. Munk Olsen, *La réception de la littérature classique au Moyen Âge (IXe–XIIe siècle)*, ed. K. Friis-Jensen (Copenhagen: Museum Tusculanum Press, 1995): 35–46.

—— *L' Étude des auteurs classiques latins aux XIe et XIIe siècles.* 3 vols. (Paris: CNRS, 1982–1989).

Murphy, J. J. ed. *Medieval Eloquence* (Berkeley and Los Angeles: University of California Press, 1978).

—— "The Rhetorical Lore of the *Boceras* in Byhrtferth's *Manual.*" In J. L. Rosier, ed., *Philological Essays: Studies in Old and Middle English Language and Literature in Honour of H. D. Meritt* (The Hague: Mouton, 1970): 111–24.

—— *Rhetoric in the Middle Ages* (Berkeley and Los Angeles: University of California Press, 1974).

—— "The Scholastic Condemnation of Rhetoric in the Commentary of Giles of Rome on the *Rhetoric* of Aristotle." In *Arts libéraux et philosophie au moyen âge* (1969): 833–41.

—— "The Teaching of Latin as a Second Language in the Twelfth Century." *HL* 7 (1980): 159–75.

Murray, O. "The Idea of the Shepherd King from Cyrus to Charlemagne." In P. Godman and O. Murray, eds., *Latin Poetry and the Classical Tradition* (Oxford: Clarendon Press 1990): 1–14.

Murru, F. "Les cas et la linguistique ancienne: le 'septième cas.'" *Lalies* 1 (1980): 67–9.

—— "À propos du *septimus casus.*" *Eos* 68 (1980): 151–4.

Mütherich, F. "Ein Illustrationszyklus zum *Anticlaudianus* des Alanus ab Insulis." *Münchner Jahrbuch der bildenden Kunst* 2 (1951): 73–88.

Neudecker, K.-J. *Das Doctrinale des Alexander de Villa-Dei und der lateinische Unterricht während des späteren Mittelalters in Deutschland* (Leipzig: Teubner, 1885).

Nifadopoulos, C. ed. *Etymologia: Studies in Ancient Etymology* (Münster: Nodus Publikationen, 2003).

Nims, M. "*Translatio:* Difficult Statement in Medieval Poetic Theory." *University of Toronto Quarterly* 43 (1974): 215–30.

Nuchelmans, G. "*Secundum/tertium adiacens*": *Vicissitudes of a Logical Distinction.* Koninklijke Nederlandse Akademie van Wetenschappen. Mededelingen van de Afdeling Letterkunde, Nieuwe Reeks, 55 no. 10 (Amsterdam and New York: Noord-Hollandsche, 1992).

—— *Theories of the Proposition: Ancient and Medieval Conceptions of the Bearers of Truth and Falsity* (Amsterdam and London: North-Holland, 1973).

O'Boyle, C. *Thirteenth- and Fourteenth-Century Copies of the Ars Medicine: A Checklist and Contents Description of the Manuscripts.* Articella Studies 1 (Cambridge: Cambridge Wellcome Unit for the History of Medicine, 1998).

O'Donnell, J. J. *Cassiodorus* (Berkeley and Los Angeles: University of California Press, 1979).

O'Donnell, J. R. "Alcuin's Priscian." In J. J. O'Meara and B. Naumann, eds., *Latin Script and Letters A.D. 400–900* (Leiden: Brill, 1976): 222–35.

—— "The Commentary of Giles of Rome on the *Rhetoric* of Aristotle." In T. A. Sandquist and M. R. Powicke, eds., *Essays in Medieval History Presented to Bertie Wilkinson* (Toronto: University of Toronto Press, 1969): 139–56.

Orme, N. *Medieval Schools: From Roman Britain to Renaissance England* (New Haven and London: Yale University Press, 2006).

Paetow, L. J. "The Crusading Ardor of John of Garland." In L. J. Paetow, ed., *The Crusades and Other Historical Essays Presented to D. C. Munro* (New York: F. S. Crofts, 1928): 207–22.

Palmer, R. B. "Bede as a Textbook Writer: A Study of his *De arte metrica*." *Speculum* 34 (1959): 573–84.

Pasnau, R. *Theories of Cognition in the Later Middle Ages* (Cambridge: Cambridge University Press, 1997).

Passalacqua, M. *I codici di Prisciano* (Rome: Storia e letteratura, 1978).

Paulmier-Foucart, M. and M.-C. Duchenne. *Vincent de Beauvais et le Grand Miroir du monde* (Turnhout: Brepols, 2004).

Pérez Castro, L. C. "Acerca de los *verba idem significantia*, la *synonymia*, y la sinonimia." *Emerità* 69 (2001): 55–62.

Perkins, N. *Hoccleve's Regiment of Princes*: *Counsel and Constraint* (Woodbridge: D. S. Brewer, 2001).

Pinborg, J. *Die Entwicklung der Sprachtheorie im Mittelalter*. Münster: Aschendorff, 1967.

—— "Some Syntactical Concepts in Medieval Grammar." in J. Pinborg, *Medieval Semantics: Selected Studies on Medieval Logic and Grammar*, ed. S. Ebbesen (London: Variorum Reprints, 1984): 496–509.

—— "Speculative Grammar." In Kretzmann et al., eds., *The Cambridge History of Later Medieval Philosophy* (1982): 254–69.

Pini, V. "La tradizione manoscritta di Guido Faba dal XIII al XV secolo." In Guido Faba, *Magistri Guidonis Rota nova*, ed. A. P. Campbell and V. Pini (Bologna: Istituto per la storia dell'Università di Bologna, 2000): 249–465.

Pinzani, R. *The Logical Grammar of Abelard* (Dordrecht: Kluwer Academic Publishers, 2003).

Pirovano, L. *Le interpretationes vergilianae di Tiberio Claudio Donato: problemi di retorica* (Rome: Herder, 2006).

Polara, G. "A proposito delle dottrine grammaticali di Virgilio Marone." In Law, ed., *History of Linguistic Thought in the Early Middle Ages* (1993): 205–22.

Préaux, J. "Le couple de 'sapientia' et 'eloquentia.'" In Chevallier, ed., *Colloque sur la Rhétorique* (1979): 171–85.

—— "Les manuscrits principaux du *De nuptiis Philologiae et Mercurii* de Martianus Capella." In G. Cambier, C. Deroux, and J. Préaux, eds., *Lettres latines du moyen âge et de la renaissance* (Brussels: Latomus, 1978): 76–128.

Purcell, W. M. "*Identitas, Similitudo*, and *Contrarietas* in Gervasius of Melkley's *Ars poetica*: A Stasis of Style." *Rhetorica* 9 (1991): 63–86.

—— "*Transsumptio*: A Rhetorical Doctrine of the Thirteenth Century." *Rhetorica* 5 (1987): 369–410.

Quadlbauer, F. *Die antike Theorie der genera dicendi im lateinischen Mittelalter* (Vienna: Hermann Böhlau, 1962).

Quain, E. A. "The Medieval *Accessus ad auctores*." *Traditio* 3 (1945): 215–64.

Quinn, B. N. "Ps-Theodolus." In Kristeller, ed., *Catalogus translationum et commentariorum* (1960–2003): 2:383–408.

Raïos, D. K. *Recherches sur le Carmen de ponderibus et mensuris* (Ioannina: Panepistimio Ioanninon, 1983).

Ramelli, I. *Tutti i commenti a Marziano Capella: Scoto Eriugena, Remigio di Auxerre, Bernardo Silvestre e Anonimi* (Milano: Bompiano 2006).

Rand, E. K. *Cicero in the Courtroom of St. Thomas Aquinas*. The Aquinas Lecture, 1945 (Milwaukee: Marquette University Press, 1946).

Rashdall, H. *The Universities of Europe in the Middle Ages*. New edition by F. M. Powicke and A. B. Emden. 3 vols. (Oxford: Clarendon, 1936).

Ray, R. "Bede and Cicero." *Anglo-Saxon England* 16 (1987): 1–15.

—— "Bede, the Exegete, as Historian." In G. Bonner, ed., *Famulus Christi: Essays in Commemoration of the Thirteenth Centenary of the Birth of the Venerable Bede* (London: SPCK, 1976): 125–40.

—— "Bede, Rhetoric, and the Creation of Christian Latin Culture." Jarrow Lecture, 1997 (Jarrow: St. Paul's Church, 1997).

Raynaud de Lage, G. *Alain de Lille: poète du XIIe siècle* (Montréal: Institut d'études médiévales; Paris: Vrin, 1951).

Reeve, M. D. and R. H. Rouse, "New Light on the Transmission of Donatus's *Commentum Terentii*." *Viator* 9 (1978): 235–49.

Reynolds, S. "*Ad auctorum expositionem*: Syntactic Theory and Interpretative Practice in the Twelfth Century." *Histoire, Épistémologie, Langage* 12 (1990): 31–51.

—— *Medieval Reading* (Cambridge: Cambridge University Press, 1996).

Richards, I. A. *The Philosophy of Rhetoric* (New York: Oxford University Press, 1936).

Richardson, H. G. "The Schools of Northampton in the Twelfth Century." *English Historical Review* 56 (1941): 595–605.

Rigg, A. G. *A History of Anglo-Latin Literature 1066–1422* (Cambridge: Cambridge University Press, 1992).

Rijk, L. M. de. *Logica modernorum: A Contribution to the History of Early Terminist Logic*, 2 vols. (Assen: Van Gorcum, 1962–7).

—— "On the Chronology of Boethius' Works on Logic" I and II. *Vivarium* 2 (1964): 1–49, 125–62.

Robert, Brother S. "Rhetoric and Dialectic According to the First Latin Commentary on the *Rhetoric* of Aristotle." *The New Scholasticism* 31 (1957): 484–98.

Robertson, D. W. "A Note On The Classical Origin of 'Circumstances' in the Medieval Confessional." *Studies in Philology* 43 (1946): 6–14.

Robins, R. H. "The Authenticity of the *Technê*: the *status quaestionis*." In V. Law and I. Sluiter, eds. *Dionysius Thrax and the Technê Grammatikê*, 2nd edn. (Münster: Nodus Publikationen, 1998): 13–26.

—— "Priscian and the Context of his Age." In I. Rosier, ed. *L'héritage des grammairiens latins de l'Antiquité aux Lumières* (Paris and Louvain: Diffusion, Peeters, 1988): 49–55.

—— *A Short History of Linguistics*, 3rd edn. (London: Longman, 1990).

Rodrigues, V. "La conception de la philosophie chez Thierry de Chartres." *Mediaevalia: Textos e Estudos* 11–12 (1997): 119–37.

Rosier, I. "La grammaire dans le '*Guide de l'étudiant*.'" In Lafleur and Carrier, eds., *L'enseignement de la philosophie au XIIIe siècle* (1997): 255–79.

—— *La grammaire spéculative des modistes* (Lille: Presses Universitaires de Lille, 1983).

—— *La parole comme acte: sur la grammaire et la sémantique au XIIIe siècle* (Paris: Vrin, 1994).

—— "Les sophismes grammaticaux au XIIIe siècle." *Medioevo: Rivista di storia della filosofia medievale* 17 (1991): 175–230.

—— "'*O Magister...*' Grammaticalité et intelligibilité selon un sophisme du XIIIe siècle." *CIMAGL* 56 (1988): 1–102.

Rosier-Catach, I. "The *Glosulae in Priscianum* and its Tradition." In McLelland and Linn, eds., *Flores Grammaticae: Essays in Memory of Vivien Law* (2005): 81–99.

—— "Modisme, pré-modisme, proto-modisme: pour une définition modulaire." In S. Ebbesen and R. L. Friedman, eds., *Medieval Analyses in Language and Cognition* (Copenhagen: Reitzels, 1999): 45–81.

—— "*Prata rident*." In A. de Libera, A. Elamrani-Jamal, and A. Galonnier, eds., *Langages et philosophie: hommage à Jean Jolivet* (Paris: Vrin, 1997): 155–76.

—— "Roger Bacon, Al-Farabi et Augustin: rhétorique, logique et philosophie morale." In Dahan and Rosier-Catach, eds., *La Rhétorique d'Aristote* (1998): 87–11.

Rouse, R. H. "The *A* Text of Seneca's Tragedies in the Thirteenth Century." *RHT* 1 (1971): 93–121.

—— "Florilegia and Latin Classical Authors in Twelfth- and Thirteenth-Century Orléans." *Viator* 10 (1979): 131–60.

—— "New Light on the Circulation of the A-Text of Seneca's Tragedies." *Journal of the Warburg and Courtauld Institutes* 40 (1977): 283–6.

—— and M. A. Rouse, "The *Florilegium Angelicum*: Its Origin, Content, and Influence." In J. J. G. Alexander and M. T. Gibson, eds., *Medieval Learning and Literature: Essays Presented to R. W. Hunt* (Oxford: Clarendon, 1976): 66–114.

Rousseau, G. S., ed. *Organic Form: The Life of an Idea* (London: Routledge and Kegan Paul, 1972).

Ruff, C. "*Desipere in loco*: Style, Memory, and the Teachable Moment." In A. Harbus and R. Poole, eds., *Verbal Encounters: Anglo-Saxon and Old Norse Studies for Roberta Frank* (Toronto: University of Toronto Press, 2005): 91–103.

Saiani, A. "La figura di Guido Faba nel Prologo autobiografico della Rota nova. Una rilettura." In Guido Faba, *Magistri Guidonis Rota nova*, ed. A. P. Campbell and V. Pini (Bologna: Istituto per la storia dell'Università di Bologna, 2000): 467–515.

Salamon, M. "Priscianus und sein Schülerkreis in Konstantinopel." *Philologus* 123 (1979): 91–6.

Salmon, P. B. "The Three Voices of Poetry in Medieval Literary Theory." *Medium Aevum* 30 (1961): 1–18.

Scaglione, A. D. *Ars grammatica: A Bibliographical Survey, Two Essays on the Grammar of the Latin and Italian Subjunctive, and a Note on the Ablative Absolute* (The Hague: Mouton, 1970).

Scanlon, L. *Narrative, Authority, and Power: The Medieval Exemplum and the Chaucerian Tradition* (Cambridge: Cambridge University Press, 1994).

Schenkeveld, D. M. "Figures and Tropes: A Border-Case between Grammar and Rhetoric." In Ueding, ed. *Rhetorik zwischen den Wissenschaften* (1991): 149–57.

—— "The Stoic *Techne peri phônês*: Studies in the History of Ancient Linguistics III." *Mnemosyne* 43 (1990): 86–108.

—— "Studies in the History of Ancient Linguistics IV: Developments in the Study of Ancient Linguistics." *Mnemosyne* 43 (1990): 289–306.

Schindel, U. *Die lateinischen Figurenlehren des 5. bis 7. Jahrhunderts und Donats Vergilkommentar (mit zwei Editionen)*. Abhandlungen der Akademie der Wissenschaften in Göttingen (Göttingen: Vandenhoeck and Ruprecht, 1975).

—— "Die Quellen von Bedas Figurenlehre." *Classica et Mediaevalia* 29 (1968): 169–86.

—— "Die Quelle von Isidors 'rhetorischer' Figurenlehre." *Rheinisches Museum* 137 (1994): 374–82.

Schmidt, P. L. "Aelius Donatus." In R. Herzog, ed., *Handbuch der lateinischen Literatur der Antike*, vol. 5 (Munich: Beck, 1989).

—— "Priscianus." In *Der Neue Pauly*, Bd 10 (2001): 338–9.

Schmidt, R. W. *The Domain of Logic According to Saint Thomas Aquinas* (The Hague: Nijhoff, 1966).

Schneider, B. *Die mittelalterlichen griechisch-lateinischen Übersetzungen der aristotelischen Rhetorik* (Berlin, New York: de Gruyter, 1971).

Schweickard, W. "'*Etymologia est origo vocabularum*' . . . Zum Verständnis der Etymologiedefinition Isidors von Sevilla." *HL* 12 (1985): 1–25.

Serbat, G., "Donat et la tradition de l'enseignement grammatical. À propos de la thèse de Louis Holtz." *Revue des études latines* 61 (1983): 56–64.

Shanzer, D. *A Philosophical and Literary Commentary on Martianus Capella's De Nuptiis Philologiae et Mercurii Book 1* (Berkeley and Los Angeles: University of California Press, 1986).

Sheridan, J. J. "The Seven Liberal Arts in Alan of Lille and Peter of Compostella." *MS* 35 (1973): 27–37.

Sicking, C. M. J. "Organische Komposition und Verwandtes," *Mnemosyne* 16 (1963): 225–42.

Siebenborn, E. *Die Lehre von der Sprachrichtigkeit und ihren Kriterien: Studien zur antiken normativen Grammatik* (Amsterdam: Grüner, 1976).

Siemiatkowska, Z. K. "Avant l'exil de Gilles de Rome: au sujet d'une dispute sur les 'theoremata de esse et essentia' de Gilles de Rome." *Mediaevalia philosophica polonorum* 7 (1960): 3–67.

Silverstein, T. "The Fabulous Cosmogony of Bernardus Silvestris." *Modern Philology* 46 (1948): 92–116.

Silvestre, H. "Le schéma 'moderne' des *accessus*." *Latomus* 16 (1957): 684–9.

—— "Les citations et reminiscences classiques dans l'oeuvre de Rupert de Deutz." *Revue d'histoire ecclésiastique* 45 (1950): 140–74.

—— "Rupert de Saint-Laurent et les auteurs classiques." In *Mélanges Félix Rousseau: Études sur l'histoire du pays mosan au moyen âge* (Brussels: La Renaissance du Livre, 1958): 541–51.

Simpson, J. *Sciences and the Self in Medieval Poetry: Alan of Lille's Anticlaudianus and John Gower's Confessio amantis* (Cambridge: Cambridge University Press, 1995).

Sirridge, M. "Robert Kilwardby as 'Scientific Grammarian,'" *Histoire, Épistémologie, Langage* 10.1 (1988): 7–28.

Sluiter, I. *Ancient Grammar in Context: Contributions to the Study of Ancient Linguistic Thought* (Amsterdam: VU University Press, 1990).

—— "Antieke grammatica: autonoom of instrument?" In J. Goedegebuuren, ed. *Nieuwe wegen in taal- en literatuurwetenschap. Handelingen van het 41ste filologencongres* (Tilburg: Tilburg University Press, 1993): 129–41.

—— "Communication, Eloquence and Entertainment in Augustine's *De doctrina christiana*." In J. den Boeft and M.L. van Poll-van de Lisdonk, eds., *The Impact of Scripture in Early Christianity* (Leiden: Brill, 1999): 245–67.

—— "The Dialectics of Genre: Some Aspects of Secondary Literature and Genre in Antiquity." In M. Depew and D. Obbink, eds. *Matrices of Genre* (Cambridge, Mass.: Harvard University Press, 2000): 183–203.

—— "The Greek Tradition." In W. van Bekkum, J. Houben, I. Sluiter, and K. Versteegh, *The Emergence of Semantics in Four Linguistic Traditions: Hebrew, Sanskrit, Greek, Arabic* (Amsterdam and Philadelphia: John Benjamins, 1997): 149–224.

—— "Language and Thought in Stoic Philosophy." In S. Auroux et al., eds., *Geschichte der Sprachwissenschaften* (Berlin: de Gruyter, 2002): 375–84.

—— "Metatexts and the Principle of Charity." In P. Schmitter and M. van der Wal, eds., *Metahistoriography: Theoretical and Methodological Aspects of the Historiography of Linguistics* (Münster: Nodus, 1998): 11–27.

—— "Persuasion, Pedagogy, Polemics: Two Case-Studies in Medieval Language Teaching." Forthcoming, *New Medieval Literatures* 11 (2009).

—— Review of Jean Lallot's translation of the *Syntax* of Apollonius Dyscolus. *Lingua* 114 (2004): 629–34.

—— Review of Terentianus Maurus, *De syllabus,* ed. and trans. J.-W. Beck. *Mnemosyne* 48 (1995): 490–3.

—— "Seven Grammarians on the Ablative Absolute." *HL* 27 (2000): 379–414.

—— "Textual Therapy. On the Relationship between Medicine and Grammar in Galen." In M. Horstmanshoff et al., eds., *Medical Education: Proceedings of the XIIth Colloquium Hippocraticum* (Leiden: Brill [forthcoming, 2009]).

—— and R. M. Rosen, "General Introduction." In R. Rosen and I. Sluiter, eds., *City, Countryside, and the Spatial Organization of Value in Classical Antiquity* (Leiden: Brill, 2006): 1–12.

Spatz, N. K. "Imagery in University Inception Sermons." In J. Hamesse et al., eds., *Medieval Sermons and Society: Cloister, City, University* (Louvain-la-Neuve: Féderation Internationale des Instituts d'Études Médiévales, 1998): 329–42.

Speer, A. "The Discovery of Nature: The Contribution of the Chartrians to Twelfth-Century Attempts to Found a *Scientia naturalis.*" *Traditio* 52 (1997): 135–51.

Spruyt, J. "Gilbert of Poitiers on the Application of Language to the Transcendent and Sublunary Domains." In Kardaun and Spruyt, eds., *The Winged Chariot* (2000): 205–36.

Squillante Saccone, M. *Le Interpretationes Vergilianae di Tiberio Claudio Donato* (Napoli: Società Editrice Napoletana 1985).

Stahl, W. H. "To a Better Understanding of Martianus Capella." *Speculum* 40 (1965): 102–15.

Staico, U. "Retorica e politica in Egidio Romano." *Documenti e studi sulla tradizione filosofica medievale* 3 (1992): 1–75.

Stammerjohann, H., et al., eds. *Lexicon grammaticorum* (Tübingen: Niemeyer, 1996).

Starr, R. J. "An Epic of Praise: Tiberius Claudius Donatus and Vergil's *Aeneid.*" *Classical Antiquity* 11 (1992): 159–74.

—— "Explaining Dido to your Son." *Classical Journal* 87 (1991): 25–34.

—— "The Flexibility of Literary Meaning and the Role of the Reader in Roman Antiquity." *Latomus* 60 (2001): 433–45.

Steinberg, J. *Accounting for Dante: Urban Readers and Writers in Late Medieval Italy* (Notre Dame, Ind.: University of Notre Dame Press, 2007).

Stock, B. *Augustine the Reader: Meditation, Self-Knowledge, and the Ethics of Interpretation* (Cambridge, Mass.: Harvard University Press, 1996).

Stok, F. "Virgil between the Middle Ages and the Renaissance." *International Journal of the Classical Tradition* 1 (1994): 15–22.

Stroh, W. "De vocis definitione quadam Stoica." In M. Baumbach et al., eds., *Mousopolos Stephanos: Festschrift für H. Görgemanns* (Heidelberg: Winter, 1998): 443–2.

Strubel, A. "'Allegoria in factis' et 'allegoria in verbis.'" *Poétique* 6 (1975): 342–7.

Sutter, C. *Aus Leben und Schriften des Magisters Boncompagno: ein Beitrag zur italienischen Kulturgeschichte im dreizehnten Jahrhundert* (Freiburg and Leipzig: Mohr, 1894).

Swerdlow, N. "'Musica dictur a moys, quod est aqua.'" *Journal of the American Musicological Society* 20 (1967): 3–9.

Swiggers, P., and A. Wouters, eds. *Grammatical Theory and Philosophy of Language in Antiquity* (Leuven: Peeters, 2002).

Szklenar, H. "Hinweis auf Magister Nicolaus de Dybin, Kreuzschulrektor in Dresden im Jahre 1369." In B. Moeller et al., *Studien zum städtischen Bildungswesen des späten Mittelalters und der frühen Neuzeit* (Göttingen: Vandenhoeck and Ruprecht, 1983): 243–55.

—— "Magister Nicolaus de Dybin als Lehrer der Rhetorik." *Daphnis: Zeitschrift für mittlere deutsche Literatur* 16 (1987): 1–12.

—— *Magister Nicolaus de Dybin: Vorstudien zu einer Edition seiner Schriften* (Munich: Artemis, 1981): 63–79.

—— "Nicolaus de Dybin commentatore del 'Laborintus.'" In C. Leonardi and E. Menestò, eds., *Retorica e poetica tra i secoli XII et XIV* (Florence: La nuova Italia, 1988): 221–37.

Tavormina, M. T., ed. *Sex, Ageing, and Death in a Medieval Medical Compendium: Trinity College Cambridge MS R. 14. 52, its Texts, Language, and Style.* 2 vols. (Tempe, Ariz.: Arizona Center for Medieval and Renaissance Studies, 2006).

Taylor, D. J. "Rethinking the History of Language Sciences in Classical Antiquity." *HL* 13 (1986): 175–90.

Taylor-Briggs, R. "Reading Between the Lines: The Textual History and Manuscript Transmission of Cicero's Rhetorical Works." In Cox and Ward, eds., *The Rhetoric of Cicero* (2006): 77–108.

Teeuwen, M. *Harmony and the Music of the Spheres: The Ars Musica in Ninth-Century Commentaries on Martianus Capella* (Leiden: Brill, 2002).

—— "The Study of Martianus Capella's *De nuptiis* in the ninth century." In A. A. MacDonald, M. W. Twomey, and G. J. Reinink, eds., *Learned Antiquity: Scholarship and Society in the Near-East, the Greco-Roman World, and the Early Medieval West* (Leuven: Peeters, 2003): 185–94.

—— *The Vocabulary of Intellectual Life in the Middle Ages* (Turnhout: Brepols, 2003).

Thomson, S. H. *The Writings of Robert Grosseteste, Bishop of Lincoln 1235–1253* (Cambridge: Cambridge University Press, 1940).

Thorndike, L. *A History of Magic and Experimental Science*, vol. 1 (New York: Columbia University Press, 1923).

—— "The Properties of Things of Nature Adapted to Sermons." *Medievalia et Humanistica* 12 (1958): 78–83.

Thurot, C. "Document relatif à l'histoire de la poésie latine au moyen-âge." In *Comptes rendus de l'Académie des inscriptions et belles-lettres* 6, 2nd ser. (Paris 1870): 258–69.

—— *Notices et extraits de divers manuscrits latins pour servir à l'histoire des doctrines grammaticales au moyen âge* (Paris, 1869; rpt. Frankfurt: Minerva, 1964).

Tilliette, J.-Y. *Des mots à la parole: une lecture de la Poetria nova de Geoffroy de Vinsauf* (Geneva: Droz, 2000).

Tsitsibakou-Vasalos, E. *Ancient Poetic Etymology. The Pelopids: Fathers and Sons* (Stuttgart: Steiner, 2007).

Tugwell, S. "Humbert of Romans, 'Compilator.'" In Lusignan and Paulmier-Foucart, eds., *Lector et compilator: Vincent de Beauvais* (1997): 47–76.

Ueding, G., ed. *Rhetorik zwischen den Wissenschaften: Geschichte, System, Praxis als Probleme des "Historischen Wörterbuchs der Rhetorik"* (Tübingen: Niemeyer, 1991).

—— ed., with G. Kalivoda and F.-H. Robling. *Historisches Wörterbuch der Rhetorik* (Tübingen : Niemeyer, 1992–).

Uhl, A. *Servius als Sprachlehrer: Zur Sprachrichtigkeit in der exegetischen Praxis des spätantiken Grammatikerunterrichts* (Göttingen: Vandenhoeck and Ruprecht 1998).

Usener, H. "Ein altes Lehrgebäude der Philologie." In Usener, *Kleine Schriften* (Leipzig-Berlin: Teubner, 1913): 2:265–314.

Valastro Canale, A. "Isidoro di Siviglia: la vis verbi come riflesso dell' omnipotenza divina." *Cuadernos de filología classica. Estudios latinos* 10 (1996): 147–76.

Valente, L. "Langage et théologie pendant la seconde moitié du XIIe siècle." In Ebbesen, ed., *Sprachtheorien in Spätantike und Mittelalter* (1995): 33–54.

Verdier, P. "L' iconographie des arts libéraux dans l'art du moyen âge jusqu'à la fin du quinzième siècle." In *Arts libéraux et philosophie au moyen âge* (1969): 305–55.

Vernet, A. "Une épitaphe inédite de Thierry de Chartres." *Recueil des travaux offert à M. Clovis Brunel*, vol. 2 (Paris: Société de l'École des Chartes, 1955): 660–70 (rpt. in A. Vernet, *Études médiévales* [Paris: Études augustiniennes, 1981], 160–70).

Viljamaa, T. "From Grammar to Rhetoric: First Exercises in Composition According to Quintilian, *Inst.* 1.9." *Arctos: Acta Philologica Fennica* 22 (1988): 179–201.

Vineis, E. "Grammatica e filosofia del linguaggio in Alcuino." *Studi e saggi linguistici* 28 (1988): 403–29.

Voigts, L. "What's the Word: Bilingualism in Late-Medieval England." *Speculum* 71 (1996): 813–26.

Vyver, A. van de. "Cassiodore et son oeuvre." *Speculum* 6 (1931): 244–92.

Waite, W. G. "Johannes de Garlandia, Poet and Musician." *Speculum* 35 (1960): 179–95.

Wallace, D. *Chaucerian Polity: Absolutist Lineages and Associational Forms in England and Italy* (Stanford: Stanford University Press, 1997).

Wallach, L. *Alcuin and Charlemagne: Studies in Carolingian History and Literature* (Ithaca: Cornell University Press, 1959).

Walzer, R. R. *Greek into Arabic: Essays on Islamic Philosophy* (Oxford: Bruno Cassirer, 1962).

Ward, J. O. *Ciceronian Rhetoric in Treatise, Scholion, and Commentary* (Turnhout: Brepols, 1995).

—— "The Date of the Commentary on Cicero's *De inventione* by Thierry of Chartres (ca. 1095–1160?) and the Cornifician Attack on the Liberal Arts." *Viator* 3 (1972): 219–73.

Ward, J. O. "Educational Crisis and the Genesis of Universities in Medieval Europe." *Teaching History* 3 (N.S.W. Australia, 1969): 5–18.

—— "From Antiquity to the Renaissance: Glosses and Commentaries on Cicero's *Rhetorica*." In Murphy, ed., *Medieval Eloquence* (1978): 25–67.

—— "Magic and Rhetoric From Antiquity to the Renaissance: Some Ruminations." *Rhetorica* 6 (1988): 57–118.

—— "The Medieval and Early Renaissance Study of Cicero's *De inventione* and the *Rhetorica ad Herennium*: Commentaries and Contexts." In Cox and Ward, eds., *The Rhetoric of Cicero* (2006): 3–75.

—— Review of Fredborg, ed., *The Latin Rhetorical Commentaries by Thierry of Chartres*. In *Rhetorica* 7 (1989): 359–68.

—— "Rhetorical Theory and the Rise and Decline of Dictamen in the Middle Ages and Early Renaissance." *Rhetorica* 19 (2001): 175–223.

—— "Rhetoric in the Faculty of Arts at the Universities of Paris and Oxford in the Middle Ages: A Summary of the Evidence." *ALMA* 54 (1996): 159–231 (Abbreviated version published in Weijers and Holtz, eds., *L'enseignement des disciplines* [1997]: 147–71).

Watson, G. *Phantasia in Classical Thought* (Galway: Galway University Press, 1988).

Webb, C. C. J. "Tenred of Dover." *English Historical Review* 30 (1915): 658–60.

Weijers, O. "The Chronology of John of Salisbury's Studies in France (*Metalogicon* II.10)." In Wilks, ed., *The World of John of Salisbury* (1984): 109–16.

—— "L'appellation des disciplines dans la classification des sciences aux XIIe et XIIIe siècles." *ALMA* 46 (1986–1987): 39–64.

—— *Le maniement du savoir: Pratiques intellectuelles à l'époque des premières universités (XIIIe–XIVe siècles)* (Turnhout: Brepols, 1996).

—— ed. *Vocabulary of Teaching and Research Between Middle Ages and Renaissance* (Turnhout: Brepols, 1995).

—— and L. Holtz, eds. *L'enseignement des disciplines à la Faculté des arts (Paris et Oxford, XIIIe–XVe siècles)* (Turnhout: Brepols, 1997).

Weisheipl, J. "Classification of the Sciences in Medieval Thought." *MS* 27 (1965): 54–90.

Wetherbee, W. *Platonism and Poetry in the Twelfth Century: The Literary Influence of the School of Chartres* (Princeton: Princeton University Press, 1972).

Wieruszowski, H. *Politics and Culture in Medieval Spain and Italy* (Rome: Edizioni di storia e letteratura, 1971).

Wilks, M. J., ed. *The World of John of Salisbury* (Oxford: Blackwell, 1984).

Williams, J. R. "The *De differentiis et derivationibus grecorum* attributed to William of Corbeil." *Viator* 3 (1972): 298–310.

Wisse, J. *Ethos and pathos from Aristotle to Cicero* (Amsterdam: Hakkert, 1989).

Witt, R. "Brunetto Latini and the Italian Tradition of *Ars Dictaminis*." *Stanford Italian Review* 2 (1983): 5–24.

Woods, M. C. "Classical Examples and References in Medieval Lectures on Poetic Composition." *Allegorica* 10 (1989): 3–12.

—— *Classroom Commentaries: Teaching the Poetria nova Across Medieval and Renaissance Europe* (Columbus: Ohio State University Press, 2009).

—— "In a Nutshell: *Verba* and *Sententia* and Matter and Form in Medieval Composition Theory." In P. Doob, C. Morse, and M. C. Woods, eds., *The Uses of Manuscripts in Literary Studies: Essays in Memory of Judson Boyce Allen* (Kalamazoo: Medieval Institute Publications, 1992): 19–40.

—— "A Medieval Rhetoric Goes to School—and to the University: The Commentaries on the *Poetria nova.*" *Rhetorica* 9 (1991): 55–65.

—— "Rape and the Pedagogical Rhetoric of Sexual Violence." In R. Copeland, ed., *Criticism and Dissent in the Middle Ages* (1996): 56–86.

—— "An Unfashionable Rhetoric in the Fifteenth Century." *The Quarterly Journal of Speech* 75 (1989): 312–20.

—— and R. Copeland. "Classroom and Confession." In D. Wallace, ed., *The Cambridge History of Medieval English Literature* (Cambridge: Cambridge University Press, 1999): 376–406.

Zedler, G. *Der älteste Buchdruck und das frühholländische Doktrinale des Alexander de Villa Dei* (Leiden: A. W. Sijthoff, 1936).

Zeeman, N. *Piers Plowman and the Medieval Discourse of Desire* (Cambridge: Cambridge University Press, 2006).

—— "The Schools Give a License to Poets." In R. Copeland, ed., *Criticism and Dissent in the Middle Ages* (1996): 151–80.

Ziolkowski, J. M. *Alan of Lille's Grammar of Sex: The Meaning of Grammar to a Twelfth-Century Intellectual* (Cambridge Mass.: Medieval Academy of America, 1985).

INDEX OF LATIN TERMS

heu [whoa!] (interjection) 287

hic, haec, hoc [this, that], (demonstrative pronoun, used to indicate morphological status, instead of (Greek) article) 186n., 189

historia [factual data, *Realien*, historical narrative] 37, 42–4, 138–9, 281, 282, 373, 393, 428–30, 478, 615, 643, 717

historia-argumentum-fabula (narrative classifications) 37, 42–4, 373, 410, 428–30, 615, 617, 643–4n., 655–6; see *argumentum; fabula*

homoeosis [likeness, comparison] (trope which illustrates something less known through likeness to something better known) 97, 268, 622 n., 733; see also *icon; parabola; paradigma*

honestum [honorable] 116

humana scientia [human science] 464

humanitas [humanity] 117

humile [low] (as *genus dicendi*) 128, 244; (as kind of *causa*) 646n.; (about subject matter (*res*)) 436; see *genera dicendi*

hypostasis [being, subsistence] 592

hypothesis, see hypothesis

icon [comparison] (pertaining to persons) 622n. (confused with *icos*)

icos, ycos, [probability, likeness to truth, verisimilitude] (from Greek *eikos*) 622 and n., 623; see also *icon*

identitas [identity] 607, 611–13

idiomata [linguistic peculiarities, idioms] 317

illustratio [vivid representation] 504 n.

imaginationes (*phantasiai*) [mental images] 24–6

immutatio [substitution] (category of change) 94, 96n., 340n.; *see* change

impressio figurae [imprint of a figure] 24; see also *similitudo*

inchoatio [beginning] 420, 421 and n., 422, 650–1; see also *exordium; initium; origo; primordium; principium*

incongruentia [irregularity] 184

incongruus [incongruent] (of ungrammatical sentence) 336; (of literary elements) *incongrua materie variatio* [incongruous variation of material] 556; *incongrua operis imperfectio* [incongruous incompleteness of the work] 556; *incongrua orationis digressio* [incongruent digression] 553; *incongrua stili mutatio* [incongruous variation in style] 554

inherentia [inherence] (of action in subject) 380; *see* inherence

initium [beginning] 420 and n., 421 and n.; see also *exordium; inchoatio; origo; primordium; principium*

insinuatio [insinuation] (division of the *exordium* in an oration) 359, 395–6, 409, 416, 418, 610–11, 615, 626–7, 633, 645–6, 761

instrumentum [instrument] (of an art; a topic in *accessus ad artem*) 385, 407, 411, 415, 470, 475–6, 478, 479, 481, 758

integer [intact] (opposed to *corruptus* [affected]) 87

intellectus [understanding] 440–1, 446, 455, 512, 514

intellegere [to understand] (one of the tasks of grammar) 154n.

intentio [intention]; *-auctoris* [author's intention] (a topic in *accessus ad auctores* or *ad artem*) 385, 388, 412, 414–15, 553, 557, 759; *-poetae* [intention of the poet] 125, 127, 138; *see* intention

interiectio [interjection] (part of speech); *see* interjection; parts of speech

interpretatio [as eloquence or expression of what is understood, paraphrase] 282, 342, 440–1; [interpretation] 343, 349n.; [translation] 356, 357

INDEX OF ANCIENT AND MEDIEVAL NAMES

GENERAL INDEX

lexicography 233, 342–3, 355–6, 532

lexis [Greek: expression] 32n., 85; *see also*
    schemata lexeos

liberal arts 4, 6–7, 13, 14, 51, 70, 148, 211–12, 232,
    233, 235, 240, 249, 273, 275, 276, 355, 390–1,
    439–41, 464, 492–3, 508, 519–30, 536, 694,
    706–23, 771, 817, 864–73; *see also* trivium;
    quadrivium; classification of knowledge;
    divisio scientiarum

license, *see licentia* and *poetica licentia*

licking, verses into shape 101

Liège 368, 390

literal speech 38; *see* proper meaning/signification

literary theory, literature, *see genus* (genre);
    inventio (literary invention from circum-
    stances); *litterae*; architecture; canon;
    composition (literary); genres of literary
    narrative; theft

loan words 351n.

logic 14–28, 190–209, 376–89, 684–5, 690–1,
    706–23, 739–40, 787–91, 871

logos [Greek: speech, discourse, reason] 32n.,
    176n., 387, 797; *see also* Greek

Lollard, Lollardy, *see* Wycliffite Bible

Lombardy, Lombards 708, 710, 711

London 607, 864–6

magic, relationship word-thing 340; and
    rhetoric, *see* rhetoric and magic

makrologia [Greek: long-windedness], see
    macrologia

manner 52, 268

Mantua 100, 102

Manuscripts
    Barcelona, Ripoll 104: 694
    Cambridge, Gonville and Caius College
        385/605: 534
    Cambridge, Trinity College R. 14. 52:
        864–5

Cambridge, University Library
    Gg.6.42: 534n.
Cambridge, University Library Nn.3.2: 820n.
Chartres, Bibl. municipale 497: 420n., 440
Chartres, Bibl. municipale 498: 440
Glasgow, Hunterian Museum V.8.14 (MS
    511): 608–9 and n.
London, BL Cotton Claudius A.x: 614n.
Munich, Staatsbibliothek Clm. 19869: 823
Munich, Staatsbibliothek Clm. 19876: 823–4
Oxford, Balliol College 263: 611n.
Oxford, Bodleian Library Canon. Class. Lat.
    201: 756
Oxford, New College 255: 699–705
Paris, BN 7420B: 699
Paris, BN lat. 7530: 69–70
Paris, BN lat. 15130: 689n.
Prague, University Library XII.B.12: 823

marriage, metaphor for acquiring knowledge,
    cf. section on Martianus Capella
    (148–66), 358n., 441

mastery 84

material concept of style 410, 496 n., 552–6,
    615, 636n., 645, 648; see *genera dicendi*

meaning, *see* form (versus meaning); semantics

medicine 232, 510, 535, 539, 673, 710n., 712–13,
    716 and n., 864; (and grammar) 152–3

meditative verbs 495 and n.

memorization (part of rhetoric), see *memoria*

memory (part of rhetoric), see *memoria*

memory, and writing 235, 386; art of 25–6;
    book of 27; exercises 506, 649n.

"mental impressions," 23–6; *see also* Aristotle,
    De interpretatione

mental suppletion (of linguistic elements)
    322

merismos [Greek: parsing] 383n.; *see* Greek

metalanguage 447, 455n.; (Greek as) 168;
    (Latin as) 816n.